ay 1 01

ppy Mothers Day,

I hope you find peace and comfort that this boo provides.

As I sit here thinking about Mothers Day and especially you, mom, I find myself in sort of a self-evaluation mode. I wonder, how many times throughout my life, have I taken you for granted? How often have I failed to say "I love you", or "Thank you", or "I appreciate you"? For all the times I should have told you, "I Love You", and "Thank You"!

It is hard to put into words how much I Appreciate you. I guess it has taken being a parent and looking to you as the role model. I am so fortunate to have a Mother like you that I can pattern my decisions for my children. I am so blessed to have you as my Mother, I love You and I miss you.

Love,

# The BOOK OF MORMON for Latter-day Saint Families

# The BOOK OF MORMON for Latter-day Saint Families

GENERAL EDITOR
Thomas R. Valletta

ASSOCIATE EDITORS

Bruce L. Andreason
Randall C. Bird
Richard O. Christensen
Lee L. Donaldson
John L. Fowles
Brian D. Garner
Gordon B. Holbrook
Dennis H Leavitt
George R. Sims

Bookcraft
Salt Lake City, Utah

**Library of Congress Cataloging-in-Publication Data**

ISBN 1-57008-684-2

Printed in the United States of America 42316-4867

10 9 8 7 6

*In loving memory of President Ezra Taft Benson,*
*who challenged us to help "flood the earth with the Book of Mormon"*
*(in Conference Report, October 1988, 4).*

# Contents

# Introduction

## *To the Young Reader*

Welcome to *The Book of Mormon for Latter-day Saint Families!* This edition of the Book of Mormon was designed especially for families with young readers. It will help you read, understand, and think about the scriptures in exciting new ways.

You will notice right away that there are many beautiful pictures and drawings to help you understand what you are reading.

In addition to the pictures, several other kinds of help can be found on every page. Whenever you see a verse number that is **colored red**, look at the bottom of the page to find any of the helps described below. (Note that on pages xvii–xxv the helps are not linked to verse numbers. Instead, red-colored superscripted numbers like this [6] precede paragraphs that have helps at the bottom of the page.)

- Many words that may be hard to understand are colored blue. That means you will find help for those words at the bottom of that page next to this picture: . While the contributors recognize the inspired nature of Joseph Smith's translation of the Book of Mormon, in some cases they have offered word helps to clarify words that may be difficult for young readers. In no way should these word helps be considered an alternate translation or a "better" rendition of Book of Mormon language. Readers should recognize that words of the Book of Mormon text often have many meanings and that the word helps may not list all those possible meanings.

- Sometimes a verse is worth a closer look. Next to the picture of the magnifying glass  you will find helpful explanations about the meaning of a verse or about the history, the people, or the customs that make that verse interesting. Some of these explanations are drawn from the Bible or the Book of Mormon itself.

- Often we can gain a better understanding of a verse by comparing it with other scriptures that talk about the same truths. The Lord has told us many things in the Doctrine and Covenants and the Pearl of Great Price that help us understand the truths revealed in the Book of Mormon. Prophets, Apostles, and other General Authorities in our day also teach us many things to help us understand the scriptures better. Next to the picture of the sun  you will find more light from modern scripture and modern Church leaders. (Note that whenever a nonscriptural source is given in the text, the full publication information for that source can be found in the "Sources Cited" section at the back of the book.)

- Sometimes the best way to understand the scriptures is to ponder them. To *ponder* the scriptures means to stop and think and pray about what you are reading so that Heavenly Father can help you learn what He wants you to learn. Next to this picture  at the bottom of the page you will find some thoughts and questions that will help you ponder what you are reading.

Heavenly Father wants you to understand His plan for you. His plan is taught in the scriptures. The helps mentioned above are just some of the ways this book will help you understand and love the scriptures.

## *A Word to Parents*

The purpose of *The Book of Mormon for Latter-day Saint Families* is not to offer a rewriting of the Book of Mormon in more modern language. The text of the Book of Mormon has not been changed. The illustrations and the reading and understanding helps are designed to complement and not replace the official LDS edition of this sacred work. The intent of this volume is to help Latter-day Saints, and especially young readers, develop a lifelong love for the Book of Mormon.

In a discourse about the great value of the scriptures, President Ezra Taft Benson counseled priesthood leaders: "Bend your efforts and your activities to stimulating meaningful scripture study among the members of the Church. Often we spend great effort in trying to increase the activity levels in our stakes. We work diligently to raise the percentages of those attending sacrament meetings. We labor to get a higher percentage of our young men on missions. We strive to improve the numbers of those marrying in the temple. All of these are commendable efforts and important to the growth of the kingdom. But when individual members and families immerse themselves in the scriptures regularly and consistently, these other areas of activity will automatically come. Testimonies will increase. Commitment will be strengthened. Families will be fortified. Personal revelation will flow" ("The Power of the Word," 81).

In addition to the helpful features mentioned under the heading "To the Young Reader" above, this edition of the Book of Mormon provides several other kinds of help for your family:

- A **glossary** explains difficult terms and concepts, such as *Redeemer* and *Sanctification*. Words found in the glossary are **colored pink** in the text.

- **Book introductions** provide help in understanding the setting and purpose of every book in the Book of Mormon.

- **Chapter introductions** provide a brief overview of each chapter in simple English. They also offer suggestions of important things to look for to give purpose to family members' reading.

- **Topic headings** are provided in the text whenever the subject changes. These headings help the young reader follow the flow of the chapter without getting lost.

Helping our young people gain a love for reading the Book of Mormon will reap lifelong benefits. It will better prepare them to participate in Primary, Sunday School, priesthood quorums, the Young Women organization, seminary, missions, and every other aspect of Church service.

President Gordon B. Hinckley said: "Read to your children. Read the story of the Son of God. Read to them from the New Testament. Read to them from the Book of Mormon. It will take time, and you are very busy, but it will prove to be a great blessing in your lives as well as in their lives. And there will grow in their hearts a great love for the Savior of the world, the only perfect man who walked the earth. He will become to them a very real living being, and His great atoning sacrifice, as they grow to manhood and womanhood, will take on a new and more glorious meaning in their lives" ("Messages of Inspiration from President Hinckley," 2).

# KINDS OF HELPS FOUND IN *THE BOOK OF MORMON FOR LATTER-DAY SAINT FAMILIES*

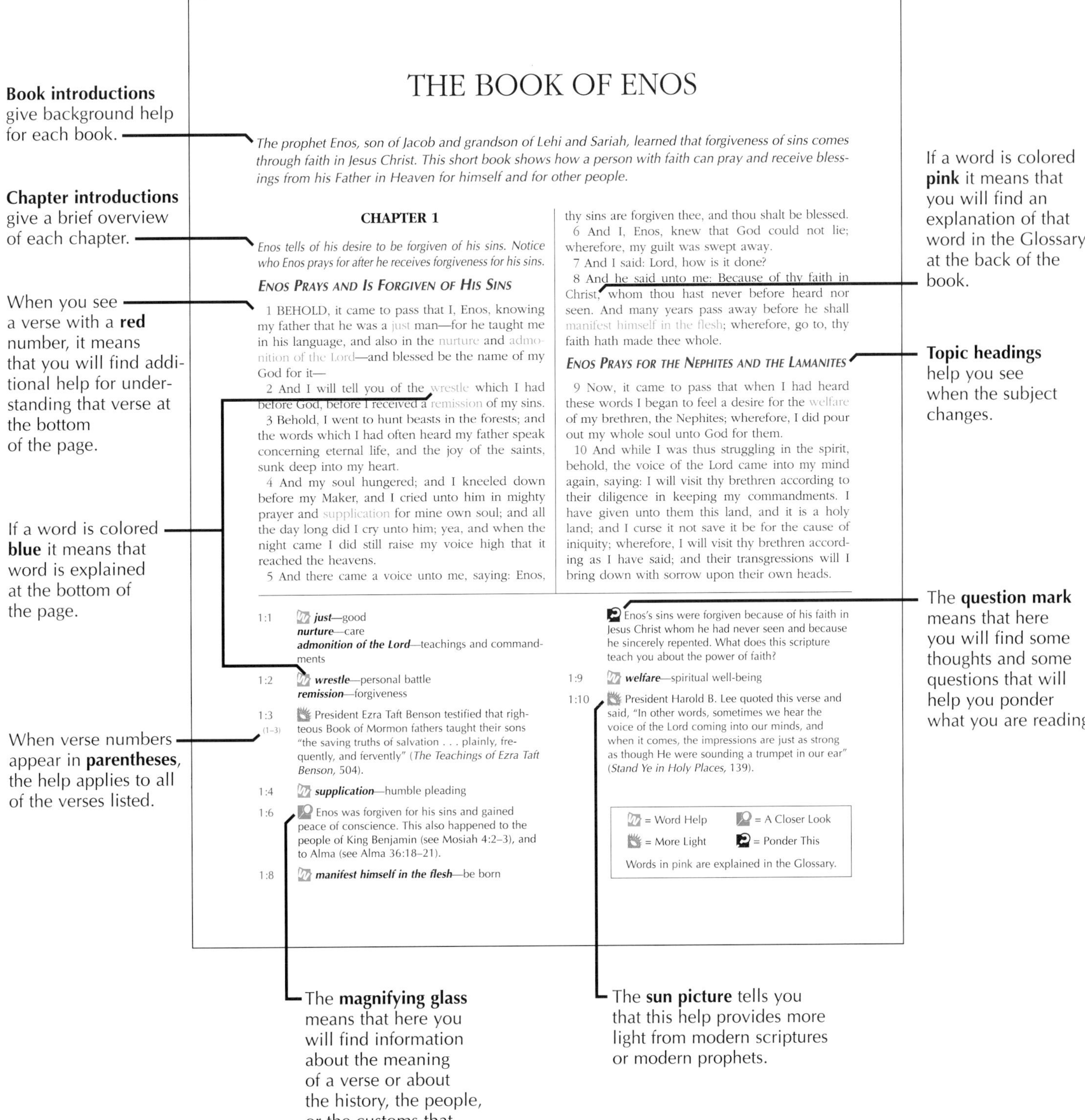


## THE BOOK OF ENOS

*The prophet Enos, son of Jacob and grandson of Lehi and Sariah, learned that forgiveness of sins comes through faith in Jesus Christ. This short book shows how a person with faith can pray and receive blessings from his Father in Heaven for himself and for other people.*

### CHAPTER 1

*Enos tells of his desire to be forgiven of his sins. Notice who Enos prays for after he receives forgiveness for his sins.*

#### *ENOS PRAYS AND IS FORGIVEN OF HIS SINS*

1 BEHOLD, it came to pass that I, Enos, knowing
my father that he was a just man—for he taught me
in his language, and also in the nurture and admonition of the Lord—and blessed be the name of my
God for it—
2 And I will tell you of the wrestle which I had
before God, before I received a remission of my sins.
3 Behold, I went to hunt beasts in the forests; and
the words which I had often heard my father speak
concerning eternal life, and the joy of the saints,
sunk deep into my heart.
4 And my soul hungered; and I kneeled down
before my Maker, and I cried unto him in mighty
prayer and supplication for mine own soul; and all
the day long did I cry unto him; yea, and when the
night came I did still raise my voice high that it
reached the heavens.
5 And there came a voice unto me, saying: Enos,
thy sins are forgiven thee, and thou shalt be blessed.
6 And I, Enos, knew that God could not lie;
wherefore, my guilt was swept away.
7 And I said: Lord, how is it done?
8 And he said unto me: Because of thy faith in
Christ, whom thou hast never before heard nor
seen. And many years pass away before he shall
manifest himself in the flesh; wherefore, go to, thy
faith hath made thee whole.

#### *ENOS PRAYS FOR THE NEPHITES AND THE LAMANITES*

9 Now, it came to pass that when I had heard
these words I began to feel a desire for the welfare
of my brethren, the Nephites; wherefore, I did pour
out my whole soul unto God for them.
10 And while I was thus struggling in the spirit,
behold, the voice of the Lord came into my mind
again, saying: I will visit thy brethren according to
their diligence in keeping my commandments. I
have given unto them this land, and it is a holy
land; and I curse it not save it be for the cause of
iniquity; wherefore, I will visit thy brethren according as I have said; and their transgressions will I
bring down with sorrow upon their own heads.

---

1:1 ***just***—good
***nurture***—care
***admonition of the Lord***—teachings and commandments

1:2 ***wrestle***—personal battle
***remission***—forgiveness

1:3 (1–3) President Ezra Taft Benson testified that righteous Book of Mormon fathers taught their sons "the saving truths of salvation . . . plainly, frequently, and fervently" (*The Teachings of Ezra Taft Benson*, 504).

1:4 ***supplication***—humble pleading

1:6 Enos was forgiven for his sins and gained peace of conscience. This also happened to the people of King Benjamin (see Mosiah 4:2–3), and to Alma (see Alma 36:18–21).

1:8 ***manifest himself in the flesh***—be born

Enos's sins were forgiven because of his faith in Jesus Christ whom he had never seen and because he sincerely repented. What does this scripture teach you about the power of faith?

1:9 ***welfare***—spiritual well-being

1:10 President Harold B. Lee quoted this verse and said, "In other words, sometimes we hear the voice of the Lord coming into our minds, and when it comes, the impressions are just as strong as though He were sounding a trumpet in our ear" (*Stand Ye in Holy Places*, 139).

= Word Help = A Closer Look
= More Light = Ponder This
Words in pink are explained in the Glossary.

JOSEPH SMITH TRANSLATING THE BOOK OF MORMON, BY DEL PARSON

*The Book of Mormon was translated by Joseph Smith from the gold plates.
Oliver Cowdery acted as Joseph's scribe.*

# Overview of the Book of Mormon

From the very first page of the Book of Mormon we learn that Heavenly Father gave us this book for at least three reasons: 1) to teach us that Jesus Christ really is the Son of God; 2) to teach us of the promises (covenants) the Lord has given His children; and 3) to teach us about the great blessings and even miracles the Lord has provided for His children. In essence, all of the stories and teachings you will read in the Book of Mormon are there to remind us of these three things (see title page of the Book of Mormon; 2 Nephi 6:12; 25:26; Mosiah 25:7–8).

The Book of Mormon begins with the story of the prophet Lehi and his family. They lived in the city of Jerusalem about six hundred years before the birth of Jesus Christ. Lehi is commanded to take his family and go into the wilderness to escape the destruction that will come upon Jerusalem because of wickedness. The Lord guides Lehi's family over the ocean to a land of promise in the Americas. From this family come two very different nations.

- The **Nephites,** in the beginning, believe in Jesus Christ and are the more righteous group.
- The **Lamanites**, in the beginning, rebel against God and become the enemies of the Nephites.

Although the Nephites and the Lamanites pass through varying periods of righteousness and wickedness, in the end the Nephites are destroyed because, despite their knowledge of the truth, they choose to disobey. The Lamanites are spared because they sin without knowing the truth.

Two other groups of people become part of the Book of Mormon story.

- The **people of Zarahemla** (sometimes called the Mulekites) leave Jerusalem about ten years after Lehi. They join the Nephites.
- The **Jaredites** are led to the Americas around the time of the Tower of Babel, almost two thousand years before Lehi's time. They completely destroy themselves in terrible wars. The last survivor of these people is found by the people of Zarahemla.

The Book of Mormon tells about the lives, testimonies, successes, and failures of these groups of people. Their experiences teach us over and over again that when people are righteous they are happy and blessed, but when they choose not to keep the commandments the Lord will not bless them and they suffer.

In the Book of Mormon you will read the words of many great prophets, such as Nephi, Jacob, Alma, Samuel, and Helaman. They teach about Heavenly Father's plan for us more clearly than the Bible does. The most important event you will read about in the Book of Mormon is Jesus Christ's personal visit to the Nephites. After His death and Resurrection in Jerusalem, Jesus came to the Nephites and set up His Church among them. He taught them many things that He was not able to tell the people in Jerusalem because of their wickedness. Because of the Savior's visit and the truths He taught them, the Book of Mormon people were united and lived in righteousness and peace for the next two hundred years.

Later, when the people became wicked again, terrible wars began. Mormon, one of the last Nephite prophets, searched through the records and put the writings we needed most into one set of gold plates called the Book of Mormon. He gave those plates to his son Moroni just before the Nephites were destroyed by the Lamanites in a great war. Moroni finished the story of the destruction of his people and hid the plates in the Hill Cumorah. It was this same Moroni who came to the Prophet Joseph Smith in 1823 and showed him where the plates were buried. Joseph Smith translated the plates by the gift and power of God, and that is how we got the Book of Mormon.

To help us understand the importance of the Book of Mormon, the Prophet Joseph Smith said, "I told the brethren that the Book of Mormon was the most correct of any book on earth, and the keystone of our religion, and a man would get nearer to God by abiding by its precepts [teachings], than by any other book" (*Teachings of the Prophet Joseph Smith,* 194).

A *keystone* is the last stone set in place in an arch. It is the stone that holds the arch together. That is what the Book of Mormon does for the Church. The Lord has promised that anyone who sincerely reads the Book of Mormon and prays about it can know by the power of the Holy Ghost that it is true (see Moroni 10:4-5). The Book of Mormon is also proof to the world that Joseph Smith truly is a prophet of God. Because Joseph Smith is a true prophet, the Church the Lord commanded him to organize really is the true Church of Jesus Christ.

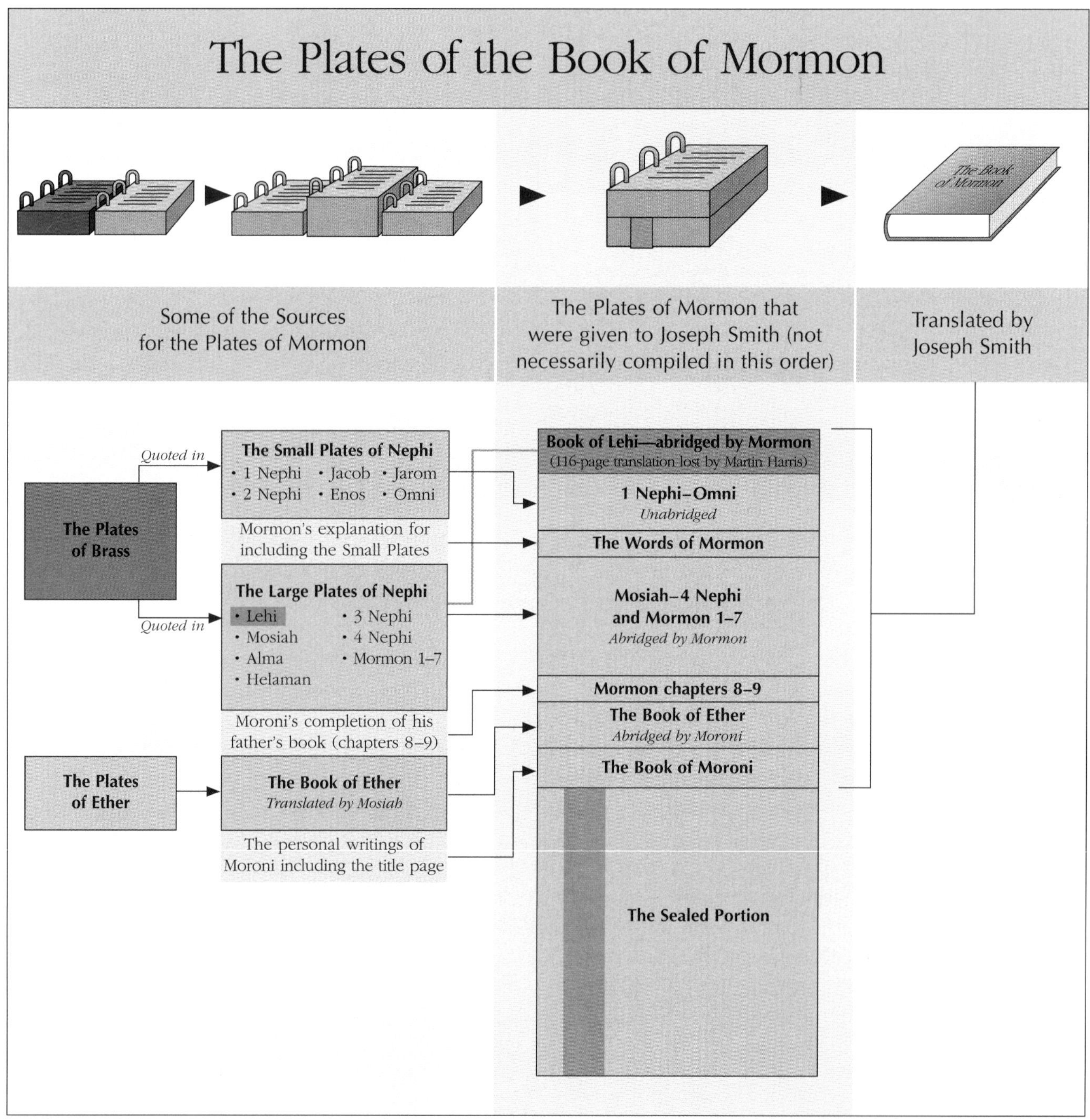

# The Book of Mormon

# Another Testament of Jesus Christ

# The Testimonies of Three Witnesses and Eight Witnesses

*These testimonies are an example of an important gospel principle: Whenever God sends vital truths to the earth, He always provides two or more witnesses that these truths come from Him. Notice the differences between what the two sets of witnesses saw and heard.*

## *The Testimony of Three Witnesses*

[1]BE it known unto all nations, kindreds, tongues, and people, unto whom this work shall come: That we, through the grace of God the Father, and our Lord Jesus Christ, have seen the plates which contain this record, which is a record of the people of Nephi, and also of the Lamanites, their brethren, and also of the people of Jared, who came from the tower of which hath been spoken. And we also know that they have been translated by the gift and power of God, for his voice hath declared it unto us; wherefore we know of a surety that the work is true. And we also testify that we have seen the engravings which are upon the plates; and they have been shown unto us by the power of God, and not of man. And we declare with words of soberness, that an angel of God came down from heaven, and he brought and laid before our eyes, that we beheld and saw the plates, and the engravings thereon; and we know that it is by the grace of God the Father, and our Lord Jesus Christ, that we beheld and bear record that these things are true. And it is marvelous in our eyes. Nevertheless, the voice of the Lord commanded us that we should bear record of it; wherefore, to be obedient unto the commandments of God, we bear testimony of these things. And we know that if we are faithful in Christ, we shall rid our garments of the blood of all men, and be found spotless before the judgment-seat of Christ, and shall dwell with him eternally in the heavens. And the honor be to the Father, and to the Son, and to the Holy Ghost, which is one God. Amen.

Oliver Cowdery
David Whitmer
Martin Harris

---

1 ***kindreds***—family groups
***engravings***—words carved or etched
***soberness***—seriousness
***found spotless***—judged to be without sin

"Rid our garments of the blood of all men" is a phrase that means to not be responsible for other people's sins.

*The Three Witnesses testified that they had, by the power of God, seen the gold plates.*

## THE TESTIMONY OF EIGHT WITNESSES

2BE it known unto all nations, kindreds, tongues, and people, unto whom this work shall come: That Joseph Smith, Jun., the translator of this work, has shown unto us the plates of which hath been spoken, which have the appearance of gold; and as many of the leaves as the said Smith has translated we did handle with our hands; and we also saw the engravings thereon, all of which has the appearance of ancient work, and of curious workmanship. And this we bear record with words of soberness, that the said Smith has shown unto us, for we have seen and hefted, and know of a surety that the said Smith has got the plates of which we have spoken. And we give our names unto the world, to witness unto the world that which we have seen. And we lie not, God bearing witness of it.

| | |
|---|---|
| CHRISTIAN WHITMER | HIRAM PAGE |
| JACOB WHITMER | JOSEPH SMITH, SEN. |
| PETER WHITMER, JUN. | HYRUM SMITH |
| JOHN WHITMER | SAMUEL H. SMITH |

2 ***kindreds***—family groups
***engravings***—words carved or etched
***curious workmanship***—skillful work
***soberness***—seriousness
***hefted***—lifted

The Three Witnesses had a miraculous experience when they saw the plates. The Eight Witnesses saw the plates without any accompanying miracles. How do the differences between these two experiences make the men's testimonies more convincing and powerful?

# The Testimony of the Prophet Joseph Smith

*In the account that follows, the Prophet Joseph Smith explains how he was given the gold plates by the angel Moroni. Look for what the angel said would happen to Joseph because of the work God had for him to do.*

## *The Angel Moroni Appears to Joseph*

[1]"ON the evening of the . . . twenty-first of September [1823] . . . I betook myself to prayer and supplication to Almighty God. . . .

[2]"While I was thus in the act of calling upon God, I discovered a light appearing in my room, which continued to increase until the room was lighter than at noonday, when immediately a personage appeared at my bedside, standing in the air, for his feet did not touch the floor.

"He had on a loose robe of most exquisite whiteness. It was a whiteness beyond anything earthly I had ever seen; nor do I believe that any earthly thing could be made to appear so exceedingly white and brilliant. His hands were naked, and his arms also, a little above the wrists; so, also, were his feet naked, as were his legs, a little above the ankles. His head and neck were also bare. I could discover that he had no other clothing on but this robe, as it was open, so that I could see into his bosom.

[3]"Not only was his robe exceedingly white, but his whole person was glorious beyond description, and his countenance truly like lightning. The room was exceedingly light, but not so very bright as immediately around his person. When I first looked upon him, I was afraid; but the fear soon left me.

[4]"He called me by name, and said unto me that he was a messenger sent from the presence of God to me, and that his name was Moroni; that God had a work for me to do; and that my name should be had for good and evil among all nations, kindreds, and tongues, or that it should be both good and evil spoken of among all people.

[5]"He said there was a book deposited, written upon gold plates, giving an account of the former inhabitants of this continent, and the source from whence they sprang. He also said that the fulness of the everlasting Gospel was contained in it, as delivered by the Savior to the ancient inhabitants;

"Also, that there were two stones in silver bows—and these stones, fastened to a breastplate, constituted what is called the Urim and Thummim—deposited with the plates; and the possession and use of these stones were what constituted *Seers* in ancient or former times; and that God had prepared them for the purpose of translating the book. . . .

---

1 ***betook***—applied
***supplication to***—humbly asking or appealing to

2 ***personage***—person

3 ***countenance***—appearance

4 This is an amazing prophecy. At this time Joseph Smith Jr. was just a seventeen-year-old boy with very little formal education. He was from a poor family living on a small farm, far away from any important cities. There was very little chance of his name being known all over the world, and yet today in almost every land people speak of Joseph Smith the Prophet.

5 ***former inhabitants of this continent***—people who used to live in the Americas
***ancient***—old

THE ANGEL MORONI APPEARS TO JOSEPH SMITH, BY TOM LOVELL

*The angel Moroni appeared to Joseph Smith in his room on September 21, 1823.*

6"Again, he told me, that when I got those plates of which he had spoken—for the time that they should be obtained was not yet fulfilled—I should not show them to any person; neither the breastplate with the Urim and Thummim; only to those to whom I should be commanded to show them; if I did I should be destroyed. While he was conversing with me about the plates, the vision was opened to my mind that I could see the place where the plates were deposited, and that so clearly and distinctly that I knew the place again when I visited it.

7"After this communication, I saw the light in the room begin to gather immediately around the person of him who had been speaking to me, and it continued to do so, until the room was again left dark, except just around him, when instantly I saw, as it were, a conduit open right up into heaven, and he ascended until he entirely disappeared, and the room was left as it had been before this heavenly light had made its appearance.

### The Angel Moroni Appears to Joseph a Second and a Third Time

8"I lay musing on the singularity of the scene, and marveling greatly at what had been told to me by this extraordinary messenger; when, in the midst of my meditation, I suddenly discovered that my room was again beginning to get lighted, and in an instant, as it were, the same heavenly messenger was again by my bedside.

9"He commenced, and again related the very same things which he had done at his first visit, without the least variation; which having done, he informed me of great judgments which were coming upon the earth, with great desolations by famine, sword, and pestilence; and that these grievous judgments would come on the earth in this generation. Having related these things, he again ascended as he had done before.

10"By this time, so deep were the impressions made on my mind, that sleep had fled from my eyes, and I lay overwhelmed in astonishment at what I had both seen and heard. But what was my surprise when again I beheld the same messenger at my bedside, and heard him rehearse or repeat over again to me the same things as before; and added a caution to me, telling me that Satan would try to tempt me (in consequence of the indigent circumstances of my father's family), to get the plates for the purpose of getting rich. This he forbade me, saying that I must have no other object in view in getting the plates but to glorify God, and must not be influenced by any other motive than that of building his kingdom; otherwise I could not get them.

"After this third visit, he again ascended into heaven as before, and I was again left to ponder on the strangeness of what I had just experienced; when almost immediately after the heavenly messenger had ascended from me the third time, the cock crowed, and I found that day was approaching, so that our interviews must have occupied the whole of that night.

---

6 ***deposited***—buried

7 ***conduit***—shaft or pillar of light

8 ***musing on the singularity***—thinking about the unusual nature
***meditation***—thinking and pondering

9 ***variation***—change
The angel Moroni prophesied that great destructions would come to the earth, including famine (hunger), war, and pestilence (disease). He said they would occur in "this generation," meaning between Joseph's day and the Second Coming of the Savior.

10 ***overwhelmed in astonishment***—overcome by surprise
***in consequence of the indigent circumstances of my father's family***—because my father's family was so poor
***be influenced by any other motive***—have any other purpose

## Joseph Goes to the Hill Cumorah

"I shortly after arose from my bed, and, as usual, went to the necessary labors of the day; but, in attempting to work as at other times, I found my strength so exhausted as to render me entirely unable. My father, who was laboring along with me, discovered something to be wrong with me, and told me to go home. I started with the intention of going to the house; but, in attempting to cross the fence out of the field where we were, my strength entirely failed me, and I fell helpless on the ground, and for a time was quite unconscious of anything.

"The first thing that I can recollect was a voice speaking unto me, calling me by name. I looked up, and beheld the same messenger standing over my head, surrounded by light as before. He then again related unto me all that he had related to me the previous night, and commanded me to go to my father and tell him of the vision and commandments which I had received.

"I obeyed; I returned to my father in the field, and rehearsed the whole matter to him. He replied to me that it was of God, and told me to go and do as commanded by the messenger. I left the field, and went to the place where the messenger had told me the plates were deposited; and owing to the distinctness of the vision which I had had concerning it, I knew the place the instant that I arrived there.

[11]"Convenient to the village of Manchester, Ontario county, New York, stands a hill of considerable size, and the most elevated of any in the neighborhood. On the west side of this hill, not far from the top, under a stone of considerable size, lay the plates, deposited in a stone box. This stone was thick and rounding in the middle on the upper side, and thinner towards the edges, so that the middle part of it was visible above the ground, but the edge all around was covered with earth.

[12]"Having removed the earth, I obtained a lever, which I got fixed under the edge of the stone, and with a little exertion raised it up. I looked in, and there indeed did I behold the plates, the Urim and Thummim, and the breastplate, as stated by the messenger. The box in which they lay was formed by laying stones together in some kind of cement. In the bottom of the box were laid two stones crossways of the box, and on these stones lay the plates and the other things with them.

"I made an attempt to take them out, but was forbidden by the messenger, and was again informed that the time for bringing them forth had not yet arrived, neither would it, until four years from that time; but he told me that I should come to that place precisely in one year from that time, and that he would there meet with me, and that I should continue to do so until the time should come for obtaining the plates.

"Accordingly, as I had been commanded, I went at the end of each year, and at each time I found the same messenger there, and

11 **Convenient to**—Near
**most elevated**—highest

12 **exertion**—effort

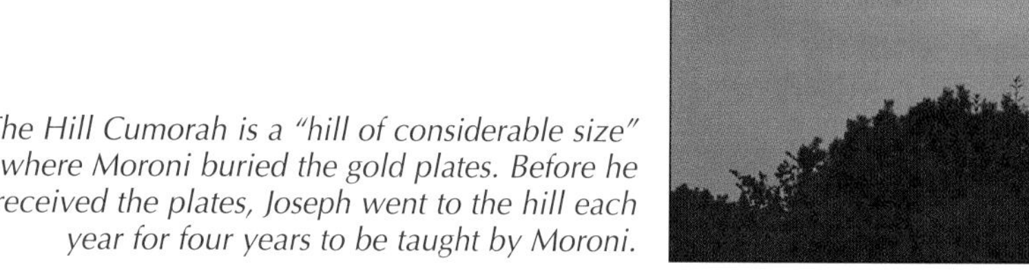

*The Hill Cumorah is a "hill of considerable size" where Moroni buried the gold plates. Before he received the plates, Joseph went to the hill each year for four years to be taught by Moroni.*

received instruction and intelligence from him at each of our interviews, respecting what the Lord was going to do, and how and in what manner His kingdom was to be conducted in the last days. . . .

## Joseph Receives the Plates

"At length the time arrived for obtaining the plates, the Urim and Thummim, and the breastplate. On the twenty-second day of September, one thousand eight hundred and twenty-seven, having gone as usual at the end of another year to the place where they were deposited, the same heavenly messenger delivered them up to me with this charge: That I should be responsible for them; that if I should let them go carelessly, or through any neglect of mine, I should be cut off; but that if I would use all my endeavors to preserve them, until he, the messenger, should call for them, they should be protected.

13"I soon found out the reason why I had received such strict charges to keep them safe, and why it was that the messenger had said that when I had done what was required at my hand, he would call for them. For no sooner was it known that I had them, than the most strenuous exertions were used to get them from me. Every stratagem that could be invented was resorted to for that purpose. The persecution became more bitter and severe than before, and multitudes were on the alert continually to get them from me if possible. But by the wisdom of God, they remained safe in my hands, until I had accomplished by them what was required at my hand. When, according to arrangements, the messenger called for them, I delivered them up to him; and he has them in his charge until this day, being the second day of May, one thousand eight hundred and thirty-eight."

*The preceding account can be found in HISTORY OF THE CHURCH 1:10–12, 13–16, 18–19, and also in Joseph Smith—History 1:29–35, 42–54, 59–60 in the Pearl of Great Price.*

---

13 W ***most strenuous exertions***—greatest efforts
***strategem***—clever plan

THE SAVIOR, BY DEL PARSON

*The Book of Mormon was written to convince the world that Jesus is the Christ.*

THE

# BOOK OF MORMON

AN ACCOUNT WRITTEN BY

# THE HAND OF MORMON

UPON PLATES
TAKEN FROM THE PLATES OF NEPHI*

### *Moroni Explains How and Why the Book of Mormon Was Written*

1 WHEREFORE, it is an abridgment of the record of the people of Nephi, and also of the Lamanites—Written to the Lamanites, who are a remnant of the house of Israel; and also to Jew and Gentile—Written by way of commandment, and also by the spirit of prophecy and of revelation—Written and sealed up, and hid up unto the Lord, that they might not be destroyed—To come forth by the gift and power of God unto the interpretation thereof—Sealed by the hand of Moroni, and hid up unto the lord, to come forth in due time by way of the Gentile—The interpretation thereof by the gift of God.

2 An abridgment taken from the Book of Ether also, which is a record of the people of Jared, who were scattered at the time the Lord confounded the language of the people, when they were building a tower to get to heaven—Which is to show unto the remnant of the House of Israel what great things the Lord hath done for their fathers; and that they may know the covenants of the Lord, that they are not cast off forever—And also to the convincing of the Jew and Gentile that JESUS is the CHRIST, the ETERNAL GOD, manifesting himself unto all nations—And now, if there are faults they are the mistakes of men; wherefore, condemn not the things of God, that ye may be found spotless at the judgment-seat of Christ.

TRANSLATED BY
JOSEPH SMITH, JUN.

---

* The title page was written by Moroni, the son of Mormon, about four hundred years after the birth of Jesus Christ. It was Moroni who came as an angel to the Prophet Joseph Smith in 1823 to tell him where the plates were buried. Joseph Smith translated the title page from the last page of the plates he received from Moroni. Notice the three purposes Moroni gives for the Book of Mormon.

1 ***an abridgment***—a shortened version
***remnant***—group who are left

Moroni tells us that the Book of Mormon was written by inspiration and revelation from God. The Bible was also written by prophets (see 2 Peter 1:20-21). One difference between the Bible and the Book of Mormon is what happened to them after the prophets finished writing them. None of the original books of the Bible exist today. We have only copies and translations made by people who were not prophets. The Book of Mormon is different. God called the Prophet Joseph Smith to be the only one to translate the gold plates and to do so by the "gift and power of God."

The spirit of prophecy is the testimony of Jesus (see Revelation 19:10). You will learn the most from your reading of the Book of Mormon by remembering and seeing Jesus throughout the book.

2 Moroni lists three reasons why God has given us the Book of Mormon. The third reason is to convince or prove to all people that "Jesus is the Christ." As you read the Book of Mormon, look for all the different ways it teaches us about Jesus Christ.

# THE FIRST BOOK OF NEPHI

## HIS REIGN AND MINISTRY

*Nephi, the son of Lehi, wrote 1 Nephi. He tells of Lehi's family leaving their home (about six hundred years before the time of the Savior's birth) and traveling through the wilderness and across an ocean to the promised land. Nephi's purpose in writing was to "persuade men to come unto the God of Abraham, and the God of Isaac, and the God of Jacob, and be saved" (1 Nephi 6:4).*

*An account of Lehi and his wife Sariah, and his four sons, being called, (beginning at the eldest) Laman, Lemuel, Sam, and Nephi. The Lord warns Lehi to depart out of the land of Jerusalem, because he prophesieth unto the people concerning their iniquity and they seek to destroy his life. He taketh three days' journey into the wilderness with his family. Nephi taketh his brethren and returneth to the land of Jerusalem after the record of the Jews. The account of their sufferings. They take the daughters of Ishmael to wife. They take their families and depart into the wilderness. Their sufferings and afflictions in the wilderness. The course of their travels. They come to the large waters, Nephi's brethren rebel against him. He confoundeth them, and buildeth a ship. They call the name of the place Bountiful. They cross the large waters into the promised land, and so forth. This is according to the account of Nephi; or in other words, I, Nephi, wrote this record.*

### CHAPTER 1

*Nephi describes his father's visions while in Jerusalem. Look for how God calls Lehi, Nephi's father, to be a prophet.*

#### NEPHI BEGINS HIS RECORD

1 I, Nephi, having been born of goodly parents, therefore I was taught somewhat in all the learning of my father; and having seen many afflictions in the course of my days, nevertheless, having been highly favored of the Lord in all my days; yea, having had a great knowledge of the goodness and the mysteries of God, therefore I make a record of my proceedings in my days.
2 Yea, I make a record in the language of my father, which consists of the learning of the Jews and the language of the Egyptians.
3 And I know that the record which I make is true; and I make it with mine own hand; and I make it according to my knowledge.

#### LEHI PRAYS FOR HIS PEOPLE

4 For it came to pass in the commencement of the first year of the reign of Zedekiah, king of Judah, (my father, Lehi, having dwelt at Jerusalem in all his days); and in that same year there came many prophets, prophesying unto the people that they must repent, or the great city Jerusalem must be destroyed.

---

1:1 ***afflictions***—trials and suffering
***mysteries of God***—truths that cannot be known except through revelation from the Lord
***proceedings***—experiences

Nephi says he had "goodly parents." This means, among other things, that his father and mother were righteous people. What is "goodly" about your parents? Nephi also states that he was highly favored of the Lord, who blessed him throughout his life with revelations, visions, and the Spirit. What blessings have you received from the Lord to help you in your life?

1:2 It is clear from this and other verses that the Nephites were familiar with some form of both the Egyptian and the Hebrew languages (see Mosiah 1:4; Mormon 9:32–33). The Prophet Joseph Smith stated that he "translated the Book of Mormon from hieroglyphics [ancient Egyptian writing], the knowledge of which was lost to the world" (*History of the Church* 6:74; see also Joseph Smith, "Church History," 707).

1:4 ***commencement***—beginning

King Zedekiah began his reign about 600 B.C. (see 1 Nephi 10:4).

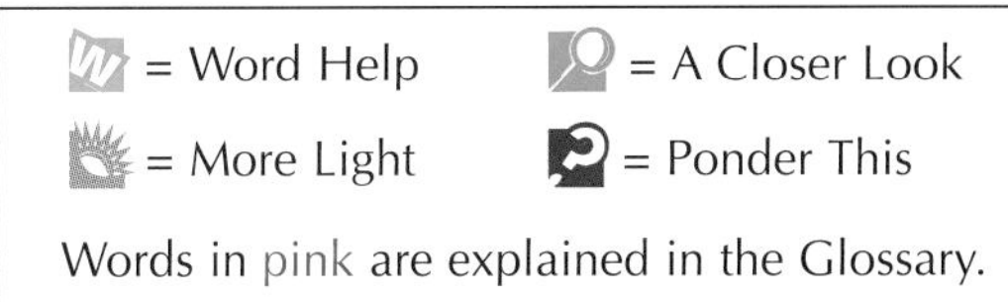

LEHI PREACHING IN JERUSALEM, BY DEL PARSON

*Lehi prophesies and calls the people of Jerusalem to repentance.*

5 Wherefore it came to pass that my father, Lehi, as he went forth prayed unto the Lord, yea, even with all his heart, in behalf of his people.

### *Lehi Sees in Vision a Pillar of Fire and Reads from a Book of Prophecy*

6 And it came to pass as he prayed unto the Lord, there came a pillar of fire and dwelt upon a rock before him; and he saw and heard much; and because of the things which he saw and heard he did quake and tremble exceedingly.

7 And it came to pass that he returned to his own house at Jerusalem; and he cast himself upon his bed, being overcome with the Spirit and the things which he had seen.

8 And being thus overcome with the Spirit, he was carried away in a vision, even that he saw the heavens open, and he thought he saw God sitting upon his throne, surrounded with numberless concourses of angels in the attitude of singing and praising their God.

9 And it came to pass that he saw One descending out of the midst of heaven, and he beheld that his luster was above that of the sun at noon-day.

10 And he also saw twelve others following him, and their brightness did exceed that of the stars in the firmament.

11 And they came down and went forth upon the face of the earth; and the first came and stood before my father, and gave unto him a book, and bade him that he should read.

---

1:6 A pillar, or column, of fire has often been used by the Lord in giving miraculous visions, guidance, and protection to His faithful followers (see Exodus 13:21–22; 14:24; Helaman 5:24, 43).

***exceedingly***—very much

1:8 ***concourses***—gatherings

1:9 ***descending***—coming down
***luster***—brightness

12 And it came to pass that as he read, he was
filled with the Spirit of the Lord.
13 And he read, saying: Wo, wo, unto Jerusalem,
for I have seen thine abominations! Yea, and many
things did my father read concerning Jerusalem—
that it should be destroyed, and the inhabitants
thereof; many should perish by the sword, and
many should be carried away captive into Babylon.
14 And it came to pass that when my father had
read and seen many great and marvelous things, he
did exclaim many things unto the Lord; such as:
Great and marvelous are thy works, O Lord God
Almighty! Thy throne is high in the heavens, and
thy power, and goodness, and mercy are over all
the inhabitants of the earth; and, because thou art
merciful, thou wilt not suffer those who come unto
thee that they shall perish!
15 And after this manner was the language of my
father in the praising of his God; for his soul did
rejoice, and his whole heart was filled, because of
the things which he had seen, yea, which the Lord
had shown unto him.
16 And now I, Nephi, do not make a full account
of the things which my father hath written, for he
hath written many things which he saw in visions
and in dreams; and he also hath written many
things which he prophesied and spake unto his
children, of which I shall not make a full account.

## Lehi Prophesies of the Destruction of Jerusalem

17 But I shall make an account of my proceedings
in my days. Behold, I make an abridgment of the
record of my father, upon plates which I have made
with mine own hands; wherefore, after I have
abridged the record of my father then will I make
an account of mine own life.
18 Therefore, I would that ye should know, that
after the Lord had shown so many marvelous things
unto my father, Lehi, yea, concerning the destruction
of Jerusalem, behold he went forth among the
people, and began to prophesy and to declare unto
them concerning the things which he had both seen
and heard.
19 And it came to pass that the Jews did mock
him because of the things which he testified of
them; for he truly testified of their wickedness and
their abominations; and he testified that the things
which he saw and heard, and also the things which
he read in the book, manifested plainly of the coming
of a Messiah, and also the redemption of the
world.
20 And when the Jews heard these things they
were angry with him; yea, even as with the
prophets of old, whom they had cast out, and
stoned, and slain; and they also sought his life, that

---

1:12 Notice that as Lehi read the book of prophecy "he was filled with the Spirit of the Lord." How does studying the scriptures make you feel?

1:13 ***Wo***—Grief, sorrow, and misery
***abominations***—acts of great evil
***perish***—die

1:14 The Lord is full of goodness and mercy. His hand is always outstretched and ready to receive those who come unto Him (see Matthew 11:28–30).

1:17 ***an abridgment***—a shortened version

1:18 The Lord showed Lehi "marvelous things" about the destruction of Jerusalem. In 1828, when Joseph Smith was busy translating the Book of Mormon, the word *marvelous* could be used to describe something that was "strange" or that excited "wonder or some degree of surprise" (Noah Webster, *An American Dictionary of the English Language* [1828], s.v. "Marvelous").

1:19 (4–19) Notice that Lehi's prophetic call follows the same pattern as the calls of many prophets in the scriptures. As Jeffrey R. Holland outlines it, Lehi "prays, has a vision, sees heavenly messengers (apparently including Jesus), receives a book, [and] is rejected by most of the people" (see "Daddy, Donna, and Nephi," 9).

1:20 Lehi testified of the people's wickedness and they became angry with him. This often happens when prophets testify of people's sins (see Helaman 13:26).

Nephi tells us that the theme of his record is to show the Lord's tender mercies over all those whom He has chosen. What examples of the Lord's tender mercies do you see in your own life?

1:20 (19–20) The term *Jew* often refers to a descendant from the tribe of Judah. However, the Book of Mormon also uses the term *Jew* to refer to any Israelite from the land or kingdom of Judah, even if not descended from the tribe of Judah (see LDS Bible Dictionary, s.v. "Jew," 713). In addition, the Book of Mormon uses the term *Jew* sometimes to refer to the entire house of Israel (see *Book of Mormon Student Manual, Religion 121 and 122,* 15).

LEHI'S FAMILY LEAVING JERUSALEM, BY SCOTT SNOW

*The Lord warned Lehi in a dream to "take his family and depart into the wilderness."*

they might take it away. But behold, I, Nephi, will show unto you that the tender mercies of the Lord are over all those whom he hath chosen, because of their faith, to make them mighty even unto the power of deliverance.

## CHAPTER 2

*Lehi's family leave their home to travel in the wilderness. Look for ways that Lehi and Nephi are obedient to Heavenly Father.*

### *Lehi Obeys the Lord's Command to Leave Jerusalem*

1 FOR behold, it came to pass that the Lord spake unto my father, yea, even in a dream, and said unto him: Blessed art thou Lehi, because of the things which thou hast done; and because thou hast been faithful and declared unto this people the things which I commanded thee, behold, they seek to take away thy life.

2 And it came to pass that the Lord commanded my father, even in a dream, that he should take his family and depart into the wilderness.

2:2 **_wilderness_**—wild land with very few people

LEHI BUILDING AN ALTAR OF STONES IN THE VALLEY OF LEMUEL, BY CLARK KELLEY PRICE

*Lehi built an altar and "gave thanks unto the Lord."*

3 And it came to pass that he was obedient unto
the word of the Lord, wherefore he did as the Lord
commanded him.
4 And it came to pass that he departed into the
wilderness. And he left his house, and the land of
his inheritance, and his gold, and his silver, and his
precious things, and took nothing with him, save it
were his family, and provisions, and tents, and
departed into the wilderness.
5 And he came down by the borders near the
shore of the Red Sea; and he traveled in the wilderness in the borders which are nearer the Red Sea;
and he did travel in the wilderness with his family,
which consisted of my mother, Sariah, and my elder

2:4 ***provisions***—supplies and food

Lehi and his family would journey in the wilderness for eight years (see 1 Nephi 17:4).

2:4 (2–4) Think of how difficult it would be to leave your house and friends, pack up your possessions, and move into the desert. What does this teach you about Lehi's faith? What difficult commandment have you obeyed?

PHOTOGRAPH BY DAVID H. GARNER

*Lehi "did travel in the wilderness with his family" in the borders near the Red Sea.*

brothers, who were Laman, Lemuel, and Sam.
6 And it came to pass that when he had traveled
three days in the wilderness, he pitched his tent in
a valley by the side of a river of water.
7 And it came to pass that he built an altar of
stones, and made an offering unto the Lord, and
gave thanks unto the Lord our God.
8 And it came to pass that he called the name of the
river, Laman, and it emptied into the Red Sea; and the
valley was in the borders near the mouth thereof.

### Lehi Counsels Laman and Lemuel to Be Faithful

9 And when my father saw that the waters of the
river emptied into the fountain of the Red Sea, he
spake unto Laman, saying: O that thou mightest be
like unto this river, continually running into the
fountain of all righteousness!
10 And he also spake unto Lemuel: O that thou mightest be like unto this valley, firm and steadfast, and
immovable in keeping the commandments of the Lord!
11 Now this he spake because of the stiffneckedness of Laman and Lemuel; for behold they did
murmur in many things against their father, because
he was a visionary man, and had led them out of
the land of Jerusalem, to leave the land of their
inheritance, and their gold, and their silver, and
their precious things, to perish in the wilderness.
And this they said he had done because of the foolish imaginations of his heart.
12 And thus Laman and Lemuel, being the eldest,
did murmur against their father. And they did murmur because they knew not the dealings of that
God who had created them.
13 Neither did they believe that Jerusalem, that
great city, could be destroyed according to the
words of the prophets. And they were like unto the
Jews who were at Jerusalem, who sought to take
away the life of my father.
14 And it came to pass that my father did speak
unto them in the valley of Lemuel, with power,
being filled with the Spirit, until their frames did
shake before him. And he did confound them, that
they durst not utter against him; wherefore, they did
as he commanded them.
15 And my father dwelt in a tent.

---

2:7 It may seem easier to refer to the "altar of stones" as a "stone altar." However, the way it is said in this verse is typical of the Hebrew language Nephi knew. Watch for other similar wording as you read the Book of Mormon (for example, see 1 Nephi 1:6; 3:3, 11, 26). This is another testimony that Joseph Smith translated the Book of Mormon by the gift and power of God.

2:9 ***fountain***—source of water

"The fountain of all righteousness" is another title for the Savior (see Ether 8:26; 12:28; Jeremiah 23:6).

2:10 Lehi's words, though possibly strange-sounding to modern Americans, fit well the feelings of those living in the deserts of the Near East. To them, the valleys, more than the mountains, represent firmness, faithfulness, safety, and that which is long lasting (see Hugh Nibley, *Lehi in the Desert,* 91–92).

2:11 ***stiffneckedness***—stubbornness or rebelliousness
***murmur***—complain or grumble
***the land of their inheritance***—the land belonging to Lehi's family

Laman and Lemuel call their father "a visionary man." They mean this in a negative and insulting way. Why do you think some people criticize and make fun of righteous men who receive revelation from the Lord?

2:13 Nephi compares Laman and Lemuel to the Jews at Jerusalem who tried to kill Lehi. Other scriptures teach us how very wicked these two brothers were (see 1 Nephi 7:16; 16:37; 17:48; 2 Nephi 5:1–2).

2:15 In the ancient Near East, to dwell in a tent was considered a great honor, especially compared to living in a house in the city. It represented living close to and trusting in the Lord. Also, the father's tent was considered the center of the whole community (see Hugh Nibley, *An Approach to the Book of Mormon,* 243; see also Hugh Nibley, *Lehi in the Desert,* 51–52).

PHOTOGRAPH BY DAVID H. GARNER

*"My father dwelt in a tent."*

### *Nephi Is Chosen by the Lord to Rule Over His Brethren*

16 And it came to pass that I, Nephi, being exceedingly young, nevertheless being large in stature, and also having great desires to know of the mysteries of God, wherefore, I did cry unto the Lord; and behold he did visit me, and did soften my heart that I did believe all the words which had been spoken by my father; wherefore, I did not rebel against him like unto my brothers.

17 And I spake unto Sam, making known unto him the things which the Lord had manifested unto me by his Holy Spirit. And it came to pass that he believed in my words.

18 But, behold, Laman and Lemuel would not hearken unto my words; and being grieved because of the hardness of their hearts I cried unto the Lord for them.

19 And it came to pass that the Lord spake unto me, saying: Blessed art thou, Nephi, because of thy faith, for thou hast sought me diligently, with lowliness of heart.

20 And inasmuch as ye shall keep my commandments, ye shall prosper, and shall be led to a land of promise; yea, even a land which I have prepared for you; yea, a land which is choice above all other lands.

21 And inasmuch as thy brethren shall rebel against thee, they shall be cut off from the presence of the Lord.

22 And inasmuch as thou shalt keep my commandments, thou shalt be made a ruler and a teacher over thy brethren.

23 For behold, in that day that they shall rebel against me, I will curse them even with a sore curse, and they shall have no power over thy seed except they shall rebel against me also.

24 And if it so be that they rebel against me, they shall be a scourge unto thy seed, to stir them up in the ways of remembrance.

## CHAPTER 3

*Nephi learns to be obedient to the commandments of God. Compare his faith with that of Laman and Lemuel.*

### *Nephi and His Brothers Return to Jerusalem to Obtain the Plates of Brass*

1 AND it came to pass that I, Nephi, returned from speaking with the Lord, to the tent of my father.

2 And it came to pass that he spake unto me, saying: Behold I have dreamed a dream, in the which the Lord hath commanded me that thou and thy brethren shall return to Jerusalem.

3 For behold, Laban hath the record of the Jews and also a genealogy of my forefathers, and they are engraven upon plates of brass.

---

2:16 ***stature***—size or height
***rebel***—oppose and fight

How was Nephi's heart softened when Lehi asked him to do something difficult? What have your parents asked of you that has been hard to accept? How might praying help change your feelings?

2:17 ***manifested***—shown

2:18 ***hearken unto***—listen to and obey
***the hardness of their hearts***—their stubbornness and their unwillingness to obey the commandments or feel the Spirit

2:19 ***lowliness of heart***—humility

2:21 (20–21) To prosper sometimes means receiving greater wealth or material possessions. It may also mean having the Spirit of the Lord. Notice that those who rebel are "cut off from the presence of the Lord" (see Alma 38:1).

2:23 ***seed***—descendants, meaning children, grandchildren, and so on

2:24 ***scourge***—punishment, chastisement, or affliction

3:2 Many evidences within the Book of Mormon show that the book really is an ancient record that has been translated into English. For example, the phrase "I have dreamed a dream" is a very unusual way of speaking in English. It is, however, a very common way of speaking in Hebrew in order to emphasize a word. Many examples of this pattern exist in the Book of Mormon (see 1 Nephi 8:2; Enos 1:13; and Alma 18:5).

3:3 ***genealogy of my forefathers***—the names and histories of my father, grandfathers, and other ancestors
***engraven***—written by being cut or impressed into metal

4 Wherefore, the Lord hath commanded me that
thou and thy brothers should go unto the house of
Laban, and seek the records, and bring them down
hither into the wilderness.
5 And now, behold thy brothers murmur, saying it
is a hard thing which I have required of them; but
behold I have not required it of them, but it is a
commandment of the Lord.
6 Therefore go, my son, and thou shalt be favored
of the Lord, because thou hast not murmured.
7 And it came to pass that I, Nephi, said unto my
father: I will go and do the things which the Lord
hath commanded, for I know that the Lord giveth
no commandments unto the children of men, save
he shall prepare a way for them that they may
accomplish the thing which he commandeth them.
8 And it came to pass that when my father had
heard these words he was exceedingly glad, for he
knew that I had been blessed of the Lord.

## *Nephi and His Brothers Fail in Their First Attempt to Get the Plates of Brass*

9 And I, Nephi, and my brethren took our journey
in the wilderness, with our tents, to go up to the
land of Jerusalem.
10 And it came to pass that when we had gone up
to the land of Jerusalem, I and my brethren did
consult one with another.
11 And we cast lots—who of us should go in unto
the house of Laban. And it came to pass that the lot
fell upon Laman; and Laman went in unto the
house of Laban, and he talked with him as he sat in
his house.
12 And he desired of Laban the records which
were engraven upon the plates of brass, which contained the genealogy of my father.
13 And behold, it came to pass that Laban was
angry, and thrust him out from his presence; and he
would not that he should have the records.
Wherefore, he said unto him: Behold thou art a robber, and I will slay thee.
14 But Laman fled out of his presence, and told
the things which Laban had done, unto us. And we
began to be exceedingly sorrowful, and my
brethren were about to return unto my father in the
wilderness.

## *The Brothers Fail a Second Time to Get the Plates*

15 But behold I said unto them that: As the Lord
liveth, and as we live, we will not go down unto our
father in the wilderness until we have accomplished
the thing which the Lord hath commanded us.
16 Wherefore, let us be faithful in keeping the
commandments of the Lord; therefore let us go
down to the land of our father's inheritance, for

---

3:4 Why do you think it was important that Lehi's family take a set of scriptures, which included their family history, with them on their journey? How important are the scriptures in your life?

3:7 Referring to this verse, Elder Spencer W. Kimball once said, "I rely upon that promise of the Lord that he will strengthen and empower me that I may be able to do this work to which I have been called" (in Conference Report, October 1943, 18).

3:7 (5–7) Nephi reacted very differently to the Lord's command than Laman and Lemuel did. How do you, personally, respond to the commandments of the Lord?

3:8 ***exceedingly***—very

3:8 (1–8) "The distance from Jerusalem to the Red Sea (the Gulf of Aqaba) is about 180 miles through hot, barren country infested anciently by many marauders [robbers]. Lehi and his family traveled three days' journey beyond this point (see 1 Nephi 2:5–6). This meant at least a twelve-to-fourteen-day trip one way" (*Book of Mormon Student Manual, Religion 121 and 122,* 5).

Why do you think the Lord would wait until Lehi's family had traveled so far out of Jerusalem before commanding them to return and get the plates of brass?

3:11 Anciently, lots were sometimes cast as a way of trying to reach a fair decision. It is not known exactly what objects were used or how it was done, but some believe that smooth stones or colorful sticks were used (see *Old Testament: 1 Kings–Malachi, Religion 302 Student Manual,* 98).

3:15 Swearing with an oath in ancient days was very significant. Elder Bruce R. McConkie stated: "Nephi and his brethren were seeking to obtain the brass plates from Laban. Their lives were in peril. Yet Nephi swore this oath [quotes 1 Nephi 3:15]. Thus Nephi made God his partner. If he failed to get the plates, it meant God had failed. And because God does not fail, it was incumbent upon [required of] Nephi to get the plates or lay down his life in the attempt" (in Conference Report, April 1982, 49–50).

NEPHI RETURNING FOR THE PLATES OF BRASS, BY ROBERT T. BARRETT

*"I will go and do the things which the Lord hath commanded."*

behold he left gold and silver, and all manner of riches. And all this he hath done because of the commandments of the Lord.

17 For he knew that Jerusalem must be destroyed, because of the wickedness of the people.

18 For behold, they have rejected the words of the prophets. Wherefore, if my father should dwell in the land after he hath been commanded to flee out of the land, behold, he would also perish. Wherefore, it must needs be that he flee out of the land.

19 And behold, it is wisdom in God that we should obtain these records, that we may preserve unto our children the language of our fathers;

20 And also that we may preserve unto them the words which have been spoken by the mouth of all the holy prophets, which have been delivered unto them by the Spirit and power of God, since the world began, even down unto this present time.

21 And it came to pass that after this manner of language did I persuade my brethren, that they might be faithful in keeping the commandments of God.

22 And it came to pass that we went down to the land of our inheritance, and we did gather together our gold, and our silver, and our precious things.

23 And after we had gathered these things together, we went up again unto the house of Laban.

24 And it came to pass that we went in unto Laban, and desired him that he would give unto us the records which were engraven upon the plates of brass, for which we would give unto him our gold, and our silver, and all our precious things.

25 And it came to pass that when Laban saw our property, and that it was exceedingly great, he did lust after it, insomuch that he thrust us out, and sent his servants to slay us, that he might obtain our property.

26 And it came to pass that we did flee before the servants of Laban, and we were obliged to leave behind our property, and it fell into the hands of Laban.

27 And it came to pass that we fled into the wilderness, and the servants of Laban did not overtake us, and we hid ourselves in the cavity of a rock.

## An Angel Protects Nephi and Sam

28 And it came to pass that Laman was angry with me, and also with my father; and also was Lemuel, for he hearkened unto the words of Laman. Wherefore Laman and Lemuel did speak many hard words unto us, their younger brothers, and they did smite us even with a rod.

29 And it came to pass as they smote us with a rod, behold, an angel of the Lord came and stood before them, and he spake unto them, saying: Why do ye smite your younger brother with a rod? Know ye not that the Lord hath chosen him to be a ruler over you, and this because of your iniquities? Behold ye shall go up to Jerusalem again, and the Lord will deliver Laban into your hands.

30 And after the angel had spoken unto us, he departed.

31 And after the angel had departed, Laman and Lemuel again began to murmur, saying: How is it possible that the Lord will deliver Laban into our hands? Behold, he is a mighty man, and he can command fifty, yea, even he can slay fifty; then why not us?

---

3:21 ***persuade***—encourage or convince

3:25 ***lust after***—strongly desire

3:26 ***obliged***—forced

3:27 ***the cavity of a rock***—a cave

3:28 ***hearkened unto***—listened to and obeyed
***smite***—hit or strike

3:29 ***smote***—hit or struck

3:31 Based on the research of Hugh Nibley, it seems likely that Laban was a military commander with a local guard of fifty and a larger force in the field (see *Lehi in the Desert,* 97–98).

Some people claim that if they could just see an angel or a miracle, then they would believe and be faithful. How did this angel's visit affect Laman and Lemuel? What do you think would have converted Laman and Lemuel? (see 1 Nephi 2:12, 16).

## CHAPTER 4

*With the help of the Lord, Nephi gets the brass plates. Watch how the Spirit of the Lord guides Nephi.*

### *Nephi Testifies to His Brothers That God Will Help Them Get the Brass Plates*

1 AND it came to pass that I spake unto my brethren, saying: Let us go up again unto Jerusalem, and let us be faithful in keeping the commandments of the Lord; for behold he is mightier than all the earth, then why not mightier than Laban and his fifty, yea, or even than his tens of thousands?

2 Therefore let us go up; let us be strong like unto Moses; for he truly spake unto the waters of the Red Sea and they divided hither and thither, and our fathers came through, out of captivity, on dry ground, and the armies of Pharaoh did follow and were drowned in the waters of the Red Sea.

3 Now behold ye know that this is true; and ye also know that an angel hath spoken unto you; wherefore can ye doubt? Let us go up; the Lord is able to deliver us, even as our fathers, and to destroy Laban, even as the Egyptians.

### *Nephi Is Led by the Spirit to Laban*

4 Now when I had spoken these words, they were yet wroth, and did still continue to murmur; nevertheless they did follow me up until we came without the walls of Jerusalem.

5 And it was by night; and I caused that they should hide themselves without the walls. And after they had hid themselves, I, Nephi, crept into the city and went forth towards the house of Laban.

6 And I was led by the Spirit, not knowing beforehand the things which I should do.

7 Nevertheless I went forth, and as I came near unto the house of Laban I beheld a man, and he had fallen to the earth before me, for he was drunken with wine.

8 And when I came to him I found that it was Laban.

9 And I beheld his sword, and I drew it forth from the sheath thereof; and the hilt thereof was of pure gold, and the workmanship thereof was exceedingly fine, and I saw that the blade thereof was of the most precious steel.

### *The Spirit Tells Nephi to Kill Laban*

10 And it came to pass that I was constrained by the Spirit that I should kill Laban; but I said in my heart: Never at any time have I shed the blood of man. And I shrunk and would that I might not slay him.

11 And the Spirit said unto me again: Behold the Lord hath delivered him into thy hands. Yea, and I also knew that he had sought to take away mine own life; yea, and he would not hearken unto the commandments of the Lord; and he also had taken away our property.

---

4:1 In 1 Nephi 3:31, Laman and Lemuel reveal their lack of faith. Nephi expresses his great faith in 1 Nephi 4:1. Why do you think Nephi has so much faith and Laman and Lemuel have so little?

4:2 Nephi used the scriptures (see Exodus 14:21–30) to try to help his brothers gain the strength and faith to return to Jerusalem. How have the scriptures given you greater strength and faith?

***hither and thither***—this way and that way
***captivity***—bondage and slavery

4:4 ***wroth***—angry

4:5 ***without***—outside

4:6 A few years after his death, Joseph Smith appeared to Brigham Young in a dream and told him: "Tell the people to be . . . sure to keep the spirit of the Lord and it will lead them right. Be careful and not turn away the small still voice; it will teach them what to do and where to go" (Journal History, 23 February 1847, 1).

PHOTOGRAPH BY G. R. SIMS

*A view of Jerusalem today from the Mount of Olives*

4:9 ***sheath***—knife or sword case
***hilt***—handle

4:10 ***constrained***—commanded
***slay***—kill

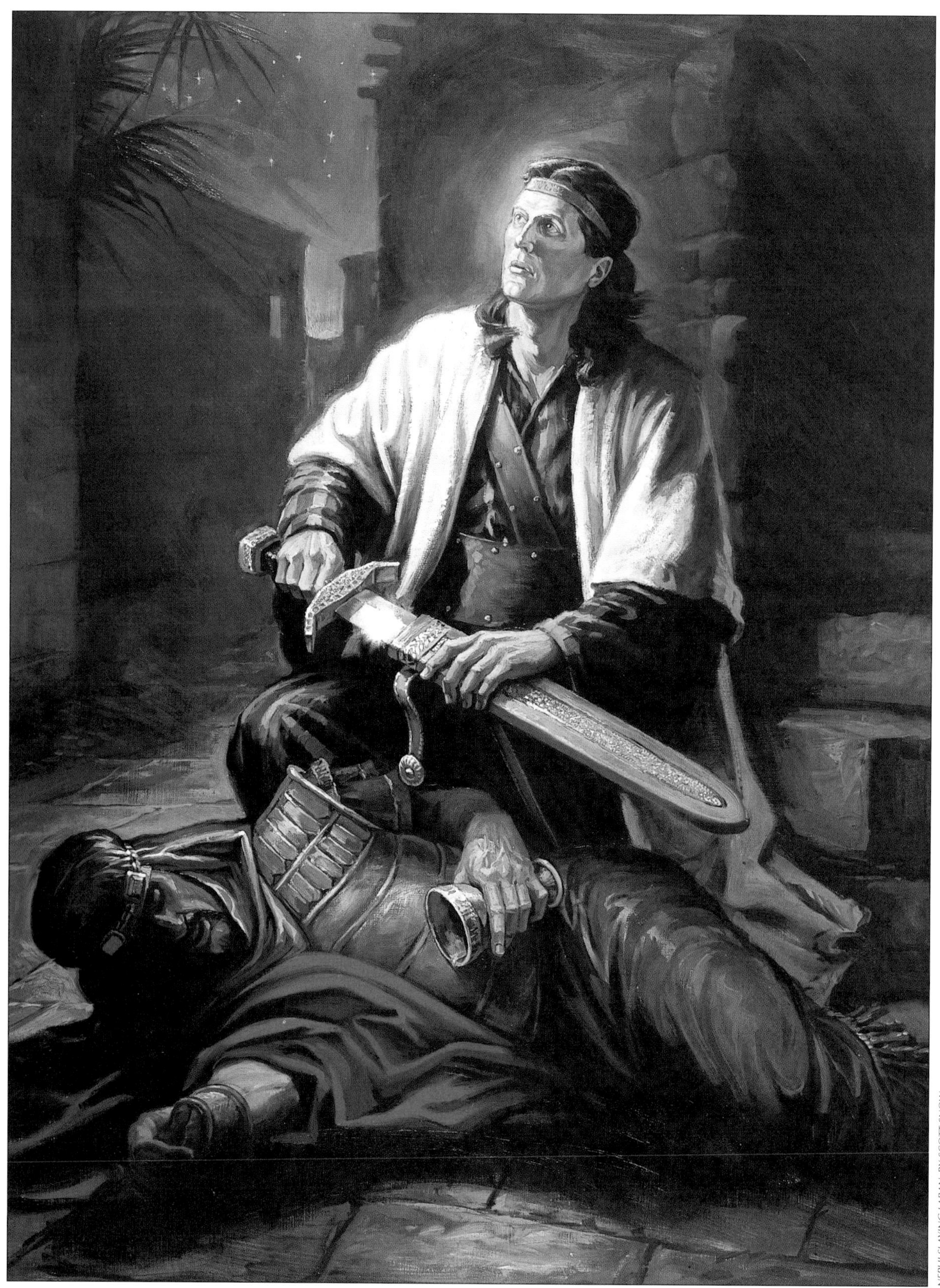

NEPHI SLAYING LABAN, BY SCOTT SNOW

*Nephi was "constrained by the Spirit" to kill Laban.*

12 And it came to pass that the Spirit said unto me again: Slay him, for the Lord hath delivered him into thy hands;
13 Behold the Lord slayeth the wicked to bring forth his righteous purposes. It is better that one man should perish than that a nation should dwindle and perish in unbelief.
14 And now, when I, Nephi, had heard these words, I remembered the words of the Lord which he spake unto me in the wilderness, saying that: Inasmuch as thy seed shall keep my commandments, they shall prosper in the land of promise.
15 Yea, and I also thought that they could not keep the commandments of the Lord according to the law of Moses, save they should have the law.
16 And I also knew that the law was engraven upon the plates of brass.
17 And again, I knew that the Lord had delivered Laban into my hands for this cause—that I might obtain the records according to his commandments.
18 Therefore I did obey the voice of the Spirit, and took Laban by the hair of the head, and I smote off his head with his own sword.

### Nephi Obtains the Plates of Brass

19 And after I had smitten off his head with his own sword, I took the garments of Laban and put them upon mine own body; yea, even every whit; and I did gird on his armor about my loins.
20 And after I had done this, I went forth unto the treasury of Laban. And as I went forth towards the treasury of Laban, behold, I saw the servant of Laban who had the keys of the treasury. And I commanded him in the voice of Laban, that he should go with me into the treasury.
21 And he supposed me to be his master, Laban, for he beheld the garments and also the sword girded about my loins.
22 And he spake unto me concerning the elders of the Jews, he knowing that his master, Laban, had been out by night among them.
23 And I spake unto him as if it had been Laban.
24 And I also spake unto him that I should carry the engravings, which were upon the plates of brass, to my elder brethren, who were without the walls.
25 And I also bade him that he should follow me.
26 And he, supposing that I spake of the brethren of the church, and that I was truly that Laban whom I had slain, wherefore he did follow me.
27 And he spake unto me many times concerning the elders of the Jews, as I went forth unto my brethren, who were without the walls.
28 And it came to pass that when Laman saw me he was exceedingly frightened, and also Lemuel and Sam. And they fled from before my presence; for they supposed it was Laban, and that he had slain me and had sought to take away their lives also.

### Zoram Joins Nephi and His Brothers

29 And it came to pass that I called after them, and they did hear me; wherefore they did cease to flee from my presence.
30 And it came to pass that when the servant of Laban beheld my brethren he began to tremble, and was about to flee from before me and return to the city of Jerusalem.
31 And now I, Nephi, being a man large in stature, and also having received much strength of the Lord, therefore I did seize upon the servant of Laban, and held him, that he should not flee.

---

4:13 ***dwindle***—become weak and fall away

4:18 ***smote***—struck

The Prophet Joseph Smith said, "Whatever God requires is right, no matter what it is, although we may not see the reason thereof till long after the events transpire [are over]" (*Teachings of the Prophet Joseph Smith,* 256).

4:19 ***whit***—little bit
***gird***—strap

4:20 ***treasury***—place for the keeping of money and valuables

4:22 The word *elders* here does not refer to priesthood officers but to "the heads of the most influential families of a city" (Hugh Nibley, *An Approach to the Book of Mormon,* 96).

4:25 ***bade***—requested

4:29 ***did cease to flee from my presence***—stopped running away from me

4:31 ***stature***—size
***seize***—grab hold

32 And it came to pass that I spake with him,
that if he would hearken unto my words, as the
Lord liveth, and as I live, even so that if he would
hearken unto our words, we would spare his life.
33 And I spake unto him, even with an oath, that he
need not fear; that he should be a free man like unto
us if he would go down in the wilderness with us.
34 And I also spake unto him, saying: Surely the
Lord hath commanded us to do this thing; and shall
we not be diligent in keeping the commandments
of the Lord? Therefore, if thou wilt go down into the
wilderness to my father thou shalt have place with
us.
35 And it came to pass that Zoram did take
courage at the words which I spake. Now Zoram
was the name of the servant; and he promised that
he would go down into the wilderness unto our
father. Yea, and he also made an oath unto us that
he would tarry with us from that time forth.
36 Now we were desirous that he should tarry
with us for this cause, that the Jews might not know
concerning our flight into the wilderness, lest they
should pursue us and destroy us.
37 And it came to pass that when Zoram had
made an oath unto us, our fears did cease concerning him.
38 And it came to pass that we took the plates of
brass and the servant of Laban, and departed into
the wilderness, and journeyed unto the tent of our
father.

## CHAPTER 5

*Living prophets and the scriptures give guidance and security to faithful Saints. Notice how Lehi's family is blessed by having both of these sources to direct them.*

### *Sariah Rejoices When Her Sons Return Safely from Jerusalem*

1 AND it came to pass that after we had come
down into the wilderness unto our father, behold,
he was filled with joy, and also my mother, Sariah,
was exceedingly glad, for she truly had mourned
because of us.
2 For she had supposed that we had perished in
the wilderness; and she also had complained
against my father, telling him that he was a visionary man; saying: Behold thou hast led us forth from
the land of our inheritance, and my sons are no
more, and we perish in the wilderness.
3 And after this manner of language had my
mother complained against my father.
4 And it had come to pass that my father spake
unto her, saying: I know that I am a visionary man;
for if I had not seen the things of God in a vision I
should not have known the goodness of God, but
had tarried at Jerusalem, and had perished with my
brethren.
5 But behold, I have obtained a land of promise,
in the which things I do rejoice; yea, and I know
that the Lord will deliver my sons out of the hands
of Laban, and bring them down again unto us in the
wilderness.
6 And after this manner of language did my father,
Lehi, comfort my mother, Sariah, concerning us,
while we journeyed in the wilderness up to the
land of Jerusalem, to obtain the record of the Jews.
7 And when we had returned to the tent of my
father, behold their joy was full, and my mother was
comforted.
8 And she spake, saying: Now I know of a surety
that the Lord hath commanded my husband to flee

---

4:32 Using the phrase "as the Lord liveth, and as I live" is one way people in ancient times made "oaths," or promises, with each other (see Numbers 14:21; Jeremiah 46:18).

4:35 ***tarry***—stay

4:36 ***pursue***—follow

4:37 When Zoram made an oath, Nephi knew Zoram would keep his promise. Why is it important to always do what you promise to do?

5:2, 8 Compare Sariah's concern in verse 2 with her testimony in verse 8. How did her discouragement turn into a stronger commitment to follow the prophet and the Lord? How have you or someone you know gained a stronger testimony of the living prophets?

5:4 ***tarried***—stayed or waited

5:6 (4–6) "These are not the words of a disaffected husband. They are the words of a husband who knows who he is and at the same time feels compassion and concern for his wife in her struggle" (Lynn Nations Johnson, review of *To Mothers & Fathers from the Book of Mormon,* 261).

into the wilderness; yea, and I also know of a surety that the Lord hath protected my sons, and delivered them out of the hands of Laban, and given them power whereby they could accomplish the thing which the Lord hath commanded them. And after this manner of language did she speak.
9 And it came to pass that they did rejoice exceedingly, and did offer sacrifice and burnt offerings unto the Lord; and they gave thanks unto the God of Israel.

### The Plates of Brass Contain Writings of Moses and Other Prophets

10 And after they had given thanks unto the God of Israel, my father, Lehi, took the records which were engraven upon the plates of brass, and he did search them from the beginning.
11 And he beheld that they did contain the five books of Moses, which gave an account of the creation of the world, and also of Adam and Eve, who were our first parents;
12 And also a record of the Jews from the beginning, even down to the commencement of the reign of Zedekiah, king of Judah;
13 And also the prophecies of the holy prophets, from the beginning, even down to the commencement of the reign of Zedekiah; and also many prophecies which have been spoken by the mouth of Jeremiah.
14 And it came to pass that my father, Lehi, also found upon the plates of brass a genealogy of his fathers; wherefore he knew that he was a descendant of Joseph; yea, even that Joseph who was the son of Jacob, who was sold into Egypt, and who was preserved by the hand of the Lord, that he might preserve his father, Jacob, and all his household from perishing with famine.
15 And they were also led out of captivity and out of the land of Egypt, by that same God who had preserved them.
16 And thus my father, Lehi, did discover the genealogy of his fathers. And Laban also was a descendant of Joseph, wherefore he and his fathers had kept the records.

### After Searching the Plates of Brass, Lehi Is Filled with the Spirit, and Prophesies

17 And now when my father saw all these things, he was filled with the Spirit, and began to prophesy concerning his seed—
18 That these plates of brass should go forth unto all nations, kindreds, tongues, and people who were of his seed.
19 Wherefore, he said that these plates of brass should never perish; neither should they be dimmed any more by time. And he prophesied many things concerning his seed.

---

5:9 From the time of Adam until the death of Christ, Israelites offered animal sacrifices as a symbol of the atoning sacrifice of Jesus Christ (see Moses 5:6–8). Since then we remember the Savior's Atonement through the ordinance of the sacrament (see Matthew 26:26–29).

The name *Israel* means "one who prevails with God," or "let God prevail." It is used several ways in the scriptures. It may refer to (1) the man Jacob, whose name was changed to Israel; (2) the family, children, or tribes of Israel (the scriptures often use the phrase "house of Israel" in this sense); (3) the land of Israel; or (4) the true believers in Christ, no matter what their family or where they live (see LDS Bible Dictionary, s.v. "Israel," 708).

5:11 This reference in the Book of Mormon adds support to the knowledge that Moses wrote the first five books of the Bible: Genesis, Exodus, Leviticus, Numbers, and Deuteronomy. This verse also affirms that Adam and Eve are indeed our first earthly parents.

5:13 (12–13) Zedekiah was the king of Judah when Lehi and his family departed in about 600 B.C. Jeremiah was one of the great prophets who lived at the same time that Lehi received his call to leave Jerusalem (see 1 Nephi 7:14).

5:14 Lehi was descended from Joseph through Joseph's son Manasseh (see Alma 10:3). This helps show how the Book of Mormon is a fulfillment of a prophecy the Lord made through the prophet Ezekiel in the Old Testament. Ezekiel said that in the last days two books would come together. One book would be the record of the Jews, which is what we today call the Bible. The other book would be a record of the tribe of Joseph, which is the Book of Mormon (see Ezekiel 37:15–17).

5:15 ***captivity***—bondage and slavery

5:18 ***kindreds, tongues***—family groups, people of various language groups

LEHI STUDYING THE PLATES OF BRASS, BY CLARK KELLEY PRICE

*Lehi "found upon the plates of brass a genealogy of his fathers; wherefore he knew that he was a descendant of Joseph."*

20 And it came to pass that thus far I and my father had kept the commandments wherewith the Lord had commanded us.

21 And we had obtained the records which the Lord had commanded us, and searched them and found that they were desirable; yea, even of great worth unto us, insomuch that we could preserve the commandments of the Lord unto our children.

22 Wherefore, it was wisdom in the Lord that we should carry them with us, as we journeyed in the wilderness towards the land of promise.

## CHAPTER 6

*Nephi writes to encourage all people to come unto Jesus Christ and be saved. Notice the commandment he gives to the record keepers who will follow him.*

### Nephi Writes Only the Things That Please God

1 AND now I, Nephi, do not give the genealogy of my fathers in this part of my record; neither at any time shall I give it after upon these plates which I am writing; for it is given in the record which has

---

5:22 (21–22) Nephi said that the plates of brass (their scriptures) were "of great worth." He discovered their worth after having "searched them." How can studying the scriptures help you appreciate them more?

been kept by my father; wherefore, I do not write it in this work.

2 For it sufficeth me to say that we are descendants of Joseph.

3 And it mattereth not to me that I am particular to give a full account of all the things of my father, for they cannot be written upon these plates, for I desire the room that I may write of the things of God.

4 For the fulness of mine intent is that I may persuade men to come unto the God of Abraham, and the God of Isaac, and the God of Jacob, and be saved.

5 Wherefore, the things which are pleasing unto the world I do not write, but the things which are pleasing unto God and unto those who are not of the world.

6 Wherefore, I shall give commandment unto my seed, that they shall not occupy these plates with things which are not of worth unto the children of men.

## CHAPTER 7

*Nephi asks Ishmael and his family to return with him into the wilderness so that Ishmael's children can marry Lehi's children. Look for ways the Lord took care of Nephi as he was on this errand.*

### *Lehi's Sons Return to Jerusalem and Get Ishmael's Family*

1 AND now I would that ye might know, that after my father, Lehi, had made an end of prophesying concerning his seed, it came to pass that the Lord spake unto him again, saying that it was not meet for him, Lehi, that he should take his family into the wilderness alone; but that his sons should take daughters to wife, that they might raise up seed unto the Lord in the land of promise.

2 And it came to pass that the Lord commanded him that I, Nephi, and my brethren, should again return unto the land of Jerusalem, and bring down Ishmael and his family into the wilderness.

3 And it came to pass that I, Nephi, did again, with my brethren, go forth into the wilderness to go up to Jerusalem.

4 And it came to pass that we went up unto the house of Ishmael, and we did gain favor in the sight of Ishmael, insomuch that we did speak unto him the words of the Lord.

5 And it came to pass that the Lord did soften the heart of Ishmael, and also his household, insomuch that they took their journey with us down into the wilderness to the tent of our father.

### *Nephi Warns His Brethren Not to Return to Jerusalem*

6 And it came to pass that as we journeyed in the wilderness, behold Laman and Lemuel, and two of the daughters of Ishmael, and the two sons of Ishmael and their families, did rebel against us; yea, against me, Nephi, and Sam, and their father, Ishmael, and his wife, and his three other daughters.

7 And it came to pass in the which rebellion, they were desirous to return unto the land of Jerusalem.

---

6:2 ***sufficeth me***—is enough for me

6:4 ***the fulness of mine intent***—my whole purpose
***persuade***—encourage or convince

6:4 (3–4) What do you see in these verses that makes the Book of Mormon different from most other books in the world? The Prophet Joseph Smith said that "the Book of Mormon was the most correct of any book on earth, . . . and a man would get nearer to God by abiding by its precepts, than by any other book" (*Teachings of the Prophet Joseph Smith,* 194).

6:5 (4–5) "The world" in this verse means people who are more interested in the things of this world than the things of God. What kinds of people do you think will like the Book of Mormon and what kinds of people will not?

6:6 ***occupy***—fill up

As you continue your study of the Book of Mormon, notice how careful the other record keepers were to write only what was pleasing to God and was of great worth. Why is the Book of Mormon important to you?

7:1 What do you think parents should do to "raise up seed [children] unto the Lord"? (see 1 Nephi 3:19–20).

7:4 ***we did gain favor in the sight of Ishmael***—Ishmael received us kindly

7:5 (4–5) These verses show why Ishmael and his family left their home and went into the wilderness. How does the Lord help you when you are obedient?

7:6 ***rebel***—oppose and fight

7:7 ***rebellion***—opposition

8 And now I, Nephi, being grieved for the hardness of their hearts, therefore I spake unto them, saying, yea, even unto Laman and unto Lemuel: Behold ye are mine elder brethren, and how is it that ye are so hard in your hearts, and so blind in your minds, that ye have need that I, your younger brother, should speak unto you, yea, and set an example for you?

9 How is it that ye have not hearkened unto the word of the Lord?

10 How is it that ye have forgotten that ye have seen an angel of the Lord?

11 Yea, and how is it that ye have forgotten what great things the Lord hath done for us, in delivering us out of the hands of Laban, and also that we should obtain the record?

12 Yea, and how is it that ye have forgotten that the Lord is able to do all things according to his will, for the children of men, if it so be that they exercise faith in him? Wherefore, let us be faithful to him.

13 And if it so be that we are faithful to him, we shall obtain the land of promise; and ye shall know at some future period that the word of the Lord shall be fulfilled concerning the destruction of Jerusalem; for all things which the Lord hath spoken concerning the destruction of Jerusalem must be fulfilled.

14 For behold, the Spirit of the Lord ceaseth soon to strive with them; for behold, they have rejected the prophets, and Jeremiah have they cast into prison. And they have sought to take away the life of my father, insomuch that they have driven him out of the land.

15 Now behold, I say unto you that if ye will return unto Jerusalem ye shall also perish with them. And now, if ye have choice, go up to the land, and remember the words which I speak unto you, that if ye go ye will also perish; for thus the Spirit of the Lord constraineth me that I should speak.

## Nephi Is Protected from His Brothers

16 And it came to pass that when I, Nephi, had spoken these words unto my brethren, they were angry with me. And it came to pass that they did lay their hands upon me, for behold, they were exceedingly wroth, and they did bind me with cords, for they sought to take away my life, that they might leave me in the wilderness to be devoured by wild beasts.

17 But it came to pass that I prayed unto the Lord, saying: O Lord, according to my faith which is in thee, wilt thou deliver me from the hands of my brethren; yea, even give me strength that I may burst these bands with which I am bound.

18 And it came to pass that when I had said these words, behold, the bands were loosed from off my hands and feet, and I stood before my brethren, and I spake unto them again.

19 And it came to pass that they were angry with me again, and sought to lay hands upon me; but behold, one of the daughters of Ishmael, yea, and

---

7:8 ***grieved***—sorrowful
***the hardness of their hearts***—their stubbornness and their unwillingness to be obedient or feel the Spirit

7:12 (10–12) Think of a time you felt very close to the Lord. What can you do to keep that feeling of closeness with the Lord?

7:13 Later, Nephi's younger brother Jacob learned from the Lord "that those who were at Jerusalem, from whence we came, have been slain and carried away captive" (2 Nephi 6:8).

7:15 ***constraineth***—commands

7:16 ***wroth***—angry

7:18 (17–18) Nephi had faith in prayer. President Gordon B. Hinckley taught: "Believe in prayer and the power of prayer. Pray to the Lord with the expectation of answers" (*Teachings of Gordon B. Hinckley,* 469).

PHOTOGRAPH BY DAVID H. GARNER

*The Judean wilderness*

DESTRUCTION OF JERUSALEM, BY GARY KAPP

*Lehi prophesied that Jerusalem would be destroyed because of its wickedness.*

also her mother, and one of the sons of Ishmael, did plead with my brethren, insomuch that they did soften their hearts; and they did cease striving to take away my life.

20 And it came to pass that they were sorrowful, because of their wickedness, insomuch that they did bow down before me, and did plead with me that I would forgive them of the thing that they had done against me.

21 And it came to pass that I did frankly forgive them all that they had done, and I did exhort them that they would pray unto the Lord their God for forgiveness. And it came to pass that they did so. And after they had done praying unto the Lord we did again travel on our journey towards the tent of our father.

22 And it came to pass that we did come down unto the tent of our father. And after I and my brethren and all the house of Ishmael had come down unto the tent of my father, they did give thanks unto the Lord their God; and they did offer sacrifice and burnt offerings unto him.

## CHAPTER 8

*Sometimes the Lord speaks to His prophets through dreams and visions. The dream given to Lehi in this chapter contains important messages for you. As you read about Lehi's dream, think about what each part of this dream represents and what you learn from it.*

### *Lehi Sees a Vision of His Family and the Tree of Life*

1 AND it came to pass that we had gathered together all manner of seeds of every kind, both of grain of every kind, and also of the seeds of fruit of every kind.

2 And it came to pass that while my father tarried in the wilderness he spake unto us, saying: Behold, I have dreamed a dream; or, in other words, I have seen a vision.

3 And behold, because of the thing which I have seen, I have reason to rejoice in the Lord because of Nephi and also of Sam; for I have reason to suppose that they, and also many of their seed, will be saved.

4 But behold, Laman and Lemuel, I fear exceedingly because of you; for behold, methought I saw in my dream, a dark and dreary wilderness.

5 And it came to pass that I saw a man, and he was dressed in a white robe; and he came and stood before me.

6 And it came to pass that he spake unto me, and bade me follow him.

7 And it came to pass that as I followed him I beheld myself that I was in a dark and dreary waste.

8 And after I had traveled for the space of many hours in darkness, I began to pray unto the Lord that he would have mercy on me, according to the multitude of his tender mercies.

---

7:21 ***frankly***—freely and honestly
***exhort***—plead with or challenge

7:22 (21–22) Why is it just as important to forgive those who have wronged us as it is to apologize and ask forgiveness when we are wrong?

8:1 Notice what Lehi and his family had been doing prior to Lehi's dramatic vision of his family and the tree of life. What do you think the gathering of the seeds of grain and of fruit has to do with the rest of the chapter?

8:2 ***tarried***—stayed or waited

8:4 ***dreary***—sad and gloomy

8:6 ***bade me***—asked me to

8:8 In scripture, darkness is often a symbol for wickedness, separation from God, and confusion (see Proverbs 4:19). Heavenly Father can deliver us from darkness if we pray to Him and have faith in His power.

LEHI'S DREAM, BY GREG K. OLSEN

*An illustration of Lehi's dream*

## Lehi Sees a Tree with White Fruit

9 And it came to pass after I had prayed unto the
Lord I beheld a large and spacious field.
10 And it came to pass that I beheld a tree, whose
fruit was desirable to make one happy.
11 And it came to pass that I did go forth and partake of the fruit thereof; and I beheld that it was
most sweet, above all that I ever before tasted. Yea,
and I beheld that the fruit thereof was white, to
exceed all the whiteness that I had ever seen.
12 And as I partook of the fruit thereof it filled my
soul with exceedingly great joy; wherefore, I began to
be desirous that my family should partake of it also;
for I knew that it was desirable above all other fruit.
13 And as I cast my eyes round about, that perhaps I might discover my family also, I beheld a
river of water; and it ran along, and it was near the
tree of which I was partaking the fruit.
14 And I looked to behold from whence it came;
and I saw the head thereof a little way off; and at
the head thereof I beheld your mother Sariah, and
Sam, and Nephi; and they stood as if they knew not
whither they should go.
15 And it came to pass that I beckoned unto them;
and I also did say unto them with a loud voice that
they should come unto me, and partake of the fruit,
which was desirable above all other fruit.

---

8:9 ***spacious***—wide open and broad

Later in this vision, Lehi refers again to the "large and spacious field, as if it had been a world" (1 Nephi 8:20).

8:10 The Prophet Joseph Smith taught: "Happiness is the object and design of our existence; and will be the end thereof, if we pursue the path that leads to it" (*Teachings of the Prophet Joseph Smith,* 255).

8:12 (11–12) These verses help us understand that the tree in Lehi's dream represents the love of God which He offers us through the Atonement of His Son, Jesus Christ, and that the fruit represents the blessings of the Atonement, including eternal life (see 1 Nephi 11:21–22; 15:36). Why do you think the fruit is described as "most sweet," "white," and something that fills a person with great joy?

8:13 Nephi later discovers that the river of water represents "the depths of hell" (see 1 Nephi 12:16).

8:15 ***beckoned***—called

16 And it came to pass that they did come unto me and partake of the fruit also.

17 And it came to pass that I was desirous that Laman and Lemuel should come and partake of the fruit also; wherefore, I cast mine eyes towards the head of the river, that perhaps I might see them.

18 And it came to pass that I saw them, but they would not come unto me and partake of the fruit.

## A Rod of Iron Leads to the Tree of Life

19 And I beheld a rod of iron, and it extended along the bank of the river, and led to the tree by which I stood.

20 And I also beheld a strait and narrow path, which came along by the rod of iron, even to the tree by which I stood; and it also led by the head of the fountain, unto a large and spacious field, as if it had been a world.

21 And I saw numberless concourses of people, many of whom were pressing forward, that they might obtain the path which led unto the tree by which I stood.

22 And it came to pass that they did come forth, and commence in the path which led to the tree.

23 And it came to pass that there arose a mist of darkness; yea, even an exceedingly great mist of darkness, insomuch that they who had commenced in the path did lose their way, that they wandered off and were lost.

24 And it came to pass that I beheld others pressing forward, and they came forth and caught hold of the end of the rod of iron; and they did press forward through the mist of darkness, clinging to the rod of iron, even until they did come forth and partake of the fruit of the tree.

25 And after they had partaken of the fruit of the tree they did cast their eyes about as if they were ashamed.

## Lehi Sees a Great and Spacious Building

26 And I also cast my eyes round about, and beheld, on the other side of the river of water, a great and spacious building; and it stood as it were in the air, high above the earth.

27 And it was filled with people, both old and young, both male and female; and their manner of dress was exceedingly fine; and they were in the attitude of mocking and pointing their fingers towards those who had come at and were partaking of the fruit.

28 And after they had tasted of the fruit they were ashamed, because of those that were scoffing at them; and they fell away into forbidden paths and were lost.

29 And now I, Nephi, do not speak all the words of my father.

30 But, to be short in writing, behold, he saw other multitudes pressing forward; and they came and caught hold of the end of the rod of iron; and they did press their way forward, continually holding fast to the rod of iron, until they came forth and fell down and partook of the fruit of the tree.

31 And he also saw other multitudes feeling their way towards that great and spacious building.

32 And it came to pass that many were drowned in the depths of the fountain; and many were lost from his view, wandering in strange roads.

---

8:18 (15–18) Why was Lehi so desirous that his family partake of the fruit? How would you feel if members of your family acted like Laman and Lemuel?

8:19 The rod of iron represents "the word of God" (see 1 Nephi 15:23–24).

8:20 ***strait***—restricted or narrow

Nephi teaches that this path leads to eternal life (see 2 Nephi 31:17–20). Why do you think this path is described as "strait and narrow"?

8:21 ***numberless concourses***—large gatherings

8:22 ***commence***—begin

8:23 The mist of darkness represents "the temptations of the devil" (see 1 Nephi 12:17).

8:26 The great and spacious building represents "the pride of the world" (1 Nephi 11:36). President Ezra Taft Benson taught that pride is "the universal sin, the great vice [evil]" and that humility is "the antidote [cure] for pride" (in Conference Report, April 1989, 6).

8:28 (24–28) Have you ever had people make fun of you because of your beliefs or because you obeyed God's commandments? What gives you strength to stay faithful at those times?

8:30 ***multitudes***—large groups of people

33 And great was the multitude that did enter into that strange building. And after they did enter into that building they did point the finger of scorn at me and those that were partaking of the fruit also; but we heeded them not.

34 These are the words of my father: For as many as heeded them, had fallen away.

35 And Laman and Lemuel partook not of the fruit, said my father.

### Lehi Asks His Family to Keep the Commandments

36 And it came to pass after my father had spoken all the words of his dream or vision, which were many, he said unto us, because of these things which he saw in a vision, he exceedingly feared for Laman and Lemuel; yea, he feared lest they should be cast off from the presence of the Lord.

37 And he did exhort them then with all the feeling of a tender parent, that they would hearken to his words, that perhaps the Lord would be merciful to them, and not cast them off; yea, my father did preach unto them.

38 And after he had preached unto them, and also prophesied unto them of many things, he bade them to keep the commandments of the Lord; and he did cease speaking unto them.

## CHAPTER 9

*Although it is a long and difficult process to engrave on metal plates, Nephi faithfully obeys the Lord's commandment to make two sets. Look for the differences between the large and small plates.*

### Nephi Makes Two Sets of Records

1 AND all these things did my father see, and hear, and speak, as he dwelt in a tent, in the valley of Lemuel, and also a great many more things, which cannot be written upon these plates.

2 And now, as I have spoken concerning these plates, behold they are not the plates upon which I make a full account of the history of my people; for the plates upon which I make a full account of my people I have given the name of Nephi; wherefore, they are called the plates of Nephi, after mine own name; and these plates also are called the plates of Nephi.

3 Nevertheless, I have received a commandment of the Lord that I should make these plates, for the special purpose that there should be an account engraven of the ministry of my people.

4 Upon the other plates should be engraven an account of the reign of the kings, and the wars and contentions of my people; wherefore these plates

---

8:33 Nephi and his family showed how to stay faithful even when others made fun of their obedience. They didn't heed, or pay attention to, the people in the building. How can this example help you remain faithful?

PHOTOGRAPH BY EDWIN M. WOOLLEY

*This stone, discovered in 1935 in Izapa, Mexico, has many of the same objects carved in it that were described in Lehi's dream.*

8:37 ***exhort***—plead with or challenge

8:38 (36–38) Why was Lehi so concerned about Laman and Lemuel? How do you feel about loved ones who are not living the gospel the way they should? How could you help them?

9:3 (2–3) "These plates" refers to the small plates of Nephi. "Upon these [small] plates were recorded the more sacred matters pertaining to the ministry—prophecies and the like (1 Nephi 9:2, 3, 5; 19:3; 2 Nephi 5:30–32; Jacob 1:1–4)" (Sidney B. Sperry, *Book of Mormon Compendium,* 16). Interestingly, these plates are not called "small" plates until Jacob 1.

9:4 The large plates "served as the official record of the Nephites from about 590 B.C. to A.D. 385. (1 Nephi 19:1–4.) During part of this period they were primarily a record of secular [civil and political] events among the descendants of Lehi, but later they contained the religious record as well. (1 Nephi 19:4; Jacob 3:13.) . . . The major books on the large plates of Nephi were as follows: Lehi, Mosiah, Alma, Helaman, [3] Nephi, [4] Nephi, and Mormon" (Daniel H. Ludlow, *A Companion to Your Study of the Book of Mormon,* 57).

are for the more part of the ministry; and the other
plates are for the more part of the reign of the kings
and the wars and contentions of my people.
5 Wherefore, the Lord hath commanded me to
make these plates for a wise purpose in him, which
purpose I know not.
6 But the Lord knoweth all things from the beginning; wherefore, he prepareth a way to accomplish
all his works among the children of men; for
behold, he hath all power unto the fulfilling of all
his words. And thus it is. Amen.

## CHAPTER 10

*Lehi and Nephi prophesy about the coming of the Messiah and His ministry, death, and Resurrection. Watch for what these prophets teach about the mission of Jesus Christ.*

### *Lehi Prophesies About the Destruction of Jerusalem*

1 AND now I, Nephi, proceed to give an account
upon these plates of my proceedings, and my reign
and ministry; wherefore, to proceed with mine
account, I must speak somewhat of the things of
my father, and also of my brethren.
2 For behold, it came to pass after my father had
made an end of speaking the words of his dream,
and also of exhorting them to all diligence, he
spake unto them concerning the Jews—
3 That after they should be destroyed, even that
great city Jerusalem, and many be carried away
captive into Babylon, according to the own due
time of the Lord, they should return again, yea,
even be brought back out of captivity; and after
they should be brought back out of captivity they
should possess again the land of their inheritance.

### *Lehi Prophesies About the Coming of John the Baptist and the Messiah*

4 Yea, even six hundred years from the time that
my father left Jerusalem, a prophet would the Lord
God raise up among the Jews—even a Messiah, or,
in other words, a Savior of the world.
5 And he also spake concerning the prophets,
how great a number had testified of these things,
concerning this Messiah, of whom he had spoken,
or this Redeemer of the world.
6 Wherefore, all mankind were in a lost and in a
fallen state, and ever would be save they should
rely on this Redeemer.

---

9:6 In a revelation to the Prophet Joseph Smith, the Lord describes Himself as "the same which knoweth all things, for all things are present before mine eyes" (D&C 38:2; see also D&C 130:7).

9:6 (5–6) Why did Nephi willingly obey the Lord and make the second set of plates even though the Lord did not tell him the reason for doing so?

The Lord did not tell Nephi why he needed to make a second set of plates. Over two thousand years later, after the Prophet Joseph Smith had translated 116 pages from the plates, Martin Harris borrowed the manuscript of the translation and lost it to wicked men. The Lord knew that these wicked men would change the writings to make any retranslation of the lost portion that Joseph Smith did look wrong by comparison. That is why He commanded Nephi to make another set of records (see Words of Mormon 1:5–7; see also the introductory notes to D&C 3 and 10; D&C 10:38–45).

10:2 ***exhorting them to all diligence***—encouraging them to be good

10:3 ***captivity***—bondage and slavery

***the land of their inheritance***—the land promised to them by the Lord

Jerusalem was destroyed in 587 B.C. by the Babylonians. Many Jews that were not killed were taken as slaves. Later, in 520 B.C., Babylon was destroyed by the Persians, at which time the Jews were freed, and many returned to Jerusalem (see LDS Bible Dictionary, s.v. "Cyrus," 651).

10:5 (4–5) Look for the different names of Jesus Christ in these verses. Each name teaches something different about Him. What do they teach you about Jesus?

10:6 No one can be saved in the celestial kingdom without the Savior (see 2 Nephi 31:21). What can you do to rely on Jesus Christ so He will save you?

10:6 (5–6) "Christ is the *Redeemer* (Isa. 41:14; 54:5; Alma 37:9; 3 Ne. 10:10; D. & C. 15:1; 18:47) because it is he who worked out the redemption, which ransoms and redeems men from the effects of the fall of Adam. He is so named nearly a score of times in both the Old Testament and the Doctrine and Covenants and more than 40 times in the Book of Mormon" (Bruce R. McConkie, *Mormon Doctrine,* 623).

7 And he spake also concerning a prophet who
should come before the Messiah, to prepare the
way of the Lord—
8 Yea, even he should go forth and cry in the
wilderness: Prepare ye the way of the Lord, and
make his paths straight; for there standeth one
among you whom ye know not; and he is mightier
than I, whose shoe's latchet I am not worthy to
unloose. And much spake my father concerning
this thing.
9 And my father said he should baptize in
Bethabara, beyond Jordan; and he also said he
should baptize with water; even that he should baptize the Messiah with water.
10 And after he had baptized the Messiah with
water, he should behold and bear record that he
had baptized the Lamb of God, who should take
away the sins of the world.
11 And it came to pass after my father had spoken
these words he spake unto my brethren concerning
the gospel which should be preached among the
Jews, and also concerning the dwindling of the Jews
in unbelief. And after they had slain the Messiah,
who should come, and after he had been slain he
should rise from the dead, and should make himself
manifest, by the Holy Ghost, unto the Gentiles.

## Lehi Prophesies the Scattering and Gathering of Israel

12 Yea, even my father spake much concerning the
Gentiles, and also concerning the house of Israel,
that they should be compared like unto an olive-
tree, whose branches should be broken off and
should be scattered upon all the face of the earth.
13 Wherefore, he said it must needs be that we
should be led with one accord into the land of promise, unto the fulfilling of the word of the Lord, that
we should be scattered upon all the face of the earth.
14 And after the house of Israel should be scattered they should be gathered together again; or, in
fine, after the Gentiles had received the fulness of

---

10:8 The job of removing people's sandals and washing their dirty feet was usually given to a servant (see Adam Clarke, *Bible Commentary* 5:616). John seems to be saying that Jesus is so great he did not feel worthy to be His servant.

10:8 (7–8) The prophet who came to prepare the way for the Lord was John the Baptist (see Matthew 3:1–3).

10:10 When John baptized Jesus he did "bear record" of Him (see John 1:32–36).

10:11 ***dwindling***—fading, shrinking or wasting away
***manifest***—known or revealed

PHOTOGRAPH BY G. R. SIMS

*Jesus was baptized by John the Baptist in the River Jordan.*

PHOTOGRAPH BY DAVID H. GARNER

*"The natural branches of the olive-tree, or the remnants of the house of Israel, should be grafted in, or come to the knowledge of the true Messiah."*

*Gentiles* is a term that means "nations." It refers to those not of the family of Israel or who do not believe in the God of Israel. In the Book of Mormon it also refers to those who come from Gentile nations, which are all nations outside the land of Israel (see LDS Bible Dictionary, s.v. "Gentile," 679).

10:13 (12–13) Lehi's family, who left Jerusalem and came to the Americas, helped to fulfill prophecies about the scattering of Israel (see Genesis 49:22–26; 2 Nephi 3:4–5; Jacob 6:1–7).

CHRIST'S BAPTISM, BY ROBERT T. BARRETT

*As Lehi prophesied, the Messiah (Jesus) would be baptized by a prophet (John the Baptist) "who should come before the Messiah, to prepare the way of the Lord."*

the Gospel, the natural branches of the olive-tree, or the remnants of the house of Israel, should be grafted in, or come to the knowledge of the true Messiah, their Lord and their Redeemer.

15 And after this manner of language did my father prophesy and speak unto my brethren, and also many more things which I do not write in this book; for I have written as many of them as were expedient for me in mine other book.

16 And all these things, of which I have spoken, were done as my father dwelt in a tent, in the valley of Lemuel.

### Nephi Desires to Know More About Jesus

17 And it came to pass after I, Nephi, having heard all the words of my father, concerning the things which he saw in a vision, and also the things which he spake by the power of the Holy Ghost, which power he received by faith on the Son of God—and the Son of God was the Messiah who should come—I, Nephi, was desirous also that I might see, and hear, and know of these things, by the power of the Holy Ghost, which is the gift of God unto all those who diligently seek him, as well in times of old as in the time that he should manifest himself unto the children of men.

18 For he is the same yesterday, to-day, and forever; and the way is prepared for all men from the foundation of the world, if it so be that they repent and come unto him.

19 For he that diligently seeketh shall find; and the mysteries of God shall be unfolded unto them, by the power of the Holy Ghost, as well in these times as in times of old, and as well in times of old as in times to come; wherefore, the course of the Lord is one eternal round.

20 Therefore remember, O man, for all thy doings thou shalt be brought into judgment.

21 Wherefore, if ye have sought to do wickedly in the days of your probation, then ye are found unclean before the judgment-seat of God; and no unclean thing can dwell with God; wherefore, ye must be cast off forever.

22 And the Holy Ghost giveth authority that I should speak these things, and deny them not.

## CHAPTER 11

*Nephi sees the vision of the tree of life. Notice how Nephi is able to understand the interpretation of his vision by learning more about the Savior. Watch for what and how this vision teaches of Jesus Christ.*

### Nephi Sees the Vision of the Tree of Life

1 FOR it came to pass after I had desired to know the things that my father had seen, and believing that the Lord was able to make them known unto me, as I sat pondering in mine heart I was caught away in the Spirit of the Lord, yea, into an exceedingly high mountain, which I never had before

---

10:14 ***the remnants***—those who are left
***grafted in***—united with or put in

10:17 Joseph Smith also promised that if we would ask God to reveal the truth to us, He would do so "by the power of His Holy Spirit. You will then know for yourselves and not for another. You will not then be dependent on man for the knowledge of God" (*Teachings of the Prophet Joseph Smith*, 11).

The visions and the inspired words of his father motivated Nephi to seek his own testimony of Jesus Christ. How have family members and friends helped you desire to seek a stronger testimony of the Lord?

10:18 ***from the foundation of the world***—from the time of the premortal life

10:19 ***mysteries of God***—truths that cannot be known except through revelation from the Lord
***unfolded***—revealed or shown

Modern revelation helps us understand the phrase "one eternal round." Doctrine and Covenants 3:2 says that "God doth not walk in crooked paths, neither doth he turn to the right hand nor to the left, neither doth he vary from that which he hath said, therefore his paths are straight, and his course is one eternal round." Doctrine and Covenants 35:1 adds that the Lord is called "the beginning and the end" and that His "course is one eternal round, the same today as yesterday, and forever."

10:20 Throughout the Book of Mormon, the words *man* and *men* nearly always mean "mankind" or "men and women."

10:21 ***in the days of your probation***—during the test of earth life

11:1 Quiet study and pondering of scriptures and the words of prophets invite additional revelation (see D&C 76:19; 138:1–2, 11).

seen, and upon which I never had before set my foot.
2 And the Spirit said unto me: Behold, what desirest thou?
3 And I said: I desire to behold the things which my father saw.
4 And the Spirit said unto me: Believest thou that thy father saw the tree of which he hath spoken?
5 And I said: Yea, thou knowest that I believe all the words of my father.
6 And when I had spoken these words, the Spirit cried with a loud voice, saying: Hosanna to the Lord, the most high God; for he is God over all the earth, yea, even above all. And blessed art thou, Nephi, because thou believest in the Son of the most high God; wherefore, thou shalt behold the things which thou hast desired.
7 And behold this thing shall be given unto thee for a sign, that after thou hast beheld the tree which bore the fruit which thy father tasted, thou shalt also behold a man descending out of heaven, and him shall ye witness; and after ye have witnessed him ye shall bear record that it is the Son of God.
8 And it came to pass that the Spirit said unto me: Look! And I looked and beheld a tree; and it was like unto the tree which my father had seen; and the beauty thereof was far beyond, yea, exceeding of all beauty; and the whiteness thereof did exceed the whiteness of the driven snow.
9 And it came to pass after I had seen the tree, I said unto the Spirit: I behold thou hast shown unto me the tree which is precious above all.
10 And he said unto me: What desirest thou?
11 And I said unto him: To know the interpretation thereof—for I spake unto him as a man speaketh; for I beheld that he was in the form of a man; yet nevertheless, I knew that it was the Spirit of the Lord; and he spake unto me as a man speaketh with another.
12 And it came to pass that he said unto me: Look! And I looked as if to look upon him, and I saw him not; for he had gone from before my presence.

## Nephi Learns of God's Great Love for His Children

13 And it came to pass that I looked and beheld the great city of Jerusalem, and also other cities. And I beheld the city of Nazareth; and in the city of Nazareth I beheld a virgin, and she was exceedingly fair and white.
14 And it came to pass that I saw the heavens open; and an angel came down and stood before me; and he said unto me: Nephi, what beholdest thou?
15 And I said unto him: A virgin, most beautiful and fair above all other virgins.
16 And he said unto me: Knowest thou the condescension of God?
17 And I said unto him: I know that he loveth his children; nevertheless, I do not know the meaning of all things.
18 And he said unto me: Behold, the virgin whom thou seest is the mother of the Son of God, after the manner of the flesh.
19 And it came to pass that I beheld that she was carried away in the Spirit; and after she had been carried away in the Spirit for the space of a time the angel spake unto me, saying: Look!
20 And I looked and beheld the virgin again, bearing a child in her arms.
21 And the angel said unto me: Behold the Lamb of God, yea, even the Son of the Eternal Father! Knowest thou the meaning of the tree which thy father saw?

---

11:6 ***Hosanna***—a shout of praise to the Lord that means "Save now!" or "Save, we pray!"

11:11 "That the Spirit of the Lord is capable of manifesting Himself in the form and figure of man, is indicated by the wonderful interview between the Spirit and Nephi, in which He revealed Himself to the prophet [Nephi], questioned him concerning his desires and belief, instructed him in the things of God, speaking face to face with the man. . . . However, the Holy Ghost does not possess a body of flesh and bones, as do both the Father and the Son, but is a personage of spirit" (James E. Talmage, *The Articles of Faith,* 159–60).

11:13 ***a virgin***—an unmarried person who is pure, righteous, and keeps the commandments

11:14 ***what beholdest thou***—what do you see

11:18 (16–18) The condescension of God, spoken of in these verses, is an expression of Heavenly Father's great love for His children. According to Elder Bruce R. McConkie, Heavenly Father "came down from his station of dominion and power to become the Father of a Son who would be born of Mary" (*A New Witness for the Articles of Faith,* 111).

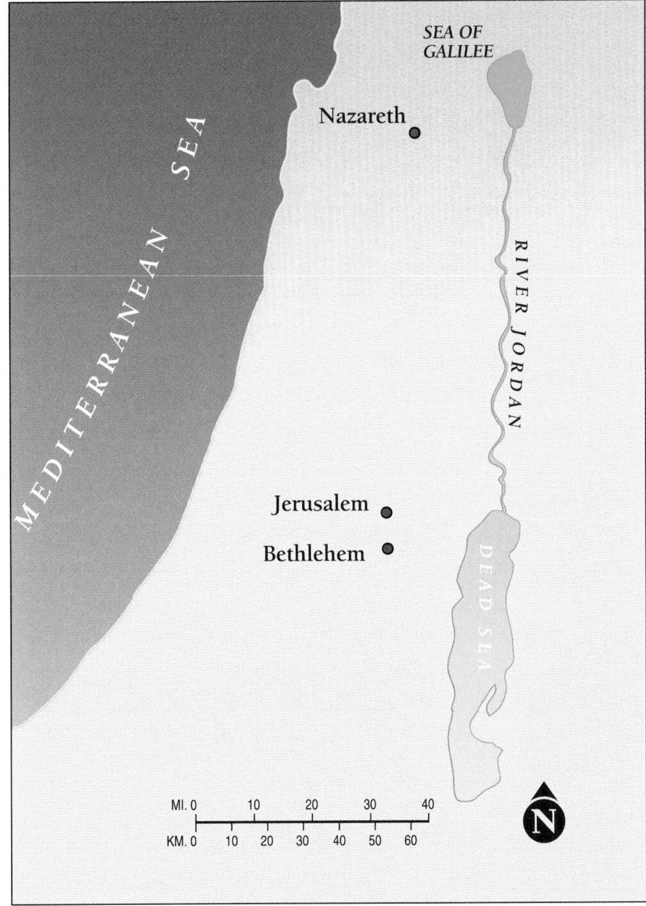


*Jesus was born in Bethlehem, near Jerusalem, but was raised in Nazareth about seventy miles to the north.*

22 And I answered him, saying: Yea, it is the love of God, which sheddeth itself abroad in the hearts of the children of men; wherefore, it is the most desirable above all things.

23 And he spake unto me, saying: Yea, and the most joyous to the soul.

24 And after he had said these words, he said unto me: Look! And I looked, and I beheld the Son of God going forth among the children of men; and I saw many fall down at his feet and worship him.

25 And it came to pass that I beheld that the rod of iron, which my father had seen, was the word of God, which led to the fountain of living waters, or to the tree of life; which waters are a representation of the love of God; and I also beheld that the tree of life was a representation of the love of God.

## Nephi Learns of the Condescension of Jesus Christ

26 And the angel said unto me again: Look and behold the condescension of God!

27 And I looked and beheld the Redeemer of the world, of whom my father had spoken; and I also beheld the prophet who should prepare the way before him. And the Lamb of God went forth and was baptized of him; and after he was baptized, I beheld the heavens open, and the Holy Ghost come down out of heaven and abide upon him in the form of a dove.

28 And I beheld that he went forth ministering unto the people, in power and great glory; and the multitudes were gathered together to hear him; and I beheld that they cast him out from among them.

29 And I also beheld twelve others following him. And it came to pass that they were carried away in the Spirit from before my face, and I saw them not.

30 And it came to pass that the angel spake unto me again, saying: Look! And I looked, and I beheld the heavens open again, and I saw angels descending upon the children of men; and they did minister unto them.

31 And he spake unto me again, saying: Look! And I looked, and I beheld the Lamb of God going forth among the children of men. And I beheld multitudes of people who were sick, and who were afflicted with all manner of diseases, and with devils and unclean spirits; and the angel spake and showed all these things unto me. And they were healed by the power of the Lamb of God; and the devils and the unclean spirits were cast out.

32 And it came to pass that the angel spake unto

11:22 (21–22) Nephi learns that the tree represents "the love of God." The Atonement of Jesus Christ is the greatest example of God's love for His children. The Savior Himself declared, "God so loved the world, that he gave his only begotten Son" (John 3:16).

11:27 The prophet who prepared the people to listen to Jesus and then baptized the Savior was John the Baptist (see Matthew 3:1–3, 13–16).

11:28 ***ministering unto***—serving, caring for, and teaching
***the multitudes***—many people

11:29 Jesus Christ chose twelve men to be His Apostles. They served as special witnesses of Him, as do the Apostles who live in our day (see 1 Nephi 12:9; D&C 107:23).

Mary holds the baby Jesus.

"SHE SHALL BRING FORTH A SON," BY LIZ LEMON SWINDLE

me again, saying: Look! And I looked and beheld
the Lamb of God, that he was taken by the people;
yea, the Son of the everlasting God was judged of
the world; and I saw and bear record.
33 And I, Nephi, saw that he was lifted up upon
the cross and slain for the sins of the world.

## *Wicked People Fight Against Jesus' Apostles*

34 And after he was slain I saw the multitudes of
the earth, that they were gathered together to fight
against the apostles of the Lamb; for thus were the
twelve called by the angel of the Lord.
35 And the multitude of the earth was gathered
together; and I beheld that they were in a large and
spacious building, like unto the building which my
father saw. And the angel of the Lord spake unto
me again, saying: Behold the world and the wisdom
thereof; yea, behold the house of Israel hath gathered together to fight against the twelve apostles of
the Lamb.
36 And it came to pass that I saw and bear
record, that the great and spacious building was
the pride of the world; and it fell, and the fall
thereof was exceedingly great. And the angel of
the Lord spake unto me again, saying: Thus shall
be the destruction of all nations, kindreds,
tongues, and people, that shall fight against the
twelve apostles of the Lamb.

# CHAPTER 12

*Nephi's vision continues. He sees Jesus Christ descend from heaven. As you read this chapter think of what it might be like to actually see the Savior.*

## *Nephi Sees the Future of the Nephites and Lamanites*

1 AND it came to pass that the angel said unto
me: Look, and behold thy seed, and also the seed
of thy brethren. And I looked and beheld the land
of promise; and I beheld multitudes of people,
yea, even as it were in number as many as the
sand of the sea.
2 And it came to pass that I beheld multitudes
gathered together to battle, one against the other;
and I beheld wars, and rumors of wars, and great
slaughters with the sword among my people.
3 And it came to pass that I beheld many generations pass away, after the manner of wars and contentions in the land; and I beheld many cities, yea,
even that I did not number them.
4 And it came to pass that I saw a mist of darkness on the face of the land of promise; and I saw
lightnings, and I heard thunderings, and earthquakes, and all manner of tumultuous noises; and I
saw the earth and the rocks, that they rent; and I
saw mountains tumbling into pieces; and I saw the

---

11:33 It was known hundreds of years before Jesus was even born that He would be crucified on a cross (see also 1 Nephi 19:10).

11:33 (26–33) The angel shows Nephi the condescension of Jesus Christ, which means that although Jesus "himself is the Lord Omnipotent, the very Being who created the earth and all things that in it are, yet being born of mortal woman, he submitted to all the trials of mortality, . . . finally being put to death" (Bruce R. McConkie, *Mormon Doctrine,* 155).

11:36 Apparently, to help show Nephi that the "great and spacious building" represents the "pride of the world," the angel shows Nephi the crucifixion of Jesus Christ (see verses 32–33). President Ezra Taft Benson said, "It was through pride that Christ was crucified." The Pharisees saw Jesus as "a threat to their position, and so they plotted His death" (in Conference Report, April 1989, 4).

11:36 (34–36) Nephi learns that among those who fight against the Apostles are those who rely only on the wisdom of the world. Why do some people who think they know a lot find it so difficult to be humble? How does having great pride make it difficult to follow Church leaders?

12:1 ***thy seed***—the Nephites
***the seed of thy brethren***—the Lamanites

12:2 ***great slaughters***—much killing and bloodshed

12:3 ***many generations***—many periods of time or many years
***contentions***—arguing and fighting

12:4 This darkness and destruction took place in the Americas when Jesus was crucified in Jerusalem (see 3 Nephi 8–10). Samuel the Lamanite, a prophet, also predicted this destruction would come (see Helaman 14:20–27).

*Nephi saw in vision that the resurrected Lord would appear on the American continent.*

plains of the earth, that they were broken up; and I saw many cities that they were sunk; and I saw many that they were burned with fire; and I saw many that did tumble to the earth, because of the quaking thereof.

## NEPHI SEES JESUS APPEAR TO THE RIGHTEOUS NEPHITES

5 And it came to pass after I saw these things, I
saw the vapor of darkness, that it passed from off the face of the earth; and behold, I saw multitudes who had not fallen because of the great and terrible judgments of the Lord.
6 And I saw the heavens open, and the Lamb of God descending out of heaven; and he came down and showed himself unto them.
7 And I also saw and bear record that the Holy Ghost fell upon twelve others; and they were ordained of God, and chosen.

---

12:5 **vapor**—mist or cloud

We learn from 3 Nephi 10:12 that the people who were not killed at this time were "the more righteous part of the people." They were those who had listened to and obeyed the prophets.

12:6 Jesus Christ is called the Lamb of God because He is the sacrifice "which taketh away the sin of the world" (John 1:29).

8 And the angel spake unto me, saying: Behold the twelve disciples of the Lamb, who are chosen to minister unto thy seed.

9 And he said unto me: Thou rememberest the twelve apostles of the Lamb? Behold they are they who shall judge the twelve tribes of Israel; wherefore, the twelve ministers of thy seed shall be judged of them; for ye are of the house of Israel.

10 And these twelve ministers whom thou beholdest shall judge thy seed. And, behold, they are righteous forever; for because of their faith in the Lamb of God their garments are made white in his blood.

11 And the angel said unto me: Look! And I looked, and beheld three generations pass away in righteousness; and their garments were white even like unto the Lamb of God. And the angel said unto me: These are made white in the blood of the Lamb, because of their faith in him.

12 And I, Nephi, also saw many of the fourth generation who passed away in righteousness.

## *Nephi Sees His Descendants Fall to Temptation and Pride*

13 And it came to pass that I saw the multitudes of the earth gathered together.

14 And the angel said unto me: Behold thy seed, and also the seed of thy brethren.

15 And it came to pass that I looked and beheld the people of my seed gathered together in multitudes against the seed of my brethren; and they were gathered together to battle.

16 And the angel spake unto me, saying: Behold the fountain of filthy water which thy father saw; yea, even the river of which he spake; and the depths thereof are the depths of hell.

17 And the mists of darkness are the temptations of the devil, which blindeth the eyes, and hardeneth the hearts of the children of men, and leadeth them away into broad roads, that they perish and are lost.

18 And the large and spacious building, which thy father saw, is vain imaginations and the pride of the children of men. And a great and a terrible gulf divideth them; yea, even the word of the justice of the Eternal God, and the Messiah who is the Lamb of God, of whom the Holy Ghost beareth record, from the beginning of the world until this time, and from this time henceforth and forever.

19 And while the angel spake these words, I beheld and saw that the seed of my brethren did contend against my seed, according to the word of the angel; and because of the pride of my seed, and the temptations of the devil, I beheld that the seed of my brethren did overpower the people of my seed.

## *Nephi Sees the Lamanites Overcome the Nephites*

20 And it came to pass that I beheld, and saw the people of the seed of my brethren that they had overcome my seed; and they went forth in multitudes upon the face of the land.

21 And I saw them gathered together in multitudes; and I saw wars and rumors of wars among them; and in wars and rumors of wars I saw many generations pass away.

22 And the angel said unto me: Behold these shall dwindle in unbelief.

---

12:11 (10–11) Notice why these Twelve Apostles are "righteous forever." Because of their faith in the Atonement of Jesus Christ, their "garments are made white," or, in other words, their sins are forgiven and they are given power to live righteously (see also Mosiah 5:2).

12:18 ***vain imaginations***—desires or thoughts with no lasting value

12:18 (16–18) The angel teaches Nephi about wickedness by showing him parts of the dream that Nephi's father, Lehi, saw. Lehi's dream included mists of darkness and a great and spacious building (see 1 Nephi 8).

12:19 ***contend***—fight

President Ezra Taft Benson said: "Pride is essentially competitive in nature. We pit our will against God's. When we direct our pride toward God, it is in the spirit of 'my will and not thine be done' " (in Conference Report, April 1989, 4).

12:20 ***overcome***—won the battle against

12:21 The Book of Mormon has sentences that repeat ideas. This is an ancient way of writing. One reason for its use is to help the reader better remember important ideas. Notice that in this verse the word *saw* is in both the first and the last phrase of the verse. Also, "wars and rumors of wars" is repeated in the middle of the verse. You will see this pattern often in the Book of Mormon; it is called *chiasmus*.

12:22 ***dwindle***—become weak and fall away

23 And it came to pass that I beheld, after they
had dwindled in unbelief they became a dark, and
loathsome, and a filthy people, full of idleness and
all manner of abominations.

## CHAPTER 13

*Nephi sees in vision the future of his people and what will happen in the promised land. He also sees the restoration of the gospel in the latter days. Look for what Heavenly Father does to help His children know the truth.*

### *The Lord Shows Nephi the Great and Abominable Church Persecuting the Saints*

1 AND it came to pass that the angel spake unto
me, saying: Look! And I looked and beheld many
nations and kingdoms.
2 And the angel said unto me: What beholdest
thou? And I said: I behold many nations and kingdoms.
3 And he said unto me: These are the nations and
kingdoms of the Gentiles.
4 And it came to pass that I saw among the
nations of the Gentiles the formation of a great
church.
5 And the angel said unto me: Behold the formation of a church which is most abominable above
all other churches, which slayeth the saints of God,
yea, and tortureth them and bindeth them down,
and yoketh them with a yoke of iron, and bringeth
them down into captivity.
6 And it came to pass that I beheld this great and
abominable church; and I saw the devil that he was
the founder of it.
7 And I also saw gold, and silver, and silks, and
scarlets, and fine-twined linen, and all manner of
precious clothing; and I saw many harlots.
8 And the angel spake unto me, saying: Behold
the gold, and the silver, and the silks, and the scarlets, and the fine-twined linen, and the precious
clothing, and the harlots, are the desires of this
great and abominable church.
9 And also for the praise of the world do they
destroy the saints of God, and bring them down
into captivity.

### *The Lord Shows Nephi That the Spirit Will Lead Columbus and Others to the Promised Land*

10 And it came to pass that I looked and beheld
many waters; and they divided the Gentiles from
the seed of my brethren.
11 And it came to pass that the angel said unto
me: Behold the wrath of God is upon the seed of
thy brethren.

---

12:23 ***loathsome***—horrible or disgusting
***idleness***—laziness
***abominations***—acts of great evil

Nephi's vision was about his descendants, or his future family. How would you feel if you knew your family would turn away from the Lord in the future? How can we help our families to remain strong in the faith and receive all the blessings of the gospel?

13:5 ***abominable***—terrible and evil
***slayeth***—kills
***tortureth***—abuses and torments
***captivity***—bondage and slavery

13:6 ***founder***—creator or builder

13:7 ***harlots***—immoral women

13:8 (4–8) Elder Bruce R. McConkie wrote, "The titles *church of the devil* and *great and abominable church* are used to identify all churches or organizations of whatever name or nature . . . which are designed to take men on a course that leads away from God and his laws and thus from salvation in the kingdom of God" (*Mormon Doctrine,* 137–38).

*The word yoke as used by the angel in 1 Nephi 13:5 is a symbol for bondage and hardship.*

13:9 Why do you think the devil and his servants are so determined to destroy the Saints of God?

NEPHI'S VISION, BY CLARK KELLEY PRICE

*While Nephi pondered the words of his father, a vision was opened to him.*

12 And I looked and beheld a man among the Gentiles, who was separated from the seed of my brethren by the many waters; and I beheld the Spirit of God, that it came down and wrought upon the man; and he went forth upon the many waters, even unto the seed of my brethren, who were in the promised land.

13 And it came to pass that I beheld the Spirit of God, that it wrought upon other Gentiles; and they went forth out of captivity, upon the many waters.

14 And it came to pass that I beheld many multitudes of the Gentiles upon the land of promise; and I beheld the wrath of God, that it was upon the seed of my brethren; and they were scattered before the Gentiles and were smitten.

## Nephi Sees the Lord Deliver Some Gentiles from All Other Nations

15 And I beheld the Spirit of the Lord, that it was upon the Gentiles, and they did prosper and obtain the land for their inheritance; and I beheld that they were white, and exceedingly fair and beautiful, like unto my people before they were slain.

16 And it came to pass that I, Nephi, beheld that the Gentiles who had gone forth out of captivity did humble themselves before the Lord; and the power of the Lord was with them.

17 And I beheld that their mother Gentiles were gathered together upon the waters, and upon the land also, to battle against them.

---

13:12 ***wrought upon***—worked on or inspired

13:12 (10–12) Referring to the man noted in these verses, President Ezra Taft Benson taught: "That man, of course, was Christopher Columbus, who testified that he was inspired in what he did" (*The Teachings of Ezra Taft Benson,* 577).

13:13 Some of the people the Spirit inspired to come to this promised land for freedom were the Puritans, one group of which was the Pilgrims.

13:14 ***smitten***—beaten

13:15 (14–15) Notice what the Lord shows Nephi about his family in the promised land before they even go there: (1) there will be fighting between his seed, or descendants, and the seed of his brothers (see 1 Nephi 2:20–24); (2) his descendants will almost all be killed by the time the Gentiles come to this promised land; and (3) the Gentiles will scatter the seed of his brothers, the Lamanites (see also 1 Nephi 13:35; 2 Nephi 1:11).

13:17 ***their mother Gentiles***—the people of the Gentile nations they came from

ILLUSTRATION BY DALE KILBOURN

*The explorer Christopher Columbus said: "Our Lord unlocked my mind, sent me upon the sea, and gave me fire for the deed. Those who heard of my enterprise called it foolish, mocked me, and laughed. But who can doubt but that the Holy Ghost inspired me?" (quoted in Ezra Taft Benson,* The Teachings of Ezra Taft Benson, *577).*

ILLUSTRATION BY GREG MICHAELS

*"The Gentiles that had gone out of captivity were delivered by the power of God out of the hands of all other nations."*

18 And I beheld that the power of God was with them, and also that the wrath of God was upon all those that were gathered together against them to battle.

19 And I, Nephi, beheld that the Gentiles that had gone out of captivity were delivered by the power of God out of the hands of all other nations.

### *Nephi Sees That the Colonists Who Come to the Promised Land Will Bring the Bible with Them*

20 And it came to pass that I, Nephi, beheld that they did prosper in the land; and I beheld a book, and it was carried forth among them.

21 And the angel said unto me: Knowest thou the meaning of the book?

22 And I said unto him: I know not.

23 And he said: Behold it proceedeth out of the mouth of a Jew. And I, Nephi, beheld it; and he said unto me: The book that thou beholdest is a record of the Jews, which contains the covenants of the Lord, which he hath made unto the house of Israel; and it also containeth many of the prophecies of the holy prophets; and it is a record like unto the engravings which are upon the plates of brass, save there are not so many; nevertheless, they contain the covenants of the Lord, which he hath made unto the house of Israel; wherefore, they are of great worth unto the Gentiles.

### *Nephi Sees That Many Plain and Precious Things Are Taken Out of the Bible*

24 And the angel of the Lord said unto me: Thou hast beheld that the book proceeded forth from the mouth of a Jew; and when it proceeded forth from the mouth of a Jew it contained the fulness of the gospel of the Lord, of whom the twelve apostles bear record; and they bear record according to the truth which is in the Lamb of God.

25 Wherefore, these things go forth from the Jews in purity unto the Gentiles, according to the truth which is in God.

26 And after they go forth by the hand of the twelve apostles of the Lamb, from the Jews unto the Gentiles, thou seest the formation of that great and abominable church, which is most abominable above all other churches; for behold, they have taken away from the gospel of the Lamb many parts which are plain and most precious; and also many covenants of the Lord have they taken away.

27 And all this have they done that they might pervert the right ways of the Lord, that they might blind the eyes and harden the hearts of the children of men.

28 Wherefore, thou seest that after the book hath gone forth through the hands of the great and abominable church, that there are many plain and precious things taken away from the book, which is the book of the Lamb of God.

29 And after these plain and precious things were taken away it goeth forth unto all the nations of the Gentiles; and after it goeth forth unto all the nations of the Gentiles, yea, even across the many waters which thou hast seen with the Gentiles which have gone forth out of captivity, thou seest—because of the many plain and precious things which have been taken out of the book, which were plain unto the understanding of the children of men, according to the plainness which is in the Lamb of God—because of these things which are taken away out of the gospel of the Lamb, an exceedingly great many do stumble, yea, insomuch that Satan hath great power over them.

### *In the Latter Days the True Gospel Will Again Be Revealed to the Gentiles*

30 Nevertheless, thou beholdest that the Gentiles who have gone forth out of captivity, and have been lifted up by the power of God above all other nations, upon the face of the land which is choice

---

13:23 ***it proceedeth out of the mouth of a Jew***—it is spoken by one who is a Jew (that is, the book comes from the Jews)

The "record of the Jews" is the Bible. Nephi learns that it is like the plates of brass that he got from Laban, but the brass plates contain more information.

13:27 ***pervert***—change or distort

13:29 Because so many plain and precious things have been taken from the Bible, there are hundreds of churches and they all disagree about what the Bible really means. How do the Book of Mormon, the Doctrine and Covenants, and the Pearl of Great Price help clear up the confusion over the meaning of the Bible?

Not all of Nephi's seed, or descendants, would be destroyed. Some would intermarry with the seed of his brothers.

above all other lands, which is the land that the Lord God hath covenanted with thy father that his seed should have for the land of their inheritance; wherefore, thou seest that the Lord God will not suffer that the Gentiles will utterly destroy the mixture of thy seed, which are among thy brethren.

31 Neither will he suffer that the Gentiles shall destroy the seed of thy brethren.

32 Neither will the Lord God suffer that the Gentiles shall forever remain in that awful state of blindness, which thou beholdest they are in, because of the plain and most precious parts of the gospel of the Lamb which have been kept back by that abominable church, whose formation thou hast seen.

33 Wherefore saith the Lamb of God: I will be merciful unto the Gentiles, unto the visiting of the remnant of the house of Israel in great judgment.

34 And it came to pass that the angel of the Lord spake unto me, saying: Behold, saith the Lamb of God, after I have visited the remnant of the house of Israel—and this remnant of whom I speak is the seed of thy father—wherefore, after I have visited them in judgment, and smitten them by the hand of the Gentiles, and after the Gentiles do stumble exceedingly, because of the most plain and precious parts of the gospel of the Lamb which have been kept back by that abominable church, which is the mother of harlots, saith the Lamb—I will be merciful unto the Gentiles in that day, insomuch that I will bring forth unto them, in mine own power, much of my gospel, which shall be plain and precious, saith the Lamb.

## *Jesus Christ Will Visit the Descendants of Nephi and Give Them His True Gospel*

35 For, behold, saith the Lamb: I will manifest myself unto thy seed, that they shall write many things which I shall minister unto them, which shall be plain and precious; and after thy seed shall be destroyed, and dwindle in unbelief, and also the seed of thy brethren, behold, these things shall be hid up, to come forth unto the Gentiles, by the gift and power of the Lamb.

36 And in them shall be written my gospel, saith the Lamb, and my rock and my salvation.

37 And blessed are they who shall seek to bring forth my Zion at that day, for they shall have the gift and the power of the Holy Ghost; and if they endure unto the end they shall be lifted up at the last day, and shall be saved in the everlasting kingdom of the Lamb; and whoso shall publish peace, yea, tidings of great joy, how beautiful upon the mountains shall they be.

## *The Book of Mormon and Other Modern Scriptures Prove to the World That the Bible Is True*

38 And it came to pass that I beheld the remnant of the seed of my brethren, and also the book of the Lamb of God, which had proceeded forth from the mouth of the Jew, that it came forth from the Gentiles unto the remnant of the seed of my brethren.

39 And after it had come forth unto them I beheld other books, which came forth by the power of the Lamb, from the Gentiles unto them, unto the

---

13:30 ***the land of their inheritance***—the land promised to them by the Lord

13:36 (35–36) The Book of Mormon restores many of the plain and precious parts of the gospel that were lost from the Bible. When Jesus visited the Nephites, He told them specific things they needed to write down so that we could have the truth today (see 3 Nephi 23:7–13).

The word *rock* in this verse refers to the gospel of Jesus Christ and its teachings. Other scriptures refer to the Savior Himself as our rock and our salvation (see 2 Samuel 22:2; Psalm 18:46; and 1 Nephi 15:15). Helaman said "that it is upon the rock of our Redeemer, who is Christ, the Son of God, that ye must build your foundation" (Helaman 5:12).

13:37 *Zion* is used several ways in the scriptures. Zion is defined as "the pure in heart" (D&C 97:21). Sometimes Zion has reference to a specific place. Enoch's city was called Zion (see Moses 7:19). Jackson County, Missouri, is also referred to as Zion (see D&C 58:49–50), and the city of New Jerusalem, which is to be built in Jackson County, will be called Zion (see D&C 45:66–67). Joseph Smith referred to Zion, in a broader sense, as all of North and South America (see *History of the Church* 6:318–19; see also LDS Bible Dictionary, s.v. "Zion," 792).

13:39 (38–39) The Lord told Moses that in the last days a prophet would be called to restore many of the truths that were lost from the Bible (see Moses 1:40–42). What books of scripture has the Lord given us in these last days? Who was the prophet that the Lord called to bring them to us?

convincing of the Gentiles and the remnant of the
seed of my brethren, and also the Jews who were
scattered upon all the face of the earth, that the
records of the prophets and of the twelve apostles
of the Lamb are true.
40 And the angel spake unto me, saying: These
last records, which thou hast seen among the
Gentiles, shall establish the truth of the first, which
are of the twelve apostles of the Lamb, and shall
make known the plain and precious things which
have been taken away from them; and shall make
known to all kindreds, tongues, and people, that
the Lamb of God is the Son of the Eternal Father,
and the Savior of the world; and that all men must
come unto him, or they cannot be saved.
41 And they must come according to the words
which shall be established by the mouth of the
Lamb; and the words of the Lamb shall be made
known in the records of thy seed, as well as in the
records of the twelve apostles of the Lamb; wherefore they both shall be established in one; for there
is one God and one Shepherd over all the earth.
42 And the time cometh that he shall manifest
himself unto all nations, both unto the Jews and
also unto the Gentiles; and after he has manifested
himself unto the Jews and also unto the Gentiles,
then he shall manifest himself unto the Gentiles and
also unto the Jews, and the last shall be first, and
the first shall be last.

## CHAPTER 14

*Nephi sees that in the last days the church of the devil will persecute the members of the Church of Jesus Christ. As you read, notice what happens to the Saints of God and what happens to wicked people.*

### An Angel Tells Nephi About Blessings and Punishments That Will Come upon the Gentiles in the Last Days

1 AND it shall come to pass, that if the Gentiles
shall hearken unto the Lamb of God in that day that
he shall manifest himself unto them in word, and
also in power, in very deed, unto the taking away
of their stumbling blocks—
2 And harden not their hearts against the Lamb of
God, they shall be numbered among the seed of thy
father; yea, they shall be numbered among the
house of Israel; and they shall be a blessed people
upon the promised land forever; they shall be no
more brought down into captivity; and the house of
Israel shall no more be confounded.
3 And that great pit, which hath been digged for
them by that great and abominable church, which
was founded by the devil and his children, that he
might lead away the souls of men down to hell—
yea, that great pit which hath been digged for the
destruction of men shall be filled by those who
digged it, unto their utter destruction, saith the Lamb

PHOTOGRAPH BY GRANT HEATON

*Modern scripture teaches the gospel and proves that the Bible is true.*

13:42 In Jesus' day the Jews were the first to receive the gospel. Later, it was taken to the Gentiles. In our day the gospel was first given to the Gentile nations, who were told to gather scattered Israel. In the end the gospel will again be taken to the Jews. That is how the first are last and the last are now first.

14:1 ***manifest***—reveal or show

These "stumbling blocks" would be created when many plain and precious truths were taken from the scriptures (see 1 Nephi 13:29).

14:2 ***captivity***—bondage and slavery
***confounded***—confused, put to shame, humiliated

14:3 ***founded***—begun
***utter***—complete

14:3 (1–3) The angel promises that if the Gentiles will "hearken unto the Lamb of God" and "harden not their hearts," they will receive the following blessings: (1) they will be included in the house of Israel; (2) they will be blessed upon their promised land forever; and (3) they will be delivered from the power of the "great and abominable church," which seeks to destroy them.

of God; not the destruction of the soul, save it be the casting of it into that hell which hath no end.

4 For behold, this is according to the captivity of the devil, and also according to the justice of God, upon all those who will work wickedness and abomination before him.

5 And it came to pass that the angel spake unto me, Nephi, saying: Thou hast beheld that if the Gentiles repent it shall be well with them; and thou also knowest concerning the covenants of the Lord unto the house of Israel; and thou also hast heard that whoso repenteth not must perish.

6 Therefore, wo be unto the Gentiles if it so be that they harden their hearts against the Lamb of God.

7 For the time cometh, saith the Lamb of God, that I will work a great and a marvelous work among the children of men; a work which shall be everlasting, either on the one hand or on the other—either to the convincing of them unto peace and life eternal, or unto the deliverance of them to the hardness of their hearts and the blindness of their minds unto their being brought down into captivity, and also into destruction, both temporally and spiritually, according to the captivity of the devil, of which I have spoken.

8 And it came to pass that when the angel had spoken these words, he said unto me: Rememberest thou the covenants of the Father unto the house of Israel? I said unto him, Yea.

9 And it came to pass that he said unto me: Look, and behold that great and abominable church, which is the mother of abominations, whose founder is the devil.

## Nephi Learns That There Are Only Two Churches

10 And he said unto me: Behold there are save two churches only; the one is the church of the Lamb of God, and the other is the church of the devil; wherefore, whoso belongeth not to the church of the Lamb of God belongeth to that great church, which is the mother of abominations; and she is the whore of all the earth.

11 And it came to pass that I looked and beheld the whore of all the earth, and she sat upon many waters; and she had dominion over all the earth, among all nations, kindreds, tongues, and people.

12 And it came to pass that I beheld the church of the Lamb of God, and its numbers were few, because of the wickedness and abominations of the whore who sat upon many waters; nevertheless, I beheld that the church of the Lamb, who were the saints of God, were also upon all the face of the earth; and their dominions upon the face of the earth were small, because of the wickedness of the great whore whom I saw.

## Nephi Sees That the Church of the Devil Will Persecute the Saints of God

13 And it came to pass that I beheld that the great mother of abominations did gather together multitudes upon the face of all the earth, among all the nations of the Gentiles, to fight against the Lamb of God.

---

14:4 ***abomination***—great evil

14:5 A covenant is an agreement between two people. In the scriptures it is usually an agreement between God and man. We promise to be obedient to God's commandments, and He promises to bless us (see LDS Bible Dictionary, s.v. "Covenant," 651).

14:6 ***wo***—grief, sorrow, and misery

14:7 The Lord also revealed to Joseph Smith that "a marvelous work is about to come forth" (D&C 4:1). Missionaries help fulfill this prophecy by sharing the gospel in every land. What can you do to be part of this "great and marvelous work"?

***temporally***—physically

14:10 In 1845 the Council of the Twelve proclaimed: "As this work progresses in its onward course, . . . no king, ruler, or subject, no community or individual, will stand *neutral.* All will . . . take sides either for or against the kingdom of God" (in James R. Clark, ed., *Messages of the First Presidency* 1:257).

***whore***—wicked and immoral person (sometimes the word is used symbolically, as it may be in this verse, to mean someone who worships false gods)

14:11 ***dominion***—power
***kindreds***—families
***tongues***—people of various language groups

14:12 ***dominions***—places of power

14 And it came to pass that I, Nephi, beheld the power of the Lamb of God, that it descended upon the saints of the church of the Lamb, and upon the covenant people of the Lord, who were scattered upon all the face of the earth; and they were armed with righteousness and with the power of God in great glory.

15 And it came to pass that I beheld that the wrath of God was poured out upon that great and abominable church, insomuch that there were wars and rumors of wars among all the nations and kindreds of the earth.

16 And as there began to be wars and rumors of wars among all the nations which belonged to the mother of abominations, the angel spake unto me, saying: Behold, the wrath of God is upon the mother of harlots; and behold, thou seest all these things—

17 And when the day cometh that the wrath of God is poured out upon the mother of harlots, which is the great and abominable church of all the earth, whose founder is the devil, then, at that day, the work of the Father shall commence, in preparing the way for the fulfilling of his covenants, which he hath made to his people who are of the house of Israel.

## *Nephi Sees the Mission of the Apostle John*

18 And it came to pass that the angel spake unto me, saying: Look!

19 And I looked and beheld a man, and he was dressed in a white robe.

20 And the angel said unto me: Behold one of the twelve apostles of the Lamb.

21 Behold, he shall see and write the remainder of these things; yea, and also many things which have been.

22 And he shall also write concerning the end of the world.

23 Wherefore, the things which he shall write are just and true; and behold they are written in the book which thou beheld proceeding out of the mouth of the Jew; and at the time they proceeded out of the mouth of the Jew, or, at the time the book proceeded out of the mouth of the Jew, the things which were written were plain and pure, and most precious and easy to the understanding of all men.

24 And behold, the things which this apostle of the Lamb shall write are many things which thou hast seen; and behold, the remainder shalt thou see.

25 But the things which thou shalt see hereafter thou shalt not write; for the Lord God hath ordained the apostle of the Lamb of God that he should write them.

26 And also others who have been, to them hath he shown all things, and they have written them; and they are sealed up to come forth in their purity, according to the truth which is in the Lamb, in the own due time of the Lord, unto the house of Israel.

27 And I, Nephi, heard and bear record, that the name of the apostle of the Lamb was John, according to the word of the angel.

28 And behold, I, Nephi, am forbidden that I should write the remainder of the things which I saw and heard; wherefore the things which I have written sufficeth me; and I have written but a small part of the things which I saw.

---

14:14 Covenant people of the Lord are people who "repent and believe in . . . the Holy One of Israel" (2 Nephi 30:2).

Even though the righteous are outnumbered, Nephi learns, they have no need to fear. How does knowing this help you?

14:15 ***wrath***—anger

14:17 ***commence***—begin

The fulfillment of God's covenant in the last days involves "the literal gathering of Israel" to the true Church and to their lands of promise, as well as Christ's personal reign upon the earth (see Articles of Faith 1:10).

14:22 (18–22) The man that Nephi saw was John the Beloved. John was one of Jesus' Twelve Apostles (see 1 Nephi 14:27; LDS Bible Dictionary, s.v. "John," 715).

14:25 ***ordained***—appointed

14:25 (23–25) The book which Nephi saw "proceeding out of the mouth of the Jew" was the Bible (see also 1 Nephi 13:23). The writings of John referred to here make up what is called the book of Revelation, the last book in the Bible. The message of Revelation is that "there will be an eventual triumph on this earth of God over the devil; a permanent victory of good over evil, of the saints over their persecutors" (LDS Bible Dictionary, s.v. "Revelation of John," 762).

14:28 ***sufficeth me***—are enough for me

29 And I bear record that I saw the things which my father saw, and the angel of the Lord did make them known unto me.

30 And now I make an end of speaking concerning the things which I saw while I was carried away in the spirit; and if all the things which I saw are not written, the things which I have written are true. And thus it is. Amen.

## CHAPTER 15

*Nephi explains Lehi's dream of the tree of life to his brothers. As you read, discover the Lord's promises and warnings to the house of Israel.*

### *Nephi's Brothers Cannot Understand Their Father's Dream*

1 AND it came to pass that after I, Nephi, had been carried away in the spirit, and seen all these things, I returned to the tent of my father.

2 And it came to pass that I beheld my brethren, and they were disputing one with another concerning the things which my father had spoken unto them.

3 For he truly spake many great things unto them, which were hard to be understood, save a man should inquire of the Lord; and they being hard in their hearts, therefore they did not look unto the Lord as they ought.

4 And now I, Nephi, was grieved because of the hardness of their hearts, and also, because of the things which I had seen, and knew they must unavoidably come to pass because of the great wickedness of the children of men.

5 And it came to pass that I was overcome because of my afflictions, for I considered that mine afflictions were great above all, because of the destruction of my people, for I had beheld their fall.

6 And it came to pass that after I had received strength I spake unto my brethren, desiring to know of them the cause of their disputations.

7 And they said: Behold, we cannot understand the words which our father hath spoken concerning the natural branches of the olive-tree, and also concerning the Gentiles.

8 And I said unto them: Have ye inquired of the Lord?

9 And they said unto me: We have not; for the Lord maketh no such thing known unto us.

10 Behold, I said unto them: How is it that ye do not keep the commandments of the Lord? How is it that ye will perish, because of the hardness of your hearts?

11 Do ye not remember the things which the Lord hath said?—If ye will not harden your hearts, and ask me in faith, believing that ye shall receive, with diligence in keeping my commandments, surely these things shall be made known unto you.

### *The Lord Promises to Gather the Scattered People of the House of Israel*

12 Behold, I say unto you, that the house of Israel was compared unto an olive-tree, by the Spirit of the Lord which was in our father; and behold are we not broken off from the house of Israel, and are we not a branch of the house of Israel?

13 And now, the thing which our father meaneth concerning the grafting in of the natural branches through the fulness of the Gentiles, is, that in the latter days, when our seed shall have dwindled in unbelief, yea, for the space of many years, and many generations after the Messiah shall be manifested in body unto the children of men, then shall the fulness of the gospel of the Messiah come unto the Gentiles, and from the Gentiles unto the remnant of our seed—

14 And at that day shall the remnant of our seed know that they are of the house of Israel, and that they are the covenant people of the Lord; and then shall they know and come to the knowledge of their forefathers, and also to the knowledge of the gospel of their Redeemer, which was ministered unto their fathers by him; wherefore, they shall come to the knowledge of their Redeemer and the

---

14:29 The things Nephi's father saw are found in 1 Nephi 8:5–35.

15:2 ***disputing***—arguing

15:4 ***grieved***—sorry or sad

15:5 ***afflictions***—trials and suffering

15:6 ***disputations***—arguments

15:11 (8–11) What do these verses explain about receiving an answer from the Lord? Do you believe the Lord answers your prayers?

15:13 ***dwindled***—become weak
***remnant of our seed***—descendants of Lehi who will survive destruction

very points of his doctrine, that they may know
how to come unto him and be saved.
15 And then at that day will they not rejoice and
give praise unto their everlasting God, their rock
and their salvation? Yea, at that day, will they not
receive the strength and nourishment from the true
vine? Yea, will they not come unto the true fold of
God?
16 Behold, I say unto you, Yea; they shall be
remembered again among the house of Israel; they
shall be grafted in, being a natural branch of the
olive-tree, into the true olive-tree.
17 And this is what our father meaneth; and he
meaneth that it will not come to pass until after they
are scattered by the Gentiles; and he meaneth that
it shall come by way of the Gentiles, that the Lord
may show his power unto the Gentiles, for the very
cause that he shall be rejected of the Jews, or of the
house of Israel.
18 Wherefore, our father hath not spoken of our
seed alone, but also of all the house of Israel, pointing to the covenant which should be fulfilled in the
latter days; which covenant the Lord made to our
father Abraham, saying: In thy seed shall all the kindreds of the earth be blessed.
19 And it came to pass that I, Nephi, spake much
unto them concerning these things; yea, I spake
unto them concerning the restoration of the Jews in
the latter days.
20 And I did rehearse unto them the words of
Isaiah, who spake concerning the restoration of the
Jews, or of the house of Israel; and after they were
restored they should no more be confounded, neither should they be scattered again. And it came to
pass that I did speak many words unto my
brethren, that they were pacified and did humble
themselves before the Lord.

### Nephi Answers His Brothers' Questions

21 And it came to pass that they did speak unto
me again, saying: What meaneth this thing which
our father saw in a dream? What meaneth the tree
which he saw?
22 And I said unto them: It was a representation
of the tree of life.
23 And they said unto me: What meaneth the rod
of iron which our father saw, that led to the tree?
24 And I said unto them that it was the word of
God; and whoso would hearken unto the word of
God, and would hold fast unto it, they would never
perish; neither could the temptations and the fiery
darts of the adversary overpower them unto blindness, to lead them away to destruction.
25 Wherefore, I, Nephi, did exhort them to give
heed unto the word of the Lord; yea, I did exhort
them with all the energies of my soul, and with all
the faculty which I possessed, that they would give
heed to the word of God and remember to keep his
commandments always in all things.
26 And they said unto me: What meaneth the river
of water which our father saw?
27 And I said unto them that the water which my
father saw was filthiness; and so much was his
mind swallowed up in other things that he beheld
not the filthiness of the water.
28 And I said unto them that it was an awful gulf,
which separated the wicked from the tree of life,
and also from the saints of God.
29 And I said unto them that it was a representation of that awful hell, which the angel said unto
me was prepared for the wicked.
30 And I said unto them that our father also saw
that the justice of God did also divide the wicked
from the righteous; and the brightness thereof was
like unto the brightness of a flaming fire, which
ascendeth up unto God forever and ever, and hath
no end.
31 And they said unto me: Doth this thing mean
the torment of the body in the days of probation, or
doth it mean the final state of the soul after the
death of the temporal body, or doth it speak of the
things which are temporal?

---

15:20 ***rehearse***—repeat or relate

15:24 Is temptation sometimes as hard to ignore as fiery darts being thrown at you? What does Nephi say will help us overcome these temptations?

15:25 ***faculty***—strength and ability

15:28 ***an awful gulf***—a large gap or space that is hard to cross

15:29 Latter-day scriptures teach that there are at least three meanings for the term *hell*. It can describe our suffering here on earth (see Alma 36:18). It can refer to a part of the spirit world where those who have not repented suffer for their sins (see Alma 40:13–14). It is also used to describe the final condition of those who completely turn away from God (see D&C 29:38).

32 And it came to pass that I said unto them that it was a representation of things both temporal and spiritual; for the day should come that they must be judged of their works, yea, even the works which were done by the temporal body in their days of probation.

### The Wicked Cannot Enter the Kingdom of God

33 Wherefore, if they should die in their wickedness they must be cast off also, as to the things which are spiritual, which are pertaining to righteousness; wherefore, they must be brought to stand before God, to be judged of their works; and if their works have been filthiness they must needs be filthy; and if they be filthy it must needs be that they cannot dwell in the kingdom of God; if so, the kingdom of God must be filthy also.
34 But behold, I say unto you, the kingdom of God is not filthy, and there cannot any unclean thing enter into the kingdom of God; wherefore there must needs be a place of filthiness prepared for that which is filthy.
35 And there is a place prepared, yea, even that awful hell of which I have spoken, and the devil is the preparator of it; wherefore the final state of the souls of men is to dwell in the kingdom of God, or to be cast out because of that justice of which I have spoken.
36 Wherefore, the wicked are rejected from the righteous, and also from that tree of life, whose fruit is most precious and most desirable above all other fruits; yea, and it is the greatest of all the gifts of God. And thus I spake unto my brethren. Amen.

## CHAPTER 16

*Lehi's family continues their journey toward the promised land. Watch for how the Lord guides them when they are obedient to Him.*

### Wicked People Do Not Like to Hear the Truth

1 AND now it came to pass that after I, Nephi, had made an end of speaking to my brethren, behold they said unto me: Thou hast declared unto us hard things, more than we are able to bear.
2 And it came to pass that I said unto them that I knew that I had spoken hard things against the wicked, according to the truth; and the righteous have I justified, and testified that they should be lifted up at the last day; wherefore, the guilty taketh the truth to be hard, for it cutteth them to the very center.
3 And now my brethren, if ye were righteous and were willing to hearken to the truth, and give heed unto it, that ye might walk uprightly before God, then ye would not murmur because of the truth, and say: Thou speakest hard things against us.
4 And it came to pass that I, Nephi, did exhort my brethren, with all diligence, to keep the commandments of the Lord.
5 And it came to pass that they did humble themselves before the Lord; insomuch that I had joy and great hopes of them, that they would walk in the paths of righteousness.
6 Now, all these things were said and done as my father dwelt in a tent in the valley which he called Lemuel.

---

15:32 ***temporal***—worldly or physical
***probation***—testing on earth

15:35 ***preparator of***—one who prepares

15:36 (33–36) What do these verses say that makes you want to be righteous and not wicked?

16:1 ***bear***—stand

16:2 ***justified***—shown to be not guilty

16:3 Why do people who are doing wrong sometimes get angry when someone tries to correct them? Nephi explains that it is the spirit of the devil that causes people to get angry at the truth (see 2 Nephi 33:5).

16:4 ***exhort***—strongly encourage

## Lehi's Sons Marry Ishmael's Daughters

7 And it came to pass that I, Nephi, took one of the daughters of Ishmael to wife; and also, my brethren took of the daughters of Ishmael to wife; and also Zoram took the eldest daughter of Ishmael to wife.

8 And thus my father had fulfilled all the commandments of the Lord which had been given unto him. And also, I, Nephi, had been blessed of the Lord exceedingly.

## The Liahona Guides Lehi's Family on Their Journey Toward the Promised Land

9 And it came to pass that the voice of the Lord spake unto my father by night, and commanded him that on the morrow he should take his journey into the wilderness.

10 And it came to pass that as my father arose in the morning, and went forth to the tent door, to his great astonishment he beheld upon the ground a round ball of curious workmanship; and it was of

ILLUSTRATION BY TED HENNINGER

*The daughters of Ishmael*

16:7 Eternal marriage is an essential part of Heavenly Father's plan (see D&C 131:1–3).

16:8 As Lehi and Nephi continued to be obedient, what did the Lord give them? What does the Lord do for you when you are obedient?

16:10 ***astonishment***—surprise and wonder

The round ball that Lehi finds outside his door is called the Liahona (see Alma 37:38). To say that it was of "curious workmanship" is a way of saying that it was "made or done skillfully or painstakingly" (*Random House Webster's College Dictionary,* s.v. "curious"). Alma later emphasized that the Lord prepared the Liahona, saying that "there cannot any man work after the manner of so curious a workmanship" (Alma 37:38–39). The Liahona—unlike a regular compass, which always points north—pointed in the direction Lehi's family should travel. Also, unlike a regular compass, the Liahona only worked according to their faith and diligence (see 1 Nephi 16:28).

The Liahona is not only a real object but also a powerful teaching symbol. For example, Alma's words suggest that the Liahona was a symbol of the "word of Christ, which will point to you a straight course to eternal bliss" (Alma 37:44). President Spencer W. Kimball compared it to our individual consciences, or the Light of Christ (see *The Teachings of Spencer W. Kimball,* 113). President Thomas S. Monson compared a patriarchal blessing to having one's own Liahona—"to guide you unerringly to your heavenly home" (in Conference Report, October 1986, 83).

ILLUSTRATION BY LESTER LEE

*The Liahona pointed the way Lehi's family should go in the wilderness.*

fine brass. And within the ball were two spindles; and the one pointed the way whither we should go into the wilderness.

11 And it came to pass that we did gather together whatsoever things we should carry into the wilderness, and all the remainder of our provisions which the Lord had given unto us; and we did take seed of every kind that we might carry into the wilderness.

12 And it came to pass that we did take our tents and depart into the wilderness, across the river Laman.

13 And it came to pass that we traveled for the space of four days, nearly a south-southeast direction, and we did pitch our tents again; and we did call the name of the place Shazer.

14 And it came to pass that we did take our bows and our arrows, and go forth into the wilderness to slay food for our families; and after we had slain food for our families we did return again to our families in the wilderness, to the place of Shazer. And we did go forth again in the wilderness, following the same direction, keeping in the most fertile parts of the wilderness, which were in the borders near the Red Sea.

15 And it came to pass that we did travel for the space of many days, slaying food by the way, with our bows and our arrows and our stones and our slings.

16 And we did follow the directions of the ball, which led us in the more fertile parts of the wilderness.

17 And after we had traveled for the space of many days, we did pitch our tents for the space of a time, that we might again rest ourselves and obtain food for our families.

## *Nephi Breaks His Bow and Everyone Suffers*

18 And it came to pass that as I, Nephi, went forth to slay food, behold, I did break my bow, which was made of fine steel; and after I did break my bow, behold, my brethren were angry with me because of the loss of my bow, for we did obtain no food.

19 And it came to pass that we did return without food to our families, and being much fatigued, because of their journeying, they did suffer much for the want of food.

20 And it came to pass that Laman and Lemuel and the sons of Ishmael did begin to murmur exceedingly, because of their sufferings and afflictions in the wilderness; and also my father began to murmur against the Lord his God; yea, and they were all exceedingly sorrowful, even that they did murmur against the Lord.

21 Now it came to pass that I, Nephi, having been afflicted with my brethren because of the loss of my bow, and their bows having lost their springs, it began to be exceedingly difficult, yea, insomuch that we could obtain no food.

22 And it came to pass that I, Nephi, did speak much unto my brethren, because they had hardened their hearts again, even unto complaining against the Lord their God.

23 And it came to pass that I, Nephi, did make out of wood a bow, and out of a straight stick, an arrow; wherefore, I did arm myself with a bow and an arrow, with a sling and with stones. And I said unto my father: Whither shall I go to obtain food?

---

16:10 ***spindles***—pointers

16:11 ***provisions***—food and other supplies

16:14 ***fertile***—plentiful

16:19 ***much fatigued***—very tired

16:21 The phrase "I, Nephi, having been afflicted with my brethren because of the loss of my bow" could be read at least two ways. It could mean that Nephi suffered along with his brothers because of the loss of his bow, or it could mean that Nephi was tormented by his brothers because of the loss of his bow.

16:22 (20–22) Does murmuring (complaining) help? How does it hurt? What are some things you could do instead of complaining when your family has troubles?

NEPHI'S BROKEN BOW, BY MICHAEL JARVIS NELSON

*"As I, Nephi, went forth to slay food, behold, I did break my bow."*

### Nephi Makes a New Bow and Seeks Spiritual Guidance

24 And it came to pass that he did inquire of the
Lord, for they had humbled themselves because of
my words; for I did say many things unto them in
the energy of my soul.
25 And it came to pass that the voice of the Lord
came unto my father; and he was truly chastened
because of his murmuring against the Lord, insomuch
that he was brought down into the depths of sorrow.

### The Liahona Works According to the Family Members' Faith, Diligence, and Heed

26 And it came to pass that the voice of the Lord
said unto him: Look upon the ball, and behold the
things which are written.
27 And it came to pass that when my father
beheld the things which were written upon the ball,
he did fear and tremble exceedingly, and also my
brethren and the sons of Ishmael and our wives.
28 And it came to pass that I, Nephi, beheld the
pointers which were in the ball, that they did work
according to the faith and diligence and heed which
we did give unto them.
29 And there was also written upon them a new
writing, which was plain to be read, which did give
us understanding concerning the ways of the Lord;
and it was written and changed from time to time,
according to the faith and diligence which we gave
unto it. And thus we see that by small means the
Lord can bring about great things.
30 And it came to pass that I, Nephi, did go forth
up into the top of the mountain, according to the
directions which were given upon the ball.
31 And it came to pass that I did slay wild beasts,
insomuch that I did obtain food for our families.
32 And it came to pass that I did return to our
tents, bearing the beasts which I had slain; and now
when they beheld that I had obtained food, how
great was their joy! And it came to pass that they
did humble themselves before the Lord, and did
give thanks unto him.

### Ishmael Dies and Part of the Family Rebels Against Lehi and Nephi

33 And it came to pass that we did again take our
journey, traveling nearly the same course as in the
beginning; and after we had traveled for the space
of many days we did pitch our tents again, that we
might tarry for the space of a time.
34 And it came to pass that Ishmael died, and was
buried in the place which was called Nahom.
35 And it came to pass that the daughters of
Ishmael did mourn exceedingly, because of the loss
of their father, and because of their afflictions in the
wilderness; and they did murmur against my father,
because he had brought them out of the land of
Jerusalem, saying: Our father is dead; yea, and we
have wandered much in the wilderness, and we
have suffered much affliction, hunger, thirst, and
fatigue; and after all these sufferings we must perish
in the wilderness with hunger.
36 And thus they did murmur against my father,
and also against me; and they were desirous to
return again to Jerusalem.

---

16:24 ***inquire***—ask

16:24 (23–24) What did Nephi do instead of murmuring? Why do you think Nephi asked his father where to hunt? What do you learn from Nephi's example? What can you learn from the way Lehi changed?

16:25 ***chastened***—scolded

16:28 ***diligence***—care and effort
***heed***—obedience

16:29 (26–29) Alma pointed out that Lehi's family had trouble in the wilderness because they "forgot to exercise their faith and diligence." Therefore, the Liahona would not work and they "did not travel a direct course, and were afflicted with hunger and thirst" (Alma 37:38–42). How has faith in Jesus Christ and diligence in keeping the commandments helped guide your life?

16:33 ***tarry***—stay

16:34 *Nahom* is a word possibly related to the Hebrew verb *naham,* which means to "be sorry, console oneself." It is a fitting name to describe the loss of a loved father.

37 And Laman said unto Lemuel and also unto the sons of Ishmael: Behold, let us slay our father, and also our brother Nephi, who has taken it upon him to be our ruler and our teacher, who are his elder brethren.

38 Now, he says that the Lord has talked with him, and also that angels have ministered unto him. But behold, we know that he lies unto us; and he tells us these things, and he worketh many things by his cunning arts, that he may deceive our eyes, thinking, perhaps, that he may lead us away into some strange wilderness; and after he has led us away, he has thought to make himself a king and a ruler over us, that he may do with us according to his will and pleasure. And after this manner did my brother Laman stir up their hearts to anger.

39 And it came to pass that the Lord was with us, yea, even the voice of the Lord came and did speak many words unto them, and did chasten them exceedingly; and after they were chastened by the voice of the Lord they did turn away their anger, and did repent of their sins, insomuch that the Lord did bless us again with food, that we did not perish.

## CHAPTER 17

*Nephi prepares to build a ship to take Lehi's family to the promised land. Watch for how the Lord helps Nephi build the ship.*

### The Lord Helps Lehi's Family Travel Through the Wilderness to Bountiful

1 AND it came to pass that we did again take our journey in the wilderness; and we did travel nearly eastward from that time forth. And we did travel and wade through much affliction in the wilderness; and our women did bear children in the wilderness.

2 And so great were the blessings of the Lord upon us, that while we did live upon raw meat in the wilderness, our women did give plenty of suck for their children, and were strong, yea, even like unto the men; and they began to bear their journeyings without murmurings.

3 And thus we see that the commandments of God must be fulfilled. And if it so be that the children of men keep the commandments of God he doth nourish them, and strengthen them, and provide means whereby they can accomplish the thing which he has commanded them; wherefore, he did provide means for us while we did sojourn in the wilderness.

4 And we did sojourn for the space of many years, yea, even eight years in the wilderness.

5 And we did come to the land which we called Bountiful, because of its much fruit and also wild honey; and all these things were prepared of the Lord that we might not perish. And we beheld the

---

16:37 ***slay***—kill

16:38 ***ministered***—appeared and given help
***cunning arts***—tricks
***deceive***—trick or fool

Why do you think Laman makes these awful claims against Nephi? What were Nephi's real goals and purposes in life? Why do the wicked so often criticize the righteous?

17:1 ***wade through much affliction***—move forward with great difficulty

17:2 ***suck***—mother's milk
***bear their journeyings***—endure their travels

17:3 ***means***—support or help

In this verse Nephi summarizes a lesson that should be learned from their experiences (see also 1 Nephi 3:7). How has Heavenly Father helped you learn to keep His commandments?

17:4 ***did sojourn***—lived and traveled

PHOTOGRAPH BY SCOT FACER PROCTOR

*Nephi's description of the land Bountiful suggests an area much like this one on the Arabian peninsula's southern coast.*

sea, which we called Irreantum, which, being interpreted, is many waters.
6 And it came to pass that we did pitch our tents
by the seashore; and notwithstanding we had suffered many afflictions and much difficulty, yea,
even so much that we cannot write them all, we
were exceedingly rejoiced when we came to the
seashore; and we called the place Bountiful,
because of its much fruit.

## The Lord Commands Nephi to Build a Ship

7 And it came to pass that after I, Nephi, had been
in the land of Bountiful for the space of many days,
the voice of the Lord came unto me, saying: Arise,
and get thee into the mountain. And it came to pass
that I arose and went up into the mountain, and
cried unto the Lord.
8 And it came to pass that the Lord spake unto
me, saying: Thou shalt construct a ship, after the
manner which I shall show thee, that I may carry
thy people across these waters.
9 And I said: Lord, whither shall I go that I may
find ore to molten, that I may make tools to construct the ship after the manner which thou hast
shown unto me?
10 And it came to pass that the Lord told me
whither I should go to find ore, that I might make
tools.
11 And it came to pass that I, Nephi, did make a
bellows wherewith to blow the fire, of the skins of
beasts; and after I had made a bellows, that I might
have wherewith to blow the fire, I did smite two
stones together that I might make fire.
12 For the Lord had not hitherto suffered that we
should make much fire, as we journeyed in the
wilderness; for he said: I will make thy food
become sweet, that ye cook it not;
13 And I will also be your light in the wilderness; and I will prepare the way before you, if it
so be that ye shall keep my commandments;
wherefore, inasmuch as ye shall keep my commandments ye shall be led towards the promised
land; and ye shall know that it is by me that ye
are led.
14 Yea, and the Lord said also that: After ye have
arrived in the promised land, ye shall know that I,
the Lord, am God; and that I, the Lord, did deliver
you from destruction; yea, that I did bring you out
of the land of Jerusalem.
15 Wherefore, I, Nephi, did strive to keep the
commandments of the Lord, and I did exhort my
brethren to faithfulness and diligence.
16 And it came to pass that I did make tools of the
ore which I did molten out of the rock.

## Nephi's Brothers Speak Against Him

17 And when my brethren saw that I was about to
build a ship, they began to murmur against me, saying: Our brother is a fool, for he thinketh that he
can build a ship; yea, and he also thinketh that he
can cross these great waters.
18 And thus my brethren did complain against me,
and were desirous that they might not labor, for
they did not believe that I could build a ship; neither would they believe that I was instructed of the
Lord.

17:5 ***being interpreted, is***—means

17:7 Nephi goes up into the mountain to pray to the Lord. The scriptures often speak of prophets going into the mountains to speak with God (see 1 Nephi 11:1; Exodus 19:20; 1 Kings 19:8).

17:8 ***manner***—way

17:9 ***ore***—rock or mineral from which metal is obtained
***molten***—melt

17:18 Nephi's brothers were not willing to help build the ship because they doubted that Nephi could do it. How does doubt and criticism get in the way of doing good deeds and helping others?

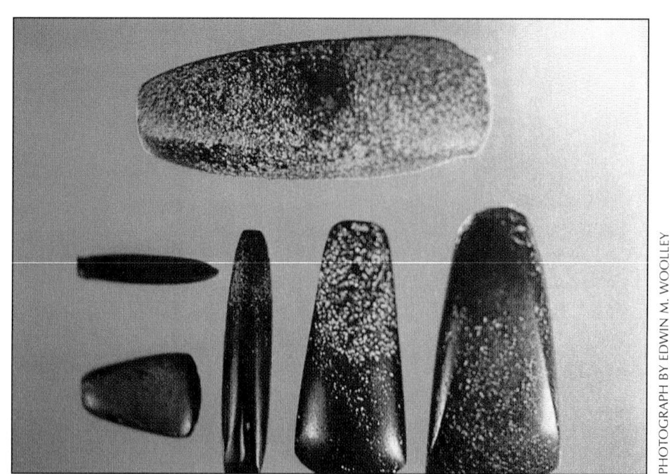
PHOTOGRAPH BY EDWIN M. WOOLLEY

*Nephi may have made tools like these to use in building a ship.*

19 And now it came to pass that I, Nephi, was exceedingly sorrowful because of the hardness of their hearts; and now when they saw that I began to be sorrowful they were glad in their hearts, insomuch that they did rejoice over me, saying: We knew that ye could not construct a ship, for we knew that ye were lacking in judgment; wherefore, thou canst not accomplish so great a work.

20 And thou art like unto our father, led away by the foolish imaginations of his heart; yea, he hath led us out of the land of Jerusalem, and we have wandered in the wilderness for these many years; and our women have toiled, being big with child; and they have borne children in the wilderness and suffered all things, save it were death; and it would have been better that they had died before they came out of Jerusalem than to have suffered these afflictions.

21 Behold, these many years we have suffered in the wilderness, which time we might have enjoyed our possessions and the land of our inheritance; yea, and we might have been happy.

22 And we know that the people who were in the land of Jerusalem were a righteous people; for they kept the statutes and judgments of the Lord, and all his commandments, according to the law of Moses; wherefore, we know that they are a righteous people; and our father hath judged them, and hath led us away because we would hearken unto his words; yea, and our brother is like unto him. And after this manner of language did my brethren murmur and complain against us.

## *Nephi Explains How God Helped the Children of Israel*

23 And it came to pass that I, Nephi, spake unto them, saying: Do ye believe that our fathers, who were the children of Israel, would have been led away out of the hands of the Egyptians if they had not hearkened unto the words of the Lord?

24 Yea, do ye suppose that they would have been led out of bondage, if the Lord had not commanded Moses that he should lead them out of bondage?

25 Now ye know that the children of Israel were in bondage; and ye know that they were laden with tasks, which were grievous to be borne; wherefore, ye know that it must needs be a good thing for them, that they should be brought out of bondage.

26 Now ye know that Moses was commanded of the Lord to do that great work; and ye know that by his word the waters of the Red Sea were divided hither and thither, and they passed through on dry ground.

27 But ye know that the Egyptians were drowned in the Red Sea, who were the armies of Pharaoh.

28 And ye also know that they were fed with manna in the wilderness.

29 Yea, and ye also know that Moses, by his word according to the power of God which was in him, smote the rock, and there came forth water, that the children of Israel might quench their thirst.

30 And notwithstanding they being led, the Lord their God, their Redeemer, going before them, leading them by day and giving light unto them by night, and doing all things for them which were expedient for man to receive, they hardened their hearts and blinded their minds, and reviled against Moses and against the true and living God.

31 And it came to pass that according to his word he did destroy them; and according to his word he did lead them; and according to his word he did do all things for them; and there was not any thing done save it were by his word.

32 And after they had crossed the river Jordan he did make them mighty unto the driving out of the

17:19 ***lacking in judgment***—not wise enough

17:20 ***toiled***—worked
***big with child***—near childbirth

17:21 (20–21) Compare these words of Laman and Lemuel with those in 1 Nephi 17:1–3 that describe how Nephi felt about their sufferings in the wilderness. Why do you think Nephi was grateful for Heavenly Father's help during their trials instead of being bitter like Laman and Lemuel?

17:22 ***statutes***—laws

17:24 ***bondage***—slavery

17:25 ***laden***—weighed down
***grievous to be borne***—very hard to endure

17:26 ***hither and thither***—this way and that way

17:28 Manna was the food that the Lord provided the children of Israel as they traveled for forty years in the wilderness (see Exodus 16).

17:30 ***expedient***—helpful or necessary
***reviled***—complained with anger

MOSES PARTING THE RED SEA, BY ROBERT T. BARRETT

*By the power of God, Moses divided the Red Sea and saved the children of Israel.*

children of the land, yea, unto the scattering them
to destruction.
33 And now, do ye suppose that the children of
this land, who were in the land of promise, who
were driven out by our fathers, do ye suppose that
they were righteous? Behold, I say unto you, Nay.
34 Do ye suppose that our fathers would have
been more choice than they if they had been righteous? I say unto you, Nay.
35 Behold, the Lord esteemeth all flesh in one; he
that is righteous is favored of God. But behold, this
people had rejected every word of God, and they
were ripe in iniquity; and the fulness of the wrath
of God was upon them; and the Lord did curse the
land against them, and bless it unto our fathers; yea,
he did curse it against them unto their destruction,
and he did bless it unto our fathers unto their
obtaining power over it.
36 Behold, the Lord hath created the earth that it
should be inhabited; and he hath created his children that they should possess it.
37 And he raiseth up a righteous nation, and
destroyeth the nations of the wicked.
38 And he leadeth away the righteous into precious lands, and the wicked he destroyeth, and
curseth the land unto them for their sakes.
39 He ruleth high in the heavens, for it is his
throne, and this earth is his footstool.

---

17:34 ***choice***—favored of the Lord

17:35 ***esteemeth all flesh in one***—values all people in the same way

When people become "ripe in iniquity," meaning very sinful, they are destroyed from off the earth. One example of this took place in the days of Noah and the Flood (see Genesis 7).

17:36 ***inhabited***—lived on

40 And he loveth those who will have him to be their God. Behold, he loved our fathers, and he covenanted with them, yea, even Abraham, Isaac, and Jacob; and he remembered the covenants which he had made; wherefore, he did bring them out of the land of Egypt.

41 And he did straiten them in the wilderness with his rod; for they hardened their hearts, even as ye have; and the Lord straitened them because of their iniquity. He sent fiery flying serpents among them; and after they were bitten he prepared a way that they might be healed; and the labor which they had to perform was to look; and because of the simpleness of the way, or the easiness of it, there were many who perished.

42 And they did harden their hearts from time to time, and they did revile against Moses, and also against God; nevertheless, ye know that they were led forth by his matchless power into the land of promise.

43 And now, after all these things, the time has come that they have become wicked, yea, nearly unto ripeness; and I know not but they are at this day about to be destroyed; for I know that the day must surely come that they must be destroyed, save a few only, who shall be led away into captivity.

## Nephi Tells His Brothers About Their Great Wickedness

44 Wherefore, the Lord commanded my father that he should depart into the wilderness; and the Jews also sought to take away his life; yea, and ye also have sought to take away his life; wherefore, ye are murderers in your hearts and ye are like unto them.

45 Ye are swift to do iniquity but slow to remember the Lord your God. Ye have seen an angel, and he spake unto you; yea, ye have heard his voice from time to time; and he hath spoken unto you in a still small voice, but ye were past feeling, that ye could not feel his words; wherefore, he has spoken unto you like unto the voice of thunder, which did cause the earth to shake as if it were to divide asunder.

46 And ye also know that by the power of his almighty word he can cause the earth that it shall pass away; yea, and ye know that by his word he can cause the rough places to be made smooth, and smooth places shall be broken up. O, then, why is it, that ye can be so hard in your hearts?

47 Behold, my soul is rent with anguish because of you, and my heart is pained; I fear lest ye shall be cast off forever. Behold, I am full of the Spirit of God, insomuch that my frame has no strength.

## Nephi, Filled with the Lord's Power, Shocks His Brothers

48 And now it came to pass that when I had spoken these words they were angry with me, and were desirous to throw me into the depths of the sea; and as they came forth to lay their hands upon me I spake unto them, saying: In the name of the Almighty God, I command you that ye touch me not, for I am filled with the power of God, even unto the consuming of my flesh; and whoso shall lay his hands upon me shall wither even as a dried reed; and he shall be as naught before the power of God, for God shall smite him.

---

17:41 ***straiten***—correct
***iniquity***—wickedness

The Lord sent fiery serpents (poisonous snakes) into the camp of the rebellious Israelites. If bitten, the people only had to look at an image of a snake Moses held up. This would teach them to look to Christ to be healed of spiritual poison, or wickedness (see Alma 33:19–22).

17:43 ***captivity***—bondage and slavery

17:44 ***sought***—tried

17:45 ***divide asunder***—tear apart

Nephi's brothers had seen an angel but continued to sin. Why is seeing an angel sometimes not enough to soften people's hearts and change their behavior? Bishop Keith B. McMullin has said that a thousand years "of experience through sight, sound, touch, taste, smell, and all the powers of the universe combined cannot approach the sublime and complete experience of one brief moment under the influence of the Holy Ghost" (in Conference Report, April 1996, 9). Furthermore, in connection with the "still small voice" mentioned in this verse, Elder Boyd K. Packer has stated, "I have come to know that inspiration comes more as a feeling than as a sound," and has observed that "it is a voice that one feels more than one hears" (*"That All May Be Edified,"* 11, 335; see also D&C 8:2).

17:47 ***rent with anguish***—torn with sorrow
***frame***—body

17:48 ***consuming***—burning up
***wither***—dry up
***naught***—nothing

49 And it came to pass that I, Nephi, said unto them that they should murmur no more against their father; neither should they withhold their labor from me, for God had commanded me that I should build a ship.

50 And I said unto them: If God had commanded me to do all things I could do them. If he should command me that I should say unto this water, be thou earth, it should be earth; and if I should say it, it would be done.

51 And now, if the Lord has such great power, and has wrought so many miracles among the children of men, how is it that he cannot instruct me, that I should build a ship?

52 And it came to pass that I, Nephi, said many things unto my brethren, insomuch that they were confounded and could not contend against me; neither durst they lay their hands upon me nor touch me with their fingers, even for the space of many days. Now they durst not do this lest they should wither before me, so powerful was the Spirit of God; and thus it had wrought upon them.

53 And it came to pass that the Lord said unto me: Stretch forth thine hand again unto thy brethren, and they shall not wither before thee, but I will shock them, saith the Lord, and this will I do, that they may know that I am the Lord their God.

54 And it came to pass that I stretched forth my hand unto my brethren, and they did not wither before me; but the Lord did shake them, even according to the word which he had spoken.

55 And now, they said: We know of a surety that the Lord is with thee, for we know that it is the power of the Lord that has shaken us. And they fell down before me, and were about to worship me, but I would not suffer them, saying: I am thy brother, yea, even thy younger brother; wherefore, worship the Lord thy God, and honor thy father and thy mother, that thy days may be long in the land which the Lord thy God shall give thee.

## CHAPTER 18

*Lehi's family travel across the sea to the promised land. Look for how they were able to build a ship and safely arrive in the promised land.*

### Nephi and His Brothers Build a Ship

1 AND it came to pass that they did worship the Lord, and did go forth with me; and we did work timbers of curious workmanship. And the Lord did show me from time to time after what manner I should work the timbers of the ship.

2 Now I, Nephi, did not work the timbers after the manner which was learned by men, neither did I build the ship after the manner of men; but I did build it after the manner which the Lord had shown unto me; wherefore, it was not after the manner of men.

3 And I, Nephi, did go into the mount oft, and I did pray oft unto the Lord; wherefore the Lord showed unto me great things.

4 And it came to pass that after I had finished the ship, according to the word of the Lord, my brethren beheld that it was good, and that the workmanship thereof was exceedingly fine; wherefore, they did humble themselves again before the Lord.

### Lehi and His Family Set Sail for the Promised Land

5 And it came to pass that the voice of the Lord came unto my father, that we should arise and go down into the ship.

6 And it came to pass that on the morrow, after we had prepared all things, much fruits and meat from the wilderness, and honey in abundance, and provisions according to that which the Lord had commanded us, we did go down into the ship, with all our loading and our seeds, and whatsoever thing

---

17:51 ***wrought***—worked

17:52 ***confounded***—confused, put to shame, or humiliated
***contend***—fight
***durst***—dared

18:1 When Nephi says that he and his brothers worked timbers of "curious workmanship," he does not mean that they prepared the ship's timbers in such a way that they looked strange or weird. He means that, following the Lord's directions, they prepared the timbers in a very special, careful, and skillful way.

18:4 (2–4) Nephi and his brothers were not shipbuilders by trade, but with God's help they were able to build a ship that sailed across the ocean. Read Luke 1:37. What are some difficult things that God might ask you to do?

18:6 ***provisions***—food and other supplies
***loading***—baggage

*NEPHI REBUKES HIS BROTHERS, BY GARY KAPP*

*Nephi shocks his brothers with the power of God.*

we had brought with us, every one according to his
age; wherefore, we did all go down into the ship,
with our wives and our children.
7 And now, my father had begat two sons in the
wilderness; the elder was called Jacob and the
younger Joseph.
8 And it came to pass after we had all gone down
into the ship, and had taken with us our provisions
and things which had been commanded us, we did
put forth into the sea and were driven forth before
the wind towards the promised land.

## *Nephi Is Bound and a Terrible Storm Nearly Sinks the Ship*

9 And after we had been driven forth before the
wind for the space of many days, behold, my
brethren and the sons of Ishmael and also their
wives began to make themselves merry, insomuch
that they began to dance, and to sing, and to speak
with much rudeness, yea, even that they did forget
by what power they had been brought thither; yea,
they were lifted up unto exceeding rudeness.
10 And I, Nephi, began to fear exceedingly lest
the Lord should be angry with us, and smite us
because of our iniquity, that we should be swallowed up in the depths of the sea; wherefore, I,
Nephi, began to speak to them with much soberness; but behold they were angry with me, saying:
We will not that our younger brother shall be a ruler
over us.
11 And it came to pass that Laman and Lemuel did
take me and bind me with cords, and they did treat
me with much harshness; nevertheless, the Lord did
suffer it that he might show forth his power, unto
the fulfilling of his word which he had spoken concerning the wicked.
12 And it came to pass that after they had bound
me insomuch that I could not move, the compass,
which had been prepared of the Lord, did cease to
work.
13 Wherefore, they knew not whither they should
steer the ship, insomuch that there arose a great
storm, yea, a great and terrible tempest, and we were
driven back upon the waters for the space of three
days; and they began to be frightened exceedingly
lest they should be drowned in the sea; nevertheless
they did not loose me.
14 And on the fourth day, which we had been
driven back, the tempest began to be exceedingly
sore.

## *The Power of God Causes Nephi's Brothers to Untie Him*

15 And it came to pass that we were about to be
swallowed up in the depths of the sea. And after we
had been driven back upon the waters for the space
of four days, my brethren began to see that the
judgments of God were upon them, and that they
must perish save that they should repent of their
iniquities; wherefore, they came unto me, and
loosed the bands which were upon my wrists, and
behold they had swollen exceedingly; and also
mine ankles were much swollen, and great was the
soreness thereof.
16 Nevertheless, I did look unto my God, and I
did praise him all the day long; and I did not murmur against the Lord because of mine afflictions.
17 Now my father, Lehi, had said many things
unto them, and also unto the sons of Ishmael; but,
behold, they did breathe out much threatenings
against anyone that should speak for me; and my
parents being stricken in years, and having suffered

---

18:9 ***speak with much rudeness***—say very impolite and evil things

After reading this verse you may think that the Lord does not approve of dancing or singing. Nephi twice says that they sinned when their dancing and singing led them to speak with much rudeness. The Lord has stated that He approves of proper dancing and singing (see D&C 136:28; Psalm 149:1–4). However, Satan can use music as an evil tool to tempt us and cause us to lose the Spirit (see the pamphlet *For the Strength of Youth,* 13–14).

18:10 ***iniquity***—sins
***soberness***—seriousness

18:12 To learn what the compass was and how it worked, see 1 Nephi 16:10, 28, and the accompanying helps.

18:14 ***sore***—terrible or intense

18:16 Nephi did not murmur or complain even though he had suffered greatly. What experiences did Nephi have with the Lord that might have helped him not to complain when hardship came? What experiences have you had that help you to be faithful during hard times?

18:17 ***stricken in years***—weak because of old age

much grief because of their children, they were brought down, yea, even upon their sick-beds.

18 Because of their grief and much sorrow, and the iniquity of my brethren, they were brought near even to be carried out of this time to meet their God; yea, their grey hairs were about to be brought down to lie low in the dust; yea, even they were near to be cast with sorrow into a watery grave.

19 And Jacob and Joseph also, being young, having need of much nourishment, were grieved because of the afflictions of their mother; and also my wife with her tears and prayers, and also my children, did not soften the hearts of my brethren that they would loose me.

20 And there was nothing save it were the power of God, which threatened them with destruction, could soften their hearts; wherefore, when they saw that they were about to be swallowed up in the depths of the sea they repented of the thing which they had done, insomuch that they loosed me.

### Nephi Sails the Ship Safely to the Promised Land

21 And it came to pass after they had loosed me, behold, I took the compass, and it did work whither I desired it. And it came to pass that I prayed unto the Lord; and after I had prayed the winds did cease, and the storm did cease, and there was a great calm.

22 And it came to pass that I, Nephi, did guide the ship, that we sailed again towards the promised land.

23 And it came to pass that after we had sailed for the space of many days we did arrive at the promised land; and we went forth upon the land, and did pitch our tents; and we did call it the promised land.

24 And it came to pass that we did begin to till the earth, and we began to plant seeds; yea, we did put all our seeds into the earth, which we had brought from the land of Jerusalem. And it came to pass that they did grow exceedingly; wherefore, we were blessed in abundance.

25 And it came to pass that we did find upon the land of promise, as we journeyed in the wilderness, that there were beasts in the forests of every kind, both the cow and the ox, and the ass and the horse, and the goat and the wild goat, and all manner of wild animals, which were for the use of men. And we did find all manner of ore, both of gold, and of silver, and of copper.

## CHAPTER 19

*Nephi makes gold plates to record the history of his people. Since space is limited and it is difficult to make plates, he has to be very selective in what he records. Nephi begins making his record about 588 B.C. and continues writing it for forty-three years (545 B.C.). Notice how his message centers on the mission of Jesus Christ.*

### Nephi Makes Metal Plates

1 AND it came to pass that the Lord commanded me, wherefore I did make plates of ore that I might engraven upon them the record of my people. And

18:21 Why was Nephi able to work the compass? Why do you think the Lord answered Nephi's prayer?

18:23 Elder Spencer W. Kimball taught: "America is no ordinary country. It is a choice land, 'choice above all other lands.' (1 Nephi 2:20.) It has a tragic and bloody past, but a glorious and peaceful future if its inhabitants really learn to serve their God. It was consecrated as a land of promise to the people of the Americas, to whom God gave these great promises" (in Conference Report, October 1961, 30).

19:1 Why do you think Nephi used metal plates to write on even though it was difficult? What does this tell you about Nephi?

*Other ancient records written on metal plates have been discovered since the publication of the Book of Mormon.*

*Lehi and his family arrive in the promised land.*

ARRIVAL IN THE PROMISED LAND, BY CLARK KELLEY PRICE

upon the plates which I made I did engraven the
record of my father, and also our journeyings in the
wilderness, and the prophecies of my father; and
also many of mine own prophecies have I engraven
upon them.
2 And I knew not at the time when I made them
that I should be commanded of the Lord to make
these plates; wherefore, the record of my father,
and the genealogy of his fathers, and the more part
of all our proceedings in the wilderness are
engraven upon those first plates of which I have
spoken; wherefore, the things which transpired
before I made these plates are, of a truth, more particularly made mention upon the first plates.
3 And after I had made these plates by way of
commandment, I, Nephi, received a commandment
that the ministry and the prophecies, the more plain
and precious parts of them, should be written upon
these plates; and that the things which were written
should be kept for the instruction of my people,

---

19:2 ***these plates***—the small plates of Nephi

19:3 (1–3) Nephi made two sets of plates: the large plates of Nephi and the small plates of Nephi. On the large plates he summarized the records of his father, Lehi. Nephi also began a detailed history of his people on the large plates. He reserved the small plates for sacred writings, prophecies, and things pertaining to the ministry. For more information on the plates of Nephi, see for 1 Nephi 9:3 and for 1 Nephi 9:4.

who should possess the land, and also for other wise purposes, which purposes are known unto the Lord.
4 Wherefore, I, Nephi, did make a record upon the other plates, which gives an account, or which gives a greater account of the wars and contentions and destructions of my people. And this have I done, and commanded my people what they should do after I was gone; and that these plates should be handed down from one generation to another, or from one prophet to another, until further commandments of the Lord.
5 And an account of my making these plates shall be given hereafter; and then, behold, I proceed according to that which I have spoken; and this I do that the more sacred things may be kept for the knowledge of my people.
6 Nevertheless, I do not write anything upon plates save it be that I think it be sacred. And now, if I do err, even did they err of old; not that I would excuse myself because of other men, but because of the weakness which is in me, according to the flesh, I would excuse myself.

## Nephi Prophesies of the Sufferings and Crucifixion of Jesus Christ

7 For the things which some men esteem to be of great worth, both to the body and soul, others set at naught and trample under their feet. Yea, even the very God of Israel do men trample under their feet; I say, trample under their feet but I would speak in other words—they set him at naught, and hearken not to the voice of his counsels.
8 And behold he cometh, according to the words of the angel, in six hundred years from the time my father left Jerusalem.
9 And the world, because of their iniquity, shall judge him to be a thing of naught; wherefore they scourge him, and he suffereth it; and they smite him, and he suffereth it. Yea, they spit upon him, and he suffereth it, because of his loving kindness and his long-suffering towards the children of men.
10 And the God of our fathers, who were led out of Egypt, out of bondage, and also were preserved in the wilderness by him, yea, the God of Abraham, and of Isaac, and the God of Jacob, yieldeth himself, according to the words of the angel, as a man, into the hands of wicked men, to be lifted up, according to the words of Zenock, and to be crucified, according to the words of Neum, and to be buried in a sepulchre, according to the words of Zenos, which he spake concerning the three days of darkness, which should be a sign given of his death unto those who should inhabit the isles of the sea, more especially given unto those who are of the house of Israel.
11 For thus spake the prophet: The Lord God surely shall visit all the house of Israel at that day, some with his voice, because of their righteousness, unto their great joy and salvation, and others with the thunderings and the lightnings of his power, by tempest, by fire, and by smoke, and vapor of darkness, and by the opening of the earth, and by mountains which shall be carried up.
12 And all these things must surely come, saith the prophet Zenos. And the rocks of the earth must rend; and because of the groanings of the earth, many of the kings of the isles of the sea shall be wrought upon by the Spirit of God, to exclaim: The God of nature suffers.
13 And as for those who are at Jerusalem, saith the prophet, they shall be scourged by all people, because they crucify the God of Israel, and turn their hearts aside, rejecting signs and wonders, and the power and glory of the God of Israel.

---

19:6 ***err***—make mistakes

19:7 ***set at naught***—put aside as worthless

Nephi teaches that there are those who "trample" Jesus Christ "under their feet" by "hearken[ing] not to the voice of his counsels." In contrast, what blessings have you received by listening to and obeying the counsel of the Lord?

19:9 ***scourge***—whip

19:10 ***sepulchre***—tomb

Zenock, Neum, and Zenos were prophets in Old Testament times. Nephi most likely studied their prophecies written on the plates of brass. It is not known why their prophecies are not in our Old Testament today, but, thankfully, the Book of Mormon preserves their witness of the mission, sufferings, and triumph of the Lord.

19:11 ***tempest***—violent storm

19:12 ***rend***—break
***wrought upon***—worked on or inspired

14 And because they turn their hearts aside, saith the prophet, and have despised the Holy One of Israel, they shall wander in the flesh, and perish, and become a hiss and a byword, and be hated among all nations.

15 Nevertheless, when that day cometh, saith the prophet, that they no more turn aside their hearts against the Holy One of Israel, then will he remember the covenants which he made to their fathers.

16 Yea, then will he remember the isles of the sea; yea, and all the people who are of the house of Israel, will I gather in, saith the Lord, according to the words of the prophet Zenos, from the four quarters of the earth.

17 Yea, and all the earth shall see the salvation of the Lord, saith the prophet; every nation, kindred, tongue and people shall be blessed.

## *The Scriptures Can Help Us to Remember the Lord*

18 And I, Nephi, have written these things unto my people, that perhaps I might persuade them that they would remember the Lord their Redeemer.

19 Wherefore, I speak unto all the house of Israel, if it so be that they should obtain these things.

20 For behold, I have workings in the spirit, which doth weary me even that all my joints are weak, for those who are at Jerusalem; for had not the Lord been merciful, to show unto me concerning them, even as he had prophets of old, I should have perished also.

21 And he surely did show unto the prophets of old all things concerning them; and also he did show unto many concerning us; wherefore, it must needs be that we know concerning them for they are written upon the plates of brass.

22 Now it came to pass that I, Nephi, did teach my brethren these things; and it came to pass that I did read many things to them, which were engraven upon the plates of brass, that they might know concerning the doings of the Lord in other lands, among people of old.

23 And I did read many things unto them which were written in the books of Moses; but that I might more fully persuade them to believe in the Lord their Redeemer I did read unto them that which was written by the prophet Isaiah; for I did liken all scriptures unto us, that it might be for our profit and learning.

24 Wherefore I spake unto them, saying: Hear ye the words of the prophet, ye who are a remnant of the house of Israel, a branch who have been broken off; hear ye the words of the prophet, which were written unto all the house of Israel, and liken them unto yourselves, that ye may have hope as well as your brethren from whom ye have been broken off; for after this manner has the prophet written.

---

19:14 ***Holy One of Israel***—Jesus Christ
***a hiss and a byword***—a despised and ridiculed people

19:18 What did Nephi write about that helps you to remember the Lord?

19:23 The books of Moses are the first five books of the Old Testament: Genesis, Exodus, Leviticus, Numbers, and Deuteronomy. The Jews in Jesus' day called these writings "the Law" or "the Torah" (see LDS Bible Dictionary, s.v. "Pentateuch," 748).

*President Ezra Taft Benson urged us to "study the Book of Mormon as individuals and families and then to do as the prophet Nephi counseled: liken the scriptures to yourselves so that it will be for your profit and learning" (in Conference Report, April 1984, 7).*

## CHAPTER 20

*Nephi quotes Isaiah 48. Isaiah explains that the Lord loves the children of Israel but that He is disappointed in them. Look for what Isaiah says that shows how much the Lord loves His children.*

### The Lord Knows All Things and Uses That Power to Show Us That He Is God

1 HEARKEN and hear this, O house of Jacob, who are called by the name of Israel, and are come forth out of the waters of Judah, or out of the waters of baptism, who swear by the name of the Lord, and make mention of the God of Israel, yet they swear not in truth nor in righteousness.
2 Nevertheless, they call themselves of the holy city, but they do not stay themselves upon the God of Israel, who is the Lord of Hosts; yea, the Lord of Hosts is his name.
3 Behold, I have declared the former things from the beginning; and they went forth out of my mouth, and I showed them. I did show them suddenly.
4 And I did it because I knew that thou art obstinate, and thy neck is an iron sinew, and thy brow brass;
5 And I have even from the beginning declared to thee; before it came to pass I showed them thee; and I showed them for fear lest thou shouldst say—Mine idol hath done them, and my graven image, and my molten image hath commanded them.
6 Thou hast seen and heard all this; and will ye not declare them? And that I have showed thee new things from this time, even hidden things, and thou didst not know them.
7 They are created now, and not from the beginning, even before the day when thou heardest them not they were declared unto thee, lest thou shouldst say—Behold I knew them.
8 Yea, and thou heardest not; yea, thou knewest not; yea, from that time thine ear was not opened; for I knew that thou wouldst deal very treacherously, and wast called a transgressor from the womb.

### Through Our Afflictions the Lord Makes Us His Chosen People

9 Nevertheless, for my name's sake will I defer mine anger, and for my praise will I refrain from thee, that I cut thee not off.
10 For, behold, I have refined thee, I have chosen thee in the furnace of affliction.
11 For mine own sake, yea, for mine own sake will I do this, for I will not suffer my name to be polluted, and I will not give my glory unto another.

---

20:1 ***swear by the name of the Lord***—make covenants in the Lord's name

The Lord calls people He has made covenants with by several names. He may call them the house of Jacob, the house of Israel, or the children of Israel; or He may simply call them Israel (see LDS Bible Dictionary, s.v. "Israel," 708).

20:2 ***stay themselves upon***—rely upon

20:4 ***obstinate***—stubborn
***thy neck is an iron sinew***—your neck is as unbending as iron
***thy brow brass***—your brow is as hard as brass

20:5 A "graven image" is an idol made from carved wood or stone. A "molten image" is an idol made from metal.

20:6 (5–6) If you heard a prophet tell of future events that later actually happened, how might that change the way you think of that prophet and the Lord's powers?

20:7 (3–7) God revealed from the beginning many things that would come to pass during mortal life. This He did so that mankind would not give credit to idols and false gods for His marvelous works. To the Prophet Joseph Smith the Lord said, "And in nothing doth man offend God, or against none is his wrath kindled, save those who confess not his hand in all things, and obey not his commandments" (D&C 59:21).

20:8 ***deal very treacherously***—act dishonestly
***transgressor from the womb***—sinner from birth

20:9 ***defer***—hold back or put off
***refrain from***—be patient with

20:10 If we rely on the Lord, our afflictions (meaning our trials and suffering) will refine us, or make us pure. That is how our trials can make us more worthy to be God's chosen people (see also D&C 98:3; 100:15–17).

20:11 ***suffer***—let
***polluted***—made unclean or unholy

## The Children of Israel Should Listen to the Lord and His Prophets

12 Hearken unto me, O Jacob, and Israel my
called, for I am he; I am the first, and I am also the
last.
13 Mine hand hath also laid the foundation of the
earth, and my right hand hath spanned the heavens.
I call unto them and they stand up together.
14 All ye, assemble yourselves, and hear; who
among them hath declared these things unto them?
The Lord hath loved him; yea, and he will fulfil his
word which he hath declared by them; and he will
do his pleasure on Babylon, and his arm shall come
upon the Chaldeans.
15 Also, saith the Lord; I the Lord, yea, I have spoken; yea, I have called him to declare, I have
brought him, and he shall make his way prosperous.
16 Come ye near unto me; I have not spoken in
secret; from the beginning, from the time that it was
declared have I spoken; and the Lord God, and his
Spirit, hath sent me.
17 And thus saith the Lord, thy Redeemer, the
Holy One of Israel; I have sent him, the Lord thy
God who teacheth thee to profit, who leadeth thee
by the way thou shouldst go, hath done it.

## Living Righteously Brings Peace

18 O that thou hadst hearkened to my commandments—then had thy peace been as a river, and thy
righteousness as the waves of the sea.
19 Thy seed also had been as the sand; the offspring of thy bowels like the gravel thereof; his
name should not have been cut off nor destroyed
from before me.
20 Go ye forth of Babylon, flee ye from the
Chaldeans, with a voice of singing declare ye, tell
this, utter to the end of the earth; say ye: The Lord
hath redeemed his servant Jacob.
21 And they thirsted not; he led them through the
deserts; he caused the waters to flow out of the
rock for them; he clave the rock also and the waters
gushed out.
22 And notwithstanding he hath done all this, and
greater also, there is no peace, saith the Lord, unto
the wicked.

---

20:13 ***laid the foundation of the earth***—created the earth
***spanned***—crossed

20:14 ***assemble yourselves***—gather yourselves together
***his arm shall come upon the Chaldeans***—the strength or power of the Lord will come against the wicked

*The Chaldeans were a mighty people in Old Testament times who symbolized wickedness.*

Ancient Babylon was a very wicked city. The people who lived there were called Chaldeans. The Lord often uses the word *Babylon* as a name for wickedness in all ages (see D&C 133:14).

20:17 (14–17) In these verses the Lord is speaking of His prophets, who have "declared" what the Lord has revealed to them. He loves them and will "fulfil" all His words which they have spoken.

20:17 (16–17) How does it make you feel to know you live in a day when prophets are upon the earth and receive the word of the Lord to teach us the ways of God?

20:19 ***the offspring of thy bowels***—your children

20:20 ***utter***—speak
***redeemed***—saved

20:21 ***clave***—split

20:22 Why does wickedness take away peace? (see also Alma 41:11).

20:22 (18–22) Elsewhere in the Book of Mormon, King Benjamin asks us to "consider on the blessed and happy state of those that keep the commandments of God. For behold, they are blessed in all things, both temporal and spiritual" (Mosiah 2:41).

## CHAPTER 21

*Nephi quotes Isaiah 49. The Lord always fulfills His promises. Israel has been scattered throughout the earth for hundreds of years, and now the promised gathering has begun. Watch for where and how Israel will be gathered.*

### Jesus Christ and His Prophet Will Gather Israel and Provide Light for the Gentiles

1 AND again: Hearken, O ye house of Israel, all
ye that are broken off and are driven out because
of the wickedness of the pastors of my people; yea,
all ye that are broken off, that are scattered abroad,
who are of my people, O house of Israel. Listen,
O isles, unto me, and hearken ye people from far;
the Lord hath called me from the womb; from the
bowels of my mother hath he made mention of my
name.
2 And he hath made my mouth like a sharp
sword; in the shadow of his hand hath he hid me,
and made me a polished shaft; in his quiver hath he
hid me;
3 And said unto me: Thou art my servant, O Israel,
in whom I will be glorified.
4 Then I said, I have labored in vain, I have spent
my strength for naught and in vain; surely my judgment is with the Lord, and my work with my God.
5 And now, saith the Lord—that formed me from
the womb that I should be his servant, to bring
Jacob again to him—though Israel be not gathered,
yet shall I be glorious in the eyes of the Lord, and
my God shall be my strength.
6 And he said: It is a light thing that thou shouldst
be my servant to raise up the tribes of Jacob, and to
restore the preserved of Israel. I will also give thee
for a light to the Gentiles, that thou mayest be my
salvation unto the ends of the earth.

### The House of Israel Will Be Gathered in the Last Days

7 Thus saith the Lord, the Redeemer of Israel, his
Holy One, to him whom man despiseth, to him
whom the nations abhorreth, to servant of rulers:
Kings shall see and arise, princes also shall worship,
because of the Lord that is faithful.
8 Thus saith the Lord: In an acceptable time have
I heard thee, O isles of the sea, and in a day of salvation have I helped thee; and I will preserve thee,
and give thee my servant for a covenant of the
people, to establish the earth, to cause to inherit the
desolate heritages;
9 That thou mayest say to the prisoners: Go forth;
to them that sit in darkness: Show yourselves. They
shall feed in the ways, and their pastures shall be in
all high places.
10 They shall not hunger nor thirst, neither shall
the heat nor the sun smite them; for he that hath
mercy on them shall lead them, even by the springs
of water shall he guide them.
11 And I will make all my mountains a way, and
my highways shall be exalted.

---

21:1 The house of Israel was scattered because of the failure of its pastors (religious leaders). In this connection, the prophet Jeremiah taught, "Therefore thus saith the Lord God of Israel against the pastors that feed my people; Ye have scattered my flock, and driven them away" (Jeremiah 23:2). Note also that in this verse the word *isles* "refers not only to islands but also to the continents of the earth (2 Ne. 10:20). It may also mean any place not immediately accessible to Israel by land" (Donald W. Parry and others, *Understanding Isaiah,* 425).

21:2 ***polished shaft***—sharp arrow
***quiver***—arrow holder

21:4 ***in vain***—uselessly
***naught***—nothing

21:7 ***abhorreth***—hate

21:8 ***desolate heritages***—empty lands of inheritance

21:9 This passage likely has more than one meaning. It may refer to those who are set free from the bondage and darkness of sin and false traditions by the light of the restored gospel of Jesus Christ (see D&C 45:28). It could also refer to Jesus Christ's visit to the spirit world while His body lay in the tomb. During this visit He organized the righteous spirits to "carry the light of the gospel to them that were in darkness" (D&C 138:30).

21:11 Israel's gathering and return shall be through what Isaiah calls exalted highways. Isaiah stated earlier, "An highway shall be there, and a way, and it shall be called The way of holiness; the unclean shall not pass over it" (Isaiah 35:8). According to Elder Bruce R. McConkie, "the way of holiness cannot be other than the strait and narrow path" (*The Millennial Messiah,* 327).

12 And then, O house of Israel, behold, these shall
come from far; and lo, these from the north and
from the west; and these from the land of Sinim.

## The Lord Will Not Forget His Children

13 Sing, O heavens; and be joyful, O earth; for the
feet of those who are in the east shall be established; and break forth into singing, O mountains;
for they shall be smitten no more; for the Lord hath
comforted his people, and will have mercy upon
his afflicted.
14 But, behold, Zion hath said: The Lord hath forsaken me, and my Lord hath forgotten me—but he
will show that he hath not.
15 For can a woman forget her sucking child, that
she should not have compassion on the son of her
womb? Yea, they may forget, yet will I not forget
thee, O house of Israel.
16 Behold, I have graven thee upon the palms of
my hands; thy walls are continually before me.
17 Thy children shall make haste against thy
destroyers; and they that made thee waste shall go
forth of thee.
18 Lift up thine eyes round about and behold; all
these gather themselves together, and they shall
come to thee. And as I live, saith the Lord, thou
shalt surely clothe thee with them all, as with an
ornament, and bind them on even as a bride.
19 For thy waste and thy desolate places, and the
land of thy destruction, shall even now be too narrow by reason of the inhabitants; and they that
swallowed thee up shall be far away.
20 The children whom thou shalt have, after thou
hast lost the first, shall again in thine ears say: The
place is too strait for me; give place to me that I
may dwell.
21 Then shalt thou say in thine heart: Who hath
begotten me these, seeing I have lost my children,
and am desolate, a captive, and removing to and
fro? And who hath brought up these? Behold, I was
left alone; these, where have they been?

## The Gentile Nations Shall Help Gather the House of Israel

22 Thus saith the Lord God: Behold, I will lift up
mine hand to the Gentiles, and set up my standard

---

21:12 In this verse the land of Sinim "may refer to Syene, in southern Egypt, also known as Aswan, where there was a large Jewish colony after the Exile. Or it may refer to the desert of Sin, which is in the peninsula of Sinai. The point is that the Lord will gather his people from wherever they have been scattered" (Donald W. Parry and others, *Understanding Isaiah,* 430).

21:12 (9–12) In 1 Nephi 22:10–12, Nephi gives us the meaning of these verses from Isaiah. Nephi says that God shall "make bare his arm in the eyes of all the nations," meaning that God will show His mighty power. The divinely restored covenants and gospel will be brought to the house of Israel. Through the gospel of Jesus Christ, Israel shall be brought out of captivity and gathered to their promised lands. They will be taught the truth and come to know that the Lord is their Savior and Redeemer.

21:16 The phrase "graven thee upon the palms of my hands" may, among other meanings, refer to the nail marks in Jesus Christ's hands made during His Atonement.

21:16 (14–16) Have you ever felt like no one cared? The Lord has promised that He will not forget us any more than a mother would forget her baby. What comfort do you feel knowing you are engraven, or written, on the palms of the Lord's hands?

21:18 The last part of this verse refers to gathered Israel as Christ's "ornament" and "bride." This symbolism is made more clear in modern revelation. Referring to the gathered Saints in the last days, Jesus Christ declares: "I will own them, and they shall be mine in that day when I shall come to make up my jewels" (D&C 101:3).

21:19 ***desolate***—empty or barren

21:20 ***strait***—narrow or tight

21:21 ***begotten***—borne

21:21 (17–21) When Israel was conquered and scattered by her enemies, her lands were empty and wasted. When the Lord shall gather Israel to her lands, her enemies shall be gone, and the lands shall be restored and crowded because of the number of people (see Isaiah 54:1–3). Gathered Israel is described as glorious by comparing her to a beautiful bride.

21:22 The "standard" that will be set up is the everlasting covenant; the fulness of the gospel of Jesus Christ; and The Church of Jesus Christ of Latter-day Saints (see D&C 45:9; D&C 115:4–5). It will be established in "a mighty nation among the Gentiles" (1 Nephi 22:7). The gospel was restored through the Prophet Joseph Smith in the United States of America.

*ORGANIZATION OF THE CHURCH—APRIL 6, 1830, BY ROBERT T. BARRETT*

*The organization of the Church in 1830 through the Prophet Joseph Smith was in fulfillment of the Lord's words: "I will lift up mine hand to the Gentiles, and set up my standard to the people."*

to the people; and they shall bring thy sons in their
arms, and thy daughters shall be carried upon their
shoulders.
23 And kings shall be thy nursing fathers, and
their queens thy nursing mothers; they shall bow
down to thee with their face towards the earth, and
lick up the dust of thy feet; and thou shalt know
that I am the Lord; for they shall not be ashamed
that wait for me.
24 For shall the prey be taken from the mighty, or
the lawful captives delivered?
25 But thus saith the Lord, even the captives of the
mighty shall be taken away, and the prey of the terrible shall be delivered; for I will contend with him
that contendeth with thee, and I will save thy children.
26 And I will feed them that oppress thee with
their own flesh; they shall be drunken with their
own blood as with sweet wine; and all flesh shall
know that I, the Lord, am thy Savior and thy
Redeemer, the Mighty One of Jacob.

21:23 In 2 Nephi 6:8–13, Nephi's brother Jacob offers extensive inspired commentary on this verse from Isaiah.

21:24 ***lawful captives***—covenant people of the Lord

"The 'prey' mentioned in Isaiah 49:24 is the house of Israel in her scattered condition. She is 'prey' or 'captive' because she has been unable throughout the centuries to return to her promised home or to claim her gospel blessings" (*Old Testament: 1 Kings–Malachi, Religion 320 Student Manual,* 194).

21:26 The wicked who persecuted the Lord's children through the years "shall war among themselves" and "be drunken with their own blood." The Lord has promised that "all that fight against Zion shall be destroyed" (1 Nephi 22:13–14).

## CHAPTER 22

*After reading to his brethren from the plates of brass, Nephi prophesies of the scattering and gathering of Israel and how the devil's kingdom will be destroyed. As you study this chapter, pay close attention to what will happen to the wicked and the great promises made to the righteous.*

### The Scattering of Israel Is Prophesied

1 AND now it came to pass that after I, Nephi, had
read these things which were engraven upon the
plates of brass, my brethren came unto me and said
unto me: What meaneth these things which ye have
read? Behold, are they to be understood according
to things which are spiritual, which shall come to
pass according to the spirit and not the flesh?
2 And I, Nephi, said unto them: Behold they were
manifest unto the prophet by the voice of the Spirit;
for by the Spirit are all things made known unto the
prophets, which shall come upon the children of
men according to the flesh.
3 Wherefore, the things of which I have read are
things pertaining to things both temporal and spiritual; for it appears that the house of Israel, sooner
or later, will be scattered upon all the face of the
earth, and also among all nations.
4 And behold, there are many who are already
lost from the knowledge of those who are at
Jerusalem. Yea, the more part of all the tribes have
been led away; and they are scattered to and fro
upon the isles of the sea; and whither they are none
of us knoweth, save that we know that they have
been led away.
5 And since they have been led away, these things
have been prophesied concerning them, and also
concerning all those who shall hereafter be scattered and be confounded, because of the Holy One
of Israel; for against him will they harden their
hearts; wherefore, they shall be scattered among all
nations and shall be hated of all men.
6 Nevertheless, after they shall be nursed by the
Gentiles, and the Lord has lifted up his hand upon
the Gentiles and set them up for a standard, and
their children have been carried in their arms, and
their daughters have been carried upon their shoulders, behold these things of which are spoken are
temporal; for thus are the covenants of the Lord
with our fathers; and it meaneth us in the days to
come, and also all our brethren who are of the
house of Israel.
7 And it meaneth that the time cometh that after all
the house of Israel have been scattered and confounded, that the Lord God will raise up a mighty
nation among the Gentiles, yea, even upon the face
of this land; and by them shall our seed be scattered.

### Israel Shall Be Gathered

8 And after our seed is scattered the Lord God will
proceed to do a marvelous work among the
Gentiles, which shall be of great worth unto our
seed; wherefore, it is likened unto their being nourished by the Gentiles and being carried in their
arms and upon their shoulders.

---

22:2 ***manifest***—revealed, made known, or shown

22:3 ***pertaining to***—concerning
***temporal***—worldly or physical

22:3 (1–3) The Joseph Smith Translation teaches that "the things of God knoweth no man, except he has the Spirit of God" (JST, 1 Corinthians 2:11).

22:4 ***to and fro***—in various places
***whither***—where

Over seven hundred years before the time of Jesus Christ, the ten tribes, which formed the northern kingdom of Israel, were conquered by the Assyrians and taken into Assyria as captives. These Israelites came to be called the "lost ten tribes." Prophecies state that they will return when they are ready to live the gospel (see LDS Bible Dictionary, s.v. "Israel, Kingdom of," 708; Articles of Faith 1:10).

22:5 The word *confounded* is usually defined today as "confused" and "bewildered." In the time that the Book of Mormon was translated into English, however, it also meant "mixed or blended in disorder," as well as "put to shame" (Noah Webster, *An American Dictionary of the English Language* [1828], s.v. "Confounded").

22:6 ***nursed***—cared for

22:7 "The 'mighty nation among the Gentiles' which the Lord was to raise up 'even upon the face of this land' evidently refers to the great nation of the United States of America" (Daniel H. Ludlow, *A Companion to Your Study of the Book of Mormon,* 121).

22:8 Elder Spencer W. Kimball taught that the Lamanites are "nourished by the Gentiles" by having the gospel and the Book of Mormon brought to them (see Conference Report, October 1959, 61–62).

9 And it shall also be of worth unto the Gentiles; and not only unto the Gentiles but unto all the house of Israel, unto the making known of the covenants of the Father of heaven unto Abraham, saying: In thy seed shall all the kindreds of the earth be blessed.

10 And I would, my brethren, that ye should know that all the kindreds of the earth cannot be blessed unless he shall make bare his arm in the eyes of the nations.

11 Wherefore, the Lord God will proceed to make bare his arm in the eyes of all the nations, in bringing about his covenants and his gospel unto those who are of the house of Israel.

12 Wherefore, he will bring them again out of captivity, and they shall be gathered together to the lands of their inheritance; and they shall be brought out of obscurity and out of darkness; and they shall know that the Lord is their Savior and their Redeemer, the Mighty One of Israel.

## All Who Fight Against Zion Will Be Destroyed

13 And the blood of that great and abominable church, which is the whore of all the earth, shall turn upon their own heads; for they shall war among themselves, and the sword of their own hands shall fall upon their own heads, and they shall be drunken with their own blood.

14 And every nation which shall war against thee, O house of Israel, shall be turned one against another, and they shall fall into the pit which they digged to ensnare the people of the Lord. And all that fight against Zion shall be destroyed, and that great whore, who hath perverted the right ways of the Lord, yea, that great and abominable church, shall tumble to the dust and great shall be the fall of it.

15 For behold, saith the prophet, the time cometh speedily that Satan shall have no more power over the hearts of the children of men; for the day soon cometh that all the proud and they who do wickedly shall be as stubble; and the day cometh that they must be burned.

16 For the time soon cometh that the fulness of the wrath of God shall be poured out upon all the children of men; for he will not suffer that the wicked shall destroy the righteous.

17 Wherefore, he will preserve the righteous by his power, even if it so be that the fulness of his wrath must come, and the righteous be preserved, even unto the destruction of their enemies by fire. Wherefore, the righteous need not fear; for thus saith the prophet, they shall be saved, even if it so be as by fire.

18 Behold, my brethren, I say unto you, that these things must shortly come; yea, even blood, and fire, and vapor of smoke must come; and it must needs be upon the face of this earth; and it cometh unto men according to the flesh if it so be that they will harden their hearts against the Holy One of Israel.

19 For behold, the righteous shall not perish; for the time surely must come that all they who fight against Zion shall be cut off.

20 And the Lord will surely prepare a way for his people, unto the fulfilling of the words of Moses, which he spake, saying: A prophet shall the Lord your God raise up unto you, like unto me; him shall ye hear in all things whatsoever he shall say unto you. And it shall come to pass that all those who will not hear that prophet shall be cut off from among the people.

21 And now I, Nephi, declare unto you, that this prophet of whom Moses spake was the Holy One of Israel; wherefore, he shall execute judgment in righteousness.

---

22:9 ***kindreds***—families

22:10 ***make bare his arm***—show His power

22:12 ***captivity***—bondage and slavery
***obscurity***—uncertainty or gloom

22:13 ***abominable***—terrible and evil

22:14 ***ensnare***—trap or capture

22:15 ***stubble***—leftover stalks after the harvest

22:16 ***wrath***—anger

22:19 "We do not say that all of the Saints will be spared and saved from the coming day of desolation. But we do say there is no promise of safety and no promise of security except for those who love the Lord and who are seeking to do all that he commands" (Bruce R. McConkie, in Conference Report, April 1979, 133).

22:19 (17–19) During the judgments of the last days, the Lord promises that "he will preserve the righteous by his power" (v. 17). Further, He promises that "the righteous shall not perish" (v. 19). How do these promises strengthen your commitment to live the gospel?

22 And the righteous need not fear, for they are
those who shall not be confounded. But it is the
kingdom of the devil, which shall be built up
among the children of men, which kingdom is
established among them which are in the flesh—
23 For the time speedily shall come that all
churches which are built up to get gain, and all
those who are built up to get power over the flesh,
and those who are built up to become popular in
the eyes of the world, and those who seek the lusts
of the flesh and the things of the world, and to do
all manner of iniquity; yea, in fine, all those who
belong to the kingdom of the devil are they who
need fear, and tremble, and quake; they are those
who must be brought low in the dust; they are
those who must be consumed as stubble; and this
is according to the words of the prophet.

## *The Holy One of Israel (Jesus Christ) Shall Lead the Righteous*

24 And the time cometh speedily that the righteous must be led up as calves of the stall, and the
Holy One of Israel must reign in dominion, and
might, and power, and great glory.
25 And he gathereth his children from the four
quarters of the earth; and he numbereth his sheep,
and they know him; and there shall be one fold and
one shepherd; and he shall feed his sheep, and in
him they shall find pasture.
26 And because of the righteousness of his
people, Satan has no power; wherefore, he cannot
be loosed for the space of many years; for he hath
no power over the hearts of the people, for they
dwell in righteousness, and the Holy One of Israel
reigneth.
27 And now behold, I, Nephi, say unto you that
all these things must come according to the flesh.
28 But, behold, all nations, kindreds, tongues, and
people shall dwell safely in the Holy One of Israel
if it so be that they will repent.
29 And now I, Nephi, make an end; for I durst not
speak further as yet concerning these things.
30 Wherefore, my brethren, I would that ye
should consider that the things which have been
written upon the plates of brass are true; and they
testify that a man must be obedient to the commandments of God.
31 Wherefore, ye need not suppose that I and my
father are the only ones that have testified, and also
taught them. Wherefore, if ye shall be obedient to
the commandments, and endure to the end, ye shall
be saved at the last day. And thus it is. Amen.

---

22:24 ***reign***—rule

22:25 (24–25) The Lord is the Good Shepherd and He knows His sheep. How does the Lord care for you as a shepherd cares for his sheep?

22:26 We learn from Doctrine and Covenants 88:110 that the space of time when Satan will not have power is a thousand years. This is sometimes referred to as the Millennium.

22:31 (30–31) Nephi concludes this book by testifying that man must be obedient to the commandments of God. Those who are obedient and endure to the end will be saved. Can you think of any additional blessings of being obedient to the commandments?

PHOTOGRAPH BY DAVID H. GARNER

*"He shall feed his sheep and in him they shall find pasture."*

# THE SECOND BOOK OF NEPHI

*The many conflicts between Lehi's children finally caused them to separate. Nephi led one group and Laman led the other. They became known as the Nephites and the Lamanites. Second Nephi contains Lehi's last teachings to his family. It also includes teachings and prophecies of Nephi and his brother Jacob. They were righteous men who tried to convince their people to believe in and follow Jesus Christ's teachings. Nephi and Jacob often quoted the words of the prophet Isaiah (taken from the brass plates) to help the people follow God. The book of 2 Nephi covers a period of time from about 588 B.C. to about 545 B.C.*

*An account of the death of Lehi. Nephi's brethren rebel against him. The Lord warns Nephi to depart into the wilderness. His journeyings in the wilderness, and so forth.**

## CHAPTER 1

*Knowing he is old and about to die, Lehi speaks to his children about the blessings that come to the righteous. He encourages them to follow the Lord. Look for the prophecies Lehi makes concerning his children and about the land of promise.*

### LEHI PROPHESIES THAT THE FAITHFUL WILL POSSESS THE PROMISED LAND

1 AND now it came to pass that after I, Nephi, had
made an end of teaching my brethren, our father,
Lehi, also spake many things unto them, and
rehearsed unto them, how great things the Lord had
done for them in bringing them out of the land of
Jerusalem.
2 And he spake unto them concerning their
rebellions upon the waters, and the mercies of
God in sparing their lives, that they were not swallowed up in the sea.
3 And he also spake unto them concerning the
land of promise, which they had obtained—how
merciful the Lord had been in warning us that we
should flee out of the land of Jerusalem.
4 For, behold, said he, I have seen a vision, in
which I know that Jerusalem is destroyed; and had
we remained in Jerusalem we should also have perished.
5 But, said he, notwithstanding our afflictions, we
have obtained a land of promise, a land which is
choice above all other lands; a land which the Lord
God hath covenanted with me should be a land for
the inheritance of my seed. Yea, the Lord hath
covenanted this land unto me, and to my children
forever, and also all those who should be led out of
other countries by the hand of the Lord.
6 Wherefore, I, Lehi, prophesy according to the
workings of the Spirit which is in me, that there
shall none come into this land save they shall be
brought by the hand of the Lord.

---

* This introduction to 2 Nephi, like that of 1 Nephi, was translated from the Book of Mormon plates.

1:1 ***rehearsed***—repeated or told

1:2 ***rebellions***—conflicts and fighting
***swallowed up***—drowned

1:3 ***the land of promise***—the land that the Lord promised to them and their children and their children's children forever, if they were righteous

1:4 Lehi's prophecy that Jerusalem would be destroyed (see 1 Nephi 1:13) was now fulfilled. In about 570 B.C. (about thirty years after Lehi's family left), the Babylonian people conquered Jerusalem. You can read about this in 2 Kings 24–25.

1:5 ***notwithstanding our afflictions***—in spite of our trials and sufferings
***choice***—favored of the Lord
***covenanted with***—promised
***seed***—descendants, meaning children, grandchildren, and so on

Words in pink are explained in the Glossary.

7 Wherefore, this land is consecrated unto him whom he shall bring. And if it so be that they shall serve him according to the commandments which he hath given, it shall be a land of liberty unto them; wherefore, they shall never be brought down into captivity; if so, it shall be because of iniquity; for if iniquity shall abound cursed shall be the land for their sakes, but unto the righteous it shall be blessed forever.
8 And behold, it is wisdom that this land should be kept as yet from the knowledge of other nations; for behold, many nations would overrun the land, that there would be no place for an inheritance.
9 Wherefore, I, Lehi, have obtained a promise, that inasmuch as those whom the Lord God shall bring out of the land of Jerusalem shall keep his commandments, they shall prosper upon the face of this land; and they shall be kept from all other nations, that they may possess this land unto themselves. And if it so be that they shall keep his commandments they shall be blessed upon the face of this land, and there shall be none to molest them, nor to take away the land of their inheritance; and they shall dwell safely forever.

### Lehi Prophesies of Wickedness and Destruction in the Promised Land

10 But behold, when the time cometh that they shall dwindle in unbelief, after they have received so great blessings from the hand of the Lord—having a knowledge of the creation of the earth, and all men, knowing the great and marvelous works of the Lord from the creation of the world; having power given them to do all things by faith; having all the commandments from the beginning, and having been brought by his infinite goodness into this precious land of promise—behold, I say, if the day shall come that they will reject the Holy One of Israel, the true Messiah, their Redeemer and their God, behold, the judgments of him that is just shall rest upon them.
11 Yea, he will bring other nations unto them, and he will give unto them power, and he will take away from them the lands of their possessions, and he will cause them to be scattered and smitten.
12 Yea, as one generation passeth to another there shall be bloodsheds, and great visitations among them; wherefore, my sons, I would that ye would remember; yea, I would that ye would hearken unto my words.
13 O that ye would awake; awake from a deep sleep, yea, even from the sleep of hell, and shake off the awful chains by which ye are bound, which are the chains which bind the children of men, that they are carried away captive down to the eternal gulf of misery and woe.

### Lehi Shares His Testimony with His Children

14 Awake! and arise from the dust, and hear the words of a trembling parent, whose limbs ye must soon lay down in the cold and silent grave, from whence no traveler can return; a few more days and I go the way of all the earth.
15 But behold, the Lord hath redeemed my soul from hell; I have beheld his glory, and I am encircled about eternally in the arms of his love.

---

1:7 **_consecrated_**—dedicated or blessed
**_liberty_**—freedom
**_captivity_**—bondage and slavery
**_iniquity_**—wickedness

1:9 **_molest_**—hurt

1:10 **_dwindle_**—become weak and fall away
**_the Holy One of Israel_**—Jesus Christ

*Messiah* means "Anointed One." The word *Christ* has the same meaning. Jesus Christ is the promised Messiah—the one chosen, set apart, and sent by God to save us. To *redeem* means to "buy back" or to "set free." Jesus Christ is our Redeemer because He willingly paid the price to buy us back and set us free from the effects of the Fall of Adam and from the burden of our own sins (see 1 Corinthians 6:20; D&C 18:11). The price He had to pay was His own blood (see 1 Peter 1:18–19).

1:11 **_smitten_**—beaten

1:12 **_hearken unto_**—listen to and obey

1:12 (10–12) The punishments Lehi spoke of were terrible, because the people had received so many blessings. The Lord teaches, "For of him unto whom much is given much is required" (D&C 82:3).

1:13 **_the eternal gulf of misery and woe_**—hell (see Glossary, s.v. "Hell")

FAMILY OF LEHI CAMPED IN PROMISED LAND, BY GARY KAPP

*The Lord promised Lehi that if he and his descendants would keep the commandments, they would prosper and "dwell safely forever" in the promised land.*

16 And I desire that ye should remember to observe the statutes and the judgments of the Lord; behold, this hath been the anxiety of my soul from the beginning.

17 My heart hath been weighed down with sorrow from time to time, for I have feared, lest for the hardness of your hearts the Lord your God should come out in the fulness of his wrath upon you, that ye be cut off and destroyed forever;

18 Or, that a cursing should come upon you for the space of many generations; and ye are visited by sword, and by famine, and are hated, and are led according to the will and captivity of the devil.

19 O my sons, that these things might not come upon you, but that ye might be a choice and a favored people of the Lord. But behold, his will be done; for his ways are righteousness forever.

20 And he hath said that: Inasmuch as ye shall keep my commandments ye shall prosper in the land; but inasmuch as ye will not keep my commandments ye shall be cut off from my presence.

## *Lehi Counsels His Sons to Be Righteous Men Who Follow Nephi's Example*

21 And now that my soul might have joy in you, and that my heart might leave this world with gladness because of you, that I might not be brought down with grief and sorrow to the grave, arise from the dust, my sons, and be men, and be determined in one mind and in one heart, united in all things, that ye may not come down into captivity;

22 That ye may not be cursed with a sore cursing; and also, that ye may not incur the displeasure of a just God upon you, unto the destruction, yea, the eternal destruction of both soul and body.

23 Awake, my sons; put on the armor of righteousness. Shake off the chains with which ye are bound, and come forth out of obscurity, and arise from the dust.

24 Rebel no more against your brother, whose views have been glorious, and who hath kept the commandments from the time that we left Jerusalem; and who hath been an instrument in the hands of God, in bringing us forth into the land of promise; for were it not for him, we must have perished with hunger in the wilderness; nevertheless, ye sought to take away his life; yea, and he hath suffered much sorrow because of you.

25 And I exceedingly fear and tremble because of you, lest he shall suffer again; for behold, ye have accused him that he sought power and authority over you; but I know that he hath not sought for power nor authority over you, but he hath sought the glory of God, and your own eternal welfare.

26 And ye have murmured because he hath been plain unto you. Ye say that he hath used sharpness; ye say that he hath been angry with you; but behold, his sharpness was the sharpness of the power of the word of God, which was in him; and that which ye call anger was the truth, according to that which is in God, which he could not restrain, manifesting boldly concerning your iniquities.

27 And it must needs be that the power of God must be with him, even unto his commanding you that ye must obey. But behold, it was not he, but it was the Spirit of the Lord which was in him, which opened his mouth to utterance that he could not shut it.

28 And now my son, Laman, and also Lemuel and Sam, and also my sons who are the sons of Ishmael, behold, if ye will hearken unto the voice of Nephi ye shall not perish. And if ye will hearken unto him I leave unto you a blessing, yea, even my first blessing.

---

1:16 ***statutes***—laws
***anxiety***—worry

1:17 ***wrath***—anger

1:19 (17–19) What words show you that Lehi loved his children? Why is it a blessing to have parents to teach us to be righteous? Can you remember a time when your parents reminded you about the importance of following God?

1:23 Referring to Lehi's counsel to "come forth out of obscurity," Elder Carlos E. Asay indicated that this phrase "instructs one to model goodness and serve as a light to others" (in Conference Report, April 1992, 59).

1:25 ***accused***—blamed

1:26 Nephi's brothers felt that he spoke to them in sharpness, or in a way that caused pain, because "the guilty taketh the truth to be hard" (1 Nephi 16:2).

1:27 ***opened his mouth to utterance***—caused him to speak

29 But if ye will not hearken unto him I take away my first blessing, yea, even my blessing, and it shall rest upon him.

## Lehi Speaks to Zoram

30 And now, Zoram, I speak unto you: Behold, thou art the servant of Laban; nevertheless, thou hast been brought out of the land of Jerusalem, and I know that thou art a true friend unto my son, Nephi, forever.
31 Wherefore, because thou hast been faithful thy seed shall be blessed with his seed, that they dwell in prosperity long upon the face of this land; and nothing, save it shall be iniquity among them, shall harm or disturb their prosperity upon the face of this land forever.
32 Wherefore, if ye shall keep the commandments of the Lord, the Lord hath consecrated this land for the security of thy seed with the seed of my son.

# CHAPTER 2

*Lehi tells his son Jacob how the Savior prepared the way for us to have eternal life. Look for how you can have eternal life and what the Savior has done to make this possible.*

## Lehi Speaks to His Son Jacob

1 AND now, Jacob, I speak unto you: Thou art my first-born in the days of my tribulation in the wilderness. And behold, in thy childhood thou hast suffered afflictions and much sorrow, because of the rudeness of thy brethren.
2 Nevertheless, Jacob, my first-born in the wilderness, thou knowest the greatness of God; and he shall consecrate thine afflictions for thy gain.
3 Wherefore, thy soul shall be blessed, and thou shalt dwell safely with thy brother, Nephi; and thy days shall be spent in the service of thy God. Wherefore, I know that thou art redeemed, because of the righteousness of thy Redeemer; for thou hast beheld that in the fulness of time he cometh to bring salvation unto men.
4 And thou hast beheld in thy youth his glory; wherefore, thou art blessed even as they unto whom he shall minister in the flesh; for the Spirit is the same, yesterday, today, and forever. And the way is prepared from the fall of man, and salvation is free.

## All People Can Be Saved Through the Atonement of Jesus Christ

5 And men are instructed sufficiently that they know good from evil. And the law is given unto men. And by the law no flesh is justified; or, by the law men are cut off. Yea, by the temporal law they were cut off; and also, by the spiritual law they perish from that which is good, and become miserable forever.
6 Wherefore, redemption cometh in and through the Holy Messiah; for he is full of grace and truth.

---

1:29 (28–29) The "first blessing" Lehi refers to is the birthright blessing, which was generally the right of the firstborn male child, based upon obedience. "This generally included a land inheritance as well as the authority to preside" (LDS Bible Dictionary, s.v. "Birthright," 625).

1:31 ***prosperity***—a state of well-being and success

1:32 ***security***—safety

2:1 Jacob was Lehi's fifth son. He was the first child born in the wilderness as the family traveled from Jerusalem to the promised land (see 1 Nephi 2:5; 18:7).

***tribulation***—hardship and struggle
***afflictions***—trials and difficulties

2:2 ***consecrate***—dedicate or bless

2:4 Jacob had the privilege of seeing the Savior (see 2 Nephi 11:2–3).

***minister in the flesh***—teach and care for when He lives on the earth

"Eternal life is freely available; salvation is free in that all may drink of the waters of life; all may come and partake; but none gains so high a reward as eternal life until he is tried and tested and found worthy, as were the ancients" (Bruce R. McConkie, *The Mortal Messiah* 3:302).

2:5 ***sufficiently***—enough
***flesh***—living creature
***justified***—shown to be not guilty
***cut off***—separated from God

2:6 ***redemption***—salvation

2:6 (5–6) Because of the Fall of Adam we all die physically. Because of our own sins we all die spiritually, meaning we are all separated from God (see 1 Nephi 15:33–34). How can the Atonement of Christ help overcome these two kinds of death?

7 Behold, he offereth himself a sacrifice for sin, to answer the ends of the law, unto all those who have a broken heart and a contrite spirit; and unto none else can the ends of the law be answered.

8 Wherefore, how great the importance to make these things known unto the inhabitants of the earth, that they may know that there is no flesh that can dwell in the presence of God, save it be through the merits, and mercy, and grace of the Holy Messiah, who layeth down his life according to the flesh, and taketh it again by the power of the Spirit, that he may bring to pass the resurrection of the dead, being the first that should rise.

9 Wherefore, he is the firstfruits unto God, inasmuch as he shall make intercession for all the children of men; and they that believe in him shall be saved.

10 And because of the intercession for all, all men come unto God; wherefore, they stand in the presence of him, to be judged of him according to the truth and holiness which is in him. Wherefore, the ends of the law which the Holy One hath given, unto the inflicting of the punishment which is affixed, which punishment that is affixed is in opposition to that of the happiness which is affixed, to answer the ends of the atonement—

## There Must Be Opposition in All Things

11 For it must needs be, that there is an opposition in all things. If not so, my first-born in the wilderness, righteousness could not be brought to pass, neither wickedness, neither holiness nor misery, neither good nor bad. Wherefore, all things must needs be a compound in one; wherefore, if it should be one body it must needs remain as dead, having no life neither death, nor corruption nor incorruption, happiness nor misery, neither sense nor insensibility.

12 Wherefore, it must needs have been created for a thing of naught; wherefore there would have been no purpose in the end of its creation. Wherefore, this thing must needs destroy the wisdom of God and his eternal purposes, and also the power, and the mercy, and the justice of God.

13 And if ye shall say there is no law, ye shall also say there is no sin. If ye shall say there is no sin, ye shall also say there is no righteousness. And if there be no righteousness there be no happiness. And if there be no righteousness nor happiness there be no punishment nor misery. And if these things are not there is no God. And if there is no God we are not, neither the earth; for there could have been no creation of things, neither to act nor to be acted upon; wherefore, all things must have vanished away.

14 And now, my sons, I speak unto you these things for your profit and learning; for there is a God, and he hath created all things, both the heavens and the earth, and all things that in them are, both things to act and things to be acted upon.

15 And to bring about his eternal purposes in the end of man, after he had created our first parents, and the beasts of the field and the fowls of the air, and in fine, all things which are created, it must needs be that there was an opposition; even the forbidden fruit in opposition to the tree of life; the one being sweet and the other bitter.

---

2:7 ***offereth***—gives
***contrite***—truly repentant

The Savior overcame physical death when He was resurrected. He also suffered and paid for our sins. What must we do to be forgiven for our sins?

2:8 ***inhabitants***—people
***merits***—worthiness or righteousness

2:9 ***intercession***—atonement

2:10 ***inflicting***—giving
***affixed***—attached

2:11 We must have opposites from which we can choose, or we would not be able to act for ourselves. Elder Bruce R. McConkie taught, "Unless there is darkness, there can be no light; unless there is vice, there can be no virtue; unless there is hate, there can be no love" (*The Mortal Messiah* 4:89).

***corruption***—decay or rot
***sense***—ability to think

2:12 ***naught***—no value

2:15 God planted the tree of knowledge of good and evil (the forbidden fruit) and the tree of life in the Garden of Eden. He told Adam and Eve that they could choose whether or not they would eat the fruit of the tree of knowledge of good and evil, "for it is given unto thee." But God also said, "Remember that I forbid it, for in the day thou eatest thereof thou shalt surely die" (see Moses 3:8–9, 15–17).

16 Wherefore, the Lord God gave unto man that he should act for himself. Wherefore, man could not act for himself save it should be that he was enticed by the one or the other.

## Adam Fell That Men Might Be

17 And I, Lehi, according to the things which I have read, must needs suppose that an angel of God, according to that which is written, had fallen from heaven; wherefore, he became a devil, having sought that which was evil before God.
18 And because he had fallen from heaven, and had become miserable forever, he sought also the misery of all mankind. Wherefore, he said unto Eve, yea, even that old serpent, who is the devil, who is the father of all lies, wherefore he said: Partake of the forbidden fruit, and ye shall not die, but ye shall be as God, knowing good and evil.
19 And after Adam and Eve had partaken of the forbidden fruit they were driven out of the garden of Eden, to till the earth.
20 And they have brought forth children; yea, even the family of all the earth.
21 And the days of the children of men were prolonged, according to the will of God, that they might repent while in the flesh; wherefore, their state became a state of probation, and their time was lengthened, according to the commandments which the Lord God gave unto the children of men. For he gave commandment that all men must repent; for he showed unto all men that they were lost, because of the transgression of their parents.
22 And now, behold, if Adam had not transgressed he would not have fallen, but he would have remained in the garden of Eden. And all things which were created must have remained in the same state in which they were after they were created; and they must have remained forever, and had no end.
23 And they would have had no children; wherefore they would have remained in a state of innocence, having no joy, for they knew no misery; doing no good, for they knew no sin.
24 But behold, all things have been done in the wisdom of him who knoweth all things.
25 Adam fell that men might be; and men are, that they might have joy.

## Because of the Savior's Atonement, All Mankind Can Choose Eternal Life or Eternal Death

26 And the Messiah cometh in the fulness of time, that he may redeem the children of men from the fall. And because that they are redeemed from the fall they have become free forever, knowing good from evil; to act for themselves and not to be acted upon, save it be by the punishment of the law at the great and last day, according to the commandments which God hath given.
27 Wherefore, men are free according to the flesh; and all things are given them which are expedient unto man. And they are free to choose liberty and eternal life, through the great Mediator of all men, or to choose captivity and death, according to the captivity and power of the devil; for he seeketh that all men might be miserable like unto himself.
28 And now, my sons, I would that ye should look to the great Mediator, and hearken unto his great commandments; and be faithful unto his words,

2:16 ***enticed***—appealed to or tempted

2:17 Lucifer rebelled against God in the premortal existence and was cast down to earth, where he became Satan, or the devil (see D&C 76:25–27; Moses 4:1–4).

***sought***—desired

2:21 ***probation***—testing
***transgression of***—breaking of a law by

2:23 (22–23) If Adam and Eve had remained in the Garden of Eden, they would have had no children. Why do you think it was so important for them to have a family?

2:25 How has Adam's decision to eat the forbidden fruit blessed you?

2:26 The Savior has redeemed us from physical death and has paid for our sins if we repent. How does this make you free?

2:27 ***expedient***—necessary

God has given us the power to act and make choices. People can do good or evil. Why do you think God gave us this ability?

2:28 A mediator is one who works to settle the differences between two people. God said that no unclean thing can enter His presence (see 1 Nephi 15:34). All of us have sinned and are not worthy to enter God's kingdom (see Romans 3:23). Jesus Christ is the great Mediator because His sacrifice makes up the difference between what we are and what we need to be to enter God's kingdom (see 1 Timothy 2:5).

ADAM AND EVE KNEELING AT AN ALTAR, BY DEL PARSON

*Adam and Eve carried out an important part of God's plan. If they had remained in the Garden of Eden they would not have progressed and Heavenly Father would not have been able to send His spirit children to the earth. That is why Lehi said, "Adam fell that men might be."*

and choose eternal life, according to the will of his Holy Spirit;

29 And not choose eternal death, according to the will of the flesh and the evil which is therein, which giveth the spirit of the devil power to captivate, to bring you down to hell, that he may reign over you in his own kingdom.

30 I have spoken these few words unto you all, my sons, in the last days of my probation; and I have chosen the good part, according to the words of the prophet. And I have none other object save it be the everlasting welfare of your souls. Amen.

## CHAPTER 3

*Lehi speaks to his son Joseph about two other important prophets also named Joseph: first, Joseph the son of Jacob, who was sold into Egypt, and second, Joseph Smith Jr., the latter-day prophet of the Restoration. As you read this chapter, look for the revelations given about and through these two Josephs.*

### Lehi Blesses His Son Joseph

1 AND now I speak unto you, Joseph, my last-born. Thou wast born in the wilderness of mine afflictions; yea, in the days of my greatest sorrow did thy mother bear thee.

2 And may the Lord consecrate also unto thee this land, which is a most precious land, for thine inheritance and the inheritance of thy seed with thy brethren, for thy security forever, if it so be that ye shall keep the commandments of the Holy One of Israel.

3 And now, Joseph, my last-born, whom I have brought out of the wilderness of mine afflictions, may the Lord bless thee forever, for thy seed shall not utterly be destroyed.

### Joseph of Egypt Prophesies of a Seer in the Latter Days

4 For behold, thou art the fruit of my loins; and I am a descendant of Joseph who was carried captive into Egypt. And great were the covenants of the Lord which he made unto Joseph.

5 Wherefore, Joseph truly saw our day. And he obtained a promise of the Lord, that out of the fruit of his loins the Lord God would raise up a righteous branch unto the house of Israel; not the Messiah, but a branch which was to be broken off, nevertheless, to be remembered in the covenants of the Lord that the Messiah should be made manifest unto them in the latter days, in the spirit of power, unto the bringing of them out of darkness unto light—yea, out of hidden darkness and out of captivity unto freedom.

---

2:29 ***flesh***—physical body
***reign***—rule

2:30 ***object***—purpose
***welfare***—good

3:1 ***afflictions***—trials or suffering
***bear***—give birth to

3:2 ***consecrate***—dedicate and bless
***thine inheritance***—your dwelling place
***security***—safety
***the Holy One of Israel***—Jesus Christ

3:3 ***utterly***—completely

3:4 "Lehi and his family were descendants of Joseph through the lineage of Manasseh, and Ishmael was a descendant of Ephraim, according to the statement of the Prophet Joseph Smith. That the Nephites were descendants of Joseph is in fulfilment of the blessings given to Joseph by his father Israel" (Joseph Fielding Smith, *Doctrines of Salvation* 3:262–63).

***the fruit of my loins***—my offspring or my descendant

A covenant is an agreement between two people. In the scriptures it is usually an agreement between God and man. We promise to be obedient to God's commandments, and He promises to bless us (see LDS Bible Dictionary, s.v. "Covenant," 651).

3:5 ***the fruit of his loins***—his offspring or his descendants
***branch***—offshoot or division
***made manifest***—shown
***captivity***—bondage and slavery

The name *Israel* means "one who prevails with God," or "let God prevail." It is used several ways in the scriptures. It may refer to (1) the man Jacob, whose name was changed to Israel; (2) the family, children, or tribes of Israel (the scriptures often use the phrase "house of Israel" in this sense); (3) the land of Israel; or (4) the true believers in Christ, no matter what their family or where they live (see LDS Bible Dictionary, s.v. "Israel," 708).

*Joseph, who was sold into Egypt, saw the latter days. He spoke of Joseph Smith when he testified, "A seer shall the Lord my God raise up, who shall be a choice seer unto the fruit of my loins."*

6 For Joseph truly testified, saying: A seer shall the Lord my God raise up, who shall be a choice seer unto the fruit of my loins.

7 Yea, Joseph truly said: Thus saith the Lord unto me: A choice seer will I raise up out of the fruit of thy loins; and he shall be esteemed highly among the fruit of thy loins. And unto him will I give commandment that he shall do a work for the fruit of thy loins, his brethren, which shall be of great worth unto them, even to the bringing of them to the knowledge of the covenants which I have made with thy fathers.

8 And I will give unto him a commandment that he shall do none other work, save the work which I shall command him. And I will make him great in mine eyes; for he shall do my work.

9 And he shall be great like unto Moses, whom I have said I would raise up unto you, to deliver my people, O house of Israel.

10 And Moses will I raise up, to deliver thy people out of the land of Egypt.

11 But a seer will I raise up out of the fruit of thy loins; and unto him will I give power to bring forth my word unto the seed of thy loins—and not to the bringing forth my word only, saith the Lord, but to the convincing them of my word, which shall have already gone forth among them.

12 Wherefore, the fruit of thy loins shall write; and the fruit of the loins of Judah shall write; and that which shall be written by the fruit of thy loins, and also that which shall be written by the fruit of the loins of Judah, shall grow together, unto the confounding of false doctrines and laying down of contentions, and establishing peace among the fruit of thy loins, and bringing them to the knowledge of their fathers in the latter days, and also to the knowledge of my covenants, saith the Lord.

13 And out of weakness he shall be made strong, in that day when my work shall commence among all my people, unto the restoring thee, O house of Israel, saith the Lord.

14 And thus prophesied Joseph, saying: Behold, that seer will the Lord bless; and they that seek to destroy him shall be confounded; for this promise, which I have obtained of the Lord, of the fruit of my loins, shall be fulfilled. Behold, I am sure of the fulfilling of this promise;

15 And his name shall be called after me; and it shall be after the name of his father. And he shall be like unto me; for the thing, which the Lord shall bring forth by his hand, by the power of the Lord shall bring my people unto salvation.

### *Joseph's Seed Will Be Preserved and Will Accept the Book of Mormon*

16 Yea, thus prophesied Joseph: I am sure of this thing, even as I am sure of the promise of Moses; for the Lord hath said unto me, I will preserve thy seed forever.

17 And the Lord hath said: I will raise up a Moses; and I will give power unto him in a rod; and I will give judgment unto him in writing. Yet I will not loose his tongue, that he shall speak much, for I will not make him mighty in speaking. But I will write unto him my law, by the finger of mine own hand; and I will make a spokesman for him.

---

3:7 ***esteemed***—valued

3:11 (6–7,11) A seer is a revelator and a prophet who can also translate ancient records. He can know of things which are past, present, and future (see Mosiah 8:13–17).

3:12 ***confounding***—disproving

3:12 (11–12) The writings of the family of Judah, one of the twelve tribes of Israel, are found in the Bible. The Book of Mormon is the record of the family of Joseph, another tribe of Israel. Commenting on the new edition of the scriptures in 1982, Elder Boyd K. Packer noted that the Bible and Book of Mormon are "woven together in such a way that as you pore over one you are drawn to the other. . . . They are indeed one in our hands. Ezekiel's prophecy now stands fulfilled" (Boyd K. Packer, in Conference Report, October 1982, 75).

3:14 ***prophesied***—declared under inspiration of the Holy Ghost
***confounded***—defeated

3:15 "The seer's name was likewise to be Joseph, and this also was to be the name of his father. That prophecy was fulfilled in Joseph Smith, Jr., son of Joseph Smith, Sr., and founder of the Church of Jesus Christ of Latter-day Saints" (Orson F. Whitney, *Saturday Night Thoughts*, 17).

3:15 (13–15) Do you have a testimony of Joseph Smith as a prophet of the Lord? How has his work blessed your life? How has knowing about Joseph Smith brought you closer to the Savior?

3:16 ***preserve***—protect or watch over

*THE BIBLE AND THE BOOK OF MORMON TESTIFY OF CHRIST,* BY GREG K. OLSEN

*The writings of Judah and the writings of Joseph would "grow together."*

18 And the Lord said unto me also: I will raise up unto the fruit of thy loins; and I will make for him a spokesman. And I, behold, I will give unto him that he shall write the writing of the fruit of thy loins, unto the fruit of thy loins; and the spokesman of thy loins shall declare it.

19 And the words which he shall write shall be the words which are expedient in my wisdom should go forth unto the fruit of thy loins. And it shall be as if the fruit of thy loins had cried unto them from the dust; for I know their faith.

20 And they shall cry from the dust; yea, even repentance unto their brethren, even after many generations have gone by them. And it shall come to pass that their cry shall go, even according to the simpleness of their words.

21 Because of their faith their words shall proceed forth out of my mouth unto their brethren who are the fruit of thy loins; and the weakness of their words will I make strong in their faith, unto the remembering of my covenant which I made unto thy fathers.

22 And now, behold, my son Joseph, after this manner did my father of old prophesy.

23 Wherefore, because of this covenant thou art blessed; for thy seed shall not be destroyed, for they shall hearken unto the words of the book.

24 And there shall rise up one mighty among them, who shall do much good, both in word and in deed, being an instrument in the hands of God, with exceeding faith, to work mighty wonders, and do that thing which is great in the sight of God, unto the bringing to pass much restoration unto the house of Israel, and unto the seed of thy brethren.

25 And now, blessed art thou, Joseph. Behold, thou art little; wherefore hearken unto the words of thy brother, Nephi, and it shall be done unto thee even according to the words which I have spoken. Remember the words of thy dying father. Amen.

## CHAPTER 4

*This chapter includes the great psalm of Nephi. It is like a song or prayer of praise to the Lord. Notice how Nephi puts his faith and trust in Jesus Christ as he faces trials.*

### *Joseph of Egypt Prophesies Concerning the Future*

1 AND now, I, Nephi, speak concerning the prophecies of which my father hath spoken, concerning Joseph, who was carried into Egypt.

2 For behold, he truly prophesied concerning all his seed. And the prophecies which he wrote, there are not many greater. And he prophesied concerning us, and our future generations; and they are written upon the plates of brass.

### *Lehi Blesses His Children and Then Dies*

3 Wherefore, after my father had made an end of speaking concerning the prophecies of Joseph, he called the children of Laman, his sons, and his daughters, and said unto them: Behold, my sons, and my daughters, who are the sons and the daughters of my first-born, I would that ye should give ear unto my words.

---

3:18 (17–18) In 1833 Sidney Rigdon was called to be a "spokesman" for the Church and for Joseph Smith (see D&C 100:11). Concerning a similar role for Oliver Cowdery, President Joseph Fielding Smith wrote: "There was another gift bestowed upon Oliver Cowdery, and that was the gift of Aaron. Like Aaron with his rod in his hand going before Moses as a spokesman, so Oliver Cowdery was to go before Joseph Smith. . . . Oliver was blessed with the great honor of holding the keys of this dispensation with Joseph Smith, and, like Aaron, did become a spokesman on numerous occasions" (*Church History and Modern Revelation* 1:52).

3:19 The phrase "cried unto them from the dust" means that through our reading of the Book of Mormon, the testimony of Jesus Christ will come to us from those who have died.

3:20 ***generations***—periods of time or years

3:21 ***proceed***—go

3:24 ***an instrument***—a tool or a means
***restoration***—restitution or bringing back of that which was lost

3:25 Nephi was a good example to his younger brother Joseph. Who is a good example in your family to follow? What are you doing to be an example to others?

4:2 ***seed***—descendants, meaning children, grandchildren, and so on

Many of the writings of Joseph are not found in our Bible today. Some of his writings were restored in the Joseph Smith Translation of the Bible (see JST, Genesis 50:24–38).

4:3 ***give ear***—listen

4 For the Lord God hath said that: Inasmuch as ye shall keep my commandments ye shall prosper in the land; and inasmuch as ye will not keep my commandments ye shall be cut off from my presence.

5 But behold, my sons and my daughters, I cannot go down to my grave save I should leave a blessing upon you; for behold, I know that if ye are brought up in the way ye should go ye will not depart from it.

6 Wherefore, if ye are cursed, behold, I leave my blessing upon you, that the cursing may be taken from you and be answered upon the heads of your parents.

7 Wherefore, because of my blessing the Lord God will not suffer that ye shall perish; wherefore, he will be merciful unto you and unto your seed forever.

8 And it came to pass that after my father had made an end of speaking to the sons and daughters of Laman, he caused the sons and daughters of Lemuel to be brought before him.

9 And he spake unto them, saying: Behold, my sons and my daughters, who are the sons and the daughters of my second son; behold I leave unto you the same blessing which I left unto the sons and daughters of Laman; wherefore, thou shalt not utterly be destroyed; but in the end thy seed shall be blessed.

10 And it came to pass that when my father had made an end of speaking unto them, behold, he spake unto the sons of Ishmael, yea, and even all his household.

11 And after he had made an end of speaking unto them, he spake unto Sam, saying: Blessed art thou, and thy seed; for thou shalt inherit the land like unto thy brother Nephi. And thy seed shall be numbered with his seed; and thou shalt be even like unto thy brother, and thy seed like unto his seed; and thou shalt be blessed in all thy days.

12 And it came to pass after my father, Lehi, had spoken unto all his household, according to the feelings of his heart and the Spirit of the Lord which was in him, he waxed old. And it came to pass that he died, and was buried.

13 And it came to pass that not many days after his death, Laman and Lemuel and the sons of Ishmael were angry with me because of the admonitions of the Lord.

14 For I, Nephi, was constrained to speak unto them, according to his word; for I had spoken many things unto them, and also my father, before his death; many of which sayings are written upon mine other plates; for a more history part are written upon mine other plates.

## Nephi Writes His Psalm

15 And upon these I write the things of my soul, and many of the scriptures which are engraven upon the plates of brass. For my soul delighteth in the scriptures, and my heart pondereth them, and writeth them for the learning and the profit of my children.

16 Behold, my soul delighteth in the things of the Lord; and my heart pondereth continually upon the things which I have seen and heard.

---

4:4 To "be cut off from" the presence of the Lord is to have the Lord's Spirit taken away. The scriptures call this "spiritual death" (Alma 42:9).

4:5 ***go down to my grave***—die

4:6 According to this verse, why is it so important to teach children to learn to obey the commandments? Have you thought much about how blessed you are to have loving family members who teach and guide you in the gospel?

4:7 ***suffer***—allow

4:9 ***utterly***—completely

4:12 ***waxed***—grew

4:13 ***admonitions***—warnings or teachings

4:14 ***constrained***—prompted or urged

The other plates referred to here are the large plates of Nephi (see 1 Nephi 19:1–4).

4:15 ***engraven upon***—written by having been cut or impressed into
***profit***—good or benefit

"As Nephi wrote of his delight in pondering the scriptures and 'the things of the Lord,' he was moved to compose a beautiful psalm (4:16–35). In these verses . . . Nephi used inspiring imagery . . . to praise God for his goodness, to lament his own weaknesses, and to declare his devotion to the Lord" (*Encyclopedia of Mormonism,* s.v. "Book of Mormon: Second Book of Nephi," 147).

Why do you think Nephi wanted his children to know the scriptures? Why do you want to know the scriptures?

17 Nevertheless, notwithstanding the great goodness of the Lord, in showing me his great and marvelous works, my heart exclaimeth: O wretched man that I am! Yea, my heart sorroweth because of my flesh; my soul grieveth because of mine iniquities.

18 I am encompassed about, because of the temptations and the sins which do so easily beset me.

19 And when I desire to rejoice, my heart groaneth because of my sins; nevertheless, I know in whom I have trusted.

20 My God hath been my support; he hath led me through mine afflictions in the wilderness; and he hath preserved me upon the waters of the great deep.

21 He hath filled me with his love, even unto the consuming of my flesh.

22 He hath confounded mine enemies, unto the causing of them to quake before me.

23 Behold, he hath heard my cry by day, and he hath given me knowledge by visions in the nighttime.

24 And by day have I waxed bold in mighty prayer before him; yea, my voice have I sent up on high; and angels came down and ministered unto me.

25 And upon the wings of his Spirit hath my body been carried away upon exceedingly high mountains. And mine eyes have beheld great things, yea, even too great for man; therefore I was bidden that I should not write them.

26 O then, if I have seen so great things, if the Lord in his condescension unto the children of men hath visited men in so much mercy, why should my heart weep and my soul linger in the valley of sorrow, and my flesh waste away, and my strength slacken, because of mine afflictions?

27 And why should I yield to sin, because of my flesh? Yea, why should I give way to temptations, that the evil one have place in my heart to destroy my peace and afflict my soul? Why am I angry because of mine enemy?

28 Awake, my soul! No longer droop in sin. Rejoice, O my heart, and give place no more for the enemy of my soul.

29 Do not anger again because of mine enemies. Do not slacken my strength because of mine afflictions.

30 Rejoice, O my heart, and cry unto the Lord, and say: O Lord, I will praise thee forever; yea, my soul will rejoice in thee, my God, and the rock of my salvation.

31 O Lord, wilt thou redeem my soul? Wilt thou deliver me out of the hands of mine enemies? Wilt thou make me that I may shake at the appearance of sin?

32 May the gates of hell be shut continually before me, because that my heart is broken and my spirit is contrite! O Lord, wilt thou not shut the gates of thy righteousness before me, that I may walk in the path of the low valley, that I may be strict in the plain road!

---

4:17 ***Nevertheless***—However
***notwithstanding***—in spite of
***exclaimeth***—cries out
***wretched***—miserable
***iniquities***—sins

4:18 ***encompassed about***—surrounded
***beset***—come upon

4:21 ***consuming***—burning up or destroying

4:22 ***confounded***—frustrated or confused
***quake***—shake

4:24 ***ministered unto***—helped

4:25 ***bidden***—told

4:26 The word *condescension* refers to the act of coming down from a higher position or level in order to do something for someone who is at a lower position or level. In this case it refers to the willingness of the Lord, an immortal and perfect being, to take notice of and bless the lives of mortal and imperfect beings.

***linger***—stay
***slacken***—weaken

4:27 ***yield***—give way or give in

4:28 ***droop***—sink or bend down

4:32 "What is a broken heart? One that is humble, one that is touched by the Spirit of the Lord, and which is willing to abide in all the covenants and the obligations which the Gospel entails" (Joseph Fielding Smith, in Conference Report, October 1941, 93). To have a spirit that is contrite is to have "a broken heart with deep sorrow for sin, a realization of the nature of wrongdoing and a desire for forgiveness through the grace of God. A contrite spirit is essential to salvation" (Joseph Fielding Smith, *Religious Truths Defined*, 273).

33 O Lord, wilt thou encircle me around in the robe of thy righteousness! O Lord, wilt thou make a way for mine escape before mine enemies! Wilt thou make my path straight before me! Wilt thou not place a stumbling block in my way—but that thou wouldst clear my way before me, and hedge not up my way, but the ways of mine enemy.
34 O Lord, I have trusted in thee, and I will trust in thee forever. I will not put my trust in the arm of flesh; for I know that cursed is he that putteth his trust in the arm of flesh. Yea, cursed is he that putteth his trust in man or maketh flesh his arm.
35 Yea, I know that God will give liberally to him that asketh. Yea, my God will give me, if I ask not amiss; therefore I will lift up my voice unto thee; yea, I will cry unto thee, my God, the rock of my righteousness. Behold, my voice shall forever ascend up unto thee, my rock and mine everlasting God. Amen.

## CHAPTER 5

*The righteous people of Nephi flee from the Lamanites. Look for how the Nephites are blessed and the Lamanites are cursed.*

### *The People of Nephi Flee into the Wilderness*

1 Behold, it came to pass that I, Nephi, did cry much unto the Lord my God, because of the anger of my brethren.
2 But behold, their anger did increase against me, insomuch that they did seek to take away my life.
3 Yea, they did murmur against me, saying: Our younger brother thinks to rule over us; and we have had much trial because of him; wherefore, now let us slay him, that we may not be afflicted more because of his words. For behold, we will not have him to be our ruler; for it belongs unto us, who are the elder brethren, to rule over this people.
4 Now I do not write upon these plates all the words which they murmured against me. But it sufficeth me to say, that they did seek to take away my life.
5 And it came to pass that the Lord did warn me, that I, Nephi, should depart from them and flee into the wilderness, and all those who would go with me.
6 Wherefore, it came to pass that I, Nephi, did take my family, and also Zoram and his family, and Sam, mine elder brother and his family, and Jacob and Joseph, my younger brethren, and also my sisters, and all those who would go with me. And all those who would go with me were those who believed in the warnings and the revelations of God; wherefore, they did hearken unto my words.
7 And we did take our tents and whatsoever things were possible for us, and did journey in the wilderness for the space of many days. And after we had journeyed for the space of many days we did pitch our tents.
8 And my people would that we should call the name of the place Nephi; wherefore, we did call it Nephi.
9 And all those who were with me did take upon them to call themselves the people of Nephi.

### *The Nephites Keep the Commandments and Are Blessed*

10 And we did observe to keep the judgments, and the statutes, and the commandments of the Lord in all things, according to the law of Moses.
11 And the Lord was with us; and we did prosper exceedingly; for we did sow seed, and we did reap again in abundance. And we began to raise flocks, and herds, and animals of every kind.

---

4:34 ***arm of flesh***—power of man

4:35 ***liberally***—generously
***amiss***—for the wrong things

4:35 (31–35) As a young missionary, Joseph F. Smith, who would become the sixth President of the Church, expressed some of the same feelings Nephi had when he wrote: "I . . . truly hope and pray that I may prove faithful to the end" (cited in Joseph Fielding Smith, comp., *Life of Joseph F. Smith,* 176).

5:1 ***cry***—pray

5:3 ***murmur***—grumble and complain
***slay***—kill
***be afflicted***—suffer

5:4 ***it sufficeth me***—it is enough

5:10 ***judgments***—declarations or decisions
***statutes***—laws

The law of Moses was made up of those laws and ordinances that the children of Israel were commanded to follow from the days of Moses until the time of Jesus Christ (see LDS Bible Dictionary, s.v. "Law of Moses," 722–23). The Nephites kept the law of Moses until Christ came to the Americas (see 3 Nephi 11).

5:11 ***prosper exceedingly***—succeed very much
***in abundance***—greatly or in large amounts

12 And I, Nephi, had also brought the records which were engraven upon the plates of brass; and also the ball, or compass, which was prepared for my father by the hand of the Lord, according to that which is written.

13 And it came to pass that we began to prosper exceedingly, and to multiply in the land.

14 And I, Nephi, did take the sword of Laban, and after the manner of it did make many swords, lest by any means the people who were now called Lamanites should come upon us and destroy us; for I knew their hatred towards me and my children and those who were called my people.

15 And I did teach my people to build buildings, and to work in all manner of wood, and of iron, and of copper, and of brass, and of steel, and of gold, and of silver, and of precious ores, which were in great abundance.

16 And I, Nephi, did build a temple; and I did construct it after the manner of the temple of Solomon save it were not built of so many precious things; for they were not to be found upon the land, wherefore, it could not be built like unto Solomon's temple. But the manner of the construction was like unto the temple of Solomon; and the workmanship thereof was exceedingly fine.

17 And it came to pass that I, Nephi, did cause my people to be industrious, and to labor with their hands.

## *The Lamanites Are Cursed Because They Break the Commandments*

18 And it came to pass that they would that I should be their king. But I, Nephi, was desirous that they should have no king; nevertheless, I did for them according to that which was in my power.

19 And behold, the words of the Lord had been fulfilled unto my brethren, which he spake concerning them, that I should be their ruler and their teacher. Wherefore, I had been their ruler and their teacher, according to the commandments of the Lord, until the time they sought to take away my life.

20 Wherefore, the word of the Lord was fulfilled which he spake unto me, saying that: Inasmuch as they will not hearken unto thy words they shall be cut off from the presence of the Lord. And behold, they were cut off from his presence.

21 And he had caused the cursing to come upon them, yea, even a sore cursing, because of their iniquity. For behold, they had hardened their hearts against him, that they had become like unto a flint; wherefore, as they were white, and exceedingly fair and delightsome, that they might not be enticing unto my people the Lord God did cause a skin of blackness to come upon them.

22 And thus saith the Lord God: I will cause that they shall be loathsome unto thy people, save they shall repent of their iniquities.

23 And cursed shall be the seed of him that mixeth with their seed; for they shall be cursed even with the same cursing. And the Lord spake it, and it was done.

24 And because of their cursing which was upon them they did become an idle people, full of mischief and subtlety, and did seek in the wilderness for beasts of prey.

25 And the Lord God said unto me: They shall be a scourge unto thy seed, to stir them up in remembrance of me; and inasmuch as they will not remember me, and hearken unto my words, they shall scourge them even unto destruction.

*An illustration of Solomon's Temple. The Nephite temple was built like this but was not as richly decorated.*

5:12 Why do you think Nephi brought the brass plates and the compass, or Liahona, with him? What does that teach you about how he felt about the Lord?

5:16 ***after the manner of***—like

5:17 ***be industrious***—work hard and be careful to get things done

5:22 ***loathsome***—disgusting, offensive, or hateful

5:23 ***mixeth with their seed***—marries them

5:24 ***mischief***—evil
***subtlety***—dishonesty and trickery

5:25 ***scourge***—torment or affliction

### Nephi Keeps Records

26 And it came to pass that I, Nephi, did consecrate Jacob and Joseph, that they should be priests and teachers over the land of my people.
27 And it came to pass that we lived after the manner of happiness.
28 And thirty years had passed away from the time we left Jerusalem.
29 And I, Nephi, had kept the records upon my plates, which I had made, of my people thus far.
30 And it came to pass that the Lord God said unto me: Make other plates; and thou shalt engraven many things upon them which are good in my sight, for the profit of thy people.
31 Wherefore, I, Nephi, to be obedient to the commandments of the Lord, went and made these plates upon which I have engraven these things.
32 And I engraved that which is pleasing unto God. And if my people are pleased with the things of God they will be pleased with mine engravings which are upon these plates.
33 And if my people desire to know the more particular part of the history of my people they must search mine other plates.
34 And it sufficeth me to say that forty years had passed away, and we had already had wars and contentions with our brethren.

## CHAPTER 6

*Jacob, Nephi's brother, quotes and explains words from Isaiah. The Jews will reject Jesus and be taken from their homeland. Look for what they must do to be gathered to their lands of inheritance.*

### Jacob Writes Under Nephi's Direction

1 THE words of Jacob, the brother of Nephi, which he spake unto the people of Nephi:
2 Behold, my beloved brethren, I, Jacob, having been called of God, and ordained after the manner of his holy order, and having been consecrated by my brother Nephi, unto whom ye look as a king or a protector, and on whom ye depend for safety, behold ye know that I have spoken unto you exceedingly many things.
3 Nevertheless, I speak unto you again; for I am desirous for the welfare of your souls. Yea, mine anxiety is great for you; and ye yourselves know that it ever has been. For I have exhorted you with all diligence; and I have taught you the words of my father; and I have spoken unto you concerning all things which are written, from the creation of the world.
4 And now, behold, I would speak unto you concerning things which are, and which are to come; wherefore, I will read you the words of Isaiah. And they are the words which my brother has desired that I should speak unto you. And I speak unto you for your sakes, that ye may learn and glorify the name of your God.
5 And now, the words which I shall read are they which Isaiah spake concerning all the house of Israel; wherefore, they may be likened unto you, for ye are of the house of Israel. And there are many things which have been spoken by Isaiah which may be likened unto you, because ye are of the house of Israel.

---

5:26 ***consecrate***—set apart

5:27 The Book of Mormon makes it clear that those who keep the commandments are happy. How do you feel when you do what Heavenly Father wants you to do?

5:31 "These plates" refers to the small plates of Nephi (see 1 Nephi 9:1–3 and the illustration on p. xiv). Nephi began making his second set of plates about 569 B.C. (see 2 Nephi 5:28).

5:34 ***sufficeth me***—is enough for me

Ten years had gone by and it was now 559 B.C.

6:2 This verse, in connection with 2 Nephi 5:26, shows that Jacob and his brother Joseph had received the Melchizedek Priesthood (see Joseph Fielding Smith, *Answers to Gospel Questions* 1:123–25; see also D&C 107:1–3; Alma 13:6, 14–16).

***consecrated***—dedicated or set apart to serve the Lord
***exceedingly***—very

6:3 ***anxiety***—concern
***exhorted you with all diligence***—encouraged or challenged you with great effort

6:4 Jacob, Nephi, and Jesus Christ have all told us to learn the words of Isaiah (see 1 Nephi 19:23; 3 Nephi 23:1).

## *Jacob Explains the Prophecies of Isaiah*

6 And now, these are the words: Thus saith the Lord God: Behold, I will lift up mine hand to the Gentiles, and set up my standard to the people; and they shall bring thy sons in their arms, and thy daughters shall be carried upon their shoulders.

7 And kings shall be thy nursing fathers, and their queens thy nursing mothers; they shall bow down to thee with their faces towards the earth, and lick up the dust of thy feet; and thou shalt know that I am the Lord; for they shall not be ashamed that wait for me.

8 And now I, Jacob, would speak somewhat concerning these words. For behold, the Lord has shown me that those who were at Jerusalem, from whence we came, have been slain and carried away captive.

9 Nevertheless, the Lord has shown unto me that they should return again. And he also has shown unto me that the Lord God, the Holy One of Israel, should manifest himself unto them in the flesh; and after he should manifest himself they should scourge him and crucify him, according to the words of the angel who spake it unto me.

10 And after they have hardened their hearts and stiffened their necks against the Holy One of Israel, behold, the judgments of the Holy One of Israel shall come upon them. And the day cometh that they shall be smitten and afflicted.

11 Wherefore, after they are driven to and fro, for thus saith the angel, many shall be afflicted in the flesh, and shall not be suffered to perish, because of the prayers of the faithful; they shall be scattered, and smitten, and hated; nevertheless, the Lord will be merciful unto them, that when they shall come to the knowledge of their Redeemer, they shall be gathered together again to the lands of their inheritance.

12 And blessed are the Gentiles, they of whom the prophet has written; for behold, if it so be that they shall repent and fight not against Zion, and do not unite themselves to that great and abominable church, they shall be saved; for the Lord God will fulfil his covenants which he has made unto his children; and for this cause the prophet has written these things.

---

6:6 *Gentiles* is a word that means "nations." It refers to those not of the family of Israel or who do not believe in the God of Israel (see LDS Bible Dictionary, s.v. "Gentile," 679).

A standard is like a flag on a tall pole. When raised it shows certain groups of people where to gather. Elder Marion G. Romney explained, "This Church is the standard which Isaiah said the Lord would set up for the people in the latter days" (in Conference Report, April 1961, 119; see also D&C 45:9).

6:7 ***nursing fathers . . . nursing mothers***—helpers and supporters
***lick up the dust of thy feet***—be made humble

People who "wait for the Lord" are those who prayerfully stay faithful until the Savior's Second Coming (see D&C 133:45).

6:8 ***captive***—prisoner

Jacob received the same revelation about Jerusalem's destruction as did Lehi (see 2 Nephi 1:4).

6:9 ***manifest***—show
***scourge***—whip

"Few details of the actual crucifixion are given us. We know however that our Lord was nailed to the cross by spikes driven through the hands and feet, as was the Roman method, and not bound only by cords as was the custom in inflicting this form of punishment among some other nations. Death by crucifixion was at once the most lingering and most painful of all forms of execution" (James E. Talmage, *Jesus the Christ,* 655).

6:10 ***smitten***—beaten
***afflicted***—made to suffer

6:10 (9–10) Though the Jews would be allowed to return to Jerusalem, they would reject and kill Jesus. As a result they would be killed and captured by the Romans (see 1 Nephi 19:10, 13–14; 2 Nephi 10:3–5).

6:11 ***suffered***—allowed or permitted

When the Jews accept Jesus as their Redeemer, then the spiritual gathering of Israel will start. "The present gathering of the Jews to Palestine is political, not spiritual, and it is not the gathering of Israel of which the prophecies speak" (Bruce R. McConkie, *A New Witness for the Articles of Faith,* 564–65).

6:12 Elder Bruce R. McConkie said that "the titles *church of the devil* and *great and abominable church* are used to identify all churches or organizations of whatever name or nature . . . which are designed to take men on a course that leads away from God and his laws and thus from salvation in the kingdom of God" (*Mormon Doctrine,* 137–38).

13 Wherefore, they that fight against Zion and the covenant people of the Lord shall lick up the dust of their feet; and the people of the Lord shall not be ashamed. For the people of the Lord are they who wait for him; for they still wait for the coming of the Messiah.

## *Israel Will Be Brought Back to Jesus Christ at His Second Coming*

14 And behold, according to the words of the prophet, the Messiah will set himself again the second time to recover them; wherefore, he will manifest himself unto them in power and great glory, unto the destruction of their enemies, when that day cometh when they shall believe in him; and none will he destroy that believe in him.
15 And they that believe not in him shall be destroyed, both by fire, and by tempest, and by earthquakes, and by bloodsheds, and by pestilence, and by famine. And they shall know that the Lord is God, the Holy One of Israel.
16 For shall the prey be taken from the mighty, or the lawful captive delivered?
17 But thus saith the Lord: Even the captives of the mighty shall be taken away, and the prey of the terrible shall be delivered; for the Mighty God shall deliver his covenant people. For thus saith the Lord: I will contend with them that contendeth with thee—
18 And I will feed them that oppress thee, with their own flesh; and they shall be drunken with their own blood as with sweet wine; and all flesh shall know that I the Lord am thy Savior and thy Redeemer, the Mighty One of Jacob.

# CHAPTER 7

*Jacob quotes Isaiah 50. Like his older brother Nephi, Jacob loved the words of Isaiah. In this chapter, Jacob uses the words of Isaiah to testify of Jesus Christ. Look for reasons why Jacob loved Isaiah's words.*

## *The Lord Does Not Give Up on His People*

1 YEA, for thus saith the Lord: Have I put thee away, or have I cast thee off forever? For thus saith the Lord: Where is the bill of your mother's divorcement? To whom have I put thee away, or to which of my creditors have I sold you? Yea, to whom have I sold you? Behold, for your iniquities have ye sold yourselves, and for your transgressions is your mother put away.
2 Wherefore, when I came, there was no man; when I called, yea, there was none to answer. O house of Israel, is my hand shortened at all that it cannot redeem, or have I no power to deliver? Behold, at my rebuke I dry up the sea, I make their rivers a wilderness and their fish to stink because the waters are dried up, and they die because of thirst.
3 I clothe the heavens with blackness, and I make sackcloth their covering.

---

6:15 Tempests (storms), earthquakes, pestilence (disease), and famine are all ways the Lord warns the wicked and unbelieving to repent (see D&C 43:25).

6:17 (16–17) The prey (house of Israel) has been captive to the mighty (gentile nations and Satan's temptations) but will be freed by the Lord's power (see Monte S. Nyman, *"Great Are the Words of Isaiah,"* 184).

6:18 ***oppress***—do wrong to or mistreat

The enemies of God's chosen people will war amongst themselves and kill each other (see 1 Nephi 22:13).

When this destruction happens, all people will know that the Savior is the God of Israel. Why is it better to learn of the Lord while there is still, in general terms, peace?

7:1 To be "put away" was the phrase used to describe a wife's being divorced by her husband. The "bill of divorcement" was the legal document used in the law of Moses for the legal separation of a husband and a wife (see Deuteronomy 24:1). Isaiah compared the Lord's relationship with the house of Israel to a marriage covenant. The Lord says He has not put away His wife, the house of Israel; nor has He sold Israel like a slave. The Lord loves His people and will not give up on them.

***my creditors***—the people I owe
***iniquities***—wickedness
***transgressions***—lawbreaking

The Lord has the power to help us through any trial. But we sometimes turn our backs on Him through sin and neglect. What does it mean to you to know that the Lord loves you even though you may sometimes forget Him?

7:2 ***rebuke***—scolding

7:3 Sackcloth was a rough cloth made of goat's hair, worn as a sign of sorrow, great trouble, or repentance (see Mosiah 11:23–25).

### *Isaiah Prophesies of the Mortal Ministry of Jesus Christ, the Messiah*

4 The Lord God hath given me the tongue of the
learned, that I should know how to speak a word
in season unto thee, O house of Israel. When ye are
weary he waketh morning by morning. He waketh
mine ear to hear as the learned.
5 The Lord God hath opened mine ear, and I was
not rebellious, neither turned away back.
6 I gave my back to the smiter, and my cheeks to
them that plucked off the hair. I hid not my face
from shame and spitting.
7 For the Lord God will help me, therefore shall
I not be confounded. Therefore have I set my face
like a flint, and I know that I shall not be
ashamed.
8 And the Lord is near, and he justifieth me. Who
will contend with me? Let us stand together. Who is
mine adversary? Let him come near me, and I will
smite him with the strength of my mouth.
9 For the Lord God will help me. And all they who
shall condemn me, behold, all they shall wax old as
a garment, and the moth shall eat them up.

### *Those Who Trust in the Lord Shall Walk in His Light*

10 Who is among you that feareth the Lord, that
obeyeth the voice of his servant, that walketh in
darkness and hath no light?
11 Behold all ye that kindle fire, that compass
yourselves about with sparks, walk in the light of
your fire and in the sparks which ye have kindled.
This shall ye have of mine hand—ye shall lie down
in sorrow.

## CHAPTER 8

*Jacob quotes Isaiah 51 and Isaiah 52:1–2. In the last days the Lord promises great blessings to the house of Israel. Watch for the promises He makes to Israel.*

### *The Lord Calls Israel to Receive Salvation*

1 HEARKEN unto me, ye that follow after righteousness. Look unto the rock from whence ye are
hewn, and to the hole of the pit from whence ye
are digged.

7:4 ***tongue***—language
***speak a word in season***—say what is needed to be said

7:5 (4–5) Jesus lived in a day when the house of Israel was spiritually tired and not listening to messages from the Father. Jesus not only listened to the Father but also did "the will of him that sent [him]" (John 4:34).

7:6 ***to the smiter***—to him who beat me
***plucked off the hair***—pulled out my beard

Isaiah saw the Son of God's mortal ministry. He tells how Jesus would suffer at the hands of both Jews and Romans. The Jews would mock, spit on, and hit Jesus. Pilate would order Jesus scourged, or whipped, before He was crucified (see Matthew 26:67; 27:26).

7:7 ***set my face like a flint***—determined to face all my trials

7:8 ***justifieth me***—declares me righteous
***adversary***—accuser or opponent
***smite him with the strength of my mouth***—challenge him with the truth

7:9 ***wax old***—wear out
***garment***—piece of clothing

7:9 (7–9) Though Jesus would face terrible trials and persecutions, with His Father's help He would complete His mission. What can Jesus' example of trusting His Father teach you about how to overcome the problems you face in life?

7:10 Isaiah's question, asked another way, might be, "Do those who fear the Lord and obey His servants walk in darkness with no light?" To which the Lord answers, "He that followeth me shall not walk in darkness, but shall have the light of life" (John 8:12).

The words "feareth the Lord" generally mean to reverence or worship God. The Lord has promised that He will be "merciful and gracious unto those who fear" Him (D&C 76:5).

7:11 ***kindle fire***—start a fire
***compass yourselves about***—surround yourselves

Isaiah warns that if we try to live by our own light instead of seeking to be led by the Spirit, we will be unhappy. When have you felt the Spirit of the Lord? What can you do to feel it more often?

2 Look unto Abraham, your father, and unto Sarah, she that bare you; for I called him alone, and blessed him.

3 For the Lord shall comfort Zion, he will comfort all her waste places; and he will make her wilderness like Eden, and her desert like the garden of the Lord. Joy and gladness shall be found therein, thanksgiving and the voice of melody.

4 Hearken unto me, my people; and give ear unto me, O my nation; for a law shall proceed from me, and I will make my judgment to rest for a light for the people.

5 My righteousness is near; my salvation is gone forth, and mine arm shall judge the people. The isles shall wait upon me, and on mine arm shall they trust.

6 Lift up your eyes to the heavens, and look upon the earth beneath; for the heavens shall vanish away like smoke, and the earth shall wax old like a garment; and they that dwell therein shall die in like manner. But my salvation shall be forever, and my righteousness shall not be abolished.

7 Hearken unto me, ye that know righteousness, the people in whose heart I have written my law, fear ye not the reproach of men, neither be ye afraid of their revilings.

8 For the moth shall eat them up like a garment, and the worm shall eat them like wool. But my righteousness shall be forever, and my salvation from generation to generation.

## *If Israel Will Turn to the Lord, He Will Give Them Great Blessings*

9 Awake, awake! Put on strength, O arm of the Lord; awake as in the ancient days. Art thou not he that hath cut Rahab, and wounded the dragon?

10 Art thou not he who hath dried the sea, the waters of the great deep; that hath made the depths of the sea a way for the ransomed to pass over?

11 Therefore, the redeemed of the Lord shall return, and come with singing unto Zion; and everlasting joy and holiness shall be upon their heads; and they shall obtain gladness and joy; sorrow and mourning shall flee away.

12 I am he; yea, I am he that comforteth you. Behold, who art thou, that thou shouldst be afraid of man, who shall die, and of the son of man, who shall be made like unto grass?

13 And forgettest the Lord thy maker, that hath stretched forth the heavens, and laid the foundations of the earth, and hast feared continually every day, because of the fury of the oppressor, as if he were ready to destroy? And where is the fury of the oppressor?

---

8:2 (1–2) To refer to the "rock" from which we were "hewn" and "the hole" from which we were "digged" is a symbolic way to show that we are related to Abraham, Sarah, and the house of Israel (see D&C 103:17).

8:3 At the Second Coming of our Lord, "the earth will be renewed and receive its paradisiacal glory" (Articles of Faith 1:10). In other words, the earth will return to the beautiful and pure conditions that existed in the Garden of Eden, and there will be peace and righteousness (see Bruce R. McConkie, *Mormon Doctrine,* 303).

8:4 Referring to this scripture in Isaiah, Elder Bruce R. McConkie wrote: "Thanks be to God, that law now has come; it is the fulness of his everlasting gospel; by it he will judge the world, and it now stands as a light for all men" (*The Millennial Messiah,* 514–15).

8:5 The "arm" of the Lord is a symbol for the power of the Lord (see D&C 90:10).

The term *isles* "refers not only to islands but also to the continents of the earth (2 Ne. 10:20). It may also mean any place not immediately accessible to Israel by land" (Donald W. Parry and others, *Understanding Isaiah,* 425).

8:7 ***reproach***—criticism
***revilings***—insults

8:9 "Rahab" and the "dragon" are symbols of Satan and his powers (see Revelation 20:2; Donald W. Parry and others, *Understanding Isaiah,* 453–54). Here the Lord teaches that He has more power than Satan and that He will defeat Satan.

8:10 The Lord saved ancient Israel by drying up a way through the Red Sea so that His "ransomed," or saved, could cross over and escape out of Egypt (see Exodus 14:21–22).

8:13 ***oppressor***—evil ruler who persecutes the righteous

8:13 (12–13) Some people are afraid to choose the right because of what others might think. How will your choices be better if you try to please the Lord rather than others?

14 The captive exile hasteneth, that he may be loosed, and that he should not die in the pit, nor that his bread should fail.

15 But I am the Lord thy God, whose waves roared; the Lord of Hosts is my name.

16 And I have put my words in thy mouth, and have covered thee in the shadow of mine hand, that I may plant the heavens and lay the foundations of the earth, and say unto Zion: Behold, thou art my people.

## God Gives Warnings to the Jews Who Live in the Latter Days

17 Awake, awake, stand up, O Jerusalem, which hast drunk at the hand of the Lord the cup of his fury—thou hast drunken the dregs of the cup of trembling wrung out—

18 And none to guide her among all the sons she hath brought forth; neither that taketh her by the hand, of all the sons she hath brought up.

## Two Prophets in the Last Days Will Teach and Comfort the Jews

19 These two sons are come unto thee, who shall be sorry for thee—thy desolation and destruction, and the famine and the sword—and by whom shall I comfort thee?

20 Thy sons have fainted, save these two; they lie at the head of all the streets; as a wild bull in a net, they are full of the fury of the Lord, the rebuke of thy God.

21 Therefore hear now this, thou afflicted, and drunken, and not with wine:

## At the Point of Their Destruction, the Lord Will Personally Save the Jews

22 Thus saith thy Lord, the Lord and thy God pleadeth the cause of his people; behold, I have taken out of thine hand the cup of trembling, the dregs of the cup of my fury; thou shalt no more drink it again.

23 But I will put it into the hand of them that afflict thee; who have said to thy soul: Bow down, that we may go over—and thou hast laid thy body as the ground and as the street to them that went over.

24 Awake, awake, put on thy strength, O Zion; put on thy beautiful garments, O Jerusalem, the holy city; for henceforth there shall no more come into thee the uncircumcised and the unclean.

---

8:14 ***The captive exile hasteneth***—The slave, who was forced to leave his home and country, hurries ***his bread should fail***—he should run out of food

8:15 The phrase "whose waves roared" refers to the Lord's power over the sea and may particularly refer to the parting of the Red Sea, which allowed the children of Israel to cross on dry ground (see 1 Nephi 4:2).

"Christ is the *Lord of Hosts* (1 Chron. 17:24; Ps. 24:10; Isa. 6:5; Zech. 14:16–17; Mal. 1:14), meaning that he is a man of war (Ex. 15:3), a God of battles (Ps. 24:8), a leader of his saints in days of conflict and carnage" (Bruce R. McConkie, *Mormon Doctrine,* 451).

8:16 ***covered thee in the shadow of mine hand***—protected thee

8:18 Isaiah prophesies of the suffering the Jewish
(17–18) people will have to endure. The "cup of his fury" and the "dregs of the cup" speak of great suffering (see James E. Talmage, *Jesus the Christ,* 620).

8:21 In the future, after the Jews have gathered to
(19–21) Jerusalem and rebuilt their city, two great prophets will be raised up to teach the people of Jerusalem (see D&C 77:15). These prophets will have great power to protect and comfort the Jews. After three and a half years, they will be killed and the Jews will again suffer (see Revelation 11:3–13).

8:23 ***them that afflict thee***—the enemies of the Jews

8:23 After the death of the two prophets, the Jews
(22–23) will almost be destroyed in a great battle. Then the Savior will come to save them, and the Jews will finally accept Jesus Christ as their Savior (see D&C 45:47–53).

8:24 ***the uncircumcised***—those who have not made covenants with the Lord

This verse refers to "those whom God should call in the last days, who should hold the power of priesthood to bring again Zion, and the redemption of Israel; and to put on her strength is to put on the authority of the priesthood, which she, Zion, has a right to by lineage; also to return to that power which she had lost" (D&C 113:8).

25 Shake thyself from the dust; arise, sit down, O Jerusalem; loose thyself from the bands of thy neck, O captive daughter of Zion.

## CHAPTER 9

*Jacob helps us understand the Atonement of Jesus Christ. President Joseph Fielding Smith said that 2 Nephi 9 "should be carefully read by every person seeking salvation"* (Answers to Gospel Questions *4:57). As you read, look for how all of our future joy and happiness comes because of the Atonement of Jesus Christ.*

### *The House of Israel Will Be Gathered to Their Promised Lands*

1 AND now, my beloved brethren, I have read these things that ye might know concerning the covenants of the Lord that he has covenanted with all the house of Israel—
2 That he has spoken unto the Jews, by the mouth of his holy prophets, even from the beginning down, from generation to generation, until the time comes that they shall be restored to the true church and fold of God; when they shall be gathered home to the lands of their inheritance, and shall be established in all their lands of promise.
3 Behold, my beloved brethren, I speak unto you these things that ye may rejoice, and lift up your heads forever, because of the blessings which the Lord God shall bestow upon your children.

### *The Atonement Delivers Us from the Effects of the Fall of Adam*

4 For I know that ye have searched much, many of you, to know of things to come; wherefore I know that ye know that our flesh must waste away and die; nevertheless, in our bodies we shall see God.
5 Yea, I know that ye know that in the body he shall show himself unto those at Jerusalem, from whence we came; for it is expedient that it should be among them; for it behooveth the great Creator that he suffereth himself to become subject unto man in the flesh, and die for all men, that all men might become subject unto him.
6 For as death hath passed upon all men, to fulfil the merciful plan of the great Creator, there must needs be a power of resurrection, and the resurrection must needs come unto man by reason of the fall; and the fall came by reason of transgression; and because man became fallen they were cut off from the presence of the Lord.

---

8:25 In this verse those of the house of Israel "are exhorted to return to the Lord from whence they have fallen; which if they do, the promise of the Lord is that he will speak to them, or give them revelation. . . .The bands of her neck are the curses of God upon her, or the remnants of Israel in their scattered condition among the Gentiles" (D&C 113:10).

9:2 Quoting the second part of this verse, Elder Bruce R. McConkie said these words mean "that the house of Joseph will be established in America, the house of Judah in Palestine, and that the Lost Tribes will come to Ephraim in America to receive their blessings in due course. (D. & C. 133.)" (*Mormon Doctrine*, 305).

9:4 The doctrine of the resurrection—meaning the reuniting of the physical body with the spirit—has been taught by true prophets since the beginning of time (see Moses 5:10; Job 19:26).

9:5 ***behooveth***—is necessary or fitting for
***become subject unto man in the flesh***—come under the power and authority of others as a mortal man

9:6 "The resurrection consists in the uniting of a spirit body with a body of flesh and bones, never again to be divided. The resurrection shall come to all, because of Christ's victory over death. Jesus Christ was the first to be resurrected on this earth (Acts 26:23; 1 Cor. 15:23; Col. 1:18; Rev. 1:5; cf. Matt. 27:52–54). Others had been brought back from death, but were restored to mortality (Mark 5:22–43; Luke 7:11–17; John 11:1–45), whereas a resurrection means to become immortal, without blood, yet with a body of flesh and bone" (LDS Bible Dictionary, s.v. "Resurrection," 761).

President Joseph Fielding Smith said: "I never speak of the part Eve took in this fall as a sin, nor do I accuse Adam of a sin. . . . It is not always a sin to transgress a law. . . . This was a transgression of the law, but not a sin in the strict sense, for it was something that Adam and Eve had to do!" (*Doctrines of Salvation* 1:114,115). Note that in Noah Webster's 1828 *An American Dictionary of the English Language, transgression* is defined as "the act of passing over or beyond any law or rule of moral duty" (s.v. "Transgression").

7 Wherefore, it must needs be an infinite atonement—save it should be an infinite atonement this corruption could not put on incorruption. Wherefore, the first judgment which came upon man must needs have remained to an endless duration. And if so, this flesh must have laid down to rot and to crumble to its mother earth, to rise no more.

8 O the wisdom of God, his mercy and grace! For behold, if the flesh should rise no more our spirits must become subject to that angel who fell from before the presence of the Eternal God, and became the devil, to rise no more.

9 And our spirits must have become like unto him, and we become devils, angels to a devil, to be shut out from the presence of our God, and to remain with the father of lies, in misery, like unto himself; yea, to that being who beguiled our first parents, who transformeth himself nigh unto an angel of light, and stirreth up the children of men unto secret combinations of murder and all manner of secret works of darkness.

10 O how great the goodness of our God, who prepareth a way for our escape from the grasp of this awful monster; yea, that monster, death and hell, which I call the death of the body, and also the death of the spirit.

11 And because of the way of deliverance of our God, the Holy One of Israel, this death, of which I have spoken, which is the temporal, shall deliver up its dead; which death is the grave.

12 And this death of which I have spoken, which is the spiritual death, shall deliver up its dead; which spiritual death is hell; wherefore, death and hell must deliver up their dead, and hell must deliver up its captive spirits, and the grave must deliver up its captive bodies, and the bodies and the spirits of men will be restored one to the other; and it is by the power of the resurrection of the Holy One of Israel.

13 O how great the plan of our God! For on the other hand, the paradise of God must deliver up the spirits of the righteous, and the grave deliver up the

---

9:7 ***this corruption could not put on incorruption***—this mortal body could not put on an immortal body

"When the prophets speak of an *infinite* atonement, they mean just that. Its effects cover all men, the earth itself and all forms of life thereon, and reach out into the endless expanses of eternity" (Bruce R. McConkie, *Mormon Doctrine,* 64).

The "first judgment which came upon man" was death, both physical and spiritual.

9:8 ***mercy***—compassion, pity

The "angel who fell" refers to Satan.

9:9 ***beguiled***—knowingly misled
***nigh unto***—close to or like

A secret combination is a group of people bound together by secret oaths to carry out the evil purposes of the group (see Helaman 6:21–31; Ether 8:19–24).

9:12 ***restored***—reunited or returned

Latter-day scriptures teach that there are at least three meanings for the term *hell.* It can describe our suffering here on earth (see Alma 36:18). It can refer to a part of the spirit world where those who have not repented suffer for their sins (see Alma 40:13–14). It is also used to describe the final condition of those who completely turn away from God (see D&C 29:38). In this verse the second meaning is apparently intended.

9:12 (10–12) "The Fall brought two kinds of death upon Adam, Eve, and their posterity: the separation of the spirit and the physical body, which the scriptures call the 'temporal death' (Alma 11:42–43); and being shut out of God's presence, which is called spiritual death (2 Ne. 9:6; D&C 29:41). Jesus Christ redeems all mankind unconditionally from the two deaths brought by the fall of Adam, raises all mankind from the grave, and restores them to God's presence for a judgment (Hel. 14:16–17). The Atonement also redeems individuals from the consequences of their own sins on conditions of repentance" (*Encyclopedia of Mormonism*, s.v. "Fall of Adam," 485).

9:13 "Paradise is that part of the spirit world in which the righteous spirits who have departed from this life await the resurrection of the body. It is a condition of happiness and peace" (LDS Bible Dictionary, s.v. "Paradise," 742).

body of the righteous; and the spirit and the body is restored to itself again, and all men become incorruptible, and immortal, and they are living souls, having a perfect knowledge like unto us in the flesh, save it be that our knowledge shall be perfect.

## *After the Resurrection, All Will Be Judged, and the Righteous Shall Inherit the Kingdom of God*

14 Wherefore, we shall have a perfect knowledge of all our guilt, and our uncleanness, and our nakedness; and the righteous shall have a perfect knowledge of their enjoyment, and their righteousness, being clothed with purity, yea, even with the robe of righteousness.

15 And it shall come to pass that when all men shall have passed from this first death unto life, insomuch as they have become immortal, they must appear before the judgment-seat of the Holy One of Israel; and then cometh the judgment, and then must they be judged according to the holy judgment of God.

16 And assuredly, as the Lord liveth, for the Lord God hath spoken it, and it is his eternal word, which cannot pass away, that they who are righteous shall be righteous still, and they who are filthy shall be filthy still; wherefore, they who are filthy are the devil and his angels; and they shall go away into everlasting fire, prepared for them; and their torment is as a lake of fire and brimstone, whose flame ascendeth up forever and ever and has no end.

17 O the greatness and the justice of our God! For he executeth all his words, and they have gone forth out of his mouth, and his law must be fulfilled.

18 But, behold, the righteous, the saints of the Holy One of Israel, they who have believed in the Holy One of Israel, they who have endured the crosses of the world, and despised the shame of it, they shall inherit the kingdom of God, which was prepared for them from the foundation of the world, and their joy shall be full forever.

19 O the greatness of the mercy of our God, the Holy One of Israel! For he delivereth his saints from that awful monster the devil, and death, and hell, and that lake of fire and brimstone, which is endless torment.

20 O how great the holiness of our God! For he knoweth all things, and there is not anything save he knows it.

## *The Righteous Will Inherit the Kingdom of God, and the Wicked Will Suffer the Penalties for Sin*

21 And he cometh into the world that he may save all men if they will hearken unto his voice; for behold, he suffereth the pains of all men, yea, the pains of every living creature, both men, women, and children, who belong to the family of Adam.

22 And he suffereth this that the resurrection might pass upon all men, that all might stand before him at the great and judgment day.

23 And he commandeth all men that they must repent, and be baptized in his name, having perfect faith in the Holy One of Israel, or they cannot be saved in the kingdom of God.

24 And if they will not repent and believe in his name, and be baptized in his name, and endure to the end, they must be damned; for the Lord God, the Holy One of Israel, has spoken it.

---

9:14 ***nakedness***—bare and poor condition

9:16 In the scriptures, a lake of fire and brimstone (sulfur) symbolizes the eternal torment of the wicked (see Revelation 14:9–11; 19:20; 20:10; Alma 12:17).

9:17 ***executeth***—carries out completely

9:18 The "crosses of the world" may refer to the trials we suffer because of our religious beliefs. Enduring these crosses means that the disciple "does not flinch when accused and scoffed at by those who would make him ashamed, for he has no real reason to be ashamed" (Neal A. Maxwell, *Wherefore, Ye Must Press Forward,* 110).

9:20 Knowing all things enables God "to give that understanding to his creatures by which they are made partakers of eternal life; and if it were not for the idea existing in the minds of men that God had all knowledge it would be impossible for them to exercise faith in him" (Joseph Smith, comp., *Lectures on Faith,* 52).

9:24 ***damned***—shut out from the presence of the Lord

9:24 (21–24) Modern revelation reminds us that the Savior "suffered the pain of all men, that all men might repent and come unto him. . . . And how great is his joy in the soul that repenteth!" (D&C 18:11,13).

How does it make you feel to know that Jesus Christ suffered pain that you might be saved? What can you do to show gratitude for His suffering?

THE GREATEST OF ALL, BY DEL PARSON

*Jesus Christ suffered "the pains of every living creature, both men, women, and children, who belong to the family of Adam."*

25 Wherefore, he has given a law; and where
there is no law given there is no punishment; and
where there is no punishment there is no condemnation; and where there is no condemnation the
mercies of the Holy One of Israel have claim upon
them, because of the atonement; for they are delivered by the power of him.
26 For the atonement satisfieth the demands of his
justice upon all those who have not the law given
to them, that they are delivered from that awful
monster, death and hell, and the devil, and the lake
of fire and brimstone, which is endless torment; and
they are restored to that God who gave them
breath, which is the Holy One of Israel.
27 But wo unto him that has the law given, yea,
that has all the commandments of God, like unto
us, and that transgresseth them, and that wasteth
the days of his probation, for awful is his state!
28 O that cunning plan of the evil one! O the vainness, and the frailties, and the foolishness of men!
When they are learned they think they are wise,
and they hearken not unto the counsel of God, for
they set it aside, supposing they know of themselves, wherefore, their wisdom is foolishness and
it profiteth them not. And they shall perish.
29 But to be learned is good if they hearken unto
the counsels of God.
30 But wo unto the rich, who are rich as to the
things of the world. For because they are rich they
despise the poor, and they persecute the meek, and
their hearts are upon their treasures; wherefore,
their treasure is their god. And behold, their treasure shall perish with them also.
31 And wo unto the deaf that will not hear; for
they shall perish.
32 Wo unto the blind that will not see; for they
shall perish also.
33 Wo unto the uncircumcised of heart, for a
knowledge of their iniquities shall smite them at the
last day.
34 Wo unto the liar, for he shall be thrust down to hell.
35 Wo unto the murderer who deliberately killeth,
for he shall die.
36 Wo unto them who commit whoredoms, for
they shall be thrust down to hell.
37 Yea, wo unto those that worship idols, for the
devil of all devils delighteth in them.
38 And, in fine, wo unto all those who die in their
sins; for they shall return to God, and behold his
face, and remain in their sins.
39 O, my beloved brethren, remember the awfulness in transgressing against that Holy God, and also
the awfulness of yielding to the enticings of that
cunning one. Remember, to be carnally-minded is

---

9:26 (25–26) The "law" is the gospel of Jesus Christ. Even those who have not the law will be "delivered from death, hell, the devil, and endless torment because of the atonement. . . . Those who die without law inherit a terrestrial kingdom. (D. & C. 76:71–72.) The wicked and rebellious go to the telestial kingdom. (D. & C. 76:98–105.)" (Bruce R. McConkie, *Doctrinal New Testament Commentary* 2:223).

9:27 To those who have been taught the gospel of Jesus Christ, the Lord has said, "For of him unto whom much is given much is required; and he who sins against the greater light shall receive the greater condemnation" (D&C 82:3).

9:28 ***cunning***—tricky
***the vainness, and the frailties***—the pride, and the weaknesses

9:29 ***be learned***—have much learning
***counsels***—words or teachings

9:30 ***despise***—hate
***persecute***—mistreat or abuse
***meek***—gentle and humble

9:31 ***wo***—suffering or grief

9:32 (31–32) These warnings are to those who refuse to see or hear spiritual truth.

9:33 The law of circumcision in the Old Testament was the sign of a covenant between God and Israel that set them apart from the world (see Genesis 17:10–11). "Uncircumcised of heart" is a phrase that describes people who do not take their covenants to heart and thus do not keep them.

9:34 ***thrust***—thrown

9:36 ***whoredoms***—acts of wickedness and immorality

9:37 ***idols***—false gods

9:39 ***yielding to the enticings of that cunning one***—giving in to the temptations of the devil
***carnally-minded***—thinking only worldly thoughts

President Gordon B. Hinckley has stated: "Each of us, with discipline and effort, has the capacity to control his thoughts and his actions. . . . We plead with people everywhere to live in accordance with the teachings of our Creator and rise above carnal attractions that often result in the tragedies that follow moral transgression" (in Conference Report, April 1987, 57, 58).

death, and to be spiritually-minded is life eternal.
40 O, my beloved brethren, give ear to my words.
Remember the greatness of the Holy One of Israel.
Do not say that I have spoken hard things against
you; for if ye do, ye will revile against the truth; for
I have spoken the words of your Maker. I know that
the words of truth are hard against all uncleanness;
but the righteous fear them not, for they love the
truth and are not shaken.

## *Jacob Invites All to Come unto Christ and to Receive His Blessings*

41 O then, my beloved brethren, come unto the
Lord, the Holy One. Remember that his paths are
righteous. Behold, the way for man is narrow, but
it lieth in a straight course before him, and the
keeper of the gate is the Holy One of Israel; and he
employeth no servant there; and there is none other
way save it be by the gate; for he cannot be
deceived, for the Lord God is his name.
42 And whoso knocketh, to him will he open; and
the wise, and the learned, and they that are rich,
who are puffed up because of their learning, and
their wisdom, and their riches—yea, they are they
whom he despiseth; and save they shall cast these
things away, and consider themselves fools before
God, and come down in the depths of humility, he
will not open unto them.
43 But the things of the wise and the prudent shall
be hid from them forever—yea, that happiness
which is prepared for the saints.
44 O, my beloved brethren, remember my words.
Behold, I take off my garments, and I shake them
before you; I pray the God of my salvation that he
view me with his all-searching eye; wherefore, ye
shall know at the last day, when all men shall be
judged of their works, that the God of Israel did
witness that I shook your iniquities from my soul,
and that I stand with brightness before him, and am
rid of your blood.
45 O, my beloved brethren, turn away from your
sins; shake off the chains of him that would bind
you fast; come unto that God who is the rock of
your salvation.
46 Prepare your souls for that glorious day when
justice shall be administered unto the righteous,
even the day of judgment, that ye may not shrink
with awful fear; that ye may not remember your
awful guilt in perfectness, and be constrained to
exclaim: Holy, holy are thy judgments, O Lord
God Almighty—but I know my guilt; I transgressed
thy law, and my transgressions are mine; and the
devil hath obtained me, that I am a prey to his
awful misery.
47 But behold, my brethren, is it expedient that I
should awake you to an awful reality of these
things? Would I harrow up your souls if your
minds were pure? Would I be plain unto you
according to the plainness of the truth if ye were
freed from sin?
48 Behold, if ye were holy I would speak unto
you of holiness; but as ye are not holy, and ye look
upon me as a teacher, it must needs be expedient
that I teach you the consequences of sin.
49 Behold, my soul abhorreth sin, and my heart
delighteth in righteousness; and I will praise the
holy name of my God.

---

9:40 ***revile against***—harshly criticize

9:41 "Christ is the *Keeper of the Gate.* He it is who shall admit men into the presence of the Father. (D. & C. 132:12.) He opens the gate to the righteous and bars it to the wicked" (Bruce R. McConkie, *Mormon Doctrine,* 409).

9:42 ***puffed up***—full of pride

9:43 ***prudent***—careful

9:44 "It was an ancient practice for the Lord's prophets to take off their garments and shake them as a sign that they were rid of the blood and sins of those to whom they had been sent to testify" (Bruce R. McConkie, *Mormon Doctrine,* 304).

9:45 ***shake off the chains***—free yourself from the slavery
***bind you fast***—tie you up so you cannot move
***the rock of your salvation***—your Savior, Jesus Christ

9:47 ***harrow up***—trouble or disturb

Jacob wants to wake us up to the "awful reality" that one day we really will be judged by Jesus Christ. Why is it so easy to forget that we will someday be judged by the Lord? How can you prepare to make your judgment before Christ a blessing instead of "an awful reality"?

9:48 ***expedient***—proper or fitting
***the consequences of***—what will happen to you because of

9:49 ***abhorreth***—hates

50 Come, my brethren, every one that thirsteth,
come ye to the waters; and he that hath no money,
come buy and eat; yea, come buy wine and milk
without money and without price.
51 Wherefore, do not spend money for that which
is of no worth, nor your labor for that which cannot satisfy. Hearken diligently unto me, and remember the words which I have spoken; and come unto
the Holy One of Israel, and feast upon that which
perisheth not, neither can be corrupted, and let
your soul delight in fatness.
52 Behold, my beloved brethren, remember the
words of your God; pray unto him continually by
day, and give thanks unto his holy name by night.
Let your hearts rejoice.
53 And behold how great the covenants of the
Lord, and how great his condescensions unto the
children of men; and because of his greatness, and
his grace and mercy, he has promised unto us that
our seed shall not utterly be destroyed, according to
the flesh, but that he would preserve them; and in
future generations they shall become a righteous
branch unto the house of Israel.
54 And now, my brethren, I would speak unto
you more; but on the morrow I will declare unto
you the remainder of my words. Amen.

## CHAPTER 10

*Jacob prophesies that the Jews will crucify Jesus and be punished for their rebellion. Look for the blessings Jacob says come to those who repent and follow the Lord.*

### Lamanites Will Be Righteous in the Last Days

1 AND now I, Jacob, speak unto you again, my
beloved brethren, concerning this righteous branch
of which I have spoken.
2 For behold, the promises which we have
obtained are promises unto us according to the
flesh; wherefore, as it has been shown unto me
that many of our children shall perish in the
flesh because of unbelief, nevertheless, God will
be merciful unto many; and our children shall
be restored, that they may come to that which
will give them the true knowledge of their
Redeemer.

### Jesus Christ Will Be Crucified by Wicked Men

3 Wherefore, as I said unto you, it must needs be
expedient that Christ—for in the last night the angel
spake unto me that this should be his name—
should come among the Jews, among those who
are the more wicked part of the world; and they
shall crucify him—for thus it behooveth our God,
and there is none other nation on earth that would
crucify their God.
4 For should the mighty miracles be wrought
among other nations they would repent, and know
that he be their God.
5 But because of priestcrafts and iniquities, they at
Jerusalem will stiffen their necks against him, that
he be crucified.

---

9:51 (50–51) Jacob uses the words of Isaiah to urge us not to waste our efforts on fleeting pleasures but to come to Jesus Christ to obtain eternal happiness (see Isaiah 55:1–3). How do you spend your time and money? How could your time and money be better spent?

9:53 For an explanation of the word *condescensions,* see for 2 Nephi 4: 26.

10:1 Family histories are sometimes compared to trees. Our "roots" would be our family who lived before us, such as our grandparents. Our "branches" would be our future family, such as our children or grandchildren. Jacob is speaking of Lehi's family in the latter days as a righteous branch (see 3 Nephi 5:22–23).

10:2 ***the flesh***—mortality
***merciful***—kind, loving, and forgiving
***restored***—returned to righteousness

10:3 *Christ* is a Greek word meaning "the Anointed One"; the Hebrew word with the same meaning is *Messiah.* Jesus is the Christ—the one chosen, set apart, and sent by God to save us (see LDS Bible Dictionary, s.v. "Christ," 633).

***behooveth***—is necessary or fitting for

For help regarding the term *crucify,* see for 2 Nephi 6:9.

10:4 ***wrought***—done

10:5 "Priestcrafts are that men preach and set themselves up for a light unto the world, that they may get gain and praise of the world; but they seek not the welfare of Zion" (2 Nephi 26:29).

***iniquities***—sins
***stiffen their necks against***—stubbornly oppose or rebel against

*Jacob said that the wicked among the Jews would crucify Jesus.*

*THE CRUCIFIXION*, BY ROBERT T. BARRETT

6 Wherefore, because of their iniquities, destructions, famines, pestilences, and bloodshed shall
come upon them; and they who shall not be
destroyed shall be scattered among all nations.

### *Blessings Will Be Restored to Israel When They Believe in Christ*

7 But behold, thus saith the Lord God: When the
day cometh that they shall believe in me, that I am
Christ, then have I covenanted with their fathers
that they shall be restored in the flesh, upon the
earth, unto the lands of their inheritance.
8 And it shall come to pass that they shall be gathered in from their long dispersion, from the isles of
the sea, and from the four parts of the earth; and
the nations of the Gentiles shall be great in the eyes
of me, saith God, in carrying them forth to the lands
of their inheritance.
9 Yea, the kings of the Gentiles shall be nursing
fathers unto them, and their queens shall become
nursing mothers; wherefore, the promises of the
Lord are great unto the Gentiles, for he hath spoken
it, and who can dispute?

### *The American Continents Will Be Blessed and Protected So That the Gospel Can Prosper and Grow*

10 But behold, this land, said God, shall be a land
of thine inheritance, and the Gentiles shall be
blessed upon the land.
11 And this land shall be a land of liberty unto the
Gentiles, and there shall be no kings upon the land,
who shall raise up unto the Gentiles.
12 And I will fortify this land against all other
nations.
13 And he that fighteth against Zion shall perish,
saith God.
14 For he that raiseth up a king against me shall
perish, for I, the Lord, the king of heaven, will be
their king, and I will be a light unto them forever,
that hear my words.
15 Wherefore, for this cause, that my covenants
may be fulfilled which I have made unto the children of men, that I will do unto them while they are
in the flesh, I must needs destroy the secret works
of darkness, and of murders, and of abominations.
16 Wherefore, he that fighteth against Zion, both
Jew and Gentile, both bond and free, both male
and female, shall perish; for they are they who are
the whore of all the earth; for they who are not for
me are against me, saith our God.
17 For I will fulfil my promises which I have made
unto the children of men, that I will do unto them
while they are in the flesh—
18 Wherefore, my beloved brethren, thus saith our
God: I will afflict thy seed by the hand of the
Gentiles; nevertheless, I will soften the hearts of the
Gentiles, that they shall be like unto a father to
them; wherefore, the Gentiles shall be blessed and
numbered among the house of Israel.
19 Wherefore, I will consecrate this land unto thy
seed, and them who shall be numbered among thy
seed, forever, for the land of their inheritance; for it
is a choice land, saith God unto me, above all other
lands, wherefore I will have all men that dwell
thereon that they shall worship me, saith God.

### *The Lord Guides Those Who Are Faithful*

20 And now, my beloved brethren, seeing that our
merciful God has given us so great knowledge concerning these things, let us remember him, and lay

---

10:6 ***pestilences***—terrible diseases

10:7 ***lands of their inheritance***—the lands promised to them by the Lord

10:8 ***dispersion***—scattering

10:8 (7–8) God's covenant, or promise, to His children is that He will forgive them if they will repent (see D&C 1:31–33). Jacob spoke of a day when the Jews would finally accept Jesus Christ and receive Heavenly Father's complete blessings.

10:9 ***nursing fathers . . . nursing mothers***—helpers and supporters

10:11 ***liberty***—freedom

10:11 (10–11) People where Joseph Smith lived enjoyed freedom of religion. How do you think freedom helped Joseph Smith restore the true Church to the earth?

10:12 ***fortify***—strengthen and protect

10:15 ***abominations***—wickedness

10:16 ***the whore of all the earth***—those who are against God and who fight against Zion

10:19 ***consecrate***—set apart, dedicate, and give

10:20 The Lord led Lehi's family to the promised land. How has the Lord led and directed your life? Why do you think we should remember these blessings?

aside our sins, and not hang down our heads, for we are not cast off; nevertheless, we have been driven out of the land of our inheritance; but we have been led to a better land, for the Lord has made the sea our path, and we are upon an isle of the sea.
21 But great are the promises of the Lord unto
them who are upon the isles of the sea; wherefore as it says isles, there must needs be more than this, and they are inhabited also by our brethren.
22 For behold, the Lord God has led away
from time to time from the house of Israel, according to his will and pleasure. And now behold, the Lord remembereth all them who have been broken off, wherefore he remembereth us also.
23 Therefore, cheer up your hearts, and remem-
ber that ye are free to act for yourselves—to choose the way of everlasting death or the way of eternal life.
24 Wherefore, my beloved brethren, reconcile
yourselves to the will of God, and not to the will of the devil and the flesh; and remember, after ye are reconciled unto God, that it is only in and through the grace of God that ye are saved.
25 Wherefore, may God raise you from death by
the power of the resurrection, and also from everlasting death by the power of the atonement, that ye may be received into the eternal kingdom of God, that ye may praise him through grace divine. Amen.

## CHAPTER 11

*Nephi testifies that he, his brother Jacob, and Isaiah all saw Jesus Christ. Note how Nephi loves to teach the importance and truthfulness of the Savior's coming.*

### Isaiah, Nephi, and Jacob Have Seen the Savior

1 AND now, Jacob spake many more things to my
people at that time; nevertheless only these things have I caused to be written, for the things which I have written sufficeth me.
2 And now I, Nephi, write more of the words of
Isaiah, for my soul delighteth in his words. For I will liken his words unto my people, and I will send them forth unto all my children, for he verily saw my Redeemer, even as I have seen him.
3 And my brother, Jacob, also has seen him as I
have seen him; wherefore, I will send their words forth unto my children to prove unto them that my words are true. Wherefore, by the words of three, God hath said, I will establish my word. Nevertheless, God sendeth more witnesses, and he proveth all his words.

### Nephi Delights in Christ and in the Plan of Salvation

4 Behold, my soul delighteth in proving unto my
people the truth of the coming of Christ; for, for this end hath the law of Moses been given; and all

---

10:22 (21–22) Besides Lehi's family, the Lord has led many other peoples to different parts of the world. For example, the Lord led the Jaredites from the land of Israel to the Americas (see Ether 1, 2, and 6).

10:23 The Lord gave unto man his agency in the Garden of Eden (see Moses 7:32). We always have the power of choice to follow God or to follow Satan.

10:24 ***reconcile yourselves to***—make yourselves one with or in harmony with

11:1 ***sufficeth***—are enough for

11:3 ***establish***—prove

Proving something is true with two or three witnesses is called the law of witnesses (see 2 Corinthians 13:1). Why are you more convinced something is true when two or three people tell you it is true?

11:4 As used in the scriptures, *types* can be historical persons, objects, rituals, or events that symbolize future events or persons of even greater importance. For example, "virtually everything in the law of Moses was, according to divine design, given to teach and testify of Christ and his atoning sacrifice (Alma 34:14)" (Joseph Fielding McConkie and others, *Doctrinal Commentary on the Book of Mormon* 2:151).

Scripture declares that "all things have their likeness, and all things are created and made to bear record" of Jesus Christ and the eternal plan of salvation (Moses 6:63).

ISAIAH, BY ROBERT T. BARRETT

*The prophet Isaiah saw many events that would take place in the latter days. Nephi included some of Isaiah's prophecies in his own record and encouraged readers to "liken them unto [themselves] and unto all men."*

things which have been given of God from the beginning of the world, unto man, are the typifying of him.

5 And also my soul delighteth in the covenants of the Lord which he hath made to our fathers; yea, my soul delighteth in his grace, and in his justice, and power, and mercy in the great and eternal plan of deliverance from death.

6 And my soul delighteth in proving unto my people that save Christ should come all men must perish.

7 For if there be no Christ there be no God; and if there be no God we are not, for there could have been no creation. But there is a God, and he is Christ, and he cometh in the fulness of his own time.

8 And now I write some of the words of Isaiah, that whoso of my people shall see these words may lift up their hearts and rejoice for all men. Now these are the words, and ye may liken them unto you and unto all men.

## CHAPTER 12

*Nephi inserts in his record some of the writings of Isaiah. In this chapter he quotes Isaiah 2. As you read and ponder, notice how Isaiah teaches against the sin of pride.*

### *Isaiah Sees a Temple Built in the Top of the Mountains*

1 THE word that Isaiah, the son of Amoz, saw concerning Judah and Jerusalem:

2 And it shall come to pass in the last days, when the mountain of the Lord's house shall be established in the top of the mountains, and shall be exalted above the hills, and all nations shall flow unto it.

3 And many people shall go and say, Come ye, and let us go up to the mountain of the Lord, to the house of the God of Jacob; and he will teach us of his ways, and we will walk in his paths; for out of Zion shall go forth the law, and the word of the Lord from Jerusalem.

---

11:5 The "great and eternal plan of deliverance from death" is also called the plan of happiness, the plan of salvation, or the gospel of Jesus Christ. It is God's plan. If we follow His plan we will be able to return to Him and be like Him (see Boyd K. Packer, *The Play and the Plan*).

11:7 (6–7) If Christ had not overcome physical death and paid for our sins, we could not return to God and be like Him (see 2 Nephi 9:7–10). How can you show the Savior your gratitude for all He's done for you?

11:8 ***liken***—compare or apply

12:2 (1–2) President Harold B. Lee stated: "The coming forth of his [the Lord's] church in these days was the beginning of the fulfillment of the ancient prophecy when 'the mountain of the Lord's house shall be established in the top of the mountains'" (in Conference Report, April 1973, 5). Elder Bruce R. McConkie noted that this scripture "has specific reference to the Salt Lake Temple and to the other temples built in the top of the Rocky Mountains, and it has a general reference to the temple yet to be built in the New Jerusalem in Jackson County, Missouri" (Bruce R. McConkie, *A New Witness for the Articles of Faith,* 539).

12:3 After Jesus Christ comes again He will rule the earth for a thousand years during what is called the Millennium. He will have two world capitals: Zion, sometimes called the New Jerusalem (Jackson County, Missouri), and Jerusalem (see D&C 57:3; 84:2–4; and Ether 13:2–11).

PHOTOGRAPH BY G. R. SIMS

*Isaiah prophesied that "the mountain of the Lord's house [would] be established in the top of the mountains." The Salt Lake Temple and other modern temples are a fulfillment of Isaiah's prophecy.*

12:3 (2–3) Isaiah foretells of people from all nations coming to the "house of the God of Jacob." Elder Neal A. Maxwell said that, "with the June 1978 revelation concerning the extension of the privileges of priesthood and temple blessings, Isaiah 2 can now be completely fulfilled" (Neal A. Maxwell, *Things As They Really Are,* 49–50).

4 And he shall judge among the nations, and shall rebuke many people: and they shall beat their swords into plow-shares, and their spears into pruning-hooks—nation shall not lift up sword against nation, neither shall they learn war any more.

## The Wicked and the Proud Will Be Humbled at the Second Coming

5 O house of Jacob, come ye and let us walk in the light of the Lord; yea, come, for ye have all gone astray, every one to his wicked ways.

6 Therefore, O Lord, thou hast forsaken thy people, the house of Jacob, because they be replenished from the east, and hearken unto soothsayers like the Philistines, and they please themselves in the children of strangers.

7 Their land also is full of silver and gold, neither is there any end of their treasures; their land is also full of horses, neither is there any end of their chariots.

8 Their land is also full of idols; they worship the work of their own hands, that which their own fingers have made.

9 And the mean man boweth not down, and the great man humbleth himself not, therefore, forgive him not.

10 O ye wicked ones, enter into the rock, and hide thee in the dust, for the fear of the Lord and the glory of his majesty shall smite thee.

11 And it shall come to pass that the lofty looks of man shall be humbled, and the haughtiness of men shall be bowed down, and the Lord alone shall be exalted in that day.

## Isaiah Describes the Second Coming

12 For the day of the Lord of Hosts soon cometh upon all nations, yea, upon every one; yea, upon the proud and lofty, and upon every one who is lifted up, and he shall be brought low.

13 Yea, and the day of the Lord shall come upon all the cedars of Lebanon, for they are high and lifted up; and upon all the oaks of Bashan;

14 And upon all the high mountains, and upon all the hills, and upon all the nations which are lifted up, and upon every people;

15 And upon every high tower, and upon every fenced wall;

16 And upon all the ships of the sea, and upon all the ships of Tarshish, and upon all pleasant pictures.

17 And the loftiness of man shall be bowed down, and the haughtiness of men shall be made low; and the Lord alone shall be exalted in that day.

---

12:4 ***plow-shares***—blades for plowing the earth

Jesus Christ is and will be the Judge among all nations of the earth (see John 5:27; Acts 10:42). He is also the "Prince of Peace" (Isaiah 9:6). When people come to know and love Him, they also come to love their fellow human beings. They willingly turn their weapons of war (swords and spears) into tools of peace (plows and knives for trimming branches).

12:5 ***Jacob***—the children of Israel

12:6 ***replenished***—fed or nourished
***soothsayers***—fortune-tellers

12:8 (5–8) This passage describes the wickedness of Israel, particularly their pride and worship of false gods. People today may not bow down to stone statues but many still worship material things, such as money and possessions. In modern revelation the Lord said: "Every man walketh in his own way, and after the image of his own god, . . . whose substance is that of an idol" (D&C 1:16).

12:9 ***mean***—common or average

12:10 ***smite thee***—cause harm to come upon you

12:11 ***lofty***—proud
***haughtiness***—great pride

12:13 The cedars of Lebanon and the oaks of Bashan "were the loftiest and most impressive trees in the ancient Middle East. They therefore symbolized not only the great beauty of the land that would be destroyed but also the proud and lofty men of the earth" (*Old Testament: Religion 302 Student Manual, 1 Kings–Malachi,* 139).

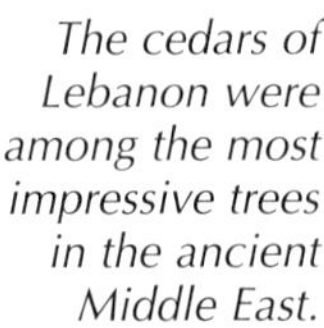

*The cedars of Lebanon were among the most impressive trees in the ancient Middle East.*

18 And the idols he shall utterly abolish.
19 And they shall go into the holes of the rocks,
and into the caves of the earth, for the fear of the
Lord shall come upon them and the glory of his
majesty shall smite them, when he ariseth to shake
terribly the earth.
20 In that day a man shall cast his idols of silver,
and his idols of gold, which he hath made for himself to worship, to the moles and to the bats;
21 To go into the clefts of the rocks, and into the
tops of the ragged rocks, for the fear of the Lord
shall come upon them and the majesty of his glory
shall smite them, when he ariseth to shake terribly
the earth.
22 Cease ye from man, whose breath is in his nos-
trils; for wherein is he to be accounted of?

## CHAPTER 13

*Nephi quotes Isaiah 3. The wickedness of Judah is described. Isaiah compares the kingdom of Judah to prideful women who love worldly fashions. Watch for what could happen to us if we are full of pride and wickedness.*

### The Ruin of Judah and Jerusalem Is Prophesied

1 FOR behold, the Lord, the Lord of Hosts, doth
take away from Jerusalem, and from Judah, the stay
and the staff, the whole staff of bread, and the
whole stay of water—
2 The mighty man, and the man of war, the judge,
and the prophet, and the prudent, and the ancient;
3 The captain of fifty, and the honorable man, and
the counselor, and the cunning artificer, and the
eloquent orator.
4 And I will give children unto them to be their
princes, and babes shall rule over them.
5 And the people shall be oppressed, every one
by another, and every one by his neighbor; the
child shall behave himself proudly against the
ancient, and the base against the honorable.
6 When a man shall take hold of his brother of the
house of his father, and shall say: Thou hast clothing, be thou our ruler, and let not this ruin come
under thy hand—
7 In that day shall he swear, saying: I will not be
a healer; for in my house there is neither bread nor
clothing; make me not a ruler of the people.
8 For Jerusalem is ruined, and Judah is fallen,
because their tongues and their doings have been
against the Lord, to provoke the eyes of his glory.
9 The show of their countenance doth witness
against them, and doth declare their sin to be even
as Sodom, and they cannot hide it. Wo unto their
souls, for they have rewarded evil unto themselves!
10 Say unto the righteous that it is well with them;
for they shall eat the fruit of their doings.
11 Wo unto the wicked, for they shall perish; for
the reward of their hands shall be upon them!
12 And my people, children are their oppressors,
and women rule over them. O my people, they
who lead thee cause thee to err and destroy the
way of thy paths.

---

12:21 (14–21) In these verses, such symbols as "high mountains," "high tower," "fenced wall," and the "ships of Tarshish" represent the riches and pride of the world. All these "shall be made low" at the Second Coming of Jesus Christ.

12:21 (20–21) Why do you think a person who has always put worldly possessions before God would want to hide those things in mole holes and bat caves when Jesus Christ comes again?

13:1 ***stay and the staff***—supply and the support

13:2 ***prudent***—careful or wise

13:3 ***cunning artificer***—skilled in magic
***eloquent orator***—skillful in casting spells of the magic arts

13:5 ***oppressed***—ruled over
***base***—rude or vulgar

13:7 ***swear***—promise

13:8 ***provoke***—anger

13:9 President David O. McKay said: "Every person who lives in this world wields an influence, whether for good or for evil. It is not what he says alone; it is not alone what he does. It is what he is. . . . Every person radiates what he or she really is. . . . It is what we are and what we *radiate* that affects the people around us" (*Man May Know for Himself,* 108).

13:12 This verse describes the social confusion that would come upon Judah (see Victor L. Ludlow, *Isaiah: Prophet, Seer and Poet,* 106). Elder Ezra Taft Benson applied this verse to our own day: "And so today, the undermining of the home and family is on the increase, with the devil anxiously working to displace the father as the head of the home and create rebellion among the children" (in Conference Report, October 1970, 21).

## *The Lord Judges Israel*

13 The Lord standeth up to plead, and standeth to
judge the people.
14 The Lord will enter into judgment with the
ancients of his people and the princes thereof; for
ye have eaten up the vineyard and the spoil of the
poor in your houses.
15 What mean ye? Ye beat my people to pieces,
and grind the faces of the poor, saith the Lord God
of Hosts.

## *The Daughters of Zion Are Cursed for Their Worldliness*

16 Moreover, the Lord saith: Because the daughters of Zion are haughty, and walk with stretched-
forth necks and wanton eyes, walking and mincing
as they go, and making a tinkling with their feet—
17 Therefore the Lord will smite with a scab the
crown of the head of the daughters of Zion, and
the Lord will discover their secret parts.
18 In that day the Lord will take away the bravery
of their tinkling ornaments, and cauls, and round
tires like the moon;
19 The chains and the bracelets, and the mufflers;
20 The bonnets, and the ornaments of the legs, and
the headbands, and the tablets, and the ear-rings;
21 The rings, and nose jewels;
22 The changeable suits of apparel, and the
mantles, and the wimples, and the crisping-pins;
23 The glasses, and the fine linen, and hoods, and
the veils.
24 And it shall come to pass, instead of sweet
smell there shall be stink; and instead of a girdle, a
rent; and instead of well set hair, baldness; and
instead of a stomacher, a girding of sackcloth; burning instead of beauty.
25 Thy men shall fall by the sword and thy mighty
in the war.

---

13:14 The vineyard represents the Lord's chosen people (see Isaiah 5:7). The rulers of Israel are supposed to be watchmen over the vineyard. Instead of guarding the Lord's vineyard, they rob the poor and eat up the vineyard (compare Matthew 21:33–41).

13:15 ***grind the faces of the poor***—mistreat and burden the poor without mercy

In our day the Lord has declared, "And remember in all things the poor and the needy, the sick and the afflicted, for he that doeth not these things, the same is not my disciple" (D&C 52:40). What do you think is a good way to bless the lives of the poor and the needy?

13:16 ***haughty***—prideful
***wanton***—lustful

The word *mincing* means "walking with short rapid steps" in such a way as to call attention to oneself (see LDS edition of the King James Bible, Isaiah 3:16, note e).

13:17 ***smite with a scab the crown of the head***—take away their beauty

In this verse the word *discover* means "reveal." The expression "discover their secret parts" is a way of saying "put them to shame" (see LDS edition of the King James Bible, Isaiah 3:17, note a).

13:18 ***bravery***—glory or show
***cauls***—hairnets
***round tires like the moon***—moon-shaped crescent necklaces

13:19 ***mufflers***—veils

13:22 ***wimples***—shawls or scarves
***crisping-pins***—money purses

13:23 ***glasses***—see-through clothing

13:24 ***a rent***—rags
***a girding of sackcloth***—a robe of rough goat's hair
***burning***—branding (given to mark someone as a slave)

A bald or shaved head in Isaiah's day often represented slavery or captivity (see Isaiah 15:2; Ezekiel 7:18).

13:24 (16–24) President Joseph Fielding Smith applied these verses to our day and warned about increasing immodesty: "It is, in my judgment, a sad reflection on the 'daughters of Zion' when they dress immodestly. Moreover, this remark pertains to the men as well as to the women. The Lord gave commandments to ancient Israel that both men and women should cover their bodies and observe the law of chastity at all times" (*Answers to Gospel Questions* 5:172–74).

26 And her gates shall lament and mourn; and she
shall be desolate, and shall sit upon the ground.

## CHAPTER 14

*Suffering in the last days will be followed by great blessings for the righteous. Watch for what great blessings come to those who stay faithful and righteous.*

### The Lord Blesses the Righteous

1 AND in that day, seven women shall take hold
of one man, saying: We will eat our own bread, and
wear our own apparel; only let us be called by thy
name to take away our reproach.
2 In that day shall the branch of the Lord be beautiful and glorious; the fruit of the earth excellent
and comely to them that are escaped of Israel.
3 And it shall come to pass, they that are left in
Zion and remain in Jerusalem shall be called holy,
every one that is written among the living in
Jerusalem—
4 When the Lord shall have washed away the
filth of the daughters of Zion, and shall have
purged the blood of Jerusalem from the midst
thereof by the spirit of judgment and by the spirit
of burning.
5 And the Lord will create upon every dwelling-
place of mount Zion, and upon her assemblies, a
cloud and smoke by day and the shining of a flaming fire by night; for upon all the glory of Zion shall
be a defence.
6 And there shall be a tabernacle for a shadow in
the daytime from the heat, and for a place of
refuge, and a covert from storm and from rain.

## CHAPTER 15

*Nephi quotes Isaiah 5. The prophet Isaiah sings a sad song, or poem, about Israel's destruction and scattering because of their wickedness. Watch for the strong warnings, as well as the wonderful promises, that the Lord gives His people.*

### Isaiah Sings the Song of the Lord's Vineyard

1 AND then will I sing to my well-beloved a song
of my beloved, touching his vineyard. My well-
beloved hath a vineyard in a very fruitful hill.

---

13:26 **her**—Jerusalem's
**desolate**—empty or defeated

13:26 (16–26) Isaiah's prophecies can be understood on several levels. The "daughters of Zion" represent Israel and Judah of old, as well as some members of the Church today. Many of the unusual words used in these verses describe ornaments, jewelry, and fashionable clothing of Isaiah's day. Isaiah warns about the danger of becoming "more concerned with . . . clothing, jewels, and personal appearance than with righteousness" (*Old Testament: Religion 302 Student Manual, 1 Kings–Malachi,* 140).

14:1 **take hold of one man**—turn to one man for help
**reproach**—shame or disgrace

This verse continues the thought of the previous chapter. The horrible war mentioned in 2 Nephi 13:25–26 results in a lack of marriageable men. "So terrible would conditions in those times be that women would offer to share a husband with others and expect no material support from him, if they could claim they were married to him" (*Old Testament: Religion 302 Student Manual, 1 Kings–Malachi,* 141).

14:2 **branch**—righteous
**comely**—beautiful

14:3 The phrases "left in Zion" and "remaineth in Jerusalem" represent those who keep the commandments.

14:4 **washed away the filth of**—made pure
**purged the blood**—cleansed the sins

14:5 When Moses led the children of Israel from Egypt, the Lord guided and protected them with a pillar of cloud by day and a pillar of fire by night (see Exodus 13:21). Isaiah used these symbols to show that the Lord will also offer guidance and protection in the latter days.

**defence**—covering or protection

14:6 **covert**—shelter

The Lord revealed that stakes are organized for "a defense, and for a refuge from the storm, and from wrath when it shall be poured out without mixture upon the whole earth" (D&C 115:6).

15:1 **my well-beloved**—the Lord Jesus Christ

2 And he fenced it, and gathered out the stones
thereof, and planted it with the choicest vine, and
built a tower in the midst of it, and also made a
wine-press therein; and he looked that it should
bring forth grapes, and it brought forth wild grapes.
3 And now, O inhabitants of Jerusalem, and men
of Judah, judge, I pray you, betwixt me and my
vineyard.
4 What could have been done more to my vineyard that I have not done in it? Wherefore, when I
looked that it should bring forth grapes it brought
forth wild grapes.
5 And now go to; I will tell you what I will do to
my vineyard—I will take away the hedge thereof,
and it shall be eaten up; and I will break down the
wall thereof, and it shall be trodden down;
6 And I will lay it waste; it shall not be pruned nor
digged; but there shall come up briers and thorns;
I will also command the clouds that they rain no
rain upon it.
7 For the vineyard of the Lord of Hosts is the
house of Israel, and the men of Judah his pleasant
plant; and he looked for judgment, and behold,
oppression; for righteousness, but behold, a cry.

## *Six Warnings of Wo Are Given to Israel*

8 Wo unto them that join house to house, till there
can be no place, that they may be placed alone in
the midst of the earth!
9 In mine ears, said the Lord of Hosts, of a truth
many houses shall be desolate, and great and fair
cities without inhabitant.
10 Yea, ten acres of vineyard shall yield one bath,
and the seed of a homer shall yield an ephah.
11 Wo unto them that rise up early in the morning, that they may follow strong drink, that continue until night, and wine inflame them!
12 And the harp, and the viol, the tabret, and pipe,
and wine are in their feasts; but they regard not the
work of the Lord, neither consider the operation of
his hands.

*The Lord used the image of a beautiful, fenced vineyard with a tower and winepress to describe the house of Israel. Such vineyards are still found in Israel today.*

15:3 ***betwixt***—between

15:4 Here the word *grapes* stands for righteousness, and the term *wild grapes* stands for wickedness.

The Lord (Jesus Christ) of the vineyard had such high hopes for His vineyard (children of Israel). He had worked hard to prepare and grow the best vines, yet only bad fruit came forth. What would you do with a garden like that—a garden in which, no matter how much you worked, only rotten fruits and vegetables grew? Compare that to raising children. How would you feel about children who ignored or disobeyed every truth you taught them?

15:5 ***trodden down***—stomped underfoot

15:7 ***he looked for judgment, and behold, oppression***—he looked for justice but saw bloodshed
***a cry***—a wild and loud outcry or a plea for help

15:8 ***Wo***—Grief, sorrow, and misery

This warning is against the selfish landowners who buy up all of the property of the poor (see LDS edition of the King James Bible, Isaiah 5:8, note c). The Lord taught people not to do this in ancient Israel (see Leviticus 25:23).

15:9 ***desolate***—empty and wasted

15:10 This verse is saying that the vineyards would not be fruitful and productive. For help with the difficult words found in this verse, see the LDS Bible Dictionary, s.v. "Weights and Measures," 788–89.

15:11 ***follow strong drink***—drink alcoholic beverages
***inflame them***—makes them drunk

13 Therefore, my people are gone into captivity,
because they have no knowledge; and their honorable men are famished, and their multitude dried
up with thirst.
14 Therefore, hell hath enlarged herself, and
opened her mouth without measure; and their
glory, and their multitude, and their pomp, and he
that rejoiceth, shall descend into it.
15 And the mean man shall be brought down, and
the mighty man shall be humbled, and the eyes of
the lofty shall be humbled.
16 But the Lord of Hosts shall be exalted in judgment, and God that is holy shall be sanctified in
righteousness.
17 Then shall the lambs feed after their manner,
and the waste places of the fat ones shall strangers
eat.
18 Wo unto them that draw iniquity with cords of
vanity, and sin as it were with a cart rope;
19 That say: Let him make speed, hasten his work,
that we may see it; and let the counsel of the Holy
One of Israel draw nigh and come, that we may
know it.
20 Wo unto them that call evil good, and good
evil, that put darkness for light, and light for darkness, that put bitter for sweet, and sweet for bitter!
21 Wo unto the wise in their own eyes and prudent in their own sight!
22 Wo unto the mighty to drink wine, and men of
strength to mingle strong drink;
23 Who justify the wicked for reward, and take
away the righteousness of the righteous from him!
24 Therefore, as the fire devoureth the stubble,
and the flame consumeth the chaff, their root shall

---

15:13 ***captivity***—bondage or slavery

According to the Prophet Joseph Smith, "a man is saved no faster than he gets knowledge, for if he does not get knowledge, he will be brought into captivity by some evil power in the other world, as evil spirits will have more knowledge, and consequently more power than many men who are on the earth. Hence it needs revelation to assist us, and give us knowledge of the things of God" (*Teachings of the Prophet Joseph Smith,* 217).

15:14 In this verse the word *hell,* which is translated from the Hebrew word *sheol,* has reference to the spirit world (see *Teachings of the Prophet Joseph Smith,* 310). Because of so much wickedness, many will die without the knowledge necessary to be saved. They will be captive in spirit prison (verse 13). In that sense "hell hath enlarged herself," or become larger, with the increase of wicked spirits.

***pomp***—noise or tumult

15:15 ***mean***—common or ordinary
***lofty***—proud

15:16 "To be *sanctified* is to become clean, pure, and spotless" (Bruce R. McConkie, *Mormon Doctrine,* 675). A person can become sanctified only through the Atonement of Jesus Christ and by obedience to the laws, ordinances, and commandments of the gospel of Jesus Christ.

15:16 (15–16) These verses testify that all mankind, especially the proud and wicked, will be humbled by the righteous judgment of Jesus Christ. How can you prepare for the time when you will be brought before the most holy and righteous person who ever walked the earth?

15:17 ***waste places of the fat ones***—deserted and ruined lands of those who were once rich

15:18 ***vanity***—pride or conceit

Isaiah warns that those who are tied to their sins are like oxen pulling their carts (see LDS edition of the King James Bible, Isaiah 5:18, note c).

15:19 There will be those who "will not believe in the Messiah until they see him" (LDS edition of the King James Bible, Isaiah 5:19, note d).

15:21 President N. Eldon Tanner said this verse was a warning to our day. He noted that when people "become learned in the worldly things . . . [they] become self-sufficient and are prepared to lean unto their own understanding, even to the point where they think they are independent of God. . . . How much wiser and better it is for man to accept the simple truths of the gospel and to accept as authority God, the Creator of the world, and his Son Jesus Christ" (in Conference Report, October 1968, 48–49).

15:23 This is a warning to those who would excuse guilty people and deprive righteous people of their legal rights (see LDS edition of the King James Bible, Isaiah 5:23, note c).

15:24 ***chaff***—worthless part of a head of wheat

Those who reject the law of the Lord and hate the word of the Lord will be burned with fire at His coming (see Isaiah 47:14), and they will "go away into everlasting fire, prepared for them; and their torment is as a lake of fire and brimstone, whose flame ascendeth up forever and ever and has no end" (2 Nephi 9:16).

be rottenness, and their blossoms shall go up as dust; because they have cast away the law of the Lord of Hosts, and despised the word of the Holy One of Israel.
25 Therefore, is the anger of the Lord kindled
against his people, and he hath stretched forth his hand against them, and hath smitten them; and the hills did tremble, and their carcasses were torn in the midst of the streets. For all this his anger is not turned away, but his hand is stretched out still.
26 And he will lift up an ensign to the nations from
far, and will hiss unto them from the end of the earth; and behold, they shall come with speed swiftly; none shall be weary nor stumble among them.
27 None shall slumber nor sleep; neither shall the
girdle of their loins be loosed, nor the latchet of their shoes be broken;
28 Whose arrows shall be sharp, and all their bows
bent, and their horses' hoofs shall be counted like flint, and their wheels like a whirlwind, their roaring like a lion.
29 They shall roar like young lions; yea, they shall
roar, and lay hold of the prey, and shall carry away safe, and none shall deliver.
30 And in that day they shall roar against them
like the roaring of the sea; and if they look unto the land, behold, darkness and sorrow, and the light is darkened in the heavens thereof.

## CHAPTER 16

*Nephi quotes Isaiah 6. Isaiah sees the Lord on His heavenly throne. Study how the Lord called Isaiah to be a prophet.*

### *Isaiah Is Made Worthy to Stand Before the Lord*

1 IN the year that king Uzziah died, I saw also the
Lord sitting upon a throne, high and lifted up, and his train filled the temple.
2 Above it stood the seraphim; each one had six
wings; with twain he covered his face, and with twain he covered his feet, and with twain he did fly.
3 And one cried unto another, and said: Holy,
holy, holy, is the Lord of Hosts; the whole earth is full of his glory.

---

15:25 ***carcasses***—dead bodies

The phrase "his hand is stretched out still" can be understood in at least two ways: (1) The punishment of the Lord is still forthcoming if His people don't repent, and (2) "in spite of all, the Lord is available if they will turn to him" (LDS edition of the King James Bible, Isaiah 9:12, note d).

15:26 ***an ensign***—a flag, banner, or standard
***hiss unto***—whistle to, call, or summon

"[The Church of Jesus Christ of Latter-day Saints] is the standard which Isaiah said the Lord would set up for the people in the latter days. This Church was given to be a light to the world and to be a standard for God's people and for the Gentiles to seek to" (Marion G. Romney, in Conference Report, April 1961, 119).

15:27 ***slumber***—nap
***girdle of their loins***—belt or sash around their waists
***latchet of their shoes be broken***—thong of their sandals break

15:28 (26–28) "Since there were no such things as trains and airplanes in that day, Isaiah could hardly have mentioned them by name, but he seems to have described them in unmistakable words. How better could 'their horses' hoofs be counted like flint, and their wheel like a whirlwind' than in the modern train? How better could 'Their roaring . . . be like a lion' than in the roar of the airplane? . . . With this manner of transportation the Lord can really 'hiss unto them from the end of the earth,' that 'they shall come with speed swiftly'" (LeGrand Richards, *A Marvelous Work and a Wonder,* 230).

15:30 (29–30) Righteous Israel will gather out of the gentile nations. No enemy will be able to stop this great gathering (see 3 Nephi 21:12–13).

16:1 The death of King Uzziah was about 740 B.C. (see LDS Bible Dictionary, s.v. "Amos," 607).

***his train***—the skirt of his robe

16:2 Seraphim "are angels who reside in the presence of God. . . . The fact that these holy beings were shown to him [Isaiah] as having wings was simply to symbolize their 'power, to move, to act, etc.' as was the case also in visions others had received. (D&C 77:4)" (Bruce R. McConkie, *Mormon Doctrine,* 702, 703).

4 And the posts of the door moved at the voice of
him that cried, and the house was filled with
smoke.
5 Then said I: Wo is unto me! for I am undone;
because I am a man of unclean lips; and I dwell in
the midst of a people of unclean lips; for mine eyes
have seen the King, the Lord of Hosts.
6 Then flew one of the seraphim unto me, having
a live coal in his hand, which he had taken with the
tongs from off the altar;
7 And he laid it upon my mouth, and said: Lo, this
has touched thy lips; and thine iniquity is taken
away, and thy sin purged.

### *Israel Rejects Isaiah, Who Is Sent to Teach About Jesus Christ*

8 Also I heard the voice of the Lord, saying:
Whom shall I send, and who will go for us? Then I
said: Here am I; send me.
9 And he said: Go and tell this people—Hear ye
indeed, but they understood not; and see ye
indeed, but they perceived not.
10 Make the heart of this people fat, and make
their ears heavy, and shut their eyes—lest they see
with their eyes, and hear with their ears, and understand with their heart, and be converted and be
healed.
11 Then said I: Lord, how long? And he said:
Until the cities be wasted without inhabitant, and
the houses without man, and the land be utterly
desolate;
12 And the Lord have removed men far away, for
there shall be a great forsaking in the midst of the
land.
13 But yet there shall be a tenth, and they shall
return, and shall be eaten, as a teil-tree, and as an
oak whose substance is in them when they cast
their leaves; so the holy seed shall be the substance
thereof.

## CHAPTER 17

*Nephi quotes Isaiah 7. Isaiah prophesies that the kingdoms of Syria and Ephraim (Israel) will go to war against the kingdom of Judah. He also prophesies of the coming of Christ. Search for what Isaiah teaches about Jesus Christ.*

### *The Kings of Syria and Israel Join Together to Battle Against the Kingdom of Judah*

1 AND it came to pass in the days of Ahaz the
son of Jotham, the son of Uzziah, king of Judah,
that Rezin, king of Syria, and Pekah the son of
Remaliah, king of Israel, went up toward Jerusalem to war against it, but could not prevail
against it.
2 And it was told the house of David, saying: Syria
is confederate with Ephraim. And his heart was
moved, and the heart of his people, as the trees of
the wood are moved with the wind.

---

16:5 ***Wo***—Grief, sorrow, and misery
***undone***—ruined or about to be destroyed

16:7 ***iniquity***—wickedness or guilt
***purged***—removed or atoned for

16:8 When called to serve his mission, Isaiah used the same words as the Savior did in the premortal world: "Here am I, send me" (see Abraham 3:27).

16:10 (9–10) Isaiah is told to teach the people clearly so that they would understand. However, like the Jews in Jesus' day, the people did not want to believe, or see, or hear the prophet's message (see Matthew 13:14–15; Acts 28:26–27).

16:11 ***utterly desolate***—completely empty

16:13 After the wicked are destroyed, a small part of Israel will remain. The imagery used here suggests that Israel is much like a tree that dies, but through its seeds more trees grow (see LDS edition of the King James Bible, Isaiah 6:13, note b).

17:1 In about 735–734 B.C. the wicked kingdoms of Syria and Israel were trying to force Judah to join them in war against the great power of Assyria. When Ahaz, the king of Judah, refused to join their fight against Assyria, they turned against Judah in an attempt to overthrow Ahaz. Judah had lost some fierce battles, and King Ahaz may have been very concerned about Judah's future (see Victor Ludlow, *Isaiah: Prophet, Seer, and Poet,* 139).

17:2 The "house of David" refers to King David's descendants who ruled the kingdom of Judah. In this case it refers to Ahaz.

***confederate***—united together

*The kingdoms of Israel and Syria attack Judah*

3 Then said the Lord unto Isaiah: Go forth now to
meet Ahaz, thou and Shearjashub thy son, at the
end of the conduit of the upper pool in the highway of the fuller's field;
4 And say unto him: Take heed, and be quiet; fear
not, neither be faint-hearted for the two tails of
these smoking firebrands, for the fierce anger of
Rezin with Syria, and of the son of Remaliah.
5 Because Syria, Ephraim, and the son of
Remaliah, have taken evil counsel against thee, saying:
6 Let us go up against Judah and vex it, and let us
make a breach therein for us, and set a king in the
midst of it, yea, the son of Tabeal.
7 Thus saith the Lord God: It shall not stand, neither shall it come to pass.
8 For the head of Syria is Damascus, and the head
of Damascus, Rezin; and within three score and five
years shall Ephraim be broken that it be not a
people.
9 And the head of Ephraim is Samaria, and the
head of Samaria is Remaliah's son. If ye will not
believe surely ye shall not be established.

## The Lord Offers a Sign to King Ahaz

10 Moreover, the Lord spake again unto Ahaz, saying:
11 Ask thee a sign of the Lord thy God; ask it
either in the depths, or in the heights above.
12 But Ahaz said: I will not ask, neither will I
tempt the Lord.
13 And he said: Hear ye now, O house of David;
is it a small thing for you to weary men, but will ye
weary my God also?

---

17:3 ***conduit***—canal or aqueduct
***fuller's field***—laundry place

The Lord sent Isaiah to this canal knowing that King Ahaz would be there checking on the water supplies and his army. Invading armies knew that control of this water source would ultimately mean control of the city (see Hoyt W. Brewster Jr., *Isaiah Plain & Simple,* 65).

17:4 In other words, "Don't be alarmed by the attack; those two kings have little fire left" (see LDS edition of the King James Bible, Isaiah 7:4, note a).

17:6 ***vex***—trouble or afflict
***let us make a breach therein for us***—let us divide up Judah

17:8 After "three score and five" (sixty-five) years, "Ephraim," the kingdom of Israel, was destroyed and taken captive by the Assyrians (see 2 Kings 17:6).

17:9 ***established***—supported

17:9 (1–9) Leaders, capitals, leading tribes or territories, and kingdoms are used interchangeably in these verses. The accompanying map might be helpful in identifying the different groups in this chapter.

17:9 (3–9) Just as He did with the kingdom of Judah, the Lord can protect us in times of danger if we are righteous and have faith. How could knowing this help you in times of trouble?

17:12 (11–12) "It is probable that Ahaz refused to ask for a sign because he had no confidence in the Lord—he was secretly depending on the aid of the king of Assyria" (Victor Ludlow, *Isaiah: Prophet, Seer, and Poet,* 142–43).

17:13 ***weary***—tire out or wear out

THE BIRTH OF CHRIST, BY ROBERT T. BARRETT

*Isaiah saw in vision the birth of Jesus Christ.*

14 Therefore, the Lord himself shall give you a
sign—Behold, a virgin shall conceive, and shall
bear a son, and shall call his name Immanuel.
15 Butter and honey shall he eat, that he may
know to refuse the evil and to choose the good.
16 For before the child shall know to refuse the
evil and choose the good, the land that thou abhorrest shall be forsaken of both her kings.

## Both Syria and Israel Will Be Captured by Egypt and Assyria

17 The Lord shall bring upon thee, and upon thy
people, and upon thy father's house, days that have
not come from the day that Ephraim departed from
Judah, the king of Assyria.
18 And it shall come to pass in that day that the
Lord shall hiss for the fly that is in the uttermost part
of Egypt, and for the bee that is in the land of
Assyria.
19 And they shall come, and shall rest all of them
in the desolate valleys, and in the holes of the
rocks, and upon all thorns, and upon all bushes.
20 In the same day shall the Lord shave with a
razor that is hired, by them beyond the river, by the
king of Assyria, the head, and the hair of the feet;
and it shall also consume the beard.
21 And it shall come to pass in that day, a man
shall nourish a young cow and two sheep;
22 And it shall come to pass, for the abundance of
milk they shall give he shall eat butter; for butter
and honey shall every one eat that is left in the
land.
23 And it shall come to pass in that day, every
place shall be, where there were a thousand vines
at a thousand silverlings, which shall be for briers
and thorns.
24 With arrows and with bows shall men come
thither, because all the land shall become briers and
thorns.
25 And all hills that shall be digged with the mattock, there shall not come thither the fear of briers
and thorns; but it shall be for the sending forth of
oxen, and the treading of lesser cattle.

---

17:14 ***a virgin shall conceive***—a young woman who is pure, chaste, and who has not had intimate relations with a mortal man will become pregnant

Jesus has many names and titles. The name *Immanuel* is a Hebrew word that means "God is with us" (see James Strong, *The Exhaustive Concordance of the Bible,* 89).

17:16 ***abhorrest***—hates

Before a child would be old enough to know the difference between right and wrong, about eight years old (see D&C 68:25), both the king of Syria and the king of Israel would lose power.

17:16 (14–16) This may be another of Isaiah's prophecies that can be understood on several levels. No matter how Ahaz may have interpreted these words of Isaiah, they stand as a beautiful prophecy of the birth of the Savior seven hundred years before He was born (see Matthew 1:23).

17:17 The time when "Ephraim departed from Judah" was after the death of King Solomon in about 975 B.C. This is when Israel was divided into the Northern and the Southern Kingdoms (see 1 Kings 12:20–21).

17:18 ***hiss***—signal or call
***for the fly***—for the attacking armies of Egypt
***for the bee***—for the attacking armies of Assyria

17:19 ***desolate valleys***—bleak or barren valleys of waste

17:20 The "razor" represents Assyria, which was beyond the Euphrates River. The Lord would use Assyria to humble Israel and Judah. The image of the razor consuming, or shaving, the hair is used because Assyrian captives were commonly humiliated by being shaved "from head to toe" (Donald W. Parry and others, *Understanding Isaiah,* 78).

17:21 ***nourish***—care for

This verse is noting that only a few survivors will remain who will be able to take care of themselves (see LDS edition of the King James Bible, Isaiah 7:21, note a).

17:22 ***abundance***—large supply

17:23 ***silverlings***—coins made of silver
***briers***—prickly weeds

17:25 ***mattock***—pick or hoe
***thither***—there
***lesser cattle***—sheep or goats

## CHAPTER 18

*Nephi quotes Isaiah 8. The king of Judah was afraid of his enemies, Israel (also called Samaria) and Syria (also called Damascus). Isaiah prophesies that the Lord will protect Judah. What does this chapter tell us about the power of the Lord and about why we should trust in Him?*

### Samaria and Damascus Will Be Conquered by Assyria

1 MOREOVER, the word of the Lord said unto me:
Take thee a great roll, and write in it with a man's
pen, concerning Maher-shalal-hash-baz.
2 And I took unto me faithful witnesses to record,
Uriah the priest, and Zechariah the son of
Jeberechiah.
3 And I went unto the prophetess; and she conceived and bare a son. Then said the Lord to me:
Call his name, Maher-shalal-hash-baz.
4 For behold, the child shall not have knowledge
to cry, My father, and my mother, before the riches
of Damascus and the spoil of Samaria shall be taken
away before the king of Assyria.
5 The Lord spake also unto me again, saying:
6 Forasmuch as this people refuseth the waters of
Shiloah that go softly, and rejoice in Rezin and
Remaliah's son;
7 Now therefore, behold, the Lord bringeth up
upon them the waters of the river, strong and many,
even the king of Assyria and all his glory; and he
shall come up over all his channels, and go over all
his banks.

### Assyria Will Attack Jerusalem, but God Will Save His People

8 And he shall pass through Judah; he shall overflow and go over, he shall reach even to the neck;
and the stretching out of his wings shall fill the
breadth of thy land, O Immanuel.
9 Associate yourselves, O ye people, and ye shall be
broken in pieces; and give ear all ye of far countries;
gird yourselves, and ye shall be broken in pieces;
gird yourselves, and ye shall be broken in pieces.

---

18:1 ***great roll***—large scroll

18:3 ***the prophetess***—my wife

18:4 (1–4) The Northern Kingdom, called Israel (Samaria), joined with Syria (Damascus) to attack the Southern Kingdom, called Judah. The Lord commanded Isaiah to name his newborn son *Maher-shalal-hash-baz,* which means "destruction comes quickly." This name was given as a prophecy that Israel and Syria would be attacked and defeated by Assyria (see verse 4).

18:6 ***Forasmuch as***—Since

The "waters of Shiloah" are the waters of a pool in the southern part of Jerusalem and anciently were the city's main water source. These waters "also represent the continuous tender care that the Lord provided for his people as he sought to lead them with gentle promptings of the Spirit. The Judean leaders rejected the Lord's advice offered through Isaiah, who foretold how . . . instead of gentle water around their knees, the raging torrent of the Assyrian army would gather around their necks (v. 8)" (Victor Ludlow, *Isaiah: Prophet, Seer, and Poet,* 148).

18:7 Ancient prophets used the image of rivers overflowing their banks to describe one nation sweeping over and conquering another (see Jeremiah 46:7–8). The "waters of the river" in this verse refer to the king of Assyria, who would attack and conquer Damascus (Syria) and Samaria (Israel).

*A modern view of the Pool of Siloam, the Greek name for Isaiah's "waters of Shiloah"*

PHOTOGRAPH BY G. R. SIMS

18:8 ***breadth***—width

18:9 ***Associate yourselves***—Join with other nations

10 Take counsel together, and it shall come to naught; speak the word, and it shall not stand; for God is with us.

11 For the Lord spake thus to me with a strong hand, and instructed me that I should not walk in the way of this people, saying:

12 Say ye not, A confederacy, to all to whom this people shall say, A confederacy; neither fear ye their fear, nor be afraid.

13 Sanctify the Lord of Hosts himself, and let him be your fear, and let him be your dread.

14 And he shall be for a sanctuary; but for a stone of stumbling, and for a rock of offense to both the houses of Israel, for a gin and a snare to the inhabitants of Jerusalem.

15 And many among them shall stumble and fall, and be broken, and be snared, and be taken.

16 Bind up the testimony, seal the law among my disciples.

17 And I will wait upon the Lord, that hideth his face from the house of Jacob, and I will look for him.

### Trust in the Lord and in the Scriptures for Guidance

18 Behold, I and the children whom the Lord hath given me are for signs and for wonders in Israel from the Lord of Hosts, which dwelleth in Mount Zion.

19 And when they shall say unto you: Seek unto them that have familiar spirits, and unto wizards that peep and mutter—should not a people seek unto their God for the living to hear from the dead?

20 To the law and to the testimony; and if they speak not according to this word, it is because there is no light in them.

21 And they shall pass through it hardly bestead and hungry; and it shall come to pass that when they shall be hungry, they shall fret themselves, and curse their king and their God, and look upward.

22 And they shall look unto the earth and behold trouble, and darkness, dimness of anguish, and shall be driven to darkness.

## CHAPTER 19

*Nephi quotes Isaiah 9. As in the previous two chapters, Isaiah warns about the military attacks coming upon Israel and Judah. Isaiah also prophesies of Jesus Christ's birth, His mortal mission, and His reign on the earth after the Second Coming. Look for all the names and titles in this chapter that refer to Jesus Christ.*

### Jesus Christ Will Bring Light into a Darkened World

1 NEVERTHELESS, the dimness shall not be such as was in her vexation, when at first he lightly afflicted the land of Zebulun, and the land of

---

18:10 (8–10) Isaiah prophesies that the king of Assyria will also overrun all the land of Judah "even to the neck," meaning to the gates of Jerusalem. The use of the name *Immanuel* (which means "God is with us") is Isaiah's way of saying that Assyria would be "broken in pieces" and that their attack on Jerusalem "shall not stand; for God is with us." The story of the fulfillment of this prophecy is found in 2 Kings 19.

18:11 ***a strong hand***—great power

18:12 This verse indicates that "Judah should not rely on secret plots with others for safety" (LDS edition of the King James Bible, Isaiah 8:12, note a).

18:13 ***Sanctify***—Praise as being holy

18:14 (13–14) The Savior will be a sanctuary (a safe place, a temple) to those who respect and reverence Him. He will be a stumbling block and a gin (trap) to the faithless because they do not walk in His ways (see also Mosiah 7:29).

18:18 Isaiah was commanded to give his two sons special names (see 2 Nephi 17:3; 18:3). Isaiah explains here that his name (which can be translated as "the Lord saves") and the names of his two sons were given as signs of what would happen to Judah and Israel (see 2 Nephi 18:1–4).

18:19 Israel was often warned against seeking advice from superstitious and Satan-inspired sources. These included sorcery and calling on the spirits of the dead (see Deuteronomy 18:9–12).

18:20 (19–20) Most people today realize it is foolish to believe in fortune-tellers of any sort, but many still trust other things more than God. Why are God and His revelations (the "law" and the "testimony") better sources of wisdom, guidance, and protection than the wisest men, the largest fortunes, or the strongest armies?

18:21 ***hardly bestead***—troubled or distressed
***fret themselves***—make themselves angry

19:1 ***vexation***—trouble
***afflicted***—caused suffering to

Naphtali, and afterwards did more grievously afflict
by the way of the Red Sea beyond Jordan in Galilee
of the nations.
2 The people that walked in darkness have seen
a great light; they that dwell in the land of the shadow of death, upon them hath the light shined.
3 Thou hast multiplied the nation, and increased
the joy—they joy before thee according to the joy
in harvest, and as men rejoice when they divide the
spoil.
4 For thou hast broken the yoke of his burden,
and the staff of his shoulder, the rod of his oppressor.
5 For every battle of the warrior is with confused
noise, and garments rolled in blood; but this shall
be with burning and fuel of fire.
6 For unto us a child is born, unto us a son is
given; and the government shall be upon his shoulder; and his name shall be called, Wonderful,
Counselor, The Mighty God, The Everlasting Father,
The Prince of Peace.
7 Of the increase of government and peace there
is no end, upon the throne of David, and upon his
kingdom to order it, and to establish it with judgment and with justice from henceforth, even forever. The zeal of the Lord of Hosts will perform
this.

## The Lord's Anger Is Against Israel

8 The Lord sent his word unto Jacob and it hath
lighted upon Israel.
9 And all the people shall know, even Ephraim
and the inhabitants of Samaria, that say in the pride
and stoutness of heart:

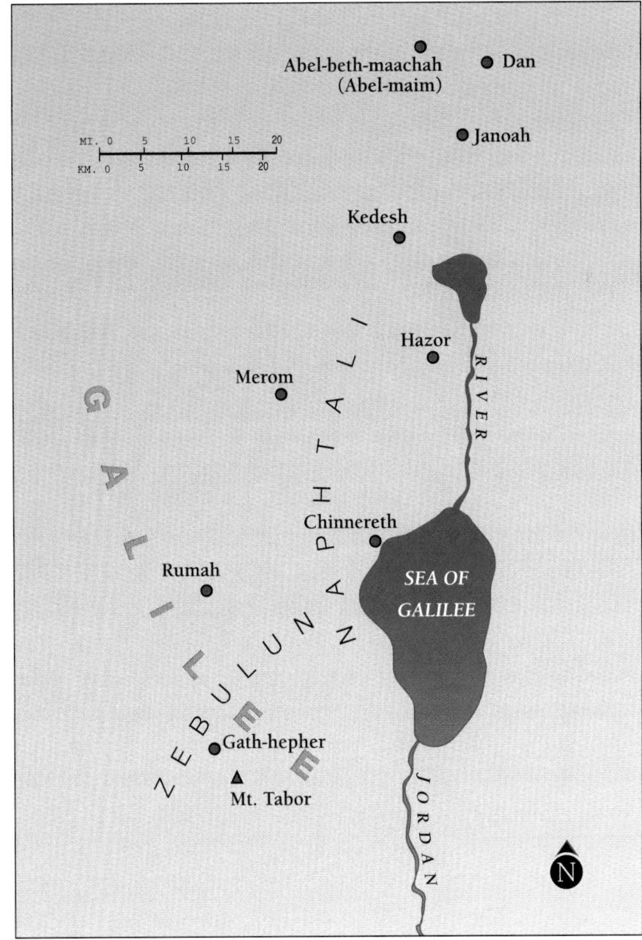


*The lands of Zebulun and Naphtali are in Galilee, where Jesus lived much of His youth.*

19:1 ***grievously***—seriously

19:2 Why do you think Christ is referred to as a "great light"? (see Mosiah 16:9; Alma 38:9; 3 Nephi 18:16). How is He a light for you?

19:3 Nephi quotes this verse of Isaiah differently from the way it currently reads in our King James Version of the Bible. In the Bible the first part of the verse reads, "Thou hast multiplied the nation, and not increased the joy," but Nephi excludes the word *not*. The version that Nephi is quoting makes the verse clearer, showing that Jesus Christ will bring gladness and joy to the nation.

19:4 A yoke, a staff, and a rod were tools used in Isaiah's day to control animals or slaves to put them in bondage. Isaiah uses these symbols to show how Jesus Christ breaks the bondage of sin and gives His followers spiritual freedom.

19:5 Isaiah speaks of war items being burned. When the Second Coming of Jesus Christ takes place, all corruptible, or perishable, things will be burned (see D&C 64:23–24; 101:24–25).

19:6 Why do you think Jesus Christ has each of these titles? What does each title teach you about the Savior?

19:7 ***zeal***—enthusiasm

19:7 (1–7) "The 'dimness' and 'darkness' were apostasy and captivity (Isa. 8:20–22); the 'great light' is Christ (Isa. 9:6–7)" (LDS edition of the King James Bible, Isaiah 9:2, note a).

19:8 ***hath lighted***—has come

19:9 ***stoutness***—boldness

10 The bricks are fallen down, but we will build with hewn stones; the sycamores are cut down, but we will change them into cedars.

11 Therefore the Lord shall set up the adversaries of Rezin against him, and join his enemies together;

12 The Syrians before and the Philistines behind; and they shall devour Israel with open mouth. For all this his anger is not turned away, but his hand is stretched out still.

13 For the people turneth not unto him that smiteth them, neither do they seek the Lord of Hosts.

14 Therefore will the Lord cut off from Israel head and tail, branch and rush in one day.

15 The ancient, he is the head; and the prophet that teacheth lies, he is the tail.

16 For the leaders of this people cause them to err; and they that are led of them are destroyed.

17 Therefore the Lord shall have no joy in their young men, neither shall have mercy on their fatherless and widows; for every one of them is a hypocrite and an evildoer, and every mouth speaketh folly. For all this his anger is not turned away, but his hand is stretched out still.

18 For wickedness burneth as the fire; it shall devour the briers and thorns, and shall kindle in the thickets of the forests, and they shall mount up like the lifting up of smoke.

19 Through the wrath of the Lord of Hosts is the land darkened, and the people shall be as the fuel of the fire; no man shall spare his brother.

20 And he shall snatch on the right hand and be hungry; and he shall eat on the left hand and they shall not be satisfied; they shall eat every man the flesh of his own arm—

21 Manasseh, Ephraim; and Ephraim, Manasseh; they together shall be against Judah. For all this his anger is not turned away, but his hand is stretched out still.

## CHAPTER 20

*Nephi quotes Isaiah 10. Isaiah describes how the Assyrians will attack Israel and Judah but will eventually be destroyed themselves. The destruction of wicked people described in this chapter follows the pattern of what will happen to the wicked at the Second Coming. Look for the similarities between what happened anciently and what will happen in the last days.*

### *The Children of Israel Become Very Wicked, and the Lord Will Not Protect Them*

1 WO unto them that decree unrighteous decrees, and that write grievousness which they have prescribed;

2 To turn away the needy from judgment, and to take away the right from the poor of my people, that widows may be their prey, and that they may rob the fatherless!

---

19:10 ***hewn***—cut

19:11 ***adversaries***—enemies

19:12 ***devour***—eat up

The phrase "his hand is stretched out still" can be understood in at least two ways: (1) The punishment of the Lord is still forthcoming if His people don't repent, and (2) "in spite of all, the Lord is available if they will turn to him" (LDS edition of the King James Bible, Isaiah 9:12, note d).

19:12 (11–12) Some of Israel's greatest enemies were the Syrians and Philistines. History tells us that Israel had to suffer at the hands of both (see also verses 17–21).

19:13 ***turneth not unto him that smiteth them***—do not repent and obey the Lord

19:16 ***err***—make mistakes

19:17 ***a hypocrite***—one who pretends to be good but is not
***speaketh folly***—talks of foolish or sinful things

19:18 ***briers***—prickly weeds
***thickets***—thick bushes

19:19 ***wrath***—anger

19:19 (18–19) "Isaiah describes the wicked as undesirable plants, such as briers, thorns, and thickets. . . . He also says that the judgements for wickedness are like a fire that devours the briers, thorns, and thickets" (Donald W. Parry and others, *Understanding Isaiah,* 101).

19:20 ***snatch***—grasp

20:1 ***Wo***—Grief, sorrow, and misery
***decree unrighteous decrees***—make unjust laws
***write grievousness which they have prescribed***—make laws that cause hardship

20:2 ***their prey***—the ones they hurt

3 And what will ye do in the day of visitation, and in the desolation which shall come from far? to whom will ye flee for help? and where will ye leave your glory?

4 Without me they shall bow down under the prisoners, and they shall fall under the slain. For all this his anger is not turned away, but his hand is stretched out still.

### The Lord Uses the Assyrians to Punish Israel

5 O Assyrian, the rod of mine anger, and the staff in their hand is their indignation.

6 I will send him against a hypocritical nation, and against the people of my wrath will I give him a charge to take the spoil, and to take the prey, and to tread them down like the mire of the streets.

### Assyria Thinks It Is Stronger Than Any Other Nation

7 Howbeit he meaneth not so, neither doth his heart think so; but in his heart it is to destroy and cut off nations not a few.

8 For he saith: Are not my princes altogether kings?

9 Is not Calno as Carchemish? Is not Hamath as Arpad? Is not Samaria as Damascus?

10 As my hand hath founded the kingdoms of the idols, and whose graven images did excel them of Jerusalem and of Samaria;

11 Shall I not, as I have done unto Samaria and her idols, so do to Jerusalem and to her idols?

### The Lord Will Humble Assyria in One Day

12 Wherefore it shall come to pass that when the Lord hath performed his whole work upon Mount Zion and upon Jerusalem, I will punish the fruit of the stout heart of the king of Assyria, and the glory of his high looks.

13 For he saith: By the strength of my hand and by my wisdom I have done these things; for I am prudent; and I have moved the borders of the people, and have robbed their treasures, and I have put down the inhabitants like a valiant man;

14 And my hand hath found as a nest the riches of the people; and as one gathereth eggs that are left have I gathered all the earth; and there was none that moved the wing, or opened the mouth, or peeped.

15 Shall the ax boast itself against him that heweth therewith? Shall the saw magnify itself against him that shaketh it? As if the rod should shake itself against them that lift it up, or as if the staff should lift up itself as if it were no wood!

16 Therefore shall the Lord, the Lord of Hosts, send among his fat ones, leanness; and under his glory he shall kindle a burning like the burning of a fire.

17 And the light of Israel shall be for a fire, and his Holy One for a flame, and shall burn and shall devour his thorns and his briers in one day;

18 And shall consume the glory of his forest, and of his fruitful field, both soul and body; and they shall be as when a standard-bearer fainteth.

19 And the rest of the trees of his forest shall be few, that a child may write them.

---

20:3 ***desolation***—ruin or destruction

20:5 ***indignation***—anger

20:6 ***a hypocritical nation***—a nation that says it is good when it is actually evil
***wrath***—anger
***charge***—command
***spoil***—valuable belongings

20:10 ***graven images***—false gods
***did excel***—were greater than

20:11 The Assyrians conquered the Northern Kingdom of Israel, whose capital city was Samaria, in about 722 B.C. (see 2 Kings 17).

20:12 ***performed***—finished
***the fruit of the stout***—the accomplishments of the strong

20:13 ***prudent***—wise
***valiant***—brave

20:16 ***send among his fat ones, leanness***—cause the healthy Assyrian troops who have much to be left with little

20:17 ***devour***—eat up

20:18 ***consume***—burn up
***a standard-bearer fainteth***—one who holds the flag falls

20:19 (15–19) The Assyrians thought they had been able to defeat and capture the ten tribes of Israel with their own strength. But as an ax or a saw works only when someone uses it, the Assyrians were able to attack the children of Israel only because God was using them to humble Israel. In time, God would allow another nation to destroy the Assyrians.

## The Remnant of Israel Will Return to the Lord and Be Saved

20 And it shall come to pass in that day, that the remnant of Israel, and such as are escaped of the house of Jacob, shall no more again stay upon him that smote them, but shall stay upon the Lord, the Holy One of Israel, in truth.

21 The remnant shall return, yea, even the remnant of Jacob, unto the mighty God.

22 For though thy people Israel be as the sand of the sea, yet a remnant of them shall return; the consumption decreed shall overflow with righteousness.

23 For the Lord God of Hosts shall make a consumption, even determined in all the land.

24 Therefore, thus saith the Lord God of Hosts: O my people that dwellest in Zion, be not afraid of the Assyrian; he shall smite thee with a rod, and shall lift up his staff against thee, after the manner of Egypt.

25 For yet a very little while, and the indignation shall cease, and mine anger in their destruction.

26 And the Lord of Hosts shall stir up a scourge for him according to the slaughter of Midian at the rock of Oreb; and as his rod was upon the sea so shall he lift it up after the manner of Egypt.

27 And it shall come to pass in that day that his burden shall be taken away from off thy shoulder, and his yoke from off thy neck, and the yoke shall be destroyed because of the anointing.

## The Assyrians Will Come into the Land of Israel

28 He is come to Aiath, he is passed to Migron; at Michmash he hath laid up his carriages.

29 They are gone over the passage; they have taken up their lodging at Geba; Ramath is afraid; Gibeah of Saul is fled.

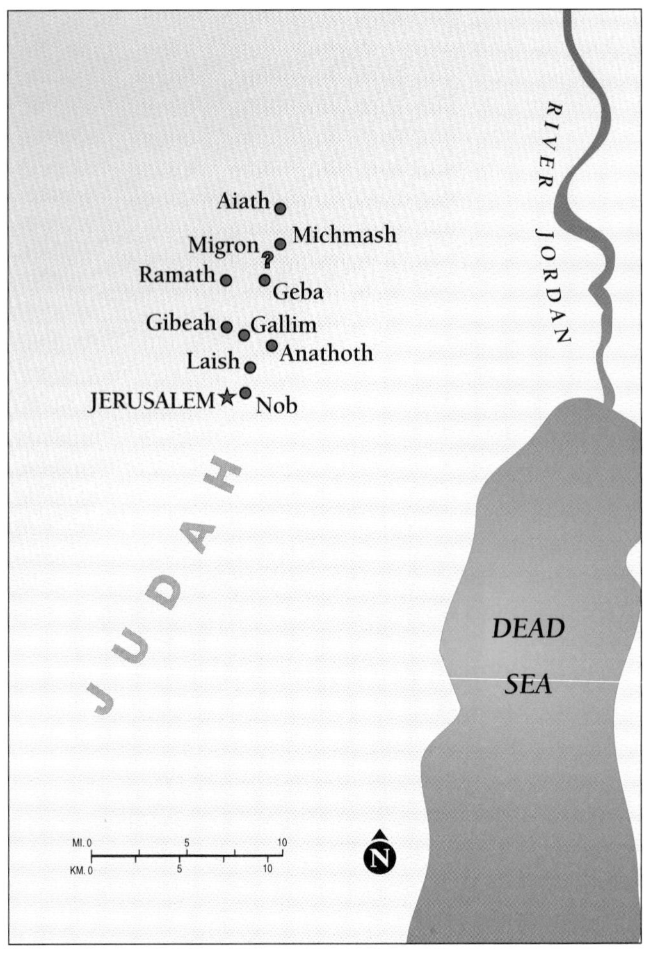


*The Assyrian forces approach and threaten Jerusalem but are defeated by the Lord of Hosts.*

30 Lift up the voice, O daughter of Gallim; cause it to be heard unto Laish, O poor Anathoth.

31 Madmenah is removed; the inhabitants of Gebim gather themselves to flee.

32 As yet shall he remain at Nob that day; he shall shake his hand against the mount of the daughter of Zion, the hill of Jerusalem.

---

20:20 ***the remnant***—those who are left
***stay***—depend

20:22 ***consumption decreed***—destruction that is ordered

20:25 ***indignation***—anger

20:26 ***scourge***—punishment

20:27 "The burden of oppression laid upon the shoulders of the Lord's people by those who oppose His work shall be removed because of the 'anointing' (divine intervention of the Messiah, even Jesus Christ)" (Hoyt Brewster, *Isaiah Plain & Simple,* 105).

20:32 (28–32) The cities mentioned in these verses are those that the Assyrian army would move through on its way to Jerusalem (see LDS edition of the King James Bible, Isaiah 10:28, note a).

### The Assyrians Will Be Cut Down

33 Behold, the Lord, the Lord of Hosts shall lop the bough with terror; and the high ones of stature shall be hewn down; and the haughty shall be humbled.
34 And he shall cut down the thickets of the forests with iron, and Lebanon shall fall by a mighty one.

## CHAPTER 21

*Nephi quotes Isaiah 11. In 1823, Joseph Smith learned from the angel Moroni that these prophecies were about to be fulfilled (see Joseph Smith—History 1:40). Watch for ways that you could help fulfill the words of Isaiah.*

### The Stem of Jesse (Jesus Christ) Judges in Righteousness

1 AND there shall come forth a rod out of the stem of Jesse, and a branch shall grow out of his roots.
2 And the Spirit of the Lord shall rest upon him, the spirit of wisdom and understanding, the spirit of counsel and might, the spirit of knowledge and of the fear of the Lord;
3 And shall make him of quick understanding in the fear of the Lord; and he shall not judge after the sight of his eyes, neither reprove after the hearing of his ears.
4 But with righteousness shall he judge the poor, and reprove with equity for the meek of the earth; and he shall smite the earth with the rod of his mouth, and with the breath of his lips shall he slay the wicked.
5 And righteousness shall be the girdle of his loins, and faithfulness the girdle of his reins.

### The Glorious Conditions of the Millennium Are Prophesied

6 The wolf also shall dwell with the lamb, and the leopard shall lie down with the kid, and the calf and the young lion and fatling together; and a little child shall lead them.
7 And the cow and the bear shall feed; their young ones shall lie down together; and the lion shall eat straw like the ox.
8 And the sucking child shall play on the hole of the asp, and the weaned child shall put his hand on the cockatrice's den.
9 They shall not hurt nor destroy in all my holy mountain, for the earth shall be full of the knowledge of the Lord, as the waters cover the sea.

---

20:33 ***lop the bough***—cut off the branches
***stature***—size
***hewn***—cut
***haughty***—proud

20:34 (33–34) In these verses, symbolic language is used to depict the Lord's actions against the enemies of Judah (see LDS edition of the King James Bible, Isaiah 10:28, note a).

21:1 ***rod***—shoot or sprout
***stem***—main shoot or trunk

Jesse was the father of King David and the ancestor of all the kings of Judah and also of Jesus Christ (see Ruth 4:17, 22).

As recorded in D&C 113:1–6, the Prophet Joseph Smith received inspired explanations of parts of Isaiah 11. For example, this scripture clearly identifies the "stem of Jesse" as Jesus Christ (see D&C 113:1–2). In addition, Elder Bruce R. McConkie explained that the "branch" spoken of in Isaiah 11:1 (or 2 Nephi 21:1) is Jesus Christ (see *The Promised Messiah,* 192).

21:3 ***reprove***—correct

21:4 ***equity***—fairness or justice

21:5 A "girdle" is a belt or sash that wraps around the waist. The "loins" and "reins" stand for a man's moral character. Thus this "stem" or "branch" (both referring to Jesus Christ) will be completely wrapped in righteousness and faithfulness.

21:6 ***fatling***—young fatted animal (such as a lamb)

21:8 ***sucking***—nursing or young
***asp***—poisonous snake
***weaned child***—toddler or a baby no longer nursing
***cockatrice's***—poisonous snake's

### *Israel and the Gentiles Shall Gather to the Lord's Ensign*

10 And in that day there shall be a root of Jesse, which shall stand for an ensign of the people; to it shall the Gentiles seek; and his rest shall be glorious.

11 And it shall come to pass in that day that the Lord shall set his hand again the second time to recover the remnant of his people which shall be left, from Assyria, and from Egypt, and from Pathros, and from Cush, and from Elam, and from Shinar, and from Hamath, and from the islands of the sea.

12 And he shall set up an ensign for the nations, and shall assemble the outcasts of Israel, and gather together the dispersed of Judah from the four corners of the earth.

13 The envy of Ephraim also shall depart, and the adversaries of Judah shall be cut off; Ephraim shall not envy Judah, and Judah shall not vex Ephraim.

14 But they shall fly upon the shoulders of the Philistines towards the west; they shall spoil them of the east together; they shall lay their hand upon Edom and Moab; and the children of Ammon shall obey them.

15 And the Lord shall utterly destroy the tongue of the Egyptian sea; and with his mighty wind he shall shake his hand over the river, and shall smite it in the seven streams, and make men go over dry shod.

16 And there shall be a highway for the remnant of his people which shall be left, from Assyria, like as it was to Israel in the day that he came up out of the land of Egypt.

## CHAPTER 22

*Nephi quotes Isaiah 12. During the Millennium all people will praise the Lord. Look for reasons why people will be so grateful for the Lord.*

### *In the Millennium All People Will Praise the Lord*

1 AND in that day thou shalt say: O Lord, I will praise thee; though thou wast angry with me thine anger is turned away, and thou comfortedest me.

2 Behold, God is my salvation; I will trust, and not be afraid; for the Lord JEHOVAH is my strength and my song; he also has become my salvation.

3 Therefore, with joy shall ye draw water out of the wells of salvation.

---

21:10 An ensign is a flag or banner mounted on a pole to be seen from great distances. It served in ancient times as a rallying point for soldiers in battle. Thus, an ensign is any object, person, or idea toward which people gather (see Isaiah 5:26).

The root of Jesse spoken of in this verse "is a descendant of Jesse, as well as of Joseph, unto whom rightly belongs the priesthood, and the keys of the kingdom, for an ensign, and for the gathering of my people in the last days" (D&C 113:6).

21:12 Elder Joseph Fielding Smith explained: "Over 125 years ago . . . the Lord set up an ensign to the nations. It was in fulfillment of the prediction made by the Prophet Isaiah. . . . That ensign was the Church of Jesus Christ of Latter-day Saints" *(Doctrines of Salvation* 3:254–55; see also D&C 45:9).

***dispersed***—scattered

21:13 ***adversaries***—enemies
***envy***—jealousy
***vex***—trouble or afflict

21:14 ***spoil***—rob

21:15 ***dry shod***—without getting their shoes or sandals wet

21:16 In another place Isaiah says that the "highway" the people will travel on when they gather to Zion is not an ordinary road. He calls it "The way of holiness," and only the righteous can travel on it (see Isaiah 35:8–10).

22:1 "In that day" means in the Millennium (see LDS edition of the King James Bible, Isaiah 12:1, note b; chapter introduction for Isaiah 11). The Millennium refers to the thousand years of peace and righteousness on the earth following the Second Coming of Jesus Christ.

22:2 *Jehovah* is the sacred name of the God of Israel and means "the *Self-existent One,* or *The Eternal*" (James E. Talmage, *Jesus the Christ,* 36). "Jesus Christ was and is Jehovah, the God of Adam and of Noah, the God of Abraham, Isaac, and Jacob, the God of Israel" (Talmage, *Jesus the Christ,* 4).

22:3 In John 4 the Savior tells a woman at a well that He has living water. Any person who drinks this "water," meaning any person who lives His teachings, will have salvation, or everlasting life (see John 4:10–14).

4 And in that day shall ye say: Praise the Lord, call upon his name, declare his doings among the people, make mention that his name is exalted.
5 Sing unto the Lord; for he hath done excellent things; this is known in all the earth.
6 Cry out and shout, thou inhabitant of Zion; for great is the Holy One of Israel in the midst of thee.

## CHAPTER 23

*Nephi quotes Isaiah 13. This chapter warns of the destruction of Babylon, which was not only an ancient empire but also a symbol of wickedness in the world. Notice what the Lord says will happen to those who break the commandments.*

### *Isaiah Foresees the Fall of the Wicked*

1 THE burden of Babylon, which Isaiah the son of Amoz did see.
2 Lift ye up a banner upon the high mountain, exalt the voice unto them, shake the hand, that they may go into the gates of the nobles.
3 I have commanded my sanctified ones, I have also called my mighty ones, for mine anger is not upon them that rejoice in my highness.
4 The noise of the multitude in the mountains like as of a great people, a tumultuous noise of the kingdoms of nations gathered together, the Lord of Hosts mustereth the hosts of the battle.
5 They come from a far country, from the end of heaven, yea, the Lord, and the weapons of his indignation, to destroy the whole land.
6 Howl ye, for the day of the Lord is at hand; it shall come as a destruction from the Almighty.
7 Therefore shall all hands be faint, every man's heart shall melt;
8 And they shall be afraid; pangs and sorrows shall take hold of them; they shall be amazed one at another; their faces shall be as flames.

### *The Lord Explains His Purpose in Punishing the Wicked*

9 Behold, the day of the Lord cometh, cruel both with wrath and fierce anger, to lay the land desolate; and he shall destroy the sinners thereof out of it.
10 For the stars of heaven and the constellations thereof shall not give their light; the sun shall be darkened in his going forth, and the moon shall not cause her light to shine.
11 And I will punish the world for evil, and the wicked for their iniquity; I will cause the arrogancy of the proud to cease, and will lay down the haughtiness of the terrible.

---

22:6 Why do you think the Millennium will be a time of peace and rejoicing? What can you do now to prepare to live with the Savior?

23:1 ***burden of Babylon***—message of doom from the Lord to Babylon

The destruction of the wicked city Babylon, prophesied in this chapter, is symbolic of the final destruction of the whole wicked world (see LDS edition of the King James Bible, Isaiah 13:1, note c; see also D&C 133:5, 7, 14).

23:2 ***banner***—battle flag
***exalt the voice***—shout
***shake the hand***—wave the hand or give a signal

23:5 ***indignation***—anger

23:5 (2–5) In these verses Isaiah sees the Lord calling the righteous and the hosts of heaven to battle against Babylon, meaning the wicked world. How can you become spiritually ready for the battle against evil?

23:6 The phrase "day of the Lord" refers to the day in which the Savior shall return, a day of great "destruction from the Almighty." It will be a day when He will punish the wicked (see *Book of Mormon Student Manual, Religion 121 and 122,* 95).

23:7 ***man's heart shall melt***—man will lose his courage

23:8 ***pangs***—pains

The phrase that "their faces shall be as flames" could mean "that the faces of sinners will burn with shame or be inflamed because of weeping" (Hoyt Brewster, *Isaiah Plain & Simple,* 128).

23:9 ***desolate***—empty

23:10 In latter-day revelation the Lord says that similar signs shall begin "not many days hence" (D&C 88:87).

23:11 ***terrible***—cruel and ruthless

12 I will make a man more precious than fine gold; even a man than the golden wedge of Ophir.
13 Therefore, I will shake the heavens, and the earth shall remove out of her place, in the wrath of the Lord of Hosts, and in the day of his fierce anger.

### Isaiah Describes What Will Happen to the Land and People During the Great Destruction

14 And it shall be as the chased roe, and as a sheep that no man taketh up; and they shall every man turn to his own people, and flee every one into his own land.
15 Every one that is proud shall be thrust through; yea, and every one that is joined to the wicked shall fall by the sword.
16 Their children also shall be dashed to pieces before their eyes; their houses shall be spoiled and their wives ravished.
17 Behold, I will stir up the Medes against them, which shall not regard silver and gold, nor shall they delight in it.
18 Their bows shall also dash the young men to pieces; and they shall have no pity on the fruit of the womb; their eyes shall not spare children.
19 And Babylon, the glory of kingdoms, the beauty of the Chaldees' excellency, shall be as when God overthrew Sodom and Gomorrah.
20 It shall never be inhabited, neither shall it be dwelt in from generation to generation: neither shall the Arabian pitch tent there; neither shall the shepherds make their fold there.
21 But wild beasts of the desert shall lie there; and their houses shall be full of doleful creatures; and owls shall dwell there, and satyrs shall dance there.
22 And the wild beasts of the islands shall cry in their desolate houses, and dragons in their pleasant palaces; and her time is near to come, and her day shall not be prolonged. For I will destroy her speedily; yea, for I will be merciful unto my people, but the wicked shall perish.

## CHAPTER 24

*Nephi quotes Isaiah 14. Isaiah prophesies that during the millennial reign the house of Israel will rest from its trials suffered at the hands of wicked nations. As you read, notice how God has power over the nations and will destroy the wicked to bring peace to the earth.*

### The Lord Will Gather the House of Israel and It Will Enjoy Peace During the Millennium

1 FOR the Lord will have mercy on Jacob, and will yet choose Israel, and set them in their own land; and the strangers shall be joined with them, and they shall cleave to the house of Jacob.

---

23:12 ***precious***—rare or valuable

The gold of Ophir was the finest gold of Isaiah's time. The prophet may be telling us that those who survive the destruction will be scarce and pure like the finest gold.

23:14 ***chased roe***—hunted deer

23:16 ***dashed to pieces***—killed

23:17 The Medes were an ancient nation that destroyed Babylon in 538 B.C. (see LDS Bible Dictionary, s.v. "Persia," 749).

23:18 ***fruit of the womb***—children
***their eyes shall not spare***—they will kill

23:21 ***doleful creatures***—jackals
***satyrs***—wild he-goats

23:22 ***dragons***—wild dogs or jackals

Notice that in this day of destruction the Lord promises to "be merciful unto [His] people." What can you do to always be one of His people?

23:22 (19–22) Babylon was the richest and most powerful nation of Isaiah's time. The Lord warned that He would destroy them as He did Sodom and Gomorrah in the Old Testament (see Genesis 19:12–25). The Lord cursed the ancient capital city of Babylon so that no one could live there.

24:1 ***strangers***—foreigners
***cleave to***—become one with or be faithful to

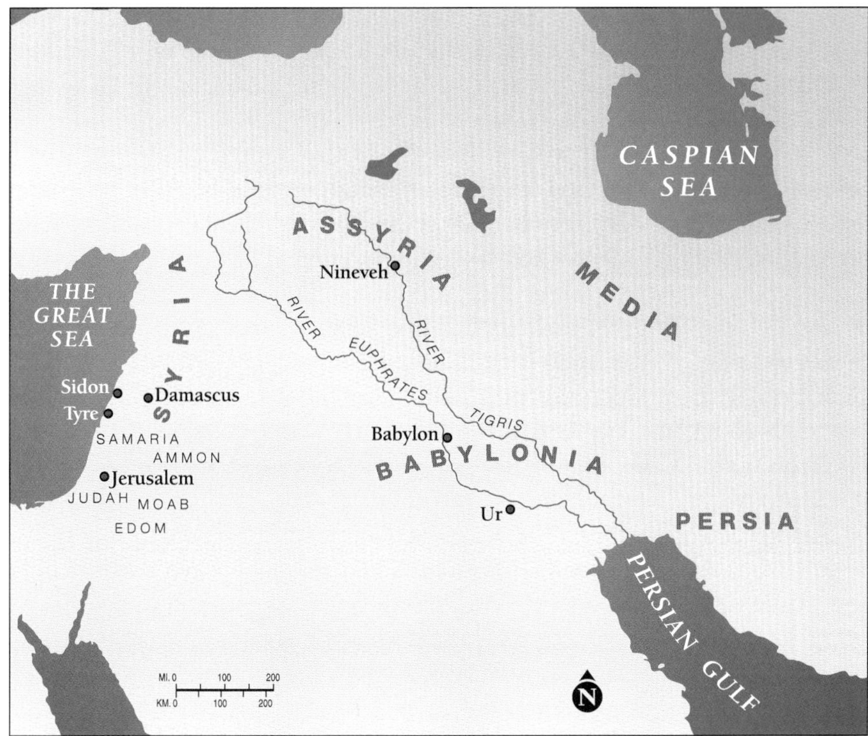


*The ancient Near East showing the Assyrian, Babylonian, and Persian Empires and their capitals.*

2 And the people shall take them and bring them
to their place; yea, from far unto the ends of the
earth; and they shall return to their lands of promise. And the house of Israel shall possess them, and the land of the Lord shall be for servants and handmaids; and they shall take them captives unto whom they were captives; and they shall rule over their oppressors.
3 And it shall come to pass in that day that the
Lord shall give thee rest, from thy sorrow, and from thy fear, and from the hard bondage wherein thou wast made to serve.

## Isaiah Prophesies the Fall of Lucifer and His Kingdom

4 And it shall come to pass in that day, that thou
shalt take up this proverb against the king of Babylon, and say: How hath the oppressor ceased, the golden city ceased!

---

24:2 ***the people***—other nations
***handmaids***—female servants
***their oppressors***—those who had ruled over them

24:3 (1–3) Victor Ludlow noted: "Historically, these verses were fulfilled when Cyrus the Great of Persia issued an order permitting all captive peoples in Babylon to return to their place of origin." These verses also refer to the gathering of Israel before and during the Millennium (see Victor Ludlow, *Isaiah: Prophet, Seer, and Poet,* 186).

24:4 ***proverb***—wise saying

The Book of Mormon includes the important phrase, "And it shall come to pass in that day." This phrase is not included in the same verse of the King James Version of Isaiah, suggesting that the Book of Mormon is applying Isaiah's prophecy to the last days.

*Babylon, known as the golden city, was used by Isaiah to represent the world.*

5 The Lord hath broken the staff of the wicked, the scepters of the rulers.

6 He who smote the people in wrath with a continual stroke, he that ruled the nations in anger, is persecuted, and none hindereth.

7 The whole earth is at rest, and is quiet; they break forth into singing.

8 Yea, the fir-trees rejoice at thee, and also the cedars of Lebanon, saying: Since thou art laid down no feller is come up against us.

9 Hell from beneath is moved for thee to meet thee at thy coming; it stirreth up the dead for thee, even all the chief ones of the earth; it hath raised up from their thrones all the kings of the nations.

10 All they shall speak and say unto thee: Art thou also become weak as we? Art thou become like unto us?

11 Thy pomp is brought down to the grave; the noise of thy viols is not heard; the worm is spread under thee, and the worms cover thee.

## Isaiah Compares the Fall of the King of Babylon to Lucifer's Fall from Heaven

12 How art thou fallen from heaven, O Lucifer, son of the morning! Art thou cut down to the ground, which did weaken the nations!

13 For thou hast said in thy heart: I will ascend into heaven, I will exalt my throne above the stars of God; I will sit also upon the mount of the congregation, in the sides of the north;

14 I will ascend above the heights of the clouds; I will be like the Most High.

15 Yet thou shalt be brought down to hell, to the sides of the pit.

16 They that see thee shall narrowly look upon thee, and shall consider thee, and shall say: Is this the man that made the earth to tremble, that did shake kingdoms?

17 And made the world as a wilderness, and destroyed the cities thereof, and opened not the house of his prisoners?

18 All the kings of the nations, yea, all of them, lie in glory, every one of them in his own house.

19 But thou art cast out of thy grave like an abominable branch, and the remnant of those that are slain, thrust through with a sword, that go down to the stones of the pit; as a carcass trodden under feet.

20 Thou shalt not be joined with them in burial, because thou hast destroyed thy land and slain thy people; the seed of evil-doers shall never be renowned.

21 Prepare slaughter for his children for the

---

24:5 The terms *staff* and *scepter* are used to symbolize the Babylonian's authority, which the Lord will destroy.

24:6 ***smote the people in wrath***—conquered the people in a furious rage
***a continual stroke***—unceasing blows
***hindereth***—stop it

24:8 ***feller***—woodsman

24:8 (4–8) Isaiah prophesies the fall of the king of Babylon. For Isaiah, the day was still in the distant future when Babylon would defeat the house of Israel in and around Jerusalem and carry them away captive. But, as Isaiah notes, Babylon would thereafter be conquered and destroyed by Cyrus and become part of the Persian empire (see LDS Bible Dictionary, s.v. "Assyria and Babylonia," 615–16). The people of the earth will "rest" and "rejoice" at the spiritual fall of Babylon.

24:9 The word *hell* in this verse may refer to the place of departed spirits; in particular, spirit prison where the wicked spirits dwell. "The inhabitants (prisoners) of hell are stirred or excited about the arrival of this once-powerful person" (Hoyt Brewster, *Isaiah Plain & Simple,* 139).

24:11 ***pomp***—glory
***viols***—stringed instruments

24:12 ***Lucifer***—Satan

24:14 (13–14) Lucifer selfishly wanted the throne of God for himself. The Lord said, "Satan rebelled against me, and sought to destroy the agency of man, which I, the Lord God, had given him, and also, that I should give unto him mine own power; by the power of mine Only Begotten, I caused that he should be cast down; and he became Satan" (Moses 4:3–4).

24:15 (12–15) The fall of the king of Babylon is compared to the fall of Lucifer. When the king of Babylon fell, the children of God on earth rejoiced; but when Lucifer, "a son of the morning," fell, the "heavens wept over him" (D&C 76:26).

24:16 ***narrowly look upon thee***—squint or stare at you

24:19 ***an abominable branch***—a rejected branch
***carcass trodden***—dead body trampled

24:20 ***seed***—children or posterity
***renowned***—famous or honored

iniquities of their fathers, that they do not rise, nor possess the land, nor fill the face of the world with cities.
22 For I will rise up against them, saith the Lord
of Hosts, and cut off from Babylon the name, and remnant, and son, and nephew, saith the Lord.
23 I will also make it a possession for the bittern,
and pools of water; and I will sweep it with the besom of destruction, saith the Lord of Hosts.

## God Controls the Destiny of Nations

24 The Lord of Hosts hath sworn, saying: Surely as
I have thought, so shall it come to pass; and as I have purposed, so shall it stand—
25 That I will bring the Assyrian in my land, and
upon my mountains tread him under foot; then shall his yoke depart from off them, and his burden depart from off their shoulders.
26 This is the purpose that is purposed upon the
whole earth; and this is the hand that is stretched out upon all nations.
27 For the Lord of Hosts hath purposed, and who
shall disannul? And his hand is stretched out, and who shall turn it back?
28 In the year that king Ahaz died was this bur-
den.
29 Rejoice not thou, whole Palestina, because the
rod of him that smote thee is broken; for out of the serpent's root shall come forth a cockatrice, and his fruit shall be a fiery flying serpent.
30 And the first-born of the poor shall feed, and
the needy shall lie down in safety; and I will kill thy root with famine, and he shall slay thy remnant.
31 Howl, O gate; cry, O city; thou, whole Pales-
tina, art dissolved; for there shall come from the north a smoke, and none shall be alone in his appointed times.
32 What shall then answer the messengers of the
nations? That the Lord hath founded Zion, and the poor of his people shall trust in it.

# CHAPTER 25

*Nephi explains why he loves Isaiah's teachings. Nephi's words, like Isaiah's, teach of the Savior. Notice the many ways Nephi teaches of Christ.*

## Nephi Teaches How to Understand Isaiah

1 NOW I, Nephi, do speak somewhat concerning
the words which I have written, which have been spoken by the mouth of Isaiah. For behold, Isaiah spake many things which were hard for many of my people to understand; for they know not concerning the manner of prophesying among the Jews.
2 For I, Nephi, have not taught them many things
concerning the manner of the Jews; for their works were works of darkness, and their doings were doings of abominations.
3 Wherefore, I write unto my people, unto all
those that shall receive hereafter these things which I write, that they may know the judgments of God, that they come upon all nations, according to the word which he hath spoken.
4 Wherefore, hearken, O my people, which are of
the house of Israel, and give ear unto my words; for

---

24:23 **bittern**—wild bird or animal
**besom**—broom

24:23 (21–23) In other words, the Lord will not allow another relative of this king to arise and continue his wickedness (see LDS edition of the King James Bible, Isaiah 14:21, note a).

24:24 **sworn**—promised

24:27 **disannul**—cancel or change His plan

24:29 Palestina was also known as Philistia and was conquered by the Assyrians along with Israel in about 722 B.C. See the map on p. 120. A cockatrice is a poisonous snake (see LDS Bible Dictionary, s.v. "Cockatrice," 647).

**fruit**—offspring

24:32 In the midst of the destruction of nations, the Lord will take care of His faithful poor and needy in Zion. Zion is where the Lord's people dwell with "one heart and one mind" having "no poor among them" (Moses 7:18).

25:1 Isaiah's words are hard for many to understand. We will better understand Isaiah if we learn how his prophecies are written and have the Holy Ghost to help us (see verse 4).

**manner**—way or method

25:2 **abominations**—great wickedness

25:4 The book of Revelation teaches that a testimony of Jesus is the spirit of prophecy (see Revelation 19:10). The spirit of prophecy makes Isaiah's words more plain to the understanding.

because the words of Isaiah are not plain unto you, nevertheless they are plain unto all those that are filled with the spirit of prophecy. But I give unto you a prophecy, according to the spirit which is in me; wherefore I shall prophesy according to the plainness which hath been with me from the time that I came out from Jerusalem with my father; for behold, my soul delighteth in plainness unto my people, that they may learn.
5 Yea, and my soul delighteth in the words of Isaiah, for I came out from Jerusalem, and mine eyes hath beheld the things of the Jews, and I know that the Jews do understand the things of the prophets, and there is none other people that understand the things which were spoken unto the Jews like unto them, save it be that they are taught after the manner of the things of the Jews.
6 But behold, I, Nephi, have not taught my children after the manner of the Jews; but behold, I, of myself, have dwelt at Jerusalem, wherefore I know concerning the regions round about; and I have made mention unto my children concerning the judgments of God, which hath come to pass among the Jews, unto my children, according to all that which Isaiah hath spoken, and I do not write them.
7 But behold, I proceed with mine own prophecy, according to my plainness; in the which I know that no man can err; nevertheless, in the days that the prophecies of Isaiah shall be fulfilled men shall know of a surety, at the times when they shall come to pass.
8 Wherefore, they are of worth unto the children of men, and he that supposeth that they are not, unto them will I speak particularly, and confine the words unto mine own people; for I know that they shall be of great worth unto them in the last days; for in that day shall they understand them; wherefore, for their good have I written them.

## The House of Israel Is Scattered Because of Wickedness and Will Be Gathered When They Choose to Believe in the Savior

9 And as one generation hath been destroyed among the Jews because of iniquity, even so have they been destroyed from generation to generation according to their iniquities; and never hath any of them been destroyed save it were foretold them by the prophets of the Lord.
10 Wherefore, it hath been told them concerning the destruction which should come upon them, immediately after my father left Jerusalem; nevertheless, they hardened their hearts; and according to my prophecy they have been destroyed, save it be those which are carried away captive into Babylon.
11 And now this I speak because of the spirit which is in me. And notwithstanding they have been carried away they shall return again, and possess the land of Jerusalem; wherefore, they shall be restored again to the land of their inheritance.
12 But, behold, they shall have wars, and rumors of wars; and when the day cometh that the Only Begotten of the Father, yea, even the Father of heaven and of earth, shall manifest himself unto them in the flesh, behold, they will reject him, because of their iniquities, and the hardness of their hearts, and the stiffness of their necks.

---

25:6 (5–6) Understanding the scriptures "is aided by a knowledge of the history, political and social conditions, educational status, and temperament of the peoples to whom the various scriptures were originally revealed. . . . Just as scientific and medical writings can be better understood by those trained in science and medicine, so those schooled in interpreting prophecies are in a better position to determine their full meanings" (Bruce R. McConkie, *Doctrinal New Testament Commentary* 1:58).

25:7 ***err***—misunderstand

25:8 ***confine***—limit

25:9 ***iniquity***—sin
***foretold them***—told them before it happened

25:10 (9–10) Prophets always warn us to repent so we will not have to experience the sadness caused by our sins. Why do so many people reject the prophets' warnings?

25:11 ***notwithstanding***—even though
***land of their inheritance***—land promised to them by the Lord

Isaiah and other prophets often taught that, because of wickedness, the house of Israel would be taken from their lands. They will be brought back when they repent and believe in Christ (see verses 14–16).

25:12 ***the hardness of their hearts***—their unwillingness to obey the commandments or feel the Spirit
***stiffness of their necks***—stubbornness or rebelliousness

13 Behold, they will crucify him; and after he is
laid in a sepulchre for the space of three days he
shall rise from the dead, with healing in his wings;
and all those who shall believe on his name shall
be saved in the kingdom of God. Wherefore, my
soul delighteth to prophesy concerning him, for I
have seen his day, and my heart doth magnify his
holy name.
14 And behold it shall come to pass that after the
Messiah hath risen from the dead, and hath manifested himself unto his people, unto as many as will
believe on his name, behold, Jerusalem shall be
destroyed again; for wo unto them that fight against
God and the people of his church.
15 Wherefore, the Jews shall be scattered among
all nations; yea, and also Babylon shall be
destroyed; wherefore, the Jews shall be scattered by
other nations.
16 And after they have been scattered, and the
Lord God hath scourged them by other nations for
the space of many generations, yea, even down
from generation to generation until they shall be
persuaded to believe in Christ, the Son of God, and
the atonement, which is infinite for all mankind—
and when that day shall come that they shall
believe in Christ, and worship the Father in his
name, with pure hearts and clean hands, and look
not forward any more for another Messiah, then, at
that time, the day will come that it must needs be
expedient that they should believe these things.
17 And the Lord will set his hand again the second
time to restore his people from their lost and fallen
state. Wherefore, he will proceed to do a marvelous
work and a wonder among the children of men.
18 Wherefore, he shall bring forth his words unto
them, which words shall judge them at the last day,
for they shall be given them for the purpose of convincing them of the true Messiah, who was rejected
by them; and unto the convincing of them that they
need not look forward any more for a Messiah to
come, for there should not any come, save it should
be a false Messiah which should deceive the
people; for there is save one Messiah spoken of by
the prophets, and that Messiah is he who should be
rejected of the Jews.

## Only Jesus Christ Can Save Mankind

19 For according to the words of the prophets, the
Messiah cometh in six hundred years from the time
that my father left Jerusalem; and according to the
words of the prophets, and also the word of the
angel of God, his name shall be Jesus Christ, the
Son of God.

PHOTOGRAPH BY G. R. SIMS

*The body of Christ was placed in a tomb like this for three days.*

25:13 ***sepulchre***—burial place

Jesus being resurrected "with healing in his wings" means that He is able to help His faithful followers overcome their sorrows, sicknesses, and sins (see Bruce R. McConkie, *The Mortal Messiah* 2:301).

25:16 ***scourged***—punished
***persuaded***—helped or taught
***infinite***—unlimited and never ending
***expedient***—necessary

Elder Dallin H. Oaks taught that we have clean hands when we do what is right and avoid doing wrong. We have pure hearts when we do what is right because we want to please Heavenly Father and our thoughts are clean (see *Pure in Heart,* 1).

25:18 (17–18) Before He comes again, Jesus will gather back to His true Church those of Israel who believe in Him. Nephi says Jesus will do this by bringing forth His words to them. Part of this "marvelous work and . . . wonder" includes the coming forth of the Book of Mormon. It teaches that Jesus is the true Messiah. What have you learned about Jesus Christ from the Book of Mormon?

25:19 This is the first mention of the name *Jesus Christ* in the Book of Mormon. The name *Jesus* means "God is help" or "Savior." *Christ* is a Greek word meaning "the Anointed One"; the Hebrew word with the same meaning is *Messiah.* Jesus is the Christ—the one chosen, set apart, and sent by God to save us (see LDS Bible Dictionary, s.v. "Jesus," 713; s.v. "Christ," 633).

HE IS RISEN, BY DEL PARSON

*"Behold, they will crucify him; and after he is laid in a sepulchre for the space of three days he shall rise from the dead, with healing in his wings."*

20 And now, my brethren, I have spoken plainly that ye cannot err. And as the Lord God liveth that brought Israel up out of the land of Egypt, and gave unto Moses power that he should heal the nations after they had been bitten by the poisonous serpents, if they would cast their eyes unto the serpent which he did raise up before them, and also gave him power that he should smite the rock and the water should come forth; yea, behold I say unto you, that as these things are true, and as the Lord God liveth, there is none other name given under heaven save it be this Jesus Christ, of which I have spoken, whereby man can be saved.

21 Wherefore, for this cause hath the Lord God promised unto me that these things which I write shall be kept and preserved, and handed down unto my seed, from generation to generation, that the promise may be fulfilled unto Joseph, that his seed should never perish as long as the earth should stand.

22 Wherefore, these things shall go from generation to generation as long as the earth shall stand; and they shall go according to the will and pleasure of God; and the nations who shall possess them shall be judged of them according to the words which are written.

23 For we labor diligently to write, to persuade our children, and also our brethren, to believe in Christ, and to be reconciled to God; for we know that it is by grace that we are saved, after all we can do.

### The Law of Moses Was Given to Ancient Israel to Teach Them of Christ

24 And, notwithstanding we believe in Christ, we keep the law of Moses, and look forward with steadfastness unto Christ, until the law shall be fulfilled.

25 For, for this end was the law given; wherefore the law hath become dead unto us, and we are made alive in Christ because of our faith; yet we keep the law because of the commandments.

26 And we talk of Christ, we rejoice in Christ, we preach of Christ, we prophesy of Christ, and we write according to our prophecies, that our children may know to what source they may look for a remission of their sins.

27 Wherefore, we speak concerning the law that our children may know the deadness of the law; and they, by knowing the deadness of the law, may look forward unto that life which is in Christ, and know for what end the law was given. And after the law is fulfilled in Christ, that they need not harden their hearts against him when the law ought to be done away.

28 And now behold, my people, ye are a stiffnecked people; wherefore, I have spoken plainly unto you, that ye cannot misunderstand. And the words which I have spoken shall stand as a testimony against you; for they are sufficient to teach any man the right way; for the right way is to believe in Christ and deny him not; for by denying him ye also deny the prophets and the law.

---

25:20 The account of healing from poisonous snakebites teaches that we can be healed by Jesus Christ (see Numbers 21:5–9; Helaman 8:13–15). The rock in the desert that brought forth saving water reminds us that Christ saves us from spiritual thirst (see Exodus 17:5–6; 1 Corinthians 10:1–4).

The name *Jesus Christ* is very special. This name is used when we are baptized, when miracles are performed, and when blessings are given. Why do you think we have been commanded not to use His name as a swear word or without thinking carefully about it?

25:21 ***his seed should never perish***—he will always have descendants or family members living

25:22 (21–22) Nephi's teachings about Christ will be saved for the latter days in the Book of Mormon. Descendants of Joseph of Egypt, the son of Israel, will take the Book of Mormon to all the world.

25:23 ***persuade***—encourage or convince
***reconciled***—brought back

25:24 ***steadfastness***—faithfulness or diligence

25:25 The members of the Church described in the Book of Mormon kept the commandments of the law of Moses while exercising great faith in Christ (see Bruce R. McConkie, *The Promised Messiah,* 426–27).

25:26 ***a remission***—forgiveness

It is only as we learn of, speak about, obey, and have faith in Jesus Christ that we can become like Him and be forgiven of our sins. What do you love most about Jesus Christ?

25:28 ***stiffnecked***—stubborn or rebellious
***sufficient***—enough
***deny***—refuse or reject

29 And now behold, I say unto you that the right way is to believe in Christ, and deny him not; and Christ is the Holy One of Israel; wherefore ye must bow down before him, and worship him with all your might, mind, and strength, and your whole soul; and if ye do this ye shall in nowise be cast out.
30 And, inasmuch as it shall be expedient, ye must keep the performances and ordinances of God until the law shall be fulfilled which was given unto Moses.

## CHAPTER 26

*Nephi prophesies of wars and destructions among the Nephites prior to Jesus Christ visiting them. Notice how the wicked reject the prophets and are destroyed while the righteous obey the prophets and come unto Jesus Christ.*

### *Nephi Prophesies of His People Before Jesus Visits America*

1 AND after Christ shall have risen from the dead he shall show himself unto you, my children, and my beloved brethren; and the words which he shall speak unto you shall be the law which ye shall do.
2 For behold, I say unto you that I have beheld that many generations shall pass away, and there shall be great wars and contentions among my people.
3 And after the Messiah shall come there shall be signs given unto my people of his birth, and also of his death and resurrection; and great and terrible shall that day be unto the wicked, for they shall perish; and they perish because they cast out the prophets, and the saints, and stone them, and slay them; wherefore the cry of the blood of the saints shall ascend up to God from the ground against them.
4 Wherefore, all those who are proud, and that do wickedly, the day that cometh shall burn them up, saith the Lord of Hosts, for they shall be as stubble.
5 And they that kill the prophets, and the saints, the depths of the earth shall swallow them up, saith the Lord of Hosts; and mountains shall cover them, and whirlwinds shall carry them away, and buildings shall fall upon them and crush them to pieces and grind them to powder.
6 And they shall be visited with thunderings, and lightnings, and earthquakes, and all manner of destructions, for the fire of the anger of the Lord shall be kindled against them, and they shall be as stubble, and the day that cometh shall consume them, saith the Lord of Hosts.
7 O the pain, and the anguish of my soul for the loss of the slain of my people! For I, Nephi, have seen it, and it well nigh consumeth me before the presence of the Lord; but I must cry unto my God: Thy ways are just.
8 But behold, the righteous that hearken unto the words of the prophets, and destroy them not, but look forward unto Christ with steadfastness for the signs which are given, notwithstanding all persecution—behold, they are they which shall not perish.

---

25:29 ***in nowise***—not

Elder Bruce R. McConkie taught that "perfect worship" is living as much as we can as Jesus Christ lived. "We honor those whom we imitate" (*The Promised Messiah,* 568). What can you do to imitate or honor Jesus Christ?

25:30 Nephi tells the members of the Church in his day to live the law of Moses until the resurrected Savior gives them His gospel (see 3 Nephi 9:17–20; 4 Nephi 1:12).

26:1 The appearance of Jesus Christ to the Nephites after His resurrection is recorded in 3 Nephi 11–27. While He was with them He gave them "the law," or the teachings of the gospel by which they should live.

26:2 ***contentions***—arguing or fighting

26:3 ***perish***—die

Elder Bruce R. McConkie explained that the cry of the Saints' blood ascending, or rising, up to God means that the Lord will some day punish those who murder or otherwise hurt the Saints (see *Mormon Doctrine,* 821).

26:4 ***stubble***—leftover stalks after the harvest

26:6 ***consume them***—burn them up

26:6 (3–6) Nephi saw the destruction of the wicked who killed the prophets prior to Jesus Christ's coming to the Nephites (see 3 Nephi 9:3–12; 10:14).

26:7 ***anguish***—sorrow or grief

26:8 ***steadfastness***—faithfulness

## Nephi Prophesies That the Resurrected Lord Will Visit His Disciples

9 But the Son of righteousness shall appear unto them; and he shall heal them, and they shall have peace with him, until three generations shall have passed away, and many of the fourth generation shall have passed away in righteousness.

10 And when these things have passed away a speedy destruction cometh unto my people; for, notwithstanding the pains of my soul, I have seen it; wherefore, I know that it shall come to pass; and they sell themselves for naught; for, for the reward of their pride and their foolishness they shall reap destruction; for because they yield unto the devil and choose works of darkness rather than light, therefore they must go down to hell.

11 For the Spirit of the Lord will not always strive with man. And when the Spirit ceaseth to strive with man then cometh speedy destruction, and this grieveth my soul.

12 And as I spake concerning the convincing of the Jews, that Jesus is the very Christ, it must needs be that the Gentiles be convinced also that Jesus is the Christ, the Eternal God;

13 And that he manifesteth himself unto all those who believe in him, by the power of the Holy Ghost; yea, unto every nation, kindred, tongue, and people, working mighty miracles, signs, and wonders, among the children of men according to their faith.

## The Nephites and Lamanites Will Weaken in Unbelief

14 But behold, I prophesy unto you concerning the last days; concerning the days when the Lord God shall bring these things forth unto the children of men.

15 After my seed and the seed of my brethren shall have dwindled in unbelief, and shall have been smitten by the Gentiles; yea, after the Lord God shall have camped against them round about, and shall have laid siege against them with a mount, and raised forts against them; and after they shall have been brought down low in the dust, even that they are not, yet the words of the righteous shall be written, and the prayers of the faithful shall be heard, and all those who have dwindled in unbelief shall not be forgotten.

16 For those who shall be destroyed shall speak unto them out of the ground, and their speech shall be low out of the dust, and their voice shall be as one that hath a familiar spirit; for the Lord God will give unto him power, that he may whisper concerning them, even as it were out of the ground; and their speech shall whisper out of the dust.

17 For thus saith the Lord God: They shall write the things which shall be done among them, and they shall be written and sealed up in a book, and those who have dwindled in unbelief shall not have them, for they seek to destroy the things of God.

18 Wherefore, as those who have been destroyed have been destroyed speedily; and the multitude of their terrible ones shall be as chaff that passeth away—yea, thus saith the Lord God: It shall be at an instant, suddenly—

---

26:10 ***naught***—nothing
***yield***—give in

26:11 ***strive with***—stay with or influence

President Harold B. Lee warned about "one of the most tragic experiences that can come to individuals—to have the Lord withdraw His Spirit from us. And when he speaks of His Spirit, it isn't just the Holy Ghost, because many of those spoken of by the prophets had not received the gift of the Holy Ghost. This Spirit to which I refer is the Light of Christ. When withdrawn, it becomes difficult for us to pray, to have direction and guidance, to withstand evil" (*Stand Ye In Holy Places,* 117–18).

26:13 ***manifesteth***—shows
***kindred, tongue***—family, language

26:15 The phrases "camped against them round about" and "laid seige against them" describe how the Lamanites will one day be surrounded and captured.

26:16 Nephi uses Isaiah's phrase "familiar spirit" to describe "the departed of his own people who, through the Book of Mormon, speak to those of the last days from the grave with a voice of warning" (Joseph Fielding McConkie and others, *Doctrinal Commentary on the Book of Mormon* 1:306).

19 And it shall come to pass, that those who have dwindled in unbelief shall be smitten by the hand of the Gentiles.

## False Churches and Secret Combinations Will Come in the Last Days

20 And the Gentiles are lifted up in the pride of their eyes, and have stumbled, because of the greatness of their stumbling block, that they have built up many churches; nevertheless, they put down the power and miracles of God, and preach up unto themselves their own wisdom and their own learning, that they may get gain and grind upon the face of the poor.

21 And there are many churches built up which cause envyings, and strifes, and malice.

22 And there are also secret combinations, even as in times of old, according to the combinations of the devil, for he is the founder of all these things; yea, the founder of murder, and works of darkness; yea, and he leadeth them by the neck with a flaxen cord, until he bindeth them with his strong cords forever.

23 For behold, my beloved brethren, I say unto you that the Lord God worketh not in darkness.

24 He doeth not anything save it be for the benefit of the world; for he loveth the world, even that he layeth down his own life that he may draw all men unto him. Wherefore, he commandeth none that they shall not partake of his salvation.

25 Behold, doth he cry unto any, saying: Depart from me? Behold, I say unto you, Nay; but he saith: Come unto me all ye ends of the earth, buy milk and honey, without money and without price.

26 Behold, hath he commanded any that they should depart out of the synagogues, or out of the houses of worship? Behold, I say unto you, Nay.

27 Hath he commanded any that they should not partake of his salvation? Behold I say unto you, Nay; but he hath given it free for all men; and he hath commanded his people that they should persuade all men to repentance.

28 Behold, hath the Lord commanded any that they should not partake of his goodness? Behold I say unto you, Nay; but all men are privileged the one like unto the other, and none are forbidden.

## The Lord Condemns Priestcraft and Commands All Men to Have Charity

29 He commandeth that there shall be no priestcrafts; for, behold, priestcrafts are that men preach and set themselves up for a light unto the world, that they may get gain and praise of the world; but they seek not the welfare of Zion.

30 Behold, the Lord hath forbidden this thing; wherefore, the Lord God hath given a commandment that all men should have charity, which charity is love. And except they should have charity they were nothing. Wherefore, if they should have charity they would not suffer the laborer in Zion to perish.

31 But the laborer in Zion shall labor for Zion; for if they labor for money they shall perish.

---

26:20 One of the reasons why the Gentiles will stumble or become confused is that precious things will be taken out of the Bible (see 1 Nephi 13:29).

26:21 ***envyings***—desires to have others' possessions or advantages
***strifes***—contentions or arguments
***malice***—desire to harm others

26:22 The first "secret combination" was between Satan and Cain, who killed his brother Abel to get his flocks (see Moses 5:28–32). "Among today's secret combinations are gangs, drug cartels, and organized crime families" (M. Russell Ballard, in Conference Report, October 1997, 51).

The flaxen cord, a lightweight rope, precedes the "chains of hell," which the devil uses to bind his followers (see 2 Nephi 28:22; Alma 12:11).

26:24 Everything the Lord does is for the benefit and salvation of the world. How can remembering this thought help you when you are going through trials?

26:28 (25–28) Jesus' life gives us the perfect example of love, concern, and service for all of Heavenly Father's children. He calls all to "come unto" Him. Salvation is offered to all, not just a select few. All can repent and partake of His goodness. How can you follow this loving example of our Lord?

26:30 Mormon taught that "charity is the pure love of Christ, and it endureth forever; and whoso is found possessed of it at the last day, it shall be well with him" (Moroni 7:47).

26:31 In our day the Lord has further counseled those who labor in Zion to "seek not for riches but for wisdom" (D&C 11:7).

26:31 (29–31) The Book of Mormon often warns about the evils of priestcrafts (see 1 Nephi 22:23; 2 Nephi 10:4–6; Alma 1:1–12).

32 And again, the Lord God hath commanded that men should not murder; that they should not lie; that they should not steal; that they should not take the name of the Lord their God in vain; that they should not envy; that they should not have malice; that they should not contend one with another; that they should not commit whoredoms; and that they should do none of these things; for whoso doeth them shall perish.

33 For none of these iniquities come of the Lord; for he doeth that which is good among the children of men; and he doeth nothing save it be plain unto the children of men; and he inviteth them all to come unto him and partake of his goodness; and he denieth none that come unto him, black and white, bond and free, male and female; and he remembereth the heathen; and all are alike unto God, both Jew and Gentile.

## CHAPTER 27

*Nephi quotes from Isaiah 29 and prophesies of a marvelous work the Lord would do in the last days. Watch for how these prophecies are fulfilled in the events surrounding the coming forth of the Book of Mormon.*

### *The Last Days Will Be a Time of Great Wickedness*

1 BUT, behold, in the last days, or in the days of the Gentiles—yea, behold all the nations of the Gentiles and also the Jews, both those who shall come upon this land and those who shall be upon other lands, yea, even upon all the lands of the earth, behold, they will be drunken with iniquity and all manner of abominations—

2 And when that day shall come they shall be visited of the Lord of Hosts, with thunder and with earthquake, and with a great noise, and with storm, and with tempest, and with the flame of devouring fire.

3 And all the nations that fight against Zion, and that distress her, shall be as a dream of a night vision; yea, it shall be unto them, even as unto a hungry man which dreameth, and behold he eateth but he awaketh and his soul is empty; or like unto a thirsty man which dreameth, and behold he drinketh but he awaketh and behold he is faint, and his soul hath appetite; yea, even so shall the multitude of all the nations be that fight against Mount Zion.

4 For behold, all ye that doeth iniquity, stay yourselves and wonder, for ye shall cry out, and cry; yea, ye shall be drunken but not with wine, ye shall stagger but not with strong drink.

5 For behold, the Lord hath poured out upon you the spirit of deep sleep. For behold, ye have closed your eyes, and ye have rejected the prophets; and your rulers, and the seers hath he covered because of your iniquity.

### *The Book of Mormon Will Come Forth*

6 And it shall come to pass that the Lord God shall bring forth unto you the words of a book, and they shall be the words of them which have slumbered.

7 And behold the book shall be sealed; and in the book shall be a revelation from God, from the beginning of the world to the ending thereof.

8 Wherefore, because of the things which are sealed up, the things which are sealed shall not be delivered in the day of the wickedness and abominations of the people. Wherefore the book shall be kept from them.

9 But the book shall be delivered unto a man, and he shall deliver the words of the book, which are the words of those who have slumbered in the dust, and he shall deliver these words unto another;

---

26:32 ***whoredoms***—wickedness and immorality

26:33 ***iniquities***—sins
***the heathen***—those who do not know the true God

27:1 ***abominations***—wickedness

27:2 ***devouring fire***—fire that destroys completely

27:3 ***distress***—trouble or bother

Those who want to destroy God's people will not be able to do so (see 1 Nephi 22:14). Nephi paraphrases Isaiah, saying they will be like a hungry man who wants to eat but only dreams about eating.

27:5 ***covered***—removed

27:6 ***slumbered***—died

MORONI DELIVERING THE GOLDEN PLATES, BY GARY KAPP

*Joseph Smith, the man Isaiah speaks of in chapter 27, verse 9, wrote: "On the twenty-second day of September, one thousand eight hundred and twenty-seven, having gone as usual at the end of another year to the place where they [the plates] were deposited, the same heavenly messenger [Moroni] delivered them up to me" (Joseph Smith—History 1:59).*

10 But the words which are sealed he shall not deliver, neither shall he deliver the book. For the book shall be sealed by the power of God, and the revelation which was sealed shall be kept in the book until the own due time of the Lord, that they may come forth; for behold, they reveal all things from the foundation of the world unto the end thereof.

11 And the day cometh that the words of the book which were sealed shall be read upon the house tops; and they shall be read by the power of Christ; and all things shall be revealed unto the children of men which ever have been among the children of men, and which ever will be even unto the end of the earth.

### The Book of Mormon Plates Will Be Seen Only by Special Witnesses

12 Wherefore, at that day when the book shall be delivered unto the man of whom I have spoken, the book shall be hid from the eyes of the world, that the eyes of none shall behold it save it be that three witnesses shall behold it, by the power of God, besides him to whom the book shall be delivered; and they shall testify to the truth of the book and the things therein.

13 And there is none other which shall view it, save it be a few according to the will of God, to bear testimony of his word unto the children of men; for the Lord God hath said that the words of the faithful should speak as if it were from the dead.

14 Wherefore, the Lord God will proceed to bring forth the words of the book; and in the mouth of as many witnesses as seemeth him good will he establish his word; and wo be unto him that rejecteth the word of God!

### The Book of Mormon Will Be Translated by the Power of God, Not the Learning of Man

15 But behold, it shall come to pass that the Lord God shall say unto him to whom he shall deliver the book: Take these words which are not sealed

---

27:11 (7–11) A part of the Book of Mormon was sealed. We learn here that the sealed part reveals the history of the world from the beginning to the end (see also Ether 4:4–7). It was sealed up or hidden from the world because of wickedness. The day will come when the sealed portion will be revealed.

27:13 (12–13) The testimonies of the Three Witnesses and the "few" other witnesses are found at the beginning of every copy of the Book of Mormon (see pp. xvii–xviii).

27:14 "Wo" means sorrow or grief. Why do you think those who refuse to believe the Book of Mormon will be sorry? How does the Book of Mormon make you happy?

PHOTOGRAPH BY DAVID H. GARNER

*The Book of Mormon was buried in the Hill Cumorah so that it could be brought forth in the last days as Isaiah prophesied.*

*Oliver Cowdery*

*David Whitmer*

*Martin Harris*

*The Lord provided witnesses to testify and establish His word. The Three Witnesses—Oliver Cowdery, David Whitmer, and Martin Harris—testified that an angel of God showed them the gold plates of the Book of Mormon.*

and deliver them to another, that he may show them unto the learned, saying: Read this, I pray thee. And the learned shall say: Bring hither the book, and I will read them.

16 And now, because of the glory of the world and to get gain will they say this, and not for the glory of God.

17 And the man shall say: I cannot bring the book, for it is sealed.

18 Then shall the learned say: I cannot read it.

19 Wherefore it shall come to pass, that the Lord God will deliver again the book and the words thereof to him that is not learned; and the man that is not learned shall say: I am not learned.

20 Then shall the Lord God say unto him: The learned shall not read them, for they have rejected them, and I am able to do mine own work; wherefore thou shalt read the words which I shall give unto thee.

21 Touch not the things which are sealed, for I will bring them forth in mine own due time; for I will show unto the children of men that I am able to do mine own work.

22 Wherefore, when thou hast read the words which I have commanded thee, and obtained the witnesses which I have promised unto thee, then shalt thou seal up the book again, and hide it up unto me, that I may preserve the words which thou hast not read, until I shall see fit in mine own wisdom to reveal all things unto the children of men.

## *The Lord Is a God of Miracles*

23 For behold, I am God; and I am a God of miracles; and I will show unto the world that I am the same yesterday, today, and forever; and I work not among the children of men save it be according to their faith.

24 And again it shall come to pass that the Lord shall say unto him that shall read the words that shall be delivered him:

25 Forasmuch as this people draw near unto me with their mouth, and with their lips do honor me, but have removed their hearts far from me, and their fear towards me is taught by the precepts of men—

26 Therefore, I will proceed to do a marvelous work among this people, yea, a marvelous work and a wonder, for the wisdom of their wise and learned shall perish, and the understanding of their prudent shall be hid.

27 And wo unto them that seek deep to hide their counsel from the Lord! And their works are in the dark; and they say: Who seeth us, and who knoweth us? And they also say: Surely, your turning of things upside down shall be esteemed as the potter's clay. But behold, I will show unto them, saith the Lord of Hosts, that I know all their works. For shall the work say of him that made it, he made me not? Or shall the thing framed say of him that framed it, he had no understanding?

---

27:18 (15–18) This prophecy of words from the Book of Mormon being taken to a "learned" man was fulfilled when Martin Harris took a copy of characters from the gold plates to Professor Charles Anthon (see Joseph Smith—History 1:63–65).

27:20 (19–20) The man called "not learned" in these verses is the Prophet Joseph Smith. He had very little regular schooling when he was young, but that did not matter. As prophesied, "learned" men could not read the gold plates. Joseph translated the Book of Mormon by the "gift and power of God" (see the Title Page to the Book of Mormon).

27:23 Here the Lord tells us that He will do miracles for us if we have faith in Him (see also Moroni 7:36–37). Some miracles are big and spectacular, others are small and personal. Can you think of some miracles God has done for your family because of your faith in Him?

27:25 Jesus Christ taught this to Joseph Smith in the First Vision (see Joseph Smith—History 1:19).

27:26 "Never in the history of the world has this truth been so greatly manifest as in the preaching of the Gospel by the weak and humble elders of the Church. They have gone forth into strength which the Lord promised them and they have confounded the wisdom of the wise and the understanding of their prudent men has been hid" (Joseph Fielding Smith, *Church History and Modern Revelation,* 149).

27:27 Evil men seek to hide their works from the Lord. This is not possible, for the Lord has revealed that He even knows their thoughts and the intents of their hearts (see D&C 6:16).

28 But behold, saith the Lord of Hosts: I will show unto the children of men that it is yet a very little while and Lebanon shall be turned into a fruitful field; and the fruitful field shall be esteemed as a forest.

29 And in that day shall the deaf hear the words of the book, and the eyes of the blind shall see out of obscurity and out of darkness.

30 And the meek also shall increase, and their joy shall be in the Lord, and the poor among men shall rejoice in the Holy One of Israel.

31 For assuredly as the Lord liveth they shall see that the terrible one is brought to naught, and the scorner is consumed, and all that watch for iniquity are cut off;

32 And they that make a man an offender for a word, and lay a snare for him that reproveth in the gate, and turn aside the just for a thing of naught.

33 Therefore, thus saith the Lord, who redeemed Abraham, concerning the house of Jacob: Jacob shall not now be ashamed, neither shall his face now wax pale.

34 But when he seeth his children, the work of my hands, in the midst of him, they shall sanctify my name, and sanctify the Holy One of Jacob, and shall fear the God of Israel.

35 They also that erred in spirit shall come to understanding, and they that murmured shall learn doctrine.

## CHAPTER 28

*Nephi sees a vision of our day. He warns us about some religions that will take people away from the truth. As you read, notice what the Lord wants you to avoid.*

### False Churches Will Be Built Up in the Last Days

1 AND now, behold, my brethren, I have spoken unto you, according as the Spirit hath constrained me; wherefore, I know that they must surely come to pass.

2 And the things which shall be written out of the book shall be of great worth unto the children of men, and especially unto our seed, which is a remnant of the house of Israel.

3 For it shall come to pass in that day that the churches which are built up, and not unto the Lord, when the one shall say unto the other: Behold, I, I am the Lord's; and the others shall say: I, I am the Lord's; and thus shall every one say that hath built up churches, and not unto the Lord—

4 And they shall contend one with another; and their priests shall contend one with another, and they shall teach with their learning, and deny the Holy Ghost, which giveth utterance.

---

27:28 Isaiah foresees that Lebanon, the northern part of the ancient land of Israel, would become fruitful once again, but not until after the coming forth of the Book of Mormon (see Hoyt Brewster, *Isaiah Plain and Simple,* 170, 171–72; compare this verse with Isaiah 29:17).

27:31 ***naught***—nothing
***the scorner is consumed***—those who mock and ridicule are destroyed

27:32 This verse describes those who treat others unfairly and deny justice to the innocent. For example, "lay a snare for him that reproveth in the gate" may mean they lay traps for those who testify against evil.

27:32 (29–32) How does the Book of Mormon help the spiritually deaf and blind hear and see the truth? How does it bring joy to the humble and teachable?

27:33 ***wax***—grow

27:34 ***sanctify***—respect or treat as sacred

27:35 Elder Bruce R. McConkie stated, "The Book of Mormon has come forth in this day so that men might 'learn doctrine' " (*Mormon Doctrine,* 204). What are some of the truths you have learned from the Book of Mormon?

28:1 ***constrained***—prompted or urged

28:2 ***remnant***—part or remainder

28:4 ***contend***—argue

28:4 (3–4) Joseph Smith described that in his day there was "an unusual excitement on the subject of religion" which created a "stir and division amongst the people. . . . A scene of great confusion and bad feeling ensued." When the Savior spoke to Joseph Smith during the First Vision in the Sacred Grove, He told Joseph that those churches "were all wrong." He specifically said, "They draw near to me with their lips, but their hearts are far from me, they teach for doctrines the commandments of men, having a form of godliness, but they deny the power thereof" (Joseph Smith—History 1:5–6, 19).

5 And they deny the power of God, the Holy One of Israel; and they say unto the people: Hearken unto us, and hear ye our precept; for behold there is no God today, for the Lord and the Redeemer hath done his work, and he hath given his power unto men;

6 Behold, hearken ye unto my precept; if they shall say there is a miracle wrought by the hand of the Lord, believe it not; for this day he is not a God of miracles; he hath done his work.

### Many Evil People Will Teach False and Foolish Doctrines

7 Yea, and there shall be many which shall say: Eat, drink, and be merry, for tomorrow we die; and it shall be well with us.

8 And there shall also be many which shall say: Eat, drink, and be merry; nevertheless, fear God—he will justify in committing a little sin; yea, lie a little, take the advantage of one because of his words, dig a pit for thy neighbor; there is no harm in this; and do all these things, for tomorrow we die; and if it so be that we are guilty, God will beat us with a few stripes, and at last we shall be saved in the kingdom of God.

9 Yea, and there shall be many which shall teach after this manner, false and vain and foolish doctrines, and shall be puffed up in their hearts, and shall seek deep to hide their counsels from the Lord; and their works shall be in the dark.

10 And the blood of the saints shall cry from the ground against them.

11 Yea, they have all gone out of the way; they have become corrupted.

12 Because of pride, and because of false teachers, and false doctrine, their churches have become corrupted, and their churches are lifted up; because of pride they are puffed up.

13 They rob the poor because of their fine sanctuaries; they rob the poor because of their fine clothing; and they persecute the meek and the poor in heart, because in their pride they are puffed up.

14 They wear stiff necks and high heads; yea, and because of pride, and wickedness, and abominations, and whoredoms, they have all gone astray save it be a few, who are the humble followers of Christ; nevertheless, they are led, that in many instances they do err because they are taught by the precepts of men.

### God Will Punish the Wicked Unless They Repent

15 O the wise, and the learned, and the rich, that are puffed up in the pride of their hearts, and all those who preach false doctrines, and all those who commit whoredoms, and pervert the right way of the Lord, wo, wo, wo be unto them, saith the Lord God Almighty, for they shall be thrust down to hell!

16 Wo unto them that turn aside the just for a thing of naught and revile against that which is good, and say that it is of no worth! For the day shall come that the Lord God will speedily visit the inhabitants of the earth; and in that day that they are fully ripe in iniquity they shall perish.

---

28:5 ***precept***—teaching

Some churches teach that God doesn't speak to man today and that His power and revelation do not exist. However, we know that God lives and that He continues to speak to His prophets and answer our prayers. How do you know that God continues to communicate with His children?

28:8 (7–8) Commenting on these verses, Elder Joseph Fielding Smith said, "Do not think it is said of the world. . . . It is said of the members of the Church" (*The Way to Perfection,* 203).

Satan fools many into thinking that it is not a sin to do a little evil, so he can destroy them (see D&C 10:25–27). What danger is there in saying that just sinning a little won't hurt anything? (see D&C 1:31).

28:9 ***vain***—empty or useless
***puffed up in their hearts***—full of pride

28:11 ***corrupted***—full of sin or error

28:13 Sometimes wicked people torment and try to hurt the righteous. Jesus said that those who suffer for His sake would be blessed with heavenly rewards (see Matthew 5:11–12).

28:14 ***abominations***—evils
***whoredoms***—immorality

The phrase "stiff necks" may refer to people who are unwilling to bow their heads in humility and reverence.

28:15 ***pervert***—change or corrupt

28:16 ***ripe in iniquity***—advanced in wickedness

28:16 (15–16) "Wo" means sorrow and grief. Why do you think the "wise," the "learned," the "rich," and the others that Nephi describes in these verses are going to be sorry when Jesus comes again?

17 But behold, if the inhabitants of the earth shall repent of their wickedness and abominations they shall not be destroyed, saith the Lord of Hosts.

## Satan Will Rage in the Hearts of Men in the Last Days

18 But behold, that great and abominable church, the whore of all the earth, must tumble to the earth, and great must be the fall thereof.
19 For the kingdom of the devil must shake, and they which belong to it must needs be stirred up unto repentance, or the devil will grasp them with his everlasting chains, and they be stirred up to anger, and perish;
20 For behold, at that day shall he rage in the hearts of the children of men, and stir them up to anger against that which is good.

## Satan Will Lead People Away from God with False Teachings

21 And others will he pacify, and lull them away into carnal security, that they will say: All is well in Zion; yea, Zion prospereth, all is well—and thus the devil cheateth their souls, and leadeth them away carefully down to hell.
22 And behold, others he flattereth away, and telleth them there is no hell; and he saith unto them: I am no devil, for there is none—and thus he whispereth in their ears, until he grasps them with his awful chains, from whence there is no deliverance.
23 Yea, they are grasped with death, and hell; and death, and hell, and the devil, and all that have been seized therewith must stand before the throne of God, and be judged according to their works, from whence they must go into the place prepared for them, even a lake of fire and brimstone, which is endless torment.
24 Therefore, wo be unto him that is at ease in Zion!
25 Wo be unto him that crieth: All is well!
26 Yea, wo be unto him that hearkeneth unto the precepts of men, and denieth the power of God, and the gift of the Holy Ghost!
27 Yea, wo be unto him that saith: We have received, and we need no more!
28 And in fine, wo unto all those who tremble, and are angry because of the truth of God! For behold, he that is built upon the rock receiveth it with gladness; and he that is built upon a sandy foundation trembleth lest he shall fall.
29 Wo be unto him that shall say: We have received the word of God, and we need no more of the word of God, for we have enough!

---

28:18 **abominable**—terrible or evil

Elder Bruce R. McConkie said, "The titles *church of the devil* and *great and abominable church* are used to identify all churches or organizations of whatever name or nature . . . which are designed to take men on a course that leads away from God and his laws and thus from salvation in the kingdom of God" (*Mormon Doctrine,* 137–38).

28:20 Doctrine and Covenants 10:63 teaches that Satan is the author of contention. President Gordon B. Hinckley said: "Let us rise above all such conduct. . . . Let us be true disciples of the Christ, observing the Golden Rule, doing unto others as we would have them do unto us" (in Conference Report, April 1998, 4).

28:22 (21–22) Satan "is working under such perfect disguise that many do not recognize either him or his methods. There is no crime he would not commit, . . . no plague he would not send, no heart he would not break, no life he would not take, no soul he would not destroy. He comes as a thief in the night; he is a wolf in sheep's clothing" (in James R. Clark, comp., *Messages of the First Presidency of The Church of Jesus Christ of Latter-day Saints* 6:179).

28:23 **brimstone**—inflammable sulfur

28:26 **precepts**—teachings

28:28 We should build upon the rock, the gospel of Jesus Christ. If we build on a sandy foundation, the teachings of Satan, we will fall (see Matthew 7:24–27).

28:29 Have you ever met anyone who has said that they already have enough of the word of God and that they do not want any more? Why is it such a great blessing to belong to a Church that is led by living prophets who receive continuing revelation?

30 For behold, thus saith the Lord God: I will give unto the children of men line upon line, precept upon precept, here a little and there a little; and blessed are those who hearken unto my precepts, and lend an ear unto my counsel, for they shall learn wisdom; for unto him that receiveth I will give more; and from them that shall say, We have enough, from them shall be taken away even that which they have.

31 Cursed is he that putteth his trust in man, or maketh flesh his arm, or shall hearken unto the precepts of men, save their precepts shall be given by the power of the Holy Ghost.

32 Wo be unto the Gentiles, saith the Lord God of Hosts! For notwithstanding I shall lengthen out mine arm unto them from day to day, they will deny me; nevertheless, I will be merciful unto them, saith the Lord God, if they will repent and come unto me; for mine arm is lengthened out all the day long, saith the Lord God of Hosts.

## CHAPTER 29

*The Bible is the word of the Lord, as is the Book of Mormon. Look for ways the Bible and the Book of Mormon work together as witnesses of Jesus Christ.*

### *In the Last Days the Book of Mormon Shall Go Forth to the Whole Earth*

1 BUT behold, there shall be many—at that day when I shall proceed to do a marvelous work among them, that I may remember my covenants which I have made unto the children of men, that I may set my hand again the second time to recover my people, which are of the house of Israel;

2 And also, that I may remember the promises which I have made unto thee, Nephi, and also unto thy father, that I would remember your seed; and that the words of your seed should proceed forth out of my mouth unto your seed; and my words shall hiss forth unto the ends of the earth, for a standard unto my people, which are of the house of Israel;

### *Many Gentiles Will Say the Only Scripture They Need Is the Bible*

3 And because my words shall hiss forth—many of the Gentiles shall say: A Bible! A Bible! We have got a Bible, and there cannot be any more Bible.

4 But thus saith the Lord God: O fools, they shall have a Bible; and it shall proceed forth from the Jews, mine ancient covenant people. And what thank they the Jews for the Bible which they receive from them? Yea, what do the Gentiles mean? Do they remember the travails, and the labors, and the pains of the Jews, and their diligence unto me, in bringing forth salvation unto the Gentiles?

5 O ye Gentiles, have ye remembered the Jews, mine ancient covenant people? Nay; but ye have cursed them, and have hated them, and have not sought to recover them. But behold, I will return all these things upon your own heads; for I the Lord have not forgotten my people.

6 Thou fool, that shall say: A Bible, we have got a Bible, and we need no more Bible. Have ye obtained a Bible save it were by the Jews?

---

28:30 ***hearken unto***—listen to and obey

M. Russell Ballard taught, "You and I can receive personal revelation for our own lives and for our families and personal responsibilities if we will live in such a way that we can be open and receptive to the whisperings of the Holy Spirit when they come" (*Our Search for Happiness,* 96–97).

28:31 The Book of Mormon promises great blessings to those who trust in the Lord (see Mosiah 4:6; 23:22; Alma 36:3).

28:32 The Lord is merciful, which means He is compassionate and loving. He stretches out His arms to those who need to repent. How does it make you feel to know that God wants everyone to come unto Him? What are you doing to stay close to the Lord?

29:2 Here the word *hiss* means whistle and suggests that the Book of Mormon will attract the attention of the world (see LDS edition of the King James Bible, Isaiah 5:26, note b).

29:4 ***proceed***—go
***travails***—efforts or work

29:5 ***recover them***—gather them back to the gospel and their promised lands

29:6 (4–6) Bruce R. McConkie asked, "If the hearts of the Christians of the world were truly centered on the Bible, as they profess, would they not have an entirely different feeling toward the Jews? Did not Jesus say that 'salvation is of the Jews'? (John 4:22.) Was not Jesus a Jew, and did not the Bible come to us through Jewish hands? Can anyone truly believe and reverence the Bible without honoring and thanking the Jews?" (*A New Witness for the Articles of Faith,* 462–63).

## *The Bible and the Book of Mormon Witness That God Speaks to All People*

7 Know ye not that there are more nations than
one? Know ye not that I, the Lord your God, have
created all men, and that I remember those who are
upon the isles of the sea; and that I rule in the heavens above and in the earth beneath; and I bring
forth my word unto the children of men, yea, even
upon all the nations of the earth?
8 Wherefore murmur ye, because that ye shall
receive more of my word? Know ye not that the testimony of two nations is a witness unto you that I
am God, that I remember one nation like unto
another? Wherefore, I speak the same words unto
one nation like unto another. And when the two
nations shall run together the testimony of the two
nations shall run together also.
9 And I do this that I may prove unto many that I
am the same yesterday, today, and forever; and that
I speak forth my words according to mine own
pleasure. And because that I have spoken one word
ye need not suppose that I cannot speak another;
for my work is not yet finished; neither shall it be
until the end of man, neither from that time henceforth and forever.
10 Wherefore, because that ye have a Bible ye
need not suppose that it contains all my words; neither need ye suppose that I have not caused more
to be written.

## *In the Last Days the Word of the Lord Will Be Available for All to Read*

11 For I command all men, both in the east and in
the west, and in the north, and in the south, and in
the islands of the sea, that they shall write the
words which I speak unto them; for out of the
books which shall be written I will judge the world,
every man according to their works, according to
that which is written.
12 For behold, I shall speak unto the Jews and
they shall write it; and I shall also speak unto the
Nephites and they shall write it; and I shall also
speak unto the other tribes of the house of Israel,
which I have led away, and they shall write it; and
I shall also speak unto all nations of the earth and
they shall write it.
13 And it shall come to pass that the Jews shall
have the words of the Nephites, and the Nephites
shall have the words of the Jews; and the Nephites
and the Jews shall have the words of the lost tribes
of Israel; and the lost tribes of Israel shall have the
words of the Nephites and the Jews.
14 And it shall come to pass that my people,
which are of the house of Israel, shall be gathered
home unto the lands of their possessions; and my
word also shall be gathered in one. And I will show
unto them that fight against my word and against
my people, who are of the house of Israel, that I am
God, and that I covenanted with Abraham that I
would remember his seed forever.

---

29:8 In 2 Corinthians 13:1 it says, "In the mouth of two or three witnesses shall every word be established." Why is it important that there be two or more witnesses that Jesus is the Savior? How does the Book of Mormon help you know that Jesus is the Son of God?

"The Bible sits on the pulpit of hundreds of different religious sects. The Book of Mormon, the record of Joseph, verifies and clarifies the Bible. It removes stumbling blocks, it restores many plain and precious things. We testify that when used together, the Bible and the Book of Mormon confound false doctrines, lay down contentions, and establish peace" (Ezra Taft Benson, *A Witness and a Warning*, 13).

29:11 Revelation 20:12 says that all people will stand before God and be judged by their works, which will have been recorded in books in heaven.

29:12 The "other tribes of the house of Israel" are the lost tribes of Israel who were taken captive by the Assyrians in 721 B.C. and who will return again in the last days (see LDS Bible Dictionary, s.v. "Israel, Kingdom of," 708; D&C 133:26–34).

29:13 ***words of the Nephites***—Book of Mormon
***words of the Jews***—Bible

## CHAPTER 30

*As they accept the gospel and make and keep covenants with the Lord, the faithful will be gathered to Zion and saved at the Second Coming. Watch for the kind of life the righteous will enjoy during the Millennium.*

### *Only Those Who Repent Are Included Among the Covenant People of God*

1 AND now behold, my beloved brethren, I would speak unto you; for I, Nephi, would not suffer that ye should suppose that ye are more righteous than the Gentiles shall be. For behold, except ye shall keep the commandments of God ye shall all likewise perish; and because of the words which have been spoken ye need not suppose that the Gentiles are utterly destroyed.

2 For behold, I say unto you that as many of the Gentiles as will repent are the covenant people of the Lord; and as many of the Jews as will not repent shall be cast off; for the Lord covenanteth with none save it be with them that repent and believe in his Son, who is the Holy One of Israel.

### *The Book of Mormon Gathers People to Christ*

3 And now, I would prophesy somewhat more concerning the Jews and the Gentiles. For after the book of which I have spoken shall come forth, and be written unto the Gentiles, and sealed up again unto the Lord, there shall be many which shall believe the words which are written; and they shall carry them forth unto the remnant of our seed.

4 And then shall the remnant of our seed know concerning us, how that we came out from Jerusalem, and that they are descendants of the Jews.

5 And the gospel of Jesus Christ shall be declared among them; wherefore, they shall be restored unto the knowledge of their fathers, and also to the knowledge of Jesus Christ, which was had among their fathers.

6 And then shall they rejoice; for they shall know that it is a blessing unto them from the hand of God; and their scales of darkness shall begin to fall from their eyes; and many generations shall not pass away among them, save they shall be a pure and a delightsome people.

7 And it shall come to pass that the Jews which are scattered also shall begin to believe in Christ; and they shall begin to gather in upon the face of the land; and as many as shall believe in Christ shall also become a delightsome people.

8 And it shall come to pass that the Lord God shall commence his work among all nations, kindreds, tongues, and people, to bring about the restoration of his people upon the earth.

### *The Lord Will Save the Righteous and Destroy the Wicked at His Second Coming*

9 And with righteousness shall the Lord God judge the poor, and reprove with equity for the meek of the earth. And he shall smite the earth with the rod of his mouth; and with the breath of his lips shall he slay the wicked.

10 For the time speedily cometh that the Lord God shall cause a great division among the people, and the wicked will he destroy; and he will spare his people, yea, even if it so be that he must destroy the wicked by fire.

---

30:1 ***suffer***—allow
***utterly***—completely

30:3 This "book" which Nephi speaks of is the Book of Mormon (see Bruce R. McConkie, *Millennial Messiah,* 228).

***remnant of our seed***—our remaining descendants

30:5 ***restored***—brought back

30:6 Nephi's statement about the Lamanites, that "their scales of darkness shall begin to fall from their eyes," means that they will begin to recognize and understand gospel truths.

***delightsome***—blessed or happy

30:8 ***commence***—begin
***kindreds, tongues***—family groups, languages

30:9 ***reprove with equity***—correct with fairness

Commenting on this verse, Elder Jeffrey R. Holland stated: "In that day the Word will come with power, and there will be incomparable power in his words. In those last days Christ's judgment will be the truth he speaks and an acknowledgment of that truth from all who hear him" (*Christ and the New Covenant,* 87).

30:10 "This refers to the day of burning that shall attend the Second Coming. 'Wherefore, the righteous need not fear; for thus saith the prophet, they shall be saved, even if it so be as by fire'" (Bruce R. McConkie, *The Millennial Messiah,* 313).

FISHERS OF MEN, BY CLARK KELLEY PRICE

*The "Lord God shall commence his work among all nations, kindreds, tongues, and people, to bring about the restoration of his people upon the earth."*

## Nephi Quotes Isaiah's Millennial Prophecies

11 And righteousness shall be the girdle of his
loins, and faithfulness the girdle of his reins.
12 And then shall the wolf dwell with the lamb;
and the leopard shall lie down with the kid, and
the calf, and the young lion, and the fatling,
together; and a little child shall lead them.
13 And the cow and the bear shall feed; their
young ones shall lie down together; and the lion
shall eat straw like the ox.
14 And the sucking child shall play on the hole of
the asp, and the weaned child shall put his hand on
the cockatrice's den.

30:11 A "girdle" is a belt or sash that wraps around the waist. The "loins" and "reins" stand for a man's moral character. Christ will be completely wrapped in righteousness and faithfulness.

30:12 ***kid***—young goat

30:14 ***sucking***—nursing or infant
***asp***—poisonous snake
***weaned child***—a toddler
***cockatrice's den***—place where a poisonous snake lives

*During the Millennium "the wolf [will] dwell with the lamb."*

15 They shall not hurt nor destroy in all my holy mountain; for the earth shall be full of the knowledge of the Lord as the waters cover the sea.

### During the Millennium the Lord Will Make Known All Things

16 Wherefore, the things of all nations shall be made known; yea, all things shall be made known unto the children of men.
17 There is nothing which is secret save it shall be revealed; there is no work of darkness save it shall be made manifest in the light; and there is nothing which is sealed upon the earth save it shall be loosed.
18 Wherefore, all things which have been revealed unto the children of men shall at that day be revealed; and Satan shall have power over the hearts of the children of men no more, for a long time. And now, my beloved brethren, I make an end of my sayings.

## CHAPTER 31

*Nephi explains the gospel plan of happiness. Look for ways the Lord sets an example for us.*

### Nephi Teaches in Plainness

1 AND now I, Nephi, make an end of my prophesying unto you, my beloved brethren. And I cannot write but a few things, which I know must surely come to pass; neither can I write but a few of the words of my brother Jacob.
2 Wherefore, the things which I have written sufficeth me, save it be a few words which I must speak concerning the doctrine of Christ; wherefore, I shall speak unto you plainly, according to the plainness of my prophesying.
3 For my soul delighteth in plainness; for after this manner doth the Lord God work among the children of men. For the Lord God giveth light unto the understanding; for he speaketh unto men according to their language, unto their understanding.

### Nephi Prophesies of Jesus' Baptism

4 Wherefore, I would that ye should remember that I have spoken unto you concerning that prophet which the Lord showed unto me, that should baptize the Lamb of God, which should take away the sins of the world.
5 And now, if the Lamb of God, he being holy, should have need to be baptized by water, to fulfil all righteousness, O then, how much more need have we, being unholy, to be baptized, yea, even by water!
6 And now, I would ask of you, my beloved brethren, wherein the Lamb of God did fulfil all righteousness in being baptized by water?
7 Know ye not that he was holy? But notwithstanding he being holy, he showeth unto the children of men that, according to the flesh he humbleth himself before the Father, and witnesseth unto the Father that he would be obedient unto him in keeping his commandments.
8 Wherefore, after he was baptized with water the Holy Ghost descended upon him in the form of a dove.

---

30:15 (12–15) In the Doctrine and Covenants, the Lord declared: "And in that day the enmity [hatred or hostility] of man, and the enmity of beasts, yea, the enmity of all flesh, shall cease from before my face" (101:26).

30:17 ***made manifest***—shown

30:18 Speaking of that great time of righteousness during the Millennium, Elder Bruce R. McConkie said: "It is not that men cannot sin, for the power is in them to do so—they have their agency—but it is that they do not sin because Satan is subject to them, and they are not enticed by his evil whisperings" (*The Millennial Messiah,* 669).

30:18 (17–18) During the Millennium all things will be restored (see Acts 3:21). "If the sealed part of the Book of Mormon has not already been revealed, it will come forth in that day" (Bruce R. McConkie, *Mormon Doctrine,* 498).

31:2 ***sufficeth me***—are enough for me

The "doctrine of Christ" is Heavenly Father's plan to have us return to His presence. The basics of this doctrine are faith, repentance, baptism by immersion for the remission of sins, and receiving the gift of the Holy Ghost (see *Articles of Faith* 1:4).

31:3 The Lord speaks to us in plainness. Why do you think the Lord wants us to understand Him?

31:8 Joseph Smith taught that at Jesus' baptism the Holy Ghost descended in the sign of a dove as a witness (see *Teachings of the Prophet Joseph Smith,* 275–76).

## Follow the Savior's Example

9 And again, it showeth unto the children of men the straitness of the path, and the narrowness of the gate, by which they should enter, he having set the example before them.

10 And he said unto the children of men: Follow thou me. Wherefore, my beloved brethren, can we follow Jesus save we shall be willing to keep the commandments of the Father?

11 And the Father said: Repent ye, repent ye, and be baptized in the name of my Beloved Son.

12 And also, the voice of the Son came unto me, saying: He that is baptized in my name, to him will the Father give the Holy Ghost, like unto me; wherefore, follow me, and do the things which ye have seen me do.

13 Wherefore, my beloved brethren, I know that if ye shall follow the Son, with full purpose of heart, acting no hypocrisy and no deception before God, but with real intent, repenting of your sins, witnessing unto the Father that ye are willing to take upon you the name of Christ, by baptism—yea, by following your Lord and your Savior down into the water, according to his word, behold, then shall ye receive the Holy Ghost; yea, then cometh the baptism of fire and of the Holy Ghost; and then can ye speak with the tongue of angels, and shout praises unto the Holy One of Israel.

14 But, behold, my beloved brethren, thus came the voice of the Son unto me, saying: After ye have repented of your sins, and witnessed unto the Father that ye are willing to keep my commandments, by the baptism of water, and have received the baptism of fire and of the Holy Ghost, and can speak with a new tongue, yea, even with the tongue of angels, and after this should deny me, it would have been better for you that ye had not known me.

15 And I heard a voice from the Father, saying: Yea, the words of my Beloved are true and faithful. He that endureth to the end, the same shall be saved.

16 And now, my beloved brethren, I know by this that unless a man shall endure to the end, in following the example of the Son of the living God, he cannot be saved.

## Endure to the End

17 Wherefore, do the things which I have told you I have seen that your Lord and your Redeemer should do; for, for this cause have they been shown unto me, that ye might know the gate by which ye should enter. For the gate by which ye should enter is repentance and baptism by water; and then cometh a remission of your sins by fire and by the Holy Ghost.

18 And then are ye in this strait and narrow path which leads to eternal life; yea, ye have entered in by the gate; ye have done according to the commandments of the Father and the Son; and ye have received the Holy Ghost, which witnesses of the Father and the Son, unto the fulfilling of the promise which he hath made, that if ye entered in by the way ye should receive.

19 And now, my beloved brethren, after ye have gotten into this strait and narrow path, I would ask if all is done? Behold, I say unto you, Nay; for ye have not come thus far save it were by the word of Christ with unshaken faith in him, relying wholly upon the merits of him who is mighty to save.

---

31:9 ***straitness***—strictness or narrowness

31:11 The Prophet Joseph Smith called baptism a "sign to God, to angels, and to heaven that we do the will of God" (*Teachings of the Prophet Joseph Smith,* 198).

31:12 In this verse the Lord invites you to follow His example. In what ways can you follow the Savior's example?

31:13 ***acting no hypocrisy***—not pretending to be good when you are not

"This baptism of fire and of the Holy Ghost here spoken of by Nephi affects the great change in the hearts of men. . . . It converts them from carnality to spirituality. It cleanses, heals, and purifies the soul. It is the sealing and sign of forgiveness" (Marion G. Romney, *Learning for the Eternities,* 133).

"True ministers always speak by the spirit of inspiration. Because they have the gift of the Holy Ghost, they can 'speak with the tongue of angels' (2 Nephi 31:13); and angels, who are but true ministers on the other side of the veil, 'speak by the power of the Holy Ghost; wherefore, they speak the word of Christ.' (2 Nephi 32:3.)" (Bruce R. McConkie, *A New Witness for the Articles of Faith,* 274).

31:17 ***remission***—forgiveness

31:19 ***merits***—works or virtues

20 Wherefore, ye must press forward with a steadfastness in Christ, having a perfect brightness of hope, and a love of God and of all men. Wherefore, if ye shall press forward, feasting upon the word of Christ, and endure to the end, behold, thus saith the Father: Ye shall have eternal life.

21 And now, behold, my beloved brethren, this is the way; and there is none other way nor name given under heaven whereby man can be saved in the kingdom of God. And now, behold, this is the doctrine of Christ, and the only and true doctrine of the Father, and of the Son, and of the Holy Ghost, which is one God, without end. Amen.

## CHAPTER 32

*The Holy Ghost will reveal to you all that you should do. As you read this chapter, watch for ways the Spirit can bless your life.*

### The Holy Ghost Teaches All Things

1 AND now, behold, my beloved brethren, I suppose that ye ponder somewhat in your hearts concerning that which ye should do after ye have entered in by the way. But, behold, why do ye ponder these things in your hearts?

2 Do ye not remember that I said unto you that after ye had received the Holy Ghost ye could speak with the tongue of angels? And now, how could ye speak with the tongue of angels save it were by the Holy Ghost?

3 Angels speak by the power of the Holy Ghost; wherefore, they speak the words of Christ. Wherefore, I said unto you, feast upon the words of Christ; for behold, the words of Christ will tell you all things what ye should do.

4 Wherefore, now after I have spoken these words, if ye cannot understand them it will be because ye ask not, neither do ye knock; wherefore, ye are not brought into the light, but must perish in the dark.

5 For behold, again I say unto you that if ye will enter in by the way, and receive the Holy Ghost, it will show unto you all things what ye should do.

6 Behold, this is the doctrine of Christ, and there will be no more doctrine given until after he shall manifest himself unto you in the flesh. And when he shall manifest himself unto you in the flesh, the things which he shall say unto you shall ye observe to do.

---

31:20 ***steadfastness***—an endurance or an unwavering faith

Nephi tells us to feast on the words of Christ. What does it mean to feast? How is feasting different from snacking? How can you feast on the scriptures?

31:20 (19–20) Quoting these verses, President Howard W. Hunter explained: "Living members recognize their duty to press forward. They are baptized as a first step of their living journey. It is a sign to God, to angels, and to heaven that they will follow God's will. . . . We are all trying, all serving, and all vowing to stand firm in the faith" (in Conference Report, April 1987, 19).

31:21 King Benjamin said, "There shall be no other name given nor any other way nor means whereby salvation can come unto the children of men, only in and through the name of Christ, the Lord Omnipotent" (Mosiah 3:17). In the New Testament, Peter similarly declared, "There is none other name under heaven given among men, whereby we must be saved" (Acts 4:12).

32:1 ***ponder***—consider seriously
***the way***—Heavenly Father's plan

32:3 (2–3) "Of all the best gifts, perhaps none is to be sought more earnestly than the ability to speak with the tongue of angels. Success in many callings depends in large measure upon the convincing power of voice and word. Without the tongue of angels, the servants of God are just ordinary men and women; but, armed with the Spirit and the words of Christ, they become 'like unto angels' and teach persuasively and powerfully" (Carlos E. Asay, *In the Lord's Service,* 172).

32:4 ***perish in the dark***—die not knowing the truth

"No message in scripture is repeated more often than the invitation, even the command, to pray—to ask. . . . Learn to pray. Pray often. Pray in your mind, in your heart. Pray on your knees" (Boyd K. Packer, in Conference Report, October 1994, 76).

32:5 The Holy Ghost can tell you what to do in every part of your life. How can you recognize when the Holy Ghost is teaching you?

32:6 ***manifest***—show

## Pray Always

7 And now I, Nephi, cannot say more; the Spirit
stoppeth mine utterance, and I am left to mourn because of the unbelief, and the wickedness, and the ignorance, and the stiffneckedness of men; for they will not search knowledge, nor understand great knowledge, when it is given unto them in plainness, even as plain as word can be.
8 And now, my beloved brethren, I perceive that
ye ponder still in your hearts; and it grieveth me that I must speak concerning this thing. For if ye would hearken unto the Spirit which teacheth a man to pray ye would know that ye must pray; for the evil spirit teacheth not a man to pray, but teacheth him that he must not pray.
9 But behold, I say unto you that ye must pray
always, and not faint; that ye must not perform any thing unto the Lord save in the first place ye shall pray unto the Father in the name of Christ, that he will consecrate thy performance unto thee, that thy performance may be for the welfare of thy soul.

## CHAPTER 33

*As Nephi finishes his record, he expresses his love for his people and testifies of Jesus Christ. Nephi testifies that his teachings are true and says, "You and I shall stand face to face . . . and ye shall know that I have been commanded . . . to write these things" (verse 11). As you read, try to feel Nephi's love for God and His children.*

## Nephi Testifies That His Words Are True

1 AND now I, Nephi, cannot write all the things
which were taught among my people; neither am I mighty in writing, like unto speaking; for when a man speaketh by the power of the Holy Ghost the power of the Holy Ghost carrieth it unto the hearts of the children of men.
2 But behold, there are many that harden their
hearts against the Holy Spirit, that it hath no place in them; wherefore, they cast many things away which are written and esteem them as things of naught.
3 But I, Nephi, have written what I have written,
and I esteem it as of great worth, and especially unto my people. For I pray continually for them by day, and mine eyes water my pillow by night, because of them; and I cry unto my God in faith, and I know that he will hear my cry.
4 And I know that the Lord God will consecrate
my prayers for the gain of my people. And the words which I have written in weakness will be made strong unto them; for it persuadeth them to do good; it maketh known unto them of their fathers; and it speaketh of Jesus, and persuadeth them to believe in him, and to endure to the end, which is life eternal.
5 And it speaketh harshly against sin, according to
the plainness of the truth; wherefore, no man will be angry at the words which I have written save he shall be of the spirit of the devil.

---

32:7 ***utterance***—ability to talk
***stiffneckedness***—stubbornness or rebelliousness

32:8 ***grieveth***—saddens or troubles

Why does the "evil spirit" teach us not to pray? How might Satan try to stop you from praying?

32:9 ***consecrate***—devote or dedicate

President Brigham Young taught: "It matters not whether you or I feel like praying, when the time comes to pray, pray. If we do not feel like it, we should pray till we do. . . . You will find that those who wait till the Spirit bids them pray, will never pray much on this earth" *(Discourses of Brigham Young,* 44).

33:2 ***esteem them as things of naught***—consider them to be worthless

33:2 (1–2) Our hearts are hardened as we give in to "the temptations of the devil" (1 Nephi 12:17; see also Helaman 16:12). The prophet Jacob teaches that "as many as will not harden their hearts shall be saved in the kingdom of God" (Jacob 6:4).

33:3 How did Nephi feel about his people? How do you think our living prophet feels about members of the Church? What does it mean to you to know that a prophet prays for you each day?

33:4 ***consecrate***—devote or dedicate
***persuadeth***—leads

To "endure to the end" is to be faithful to your covenants and to keep the commandments until you die. Elder Neal A. Maxwell said, "Enduring is vital, and those who so last will be first spiritually!" (*The Neal A. Maxwell Quote Book,* 100).

33:5 "The Bible bears witness of the Book of Mormon, and the Book of Mormon testifies of the Bible. They are both true; they both came from God; neither is false, and both are accepted by true believers. Those who believe one believe the other, and those who reject one reject, in a very real sense the other" (Bruce R. McConkie, *A New Witness for the Articles of Faith,* 394).

## Nephi's Words Testify of Jesus Christ

6 I glory in plainness; I glory in truth; I glory in my Jesus, for he hath redeemed my soul from hell.
7 I have charity for my people, and great faith in Christ that I shall meet many souls spotless at his judgment-seat.
8 I have charity for the Jew—I say Jew, because I mean them from whence I came.
9 I also have charity for the Gentiles. But behold, for none of these can I hope except they shall be reconciled unto Christ, and enter into the narrow gate, and walk in the strait path which leads to life, and continue in the path until the end of the day of probation.
10 And now, my beloved brethren, and also Jew, and all ye ends of the earth, hearken unto these words and believe in Christ; and if ye believe not in these words believe in Christ. And if ye shall believe in Christ ye will believe in these words, for they are the words of Christ, and he hath given them unto me; and they teach all men that they should do good.

## Nephi's Words Are True and Shall Stand As a Witness Before God

11 And if they are not the words of Christ, judge ye—for Christ will show unto you, with power and great glory, that they are his words, at the last day; and you and I shall stand face to face before his bar; and ye shall know that I have been commanded of him to write these things, notwithstanding my weakness.
12 And I pray the Father in the name of Christ that many of us, if not all, may be saved in his kingdom at that great and last day.
13 And now, my beloved brethren, all those who are of the house of Israel, and all ye ends of the earth, I speak unto you as the voice of one crying from the dust: Farewell until that great day shall come.
14 And you that will not partake of the goodness of God, and respect the words of the Jews, and also my words, and the words which shall proceed forth out of the mouth of the Lamb of God, behold, I bid you an everlasting farewell, for these words shall condemn you at the last day.
15 For what I seal on earth, shall be brought against you at the judgment bar; for thus hath the Lord commanded me, and I must obey. Amen.

---

33:9 ***reconciled***—brought back together

The "day of probation" is "the day of [our] repentance" or the time we have on earth to be brought back to God (Alma 34:33). Amulek testified that "this life is the time for men to prepare to meet God" and warned us not to delay our repentance (Alma 34:32).

33:9 (7–9) "Charity is the pure love of Christ, and it endureth forever. . . . Pray unto the Father with all the energy of heart, that ye may be filled with this love" (Moroni 7:47–48).

33:10 The scriptures "teach all men that they should do good." What are some of your favorite scriptures that remind you to do good?

33:11 ***his bar***—the place where God judges us

33:13 (12–13) Nephi describes the judgment day as "that great day." Judgment before God will be a great day for the righteous because they will receive their rewards. However, to the wicked it will be a "dreadful day" because they will be punished for their sins (see Malachi 4:5; Mosiah 3:25–27).

33:14 ***condemn you***—pronounce you guilty

33:15 "Though men may reject the teachings of the apostles and prophets concerning Jesus Christ and his gospel, yet those very teachings shall rise to condemn the unbelievers in the day of judgment. That is, the words of the apostles and prophets shall stand as a testimony against unbelievers at the judgment bar of Christ" (Bruce R. McConkie, *Doctrinal New Testament Commentary* 1:330).

# THE BOOK OF JACOB

## THE BROTHER OF NEPHI

*Jacob was a younger brother of Nephi. He was a faithful teacher of the gospel and one to whom angels appeared. Like his brother Nephi, Jacob also saw the Redeemer, Jesus Christ (see 2 Nephi 11:3). In this book he invites us all to leave our sins behind and come unto Christ.*

*The words of his preaching unto his brethren. He confoundeth a man who seeketh to overthrow the doctrine of Christ. A few words concerning the history of the people of Nephi.**

### CHAPTER 1

*Jacob persuades men to come unto Christ and partake of His goodness. Look for his love for the Savior as you read his words.*

#### *Jacob Writes Only That Which Is Sacred upon the Small Plates*

1 FOR behold, it came to pass that fifty and five
years had passed away from the time that Lehi left
Jerusalem; wherefore, Nephi gave me, Jacob, a
commandment concerning the small plates, upon
which these things are engraven.
2 And he gave me, Jacob, a commandment that I
should write upon these plates a few of the things
which I considered to be most precious; that I
should not touch, save it were lightly, concerning
the history of this people which are called the
people of Nephi.
3 For he said that the history of his people should
be engraven upon his other plates, and that I
should preserve these plates and hand them down
unto my seed, from generation to generation.
4 And if there were preaching which was sacred,
or revelation which was great, or prophesying, that
I should engraven the heads of them upon these
plates, and touch upon them as much as it were
possible, for Christ's sake, and for the sake of our
people.

#### *Jacob and Nephi Write to Persuade Men to Believe in Christ*

5 For because of faith and great anxiety, it truly
had been made manifest unto us concerning our
people, what things should happen unto them.
6 And we also had many revelations, and the
spirit of much prophecy; wherefore, we knew of
Christ and his kingdom, which should come.
7 Wherefore we labored diligently among our
people, that we might persuade them to come unto
Christ, and partake of the goodness of God, that
they might enter into his rest, lest by any means he
should swear in his wrath they should not enter in,
as in the provocation in the days of temptation
while the children of Israel were in the wilderness.

---

* This introduction to Jacob was translated from the Book of Mormon plates.

1:1 When Lehi left Jerusalem about 589 B.C., Jeremiah was the prophet, and Zedekiah was the king of Judah (see 1 Nephi 1:4–5).

1:2 ***touch***—write

1:3 ***engraven***—written by being cut or impressed into metal
***his other plates***—the large plates of Nephi
***these plates***—the small plates of Nephi
***seed***—descendants, meaning children, grandchildren, and so on

1:4 ***heads of them***—the most important revelations and prophecies

1:5 ***anxiety***—concern

1:7 This "provocation" refers to the days of Moses when the children of Israel rebelled against God and made and worshiped a gold calf—refusing to accept Jehovah's invitation to come to Him and receive great priesthood blessings (see Exodus 32; D&C 84:23–25).

= Word Help = A Closer Look
= More Light = Ponder This
Words in pink are explained in the Glossary.

JESUS CHRIST, BY ROBERT T. BARRETT

*Jacob and Nephi "labored diligently" to persuade men to "come unto Christ, and partake of the goodness of God."*

8 Wherefore, we would to God that we could persuade all men not to rebel against God, to provoke him to anger, but that all men would believe in Christ, and view his death, and suffer his cross and bear the shame of the world; wherefore, I, Jacob, take it upon me to fulfil the commandment of my brother Nephi.

## Jacob Notes Nephi's Death and the Problems Between the Nephites and Lamanites

9 Now Nephi began to be old, and he saw that he must soon die; wherefore, he anointed a man to be a king and a ruler over his people now, according to the reigns of the kings.

10 The people having loved Nephi exceedingly, he having been a great protector for them, having wielded the sword of Laban in their defence, and having labored in all his days for their welfare—

11 Wherefore, the people were desirous to retain in remembrance his name. And whoso should reign in his stead were called by the people, second Nephi, third Nephi, and so forth, according to the reigns of the kings; and thus they were called by the people, let them be of whatever name they would.

12 And it came to pass that Nephi died.

13 Now the people which were not Lamanites were Nephites; nevertheless, they were called Nephites, Jacobites, Josephites, Zoramites, Lamanites, Lemuelites, and Ishmaelites.

14 But I, Jacob, shall not hereafter distinguish them by these names, but I shall call them Lamanites that seek to destroy the people of Nephi, and those who are friendly to Nephi I shall call Nephites, or the people of Nephi, according to the reigns of the kings.

## The Nephites Grow in Wickedness

15 And now it came to pass that the people of Nephi, under the reign of the second king, began to grow hard in their hearts, and indulge themselves somewhat in wicked practices, such as like unto David of old desiring many wives and concubines, and also Solomon, his son.

16 Yea, and they also began to search much gold and silver, and began to be lifted up somewhat in pride.

17 Wherefore I, Jacob, gave unto them these words as I taught them in the temple, having first obtained mine errand from the Lord.

18 For I, Jacob, and my brother Joseph had been consecrated priests and teachers of this people, by the hand of Nephi.

---

1:8 Do you usually enjoy having your mistakes corrected? How can you become better at receiving correction?

President Joseph Fielding Smith once asked, "How many members of the Church, when partaking of the emblems of the sacrament, try to visualize the extreme suffering of the Son of God as he went through his torment in our behalf in the Garden of Gethsemane?" (*Answers to Gospel Questions* 5:9).

1:9 Anointing is the process of pouring oil on a person's head. Anciently it was used to bless the sick, anoint kings, and set people apart in sacred positions (see LDS Bible Dictionary, s.v. "Anoint," 609).

1:10 ***wielded***—used or handled with skill

Laban lived in Jerusalem at the same time as Nephi. He possessed a unique sword. "The hilt thereof was of pure gold, and the workmanship thereof was exceedingly fine, and . . . the blade thereof was of the most precious steel" (1 Nephi 4:9).

1:11 ***reign***—rule

1:14 ***distinguish***—separate

1:15 ***indulge themselves***—take pleasure in

In the Old Testament, a concubine was a woman who belonged to a man in a relationship similar to but not equal to that of a legal wife. There were laws protecting concubines (see Exodus 21:7; Deuteronomy 21:10–14), but they usually had very little authority in the family. Generally, a concubine's main purpose was to bear children (see *Easton's Bible Dictionary,* s.v. "Concubine").

1:17 ***errand***—assignment or mission

The Nephites built a temple shortly after they arrived in the land of Nephi (see 2 Nephi 5:16). Nearly five hundred years later, the Nephites still had temples. It was at the temple in the city Bountiful where the people were assembled when the resurrected Lord appeared (see 3 Nephi 11:1).

1:18 Nephi consecrated (set apart) his brothers as priests and teachers soon after they arrived in the land of Nephi (see 2 Nephi 5:26).

19 And we did magnify our office unto the Lord,
taking upon us the responsibility, answering the
sins of the people upon our own heads if we did
not teach them the word of God with all diligence;
wherefore, by laboring with our might their blood
might not come upon our garments; otherwise their
blood would come upon our garments, and we
would not be found spotless at the last day.

## CHAPTER 2

*Jacob teaches in the temple. He warns his people against two terrible sins. As you read, notice what kind of suffering these sins cause.*

### JACOB TEACHES WHAT GOD HAS COMMANDED HIM TO SAY

1 THE words which Jacob, the brother of Nephi,
spake unto the people of Nephi, after the death of
Nephi:
2 Now, my beloved brethren, I, Jacob, according
to the responsibility which I am under to God, to
magnify mine office with soberness, and that I
might rid my garments of your sins, I come up into
the temple this day that I might declare unto you
the word of God.
3 And ye yourselves know that I have hitherto
been diligent in the office of my calling; but I this
day am weighed down with much more desire and
anxiety for the welfare of your souls than I have
hitherto been.
4 For behold, as yet, ye have been obedient unto
the word of the Lord, which I have given unto you.
5 But behold, hearken ye unto me, and know that
by the help of the all-powerful Creator of heaven
and earth I can tell you concerning your thoughts,
how that ye are beginning to labor in sin, which sin
appeareth very abominable unto me, yea, and
abominable unto God.
6 Yea, it grieveth my soul and causeth me to
shrink with shame before the presence of my
Maker, that I must testify unto you concerning the
wickedness of your hearts.
7 And also it grieveth me that I must use so
much boldness of speech concerning you, before
your wives and your children, many of whose
feelings are exceedingly tender and chaste and
delicate before God, which thing is pleasing unto
God;
8 And it supposeth me that they have come up
hither to hear the pleasing word of God, yea, the
word which healeth the wounded soul.

---

1:19 President Hinckley quoted this verse and then declared: "To every officer, to every teacher in this Church who acts in a priesthood office, there comes the sacred responsibility of magnifying that priesthood calling. Each of us is responsible for the welfare and the growth and development of others. We do not live only unto ourselves. If we are to magnify our callings, we cannot live only unto ourselves. As we serve with diligence, as we teach with faith and testimony, as we lift and strengthen and build convictions of righteousness in those whose lives we touch, we magnify our priesthood" (in Conference Report, April 1989, 61).

2:2 ***magnify mine office with soberness***—faithfully and seriously do my duty (see also for Jacob 1:19)

"It was an ancient practice for the Lord's prophets to take off their garments and shake them as a sign that they were rid of the blood and sins of those to whom they had been sent to testify. (2 Ne. 9:44; Jacob 1:19; 2:2; Mosiah 2:28; Mormon 9:35.)" (Bruce R. McConkie, *Mormon Doctrine,* 304).

2:3 ***hitherto been diligent***—up to this time been faithful

2:5 Only God has the power to know our thoughts (see D&C 6:16). At times God reveals the thoughts of others to His servants (see Alma 18:20–35). This is called the power of discernment (see D&C 46:27). Elder Boyd K. Packer said, "This power of discernment is a very real spiritual gift. It is often conferred as a blessing upon men ordained as bishops, stake presidents, and so forth" (*"That All May Be Edified": Talks, Sermons & Commentary by Boyd K. Packer,* 34).

***abominable***—terribly evil

2:6 ***grieveth my soul***—makes me very sad
***shrink with shame***—withdraw or move back in embarrassment

2:7 ***chaste***—pure and clean

2:8 ***it supposeth me***—I believe or assume

9 Wherefore, it burdeneth my soul that I should be constrained, because of the strict commandment which I have received from God, to admonish you according to your crimes, to enlarge the wounds of those who are already wounded, instead of consoling and healing their wounds; and those who have not been wounded, instead of feasting upon the pleasing word of God have daggers placed to pierce their souls and wound their delicate minds.

10 But, notwithstanding the greatness of the task, I must do according to the strict commands of God, and tell you concerning your wickedness and abominations, in the presence of the pure in heart, and the broken heart, and under the glance of the piercing eye of the Almighty God.

11 Wherefore, I must tell you the truth according to the plainness of the word of God. For behold, as I inquired of the Lord, thus came the word unto me, saying: Jacob, get thou up into the temple on the morrow, and declare the word which I shall give thee unto this people.

## *Jacob Warns His People Against Pride*

12 And now behold, my brethren, this is the word which I declare unto you, that many of you have begun to search for gold, and for silver, and for all manner of precious ores, in the which this land, which is a land of promise unto you and to your seed, doth abound most plentifully.

13 And the hand of providence hath smiled upon you most pleasingly, that you have obtained many riches; and because some of you have obtained more abundantly than that of your brethren ye are lifted up in the pride of your hearts, and wear stiff necks and high heads because of the costliness of your apparel, and persecute your brethren because ye suppose that ye are better than they.

14 And now, my brethren, do ye suppose that God justifieth you in this thing? Behold, I say unto you, Nay. But he condemneth you, and if ye persist in these things his judgments must speedily come unto you.

---

2:9 ***constrained***—required or forced
***admonish***—warn or scold
***consoling***—comforting
***daggers***—knives

It is often the burden of the prophet to tell us what we need to hear even if he knows we do not want to hear it (see 1 Nephi 1:19; Helaman 13:26).

2:9 (6–9) Why do you think Jacob is so sorry for having to be so direct and bold in speaking about the sins of his people? Why does it make the people who love us sad when we sin?

2:10 ***abominations***—wickedness

Some people think that no one knows the things they do in secret. Jacob reminds his people that the "piercing eye" of God sees all things (see 2 Nephi 9:20; D&C 38:2).

2:12 ***precious ores***—valuable metals

2:13 ***the hand of providence***—God
***obtained more abundantly***—received more wealth
***the costliness of your apparel***—the expensiveness of your clothes

2:14 ***persist***—continue

2:14 (13–14) President Ezra Taft Benson quoted C. S. Lewis about the sin of pride: "Pride gets no pleasure out of having something, only out of having more of it than the next man" (in Conference Report, April 1989, 4).

*Palenque sculpture depicting royalty. In Jacob's day, many who were more famous or more wealthy than their neighbors became proud and wore "stiff necks and high heads."*

PHOTOGRAPH BY EDWIN M. WOOLLEY

Jacob said some of his people thought that if their clothes cost a lot of money that made them better than people whose clothes were less expensive. Does it make someone a better person if they wear expensive clothes? Why do you think some people make fun of those whose clothes are not like theirs?

15 O that he would show you that he can pierce
you, and with one glance of his eye he can smite
you to the dust!
16 O that he would rid you from this iniquity and
abomination. And, O that ye would listen unto the
word of his commands, and let not this pride of
your hearts destroy your souls!
17 Think of your brethren like unto yourselves,
and be familiar with all and free with your substance, that they may be rich like unto you.
18 But before ye seek for riches, seek ye for the
kingdom of God.
19 And after ye have obtained a hope in Christ ye
shall obtain riches, if ye seek them; and ye will seek
them for the intent to do good—to clothe the naked,
and to feed the hungry, and to liberate the captive,
and administer relief to the sick and the afflicted.
20 And now, my brethren, I have spoken unto
you concerning pride; and those of you which have
afflicted your neighbor, and persecuted him
because ye were proud in your hearts, of the things
which God hath given you, what say ye of it?
21 Do ye not suppose that such things are abominable unto him who created all flesh? And the one
being is as precious in his sight as the other. And all
flesh is of the dust; and for the selfsame end hath
he created them, that they should keep his commandments and glorify him forever.
22 And now I make an end of speaking unto you
concerning this pride. And were it not that I must
speak unto you concerning a grosser crime, my
heart would rejoice exceedingly because of you.

## Unfaithfulness in Marriage Is a Serious Sin

23 But the word of God burdens me because of
your grosser crimes. For behold, thus saith the Lord:
This people begin to wax in iniquity; they understand not the scriptures, for they seek to excuse
themselves in committing whoredoms, because of
the things which were written concerning David,
and Solomon his son.
24 Behold, David and Solomon truly had many
wives and concubines, which thing was abominable before me, saith the Lord.
25 Wherefore, thus saith the Lord, I have led this
people forth out of the land of Jerusalem, by the
power of mine arm, that I might raise up unto me a
righteous branch from the fruit of the loins of Joseph.
26 Wherefore, I the Lord God will not suffer that
this people shall do like unto them of old.
27 Wherefore, my brethren, hear me, and heark-
en to the word of the Lord: For there shall not any
man among you have save it be one wife; and concubines he shall have none;
28 For I, the Lord God, delight in the chastity of
women. And whoredoms are an abomination
before me; thus saith the Lord of Hosts.
29 Wherefore, this people shall keep my commandments, saith the Lord of Hosts, or cursed be
the land for their sakes.
30 For if I will, saith the Lord of Hosts, raise up
seed unto me, I will command my people; otherwise they shall hearken unto these things.
31 For behold, I, the Lord, have seen the sorrow,

---

2:16 The Lord warns us in modern revelation: "Beware of pride, lest ye become as the Nephites of old" (D&C 38:39).

2:17 ***free with your substance***—generous in sharing your riches

2:19 ***liberate***—set free

2:19 (18–19) Jacob teaches that righteous people use their riches to do good instead of just using them for themselves. That is what it will be like in Zion (see Moses 7:18; 4 Nephi 1:2–3). What could this world offer that would be better than living in Zion?

2:20 ***afflicted***—tormented or mistreated

2:21 ***selfsame***—same

The phrase "all flesh is of the dust" refers to the creation of our mortal bodies (see Moses 3:7). Elder Russell M. Nelson noted that "compounds derived from dust—elements of the earth—are combined to make each living cell in our bodies" (in Conference Report, April 1987, 10).

2:22 ***grosser crime***—more serious sin

2:23 ***wax in iniquity***—grow in wickedness
***whoredoms***—wickedness and immorality

2:28 ***chastity***—sexual purity

2:30 The Lord explains that one reason plural marriage might be commanded is to "raise up seed unto me," meaning to rear righteous children. If God does not command it, plural marriage is forbidden.

2:30 (24–30) From modern revelation we understand why Jacob condemned David and Solomon for having married many wives and concubines without the Lord's approval. It is a sin to take plural wives when God has not specifically commanded it. Abraham, for example, had plural wives and was not condemned because God had commanded it (see D&C 132:37–39).

and heard the mourning of the daughters of my people in the land of Jerusalem, yea, and in all the lands of my people, because of the wickedness and abominations of their husbands.
32 And I will not suffer, saith the Lord of Hosts,
that the cries of the fair daughters of this people, which I have led out of the land of Jerusalem, shall come up unto me against the men of my people, saith the Lord of Hosts.
33 For they shall not lead away captive the daugh-
ters of my people because of their tenderness, save I shall visit them with a sore curse, even unto destruction; for they shall not commit whoredoms, like unto them of old, saith the Lord of Hosts.
34 And now behold, my brethren, ye know that
these commandments were given to our father, Lehi; wherefore, ye have known them before; and ye have come unto great condemnation; for ye have done these things which ye ought not to have done.
35 Behold, ye have done greater iniquities than
the Lamanites, our brethren. Ye have broken the hearts of your tender wives, and lost the confidence of your children, because of your bad examples before them; and the sobbings of their hearts ascend up to God against you. And because of the strictness of the word of God, which cometh down against you, many hearts died, pierced with deep wounds.

## CHAPTER 3

*Jacob continues the warning against sin. As you read these words, notice why he said the Lamanites were more righteous than the Nephites.*

### *The Pure in Heart Feast on God's Love*

1 BUT behold, I, Jacob, would speak unto you
that are pure in heart. Look unto God with firmness of mind, and pray unto him with exceeding faith, and he will console you in your afflictions, and he will plead your cause, and send down justice upon those who seek your destruction.
2 O all ye that are pure in heart, lift up your heads
and receive the pleasing word of God, and feast upon his love; for ye may, if your minds are firm, forever.

### *The Nephites Are More Wicked than the Lamanites*

3 But, wo, wo, unto you that are not pure in heart,
that are filthy this day before God; for except ye repent the land is cursed for your sakes; and the Lamanites, which are not filthy like unto you, nevertheless they are cursed with a sore cursing, shall scourge you even unto destruction.
4 And the time speedily cometh, that except ye
repent they shall possess the land of your inheritance, and the Lord God will lead away the righteous out from among you.
5 Behold, the Lamanites your brethren, whom ye
hate because of their filthiness and the cursing which hath come upon their skins, are more righteous than you; for they have not forgotten the commandment of the Lord, which was given unto our father—that they should have save it were one wife, and concubines they should have none, and there should not be whoredoms committed among them.
6 And now, this commandment they observe to
keep; wherefore, because of this observance, in

---

2:34 ***come unto great condemnation***—been judged guilty by God

2:35 ***iniquities***—sins or wickedness

Because the men sinned, their wives and children are brokenhearted. It is especially painful for them that Jacob must speak so strongly against those sins in public. See also for Jacob 2:6–9.

3:1 ***with firmness of mind***—not doubting

This life doesn't always seem fair, but God will console (comfort) the faithful in their trials. More importantly, if we are faithful, Jesus Christ will stand with us and plead our cause before Heavenly Father (see D&C 45:3–5).

3:2 Jacob calls the word of God "pleasing." How do the scriptures and the words of living prophets make you feel? How often do you feast on, or read, them?

3:3 ***wo***—sorrow

3:4 Mosiah I fulfilled Jacob's prophecy when he led the righteous out from among the wicked Nephites (see Omni 1:12–13).

3:5 ***whoredoms***—wickedness and immorality

keeping this commandment, the Lord God will not destroy them, but will be merciful unto them; and one day they shall become a blessed people.

7 Behold, their husbands love their wives, and their wives love their husbands; and their husbands and their wives love their children; and their unbelief and their hatred towards you is because of the iniquity of their fathers; wherefore, how much better are you than they, in the sight of your great Creator?

8 O my brethren, I fear that unless ye shall repent of your sins that their skins will be whiter than yours, when ye shall be brought with them before the throne of God.

9 Wherefore, a commandment I give unto you, which is the word of God, that ye revile no more against them because of the darkness of their skins; neither shall ye revile against them because of their filthiness; but ye shall remember your own filthiness, and remember that their filthiness came because of their fathers.

10 Wherefore, ye shall remember your children, how that ye have grieved their hearts because of the example that ye have set before them; and also, remember that ye may, because of your filthiness, bring your children unto destruction, and their sins be heaped upon your heads at the last day.

### The Wicked Stand in Danger of the Second Death

11 O my brethren, hearken unto my words; arouse the faculties of your souls; shake yourselves that ye may awake from the slumber of death; and loose yourselves from the pains of hell that ye may not become angels to the devil, to be cast into that lake of fire and brimstone which is the second death.

12 And now I, Jacob, spake many more things unto the people of Nephi, warning them against fornication and lasciviousness, and every kind of sin, telling them the awful consequences of them.

13 And a hundredth part of the proceedings of this people, which now began to be numerous, cannot be written upon these plates; but many of their proceedings are written upon the larger plates, and their wars, and their contentions, and the reigns of their kings.

14 These plates are called the plates of Jacob, and they were made by the hand of Nephi. And I make an end of speaking these words.

## CHAPTER 4

*Jacob promised that through the Atonement of Jesus Christ we can be made clean through repentance and that all will be resurrected. As you read, look for the wonderful hope and blessings that come through the Atonement of Jesus Christ.*

### All the Prophets Worshiped Heavenly Father in the Name of Christ

1 NOW behold, it came to pass that I, Jacob, having ministered much unto my people in word, (and I cannot write but a little of my words, because of the difficulty of engraving our words upon plates) and we know that the things which we write upon plates must remain;

2 But whatsoever things we write upon anything save it be upon plates must perish and vanish away;

---

3:9 ***revile***—say bad things

3:9 (5–9) The Lord judges people on how well they live the light or truth they have been given (see D&C 82:3). The Lamanites did not know as much truth as the Nephites did, but they did a better job of living what they knew. Therefore, in the Lord's eyes they were more righteous than the Nephites. How well do you live the truth you have been given?

3:10 Parents are responsible to teach their children the "doctrine of repentance, faith in Christ the Son of the living God, and of baptism and the gift of the Holy Ghost . . . [and] to pray, and to walk uprightly before the Lord" (D&C 68:25–28).

3:11 ***faculties of your souls***—your spiritual awareness

At the final judgment those who refuse to repent are shut out forever from the presence of God. That is called the "second death" (see Helaman 14:15–18).

3:12 ***lasciviousness***—immorality and unchastity

3:13 ***proceedings***—actions or activities

4:1 ***ministered***—served and taught

4:2 ***perish and vanish***—disappear

but we can write a few words upon plates, which
will give our children, and also our beloved
brethren, a small degree of knowledge concerning
us, or concerning their fathers—
3 Now in this thing we do rejoice; and we labor
diligently to engraven these words upon plates,
hoping that our beloved brethren and our children
will receive them with thankful hearts, and look
upon them that they may learn with joy and not
with sorrow, neither with contempt, concerning
their first parents.
4 For, for this intent have we written these things,
that they may know that we knew of Christ, and we
had a hope of his glory many hundred years before
his coming; and not only we ourselves had a hope
of his glory, but also all the holy prophets which
were before us.
5 Behold, they believed in Christ and worshiped
the Father in his name, and also we worship the
Father in his name. And for this intent we keep the
law of Moses, it pointing our souls to him; and for
this cause it is sanctified unto us for righteousness,
even as it was accounted unto Abraham in the
wilderness to be obedient unto the commands of
God in offering up his son Isaac, which is a similitude of God and his Only Begotten Son.
6 Wherefore, we search the prophets, and we have
many revelations and the spirit of prophecy; and having all these witnesses we obtain a hope, and our
faith becometh unshaken, insomuch that we truly can
command in the name of Jesus and the very trees
obey us, or the mountains, or the waves of the sea.
7 Nevertheless, the Lord God showeth us our
weakness that we may know that it is by his grace,
and his great condescensions unto the children of
men, that we have power to do these things.

## We Should Listen to and Do All That the Lord Commands Us

8 Behold, great and marvelous are the works of
the Lord. How unsearchable are the depths of the
mysteries of him; and it is impossible that man
should find out all his ways. And no man knoweth
of his ways save it be revealed unto him; wherefore, brethren, despise not the revelations of God.

---

4:3 ***contempt***—disrespect

4:3 (1–3) These verses explain how much work the record keepers of the Book of Mormon did so that you might read their words. Why do you think it was so important to these record keepers that you read what they had to say? How do the words they wrote help you?

4:5 ***a similitude of***—similar to or like

The law of Moses was the list of the laws and ordinances that the children of Israel were commanded to follow from the days of Moses until the time of Jesus Christ (see LDS Bible Dictionary, s.v. "Law of Moses," 722–23).

4:5 (4–5) "All of the holy prophets worshiped the Father in the name of the Son! There is no other way. The first and great commandment, revealed anew in our day but given to the Lord's people in all dispensations, is: 'Thou shalt love the Lord thy God with all thy heart, with all thy might, mind, and strength; and in the name of Jesus Christ thou shalt serve him.' (D&C 59:5.)" (Bruce R. McConkie, *The Promised Messiah,* 559).

4:6 We "search the prophets" by studying the scriptures. "Thus the scriptures become a road map, a set of divine directions to assist us on our journey through mortality and our return trip home. Just as a road map that is not read, scriptures that are not searched are of little value to us in providing directions" (L. Lionel Kendrick, in Conference Report, April 1993, 13).

"The testimony of Jesus is the spirit of prophecy" (Revelation 19:10).

4:7 Compared to God, we are weak. We receive power because God is kind and gracious enough, or in other words condescends, to bless us with His power. It was Ammon, the son of Mosiah, who said, "I know that I am nothing; as to my strength I am weak" and that only "in [God's] strength I can do all things" (Alma 26:12).

The grace of God refers to the divine help given to us by God through the Atonement of Jesus Christ. It provides us with the power needed to repent, keep the commandments, and become like God (see LDS Bible Dictionary, s.v. "Grace," 697; see also 2 Nephi 25:23).

4:8 ***the mysteries of him***—truths known only through revelation from God
***despise***—hate

President Gordon B. Hinckley explains: "Of course we believe in the cultivation [improvement] of the mind, but the intellect is not the only source of knowledge. There is a promise, given under inspiration from the Almighty, set forth in these beautiful words: 'God shall give unto you knowledge by his Holy Spirit, yea, by the unspeakable gift of the Holy Ghost.' (D&C 121:26.)" (*Faith, the Essence of True Religion,* 78).

SACRIFICE OF ISAAC, BY JERRY HARSTON

*Abraham was commanded to sacrifice his son, Isaac, which symbolized God offering His Only Begotten Son, Jesus Christ.*

9 For behold, by the power of his word man came upon the face of the earth, which earth was created by the power of his word. Wherefore, if God being able to speak and the world was, and to speak and man was created, O then, why not able to command the earth, or the workmanship of his hands upon the face of it, according to his will and pleasure?
10 Wherefore, brethren, seek not to counsel the Lord, but to take counsel from his hand. For behold, ye yourselves know that he counseleth in wisdom, and in justice, and in great mercy, over all his works.

## Through the Atonement of Jesus Christ We Can Live Again with God

11 Wherefore, beloved brethren, be reconciled unto him through the atonement of Christ, his Only Begotten Son, and ye may obtain a resurrection, according to the power of the resurrection which is in Christ, and be presented as the first-fruits of Christ unto God, having faith, and obtained a good hope of glory in him before he manifesteth himself in the flesh.
12 And now, beloved, marvel not that I tell you

---

4:10 The Lord knows all things. Should we tell Him what to do? How can you show your willingness to listen to and obey Him?

4:11 ***be reconciled unto him***—be brought back together with God
***manifesteth***—shows

Because of the power of the Atonement, we can repent and be made worthy to dwell in God's presence. Because of the power of Christ's Resurrection we can be among the first to be resurrected (first-fruits) and to be presented to Heavenly Father (see D&C 88:96–98).

these things; for why not speak of the atonement of Christ, and attain to a perfect knowledge of him, as to attain to the knowledge of a resurrection and the world to come?

13 Behold, my brethren, he that prophesieth, let him prophesy to the understanding of men; for the Spirit speaketh the truth and lieth not. Wherefore, it speaketh of things as they really are, and of things as they really will be; wherefore, these things are manifested unto us plainly, for the salvation of our souls. But behold, we are not witnesses alone in these things; for God also spake them unto prophets of old.

## *The Jews Will Suffer for Rejecting Jesus Christ*

14 But behold, the Jews were a stiffnecked people; and they despised the words of plainness, and killed the prophets, and sought for things that they could not understand. Wherefore, because of their blindness, which blindness came by looking beyond the mark, they must needs fall; for God hath taken away his plainness from them, and delivered unto them many things which they cannot understand, because they desired it. And because they desired it God hath done it, that they may stumble.

15 And now I, Jacob, am led on by the Spirit unto prophesying; for I perceive by the workings of the Spirit which is in me, that by the stumbling of the Jews they will reject the stone upon which they might build and have safe foundation.

16 But behold, according to the scriptures, this stone shall become the great, and the last, and the only sure foundation, upon which the Jews can build.

17 And now, my beloved, how is it possible that these, after having rejected the sure foundation, can ever build upon it, that it may become the head of their corner?

18 Behold, my beloved brethren, I will unfold this mystery unto you; if I do not, by any means, get shaken from my firmness in the Spirit, and stumble because of my over anxiety for you.

# CHAPTER 5

*The prophet Zenos compares the children of Israel to a tame olive tree and the Gentiles to wild olive trees. Look for all that the Lord does to help His trees grow good fruit.*

## *The Master Cares for the Tame Olive Tree When They (the Children of Israel) Begin to Become Evil*

1 BEHOLD, my brethren, do ye not remember to have read the words of the prophet Zenos, which he spake unto the house of Israel, saying:

2 Hearken, O ye house of Israel, and hear the words of me, a prophet of the Lord.

---

4:12 ***attain to***—obtain

4:13 Many people are confused about what is most important in life. Who will tell us "things as they really are"? How can you listen to Him?

4:14 ***stiffnecked***—stubborn
***despised***—hated

4:15 ***perceive***—see or understand

4:15 (14–15) The gospel is plain and simple. The Jews rejected the simple gospel and God's plan by "'looking beyond the mark' (Jacob 4:14)—the mark of Christ, who is at the center of it all" (Neal A. Maxwell, *"Not My Will, But Thine,"* 7). When Jesus came into the world, the Jews "stumbled" over Him like a stone in their path because they were looking beyond Him for some other kind of Messiah.

4:18 ***over anxiety***—serious concern

4:18 (16–18) Jesus Christ is the only stone or rock upon which we can build to keep us safe from Satan's storms and to help us obtain salvation (see Matthew 7:24–27; Helaman 5:12). In the last days even the Jews will "come to the knowledge of their Redeemer" and be saved (see 2 Nephi 6:11).

5:1 Zenos was an Israelite prophet often quoted in the Book of Mormon (see 1 Nephi 19:10–17; Alma 33:3–15; Helaman 8:19; 15:11; 3 Nephi 10:16). All we know of his personal life is that he was killed because he testified boldly of what God revealed to him (see Helaman 8:19).

5:2 ***Hearken***—Listen to and obey

3 For behold, thus saith the Lord, I will liken thee, O house of Israel, like unto a tame olive-tree, which a man took and nourished in his vineyard; and it grew, and waxed old, and began to decay.

4 And it came to pass that the master of the vineyard went forth, and he saw that his olive-tree began to decay; and he said: I will prune it, and dig about it, and nourish it, that perhaps it may shoot forth young and tender branches, and it perish not.

5 And it came to pass that he pruned it, and digged about it, and nourished it according to his word.

### *The Master (God) and His Servant (the Prophets) Graft Wild Olive Tree Branches (the Gentiles) into the Tame Olive Tree (the House of Israel)*

6 And it came to pass that after many days it began to put forth somewhat a little, young and tender branches; but behold, the main top thereof began to perish.

7 And it came to pass that the master of the vineyard saw it, and he said unto his servant: It grieveth me that I should lose this tree; wherefore, go and pluck the branches from a wild olive-tree, and bring them hither unto me; and we will pluck off those main branches which are beginning to wither away, and we will cast them into the fire that they may be burned.

8 And behold, saith the Lord of the vineyard, I take away many of these young and tender branches, and I will graft them whithersoever I will; and it mattereth not that if it so be that the root of this tree will perish, I may preserve the fruit thereof unto myself; wherefore, I will take these young and tender branches, and I will graft them whithersoever I will.

9 Take thou the branches of the wild olive-tree, and graft them in, in the stead thereof; and these which I have plucked off I will cast into the fire and burn them, that they may not cumber the ground of my vineyard.

10 And it came to pass that the servant of the Lord of the vineyard did according to the word of the Lord of the vineyard, and grafted in the branches of the wild olive-tree.

11 And the Lord of the vineyard caused that it should be digged about, and pruned, and nourished, saying unto his servant: It grieveth me that I should lose this tree; wherefore, that perhaps I might preserve the roots thereof that they perish not, that I might preserve them unto myself, I have done this thing.

12 Wherefore, go thy way; watch the tree, and nourish it, according to my words.

---

PHOTOGRAPH BY DAVID H. GARNER

*The Lord likened the house of Israel to a tame olive tree.*

5:3 ***liken***—compare or apply
***his vineyard***—the place where the olive trees are planted
***waxed***—grew
***decay***—die or rot

5:4 ***prune it***—cut off the rotten limbs
***perish***—die

5:6 ***put forth***—sprout or grow

5:7 ***grieveth me***—makes me very sad
***pluck***—take or pick
***hither***—here
***wither***—shrivel or wilt

5:8 (6–8) The "young and tender" branches appear to be small groups of the children of Israel who were willing to obey the Lord. Elder Joseph Fielding Smith said, "Now in that parable the olive tree is the House of Israel. . . . In its native land it began to die. So the Lord took branches like the Nephites, like the lost tribes, and like others that the Lord led off that we do not know anything about, to other parts of the earth. He planted them all over his vineyard, which is the world" (*Answers to Gospel Questions* 4:204).

5:8 (7–8) The "master of the vineyard" and the "Lord of the vineyard" are the same person.

5:9 ***stead***—place
***cumber***—get in the way or clutter

5:11 ***preserve***—save

13 And these will I place in the nethermost part of my vineyard, whithersoever I will, it mattereth not unto thee; and I do it that I may preserve unto myself the natural branches of the tree; and also, that I may lay up fruit thereof against the season, unto myself; for it grieveth me that I should lose this tree and the fruit thereof.

14 And it came to pass that the Lord of the vineyard went his way, and hid the natural branches of the tame olive-tree in the nethermost parts of the vineyard, some in one and some in another, according to his will and pleasure.

### *After a Long Time, the Master and His Servant Discover That the Tame Olive Tree and All But One of the Natural Branches They Had Planted in the Nethermost Parts of the Vineyard Have Grown Good Fruit*

15 And it came to pass that a long time passed away, and the Lord of the vineyard said unto his servant: Come, let us go down into the vineyard, that we may labor in the vineyard.

16 And it came to pass that the Lord of the vineyard, and also the servant, went down into the vineyard to labor. And it came to pass that the servant said unto his master: Behold, look here; behold the tree.

17 And it came to pass that the Lord of the vineyard looked and beheld the tree in the which the wild olive branches had been grafted; and it had sprung forth and begun to bear fruit. And he beheld that it was good; and the fruit thereof was like unto the natural fruit.

18 And he said unto the servant: Behold, the branches of the wild tree have taken hold of the moisture of the root thereof, that the root thereof hath brought forth much strength; and because of the much strength of the root thereof the wild branches have brought forth tame fruit. Now, if we had not grafted in these branches, the tree thereof would have perished. And now, behold, I shall lay up much fruit, which the tree thereof hath brought forth; and the fruit thereof I shall lay up against the season, unto mine own self.

19 And it came to pass that the Lord of the vineyard said unto the servant: Come, let us go to the nethermost part of the vineyard, and behold if the natural branches of the tree have not brought forth much fruit also, that I may lay up of the fruit thereof against the season, unto mine own self.

20 And it came to pass that they went forth whither the master had hid the natural branches of the tree, and he said unto the servant: Behold these; and he beheld the first that it had brought forth much fruit; and he beheld also that it was good. And he said unto the servant: Take of the fruit thereof, and lay it up against the season, that I may preserve it unto mine own self; for behold, said he, this long time have I nourished it, and it hath brought forth much fruit.

21 And it came to pass that the servant said unto his master: How comest thou hither to plant this tree, or this branch of the tree? For behold, it was the poorest spot in all the land of thy vineyard.

22 And the Lord of the vineyard said unto him: Counsel me not; I knew that it was a poor spot of ground; wherefore, I said unto thee, I have nourished it this long time, and thou beholdest that it hath brought forth much fruit.

23 And it came to pass that the Lord of the vineyard said unto his servant: Look hither; behold I have planted another branch of the tree also; and thou knowest that this spot of ground was poorer than the first. But, behold the tree. I have nourished it this long time, and it hath brought forth much fruit; therefore, gather it, and lay it up against the season, that I may preserve it unto mine own self.

24 And it came to pass that the Lord of the vineyard said again unto his servant: Look hither, and behold another branch also, which I have planted; behold that I have nourished it also, and it hath brought forth fruit.

25 And he said unto the servant: Look hither and behold the last. Behold, this have I planted in a good spot of ground; and I have nourished it this long time, and only a part of the tree hath brought forth tame fruit, and the other part of the tree hath brought forth wild fruit; behold, I have nourished this tree like unto the others.

---

5:13 ***nethermost***—lowest or furthest
***whithersoever***—wherever
***lay***—store

5:17 ***sprung forth***—grown

26 And it came to pass that the Lord of the vineyard said unto the servant: Pluck off the branches
that have not brought forth good fruit, and cast
them into the fire.
27 But behold, the servant said unto him: Let us
prune it, and dig about it, and nourish it a little
longer, that perhaps it may bring forth good fruit
unto thee, that thou canst lay it up against the season.
28 And it came to pass that the Lord of the vineyard and the servant of the Lord of the vineyard did
nourish all the fruit of the vineyard.

## After a Long Time, the Master and His Servant Discover That All of the Olive Trees Are Growing Bad Fruit

29 And it came to pass that a long time had passed
away, and the Lord of the vineyard said unto his
servant: Come, let us go down into the vineyard,
that we may labor again in the vineyard. For
behold, the time draweth near, and the end soon
cometh; wherefore, I must lay up fruit against the
season, unto mine own self.
30 And it came to pass that the Lord of the vineyard and the servant went down into the vineyard;
and they came to the tree whose natural branches
had been broken off, and the wild branches had
been grafted in; and behold all sorts of fruit did
cumber the tree.
31 And it came to pass that the Lord of the vineyard did taste of the fruit, every sort according to its
number. And the Lord of the vineyard said: Behold,
this long time have we nourished this tree, and I
have laid up unto myself against the season much
fruit.
32 But behold, this time it hath brought forth
much fruit, and there is none of it which is good.
And behold, there are all kinds of bad fruit; and it
profiteth me nothing, notwithstanding all our labor;
and now it grieveth me that I should lose this tree.
33 And the Lord of the vineyard said unto the
servant: What shall we do unto the tree, that I may
preserve again good fruit thereof unto mine own
self?
34 And the servant said unto his master: Behold,
because thou didst graft in the branches of the wild
olive-tree they have nourished the roots, that they
are alive and they have not perished; wherefore
thou beholdest that they are yet good.
35 And it came to pass that the Lord of the vineyard said unto his servant: The tree profiteth me
nothing, and the roots thereof profit me nothing so
long as it shall bring forth evil fruit.
36 Nevertheless, I know that the roots are good,
and for mine own purpose I have preserved them;
and because of their much strength they have
hitherto brought forth, from the wild branches,
good fruit.
37 But behold, the wild branches have grown and
have overrun the roots thereof; and because that
the wild branches have overcome the roots thereof
it hath brought forth much evil fruit; and because
that it hath brought forth so much evil fruit thou
beholdest that it beginneth to perish; and it will
soon become ripened, that it may be cast into the
fire, except we should do something for it to preserve it.
38 And it came to pass that the Lord of the vineyard said unto his servant: Let us go down into the
nethermost parts of the vineyard, and behold if the
natural branches have also brought forth evil fruit.
39 And it came to pass that they went down into
the nethermost parts of the vineyard. And it came
to pass that they beheld that the fruit of the natural
branches had become corrupt also; yea, the first
and the second and also the last; and they had all
become corrupt.
40 And the wild fruit of the last had overcome that
part of the tree which brought forth good fruit, even
that the branch had withered away and died.
41 And it came to pass that the Lord of the vineyard wept, and said unto the servant: What could I
have done more for my vineyard?

---

5:29 The end that "soon cometh" is the end of the world or the time of the destruction of the wicked (see Joseph Smith—Matthew 1:4).

5:32 The period of time between the death of Jesus' Apostles and the Restoration through the Prophet Joseph Smith was a period of spiritual darkness. It appears to be this time period Zenos is referring to when none of the trees bore good fruit (see Jacob 5:29–48).

5:36 ***hitherto***—up to this time

5:39 ***corrupt***—evil

5:41 The Lord asks what more He could have done for His vineyard. What would you say to Him?

42 Behold, I knew that all the fruit of the vineyard, save it were these, had become corrupted. And now these which have once brought forth good fruit have also become corrupted; and now all the trees of my vineyard are good for nothing save it be to be hewn down and cast into the fire.

43 And behold this last, whose branch hath withered away, I did plant in a good spot of ground; yea, even that which was choice unto me above all other parts of the land of my vineyard.

44 And thou beheldest that I also cut down that which cumbered this spot of ground, that I might plant this tree in the stead thereof.

45 And thou beheldest that a part thereof brought forth good fruit, and a part thereof brought forth wild fruit; and because I plucked not the branches thereof and cast them into the fire, behold, they have overcome the good branch that it hath withered away.

46 And now, behold, notwithstanding all the care which we have taken of my vineyard, the trees thereof have become corrupted, that they bring forth no good fruit; and these I had hoped to preserve, to have laid up fruit thereof against the season, unto mine own self. But, behold, they have become like unto the wild olive-tree, and they are of no worth but to be hewn down and cast into the fire; and it grieveth me that I should lose them.

47 But what could I have done more in my vineyard? Have I slackened mine hand, that I have not nourished it? Nay, I have nourished it, and I have digged about it, and I have pruned it, and I have dunged it; and I have stretched forth mine hand almost all the day long, and the end draweth nigh. And it grieveth me that I should hew down all the trees of my vineyard, and cast them into the fire that they should be burned. Who is it that has corrupted my vineyard?

48 And it came to pass that the servant said unto his master: Is it not the loftiness of thy vineyard—have not the branches thereof overcome the roots which are good? And because the branches have overcome the roots thereof, behold they grew faster than the strength of the roots, taking strength unto themselves. Behold, I say, is not this the cause that the trees of thy vineyard have become corrupted?

## *The Master and His Servant Decide What They Will Do to Give All of the Olive Trees One More Chance to Grow Good Fruit*

49 And it came to pass that the Lord of the vineyard said unto the servant: Let us go to and hew down the trees of the vineyard and cast them into the fire, that they shall not cumber the ground of my vineyard, for I have done all. What could I have done more for my vineyard?

50 But, behold, the servant said unto the Lord of the vineyard: Spare it a little longer.

51 And the Lord said: Yea, I will spare it a little longer, for it grieveth me that I should lose the trees of my vineyard.

52 Wherefore, let us take of the branches of these which I have planted in the nethermost parts of my vineyard, and let us graft them into the tree from whence they came; and let us pluck from the tree those branches whose fruit is most bitter, and graft in the natural branches of the tree in the stead thereof.

53 And this will I do that the tree may not perish, that, perhaps, I may preserve unto myself the roots thereof for mine own purpose.

54 And, behold, the roots of the natural branches of the tree which I planted whithersoever I would are yet alive; wherefore, that I may preserve them also for mine own purpose, I will take of the branches of this tree, and I will graft them in unto them. Yea, I will graft in unto them the branches of their mother tree, that I may preserve the roots also unto mine own self, that when they shall be sufficiently strong perhaps they may bring forth good fruit unto me, and I may yet have glory in the fruit of my vineyard.

55 And it came to pass that they took from the natural tree which had become wild, and grafted in unto the natural trees, which also had become wild.

56 And they also took of the natural trees which

5:42 ***hewn***—cut

5:47 ***slackened mine hand***—lessened my effort
***dunged***—nourished and fertilized
***draweth nigh***—is near

5:48 ***loftiness***—height

5:50 ***Spare***—Save

5:54 ***sufficiently strong***—strong enough that

5:55 (54–55) The "mother tree" is the tame olive tree first mentioned in Jacob 5:3. The Lord will take branches from the scattered trees and graft them into the mother tree. He will also take branches from the mother tree and graft them into the roots of the scattered trees.

had become wild, and grafted into their mother tree.

57 And the Lord of the vineyard said unto the servant: Pluck not the wild branches from the trees, save it be those which are most bitter; and in them ye shall graft according to that which I have said.

58 And we will nourish again the trees of the vineyard, and we will trim up the branches thereof; and we will pluck from the trees those branches which are ripened, that must perish, and cast them into the fire.

59 And this I do that, perhaps, the roots thereof may take strength because of their goodness; and because of the change of the branches, that the good may overcome the evil.

60 And because that I have preserved the natural branches and the roots thereof, and that I have grafted in the natural branches again into their mother tree, and have preserved the roots of their mother tree, that, perhaps, the trees of my vineyard may bring forth again good fruit and that I may have joy again in the fruit of my vineyard, and, perhaps, that I may rejoice exceedingly that I have preserved the roots and the branches of the first fruit—

61 Wherefore, go to, and call servants, that we may labor diligently with our might in the vineyard, that we may prepare the way, that I may bring forth again the natural fruit, which natural fruit is good and the most precious above all other fruit.

62 Wherefore, let us go to and labor with our might this last time, for behold the end draweth nigh, and this is for the last time that I shall prune my vineyard.

63 Graft in the branches; begin at the last that they may be first, and that the first may be last, and dig about the trees, both old and young, the first and the last; and the last and the first, that all may be nourished once again for the last time.

64 Wherefore, dig about them, and prune them, and dung them once more, for the last time, for the end draweth nigh. And if it be so that these last grafts shall grow, and bring forth the natural fruit, then shall ye prepare the way for them, that they may grow.

65 And as they begin to grow ye shall clear away the branches which bring forth bitter fruit, according to the strength of the good and the size thereof; and ye shall not clear away the bad thereof all at once, lest the roots thereof should be too strong for the graft, and the graft thereof shall perish, and I lose the trees of my vineyard.

66 For it grieveth me that I should lose the trees of my vineyard; wherefore ye shall clear away the bad according as the good shall grow, that the root and the top may be equal in strength, until the good shall overcome the bad, and the bad be hewn down and cast into the fire, that they cumber not the ground of my vineyard; and thus will I sweep away the bad out of my vineyard.

67 And the branches of the natural tree will I graft in again into the natural tree;

68 And the branches of the natural tree will I graft into the natural branches of the tree; and thus will I bring them together again, that they shall bring forth the natural fruit, and they shall be one.

69 And the bad shall be cast away, yea, even out of all the land of my vineyard; for behold, only this once will I prune my vineyard.

## *The Master's Servant and Other Servants Work in the Vineyard to Save the Olive Trees and to Gather Much Good Fruit*

70 And it came to pass that the Lord of the vineyard sent his servant; and the servant went and did as the Lord had commanded him, and brought other servants; and they were few.

71 And the Lord of the vineyard said unto them: Go to, and labor in the vineyard, with your might. For behold, this is the last time that I shall nourish my vineyard; for the end is nigh at hand, and the season speedily cometh; and if ye labor with your might with me ye shall have joy in the fruit which I shall lay up unto myself against the time which will soon come.

---

5:57 ***bitter***—bad or evil

5:62 (61–62) The Lord is describing the last time He will gather and care for His olive trees. During this final effort, He is going to call other "servants" to assist in the work. What can you do as one of His servants to help the Lord in His work?

5:68 (67–68) Father Lehi also compared the scattering and gathering of Israel to the branches of an olive tree. He explained that the "natural branches" were the "remnants of the house of Israel." He also explained that when they are gathered and "grafted in," it is symbolic of the children of Israel coming "to the knowledge of the true Messiah" (see 1 Nephi 10:14).

5:71 Doctrine and Covenants 18:15 says that if we "should labor all [our] days in crying repentance unto this people," and bring even one person unto Christ, "how great shall be [our] joy with him in the kingdom of [our] Father!"

72 And it came to pass that the servants did go
and labor with their mights; and the Lord of the
vineyard labored also with them; and they did obey
the commandments of the Lord of the vineyard in
all things.
73 And there began to be the natural fruit again in
the vineyard; and the natural branches began to
grow and thrive exceedingly; and the wild branches began to be plucked off and to be cast away; and
they did keep the root and the top thereof equal,
according to the strength thereof.

### *The Trees Grow Good Fruit and the Master Blesses His Servants*

74 And thus they labored, with all diligence,
according to the commandments of the Lord of the
vineyard, even until the bad had been cast away
out of the vineyard, and the Lord had preserved
unto himself that the trees had become again the
natural fruit; and they became like unto one body;
and the fruits were equal; and the Lord of the vineyard had preserved unto himself the natural fruit,
which was most precious unto him from the beginning.
75 And it came to pass that when the Lord of the
vineyard saw that his fruit was good, and that his
vineyard was no more corrupt, he called up his servants, and said unto them: Behold, for this last time
have we nourished my vineyard; and thou beholdest that I have done according to my will; and I
have preserved the natural fruit, that it is good,
even like as it was in the beginning. And blessed art
thou; for because ye have been diligent in laboring
with me in my vineyard, and have kept my commandments, and have brought unto me again the
natural fruit, that my vineyard is no more corrupted, and the bad is cast away, behold ye shall
have joy with me because of the fruit of my vineyard.

### *The Master Will Gather Good Fruit and Burn the Bad*

76 For behold, for a long time will I lay up of the
fruit of my vineyard unto mine own self against the
season, which speedily cometh; and for the last
time have I nourished my vineyard, and pruned it,
and dug about it, and dunged it; wherefore I will
lay up unto mine own self of the fruit, for a long
time, according to that which I have spoken.
77 And when the time cometh that evil fruit shall
again come into my vineyard, then will I cause the
good and the bad to be gathered; and the good will
I preserve unto myself, and the bad will I cast away
into its own place. And then cometh the season and
the end; and my vineyard will I cause to be burned
with fire.

## CHAPTER 6

*Jacob continues to recall the teachings of Zenos and testifies about the Second Coming of Jesus Christ. Look for what we must do to avoid the terrible judgments that will come upon the wicked.*

### *In the Last Days the Lord Will Save His People*

1 AND now, behold, my brethren, as I said unto
you that I would prophesy, behold, this is my
prophecy—that the things which this prophet
Zenos spake, concerning the house of Israel, in the
which he likened them unto a tame olive-tree, must
surely come to pass.

---

5:74 ***diligence***—care and effort

5:75 What are some of the blessings you have received when you have tried to help people be faithful members of the Church?

5:77 In a similar story called the parable of the wheat and the tares (weeds), the Savior described how in the last days the tares will be gathered to be burned and the wheat will be gathered and saved (see Matthew 13:24–30; D&C 86:1–11).

5:77 (2–77) Zenos spoke about olive trees and their fruit to teach us about all that the Lord has done and continues to do to save His children. What have you learned about the Lord in Jacob 5 that helps you better understand His love for you and all of His children?

6:1 ***likened***—compared or applied

A prophet is a messenger of God who preaches righteousness and tells of the punishments that come from sin (see LDS Bible Dictionary, s.v. "Prophet," 754). Prophets also prophesy, or foretell the future.

Zenos's teachings about the tame olive tree are found in Jacob 5:3–7.

2 And the day that he shall set his hand again the second time to recover his people, is the day, yea, even the last time, that the servants of the Lord shall go forth in his power, to nourish and prune his vineyard; and after that the end soon cometh.

3 And how blessed are they who have labored diligently in his vineyard; and how cursed are they who shall be cast out into their own place! And the world shall be burned with fire.

4 And how merciful is our God unto us, for he remembereth the house of Israel, both roots and branches; and he stretches forth his hands unto them all the day long; and they are a stiffnecked and a gainsaying people; but as many as will not harden their hearts shall be saved in the kingdom of God.

## At the Second Coming the Earth Will Be Cleansed with Fire

5 Wherefore, my beloved brethren, I beseech of you in words of soberness that ye would repent, and come with full purpose of heart, and cleave unto God as he cleaveth unto you. And while his arm of mercy is extended towards you in the light of the day, harden not your hearts.

6 Yea, today, if ye will hear his voice, harden not your hearts; for why will ye die?

7 For behold, after ye have been nourished by the good word of God all the day long, will ye bring forth evil fruit, that ye must be hewn down and cast into the fire?

## Jacob Preaches Repentance and Asks Us to Follow Christ

8 Behold, will ye reject these words? Will ye reject the words of the prophets; and will ye reject all the words which have been spoken concerning Christ, after so many have spoken concerning him; and deny the good word of Christ, and the power of God, and the gift of the Holy Ghost, and quench the Holy Spirit, and make a mock of the great plan of redemption, which hath been laid for you?

9 Know ye not that if ye will do these things, that the power of the redemption and the resurrection, which is in Christ, will bring you to stand with shame and awful guilt before the bar of God?

10 And according to the power of justice, for justice cannot be denied, ye must go away into that lake of fire and brimstone, whose flames are unquenchable, and whose smoke ascendeth up forever and ever, which lake of fire and brimstone is endless torment.

---

6:2 ***set his hand***—begin
***recover***—bring back or save

In the last days the Lord will call servants to help care for His vineyard, which is this world. These servants include the prophets and the missionaries (see D&C 1:14; 4:1–4).

6:3 Those who labor diligently for the Lord will be greatly blessed. What are you doing to be a faithful servant of the Lord? What blessings have you received from Him?

6:4 ***merciful***—kind, loving, and forgiving
***stiffnecked***—stubborn or rebellious
***gainsaying people***—those who turn against God

Tree roots and branches sometimes represent families. Branches remind us of family members who spread out to live in distant lands. Heavenly Father remembers all members of His family wherever they live.

6:5 ***beseech***—strongly ask or beg
***words of soberness***—serious words
***cleave***—hold to or support

Mercy is love and kindness. In what ways has God reached out His arms to you in love and kindness?

6:7 Those who bring forth evil fruit, or who do evil works, will be destroyed by fire at the Second Coming (see D&C 63:34).

6:8 ***reject***—refuse to receive
***deny***—not accept
***quench***—stop or put an end to or extinguish
***make a mock***—make fun of

6:9 After we die, we will be judged by Jesus Christ (see John 5:22). The bar of God is the place where we will be judged. Those who are wicked will be fearful and ashamed.

6:10 "Justice" refers to an eternal law, which states that when a commandment is broken a penalty results (see Alma 42:22).

In the scriptures, a lake of fire and brimstone (sulfur) symbolizes the eternal torment of the wicked (see Revelation 14:9–11; 19:20; 20:10; Alma 12:17).

11 O then, my beloved brethren, repent ye, and enter in at the strait gate, and continue in the way which is narrow, until ye shall obtain eternal life.

12 O be wise; what can I say more?

13 Finally, I bid you farewell, until I shall meet you before the pleasing bar of God, which bar striketh the wicked with awful dread and fear. Amen.

## CHAPTER 7

*Satan tries to use his followers to destroy people's faith in Jesus. As you read this chapter, look for how Jacob overcomes Sherem's attempt to convince him and the Nephites not to believe in Jesus Christ and His Atonement.*

### *Sherem Preaches That There Should Be No Christ*

1 AND now it came to pass after some years had passed away, there came a man among the people of Nephi, whose name was Sherem.

2 And it came to pass that he began to preach among the people, and to declare unto them that there should be no Christ. And he preached many things which were flattering unto the people; and this he did that he might overthrow the doctrine of Christ.

3 And he labored diligently that he might lead away the hearts of the people, insomuch that he did lead away many hearts; and he knowing that I, Jacob, had faith in Christ who should come, he sought much opportunity that he might come unto me.

4 And he was learned, that he had a perfect knowledge of the language of the people; wherefore, he could use much flattery, and much power of speech, according to the power of the devil.

### *Sherem Argues with Jacob*

5 And he had hope to shake me from the faith, notwithstanding the many revelations and the many things which I had seen concerning these things; for I truly had seen angels, and they had ministered unto me. And also, I had heard the voice of the Lord speaking unto me in very word, from time to time; wherefore, I could not be shaken.

6 And it came to pass that he came unto me, and on this wise did he speak unto me, saying: Brother Jacob, I have sought much opportunity that I might speak unto you; for I have heard and also know that thou goest about much, preaching that which ye call the gospel, or the doctrine of Christ.

7 And ye have led away much of this people that they pervert the right way of God, and keep not the law of Moses which is the right way; and convert the law of Moses into the worship of a being which ye say shall come many hundred years hence. And now behold, I, Sherem, declare unto you that this is blasphemy; for no man knoweth of such things; for he cannot tell of things to come. And after this manner did Sherem contend against me.

---

6:11 The strait gate and a narrow path lead to heaven. Why do you want to follow this path? How might you help others get on that path?

7:2 ***overthrow***—cause the downfall of

"An antichrist is an opponent of Christ; he is one who is in opposition to the true gospel, the true Church, and the true plan of salvation. (1 John 2:19; 4:4–6.) He is one who offers salvation to men on some other terms than those laid down by Christ. Sherem (Jacob 7:1–23), Nehor (Alma 1:2–16), and Korihor (Alma 30:6–60) were antichrists who spread their delusions [falsehoods] among the Nephites" (Bruce R. McConkie, *Mormon Doctrine,* 39).

7:3 ***labored diligently***—worked hard
***sought much opportunity***—often tried

7:4 ***learned***—smart

7:5 ***notwithstanding***—in spite of
***ministered***—appeared to and given help

Sherem did not influence Jacob with his false doctrine because Jacob had a strong testimony of Jesus Christ. Jacob had the gift of the Holy Ghost and had received many revelations. How can the Holy Ghost help you when you are confronted by those who teach false doctrine?

7:6 ***on this wise***—in this way

7:7 ***pervert***—corrupt
***convert***—change

Blasphemy is falsely claiming to be like God or speaking evil of God or of sacred things (see LDS Bible Dictionary, s.v. "Blasphemy," 625–26).

Sherem argues that no one can predict things to come. Korihor, another antichrist, preached the same thing during his encounter with Alma (see Alma 30:15).

8 But behold, the Lord God poured in his Spirit
into my soul, insomuch that I did confound him in
all his words.
9 And I said unto him: Deniest thou the Christ
who shall come? And he said: If there should be a
Christ, I would not deny him; but I know that there
is no Christ, neither has been, nor ever will be.
10 And I said unto him: Believest thou the scriptures? And he said, Yea.
11 And I said unto him: Then ye do not understand them; for they truly testify of Christ. Behold, I
say unto you that none of the prophets have written, nor prophesied, save they have spoken concerning this Christ.
12 And this is not all—it has been made manifest
unto me, for I have heard and seen; and it also has
been made manifest unto me by the power of the
Holy Ghost; wherefore, I know if there should be
no atonement made all mankind must be lost.

## Sherem Demands That Jacob Show Him a Sign

13 And it came to pass that he said unto me: Show
me a sign by this power of the Holy Ghost, in the
which ye know so much.
14 And I said unto him: What am I that I should
tempt God to show unto thee a sign in the thing
which thou knowest to be true? Yet thou wilt deny
it, because thou art of the devil. Nevertheless, not my
will be done; but if God shall smite thee, let that be
a sign unto thee that he has power, both in heaven
and in earth; and also, that Christ shall come. And
thy will, O Lord, be done, and not mine.
15 And it came to pass that when I, Jacob, had
spoken these words, the power of the Lord came
upon him, insomuch that he fell to the earth. And it
came to pass that he was nourished for the space
of many days.

## Sherem Gives His Final Speech

16 And it came to pass that he said unto the
people: Gather together on the morrow, for I shall
die; wherefore, I desire to speak unto the people
before I shall die.
17 And it came to pass that on the morrow the multitude were gathered together; and he spake plainly
unto them and denied the things which he had
taught them, and confessed the Christ, and the power
of the Holy Ghost, and the ministering of angels.
18 And he spake plainly unto them, that he had
been deceived by the power of the devil. And he
spake of hell, and of eternity, and of eternal punishment.
19 And he said: I fear lest I have committed the
unpardonable sin, for I have lied unto God; for I
denied the Christ, and said that I believed the scriptures; and they truly testify of him. And because I
have thus lied unto God I greatly fear lest my case
shall be awful; but I confess unto God.
20 And it came to pass that when he had said
these words he could say no more, and he gave up
the ghost.

---

7:8 ***confound***—confuse or defeat

7:11 In John 5:39, Jesus Christ taught that everyone should search the scriptures because they do testify of Him. What have the scriptures taught you about Jesus Christ?

7:12 ***made manifest***—been shown

"The atonement of the Master is the central point of world history. Without it, the whole purpose for the creation of earth and our living upon it would fail" (Marion G. Romney, in Conference Report, October 1953, 34–35).

7:13 The Lord states in the Doctrine and Covenants that "faith cometh not by signs, but signs follow those that believe. Yea, signs come by faith, not by the will of men, nor as they please, but by the will of God" (D&C 63:9–10).

7:15 ***nourished***—sustained

7:16 ***on the morrow***—tomorrow

7:18 ***deceived***—tricked or fooled

Latter-day scriptures teach that there are at least three meanings for the term *hell*. It can describe our suffering here on earth (see Alma 36:18). It can refer to a part of the spirit world where those who have not repented suffer for their sins (see Alma 40:13–14). It is also used to describe the final condition of those who completely turn away from God (see D&C 29:38).

7:19 The unpardonable sin is the sin of denying the Holy Ghost, a sin that cannot be forgiven (see D&C 76:34–35).

7:20 ***gave up the ghost***—died

JACOB AND ENOS, BY SCOTT SNOW

Before Jacob died, he gave the record of his people to Enos, his son.

21 And when the multitude had witnessed that he spake these things as he was about to give up the ghost, they were astonished exceedingly; insomuch that the power of God came down upon them, and they were overcome that they fell to the earth.
22 Now, this thing was pleasing unto me, Jacob, for I had requested it of my Father who was in heaven; for he had heard my cry and answered my prayer.
23 And it came to pass that peace and the love of God was restored again among the people; and they searched the scriptures, and hearkened no more to the words of this wicked man.

## Lamanites Reject the Truth

24 And it came to pass that many means were devised to reclaim and restore the Lamanites to the knowledge of the truth; but it all was vain, for they delighted in wars and bloodshed, and they had an eternal hatred against us, their brethren. And they sought by the power of their arms to destroy us continually.
25 Wherefore, the people of Nephi did fortify against them with their arms, and with all their might, trusting in the God and rock of their salvation; wherefore, they became as yet, conquerors of their enemies.

7:21 **astonished exceedingly**—very surprised

7:24 **means were devised**—plans were made
**reclaim**—bring back
**arms**—weapons

7:25 **fortify**—strengthen themselves

The Nephites prepared for battle with their enemies physically by arming themselves and spiritually by trusting in God. How can you prepare yourself physically and spiritually for the trials you will have?

26 And it came to pass that I, Jacob, began to be
old; and the record of this people being kept on the
other plates of Nephi, wherefore, I conclude this
record, declaring that I have written according to the
best of my knowledge, by saying that the time
passed away with us, and also our lives passed away
like as it were unto us a dream, we being a lone-
some and a solemn people, wanderers, cast out from
Jerusalem, born in tribulation, in a wilderness, and
hated of our brethren, which caused wars and contentions; wherefore, we did mourn out our days.
27 And I, Jacob, saw that I must soon go down to
my grave; wherefore, I said unto my son Enos: Take
these plates. And I told him the things which my
brother Nephi had commanded me, and he promised obedience unto the commands. And I make an
end of my writing upon these plates, which writing
has been small; and to the reader I bid farewell,
hoping that many of my brethren may read my
words. Brethren, adieu.

7:26 **W** ***solemn***—joyless
***tribulation***—hard times

7:27 **W** ***adieu***—farewell

# THE BOOK OF ENOS

*The prophet Enos, son of Jacob and grandson of Lehi and Sariah, learned that forgiveness of sins comes through faith in Jesus Christ. This short book shows how a person with faith can pray and receive blessings from his Father in Heaven for himself and for other people.*

## CHAPTER 1

*Enos tells of his desire to be forgiven of his sins. Notice who Enos prays for after he receives forgiveness for his sins.*

### Enos Prays and Is Forgiven of His Sins

1 BEHOLD, it came to pass that I, Enos, knowing
my father that he was a just man—for he taught me
in his language, and also in the nurture and admonition of the Lord—and blessed be the name of my
God for it—
2 And I will tell you of the wrestle which I had
before God, before I received a remission of my sins.
3 Behold, I went to hunt beasts in the forests; and
the words which I had often heard my father speak
concerning eternal life, and the joy of the saints,
sunk deep into my heart.
4 And my soul hungered; and I kneeled down
before my Maker, and I cried unto him in mighty
prayer and supplication for mine own soul; and all
the day long did I cry unto him; yea, and when the
night came I did still raise my voice high that it
reached the heavens.
5 And there came a voice unto me, saying: Enos,
thy sins are forgiven thee, and thou shalt be blessed.
6 And I, Enos, knew that God could not lie;
wherefore, my guilt was swept away.
7 And I said: Lord, how is it done?
8 And he said unto me: Because of thy faith in
Christ, whom thou hast never before heard nor
seen. And many years pass away before he shall
manifest himself in the flesh; wherefore, go to, thy
faith hath made thee whole.

### Enos Prays for the Nephites and the Lamanites

9 Now, it came to pass that when I had heard
these words I began to feel a desire for the welfare
of my brethren, the Nephites; wherefore, I did pour
out my whole soul unto God for them.
10 And while I was thus struggling in the spirit,
behold, the voice of the Lord came into my mind
again, saying: I will visit thy brethren according to
their diligence in keeping my commandments. I
have given unto them this land, and it is a holy
land; and I curse it not save it be for the cause of
iniquity; wherefore, I will visit thy brethren according as I have said; and their transgressions will I
bring down with sorrow upon their own heads.

---

1:1 ***just***—good
***nurture***—care
***admonition of the Lord***—teachings and commandments

1:2 ***wrestle***—personal battle
***remission***—forgiveness

1:3 (1–3) President Ezra Taft Benson testified that righteous Book of Mormon fathers taught their sons "the saving truths of salvation . . . plainly, frequently, and fervently" (*The Teachings of Ezra Taft Benson,* 504).

1:4 ***supplication***—humble pleading

1:6 Enos was forgiven for his sins and gained peace of conscience. This also happened to the people of King Benjamin (see Mosiah 4:2–3), and to Alma (see Alma 36:18–21).

1:8 ***manifest himself in the flesh***—be born

Enos's sins were forgiven because of his faith in Jesus Christ whom he had never seen and because he sincerely repented. What does this scripture teach you about the power of faith?

1:9 ***welfare***—spiritual well-being

1:10 President Harold B. Lee quoted this verse and said, "In other words, sometimes we hear the voice of the Lord coming into our minds, and when it comes, the impressions are just as strong as though He were sounding a trumpet in our ear" (*Stand Ye in Holy Places,* 139).

ENOS PRAYING, BY ROBERT T. BARRETT

*"And my soul hungered; and I kneeled down before my Maker, and I cried unto him in mighty prayer."*

11 And after I, Enos, had heard these words, my
faith began to be unshaken in the Lord; and I
prayed unto him with many long strugglings for my
brethren, the Lamanites.
12 And it came to pass that after I had prayed and
labored with all diligence, the Lord said unto me: I
will grant unto thee according to thy desires,
because of thy faith.
13 And now behold, this was the desire which I
desired of him—that if it should so be, that my
people, the Nephites, should fall into transgression,
and by any means be destroyed, and the Lamanites
should not be destroyed, that the Lord God would
preserve a record of my people, the Nephites; even
if it so be by the power of his holy arm, that it might
be brought forth at some future day unto the
Lamanites, that, perhaps, they might be brought
unto salvation—
14 For at the present our strugglings were vain in
restoring them to the true faith. And they swore in
their wrath that, if it were possible, they would
destroy our records and us, and also all the traditions of our fathers.
15 Wherefore, I knowing that the Lord God was
able to preserve our records, I cried unto him continually, for he had said unto me: Whatsoever thing
ye shall ask in faith, believing that ye shall receive
in the name of Christ, ye shall receive it.
16 And I had faith, and I did cry unto God that he
would preserve the records; and he covenanted
with me that he would bring them forth unto the
Lamanites in his own due time.
17 And I, Enos, knew it would be according to the
covenant which he had made; wherefore my soul
did rest.
18 And the Lord said unto me: Thy fathers have
also required of me this thing; and it shall be done
unto them according to their faith; for their faith
was like unto thine.

## Enos Sees Great Wars Between the Nephites and the Lamanites

19 And now it came to pass that I, Enos, went
about among the people of Nephi, prophesying of
things to come, and testifying of the things which I
had heard and seen.
20 And I bear record that the people of Nephi did
seek diligently to restore the Lamanites unto the
true faith in God. But our labors were vain; their
hatred was fixed, and they were led by their evil
nature that they became wild, and ferocious, and a
blood-thirsty people, full of idolatry and filthiness;
feeding upon beasts of prey; dwelling in tents, and
wandering about in the wilderness with a short skin
girdle about their loins and their heads shaven; and
their skill was in the bow, and in the cimeter, and
the ax. And many of them did eat nothing save it
was raw meat; and they were continually seeking to
destroy us.

---

1:11 ***unshaken***—firm or strong

1:12 Enos prayed with great faith. Elder Bruce R. McConkie taught that "faith is the power which brings answers to prayers" (*Doctrinal New Testament Commentary* 1:542).

1:14 ***strugglings were vain***—efforts did no good
***restoring them***—bringing them back
***traditions***—teachings

1:17 A covenant is an agreement between two people. In the scriptures it is usually an agreement between God and man. We agree to be obedient to God's commandments, and He agrees to bless us (see LDS Bible Dictionary, s.v.,"Covenant," 651).

1:18 ***required of me***—asked me

1:20 ***fixed***—firmly set
***ferocious***—savage
***idolatry***—worship of false gods
***cimeter***—short, curved sword

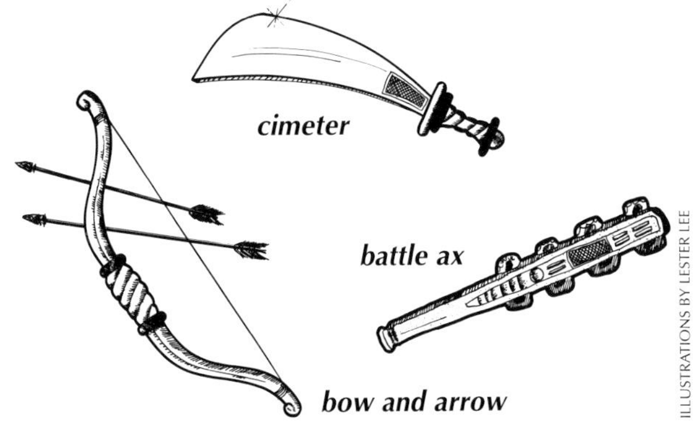


*The Lamanites were a hard and ferocious people whose "skill was in the bow, and in the cimeter, and the ax."*

21 And it came to pass that the people of Nephi
did till the land, and raise all manner of grain, and
of fruit, and flocks of herds, and flocks of all manner of cattle of every kind, and goats, and wild
goats, and also many horses.
22 And there were exceedingly many prophets
among us. And the people were a stiffnecked
people, hard to understand.
23 And there was nothing save it was exceeding
harshness, preaching and prophesying of wars,
and contentions, and destructions, and continually reminding them of death, and the duration of
eternity, and the judgments and the power of
God, and all these things—stirring them up continually to keep them in the fear of the Lord. I say
there was nothing short of these things, and
exceedingly great plainness of speech, would
keep them from going down speedily to destruction. And after this manner do I write concerning
them.
24 And I saw wars between the Nephites and
Lamanites in the course of my days.

## Enos Testifies Concerning the Blessings He Will Receive

25 And it came to pass that I began to be old, and
an hundred and seventy and nine years had passed
away from the time that our father Lehi left
Jerusalem.
26 And I saw that I must soon go down to my
grave, having been wrought upon by the power of
God that I must preach and prophesy unto this
people, and declare the word according to the truth
which is in Christ. And I have declared it in all my
days, and have rejoiced in it above that of the
world.
27 And I soon go to the place of my rest, which is
with my Redeemer; for I know that in him I shall
rest. And I rejoice in the day when my mortal shall
put on immortality, and shall stand before him; then
shall I see his face with pleasure, and he will say
unto me: Come unto me, ye blessed, there is a
place prepared for you in the mansions of my
Father. Amen.

---

1:21 ***till***—plow and plant

1:22 ***stiffnecked***—stubborn

1:23 ***harshness***—strong words
***duration***—length

1:26 ***wrought upon***—worked on or changed

1:27 ***mortal***—earthly body that can die
***immortality***—a resurrected body that cannot die

"Some accept the divine invitation and attempt to come unto Christ. Others refuse his entreaty and turn away. But, the day will come when all will stand before Christ, whether they are ready or not, and be judged" (Carlos E. Asay, *In the Lord's Service,* 150).

# THE BOOK OF JAROM

*Jarom, Lehi's great-grandson, writes a small book that tells of the Nephite's struggle to keep the Lord's commandments. Obedience to the law of Moses helped them to have faith in Jesus Christ.*

## CHAPTER 1

*There are both righteous and wicked people among the Nephites. Notice what the prophets and teachers do to keep the Nephites humble.*

### THERE ARE BOTH WICKED AND RIGHTEOUS AMONG THE NEPHITES

1 NOW behold, I, Jarom, write a few words according to the commandment of my father, Enos, that our genealogy may be kept.

2 And as these plates are small, and as these things are written for the intent of the benefit of our brethren the Lamanites, wherefore, it must needs be that I write a little; but I shall not write the things of my prophesying, nor of my revelations. For what could I write more than my fathers have written? For have not they revealed the plan of salvation? I say unto you, Yea; and this sufficeth me.

3 Behold, it is expedient that much should be done among this people, because of the hardness of their hearts, and the deafness of their ears, and the blindness of their minds, and the stiffness of their necks; nevertheless, God is exceedingly merciful unto them, and has not as yet swept them off from the face of the land.

4 And there are many among us who have many revelations, for they are not all stiffnecked. And as many as are not stiffnecked and have faith, have communion with the Holy Spirit, which maketh manifest unto the children of men, according to their faith.

### THE LORD PROTECTS AND BLESSES THE NEPHITES

5 And now, behold, two hundred years had passed away, and the people of Nephi had waxed strong in the land. They observed to keep the law of Moses and the sabbath day holy unto the Lord. And they profaned not; neither did they blaspheme. And the laws of the land were exceedingly strict.

---

1:1 ***our genealogy***—the names and history of our fathers, grandfathers, and other ancestors

The Lord's people have always kept a record or a journal (see Moses 6:4–6). What special thoughts and experiences should you put in your record?

1:2 ***intent***—purpose
***prophesying***—speaking the things of the Lord
***sufficeth***—is enough for

Heavenly Father's plan to help us return to Him has several different titles in the Book of Mormon. It is called the "merciful plan" (2 Nephi 9:6), the "plan of our God" (2 Nephi 9:13), the "plan of deliverance" (2 Nephi 11:5), the "plan of redemption" (Alma 22:13), and the "plan of happiness" (Alma 42:8).

1:3 ***expedient***—necessary
***exceedingly***—very

Prophets sometimes use different parts of the body as symbols to describe people's spiritual problems (see Moses 6:27). In this verse, Jarom uses phrases such as *hard hearts, deaf ears, blind minds,* and *stiff necks* to describe the spiritual sickness of his people.

1:4 ***stiffnecked***—stubborn or rebellious
***have communion with***—receive revelation from
***maketh manifest***—gives knowledge

1:5 ***waxed***—grown
***profaned not***—did not speak in an irreverent manner
***blaspheme***—falsely claim to be like God or speak evil of God

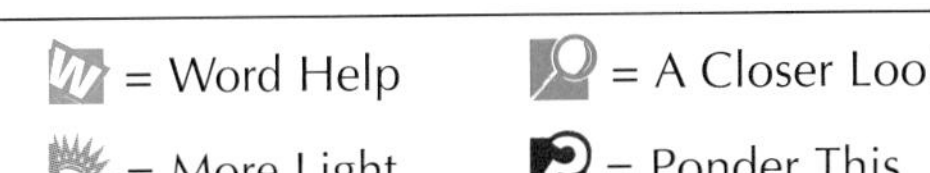


Words in pink are explained in the Glossary.

6 And they were scattered upon much of the face
of the land, and the Lamanites also. And they were
exceedingly more numerous than were they of the
Nephites; and they loved murder and would drink
the blood of beasts.
7 And it came to pass that they came many times
against us, the Nephites, to battle. But our kings
and our leaders were mighty men in the faith of the
Lord; and they taught the people the ways of the
Lord; wherefore, we withstood the Lamanites and
swept them away out of our lands, and began to
fortify our cities, or whatsoever place of our inheritance.
8 And we multiplied exceedingly, and spread
upon the face of the land, and became exceedingly rich in gold, and in silver, and in precious things,
and in fine workmanship of wood, in buildings,
and in machinery, and also in iron and copper, and
brass and steel, making all manner of tools of every
kind to till the ground, and weapons of war—yea,
the sharp pointed arrow, and the quiver, and the
dart, and the javelin, and all preparations for war.
9 And thus being prepared to meet the Lamanites,
they did not prosper against us. But the word of the
Lord was verified, which he spake unto our fathers,
saying that: Inasmuch as ye will keep my commandments ye shall prosper in the land.
10 And it came to pass that the prophets of the
Lord did threaten the people of Nephi, according to
the word of God, that if they did not keep the commandments, but should fall into transgression, they
should be destroyed from off the face of the land.

## Church Leaders Persuade the Nephites to Look to the Lord

11 Wherefore, the prophets, and the priests, and
the teachers, did labor diligently, exhorting with all
long-suffering the people to diligence; teaching the
law of Moses, and the intent for which it was given;
persuading them to look forward unto the Messiah,
and believe in him to come as though he already
was. And after this manner did they teach them.
12 And it came to pass that by so doing they kept
them from being destroyed upon the face of the
land; for they did prick their hearts with the word,
continually stirring them up unto repentance.
13 And it came to pass that two hundred and
thirty and eight years had passed away—after the
manner of wars, and contentions, and dissensions,
for the space of much of the time.
14 And I, Jarom, do not write more, for the plates
are small. But behold, my brethren, ye can go to the
other plates of Nephi; for behold, upon them the
records of our wars are engraven, according to the
writings of the kings, or those which they caused to
be written.
15 And I deliver these plates into the hands of my
son Omni, that they may be kept according to the
commandments of my fathers.

---

1:7 ***fortify***—build defenses around

1:8 Machinery can be any type of complicated work (see Noah Webster, *American Dictionary of the English Language,* 1828, s.v. "Machinery").

1:9 ***prosper***—succeed or do well
***verified***—proved true

1:11 ***exhorting***—strongly encouraging

1:12 A prick is a stick with a sharp metal point used anciently to poke an animal to turn its course (see LDS Bible Dictionary, s.v. "Goads," 681).

1:12 (11–12) Jarom says that the preaching of the prophets kept the Nephites from being destroyed. When do you get to hear the prophets speak? How does following them bless your life?

1:13 ***contentions***—arguing and fighting
***dissensions***—disagreements

1:14 To engrave is to write by cutting, etching, or impressing into metal.

# THE BOOK OF OMNI

*The Book of Omni covers a period of time of more than one hundred thirty years and contains the writings of five Nephite record keepers. The last writer in the book, Amaleki, after inviting all to come unto Christ, delivers the plates to King Benjamin.*

## CHAPTER 1

*Five writers each give a brief report of the events of their day and then pass the record on. Notice how the Lord continues to save and bless the righteous Nephites.*

### *The Records Pass from Omni to Amaron to Chemish to Abinadom*

1 BEHOLD, it came to pass that I, Omni, being
commanded by my father, Jarom, that I should
write somewhat upon these plates, to preserve our
genealogy—
2 Wherefore, in my days, I would that ye should
know that I fought much with the sword to preserve my people, the Nephites, from falling into the
hands of their enemies, the Lamanites. But behold,
I of myself am a wicked man, and I have not kept
the statutes and the commandments of the Lord as
I ought to have done.
3 And it came to pass that two hundred and seventy and six years had passed away, and we had
many seasons of peace; and we had many seasons
of serious war and bloodshed. Yea, and in fine, two
hundred and eighty and two years had passed
away, and I had kept these plates according to the
commandments of my fathers; and I conferred them
upon my son Amaron. And I make an end.
4 And now I, Amaron, write the things whatsoever
I write, which are few, in the book of my father.
5 Behold, it came to pass that three hundred and
twenty years had passed away, and the more
wicked part of the Nephites were destroyed.
6 For the Lord would not suffer, after he had led
them out of the land of Jerusalem and kept and
preserved them from falling into the hands of their
enemies, yea, he would not suffer that the words
should not be verified, which he spake unto our
fathers, saying that: Inasmuch as ye will not keep
my commandments ye shall not prosper in the land.
7 Wherefore, the Lord did visit them in great judgment; nevertheless, he did spare the righteous that
they should not perish, but did deliver them out of
the hands of their enemies.
8 And it came to pass that I did deliver the plates
unto my brother Chemish.
9 Now I, Chemish, write what few things I write,
in the same book with my brother; for behold, I
saw the last which he wrote, that he wrote it with
his own hand; and he wrote it in the day that he
delivered them unto me. And after this manner
we keep the records, for it is according to the
commandments of our fathers. And I make an
end.
10 Behold, I, Abinadom, am the son of Chemish.
Behold, it came to pass that I saw much war and
contention between my people, the Nephites, and
the Lamanites; and I, with my own sword, have
taken the lives of many of the Lamanites in the
defence of my brethren.
11 And behold, the record of this people is
engraven upon plates which is had by the kings,
according to the generations; and I know of no revelation save that which has been written, neither
prophecy; wherefore, that which is sufficient is
written. And I make an end.

---

1:1 — ***somewhat***—a little
***our genealogy***—the names and history of our fathers, grandfathers, and other ancestors

1:2 — ***statutes***—laws

1:3 — ***conferred them upon***—gave them to

1:7 (6–7) — Notice how the Lord continues to fulfill His promise to Nephi that the Nephites will prosper in the land if they keep His commandments (see 1 Nephi 2:20; Jarom 1:9).

= Word Help | = A Closer Look
= More Light | = Ponder This
Words in pink are explained in the Glossary.

## King Mosiah Discovers the People of Zarahemla and Learns of the Jaredites

12 Behold, I am Amaleki, the son of Abinadom. Behold, I will speak unto you somewhat concerning Mosiah, who was made king over the land of Zarahemla; for behold, he being warned of the Lord that he should flee out of the land of Nephi, and as many as would hearken unto the voice of the Lord should also depart out of the land with him, into the wilderness—

13 And it came to pass that he did according as the Lord had commanded him. And they departed out of the land into the wilderness, as many as would hearken unto the voice of the Lord; and they were led by many preachings and prophesyings. And they were admonished continually by the word of God; and they were led by the power of his arm, through the wilderness until they came down into the land which is called the land of Zarahemla.

14 And they discovered a people, who were called the people of Zarahemla. Now, there was great rejoicing among the people of Zarahemla; and also Zarahemla did rejoice exceedingly, because the Lord had sent the people of Mosiah with the plates of brass which contained the record of the Jews.

15 Behold, it came to pass that Mosiah discovered that the people of Zarahemla came out from Jerusalem at the time that Zedekiah, king of Judah, was carried away captive into Babylon.

16 And they journeyed in the wilderness, and were brought by the hand of the Lord across the great waters, into the land where Mosiah discovered them; and they had dwelt there from that time forth.

17 And at the time that Mosiah discovered them, they had become exceedingly numerous. Nevertheless, they had had many wars and serious contentions, and had fallen by the sword from time to time; and their language had become corrupted; and they had brought no records with them; and they denied the being of their Creator; and Mosiah, nor the people of Mosiah, could understand them.

18 But it came to pass that Mosiah caused that they should be taught in his language. And it came to pass that after they were taught in the language of Mosiah, Zarahemla gave a genealogy of his fathers, according to his memory; and they are written, but not in these plates.

19 And it came to pass that the people of Zarahemla, and of Mosiah, did unite together; and Mosiah was appointed to be their king.

20 And it came to pass in the days of Mosiah, there was a large stone brought unto him with engravings on it; and he did interpret the engravings by the gift and power of God.

---

1:12 ***wilderness***—wild land with very few people

1:14 The plates of brass were the Old Testament scriptures that Nephi obtained from Laban in Jerusalem. They contained Lehi's genealogy, the five books of Moses, the record of the Jews, and many prophecies of the holy prophets up to the time of Jeremiah (see 1 Nephi 5:10–14).

1:14 (12–14) The name *Zarahemla* has several meanings in these verses. It refers to (1) the land discovered by Mosiah and his people (verse 13); (2) the people who lived there (verse 14); and (3) the man who was their leader (verse 14).

1:17 ***contentions***—arguing and fighting

1:18 ***these plates***—the small plates of Nephi

1:20 ***interpret***—translate or explain

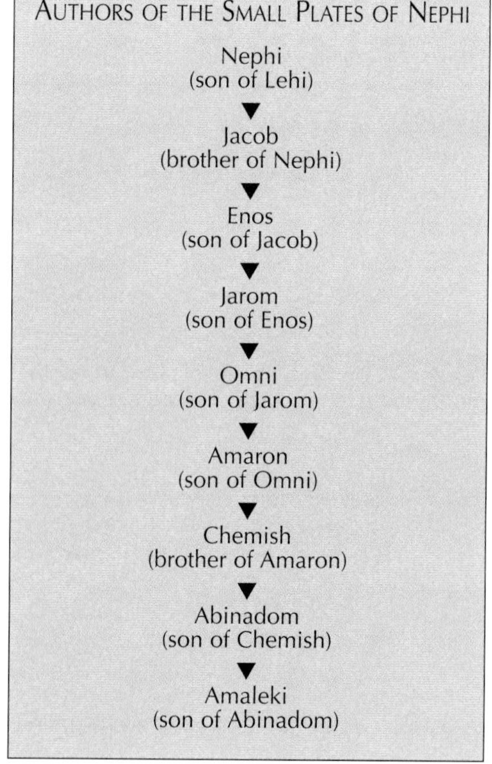

21 And they gave an account of one Coriantumr,
and the slain of his people. And Coriantumr was
discovered by the people of Zarahemla; and he
dwelt with them for the space of nine moons.
22 It also spake a few words concerning his
fathers. And his first parents came out from the
tower, at the time the Lord confounded the language of the people; and the severity of the Lord
fell upon them according to his judgments, which
are just; and their bones lay scattered in the land
northward.

## Amaleki Gives the Plates to King Benjamin

23 Behold, I, Amaleki, was born in the days of
Mosiah; and I have lived to see his death; and
Benjamin, his son, reigneth in his stead.
24 And behold, I have seen, in the days of king
Benjamin, a serious war and much bloodshed
between the Nephites and the Lamanites. But
behold, the Nephites did obtain much advantage
over them; yea, insomuch that king Benjamin did
drive them out of the land of Zarahemla.
25 And it came to pass that I began to be old; and,
having no seed, and knowing king Benjamin to be
a just man before the Lord, wherefore, I shall deliver up these plates unto him, exhorting all men to
come unto God, the Holy One of Israel, and believe
in prophesying, and in revelations, and in the ministering of angels, and in the gift of speaking with
tongues, and in the gift of interpreting languages,
and in all things which are good; for there is nothing which is good save it comes from the Lord: and
that which is evil cometh from the devil.
26 And now, my beloved brethren, I would that
ye should come unto Christ, who is the Holy One
of Israel, and partake of his salvation, and the
power of his redemption. Yea, come unto him, and
offer your whole souls as an offering unto him, and
continue in fasting and praying, and endure to the
end; and as the Lord liveth ye will be saved.

## A Colony of Nephites Returns to the Land of Nephi

27 And now I would speak somewhat concerning
a certain number who went up into the wilderness
to return to the land of Nephi; for there was a large
number who were desirous to possess the land of
their inheritance.
28 Wherefore, they went up into the wilderness.
And their leader being a strong and mighty man,
and a stiffnecked man, wherefore he caused a contention among them; and they were all slain, save
fifty, in the wilderness, and they returned again to
the land of Zarahemla.
29 And it came to pass that they also took others
to a considerable number, and took their journey
again into the wilderness.
30 And I, Amaleki, had a brother, who also went
with them; and I have not since known concerning
them. And I am about to lie down in my grave; and
these plates are full. And I make an end of my
speaking.

---

1:21 The story of Coriantumr and the destruction of his people (the Jaredites) is found in the Book of Ether.

1:22 ***tower***—Tower of Babel

1:25 The term *seed* refers to descendants, meaning children, grandchildren and so on.

Prophecy, revelation, the help of angels, speaking in tongues (other languages), and understanding languages are all gifts of the Spirit. The Lord gives them to His people to help them do His work (see D&C 46:8–33).

1:26 An offering is something given to God as an act of worship or sacrifice. What could you do to "offer" your soul to Jesus Christ? Would it be worth it if in return you are redeemed (rescued from sin) and saved in the celestial kingdom?

1:28 You can read more about what happened to this group in Mosiah chapters 9–22.

# WORDS OF MORMON

*Mormon is about to give the records to his son, Moroni. He explains where the records of 1 Nephi, 2 Nephi, Jacob, Enos, Jarom, and Omni came from and what other records he included with the plates that would someday become the Book of Mormon.*

## CHAPTER 1

*Mormon expresses the need to always trust the Lord because He knows all things. Watch for how God guided Mormon to include all the records that would be needed for the eventual coming forth and translation of the Book of Mormon.*

### Mormon Includes the Small Plates of Nephi in the Book of Mormon for a Wise Purpose

1 AND now I, Mormon, being about to deliver up
the record which I have been making into the
hands of my son Moroni, behold I have witnessed
almost all the destruction of my people, the
Nephites.
2 And it is many hundred years after the coming
of Christ that I deliver these records into the hands
of my son; and it supposeth me that he will witness
the entire destruction of my people. But may God
grant that he may survive them, that he may write
somewhat concerning them, and somewhat concerning Christ, that perhaps some day it may profit
them.
3 And now, I speak somewhat concerning that
which I have written; for after I had made an
abridgment from the plates of Nephi, down to the
reign of this king Benjamin, of whom Amaleki
spake, I searched among the records which had
been delivered into my hands, and I found these
plates, which contained this small account of the
prophets, from Jacob down to the reign of this king
Benjamin, and also many of the words of Nephi.
4 And the things which are upon these plates
pleasing me, because of the prophecies of the coming of Christ; and my fathers knowing that many of
them have been fulfilled; yea, and I also know that
as many things as have been prophesied concerning us down to this day have been fulfilled, and as
many as go beyond this day must surely come to
pass—
5 Wherefore, I chose these things, to finish my
record upon them, which remainder of my record I
shall take from the plates of Nephi; and I cannot
write the hundredth part of the things of my
people.
6 But behold, I shall take these plates, which contain these prophesyings and revelations, and put
them with the remainder of my record, for they are
choice unto me; and I know they will be choice
unto my brethren.

---

1:1 ***witnessed***—seen

1:2 ***it supposeth me***—I suppose
***survive***—outlive
***profit***—bless or help

Mormon is the main compiler of the gold plates. He lived nearly four hundred years after Christ, during the time when the Nephites were being destroyed by the Lamanites (see Mormon 6:5–7). Mormon's son, Moroni, finished the record, buried the plates in the earth, and later appeared to Joseph Smith on September 21, 1823 (see Joseph Smith—History 1:29–34).

1:3 ***abridgment***—shortened or condensed version

The plates of Nephi that Mormon first worked with are called the large plates of Nephi. Later, Mormon found the small plates of Nephi. These smaller plates contained the books of 1 Nephi, 2 Nephi, Jacob, Enos, Jarom, and Omni (see 1 Nephi 9:1–6).

1:4 ***been fullfilled***—taken place or happened
***concerning***—about

1:5 ***remainder of***—the rest of

MORMON ABRIDGING THE PLATES, BY TOM LOVELL

*Mormon could include only a small part of the history of his people in his abridgement. He was guided by the Spirit to know what he should include.*

7 And I do this for a wise purpose; for thus it whispereth me, according to the workings of the Spirit of the Lord which is in me. And now, I do not know all things; but the Lord knoweth all things which are to come; wherefore, he worketh in me to do according to his will.
8 And my prayer to God is concerning my brethren, that they may once again come to the knowledge of God, yea, the redemption of Christ; that they may once again be a delightsome people.

## Mormon Tells the History of the Sacred Records from Which He Abridged the Book of Mormon

9 And now I, Mormon, proceed to finish out my record, which I take from the plates of Nephi; and I make it according to the knowledge and the understanding which God has given me.
10 Wherefore, it came to pass that after Amaleki had delivered up these plates into the hands of king Benjamin, he took them and put them with the other plates, which contained records which had been handed down by the kings, from generation to generation until the days of king Benjamin.
11 And they were handed down from king Benjamin, from generation to generation until they have fallen into my hands. And I, Mormon, pray to God that they may be preserved from this time henceforth. And I know that they will be preserved; for there are great things written upon them, out of which my people and their brethren shall be judged at the great and last day, according to the word of God which is written.

## Mormon Tells More About King Benjamin's Time

12 And now, concerning this king Benjamin—he had somewhat of contentions among his own people.
13 And it came to pass also that the armies of the Lamanites came down out of the land of Nephi, to battle against his people. But behold, king Benjamin gathered together his armies, and he did stand against them; and he did fight with the strength of his own arm, with the sword of Laban.
14 And in the strength of the Lord they did contend against their enemies, until they had slain many thousands of the Lamanites. And it came to pass that they did contend against the Lamanites until they had driven them out of all the lands of their inheritance.
15 And it came to pass that after there had been false Christs, and their mouths had been shut, and they punished according to their crimes;
16 And after there had been false prophets, and false preachers and teachers among the people, and all these having been punished according to their crimes; and after there having been much contention and many dissensions away unto the Lamanites, behold, it came to pass that king Benjamin, with the assistance of the holy prophets who were among his people—

---

1:7 Doctrine and Covenants 10:1–19, 30–47 explains the "wise purpose" mentioned here. Joseph Smith first translated material from the Book of Lehi, which was taken from the large plates of Nephi. But this translation was stolen by wicked men who wanted to discredit Joseph Smith. God protected Joseph Smith from criticism by having him translate the small plates of Nephi in place of what had been stolen.

1:8 Who are Mormon's brethren who are living today? How can you help fulfill Mormon's hope that his people will "once again be a delightsome people"?

1:11 ***preserved***—kept safe

Revelation 20:12 explains that all people will be judged by their works, which are written in books. What would you like to have written about you?

1:12 ***contentions***—arguments and fights

1:14 King Benjamin and his people are able to defeat the Lamanites in battle because they have the "strength of the Lord." What has the Lord given you strength to do?

***of their inheritance***—that belonged to the Nephites

1:16 ***dissensions away unto***—Nephites joining the side of

17 For behold, king Benjamin was a holy man, and he did reign over his people in righteousness; and there were many holy men in the land, and they did speak the word of God with power and with authority; and they did use much sharpness because of the stiffneckedness of the people—

18 Wherefore, with the help of these, king Benjamin, by laboring with all the might of his body and the faculty of his whole soul, and also the prophets, did once more establish peace in the land.

---

1:17 ***sharpness***—clear and direct language
***stiffneckedness***—stubbornness and rebellion

1:18 ***faculty***—ability

# THE BOOK OF MOSIAH

*In this book you will read about King Benjamin and King Mosiah II, who were Nephite kings in the land of Zarahemla (see the accompanying map). You will also read about Zeniff, Noah, and Limhi, who were kings of a group of Nephites living among the Lamanites in the land of Nephi. Most of these kings were good; King Noah was not. What happened to the people under these kings is a powerful illustration of the Lord's promise that "if ye shall keep the commandments . . . ye shall prosper in the land, and your enemies shall have no power over you" (Mosiah 2:31). The Book of Mosiah covers almost forty years of Nephite history, from about 130 B.C. to 91 B.C.*

## CHAPTER 1

*King Benjamin teaches his sons about the importance of the scriptures. He also prepares to give the kingdom to his son Mosiah II. Notice what a righteous king does to prepare his son to rule over the people.*

### *THE SCRIPTURES HELP THE NEPHITES UNDERSTAND GOD AND HIS COMMANDMENTS*

1 AND now there was no more contention in all
the land of Zarahemla, among all the people who
belonged to king Benjamin, so that king Benjamin
had continual peace all the remainder of his days.
2 And it came to pass that he had three sons; and
he called their names Mosiah, and Helorum, and
Helaman. And he caused that they should be taught
in all the language of his fathers, that thereby they
might become men of understanding; and that they
might know concerning the prophecies which had
been spoken by the mouths of their fathers, which
were delivered them by the hand of the Lord.
3 And he also taught them concerning the records
which were engraven on the plates of brass, saying:
My sons, I would that ye should remember that
were it not for these plates, which contain these
records and these commandments, we must have
suffered in ignorance, even at this present time, not
knowing the mysteries of God.
4 For it were not possible that our father, Lehi,
could have remembered all these things, to have
taught them to his children, except it were for the
help of these plates; for he having been taught in
the language of the Egyptians therefore he could
read these engravings, and teach them to his children, that thereby they could teach them to their
children, and so fulfilling the commandments of
God, even down to this present time.
5 I say unto you, my sons, were it not for these
things, which have been kept and preserved by the
hand of God, that we might read and understand of
his mysteries, and have his commandments always
before our eyes, that even our fathers would have
dwindled in unbelief, and we should have been
like unto our brethren, the Lamanites, who know
nothing concerning these things, or even do not
believe them when they are taught them, because
of the traditions of their fathers, which are not correct.
6 O my sons, I would that ye should remember
that these sayings are true, and also that these
records are true. And behold, also the plates of
Nephi, which contain the records and the sayings of
our fathers from the time they left Jerusalem until

---

1:1 ***contention***—arguing and fighting
***remainder***—rest

1:2 For more about the language of his fathers, see for 1 Nephi 1:2.

1:3 ***mysteries of God***—truths known only through revelation from God

What does King Benjamin teach his children? How is that like the way your parents teach you?

1:5 ***dwindled***—become weak or fallen away
***traditions***—teachings and practices

Words in pink are explained in the Glossary.

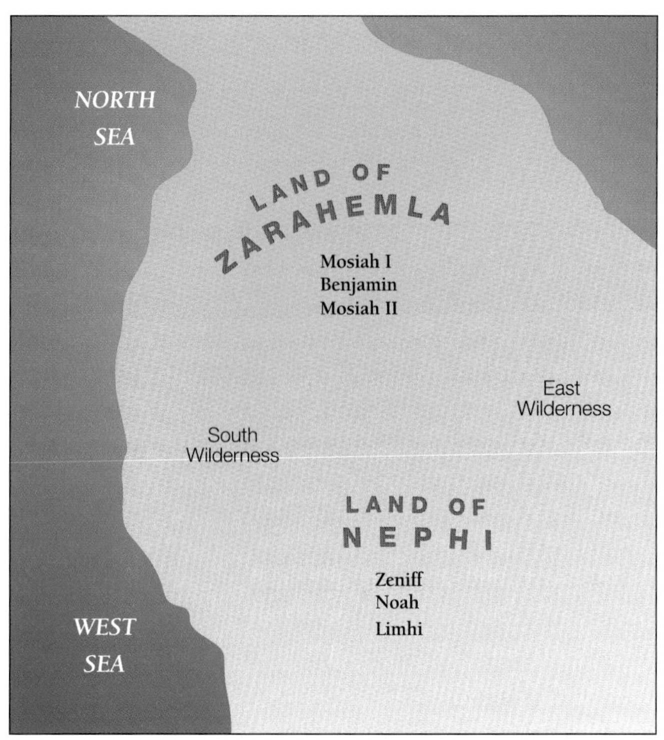


*The book of Mosiah explains that for many years there were two Nephite kingdoms.*

now, and they are true; and we can know of their
surety because we have them before our eyes.
7 And now, my sons, I would that ye should
remember to search them diligently, that ye may
profit thereby; and I would that ye should keep the
commandments of God, that ye may prosper in the
land according to the promises which the Lord
made unto our fathers.
8 And many more things did king Benjamin teach
his sons, which are not written in this book.

## Benjamin Wants His People to Gather and Make Covenants with the Lord

9 And it came to pass that after king Benjamin had
made an end of teaching his sons, that he waxed old,
and he saw that he must very soon go the way of all
the earth; therefore, he thought it expedient that he
should confer the kingdom upon one of his sons.
10 Therefore, he had Mosiah brought before him;
and these are the words which he spake unto him,
saying: My son, I would that ye should make a
proclamation throughout all this land among all this
people, or the people of Zarahemla, and the people
of Mosiah who dwell in the land, that thereby they
may be gathered together; for on the morrow I shall
proclaim unto this my people out of mine own
mouth that thou art a king and a ruler over this
people, whom the Lord our God hath given us.
11 And moreover, I shall give this people a name,
that thereby they may be distinguished above all
the people which the Lord God hath brought out of
the land of Jerusalem; and this I do because they
have been a diligent people in keeping the commandments of the Lord.
12 And I give unto them a name that never shall
be blotted out, except it be through transgression.
13 Yea, and moreover I say unto you, that if this
highly favored people of the Lord should fall into
transgression, and become a wicked and an adulterous people, that the Lord will deliver them up,
that thereby they become weak like unto their
brethren; and he will no more preserve them by his
matchless and marvelous power, as he has hitherto
preserved our fathers.
14 For I say unto you, that if he had not extended his arm in the preservation of our fathers they
must have fallen into the hands of the Lamanites,
and become victims to their hatred.

## Benjamin Gives Responsibility for the Nephite Kingdom to Mosiah II

15 And it came to pass that after king Benjamin had
made an end of these sayings to his son, that he gave
him charge concerning all the affairs of the kingdom.

---

1:9 **waxed**—grew
**expedient**—necessary
**confer**—give

1:11 Receiving a name is very important in the gospel. When people take upon themselves a name, it represents whom they will follow and try to become like. In Mosiah 5:7–11 King Benjamin tells them the name he wants to give them.

1:12 **blotted out**—erased, wiped out, or canceled

1:13 **a wicked and an adulterous**—sinful and immoral

When the Prophet Joseph Smith was translating the Book of Mormon, one of the meanings of the word *transgression* was "the act of passing over or beyond any law or rule of moral duty" (Noah Webster, *An American Dictionary of the English Language,* s.v. "Transgression"). In the scriptures, *transgression* generally means the breaking of spiritual law.

16 And moreover, he also gave him charge concerning the records which were engraven on the
plates of brass; and also the plates of Nephi; and
also, the sword of Laban, and the ball or director,
which led our fathers through the wilderness,
which was prepared by the hand of the Lord that
thereby they might be led, every one according to
the heed and diligence which they gave unto him.
17 Therefore, as they were unfaithful they did not
prosper nor progress in their journey, but were
driven back, and incurred the displeasure of God
upon them; and therefore they were smitten with
famine and sore afflictions, to stir them up in
remembrance of their duty.
18 And now, it came to pass that Mosiah went and
did as his father had commanded him, and proclaimed unto all the people who were in the land
of Zarahemla that thereby they might gather themselves together, to go up to the temple to hear the
words which his father should speak unto them.

# CHAPTER 2

*King Benjamin begins his great final message to the people. As you read, watch for reasons why we should always serve our Heavenly Father.*

## *The People Gather Around the Temple to Hear King Benjamin's Speech*

1 AND it came to pass that after Mosiah had done
as his father had commanded him, and had made a
proclamation throughout all the land, that the
people gathered themselves together throughout all
the land, that they might go up to the temple to
hear the words which king Benjamin should speak
unto them.
2 And there were a great number, even so many
that they did not number them; for they had multiplied exceedingly and waxed great in the land.
3 And they also took of the firstlings of their

ILLUSTRATION BY TED HENNINGER

*The brass plates and the sword of Laban were two things that reminded King Benjamin's people of the faithfulness of their ancestors and of the many blessings that God had given them.*

PHOTOGRAPH BY EDWIN M. WOOLLEY

*Ancient ruins in Mesoamerica*

1:16 King Benjamin gives Mosiah some important reminders of Nephite history. Each of these items represents an example of a former prophet's faithfulness and the Lord's blessings to him.

1:17 ***incurred***—brought
***afflictions***—trials and suffering

1:18 Speaking of the significance of holy temples, President Gordon B. Hinckley stated: "Surely these temples are unique among all buildings. They are houses of instruction. They are places of covenants and promises" (*Be Thou an Example,* 133).

2:1 ***a proclamation***—an official announcement

2:2 ***multiplied exceedingly***—greatly increased in number
***waxed***—grew

2:3 ***firstlings***—first-born

From the days of Adam and Eve to the death of Jesus Christ, God's children were commanded to offer sacrifices and burnt offerings. They did this as a reminder that the Savior would come to earth and sacrifice His life for all of God's children (see Moses 5:4–7).

flocks, that they might offer sacrifice and burnt
offerings according to the law of Moses;
4 And also that they might give thanks to the
Lord their God, who had brought them out of the
land of Jerusalem, and who had delivered them
out of the hands of their enemies, and had appointed just men to be their teachers, and also a
just man to be their king, who had established
peace in the land of Zarahemla, and who had
taught them to keep the commandments of God,
that they might rejoice and be filled with love
towards God and all men.
5 And it came to pass that when they came up to
the temple, they pitched their tents round about,
every man according to his family, consisting of his
wife, and his sons, and his daughters, and their
sons, and their daughters, from the eldest down to
the youngest, every family being separate one from
another.
6 And they pitched their tents round about the
temple, every man having his tent with the door
thereof towards the temple, that thereby they might
remain in their tents and hear the words which king
Benjamin should speak unto them;
7 For the multitude being so great that king
Benjamin could not teach them all within the walls
of the temple, therefore he caused a tower to be
erected, that thereby his people might hear the
words which he should speak unto them.
8 And it came to pass that he began to speak to
his people from the tower; and they could not all
hear his words because of the greatness of the multitude; therefore he caused that the words which he
spake should be written and sent forth among those
that were not under the sound of his voice, that
they might also receive his words.

## King Benjamin Explains How and Why He Has Served the People

9 And these are the words which he spake and
caused to be written, saying: My brethren, all ye
that have assembled yourselves together, you that
can hear my words which I shall speak unto you
this day; for I have not commanded you to come up
hither to trifle with the words which I shall speak,
but that you should hearken unto me, and open
your ears that ye may hear, and your hearts that ye
may understand, and your minds that the mysteries
of God may be unfolded to your view.
10 I have not commanded you to come up hither
that ye should fear me, or that ye should think that
I of myself am more than a mortal man.
11 But I am like as yourselves, subject to all manner of infirmities in body and mind; yet I have been
chosen by this people, and consecrated by my
father, and was suffered by the hand of the Lord
that I should be a ruler and a king over this people;
and have been kept and preserved by his matchless
power, to serve you with all the might, mind and
strength which the Lord hath granted unto me.
12 I say unto you that as I have been suffered to
spend my days in your service, even up to this time,
and have not sought gold nor silver nor any manner of riches of you;
13 Neither have I suffered that ye should be confined in dungeons, nor that ye should make slaves
one of another, nor that ye should murder, or plunder, or steal, or commit adultery; nor even have I
suffered that ye should commit any manner of
wickedness, and have taught you that ye should
keep the commandments of the Lord, in all things
which he hath commanded you—

---

2:4 ***appointed just men***—chosen good men
***established***—built

2:5 ***consisting of***—including

2:7 ***multitude***—crowd
***erected***—built

2:9 ***assembled***—gathered
***hither***—here
***trifle with***—take lightly
***hearken unto***—listen to and obey

King Benjamin asks his listeners to open their ears, hearts, and minds so they can learn the ways of God. How can you open your ears, heart, and mind to the message of King Benjamin?

2:10 ***mortal***—physical

2:11 ***subject to***—under the influence of
***infirmities***—weaknesses and diseases
***consecrated***—set apart
***suffered***—allowed
***preserved***—protected

2:13 ***confined***—kept
***plunder***—rob
***commit adultery***—use the sacred creative powers with someone who is not your husband or wife

14 And even I, myself, have labored with mine own hands that I might serve you, and that ye should not be laden with taxes, and that there should nothing come upon you which was grievous to be borne—and of all these things which I have spoken, ye yourselves are witnesses this day.

15 Yet, my brethren, I have not done these things that I might boast, neither do I tell these things that thereby I might accuse you; but I tell you these things that ye may know that I can answer a clear conscience before God this day.

16 Behold, I say unto you that because I said unto you that I had spent my days in your service, I do not desire to boast, for I have only been in the service of God.

17 And behold, I tell you these things that ye may learn wisdom; that ye may learn that when ye are in the service of your fellow beings ye are only in the service of your God.

## King Benjamin Explains Why People Should Serve Their Heavenly King

18 Behold, ye have called me your king; and if I, whom ye call your king, do labor to serve you, then ought not ye to labor to serve one another?

19 And behold also, if I, whom ye call your king, who has spent his days in your service, and yet has been in the service of God, do merit any thanks from you, O how you ought to thank your heavenly King!

20 I say unto you, my brethren, that if you should render all the thanks and praise which your whole soul has power to possess, to that God who has created you, and has kept and preserved you, and has caused that ye should rejoice, and has granted that ye should live in peace one with another—

21 I say unto you that if ye should serve him who has created you from the beginning, and is preserving you from day to day, by lending you breath, that ye may live and move and do according to your own will, and even supporting you from one moment to another—I say, if ye should serve him with all your whole souls yet ye would be unprofitable servants.

22 And behold, all that he requires of you is to keep his commandments; and he has promised you that if ye would keep his commandments ye should prosper in the land; and he never doth vary from that which he hath said; therefore, if ye do keep his commandments he doth bless you and prosper you.

---

*King Benjamin served his people by working with his own hands.*

2:14 ***laden***—loaded down
***grievous to be borne***—very hard to carry

2:15 ***boast***—brag
***accuse***—blame

A person who has a clear conscience feels at peace in his life because he has repented of his sins and has no guilty feelings. Enos, like King Benjamin, had a clear conscience, and his "guilt was swept away" (Enos 1:6).

2:17 What can you do for other people that would also be of service to God?

2:17 (16–17) By serving others, President Marion G. Romney explained, "we experience the only true and lasting happiness. Service is not something we endure on this earth so we can earn the right to live in the celestial kingdom. Service is the very fiber of which an exalted life in the celestial kingdom is made" (in Conference Report, October 1982, 135).

2:18 ***ought not ye to***—shouldn't you

Serving others is so important that we cannot love and serve God unless we love and serve others (see 1 John 4:20–21).

2:19 ***do merit***—have earned

It is a commandment from God that we thank Him in all things (see D&C 59:7, 21).

2:20 ***render***—give
***granted***—allowed

2:21 Someone who is unprofitable continues to get further and further in debt and ends up owing more and more. Why do you owe God more each day of your life?

KING BENJAMIN PREACHES TO THE NEPHITES, BY GARY KAPP

King Benjamin "caused a tower to be erected, that thereby his people might hear the words which he should speak unto them."

23 And now, in the first place, he hath created you, and granted unto you your lives, for which ye are indebted unto him.
24 And secondly, he doth require that ye should do as he hath commanded you; for which if ye do, he doth immediately bless you; and therefore he hath paid you. And ye are still indebted unto him, and are, and will be, forever and ever; therefore, of what have ye to boast?
25 And now I ask, can ye say aught of yourselves? I answer you, Nay. Ye cannot say that ye are even as much as the dust of the earth; yet ye were created of the dust of the earth; but behold, it belongeth to him who created you.
26 And I, even I, whom ye call your king, am no better than ye yourselves are; for I am also of the dust. And ye behold that I am old, and am about to yield up this mortal frame to its mother earth.

## King Benjamin Explains What Happens to People Who Rebel Against God

27 Therefore, as I said unto you that I had served you, walking with a clear conscience before God, even so I at this time have caused that ye should assemble yourselves together, that I might be found blameless, and that your blood should not come upon me, when I shall stand to be judged of God of the things whereof he hath commanded me concerning you.

---

2:24 (22–24) We should always remember and be thankful for the blessings that God has given us. What does He ask from us?

2:25 ***aught***—anything at all
***Nay***—No

2:26 ***yield***—give
***mortal frame***—physical body

2:27 ***blameless***—without sin

28 I say unto you that I have caused that ye
should assemble yourselves together that I might
rid my garments of your blood, at this period of
time when I am about to go down to my grave, that
I might go down in peace, and my immortal spirit
may join the choirs above in singing the praises of
a just God.
29 And moreover, I say unto you that I have
caused that ye should assemble yourselves together, that I might declare unto you that I can no
longer be your teacher, nor your king;
30 For even at this time, my whole frame doth
tremble exceedingly while attempting to speak unto
you; but the Lord God doth support me, and hath suffered me that I should speak unto you, and hath
commanded me that I should declare unto you this
day, that my son Mosiah is a king and a ruler over you.
31 And now, my brethren, I would that ye should
do as ye have hitherto done. As ye have kept my
commandments, and also the commandments of
my father, and have prospered, and have been kept
from falling into the hands of your enemies, even
so if ye shall keep the commandments of my son,
or the commandments of God which shall be delivered unto you by him, ye shall prosper in the land,
and your enemies shall have no power over you.
32 But, O my people, beware lest there shall arise
contentions among you, and ye list to obey the evil
spirit, which was spoken of by my father Mosiah.
33 For behold, there is a wo pronounced upon
him who listeth to obey that spirit; for if he listeth
to obey him, and remaineth and dieth in his sins,
the same drinketh damnation to his own soul; for
he receiveth for his wages an everlasting punishment, having transgressed the law of God contrary
to his own knowledge.
34 I say unto you, that there are not any among
you, except it be your little children that have not
been taught concerning these things, but what
knoweth that ye are eternally indebted to your
heavenly Father, to render to him all that you
have and are; and also have been taught concerning the records which contain the prophecies
which have been spoken by the holy prophets,
even down to the time our father, Lehi, left
Jerusalem;
35 And also, all that has been spoken by our
fathers until now. And behold, also, they spake that
which was commanded them of the Lord; therefore,
they are just and true.
36 And now, I say unto you, my brethren, that
after ye have known and have been taught all these
things, if ye should transgress and go contrary to
that which has been spoken, that ye do withdraw
yourselves from the Spirit of the Lord, that it may
have no place in you to guide you in wisdom's
paths that ye may be blessed, prospered, and preserved—
37 I say unto you, that the man that doeth this, the
same cometh out in open rebellion against God;
therefore he listeth to obey the evil spirit, and
becometh an enemy to all righteousness; therefore,
the Lord has no place in him, for he dwelleth not in
unholy temples.

---

2:28 ***immortal***—undying or everlasting

King Benjamin understood that God had commanded him to teach his people the truth. If he failed to do so, he would be partly responsible for their sins (see also Jacob 1:19). In his last speech he wanted to make sure they understood the truth so he would not be guilty. The Lord has told parents in the Church that they have the same duty to teach their children the truth (see D&C 68:25–28).

2:30 ***tremble***—shake

2:31 ***hitherto***—so far

2:32 ***beware lest***—be careful or
***contentions***—arguing and fighting
***list***—choose

2:33 ***a wo pronounced***—a warning given of grief, sorrow, and misery
***transgressed***—broken

Damnation is a very serious punishment. People who are damned cannot move forward. They are like water that has been flowing down a river but is stopped by a dam. Their progress is stopped.

2:34 ***indebted to***—owing
***render***—give
***concerning***—about

2:36 ***contrary to***—against

2:37 The Apostle Paul explains that our bodies are a temple, or a place where the Holy Spirit can come (see 1 Corinthians 6:19).

38 Therefore if that man repenteth not, and remaineth and dieth an enemy to God, the demands of divine justice do awaken his immortal soul to a lively sense of his own guilt, which doth cause him to shrink from the presence of the Lord, and doth fill his breast with guilt, and pain, and anguish, which is like an unquenchable fire, whose flame ascendeth up forever and ever.
39 And now I say unto you, that mercy hath no claim on that man; therefore his final doom is to endure a never-ending torment.
40 O, all ye old men, and also ye young men, and you little children who can understand my words, for I have spoken plainly unto you that ye might understand, I pray that ye should awake to a remembrance of the awful situation of those that have fallen into transgression.
41 And moreover, I would desire that ye should consider on the blessed and happy state of those that keep the commandments of God. For behold, they are blessed in all things, both temporal and spiritual; and if they hold out faithful to the end they are received into heaven, that thereby they may dwell with God in a state of never-ending happiness. O remember, remember that these things are true; for the Lord God hath spoken it.

## CHAPTER 3

*King Benjamin tells his people what he learned from an angel. Watch for what the angel teaches King Benjamin about Jesus Christ and His Atonement.*

### An Angel Teaches King Benjamin About Jesus Christ's Life and Atonement

1 AND again my brethren, I would call your attention, for I have somewhat more to speak unto you; for behold, I have things to tell you concerning that which is to come.
2 And the things which I shall tell you are made known unto me by an angel from God. And he said unto me: Awake; and I awoke, and behold he stood before me.
3 And he said unto me: Awake, and hear the words which I shall tell thee; for behold, I am come to declare unto you the glad tidings of great joy.
4 For the Lord hath heard thy prayers, and hath judged of thy righteousness, and hath sent me to declare unto thee that thou mayest rejoice; and that thou mayest declare unto thy people, that they may also be filled with joy.

---

2:38 ***anguish***—deep sorrow
***an unquenchable fire***—a fire that cannot be put out
***ascendeth***—rises

2:39 ***claim***—power or hold
***doom***—reward or fate
***torment***—punishment

2:39 (38–39) Elder Bruce R. McConkie wrote: " 'Mercy hath no claim' on any man unless and until he repents and turns to the Lord. (Mosiah 2:38–39.) However, *'If ye will repent, and harden not your hearts,'* saith God, *'then will I have mercy upon you, through mine Only Begotten Son; Therefore, whosoever repenteth, and hardeneth not his heart, he shall have claim on mercy through mine Only Begotten Son, unto a remission of his sins; and these shall enter into my rest.'* (Alma 12:33–34.) Mercy is thus for the repentant, the faithful, the obedient, those who love and serve God. All others fail to escape the clutches of justice" (*Mormon Doctrine,* 485–86).

2:41 ***temporal***—physical

2:41 (39–41) King Benjamin explains that we are deciding right now whether in our next life we will have "never-ending torment" or "never-ending happiness." What must you do to have never-ending happiness in the next life?

3:3 ***tidings***—news or reports

3:3 (2–3) Years later, on the night before the Savior's birth, an angel shares this same message of joy to shepherds watching their flocks near Bethlehem (see Luke 2:10). Why do you think the birth of Jesus Christ was a cause for so much joy?

3:4 ***declare unto***—tell

The Lord answered King Benjamin's prayer because of his righteousness. What could you do to improve your personal righteousness so you can pray with greater faith?

CHRIST HEALING THE MAN WITH THE WITHERED HAND, BY ROBERT T. BARRETT

*An angel told King Benjamin that Christ would come to the earth and work "mighty miracles, such as healing the sick . . . and curing all manner of diseases."*

5 For behold, the time cometh, and is not far distant, that with power, the Lord Omnipotent who reigneth, who was, and is from all eternity to all eternity, shall come down from heaven among the children of men, and shall dwell in a tabernacle of clay, and shall go forth amongst men, working mighty miracles, such as healing the sick, raising the dead, causing the lame to walk, the blind to receive their sight, and the deaf to hear, and curing all manner of diseases.

6 And he shall cast out devils, or the evil spirits which dwell in the hearts of the children of men.

7 And lo, he shall suffer temptations, and pain of body, hunger, thirst, and fatigue, even more than man can suffer, except it be unto death; for behold, blood cometh from every pore, so great shall be his anguish for the wickedness and the abominations of his people.

8 And he shall be called Jesus Christ, the Son of God, the Father of heaven and earth, the Creator of all things from the beginning; and his mother shall be called Mary.

9 And lo, he cometh unto his own, that salvation might come unto the children of men even through faith on his name; and even after all this they shall consider him a man, and say that he hath a devil, and shall scourge him, and shall crucify him.

10 And he shall rise the third day from the dead; and behold, he standeth to judge the world; and behold, all these things are done that a righteous judgment might come upon the children of men.

11 For behold, and also his blood atoneth for the sins of those who have fallen by the transgression of Adam, who have died not knowing the will of God concerning them, or who have ignorantly sinned.

12 But wo, wo unto him who knoweth that he rebelleth against God! For salvation cometh to none such except it be through repentance and faith on the Lord Jesus Christ.

13 And the Lord God hath sent his holy prophets among all the children of men, to declare these things to every kindred, nation, and tongue, that thereby whosoever should believe that Christ should come, the same might receive remission of their sins, and rejoice with exceedingly great joy, even as though he had already come among them.

14 Yet the Lord God saw that his people were a stiffnecked people, and he appointed unto them a law, even the law of Moses.

---

3:5 ***Omnipotent***—who has all power
***reigneth***—rules as king
***is from all eternity to all eternity***—lives forever
***tabernacle of clay***—physical body

3:5 (1–5) King Benjamin knows about the future because he is a prophet. He tells his people about the first coming of Jesus. We also have prophets today. What have our prophets said about the Second Coming of Jesus Christ and how we should prepare for it?

3:6 (5–6) In Matthew 8–9 we can read of many miracles that show the power of Jesus Christ over the elements, over sickness, over death, and over the devil.

3:7 Through the Atonement, Jesus Christ suffered for everything that causes us pain, sorrow, sickness, and affliction, as well as for our sins (see Alma 7:11–13). This suffering was so intense that it caused Jesus, "the greatest of all, to tremble because of pain, and to bleed at every pore, and to suffer both body and spirit" (D&C 19:18).

***abominations***—great evil

3:8 Jesus has many names and titles. Each of His names teaches us something about Him and His mission. What do the names in this verse teach us about Him?

3:9 "Full salvation, often called eternal life or exaltation, is to be like God, to be a son of God, a joint-heir with Christ, receiving, inheriting, and possessing, as he does, the fulness of the kingdom of the Father" (Bruce R. McConkie, *A New Witness for the Articles of Faith,* 144).

3:10 Jesus was the first to be resurrected (see 1 Corinthians 15:20–22). As a result of His resurrection, every person will also be resurrected and live forever with a perfect body (see Alma 11:43–44).

3:11 (10–11) Jesus came to earth and experienced the challenges of mortality. By doing that and suffering the Atonement, He came to know firsthand how difficult life can be and therefore is completely fair and understanding as our eternal judge (see Alma 7:11–13).

3:12 ***wo***—sorrow and misery

3:13 ***remission***—forgiveness
***exceedingly***—very

3:14 ***stiffnecked***—stubborn
***appointed***—gave

15 And many signs, and wonders, and types, and
shadows showed he unto them, concerning his coming; and also holy prophets spake unto them concerning his coming; and yet they hardened their hearts, and understood not that the law of Moses availeth nothing except it were through the atonement of his blood.

## Natural Man Is an Enemy to God

16 And even if it were possible that little children
could sin they could not be saved; but I say unto you they are blessed; for behold, as in Adam, or by nature, they fall, even so the blood of Christ atoneth for their sins.
17 And moreover, I say unto you, that there shall
be no other name given nor any other way nor means whereby salvation can come unto the children of men, only in and through the name of Christ, the Lord Omnipotent.
18 For behold he judgeth, and his judgment is
just; and the infant perisheth not that dieth in his infancy; but men drink damnation to their own souls except they humble themselves and become as little children, and believe that salvation was, and is, and is to come, in and through the atoning blood of Christ, the Lord Omnipotent.
19 For the natural man is an enemy to God, and
has been from the fall of Adam, and will be, forever and ever, unless he yields to the enticings of the Holy Spirit, and putteth off the natural man and becometh a saint through the atonement of Christ the Lord, and becometh as a child, submissive, meek, humble, patient, full of love, willing to submit to all things which the Lord seeth fit to inflict upon him, even as a child doth submit to his father.

## God's Mercy Cannot Save Those Who Rebel Against the Truth

20 And moreover, I say unto you, that the time
shall come when the knowledge of a Savior shall spread throughout every nation, kindred, tongue, and people.
21 And behold, when that time cometh, none shall
be found blameless before God, except it be little children, only through repentance and faith on the name of the Lord God Omnipotent.
22 And even at this time, when thou shalt have
taught thy people the things which the Lord thy God hath commanded thee, even then are they found no more blameless in the sight of God, only according to the words which I have spoken unto thee.
23 And now I have spoken the words which the
Lord God hath commanded me.
24 And thus saith the Lord: They shall stand as a
bright testimony against this people, at the judgment day; whereof they shall be judged, every man according to his works, whether they be good, or whether they be evil.

---

3:15 ***wonders***—miracles
***availeth nothing***—was good for nothing

Types and shadows are actual objects, events, people, or rituals that teach spiritual truths about Jesus Christ and the eternal plan of God. For example, the Liahona not only is an actual object that directs Lehi's family to the promised land but also typifies, or represents, the words of Christ, which can lead us to the eternal land of promise if we are faithful (see Alma 37:38–45).

3:18 ***just***—fair

The "infant perisheth not that dieth in his infancy" means that "all children who die before they arrive at the years of accountability are saved in the celestial kingdom of heaven" (D&C 137:10; see also D&C 29:46).

3:18 (11–18) The Atonement of Jesus Christ saves those who sinned without knowing the gospel (verse 11), "little children" (verse 16), and those who humble themselves and become as believing and obedient as little children (verse 18).

3:19 ***submissive***—willingly obedient
***meek***—gentle
***submit to***—obey
***inflict***—allow to come

A "natural man" is one who yields, or gives in, to the temptations of this fallen world (see James 4:4; Ether 3:2). One who yields to the enticings (whisperings) of the Spirit and puts off (changes) the natural man can become a "Saint." When someone has been able to change himself through the Atonement from the natural man to a Saint, he is born again and has a desire to only do what is right (see Mosiah 5:2).

Think about the times in your life when you have felt the Spirit touch your heart. Does the Spirit help you feel more patient and loving? How do you think your life would be better if you felt close to the Spirit more often?

3:24 We will be judged not only by our works but also by our words and thoughts (see Mosiah 4:30).

25 And if they be evil they are consigned to an awful view of their own guilt and abominations, which doth cause them to shrink from the presence of the Lord into a state of misery and endless torment, from whence they can no more return; therefore they have drunk damnation to their own souls.
26 Therefore, they have drunk out of the cup of the wrath of God, which justice could no more deny unto them than it could deny that Adam should fall because of his partaking of the forbidden fruit; therefore, mercy could have claim on them no more forever.
27 And their torment is as a lake of fire and brimstone, whose flames are unquenchable, and whose smoke ascendeth up forever and ever. Thus hath the Lord commanded me. Amen.

## CHAPTER 4

*King Benjamin teaches what his people must do to be saved. Notice how those who trust and obey the Lord will treat others.*

### Salvation Comes to Each of Us Through the Atonement

1 AND now, it came to pass that when king Benjamin had made an end of speaking the words which had been delivered unto him by the angel of the Lord, that he cast his eyes round about on the multitude, and behold they had fallen to the earth, for the fear of the Lord had come upon them.
2 And they had viewed themselves in their own carnal state, even less than the dust of the earth. And they all cried aloud with one voice, saying: O have mercy, and apply the atoning blood of Christ that we may receive forgiveness of our sins, and our hearts may be purified; for we believe in Jesus Christ, the Son of God, who created heaven and earth, and all things; who shall come down among the children of men.
3 And it came to pass that after they had spoken these words the Spirit of the Lord came upon them, and they were filled with joy, having received a remission of their sins, and having peace of conscience, because of the exceeding faith which they had in Jesus Christ who should come, according to the words which king Benjamin had spoken unto them.
4 And king Benjamin again opened his mouth and began to speak unto them, saying: My friends and my brethren, my kindred and my people, I would again call your attention, that ye may hear and understand the remainder of my words which I shall speak unto you.
5 For behold, if the knowledge of the goodness of God at this time has awakened you to a sense of your nothingness, and your worthless and fallen state—

---

3:25 ***consigned to***—given
***abominations***—great evil
***drunk damnation to***—stopped the progression of

3:26 ***drunk out of the cup of the wrath***—experienced the anger
***deny unto***—refuse to give
***mercy could have claim on them no more***—there could be no more forgiveness for them

3:27 ***brimstone, whose flames are unquenchable***—hot coals that cannot be cooled
***ascendeth***—rises

4:1 ***delivered***—given
***cast his eyes***—looked
***the fear of***—reverence for

4:2 ***carnal***—earthly

When we have sinned, we often feel like King Benjamin's people, who felt unworthy and "less than the dust of the earth." The only way to change this feeling is to repent and "pray until you have the peace of conscience because of your faith in Jesus Christ's atonement, and you will know that your sins then have been forgiven" (Marion G. Romney, as quoted in Harold B. Lee, *Stand Ye in Holy Places,* 211).

4:3 ***remission***—forgiveness

"If the time comes when you have done all that you can to repent of your sins, whoever you are, wherever you are, and have made amends and restitution to the best of your ability . . . if you seek for and you find that peace of conscience, by that token [sign] you may know that the Lord has accepted of your repentance. . . . The miracle of forgiveness is available to all of those who turn from their evil doings and return no more" (Harold B. Lee, in Conference Report, April 1973, 177–78).

4:4 ***kindred***—family
***remainder***—rest

4:5 ***fallen state***—sinful condition

6 I say unto you, if ye have come to a knowledge
of the goodness of God, and his matchless power,
and his wisdom, and his patience, and his long-
suffering towards the children of men; and also, the
atonement which has been prepared from the foundation of the world, that thereby salvation might
come to him that should put his trust in the Lord,
and should be diligent in keeping his commandments, and continue in the faith even unto the end
of his life, I mean the life of the mortal body—
7 I say, that this is the man who receiveth salvation,
through the atonement which was prepared from
the foundation of the world for all mankind, which
ever were since the fall of Adam, or who are, or
who ever shall be, even unto the end of the world.
8 And this is the means whereby salvation cometh.
And there is none other salvation save this which
hath been spoken of; neither are there any conditions whereby man can be saved except the conditions which I have told you.

## We Must Believe in God to Be Saved

9 Believe in God; believe that he is, and that he
created all things, both in heaven and in earth;
believe that he has all wisdom, and all power, both
in heaven and in earth; believe that man doth not
comprehend all the things which the Lord can comprehend.
10 And again, believe that ye must repent of your
sins and forsake them, and humble yourselves
before God; and ask in sincerity of heart that he
would forgive you; and now, if you believe all these
things see that ye do them.
11 And again I say unto you as I have said
before, that as ye have come to the knowledge of
the glory of God, or if ye have known of his goodness and have tasted of his love, and have
received a remission of your sins, which causeth
such exceedingly great joy in your souls, even so
I would that ye should remember, and always
retain in remembrance, the greatness of God, and
your own nothingness, and his goodness and
long-suffering towards you, unworthy creatures,
and humble yourselves even in the depths of
humility, calling on the name of the Lord daily,
and standing steadfastly in the faith of that which
is to come, which was spoken by the mouth of the
angel.
12 And behold, I say unto you that if ye do this ye
shall always rejoice, and be filled with the love of
God, and always retain a remission of your sins;
and ye shall grow in the knowledge of the glory of
him that created you, or in the knowledge of that
which is just and true.
13 And ye will not have a mind to injure one
another, but to live peaceably, and to render to
every man according to that which is his due.
14 And ye will not suffer your children that they
go hungry, or naked; neither will ye suffer that they
transgress the laws of God, and fight and quarrel
one with another, and serve the devil, who is the
master of sin, or who is the evil spirit which hath
been spoken of by our fathers, he being an enemy
to all righteousness.
15 But ye will teach them to walk in the ways of
truth and soberness; ye will teach them to love one
another, and to serve one another.

---

4:8 (6–8) King Benjamin teaches that Christ's Atonement is the only means whereby men can receive salvation. Similarly, Alma explains that without this infinite and eternal Atonement all would have perished (see Alma 34:9–14).

4:9 ***comprehend***—understand

4:10 ***forsake***—leave

4:10 (9–10) King Benjamin gives his people five things they need to believe and adds, "If you believe all these things see that ye do them." Elder Bruce R. McConkie wrote, "Belief, humble belief, is the foundation of all righteousness and the beginning of spiritual progression" (*A New Witness for the Articles of Faith,* 21).

4:11 ***tasted***—felt
***retain***—keep
***steadfastly***—firm

4:14 ***transgress***—break

4:15 ***soberness***—reverence

4:15 (14–15) When we fight and argue with our brother or sister, whose spirit are we inviting? What does King Benjamin tell parents to teach? How would this help your family?

## Caring for the Poor Helps Us Maintain Forgiveness of Our Sins

16 And also, ye yourselves will succor those that stand in need of your succor; ye will administer of your substance unto him that standeth in need; and ye will not suffer that the beggar putteth up his petition to you in vain, and turn him out to perish.
17 Perhaps thou shalt say: The man has brought upon himself his misery; therefore I will stay my hand, and will not give unto him of my food, nor impart unto him of my substance that he may not suffer, for his punishments are just—
18 But I say unto you, O man, whosoever doeth this the same hath great cause to repent; and except he repenteth of that which he hath done he perisheth forever, and hath no interest in the kingdom of God.
19 For behold, are we not all beggars? Do we not all depend upon the same Being, even God, for all the substance which we have, for both food and raiment, and for gold, and for silver, and for all the riches which we have of every kind?
20 And behold, even at this time, ye have been calling on his name, and begging for a remission of your sins. And has he suffered that ye have begged in vain? Nay; he has poured out his Spirit upon you, and has caused that your hearts should be filled with joy, and has caused that your mouths should be stopped that ye could not find utterance, so exceedingly great was your joy.
21 And now, if God, who has created you, on whom you are dependent for your lives and for all that ye have and are, doth grant unto you whatsoever ye ask that is right, in faith, believing that ye shall receive, O then, how ye ought to impart of the substance that ye have one to another.
22 And if ye judge the man who putteth up his petition to you for your substance that he perish not, and condemn him, how much more just will be your condemnation for withholding your substance, which doth not belong to you but to God, to whom also your life belongeth; and yet ye put up no petition, nor repent of the thing which thou hast done.
23 I say unto you, wo be unto that man, for his substance shall perish with him; and now, I say these things unto those who are rich as pertaining to the things of this world.
24 And again, I say unto the poor, ye who have not and yet have sufficient, that ye remain from day to day; I mean all you who deny the beggar, because ye have not; I would that ye say in your hearts that: I give not because I have not, but if I had I would give.
25 And now, if ye say this in your hearts ye remain guiltless, otherwise ye are condemned; and your condemnation is just for ye covet that which ye have not received.
26 And now, for the sake of these things which I have spoken unto you—that is, for the sake of retaining a remission of your sins from day to day, that ye may walk guiltless before God—I would that ye should impart of your substance to the poor, every man according to that which he hath, such as feeding the hungry, clothing the naked, visiting the sick and administering to their relief, both spiritually and temporally, according to their wants.

## We Should Do All Things in Wisdom and Order

27 And see that all these things are done in wisdom and order; for it is not requisite that a man should run faster than he has strength. And again,

4:16 ***succor***—help
***administer of your substance***—give some of what you have
***putteth up his petition to you***—shall ask for your help

4:17 ***impart***—give

4:18 (17–18) Benjamin teaches that the person who refuses to share with the poor and needy "hath no interest in the kingdom of God." Jesus also teaches a rich young man that if he would give to the poor, he would "have treasure in heaven" (Mark 10:21).

4:19 ***raiment***—clothing

4:20 ***could not find utterance***—were speechless

4:24 (22–24) We will be condemned, or punished, for not sharing. One reason is that all that we have comes to us from God. How can knowing this help you to share more willingly? If you really don't have much to share, what can you say in your heart?

4:25 ***covet***—desire unrighteously

4:27 The prize that we should all be trying to win is eternal life. As President Lorenzo Snow taught, "The reward for righteousness is exaltation" (*Improvement Era,* 22:651). *Exaltation* is another word for eternal life.

***requisite***—required

it is expedient that he should be diligent, that thereby he might win the prize; therefore, all things must be done in order.

28 And I would that ye should remember, that whosoever among you borroweth of his neighbor should return the thing that he borroweth, according as he doth agree, or else thou shalt commit sin; and perhaps thou shalt cause thy neighbor to commit sin also.

29 And finally, I cannot tell you all the things whereby ye may commit sin; for there are divers ways and means, even so many that I cannot number them.

30 But this much I can tell you, that if ye do not watch yourselves, and your thoughts, and your words, and your deeds, and observe the commandments of God, and continue in the faith of what ye have heard concerning the coming of our Lord, even unto the end of your lives, ye must perish. And now, O man, remember, and perish not.

## CHAPTER 5

*King Benjamin's people believe his words. They willingly enter into a covenant with God to be obedient to His commandments. Look for the blessings that are promised to those who keep their covenants.*

### The People Feel the Spirit, Believe King Benjamin's Words, and Desire to Follow the Lord

1 AND now, it came to pass that when king Benjamin had thus spoken to his people, he sent among them, desiring to know of his people if they believed the words which he had spoken unto them.

2 And they all cried with one voice, saying: Yea, we believe all the words which thou hast spoken unto us; and also, we know of their surety and truth, because of the Spirit of the Lord Omnipotent, which has wrought a mighty change in us, or in our hearts, that we have no more disposition to do evil, but to do good continually.

3 And we, ourselves, also, through the infinite goodness of God, and the manifestations of his Spirit, have great views of that which is to come; and were it expedient, we could prophesy of all things.

4 And it is the faith which we have had on the things which our king has spoken unto us that has brought us to this great knowledge, whereby we do rejoice with such exceedingly great joy.

5 And we are willing to enter into a covenant with our God to do his will, and to be obedient to his commandments in all things that he shall command us, all the remainder of our days, that we may not bring upon ourselves a never-ending torment, as has been spoken by the angel, that we may not drink out of the cup of the wrath of God.

### We Become Sons and Daughters of Christ by Faith and Obedience

6 And now, these are the words which king Benjamin desired of them; and therefore he said unto them: Ye have spoken the words that I desired; and the covenant which ye have made is a righteous covenant.

---

4:27 ***expedient***—necessary

4:29 ***divers***—many

4:30 ***perish***—die

"Your thoughts will determine your actions, and so they must be controlled" (*The Teachings of Ezra Taft Benson,* 197). Alma taught that our words and our thoughts will be considered when we are judged (see Alma 12:14).

5:2 ***cried***—declared or shouted
***Omnipotent***—who has all power
***wrought***—brought about or worked
***disposition***—desire or intention

The Prophet Joseph Smith taught, "The nearer man approaches perfection, the clearer are his views, and the greater his enjoyments, till he has overcome the evils of his life and lost every desire for sin" (*Teachings of the Prophet Joseph Smith,* 51).

5:3 ***infinite***—unending or eternal
***manifestations***—clear displays
***expedient***—necessary

5:4 ***exceedingly***—very

5:5 A covenant is an agreement between two people. In the scriptures it is usually an agreement between God and man. God promises to bless us when we agree to be obedient to His commandments (see LDS Bible Dictionary, s.v. "Covenant," 651).

***remainder of our days***—rest of our lives
***torment***—punishment
***drink out of the cup of the wrath***—experience the anger

7 And now, because of the covenant which ye have made ye shall be called the children of Christ, his sons, and his daughters; for behold, this day he hath spiritually begotten you; for ye say that your hearts are changed through faith on his name; therefore, ye are born of him and have become his sons and his daughters.

8 And under this head ye are made free, and there is no other head whereby ye can be made free. There is no other name given whereby salvation cometh; therefore, I would that ye should take upon you the name of Christ, all you that have entered into the covenant with God that ye should be obedient unto the end of your lives.

9 And it shall come to pass that whosoever doeth this shall be found at the right hand of God, for he shall know the name by which he is called; for he shall be called by the name of Christ.

10 And now it shall come to pass, that whosoever shall not take upon him the name of Christ must be called by some other name; therefore, he findeth himself on the left hand of God.

### *King Benjamin Encourages the People to Remain Faithful*

11 And I would that ye should remember also, that this is the name that I said I should give unto you that never should be blotted out, except it be through transgression; therefore, take heed that ye do not transgress, that the name be not blotted out of your hearts.

12 I say unto you, I would that ye should remember to retain the name written always in your hearts, that ye are not found on the left hand of God, but that ye hear and know the voice by which ye shall be called, and also, the name by which he shall call you.

13 For how knoweth a man the master whom he has not served, and who is a stranger unto him, and is far from the thoughts and intents of his heart?

14 And again, doth a man take an ass which belongeth to his neighbor, and keep him? I say unto you, Nay; he will not even suffer that he shall feed among his flocks, but will drive him away, and cast him out. I say unto you, that even so shall it be among you if ye know not the name by which ye are called.

15 Therefore, I would that ye should be steadfast and immovable, always abounding in good works, that Christ, the Lord God Omnipotent, may seal you his, that you may be brought to heaven, that ye may have everlasting salvation and eternal life, through the wisdom, and power, and justice, and mercy of him who created all things, in heaven and in earth, who is God above all. Amen.

## CHAPTER 6

*Mosiah replaces his father, King Benjamin, as king. Look for ways King Mosiah follows his father's good example.*

---

5:7 ***spiritually begotten you***—given you spiritual life

Heavenly Father is the Father of our spirits, but when we enter into and keep our covenants with God, Jesus Christ becomes our spiritual father. This is sometimes called being born again. "We are, then, because of his great love and because of our desire to be guided by his light, part of the family of Christ" (Aileen H. Clyde, in Conference Report, April 1995, 36).

5:7 (6–7) What covenants have you made with God? Why do you think it is important that you remain true to those promises?

5:8 ***head***—name

5:10 (9–10) Anciently the right hand was a symbol for something favorable and the left hand was a symbol for something unfavorable (see Isaiah 41:10; Matthew 25:31–46). Those on the "right hand of God" are considered to be the righteous.

5:11 ***blotted***—forgotten or erased

5:12 ***retain***—keep

5:13 "Service is a means of knowing and becoming closer to the Savior" (Carlos E. Asay, *Family Pecan Trees: Planting a Legacy of Faith at Home,* 181).

5:14 ***Nay***—No

5:15 ***steadfast and immovable***—strong, faithful, and endure to the end

## King Mosiah Serves as a Righteous Example to His People

1 AND now, king Benjamin thought it was expedient, after having finished speaking to the people,
that he should take the names of all those who had
entered into a covenant with God to keep his commandments.
2 And it came to pass that there was not one soul,
except it were little children, but who had entered
into the covenant and had taken upon them the
name of Christ.
3 And again, it came to pass that when king
Benjamin had made an end of all these things, and
had consecrated his son Mosiah to be a ruler and a
king over his people, and had given him all the
charges concerning the kingdom, and also had
appointed priests to teach the people, that thereby
they might hear and know the commandments of
God, and to stir them up in remembrance of the
oath which they had made, he dismissed the multitude, and they returned, every one, according to
their families, to their own houses.
4 And Mosiah began to reign in his father's stead.
And he began to reign in the thirtieth year of his
age, making in the whole, about four hundred and
seventy-six years from the time that Lehi left
Jerusalem.
5 And king Benjamin lived three years and he died.
6 And it came to pass that king Mosiah did walk
in the ways of the Lord, and did observe his judgments and his statutes, and did keep his commandments in all things whatsoever he commanded him.
7 And king Mosiah did cause his people that they
should till the earth. And he also, himself, did till
the earth, that thereby he might not become burdensome to his people, that he might do according
to that which his father had done in all things. And
there was no contention among all his people for
the space of three years.

# CHAPTER 7

*Ammon and his brethren discover Limhi and his people. Watch for how the Lord protects Ammon and softens Limhi's heart.*

## Ammon Leads a Search Party to the Land of Lehi-Nephi

1 AND now, it came to pass that after king Mosiah
had had continual peace for the space of three
years, he was desirous to know concerning the
people who went up to dwell in the land of Lehi-
Nephi, or in the city of Lehi-Nephi; for his people
had heard nothing from them from the time they
left the land of Zarahemla; therefore, they wearied
him with their teasings.
2 And it came to pass that king Mosiah granted
that sixteen of their strong men might go up to the
land of Lehi-Nephi, to inquire concerning their
brethren.

---

6:1 ***expedient***—good or desirable

6:2 ***soul***—person

6:3 ***made an end of***—finished
***consecrated***—set apart
***charges***—duties
***appointed***—called and ordained
***oath***—promise
***dismissed***—sent away

6:3 (1–3) Names are written down of people who promised to keep God's commandments. Priesthood holders are assigned to teach the gospel and remind Church members of their promises. How do your home teachers help you learn and remember the commandments?

6:4 ***reign***—rule as king
***stead***—place

6:6 ***statutes***—laws

6:7 ***till the earth***—plant and harvest crops
***burdensome***—a weight

President David O. McKay counseled: "Learn to like your work. Learn to say, 'This is my work, my glory, not my doom.' God has blessed us with the privilege of working. When he said, 'Earn thy bread by the sweat of thy brow,' he gave us a blessing. Men and women have accepted it. Too much leisure is dangerous. Work is a divine gift" (*Gospel Ideals*, 497).

7:1 ***wearied him with their teasings***—continued to ask and beg for information

7:2 (1–2) The land of Lehi-Nephi is where Lehi's family first lived after they arrived in the promised land (see 1 Nephi 18:23). The Nephites left that area under King Mosiah I and traveled to the land of Zarahemla (see Omni 1:12–13). King Mosiah sent the sixteen men to Lehi-Nephi in about 121 B.C.

KING BENJAMIN ORDAINING MOSIAH, BY ROBERT T. BARRETT

*King Benjamin "consecrated his son Mosiah to be a ruler and a king over his people."*

3 And it came to pass that on the morrow they started to go up, having with them one Ammon, he being a strong and mighty man, and a descendant of Zarahemla; and he was also their leader.

4 And now, they knew not the course they should travel in the wilderness to go up to the land of Lehi-Nephi; therefore they wandered many days in the wilderness, even forty days did they wander.

5 And when they had wandered forty days they came to a hill, which is north of the land of Shilom, and there they pitched their tents.

6 And Ammon took three of his brethren, and their names were Amaleki, Helem, and Hem, and they went down into the land of Nephi.

### Ammon Is Taken Prisoner and Questioned

7 And behold, they met the king of the people who were in the land of Nephi, and in the land of Shilom; and they were surrounded by the king's guard, and were taken, and were bound, and were committed to prison.

8 And it came to pass when they had been in prison two days they were again brought before the king, and their bands were loosed; and they stood before the king, and were permitted, or rather commanded, that they should answer the questions which he should ask them.

9 And he said unto them: Behold, I am Limhi, the son of Noah, who was the son of Zeniff, who came up out of the land of Zarahemla to inherit this land, which was the land of their fathers, who was made a king by the voice of the people.

10 And now, I desire to know the cause whereby ye were so bold as to come near the walls of the city, when I, myself, was with my guards without the gate?

11 And now, for this cause have I suffered that ye should be preserved, that I might inquire of you, or else I should have caused that my guards should have put you to death. Ye are permitted to speak.

12 And now, when Ammon saw that he was permitted to speak, he went forth and bowed himself before the king; and rising again he said: O king, I am very thankful before God this day that I am yet alive, and am permitted to speak; and I will endeavor to speak with boldness;

13 For I am assured that if ye had known me ye would not have suffered that I should have worn these bands. For I am Ammon, and am a descendant of Zarahemla, and have come up out of the land of Zarahemla to inquire concerning our brethren, whom Zeniff brought up out of that land.

14 And now, it came to pass that after Limhi had heard the words of Ammon, he was exceedingly glad, and said: Now, I know of a surety that my brethren who were in the land of Zarahemla are yet alive. And now, I will rejoice; and on the morrow I will cause that my people shall rejoice also.

15 For behold, we are in bondage to the Lamanites, and are taxed with a tax which is grievous to be borne. And now, behold, our brethren will deliver us out of our bondage, or out of the hands of the Lamanites, and we will be their slaves; for it is better that we be slaves to the Nephites than to pay tribute to the king of the Lamanites.

16 And now, king Limhi commanded his guards that they should no more bind Ammon nor his brethren, but caused that they should go to the hill which was north of Shilom, and bring their brethren into the city, that thereby they might eat, and drink, and rest themselves from the labors of their journey; for they had suffered many things; they had suffered hunger, thirst, and fatigue.

### Limhi Speaks to His People

17 And now, it came to pass on the morrow that king Limhi sent a proclamation among all his people, that thereby they might gather themselves together to the temple to hear the words which he should speak unto them.

18 And it came to pass that when they had gathered themselves together that he spake unto them in this wise, saying: O ye, my people, lift up your heads and be comforted; for behold, the time is at hand, or is not far distant, when we shall no longer be in subjection to our enemies, notwithstanding our many strugglings, which have been in vain; yet I trust there remaineth an effectual struggle to be made.

---

7:3 ***morrow***—next day

7:12 ***endeavor***—try

7:15 ***grievous to be borne***—very hard to pay
***bondage***—slavery
***tribute***—taxes

7:16 ***fatigue***—great tiredness

7:18 ***in subjection to***—under the power of
***in vain***—useless
***an effectual***—a successful

19 Therefore, lift up your heads, and rejoice, and
put your trust in God, in that God who was the God
of Abraham, and Isaac, and Jacob; and also, that
God who brought the children of Israel out of the
land of Egypt, and caused that they should walk
through the Red Sea on dry ground, and fed them
with manna that they might not perish in the wilderness; and many more things did he do for them.
20 And again, that same God has brought our
fathers out of the land of Jerusalem, and has kept
and preserved his people even until now; and
behold, it is because of our iniquities and abominations that he has brought us into bondage.
21 And ye all are witnesses this day, that Zeniff,
who was made king over this people, he being
over-zealous to inherit the land of his fathers, therefore being deceived by the cunning and craftiness
of king Laman, who having entered into a treaty
with king Zeniff, and having yielded up into his
hands the possessions of a part of the land, or even
the city of Lehi-Nephi, and the city of Shilom; and
the land round about—
22 And all this he did, for the sole purpose of
bringing this people into subjection or into
bondage. And behold, we at this time do pay tribute to the king of the Lamanites, to the amount of
one half of our corn, and our barley, and even all
our grain of every kind, and one half of the increase
of our flocks and our herds; and even one half of
all we have or possess the king of the Lamanites
doth exact of us, or our lives.
23 And now, is not this grievous to be borne? And
is not this, our affliction, great? Now behold, how
great reason we have to mourn.
24 Yea, I say unto you, great are the reasons
which we have to mourn; for behold how many of
our brethren have been slain, and their blood has
been spilt in vain, and all because of iniquity.
25 For if this people had not fallen into transgression the Lord would not have suffered that this
great evil should come upon them. But behold,
they would not hearken unto his words; but there
arose contentions among them, even so much that
they did shed blood among themselves.
26 And a prophet of the Lord have they slain; yea,
a chosen man of God, who told them of their
wickedness and abominations, and prophesied of
many things which are to come, yea, even the coming of Christ.
27 And because he said unto them that Christ was
the God, the Father of all things, and said that he
should take upon him the image of man, and it
should be the image after which man was created
in the beginning; or in other words, he said that
man was created after the image of God, and that
God should come down among the children of
men, and take upon him flesh and blood, and go
forth upon the face of the earth—
28 And now, because he said this, they did put
him to death; and many more things did they do
which brought down the wrath of God upon them.
Therefore, who wondereth that they are in bondage,
and that they are smitten with sore afflictions?
29 For behold, the Lord hath said: I will not succor
my people in the day of their transgression; but I will
hedge up their ways that they prosper not; and their
doings shall be as a stumbling block before them.
30 And again, he saith: If my people shall sow
filthiness they shall reap the chaff thereof in the
whirlwind; and the effect thereof is poison.

---

7:19 Manna is the food the Lord miraculously provided for the children of Israel while they were in the wilderness with Moses (see Exodus 16:14–15).

7:20 ***iniquities and abominations***—sins

7:21 ***over-zealous***—too anxious
***yielded up***—given

7:22 ***doth exact of***—takes from

7:28 ***smitten***—tormented

7:28 (25–28) Like Abinadi, many prophets have been killed or persecuted for teaching the truth. Why do you think the wicked want to kill those who teach and testify of Jesus Christ?

7:29 ***succor***—run to help
***hedge up their ways***—make their life difficult

PHOTOGRAPH BY DAVID H. GARNER

*Chaff is the husk that surrounds a kernel of wheat. With the help of the wind, it is separated from the wheat before the wheat is eaten.*

31 And again he saith: If my people shall sow
filthiness they shall reap the east wind, which
bringeth immediate destruction.
32 And now, behold, the promise of the Lord is
fulfilled, and ye are smitten and afflicted.
33 But if ye will turn to the Lord with full purpose
of heart, and put your trust in him, and serve him
with all diligence of mind, if ye do this, he will,
according to his own will and pleasure, deliver you
out of bondage.

## CHAPTER 8

*Ammon tells Limhi's people what has happened in Zarahemla. Limhi tells Ammon about twenty-four gold plates his people found. See what you can learn about the importance of prophets, seers, and scriptures.*

### Ammon Teaches the Words of King Benjamin

1 AND it came to pass that after king Limhi had
made an end of speaking to his people, for he
spake many things unto them and only a few of
them have I written in this book, he told his people
all the things concerning their brethren who were
in the land of Zarahemla.
2 And he caused that Ammon should stand up
before the multitude, and rehearse unto them all
that had happened unto their brethren from the
time that Zeniff went up out of the land even until
the time that he himself came up out of the land.
3 And he also rehearsed unto them the last words
which king Benjamin had taught them, and
explained them to the people of king Limhi, so that
they might understand all the words which he spake.
4 And it came to pass that after he had done all
this, that king Limhi dismissed the multitude, and
caused that they should return every one unto his
own house.

### Limhi Tells of Finding the Jaredite Record

5 And it came to pass that he caused that the plates
which contained the record of his people from the
time that they left the land of Zarahemla, should be
brought before Ammon, that he might read them.
6 Now, as soon as Ammon had read the record, the
king inquired of him to know if he could interpret
languages, and Ammon told him that he could not.
7 And the king said unto him: Being grieved for
the afflictions of my people, I caused that forty and
three of my people should take a journey into the
wilderness, that thereby they might find the land of
Zarahemla, that we might appeal unto our brethren
to deliver us out of bondage.
8 And they were lost in the wilderness for the
space of many days, yet they were diligent, and
found not the land of Zarahemla but returned to this
land, having traveled in a land among many waters,
having discovered a land which was covered with
bones of men, and of beasts, and was also covered
with ruins of buildings of every kind, having discovered a land which had been peopled with a
people who were as numerous as the hosts of Israel.

---

7:31 The "east wind" refers to the hot, dry wind often mentioned in the Old Testament that blows across the desert, destroying crops and bringing sandstorms. It often represents destruction (see Genesis 41:6, 23; Job 27:21; Isaiah 27:8).

7:33 Limhi tells his people that the only way they can escape their problems is by turning to the Lord. How does turning to the Lord help you with your own problems?

8:2 ***rehearse***—tell

8:3 King Benjamin taught of the Savior, His mission, our need for Him, and how we must live so we can be blessed by Him (see Mosiah 2–5).

8:6 ***inquired***—asked
***interpret languages***—understand or explain words from other languages

8:7 ***Being grieved***—Feeling deep sorrow
***afflictions***—trials and sufferings
***appeal unto***—ask
***bondage***—slavery

8:8 ***diligent***—not willing to give up
***hosts***—armies

PHOTOGRAPH BY EDWIN M. WOOLLEY

*Limhi's people found a land where many people had lived and died. Ruins, or remains of buildings, that may have looked like this were also in the land.*

9 And for a testimony that the things that they had said are true they have brought twenty-four plates which are filled with engravings, and they are of pure gold.

10 And behold, also, they have brought breastplates, which are large, and they are of brass and of copper, and are perfectly sound.

11 And again, they have brought swords, the hilts thereof have perished, and the blades thereof were cankered with rust; and there is no one in the land that is able to interpret the language or the engravings that are on the plates. Therefore I said unto thee: Canst thou translate?

12 And I say unto thee again: Knowest thou of any one that can translate? For I am desirous that these records should be translated into our language; for, perhaps, they will give us a knowledge of a remnant of the people who have been destroyed, from whence these records came; or, perhaps, they will give us a knowledge of this very people who have been destroyed; and I am desirous to know the cause of their destruction.

## A Seer Is a Revelator and a Prophet

13 Now Ammon said unto him: I can assuredly tell thee, O king, of a man that can translate the records; for he has wherewith that he can look, and translate all records that are of ancient date; and it is a gift from God. And the things are called interpreters, and no man can look in them except he be commanded, lest he should look for that he ought not and he should perish. And whosoever is commanded to look in them, the same is called seer.

14 And behold, the king of the people who are in the land of Zarahemla is the man that is commanded to do these things, and who has this high gift from God.

15 And the king said that a seer is greater than a prophet.

16 And Ammon said that a seer is a revelator and a prophet also; and a gift which is greater can no man have, except he should possess the power of God, which no man can; yet a man may have great power given him from God.

17 But a seer can know of things which are past, and also of things which are to come, and by them shall all things be revealed, or, rather, shall secret things be made manifest, and hidden things shall come to light, and things which are not known shall be made known by them, and also things shall be made known by them which otherwise could not be known.

PHOTOGRAPH BY MARTY MAYO

*Engravings are writings cut or impressed into metal.*

8:11 ***hilts***—handles
***cankered***—damaged
***Canst thou***—Can you
***translate***—understand or explain words from another language

8:12 ***a remnant***—those who are left

8:13 Anciently these interpreters were called the Urim and Thummim. Those who possessed and used them were "seers" (see Joseph Smith—History 1:35; LDS Bible Dictionary, s.v. "Urim and Thummim," 786–87).

8:17 ***made manifest***—shown

8:17 (15–17) Ammon explains to King Limhi some of the differences between a prophet and a seer. President Ezra Taft Benson taught: "Have you ever thought about the significance of those terms? Prophet: An inspired teacher of known truths. Seer: One who sees with spiritual eyes—one who foresees the future. Revelator: A revealer of new truth" (*The Teachings of Ezra Taft Benson,* 141).

The President of the Church today is a prophet, seer, and revelator. How does it make you feel to know the Church is led by such a holy man? How does knowing of his priesthood power help you follow him better?

18 Thus God has provided a means that man, through faith, might work mighty miracles; therefore he becometh a great benefit to his fellow beings.

19 And now, when Ammon had made an end of speaking these words the king rejoiced exceedingly, and gave thanks to God, saying: Doubtless a great mystery is contained within these plates, and these interpreters were doubtless prepared for the purpose of unfolding all such mysteries to the children of men.

20 O how marvelous are the works of the Lord, and how long doth he suffer with his people; yea, and how blind and impenetrable are the understandings of the children of men; for they will not seek wisdom, neither do they desire that she should rule over them!

21 Yea, they are as a wild flock which fleeth from the shepherd, and scattereth, and are driven, and are devoured by the beasts of the forest.

THE RECORD OF ZENIFF—*An account of his people, from the time they left the land of Zarahemla until the time that they were delivered out of the hands of the Lamanites. Comprising chapters 9 to 22 inclusive.**

## CHAPTER 9

*Zeniff and his followers move back to the land of Nephi. Their journey takes place about 200 B.C. As you read this chapter, look for reasons why they grew weaker both physically and spiritually.*

### Zeniff Leads a Group Back to the Land of Nephi

1 I, Zeniff, having been taught in all the language of the Nephites, and having had a knowledge of the land of Nephi, or of the land of our fathers' first inheritance, and having been sent as a spy among the Lamanites that I might spy out their forces, that our army might come upon them and destroy them—but when I saw that which was good among them I was desirous that they should not be destroyed.

2 Therefore, I contended with my brethren in the wilderness, for I would that our ruler should make a treaty with them; but he being an austere and a blood-thirsty man commanded that I should be slain; but I was rescued by the shedding of much blood; for father fought against father, and brother against brother, until the greater number of our army was destroyed in the wilderness; and we returned, those of us that were spared, to the land of Zarahemla, to relate that tale to their wives and their children.

3 And yet, I being over-zealous to inherit the land of our fathers, collected as many as were desirous to go up to possess the land, and started again on our journey into the wilderness to go up to the land; but we were smitten with famine and sore afflictions; for we were slow to remember the Lord our God.

---

8:18 ***means***—way

8:19 ***Doubtless***—Certainly
***unfolding***—revealing or showing

8:20 ***impenetrable***—unknowable

8:21 ***fleeth***—runs away
***devoured***—eaten

PHOTOGRAPH BY CHURCH EDUCATIONAL SYSTEM

*These sheep are following their shepherd. Ammon said that the children of men were like sheep who ran away from their shepherd, became scattered, and placed themselves in danger.*

The scriptures often speak of Jesus as the Shepherd and His followers as sheep. We are safe from temptation and sin (the beasts of the forest) only when we follow our Shepherd. How has studying the Book of Mormon helped you follow your Shepherd?

* The record of Zeniff covers a time span from about 200 to 121 B.C. This introduction, excluding the last sentence, was translated from the gold plates.

9:1 At this point in the Book of Mormon account, there are two Nephite kingdoms existing at the same time: one in the land of Zarahemla and the other in the land of Lehi-Nephi, where Lehi and his family first landed.

9:2 ***contended***—argued
***an austere***—hard and strict
***blood-thirsty man***—man who enjoyed killing
***spared***—not killed
***tale***—story

9:3 ***over-zealous***—too eager
***inherit***—gain or possess
***smitten***—punished or hit
***sore***—terrible

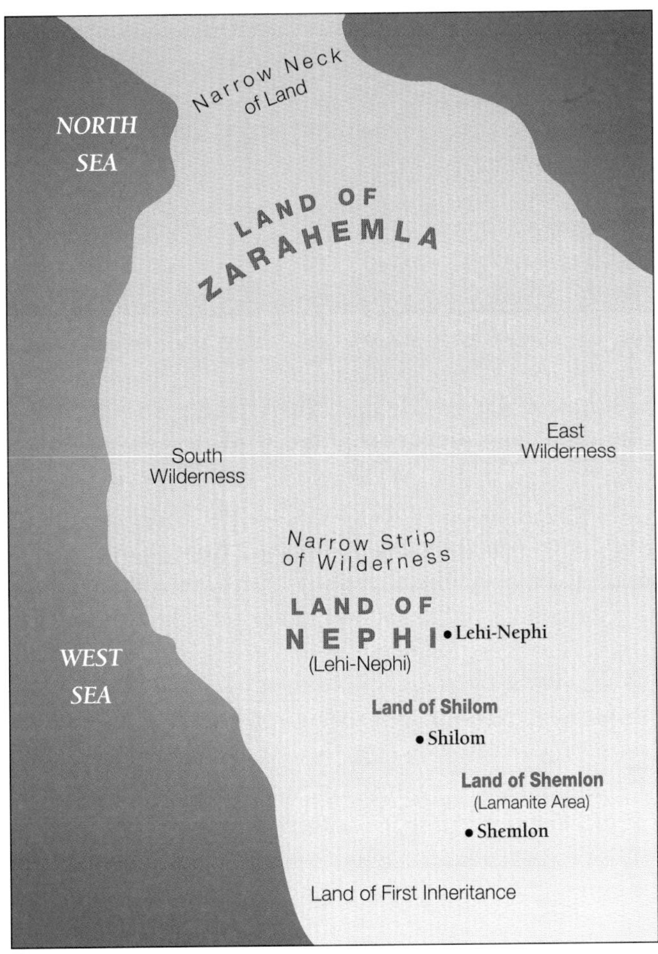


*The people of Zeniff moved from Zarahemla back to the land of Nephi.*

## Zeniff Is Deceived by the Lamanite King

4 Nevertheless, after many days' wandering in the wilderness we pitched our tents in the place where our brethren were slain, which was near to the land of our fathers.

5 And it came to pass that I went again with four of my men into the city, in unto the king, that I might know of the disposition of the king, and that I might know if I might go in with my people and possess the land in peace.

6 And I went in unto the king, and he covenanted with me that I might possess the land of Lehi-Nephi, and the land of Shilom.

7 And he also commanded that his people should depart out of the land, and I and my people went into the land that we might possess it.

8 And we began to build buildings, and to repair the walls of the city, yea, even the walls of the city of Lehi-Nephi, and the city of Shilom.

9 And we began to till the ground, yea, even with all manner of seeds, with seeds of corn, and of wheat, and of barley, and with neas, and with sheum, and with seeds of all manner of fruits; and we did begin to multiply and prosper in the land.

10 Now it was the cunning and the craftiness of king Laman, to bring my people into bondage, that he yielded up the land that we might possess it.

## The Lamanites Attack the People of Zeniff

11 Therefore it came to pass, that after we had dwelt in the land for the space of twelve years that king Laman began to grow uneasy, lest by any means my people should wax strong in the land, and that they could not overpower them and bring them into bondage.

12 Now they were a lazy and an idolatrous people; therefore they were desirous to bring us into bondage, that they might glut themselves with the labors of our hands; yea, that they might feast themselves upon the flocks of our fields.

13 Therefore it came to pass that king Laman began to stir up his people that they should contend with my people; therefore there began to be wars and contentions in the land.

14 For, in the thirteenth year of my reign in the land of Nephi, away on the south of the land of Shilom, when my people were watering and feeding their flocks, and tilling their lands, a numerous host of Lamanites came upon them and began to slay them, and to take off their flocks, and the corn of their fields.

15 Yea, and it came to pass that they fled, all that were not overtaken, even into the city of Nephi, and did call upon me for protection.

16 And it came to pass that I did arm them with bows, and with arrows, with swords, and with cimeters, and with clubs, and with slings, and with all manner of weapons which we could invent, and I and my people did go forth against the Lamanites to battle.

---

9:5 ***disposition***—feelings and thoughts

9:10 ***cunning***—trickery
***bondage***—slavery
***yielded***—gave

9:11 ***wax***—become

9:12 ***idolatrous***—idol-worshiping
***glut***—overfeed

9:16 ***cimeters***—short, curved swords
***manner***—kinds

17 Yea, in the strength of the Lord did we go forth to battle against the Lamanites; for I and my people did cry mightily to the Lord that he would deliver us out of the hands of our enemies, for we were awakened to a remembrance of the deliverance of our fathers.

18 And God did hear our cries and did answer our prayers; and we did go forth in his might; yea, we did go forth against the Lamanites, and in one day and a night we did slay three thousand and forty-three; we did slay them even until we had driven them out of our land.

19 And I, myself, with mine own hands, did help to bury their dead. And behold, to our great sorrow and lamentation, two hundred and seventy-nine of our brethren were slain.

## CHAPTER 10

*The Lamanites begin a war against Zeniff's people. As you read and ponder this chapter, look for reasons why the Nephites, who had fewer people, were able to defeat a larger group of Lamanites.*

### *Zeniff Prepares His People to Defend Themselves Against the Lamanites*

1 AND it came to pass that we again began to establish the kingdom and we again began to possess the land in peace. And I caused that there should be weapons of war made of every kind, that thereby I might have weapons for my people against the time the Lamanites should come up again to war against my people.

2 And I set guards round about the land, that the Lamanites might not come upon us again unawares and destroy us; and thus I did guard my people and my flocks, and keep them from falling into the hands of our enemies.

3 And it came to pass that we did inherit the land of our fathers for many years, yea, for the space of twenty and two years.

4 And I did cause that the men should till the ground, and raise all manner of grain and all manner of fruit of every kind.

5 And I did cause that the women should spin, and toil, and work, and work all manner of fine linen, yea, and cloth of every kind, that we might clothe our nakedness; and thus we did prosper in the land—thus we did have continual peace in the land for the space of twenty and two years.

6 And it came to pass that king Laman died, and his son began to reign in his stead. And he began to stir his people up in rebellion against my people; therefore they began to prepare for war, and to come up to battle against my people.

7 But I had sent my spies out round about the land of Shemlon, that I might discover their preparations, that I might guard against them, that they might not come upon my people and destroy them.

8 And it came to pass that they came up upon the north of the land of Shilom, with their numerous hosts, men armed with bows, and with arrows, and with swords, and with cimeters, and with stones, and with slings; and they had their heads shaved that they were naked; and they were girded with a leathern girdle about their loins.

PHOTOGRAPH BY EDWIN M. WOOLLEY

*Zeniff caused his people to make weapons of war so they would be prepared to defend themselves against the Lamanites. Their weapons may have been similar to these ceremonial knives.*

9:17 How did the Lord help Zeniff and his people? What are some ways the "strength of the Lord" has helped you?

9:19 ***lamentation***—crying and mourning

10:1 ***establish***—build

10:2 ***unawares***—by surprise

10:4 ***till***—plow

10:5 ***spin, and toil***—make thread and labor
***prosper***—succeed

10:6 ***reign***—rule

10:8 ***numerous hosts***—large armies
***were girded with a leathern girdle about their loins***—had tied a leather belt around their waists

9 And it came to pass that I caused that the women and children of my people should be hid in the wilderness; and I also caused that all my old men that could bear arms, and also all my young men that were able to bear arms, should gather themselves together to go to battle against the Lamanites; and I did place them in their ranks, every man according to his age.

### *Lamanites Teach Their Children to Hate the Nephites*

10 And it came to pass that we did go up to battle against the Lamanites; and I, even I, in my old age, did go up to battle against the Lamanites. And it came to pass that we did go up in the strength of the Lord to battle.

11 Now, the Lamanites knew nothing concerning the Lord, nor the strength of the Lord, therefore they depended upon their own strength. Yet they were a strong people, as to the strength of men.

12 They were a wild, and ferocious, and a blood-thirsty people, believing in the tradition of their fathers, which is this—Believing that they were driven out of the land of Jerusalem because of the iniquities of their fathers, and that they were wronged in the wilderness by their brethren, and they were also wronged while crossing the sea;

13 And again, that they were wronged while in the land of their first inheritance, after they had crossed the sea, and all this because that Nephi was more faithful in keeping the commandments of the Lord—therefore he was favored of the Lord, for the Lord heard his prayers and answered them, and he took the lead of their journey in the wilderness.

14 And his brethren were wroth with him because they understood not the dealings of the Lord; they were also wroth with him upon the waters because they hardened their hearts against the Lord.

15 And again, they were wroth with him when they had arrived in the promised land, because they said that he had taken the ruling of the people out of their hands; and they sought to kill him.

16 And again, they were wroth with him because he departed into the wilderness as the Lord had commanded him, and took the records which were engraven on the plates of brass, for they said that he robbed them.

17 And thus they have taught their children that they should hate them, and that they should murder them, and that they should rob and plunder them, and do all they could to destroy them; therefore they have an eternal hatred towards the children of Nephi.

18 For this very cause has king Laman, by his cunning, and lying craftiness, and his fair promises, deceived me, that I have brought this my people up into this land, that they may destroy them; yea, and we have suffered these many years in the land.

### *Zeniff's People Battle the Lamanites*

19 And now I, Zeniff, after having told all these things unto my people concerning the Lamanites, I did stimulate them to go to battle with their might, putting their trust in the Lord; therefore, we did contend with them, face to face.

---

10:9 ***bear arms***—carry weapons
***ranks***—order

10:11 (10–11) The Lamanites "depended upon their own strength" (verse 11), but the Nephites went to battle "in the strength of the Lord" (verse 10). Who do you think won? Why does life go better for you when you rely on the Lord rather than on your own strength?

10:12 ***ferocious***—cruel
***tradition***—teachings
***iniquities***—sins

10:13 ***inheritance***—reward

10:13 (11–13) These verses show how Satan takes away the Spirit through disobedience and causes people to hate because of the false teachings of their fathers (see D&C 93:39).

10:14 ***wroth***—angry
***dealings***—workings

10:15 Do you remember why Laman and Lemuel did not understand the ways of God and Nephi did? (see 1 Nephi 15:8–10).

***sought***—tried

10:16 ***engraven***—written by being cut or impressed into metal

10:17 ***plunder them***—steal from them in time of war

The Lamanites taught their children to hate the Nephites. The Lord has commanded parents to teach their children light and truth or stand condemned before Him (see D&C 93:40–42; 68:25).

10:18 ***cunning***—cleverness
***craftiness***—trickery

10:19 ***stimulate***—encourage or urge
***contend***—fight

20 And it came to pass that we did drive them again out of our land; and we slew them with a great slaughter, even so many that we did not number them.

21 And it came to pass that we returned again to our own land, and my people again began to tend their flocks, and to till their ground.

22 And now I, being old, did confer the kingdom upon one of my sons; therefore, I say no more. And may the Lord bless my people. Amen.

## CHAPTER 11

*Zeniff gives the kingdom to his son Noah. King Noah turns his people to wickedness. He rules from about 160 B.C. to 145 B.C. Notice the different ways the Lord tries to help the people repent.*

### King Noah Taxes His People to Support His Wickedness

1 AND now it came to pass that Zeniff conferred the kingdom upon Noah, one of his sons; therefore Noah began to reign in his stead; and he did not walk in the ways of his father.

2 For behold, he did not keep the commandments of God, but he did walk after the desires of his own heart. And he had many wives and concubines. And he did cause his people to commit sin, and do that which was abominable in the sight of the Lord. Yea, and they did commit whoredoms and all manner of wickedness.

3 And he laid a tax of one fifth part of all they possessed, a fifth part of their gold and of their silver, and a fifth part of their ziff, and of their copper, and of their brass and their iron; and a fifth part of their fatlings; and also a fifth part of all their grain.

4 And all this did he take to support himself, and his wives and his concubines; and also his priests, and their wives and their concubines; thus he had changed the affairs of the kingdom.

5 For he put down all the priests that had been consecrated by his father, and consecrated new ones in their stead, such as were lifted up in the pride of their hearts.

6 Yea, and thus they were supported in their laziness, and in their idolatry, and in their whoredoms,

---

10:20 **slew**—killed
**slaughter**—destruction

10:22 **confer the kingdom upon**—transfer the kingdom to

Zeniff turns his kingdom over to Noah around 160 B.C.

11:1 **conferred the kingdom upon**—gave the kingdom to
**reign**—rule

11:2 In the Old Testament, a concubine was a woman who belonged to a man in a relationship similar but not equal to that of a legal wife. There were laws protecting concubines (see Exodus 21:7; Deuteronomy 21:10–14), but they usually had very little authority in the family. Generally, a concubine's main purpose was to bear children (see *Easton's Bible Dictionary,* s.v. "Concubine"). The Lord had not allowed the Nephites to have plural wives or concubines (see Jacob 2:23–33).

**abominable**—evil
**whoredoms**—use the sacred creative powers with someone who was not their husband or wife

11:3 We do not know what kind of metal "ziff" was, but a very similar word in Hebrew, *ziyv,* means brightness or shining (see Daniel 2:31, where it is translated "brightness").

**fatlings**—young animals raised for food

11:5 **consecrated**—ordained or set apart
**stead**—place

11:6 (3–6) How would you like to have lived at the time of King Noah? How would life under King Noah be different from life under King Mosiah (in Mosiah 2:12–14)? What does that tell you about the importance of keeping the Lord's commandments?

PHOTOGRAPH BY SCOT FACER PROCTOR

*Ancient American royalty, as depicted in a mural in a temple in Bonampak, Mexico. These men in their fine clothing may resemble King Noah's wicked priests.*

by the taxes which king Noah had put upon his people; thus did the people labor exceedingly to support iniquity.

7 Yea, and they also became idolatrous, because they were deceived by the vain and flattering words of the king and priests; for they did speak flattering things unto them.

8 And it came to pass that king Noah built many elegant and spacious buildings; and he ornamented them with fine work of wood, and of all manner of precious things, of gold, and of silver, and of iron, and of brass, and of ziff, and of copper;

9 And he also built him a spacious palace, and a throne in the midst thereof, all of which was of fine wood and was ornamented with gold and silver and with precious things.

10 And he also caused that his workmen should work all manner of fine work within the walls of the temple, of fine wood, and of copper, and of brass.

11 And the seats which were set apart for the high priests, which were above all the other seats, he did ornament with pure gold; and he caused a breastwork to be built before them, that they might rest their bodies and their arms upon while they should speak lying and vain words to his people.

12 And it came to pass that he built a tower near the temple; yea, a very high tower, even so high that he could stand upon the top thereof and overlook the land of Shilom, and also the land of Shemlon, which was possessed by the Lamanites; and he could even look over all the land round about.

13 And it came to pass that he caused many buildings to be built in the land Shilom; and he caused a great tower to be built on the hill north of the land Shilom, which had been a resort for the children of Nephi at the time they fled out of the land; and thus he did do with the riches which he obtained by the taxation of his people.

14 And it came to pass that he placed his heart upon his riches, and he spent his time in riotous living with his wives and his concubines; and so did also his priests spend their time with harlots.

15 And it came to pass that he planted vineyards round about in the land; and he built wine-presses, and made wine in abundance; and therefore he became a wine-bibber, and also his people.

## King Noah's Armies Delight in Bloodshed

16 And it came to pass that the Lamanites began to come in upon his people, upon small numbers, and to slay them in their fields, and while they were tending their flocks.

17 And king Noah sent guards round about the land to keep them off; but he did not send a sufficient number, and the Lamanites came upon them and killed them, and drove many of their flocks out of the land; thus the Lamanites began to destroy them, and to exercise their hatred upon them.

PHOTOGRAPH BY SCOT FACER PROCTOR

*This structure, built for astronomical observation, is an example of the kind of towers that may have existed in Book of Mormon times.*

11:6 ***iniquity***—sin and wickedness

11:7 ***idolatrous***—worshipers of false gods
***vain***—empty and useless
***flattering***—falsely praising

11:9 ***spacious***—large

11:11 ***breastwork***—low wall

11:14 ***riotous***—wild and sinful
***harlots***—wicked women

11:15 ***a wine-bibber***—a person who drinks much wine

11:17 (16–17) Notice how the Lamanites gain more power whenever the Nephites are not righteous. That is just what the Lord prophesied in 1 Nephi 2:21–24.

18 And it came to pass that king Noah sent his armies against them, and they were driven back, or they drove them back for a time; therefore, they returned rejoicing in their spoil.
19 And now, because of this great victory they were lifted up in the pride of their hearts; they did boast in their own strength, saying that their fifty could stand against thousands of the Lamanites; and thus they did boast, and did delight in blood, and the shedding of the blood of their brethren, and this because of the wickedness of their king and priests.

### *Abinadi Warns the People to Repent or Face Bondage*

20 And it came to pass that there was a man among them whose name was Abinadi; and he went forth among them, and began to prophesy, saying: Behold, thus saith the Lord, and thus hath he commanded me, saying, Go forth, and say unto this people, thus saith the Lord—Wo be unto this people, for I have seen their abominations, and their wickedness, and their whoredoms; and except they repent I will visit them in mine anger.
21 And except they repent and turn to the Lord their God, behold, I will deliver them into the hands of their enemies; yea, and they shall be brought into bondage; and they shall be afflicted by the hand of their enemies.
22 And it shall come to pass that they shall know that I am the Lord their God, and am a jealous God, visiting the iniquities of my people.
23 And it shall come to pass that except this people repent and turn unto the Lord their God, they shall be brought into bondage; and none shall deliver them, except it be the Lord the Almighty God.
24 Yea, and it shall come to pass that when they shall cry unto me I will be slow to hear their cries; yea, and I will suffer them that they be smitten by their enemies.
25 And except they repent in sackcloth and ashes, and cry mightily to the Lord their God, I will not hear their prayers, neither will I deliver them out of their afflictions; and thus saith the Lord, and thus hath he commanded me.
26 Now it came to pass that when Abinadi had spoken these words unto them they were wroth with him, and sought to take away his life; but the Lord delivered him out of their hands.
27 Now when king Noah had heard of the words which Abinadi had spoken unto the people, he was also wroth; and he said: Who is Abinadi, that I and my people should be judged of him, or who is the Lord, that shall bring upon my people such great affliction?
28 I command you to bring Abinadi hither, that I may slay him, for he has said these things that he might stir up my people to anger one with another, and to raise contentions among my people; therefore I will slay him.
29 Now the eyes of the people were blinded; therefore they hardened their hearts against the words of Abinadi, and they sought from that time forward to take him. And king Noah hardened his heart against the word of the Lord, and he did not repent of his evil doings.

## CHAPTER 12

*Abinadi defends himself before King Noah and his wicked priests. Watch for actions that show Abinadi's faith and courage.*

---

11:21 ***bondage***—slavery
***afflicted***—tormented and mistreated

11:22 God is jealous, which means He demands that we love and serve Him and worship nothing else. He knows that we cannot be saved or be happy if we do not put Him first (see Exodus 20:3–6; 34:14).

11:24 ***smitten***—beaten

11:25 Sackcloth is a rough cloth made from goat hair. In ancient times people wore sackcloth and put ashes on their heads when they were very sad.

11:27 King Noah, Cain, and Pharaoh, king of Egypt, all asked the same foolish question: "Who is the Lord?" (see Moses 5:16; Exodus 5:2). When you remember what happened to Cain and to Pharaoh, what do you think might happen to King Noah? (see Mosiah 19:20).

*Sitting in sackcloth*

## *Abinadi Prophesies the Destruction of King Noah and His People*

1 AND it came to pass that after the space of two
years that Abinadi came among them in disguise,
that they knew him not, and began to prophesy
among them, saying: Thus has the Lord commanded me, saying—Abinadi, go and prophesy
unto this my people, for they have hardened their
hearts against my words; they have repented not
of their evil doings; therefore, I will visit them in
my anger, yea, in my fierce anger will I visit them
in their iniquities and abominations.
2 Yea, wo be unto this generation! And the Lord
said unto me: Stretch forth thy hand and prophesy,
saying: Thus saith the Lord, it shall come to pass that
this generation, because of their iniquities, shall be
brought into bondage, and shall be smitten on the
cheek; yea, and shall be driven by men, and shall be
slain; and the vultures of the air, and the dogs, yea,
and the wild beasts, shall devour their flesh.
3 And it shall come to pass that the life of king
Noah shall be valued even as a garment in a hot
furnace; for he shall know that I am the Lord.
4 And it shall come to pass that I will smite this
my people with sore afflictions, yea, with famine
and with pestilence; and I will cause that they shall
howl all the day long.
5 Yea, and I will cause that they shall have burdens lashed upon their backs; and they shall be
driven before like a dumb ass.
6 And it shall come to pass that I will send forth
hail among them, and it shall smite them; and they
shall also be smitten with the east wind; and
insects shall pester their land also, and devour
their grain.
7 And they shall be smitten with a great pestilence—and all this will I do because of their iniquities and abominations.
8 And it shall come to pass that except they repent
I will utterly destroy them from off the face of the
earth; yet they shall leave a record behind them,
and I will preserve them for other nations which
shall possess the land; yea, even this will I do that
I may discover the abominations of this people to
other nations. And many things did Abinadi prophesy against this people.

## *Abinadi Is Cast into Prison*

9 And it came to pass that they were angry with
him; and they took him and carried him bound
before the king, and said unto the king: Behold, we
have brought a man before thee who has prophesied evil concerning thy people, and saith that God
will destroy them.

---

12:1 "Harden their hearts" is a scriptural phrase that means a person will not listen to things that are spiritual. The Lord revealed to the Prophet Joseph Smith that the wicked "will not hear my voice but harden their hearts" (D&C 38:6).

***iniquities***—sins
***abominations***—great evils

12:2 ***generation***—people
***devour***—eat

12:3 In fulfillment of this prophecy King Noah is put to death by fire by his own people (see Mosiah 19:20).

***garment***—piece of clothing

12:4 ***sore afflictions***—misery and terrible suffering
***pestilence***—disease
***howl***—scream

12:5 ***lashed***—tied

12:6 ***pester***—bother

In the Bible the "east wind" is a wind that often brings with it destruction and violence (see Joseph Fielding McConkie and others, *Doctrinal Commentary on the Book of Mormon* 2:187).

ILLUSTRATION BY TED HENNINGER

*Abinadi and wicked King Noah*

10 And he also prophesieth evil concerning thy
life, and saith that thy life shall be as a garment in
a furnace of fire.
11 And again, he saith that thou shalt be as a stalk,
even as a dry stalk of the field, which is run over
by the beasts and trodden under foot.
12 And again, he saith thou shalt be as the blossoms of a thistle, which, when it is fully ripe, if the
wind bloweth, it is driven forth upon the face of the
land. And he pretendeth the Lord hath spoken it.
And he saith all this shall come upon thee except
thou repent, and this because of thine iniquities.
13 And now, O king, what great evil hast thou
done, or what great sins have thy people committed, that we should be condemned of God or
judged of this man?
14 And now, O king, behold, we are guiltless, and
thou, O king, hast not sinned; therefore, this man
has lied concerning you, and he has prophesied in
vain.
15 And behold, we are strong, we shall not come
into bondage, or be taken captive by our enemies;
yea, and thou hast prospered in the land, and thou
shalt also prosper.
16 Behold, here is the man, we deliver him into
thy hands; thou mayest do with him as seemeth
thee good.
17 And it came to pass that king Noah caused that
Abinadi should be cast into prison; and he commanded that the priests should gather themselves
together that he might hold a council with them
what he should do with him.

## Abinadi Defends Himself Before the Wicked Priests of King Noah

18 And it came to pass that they said unto the
king: Bring him hither that we may question him;
and the king commanded that he should be
brought before them.
19 And they began to question him, that they
might cross him, that thereby they might have
wherewith to accuse him; but he answered them
boldly, and withstood all their questions, yea, to
their astonishment; for he did withstand them in all
their questions, and did confound them in all their
words.
20 And it came to pass that one of them said unto
him: What meaneth the words which are written,
and which have been taught by our fathers, saying:
21 How beautiful upon the mountains are the feet
of him that bringeth good tidings; that publisheth
peace; that bringeth good tidings of good; that publisheth salvation; that saith unto Zion, Thy God
reigneth;
22 Thy watchmen shall lift up the voice; with the
voice together shall they sing; for they shall see eye
to eye when the Lord shall bring again Zion;
23 Break forth into joy; sing together ye waste
places of Jerusalem; for the Lord hath comforted his
people, he hath redeemed Jerusalem;
24 The Lord hath made bare his holy arm in the
eyes of all the nations, and all the ends of the earth
shall see the salvation of our God?
25 And now Abinadi said unto them: Are you
priests, and pretend to teach this people, and to
understand the spirit of prophesying, and yet desire
to know of me what these things mean?
26 I say unto you, wo be unto you for perverting
the ways of the Lord! For if ye understand these
things ye have not taught them; therefore, ye have
perverted the ways of the Lord.
27 Ye have not applied your hearts to understanding; therefore, ye have not been wise.
Therefore, what teach ye this people?
28 And they said: We teach the law of Moses.
29 And again he said unto them: If ye teach the
law of Moses why do ye not keep it? Why do ye set
your hearts upon riches? Why do ye commit whoredoms and spend your strength with harlots, yea,
and cause this people to commit sin, that the Lord
has cause to send me to prophesy against this
people, yea, even a great evil against this people?

---

12:11 ***stalk***—stem of a plant
***trodden***—trampled or walked upon

12:13 ***condemned***—found guilty

12:14 ***in vain***—without effect

12:19 ***cross***—trick
***withstood***—answered

12:21 ***publisheth***—makes known

These verses contain the words of Isaiah as found in Isaiah 52:7–10. Verse 21 refers to Jesus Christ. How does the Savior publish peace and bring good news to us today?

12:22 ***watchmen***—guards

12:29 ***whoredoms***—wickedness and immorality

30 Know ye not that I speak the truth? Yea, ye
know that I speak the truth; and you ought to
tremble before God.
31 And it shall come to pass that ye shall be smitten for your iniquities, for ye have said that ye teach
the law of Moses. And what know ye concerning
the law of Moses? Doth salvation come by the law
of Moses? What say ye?
32 And they answered and said that salvation did
come by the law of Moses.

### Abinadi Begins Teaching the Ten Commandments

33 But now Abinadi said unto them: I know if ye
keep the commandments of God ye shall be
saved; yea, if ye keep the commandments which
the Lord delivered unto Moses in the mount of
Sinai, saying:
34 I am the Lord thy God, who hath brought thee
out of the land of Egypt, out of the house of
bondage.
35 Thou shalt have no other God before me.
36 Thou shalt not make unto thee any graven
image, or any likeness of any thing in heaven
above, or things which are in the earth beneath.
37 Now Abinadi said unto them, Have ye done all
this? I say unto you, Nay, ye have not. And have ye
taught this people that they should do all these
things? I say unto you, Nay, ye have not.

## CHAPTER 13

*Abinadi teaches the Ten Commandments and is protected by the Lord's power. Notice why he says the commandments alone cannot save us.*

### Abinadi Is Protected by the Lord

1 AND now when the king had heard these
words, he said unto his priests: Away with this fellow, and slay him; for what have we to do with
him, for he is mad.
2 And they stood forth and attempted to lay their
hands on him; but he withstood them, and said
unto them:
3 Touch me not, for God shall smite you if ye lay
your hands upon me, for I have not delivered the
message which the Lord sent me to deliver; neither
have I told you that which ye requested that I
should tell; therefore, God will not suffer that I shall
be destroyed at this time.
4 But I must fulfil the commandments wherewith
God has commanded me; and because I have told
you the truth ye are angry with me. And again,
because I have spoken the word of God ye have
judged me that I am mad.
5 Now it came to pass after Abinadi had spoken
these words that the people of king Noah durst not
lay their hands on him, for the Spirit of the Lord
was upon him; and his face shone with exceeding
luster, even as Moses' did while in the mount of
Sinai, while speaking with the Lord.
6 And he spake with power and authority from
God; and he continued his words, saying:
7 Ye see that ye have not power to slay me, therefore I finish my message. Yea, and I perceive that it
cuts you to your hearts because I tell you the truth
concerning your iniquities.
8 Yea, and my words fill you with wonder and
amazement, and with anger.
9 But I finish my message; and then it matters not
whither I go, if it so be that I am saved.

---

12:31 ***smitten***—punished

12:36 ***graven image***—carved idol

13:1 ***slay***—kill
***mad***—insane or cannot think clearly

13:3 ***smite***—strike you down
***suffer***—allow

13:5 ***durst not***—did not dare
***luster***—brightness

13:5 (2–5) The Lord's power stopped King Noah's men from hurting Abinadi until the prophet finished giving God's message. What messengers does the Lord watch over and protect today?

13:7 ***perceive***—know or can tell
***iniquities***—sins

Elder Neal A. Maxwell taught that "when prophets speak 'hard things against the wicked, according to the truth,'. . . [there] is kindness in this pain, for as truth, the Lord's laser, cuts through to all but the hardest of hearts, so the healing light of the gospel is let in" (*Things As They Really Are,* 79).

MOSES AND THE TEN COMMANDMENTS, BY ROBERT T. BARRETT

*The Lord delivered the Ten Commandments to Moses on Mount Sinai.
Abinadi taught the wicked priests of King Noah that if they kept the commandments, they would be saved.*

10 But this much I tell you, what you do with me,
after this, shall be as a type and a shadow of things
which are to come.

## *Abinadi Teaches the Ten Commandments*

11 And now I read unto you the remainder of the
commandments of God, for I perceive that they are
not written in your hearts; I perceive that ye have
studied and taught iniquity the most part of your
lives.
12 And now, ye remember that I said unto you:
Thou shall not make unto thee any graven image,
or any likeness of things which are in heaven
above, or which are in the earth beneath, or which
are in the water under the earth.
13 And again: Thou shalt not bow down thyself
unto them, nor serve them; for I the Lord thy God
am a jealous God, visiting the iniquities of the
fathers upon the children, unto the third and fourth
generations of them that hate me;
14 And showing mercy unto thousands of them
that love me and keep my commandments.
15 Thou shalt not take the name of the Lord thy
God in vain; for the Lord will not hold him guiltless
that taketh his name in vain.
16 Remember the sabbath day, to keep it holy.
17 Six days shalt thou labor, and do all thy work;
18 But the seventh day, the sabbath of the Lord
thy God, thou shalt not do any work, thou, nor thy
son, nor thy daughter, thy man-servant, nor thy
maid-servant, nor thy cattle, nor thy stranger that is
within thy gates;
19 For in six days the Lord made heaven and
earth, and the sea, and all that in them is; wherefore the Lord blessed the sabbath day, and hallowed it.
20 Honor thy father and thy mother, that thy days
may be long upon the land which the Lord thy God
giveth thee.
21 Thou shalt not kill.
22 Thou shalt not commit adultery. Thou shalt not
steal.
23 Thou shalt not bear false witness against thy
neighbor.
24 Thou shalt not covet thy neighbor's house,
thou shalt not covet thy neighbor's wife, nor his
man-servant, nor his maid-servant, nor his ox, nor
his ass, nor anything that is thy neighbor's.

## *The Law of Moses Points to Christ*

25 And it came to pass that after Abinadi had
made an end of these sayings that he said unto
them: Have ye taught this people that they should
observe to do all these things for to keep these
commandments?
26 I say unto you, Nay; for if ye had, the Lord
would not have caused me to come forth and to
prophesy evil concerning this people.

PHOTOGRAPH BY EDWIN M. WOOLLEY

*Graven images are common among the ancient ruins of Central and South America.*

13:10 For more about types and shadows, see for Mosiah 3:15.

13:11 Elder Russell M. Nelson explained that "when we know who we are and what God expects of us—when his 'law [is] written in [our] hearts'—we are spiritually protected" (in Conference Report, April 1995, 44).

13:12 ***graven image***—carved statue

13:15 ***in vain***—insincerely

13:19 ***hallowed it***—made it holy or sacred

13:22 ***adultery***—use of the sacred creative powers with someone other than your husband or wife

13:23 ***bear false witness***—lie or say things that are not true

13:24 ***covet***—unrighteously desire

27 And now ye have said that salvation cometh by
the law of Moses. I say unto you that it is expedient that ye should keep the law of Moses as yet; but
I say unto you, that the time shall come when it
shall no more be expedient to keep the law of
Moses.
28 And moreover, I say unto you, that salvation
doth not come by the law alone; and were it not for
the atonement, which God himself shall make for
the sins and iniquities of his people, that they must
unavoidably perish, notwithstanding the law of
Moses.
29 And now I say unto you that it was expedient
that there should be a law given to the children of
Israel, yea, even a very strict law; for they were a
stiffnecked people, quick to do iniquity, and slow
to remember the Lord their God;
30 Therefore there was a law given them, yea, a
law of performances and of ordinances, a law
which they were to observe strictly from day to day,
to keep them in remembrance of God and their
duty towards him.
31 But behold, I say unto you, that all these things
were types of things to come.
32 And now, did they understand the law? I say unto
you, Nay, they did not all understand the law; and this
because of the hardness of their hearts; for they
understood not that there could not any man be
saved except it were through the redemption of God.
33 For behold, did not Moses prophesy unto them
concerning the coming of the Messiah, and that
God should redeem his people? Yea, and even all
the prophets who have prophesied ever since the
world began—have they not spoken more or less
concerning these things?
34 Have they not said that God himself should
come down among the children of men, and take
upon him the form of man, and go forth in mighty
power upon the face of the earth?
35 Yea, and have they not said also that he should
bring to pass the resurrection of the dead, and that
he, himself, should be oppressed and afflicted?

## CHAPTER 14

*Before being put to death, the prophet Abinadi quotes Isaiah 53, a powerful chapter about Jesus Christ and His Atonement. Notice what the Savior suffered for besides the sins of all mankind as He worked out the Atonement.*

### *Jesus the Son of God Experiences Mortal Life*

1 YEA, even doth not Isaiah say: Who hath
believed our report, and to whom is the arm of the
Lord revealed?
2 For he shall grow up before him as a tender
plant, and as a root out of dry ground; he hath no
form nor comeliness; and when we shall see him
there is no beauty that we should desire him.

---

13:27 ***expedient***—necessary

13:28 ***perish***—be lost

Heavenly Father knew we would make mistakes. He sent His Son Jesus Christ to pay for our sins if we would believe Him and obey Him. What does that teach you about how much Heavenly Father and Jesus Christ love you?

13:29 ***stiffnecked***—rebellious

13:31 Elder Bruce R. McConkie told us that "for more than 1400 years the Lord required Israel to perform rites and ordinances in such a way as to point attention forward to Christ and his atonement" (*Doctrinal New Testament Commentary* 3:180).

13:32 ***through the redemption of God***—by Jesus' paying for our sins

13:33 ***prophesy***—tell of future events

13:35 ***oppressed***—burdened or abused
***afflicted***—mistreated

14:1 Isaiah was an Old Testament prophet who was sent to call the kingdom of Judah to repentance from 740 to 701 B.C. "The bulk of Isaiah's prophecies deal with the coming of the Redeemer" (LDS Bible Dictionary, s.v. "Isaiah," 707).

***arm***—strength
***revealed***—shown

14:2 ***form***—beauty
***comeliness***—glory or attractiveness

" 'He,' the Messiah, . . . grew up and lived as other men live, subject to the ills and troubles of mortality. . . . There is no . . . dynamic appearance, no halo around his head, thunders do not roll and lightnings do not flash at his appearance. . . . He is a man among men, appearing, speaking, dressing, seeming in all outward respects as they are" (Bruce R. McConkie, *The Promised Messiah*, 477–78).

3 He is despised and rejected of men; a man of
sorrows, and acquainted with grief; and we hid as
it were our faces from him; he was despised, and
we esteemed him not.

## *Through Suffering the Pains, Sins, and Sorrows of the World, Jesus Worked Out the Atonement*

4 Surely he has borne our griefs, and carried our
sorrows; yet we did esteem him stricken, smitten of
God, and afflicted.
5 But he was wounded for our transgressions, he
was bruised for our iniquities; the chastisement of
our peace was upon him; and with his stripes we
are healed.
6 All we, like sheep, have gone astray; we have
turned every one to his own way; and the Lord hath
laid on him the iniquities of us all.
7 He was oppressed, and he was afflicted, yet
he opened not his mouth; he is brought as a lamb
to the slaughter, and as a sheep before her shearers is dumb so he opened not his mouth.
8 He was taken from prison and from judgment;
and who shall declare his generation? For he was
cut off out of the land of the living; for the transgressions of my people was he stricken.
9 And he made his grave with the wicked, and
with the rich in his death; because he had done no
evil, neither was any deceit in his mouth.
10 Yet it pleased the Lord to bruise him; he hath
put him to grief; when thou shalt make his soul an
offering for sin he shall see his seed, he shall prolong his days, and the pleasure of the Lord shall
prosper in his hand.
11 He shall see the travail of his soul, and shall be
satisfied; by his knowledge shall my righteous servant justify many; for he shall bear their iniquities.

---

14:3 ***despised***—hated
***acquainted with***—familiar with
***esteemed***—valued

14:4 ***borne***—carried
***griefs***—disappointments
***stricken, smitten of God, and afflicted***—struck, beaten of God, and tormented

14:5 ***iniquities***—sins
***chastisement***—scolding
***stripes***—whipping

14:5 (3–5) Jesus Christ took upon Himself the pains, sins, and sorrows of all people (see Alma 7:11–13). This action is called the Atonement. The Atonement was very difficult and painful for Jesus (see D&C 19:16–19), but because of the Atonement, all of us can overcome our pains, sins, and sorrows (see Matthew 11:28–30).

14:5 (4–5) How does it make you feel to know that Jesus suffered for you?

14:6 We are like sheep, and Jesus is like our shepherd (see John 10:14).

***gone astray***—become lost

14:7 ***oppressed***—mistreated

When Jesus was tried before King Herod (see Luke 23:8–11) and the second time before Pontius Pilate (see Matthew 27:13–14), Jesus did not say a word to them. Symbolically, Jesus was Heavenly Father's Lamb (see John 1:29, 36) and was the last sacrifice under the law of Moses (see Alma 34:10–15). "Shearers" are people who cut wool off sheep.

14:8 Elder Bruce R. McConkie said this verse means " 'Who will reveal his genealogy? Who will give the source from [where] he [came]? Who will announce the divinity of the mortal Messiah?' . . . 'Whose son is he?' " (*BYU Studies* 16 [Summer 1976]: 554–55).

14:10 Whoever hears and obeys the words of the prophets and believes that Jesus is the Christ is His child (see Mosiah 15:10–13).

***prolong***—make longer
***prosper in his hand***—make successful the things He does

14:11 ***travail***—suffering
***bear their iniquities***—suffer and pay for their sins

A person who is "justified" has had his sins forgiven and stands approved of God. Our sins can be forgiven because of the Savior's Atonement. The Lord has declared, "The righteous have I justified, and testified that they should be lifted up at the last day" (1 Nephi 16:2).

*CHRIST AND PILATE*, BY ROBERT T. BARRETT

*As Isaiah prophesied, Jesus Christ was "acquainted with grief." He was "taken from prison and from judgment," and when He was condemned to die, He went as a "lamb to the slaughter."*

12 Therefore will I divide him a portion with the great, and he shall divide the spoil with the strong; because he hath poured out his soul unto death; and he was numbered with the transgressors; and he bore the sins of many, and made intercession for the transgressors.

## CHAPTER 15

*Abinadi teaches that the Savior will redeem all who obey the words of the prophets. Look for what Jesus Christ does for us and what we must do for ourselves to be saved in the kingdom of heaven.*

### *Abinadi Explains How Jesus Christ Can Be Called Both Father and Son*

1 AND now Abinadi said unto them: I would that ye should understand that God himself shall come down among the children of men, and shall redeem his people.

2 And because he dwelleth in flesh he shall be called the Son of God, and having subjected the flesh to the will of the Father, being the Father and the Son—

3 The Father, because he was conceived by the power of God; and the Son, because of the flesh; thus becoming the Father and Son—

4 And they are one God, yea, the very Eternal Father of heaven and of earth.

### *Abinadi Prophesies of Jesus Christ's Mortal Ministry*

5 And thus the flesh becoming subject to the Spirit, or the Son to the Father, being one God, suffereth temptation, and yieldeth not to the temptation, but suffereth himself to be mocked, and scourged, and cast out, and disowned by his people.

6 And after all this, after working many mighty miracles among the children of men, he shall be led, yea, even as Isaiah said, as a sheep before the shearer is dumb, so he opened not his mouth.

7 Yea, even so he shall be led, crucified, and slain, the flesh becoming subject even unto death, the will of the Son being swallowed up in the will of the Father.

8 And thus God breaketh the bands of death, having gained the victory over death; giving the Son power to make intercession for the children of men—

---

14:12 ***divide him a portion***—share with Him a part
***made intercession for the transgressors***—made a way for sinners to repent

14:12 (9–12) Jesus "made his grave with the wicked" when He was crucified between two thieves (see Matthew 27:38). He was "with the rich in his death" when He was buried in the tomb of a rich man named Joseph of Arimathea (see Matthew 27:57). Not only was there no "deceit in his mouth" but when Jesus was crucified He said, "Father, forgive them; for they know not what they do" (Luke 23:34).

15:1 Jesus Christ was the God of the Old Testament and was known as Jehovah (see D&C 110:1–4). He led Lehi's family to the promised land. When Abinadi taught that "God himself shall come down among the children of men," he was referring to Jesus' mortal ministry.

***redeem his people***—save His people from sin and death

15:2 ***dwelleth***—lives
***flesh***—a physical body

15:4 (3–4) In 1916 the First Presidency of the Church explained that there are several ways in which Jesus can be called the Father. One way is that Jesus was "conceived" or born, in both body and spirit, a literal Son of God (see verse 3). Jesus was given all that was needed to become just like the Father. Another way in which He is the Father is that He is the Creator of "heaven and the earth" (verse 4; see James E. Talmage, *The Articles of Faith,* 466–73).

15:5 ***yieldeth not***—does not give in
***mocked***—made fun of
***scourged***—whipped

15:6 ***dumb***—silent

15:7 ***subject***—obedient

15:8 ***bands***—chains
***make intercession***—atone

9 Having ascended into heaven, having the bowels of mercy; being filled with compassion towards the children of men; standing betwixt them and justice; having broken the bands of death, taken upon himself their iniquity and their transgressions, having redeemed them, and satisfied the demands of justice.

### *The Atonement of Jesus Christ Will Save All Those Who Obey the Words of the Prophets*

10 And now I say unto you, who shall declare his generation? Behold, I say unto you, that when his soul has been made an offering for sin he shall see his seed. And now what say ye? And who shall be his seed?

11 Behold I say unto you, that whosoever has heard the words of the prophets, yea, all the holy prophets who have prophesied concerning the coming of the Lord—I say unto you, that all those who have hearkened unto their words, and believed that the Lord would redeem his people, and have looked forward to that day for a remission of their sins, I say unto you, that these are his seed, or they are the heirs of the kingdom of God.

12 For these are they whose sins he has borne; these are they for whom he has died, to redeem them from their transgressions. And now, are they not his seed?

13 Yea, and are not the prophets, every one that has opened his mouth to prophesy, that has not fallen into transgression, I mean all the holy prophets ever since the world began? I say unto you that they are his seed.

### *Abinadi Explains How Beautiful Are the Feet of Those Who Speak the Truth About Salvation*

14 And these are they who have published peace, who have brought good tidings of good, who have published salvation; and said unto Zion: Thy God reigneth!

15 And O how beautiful upon the mountains were their feet!

16 And again, how beautiful upon the mountains are the feet of those that are still publishing peace!

17 And again, how beautiful upon the mountains are the feet of those who shall hereafter publish peace, yea, from this time henceforth and forever!

18 And behold, I say unto you, this is not all. For O how beautiful upon the mountains are the feet of him that bringeth good tidings, that is the founder of peace, yea, even the Lord, who has redeemed his people; yea, him who has granted salvation unto his people;

---

15:9 ***bowels***—feelings
***betwixt***—between
***iniquity***—sin

The Savior can give us mercy if we repent because He suffered for our sins. The law of mercy will not force us to suffer for the sins we repent of because Jesus has already suffered for them. Alma said that "mercy cometh because of the atonement" (Alma 42:23).

15:11 ***remission***—forgiveness
***heirs of***—people who inherit

15:11 (10–11) Elder Neal A. Maxwell taught, "When we take upon ourselves [Jesus'] name and covenant to keep His commandments, it is then that we become His sons and daughters, 'the children of Christ' " (*Men and Women of Christ,* 37).

15:12 ***borne***—carried

15:14 ***tidings***—news
***published***—declared or told people about

15:18 ***founder of***—person who began
***granted***—given

PHOTOGRAPH BY JOHN LUKE

*"How beautiful . . . are the feet of those who shall hereafter publish peace."*

19 For were it not for the redemption which he hath made for his people, which was prepared from the foundation of the world, I say unto you, were it not for this, all mankind must have perished.
20 But behold, the bands of death shall be broken, and the Son reigneth, and hath power over the dead; therefore, he bringeth to pass the resurrection of the dead.

### Abinadi Tells Who Will Be Resurrected at the Time of Christ's Resurrection

21 And there cometh a resurrection, even a first resurrection; yea, even a resurrection of those that have been, and who are, and who shall be, even until the resurrection of Christ—for so shall he be called.
22 And now, the resurrection of all the prophets, and all those that have believed in their words, or all those that have kept the commandments of God, shall come forth in the first resurrection; therefore, they are the first resurrection.
23 They are raised to dwell with God who has redeemed them; thus they have eternal life through Christ, who has broken the bands of death.
24 And these are those who have part in the first resurrection; and these are they that have died before Christ came, in their ignorance, not having salvation declared unto them. And thus the Lord bringeth about the restoration of these; and they have a part in the first resurrection, or have eternal life, being redeemed by the Lord.
25 And little children also have eternal life.

### Wicked People Will Not Be Redeemed

26 But behold, and fear, and tremble before God, for ye ought to tremble; for the Lord redeemeth none such that rebel against him and die in their sins; yea, even all those that have perished in their sins ever since the world began, that have wilfully rebelled against God, that have known the commandments of God, and would not keep them; these are they that have no part in the first resurrection.
27 Therefore ought ye not to tremble? For salvation cometh to none such; for the Lord hath redeemed none such; yea, neither can the Lord redeem such; for he cannot deny himself; for he cannot deny justice when it has its claim.

### In the Last Days, Salvation Will Be Spoken to All People

28 And now I say unto you that the time shall come that the salvation of the Lord shall be declared to every nation, kindred, tongue, and people.
29 Yea, Lord, thy watchmen shall lift up their voice; with the voice together shall they sing; for they shall see eye to eye, when the Lord shall bring again Zion.
30 Break forth into joy, sing together, ye waste places of Jerusalem; for the Lord hath comforted his people, he hath redeemed Jerusalem.
31 The Lord hath made bare his holy arm in the eyes of all the nations; and all the ends of the earth shall see the salvation of our God.

## CHAPTER 16

*Abinadi boldly teaches King Noah and his priests that because of the Atonement of Jesus Christ the righteous will be resurrected and live in endless happiness. The wicked will also be resurrected and live forever, but they will not enjoy the same blessings of happiness.*

### God Will Save Those Who Repent of Their Sins

1 AND now, it came to pass that after Abinadi had spoken these words he stretched forth his hand and said: The time shall come when all shall see the salvation of the Lord; when every nation, kindred, tongue, and people shall see eye to eye and shall confess before God that his judgments are just.

---

15:19 ***foundation***—beginnings

15:22 ***come forth***—be resurrected

15:23 Through the Prophet Joseph Smith the Lord explained that eternal life is God's life (see D&C 19:7–12). People who receive eternal life will live in the highest degree of the celestial kingdom (see D&C 131:1–4).

15:24 ***in their ignorance***—not knowing the truth
***restoration***—gathering back

15:26 ***wilfully rebelled***—knowingly chosen to rebel

15:27 ***deny***—go against

15:31 (29–31) Abinadi quotes Isaiah 52:8–10. In the last days, the Lord shall gather His children safely to Zion, and all the world will know that God has saved His children.

"FOR AS IN ADAM ALL DIE, EVEN SO IN CHRIST SHALL ALL BE MADE ALIVE," BY ROBERT T. BARRETT

*Abinadi proclaimed: "How beautiful . . . are the feet of him that bringeth good tidings" (Mosiah 15:8). Christ, who bears the marks of His death on His feet, bringeth good tidings of salvation and resurrection to all men.*

2 And then shall the wicked be cast out, and they
shall have cause to howl, and weep, and wail, and
gnash their teeth; and this because they would not
hearken unto the voice of the Lord; therefore the
Lord redeemeth them not.
3 For they are carnal and devilish, and the devil
has power over them; yea, even that old serpent
that did beguile our first parents, which was the
cause of their fall; which was the cause of all
mankind becoming carnal, sensual, devilish, knowing evil from good, subjecting themselves to the
devil.
4 Thus all mankind were lost; and behold, they
would have been endlessly lost were it not that
God redeemed his people from their lost and fallen
state.
5 But remember that he that persists in his own
carnal nature, and goes on in the ways of sin and
rebellion against God, remaineth in his fallen state
and the devil hath all power over him. Therefore,
he is as though there was no redemption made,
being an enemy to God; and also is the devil an
enemy to God.
6 And now if Christ had not come into the
world, speaking of things to come as though they
had already come, there could have been no
redemption.

## We Will All Be Resurrected to Either Endless Life or Endless Damnation

7 And if Christ had not risen from the dead, or
have broken the bands of death that the grave
should have no victory, and that death should have
no sting, there could have been no resurrection.
8 But there is a resurrection, therefore the grave
hath no victory, and the sting of death is swallowed
up in Christ.
9 He is the light and the life of the world; yea, a
light that is endless, that can never be darkened;
yea, and also a life which is endless, that there can
be no more death.
10 Even this mortal shall put on immortality, and
this corruption shall put on incorruption, and shall
be brought to stand before the bar of God, to be
judged of him according to their works whether
they be good or whether they be evil—
11 If they be good, to the resurrection of endless
life and happiness; and if they be evil, to the resurrection of endless damnation, being delivered up to
the devil, who hath subjected them, which is
damnation—
12 Having gone according to their own carnal
wills and desires; having never called upon the
Lord while the arms of mercy were extended

---

16:2 ***wail***—cry loudly
***gnash***—grit or grind

16:3 To beguile is to deceive, trick, or fool. Satan's mission is "to deceive and to blind men" that he might "lead them captive at his will" (Moses 4:4). He began by deceiving our "first parents," Adam and Eve, and they fell; however, Heavenly Father knew Satan's plan and sent His Son, Jesus Christ, to save His children from sin and death. The Father's plan is known as the plan of salvation or happiness.

16:4 To "redeem" means to buy back or to set free. Jesus Christ is our Redeemer because He willingly paid the price to buy us back and set us free from the effects of the Fall of Adam and the burden of our own sins (see 1 Corinthians 6:20; D&C 18:11). The price He had to pay was His own life (see 1 Peter 1:18–19).

If it were not for Jesus Christ's Atonement, we would be lost forever and not be allowed to return to Heavenly Father's presence. How does knowing that make you feel about Jesus Christ?

16:6 ***redemption***—salvation

16:9 (7–9) President Gordon B. Hinckley said: "Whenever the cold hand of death strikes, there shines through the gloom and the darkness of that hour the triumphant figure of the Lord Jesus Christ, He, the Son of God, who by His matchless and eternal power overcame death. He is the Redeemer of the world" (in Conference Report, April 1996, 92; see also 1 Corinthians 15:20–21).

16:10 ***corruption***—imperfect mortal body
***incorruption***—a perfect, resurrected body

16:11 ***subjected them***—brought them under his control

16:12 (10–12) All will be judged and receive a reward for the kind of life they lived here on the earth. Those who lived wicked lives and refuse to accept the Lord's mercy will suffer damnation. "Damnation is the opposite of salvation" and those who suffer it shall "be limited in their progress and privileges" (LDS Bible Dictionary, s.v. "Damnation," 652).

towards them; for the arms of mercy were extended towards them, and they would not; they being warned of their iniquities and yet they would not depart from them; and they were commanded to repent and yet they would not repent.

### *Abinadi Warns King Noah and His Priests to Repent*

13 And now, ought ye not to tremble and repent of your sins, and remember that only in and through Christ ye can be saved?
14 Therefore, if ye teach the law of Moses, also teach that it is a shadow of those things which are to come—
15 Teach them that redemption cometh through Christ the Lord, who is the very Eternal Father. Amen.

## CHAPTER 17

*Alma, one of King Noah's priests, believes Abinadi's words, but wicked King Noah commands that Abinadi be burned to death. As you read this chapter, look for how Abinadi showed courage and faith while facing such danger.*

### *Alma Believes Abinadi's Words and Is Cast Out from Noah's People*

1 AND now it came to pass that when Abinadi had finished these sayings, that the king commanded that the priests should take him and cause that he should be put to death.
2 But there was one among them whose name was Alma, he also being a descendant of Nephi. And he was a young man, and he believed the words which Abinadi had spoken, for he knew concerning the iniquity which Abinadi had testified against them; therefore he began to plead with the king that he would not be angry with Abinadi, but suffer that he might depart in peace.
3 But the king was more wroth, and caused that Alma should be cast out from among them, and sent his servants after him that they might slay him.
4 But he fled from before them and hid himself that they found him not. And he being concealed for many days did write all the words which Abinadi had spoken.

### *Abinadi Is Imprisoned and Then Brought Before King Noah*

5 And it came to pass that the king caused that his guards should surround Abinadi and take him; and they bound him and cast him into prison.
6 And after three days, having counseled with his priests, he caused that he should again be brought before him.
7 And he said unto him: Abinadi, we have found an accusation against thee, and thou art worthy of death.
8 For thou hast said that God himself should come down among the children of men; and now, for this cause thou shalt be put to death unless thou wilt recall all the words which thou hast spoken evil concerning me and my people.
9 Now Abinadi said unto him: I say unto you, I will not recall the words which I have spoken unto you concerning this people, for they are true; and that ye may know of their surety I have suffered myself that I have fallen into your hands.

---

16:13 Abinadi taught Noah's priests to repent, or "tremble" before God. Why is it important for you to repent of your sins?

16:14 ***shadow***—likeness or symbol

16:15 To discover various ways in which Jesus Christ is considered "the very Eternal Father," see for Mosiah 15:2–5.

17:2 ***iniquity***—sins and wickedness
***plead with***—beg
***suffer that he might depart***—allow him to leave

Alma knew Abinadi's teachings were true. Whose teachings have you heard that you know are true? How do you know they are true? What difference do those teachings make in your life?

17:3 ***wroth***—angry
***slay***—kill

17:4 ***fled***—ran away
***concealed***—hidden

17:5 ***bound him***—tied him up

17:7 ***an accusation***—a charge of committing crime

17:8 ***recall***—take back

17:9 ***suffered myself that I have fallen***—allowed myself to fall

10 Yea, and I will suffer even until death, and I will not recall my words, and they shall stand as a testimony against you. And if ye slay me ye will shed innocent blood, and this shall also stand as a testimony against you at the last day.

## Abinadi Is Put to Death by Fire

11 And now king Noah was about to release him, for he feared his word; for he feared that the judgments of God would come upon him.
12 But the priests lifted up their voices against him, and began to accuse him, saying: He has reviled the king. Therefore the king was stirred up in anger against him, and he delivered him up that he might be slain.
13 And it came to pass that they took him and bound him, and scourged his skin with faggots, yea, even unto death.
14 And now when the flames began to scorch him, he cried unto them, saying:
15 Behold, even as ye have done unto me, so shall it come to pass that thy seed shall cause that many shall suffer the pains that I do suffer, even the pains of death by fire; and this because they believe in the salvation of the Lord their God.
16 And it will come to pass that ye shall be afflicted with all manner of diseases because of your iniquities.
17 Yea, and ye shall be smitten on every hand, and shall be driven and scattered to and fro, even as a wild flock is driven by wild and ferocious beasts.
18 And in that day ye shall be hunted, and ye shall be taken by the hand of your enemies, and then ye shall suffer, as I suffer, the pains of death by fire.
19 Thus God executeth vengeance upon those that destroy his people. O God, receive my soul.
20 And now, when Abinadi had said these words, he fell, having suffered death by fire; yea, having been put to death because he would not deny the commandments of God, having sealed the truth of his words by his death.

# CHAPTER 18

*Alma hides from King Noah but continues to teach the truth secretly to those who will listen. Notice the sacrifices Alma's people are willing to make to accept the gospel of Jesus Christ.*

## Alma Teaches the Words of Abinadi

1 AND now, it came to pass that Alma, who had fled from the servants of king Noah, repented of his sins and iniquities, and went about privately among the people, and began to teach the words of Abinadi—
2 Yea, concerning that which was to come, and also concerning the resurrection of the dead, and the redemption of the people, which was to be brought to pass through the power, and sufferings, and death of Christ, and his resurrection and ascension into heaven.

---

17:10 Abinadi was even willing to suffer death rather than deny his testimony of Jesus Christ. Jesus taught that "blessed are they which are persecuted for righteousness' sake: for theirs is the kingdom of heaven" (Matthew 5:10).

17:12 ***reviled***—mocked or made fun of
***slain***—killed

17:13 ***faggots***—a bundle of sticks

17:14 ***scorch***—burn

17:15 Abinadi prophesied that King Noah's seed, meaning his children, grandchildren, and so on, would cause many other believers also to suffer death by fire. This prophecy is fulfilled in Alma 25:7–12.

17:16 ***afflicted***—cursed
***iniquities***—sins

17:17 ***to and fro***—here and there

17:18 (17–18) Abinadi spoke of the punishments of God that would come upon King Noah and his people. Eventually King Noah's people were hunted by the Lamanites (see Mosiah 19), and King Noah died by fire in the same way Abinadi had (see Mosiah 19:20).

17:19 ***executeth vengeance upon***—punishes

17:20 The Lord has promised, "And whoso layeth down his life in my cause, for my name's sake, shall find it again, even life eternal" (D&C 98:13).

18:1 ***iniquities***—wickedness

18:2 ***concerning***—about
***redemption***—salvation
***ascension***—rising

ABINADI AT THE STAKE, BY RON CROSBY

*King Noah and his wicked priests burn Abinadi at the stake because he will not take back the words that he has spoken.*

3 And as many as would hear his word he did
teach. And he taught them privately, that it might
not come to the knowledge of the king. And many
did believe his words.
4 And it came to pass that as many as did believe
him did go forth to a place which was called
Mormon, having received its name from the king,
being in the borders of the land having been infested, by times or at seasons, by wild beasts.
5 Now, there was in Mormon a fountain of pure
water, and Alma resorted thither, there being near
the water a thicket of small trees, where he did hide
himself in the daytime from the searches of the king.
6 And it came to pass that as many as believed
him went thither to hear his words.

## Alma Teaches the Covenant of Baptism

7 And it came to pass after many days there were
a goodly number gathered together at the place of
Mormon, to hear the words of Alma. Yea, all were
gathered together that believed on his word, to hear
him. And he did teach them, and did preach unto
them repentance, and redemption, and faith on the
Lord.
8 And it came to pass that he said unto them:
Behold, here are the waters of Mormon (for thus
were they called) and now, as ye are desirous to
come into the fold of God, and to be called his
people, and are willing to bear one another's burdens, that they may be light;
9 Yea, and are willing to mourn with those that
mourn; yea, and comfort those that stand in need
of comfort, and to stand as witnesses of God at all
times and in all things, and in all places that ye may
be in, even until death, that ye may be redeemed of
God, and be numbered with those of the first resurrection, that ye may have eternal life—
10 Now I say unto you, if this be the desire of your
hearts, what have you against being baptized in the
name of the Lord, as a witness before him that ye
have entered into a covenant with him, that ye will
serve him and keep his commandments, that he may
pour out his Spirit more abundantly upon you?
11 And now when the people had heard these
words, they clapped their hands for joy, and
exclaimed: This is the desire of our hearts.
12 And now it came to pass that Alma took
Helam, he being one of the first, and went and
stood forth in the water, and cried, saying: O Lord,
pour out thy Spirit upon thy servant, that he may do
this work with holiness of heart.

---

18:4 The Prophet Joseph Smith explained that the word *Mormon* literally means "more good" (*Teachings of the Prophet Joseph Smith,* 300).

***infested***—overrun

18:5 ***resorted thither***—went there
***thicket***—thick growth

18:7 ***goodly***—large

18:8 A sheepfold is a place of safety where a shepherd keeps his sheep at night and in times of danger to protect them from harm. This verse uses the term "fold of God" to describe the spiritual protection the Church offers its members.

***bear one another's burdens***—help each other in our troubles

18:9 President Ezra Taft Benson explained what it means to stand as witnesses of God: "When our actions are honorable, we bring credit to His Church and kingdom; when they are not, it reflects on the entire Church" (*Teachings of Ezra Taft Benson,* 331).

18:10 ***abundantly***—fully

18:10 (8–10) Alma lists some of the promises we make to Heavenly Father when we are baptized and the blessings He promises us in return. How can keeping these covenants with God help other people? Why are the promised blessings worth any effort?

PHOTOGRAPH BY SCOT FACER PROCTOR

*Alma baptized many people at the waters of Mormon, which may have looked like these waters in Guatemala.*

13 And when he had said these words, the Spirit of the Lord was upon him, and he said: Helam, I baptize thee, having authority from the Almighty God, as a testimony that ye have entered into a covenant to serve him until you are dead as to the mortal body; and may the Spirit of the Lord be poured out upon you; and may he grant unto you eternal life, through the redemption of Christ, whom he has prepared from the foundation of the world.
14 And after Alma had said these words, both Alma and Helam were buried in the water; and they arose and came forth out of the water rejoicing, being filled with the Spirit.
15 And again, Alma took another, and went forth a second time into the water, and baptized him according to the first, only he did not bury himself again in the water.
16 And after this manner he did baptize every one that went forth to the place of Mormon; and they were in number about two hundred and four souls; yea, and they were baptized in the waters of Mormon, and were filled with the grace of God.

### *Alma Organizes the Church of Christ*

17 And they were called the church of God, or the church of Christ, from that time forward. And it came to pass that whosoever was baptized by the power and authority of God was added to his church.
18 And it came to pass that Alma, having authority from God, ordained priests; even one priest to every fifty of their number did he ordain to preach unto them, and to teach them concerning the things pertaining to the kingdom of God.
19 And he commanded them that they should teach nothing save it were the things which he had taught, and which had been spoken by the mouth of the holy prophets.
20 Yea, even he commanded them that they should preach nothing save it were repentance and faith on the Lord, who had redeemed his people.
21 And he commanded them that there should be no contention one with another, but that they should look forward with one eye, having one faith and one baptism, having their hearts knit together in unity and in love one towards another.
22 And thus he commanded them to preach. And thus they became the children of God.
23 And he commanded them that they should observe the sabbath day, and keep it holy, and also every day they should give thanks to the Lord their God.

### *Church Members Support Each Other in All Things*

24 And he also commanded them that the priests whom he had ordained should labor with their own hands for their support.
25 And there was one day in every week that was set apart that they should gather themselves together to teach the people, and to worship the Lord their God, and also, as often as it was in their power, to assemble themselves together.
26 And the priests were not to depend upon the people for their support; but for their labor they were to receive the grace of God, that they might wax strong in the Spirit, having the knowledge of God, that they might teach with power and authority from God.

---

18:13 The baptismal prayer we use today was revealed to the Prophet Joseph Smith and is recorded in Doctrine and Covenants 20:73.

***the foundation of the world***—the premortal life or the beginning

18:15 (14–15) Because Alma held the priesthood, he had already been baptized. "When Alma baptized himself with Helam that was not a case of Alma baptizing himself, but merely as a token [or sign] to the Lord of his humility and full repentance" (Joseph Fielding Smith, *Answers to Gospel Questions* 3:203).

18:16 Grace is the divine help given by God through the Atonement of Jesus Christ. It provides us with the power needed to repent, keep the commandments, and become like God (see LDS Bible Dictionary, s.v. "Grace," 697; see also 2 Nephi 25:23).

18:21 ***knit***—tied

Alma teaches members of the Church to avoid contention or arguments and have love for Christ and each other. Elder Neal A. Maxwell suggested that " 'one eye, . . . one faith, and one baptism,' which brings unity and love" means that our eye is "*single* to the glory of God" (*Notwithstanding My Weakness*, 27).

18:25 ***assemble***—gather

18:26 ***wax***—grow

27 And again Alma commanded that the people of the church should impart of their substance, every one according to that which he had; if he have more abundantly he should impart more abundantly; and of him that had but little, but little should be required; and to him that had not should be given.

28 And thus they should impart of their substance of their own free will and good desires towards God, and to those priests that stood in need, yea, and to every needy, naked soul.

29 And this he said unto them, having been commanded of God; and they did walk uprightly before God, imparting to one another both temporally and spiritually according to their needs and their wants.

30 And now it came to pass that all this was done in Mormon, yea, by the waters of Mormon, in the forest that was near the waters of Mormon; yea, the place of Mormon, the waters of Mormon, the forest of Mormon, how beautiful are they to the eyes of them who there came to the knowledge of their Redeemer; yea, and how blessed are they, for they shall sing to his praise forever.

### *Alma's People Flee from King Noah into the Wilderness*

31 And these things were done in the borders of the land, that they might not come to the knowledge of the king.

32 But behold, it came to pass that the king, having discovered a movement among the people, sent his servants to watch them. Therefore on the day that they were assembling themselves together to hear the word of the Lord they were discovered unto the king.

33 And now the king said that Alma was stirring up the people to rebellion against him; therefore he sent his army to destroy them.

34 And it came to pass that Alma and the people of the Lord were apprised of the coming of the king's army; therefore they took their tents and their families and departed into the wilderness.

35 And they were in number about four hundred and fifty souls.

## CHAPTER 19

*King Noah's people are captured by the Lamanites, and King Noah dies by fire. Watch for the fulfillment of Abinadi's words to King Noah.*

### *Gideon Confronts King Noah*

1 AND it came to pass that the army of the king returned, having searched in vain for the people of the Lord.

2 And now behold, the forces of the king were small, having been reduced, and there began to be a division among the remainder of the people.

3 And the lesser part began to breathe out threatenings against the king, and there began to be a great contention among them.

4 And now there was a man among them whose name was Gideon, and he being a strong man and an enemy to the king, therefore he drew his sword, and swore in his wrath that he would slay the king.

5 And it came to pass that he fought with the king; and when the king saw that he was about to overpower him, he fled and ran and got upon the tower which was near the temple.

6 And Gideon pursued after him and was about to get upon the tower to slay the king, and the king cast his eyes round about towards the land of Shemlon, and behold, the army of the Lamanites were within the borders of the land.

7 And now the king cried out in the anguish of his soul, saying: Gideon, spare me, for the Lamanites are upon us, and they will destroy us; yea, they will destroy my people.

---

18:27 ***impart***—give
***substance***—wealth or materials
***more abundantly***—a lot more

18:28 (27–28) These verses speak of sharing the blessings we receive from Heavenly Father with those who are in need. How can you share what you have with others?

18:29 ***uprightly***—righteously
***temporally***—with physical things

18:33 ***to rebellion***—in opposition

18:34 ***apprised***—told or warned

18:35 The account of what happened to Alma and his people is found in Mosiah 23–24.

19:1 ***in vain***—without success

19:2 ***remainder***—rest

19:3 ***contention***—arguing and fighting

19:7 ***anguish***—pain and worry

8 And now the king was not so much concerned about his people as he was about his own life; nevertheless, Gideon did spare his life.

## *Lamanites Capture Limhi, the Son of King Noah, and His People*

9 And the king commanded the people that they should flee before the Lamanites, and he himself did go before them, and they did flee into the wilderness, with their women and their children.

10 And it came to pass that the Lamanites did pursue them, and did overtake them, and began to slay them.

11 Now it came to pass that the king commanded them that all the men should leave their wives and their children, and flee before the Lamanites.

12 Now there were many that would not leave them, but had rather stay and perish with them. And the rest left their wives and their children and fled.

13 And it came to pass that those who tarried with their wives and their children caused that their fair daughters should stand forth and plead with the Lamanites that they would not slay them.

14 And it came to pass that the Lamanites had compassion on them, for they were charmed with the beauty of their women.

15 Therefore the Lamanites did spare their lives, and took them captives and carried them back to the land of Nephi, and granted unto them that they might possess the land, under the conditions that they would deliver up king Noah into the hands of the Lamanites, and deliver up their property, even one half of all they possessed, one half of their gold, and their silver, and all their precious things, and thus they should pay tribute to the king of the Lamanites from year to year.

16 And now there was one of the sons of the king among those that were taken captive, whose name was Limhi.

17 And now Limhi was desirous that his father should not be destroyed; nevertheless, Limhi was not ignorant of the iniquities of his father, he himself being a just man.

## *King Noah's People Put Him to Death*

18 And it came to pass that Gideon sent men into the wilderness secretly, to search for the king and those that were with him. And it came to pass that they met the people in the wilderness, all save the king and his priests.

19 Now they had sworn in their hearts that they would return to the land of Nephi, and if their wives and their children were slain, and also those that had tarried with them, that they would seek revenge, and also perish with them.

20 And the king commanded them that they should not return; and they were angry with the king, and caused that he should suffer, even unto death by fire.

21 And they were about to take the priests also and put them to death, and they fled before them.

22 And it came to pass that they were about to return to the land of Nephi, and they met the men of Gideon. And the men of Gideon told them of all that had happened to their wives and their children; and that the Lamanites had granted unto them that they might possess the land by paying a tribute to the Lamanites of one half of all they possessed.

---

19:8 ***nevertheless***—but

King Noah is selfish and concerned only for his own life. Notice King Noah's other selfish acts in verses 10–12 and 18–20. How does selfishness hurt others?

19:12 ***perish***—die

19:13 ***tarried***—stayed
***plead with***—beg

19:14 ***compassion***—mercy
***charmed***—pleased

19:15 ***tribute***—taxes

These events fulfill Abinadi's prophecy that the people would be brought into bondage because they would not repent (see Mosiah 12:1–2).

19:17 ***was desirous***—wished
***was not ignorant***—knew
***iniquities***—wickedness

19:19 ***tarried***—stayed
***seek revenge***—get even

19:20 Abinadi's prophecy that King Noah would also die by flames, as Abinadi did, is fulfilled (see Mosiah 12:3; 17:15–18).

In this chapter you have read about the fulfillment of two of Abinadi's prophecies (verses 15, 20). What does that tell you about the Lord's prophets? What do you think you should do about the things our modern prophets are telling us?

23 And the people told the men of Gideon that they had slain the king, and his priests had fled from them farther into the wilderness.

24 And it came to pass that after they had ended the ceremony, that they returned to the land of Nephi, rejoicing, because their wives and their children were not slain; and they told Gideon what they had done to the king.

25 And it came to pass that the king of the Lamanites made an oath unto them, that his people should not slay them.

26 And also Limhi, being the son of the king, having the kingdom conferred upon him by the people, made oath unto the king of the Lamanites that his people should pay tribute unto him, even one half of all they possessed.

27 And it came to pass that Limhi began to establish the kingdom and to establish peace among his people.

28 And the king of the Lamanites set guards round about the land, that he might keep the people of Limhi in the land, that they might not depart into the wilderness; and he did support his guards out of the tribute which he did receive from the Nephites.

29 And now king Limhi did have continual peace in his kingdom for the space of two years, that the Lamanites did not molest them nor seek to destroy them.

## CHAPTER 20

*Rejecting true prophets always brings suffering and heartache. Watch for how Abinadi's prophecies come to pass.*

### *The Wicked Priests of King Noah Carry Away Twenty-Four Daughters of the Lamanites*

1 NOW there was a place in Shemlon where the daughters of the Lamanites did gather themselves together to sing, and to dance, and to make themselves merry.

2 And it came to pass that there was one day a small number of them gathered together to sing and to dance.

3 And now the priests of king Noah, being ashamed to return to the city of Nephi, yea, and also fearing that the people would slay them, therefore they durst not return to their wives and their children.

4 And having tarried in the wilderness, and having discovered the daughters of the Lamanites, they laid and watched them;

5 And when there were but few of them gathered together to dance, they came forth out of their secret places and took them and carried them into the wilderness; yea, twenty and four of the daughters of the Lamanites they carried into the wilderness.

### *The Lamanites Attack the People of Limhi*

6 And it came to pass that when the Lamanites found that their daughters had been missing, they were angry with the people of Limhi, for they thought it was the people of Limhi.

7 Therefore they sent their armies forth; yea, even the king himself went before his people; and they went up to the land of Nephi to destroy the people of Limhi.

---

19:24 ***ceremony***—ritual

19:25 ***an oath***—a promise

19:26 Zeniff, Noah's father, gave the kingdom to Noah (see Mosiah 10:22–11:1). But Limhi, Noah's son, received the kingdom from the people.

19:29 ***molest***—hurt

20:1 ***merry***—happy

20:3 The wicked priests of King Noah felt fear and shame because they ran away and left their wives and children in the hands of the attacking Lamanites (see Mosiah 19:11, 20–21).

***slay***—kill
***durst not***—did not dare

20:4 ***tarried***—stayed

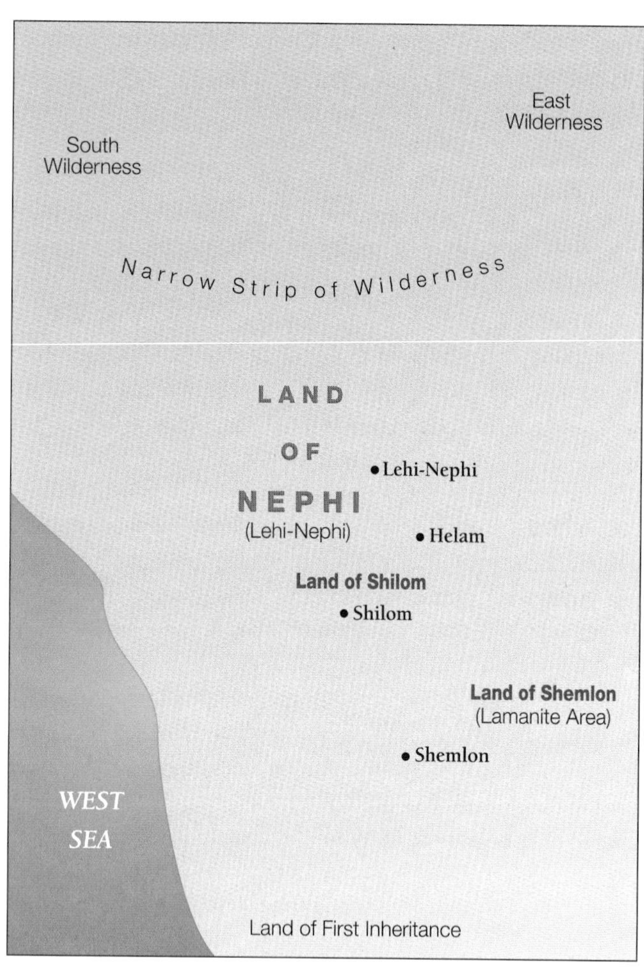


*Settlements in the Land of Nephi*

8 And now Limhi had discovered them from the
tower, even all their preparations for war did he discover; therefore he gathered his people together,
and laid wait for them in the fields and in the forests.
9 And it came to pass that when the Lamanites
had come up, that the people of Limhi began to fall
upon them from their waiting places, and began to
slay them.
10 And it came to pass that the battle became
exceedingly sore, for they fought like lions for their
prey.

## The People of Limhi Defeat the Lamanites

11 And it came to pass that the people of Limhi
began to drive the Lamanites before them; yet they
were not half so numerous as the Lamanites. But
they fought for their lives, and for their wives, and
for their children; therefore they exerted themselves
and like dragons did they fight.
12 And it came to pass that they found the king of
the Lamanites among the number of their dead; yet he
was not dead, having been wounded and left upon
the ground, so speedy was the flight of his people.
13 And they took him and bound up his wounds,
and brought him before Limhi, and said: Behold,
here is the king of the Lamanites; he having
received a wound has fallen among their dead, and
they have left him; and behold, we have brought
him before you; and now let us slay him.

## The King of the Lamanites Pleads in Behalf of the People of Limhi

14 But Limhi said unto them: Ye shall not slay
him, but bring him hither that I may see him. And
they brought him. And Limhi said unto him: What
cause have ye to come up to war against my
people? Behold, my people have not broken the
oath that I made unto you; therefore, why should
ye break the oath which ye made unto my people?
15 And now the king said: I have broken the oath
because thy people did carry away the daughters of
my people; therefore, in my anger I did cause my
people to come up to war against thy people.
16 And now Limhi had heard nothing concerning
this matter; therefore he said: I will search among
my people and whosoever has done this thing shall
perish. Therefore he caused a search to be made
among his people.
17 Now when Gideon had heard these things, he
being the king's captain, he went forth and said unto
the king: I pray thee forbear, and do not search this
people, and lay not this thing to their charge.

---

20:9 ***fall upon***—attack

20:10 ***sore***—terrible
***prey***—food

20:11 ***numerous***—many
***exerted themselves***—fought with all their strength

20:13 ***bound***—bandaged

20:14 ***hither***—here
***What cause***—Why

20:16 ***perish***—die

20:17 Gideon is the righteous man who challenged wicked King Noah in Mosiah 19:1–8.

***forbear***—do not do this
***lay not this thing to their charge***—don't blame our people for taking the Lamanite daughters

18 For do ye not remember the priests of thy father, whom this people sought to destroy? And are they not in the wilderness? And are not they the ones who have stolen the daughters of the Lamanites?

19 And now, behold, and tell the king of these things, that he may tell his people that they may be pacified towards us; for behold they are already preparing to come against us; and behold also there are but few of us.

20 And behold, they come with their numerous hosts; and except the king doth pacify them towards us we must perish.

21 For are not the words of Abinadi fulfilled, which he prophesied against us—and all this because we would not hearken unto the words of the Lord, and turn from our iniquities?

22 And now let us pacify the king, and we fulfil the oath which we have made unto him; for it is better that we should be in bondage than that we should lose our lives; therefore, let us put a stop to the shedding of so much blood.

23 And now Limhi told the king all the things concerning his father, and the priests that had fled into the wilderness, and attributed the carrying away of their daughters to them.

24 And it came to pass that the king was pacified towards his people; and he said unto them: Let us go forth to meet my people, without arms; and I swear unto you with an oath that my people shall not slay thy people.

25 And it came to pass that they followed the king, and went forth without arms to meet the Lamanites. And it came to pass that they did meet the Lamanites; and the king of the Lamanites did bow himself down before them, and did plead in behalf of the people of Limhi.

26 And when the Lamanites saw the people of Limhi, that they were without arms, they had compassion on them and were pacified towards them, and returned with their king in peace to their own land.

## CHAPTER 21

*Limhi and his people struggle to free themselves from Lamanite bondage. Watch for what happens to them because they turned away from the Lord.*

### Limhi and His People Lose Three Wars in Their Attempts to Escape from the Lamanites

1 AND it came to pass that Limhi and his people returned to the city of Nephi, and began to dwell in the land again in peace.

2 And it came to pass that after many days the Lamanites began again to be stirred up in anger against the Nephites, and they began to come into the borders of the land round about.

3 Now they durst not slay them, because of the oath which their king had made unto Limhi; but they would smite them on their cheeks, and exercise authority over them; and began to put heavy burdens upon their backs, and drive them as they would a dumb ass—

4 Yea, all this was done that the word of the Lord might be fulfilled.

---

20:19 ***pacified***—no longer angry

20:20 ***numerous hosts***—large army

20:21 In Mosiah 12:2 Abinadi prophesied that King Noah's people would be beaten, killed, and enslaved because of their wickedness. By Limhi's day these prophecies had been fulfilled. The Lord promises that all of His prophecies will be fulfilled (see D&C 1:38).

The phrase "turn from our iniquities" means to "repent of our sins." The Hebrew word meaning "repent" means "to turn" away from a bad or evil direction, so a new direction would be one that leads to the Lord (see James Strong, *The Exhaustive Concordance of the Bible,* 113).

20:22 ***bondage***—slavery
***shedding of so much blood***—killing of so many people

20:22 (14–22) In Mosiah 19:25–26 the king of the Lamanites had made an oath, or a promise, with the people of Limhi that if Limhi's people continued to pay tribute of one-half of everything they had, then the Lamanites would not kill them.

20:23 ***attributed***—blamed

20:24 ***arms***—weapons
***swear***—promise

20:26 (24–26) The king of the Lamanites kept his promise. Why is it important to keep our promises?

21:3 ***durst***—dared

21:4 A few years earlier, the Lord's prophet Abinadi had warned these same Nephites that if they did not repent of their wicked ways they would be mistreated, forced into slavery, and even killed (see Mosiah 12:2).

THE RETURN, BY DAVID HOFFT

*The people of Limhi murmured "because of their afflictions." They asked Limhi to let them go to battle against the Lamanites, but were defeated and suffered many losses.*

5 And now the afflictions of the Nephites were great, and there was no way that they could deliver themselves out of their hands, for the Lamanites had surrounded them on every side.

6 And it came to pass that the people began to murmur with the king because of their afflictions; and they began to be desirous to go against them to battle. And they did afflict the king sorely with their complaints; therefore he granted unto them that they should do according to their desires.

7 And they gathered themselves together again, and put on their armor, and went forth against the Lamanites to drive them out of their land.

8 And it came to pass that the Lamanites did beat them, and drove them back, and slew many of them.

9 And now there was a great mourning and lamentation among the people of Limhi, the widow mourning for her husband, the son and the daughter mourning for their father, and the brothers for their brethren.

10 Now there were a great many widows in the land, and they did cry mightily from day to day, for a great fear of the Lamanites had come upon them.

11 And it came to pass that their continual cries did stir up the remainder of the people of Limhi to anger against the Lamanites; and they went again to battle, but they were driven back again, suffering much loss.

12 Yea, they went again even the third time, and suffered in the like manner; and those that were not slain returned again to the city of Nephi.

## Limhi's People Humble Themselves Before the Lord

13 And they did humble themselves even to the dust, subjecting themselves to the yoke of bondage, submitting themselves to be smitten, and to be driv-

---

21:5 W ***afflictions***—trials and suffering

21:6 W ***murmur***—grumble and complain

21:9 W ***mourning and lamentation***—sadness and crying
***widow***—woman whose husband was dead

21:13 W ***subjecting***—forcing
***submitting***—allowing

en to and fro, and burdened, according to the
desires of their enemies.
14 And they did humble themselves even in the
depths of humility; and they did cry mightily to
God; yea, even all the day long did they cry unto
their God that he would deliver them out of their
afflictions.
15 And now the Lord was slow to hear their cry
because of their iniquities; nevertheless the Lord
did hear their cries, and began to soften the hearts
of the Lamanites that they began to ease their burdens; yet the Lord did not see fit to deliver them out
of bondage.
16 And it came to pass that they began to prosper
by degrees in the land, and began to raise grain
more abundantly, and flocks, and herds, that they
did not suffer with hunger.
17 Now there was a great number of women, more
than there was of men; therefore king Limhi commanded that every man should impart to the support
of the widows and their children, that they might not
perish with hunger; and this they did because of the
greatness of their number that had been slain.
18 Now the people of Limhi kept together in a
body as much as it was possible, and secured their
grain and their flocks;
19 And the king himself did not trust his person
without the walls of the city, unless he took his
guards with him, fearing that he might by some
means fall into the hands of the Lamanites.
20 And he caused that his people should watch
the land round about, that by some means they
might take those priests that fled into the wilderness, who had stolen the daughters of the
Lamanites, and that had caused such a great
destruction to come upon them.
21 For they were desirous to take them that they
might punish them; for they had come into the land
of Nephi by night, and carried off their grain and
many of their precious things; therefore they laid
wait for them.
22 And it came to pass that there was no more disturbance between the Lamanites and the people of
Limhi, even until the time that Ammon and his
brethren came into the land.

## Limhi and His People Tell Their Story to Ammon and His Men

23 And the king having been without the gates of
the city with his guard, discovered Ammon and his
brethren; and supposing them to be priests of Noah
therefore he caused that they should be taken, and
bound, and cast into prison. And had they been the
priests of Noah he would have caused that they
should be put to death.

A yoke is a tool used for oxen and other laboring animals.

21:14 (13–14) The scriptures teach that it is better to choose to be humble rather than to be forced to be humble. In other words, "blessed is he that believeth in the word of God, and is baptized without stubbornness of heart" (Alma 32:16).

21:15 ***iniquities***—sins

If we are slow to obey the Lord, He may be slow to answer our prayers (see D&C 101:7).

21:16 ***more abundantly***—in larger amounts

21:17 ***impart***—give

21:18 ***secured***—kept safe

21:22 Ammon and his brethren enter the land of Nephi about 121 B.C.

21:23 ***supposing***—thinking

24 But when he found that they were not, but that
they were his brethren, and had come from the
land of Zarahemla, he was filled with exceedingly
great joy.
25 Now king Limhi had sent, previous to the coming of Ammon, a small number of men to search for
the land of Zarahemla; but they could not find it,
and they were lost in the wilderness.
26 Nevertheless, they did find a land which had
been peopled; yea, a land which was covered with
dry bones; yea, a land which had been peopled and
which had been destroyed; and they, having supposed it to be the land of Zarahemla, returned to the
land of Nephi, having arrived in the borders of the
land not many days before the coming of Ammon.
27 And they brought a record with them, even a
record of the people whose bones they had found;
and it was engraven on plates of ore.
28 And now Limhi was again filled with joy on
learning from the mouth of Ammon that king Mosiah
had a gift from God, whereby he could interpret
such engravings; yea, and Ammon also did rejoice.
29 Yet Ammon and his brethren were filled with
sorrow because so many of their brethren had been
slain;
30 And also that king Noah and his priests had
caused the people to commit so many sins and iniquities against God; and they also did mourn for the
death of Abinadi; and also for the departure of
Alma and the people that went with him, who had
formed a church of God through the strength and
power of God, and faith on the words which had
been spoken by Abinadi.
31 Yea, they did mourn for their departure, for
they knew not whither they had fled. Now they
would have gladly joined with them, for they themselves had entered into a covenant with God to
serve him and keep his commandments.
32 And now since the coming of Ammon, king
Limhi had also entered into a covenant with God,
and also many of his people, to serve him and keep
his commandments.
33 And it came to pass that king Limhi and many
of his people were desirous to be baptized; but
there was none in the land that had authority from
God. And Ammon declined doing this thing, considering himself an unworthy servant.
34 Therefore they did not at that time form themselves into a church, waiting upon the Spirit of the
Lord. Now they were desirous to become even as
Alma and his brethren, who had fled into the
wilderness.
35 They were desirous to be baptized as a witness
and a testimony that they were willing to serve God
with all their hearts; nevertheless they did prolong
the time; and an account of their baptism shall be
given hereafter.
36 And now all the study of Ammon and his
people, and king Limhi and his people, was to
deliver themselves out of the hands of the
Lamanites and from bondage.

## CHAPTER 22

*Gideon thinks up a plan to help his people escape from the Lamanites. Watch how Gideon's plan works and how the Lord blesses the people so they can escape.*

### Gideon Presents His Plan to Deliver the People of Limhi

1 AND now it came to pass that Ammon and king
Limhi began to consult with the people how they
should deliver themselves out of bondage; and
even they did cause that all the people should
gather themselves together; and this they did that
they might have the voice of the people concerning
the matter.
2 And it came to pass that they could find no way
to deliver themselves out of bondage, except it
were to take their women and children, and their
flocks, and their herds, and their tents, and depart
into the wilderness; for the Lamanites being so
numerous, it was impossible for the people of
Limhi to contend with them, thinking to deliver
themselves out of bondage by the sword.

---

21:27 ***ore***—rock or mineral from which metal is obtained

21:28 ***interpret***—translate or explain

21:30 ***departure***—leaving

21:33 ***declined doing***—would not do

21:35 The people of Limhi wanted to be baptized to show their willingness to serve the Lord. How does baptism show that a person is willing to serve the Lord?

***prolong***—delay

22:2 ***contend***—fight

3 Now it came to pass that Gideon went forth and
stood before the king, and said unto him: Now O
king, thou hast hitherto hearkened unto my words
many times when we have been contending with
our brethren, the Lamanites.
4 And now O king, if thou hast not found me to
be an unprofitable servant, or if thou hast hitherto
listened to my words in any degree, and they have
been of service to thee, even so I desire that thou
wouldst listen to my words at this time, and I will
be thy servant and deliver this people out of
bondage.
5 And the king granted unto him that he might
speak. And Gideon said unto him:
6 Behold the back pass, through the back wall, on
the back side of the city. The Lamanites, or the
guards of the Lamanites, by night are drunken;
therefore let us send a proclamation among all this
people that they gather together their flocks and
herds, that they may drive them into the wilderness
by night.
7 And I will go according to thy command and
pay the last tribute of wine to the Lamanites, and
they will be drunken; and we will pass through the
secret pass on the left of their camp when they are
drunken and asleep.
8 Thus we will depart with our women and our
children, our flocks, and our herds into the wilderness; and we will travel around the land of Shilom.

## Limhi's People Are Delivered from the Lamanites

9 And it came to pass that the king hearkened
unto the words of Gideon.
10 And king Limhi caused that his people should
gather their flocks together; and he sent the tribute
of wine to the Lamanites; and he also sent more
wine, as a present unto them; and they did drink
freely of the wine which king Limhi did send unto
them.
11 And it came to pass that the people of king
Limhi did depart by night into the wilderness with
their flocks and their herds, and they went round
about the land of Shilom in the wilderness, and
bent their course towards the land of Zarahemla,
being led by Ammon and his brethren.
12 And they had taken all their gold, and silver,
and their precious things, which they could carry,
and also their provisions with them, into the wilderness; and they pursued their journey.
13 And after being many days in the wilderness
they arrived in the land of Zarahemla, and joined
Mosiah's people, and became his subjects.

---

22:3 Gideon was a faithful, strong man who earlier had attempted to end wicked King Noah's reign (see Mosiah 19:4–8, 18).

***hitherto hearkened***—listened before

22:4 ***an unprofitable***—a weak or poor

22:6 ***a proclamation***—an announcement

22:7 ***tribute***—payment

22:8 (1–8) Years earlier, Abinadi had warned Limhi's people that God would deliver them from bondage (slavery) only if they repented (see Mosiah 11:23). They finally cried "mightily to God," and He heard their prayers (see Mosiah 21:14–16). The Lord did not do all the work for them, however. He allowed them to choose their own plan of escape. The Lord told Joseph Smith that "it is not meet that I should command in all things" and the Saints should "do many things of their own free will, and bring to pass much righteousness" (D&C 58:26–27).

22:12 ***provisions***—food and other supplies
***pursued***—continued

22:13 ***his subjects***—people who were under his authority

*The people of Limhi escaped through a "back pass" that may have been like this one.*

PHOTOGRAPH BY SCOT FACER PROCTOR

14 And it came to pass that Mosiah received them with joy; and he also received their records, and also the records which had been found by the people of Limhi.
15 And now it came to pass when the Lamanites had found that the people of Limhi had departed out of the land by night, that they sent an army into the wilderness to pursue them;
16 And after they had pursued them two days, they could no longer follow their tracks; therefore they were lost in the wilderness.

*An account of Alma and the people of the Lord, who were driven into the wilderness by the people of King Noah. Comprising chapters 23 and 24.**

## CHAPTER 23

*Alma and his followers escape the armies of King Noah. Alma refuses to be king. The Lamanites conquer and rule over Alma and his people. Look for how the prophecy of Abinadi in Mosiah 11:23–25 is fulfilled.*

### Alma's People Escape into the Wilderness

1 NOW Alma, having been warned of the Lord that the armies of king Noah would come upon them, and having made it known to his people, therefore they gathered together their flocks, and took of their grain, and departed into the wilderness before the armies of king Noah.
2 And the Lord did strengthen them, that the people of king Noah could not overtake them to destroy them.
3 And they fled eight days' journey into the wilderness.
4 And they came to a land, yea, even a very beautiful and pleasant land, a land of pure water.
5 And they pitched their tents, and began to till the ground, and began to build buildings; yea, they were industrious, and did labor exceedingly.

### Alma Refuses to Be King

6 And the people were desirous that Alma should be their king, for he was beloved by his people.
7 But he said unto them: Behold, it is not expedient that we should have a king; for thus saith the Lord: Ye shall not esteem one flesh above another, or one man shall not think himself above another; therefore I say unto you it is not expedient that ye should have a king.
8 Nevertheless, if it were possible that ye could always have just men to be your kings it would be well for you to have a king.

---

22:14 When Limhi's people joined with the people of King Mosiah in the land of Zarahemla, they brought with them their own records, and other records they had found known "as the records of Ether" (see Daniel H. Ludlow, *A Companion to Your Study of the Book of Mormon,* 188).

22:16 The Lamanites were unable to follow the tracks left by Limhi's people and all of their flocks and herds. What part might the Lord have played in helping Limhi's people escape? What does that teach you about the Lord's power to help His people?

* These chapters take us back in time and tell us what happened to the people who fled into the wilderness with Alma to escape the armies of King Noah. These events occurred between 145 and 121 B.C. The first sentence of this introduction was translated from the gold plates.

23:5 Being industrious, or hardworking, has always been expected of the Lord's people (see Genesis 3:19). In our own day the prophets have declared: "The aim of the Church is to help the people to help themselves. Work is to be re-enthroned as the ruling principle of the lives of our Church membership" (Heber J. Grant, in Conference Report, October 1936, 3).

PHOTOGRAPH BY EDWIM M. WOOLLEY

*The Lord led Alma's people to "a very beautiful and pleasant land, a land of pure water." It may have resembled this land in Guatemala.*

23:7 ***expedient***—helpful or necessary
***esteem***—respect or value

9 But remember the iniquity of king Noah and his priests; and I myself was caught in a snare, and did many things which were abominable in the sight of the Lord, which caused me sore repentance;

10 Nevertheless, after much tribulation, the Lord did hear my cries, and did answer my prayers, and has made me an instrument in his hands in bringing so many of you to a knowledge of his truth.

11 Nevertheless, in this I do not glory, for I am unworthy to glory of myself.

12 And now I say unto you, ye have been oppressed by king Noah, and have been in bondage to him and his priests, and have been brought into iniquity by them; therefore ye were bound with the bands of iniquity.

13 And now as ye have been delivered by the power of God out of these bonds; yea, even out of the hands of king Noah and his people, and also from the bonds of iniquity, even so I desire that ye should stand fast in this liberty wherewith ye have been made free, and that ye trust no man to be a king over you.

## Alma Organizes the Church of Jesus Christ

14 And also trust no one to be your teacher nor your minister, except he be a man of God, walking in his ways and keeping his commandments.

15 Thus did Alma teach his people, that every man should love his neighbor as himself, that there should be no contention among them.

16 And now, Alma was their high priest, he being the founder of their church.

17 And it came to pass that none received authority to preach or to teach except it were by him from God. Therefore he consecrated all their priests and all their teachers; and none were consecrated except they were just men.

18 Therefore they did watch over their people, and did nourish them with things pertaining to righteousness.

## Alma's People Are Put in Bondage to the Lamanites

19 And it came to pass that they began to prosper exceedingly in the land; and they called the land Helam.

20 And it came to pass that they did multiply and prosper exceedingly in the land of Helam; and they built a city, which they called the city of Helam.

21 Nevertheless the Lord seeth fit to chasten his people; yea, he trieth their patience and their faith.

22 Nevertheless—whosoever putteth his trust in him the same shall be lifted up at the last day. Yea, and thus it was with this people.

23 For behold, I will show unto you that they were brought into bondage, and none could deliver them but the Lord their God, yea, even the God of Abraham and Isaac and of Jacob.

24 And it came to pass that he did deliver them, and he did show forth his mighty power unto them, and great were their rejoicings.

---

23:9 ***iniquity***—wickedness
***snare***—trap
***abominable***—terrible and evil

23:10 ***tribulation***—suffering and sorrow

23:10 (9–10) This is the first we read of Alma's struggle to repent after being one of King Noah's priests. What do you think he would tell you about the value of keeping the commandments?

23:12 ***oppressed***—abused and overworked

When a person repeatedly gives in to temptation, sin can become a habit as strong as iron bands or chains. In scripture, sin is sometimes called the "bands of iniquity" or the "chains of hell" (see 2 Nephi 1:23; Alma 12:11).

23:14 Alma and his people suffered because of King Noah and his wicked priests. Why is it important to follow only teachers who keep the Lord's commandments?

23:15 ***contention***—arguing or fighting

23:17 ***consecrated***—ordained or set apart

"Book of Mormon prophets gave the title *priest* to officers known in this dispensation as *high priests*. That is, they were priests of the Melchizedek Priesthood. . . . Since there was no Aaronic Priesthood among the Nephites in Alma's day . . . , there was no need to distinguish between priests of the lesser and greater priesthoods" (Bruce R. McConkie, *Mormon Doctrine,* 599; see also Alma 13:1–20).

23:18 ***nourish***—care for

23:19 ***prosper exceedingly***—succeed very much

23:21 ***chasten***—test or punish

23:24 (21–24) In mortality, we must learn to have "patient faith in God and his unfolding purposes. We read in Mosiah about how the Lord simultaneously tries the *patience* of his people even as he tries their faith (see Mosiah 23:21). One is not only to endure—but to endure well and gracefully those things which the Lord 'seeth fit to inflict upon [us]' (Mosiah 3:19)" (Neal A. Maxwell, "Patience," 28).

25 For behold, it came to pass that while they were in the land of Helam, yea, in the city of Helam, while tilling the land round about, behold an army of the Lamanites was in the borders of the land.

26 Now it came to pass that the brethren of Alma fled from their fields, and gathered themselves together in the city of Helam; and they were much frightened because of the appearance of the Lamanites.

27 But Alma went forth and stood among them, and exhorted them that they should not be frightened, but that they should remember the Lord their God and he would deliver them.

28 Therefore they hushed their fears, and began to cry unto the Lord that he would soften the hearts of the Lamanites, that they would spare them, and their wives, and their children.

29 And it came to pass the the Lord did soften the hearts of the Lamanites. And Alma and his brethren went forth and delivered themselves up into their hands; and the Lamanites took possession of the land of Helam.

30 Now the armies of the Lamanites, which had followed after the people of king Limhi, had been lost in the wilderness for many days.

31 And behold, they had found those priests of king Noah, in a place which they called Amulon; and they had begun to possess the land of Amulon and had begun to till the ground.

32 Now the name of the leader of those priests was Amulon.

33 And it came to pass that Amulon did plead with the Lamanites; and he also sent forth their wives, who were the daughters of the Lamanites, to plead with their brethren, that they should not destroy their husbands.

34 And the Lamanites had compassion on Amulon and his brethren, and did not destroy them, because of their wives.

35 And Amulon and his brethren did join the Lamanites, and they were traveling in the wilderness in search of the land of Nephi when they discovered the land of Helam, which was possessed by Alma and his brethren.

36 And it came to pass that the Lamanites promised unto Alma and his brethren, that if they would show them the way which led to the land of Nephi that they would grant unto them their lives and their liberty.

37 But after Alma had shown them the way that led to the land of Nephi the Lamanites would not keep their promise; but they set guards round about the land of Helam, over Alma and his brethren.

38 And the remainder of them went to the land of Nephi; and a part of them returned to the land of Helam, and also brought with them the wives and the children of the guards who had been left in the land.

39 And the king of the Lamanites had granted unto Amulon that he should be a king and a ruler over his people, who were in the land of Helam; nevertheless he should have no power to do anything contrary to the will of the king of the Lamanites.

## CHAPTER 24

*The wicked priest Amulon and the Lamanites mistreat and abuse Alma and his people. Because of their faithfulness, the people of Alma are freed from bondage and led by the Lord to the land of Zarahemla. Look for how the Lord blesses those who are faithful.*

### AMULON AND HIS PEOPLE TEACH THE NEPHITE LANGUAGE TO THE LAMANITES

1 AND it came to pass that Amulon did gain favor in the eyes of the king of the Lamanites; therefore, the king of the Lamanites granted unto him and his brethren that they should be appointed teachers over his people, yea, even over the people who were in the land of Shemlon, and in the land of Shilom, and in the land of Amulon.

2 For the Lamanites had taken possession of all these lands; therefore, the king of the Lamanites had appointed kings over all these lands.

---

23:27 ***exhorted***—strongly encouraged

23:33 (31–33) The story of the wicked priests of King Noah and how they took Lamanite wives is found in Mosiah 20.

23:37 (36–37) Have you noticed how often the wicked break their promises? Who can you trust to always keep promises? (see Enos 1:6; D&C 1:37–38).

23:39 ***contrary to***—against

24:1 ***favor***—respect and friendship
***appointed***—assigned as

3 And now the name of the king of the Lamanites was Laman, being called after the name of his father; and therefore he was called king Laman. And he was king over a numerous people.
4 And he appointed teachers of the brethren of Amulon in every land which was possessed by his people; and thus the language of Nephi began to be taught among all the people of the Lamanites.
5 And they were a people friendly one with another; nevertheless they knew not God; neither did the brethren of Amulon teach them anything concerning the Lord their God, neither the law of Moses; nor did they teach them the words of Abinadi;
6 But they taught them that they should keep their record, and that they might write one to another.

## Amulon Persecutes Alma and His Followers

7 And thus the Lamanites began to increase in riches, and began to trade one with another and wax great, and began to be a cunning and a wise people, as to the wisdom of the world, yea, a very cunning people, delighting in all manner of wickedness and plunder, except it were among their own brethren.
8 And now it came to pass that Amulon began to exercise authority over Alma and his brethren, and began to persecute him, and cause that his children should persecute their children.
9 For Amulon knew Alma, that he had been one of the king's priests, and that it was he that believed the words of Abinadi and was driven out before the king, and therefore he was wroth with him; for he was subject to king Laman, yet he exercised authority over them, and put tasks upon them, and put task-masters over them.
10 And it came to pass that so great were their afflictions that they began to cry mightily to God.
11 And Amulon commanded them that they should stop their cries; and he put guards over them to watch them, that whosoever should be found calling upon God should be put to death.
12 And Alma and his people did not raise their voices to the Lord their God, but did pour out their hearts to him; and he did know the thoughts of their hearts.

## The Lord Hears the Cries of Alma and His People and Delivers Them from Bondage

13 And it came to pass that the voice of the Lord came to them in their afflictions, saying: Lift up your heads and be of good comfort, for I know of the covenant which ye have made unto me; and I will covenant with my people and deliver them out of bondage.
14 And I will also ease the burdens which are put upon your shoulders, that even you cannot feel them upon your backs, even while you are in bondage; and this will I do that ye may stand as witnesses for me hereafter, and that ye may know of a surety that I, the Lord God, do visit my people in their afflictions.

---

24:3 ***numerous***—large number of

24:4 ***possessed***—held

That Amulon's brethren teach the Lamanites the Nephite language "takes on added significance later in the Book of Mormon when we read about the missionary efforts between these two groups" (Daniel H. Ludlow, *A Companion to Your Study of the Book of Mormon,* 190).

24:7 ***wax***—grow
***cunning***—skillful
***delighting in***—enjoying
***plunder***—robbing

24:8 ***persecute***—mistreat or abuse

24:9 ***wroth***—angry
***tasks***—heavy workloads
***task-masters***—rulers

Jesus taught that when we are sad or worried and carry heavy burdens, we should "come unto" Him. He promised that He would lighten our burdens and give us rest (see Matthew 11:28). When have you felt the Lord lifting worries and cares from your life?

24:11 Amulon commanded Alma and his people not to pray. What kind of person would want you not to pray? (see 2 Nephi 32:8). Why do you think it is important to pray often?

24:13 ***bondage***—slavery

24:14 ***burdens***—heavy loads

15 And now it came to pass that the burdens which were laid upon Alma and his brethren were made light; yea, the Lord did strengthen them that they could bear up their burdens with ease, and they did submit cheerfully and with patience to all the will of the Lord.

16 And it came to pass that so great was their faith and their patience that the voice of the Lord came unto them again, saying: Be of good comfort, for on the morrow I will deliver you out of bondage.

17 And he said unto Alma: Thou shalt go before this people, and I will go with thee and deliver this people out of bondage.

18 Now it came to pass that Alma and his people in the night-time gathered their flocks together, and also of their grain; yea, even all the night-time were they gathering their flocks together.

19 And in the morning the Lord caused a deep sleep to come upon the Lamanites, yea, and all their task-masters were in a profound sleep.

20 And Alma and his people departed into the wilderness; and when they had traveled all day they pitched their tents in a valley, and they called the valley Alma, because he led their way in the wilderness.

21 Yea, and in the valley of Alma they poured out their thanks to God because he had been merciful unto them, and eased their burdens, and had delivered them out of bondage; for they were in bondage, and none could deliver them except it were the Lord their God.

22 And they gave thanks to God, yea, all their men and all their women and all their children that could speak lifted their voices in the praises of their God.

23 And now the Lord said unto Alma: Haste thee and get thou and this people out of this land, for the Lamanites have awakened and do pursue thee; therefore get thee out of this land, and I will stop the Lamanites in this valley that they come no further in pursuit of this people.

24 And it came to pass that they departed out of the valley, and took their journey into the wilderness.

25 And after they had been in the wilderness twelve days they arrived in the land of Zarahemla; and king Mosiah did also receive them with joy.

## CHAPTER 25

*King Mosiah reads the records of Zeniff to his people, and Alma builds up the Church. Watch for how reading sacred records touches the people's hearts.*

### *King Mosiah Gathers His People*

1 AND now king Mosiah caused that all the people should be gathered together.

PHOTOGRAPH BY DAVID H. GARNER

*Alma's people "gathered their flocks together."*

24:15 "The Lord . . . loves us . . . , comforts and strengthens us, and enables us to bear our afflictions with patience and fortitude" (George Q. Cannon, in *Collected Discourses* 2:176, February 15, 1891).

***submit***—obey

24:16 ***morrow***—next day

24:19 ***profound***—heavy

24:21 After the Nephites are freed from the Lamanites, the first thing they do is pray and give thanks to God. Do you remember to thank Heavenly Father when you are blessed? What are some blessings you are thankful for?

24:23 ***Haste thee***—Hurry up
***pursue***—chase

24:25 Alma and his people arrive in Zarahemla about 120 B.C.

2 Now there were not so many of the children of Nephi, or so many of those who were descendants of Nephi, as there were of the people of Zarahemla, who was a descendant of Mulek, and those who came with him into the wilderness.

3 And there were not so many of the people of Nephi and of the people of Zarahemla as there were of the Lamanites; yea, they were not half so numerous.

4 And now all the people of Nephi were assembled together, and also all the people of Zarahemla, and they were gathered together in two bodies.

### King Mosiah Reads the Records to His People

5 And it came to pass that Mosiah did read, and caused to be read, the records of Zeniff to his people; yea, he read the records of the people of Zeniff, from the time they left the land of Zarahemla until they returned again.

6 And he also read the account of Alma and his brethren, and all their afflictions, from the time they left the land of Zarahemla until the time they returned again.

7 And now, when Mosiah had made an end of reading the records, his people who tarried in the land were struck with wonder and amazement.

8 For they knew not what to think; for when they beheld those that had been delivered out of bondage they were filled with exceedingly great joy.

9 And again, when they thought of their brethren who had been slain by the Lamanites they were filled with sorrow, and even shed many tears of sorrow.

10 And again, when they thought of the immediate goodness of God, and his power in delivering Alma and his brethren out of the hands of the Lamanites and of bondage, they did raise their voices and give thanks to God.

11 And again, when they thought upon the Lamanites, who were their brethren, of their sinful and polluted state, they were filled with pain and anguish for the welfare of their souls.

12 And it came to pass that those who were the children of Amulon and his brethren, who had taken to wife the daughters of the Lamanites, were displeased with the conduct of their fathers, and they would no longer be called by the names of their fathers, therefore they took upon themselves the name of Nephi, that they might be called the children of Nephi and be numbered among those who were called Nephites.

13 And now all the people of Zarahemla were numbered with the Nephites, and this because the kingdom had been conferred upon none but those who were descendants of Nephi.

14 And now it came to pass that when Mosiah had made an end of speaking and reading to the people, he desired that Alma should also speak to the people.

### Alma Preaches, Baptizes, and Organizes the Church in Zarahemla

15 And Alma did speak unto them, when they were assembled together in large bodies, and he went from one body to another, preaching unto the people repentance and faith on the Lord.

16 And he did exhort the people of Limhi and his brethren, all those that had been delivered out of bondage, that they should remember that it was the Lord that did deliver them.

---

25:2 ***descendants***—children, grandchildren, and so on

Mulek was the son of Zedekiah, the last king of Judah. The Bible records that Zedekiah's sons were killed by the Babylonians (see 2 Kings 25:7), but in Mosiah 25:2 we learn that Mulek was not killed. President Joseph Fielding Smith told us that "Mulek, son of Zedekiah, was spared by the power of the Lord and with other fugitives was directed across the 'great waters' to [America]" (*Doctrines of Salvation* 3:322–23).

25:6 ***afflictions***—trials or sufferings

25:7 ***tarried***—lived

25:8 ***bondage***—slavery
***exceedingly***—very

25:15 ***large bodies***—large groups of people

25:16 ***exhort***—strongly encourage

Alma reminds the people that it was the power of God that delivered them from slavery. Notice that this is just what Abinadi prophesied would happen to them (see Mosiah 11:23).

17 And it came to pass that after Alma had taught the people many things, and had made an end of speaking to them, that king Limhi was desirous that he might be baptized; and all his people were desirous that they might be baptized also.

18 Therefore, Alma did go forth into the water and did baptize them; yea, he did baptize them after the manner he did his brethren in the waters of Mormon; yea, and as many as he did baptize did belong to the church of God; and this because of their belief on the words of Alma.

19 And it came to pass that king Mosiah granted unto Alma that he might establish churches throughout all the land of Zarahemla; and gave him power to ordain priests and teachers over every church.

20 Now this was done because there were so many people that they could not all be governed by one teacher; neither could they all hear the word of God in one assembly;

21 Therefore they did assemble themselves together in different bodies, being called churches; every church having their priests and their teachers, and every priest preaching the word according as it was delivered to him by the mouth of Alma.

22 And thus, notwithstanding there being many churches they were all one church, yea, even the church of God; for there was nothing preached in all the churches except it were repentance and faith in God.

23 And now there were seven churches in the land of Zarahemla. And it came to pass that whosoever were desirous to take upon them the name of Christ, or of God, they did join the churches of God;

24 And they were called the people of God. And the Lord did pour out his Spirit upon them, and they were blessed, and prospered in the land.

## CHAPTER 26

*Alma learns from the Lord how to help those who have fallen into sin. Notice the Lord's concern is all for His children, including those who may have wandered from the Church.*

### *Members of the Church Are Led into Sin by Unbelievers*

1 NOW it came to pass that there were many of the rising generation that could not understand the words of king Benjamin, being little children at the time he spake unto his people; and they did not believe the tradition of their fathers.

2 They did not believe what had been said concerning the resurrection of the dead, neither did they believe concerning the coming of Christ.

3 And now because of their unbelief they could not understand the word of God; and their hearts were hardened.

4 And they would not be baptized; neither would they join the church. And they were a separate people as to their faith, and remained so ever after, even in their carnal and sinful state; for they would not call upon the Lord their God.

5 And now in the reign of Mosiah they were not half so numerous as the people of God; but because of the dissensions among the brethren they became more numerous.

6 For it came to pass that they did deceive many with their flattering words, who were in the church, and did cause them to commit many sins; therefore it became expedient that those who committed sin, that were in the church, should be admonished by the church.

---

25:19 Mosiah held the keys of the kingdom, and so Alma acted under his direction as he organized churches throughout the land (see Joseph Fielding McConkie and others, *Doctrinal Commentary on the Book of Mormon* 2:291).

25:24 (19–24) Churches were organized under the direction of priesthood leaders, and people who wanted to "take upon them the name of Christ" joined the churches. How is that like being baptized into the Church today? What would you tell a friend who wanted to know how to follow Jesus Christ?

26:1 ***rising generation***—younger people
***tradition***—teachings or beliefs

26:4 ***carnal***—worldly

26:4 (3–4) Why must you first believe the word of God before you can understand it? The Apostle Paul explains that the things of God can only be understood by the Spirit of God (see 1 Corinthians 2:11). What can you do to invite the Spirit into your life?

26:5 ***dissensions***—disagreements

26:6 ***deceive***—mislead or fool
***flattering words***—false praise
***expedient***—necessary
***admonished***—warned or scolded

## The Leaders Try to Decide How to Work with Members Who Sin

7 And it came to pass that they were brought before the priests, and delivered up unto the priests by the teachers; and the priests brought them before Alma, who was the high priest.
8 Now king Mosiah had given Alma the authority over the church.
9 And it came to pass that Alma did not know concerning them; but there were many witnesses against them; yea, the people stood and testified of their iniquity in abundance.
10 Now there had not any such thing happened before in the church; therefore Alma was troubled in his spirit, and he caused that they should be brought before the king.
11 And he said unto the king: Behold, here are many whom we have brought before thee, who are accused of their brethren; yea, and they have been taken in divers iniquities. And they do not repent of their iniquities; therefore we have brought them before thee, that thou mayest judge them according to their crimes.
12 But king Mosiah said unto Alma: Behold, I judge them not; therefore I deliver them into thy hands to be judged.
13 And now the spirit of Alma was again troubled; and he went and inquired of the Lord what he should do concerning this matter, for he feared that he should do wrong in the sight of God.

## The Lord Blesses Alma and Instructs Him How to Work with Members Who Sin

14 And it came to pass that after he had poured out his whole soul to God, the voice of the Lord came to him, saying:
15 Blessed art thou, Alma, and blessed are they who were baptized in the waters of Mormon. Thou art blessed because of thy exceeding faith in the words alone of my servant Abinadi.
16 And blessed are they because of their exceeding faith in the words alone which thou hast spoken unto them.
17 And blessed art thou because thou hast established a church among this people; and they shall be established, and they shall be my people.
18 Yea, blessed is this people who are willing to bear my name; for in my name shall they be called; and they are mine.
19 And because thou hast inquired of me concerning the transgressor, thou art blessed.
20 Thou art my servant; and I covenant with thee that thou shalt have eternal life; and thou shalt serve me and go forth in my name, and shalt gather together my sheep.
21 And he that will hear my voice shall be my sheep; and him shall ye receive into the church, and him will I also receive.
22 For behold, this is my church; whosoever is baptized shall be baptized unto repentance. And whomsoever ye receive shall believe in my name; and him will I freely forgive.

---

26:7 The person in the Church today who has authority, power, and responsibility over the Church is the President and prophet (see D&C 28:2–3; 43:3–4).

26:9 ***iniquity in abundance***—sins in large numbers

26:11 ***accused of***—blamed for doing wrong by
***divers***—many

26:13 ***inquired***—asked

26:17 ***established***—strengthened

26:18 ***bear my name***—take my name upon them

26:19 ***transgressor***—sinner

26:20 ***covenant with thee***—promise you

Alma's faithfulness was rewarded with the promise of eternal life. "Every member of the Church has the promise of eternal life on the condition of obedience to the laws and ordinances of the gospel" (Bruce R. McConkie, *Doctrinal New Testament Commentary* 3:382).

26:22 Alma learns that the Lord freely forgives people who truly repent and are baptized. How would knowing that give someone additional desire and strength to repent of his sins?

23 For it is I that taketh upon me the sins of the
world; for it is I that hath created them; and it is I
that granteth unto him that believeth unto the end
a place at my right hand.
24 For behold, in my name are they called; and if
they know me they shall come forth, and shall have
a place eternally at my right hand.
25 And it shall come to pass that when the second
trump shall sound then shall they that never knew
me come forth and shall stand before me.
26 And then shall they know that I am the Lord
their God, that I am their Redeemer; but they would
not be redeemed.
27 And then I will confess unto them that I never
knew them; and they shall depart into everlasting
fire prepared for the devil and his angels.
28 Therefore I say unto you, that he that will not
hear my voice, the same shall ye not receive into
my church, for him I will not receive at the last day.
29 Therefore I say unto you, Go; and whosoever
transgresseth against me, him shall ye judge according
to the sins which he has committed; and if he
confess his sins before thee and me, and repenteth
in the sincerity of his heart, him shall ye forgive,
and I will forgive him also.
30 Yea, and as often as my people repent will I
forgive them their trespasses against me.
31 And ye shall also forgive one another your
trespasses; for verily I say unto you, he that forgiveth
not his neighbor's trespasses when he says
that he repents, the same hath brought himself
under condemnation.
32 Now I say unto you, Go; and whosoever will
not repent of his sins the same shall not be numbered
among my people; and this shall be observed
from this time forward.

---

26:23 ***granteth***—gives

26:24 To know the Lord, we must keep His commandments (see 1 John 2:3).

26:27 ***confess***—declare

Jesus Christ taught this about the judgment of the wicked: "Many will say to me in that day, Lord, Lord, have we not prophesied in thy name? and in thy name have cast out devils? and in thy name done many wonderful works? And then will I profess unto them, I never knew you: depart from me, ye that work iniquity" (Matthew 7:22–23; see also JST, Matthew 7:31–33).

26:27 (25–27) The "second trump" refers to the announcement of the second resurrection or the resurrection of the unjust (see D&C 76:81–86).

26:30 (29–30) The Lord will forgive us of our trespasses or sins as often as we sincerely or truly repent; however, Joseph Smith warned: "Repentance is a thing that cannot be trifled [played] with every day. Daily transgression and daily repentance is not . . . pleasing to God" (*Teachings of the Prophet Joseph Smith,* 148).

26:31 The Lord declares that if we do not forgive other people for their sins, we stand condemned and have committed a greater sin than they have (see D&C 64:9–10). The Lord promises, however, that "if ye forgive men their trespasses your heavenly Father will also forgive you" (3 Nephi 13:14).

***condemnation***—punishment

26:32 Leaders of the Church are directed to protect Church members from those who refuse to repent. Elder Dallin H. Oaks writes: "While saving souls is the primary purpose of church discipline, there are two secondary purposes, both supportive of the primary purpose and each important in its own right: protecting the flock and preserving the good name and influence of the Church" (*The Lord's Way,* 227).

PHOTOGRAPH BY G. R. SIMS

*When the angels sound the "second trump," it will signal the second resurrection—the resurrection of those who "never knew" the Lord.*

## Alma Judges the People

33 And it came to pass when Alma had heard these
words he wrote them down that he might have
them, and that he might judge the people of that
church according to the commandments of God.
34 And it came to pass that Alma went and judged
those that had been taken in iniquity, according to
the word of the Lord.
35 And whosoever repented of their sins and did
confess them, them he did number among the
people of the church;
36 And those that would not confess their sins and
repent of their iniquity, the same were not numbered among the people of the church, and their
names were blotted out.
37 And it came to pass that Alma did regulate all
the affairs of the church; and they began again to
have peace and to prosper exceedingly in the
affairs of the church, walking circumspectly before
God, receiving many, and baptizing many.
38 And now all these things did Alma and his fellow laborers do who were over the church, walking in all diligence, teaching the word of God in all
things, suffering all manner of afflictions, being persecuted by all those who did not belong to the
church of God.
39 And they did admonish their brethren; and they
were also admonished, every one by the word of
God, according to his sins, or to the sins which he
had committed, being commanded of God to pray
without ceasing, and to give thanks in all things.

# CHAPTER 27

*Alma the Younger and the four sons of Mosiah are among the unbelievers who go about persecuting the faithful members of the Church. Look for how the Lord answers the prayers of the faithful.*

## King Mosiah Forbids Persecution and Inequality

1 AND now it came to pass that the persecutions
which were inflicted on the church by the unbelievers became so great that the church began to
murmur, and complain to their leaders concerning
the matter; and they did complain to Alma. And
Alma laid the case before their king, Mosiah. And
Mosiah consulted with his priests.
2 And it came to pass that king Mosiah sent a
proclamation throughout the land round about that
there should not any unbeliever persecute any of
those who belonged to the church of God.
3 And there was a strict command throughout all
the churches that there should be no persecutions
among them, that there should be an equality
among all men;
4 That they should let no pride nor haughtiness
disturb their peace; that every man should esteem
his neighbor as himself, laboring with their own
hands for their support.
5 Yea, and all their priests and teachers should labor
with their own hands for their support, in all cases
save it were in sickness, or in much want; and doing
these things, they did abound in the grace of God.

---

26:35 The Savior states that "he who has repented of his sins, the same is forgiven, and I, the Lord, remember them no more. By this ye may know if a man repenteth of his sins—behold, he will confess them and forsake them" (D&C 58:42–43).

26:36 According to President Spencer W. Kimball: "The scriptures speak of Church members being 'cast out' or 'cut off,' or having their names 'blotted out.' This means excommunication. This dread action means the total severance of the individual from the Church. The person who is excommunicated loses his membership in the Church and all attendant blessings" (*The Teachings of Spencer W. Kimball,* 100).

26:37 ***regulate***—direct or control
***prosper exceedingly***—succeed very much
***circumspectly***—correctly and wisely

26:38 ***afflictions***—trials or suffering

26:39 ***admonish***—warn or encourage

Why is it so important to give thanks to God "in all things"? (see D&C 59:20–21).

27:1 ***persecutions***—mistreatment and abuse
***inflicted***—imposed

27:2 ***a proclamation***—an official announcement

27:3 ***an equality***—fairness

27:4 ***haughtiness***—arrogance
***laboring***—working

Jesus said we should love our neighbor as we would love ourselves. He called this the second great commandment (see Matthew 22:36–40).

27:5 ***save***—except
***abound***—overflow

6 And there began to be much peace again in the
land; and the people began to be very numerous,
and began to scatter abroad upon the face of the
earth, yea, on the north and on the south, on the
east and on the west, building large cities and villages in all quarters of the land.
7 And the Lord did visit them and prosper them,
and they became a large and wealthy people.

## An Angel Calls upon Alma to Repent

8 Now the sons of Mosiah were numbered among
the unbelievers; and also one of the sons of Alma
was numbered among them, he being called Alma,
after his father; nevertheless, he became a very
wicked and an idolatrous man. And he was a man
of many words, and did speak much flattery to the
people; therefore he led many of the people to do
after the manner of his iniquities.
9 And he became a great hinderment to the prosperity of the church of God; stealing away the
hearts of the people; causing much dissension
among the people; giving a chance for the enemy
of God to exercise his power over them.
10 And now it came to pass that while he was
going about to destroy the church of God, for he
did go about secretly with the sons of Mosiah seeking to destroy the church, and to lead astray the
people of the Lord, contrary to the commandments
of God, or even the king—
11 And as I said unto you, as they were going
about rebelling against God, behold, the angel of
the Lord appeared unto them; and he descended as
it were in a cloud; and he spake as it were with a
voice of thunder, which caused the earth to shake
upon which they stood;
12 And so great was their astonishment, that they
fell to the earth, and understood not the words
which he spake unto them.
13 Nevertheless he cried again, saying: Alma, arise
and stand forth, for why persecutest thou the
church of God? For the Lord hath said: This is my
church, and I will establish it; and nothing shall
overthrow it, save it is the transgression of my
people.
14 And again, the angel said: Behold, the Lord
hath heard the prayers of his people, and also the
prayers of his servant, Alma, who is thy father; for
he has prayed with much faith concerning thee that
thou mightest be brought to the knowledge of the
truth; therefore, for this purpose have I come to
convince thee of the power and authority of God,
that the prayers of his servants might be answered
according to their faith.

PHOTOGRAPH BY EDWIN M. WOOLLEY

*The Nephites built many villages and large cities. They may have been similar to this ancient site in Teotihuacán.*

27:6 ***quarters***—parts

27:7 ***prosper***—bless

27:8 ***idolatrous***—idol-worshiping
***speak much flattery to the people***—tell the people what they wanted to hear, whether it was right or wrong
***after the manner of his iniquities***—the same sins he did

27:9 ***hinderment to the prosperity***—block to the success

Arguing and fighting give Satan, the "enemy of God," a chance to gain power over us (see 3 Nephi 11:29). What can you do to help stop contention in your home?

27:10 ***lead astray***—guide into error
***contrary to***—against

27:11 ***descended***—came down

27:12 ***astonishment***—surprise and wonder

27:13 ***establish***—support
***save it is the transgression***—except for the wickedness

27:14 "We learn that there is majestic, undeniable power in the love and prayer of a parent. The angel who appeared to Alma and the sons of Mosiah did not come in response to any righteousness on their part, though their souls were still precious in the sight of God. He came in response to the prayers of a faithful parent" (Jeffrey R. Holland, *However Long and Hard the Road,* 81).

CONVERSION OF ALMA THE YOUNGER, BY GARY KAPP

*An angel appeared to Alma and the sons of Mosiah and told them to "seek to destroy the church no more."*

15 And now behold, can ye dispute the power of
God? For behold, doth not my voice shake the
earth? And can ye not also behold me before you?
And I am sent from God.
16 Now I say unto thee: Go, and remember the
captivity of thy fathers in the land of Helam, and in
the land of Nephi; and remember how great things
he has done for them; for they were in bondage,
and he has delivered them. And now I say unto
thee, Alma, go thy way, and seek to destroy the
church no more, that their prayers may be
answered, and this even if thou wilt of thyself be
cast off.
17 And now it came to pass that these were the
last words which the angel spake unto Alma, and
he departed.

---

27:15 **dispute**—argue about

27:16 Just as the Lord delivered Alma's fathers from captivity and bondage, so He would deliver Alma, upon conditions of repentance, from bondage to sin and captivity to the devil (see Mosiah 24:16–21; 27:24–32).

**bondage**—slavery
***cast off***—destroyed

## Alma Repents and Is Forgiven

18 And now Alma and those that were with him
fell again to the earth, for great was their astonishment; for with their own eyes they had beheld an
angel of the Lord; and his voice was as thunder,
which shook the earth; and they knew that there
was nothing save the power of God that could
shake the earth and cause it to tremble as though it
would part asunder.
19 And now the astonishment of Alma was so
great that he became dumb, that he could not open
his mouth; yea, and he became weak, even that he
could not move his hands; therefore he was taken
by those that were with him, and carried helpless,
even until he was laid before his father.
20 And they rehearsed unto his father all that had
happened unto them; and his father rejoiced, for he
knew that it was the power of God.
21 And he caused that a multitude should be gathered together that they might witness what the Lord
had done for his son, and also for those that were
with him.
22 And he caused that the priests should assemble
themselves together; and they began to fast, and to
pray to the Lord their God that he would open the
mouth of Alma, that he might speak, and also that
his limbs might receive their strength—that the eyes
of the people might be opened to see and know of
the goodness and glory of God.
23 And it came to pass after they had fasted and
prayed for the space of two days and two nights,
the limbs of Alma received their strength, and he
stood up and began to speak unto them, bidding
them to be of good comfort:
24 For, said he, I have repented of my sins, and have been
redeemed of the Lord; behold I am born of the Spirit.
25 And the Lord said unto me: Marvel not that all
mankind, yea, men and women, all nations, kindreds, tongues and people, must be born again; yea,
born of God, changed from their carnal and fallen
state, to a state of righteousness, being redeemed of
God, becoming his sons and daughters;
26 And thus they become new creatures; and
unless they do this, they can in nowise inherit the
kingdom of God.
27 I say unto you, unless this be the case, they
must be cast off; and this I know, because I was
like to be cast off.
28 Nevertheless, after wading through much tribulation, repenting nigh unto death, the Lord in mercy
hath seen fit to snatch me out of an everlasting
burning, and I am born of God.
29 My soul hath been redeemed from the gall of
bitterness and bonds of iniquity. I was in the darkest
abyss; but now I behold the marvelous light of

---

27:18 ***part asunder***—split apart

27:19 ***dumb***—unable to speak

27:20 ***rehearsed unto***—told

27:21 ***witness***—see

27:22 ***limbs***—arms and legs

When the scriptures speak of "the eyes of [our] understanding" being opened, they aren't saying that we physically open our eyes. Instead, they mean that we understand spiritual things (see D&C 138:11).

27:23 ***bidding***—telling

Fasting can add strength to our righteous prayers (see Matthew 17:14–21).

27:25 ***Marvel***—Wonder
***kindreds***—family groups
***tongues***—languages
***carnal***—earthly

27:26 (24–26) President Ezra Taft Benson said: "When we have undergone this mighty change, which is brought about only through faith in Jesus Christ and through the operation of the Spirit upon us, it is as though we have become a new person. Thus, the change is likened to a new birth. . . . You have forsaken lives of sin, sometimes deep and offensive sin, and through applying the blood of Christ in your lives, have become clean. You have no more disposition to return to your old ways. You are in reality a new person. This is what is meant by a change of heart" ("A Mighty Change of Heart," 4).

27:28 ***tribulation***—trouble and misery

27:29 ***abyss***—pit

The phrase "gall of bitterness and bonds of iniquity" is used four times in the Book of Mormon (see Mosiah 27:29; Alma 41:11; Mormon 8:31; Moroni 8:14). *Gall* was a bitter and sometimes poisonous herb or drink. The word is used in the Old Testament to describe those who turn away from God (see Deuteronomy 29:18). The phrase "bonds of iniquity" refers to the cords or chains of wickedness and sin (see Proverbs 5:22; Isaiah 58:6).

*ALMA THE YOUNGER*, BY ROBERT T. BARRETT

*After his father and the priests had fasted for two days and two nights, "the limbs of Alma received their strength."*

God. My soul was racked with eternal torment; but I am snatched, and my soul is pained no more.

30 I rejected my Redeemer, and denied that which had been spoken of by our fathers; but now that they may foresee that he will come, and that he remembereth every creature of his creating, he will make himself manifest unto all.

31 Yea, every knee shall bow, and every tongue confess before him. Yea, even at the last day, when all men shall stand to be judged of him, then shall they confess that he is God; then shall they confess, who live without God in the world, that the judgment of an everlasting punishment is just upon them; and they shall quake, and tremble, and shrink beneath the glance of his all-searching eye.

## Alma and the Sons of Mosiah Teach the Gospel

32 And now it came to pass that Alma began from this time forward to teach the people, and those who were with Alma at the time the angel appeared unto them, traveling round about through all the land, publishing to all the people the things which they had heard and seen, and preaching the word of God in much tribulation, being greatly persecuted by those who were unbelievers, being smitten by many of them.

33 But notwithstanding all this, they did impart much consolation to the church, confirming their faith, and exhorting them with long-suffering and much travail to keep the commandments of God.

34 And four of them were the sons of Mosiah; and their names were Ammon, and Aaron, and Omner, and Himni; these were the names of the sons of Mosiah.

35 And they traveled throughout all the land of Zarahemla, and among all the people who were under the reign of king Mosiah, zealously striving to repair all the injuries which they had done to the church, confessing all their sins, and publishing all the things which they had seen, and explaining the prophecies and the scriptures to all who desired to hear them.

36 And thus they were instruments in the hands of God in bringing many to the knowledge of the truth, yea, to the knowledge of their Redeemer.

37 And how blessed are they! For they did publish peace; they did publish good tidings of good; and they did declare unto the people that the Lord reigneth.

---

27:29 (28–29) Alma describes the pain of his experience in more detail to his son Helaman in Alma 36:18–20, 23–26. Elder J. Richard Clarke noted that "repentance is not easy. 'Godly sorrow' brings one to the depth of humility. This is why the gift of forgiveness is so sweet and draws the transgressor so close to the Savior with a special bond of affection" ("Confession, a Requirement for Forgiveness," in *Repentance,* 92).

27:30 ***denied***—refused or rejected
***foresee***—understand or anticipate
***manifest***—known

27:31 ***just***—fair

27:32 ***publishing***—making known
***tribulation***—trouble and misery
***smitten***—hit or beaten

27:33 ***impart much consolation to***—share much comfort with
***confirming***—strengthening
***exhorting***—strongly encouraging
***much travail***—many trials

27:34 (32–34) "If you have made a serious mistake in your life and Satan would have you believe that your opportunity for true joy and happiness is past, study the lives of Alma the younger and his companions, the sons of Mosiah. (See Mosiah 27; Alma 5:3–62.)" (Richard G. Scott, "The Power of the Book of Mormon in My Life," 10).

27:35 ***zealously striving***—trying very hard

27:37 ***tidings***—news
***reigneth***—rules

27:37 (35–37) "After conversion comes the desire to share—not so much out of a sense of duty, even though that responsibility falls on the priesthood, but out of a sincere love and appreciation for that which has been received. When such a 'pearl of great price' comes into our lives, we cannot be content just to admire it by ourselves. It must be shared! And here is the great joy and happiness of the gift!" (L. Tom Perry, in Conference Report, April 1984, 106).

## CHAPTER 28

*King Mosiah's sons are cleansed of their past sins and desire to serve missions among the Lamanites. The Lord tells Mosiah to let them go and that many will believe them. They begin their missionary journey about 92 B.C. See what you can learn about the proper attitude we need to have to serve a mission.*

### Mosiah's Sons Desire to Serve Missions

1 NOW it came to pass that after the sons of Mosiah had done all these things, they took a small number with them and returned to their father, the king, and desired of him that he would grant unto them that they might, with these whom they had selected, go up to the land of Nephi that they might preach the things which they had heard, and that they might impart the word of God to their brethren, the Lamanites—
2 That perhaps they might bring them to the knowledge of the Lord their God, and convince them of the iniquity of their fathers; and that perhaps they might cure them of their hatred towards the Nephites, that they might also be brought to rejoice in the Lord their God, that they might become friendly to one another, and that there should be no more contentions in all the land which the Lord their God had given them.
3 Now they were desirous that salvation should be declared to every creature, for they could not bear that any human soul should perish; yea, even the very thoughts that any soul should endure endless torment did cause them to quake and tremble.
4 And thus did the Spirit of the Lord work upon them, for they were the very vilest of sinners. And the Lord saw fit in his infinite mercy to spare them; nevertheless they suffered much anguish of soul because of their iniquities, suffering much and fearing that they should be cast off forever.
5 And it came to pass that they did plead with their father many days that they might go up to the land of Nephi.
6 And king Mosiah went and inquired of the Lord if he should let his sons go up among the Lamanites to preach the word.
7 And the Lord said unto Mosiah: Let them go up, for many shall believe on their words, and they shall have eternal life; and I will deliver thy sons out of the hands of the Lamanites.
8 And it came to pass that Mosiah granted that they might go and do according to their request.
9 And they took their journey into the wilderness to go up to preach the word among the Lamanites; and I shall give an account of their proceedings hereafter.

### King Mosiah Translates the Jaredite Plates

10 Now king Mosiah had no one to confer the kingdom upon, for there was not any of his sons who would accept of the kingdom.
11 Therefore he took the records which were engraven on the plates of brass, and also the plates of Nephi, and all the things which he had kept and preserved according to the commandments of God, after having translated and caused to be written the records which were on the plates of gold which had been found by the people of Limhi, which were delivered to him by the hand of Limhi;

---

28:1 ***grant unto***—allow
***impart***—teach

28:2 ***iniquity***—sins
***contentions***—arguing and fighting

For many generations the Lamanites taught their children to hate the Nephites. They believed they had been wronged by Nephi and others during their journey to the promised land (see Mosiah 10:12–17).

28:3 ***bear***—stand
***perish***—die spiritually
***quake and tremble***—shake with fear

28:4 ***very vilest***—most evil
***infinite***—endless

28:4 (3–4) Jesus Christ declared, "Remember the worth of souls is great in the sight of God," and He "suffered death in the flesh . . . that all men might repent and come unto him" (D&C 18:10–11).

28:6 ***inquired of***—asked

28:7 The Lord promised Mosiah that his sons would be safe and would also receive eternal life for their efforts. What blessings come to missionaries today?

28:9 ***proceedings***—experiences

28:10 ***confer the kingdom upon***—give the responsibility for the kingdom to

28:11 ***preserved***—protected

12 And this he did because of the great anxiety of
his people; for they were desirous beyond measure
to know concerning those people who had been
destroyed.
13 And now he translated them by the means of
those two stones which were fastened into the two
rims of a bow.
14 Now these things were prepared from the
beginning, and were handed down from generation to generation, for the purpose of interpreting
languages;
15 And they have been kept and preserved by the
hand of the Lord, that he should discover to every
creature who should possess the land the iniquities
and abominations of his people;
16 And whosoever has these things is called seer,
after the manner of old times.
17 Now after Mosiah had finished translating these
records, behold, it gave an account of the people
who were destroyed, from the time that they were
destroyed back to the building of the great tower,
at the time the Lord confounded the language of
the people and they were scattered abroad upon
the face of all the earth, yea, and even from that
time back until the creation of Adam.
18 Now this account did cause the people of
Mosiah to mourn exceedingly, yea, they were filled
with sorrow; nevertheless it gave them much
knowledge, in the which they did rejoice.
19 And this account shall be written hereafter; for
behold, it is expedient that all people should know
the things which are written in this account.
20 And now, as I said unto you, that after king
Mosiah had done these things, he took the plates of
brass, and all the things which he had kept, and
conferred them upon Alma, who was the son of
Alma; yea, all the records, and also the interpreters,
and conferred them upon him, and commanded
him that he should keep and preserve them, and
also keep a record of the people, handing them
down from one generation to another, even as they
had been handed down from the time that Lehi left
Jerusalem.

## CHAPTER 29

*Mosiah convinces the people of the dangers of being ruled by a king. The people choose to be led by judges instead of a king. Alma is chosen to be the first chief judge. Look for the dangers of being led by an unrighteous king.*

### Mosiah's Sons Refuse to Be King

1 NOW when Mosiah had done this he sent out
throughout all the land, among all the people,
desiring to know their will concerning who should
be their king.
2 And it came to pass that the voice of the people
came, saying: We are desirous that Aaron thy son
should be our king and our ruler.
3 Now Aaron had gone up to the land of Nephi,
therefore the king could not confer the kingdom
upon him; neither would Aaron take upon him the
kingdom; neither were any of the sons of Mosiah
willing to take upon them the kingdom.
4 Therefore king Mosiah sent again among the
people; yea, even a written word sent he among
the people. And these were the words that were
written, saying:

---

28:12 ***anxiety***—concern

28:14 ***interpreting***—translating

28:15 ***iniquities and abominations***—wickedness

28:16 A seer knows the past, present, and future. He is authorized to see with spiritual eyes things that God has hidden from the world (see 1 Samuel 9:9; Mosiah 8:13).

28:16 (13–16) These "two stones" are also known as the Urim and Thummin (see LDS Bible Dictionary, s.v. "Urim and Thummin," 786–87). They were used to help prophets translate and interpret languages. More than one set of such stones existed and were used anciently by such seers as Abraham and Aaron. Mosiah's seer stones had been sealed up by the brother of Jared (see Ether 3:22–23) and were the same ones used by Joseph Smith in translating the Book of Mormon from the gold plates (see D&C 17:1).

28:17 ***confounded***—confused

28:18 ***mourn exceedingly***—feel very sad

28:19 ***expedient***—necessary or important

28:20 Why do you think it was important to keep a written record and hand it down from one generation to another? How might you benefit if you had a record of your great-grandfather's life?

29:3 ***confer the kingdom upon***—give the responsibility for the kingdom to

5 Behold, O ye my people, or my brethren, for I esteem you as such, I desire that ye should consider the cause which ye are called to consider—for ye are desirous to have a king.
6 Now I declare unto you that he to whom the kingdom doth rightly belong has declined, and will not take upon him the kingdom.
7 And now if there should be another appointed in his stead, behold I fear there would rise contentions among you. And who knoweth but what my son, to whom the kingdom doth belong, should turn to be angry and draw away a part of this people after him, which would cause wars and contentions among you, which would be the cause of shedding much blood and perverting the way of the Lord, yea, and destroy the souls of many people.
8 Now I say unto you let us be wise and consider these things, for we have no right to destroy my son, neither should we have any right to destroy another if he should be appointed in his stead.
9 And if my son should turn again to his pride and vain things he would recall the things which he had said, and claim his right to the kingdom, which would cause him and also this people to commit much sin.

## Mosiah Warns of the Dangers of Being Led by a King

10 And now let us be wise and look forward to these things, and do that which will make for the peace of this people.
11 Therefore I will be your king the remainder of my days; nevertheless, let us appoint judges, to judge this people according to our law; and we will newly arrange the affairs of this people, for we will appoint wise men to be judges, that will judge this people according to the commandments of God.
12 Now it is better that a man should be judged of God than of man, for the judgments of God are always just, but the judgments of man are not always just.
13 Therefore, if it were possible that you could have just men to be your kings, who would establish the laws of God, and judge this people according to his commandments, yea, if ye could have men for your kings who would do even as my father Benjamin did for this people—I say unto you, if this could always be the case then it would be expedient that ye should always have kings to rule over you.
14 And even I myself have labored with all the power and faculties which I have possessed, to teach you the commandments of God, and to establish peace throughout the land, that there should be no wars nor contentions, no stealing, nor plundering, nor murdering, nor any manner of iniquity;
15 And whosoever has committed iniquity, him have I punished according to the crime which he has committed, according to the law which has been given to us by our fathers.
16 Now I say unto you, that because all men are not just it is not expedient that ye should have a king or kings to rule over you.
17 For behold, how much iniquity doth one wicked king cause to be committed, yea, and what great destruction!
18 Yea, remember king Noah, his wickedness and his abominations, and also the wickedness and abominations of his people. Behold what great

---

29:5 **esteem**—value

29:6 **declined**—said no

29:7 **stead**—place
**contentions**—arguing and fighting
**perverting**—changing or distorting

29:9 **vain**—useless
**recall**—take back

29:11 **appoint**—select or choose
**newly arrange the affairs**—make changes in the government

In Old Testament times the people were ruled by judges for several hundred years. An account of these rulers is found in the book of Judges.

29:13 It would only be expedient, or wise, to have kings to rule if you could always be sure that they would be righteous; however, the Lord teaches that men often become wicked when given power over others (see D&C 121:34–36, 39–40).

29:14 Mosiah, like his father, King Benjamin, was a righteous king (see Mosiah 2:14–16). He used his power and faculties (abilities) to help the people avoid wars, contentions, stealing, plundering, and all kinds of iniquity.

29:17 Just as one person can cause much iniquity or sin, one person can also bring about much righteousness. How could you help the people you know and love to be good?

29:18 **abominations**—acts of great evil

destruction did come upon them; and also because of their iniquities they were brought into bondage.
19 And were it not for the interposition of their all-wise Creator, and this because of their sincere repentance, they must unavoidably remain in bondage until now.
20 But behold, he did deliver them because they did humble themselves before him; and because they cried mightily unto him he did deliver them out of bondage; and thus doth the Lord work with his power in all cases among the children of men, extending the arm of mercy towards them that put their trust in him.
21 And behold, now I say unto you, ye cannot dethrone an iniquitous king save it be through much contention, and the shedding of much blood.
22 For behold, he has his friends in iniquity, and he keepeth his guards about him; and he teareth up the laws of those who have reigned in righteousness before him; and he trampleth under his feet the commandments of God;
23 And he enacteth laws, and sendeth them forth among his people, yea, laws after the manner of his own wickedness; and whosoever doth not obey his laws he causeth to be destroyed; and whosoever doth rebel against him he will send his armies against them to war, and if he can he will destroy them; and thus an unrighteous king doth pervert the ways of all righteousness.
24 And now behold I say unto you, it is not expedient that such abominations should come upon you.

## Mosiah Counsels the People to Choose Judges to Rule over Them

25 Therefore, choose you by the voice of this people, judges, that ye may be judged according to the laws which have been given you by our fathers, which are correct, and which were given them by the hand of the Lord.
26 Now it is not common that the voice of the people desireth anything contrary to that which is right; but it is common for the lesser part of the people to desire that which is not right; therefore this shall ye observe and make it your law—to do your business by the voice of the people.
27 And if the time comes that the voice of the people doth choose iniquity, then is the time that the judgments of God will come upon you; yea, then is the time he will visit you with great destruction even as he has hitherto visited this land.
28 And now if ye have judges, and they do not judge you according to the law which has been given, ye can cause that they may be judged of a higher judge.
29 If your higher judges do not judge righteous judgments, ye shall cause that a small number of your lower judges should be gathered together, and they shall judge your higher judges, according to the voice of the people.
30 And I command you to do these things in the fear of the Lord; and I command you to do these things, and that ye have no king; that if these people commit sins and iniquities they shall be answered upon their own heads.

---

29:19 ***interposition***—help or intervention
***unavoidably***—surely

29:20 The Lord forgives and saves those who trust Him. Proverbs 3:5–6 teaches us to "trust in the Lord with all [our] heart . . . and he shall direct [our] paths."

29:21 The prophet Samuel also warned against being ruled by a king. He knew that kings could be removed from their thrones only by fighting and bloodshed (see 1 Samuel 8:10–18).

29:22 ***reigned***—ruled
***trampleth***—walks or stomps

29:23 ***enacteth***—makes

29:24 ***expedient***—good

Like Mosiah, our prophets counsel us today in righteousness. What counsel has the prophet recently given the Church members? How are you striving to follow this counsel?

29:25 Mosiah teaches his people that they should choose their leaders "by the voice of [the] people" and that the leaders should govern according to laws "given them by the hand of the Lord." How would these same principles help your nation or community today?

29:26 ***contrary***—opposite

29:27 ***hitherto***—before now

Is this warning important today? How can you help your nation and community avoid destruction?

29:30 ***answered upon their own heads***—punished for their own sins

31 For behold I say unto you, the sins of many people have been caused by the iniquities of their kings; therefore their iniquities are answered upon the heads of their kings.

32 And now I desire that this inequality should be no more in this land, especially among this my people; but I desire that this land be a land of liberty, and every man may enjoy his rights and privileges alike, so long as the Lord sees fit that we may live and inherit the land, yea, even as long as any of our posterity remains upon the face of the land.

33 And many more things did king Mosiah write unto them, unfolding unto them all the trials and troubles of a righteous king, yea, all the travails of soul for their people, and also all the murmurings of the people to their king; and he explained it all unto them.

34 And he told them that these things ought not to be; but that the burden should come upon all the people, that every man might bear his part.

35 And he also unfolded unto them all the disadvantages they labored under, by having an unrighteous king to rule over them;

36 Yea, all his iniquities and abominations, and all the wars, and contentions, and bloodshed, and the stealing, and the plundering, and the committing of whoredoms, and all manner of iniquities which cannot be enumerated—telling them that these things ought not to be, that they were expressly repugnant to the commandments of God.

## Alma Is Appointed As the First Chief Judge

37 And now it came to pass, after king Mosiah had sent these things forth among the people they were convinced of the truth of his words.

38 Therefore they relinquished their desires for a king, and became exceedingly anxious that every man should have an equal chance throughout all the land; yea, and every man expressed a willingness to answer for his own sins.

39 Therefore, it came to pass that they assembled themselves together in bodies throughout the land, to cast in their voices concerning who should be their judges, to judge them according to the law which had been given them; and they were exceedingly rejoiced because of the liberty which had been granted unto them.

40 And they did wax strong in love towards Mosiah; yea, they did esteem him more than any other man; for they did not look upon him as a tyrant who was seeking for gain, yea, for that lucre which doth corrupt the soul; for he had not exacted riches of them, neither had he delighted in the shedding of blood; but he had established peace in the land, and he had granted unto his people that they should be delivered from all manner of bondage; therefore they did esteem him, yea, exceedingly, beyond measure.

41 And it came to pass that they did appoint judges to rule over them, or to judge them according to the law; and this they did throughout all the land.

42 And it came to pass that Alma was appointed to be the first chief judge, he being also the high priest, his father having conferred the office upon him, and having given him the charge concerning all the affairs of the church.

43 And now it came to pass that Alma did walk in the ways of the Lord, and he did keep his commandments, and he did judge righteous judgments; and there was continual peace through the land.

---

29:33 ***travails of soul***—pains of his heart

29:34 ***ought not to***—should not
***burden***—heavy load

29:36 ***whoredoms***—wickedness and immorality
***enumerated***—listed
***expressly repugnant***—clearly disobedient

29:38 ***relinquished***—gave up

29:39 ***bodies***—groups
***liberty***—freedom

29:40 ***wax***—grow
***tyrant***—wicked and cruel leader
***lucre***—wealth
***exacted***—demanded

"True pupils will always revere [honor] a true tutor!" (Neal A. Maxwell, *We Will Prove Them Herewith*, 24).

29:42 ***conferred the office upon***—given the office to

29:43 (42–43) "Alma, by the voice of the people, 'was appointed to be the first chief judge.' In this capacity he was both chief justice and administrative head of state. As chief justice, the record says, 'he did judge righteous judgments.' (Mosiah 29:42–43.)" (Marion G. Romney, *Learning for the Eternities*, 67).

44 And thus commenced the reign of the judges
throughout all the land of Zarahemla, among all the
people who were called the Nephites; and Alma
was the first and chief judge.
45 And now it came to pass that his father died,
being eighty and two years old, having lived to fulfil the commandments of God.

46 And it came to pass that Mosiah died also, in
the thirty and third year of his reign, being sixty and
three years old; making in the whole, five hundred
and nine years from the time Lehi left Jerusalem.
47 And thus ended the reign of the kings over the
people of Nephi; and thus ended the days of Alma,
who was the founder of their church.

---

29:45 (43–45) Do you know anyone today that can be described as Alma is described in these verses? How would you like these comments made about your life?

29:47 ***founder***—builder

# THE BOOK OF ALMA

## THE SON OF ALMA

*Alma, often called Alma the Younger, became a powerful missionary and teacher after his conversion (see Mosiah 27). The book of Alma covers less than forty years of history, from about 91 B.C. to 53 B.C. The first half of the book tells of the missionary labors of Alma the Younger and the sons of King Mosiah. The second half tells of the terrible wars between the Lamanites and the Nephites. An important teaching in the book of Alma is that the word of God, which includes the scriptures, is more powerful than the sword in bringing people to the Lord. Rejection of God's word often leads, however, to war and bloodshed.*

*The account of Alma, who was the son of Alma, the first and chief judge over the people of Nephi, and also the high priest over the Church. An account of the reign of the judges, and the wars and contentions among the people. And also an account of a war between the Nephites and the Lamanites, according to the record of Alma, the first and chief judge.**

### CHAPTER 1

*Nehor, an enemy to the Church, tries to lead the people away from the truth with false teachings and with the sword. He is executed for his crime. Notice the effect of Nehor's teachings on the Church.*

#### NEHOR TEACHES FALSE DOCTRINE AND SLAYS GIDEON

1 NOW it came to pass that in the first year of the
reign of the judges over the people of Nephi, from
this time forward, king Mosiah having gone the way
of all the earth, having warred a good warfare,
walking uprightly before God, leaving none to
reign in his stead; nevertheless he had established
laws, and they were acknowledged by the people;
therefore they were obliged to abide by the laws
which he had made.
2 And it came to pass that in the first year of the
reign of Alma in the judgment-seat, there was a
man brought before him to be judged, a man who
was large, and was noted for his much strength.
3 And he had gone about among the people,
preaching to them that which he termed to be the
word of God, bearing down against the church;
declaring unto the people that every priest and
teacher ought to become popular; and they ought
not to labor with their hands, but that they ought to
be supported by the people.
4 And he also testified unto the people that all
mankind should be saved at the last day, and that

---

* This introduction to the book of Alma was translated from the Book of Mormon plates.

1:1 At this point, time begins to be measured from the beginning of the reign of the judges. This ends five hundred years of rule by Nephite kings (see Jacob 1:9–11).

***gone the way of all the earth***—died
***walking uprightly before God***—keeping the Lord's commandments

1:2 ***judgment-seat***—office of chief judge

1:3 ***bearing down***—speaking out

"Nehor's words appealed to many of the people; they were easy words because they required neither obedience nor sacrifice. As we face many decisions in life, the easy and popular messages of the world will seem appealing. But when these worldly messages contradict gospel teachings and the still, small voice of the Spirit, we can be 100 percent confident they are wrong. Still, it will take great courage to choose the right" (L. Tom Perry, *Living with Enthusiasm,* 108–9).

1:4 What we believe affects the way we behave. Nehor teaches that all men will be saved at the last day no matter what they have done. If a person really believed this, how do you think he would behave?

= Word Help | = A Closer Look
= More Light | = Ponder This

Words in pink are explained in the Glossary.

they need not fear nor tremble, but that they might
lift up their heads and rejoice; for the Lord had created all men, and had also redeemed all men; and,
in the end, all men should have eternal life.
5 And it came to pass that he did teach these
things so much that many did believe on his words,
even so many that they began to support him and
give him money.
6 And he began to be lifted up in the pride of his
heart, and to wear very costly apparel, yea, and
even began to establish a church after the manner
of his preaching.
7 And it came to pass as he was going, to preach
to those who believed on his word, he met a man
who belonged to the church of God, yea, even one
of their teachers; and he began to contend with him
sharply, that he might lead away the people of the
church; but the man withstood him, admonishing
him with the words of God.
8 Now the name of the man was Gideon; and it
was he who was an instrument in the hands of God
in delivering the people of Limhi out of bondage.
9 Now, because Gideon withstood him with the
words of God he was wroth with Gideon, and drew
his sword and began to smite him. Now Gideon
being stricken with many years, therefore he was
not able to withstand his blows, therefore he was
slain by the sword.
10 And the man who slew him was taken by the
people of the church, and was brought before
Alma, to be judged according to the crimes which
he had committed.

## Nehor Is Tried and Put to Death

11 And it came to pass that he stood before Alma
and pleaded for himself with much boldness.
12 But Alma said unto him: Behold, this is the
first time that priestcraft has been introduced
among this people. And behold, thou art not only
guilty of priestcraft, but hast endeavored to
enforce it by the sword; and were priestcraft to be
enforced among this people it would prove their
entire destruction.
13 And thou hast shed the blood of a righteous
man, yea, a man who has done much good among
this people; and were we to spare thee his blood
would come upon us for vengeance.
14 Therefore thou art condemned to die, according to the law which has been given us by Mosiah,
our last king; and it has been acknowledged by this
people; therefore this people must abide by the
law.
15 And it came to pass that they took him; and his
name was Nehor; and they carried him upon the
top of the hill Manti, and there he was caused, or
rather did acknowledge, between the heavens and
the earth, that what he had taught to the people
was contrary to the word of God; and there he suffered an ignominious death.

## Priestcraft, False Doctrine, and Persecution Spread Among the Nephites

16 Nevertheless, this did not put an end to the
spreading of priestcraft through the land; for there
were many who loved the vain things of the world,
and they went forth preaching false doctrines; and
this they did for the sake of riches and honor.
17 Nevertheless, they durst not lie, if it were
known, for fear of the law, for liars were punished;
therefore they pretended to preach according to
their belief; and now the law could have no power
on any man for his belief.

---

1:6 Elder Bruce R. McConkie points out that "the Nephite prophets repeatedly indentified the wearing of costly clothing with apostasy and failure to live by gospel standards. (Jacob 2:13; Alma 1:6, 32; 4:6; 5:53; 31:27–28; 4 Nephi 24; Mormon 8:36–37.)" (*Doctrinal New Testament Commentary* 3:79).

1:7 ***contend with him***—argue with him
***withstood***—opposed or resisted
***admonishing***—strongly warning

1:8 ***bondage***—slavery or captivity

1:9 ***wroth***—angry
***stricken with many years***—very old

Gideon, a man of great courage, uses the scriptures to oppose Nehor's wicked teachings. How do people feel when they are caught in their lies?

1:12 Nephi defines priestcraft as preaching for personal gain and praise (see 2 Nephi 26:29). This is the first time that priestcraft appears in the Book of Mormon. Alma warns that this terrible sin can destroy the Nephites.

1:13 ***vengeance***—punishment

1:15 ***ignominious***—shameful

1:17 ***durst***—dared

ALMA THE YOUNGER, BY SCOTT SNOW

*Alma knew that if priestcraft became a part of Nephite society "it would prove their entire destruction." He was faced with the problem of how to put an end to the wicked practice.*

18 And they durst not steal, for fear of the law, for
such were punished; neither durst they rob, nor murder, for he that murdered was punished unto death.
19 But it came to pass that whosoever did not
belong to the church of God began to persecute
those that did belong to the church of God, and had
taken upon them the name of Christ.
20 Yea, they did persecute them, and afflict them
with all manner of words, and this because of their
humility; because they were not proud in their own
eyes, and because they did impart the word of God,
one with another, without money and without price.
21 Now there was a strict law among the people
of the church, that there should not any man,
belonging to the church, arise and persecute those
that did not belong to the church, and that there
should be no persecution among themselves.
22 Nevertheless, there were many among them
who began to be proud, and began to contend
warmly with their adversaries, even unto blows;
yea, they would smite one another with their fists.

## Church Members Who Are Patient in Trials and Suffering Are Blessed

23 Now this was in the second year of the reign
of Alma, and it was a cause of much affliction to the
church; yea, it was the cause of much trial with the
church.
24 For the hearts of many were hardened, and their
names were blotted out, that they were remembered no more among the people of God. And also
many withdrew themselves from among them.
25 Now this was a great trial to those that did
stand fast in the faith; nevertheless, they were steadfast and immovable in keeping the commandments
of God, and they bore with patience the persecution which was heaped upon them.
26 And when the priests left their labor to impart
the word of God unto the people, the people also
left their labors to hear the word of God. And when
the priest had imparted unto them the word of God
they all returned again diligently unto their labors;
and the priest, not esteeming himself above his
hearers, for the preacher was no better than the
hearer, neither was the teacher any better than the
learner; and thus they were all equal, and they did
all labor, every man according to his strength.
27 And they did impart of their substance, every
man according to that which he had, to the poor,
and the needy, and the sick, and the afflicted; and
they did not wear costly apparel, yet they were neat
and comely.
28 And thus they did establish the affairs of the
church; and thus they began to have continual
peace again, notwithstanding all their persecutions.
29 And now, because of the steadiness of the
church they began to be exceedingly rich, having
abundance of all things whatsoever they stood in
need—an abundance of flocks and herds, and
fatlings of every kind, and also abundance of grain,
and of gold, and of silver, and of precious things,
and abundance of silk and fine-twined linen, and
all manner of good homely cloth.

---

1:18 (17–18) Nephite law only punished people for their acts, not for their beliefs. Why is it important that people be given the freedom to choose their own beliefs?

1:19 ***persecute***—mistreat or abuse

*Christ* is a Greek word meaning "the Anointed One"; the Hebrew word with the same meaning is *Messiah.* Jesus is the Christ—the one chosen, set apart, and sent by God to save us (see LDS Bible Dictionary, s.v. "Christ," 633).

1:20 ***impart***—give or spread

1:21 Alma's people are forbidden to persecute those who do not belong to the Church. How should you treat people who are not members of The Church of Jesus Christ of Latter-day Saints?

1:22 ***contend warmly***—argue angrily

1:23 ***affliction***—suffering

1:24 ***blotted out***—erased or removed

1:25 The humble Church members suffered persecution from those who were not members (verses 19–20). An even greater sorrow was caused when some Church members became so angry over the persecution that they would fight each other with words and fists. Their hearts became hard, they lost the Spirit, and they left the Church. How would you feel if someone you loved fell away from the Church? What could you do to help them come back?

1:26 ***impart***—give or spread
***esteeming***—valuing

1:27 ***comely***—appropriate and pleasing to look at

1:29 ***an abundance***—plenty
***homely***—plain

30 And thus, in their prosperous circumstances, they did not send away any who were naked, or that were hungry, or that were athirst, or that were sick, or that had not been nourished; and they did not set their hearts upon riches; therefore they were liberal to all, both old and young, both bond and free, both male and female, whether out of the church or in the church, having no respect to persons as to those who stood in need.

31 And thus they did prosper and become far more wealthy than those who did not belong to their church.

32 For those who did not belong to their church did indulge themselves in sorceries, and in idolatry or idleness, and in babblings, and in envyings and strife; wearing costly apparel; being lifted up in the pride of their own eyes; persecuting, lying, thieving, robbing, committing whoredoms, and murdering, and all manner of wickedness; nevertheless, the law was put in force upon all those who did transgress it, inasmuch as it was possible.

33 And it came to pass that by thus exercising the law upon them, every man suffering according to that which he had done, they became more still, and durst not commit any wickedness if it were known; therefore, there was much peace among the people of Nephi until the fifth year of the reign of the judges.

## CHAPTER 2

*Priestcraft continues to trouble the Nephites. Amlici, "a very cunning man," seeks to destroy the Church and make himself king over the people. Watch for how the Lord preserves His people when they trust in Him.*

### Amlici Is Rejected as King

1 AND it came to pass in the commencement of the fifth year of their reign there began to be a contention among the people; for a certain man, being called Amlici, he being a very cunning man, yea, a wise man as to the wisdom of the world, he being after the order of the man that slew Gideon by the sword, who was executed according to the law—

2 Now this Amlici had, by his cunning, drawn away much people after him; even so much that they began to be very powerful; and they began to endeavor to establish Amlici to be a king over the people.

3 Now this was alarming to the people of the church, and also to all those who had not been drawn away after the persuasions of Amlici; for they knew that according to their law that such things must be established by the voice of the people.

4 Therefore, if it were possible that Amlici should gain the voice of the people, he, being a wicked man, would deprive them of their rights and privileges of the church; for it was his intent to destroy the church of God.

5 And it came to pass that the people assembled themselves together throughout all the land, every man according to his mind, whether it were for or against Amlici, in separate bodies, having much dispute and wonderful contentions one with another.

6 And thus they did assemble themselves together to cast in their voices concerning the matter; and they were laid before the judges.

7 And it came to pass that the voice of the people came against Amlici, that he was not made king over the people.

---

1:30 ***prosperous circumstances***—blessed and wealthy condition
***liberal***—generous

1:31 (29–31) Elder Dean L. Larsen taught that the "scriptures contain many evidences of the Lord's willingness to prosper his people with the riches of the earth when they demonstrate that they will use this abundance prudently [wisely], with humility and charity, always acknowledging the source of their blessings" (in Conference Report, October 1992, 57).

1:32 ***indulge themselves in***—give in to or practice
***idolatry***—worshiping false gods
***babblings***—speaking foolishness or gossiping
***envyings and strife***—jealousy and arguments
***whoredoms***—immorality

2:1 ***reign***—rule
***a contention***—argument
***cunning***—tricky

2:2 ***endeavor to establish***—try to make

2:3 ***persuasions***—convincing ideas

2:4 ***deprive them of***—take from them

2:5 ***dispute***—to argue about
***wonderful***—astonishing or surprising

2:6 The term "cast in their voices" is a phrase that means to shout or speak your opinion. Here, it means the people expressed their voice or vote on a subject.

## Amlici Causes a War Between Nephite Groups

8 Now this did cause much joy in the hearts of those who were against him; but Amlici did stir up those who were in his favor to anger against those who were not in his favor.

9 And it came to pass that they gathered themselves together, and did consecrate Amlici to be their king.

10 Now when Amlici was made king over them he commanded them that they should take up arms against their brethren; and this he did that he might subject them to him.

11 Now the people of Amlici were distinguished by the name of Amlici, being called Amlicites; and the remainder were called Nephites, or the people of God.

12 Therefore the people of the Nephites were aware of the intent of the Amlicites, and therefore they did prepare to meet them; yea, they did arm themselves with swords, and with cimeters, and with bows, and with arrows, and with stones, and with slings, and with all manner of weapons of war, of every kind.

13 And thus they were prepared to meet the Amlicites at the time of their coming. And there were appointed captains, and higher captains, and chief captains, according to their numbers.

14 And it came to pass that Amlici did arm his men with all manner of weapons of war of every kind; and he also appointed rulers and leaders over his people, to lead them to war against their brethren.

15 And it came to pass that the Amlicites came upon the hill Amnihu, which was east of the river Sidon, which ran by the land of Zarahemla, and there they began to make war with the Nephites.

16 Now Alma, being the chief judge and the governor of the people of Nephi, therefore he went up with his people, yea, with his captains, and chief captains, yea, at the head of his armies, against the Amlicites to battle.

17 And they began to slay the Amlicites upon the hill east of Sidon. And the Amlicites did contend with the Nephites with great strength, insomuch that many of the Nephites did fall before the Amlicites.

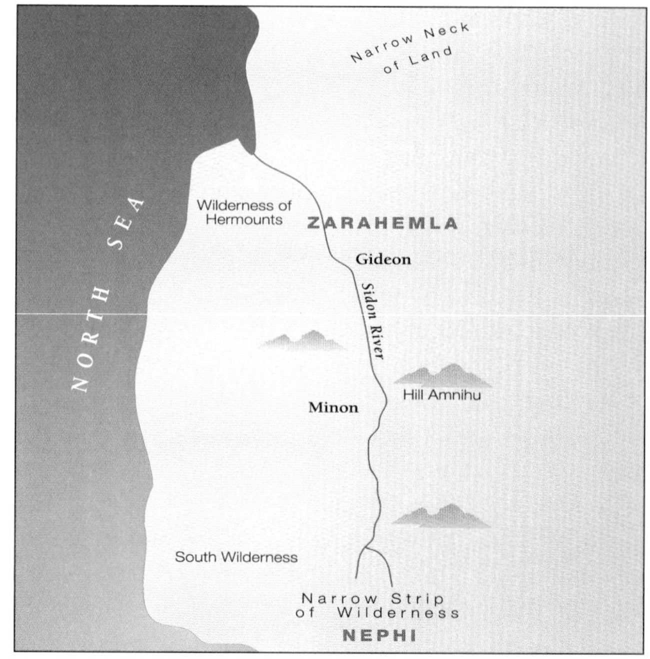


*The hill Amnihu was "east of the river Sidon, which ran by the land of Zarahemla."*

18 Nevertheless the Lord did strengthen the hand of the Nephites, that they slew the Amlicites with great slaughter, that they began to flee before them.

19 And it came to pass that the Nephites did pursue the Amlicites all that day, and did slay them with much slaughter, insomuch that there were slain of the Amlicites twelve thousand five hundred thirty and two souls; and there were slain of the Nephites six thousand five hundred sixty and two souls.

20 And it came to pass that when Alma could pursue the Amlicites no longer he caused that his people should pitch their tents in the valley of Gideon, the valley being called after that Gideon who was slain by the hand of Nehor with the sword; and in this valley the Nephites did pitch their tents for the night.

---

2:9 **_consecrate_**—appoint

2:10 **_arms_**—weapons

2:11 **_distinguished_**—identified

2:12 **_intent_**—purpose or desire

2:16 **_at the head_**—in front

2:17 **_did contend_**—fought

2:19 **_pursue_**—chase

In one day, nineteen thousand Amlicites and Nephites died in battle. Could this great tragedy have been avoided? Why do people and nations fight with one another?

21 And Alma sent spies to follow the remnant of
the Amlicites, that he might know of their plans and
their plots, whereby he might guard himself against
them, that he might preserve his people from being
destroyed.
22 Now those whom he had sent out to watch the
camp of the Amlicites were called Zeram, and
Amnor, and Manti, and Limher; these were they
who went out with their men to watch the camp of
the Amlicites.
23 And it came to pass that on the morrow they
returned into the camp of the Nephites in great
haste, being greatly astonished, and struck with
much fear, saying:

### The Amlicites Join the Lamanites but Are Defeated by the Nephites

24 Behold, we followed the camp of the Amlicites,
and to our great astonishment, in the land of Minon,
above the land of Zarahemla, in the course of the
land of Nephi, we saw a numerous host of the
Lamanites; and behold, the Amlicites have joined
them;
25 And they are upon our brethren in that land;
and they are fleeing before them with their flocks,
and their wives, and their children, towards our
city; and except we make haste they obtain possession of our city, and our fathers, and our wives, and
our children be slain.
26 And it came to pass that the people of Nephi
took their tents, and departed out of the valley of
Gideon towards their city, which was the city of
Zarahemla.
27 And behold, as they were crossing the river
Sidon, the Lamanites and the Amlicites, being as
numerous almost, as it were, as the sands of the
sea, came upon them to destroy them.
28 Nevertheless, the Nephites being strengthened
by the hand of the Lord, having prayed mightily to
him that he would deliver them out of the hands of
their enemies, therefore the Lord did hear their
cries, and did strengthen them, and the Lamanites
and the Amlicites did fall before them.

### Alma and His People Drive the Amlicites and Lamanites from the Land

29 And it came to pass that Alma fought with
Amlici with the sword, face to face; and they did
contend mightily, one with another.
30 And it came to pass that Alma, being a man of
God, being exercised with much faith, cried, saying:
O Lord, have mercy and spare my life, that I may
be an instrument in thy hands to save and preserve
this people.
31 Now when Alma had said these words he contended again with Amlici; and he was strengthened,
insomuch that he slew Amlici with the sword.
32 And he also contended with the king of the
Lamanites; but the king of the Lamanites fled back
from before Alma and sent his guards to contend
with Alma.
33 But Alma, with his guards, contended with the
guards of the king of the Lamanites until he slew
and drove them back.
34 And thus he cleared the ground, or rather the
bank, which was on the west of the river Sidon,
throwing the bodies of the Lamanites who had
been slain into the waters of Sidon, that thereby his

2:21 W ***the remnant***—those that were left

2:23 W ***in great haste***—with great speed

2:24 W ***a numerous host***—large numbers

2:25 W ***obtain possession***—get control

2:30 W ***exercised***—inspired

PHOTOGRAPH BY EDWIN M. WOOLLEY

*This river in Sumadarow Canyon has been identified by some as a possible site for the river the Nephites called Sidon.*

people might have room to cross and contend with the Lamanites and the Amlicites on the west side of the river Sidon.

35 And it came to pass that when they had all crossed the river Sidon that the Lamanites and the Amlicites began to flee before them, notwithstanding they were so numerous that they could not be numbered.

36 And they fled before the Nephites towards the wilderness which was west and north, away beyond the borders of the land; and the Nephites did pursue them with their might, and did slay them.

37 Yea, they were met on every hand, and slain and driven, until they were scattered on the west, and on the north, until they had reached the wilderness, which was called Hermounts; and it was that part of the wilderness which was infested by wild and ravenous beasts.

38 And it came to pass that many died in the wilderness of their wounds, and were devoured by those beasts and also the vultures of the air; and their bones have been found, and have been heaped up on the earth.

## CHAPTER 3

*The Nephites have just finished fighting a terrible war with the Lamanites because of the wickedness of the Amlicites. Look for what Mormon teaches us about what happens to those who choose wickedness.*

### *The Many Nephites Who Died in Battle Are Buried*

1 AND it came to pass that the Nephites who were not slain by the weapons of war, after having buried those who had been slain—now the number of the slain were not numbered, because of the greatness of their number—after they had finished burying their dead they all returned to their lands, and to their houses, and their wives, and their children.

2 Now many women and children had been slain with the sword, and also many of their flocks and their herds; and also many of their fields of grain were destroyed, for they were trodden down by the hosts of men.

3 And now as many of the Lamanites and the Amlicites who had been slain upon the bank of the river Sidon were cast into the waters of Sidon; and behold their bones are in the depths of the sea, and they are many.

### *The Amlicites Mark Themselves and Are Cursed Like the Lamanites*

4 And the Amlicites were distinguished from the Nephites, for they had marked themselves with red in their foreheads after the manner of the Lamanites; nevertheless they had not shorn their heads like unto the Lamanites.

5 Now the heads of the Lamanites were shorn; and they were naked, save it were skin which was girded about their loins, and also their armor, which was girded about them, and their bows, and their arrows, and their stones, and their slings, and so forth.

6 And the skins of the Lamanites were dark, according to the mark which was set upon their fathers, which was a curse upon them because of their transgression and their rebellion against their brethren, who consisted of Nephi, Jacob, and Joseph, and Sam, who were just and holy men.

---

2:35 ***notwithstanding***—even though

2:36 ***wilderness***—wild land with very few people

2:37 ***infested by***—full of
***ravenous***—very hungry

2:38 ***devoured***—eaten up

3:2 ***trodden down***—trampled
***hosts***—large number

3:4 ***distinguished***—made different
***shorn***—shaved

The Amlicites marked their foreheads with red "after the manner of the Lamanites." Some have suggested that this passage provides "a clue concerning the origin of painted war faces among this people, which continued to the coming of the white man some 1600 years later" (Daniel H. Ludlow, *A Companion to Your Study of the Book of Mormon,* 195).

3:5 ***girded***—fastened or worn

3:6 ***transgression***—disobedience

A curse is a punishment from God. Laman and Lemuel were punished for rebelling against their righteous father and brethren (see 1 Nephi 2:23; 2 Nephi 5:21–24). They were "cut off from the presence of the Lord" (2 Nephi 5:20). This punishment continued with the Lamanites only as long as they rebelled against God (see Words of Mormon 1:8; Mormon 5:17).

7 And their brethren sought to destroy them, therefore they were cursed; and the Lord God set a mark
upon them, yea, upon Laman and Lemuel, and also
the sons of Ishmael, and Ishmaelitish women.
8 And this was done that their seed might be distinguished from the seed of their brethren, that
thereby the Lord God might preserve his people,
that they might not mix and believe in incorrect traditions which would prove their destruction.
9 And it came to pass that whosoever did mingle
his seed with that of the Lamanites did bring the
same curse upon his seed.
10 Therefore, whosoever suffered himself to be
led away by the Lamanites was called under that
head, and there was a mark set upon him.
11 And it came to pass that whosoever would not
believe in the tradition of the Lamanites, but
believed those records which were brought out of
the land of Jerusalem, and also in the tradition of
their fathers, which were correct, who believed in
the commandments of God and kept them, were
called the Nephites, or the people of Nephi, from
that time forth—
12 And it is they who have kept the records which
are true of their people, and also of the people of
the Lamanites.
13 Now we will return again to the Amlicites, for
they also had a mark set upon them; yea, they set
the mark upon themselves, yea, even a mark of red
upon their foreheads.
14 Thus the word of God is fulfilled, for these are
the words which he said to Nephi: Behold, the
Lamanites have I cursed, and I will set a mark on
them that they and their seed may be separated
from thee and thy seed, from this time henceforth
and forever, except they repent of their wickedness
and turn to me that I may have mercy upon them.
15 And again: I will set a mark upon him that min-
gleth his seed with thy brethren, that they may be
cursed also.
16 And again: I will set a mark upon him that
fighteth against thee and thy seed.
17 And again, I say he that departeth from thee
shall no more be called thy seed; and I will bless
thee, and whomsoever shall be called thy seed,
henceforth and forever; and these were the
promises of the Lord unto Nephi and to his
seed.
18 Now the Amlicites knew not that they were fulfilling the words of God when they began to mark
themselves in their foreheads; nevertheless they
had come out in open rebellion against God; therefore it was expedient that the curse should fall upon
them.
19 Now I would that ye should see that they
brought upon themselves the curse; and even so
doth every man that is cursed bring upon himself
his own condemnation.

## The Nephites Drive Away Another Lamanite Army

20 Now it came to pass that not many days after
the battle which was fought in the land of
Zarahemla, by the Lamanites and the Amlicites, that
there was another army of the Lamanites came in
upon the people of Nephi, in the same place where
the first army met the Amlicites.
21 And it came to pass that there was an army sent
to drive them out of their land.
22 Now Alma himself being afflicted with a
wound did not go up to battle at this time against
the Lamanites;
23 But he sent up a numerous army against them;
and they went up and slew many of the Lamanites,
and drove the remainder of them out of the borders
of their land.
24 And then they returned again and began to
establish peace in the land, being troubled no more
for a time with their enemies.
25 Now all these things were done, yea, all these
wars and contentions were commenced and ended
in the fifth year of the reign of the judges.

3:8 ***seed***—descendants, meaning children, grandchildren and so on

3:9 ***mingle his seed***—marry and have children

3:10 ***was called under that head***—became a part of that group

3:18 ***expedient***—necessary

3:19 ***condemnation***—punishment

3:22 ***being afflicted***—suffering

3:25 ***commenced***—begun

26 And in one year were thousands and tens of thousands of souls sent to the eternal world, that they might reap their rewards according to their works, whether they were good or whether they were bad, to reap eternal happiness or eternal misery, according to the spirit which they listed to obey, whether it be a good spirit or a bad one.

27 For every man receiveth wages of him whom he listeth to obey, and this according to the words of the spirit of prophecy; therefore let it be according to the truth. And thus endeth the fifth year of the reign of the judges.

## CHAPTER 4

*Alma gives up his job as chief judge, or as leader of his country, to spend all his time preaching the word of God to members of the Church. Look for reasons why Alma felt it was necessary to spend all of his time preaching to the people.*

### *Many Nephites Are Humbled Because of the War and Are Baptized into the Church*

1 NOW it came to pass in the sixth year of the reign of the judges over the people of Nephi, there were no contentions nor wars in the land of Zarahemla;

2 But the people were afflicted, yea, greatly afflicted for the loss of their brethren, and also for the loss of their flocks and herds, and also for the loss of their fields of grain, which were trodden under foot and destroyed by the Lamanites.

3 And so great were their afflictions that every soul had cause to mourn; and they believed that it was the judgments of God sent upon them because of their wickedness and their abominations; therefore they were awakened to a remembrance of their duty.

4 And they began to establish the church more fully; yea, and many were baptized in the waters of Sidon and were joined to the church of God; yea, they were baptized by the hand of Alma, who had been consecrated the high priest over the people of the church, by the hand of his father Alma.

5 And it came to pass in the seventh year of the reign of the judges there were about three thousand five hundred souls that united themselves to the church of God and were baptized. And thus ended the seventh year of the reign of the judges over the people of Nephi; and there was continual peace in all that time.

### *Many Church Members Become Rich, Proud, and Wicked*

6 And it came to pass in the eighth year of the reign of the judges, that the people of the church began to wax proud, because of their exceeding

---

3:26 ***eternal world***—spirit world
***reap***—receive
***listed***—chose

3:27 ***wages***—rewards

3:27 (26–27) Mormon testifies that in the next life the wicked receive eternal misery and the righteous have eternal happiness. What are you doing right now to choose eternal happiness instead of eternal misery?

4:1 ***contentions***—arguments or fights

4:2 ***were afflicted***—suffered
***trodden***—stomped down

4:3 ***soul***—person
***mourn***—feel sad or cry
***abominations***—acts of great evil
***were awakened to a rememberance of***—once again remembered

The Nephites decided to do good because they knew they were being punished for the wicked things they had done. Is that the only reason to be good? Why do you choose to do good?

4:4 ***establish***—organize and strengthen
***consecrated***—ordained

4:6 ***wax***—grow

*A modern Guatemalan woman in her humble native dress. Clothing is often an outward expression of who we are. In Alma's day the humble followers of Christ were persecuted by the rich and proud.*

PHOTOGRAPH BY EDWIN M. WOOLLEY

riches, and their fine silks, and their fine-twined
linen, and because of their many flocks and herds,
and their gold and their silver, and all manner of
precious things, which they had obtained by their
industry; and in all these things were they lifted up
in the pride of their eyes, for they began to wear
very costly apparel.
7 Now this was the cause of much affliction to
Alma, yea, and to many of the people whom Alma
had consecrated to be teachers, and priests, and
elders over the church; yea, many of them were
sorely grieved for the wickedness which they saw
had begun to be among their people.
8 For they saw and beheld with great sorrow that
the people of the church began to be lifted up in
the pride of their eyes, and to set their hearts upon
riches and upon the vain things of the world, that
they began to be scornful, one towards another,
and they began to persecute those that did not
believe according to their own will and pleasure.
9 And thus, in this eighth year of the reign of the
judges, there began to be great contentions among
the people of the church; yea, there were envyings,
and strife, and malice, and persecutions, and pride,
even to exceed the pride of those who did not
belong to the church of God.
10 And thus ended the eighth year of the reign of
the judges; and the wickedness of the church was a
great stumbling-block to those who did not belong
to the church; and thus the church began to fail in
its progress.
11 And it came to pass in the commencement of
the ninth year, Alma saw the wickedness of the
church, and he saw also that the example of the
church began to lead those who were unbelievers
on from one piece of iniquity to another, thus
bringing on the destruction of the people.
12 Yea, he saw great inequality among the people,
some lifting themselves up with their pride, despising others, turning their backs upon the needy and
the naked and those who were hungry, and those
who were athirst, and those who were sick and
afflicted.
13 Now this was a great cause for lamentations
among the people, while others were abasing
themselves, succoring those who stood in need of
their succor, such as imparting their substance to
the poor and the needy, feeding the hungry, and
suffering all manner of afflictions, for Christ's sake,
who should come according to the spirit of
prophecy;
14 Looking forward to that day, thus retaining a
remission of their sins; being filled with great joy
because of the resurrection of the dead, according
to the will and power and deliverance of Jesus
Christ from the bands of death.

---

4:6 ***fine-twined linen***—finely woven cloth
***industry***—energy and hard work
***costly apparel***—expensive clothing

4:7 ***sorely grieved***—very sad

4:8 ***vain***—useless or foolish
***persecute***—mistreat and abuse

Alma and the righteous people were sad because many of the members of the Church began to scorn, or to dislike, and even hate other members of the Church. How should you think about and treat other people?

4:8 (6–8) President Ezra Taft Benson taught, "In the scriptures there is no such thing as righteous pride" (in Conference Report, April 1989, 3).

4:9 ***envyings***—desires to have others' possessions
***strife, and malice***—arguments and hatred
***to exceed***—more than

4:10 A stumbling-block is something that is in the way and causes people to stumble as they pass. The wickedness of the members of the Church was causing nonmembers to stumble or to think that it was all right to sin. What can you do to make sure you are never a stumbling-block to nonmembers?

4:11 ***commencement***—beginning
***iniquity***—sin

4:12 ***despising***—hating

In Alma 34:28–29, Alma explains that if members of the Church do not take care of the poor and the needy, none of the good things they do will help them get into heaven.

4:13 ***lamentations***—sadness and crying
***abasing***—humbling
***succoring***—comforting and helping
***imparting***—sharing or giving
***substance***—belongings and wealth

4:14 ***retaining***—keeping
***remission***—forgiveness

### A New Chief Judge Is Chosen to Replace Alma

15 And now it came to pass that Alma, having seen the afflictions of the humble followers of God, and the persecutions which were heaped upon them by the remainder of his people, and seeing all their inequality, began to be very sorrowful; nevertheless the Spirit of the Lord did not fail him.
16 And he selected a wise man who was among the elders of the church, and gave him power according to the voice of the people, that he might have power to enact laws according to the laws which had been given, and to put them in force according to the wickedness and the crimes of the people.
17 Now this man's name was Nephihah, and he was appointed chief judge; and he sat in the judgment-seat to judge and to govern the people.
18 Now Alma did not grant unto him the office of being high priest over the church, but he retained the office of high priest unto himself; but he delivered the judgment-seat unto Nephihah.

### Alma Spends His Time Preaching the Word of God and Bearing Testimony to the People

19 And this he did that he himself might go forth among his people, or among the people of Nephi, that he might preach the word of God unto them, to stir them up in remembrance of their duty, and that he might pull down, by the word of God, all the pride and craftiness and all the contentions which were among his people, seeing no way that he might reclaim them save it were in bearing down in pure testimony against them.
20 And thus in the commencement of the ninth year of the reign of the judges over the people of Nephi, Alma delivered up the judgment-seat to Nephihah, and confined himself wholly to the high priesthood of the holy order of God, to the testimony of the word, according to the spirit of revelation and prophecy.

*The words which Alma, the High Priest according to the holy order of God, delivered to the people in their cities and villages throughout the land. Comprising chapter 5.**

## CHAPTER 5

*This chapter records the message of Alma to the members of the Church as he visits different Nephite cities. He teaches what is needed to receive eternal life. Look for Alma's questions and what he tells us is necessary to receive eternal life.*

### Alma Uses the Power of the Word to Teach the People

1 NOW it came to pass that Alma began to deliver the word of God unto the people, first in the land of Zarahemla, and from thence throughout all the land.
2 And these are the words which he spake to the people in the church which was established in the city of Zarahemla, according to his own record, saying:
3 I, Alma, having been consecrated by my father, Alma, to be a high priest over the church of God, he having power and authority from God to do

---

4:15 ***heaped upon them by the remainder***—piled on them by the rest

4:16 ***enact***—make

4:18 "God's chief representative on earth, the one who holds the highest spiritual position in his kingdom in any age, is called *the high priest*" (see Bruce R. McConkie, *Mormon Doctrine,* 355–56).

Before the priesthood was called the Melchizedek Priesthood, "it was called *the Holy Priesthood, after the Order of the Son of God*" (D&C 107:3).

4:19 Why do you think the most powerful way Alma could help his people was to preach the word of the Lord to them and bear "pure testimony against them"? How have others' testimonies helped you?

***reclaim them***—bring them back to the gospel

4:20 ***commencement***—beginning
***confined***—limited

* This introduction to chapter 5, except for the second sentence, was translated from the Book of Mormon plates.

5:1 ***deliver***—teach
***thence***—there

5:2 ***established***—organized

5:3 ***consecrated***—ordained

President J. Reuben Clark Jr. explained that "the Presiding High Priest [is] the President of the Church" (James R. Clark, *Messages of the First Presidency* 5:319).

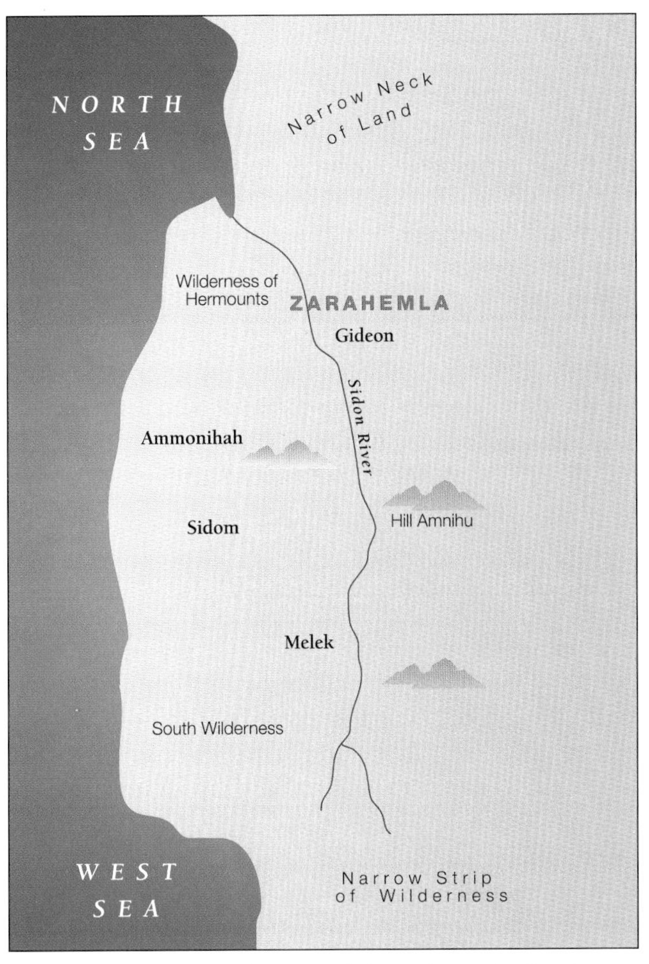


*Alma preaches the gospel throughout the land.*

these things, behold, I say unto you that he began
to establish a church in the land which was in the
borders of Nephi; yea, the land which was called
the land of Mormon; yea, and he did baptize his
brethren in the waters of Mormon.
4 And behold, I say unto you, they were delivered
out of the hands of the people of king Noah, by the
mercy and power of God.
5 And behold, after that, they were brought into
bondage by the hands of the Lamanites in the
wilderness; yea, I say unto you, they were in captivity, and again the Lord did deliver them out of
bondage by the power of his word; and we were
brought into this land, and here we began to establish the church of God throughout this land also.
6 And now behold, I say unto you, my brethren,
you that belong to this church, have you sufficiently retained in remembrance the captivity of
your fathers? Yea, and have you sufficiently retained
in remembrance his mercy and long-suffering
towards them? And moreover, have ye sufficiently
retained in remembrance that he has delivered their
souls from hell?
7 Behold, he changed their hearts; yea, he awakened them out of a deep sleep, and they awoke
unto God. Behold, they were in the midst of darkness; nevertheless, their souls were illuminated by
the light of the everlasting word; yea, they were
encircled about by the bands of death, and the
chains of hell, and an everlasting destruction did
await them.
8 And now I ask of you, my brethren, were they
destroyed? Behold, I say unto you, Nay, they were not.
9 And again I ask, were the bands of death broken, and the chains of hell which encircled them
about, were they loosed? I say unto you, Yea, they
were loosed, and their souls did expand, and they
did sing redeeming love. And I say unto you that
they are saved.

## *Alma Explains the Need of Being Born Again in Order to Gain Eternal Life*

10 And now I ask of you on what conditions are
they saved? Yea, what grounds had they to hope for
salvation? What is the cause of their being loosed
from the bands of death, yea, and also the chains of
hell?

---

5:4 ***delivered out of***—rescued from

5:5 ***captivity***—bondage and slavery

5:6 ***sufficiently retained in remembrance***—fully remembered
***long-suffering***—loving patience

5:7 ***midst***—middle
***illuminated***—enlightened

The phrase "chains of hell" is defined in Alma 12:11.

5:7 (6–7) Latter-day scriptures teach that there are at least three meanings for the term *hell*. It can describe our suffering here on earth (see Alma 36:18). It can refer to a part of the spirit world where those who have not repented suffer for their sins (see Alma 40:13–14). It is also used to describe the final condition of those who completely turn away from God (see D&C 29:38).

5:8 ***Nay***—No

5:9 ***did expand***—grew

5:10 ***grounds***—reasons

11 Behold, I can tell you—did not my father Alma believe in the words which were delivered by the mouth of Abinadi? And was he not a holy prophet? Did he not speak the words of God, and my father Alma believe them?

12 And according to his faith there was a mighty change wrought in his heart. Behold I say unto you that this is all true.

13 And behold, he preached the word unto your fathers, and a mighty change was also wrought in their hearts, and they humbled themselves and put their trust in the true and living God. And behold, they were faithful until the end; therefore they were saved.

## Alma Asks Questions That Help Us Understand What It Is Like to Be Born Again

14 And now behold, I ask of you, my brethren of the church, have ye spiritually been born of God? Have ye received his image in your countenances? Have ye experienced this mighty change in your hearts?

15 Do ye exercise faith in the redemption of him who created you? Do you look forward with an eye of faith, and view this mortal body raised in immortality, and this corruption raised in incorruption, to stand before God to be judged according to the deeds which have been done in the mortal body?

16 I say unto you, can you imagine to yourselves that ye hear the voice of the Lord, saying unto you, in that day: Come unto me ye blessed, for behold, your works have been the works of righteousness upon the face of the earth?

17 Or do ye imagine to yourselves that ye can lie unto the Lord in that day, and say—Lord, our works have been righteous works upon the face of the earth—and that he will save you?

18 Or otherwise, can ye imagine yourselves brought before the tribunal of God with your souls filled with guilt and remorse, having a remembrance of all your guilt, yea, a perfect remembrance of all your wickedness, yea, a remembrance that ye have set at defiance the commandments of God?

19 I say unto you, can ye look up to God at that day with a pure heart and clean hands? I say unto you, can you look up, having the image of God engraven upon your countenances?

20 I say unto you, can ye think of being saved when you have yielded yourselves to become subjects to the devil?

21 I say unto you, ye will know at that day that ye cannot be saved; for there can no man be saved except his garments are washed white; yea, his garments must be purified until they are cleansed from all stain, through the blood of him of whom it has been spoken by our fathers, who should come to redeem his people from their sins.

22 And now I ask of you, my brethren, how will any of you feel, if ye shall stand before the bar of God, having your garments stained with blood and all manner of filthiness? Behold, what will these things testify against you?

---

5:11 ***delivered***—preached

5:14 ***countenances***—faces or appearances

"Sometimes men are born again miraculously and suddenly, as was Alma. . . . But for most members of the Church the spiritual rebirth is a process that goes on gradually . . . degree by degree" (Bruce R. McConkie, *The Promised Messiah,* 351).

5:15 ***raised in immortality***—resurrected
***this corruption raised in incorruption***—this mortal body made immortal

5:17 (15–17) After the resurrection, we will be brought before the Lord to be judged (see Alma 11:44). At the final Judgment we will be judged by our thoughts, our words, and our deeds, or what we have done (see Mosiah 4:30).

5:18 ***tribunal***—judgment place
***remorse***—sorrow or regret
***set at defiance***—rebelled against

When the wicked think about coming into the presence of the Lord to be judged, they will feel so badly that they will wish the mountains could bury them and hide them from His presence (see Revelation 6:15–17).

5:19 ***engraven upon***—carved or impressed into

5:20 ***yielded***—allowed
***subjects***—servants

5:21 ***purified***—made pure
***stain***—dirty marks

5:22 ***bar***—judgment place

5:22 (21–22) Having your "garments . . . washed white" is a symbolic way of saying that your sins are forgiven. Our sins are washed white by the blood of Christ's Atonement (see Isaiah 1:18).

23 Behold will they not testify that ye are murderers, yea, and also that ye are guilty of all manner of wickedness?

24 Behold, my brethren, do ye suppose that such an one can have a place to sit down in the kingdom of God, with Abraham, with Isaac, and with Jacob, and also all the holy prophets, whose garments are cleansed and are spotless, pure and white?

25 I say unto you, Nay; except ye make our Creator a liar from the beginning, or suppose that he is a liar from the beginning, ye cannot suppose that such can have place in the kingdom of heaven; but they shall be cast out for they are the children of the kingdom of the devil.

26 And now behold, I say unto you, my brethren, if ye have experienced a change of heart, and if ye have felt to sing the song of redeeming love, I would ask, can ye feel so now?

27 Have ye walked, keeping yourselves blameless before God? Could ye say, if ye were called to die at this time, within yourselves, that ye have been sufficiently humble? That your garments have been cleansed and made white through the blood of Christ, who will come to redeem his people from their sins?

28 Behold, are ye stripped of pride? I say unto you, if ye are not ye are not prepared to meet God. Behold ye must prepare quickly; for the kingdom of heaven is soon at hand, and such an one hath not eternal life.

29 Behold, I say, is there one among you who is not stripped of envy? I say unto you that such an one is not prepared; and I would that he should prepare quickly, for the hour is close at hand, and he knoweth not when the time shall come; for such an one is not found guiltless.

30 And again I say unto you, is there one among you that doth make a mock of his brother, or that heapeth upon him persecutions?

31 Wo unto such an one, for he is not prepared, and the time is at hand that he must repent or he cannot be saved!

32 Yea, even wo unto all ye workers of iniquity; repent, repent, for the Lord God hath spoken it!

## *Eternal Life Is Offered to All Through the Name of Jesus Christ*

33 Behold, he sendeth an invitation unto all men, for the arms of mercy are extended towards them, and he saith: Repent, and I will receive you.

34 Yea, he saith: Come unto me and ye shall partake of the fruit of the tree of life; yea, ye shall eat and drink of the bread and the waters of life freely;

35 Yea, come unto me and bring forth works of righteousness, and ye shall not be hewn down and cast into the fire—

36 For behold, the time is at hand that whosoever bringeth forth not good fruit, or whosoever doeth not the works of righteousness, the same have cause to wail and mourn.

37 O ye workers of iniquity; ye that are puffed up in the vain things of the world, ye that have professed to have known the ways of righteousness nevertheless have gone astray, as sheep having no shepherd, notwithstanding a shepherd hath called after you and is still calling after you, but ye will not hearken unto his voice!

---

5:25 (24–25) "No unclean thing can dewll with God" (1 Nephi 10:21).

5:26 "Spirituality, that condition of closeness with the Lord through his Spirit, is like manna to us. We cannot live well without it, and it must be gathered every day. It isn't enough to have known, to have read, to have given, to have prayed, to have obeyed" (Marion D. Hanks, "An Attitude—The Weightier Matters," 71).

5:27 ***sufficiently humble***—humble enough

5:28 ***are ye stripped of pride?***—have you gotten rid of pride?

5:28 (27–28) President James E. Faust taught that pride is an enemy "to the full enjoyment of the Spirit of God" (in Conference Report, April 1994, 4).

5:29 ***envy***—jealousy

5:30 ***a mock***—fun
***persecutions***—abuses and mistreatment

5:31 ***Wo***—Grief, sorrow, and misery

5:32 ***iniquity***—sin

5:33 ***mercy***—loving kindness
***extended***—opened

5:34 Jesus Christ is the bread of life (see John 6:48) and the living water (see John 7:37).

5:35 ***hewn***—cut

5:37 ***vain***—useless or foolish
***professed***—claimed
***astray***—out of the right way
***hearken unto***—listen to and obey

THE LOST SHEEP, BY DEL PARSON

*Jesus Christ is the Good Shepherd.*

38 Behold, I say unto you, that the good shepherd
doth call you; yea, and in his own name he doth
call you, which is the name of Christ; and if ye will
not hearken unto the voice of the good shepherd,
to the name by which ye are called, behold, ye are
not the sheep of the good shepherd.
39 And now if ye are not the sheep of the good
shepherd, of what fold are ye? Behold, I say unto
you, that the devil is your shepherd, and ye are of
his fold; and now, who can deny this? Behold, I say
unto you, whosoever denieth this is a liar and a
child of the devil.
40 For I say unto you that whatsoever is good
cometh from God, and whatsoever is evil cometh
from the devil.
41 Therefore, if a man bringeth forth good works he
hearkeneth unto the voice of the good shepherd, and
he doth follow him; but whosoever bringeth forth evil
works, the same becometh a child of the devil, for
he hearkeneth unto his voice, and doth follow him.

---

5:39 ***deny this***—say otherwise

5:39 (37–39) "Christ is the *Shepherd* (Gen. 49:24; Ps. 23; 1 Pet. 2:25; Morm. 5:17), the *Chief Shepherd* (1 Pet. 5:4), the *Great Shepherd* (Heb. 13:20), the *True Shepherd* (Hela. 15:13), the *Shepherd of Israel* (Ps. 80:1), the *Good Shepherd* (D. & C. 50:44; John 10:7–18; Alma 5:38-60; Hela. 7:18.) His saints are the sheep; his sheepfold is the Church of Jesus Christ; and the day will come when there will be 'one God and one Shepherd over all the earth' (1 Ne. 13:41), 'and he shall feed his sheep, and in him they shall find pasture.' (1 Ne. 22:25.)" (Bruce R. McConkie, *Mormon Doctrine,* 328).

42 And whosoever doeth this must receive his wages of him; therefore, for his wages he receiveth death, as to things pertaining unto righteousness, being dead unto all good works.

## There Is Value in Having More Than One Witness to the Truth

43 And now, my brethren, I would that ye should hear me, for I speak in the energy of my soul; for behold, I have spoken unto you plainly that ye cannot err, or have spoken according to the commandments of God.

44 For I am called to speak after this manner, according to the holy order of God, which is in Christ Jesus; yea, I am commanded to stand and testify unto this people the things which have been spoken by our fathers concerning the things which are to come.

45 And this is not all. Do ye not suppose that I know of these things myself? Behold, I testify unto you that I do know that these things whereof I have spoken are true. And how do ye suppose that I know of their surety?

46 Behold, I say unto you they are made known unto me by the Holy Spirit of God. Behold, I have fasted and prayed many days that I might know these things of myself. And now I do know of myself that they are true; for the Lord God hath made them manifest unto me by his Holy Spirit; and this is the spirit of revelation which is in me.

47 And moreover, I say unto you that it has thus been revealed unto me, that the words which have been spoken by our fathers are true, even so according to the spirit of prophecy which is in me, which is also by the manifestation of the Spirit of God.

48 I say unto you, that I know of myself that whatsoever I shall say unto you, concerning that which is to come, is true; and I say unto you, that I know that Jesus Christ shall come, yea, the Son, the Only Begotten of the Father, full of grace, and mercy, and truth. And behold, it is he that cometh to take away the sins of the world, yea, the sins of every man who steadfastly believeth on his name.

49 And now I say unto you that this is the order after which I am called, yea, to preach unto my beloved brethren, yea, and every one that dwelleth in the land; yea, to preach unto all, both old and young, both bond and free; yea, I say unto you the aged, and also the middle aged, and the rising generation; yea, to cry unto them that they must repent and be born again.

## By Repenting and Living Righteously, We Show the Lord We Accept Him

50 Yea, thus saith the Spirit: Repent, all ye ends of the earth, for the kingdom of heaven is soon at hand; yea, the Son of God cometh in his glory, in his might, majesty, power, and dominion. Yea, my beloved brethren, I say unto you, that the Spirit saith: Behold the glory of the King of all the earth; and also the King of heaven shall very soon shine forth among all the children of men.

---

5:42 ***wages***—payment or reward
***pertaining***—having to do with

5:43 ***err***—misunderstand or make a mistake

5:44 ***after this manner***—in this way

The words *holy order of God* and sometimes just the word *order* are used in the scriptures to speak about the priesthood of Jesus Christ (see D&C 107:3).

5:46 ***hath made them manifest***—has shown them

We can learn the truth of "all things" through the power of the Holy Ghost (see 2 Nephi 32:5; Moroni 10:5).

5:47 ***it has thus been revealed***—it has been shown in this way
***manifestation***—witness

5:48 This is Alma's testimony of Jesus Christ. Do you have a testimony of Jesus Christ? When can you share your testimony?

*Grace* is divine help given by God through the Atonement of Jesus Christ. It provides us with the power needed to repent, keep the commandments, and become like God (see LDS Bible Dictionary, s.v. "Grace," 697; see also 2 Nephi 25:23).

***mercy***—kindness and forgiveness
***steadfastly***—strongly and constantly

5:49 ***dwelleth***—lives
***bond***—slave
***rising generation***—children

5:50 ***dominion***—authority

51 And also the Spirit saith unto me, yea, crieth
unto me with a mighty voice, saying: Go forth and
say unto this people—Repent, for except ye repent
ye can in nowise inherit the kingdom of heaven.
52 And again I say unto you, the Spirit saith:
Behold, the ax is laid at the root of the tree; therefore every tree that bringeth not forth good fruit
shall be hewn down and cast into the fire, yea,
a fire which cannot be consumed, even an
unquenchable fire. Behold, and remember, the
Holy One hath spoken it.
53 And now my beloved brethren, I say unto you,
can ye withstand these sayings; yea, can ye lay
aside these things, and trample the Holy One under
your feet; yea, can ye be puffed up in the pride of
your hearts; yea, will ye still persist in the wearing
of costly apparel and setting your hearts upon the
vain things of the world, upon your riches?
54 Yea, will ye persist in supposing that ye are
better one than another; yea, will ye persist in the
persecution of your brethren, who humble themselves and do walk after the holy order of God,
wherewith they have been brought into this church,
having been sanctified by the Holy Spirit, and they
do bring forth works which are meet for repentance—
55 Yea, and will you persist in turning your backs
upon the poor, and the needy, and in withholding
your substance from them?
56 And finally, all ye that will persist in your
wickedness, I say unto you that these are they who
shall be hewn down and cast into the fire except
they speedily repent.
57 And now I say unto you, all you that are
desirous to follow the voice of the good shepherd,
come ye out from the wicked, and be ye separate,
and touch not their unclean things; and behold,
their names shall be blotted out, that the names of
the wicked shall not be numbered among the
names of the righteous, that the word of God may
be fulfilled, which saith: The names of the wicked
shall not be mingled with the names of my people;
58 For the names of the righteous shall be written
in the book of life, and unto them will I grant an
inheritance at my right hand. And now, my
brethren, what have ye to say against this? I say
unto you, if ye speak against it, it matters not, for
the word of God must be fulfilled.
59 For what shepherd is there among you having
many sheep doth not watch over them, that the
wolves enter not and devour his flock? And
behold, if a wolf enter his flock doth he not drive
him out? Yea, and at the last, if he can, he will
destroy him.
60 And now I say unto you that the good shepherd doth call after you; and if you will hearken
unto his voice he will bring you into his fold, and
ye are his sheep; and he commandeth you that ye
suffer no ravenous wolf to enter among you, that ye
may not be destroyed.
61 And now I, Alma, do command you in the language of him who hath commanded me, that ye
observe to do the words which I have spoken unto
you.
62 I speak by way of command unto you that
belong to the church; and unto those who do not
belong to the church I speak by way of invitation,
saying: Come and be baptized unto repentance,
that ye also may be partakers of the fruit of the tree
of life.

---

5:51 Repentance is such an important message that the Lord has said, "Say nothing but repentance unto this generation" (D&C 6:9).

5:52 ***consumed, even an unquenchable***—burned, even a never–ending

5:53 ***withstand***—resist
***costly apparel***—expensive clothes
***vain***—useless or foolish

5:54 "To be *sanctified* is to become clean, pure, and spotless" (Bruce R. McConkie, *Mormon Doctrine,* 675). A person can become sanctified only through the Atonement of Jesus Christ and by obedience to the laws, ordinances, and commandments of the gospel of Jesus Christ.

5:57 ***mingled***—mixed

5:58 ***grant an inheritance***—give a reward or a place

5:59 ***devour***—eat hungrily

5:60 ***ravenous***—very hungry

## CHAPTER 6

*Alma begins to build up and strengthen the Church in Zarahemla. Watch for the ordinances he performs and the doctrines he teaches, which we also do and teach in the Church today.*

### Alma Builds Up and Strengthens the Church in Zarahemla

1 AND now it came to pass that after Alma had made an end of speaking unto the people of the church, which was established in the city of Zarahemla, he ordained priests and elders, by laying on his hands according to the order of God, to preside and watch over the church.
2 And it came to pass that whosoever did not belong to the church who repented of their sins were baptized unto repentance, and were received into the church.
3 And it also came to pass that whosoever did belong to the church that did not repent of their wickedness and humble themselves before God—I mean those who were lifted up in the pride of their hearts—the same were rejected, and their names were blotted out, that their names were not numbered among those of the righteous.
4 And thus they began to establish the order of the church in the city of Zarahemla.

### Alma Declares the Gospel in Gideon

5 Now I would that ye should understand that the word of God was liberal unto all, that none were deprived of the privilege of assembling themselves together to hear the word of God.
6 Nevertheless the children of God were commanded that they should gather themselves together oft, and join in fasting and mighty prayer in behalf of the welfare of the souls of those who knew not God.
7 And now it came to pass that when Alma had made these regulations he departed from them, yea, from the church which was in the city of Zarahemla, and went over upon the east of the river Sidon, into the valley of Gideon, there having been a city built, which was called the city of Gideon, which was in the valley that was called Gideon, being called after the man who was slain by the hand of Nehor with the sword.
8 And Alma went and began to declare the word of God unto the church which was established in the valley of Gideon, according to the revelation of the truth of the word which had been spoken by his fathers, and according to the spirit of prophecy which was in him, according to the testimony of Jesus Christ, the Son of God, who should come to redeem his people from their sins, and the holy order by which he was called. And thus it is written. Amen.

*The words of Alma which he delivered to the people in Gideon, according to his own record. Comprising chapter 7.**

---

6:1 To be *ordained* means to be given priesthood authority and to be appointed to serve in an office in that priesthood by one who already holds the priesthood. "The order of God" is another name for the Melchizedek Priesthood (see Articles of Faith 1:5; D&C 107:3).

**preside**—lead or direct

6:3 **blotted out**—erased or removed

6:3 (2–3) Why do you think Heavenly Father wants the members of His Church to repent and be humble?

6:5 **liberal**—freely given
**deprived of**—refused or denied

6:6 Along with fasting and praying, what could you do to help those around you who don't know about God?

6:7 **regulations**—rules

6:8 John the Revelator taught that if you have the testimony of Jesus Christ, then you also have the spirit of prophecy (see Revelation 19:10).

To *redeem* means to "buy back" or to "set free." Jesus Christ is our Redeemer because He willingly paid the price to buy us back and set us free from the effects of the Fall of Adam and from the burden of our own sins (see 1 Corinthians 6:20). The price He had to pay was His own blood (see 1 Peter 1:18–19).

* This introduction, except for the second sentence, was translated from the Book of Mormon plates.

## CHAPTER 7

*Alma shares his testimony with the people in Gideon. He explains what we must do to be clean and to be worthy to enter the kingdom of heaven. See if you can find what Alma prophesies concerning the birth of Jesus Christ.*

### Alma Desires That the People of Gideon Be Humble, Obedient, and Believing

1 BEHOLD my beloved brethren, seeing that I have been permitted to come unto you, therefore I attempt to address you in my language; yea, by my own mouth, seeing that it is the first time that I have spoken unto you by the words of my mouth, I having been wholly confined to the judgment-seat, having had much business that I could not come unto you.
2 And even I could not have come now at this time were it not that the judgment-seat hath been given to another, to reign in my stead; and the Lord in much mercy hath granted that I should come unto you.
3 And behold, I have come having great hopes and much desire that I should find that ye had humbled yourselves before God, and that ye had continued in the supplicating of his grace, that I should find that ye were blameless before him, that I should find that ye were not in the awful dilemma that our brethren were in at Zarahemla.
4 But blessed be the name of God, that he hath given me to know, yea, hath given unto me the exceedingly great joy of knowing that they are established again in the way of his righteousness.
5 And I trust, according to the Spirit of God which is in me, that I shall also have joy over you; nevertheless I do not desire that my joy over you should come by the cause of so much afflictions and sorrow which I have had for the brethren at Zarahemla, for behold, my joy cometh over them after wading through much affliction and sorrow.
6 But behold, I trust that ye are not in a state of so much unbelief as were your brethren; I trust that ye are not lifted up in the pride of your hearts; yea, I trust that ye have not set your hearts upon riches and the vain things of the world; yea, I trust that you do not worship idols, but that ye do worship the true and the living God, and that ye look forward for the remission of your sins, with an everlasting faith, which is to come.

### Alma Prophesies of the Birth of Jesus Christ

7 For behold, I say unto you there be many things to come; and behold, there is one thing which is of more importance than they all—for behold, the time is not far distant that the Redeemer liveth and cometh among his people.
8 Behold, I do not say that he will come among us at the time of his dwelling in his mortal tabernacle; for behold, the Spirit hath not said unto me that this should be the case. Now as to this thing I do not know; but this much I do know, that the Lord God hath power to do all things which are according to his word.
9 But behold, the Spirit hath said this much unto me, saying: Cry unto this people, saying—Repent ye, and prepare the way of the Lord, and walk in his paths, which are straight; for behold, the kingdom

---

7:1 ***permitted***—allowed
***wholly confined to***—spending all my time at

7:2 Alma now had time to preach because Nephihah had been appointed chief judge in his place (see Alma 4:17–18).

***reign***—rule
***stead***—place

7:3 ***supplicating of***—praying for
***dilemma***—trouble or difficulty

7:4 ***exceedingly***—very

7:5 ***afflictions***—trials and suffering
***wading through***—experiencing and enduring

7:6 ***vain***—useless and foolish
***remission***—forgiveness

Alma counsels the people not to set their hearts upon riches and the things of the world. How can you avoid setting your heart on the things of the world?

7:7 Alma teaches that the message of Jesus Christ is the most important one of all. What do you think makes Jesus Christ's message so important?

7:8 "The time of his dwelling in his mortal tabernacle" refers to the time of Jesus Christ's mortal life. The events in Alma 7 occur about 83 years before Jesus Christ's birth.

7:9 ***Cry***—Call or declare

of heaven is at hand, and the Son of God cometh
upon the face of the earth.
10 And behold, he shall be born of Mary, at
Jerusalem which is the land of our forefathers, she
being a virgin, a precious and chosen vessel, who
shall be overshadowed and conceive by the power
of the Holy Ghost, and bring forth a son, yea, even
the Son of God.
11 And he shall go forth, suffering pains and afflictions and temptations of every kind; and this that
the word might be fulfilled which saith he will take
upon him the pains and the sicknesses of his
people.

## *Alma Testifies That Jesus Will Atone for Our Sins and Die for Us*

12 And he will take upon him death, that he may
loose the bands of death which bind his people;
and he will take upon him their infirmities, that his
bowels may be filled with mercy, according to the
flesh, that he may know according to the flesh
how to succor his people according to their infirmities.
13 Now the Spirit knoweth all things; nevertheless
the Son of God suffereth according to the flesh that
he might take upon him the sins of his people, that
he might blot out their transgressions according to
the power of his deliverance; and now behold, this
is the testimony which is in me.

## *To Enter the Kingdom of God We Must Repent and Keep the Commandments*

14 Now I say unto you that ye must repent, and
be born again; for the Spirit saith if ye are not born
again ye cannot inherit the kingdom of heaven;
therefore come and be baptized unto repentance,
that ye may be washed from your sins, that ye may
have faith on the Lamb of God, who taketh away
the sins of the world, who is mighty to save and to
cleanse from all unrighteousness.

---

7:10 Bethlehem, where Jesus Christ was born, was a small village some six miles from the city of Jerusalem. It was within the area referred to by the people of that day as "the land of Jerusalem" (see Hugh Nibley, *An Approach to the Book of Mormon,* 101–2).

***virgin***—woman who is pure, chaste, and who has not had intimate relations with a man
***vessel***—one to carry the unborn child until birth

"When Jesus was born into mortality, his parents were God the Eternal Father (see 1 Nephi 11:21) and Mary, whom Nephi saw in a heavenly vision as 'a virgin, most beautiful and fair above all other virgins' (15). He is God's Only Begotten Son, the only one who ever has or ever will be born on earth of such parentage" (Joseph B. Wirthlin, in Conference Report, October 1993, 5).

Mary " 'was carried away in the Spirit' (1 Ne. 11:18–19), was 'overshadowed' and conceived 'by the power of the Holy Ghost' (Alma 7:9–10)—but the Holy Ghost is not the Father of Christ—and when the Child was born, he was 'the Son of the Eternal Father.' (1 Ne. 11:21.)" (Bruce R. McConkie, *Mormon Doctrine,* 743).

7:12 ***infirmities***—sicknesses or weaknesses
***bowels***—inner feelings
***succor***—bless, comfort, and help

7:12 (11–12) Jesus not only suffered for our sins, but also for our pains, sicknesses, and temptations. Have you been healed from any of these things through the power of Jesus Christ? What does this teach you about His love for you?

7:13 ***blot out***—wipe out
***transgressions***—sins

"Forgiveness is available because of the atoning sacrifice of the Great Jehovah. Forgiveness is available because Christ the Lord sweat great drops of blood in Gethsemane as he bore the incalculable [impossible to measure] weight of the sins of all who ever had or ever would repent" (Bruce R. McConkie, *The Promised Messiah,* 337–38).

7:14 "To gain salvation in the celestial kingdom men must be *born again* (Alma 7:14); born of water and of the Spirit (John 3:1–13); born of God, so that they are changed from their 'carnal and fallen state, to a state of righteousness' becoming new creatures of the Holy Ghost. (Mosiah 27:24–29.) They must become newborn babes in Christ (1 Pet. 2:2); they must be 'spiritually begotten' of God, be born of Christ, thus becoming his sons and daughters. (Mosiah 5:7.)" (Bruce R. McConkie, *Mormon Doctrine,* 100–101).

15 Yea, I say unto you come and fear not, and lay aside every sin, which easily doth beset you, which doth bind you down to destruction, yea, come and go forth, and show unto your God that ye are willing to repent of your sins and enter into a covenant with him to keep his commandments, and witness it unto him this day by going into the waters of baptism.

16 And whosoever doeth this, and keepeth the commandments of God from thenceforth, the same will remember that I say unto him, yea, he will remember that I have said unto him, he shall have eternal life, according to the testimony of the Holy Spirit, which testifieth in me.

17 And now my beloved brethren, do you believe these things? Behold, I say unto you, yea, I know that ye believe them; and the way that I know that ye believe them is by the manifestation of the Spirit which is in me. And now because your faith is strong concerning that, yea, concerning the things which I have spoken, great is my joy.

18 For as I said unto you from the beginning, that I had much desire that ye were not in the state of dilemma like your brethren, even so I have found that my desires have been gratified.

19 For I perceive that ye are in the paths of righteousness; I perceive that ye are in the path which leads to the kingdom of God; yea, I perceive that ye are making his paths straight.

20 I perceive that it has been made known unto you, by the testimony of his word, that he cannot walk in crooked paths; neither doth he vary from that which he hath said; neither hath he a shadow of turning from the right to the left, or from that which is right to that which is wrong; therefore, his course is one eternal round.

21 And he doth not dwell in unholy temples; neither can filthiness or anything which is unclean be received into the kingdom of God; therefore I say unto you the time shall come, yea, and it shall be at the last day, that he who is filthy shall remain in his filthiness.

## Alma Asks the People of Gideon to Follow the Lord

22 And now my beloved brethren, I have said these things unto you that I might awaken you to a sense of your duty to God, that ye may walk blameless before him, that ye may walk after the holy order of God, after which ye have been received.

23 And now I would that ye should be humble, and be submissive and gentle; easy to be entreated; full of patience and long-suffering; being temperate in all things; being diligent in keeping the commandments of God at all times; asking for whatsoever

---

7:15 **beset**—surround or trouble

A covenant is an agreement between two people. In the scriptures it is usually an agreement between God and man. We promise to be obedient to God's commandments, and He promises to bless us (see LDS Bible Dictionary, s.v., "Covenant," 651).

What do you think it means to "lay aside every sin"? What are you doing to show Heavenly Father that you "are willing to repent of your sins and enter into a covenant with Him to keep His commandments?"

7:17 **manifestation**—witness or testimony

7:18 **dilemma**—trouble
**gratified**—satisfied

7:19 **perceive**—can see

7:20 "Just as a ring has no beginning or ending, and as [the Lord's] priesthood has neither 'beginning of days or end of years' (Alma 13:7), so is the course of God one eternal round" (Hoyt Brewster, *Doctrine and Covenants Encyclopedia,* s.v. "One Eternal Round").

*God does not dwell in unholy temples, and He cannot receive into His kingdom anything that is unclean. For this reason, only those who are worthy can enter His temples.*

PHOTOGRAPH BY G. R. SIMS

7:22 Only those who are cleansed from sin can return to live with God. We become cleansed from our sins through the Atonement of Jesus Christ. What are you doing to remain clean and pure?

things ye stand in need, both spiritual and temporal; always returning thanks unto God for whatsoever things ye do receive.
24 And see that ye have faith, hope, and charity,
and then ye will always abound in good works.
25 And may the Lord bless you, and keep your
garments spotless, that ye may at last be brought to
sit down with Abraham, Isaac, and Jacob, and the
holy prophets who have been ever since the world
began, having your garments spotless even as their
garments are spotless, in the kingdom of heaven to
go no more out.
26 And now my beloved brethren, I have spoken
these words unto you according to the Spirit which
testifieth in me; and my soul doth exceedingly
rejoice, because of the exceeding diligence and
heed which ye have given unto my word.
27 And now, may the peace of God rest upon
you, and upon your houses and lands, and upon
your flocks and herds, and all that you possess,
your women and your children, according to your
faith and good works, from this time forth and forever. And thus I have spoken. Amen.

## CHAPTER 8

*Alma has missionary success in Melek but is rejected in Ammonihah. Look for how the Lord provides Alma with a missionary companion.*

### Alma Returns to Melek, Preaches, and Baptizes

1 AND now it came to pass that Alma returned from
the land of Gideon, after having taught the people of
Gideon many things which cannot be written, having
established the order of the church, according as he
had before done in the land of Zarahemla, yea, he
returned to his own house at Zarahemla to rest himself from the labors which he had performed.
2 And thus ended the ninth year of the reign of
the judges over the people of Nephi.
3 And it came to pass in the commencement of
the tenth year of the reign of the judges over the
people of Nephi, that Alma departed from thence
and took his journey over into the land of Melek,
on the west of the river Sidon, on the west by the
borders of the wilderness.
4 And he began to teach the people in the land of
Melek according to the holy order of God, by which
he had been called; and he began to teach the
people throughout all the land of Melek.
5 And it came to pass that the people came to him
throughout all the borders of the land which was by
the wilderness side. And they were baptized
throughout all the land;

### Alma's Message Is Rejected at Ammonihah

6 So that when he had finished his work at Melek
he departed thence, and traveled three days' journey on the north of the land of Melek; and he came
to a city which was called Ammonihah.
7 Now it was the custom of the people of Nephi
to call their lands, and their cities, and their villages,
yea, even all their small villages, after the name of
him who first possessed them; and thus it was with
the land of Ammonihah.

7:25 "Clean garments are a sign of cleanliness, perfection, and salvation. To gain salvation men must wash their garments in the blood of the Lamb" (Bruce R. McConkie, *Mormon Doctrine,* 304).

8:1 The order, or organization, of the Church is directed by the priesthood. Anyone "with the spirit of this Gospel will understand that God has established an order in His Church, for its guidance and government" (Charles W. Penrose, in Conference Report, October 1915, 40).

8:2 ***reign***—rule

8:3 ***commencement***—beginning
***thence***—there

8:4 The phrase "holy order of God" is a scriptural way to say priesthood of God (see D&C 107:3).

8:7  ***possessed***—settled

PHOTOGRAPH BY REGNAL GARFF

*This modern-day hut found in Central America might look like the dwellings used in Book of Mormon times.*

8 And it came to pass that when Alma had come
to the city of Ammonihah he began to preach the
word of God unto them.
9 Now Satan had gotten great hold upon the
hearts of the people of the city of Ammonihah;
therefore they would not hearken unto the words
of Alma.
10 Nevertheless Alma labored much in the spirit,
wrestling with God in mighty prayer, that he would
pour out his Spirit upon the people who were in
the city; that he would also grant that he might baptize them unto repentance.
11 Nevertheless, they hardened their hearts, saying unto him: Behold, we know that thou art Alma;
and we know that thou art high priest over the
church which thou hast established in many parts
of the land, according to your tradition; and we are
not of thy church, and we do not believe in such
foolish traditions.
12 And now we know that because we are not of
thy church we know that thou hast no power over
us; and thou hast delivered up the judgment-seat
unto Nephihah; therefore thou art not the chief
judge over us.
13 Now when the people had said this, and withstood all his words, and reviled him, and spit upon
him, and caused that he should be cast out of their
city, he departed thence and took his journey
towards the city which was called Aaron.

## Alma Is Commanded to Return to Ammonihah

14 And it came to pass that while he was journeying thither, being weighed down with sorrow, wading through much tribulation and anguish of soul,
because of the wickedness of the people who were
in the city of Ammonihah, it came to pass while
Alma was thus weighed down with sorrow, behold
an angel of the Lord appeared unto him, saying:
15 Blessed art thou, Alma; therefore, lift up thy
head and rejoice, for thou hast great cause to
rejoice; for thou hast been faithful in keeping the
commandments of God from the time which thou
receivedst thy first message from him. Behold, I am
he that delivered it unto you.
16 And behold, I am sent to command thee that
thou return to the city of Ammonihah, and preach
again unto the people of the city; yea, preach unto
them. Yea, say unto them, except they repent the
Lord God will destroy them.
17 For behold, they do study at this time that they
may destroy the liberty of thy people, (for thus saith
the Lord) which is contrary to the statutes, and
judgments, and commandments which he has given
unto his people.
18 Now it came to pass that after Alma had
received his message from the angel of the Lord he
returned speedily to the land of Ammonihah. And
he entered the city by another way, yea, by the way
which is on the south of the city of Ammonihah.

---

8:10 ***labored***—struggled or worked

Alma, like Enos (see Enos 1:2), wrestled or struggled to receive an answer to his prayers. What do you think it means to wrestle with God in mighty prayer? How would you describe your prayers?

8:11 These people of Ammonihah behaved just the way Jacob described centuries earlier: "When they are learned they think they are wise, and they hearken not unto the counsel of God" (2 Nephi 9:28).

8:12 ***judgment-seat***—office of the chief judge

8:13 ***withstood***—resisted or opposed
***reviled him***—complained with anger against him

8:14 "Both the righteous and the wicked suffer *anguish* of soul, meaning excruciating [intense] distress and extreme pain of body and mind. The righteous suffer anguish in this life because of the sins and rebellion of their brethren. (1 Ne. 17:47; 2 Ne. 26:7; Mosiah 25:11; Alma 8:14; Morm. 6:16.) Christ himself suffered until blood came from every pore, so great was 'his anguish for the wickedness and the abominations of his people.' (Mosiah 3:7)" (Bruce R. McConkie, *Mormon Doctrine,* 38).

Elder Jeffrey R. Holland said that "one of the profound themes of the Book of Mormon . . . is the role and prevalence and central participation of angels in the everlasting gospel story. Especially to those who lived in trust before Christ came" ("A Standard unto My People," 11).

8:16 The people of Ammonihah who do not repent will eventually be destroyed by a Lamanite army (see Alma 16:1–3).

## *Alma Meets Amulek*

19 And as he entered the city he was an hungered, and he said to a man: Will ye give to an humble servant of God something to eat?

20 And the man said unto him: I am a Nephite, and I know that thou art a holy prophet of God, for thou art the man whom an angel said in a vision: Thou shalt receive. Therefore, go with me into my house and I will impart unto thee of my food; and I know that thou wilt be a blessing unto me and my house.

21 And it came to pass that the man received him into his house; and the man was called Amulek; and he brought forth bread and meat and set before Alma.

22 And it came to pass that Alma ate bread and was filled; and he blessed Amulek and his house, and he gave thanks unto God.

23 And after he had eaten and was filled he said unto Amulek: I am Alma, and am the high priest over the church of God throughout the land.

24 And behold, I have been called to preach the word of God among all this people, according to the spirit of revelation and prophecy; and I was in this land and they would not receive me, but they cast me out and I was about to set my back towards this land forever.

25 But behold, I have been commanded that I should turn again and prophesy unto this people, yea, and to testify against them concerning their iniquities.

26 And now, Amulek, because thou hast fed me and taken me in, thou art blessed; for I was an hungered, for I had fasted many days.

27 And Alma tarried many days with Amulek before he began to preach unto the people.

## *Amulek Is Called to Preach the Gospel*

28 And it came to pass that the people did wax more gross in their iniquities.

29 And the word came to Alma, saying: Go; and also say unto my servant Amulek, go forth and prophesy unto this people, saying—Repent ye, for thus saith the Lord, except ye repent I will visit this people in mine anger; yea, and I will not turn my fierce anger away.

30 And Alma went forth, and also Amulek, among the people, to declare the words of God unto them; and they were filled with the Holy Ghost.

31 And they had power given unto them, insomuch that they could not be confined in dungeons; neither was it possible that any man could slay them; nevertheless they did not exercise their power until they were bound in bands and cast into prison. Now, this was done that the Lord might show forth his power in them.

32 And it came to pass that they went forth and began to preach and to prophesy unto the people, according to the spirit and power which the Lord had given them.

*The words of Alma, and also the words of Amulek, which were declared unto the people who were in the land of Ammonihah. And also they are cast into prison, and delivered by the miraculous power of God which was in them, according to the record of Alma. Comprising chapters 9 to 14 inclusive.**

## CHAPTER 9

*Only destruction and sadness awaits a richly blessed people who turn away from the Lord, reject His prophets and teachings, and refuse to repent. Watch for how the people of Ammonihah respond to Alma's warnings.*

---

8:20 ***impart***—give or share

Amulek serves Alma by caring for and feeding him. When we serve others we are in the service of God (see Mosiah 2:17). What have you done to serve others who are in need?

8:23 "God's chief representative on earth, the one who holds the highest spiritual position in his kingdom in any age, is called *the high priest*" (Bruce R. McConkie, *Mormon Doctrine,* 355–56).

8:25 ***iniquities***—sins

8:26 Why do you think Alma fasted? What blessings have you received from fasting?

8:27 ***tarried***—remained

8:28 ***did wax***—grew or became
***gross***—serious or disgusting

8:31 ***confined***—kept
***bound in bands***—tied up in ropes or chains

* This introduction to chapters 9–14, except for the last sentence, was translated from the Book of Mormon plates.

## Alma Commands the People of Ammonihah to Repent

1 AND again, I, Alma, having been commanded of God that I should take Amulek and go forth and preach again unto this people, or the people who were in the city of Ammonihah, it came to pass as I began to preach unto them, they began to contend with me, saying:
2 Who art thou? Suppose ye that we shall believe the testimony of one man, although he should preach unto us that the earth should pass away?
3 Now they understood not the words which they spake; for they knew not that the earth should pass away.
4 And they said also: We will not believe thy words if thou shouldst prophesy that this great city should be destroyed in one day.
5 Now they knew not that God could do such marvelous works, for they were a hard-hearted and a stiffnecked people.
6 And they said: Who is God, that sendeth no more authority than one man among this people, to declare unto them the truth of such great and marvelous things?
7 And they stood forth to lay their hands on me; but behold, they did not. And I stood with boldness to declare unto them, yea, I did boldly testify unto them, saying:
8 Behold, O ye wicked and perverse generation, how have ye forgotten the tradition of your fathers; yea, how soon ye have forgotten the commandments of God.
9 Do ye not remember that our father, Lehi, was brought out of Jerusalem by the hand of God? Do ye not remember that they were all led by him through the wilderness?
10 And have ye forgotten so soon how many times he delivered our fathers out of the hands of their enemies, and preserved them from being destroyed, even by the hands of their own brethren?
11 Yea, and if it had not been for his matchless power, and his mercy, and his long-suffering towards us, we should unavoidably have been cut off from the face of the earth long before this period of time, and perhaps been consigned to a state of endless misery and woe.
12 Behold, now I say unto you that he commandeth you to repent; and except ye repent, ye can in nowise inherit the kingdom of God. But behold, this is not all—he has commanded you to repent, or he will utterly destroy you from off the face of the earth; yea, he will visit you in his anger, and in his fierce anger he will not turn away.
13 Behold, do ye not remember the words which he spake unto Lehi, saying that: Inasmuch as ye shall keep my commandments, ye shall prosper in the land? And again it is said that: Inasmuch as ye will not keep my commandments ye shall be cut off from the presence of the Lord.

## The Lord Promises That the Lamanites Will Believe in the Last Days

14 Now I would that ye should remember, that inasmuch as the Lamanites have not kept the commandments of God, they have been cut off from the presence of the Lord. Now we see that the word of the Lord has been verified in this thing, and the Lamanites have been cut off from his presence,

---

9:5 ***a hard-hearted***—an unfeeling
***stiffnecked***—rebellious and stubborn

9:6 (2–6) The people of Ammonihah wanted to reject Alma's testimony because they thought he was alone. Notice their surprise in the next chapter when Amulek speaks as a second witness (see Alma 10:12).

9:8 ***wicked and perverse generation***—stubbornly wicked people

9:10 ***preserved***—protected or saved

9:10 (8–10) The Lord has said we offend God when we "confess not his hand in all things, and obey not his commandments" (D&C 59:21). How could remembering Heavenly Father's blessings and thanking Him each day have helped the people of Ammonihah to be more righteous? What are the blessings for which you are grateful?

9:11 ***long-suffering***—patience
***unavoidably have been cut off***—surely have been destroyed
***consigned***—sent
***misery and woe***—suffering and sorrow

9:12 ***inherit***—receive
***utterly***—completely

9:14 ***verified***—proven correct

When the Prophet Joseph Smith was translating the Book of Mormon, one of the meanings of the word *transgression* was "the act of passing over or beyond any law or rule of moral duty" (Noah Webster, *An American Dictionary of the English Language,* s.v. "Transgression").

from the beginning of their transgressions in the land.

15 Nevertheless I say unto you, that it shall be more tolerable for them in the day of judgment than for you, if ye remain in your sins, yea, and even more tolerable for them in this life than for you, except ye repent.

16 For there are many promises which are extended to the Lamanites; for it is because of the traditions of their fathers that caused them to remain in their state of ignorance; therefore the Lord will be merciful unto them and prolong their existence in the land.

17 And at some period of time they will be brought to believe in his word, and to know of the incorrectness of the traditions of their fathers; and many of them will be saved, for the Lord will be merciful unto all who call on his name.

## *Alma Warns the People to Repent or Be Destroyed by the Lamanites*

18 But behold, I say unto you that if ye persist in your wickedness that your days shall not be prolonged in the land, for the Lamanites shall be sent upon you; and if ye repent not they shall come in a time when you know not, and ye shall be visited with utter destruction; and it shall be according to the fierce anger of the Lord.

19 For he will not suffer you that ye shall live in your iniquities, to destroy his people. I say unto you, Nay; he would rather suffer that the Lamanites might destroy all his people who are called the people of Nephi, if it were possible that they could fall into sins and transgressions, after having had so much light and so much knowledge given unto them of the Lord their God;

20 Yea, after having been such a highly favored people of the Lord; yea, after having been favored above every other nation, kindred, tongue, or people; after having had all things made known unto them, according to their desires, and their faith, and prayers, of that which has been, and which is, and which is to come;

21 Having been visited by the Spirit of God; having conversed with angels, and having been spoken unto by the voice of the Lord; and having the spirit of prophecy, and the spirit of revelation, and also many gifts, the gift of speaking with tongues, and the gift of preaching, and the gift of the Holy Ghost, and the gift of translation;

22 Yea, and after having been delivered of God out of the land of Jerusalem, by the hand of the Lord; having been saved from famine, and from sickness, and all manner of diseases of every kind; and they having waxed strong in battle, that they might not be destroyed; having been brought out of bondage time after time, and having been kept and preserved until now; and they have been prospered until they are rich in all manner of things—

23 And now behold I say unto you, that if this people, who have received so many blessings from the hand of the Lord, should transgress contrary to the light and knowledge which they do have, I say unto you that if this be the case, that if they should fall into transgression, it would be far more tolerable for the Lamanites than for them.

24 For behold, the promises of the Lord are extended to the Lamanites, but they are not unto you if ye transgress; for has not the Lord expressly promised and firmly decreed, that if ye will

---

9:15 ***tolerable***—bearable

9:16 Traditions are the stories and teachings that tell us about our ancestors (our parents, grandparents, and so on). The people of Ammonihah had forgotten the true stories of how God had saved and blessed their ancestors (see verses 8–11). The Lamanites, on the other hand, remembered and believed the false traditions that had been passed down since the time of Laman and Lemuel (see Mosiah 10:12–17). Changing the truth into false traditions is one of the ways Satan tricks people into committing sin (see D&C 93:39).

***ignorance***—spiritual darkness
***prolong their existence***—allow them to continue

9:18 ***persist***—continue

9:19 ***iniquities***—sins or wickedness

9:21 ***conversed***—talked

9:22 ***famine***—starvation
***waxed strong***—grown stronger
***bondage***—slavery

9:23 ***contrary to***—in spite of or against

9:23 (19–23) The people of Ammonihah knew of the gospel and yet chose not to live it. This choice left them open to the punishments of God. Brigham Young said, "When light comes, if the people reject that light, it will condemn them, and will add to their sorrow and affliction" (*Discourses of Brigham Young,* 226).

9:24 ***decreed***—ruled

rebel against him that ye shall utterly be destroyed from off the face of the earth?

25 And now for this cause, that ye may not be destroyed, the Lord has sent his angel to visit many of his people, declaring unto them that they must go forth and cry mightily unto this people, saying: Repent ye, for the kingdom of heaven is nigh at hand;

## *Alma Prophesies That Jesus Will Come and Redeem Those Who Believe in Him*

26 And not many days hence the Son of God shall come in his glory; and his glory shall be the glory of the Only Begotten of the Father, full of grace, equity, and truth, full of patience, mercy, and long-suffering, quick to hear the cries of his people and to answer their prayers.

27 And behold, he cometh to redeem those who will be baptized unto repentance, through faith on his name.

28 Therefore, prepare ye the way of the Lord, for the time is at hand that all men shall reap a reward of their works, according to that which they have been—if they have been righteous they shall reap the salvation of their souls, according to the power and deliverance of Jesus Christ; and if they have been evil they shall reap the damnation of their souls, according to the power and captivation of the devil.

29 Now behold, this is the voice of the angel, crying unto the people.

30 And now, my beloved brethren, for ye are my brethren, and ye ought to be beloved, and ye ought to bring forth works which are meet for repentance, seeing that your hearts have been grossly hardened against the word of God, and seeing that ye are a lost and a fallen people.

31 Now it came to pass that when I, Alma, had spoken these words, behold, the people were wroth with me because I said unto them that they were a hard-hearted and a stiffnecked people.

32 And also because I said unto them that they were a lost and a fallen people they were angry with me, and sought to lay their hands upon me, that they might cast me into prison.

33 But it came to pass that the Lord did not suffer them that they should take me at that time and cast me into prison.

34 And it came to pass that Amulek went and stood forth, and began to preach unto them also. And now the words of Amulek are not all written, nevertheless a part of his words are written in this book.

# CHAPTER 10

*Amulek tells how an angel of the Lord appeared and directed him to help the prophet Alma. Amulek proclaims the gospel and answers the wicked men who try to stop him. See how the Lord helps Amulek teach with power.*

## *Amulek Tells Who He Is and How He Was Called*

1 NOW these are the words which Amulek preached unto the people who were in the land of Ammonihah, saying:

2 I am Amulek; I am the son of Giddonah, who was the son of Ishmael, who was a descendant of Aminadi; and it was the same Aminadi who interpreted the writing which was upon the wall of the temple, which was written by the finger of God.

---

9:25 Sending angels is one of the many ways God tries to warn His children to repent. In modern revelation the Lord lists other means, such as thunder, lightning, earthquakes, and famines (see D&C 87:6). The wicked people living in the last days, just as the people of Ammonihah, will be destroyed because no matter how the Lord invites them to come unto Him they will not.

9:26 ***hence***—in the future
***equity***—fairness or justice

9:28 ***reap***—harvest or receive
***captivation***—enslavement

"Damnation is the opposite of salvation" and those who suffer it shall "be limited in their progress and privileges" (LDS Bible Dictionary, s.v. "Damnation," 652).

9:30 ***meet***—the evidence of
***grossly***—totally or entirely

9:33 The Lord protected Alma just as He earlier did Nephi (see 1 Nephi 17:48) and Abinadi (see Mosiah 13:1–5). What does this teach you about the Lord's power to help His servants complete their assignments?

10:2 Our present Book of Mormon does not relate the story of Aminadi interpreting the writing done by the finger of God on a temple wall. The Old Testament records a similar story in Daniel 5:5.

3 And Aminadi was a descendant of Nephi, who was the son of Lehi, who came out of the land of Jerusalem, who was a descendant of Manasseh, who was the son of Joseph who was sold into Egypt by the hands of his brethren.
4 And behold, I am also a man of no small reputation among all those who know me; yea, and behold, I have many kindreds and friends, and I have also acquired much riches by the hand of my industry.
5 Nevertheless, after all this, I never have known much of the ways of the Lord, and his mysteries and marvelous power. I said I never had known much of these things; but behold, I mistake, for I have seen much of his mysteries and his marvelous power; yea, even in the preservation of the lives of this people.
6 Nevertheless, I did harden my heart, for I was called many times and I would not hear; therefore I knew concerning these things, yet I would not know; therefore I went on rebelling against God, in the wickedness of my heart, even until the fourth day of this seventh month, which is in the tenth year of the reign of the judges.
7 As I was journeying to see a very near kindred, behold an angel of the Lord appeared unto me and said: Amulek, return to thine own house, for thou shalt feed a prophet of the Lord; yea, a holy man, who is a chosen man of God; for he has fasted many days because of the sins of this people, and he is an hungered, and thou shalt receive him into thy house and feed him, and he shall bless thee and thy house; and the blessing of the Lord shall rest upon thee and thy house.
8 And it came to pass that I obeyed the voice of the angel, and returned towards my house. And as I was going thither I found the man whom the angel said unto me: Thou shalt receive into thy house—and behold it was this same man who has been speaking unto you concerning the things of God.
9 And the angel said unto me he is a holy man; wherefore I know he is a holy man because it was said by an angel of God.
10 And again, I know that the things whereof he hath testified are true; for behold I say unto you, that as the Lord liveth, even so has he sent his angel to make these things manifest unto me; and this he has done while this Alma hath dwelt at my house.
11 For behold, he hath blessed mine house, he hath blessed me, and my women, and my children, and my father and my kinsfolk; yea, even all my kindred hath he blessed, and the blessing of the Lord hath rested upon us according to the words which he spake.

10:3 The story of Joseph being sold by his brothers as a slave into Egypt is found in Genesis 37.

10:4 ***of no small reputation***—who is well known
***kindreds***—family members
***acquired***—obtained
***the hand of my industry***—my hard work

10:5 ***preservation***—saving

10:6 Earlier in his life Amulek had not followed "the things of the Spirit because, though he was basically good, he was preoccupied [busy] with the cares of the world" (Neal A. Maxwell, *Meek and Lowly,* 12)

10:6 (5–6) Amulek admitted he had seen the miracles and power of the Lord, but he would not allow himself to feel, hear, or know these things came from God. President Hunter taught us to look for God's hand in our lives: "Are not the greatest *miracles* the fact that we have life and limb and sight and speech in the first place? Yes, there will always be plenty of miracles if we have eyes to see and ears to hear" (*The Teachings of Howard W. Hunter,* 115).

10:7 The word *holy* in Hebrew means "committed" or "consecrated" (see 2 Nephi 9:20, note a). Those who are committed do what they promise to do. Consecrated individuals commit themselves to serve the Lord.

The angel told Amulek that helping Alma would bring blessings to him and his family. In what ways does the Lord bless you when you help others?

10:8 ***thither***—there

10:10 ***manifest***—known

We, too, can learn from angels. Elder Dallin H. Oaks taught: "Angelic messages can be delivered by a voice or merely by thoughts or feelings communicated to the mind. . . . Most angelic communications are felt or heard rather than seen" (in Conference Report, October 1998, 51).

10:11 ***kinsfolk***—relatives

## Lawyers Try to Trick Amulek with Their Questions

12 And now, when Amulek had spoken these words the people began to be astonished, seeing there was more than one witness who testified of the things whereof they were accused, and also of the things which were to come, according to the spirit of prophecy which was in them.

13 Nevertheless, there were some among them who thought to question them, that by their cunning devices they might catch them in their words, that they might find witness against them, that they might deliver them to their judges that they might be judged according to the law, and that they might be slain or cast into prison, according to the crime which they could make appear or witness against them.

14 Now it was those men who sought to destroy them, who were lawyers, who were hired or appointed by the people to administer the law at their times of trials, or at the trials of the crimes of the people before the judges.

15 Now these lawyers were learned in all the arts and cunning of the people; and this was to enable them that they might be skilful in their profession.

16 And it came to pass that they began to question Amulek, that thereby they might make him cross his words, or contradict the words which he should speak.

## Amulek Tells of the Wickedness of the People in Ammonihah

17 Now they knew not that Amulek could know of their designs. But it came to pass as they began to question him, he perceived their thoughts, and he said unto them: O ye wicked and perverse generation, ye lawyers and hypocrites, for ye are laying the foundations of the devil; for ye are laying traps and snares to catch the holy ones of God.

18 Ye are laying plans to pervert the ways of the righteous, and to bring down the wrath of God upon your heads, even to the utter destruction of this people.

19 Yea, well did Mosiah say, who was our last king, when he was about to deliver up the kingdom, having no one to confer it upon, causing that this people should be governed by their own voices—yea, well did he say that if the time should come that the voice of this people should choose iniquity, that is, if the time should come that this people should fall into transgression, they would be ripe for destruction.

20 And now I say unto you that well doth the Lord judge of your iniquities; well doth he cry unto this people, by the voice of his angels: Repent ye, repent, for the kingdom of heaven is at hand.

21 Yea, well doth he cry, by the voice of his angels that: I will come down among my people, with equity and justice in my hands.

---

10:12 ***astonished***—surprised or amazed

10:13 ***devices***—schemes or plans

10:14 ***administer***—enforce

10:15 ***arts***—tactics or tricks

10:16 (13–16) These wicked lawyers wanted to make Alma and Amulek say words that were against the law so they could put them in prison or have them killed. Wicked religious leaders tried to do the same thing to Jesus (see Mark 14:55–64).

10:17 ***designs***—plans
***perceived***—knew
***wicked and perverse generation***—stubbornly wicked people
***hypocrites***—people who pretend to be good but are not

In 1828, about the time Joseph Smith translated the Book of Mormon, the word *snare* meant a trap used "for catching animals, particularly fowls, by the leg. It consists of a cord or string with slip-knots, in which the leg is entangled. A snare is not a net." Figuratively, a snare is "any thing by which one is entangled and brought into trouble" (Noah Webster, *An American Dictionary of the English Language,* 1828, s.v. "Snare").

10:18 ***pervert***—corrupt or change
***wrath***—anger

10:19 ***confer it upon***—give it to
***iniquity***—sin
***ripe for destruction***—about to be destroyed

King Mosiah's warning is found in Mosiah 29:27. This warning was later fulfilled with the destruction of the people of Ammonihah (see Alma 16:9).

10:20 ***kingdom of heaven is at hand***—Lord's true Church is on the earth

10:21 ***equity and justice***—fair judgments and punishments

22 Yea, and I say unto you that if it were not for the prayers of the righteous, who are now in the land, that ye would even now be visited with utter destruction; yet it would not be by flood, as were the people in the days of Noah, but it would be by famine, and by pestilence, and the sword.

23 But it is by the prayers of the righteous that ye are spared; now therefore, if ye will cast out the righteous from among you then will not the Lord stay his hand; but in his fierce anger he will come out against you; then ye shall be smitten by famine, and by pestilence, and by the sword; and the time is soon at hand except ye repent.

24 And now it came to pass that the people were more angry with Amulek, and they cried out, saying: This man doth revile against our laws which are just, and our wise lawyers whom we have selected.

25 But Amulek stretched forth his hand, and cried the mightier unto them, saying: O ye wicked and perverse generation, why hath Satan got such great hold upon your hearts? Why will ye yield yourselves unto him that he may have power over you, to blind your eyes, that ye will not understand the words which are spoken, according to their truth?

26 For behold, have I testified against your law? Ye do not understand; ye say that I have spoken against your law; but I have not, but I have spoken in favor of your law, to your condemnation.

27 And now behold, I say unto you, that the foundation of the destruction of this people is beginning to be laid by the unrighteousness of your lawyers and your judges.

28 And now it came to pass that when Amulek had spoken these words the people cried out against him, saying: Now we know that this man is a child of the devil, for he hath lied unto us; for he hath spoken against our law. And now he says that he has not spoken against it.

29 And again, he has reviled against our lawyers, and our judges.

30 And it came to pass that the lawyers put it into their hearts that they should remember these things against him.

31 And there was one among them whose name was Zeezrom. Now he was the foremost to accuse Amulek and Alma, he being one of the most expert among them, having much business to do among the people.

32 Now the object of these lawyers was to get gain; and they got gain according to their employ.

## CHAPTER 11

*Zeezrom fails in his attempt to bribe and deceive Amulek. Amulek rebukes him and testifies boldly about Jesus Christ and the plan of redemption. Watch for the great truths Amulek teaches about the Resurrection.*

### The Nephite Judges Were Paid According to Their Labor

1 NOW it was in the law of Mosiah that every man who was a judge of the law, or those who were appointed to be judges, should receive wages according to the time which they labored to judge those who were brought before them to be judged.

2 Now if a man owed another, and he would not pay that which he did owe, he was complained of

---

10:22 ***utter***—complete
***pestilence***—terrible disease

"Our world is now much the same as it was in the days of the Nephite prophet [Amulek]. . . . Of course, there are many many upright and faithful who live all the commandments and whose lives and prayers keep the world from destruction" (Spencer W. Kimball, in Conference Report, April 1971, 7).

10:23 ***spared***—kept alive
***stay***—stop

"It seems to me that what we need in this fair land of ours is a shining example of prayerfulness, and the Latter-day Saints are the people who are chosen to exemplify to the world the power of prayer. Every Latter-day Saint home should be a house of God, where the altar of prayer is ever in use and where the proper example is set to our children in supplicating God for divine guidance in all of our endeavors" (Joseph L. Wirthlin, in Conference Report, April 1949, 159).

10:24 ***revile against***—harshly criticize

10:25 ***yield***—surrender or give

10:26 ***to your condemnation***—proving you are guilty

10:27 ***foundation***—start

10:31 ***foremost***—most important

11:1 ***wages***—payment

11:2 ***complained of***—reported

to the judge; and the judge executed authority, and
sent forth officers that the man should be brought
before him; and he judged the man according to the
law and the evidences which were brought against
him, and thus the man was compelled to pay that
which he owed, or be stripped, or be cast out from
among the people as a thief and a robber.
3 And the judge received for his wages according
to his time—a senine of gold for a day, or a senum
of silver, which is equal to a senine of gold; and this
is according to the law which was given.
4 Now these are the names of the different pieces
of their gold, and of their silver, according to their
value. And the names are given by the Nephites, for
they did not reckon after the manner of the Jews
who were at Jerusalem; neither did they measure
after the manner of the Jews; but they altered their
reckoning and their measure, according to the
minds and the circumstances of the people, in
every generation, until the reign of the judges, they
having been established by king Mosiah.
5 Now the reckoning is thus—a senine of gold, a
seon of gold, a shum of gold, and a limnah of gold.
6 A senum of silver, an amnor of silver, an ezrom
of silver, and an onti of silver.
7 A senum of silver was equal to a senine of gold,
and either for a measure of barley, and also for a
measure of every kind of grain.
8 Now the amount of a seon of gold was twice the
value of a senine.
9 And a shum of gold was twice the value of a seon.
10 And a limnah of gold was the value of them all.
11 And an amnor of silver was as great as two
senums.
12 And an ezrom of silver was as great as four
senums.
13 And an onti was as great as them all.
14 Now this is the value of the lesser numbers of
their reckoning—
15 A shiblon is half of a senum; therefore, a shiblon
for half a measure of barley.
16 And a shiblum is a half of a shiblon.
17 And a leah is the half of a shiblum.
18 Now this is their number, according to their
reckoning.
19 Now an antion of gold is equal to three shiblons.
20 Now, it was for the sole purpose to get gain,
because they received their wages according to
their employ, therefore, they did stir up the people
to riotings, and all manner of disturbances and
wickedness, that they might have more employ,
that they might get money according to the suits
which were brought before them; therefore they
did stir up the people against Alma and Amulek.

## Amulek Says That Zeezrom Is a Wicked Man

21 And this Zeezrom began to question Amulek,
saying: Will ye answer me a few questions which I
shall ask you? Now Zeezrom was a man who was
expert in the devices of the devil, that he might
destroy that which was good; therefore, he said
unto Amulek: Will ye answer the questions which I
shall put unto you?

11:2 ***executed authority***—used his power
***evidences***—proofs of what he had done wrong
***compelled***—forced

11:4 ***reckon***—count their money
***altered***—changed
***generation***—period of time
***established***—set

The term *Jew* often refers to a descendant from the tribe of Judah. However, the Book of Mormon also uses the term *Jew* to refer to any Israelite from the land or kingdom of Judah, even if not descended from the tribe of Judah (see LDS Bible Dictionary, s.v. "Jew," 713). In addition, the Book of Mormon sometimes uses the term *Jews* to refer to the entire house of Israel (see *Book of Mormon Student Manual, Religion 121 and 122,* 15).

11:20 ***sole***—only
***gain***—more money
***employ***—work or job
***riotings***—violent or wild behavior
***suits***—legal actions

11:21 ***devices***—tricks or ways

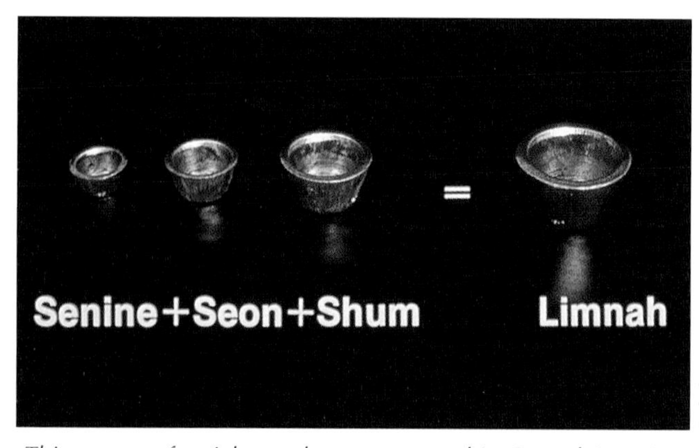


*This system of weights and measures used in Central America today is similar to the Nephite monetary system.*

22 And Amulek said unto him: Yea, if it be
according to the Spirit of the Lord, which is in me;
for I shall say nothing which is contrary to the
Spirit of the Lord. And Zeezrom said unto him:
Behold, here are six onties of silver, and all these
will I give thee if thou wilt deny the existence of a
Supreme Being.
23 Now Amulek said: O thou child of hell, why
tempt ye me? Knowest thou that the righteous yieldeth to no such temptations?
24 Believest thou that there is no God? I say unto
you, Nay, thou knowest that there is a God, but
thou lovest that lucre more than him.
25 And now thou hast lied before God unto me.
Thou saidst unto me—Behold these six onties,
which are of great worth, I will give unto thee—
when thou hadst it in thy heart to retain them from
me; and it was only thy desire that I should deny
the true and living God, that thou mightest have
cause to destroy me. And now behold, for this great
evil thou shalt have thy reward.

## Amulek Explains That We Cannot Be Saved in Our Sins

26 And Zeezrom said unto him: Thou sayest there
is a true and living God?
27 And Amulek said: Yea, there is a true and living God.
28 Now Zeezrom said: Is there more than one
God?
29 And he answered, No.
30 Now Zeezrom said unto him again: How
knowest thou these things?
31 And he said: An angel hath made them known
unto me.
32 And Zeezrom said again: Who is he that shall
come? Is it the Son of God?
33 And he said unto him, Yea.
34 And Zeezrom said again: Shall he save his
people in their sins? And Amulek answered and
said unto him: I say unto you he shall not, for it is
impossible for him to deny his word.
35 Now Zeezrom said unto the people: See that ye
remember these things; for he said there is but one
God; yet he saith that the Son of God shall come,
but he shall not save his people—as though he had
authority to command God.
36 Now Amulek saith again unto him: Behold
thou hast lied, for thou sayest that I spake as
though I had authority to command God because I
said he shall not save his people in their sins.
37 And I say unto you again that he cannot save
them in their sins; for I cannot deny his word, and
he hath said that no unclean thing can inherit the
kingdom of heaven; therefore, how can ye be
saved, except ye inherit the kingdom of heaven?
Therefore, ye cannot be saved in your sins.
38 Now Zeezrom saith again unto him: Is the Son
of God the very Eternal Father?
39 And Amulek said unto him: Yea, he is the very
Eternal Father of heaven and of earth, and all things
which in them are; he is the beginning and the end,
the first and the last;

---

11:22 ***contrary to***—against
***a Supreme Being***—God

11:23 ***yieldeth***—give in

11:24 ***lucre***—wealth or money

11:25 ***retain***—keep

11:25 (21–25) Amulek was not afraid to speak because he knew what he was saying was true and he had the help of the Spirit of the Lord. What can you learn from this story that can help you in your life?

11:28 "Zeezrom, in his eagerness to trap Amulek in his own words, asks whether there is more than one God. Amulek answers that there is not. Amulek is, of course, speaking entirely of the Savior, of the Lord Jehovah; he is not making reference to our Father in Heaven or to the Godhead" (Joseph Fielding McConkie and others, *Doctrinal Commentary on the Book of Mormon* 3:75).

11:35 ***authority***—power

11:37 ***inherit***—obtain

When we sin, we become spiritually unclean and cannot live with God (see 1 Nephi 10:21). To become clean again, we must have faith in Christ, repent of our sins, be baptized, and receive the gift of the Holy Ghost.

11:37 (34–37) "Even the Omnipotent [all-powerful] One, the Lord Jehovah, cannot save his people *in* their sins. He came on a search-and-rescue mission to save people *from* their sins" (Joseph Fielding McConkie and others, *Doctrinal Commentary on the Book of Mormon* 3:76; see also Helaman 5:10–11).

11:39 Jesus Christ is the Creator or Father of heaven and the earth (see Moses 1:31–33).

40 And he shall come into the world to redeem his
people; and he shall take upon him the transgressions of those who believe on his name; and these
are they that shall have eternal life, and salvation
cometh to none else.
41 Therefore the wicked remain as though there
had been no redemption made, except it be the
loosing of the bands of death; for behold, the day
cometh that all shall rise from the dead and stand
before God, and be judged according to their
works.

### Amulek Tells Zeezrom That All People Will Be Resurrected and Judged by Their Works

42 Now, there is a death which is called a temporal death; and the death of Christ shall loose the
bands of this temporal death, that all shall be raised
from this temporal death.
43 The spirit and the body shall be reunited again
in its perfect form; both limb and joint shall be
restored to its proper frame, even as we now are at
this time; and we shall be brought to stand before
God, knowing even as we know now, and have a
bright recollection of all our guilt.
44 Now, this restoration shall come to all, both old
and young, both bond and free, both male and
female, both the wicked and the righteous; and
even there shall not so much as a hair of their heads
be lost; but every thing shall be restored to its perfect frame, as it is now, or in the body, and shall be
brought and be arraigned before the bar of Christ
the Son, and God the Father, and the Holy Spirit,
which is one Eternal God, to be judged according
to their works, whether they be good or whether
they be evil.
45 Now, behold, I have spoken unto you concerning the death of the mortal body, and also concerning the resurrection of the mortal body. I say
unto you that this mortal body is raised to an
immortal body, that is from death, even from the
first death unto life, that they can die no more; their
spirits uniting with their bodies, never to be divided;
thus the whole becoming spiritual and immortal,
that they can no more see corruption.
46 Now, when Amulek had finished these words
the people began again to be astonished, and also
Zeezrom began to tremble. And thus ended the
words of Amulek, or this is all that I have written.

## CHAPTER 12

*Our Heavenly Father's plan of happiness makes it possible for us to return to His presence. As you read this chapter, look for what Alma teaches we must do in this life so we can return to our Father in Heaven.*

### Alma Speaks Against Zeezrom's Evil Plan

1 NOW Alma, seeing that the words of Amulek
had silenced Zeezrom, for he beheld that Amulek
had caught him in his lying and deceiving to
destroy him, and seeing that he began to tremble
under a consciousness of his guilt, he opened his
mouth and began to speak unto him, and to establish the words of Amulek, and to explain things
beyond, or to unfold the scriptures beyond that
which Amulek had done.
2 Now the words that Alma spake unto Zeezrom
were heard by the people round about; for the multitude was great, and he spake on this wise:

---

11:41 ***loosing of the bands of death***—overcoming of death through the Resurrection

11:42 ***temporal***—physical

11:43 ***reunited***—brought back together
***bright recollection***—clear memory
***our guilt***—the pain in our hearts and minds for our sins

11:44 ***bond***—slaves
***arraigned before the bar of***—judged before

When we are resurrected, not only will our spirit and our body be restored, or brought back together, but also our memory of all that we have done on earth will be restored to our minds (see 2 Nephi 9:14). Revelation 20:12 says that the dead will stand before God and books that contain a record of what they did on earth will be opened, and each will be judged by their works.

11:45 ***mortal***—physical
***an immortal body***—a resurrected body
***corruption***—death and decay

11:46 ***astonished***—surprised or amazed

12:1 ***consciousness***—knowledge
***unfold***—make known

12:2 ***on this wise***—in this way

3 Now Zeezrom, seeing that thou hast been taken
in thy lying and craftiness, for thou hast not lied
unto men only but thou hast lied unto God; for
behold, he knows all thy thoughts, and thou seest
that thy thoughts are made known unto us by his
Spirit;
4 And thou seest that we know that thy plan was
a very subtle plan, as to the subtlety of the devil, for
to lie and to deceive this people that thou mightest
set them against us, to revile us and to cast us out—
5 Now this was a plan of thine adversary, and he
hath exercised his power in thee. Now I would that
ye should remember that what I say unto thee I say
unto all.
6 And behold I say unto you all that this was a
snare of the adversary, which he has laid to catch
this people, that he might bring you into subjection
unto him, that he might encircle you about with his
chains, that he might chain you down to everlasting
destruction, according to the power of his captivity.
7 Now when Alma had spoken these words,
Zeezrom began to tremble more exceedingly, for
he was convinced more and more of the power of
God; and he was also convinced that Alma and
Amulek had a knowledge of him, for he was convinced that they knew the thoughts and intents of
his heart; for power was given unto them that they
might know of these things according to the spirit
of prophecy.
8 And Zeezrom began to inquire of them diligently,
that he might know more concerning the kingdom
of God. And he said unto Alma: What does this
mean which Amulek hath spoken concerning the
resurrection of the dead, that all shall rise from the
dead, both the just and the unjust, and are brought
to stand before God to be judged according to their
works?

## The Mysteries of God Are Unfolded to the Faithful and Obedient

9 And now Alma began to expound these things
unto him, saying: It is given unto many to know the
mysteries of God; nevertheless they are laid under
a strict command that they shall not impart only
according to the portion of his word which he doth
grant unto the children of men, according to the
heed and diligence which they give unto him.
10 And therefore, he that will harden his heart, the
same receiveth the lesser portion of the word; and
he that will not harden his heart, to him is given the
greater portion of the word, until it is given unto
him to know the mysteries of God until he know
them in full.
11 And they that will harden their hearts, to them
is given the lesser portion of the word until they
know nothing concerning his mysteries; and then
they are taken captive by the devil, and led by his
will down to destruction. Now this is what is meant
by the chains of hell.

---

12:3 ***craftiness***—deceptive or tricky ways

Elder Bruce R. McConkie stated: "The Lord can and does on occasion reveal to his prophets the thoughts and intents of the hearts of men. 'By the help of the all-powerful Creator of heaven and earth,' Jacob said to his Nephite brethren, 'I can tell you concerning your thoughts' (Jacob. 2:5; Alma 10:17)" (*Mormon Doctrine,* 777).

12:4 ***subtle***—sly or deceptive
***revile***—criticize

12:5 ***thine adversary***—Satan

12:6 ***snare***—trap
***into subjection unto him***—under his control

12:8 ***just and the unjust***—righteous and the unrighteous

12:9 ***expound***—explain
***impart***—teach or share
***heed***—attention or obedience

"A mystery is . . . some truth which is not understood. All the principles of the gospel and all truth pertaining to the salvation of men are simple when understood. Until it is understood, however, a simple truth may be a great mystery. *Gospel truths appeal more to the spirit. . . .* Revelations through the Spirit of the Lord, many times, cannot be explained" (Joseph Fielding Smith, *Doctrines of Salvation* 1:296).

12:11 (10–11) Using these verses, President Ezra Taft Benson taught that "pride is a damning sin in the true sense of that word. It limits or stops progression (see Alma 12:10–11). The proud are not easily taught (see 1 Nephi 15:3, 7–11). They won't change their minds to accept truths, because to do so implies they have been wrong" (in Conference Report, April 1989, 5).

## PEOPLE WILL BE JUDGED BY THEIR WORDS, WORKS, AND THOUGHTS

12 And Amulek hath spoken plainly concerning death, and being raised from this mortality to a state of immortality, and being brought before the bar of God, to be judged according to our works.

13 Then if our hearts have been hardened, yea, if we have hardened our hearts against the word, insomuch that it has not been found in us, then will our state be awful, for then we shall be condemned.

14 For our words will condemn us, yea, all our works will condemn us; we shall not be found spotless; and our thoughts will also condemn us; and in this awful state we shall not dare to look up to our God; and we would fain be glad if we could command the rocks and the mountains to fall upon us to hide us from his presence.

15 But this cannot be; we must come forth and stand before him in his glory, and in his power, and in his might, majesty, and dominion, and acknowledge to our everlasting shame that all his judgments are just; that he is just in all his works, and that he is merciful unto the children of men, and that he has all power to save every man that believeth on his name and bringeth forth fruit meet for repentance.

16 And now behold, I say unto you then cometh a death, even a second death, which is a spiritual death; then is a time that whosoever dieth in his sins, as to a temporal death, shall also die a spiritual death; yea, he shall die as to things pertaining unto righteousness.

17 Then is the time when their torments shall be as a lake of fire and brimstone, whose flame ascendeth up forever and ever; and then is the time that they shall be chained down to an everlasting destruction, according to the power and captivity of Satan, he having subjected them according to his will.

18 Then, I say unto you, they shall be as though there had been no redemption made; for they cannot be redeemed according to God's justice; and they cannot die, seeing there is no more corruption.

## MORTAL LIFE IS A TIME OF TESTING FOR GOD'S CHILDREN

19 Now it came to pass that when Alma had made an end of speaking these words, the people began to be more astonished;

20 But there was one Antionah, who was a chief ruler among them, came forth and said unto him: What is this that thou hast said, that man should rise from the dead and be changed from this mortal to an immortal state, that the soul can never die?

21 What does the scripture mean, which saith that God placed cherubim and a flaming sword on the east of the garden of Eden, lest our first parents should enter and partake of the fruit of the tree of life, and live forever? And thus we see that there was no possible chance that they should live forever.

---

12:12 ***immortality***—a resurrected body that cannot die
***bar of God***—place where God judges us

12:13 ***condemned***—declared guilty

12:15 To say a person brings "forth fruit meet for repentance" means he does what he has to do to repent of his sins. What must a person do to repent and be forgiven for his sins?

12:16 ***temporal***—physical

12:17 ***torments***—suffering
***ascendeth***—rises

The Prophet Joseph Smith said, "A man is his own tormenter and his own condemner. Hence the saying, They shall go into the lake that burns with fire and brimstone. The torment of disappointment in the mind of man is as exquisite as a lake burning with fire and brimstone" (*Teachings of the Prophet Joseph Smith,* 357).

12:18 ***corruption***—decay or death

12:18 (15–18) "It is very clear in the Doctrine and Covenants 76:30–37, that the only persons who will be completely overcome by this dreadful fate [the second death] are the sons of perdition, who go with the devil and his angels into 'outer darkness' " (Joseph Fielding Smith, *Answers to Gospel Questions* 1:76).

12:21 ***partake***—eat

*Cherubim* is a plural word meaning heavenly beings. "In the account of the Fall, cherubim are represented as keeping 'the way of the tree of life' (Gen. 3:24)" (LDS Bible Dictionary, s.v. "Cherubim," 632).

Our "first parents" were Adam and Eve (see Moses 2–4).

22 Now Alma said unto him: This is the thing which I was about to explain. Now we see that Adam did fall by the partaking of the forbidden fruit, according to the word of God; and thus we see, that by his fall, all mankind became a lost and fallen people.

23 And now behold, I say unto you that if it had been possible for Adam to have partaken of the fruit of the tree of life at that time, there would have been no death, and the word would have been void, making God a liar, for he said: If thou eat thou shalt surely die.

24 And we see that death comes upon mankind, yea, the death which has been spoken of by Amulek, which is the temporal death; nevertheless there was a space granted unto man in which he might repent; therefore this life became a probationary state; a time to prepare to meet God; a time to prepare for that endless state which has been spoken of by us, which is after the resurrection of the dead.

## All of God's Children Will Be Resurrected Because of the Plan of Redemption

25 Now, if it had not been for the plan of redemption, which was laid from the foundation of the world, there could have been no resurrection of the dead; but there was a plan of redemption laid, which shall bring to pass the resurrection of the dead, of which has been spoken.

26 And now behold, if it were possible that our first parents could have gone forth and partaken of the tree of life they would have been forever miserable, having no preparatory state; and thus the plan of redemption would have been frustrated, and the word of God would have been void, taking none effect.

27 But behold, it was not so; but it was appointed unto men that they must die; and after death, they must come to judgment, even that same judgment of which we have spoken, which is the end.

28 And after God had appointed that these things should come unto man, behold, then he saw that it was expedient that man should know concerning the things whereof he had appointed unto them;

29 Therefore he sent angels to converse with them, who caused men to behold of his glory.

30 And they began from that time forth to call on his name; therefore God conversed with men, and made known unto them the plan of redemption, which had been prepared from the foundation of the world; and this he made known unto them according to their faith and repentance and their holy works.

31 Wherefore, he gave commandments unto men, they having first transgressed the first commandments as to things which were temporal, and becoming as Gods, knowing good from evil,

---

12:22 "The fall of Adam is one of the most important occurrences in the history of man. Before the fall, Adam and Eve had physical bodies but no blood. There was no sin, no death, and no children among any of the earthly creations." The Fall brought mortality and "both physical and spiritual death into the world upon all mankind (Hel. 14:16–17). . . . It was a necessary step in the progress of man, and provisions for a Savior had been made even before the fall had occurred. Jesus Christ came to atone for the fall of Adam and also for man's individual sins" (LDS Bible Dictionary, s.v. "Fall of Adam," 670).

12:23 ***void***—useless

12:24 ***space***—length of time

"In mortality we are on probation. We are here to be tried, tested, and proved in all things, to see whether we will be obedient to that which the Lord commands us to do. (See Abraham 3:25; 2 Nephi 2:21; Alma 42:4)" (Joseph Fielding McConkie and others, *Doctrinal Commentary on the Book of Mormon* 3:88).

12:25 "The means provided for our redemption from death were prepared in the plan of salvation before Adam and Eve were sent to the earth, and Jesus Christ volunteered to come and atone for this transgression and thus gain the victory over the devil" (Joseph Fielding Smith, *Answers to Gospel Questions* 1:32).

12:26 ***miserable***—unhappy and without hope

The term "preparatory state" refers to our lives upon this earth and the time allowed us to prepare to return to our Father in Heaven (see Alma 34:32).

12:28 ***expedient***—necessary

12:29 ***converse***—talk

12:31 The transgression of the first commandment was Adam and Eve's partaking of the forbidden fruit and being cast out of the Garden of Eden (see Genesis 3).

placing themselves in a state to act, or being placed
in a state to act according to their wills and pleasures, whether to do evil or to do good—
32 Therefore God gave unto them commandments, after having made known unto them the
plan of redemption, that they should not do evil,
the penalty thereof being a second death, which
was an everlasting death as to things pertaining
unto righteousness; for on such the plan of redemption could have no power, for the works of justice
could not be destroyed, according to the supreme
goodness of God.
33 But God did call on men, in the name of his
Son, (this being the plan of redemption which was
laid) saying: If ye will repent and harden not your
hearts, then will I have mercy upon you, through
mine Only Begotten Son;
34 Therefore, whosoever repenteth, and hardeneth not his heart, he shall have claim on mercy
through mine Only Begotten Son, unto a remission of his sins; and these shall enter into my
rest.
35 And whosoever will harden his heart and will
do iniquity, behold, I swear in my wrath that he
shall not enter into my rest.
36 And now, my brethren, behold I say unto you,
that if ye will harden your hearts ye shall not enter
into the rest of the Lord; therefore your iniquity provoketh him that he sendeth down his wrath upon
you as in the first provocation, yea, according to his
word in the last provocation as well as the first, to
the everlasting destruction of your souls; therefore,
according to his word, unto the last death, as well
as the first.
37 And now, my brethren, seeing we know these
things, and they are true, let us repent, and harden
not our hearts, that we provoke not the Lord our
God to pull down his wrath upon us in these his
second commandments which he has given unto
us; but let us enter into the rest of God, which is
prepared according to his word.

## CHAPTER 13

*Alma tells his people that the holy priesthood is eternal and helps us learn about Jesus Christ. Look for how the priesthood also helps us become like Christ.*

### Righteous Priesthood Holders Were Called to Hold the Priesthood Before They Were Born

1 AND again, my brethren, I would cite your
minds forward to the time when the Lord God gave
these commandments unto his children; and I
would that ye should remember that the Lord God
ordained priests, after his holy order, which was
after the order of his Son, to teach these things unto
the people.
2 And those priests were ordained after the order
of his Son, in a manner that thereby the people
might know in what manner to look forward to his
Son for redemption.

---

12:32 God gave commandments to His children, "after having made known unto them the plan of redemption." How does learning and understanding Heavenly Father's plan help you keep the commandments?

12:34 ***claim on***—the right to receive
***remission***—forgiveness

One modern revelation defines the "rest" of the Lord as "the fulness of his glory" (D&C 84:24). President Joseph F. Smith added that, in this life, God's rest "means entering into the knowledge and love of God, having faith in his purpose and in his plan, to such an extent that we know we are right" (*Gospel Doctrine,* 58).

12:36 ***provoketh***—angers
***provocation***—offense

13:1 The phrase "cite your minds forward" means to direct your attention to an earlier time. Alma is referring to the time when God gave commandments to Adam and Eve and their children (see Alma 12:31–37).

***ordained***—called and gave authority to

13:2 ***manner***—way

13:2 (1–2) The Melchizedek Priesthood, "the higher priesthood, is defined as the priesthood after the holiest order of God, or the Holy Priesthood after the Order of the Son of God (see Alma 13:18; Hel. 8:18; D&C 107:2–4)" (Boyd K. Packer, "The Holy Temple," 34).

3 And this is the manner after which they were ordained—being called and prepared from the foundation of the world according to the foreknowledge of God, on account of their exceeding faith and good works; in the first place being left to choose good or evil; therefore they having chosen good, and exercising exceedingly great faith, are called with a holy calling, yea, with that holy calling which was prepared with, and according to, a preparatory redemption for such.
4 And thus they have been called to this holy calling on account of their faith, while others would reject the Spirit of God on account of the hardness of their hearts and blindness of their minds, while, if it had not been for this they might have had as great privilege as their brethren.
5 Or in fine, in the first place they were on the same standing with their brethren; thus this holy calling being prepared from the foundation of the world for such as would not harden their hearts, being in and through the atonement of the Only Begotten Son, who was prepared—
6 And thus being called by this holy calling, and ordained unto the high priesthood of the holy order of God, to teach his commandments unto the children of men, that they also might enter into his rest—

## *The Eternal Priesthood Helps Us Gain Salvation*

7 This high priesthood being after the order of his Son, which order was from the foundation of the world; or in other words, being without beginning of days or end of years, being prepared from eternity to all eternity, according to his foreknowledge of all things—
8 Now they were ordained after this manner—being called with a holy calling, and ordained with a holy ordinance, and taking upon them the high priesthood of the holy order, which calling, and ordinance, and high priesthood, is without beginning or end—
9 Thus they become high priests forever, after the order of the Son, the Only Begotten of the Father, who is without beginning of days or end of years, who is full of grace, equity, and truth. And thus it is. Amen.
10 Now, as I said concerning the holy order, or this high priesthood, there were many who were ordained and became high priests of God; and it was on account of their exceeding faith and repentance, and their righteousness before God, they choosing to repent and work righteousness rather than to perish;

---

13:3 ***foundation***—beginning

The foreknowledge of God means that "the Lord knoweth all things which are to come" (Words of Mormon 1:7).

These priesthood holders were called in the premortal life with "a holy calling which was prepared with, and according to" the Atonement of Jesus Christ.

Priesthood holders are "called and prepared from the foundation of the world" to hold this priesthood. The Prophet Joseph Smith explained that "every man who has a calling to minister to the inhabitants of the world was ordained to that very purpose in the Grand Council of heaven before this world was" (*Teachings of the Prophet Joseph Smith,* 365).

13:5 ***Or in fine***—In other words
***on the same standing***—equal

13:5 (3–5) The Lord gave to man his agency in the premortal life. "This great gift of agency, that is the privilege given to man to make his own choice, has never been revoked, and it never will be. It is an eternal principle giving freedom of thought and action to every soul" (Joseph Fielding Smith, *Answers to Gospel Questions* 2:20).

13:6 See on the "rest" of the Lord for Alma 12:34.

13:8 An "ordinance" is a sacred ceremony in which people enter covenants with God to aid in their eternal progression (see *Gospel Principles,* s.v. "Ordinances," 380).

13:8 (7–8) The Prophet Joseph Smith taught that "the Priesthood is an everlasting principle, and existed with God from eternity, and will to eternity, without beginning of days or end of years" (*Teachings of the Prophet Joseph Smith,* 157).

13:9 ***equity***—fairness or justice

13:10 ***perish***—die physically or spiritually

11 Therefore they were called after this holy order, and were sanctified, and their garments were washed white through the blood of the Lamb.

12 Now they, after being sanctified by the Holy Ghost, having their garments made white, being pure and spotless before God, could not look upon sin save it were with abhorrence; and there were many, exceedingly great many, who were made pure and entered into the rest of the Lord their God.

13 And now, my brethren, I would that ye should humble yourselves before God, and bring forth fruit meet for repentance, that ye may also enter into that rest.

## *Melchizedek Leads His People by Faith and the Power of the Priesthood*

14 Yea, humble yourselves even as the people in the days of Melchizedek, who was also a high priest after this same order which I have spoken, who also took upon him the high priesthood forever.

15 And it was this same Melchizedek to whom Abraham paid tithes; yea, even our father Abraham paid tithes of one-tenth part of all he possessed.

16 Now these ordinances were given after this manner, that thereby the people might look forward on the Son of God, it being a type of his order, or it being his order, and this that they might look forward to him for a remission of their sins, that they might enter into the rest of the Lord.

17 Now this Melchizedek was a king over the land of Salem; and his people had waxed strong in iniquity and abomination; yea, they had all gone astray; they were full of all manner of wickedness;

18 But Melchizedek having exercised mighty faith, and received the office of the high priesthood according to the holy order of God, did preach repentance unto his people. And behold, they did repent; and Melchizedek did establish peace in the land in his days; therefore he was called the prince of peace, for he was the king of Salem; and he did reign under his father.

19 Now, there were many before him, and also there were many afterwards, but none were greater; therefore, of him they have more particularly made mention.

20 Now I need not rehearse the matter; what I have said may suffice. Behold, the scriptures are before you; if ye will wrest them it shall be to your own destruction.

## *Alma Pleads with His People to Repent*

21 And now it came to pass that when Alma had said these words unto them, he stretched forth his hand unto them and cried with a mighty voice, saying: Now is the time to repent, for the day of salvation draweth nigh;

22 Yea, and the voice of the Lord, by the mouth of angels, doth declare it unto all nations; yea, doth declare it, that they may have glad tidings of great joy; yea, and he doth sound these glad tidings among all his people, yea, even to them that are scattered abroad upon the face of the earth; wherefore they have come unto us.

23 And they are made known unto us in plain terms, that we may understand, that we cannot err; and this because of our being wanderers in a strange land; therefore, we are thus highly favored, for we have these glad tidings declared unto us in all parts of our vineyard.

---

13:12 ***abhorrence***—disgust or hatred

13:12 (11–12) As we get closer to Heavenly Father, by our faith and obedience, a "mighty change" gradually occurs in our hearts. We lose the desire to sin and grow in our desire to always do good (see Mosiah 5:2; Alma 5:14; 19:33).

13:13 ***fruit meet for repentance***—good works that show you have repented

13:16 ***remission***—forgiveness

Alma explains that the way priesthood holders are called and serve is a "type," or example, intended to remind us of the calling and service of Jesus Christ (see also verse 2). What do you see in the life and service of your Church leaders that reminds you of Jesus Christ?

13:17 ***waxed***—grown

13:18 ***reign***—rule

13:20 ***wrest***—change or misinterpret

13:20 (14–20) To learn more about the great prophet Melchizedek see "Melchizedek" in the LDS Bible Dictionary. Refer also to the Joseph Smith Translation for Genesis 14:25–40 in the appendix of the LDS edition of the King James Bible, 797.

13:21 ***draweth nigh***—is coming close

13:22 ***tidings***—news

13:23 ***err***—make a mistake or misunderstand

MELCHIZEDEK ORDAINING ABRAHAM, BY GARY KAPP

*Melchizedek, the king of Salem, was a mighty and faithful high priest.*
*Melchizedek was Abraham's priesthood leader and is shown here blessing Abraham.*

24 For behold, angels are declaring it unto many
at this time in our land; and this is for the purpose
of preparing the hearts of the children of men to
receive his word at the time of his coming in his
glory.
25 And now we only wait to hear the joyful news
declared unto us by the mouth of angels, of his
coming; for the time cometh, we know not how
soon. Would to God that it might be in my day; but
let it be sooner or later, in it I will rejoice.
26 And it shall be made known unto just and holy
men, by the mouth of angels, at the time of his
coming, that the words of our fathers may be fulfilled, according to that which they have spoken
concerning him, which was according to the spirit
of prophecy which was in them.
27 And now, my brethren, I wish from the inmost
part of my heart, yea, with great anxiety even unto
pain, that ye would hearken unto my words, and
cast off your sins, and not procrastinate the day of
your repentance;
28 But that ye would humble yourselves before
the Lord, and call on his holy name, and watch and
pray continually, that ye may not be tempted above
that which ye can bear, and thus be led by the Holy
Spirit, becoming humble, meek, submissive,
patient, full of love and all long-suffering;
29 Having faith on the Lord; having a hope that ye
shall receive eternal life; having the love of God
always in your hearts, that ye may be lifted up at
the last day and enter into his rest.
30 And may the Lord grant unto you repentance,
that ye may not bring down his wrath upon you,
that ye may not be bound down by the chains of
hell, that ye may not suffer the second death.
31 And Alma spake many more words unto the
people, which are not written in this book.

## CHAPTER 14

*Alma and Amulek are imprisoned and many of the righteous are killed. Look for what Alma says about why bad things sometimes happen to good people.*

### *Alma and Amulek Are Brought Before the Chief Judge for Teaching the Truth*

1 AND it came to pass after he had made an end
of speaking unto the people many of them did
believe on his words, and began to repent, and to
search the scriptures.
2 But the more part of them were desirous that
they might destroy Alma and Amulek; for they were
angry with Alma, because of the plainness of his
words unto Zeezrom; and they also said that
Amulek had lied unto them, and had reviled against
their law and also against their lawyers and judges.

---

13:26 The "spirit of prophecy" is a spiritual gift (see D&C 46:22). It is given to prophets and can be received by all those who have a testimony of Jesus Christ and are faithful (see Revelation 19:10).

13:26 (24–26) Alma teaches that the Lord sends angels to prepare people for Jesus Christ's first coming on earth. The Prophet Joseph Smith taught that the Lord is also sending angels in our day to prepare people for the Second Coming of Jesus Christ (see D&C 20:6–10; 43:24–25).

13:27 ***anxiety***—concern
***procrastinate***—put off or delay

Alma tells the people of his deep love and concern for them. He asks them to repent. What have you heard our living prophets say that shows you that they feel the same way about us?

13:28 Notice the process Alma gives his people in this verse for overcoming temptation: (1) be humble, (2) watch and pray continually for strength, and (3) follow the whisperings of the Holy Spirit. Following Alma's process will help you become humble, meek (teachable), submissive (willing to obey), patient, full of love, and all long-suffering (enduring trials faithfully). In which parts of this process could you improve to better resist temptation?

13:30 ***wrath***—anger and punishment

"After the separation of body and spirit, which is the natural death, the wicked and ungodly die a second death, a spiritual death, meaning they are cast out of the presence of the Lord and are dead as pertaining to the things of righteousness, which are the things of the Spirit" (Bruce R. McConkie, *Doctrinal New Testament Commentary* 3:583–84; see also D&C 63:17–18).

14:2 ***reviled against***—criticized and insulted

3 And they were also angry with Alma and Amulek; and because they had testified so plainly against their wickedness, they sought to put them away privily.

4 But it came to pass that they did not; but they took them and bound them with strong cords, and took them before the chief judge of the land.

5 And the people went forth and witnessed against them—testifying that they had reviled against the law, and their lawyers and judges of the land, and also of all the people that were in the land; and also testified that there was but one God, and that he should send his Son among the people, but he should not save them; and many such things did the people testify against Alma and Amulek. Now this was done before the chief judge of the land.

6 And it came to pass that Zeezrom was astonished at the words which had been spoken; and he also knew concerning the blindness of the minds, which he had caused among the people by his lying words; and his soul began to be harrowed up under a consciousness of his own guilt; yea, he began to be encircled about by the pains of hell.

7 And it came to pass that he began to cry unto the people, saying: Behold, I am guilty, and these men are spotless before God. And he began to plead for them from that time forth; but they reviled him, saying: Art thou also possessed with the devil? And they spit upon him, and cast him out from among them, and also all those who believed in the words which had been spoken by Alma and Amulek; and they cast them out, and sent men to cast stones at them.

8 And they brought their wives and children together, and whosoever believed or had been taught to believe in the word of God they caused that they should be cast into the fire; and they also brought forth their records which contained the holy scriptures, and cast them into the fire also, that they might be burned and destroyed by fire.

## Alma and Amulek Are Forced to Watch Righteous People Burn to Death

9 And it came to pass that they took Alma and Amulek, and carried them forth to the place of martyrdom, that they might witness the destruction of those who were consumed by fire.

10 And when Amulek saw the pains of the women and children who were consuming in the fire, he also was pained; and he said unto Alma: How can we witness this awful scene? Therefore let us stretch forth our hands, and exercise the power of God which is in us, and save them from the flames.

11 But Alma said unto him: The Spirit constraineth me that I must not stretch forth mine hand; for behold the Lord receiveth them up unto himself, in glory; and he doth suffer that they may do this thing, or that the people may do this thing unto them, according to the hardness of their hearts, that the judgments which he shall exercise upon them in his wrath may be just; and the blood of the innocent shall stand as a witness against them, yea, and cry mightily against them at the last day.

12 Now Amulek said unto Alma: Behold, perhaps they will burn us also.

---

14:3 ***put them away privily***—get rid of them privately or secretly

Nephi taught that when the wicked hear the truth they become angry because of the guilt they feel (see 1 Nephi 16:1–2).

14:6 ***astonished***—surprised or amazed
***harrowed up***—greatly troubled
***a consciousness***—an awareness or a knowledge
***encircled***—surrounded

14:7 ***spotless***—without sin
***possessed with***—controlled by

14:8 (7–8) Amulek told the wicked people of Ammonihah that it was only the prayers of the righteous among them that kept them from being destroyed. He told them that if they ever cast out the righteous they would be destroyed (see Alma 10:22–23). Now the wicked drive away and burn all the righteous in their city. To find out how Amulek's prophecy is fulfilled see Alma 16:1–3.

14:9 ***martyrdom***—the murder of those who believe in God
***consumed***—burned entirely

14:11 ***constraineth me***—prevents me
***wrath***—anger

Alma testifies "the Lord receiveth . . . unto himself, in glory" these righteous Saints who suffer a horrible death for their testimonies. In what ways does it help you to know that the Lord loves, comforts, and blesses the righteous and faithful who suffer in this life?

14:11 (9–11) The Lord sometimes allows the righteous to be killed because they enter into the rest of the Lord, and it provides a way to judge those who do such a terrible deed (see Alma 60:13).

13 And Alma said: Be it according to the will of
the Lord. But, behold, our work is not finished;
therefore they burn us not.

### ALMA AND AMULEK ARE MOCKED, BEATEN, AND MISTREATED

14 Now it came to pass that when the bodies of
those who had been cast into the fire were consumed, and also the records which were cast in
with them, the chief judge of the land came and
stood before Alma and Amulek, as they were
bound; and he smote them with his hand upon
their cheeks, and said unto them: After what ye
have seen, will ye preach again unto this people,
that they shall be cast into a lake of fire and brimstone?
15 Behold, ye see that ye had not power to save
those who had been cast into the fire; neither has
God saved them because they were of thy faith.
And the judge smote them again upon their cheeks,
and asked: What say ye for yourselves?
16 Now this judge was after the order and faith of
Nehor, who slew Gideon.
17 And it came to pass that Alma and Amulek
answered him nothing; and he smote them again,
and delivered them to the officers to be cast into
prison.
18 And when they had been cast into prison three
days, there came many lawyers, and judges, and
priests, and teachers, who were of the profession of
Nehor; and they came in unto the prison to see
them, and they questioned them about many
words; but they answered them nothing.
19 And it came to pass that the judge stood before
them, and said: Why do ye not answer the words
of this people? Know ye not that I have power to
deliver you up unto the flames? And he commanded them to speak; but they answered nothing.
20 And it came to pass that they departed and
went their ways, but came again on the morrow;
and the judge also smote them again on their
cheeks. And many came forth also, and smote
them, saying: Will ye stand again and judge this
people, and condemn our law? If ye have such
great power why do ye not deliver yourselves?
21 And many such things did they say unto them,
gnashing their teeth upon them, and spitting upon
them, and saying: How shall we look when we are
damned?
22 And many such things, yea, all manner of such
things did they say unto them; and thus they did mock
them for many days. And they did withhold food from
them that they might hunger, and water that they
might thirst; and they also did take from them their
clothes that they were naked; and thus they were
bound with strong cords, and confined in prison.

### ALMA AND AMULEK ARE SET FREE BY THE POWER OF GOD

23 And it came to pass after they had thus suffered
for many days, (and it was on the twelfth day, in
the tenth month, in the tenth year of the reign of
the judges over the people of Nephi) that the chief
judge over the land of Ammonihah and many of
their teachers and their lawyers went in unto the
prison where Alma and Amulek were bound with
cords.
24 And the chief judge stood before them, and
smote them again, and said unto them: If ye have
the power of God deliver yourselves from these
bands, and then we will believe that the Lord will
destroy this people according to your words.

---

14:13 The Lord protects His servants until they have finished their work on the earth (see D&C 122:9).

14:14 ***brimstone***—hot burning sulphur

14:18 (16–18) Nehor killed a servant of the Lord named Gideon (Alma 1:9). The "profession of Nehor" was the belief that religious leaders should be paid by the people and that the righteous and the wicked would all be saved. (For more information on the "Nehors," see Alma 1:1-16.)

14:20 ***condemn***—criticize

14:21 ***gnashing their teeth***—biting or grinding in a rage

14:22 ***mock***—make fun of
***confined***—locked up

14:22 (17–22) Alma and Amulek were terribly mistreated by these wicked people. Many of the Lord's servants have been persecuted and even killed. Why do the wicked respond in these ways to the gospel of Jesus Christ?

ALMA AND AMULEK IN PRISON, BY GARY KAPP

*After Alma and Amulek prayed for deliverance, the prison walls "fell to the earth" and killed the wicked people. Alma and Amulek, however, "came forth out of the prison, and they were not hurt."*

25 And it came to pass that they all went forth and smote them, saying the same words, even until the last; and when the last had spoken unto them the power of God was upon Alma and Amulek, and they rose and stood upon their feet.

26 And Alma cried, saying: How long shall we suffer these great afflictions, O Lord? O Lord, give us strength according to our faith which is in Christ, even unto deliverance. And they broke the cords with which they were bound; and when the people saw this, they began to flee, for the fear of destruction had come upon them.

27 And it came to pass that so great was their fear that they fell to the earth, and did not obtain the outer door of the prison; and the earth shook mightily, and the walls of the prison were rent in twain, so that they fell to the earth; and the chief judge, and the lawyers, and priests, and teachers, who smote upon Alma and Amulek, were slain by the fall thereof.

---

14:26 ***afflictions***—trials and sufferings

Referring to Alma's prayer, Elder Gene R. Cook said: "Note that they did not have faith in their own strength; they trusted in the Lord and relied on his strength. It is faith in Christ that will deliver us from our own bonds; it is increasing our faith in Christ that will give us added power in prayer" (*Receiving Answers to Our Prayers,* 18).

14:27 ***rent in twain***—torn in pieces

14:27 (24–27) The Lord revealed to Joseph Smith that those who seek for signs, but have no faith, may see signs, but the signs will not save or bless them (see D&C 63:7–12).

28 And Alma and Amulek came forth out of the prison, and they were not hurt; for the Lord had granted unto them power, according to their faith which was in Christ. And they straightway came forth out of the prison; and they were loosed from their bands; and the prison had fallen to the earth, and every soul within the walls thereof, save it were Alma and Amulek, was slain; and they straightway came forth into the city.

29 Now the people having heard a great noise came running together by multitudes to know the cause of it; and when they saw Alma and Amulek coming forth out of the prison, and the walls thereof had fallen to the earth, they were struck with great fear, and fled from the presence of Alma and Amulek even as a goat fleeth with her young from two lions; and thus they did flee from the presence of Alma and Amulek.

## CHAPTER 15

*Zeezrom suffers greatly for his wickedness. He repents of his sins, expresses faith in the Lord, and is healed both physically and spiritually. Alma and Amulek establish the Church in Sidom. Look for the cause of Zeezrom's sickness and how he is healed.*

### *Alma and Amulek Find Zeezrom Sick from His Sins*

1 AND it came to pass that Alma and Amulek were commanded to depart out of that city; and they departed, and came out even into the land of Sidom; and behold, there they found all the people who had departed out of the land of Ammonihah, who had been cast out and stoned, because they believed in the words of Alma.

2 And they related unto them all that had happened unto their wives and children, and also concerning themselves, and of their power of deliverance.

3 And also Zeezrom lay sick at Sidom, with a burning fever, which was caused by the great tribulations of his mind on account of his wickedness, for he supposed that Alma and Amulek were no more; and he supposed that they had been slain because of his iniquity. And this great sin, and his many other sins, did harrow up his mind until it did become exceedingly sore, having no deliverance; therefore he began to be scorched with a burning heat.

4 Now, when he heard that Alma and Amulek were in the land of Sidom, his heart began to take courage; and he sent a message immediately unto them, desiring them to come unto him.

5 And it came to pass that they went immediately, obeying the message which he had sent unto them; and they went in unto the house unto Zeezrom; and they found him upon his bed, sick, being very low with a burning fever; and his mind also was exceedingly sore because of his iniquities; and when he saw them he stretched forth his hand, and besought them that they would heal him.

### *Alma Blesses and Baptizes Zeezrom*

6 And it came to pass that Alma said unto him, taking him by the hand: Believest thou in the power of Christ unto salvation?

---

15:1 It is not always easy to follow the Lord's prophets. Have you been tried or persecuted for following the prophet? In what ways?

15:3 Some physical illnesses, like Zeezrom's, are related to spiritual problems. Elder Boyd K. Packer explained, "There are spiritual disorders, too, and spiritual diseases that can cause intense suffering. The body and the spirit of man are bound together. Often, very often, when there are disorders, it is very difficult to tell which is which" (in Conference Report, October 1977, 89).

***tribulations***—concern or uneasiness
***no more***—dead
***iniquity***—sin
***harrow up***—trouble or disturb
***deliverance***—escape or relief

Sorrow for one's sins can make a person feel as though he is being scorched or burned with great heat (see Revelation 16:9). This burning, according to President Ezra Taft Benson, "is a deep, burning, and heartfelt sorrow for sin that will drive us to our knees in humility and tears—a deep, heartfelt sorrow for sin that produces a reformation of life" (*The Teachings of Ezra Taft Benson,* 74).

15:5 ***exceedingly***—very
***besought***—begged

15:6 Before Alma blesses Zeezrom, the prophet asks Zeezrom if he believes in the redeeming power of Jesus Christ. Elder Bruce R. McConkie explained that "faith and miracles go together, always and everlastingly. And faith precedes the miracle" (*The Mortal Messiah* 2:287).

7 And he answered and said: Yea, I believe all the words that thou hast taught.

8 And Alma said: If thou believest in the redemption of Christ thou canst be healed.

9 And he said: Yea, I believe according to thy words.

10 And then Alma cried unto the Lord, saying: O Lord our God, have mercy on this man, and heal him according to his faith which is in Christ.

11 And when Alma had said these words, Zeezrom leaped upon his feet, and began to walk; and this was done to the great astonishment of all the people; and the knowledge of this went forth throughout all the land of Sidom.

12 And Alma baptized Zeezrom unto the Lord; and he began from that time forth to preach unto the people.

## Alma Establishes the Church in Sidom

13 And Alma established a church in the land of Sidom, and consecrated priests and teachers in the land, to baptize unto the Lord whosoever were desirous to be baptized.

14 And it came to pass that they were many; for they did flock in from all the region round about Sidom, and were baptized.

15 But as to the people that were in the land of Ammonihah, they yet remained a hard-hearted and a stiffnecked people; and they repented not of their sins, ascribing all the power of Alma and Amulek to the devil; for they were of the profession of Nehor, and did not believe in the repentance of their sins.

## Alma Provides for Amulek's Needs

16 And it came to pass that Alma and Amulek, Amulek having forsaken all his gold, and silver, and his precious things, which were in the land of Ammonihah, for the word of God, he being rejected by those who were once his friends and also by his father and his kindred;

17 Therefore, after Alma having established the church at Sidom, seeing a great check, yea, seeing that the people were checked as to the pride of their hearts, and began to humble themselves before God, and began to assemble themselves together at their sanctuaries to worship God before the altar, watching and praying continually, that they might be delivered from Satan, and from death, and from destruction—

18 Now as I said, Alma having seen all these things, therefore he took Amulek and came over to the land of Zarahemla, and took him to his own house, and did administer unto him in his tribulations, and strengthened him in the Lord.

19 And thus ended the tenth year of the reign of the judges over the people of Nephi.

---

15:10 ***mercy***—compassion

15:11 ***astonishment***—surprise or amazement

15:12 (11–12) A *Church News* editorial commented on Zeezrom's conversion: "Following . . . sincere and honest repentance, he was baptized into the church—thereby beginning his journey to receive all the promised blessings of our Savior's atonement. (See Alma 15:12.) The story is miraculous; the steps, however, are simple: faith, repentance, baptism and receiving of the Holy Ghost" ("His Atoning Sacrifice," *Church News,* 23 March 1991, 16).

15:13 Elder Bruce R. McConkie explained that "among the Nephites it was the practice to consecrate priests and teachers, give them administrative responsibility, and send them out to preach, teach, and baptize" (*Mormon Doctrine,* 598). These priests and teachers held the Melchizedek Priesthood (see Joseph Fielding Smith, *Doctrines of Salvation* 3:87).

15:14 ***flock***—gather

15:15 ***hard-hearted***—disobedient or unfeeling
***stiffnecked***—stubborn, rebellious
***ascribing***—crediting

15:17 ***checked***—stopped
***sanctuaries***—places of worship

15:18 ***administer unto***—help and comfort
***tribulations***—troubles and misery

15:18 (16–18) Amulek gave up his wealth, friends, and family to accept the gospel. What would you be willing to give up to follow the Savior's teachings?

15:19 ***reign***—rule

15:19 (18–19) There are times when we give to others and times when we receive. Amulek shares his home and food when Alma needs help (see Alma 8:19–27). Now Alma shares his home and food because Amulek has given up all of his wealth, family, and friends for the gospel. How do you feel when you give help to others? How do you feel toward those who help you?

## CHAPTER 16

*After many battles between the Nephites and Lamanites, there are three years of peace. During this time Alma and Amulek, and many other priests, preach the gospel with much success. As you read, look for what the missionaries taught that had such a great impact on the people.*

### *The Lamanites Destroy Ammonihah and Take Many Nephite Prisoners*

1 AND it came to pass in the eleventh year of the reign of the judges over the people of Nephi, on the fifth day of the second month, there having been much peace in the land of Zarahemla, there having been no wars nor contentions for a certain number of years, even until the fifth day of the second month in the eleventh year, there was a cry of war heard throughout the land.

2 For behold, the armies of the Lamanites had come in upon the wilderness side, into the borders of the land, even into the city of Ammonihah, and began to slay the people and destroy the city.

3 And now it came to pass, before the Nephites could raise a sufficient army to drive them out of the land, they had destroyed the people who were in the city of Ammonihah, and also some around the borders of Noah, and taken others captive into the wilderness.

### *Zoram Leads the Nephites to Victory over the Lamanites*

4 Now it came to pass that the Nephites were desirous to obtain those who had been carried away captive into the wilderness.

5 Therefore, he that had been appointed chief captain over the armies of the Nephites, (and his name was Zoram, and he had two sons, Lehi and Aha)—now Zoram and his two sons, knowing that Alma was high priest over the church, and having heard that he had the spirit of prophecy, therefore they went unto him and desired of him to know whither the Lord would that they should go into the wilderness in search of their brethren, who had been taken captive by the Lamanites.

6 And it came to pass that Alma inquired of the Lord concerning the matter. And Alma returned and said unto them: Behold, the Lamanites will cross the river Sidon in the south wilderness, away up beyond the borders of the land of Manti. And behold there shall ye meet them, on the east of the river Sidon, and there the Lord will deliver unto thee thy brethren who have been taken captive by the Lamanites.

7 And it came to pass that Zoram and his sons crossed over the river Sidon, with their armies, and marched away beyond the borders of Manti into the south wilderness, which was on the east side of the river Sidon.

---

16:1 ***contentions***—arguing and fighting

16:3 ***sufficient***—large and powerful enough
***captive***—prisoner

16:3 (2–3) Amulek had warned the people of Ammonihah that if they ever "cast out the righteous" they would be destroyed (see Alma 10:22–23). Despite the warning, they did cast out the righteous (see Alma 15:1). Just as was prophesied, the Lamanites completely destroyed the once great city of Ammonihah in about 81 B.C.

16:4 ***obtain***—bring back or rescue

16:5 ***whither***—where

Zoram, Nephite chief captain, asks Alma for guidance because he knows that Alma is a prophet. Do you believe our prophet today can give you help and guidance? Why is it important to follow his counsel and direction?

PHOTOGRAPH BY SCOT FACER PROCTOR

*The river Sidon might have looked like this river in Guatemala.*

8 And they came upon the armies of the Lamanites,
and the Lamanites were scattered and driven into
the wilderness; and they took their brethren who
had been taken captive by the Lamanites, and there
was not one soul of them had been lost that were
taken captive. And they were brought by their
brethren to possess their own lands.
9 And thus ended the eleventh year of the judges,
the Lamanites having been driven out of the land,
and the people of Ammonihah were destroyed; yea,
every living soul of the Ammonihahites was
destroyed, and also their great city, which they said
God could not destroy, because of its greatness.
10 But behold, in one day it was left desolate; and
the carcases were mangled by dogs and wild beasts
of the wilderness.
11 Nevertheless, after many days their dead bodies were heaped up upon the face of the earth, and
they were covered with a shallow covering. And
now so great was the scent thereof that the people
did not go in to possess the land of Ammonihah for
many years. And it was called Desolation of Nehors;
for they were of the profession of Nehor, who were
slain; and their lands remained desolate.

## Alma, Amulek, and Others Preach the Gospel to All Who Will Listen

12 And the Lamanites did not come again to war
against the Nephites until the fourteenth year of the
reign of the judges over the people of Nephi. And
thus for three years did the people of Nephi have
continual peace in all the land.
13 And Alma and Amulek went forth preaching
repentance to the people in their temples, and in
their sanctuaries, and also in their synagogues,
which were built after the manner of the Jews.
14 And as many as would hear their words, unto
them they did impart the word of God, without any
respect of persons, continually.
15 And thus did Alma and Amulek go forth, and
also many more who had been chosen for the
work, to preach the word throughout all the land.
And the establishment of the church became general throughout the land, in all the region round
about, among all the people of the Nephites.
16 And there was no inequality among them; the
Lord did pour out his Spirit on all the face of the
land to prepare the minds of the children of men,

---

16:8 ***to possess***—to regain

16:10 ***desolate***—empty or without life
***carcases***—dead bodies
***mangled***—destroyed and eaten

16:10 (9–10) The people of Ammonihah placed their trust in themselves and boasted that even God could not destroy their great city, but it was destroyed in one day. What are some of the things people of today put their trust in, other than God? Why is it important to place your trust in God?

16:11 ***scent***—smell
***Desolation***—Ruin or destruction

Nehor was a wicked man who taught false doctrine (see Alma 1:2–5, 15). To be "of the profession of Nehor" meant that you were a follower of Nehor's wicked teachings and bad example. Because their self-centered beliefs caused the destruction of the people of Ammonihah, their land was called "Desolation of Nehors."

16:13 ***sanctuaries***—places of worship
***synagogues***—buildings used for religious gatherings

16:14 ***impart***—preach

God is no respecter of persons. That means He judges all people according to the same laws, from "the newest convert [to] members of the First Presidency" (Robert L. Simpson, in Conference Report, October 1976, 150–51).

16:16 Moses 7:18 tells about people who were equal in all things. The Lord called them *Zion,* "because they were of one heart and one mind, and dwelt in righteousness; and there was no poor among them."

PHOTOGRAPH BY DAVID H. GARNER

*Nephite places of worship were "built after the manner of the Jews." They might have looked like this ancient Jewish synagogue, which still stands in the city of Nazareth.*

or to prepare their hearts to receive the word which should be taught among them at the time of his coming—
17 That they might not be hardened against the word, that they might not be unbelieving, and go on to destruction, but that they might receive the word with joy, and as a branch be grafted into the true vine, that they might enter into the rest of the Lord their God.

### Alma and Other Priests Preach Against Evil and Testify of Christ

18 Now those priests who did go forth among the people did preach against all lyings, and deceivings, and envyings, and strifes, and malice, and revilings, and stealing, robbing, plundering, murdering, committing adultery, and all manner of lasciviousness, crying that these things ought not so to be—
19 Holding forth things which must shortly come; yea, holding forth the coming of the Son of God, his sufferings and death, and also the resurrection of the dead.
20 And many of the people did inquire concerning the place where the Son of God should come; and they were taught that he would appear unto them after his resurrection; and this the people did hear with great joy and gladness.
21 And now after the church had been established throughout all the land—having got the victory over the devil, and the word of God being preached in its purity in all the land, and the Lord pouring out his blessings upon the people—thus ended the fourteenth year of the reign of the judges over the people of Nephi.

*An account of the sons of Mosiah, who rejected their rights to the kingdom for the word of God, and went up to the land of Nephi to preach to the Lamanites; their sufferings and deliverance—according to the record of Alma. Comprising chapters 17 to 26 inclusive.**

## CHAPTER 17

*Alma meets his friends, the sons of Mosiah, as they are returning home from successful missions among the Lamanites. He rejoices that they are all still faithful and strong in their testimonies of the Lord. Look for ways these great missionaries prepared for their missions.*

### The Sons of Mosiah Prepare Spiritually to Serve a Mission Among the Lamanites

1 AND now it came to pass that as Alma was journeying from the land of Gideon southward, away to the land of Manti, behold, to his astonishment, he met with the sons of Mosiah journeying towards the land of Zarahemla.
2 Now these sons of Mosiah were with Alma at the time the angel first appeared unto him; therefore Alma did rejoice exceedingly to see his brethren; and what added more to his joy, they were still his

---

16:17 Alma had taught the people of Ammonihah how to enter the Lord's rest (see Alma 12:34–37), but like the people that Moses led, they rejected it. Alma did not want to see this happen again with the Nephites. For additional insight on the "rest of the Lord" see for Alma 12:34.

16:17 (16–17) Prophets have compared the house of Israel to an olive tree. Nephi explained to his brothers that they were a branch "broken off from the house of Israel" and would one day be grafted in or joined again with the other tribes of Israel (see 1 Nephi 15:12–16).

16:18 ***deceivings***—falsehoods
***envyings***—desires to have others' possessions
***strifes***—arguments and fighting
***malice***—desires to hurt others
***revilings***—insults
***plundering***—stealing
***lasciviousness***—immorality and unchastity

16:19 ***Holding forth***—Proclaiming or announcing

16:20 This prophecy was fulfilled when the Savior appeared to the Nephites shortly after His Resurrection. You can read about that visit in 3 Nephi 11–30.

* This introduction to chapters 17–26, except for the last sentence, was translated from the Book of Mormon plates.

17:1 ***astonishment***—surprise and wonder

The sons of Mosiah had completed a fourteen-year mission among the Lamanites and are on their way to the land of Zarahemla when they meet their friend Alma (see Alma 17:1, 4).

17:2 Alma had not seen his friends for fourteen years while they served faithful missions (see Alma 17:4). Besides seeing them again, what "added more to his joy"? Whom do you know who is serving or has served as a missionary? How excited were you or will you be when they return?

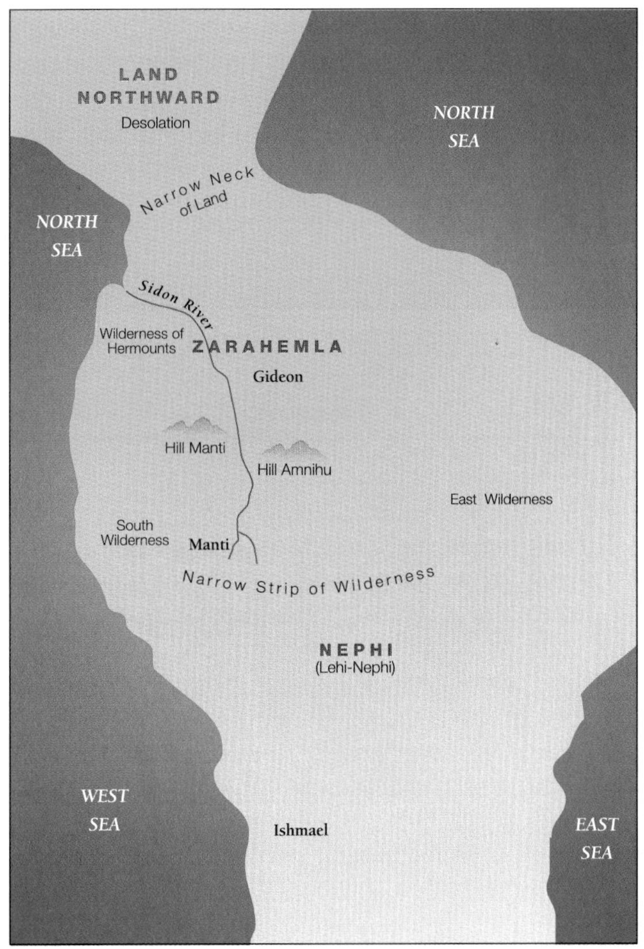


*The sons of Mosiah journeyed to the land of the Lamanites to preach the gospel. Ammon went to the land of Ishmael. After fourteen years, the sons of Mosiah returned to Zarahemla. On their way, they met Alma and had a joyful reunion.*

brethren in the Lord; yea, and they had waxed
strong in the knowledge of the truth; for they were
men of a sound understanding and they had
searched the scriptures diligently, that they might
know the word of God.
3 But this is not all; they had given themselves to
much prayer, and fasting; therefore they had the
spirit of prophecy, and the spirit of revelation, and
when they taught, they taught with power and
authority of God.
4 And they had been teaching the word of God
for the space of fourteen years among the
Lamanites, having had much success in bringing
many to the knowledge of the truth; yea, by the
power of their words many were brought before
the altar of God, to call on his name and confess
their sins before him.
5 Now these are the circumstances which attended them in their journeyings, for they had
many afflictions; they did suffer much, both in body
and in mind, such as hunger, thirst and fatigue, and
also much labor in the spirit.

## The Sons of Mosiah Set Out on Their Mission to the Lamanites

6 Now these were their journeyings: Having taken
leave of their father, Mosiah, in the first year of the
judges; having refused the kingdom which their
father was desirous to confer upon them, and also
this was the minds of the people;
7 Nevertheless they departed out of the land of

---

17:2 "To obtain the Spirit, you will have to search the scriptures daily. The Book of Mormon tells us about some of the most successful missionaries who have gone forth to preach the gospel—Ammon, Aaron, Omner, and Himni—the four sons of Mosiah. They were men of God who had prepared themselves to do the work. Their example is worthy of emulation" (Ezra Taft Benson, "Keys to Successful Member-Missionary Work," 5).

***waxed***—grown
***sound***—good

17:3 "The Saints by fasting and praying can sanctify the soul and elevate the spirit to Christlike perfection, and thus the body would be brought into subjection to the spirit, promote communion with the Holy Ghost, and insure spiritual strength and power to the individual. By observing fasting and prayer in its true spirit, the Latter-day Saints cannot be overpowered by Satan tempting them to evil" (Delbert L. Stapley, in Conference Report, October 1951, 123).

17:4 ***were brought before the altar of God***—entered into covenants with the Lord

17:5 ***afflictions***—trials
***fatigue***—being worn out

17:6 ***taken leave of***—left
***to confer upon them***—to give them
***minds***—desires

17:6 (4–6) Alma reunites with the sons of Mosiah in about 77 B.C. after their Lamanite missions (see Alma 28:8). At this point, we begin an account of the fourteen-year missions of the sons of Mosiah, which began around 91 B.C.

Zarahemla, and took their swords, and their spears, and their bows, and their arrows, and their slings; and this they did that they might provide food for themselves while in the wilderness.

8 And thus they departed into the wilderness with their numbers which they had selected, to go up to the land of Nephi, to preach the word of God unto the Lamanites.

9 And it came to pass that they journeyed many days in the wilderness, and they fasted much and prayed much that the Lord would grant unto them a portion of his Spirit to go with them, and abide with them, that they might be an instrument in the hands of God to bring, if it were possible, their brethren, the Lamanites, to the knowledge of the truth, to the knowledge of the baseness of the traditions of their fathers, which were not correct.

10 And it came to pass that the Lord did visit them with his Spirit, and said unto them: Be comforted. And they were comforted.

11 And the Lord said unto them also: Go forth among the Lamanites, thy brethren, and establish my word; yet ye shall be patient in long-suffering and afflictions, that ye may show forth good examples unto them in me, and I will make an instrument of thee in my hands unto the salvation of many souls.

12 And it came to pass that the hearts of the sons of Mosiah, and also those who were with them, took courage to go forth unto the Lamanites to declare unto them the word of God.

13 And it came to pass when they had arrived in the borders of the land of the Lamanites, that they separated themselves and departed one from another, trusting in the Lord that they should meet again at the close of their harvest; for they supposed that great was the work which they had undertaken.

14 And assuredly it was great, for they had undertaken to preach the word of God to a wild and a hardened and a ferocious people; a people who delighted in murdering the Nephites, and robbing and plundering them; and their hearts were set upon riches, or upon gold and silver, and precious stones; yet they sought to obtain these things by murdering and plundering, that they might not labor for them with their own hands.

15 Thus they were a very indolent people, many of whom did worship idols, and the curse of God had fallen upon them because of the traditions of their fathers; notwithstanding the promises of the Lord were extended unto them on the conditions of repentance.

16 Therefore, this was the cause for which the sons of Mosiah had undertaken the work, that perhaps they might bring them unto repentance; that perhaps they might bring them to know of the plan of redemption.

17 Therefore they separated themselves one from another, and went forth among them, every man alone, according to the word and power of God which was given unto him.

---

17:9 ***an instrument***—a tool
***baseness***—wickedness

17:10 Can you remember when the Spirit brought you comfort at a hard time in your life?

17:11 "We must have patience in order to withstand pain and grief without complaint or discouragement, which detract from the Spirit. It's necessary to have patience in the face of tribulation and persecution for the cause of truth, which sets an example because the manner in which we bear our cross will be an influence to others to help lighten their load" (Angel Abrea, in Conference Report, April 1992, 34).

***establish***—set forth or teach
***long-suffering***—enduring trials faithfully

17:13 The harvest being referred to here has to do with missionary work. The Lord also compared missionary work to a harvest in our day (see D&C 4:4).

***undertaken***—begun or set about to do

17:14 ***plundering***—spoiling or wrecking

17:15 ***indolent***—lazy
***idols***—false gods

The curse that fell upon the Lamanites is described in 2 Nephi 5:21–24.

17:17 (16–17) It was important for the sons of Mosiah to teach the plan of redemption to the Lamanites, for as Elder Boyd K. Packer has explained, "The Plan of Redemption, as contained in the standard works, must be the foundation of all that we do as members of His church" (*Our Father's Plan,* 58).

## Ammon Travels to the Land of Ishmael and Becomes a Servant to King Lamoni

18 Now Ammon being the chief among them, or rather he did administer unto them, and he departed from them, after having blessed them according to their several stations, having imparted the word of God unto them, or administered unto them before his departure; and thus they took their several journeys throughout the land.

19 And Ammon went to the land of Ishmael, the land being called after the sons of Ishmael, who also became Lamanites.

20 And as Ammon entered the land of Ishmael, the Lamanites took him and bound him, as was their custom to bind all the Nephites who fell into their hands, and carry them before the king; and thus it was left to the pleasure of the king to slay them, or to retain them in captivity, or to cast them into prison, or to cast them out of his land, according to his will and pleasure.

21 And thus Ammon was carried before the king who was over the land of Ishmael; and his name was Lamoni; and he was a descendant of Ishmael.

22 And the king inquired of Ammon if it were his desire to dwell in the land among the Lamanites, or among his people.

23 And Ammon said unto him: Yea, I desire to dwell among this people for a time; yea, and perhaps until the day I die.

24 And it came to pass that king Lamoni was much pleased with Ammon, and caused that his bands should be loosed; and he would that Ammon should take one of his daughters to wife.

25 But Ammon said unto him: Nay, but I will be thy servant. Therefore Ammon became a servant to king Lamoni. And it came to pass that he was set among other servants to watch the flocks of Lamoni, according to the custom of the Lamanites.

## Ammon Shows Forth the Power of God by Saving the King's Flocks

26 And after he had been in the service of the king three days, as he was with the Lamanitish servants going forth with their flocks to the place of water, which was called the water of Sebus, and all the Lamanites drive their flocks hither, that they may have water—

27 Therefore, as Ammon and the servants of the king were driving forth their flocks to this place of water, behold, a certain number of the Lamanites, who had been with their flocks to water, stood and scattered the flocks of Ammon and the servants of the king, and they scattered them insomuch that they fled many ways.

28 Now the servants of the king began to murmur, saying: Now the king will slay us, as he has our brethren because their flocks were scattered by the wickedness of these men. And they began to weep exceedingly, saying: Behold, our flocks are scattered already.

---

17:18 ***several stations***—circumstances

17:20 ***retain***—keep

17:24 ***bands***—ropes

17:25 (21–25) "As with Ammon, the only desire of our army of modern missionaries is to serve their fellowmen" (L. Tom Perry, in Conference Report, October 1989, 89).

17:26 ***hither***—there

17:28 ***murmur***—mourn

ILLUSTRATION BY TED HENNINGER

*Ammon was a faithful servant to King Lamoni.*

29 Now they wept because of the fear of being slain. Now when Ammon saw this his heart was swollen within him with joy; for, said he, I will show forth my power unto these my fellow-servants, or the power which is in me, in restoring these flocks unto the king, that I may win the hearts of these my fellow-servants, that I may lead them to believe in my words.
30 And now, these were the thoughts of Ammon, when he saw the afflictions of those whom he termed to be his brethren.
31 And it came to pass that he flattered them by his words, saying: My brethren, be of good cheer and let us go in search of the flocks, and we will gather them together and bring them back unto the place of water; and thus we will preserve the flocks unto the king and he will not slay us.
32 And it came to pass that they went in search of the flocks, and they did follow Ammon, and they rushed forth with much swiftness and did head the flocks of the king, and did gather them together again to the place of water.
33 And those men again stood to scatter their flocks; but Ammon said unto his brethren: Encircle the flocks round about that they flee not; and I go and contend with these men who do scatter our flocks.
34 Therefore, they did as Ammon commanded them, and he went forth and stood to contend with those who stood by the waters of Sebus; and they were in number not a few.
35 Therefore they did not fear Ammon, for they supposed that one of their men could slay him according to their pleasure, for they knew not that the Lord had promised Mosiah that he would deliver his sons out of their hands; neither did they know anything concerning the Lord; therefore they delighted in the destruction of their brethren; and for this cause they stood to scatter the flocks of the king.
36 But Ammon stood forth and began to cast stones at them with his sling; yea, with mighty power he did sling stones amongst them; and thus he slew a certain number of them insomuch that they began to be astonished at his power; nevertheless they were angry because of the slain of their brethren, and they were determined that he should fall; therefore, seeing that they could not hit him with their stones, they came forth with clubs to slay him.
37 But behold, every man that lifted his club to smite Ammon, he smote off their arms with his sword; for he did withstand their blows by smiting their arms with the edge of his sword, insomuch that they began to be astonished, and began to flee before him; yea, and they were not few in number; and he caused them to flee by the strength of his arm.
38 Now six of them had fallen by the sling, but he slew none save it were their leader with his sword; and he smote off as many of their arms as were lifted against him, and they were not a few.
39 And when he had driven them afar off, he returned and they watered their flocks and returned them to the pasture of the king, and then went in unto the king, bearing the arms which had been smitten off by the sword of Ammon, of those who sought to slay him; and they were carried in unto the king for a testimony of the things which they had done.

---

17:29 President Spencer W. Kimball taught, "Difficulties are often opportunities for service" (*The Teachings of Spencer W. Kimball*, 254). Ammon saw this difficult situation as an opportunity to show God's power in restoring or bringing back the king's sheep. He believed this would give him a chance to teach the gospel to the king.

17:31 "Ammon teaches us that no matter our circumstances, we can be an example to others, we can lift them, we can inspire them to seek righteousness, and we can bear testimony to all of the power of Jesus Christ" (Robert D. Hales, in Conference Report, April 1997, 113).

***flattered***—encouraged
***preserve***—save

17:35 After Mosiah's sons had requested to serve a mission among their enemies the Lamanites, King Mosiah asked the Lord "if he should let his sons go." The Lord revealed that they would not only have a successful mission but that they would all return safely, and also that they would eventually be blessed with "eternal life" (Mosiah 28:6–7).

17:36 ***astonished***—surprised or amazed

17:37 ***smote***—cut

17:39 ***bearing***—carrying

17:39 (36–39) How does this story show that the Lord blessed Ammon with strength to accomplish good? How can this help you when the Lord asks you to do something for Him?

## CHAPTER 18

*Ammon teaches the plan of salvation to King Lamoni. Look for what Ammon does and says that convinces Lamoni to listen to him.*

### *King Lamoni Thinks Ammon Is the Great Spirit*

1 AND it came to pass that king Lamoni caused that
his servants should stand forth and testify to all the
things which they had seen concerning the matter.
2 And when they had all testified to the things
which they had seen, and he had learned of the
faithfulness of Ammon in preserving his flocks, and
also of his great power in contending against those
who sought to slay him, he was astonished exceedingly, and said: Surely, this is more than a man.
Behold, is not this the Great Spirit who doth send
such great punishments upon this people, because
of their murders?
3 And they answered the king, and said: Whether
he be the Great Spirit or a man, we know not; but
this much we do know, that he cannot be slain by
the enemies of the king; neither can they scatter the
king's flocks when he is with us, because of his
expertness and great strength; therefore, we know
that he is a friend to the king. And now, O king, we
do not believe that a man has such great power, for
we know he cannot be slain.
4 And now, when the king heard these words, he
said unto them: Now I know that it is the Great
Spirit; and he has come down at this time to preserve your lives, that I might not slay you as I did
your brethren. Now this is the Great Spirit of whom
our fathers have spoken.
5 Now this was the tradition of Lamoni, which he
had received from his father, that there was a Great
Spirit. Notwithstanding they believed in a Great
Spirit, they supposed that whatsoever they did was
right; nevertheless, Lamoni began to fear exceedingly, with fear lest he had done wrong in slaying
his servants;
6 For he had slain many of them because their
brethren had scattered their flocks at the place of
water; and thus, because they had had their flocks
scattered they were slain.
7 Now it was the practice of these Lamanites to
stand by the waters of Sebus to scatter the flocks of
the people, that thereby they might drive away
many that were scattered unto their own land, it
being a practice of plunder among them.
8 And it came to pass that king Lamoni inquired
of his servants, saying: Where is this man that has
such great power?
9 And they said unto him: Behold, he is feeding
thy horses. Now the king had commanded his servants, previous to the time of the watering of their
flocks, that they should prepare his horses and
chariots, and conduct him forth to the land of
Nephi; for there had been a great feast appointed at
the land of Nephi, by the father of Lamoni, who
was king over all the land.
10 Now when king Lamoni heard that Ammon
was preparing his horses and his chariots he was
more astonished, because of the faithfulness of
Ammon, saying: Surely there has not been any servant among all my servants that has been so faithful as this man; for even he doth remember all my
commandments to execute them.
11 Now I surely know that this is the Great Spirit,
and I would desire him that he come in unto me,
but I durst not.

---

18:2 ***preserving***—saving
***contending***—fighting
***astonished exceedingly***—very surprised

18:3 ***expertness***—great skill

18:4 "According to Lamanite traditions, God is the Great Spirit. It is obvious that by this designation the Lamanites had in mind a personal being, for King Lamoni mistakenly supposed that Ammon was the Great Spirit. (Alma 18:2–28; 19:25–27.) . . . This same Lamanite concept that God is the Great Spirit has existed among the American Indians in modern times" (Bruce R. McConkie, *Mormon Doctrine,* 340).

18:5 ***tradition***—belief
***Notwithstanding***—But even though

18:7 ***plunder***—robbery

18:9 ***previous to***—before
***conduct***—take
***appointed***—decreed

18:10 ***execute***—do

18:11 ***durst***—dare

18:11 (10–11) Lamoni has never seen a more faithful servant than Ammon. In Alma 17:11, God told Ammon and his brothers and friends to "show forth good examples" before the Lamanites. How did Ammon's faithful service prepare the king to be taught? What can you do to set a good example for others?

## Ammon Answers King Lamoni's Questions

12 And it came to pass that when Ammon had made ready the horses and the chariots for the king and his servants, he went in unto the king, and he saw that the countenance of the king was changed; therefore he was about to return out of his presence.

13 And one of the king's servants said unto him, Rabbanah, which is, being interpreted, powerful or great king, considering their kings to be powerful; and thus he said unto him: Rabbanah, the king desireth thee to stay.

14 Therefore Ammon turned himself unto the king, and said unto him: What wilt thou that I should do for thee, O king? And the king answered him not for the space of an hour, according to their time, for he knew not what he should say unto him.

15 And it came to pass that Ammon said unto him again: What desirest thou of me? But the king answered him not.

16 And it came to pass that Ammon, being filled with the Spirit of God, therefore he perceived the thoughts of the king. And he said unto him: Is it because thou hast heard that I defended thy servants and thy flocks, and slew seven of their brethren with the sling and with the sword, and smote off the arms of others, in order to defend thy flocks and thy servants; behold, is it this that causeth thy marvelings?

17 I say unto you, what is it, that thy marvelings are so great? Behold, I am a man, and am thy servant; therefore, whatsoever thou desirest which is right, that will I do.

18 Now when the king had heard these words, he marveled again, for he beheld that Ammon could discern his thoughts; but notwithstanding this, king Lamoni did open his mouth, and said unto him: Who art thou? Art thou that Great Spirit, who knows all things?

19 Ammon answered and said unto him: I am not.

20 And the king said: How knowest thou the thoughts of my heart? Thou mayest speak boldly, and tell me concerning these things; and also tell me by what power ye slew and smote off the arms of my brethren that scattered my flocks—

21 And now, if thou wilt tell me concerning these things, whatsoever thou desirest I will give unto thee; and if it were needed, I would guard thee with my armies; but I know that thou art more powerful than all they; nevertheless, whatsoever thou desirest of me I will grant it unto thee.

22 Now Ammon being wise, yet harmless, he said unto Lamoni: Wilt thou hearken unto my words, if I tell thee by what power I do these things? And this is the thing that I desire of thee.

23 And the king answered him, and said: Yea, I will believe all thy words. And thus he was caught with guile.

24 And Ammon began to speak unto him with boldness, and said unto him: Believest thou that there is a God?

25 And he answered, and said unto him: I do not know what that meaneth.

26 And then Ammon said: Believest thou that there is a Great Spirit?

27 And he said, Yea.

28 And Ammon said: This is God. And Ammon said unto him again: Believest thou that this Great Spirit, who is God, created all things which are in heaven and in the earth?

29 And he said: Yea, I believe that he created all things which are in the earth; but I do not know the heavens.

30 And Ammon said unto him: The heavens is a place where God dwells and all his holy angels.

31 And king Lamoni said: Is it above the earth?

---

18:12 ***countenance***—appearance

18:16 Ammon knew and understood King Lamoni's thoughts by the power of the Spirit. This is sometimes called discernment. According to Elder Boyd K. Packer: "This power of discernment is a very real spiritual gift. It is often conferred as a blessing upon men ordained as bishops, stake presidents, and so forth. Many can bear witness to the fact that they do not have to hear or to see all that they know, that they can discern thoughts when the purpose of their office is served" (*That All May Be Edified,* 34).

***perceived***—knew with the help of the Spirit
***defended***—protected
***marvelings***—surprise or wonder

18:18 ***discern***—know or understand

18:20 ***smote***—cut

18:23 ***with guile***—with stratagem or according to Ammon's plan

AMMON BEFORE KING LAMONI, BY GARY KAPP

Ammon and King Lamoni

32 And Ammon said: Yea, and he looketh down
upon all the children of men; and he knows all the
thoughts and intents of the heart; for by his hand
were they all created from the beginning.
33 And king Lamoni said: I believe all these
things which thou hast spoken. Art thou sent from
God?
34 Ammon said unto him: I am a man; and man
in the beginning was created after the image of
God, and I am called by his Holy Spirit to teach
these things unto this people, that they may be
brought to a knowledge of that which is just and
true;
35 And a portion of that Spirit dwelleth in me,
which giveth me knowledge, and also power
according to my faith and desires which are in God.

## Ammon Teaches Lamoni the Plan of Salvation

36 Now when Ammon had said these words, he
began at the creation of the world, and also the creation of Adam, and told him all the things concerning the fall of man, and rehearsed and laid before him the records and the holy scriptures of the people, which had been spoken by the prophets, even down to the time that their father, Lehi, left Jerusalem.

18:32 ***intents***—purposes or motives

18:35 ***portion***—part

18:36 ***rehearsed***—went over

37 And he also rehearsed unto them (for it was
unto the king and to his servants) all the journeyings of their fathers in the wilderness, and all their
sufferings with hunger and thirst, and their travail,
and so forth.
38 And he also rehearsed unto them concerning
the rebellions of Laman and Lemuel, and the sons
of Ishmael, yea, all their rebellions did he relate
unto them; and he expounded unto them all the
records and scriptures from the time that Lehi left
Jerusalem down to the present time.
39 But this is not all; for he expounded unto them
the plan of redemption, which was prepared from
the foundation of the world; and he also made
known unto them concerning the coming of Christ,
and all the works of the Lord did he make known
unto them.

### *King Lamoni Believes Ammon and Desires to Be Forgiven*

40 And it came to pass that after he had said all
these things, and expounded them to the king, that
the king believed all his words.
41 And he began to cry unto the Lord, saying: O
Lord, have mercy; according to thy abundant mercy
which thou hast had upon the people of Nephi,
have upon me, and my people.
42 And now, when he had said this, he fell unto
the earth, as if he were dead.
43 And it came to pass that his servants took him
and carried him in unto his wife, and laid him upon
a bed; and he lay as if he were dead for the space
of two days and two nights; and his wife, and his
sons, and his daughters mourned over him, after the
manner of the Lamanites, greatly lamenting his loss.

## CHAPTER 19

*King Lamoni, overcome by the Spirit, lies for three days as though he is dead. After arising and powerfully testifying of Jesus Christ, he collapses again. This time he is joined by his queen, their servants, and Ammon. Watch for how the Lamanite woman Abish bravely uses this miracle to share her testimony of the gospel.*

### *King Lamoni Is Overcome by the Spirit for Three Days*

1 AND it came to pass that after two days and two
nights they were about to take his body and lay it
in a sepulchre, which they had made for the purpose of burying their dead.
2 Now the queen having heard of the fame of
Ammon, therefore she sent and desired that he
should come in unto her.
3 And it came to pass that Ammon did as he was
commanded, and went in unto the queen, and
desired to know what she would that he should do.

---

18:37 **travail**—labor and pain

18:38 **rebellions**—conflicts and fighting
***expounded***—explained

18:39 **foundation**—beginning

"Teaching that salvation was in Christ, and then bearing testimony that such teachings were true, was the perfect missionary approach then as it is now. . . . When prophets and missionaries bear record of Christ and his gospel, such has the effect of dividing the people. They either believe and obey, or disbelieve and disobey" (Bruce R. McConkie, *The Promised Messiah,* 82–83).

18:39 (36–39) "The Book of Mormon Saints knew that the plan of redemption must start with the account of the fall of Adam. . . . Just as a man does not really desire food until he is hungry, so he does not desire the salvation of Christ until he knows why he needs Christ. No one adequately and properly knows why he needs Christ until he understands and accepts the doctrine of the Fall and its effect upon all mankind. And no other book in the world explains this vital doctrine nearly as well as the Book of Mormon" (Ezra Taft Benson, in Conference Report, April 1987, 106).

18:41 **mercy**—compassion
***abundant***—great

18:42 An explanation for what happened to King Lamoni can be found in Alma 19:6. For additional help see for Alma 19:6 and for Alma 19:13–15.

18:43 **mourned**—felt sorrow
***lamenting his loss***—expressing sadness because they thought he was dead

19:1 **sepulchre**—tomb

19:2 **fame**—reputation

4 And she said unto him: The servants of my husband have made it known unto me that thou art a prophet of a holy God, and that thou hast power to do many mighty works in his name;

5 Therefore, if this is the case, I would that ye should go in and see my husband, for he has been laid upon his bed for the space of two days and two nights; and some say that he is not dead, but others say that he is dead and that he stinketh, and that he ought to be placed in the sepulchre; but as for myself, to me he doth not stink.

6 Now, this was what Ammon desired, for he knew that king Lamoni was under the power of God; he knew that the dark veil of unbelief was being cast away from his mind, and the light which did light up his mind, which was the light of the glory of God, which was a marvelous light of his goodness—yea, this light had infused such joy into his soul, the cloud of darkness having been dispelled, and that the light of everlasting life was lit up in his soul, yea, he knew that this had overcome his natural frame, and he was carried away in God—

7 Therefore, what the queen desired of him was his only desire. Therefore, he went in to see the king according as the queen had desired him; and he saw the king, and he knew that he was not dead.

8 And he said unto the queen: He is not dead, but he sleepeth in God, and on the morrow he shall rise again; therefore bury him not.

9 And Ammon said unto her: Believest thou this? And she said unto him: I have had no witness save thy word, and the word of our servants; nevertheless I believe that it shall be according as thou hast said.

10 And Ammon said unto her: Blessed art thou because of thy exceeding faith; I say unto thee, woman, there has not been such great faith among all the people of the Nephites.

11 And it came to pass that she watched over the bed of her husband, from that time even until that time on the morrow which Ammon had appointed that he should rise.

## The King's Household and Ammon Are All Overcome by the Spirit

12 And it came to pass that he arose, according to the words of Ammon; and as he arose, he stretched forth his hand unto the woman, and said: Blessed be the name of God, and blessed art thou.

13 For as sure as thou livest, behold, I have seen my Redeemer; and he shall come forth, and be born of a woman, and he shall redeem all mankind who believe on his name. Now, when he had said these words, his heart was swollen within him, and he sunk again with joy; and the queen also sunk down, being overpowered by the Spirit.

14 Now Ammon seeing the Spirit of the Lord poured out according to his prayers upon the Lamanites, his brethren, who had been the cause of so much mourning among the Nephites, or among all the people of God because of their iniquities and their traditions, he fell upon his knees, and began to pour out his soul in prayer and thanksgiving to God for what he had done for his brethren; and he was also overpowered with joy; and thus they all three had sunk to the earth.

---

19:6 ***veil***—covering
***cast***—thrown
***infused***—filled
***dispelled***—taken away

Referring to this verse, Elder Bruce R. McConkie stated: "We have no better illustration of the full operation of the light of Christ upon an investigator of the gospel than what happened to King Lamoni. . . . Thereafter, Lamoni was baptized and received the gift of the Holy Ghost" (*A New Witness for the Articles of Faith,* 261).

19:9 ***save***—except

19:10 (9–10) Ammon tells the queen that "there has not been such great faith among all the . . . Nephites" (Alma 19:10). Her faith and the faith of her servant Abish save the life of the king and help convert many Lamanites to the Lord. How can you increase your faith in the Lord? How can your faith bless the lives of others?

19:11 ***on the morrow***—the next day
***appointed***—declared

19:14 ***mourning***—sadness and sorrow
***iniquities***—sins
***traditions***—beliefs

15 Now, when the servants of the king had seen that they had fallen, they also began to cry unto God, for the fear of the Lord had come upon them also, for it was they who had stood before the king and testified unto him concerning the great power of Ammon.

16 And it came to pass that they did call on the name of the Lord, in their might, even until they had all fallen to the earth, save it were one of the Lamanitish women, whose name was Abish, she having been converted unto the Lord for many years, on account of a remarkable vision of her father—

17 Thus, having been converted to the Lord, and never having made it known, therefore, when she saw that all the servants of Lamoni had fallen to the earth, and also her mistress, the queen, and the king, and Ammon lay prostrate upon the earth, she knew that it was the power of God; and supposing that this opportunity, by making known unto the people what had happened among them, that by beholding this scene it would cause them to believe in the power of God, therefore she ran forth from house to house, making it known unto the people.

## Ammon's Life Is Saved by the Lord

18 And they began to assemble themselves together unto the house of the king. And there came a multitude, and to their astonishment they beheld the king, and the queen, and their servants prostrate upon the earth, and they all lay there as though they were dead; and they also saw Ammon, and behold, he was a Nephite.

19 And now the people began to murmur among themselves; some saying that it was a great evil that had come upon them, or upon the king and his house, because he had suffered that the Nephite should remain in the land.

20 But others rebuked them, saying: The king hath brought this evil upon his house, because he slew his servants who had had their flocks scattered at the waters of Sebus.

21 And they were also rebuked by those men who had stood at the waters of Sebus and scattered the flocks which belonged to the king, for they were angry with Ammon because of the number which he had slain of their brethren at the waters of Sebus, while defending the flocks of the king.

22 Now, one of them, whose brother had been slain with the sword of Ammon, being exceedingly angry with Ammon, drew his sword and went forth that he might let it fall upon Ammon, to slay him; and as he lifted the sword to smite him, behold, he fell dead.

23 Now we see that Ammon could not be slain, for the Lord had said unto Mosiah, his father: I will spare him, and it shall be unto him according to thy faith—therefore, Mosiah trusted him unto the Lord.

24 And it came to pass that when the multitude beheld that the man had fallen dead, who lifted the sword to slay Ammon, fear came upon them all, and they durst not put forth their hands to touch him or any of those who had fallen; and they began to marvel again among themselves what could be the cause of this great power, or what all these things could mean.

---

19:15 ***fear***—reverence

19:15 (13–15) The king, queen, their servants, and Ammon all sink down, or fall to the ground, and are overpowered by the Spirit. During this sleeplike condition they receive revelation from Heavenly Father. The scriptures speak of other righteous people who also had similar experiences, such as Ezekiel (see Ezekiel 3:14), Peter (see Acts 10:10–11), Paul (see Acts 22:17–21), Lehi (see 1 Nephi 1:7–8), Alma (see Mosiah 27:19), and King Lamoni's father (see Alma 22:18).

19:16 Abish is one of only four women noted by name in the Book of Mormon (see also 1 Nephi 2:5; Mosiah 3:8; Alma 39:3). This brave Lamanite convert plays an important role in the spiritual rebirth of many of her people.

19:17 ***mistress***—ruler
***prostrate***—flat

19:19 ***suffered***—allowed

19:20 ***rebuked***—scolded

19:21 ***slain***—killed

19:22 ***smite***—strike

19:23 The Lord promised Ammon's father that Ammon and his brothers would be delivered out of the hands of the Lamanites (see Mosiah 28:7).

19:24 ***durst***—dared
***marvel***—wonder

ABISH, THE LAMANITE WOMAN, BY ROBERT T. BARRETT

*Abish was a courageous Lamanite convert. When the people became angry, thinking that the king and queen were dead, Abish "went and took the queen by the hand, that perhaps she might raise her from the ground."*

## All Who Were Carried Away by the Spirit Awake and Begin to Teach the Gospel

25 And it came to pass that there were many among them who said that Ammon was the Great Spirit, and others said he was sent by the Great Spirit;

26 But others rebuked them all, saying that he was a monster, who had been sent from the Nephites to torment them.

27 And there were some who said that Ammon was sent by the Great Spirit to afflict them because of their iniquities; and that it was the Great Spirit that had always attended the Nephites, who had ever delivered them out of their hands; and they said that it was this Great Spirit who had destroyed so many of their brethren, the Lamanites.

28 And thus the contention began to be exceedingly sharp among them. And while they were thus contending, the woman servant who had caused the multitude to be gathered together came, and when she saw the contention which was among the multitude she was exceedingly sorrowful, even unto tears.

29 And it came to pass that she went and took the queen by the hand, that perhaps she might raise her from the ground; and as soon as she touched her hand she arose and stood upon her feet, and cried with a loud voice, saying: O blessed Jesus, who has saved me from an awful hell! O blessed God, have mercy on this people!

---

19:26 W ***torment***—punish

19:27 W ***afflict***—cause suffering to

19:28 W ***contention***—arguing

30 And when she had said this, she clasped her hands, being filled with joy, speaking many words which were not understood; and when she had done this, she took the king, Lamoni, by the hand, and behold he arose and stood upon his feet.

31 And he, immediately, seeing the contention among his people, went forth and began to rebuke them, and to teach them the words which he had heard from the mouth of Ammon; and as many as heard his words believed, and were converted unto the Lord.

32 But there were many among them who would not hear his words; therefore they went their way.

33 And it came to pass that when Ammon arose he also administered unto them, and also did all the servants of Lamoni; and they did all declare unto the people the selfsame thing—that their hearts had been changed; that they had no more desire to do evil.

34 And behold, many did declare unto the people that they had seen angels and had conversed with them; and thus they had told them things of God, and of his righteousness.

35 And it came to pass that there were many that did believe in their words; and as many as did believe were baptized; and they became a righteous people, and they did establish a church among them.

36 And thus the work of the Lord did commence among the Lamanites; thus the Lord did begin to pour out his Spirit upon them; and we see that his arm is extended to all people who will repent and believe on his name.

## CHAPTER 20

*The Lord reveals to Ammon that his brethren are in prison in the land of Middoni. On the way to help them Ammon meets King Lamoni's father. Notice what Ammon does that eventually leads to his brethren's release.*

### The Lord Sends Ammon to Deliver His Brethren from Prison

1 AND it came to pass that when they had established a church in that land, that king Lamoni desired that Ammon should go with him to the land of Nephi, that he might show him unto his father.

2 And the voice of the Lord came to Ammon, saying: Thou shalt not go up to the land of Nephi, for behold, the king will seek thy life; but thou shalt go to the land of Middoni; for behold, thy brother Aaron, and also Muloki and Ammah are in prison.

3 Now it came to pass that when Ammon had heard this, he said unto Lamoni: Behold, my brother and brethren are in prison at Middoni, and I go that I may deliver them.

4 Now Lamoni said unto Ammon: I know, in the strength of the Lord thou canst do all things. But behold, I will go with thee to the land of Middoni; for the king of the land of Middoni, whose name is Antiomno, is a friend unto me; therefore I go to the land of Middoni, that I may flatter the king of the land, and he will cast thy brethren out of prison. Now Lamoni said unto him: Who told thee that thy brethren were in prison?

5 And Ammon said unto him: No one hath told me, save it be God; and he said unto me—Go and deliver thy brethren, for they are in prison in the land of Middoni.

6 Now when Lamoni had heard this he caused that his servants should make ready his horses and his chariots.

7 And he said unto Ammon: Come, I will go with thee down to the land of Middoni, and there I will plead with the king that he will cast thy brethren out of prison.

---

19:31 ***rebuke***—correct

19:33 ***administered unto***—taught

When our hearts are changed and we no longer want to do evil, we are truly converted (see Mosiah 5:2). Are there some temptations you have struggled with in the past that the Lord has helped you overcome?

19:36 ***commence***—begin

20:1 ***established***—started

20:3 (2–3) Ammon hears the voice of the Lord. This is called "the spirit of revelation" and often comes to your mind and heart (see D&C 8:2–3).

20:4 ***thou canst***—you can
***flatter***—please or win favor from
***cast***—release

What had Ammon done to make Lamoni believe that Ammon could do all things? (see Alma 18:2, 9–10). How can the strength of the Lord help you accomplish your righteous goals?

## Ammon and Lamoni Meet Lamoni's Father

8 And it came to pass that as Ammon and Lamoni
were journeying thither, they met the father of
Lamoni, who was king over all the land.
9 And behold, the father of Lamoni said unto him:
Why did ye not come to the feast on that great day
when I made a feast unto my sons, and unto my
people?
10 And he also said: Whither art thou going with
this Nephite, who is one of the children of a liar?
11 And it came to pass that Lamoni rehearsed unto
him whither he was going, for he feared to offend
him.
12 And he also told him all the cause of his tarrying in his own kingdom, that he did not go unto his
father to the feast which he had prepared.
13 And now when Lamoni had rehearsed unto
him all these things, behold, to his astonishment,
his father was angry with him, and said: Lamoni,
thou art going to deliver these Nephites, who are
sons of a liar. Behold, he robbed our fathers; and
now his children are also come amongst us that
they may, by their cunning and their lyings, deceive
us, that they again may rob us of our property.
14 Now the father of Lamoni commanded him that
he should slay Ammon with the sword. And he also
commanded him that he should not go to the land
of Middoni, but that he should return with him to
the land of Ishmael.
15 But Lamoni said unto him: I will not slay
Ammon, neither will I return to the land of Ishmael,
but I go to the land of Middoni that I may release
the brethren of Ammon, for I know that they are
just men and holy prophets of the true God.
16 Now when his father had heard these words,
he was angry with him, and he drew his sword that
he might smite him to the earth.
17 But Ammon stood forth and said unto him:
Behold, thou shalt not slay thy son; nevertheless, it
were better that he should fall than thee, for
behold, he has repented of his sins; but if thou
shouldst fall at this time, in thine anger, thy soul
could not be saved.
18 And again, it is expedient that thou shouldst
forbear; for if thou shouldst slay thy son, he being
an innocent man, his blood would cry from the
ground to the Lord his God, for vengeance to come
upon thee; and perhaps thou wouldst lose thy soul.
19 Now when Ammon had said these words unto
him, he answered him, saying: I know that if I
should slay my son, that I should shed innocent
blood; for it is thou that hast sought to destroy him.
20 And he stretched forth his hand to slay
Ammon. But Ammon withstood his blows, and also
smote his arm that he could not use it.
21 Now when the king saw that Ammon could
slay him, he began to plead with Ammon that he
would spare his life.
22 But Ammon raised his sword, and said unto
him: Behold, I will smite thee except thou wilt grant
unto me that my brethren may be cast out of prison.

---

20:8 ***journeying thither***—traveling there

20:10 ***Whither***—Where

20:11 ***rehearsed***—told

20:12 ***tarrying***—staying

20:13 ***cunning***—trickery

20:14 (10–14) The father of Lamoni hated the Nephites. The Lamanites had hated the Nephites for many generations (see Mosiah 10:11–17).

20:15 ***just***—fair or righteous

20:16 ***smite him to the earth***—kill him

20:18 ***expedient***—necessary
***forbear***—stop
***vengeance***—punishment

20:18 (17–18) "Anger is not an expression of strength. It is an indication of one's inability to control his thoughts, words, his emotions. . . . When the weakness of anger takes over, the strength of reason leaves" (Gordon B. Hinckley, in Conference Report, October 1991, 71).

20:19 ***sought***—tried

20:20 ***withstood***—defended himself against
***smote***—cut

20:22 ***grant***—give

## Ammon's Brethren Are Released from Prison

23 Now the king, fearing he should lose his life, said: If thou wilt spare me I will grant unto thee whatsoever thou wilt ask, even to half of the kingdom.

24 Now when Ammon saw that he had wrought upon the old king according to his desire, he said unto him: If thou wilt grant that my brethren may be cast out of prison, and also that Lamoni may retain his kingdom, and that ye be not displeased with him, but grant that he may do according to his own desires in whatsoever thing he thinketh, then will I spare thee; otherwise I will smite thee to the earth.

25 Now when Ammon had said these words, the king began to rejoice because of his life.

26 And when he saw that Ammon had no desire to destroy him, and when he also saw the great love he had for his son Lamoni, he was astonished exceedingly, and said: Because this is all that thou hast desired, that I would release thy brethren, and suffer that my son Lamoni should retain his kingdom, behold, I will grant unto you that my son may retain his kingdom from this time and forever; and I will govern him no more—

27 And I will also grant unto thee that thy brethren may be cast out of prison, and thou and thy brethren may come unto me, in my kingdom; for I shall greatly desire to see thee. For the king was greatly astonished at the words which he had spoken, and also at the words which had been spoken by his son Lamoni, therefore he was desirous to learn them.

28 And it came to pass that Ammon and Lamoni proceeded on their journey towards the land of Middoni. And Lamoni found favor in the eyes of the king of the land; therefore the brethren of Ammon were brought forth out of prison.

29 And when Ammon did meet them he was exceedingly sorrowful, for behold they were naked, and their skins were worn exceedingly because of being bound with strong cords. And they also had suffered hunger, thirst, and all kinds of afflictions; nevertheless they were patient in all their sufferings.

30 And, as it happened, it was their lot to have fallen into the hands of a more hardened and a more stiffnecked people; therefore they would not hearken unto their words, and they had cast them out, and had smitten them, and had driven them from house to house, and from place to place, even until they had arrived in the land of Middoni; and there they were taken and cast into prison, and bound with strong cords, and kept in prison for many days, and were delivered by Lamoni and Ammon.

*An account of the preaching of Aaron, and Muloki, and their brethren, to the Lamanites. Comprising chapters 21 to 26 inclusive.**

# CHAPTER 21

*This chapter begins the story of Aaron, Muloki, and their companions preaching the gospel to the Lamanites. Note how the Lord blesses them for their efforts.*

## Aaron Teaches the Wicked Nephites Who Live Among the Lamanites

1 NOW when Ammon and his brethren separated themselves in the borders of the land of the Lamanites, behold Aaron took his journey towards the land which was called by the Lamanites, Jerusalem, calling it after the land of their fathers' nativity; and it was away joining the borders of Mormon.

---

20:23 The father of Lamoni is so afraid of Ammon, he is willing to give up half of his kingdom if Ammon will spare his life. Later in the story when Aaron teaches him, he becomes willing to give up all that he possesses, including his sins, to gain the kingdom of God. All of us must be willing to give up our sins and repent to fully receive of the Spirit of the Lord (see Alma 22:15–18).

20:24 ***wrought upon***—changed
***retain***–keep

20:26 ***suffer***—allow

20:28 ***proceeded***—continued

20:30 ***lot***—fate

* The first sentence of this introduction to chapter 21 was translated from the Book of Mormon plates.

21:1 Ammon and the sons of Mosiah and their friends each went in separate directions to teach the gospel to the Lamanites (see Alma 17:16–18).

***nativity***—birth

2 Now the Lamanites and the Amalekites and the people of Amulon had built a great city, which was called Jerusalem.

3 Now the Lamanites of themselves were sufficiently hardened, but the Amalekites and the Amulonites were still harder; therefore they did cause the Lamanites that they should harden their hearts, that they should wax strong in wickedness and their abominations.

4 And it came to pass that Aaron came to the city of Jerusalem, and first began to preach to the Amalekites. And he began to preach to them in their synagogues, for they had built synagogues after the order of the Nehors; for many of the Amalekites and the Amulonites were after the order of the Nehors.

5 Therefore, as Aaron entered into one of their synagogues to preach unto the people, and as he was speaking unto them, behold there arose an Amalekite and began to contend with him, saying: What is that thou hast testified? Hast thou seen an angel? Why do not angels appear unto us? Behold are not this people as good as thy people?

6 Thou also sayest, except we repent we shall perish. How knowest thou the thought and intent of our hearts? How knowest thou that we have cause to repent? How knowest thou that we are not a righteous people? Behold, we have built sanctuaries, and we do assemble ourselves together to worship God. We do believe that God will save all men.

7 Now Aaron said unto him: Believest thou that the Son of God shall come to redeem mankind from their sins?

8 And the man said unto him: We do not believe that thou knowest any such thing. We do not believe in these foolish traditions. We do not believe that thou knowest of things to come, neither do we believe that thy fathers and also that our fathers did know concerning the things which they spake, of that which is to come.

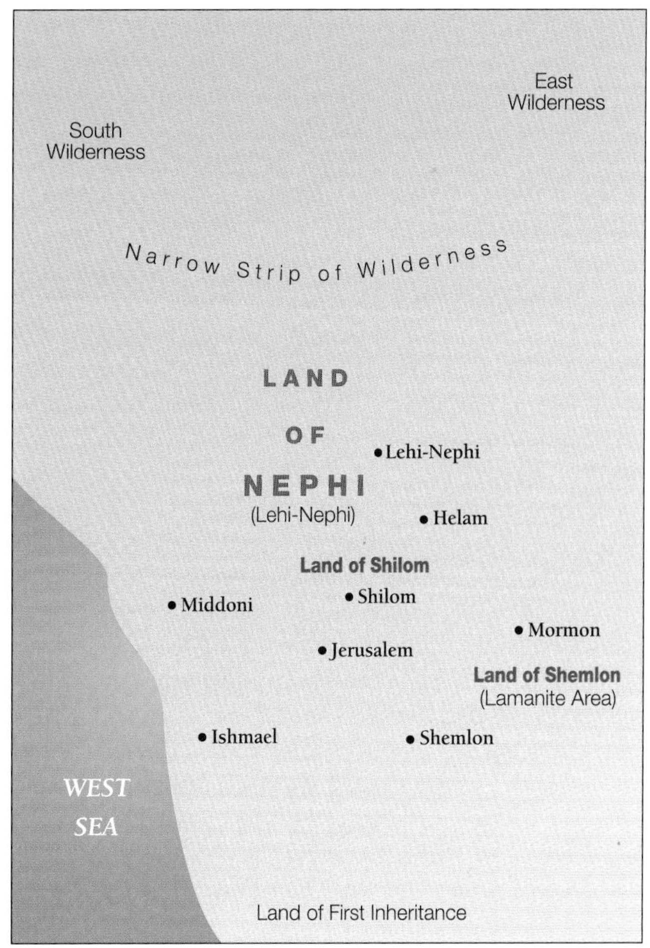


*The sons of Mosiah taught the gospel to the Lamanites in the land of Nephi.*

9 Now Aaron began to open the scriptures unto them concerning the coming of Christ, and also concerning the resurrection of the dead, and that there could be no redemption for mankind save it were through the death and sufferings of Christ, and the atonement of his blood.

---

21:2 Not to be confused with the Jerusalem located in Israel, this Jerusalem was a Lamanite city built within the borders of the land of Nephi. The Amulonites and Amalekites, wicked groups of Nephites, helped build the city (see Joseph Fielding McConkie and others, *Doctrinal Commentary on the Book of Mormon* 3:151–52).

21:3 ***sufficiently***—quite
***wax***—grow
***abominations***—great evildoings

21:4 ***synagogues***—churches

21:5 ***contend***—argue

21:6 ***intent***—desire
***sanctuaries***—places of worship
***assemble***—gather

21:8 (4–8) The order of Nehors began with the anti-Christ named Nehor (see Alma 1:1–16). Verses 6–8 show some of their false beliefs.

21:9 ***save***—except

10 And it came to pass as he began to expound
these things unto them they were angry with him,
and began to mock him; and they would not hear
the words which he spake.

### *The Sons of Mosiah and Their Friends Are Treated Badly As They Preach the Gospel to the Lamanites*

11 Therefore, when he saw that they would not
hear his words, he departed out of their synagogue, and came over to a village which was called
Ani-Anti, and there he found Muloki preaching the
word unto them; and also Ammah and his
brethren. And they contended with many about the
word.
12 And it came to pass that they saw that the
people would harden their hearts, therefore they
departed and came over into the land of Middoni.
And they did preach the word unto many, and few
believed on the words which they taught.
13 Nevertheless, Aaron and a certain number of
his brethren were taken and cast into prison, and
the remainder of them fled out of the land of
Middoni unto the regions round about.
14 And those who were cast into prison suffered
many things, and they were delivered by the hand
of Lamoni and Ammon, and they were fed and
clothed.
15 And they went forth again to declare the word,
and thus they were delivered for the first time out
of prison; and thus they had suffered.
16 And they went forth whithersoever they were
led by the Spirit of the Lord, preaching the word of
God in every synagogue of the Amalekites, or in
every assembly of the Lamanites where they could
be admitted.
17 And it came to pass that the Lord began to
bless them, insomuch that they brought many to the
knowledge of the truth; yea, they did convince
many of their sins, and of the traditions of their
fathers, which were not correct.

### *Ammon and Lamoni Return to the Land of Ishmael to Strengthen the Church*

18 And it came to pass that Ammon and Lamoni
returned from the land of Middoni to the land of
Ishmael, which was the land of their inheritance.
19 And king Lamoni would not suffer that Ammon
should serve him, or be his servant.
20 But he caused that there should be synagogues
built in the land of Ishmael, and he caused that his
people, or the people who were under his reign,
should assemble themselves together.
21 And he did rejoice over them, and he did teach
them many things. And he did also declare unto
them that they were a people who were under him,
and that they were a free people, that they were
free from the oppressions of the king, his father; for
that his father had granted unto him that he might
reign over the people who were in the land of
Ishmael, and in all the land round about.
22 And he also declared unto them that they might
have the liberty of worshiping the Lord their God
according to their desires, in whatsoever place they
were in, if it were in the land which was under the
reign of king Lamoni.

---

21:10 ***expound***—explain
***mock***—make fun of

21:12 Brigham Young taught that the phrase "harden their hearts" means people "shut their ears, stop them up tight, close their eyes, and are determined to hear nothing that is true concerning this people, or the doctrines we preach. . . . They reject the truth and receive lies" (in *Journal of Discourses* 4:371).

21:12 (5–12) Not everyone who hears the gospel message believes it. Why do you think many people today don't accept the message of Christ?

21:13 ***remainder***—rest
***regions***—places

21:14 ***delivered***—brought out or freed

You can read about King Lamoni and Ammon rescuing Aaron and his brethren from prison in Alma 20:2, 7, 28–30.

21:16 ***whithersoever***—wherever
***assembly***—gathering

21:19 ***suffer***—allow

21:20 ***reign***—rule

21:22 The freedom to worship according to one's own conscience is one of the basic principles of the gospel explained in Article of Faith 11.

23 And Ammon did preach unto the people of
king Lamoni; and it came to pass that he did teach them all things concerning things pertaining to righteousness. And he did exhort them daily, with all diligence; and they gave heed unto his word, and they were zealous for keeping the commandments of God.

## CHAPTER 22

*Aaron and his brethren teach the Lamanite king. He is converted to the gospel. Look for the miraculous way in which the Lord prepares the king's heart to receive the truth.*

### *Aaron Is Led by the Spirit to King Lamoni's Father*

1 NOW, as Ammon was thus teaching the people
of Lamoni continually, we will return to the account of Aaron and his brethren; for after he departed from the land of Middoni he was led by the Spirit to the land of Nephi, even to the house of the king which was over all the land save it were the land of Ishmael; and he was the father of Lamoni.
2 And it came to pass that he went in unto him
into the king's palace, with his brethren, and bowed himself before the king, and said unto him: Behold, O king, we are the brethren of Ammon, whom thou hast delivered out of prison.
3 And now, O king, if thou wilt spare our lives,
we will be thy servants. And the king said unto them: Arise, for I will grant unto you your lives, and I will not suffer that ye shall be my servants; but I will insist that ye shall administer unto me; for I have been somewhat troubled in mind because of the generosity and the greatness of the words of thy brother Ammon; and I desire to know the cause why he has not come up out of Middoni with thee.
4 And Aaron said unto the king: Behold, the Spirit
of the Lord has called him another way; he has gone to the land of Ishmael, to teach the people of Lamoni.
5 Now the king said unto them: What is this that
ye have said concerning the Spirit of the Lord? Behold, this is the thing which doth trouble me.
6 And also, what is this that Ammon said—If ye
will repent ye shall be saved, and if ye will not repent, ye shall be cast off at the last day?
7 And Aaron answered him and said unto him:
Believest thou that there is a God? And the king said: I know that the Amalekites say that there is a God, and I have granted unto them that they should build sanctuaries, that they may assemble themselves together to worship him. And if now thou sayest there is a God, behold I will believe.
8 And now when Aaron heard this, his heart
began to rejoice, and he said: Behold, assuredly as thou livest, O king, there is a God.
9 And the king said: Is God that Great Spirit that
brought our fathers out of the land of Jerusalem?
10 And Aaron said unto him: Yea, he is that Great
Spirit, and he created all things both in heaven and in earth. Believest thou this?
11 And he said: Yea, I believe that the Great Spirit
created all things, and I desire that ye should tell me concerning all these things, and I will believe thy words.
12 And it came to pass that when Aaron saw that
the king would believe his words, he began from the creation of Adam, reading the scriptures unto the king—how God created man after his own image, and that God gave him commandments, and that because of transgression, man had fallen.

---

21:23 ***pertaining to***—about
***all diligence***—great effort
***gave heed unto***—obeyed
***zealous***—enthusiastic

Ammon continued to teach the gospel to these new converts after their baptism. Why is it so important to teach and support new converts to the Church?

22:1 In this chapter Aaron and his brethren follow the guidance of the Spirit and have great success. Can you think of times in your life when you were blessed because you listened to the promptings of the Holy Ghost?

22:3 ***administer unto***—teach and comfort
***generosity***—kindness

22:6 ***cast off***—cut off or kicked out

22:7 ***sanctuaries***—places of worship

22:8 ***assuredly***—as sure

22:9 The king remembers the story of God bringing father Lehi and his children out of the land of Jerusalem (see 1 Nephi 2).

13 And Aaron did expound unto him the scriptures from the creation of Adam, laying the fall of man before him, and their carnal state and also the plan of redemption, which was prepared from the foundation of the world, through Christ, for all whosoever would believe on his name.

14 And since man had fallen he could not merit anything of himself; but the sufferings and death of Christ atone for their sins, through faith and repentance, and so forth; and that he breaketh the bands of death, that the grave shall have no victory, and that the sting of death should be swallowed up in the hopes of glory; and Aaron did expound all these things unto the king.

15 And it came to pass that after Aaron had expounded these things unto him, the king said: What shall I do that I may have this eternal life of which thou hast spoken? Yea, what shall I do that I may be born of God, having this wicked spirit rooted out of my breast, and receive his Spirit, that I may be filled with joy, that I may not be cast off at the last day? Behold, said he, I will give up all that I possess, yea, I will forsake my kingdom, that I may receive this great joy.

16 But Aaron said unto him: If thou desirest this thing, if thou wilt bow down before God, yea, if thou wilt repent of all thy sins, and will bow down before God, and call on his name in faith, believing that ye shall receive, then shalt thou receive the hope which thou desirest.

## The Lamanite King Is Converted

17 And it came to pass that when Aaron had said these words, the king did bow down before the Lord, upon his knees; yea, even he did prostrate himself upon the earth, and cried mightily, saying:

18 O God, Aaron hath told me that there is a God; and if there is a God, and if thou art God, wilt thou make thyself known unto me, and I will give away all my sins to know thee, and that I may be raised from the dead, and be saved at the last day. And now when the king had said these words, he was struck as if he were dead.

19 And it came to pass that his servants ran and told the queen all that had happened unto the king. And she came in unto the king; and when she saw him lay as if he were dead, and also Aaron and his brethren standing as though they had been the cause of his fall, she was angry with them, and commanded that her servants, or the servants of the king, should take them and slay them.

20 Now the servants had seen the cause of the king's fall, therefore they durst not lay their hands on Aaron and his brethren; and they pled with the queen saying: Why commandest thou that we should slay these men, when behold one of them is mightier than us all? Therefore we shall fall before them.

21 Now when the queen saw the fear of the servants she also began to fear exceedingly, lest there

---

22:13 ***expound***—explain
***carnal state***—worldly condition

22:14 ***merit***—earn
***sting***—pain

There are two deaths—the physical death of the body and a spiritual death when we are cut off from the Lord. The hopes of glory are to overcome both deaths. We can receive this glory by repenting. President Spencer W. Kimball explained that "true repentance is rewarded by forgiveness, but sin brings the sting of death" (in Conference Report, October 1977, 6).

22:14 (12–14) President Ezra Taft Benson explained why Aaron taught the king about the Fall before teaching about Jesus Christ: "Just as a man does not really desire food until he is hungry, so he does not desire the salvation of Christ until he knows why he needs Christ. No one adequately and properly knows why he needs Christ until he understands and accepts the doctrine of the Fall and its effect upon all mankind (in Conference Report, April 1987, 106).

22:15 ***rooted out***—taken out

In Alma 20 when the king was afraid Ammon was going to kill him, he was willing to give "half of the kingdom" to save his mortal life (Alma 20:23). Notice what the king is now willing to give for the joy of eternal life.

22:17 ***prostrate himself***—lay down

22:18 President Ezra Taft Benson notes that "each of us must surrender our sins if we are to really know Christ. For we do not know Him until we become like Him. There are some, like this king, who must pray until they, too, have 'a wicked spirit rooted' from them so they can find the same joy" (in Conference Report, October 1983, 63).

22:20 ***durst***—dared

should some evil come upon her. And she commanded her servants that they should go and call the people, that they might slay Aaron and his brethren.

22 Now when Aaron saw the determination of the queen, he, also knowing the hardness of the hearts of the people, feared lest that a multitude should assemble themselves together, and there should be a great contention and a disturbance among them; therefore he put forth his hand and raised the king from the earth, and said unto him: Stand. And he stood upon his feet, receiving his strength.

23 Now this was done in the presence of the queen and many of the servants. And when they saw it they greatly marveled, and began to fear. And the king stood forth, and began to minister unto them. And he did minister unto them, insomuch that his whole household were converted unto the Lord.

24 Now there was a multitude gathered together because of the commandment of the queen, and there began to be great murmurings among them because of Aaron and his brethren.

25 But the king stood forth among them and administered unto them. And they were pacified towards Aaron and those who were with him.

26 And it came to pass that when the king saw that the people were pacified, he caused that Aaron and his brethren should stand forth in the midst of the multitude, and that they should preach the word unto them.

## A Description of the Lamanite King's Land Is Set Forth

27 And it came to pass that the king sent a proclamation throughout all the land, amongst all his people who were in all his land, who were in all the regions round about, which was bordering even to the sea, on the east and on the west, and which was divided from the land of Zarahemla by a narrow strip of wilderness, which ran from the sea east even to the sea west, and round about on the borders of the seashore, and the borders of the wilderness which was on the north by the land of Zarahemla, through the borders of Manti, by the head of the river Sidon, running from the east towards the west—and thus were the Lamanites and the Nephites divided.

28 Now, the more idle part of the Lamanites lived in the wilderness, and dwelt in tents; and they were spread through the wilderness on the west, in the land of Nephi; yea, and also on the west of the land of Zarahemla, in the borders by the seashore, and on the west in the land of Nephi, in the place of their fathers' first inheritance, and thus bordering along by the seashore.

29 And also there were many Lamanites on the east by the seashore, whither the Nephites had driven them. And thus the Nephites were nearly surrounded by the Lamanites; nevertheless the Nephites had taken possession of all the northern parts of the land bordering on the wilderness, at the head of the river Sidon, from the east to the west, round about on the wilderness side; on the north, even until they came to the land which they called Bountiful.

30 And it bordered upon the land which they called Desolation, it being so far northward that it came into the land which had been peopled and been destroyed, of whose bones we have spoken, which was discovered by the people of Zarahemla, it being the place of their first landing.

31 And they came from there up into the south wilderness. Thus the land on the northward was called Desolation, and the land on the southward was called Bountiful, it being the wilderness which is filled with all manner of wild animals of every kind, a part of which had come from the land northward for food.

32 And now, it was only the distance of a day and a half's journey for a Nephite, on the line Bountiful and the land Desolation, from the east to the west sea; and thus the land of Nephi and the land of Zarahemla were nearly surrounded by water, there being a small neck of land between the land northward and the land southward.

---

22:22 ***determination***—plans
***contention***—argument or fight

22:23 ***minister unto***—help

22:25 ***were pacified***—lost their anger

22:26 ***midst***—middle

22:27 ***a proclamation***—an announcement

22:28 ***idle***—lazy

22:30 The land called Desolation is where the Jaredites in the book of Ether are destroyed (see Ether 14–15).

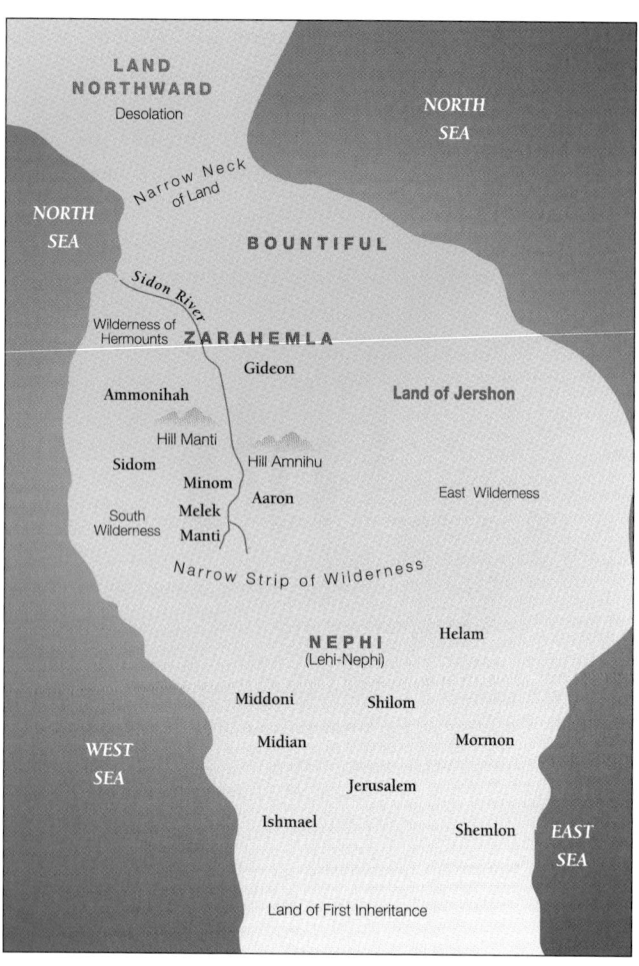


*Relative geographic locations in the Book of Mormon between 90 and 77 B.C.*

33 And it came to pass that the Nephites had inhabited the land Bountiful, even from the east unto the west sea, and thus the Nephites in their wisdom, with their guards and their armies, had hemmed in the Lamanites on the south, that thereby they should have no more possession on the north, that they might not overrun the land northward.
34 Therefore the Lamanites could have no more possessions only in the land of Nephi, and the wilderness round about. Now this was wisdom in the Nephites—as the Lamanites were an enemy to them, they would not suffer their afflictions on every hand, and also that they might have a country whither they might flee, according to their desires.
35 And now I, after having said this, return again to the account of Ammon and Aaron, Omner and Himni, and their brethren.

## CHAPTER 23

*Aaron and his brethren are allowed to teach the gospel to the Lamanites. The Lamanites in seven lands and cities accept the gospel. Look for some of the ways these Lamanites change their lives when they accept the truth.*

### The King of the Lamanites Declares Freedom of Religion

1 BEHOLD, now it came to pass that the king of the Lamanites sent a proclamation among all his people, that they should not lay their hands on Ammon, or Aaron, or Omner, or Himni, nor either of their brethren who should go forth preaching the word of God, in whatsoever place they should be, in any part of their land.
2 Yea, he sent a decree among them, that they should not lay their hands on them to bind them, or to cast them into prison; neither should they spit upon them, nor smite them, nor cast them out of their synagogues, nor scourge them; neither should they cast stones at them, but that they should have free access to their houses, and also their temples, and their sanctuaries.
3 And thus they might go forth and preach the word according to their desires, for the king had been converted unto the Lord, and all his household; therefore he sent his proclamation throughout

22:33 ***hemmed in***—contained

22:34 ***affictions***—trials or sufferings

23:1 ***proclamation***—message

23:2 ***synagogues***—churches
***scourge***—whip
***free access***—freedom to go
***sanctuaries***—holy places

23:3 The Lamanites had taught their children many false stories about what happened to their ancestors since the time they left Jerusalem (see Mosiah 10:12–17). Because of these false traditions the Lamanites hated the Nephites and previously would not listen to the missionaries. Satan uses this same plan today to keep people from listening to the truth (see D&C 93:38–39).

the land unto his people, that the word of God might have no obstruction, but that it might go forth throughout all the land, that his people might be convinced concerning the wicked traditions of their fathers, and that they might be convinced that they were all brethren, and that they ought not to murder, nor to plunder, nor to steal, nor to commit adultery, nor to commit any manner of wickedness.

## Thousands of Lamanites Are Converted to the Lord

4 And now it came to pass that when the king had sent forth this proclamation, that Aaron and his brethren went forth from city to city, and from one house of worship to another, establishing churches, and consecrating priests and teachers throughout the land among the Lamanites, to preach and to teach the word of God among them; and thus they began to have great success.
5 And thousands were brought to the knowledge of the Lord, yea, thousands were brought to believe in the traditions of the Nephites; and they were taught the records and prophecies which were handed down even to the present time.
6 And as sure as the Lord liveth, so sure as many as believed, or as many as were brought to the knowledge of the truth, through the preaching of Ammon and his brethren, according to the spirit of revelation and of prophecy, and the power of God working miracles in them—yea, I say unto you, as the Lord liveth, as many of the Lamanites as believed in their preaching, and were converted unto the Lord, never did fall away.
7 For they became a righteous people; they did lay down the weapons of their rebellion, that they did not fight against God any more, neither against any of their brethren.
8 Now, these are they who were converted unto the Lord:
9 The people of the Lamanites who were in the land of Ishmael;
10 And also of the people of the Lamanites who were in the land of Middoni;
11 And also of the people of the Lamanites who were in the city of Nephi;
12 And also of the people of the Lamanites who were in the land of Shilom, and who were in the land of Shemlon, and in the city of Lemuel, and in the city of Shimnilom.
13 And these are the names of the cities of the Lamanites which were converted unto the Lord; and these are they that laid down the weapons of their rebellion, yea, all their weapons of war; and they were all Lamanites.
14 And the Amalekites were not converted, save only one; neither were any of the Amulonites; but they did harden their hearts, and also the hearts of the Lamanites in that part of the land wheresoever they dwelt, yea, and all their villages and all their cities.
15 Therefore, we have named all the cities of the Lamanites in which they did repent and come to the knowledge of the truth, and were converted.

## The Converted Lamanites Desire a New Name

16 And now it came to pass that the king and those who were converted were desirous that they might have a name, that thereby they might be distinguished from their brethren; therefore the king consulted with Aaron and many of their priests, concerning the name that they should take upon them, that they might be distinguished.
17 And it came to pass that they called their names Anti-Nephi-Lehies; and they were called by this name and were no more called Lamanites.

---

23:3 ***have no obstruction***—not be stopped
***plunder***—rob
***commit adultery***—misuse the sacred creative powers with someone other than their husband or wife

23:4 ***establishing***—organizing
***consecrating***—calling and giving authority to

23:7 (6–7) When these Lamanites learned the truth and were converted, they put away "the weapons of their rebellion." What weapons of rebellion do people use today to fight against God? (see Mosiah 2:36–37). What could you do to become more "converted unto the Lord"?

23:16 ***distinguished***—different
***consulted***—talked

23:17 The Book of Mormon does not tell us why these converted Lamanites chose the name Anti-Nephi-Lehies. One meaning of the word *anti* at the time of Joseph Smith was "mirror image of." Perhaps these new believers wanted to be just like Lehi and Nephi, their righteous ancestors (see Joseph Fielding McConkie and others, *Doctrinal Commentary on the Book of Mormon* 3:165).

18 And they began to be a very industrious people; yea, and they were friendly with the Nephites; therefore, they did open a correspondence with them, and the curse of God did no more follow them.

## CHAPTER 24

*The Lamanites attack and kill many of the people of Anti-Nephi-Lehi. The converted people of Anti-Nephi-Lehi refuse to defend themselves by fighting the Lamanites. Watch for why the people of Anti-Nephi-Lehi are willing to die rather than kill other Lamanites.*

### The Lamanites Attack the People of Anti-Nephi-Lehi

1 AND it came to pass that the Amalekites and the Amulonites and the Lamanites who were in the land of Amulon, and also in the land of Helam, and who were in the land of Jerusalem, and in fine, in all the land round about, who had not been converted and had not taken upon them the name of Anti-Nephi-Lehi, were stirred up by the Amalekites and by the Amulonites to anger against their brethren.
2 And their hatred became exceedingly sore against them, even insomuch that they began to rebel against their king, insomuch that they would not that he should be their king; therefore, they took up arms against the people of Anti-Nephi-Lehi.
3 Now the king conferred the kingdom upon his son, and he called his name Anti-Nephi-Lehi.
4 And the king died in that selfsame year that the Lamanites began to make preparations for war against the people of God.

### The People of Anti-Nephi-Lehi Rejoice in Christ

5 Now when Ammon and his brethren and all those who had come up with him saw the preparations of the Lamanites to destroy their brethren, they came forth to the land of Midian, and there Ammon met all his brethren; and from thence they came to the land of Ishmael that they might hold a council with Lamoni and also with his brother Anti-Nephi-Lehi, what they should do to defend themselves against the Lamanites.
6 Now there was not one soul among all the people who had been converted unto the Lord that would take up arms against their brethren; nay, they would not even make any preparations for war; yea, and also their king commanded them that they should not.
7 Now, these are the words which he said unto the people concerning the matter: I thank my God, my beloved people, that our great God has in goodness sent these our brethren, the Nephites, unto us to preach unto us, and to convince us of the traditions of our wicked fathers.
8 And behold, I thank my great God that he has given us a portion of his Spirit to soften our hearts, that we have opened a correspondence with these brethren, the Nephites.
9 And behold, I also thank my God, that by opening this correspondence we have been convinced of our sins, and of the many murders which we have committed.

---

23:18 ***industrious***—hard-working
***open a correspondence with***—write to or do business with

The Lamanites were cursed by God for their rebellion in the days of Laman and Lemuel. The cursing included being cut off from the Spirit of God (see 2 Nephi 5:20–24). This curse was taken from the Anti-Nephi-Lehies because of their righteousness. "That is, they had their sins remitted, had their souls reoriented toward the things of God, and began to enjoy rich outpourings of his Spirit" (Joseph Fielding McConkie and others, *Doctrinal Commentary on the Book of Mormon* 3:166).

24:2 ***exceedingly sore***—very strong
***took up arms against***—prepared for war with

24:3 ***conferred the kingdom upon***—gave the kingdom to

24:5 ***thence***—there

24:6 The Anti-Nephi-Lehies would not go to war because they made sacred covenants to never kill again. What covenants have you made? What sacrifices would you be willing to make to keep your covenants?

24:7 The Lord's missionaries are loved by those they teach. Jesus said, "How beautiful upon the mountains are the feet of him that bringeth good tidings unto them, that publisheth peace; that bringeth good tidings unto them" (3 Nephi 20:40). Those who teach the gospel also have a strong love for those they teach (see D&C 18:15–16).

24:8 ***correspondence***—communication

10 And I also thank my God, yea, my great God, that he hath granted unto us that we might repent of these things, and also that he hath forgiven us of those our many sins and murders which we have committed, and taken away the guilt from our hearts, through the merits of his Son.

## *The People of Anti-Nephi-Lehi Refuse to Fight the Lamanites*

11 And now behold, my brethren, since it has been all that we could do, (as we were the most lost of all mankind) to repent of all our sins and the many murders which we have committed, and to get God to take them away from our hearts, for it was all we could do to repent sufficiently before God that he would take away our stain—
12 Now, my best beloved brethren, since God hath taken away our stains, and our swords have become bright, then let us stain our swords no more with the blood of our brethren.
13 Behold, I say unto you, Nay, let us retain our swords that they be not stained with the blood of our brethren; for perhaps, if we should stain our swords again they can no more be washed bright through the blood of the Son of our great God, which shall be shed for the atonement of our sins.
14 And the great God has had mercy on us, and made these things known unto us that we might not perish; yea, and he has made these things known unto us beforehand, because he loveth our souls as well as he loveth our children; therefore, in his mercy he doth visit us by his angels, that the plan of salvation might be made known unto us as well as unto future generations.
15 Oh, how merciful is our God! And now behold, since it has been as much as we could do to get our stains taken away from us, and our swords are made bright, let us hide them away that they may be kept bright, as a testimony to our God at the last day, or at the day that we shall be brought to stand before him to be judged, that we have not stained our swords in the blood of our brethren since he imparted his word unto us and has made us clean thereby.
16 And now, my brethren, if our brethren seek to destroy us, behold, we will hide away our swords, yea, even we will bury them deep in the earth, that they may be kept bright, as a testimony that we have never used them, at the last day; and if our brethren destroy us, behold, we shall go to our God and shall be saved.
17 And now it came to pass that when the king had made an end of these sayings, and all the people were assembled together, they took their swords, and all the weapons which were used for the shedding of man's blood, and they did bury them up deep in the earth.
18 And this they did, it being in their view a testimony to God, and also to men, that they never would use weapons again for the shedding of man's blood; and this they did, vouching and covenanting with God, that rather than shed the blood of their brethren they would give up their own lives; and rather than take away from a brother they would give unto him; and rather than spend their days in idleness they would labor abundantly with their hands.

---

24:10 ***merits***—righteous works

"Because of the false traditions of their fathers, before their conversion these Lamanites had taken life in unrighteous wars. Though such needless killing is a sin of the gravest magnitude, it is not the same as the willful and premeditated [thought-out] taking of life that . . . is called first-degree murder; or that is spoken of in the scriptures as being 'sin unto death' (1 John 5:16–17), meaning a person cannot, even through repentance, obtain a glory greater than that of the telestial kingdom in the worlds to come" (Joseph Fielding McConkie and others, *Doctrinal Commentary on the Book of Mormon* 3:167–68).

24:11 ***sufficiently***—enough

24:13 The Lord, speaking of those who return to sins already repented of, said, "Unto that soul who sinneth shall the former sins return, saith the Lord your God" (see D&C 82:7).

24:14 ***mercy on***—compassion or love

24:15 ***imparted his word***—taught the gospel

24:15 (11–15) The "stain" spoken of here is a symbol for how sin makes us unclean (see Isaiah 1:18). Their "swords" being made "bright" is also a symbol of the powers of the Atonement to wash the blood of those killed, or the sin, from their swords.

24:16 The Anti-Nephi-Lehies buried their weapons. What could you "bury" or get rid of in your life that would help you to remain "firm" in the faith? (See Alma 24:19).

24:18 ***it being in their view***—as
***vouching***—promising
***idleness***—laziness
***labor abundantly***—work hard

THE ANTI-NEPHI-LEHIES BURYING THEIR SWORDS, BY DEL PARSON

*The Anti-Nephi-Lehies bury their weapons of war.*

19 And thus we see that, when these Lamanites were brought to believe and to know the truth, they were firm, and would suffer even unto death rather than commit sin; and thus we see that they buried their weapons of peace, or they buried the weapons of war, for peace.

## *Many Lamanites Are Converted by the Example of the People of Anti-Nephi-Lehi*

20 And it came to pass that their brethren, the Lamanites, made preparations for war, and came up to the land of Nephi for the purpose of destroying the king, and to place another in his stead, and also of destroying the people of Anti-Nephi-Lehi out of the land.
21 Now when the people saw that they were coming against them they went out to meet them, and prostrated themselves before them to the earth, and began to call on the name of the Lord; and thus they were in this attitude when the Lamanites began to fall upon them, and began to slay them with the sword.
22 And thus without meeting any resistance, they did slay a thousand and five of them; and we know that they are blessed, for they have gone to dwell with their God.
23 Now when the Lamanites saw that their brethren would not flee from the sword, neither would they turn aside to the right hand or to the left, but that they would lie down and perish, and praised God even in the very act of perishing under the sword—
24 Now when the Lamanites saw this they did forbear from slaying them; and there were many whose hearts had swollen in them for those of their brethren who had fallen under the sword, for they repented of the things which they had done.
25 And it came to pass that they threw down their weapons of war, and they would not take them again, for they were stung for the murders which they had committed; and they came down even as their brethren, relying upon the mercies of those whose arms were lifted to slay them.
26 And it came to pass that the people of God were joined that day by more than the number who had been slain; and those who had been slain were righteous people, therefore we have no reason to doubt but what they were saved.
27 And there was not a wicked man slain among them; but there were more than a thousand brought to the knowledge of the truth; thus we see that the Lord worketh in many ways to the salvation of his people.
28 Now the greatest number of those of the Lamanites who slew so many of their brethren were Amalekites and Amulonites, the greatest number of whom were after the order of the Nehors.
29 Now, among those who joined the people of the Lord, there were none who were Amalekites or Amulonites, or who were of the order of Nehor, but they were actual descendants of Laman and Lemuel.
30 And thus we can plainly discern, that after a people have been once enlightened by the Spirit of God, and have had great knowledge of things pertaining to righteousness, and then have fallen away into sin and transgression, they become more hardened, and thus their state becomes worse than though they had never known these things.

---

24:19 (17–19) The Anti-Nephi-Lehies knew that an army of the Lamanites was about to attack them, and yet they buried their weapons. In the face of fear they showed great courage. What times in your life have you had to make courageous choices to do what is right, even though you were afraid?

24:21 ***prostrated***—bowed

24:22 ***meeting any resistance***—anyone fighting back

24:22 (21–22) The Lord sometimes allows the righteous to suffer that His judgments might come upon the wicked (see Alma 60:13).

24:23 ***flee***—run away

24:24 ***forbear from***—stop
***whose hearts had swollen in them***—who were very sad

24:25 ***relying***—depending

Many Lamanites were greatly affected by the example of the people of Anti-Nephi-Lehi. In what areas of your life can you resolve to be an example to others?

24:28 The "order of Nehors" was a priestcraft—an imitation of the true priesthood. Some of their false beliefs included priests teaching for money and gain, that there would be no Christ, no Atonement, and no life after death (see Alma 1:3–4; 21:4, 7–10).

24:29 ***descendants***—children, grandchildren, and so on

24:30 ***discern***—see
***enlightened***—inspired
***pertaining to***—about

24:30 (29–30) Why do you think people who have the gospel and then fall away from it become harder to convert than people who have never heard about it?

## CHAPTER 25

*The children of King Noah's wicked priests are killed. Many more Lamanites join with the righteous Lamanites who call themselves the Anti-Nephi-Lehies. Compare what the Lamanites were like before and after they joined the Anti-Nephi-Lehies.*

### *The Children of King Noah's Wicked Priests Are Killed*

1 AND behold, now it came to pass that those Lamanites were more angry because they had slain their brethren; therefore they swore vengeance upon the Nephites; and they did no more attempt to slay the people of Anti-Nephi-Lehi at that time.

2 But they took their armies and went over into the borders of the land of Zarahemla, and fell upon the people who were in the land of Ammonihah and destroyed them.

3 And after that, they had many battles with the Nephites, in the which they were driven and slain.

4 And among the Lamanites who were slain were almost all the seed of Amulon and his brethren, who were the priests of Noah, and they were slain by the hands of the Nephites;

5 And the remainder, having fled into the east wilderness, and having usurped the power and authority over the Lamanites, caused that many of the Lamanites should perish by fire because of their belief—

6 For many of them, after having suffered much loss and so many afflictions, began to be stirred up in remembrance of the words which Aaron and his brethren had preached to them in their land; therefore they began to disbelieve the traditions of their fathers, and to believe in the Lord, and that he gave great power unto the Nephites; and thus there were many of them converted in the wilderness.

7 And it came to pass that those rulers who were the remnant of the children of Amulon caused that they should be put to death, yea, all those that believed in these things.

8 Now this martyrdom caused that many of their brethren should be stirred up to anger; and there began to be contention in the wilderness; and the Lamanites began to hunt the seed of Amulon and his brethren and began to slay them; and they fled into the east wilderness.

9 And behold they are hunted at this day by the Lamanites. Thus the words of Abinadi were brought to pass, which he said concerning the seed of the priests who caused that he should suffer death by fire.

10 For he said unto them: What ye shall do unto me shall be a type of things to come.

11 And now Abinadi was the first that suffered death by fire because of his belief in God; now this is what he meant, that many should suffer death by fire, according as he had suffered.

12 And he said unto the priests of Noah that their seed should cause many to be put to death, in the like manner as he was, and that they should be scattered abroad and slain, even as a sheep having no shepherd is driven and slain by wild beasts; and now behold, these words were verified, for they were driven by the Lamanites, and they were hunted, and they were smitten.

### *Many Lamanites Repent and Join the Anti-Nephi-Lehies*

13 And it came to pass that when the Lamanites saw that they could not overpower the Nephites they returned again to their own land; and many of them came over to dwell in the land of Ishmael and the land of Nephi, and did join themselves to the people of God, who were the people of Anti-Nephi-Lehi.

---

25:1 ***swore vengeance upon***—promised they would kill
***attempt***—try

25:4 The account of Amulon and the other wicked priests of King Noah is found in Mosiah 20:1–5; 23:30–39; 24:1–20.

25:5 ***remainder***—rest
***usurped***—taken

25:6 ***afflictions***—trials and suffering

25:7 ***remnant***—remaining part

25:8 ***martyrdom***—killing of good people
***contention***—arguing and fighting

25:10 ***a type***—an example

25:12 ***verified***—proven to be true

25:13 ***dwell***—live

14 And they did also bury their weapons of war,
according as their brethren had, and they began to
be a righteous people; and they did walk in the
ways of the Lord, and did observe to keep his commandments and his statutes.
15 Yea, and they did keep the law of Moses; for
it was expedient that they should keep the law of
Moses as yet, for it was not all fulfilled. But
notwithstanding the law of Moses, they did look
forward to the coming of Christ, considering that
the law of Moses was a type of his coming, and
believing that they must keep those outward performances until the time that he should be revealed
unto them.
16 Now they did not suppose that salvation came
by the law of Moses; but the law of Moses did serve
to strengthen their faith in Christ; and thus they did
retain a hope through faith, unto eternal salvation,
relying upon the spirit of prophecy, which spake of
those things to come.
17 And now behold, Ammon, and Aaron, and
Omner, and Himni, and their brethren did rejoice
exceedingly, for the success which they had had
among the Lamanites, seeing that the Lord had
granted unto them according to their prayers, and
that he had also verified his word unto them in
every particular.

## CHAPTER 26

*Ammon speaks to his brethren about the power and goodness of God. Ammon teaches that all glory and honor belongs to God. Look for the blessings which come to mankind because of the power of God.*

### Ammon Speaks of the Blessings He Received As a Missionary

1 AND now, these are the words of Ammon to his
brethren, which say thus: My brothers and my
brethren, behold I say unto you, how great reason
have we to rejoice; for could we have supposed when
we started from the land of Zarahemla that God
would have granted unto us such great blessings?
2 And now, I ask, what great blessings has he
bestowed upon us? Can ye tell?
3 Behold, I answer for you; for our brethren, the
Lamanites, were in darkness, yea, even in the darkest abyss, but behold, how many of them are
brought to behold the marvelous light of God! And
this is the blessing which hath been bestowed upon
us, that we have been made instruments in the
hands of God to bring about this great work.
4 Behold, thousands of them do rejoice, and have
been brought into the fold of God.

---

25:14 ***statutes***—laws

25:15 ***expedient***—necessary or helpful

The law of Moses required many "outward performances." These performances included sacrificing animals and participating in special feasts. When Jesus lived on earth, He fulfilled the law of Moses and commanded the people to live the law of the gospel (see Matthew 5:17).

25:16 ***suppose***—think
***retain***—keep
***relying***—depending

25:17 ***granted***—given
***particular***—way

26:1 ***rejoice***—be thankful and happy

26:2 ***bestowed upon***—given

A church hymn teaches us, "Count your many blessings, name them one by one" ("Count Your Blessings," *Hymns,* no. 241). What blessings has the Lord given you? How does thinking about those blessings make you feel?

26:3 ***abyss***—pit of spiritual darkness

An instrument is a tool. God can use a worthy and willing person, like a missionary, "as an instrument to accomplish His work" (Ezra Taft Benson, in Conference Report, April 1984, 63).

26:4 ***fold***—Church

5 Behold, the field was ripe, and blessed are ye, for ye did thrust in the sickle, and did reap with your might, yea, all the day long did ye labor; and behold the number of your sheaves! And they shall be gathered into the garners, that they are not wasted.

6 Yea, they shall not be beaten down by the storm at the last day; yea, neither shall they be harrowed up by the whirlwinds; but when the storm cometh they shall be gathered together in their place, that the storm cannot penetrate to them; yea, neither shall they be driven with fierce winds whithersoever the enemy listeth to carry them.

7 But behold, they are in the hands of the Lord of the harvest, and they are his; and he will raise them up at the last day.

8 Blessed be the name of our God; let us sing to his praise, yea, let us give thanks to his holy name, for he doth work righteousness forever.

9 For if we had not come up out of the land of Zarahemla, these our dearly beloved brethren, who have so dearly beloved us, would still have been racked with hatred against us, yea, and they would also have been strangers to God.

## Ammon Tells Aaron That Their Missionary Success Came Because of God's Power

10 And it came to pass that when Ammon had said these words, his brother Aaron rebuked him, saying: Ammon, I fear that thy joy doth carry thee away unto boasting.

11 But Ammon said unto him: I do not boast in my own strength, nor in my own wisdom; but behold, my joy is full, yea, my heart is brim with joy, and I will rejoice in my God.

12 Yea, I know that I am nothing; as to my strength I am weak; therefore I will not boast of myself, but I will boast of my God, for in his strength I can do all things; yea, behold, many mighty miracles we have wrought in this land, for which we will praise his name forever.

13 Behold, how many thousands of our brethren has he loosed from the pains of hell; and they are brought to sing redeeming love, and this because of the power of his word which is in us, therefore have we not great reason to rejoice?

*After wheat ripens, it is cut down and gathered into sheaves.*

PHOTOGRAPH BY EDWIN M. WOOLLEY

26:5 A field that is ripe is ready to be harvested or picked. Sheaves are the bundles of grain that are gathered. This is a common way scriptures describe people who are ready to accept the gospel or join the Church.

26:6 ***harrowed up***—troubled or disturbed
***penetrate to***—reach
***listeth***—desires

26:7 President Ezra Taft Benson defines the harvest as the "harvest of souls" (see *The Teachings of Ezra Taft Benson,* 79). Ammon is teaching us that the Lord is in charge; all souls belong to Him.

26:8 ***doth***—does

26:9 ***racked***—tortured

Strangers to God are people who don't know God or His plan of happiness. Missionaries help teach these people the truth. Would you enjoy being a missionary and helping people in this way? Why?

26:10 ***rebuked***—scolded
***boasting***—bragging

26:11 ***brim***—full

26:12 ***wrought***—worked

26:13 Receiving Jesus Christ's Atonement in our life makes us feel happy and filled with love. In Alma 5:26, Alma asks us to consider if we can feel that love right now in our lives. Can you?

To "sing redeeming love" is to give praise and thanksgiving for the Atonement of Jesus Christ. One way to praise God is through song. D&C 25:12 teaches that the song of the righteous is a prayer unto the Lord.

## Ammon Praises God Because He Was Delivered by God from Sin

14 Yea, we have reason to praise him forever, for he is the Most High God, and has loosed our brethren from the chains of hell.

15 Yea, they were encircled about with everlasting darkness and destruction; but behold, he has brought them into his everlasting light, yea, into everlasting salvation; and they are encircled about with the matchless bounty of his love; yea, and we have been instruments in his hands of doing this great and marvelous work.

16 Therefore, let us glory, yea, we will glory in the Lord; yea, we will rejoice, for our joy is full; yea, we will praise our God forever. Behold, who can glory too much in the Lord? Yea, who can say too much of his great power, and of his mercy, and of his long-suffering towards the children of men? Behold, I say unto you, I cannot say the smallest part which I feel.

17 Who could have supposed that our God would have been so merciful as to have snatched us from our awful, sinful, and polluted state?

18 Behold, we went forth even in wrath, with mighty threatenings to destroy his church.

19 Oh then, why did he not consign us to an awful destruction, yea, why did he not let the sword of his justice fall upon us, and doom us to eternal despair?

20 Oh, my soul, almost as it were, fleeth at the thought. Behold, he did not exercise his justice upon us, but in his great mercy hath brought us over that everlasting gulf of death and misery, even to the salvation of our souls.

21 And now behold, my brethren, what natural man is there that knoweth these things? I say unto you, there is none that knoweth these things, save it be the penitent.

22 Yea, he that repenteth and exerciseth faith, and bringeth forth good works, and prayeth continually without ceasing—unto such it is given to know the mysteries of God; yea, unto such it shall be given to reveal things which never have been revealed; yea, and it shall be given unto such to bring thousands of souls to repentance, even as it has been given unto us to bring these our brethren to repentance.

## Ammon Reminds His Brothers About Some of Their Missionary Experiences

23 Now do ye remember, my brethren, that we said unto our brethren in the land of Zarahemla, we go up to the land of Nephi, to preach unto our brethren, the Lamanites, and they laughed us to scorn?

24 For they said unto us: Do ye suppose that ye can bring the Lamanites to the knowledge of the truth? Do ye suppose that ye can convince the Lamanites of the incorrectness of the traditions of their fathers, as stiffnecked a people as they are; whose hearts delight in the shedding of blood; whose days have been spent in the grossest iniquity; whose ways have been the ways of a transgressor from the beginning? Now my brethren, ye remember that this was their language.

---

26:15 Many times the Book of Mormon prophets teach by contrast. Notice in this verse how the darkness and destruction is contrasted with light and love.

26:16 Ammon is using the word *glory* to give praise. The word *glory* in Hebrew is *halal,* from which we get the word *hallelujah.* It means to praise or give thanks (see LDS Bible Dictionary, s.v. "Hallelujah," 698).

***long-suffering***—patience

26:17 ***snatched***—taken

26:18 ***wrath***—anger

26:19 ***consign***—agree to deliver
***doom***—penalize
***despair***—pain or misery

26:20 ***fleeth at***—avoids or runs from

26:21 ***penitent***—repentant

Elder Rulon S. Wells asks: "How can the garden grow in darkness? How can the trees blossom and produce their luscious fruit? Or how can the fields grow and ripen into golden harvests, unless the *sun* shall shine upon them? How can we know or understand the things of God without the light of his Holy Spirit? . . . Hence, there is need to obtain the gift of the Holy Ghost which in the gospel of our Lord is bestowed upon repentant and baptized believers by the laying on of hands" (in Conference Report, October 1927, 57).

26:23 ***laughed us to scorn***—rejected us and made fun of us

26:24 ***stiffnecked***—stubborn or rebellious
***grossest iniquity***—most evil of sins
***transgressor***—sinner

25 And moreover they did say: Let us take up arms against them, that we destroy them and their iniquity out of the land, lest they overrun us and destroy us.

26 But behold, my beloved brethren, we came into the wilderness not with the intent to destroy our brethren, but with the intent that perhaps we might save some few of their souls.

27 Now when our hearts were depressed, and we were about to turn back, behold, the Lord comforted us, and said: Go amongst thy brethren, the Lamanites, and bear with patience thine afflictions, and I will give unto you success.

28 And now behold, we have come, and been forth amongst them; and we have been patient in our sufferings, and we have suffered every privation; yea, we have traveled from house to house, relying upon the mercies of the world—not upon the mercies of the world alone but upon the mercies of God.

29 And we have entered into their houses and taught them, and we have taught them in their streets; yea, and we have taught them upon their hills; and we have also entered into their temples and their synagogues and taught them; and we have been cast out, and mocked, and spit upon, and smote upon our cheeks; and we have been stoned, and taken and bound with strong cords, and cast into prison; and through the power and wisdom of God we have been delivered again.

30 And we have suffered all manner of afflictions, and all this, that perhaps we might be the means of saving some soul; and we supposed that our joy would be full if perhaps we could be the means of saving some.

31 Now behold, we can look forth and see the fruits of our labors; and are they few? I say unto you, Nay, they are many; yea, and we can witness of their sincerity, because of their love towards their brethren and also towards us.

32 For behold, they had rather sacrifice their lives than even to take the life of their enemy; and they have buried their weapons of war deep in the earth, because of their love towards their brethren.

33 And now behold I say unto you, has there been so great love in all the land? Behold, I say unto you, Nay, there has not, even among the Nephites.

34 For behold, they would take up arms against their brethren; they would not suffer themselves to be slain. But behold how many of these have laid down their lives; and we know that they have gone to their God, because of their love and of their hatred to sin.

## *We Can Rejoice Because of the Goodness of God*

35 Now have we not reason to rejoice? Yea, I say unto you, there never were men that had so great reason to rejoice as we, since the world began; yea, and my joy is carried away, even unto boasting in my God; for he has all power, all wisdom, and all understanding; he comprehendeth all things, and he is a merciful Being, even unto salvation, to those who will repent and believe on his name.

36 Now if this is boasting, even so will I boast; for this is my life and my light, my joy and my salvation, and my redemption from everlasting wo. Yea, blessed is the name of my God, who has been mindful of this people, who are a branch of the tree of Israel, and has been lost from its body in a strange land; yea, I say, blessed be the name of my God, who has been mindful of us, wanderers in a strange land.

37 Now my brethren, we see that God is mindful of every people, whatsoever land they may be in; yea, he numbereth his people, and his bowels of mercy are over all the earth. Now this is my joy, and my great thanksgiving; yea, and I will give thanks unto my God forever. Amen.

---

26:27 Sometimes preaching the gospel can be difficult. Ammon and his brethren were about to quit, but the Lord blessed and strengthened them. When has it been difficult for you to follow the gospel? What helps you to remain faithful?

26:28 ***privation***—loss of our comforts or belongings

26:29 ***smote***—struck or hit

26:30 Ammon wanted to help bring people to the gospel. He knew that "the worth of souls is great in the sight of God" (D&C 18:10).

26:31 ***fruits of our labors***—people we have taught who were converted to the gospel

26:34 ***suffer***—allow

26:35 ***comprehendeth***—knows and understands

26:37 ***bowels of mercy***—feelings of love and kindness

## CHAPTER 27

*The people of Anti-Nephi-Lehi are attacked and again refuse to use any weapons, even in their own defense. Many are easily killed by the wicked Lamanites. The Lord commands Ammon to lead them to safety among the Nephites. Notice how the Nephites receive them.*

### *Ammon Asks the Lord How to Save the Anti-Nephi-Lehies*

1 NOW it came to pass that when those Lamanites who had gone to war against the Nephites had found, after their many struggles to destroy them, that it was in vain to seek their destruction, they returned again to the land of Nephi.

2 And it came to pass that the Amalekites, because of their loss, were exceedingly angry. And when they saw that they could not seek revenge from the Nephites, they began to stir up the people in anger against their brethren, the people of Anti-Nephi-Lehi; therefore they began again to destroy them.

3 Now this people again refused to take their arms, and they suffered themselves to be slain according to the desires of their enemies.

4 Now when Ammon and his brethren saw this work of destruction among those whom they so dearly beloved, and among those who had so dearly beloved them—for they were treated as though they were angels sent from God to save them from everlasting destruction—therefore, when Ammon and his brethren saw this great work of destruction, they were moved with compassion, and they said unto the king:

5 Let us gather together this people of the Lord, and let us go down to the land of Zarahemla to our brethren the Nephites, and flee out of the hands of our enemies, that we be not destroyed.

6 But the king said unto them: Behold, the Nephites will destroy us, because of the many murders and sins we have committed against them.

7 And Ammon said: I will go and inquire of the Lord, and if he say unto us, go down unto our brethren, will ye go?

8 And the king said unto him: Yea, if the Lord saith unto us go, we will go down unto our brethren, and we will be their slaves until we repair unto them the many murders and sins which we have committed against them.

9 But Ammon said unto him: It is against the law of our brethren, which was established by my father, that there should be any slaves among them; therefore let us go down and rely upon the mercies of our brethren.

10 But the king said unto him: Inquire of the Lord, and if he saith unto us go, we will go; otherwise we will perish in the land.

11 And it came to pass that Ammon went and inquired of the Lord, and the Lord said unto him:

12 Get this people out of this land, that they perish not; for Satan has great hold on the hearts of the Amalekites, who do stir up the Lamanites to anger against their brethren to slay them; therefore get thee out of this land; and blessed are this people in this generation, for I will preserve them.

### *Ammon and His Brothers Meet Alma on Their Way Home*

13 And now it came to pass that Ammon went and told the king all the words which the Lord had said unto him.

14 And they gathered together all their people, yea, all the people of the Lord, and did gather together all their flocks and herds, and departed out of the land, and came into the wilderness which divided the land of Nephi from the land of Zarahemla, and came over near the borders of the land.

---

27:1 ***in vain to seek their destruction***—useless to try to kill them

27:2 ***seek revenge from***—get even with

27:3 ***suffered***—allowed

27:4 Many times missionaries are loved by the people they teach. Why did the Lamanite converts treat Ammon and his brethren "as though they were angels"? Is there anyone in your life that is like an angel to you? Is there anyone you could help or for whom you could be an "angel"?

27:7 ***inquire of***—ask

27:8 ***repair unto them***—make up for the damage done to them by

27:9 ***established***—set up
***rely upon the mercies***—count on the kindness

27:12 ***in this generation***—at this time
***preserve***—protect or save

15 And it came to pass that Ammon said unto
them: Behold, I and my brethren will go forth into
the land of Zarahemla, and ye shall remain here
until we return; and we will try the hearts of our
brethren, whether they will that ye shall come into
their land.
16 And it came to pass that as Ammon was going
forth into the land, that he and his brethren met
Alma, over in the place of which has been spoken;
and behold, this was a joyful meeting.
17 Now the joy of Ammon was so great even that
he was full; yea, he was swallowed up in the joy of
his God, even to the exhausting of his strength; and
he fell again to the earth.
18 Now was not this exceeding joy? Behold, this
is joy which none receiveth save it be the truly penitent and humble seeker of happiness.
19 Now the joy of Alma in meeting his brethren
was truly great, and also the joy of Aaron, of
Omner, and Himni; but behold their joy was not
that to exceed their strength.

## The Nephites Provide a Safe Home for the Lamanite Converts

20 And now it came to pass that Alma conducted
his brethren back to the land of Zarahemla; even to
his own house. And they went and told the chief
judge all the things that had happened unto them
in the land of Nephi, among their brethren, the
Lamanites.
21 And it came to pass that the chief judge sent a
proclamation throughout all the land, desiring the
voice of the people concerning the admitting their
brethren, who were the people of Anti-Nephi-Lehi.
22 And it came to pass that the voice of the
people came, saying: Behold, we will give up the
land of Jershon, which is on the east by the sea,
which joins the land Bountiful, which is on the
south of the land Bountiful; and this land Jershon is
the land which we will give unto our brethren for
an inheritance.
23 And behold, we will set our armies between
the land Jershon and the land Nephi, that we may
protect our brethren in the land Jershon; and this
we do for our brethren, on account of their fear to
take up arms against their brethren lest they should
commit sin; and this their great fear came because
of their sore repentance which they had, on
account of their many murders and their awful
wickedness.
24 And now behold, this will we do unto our
brethren, that they may inherit the land Jershon;
and we will guard them from their enemies with
our armies, on condition that they will give us a
portion of their substance to assist us that we may
maintain our armies.

## The Anti-Nephi-Lehies Become Known as the People of Ammon

25 Now, it came to pass that when Ammon had
heard this, he returned to the people of Anti-Nephi-
Lehi, and also Alma with him, into the wilderness,
where they had pitched their tents, and made
known unto them all these things. And Alma also
related unto them his conversion, with Ammon and
Aaron, and his brethren.

---

27:15 ***try the hearts***—find out the feelings

Ammon's plan was to talk to the Nephites, tell them about the people of Anti-Nephi-Lehi, and find out if the Nephites would allow these converts to live in their land. Since the Lamanites were the sworn enemy of the Nephites, this decision might not have been so simple (see Enos 1:20).

27:17 ***swallowed up***—overcome
***exhausting***—draining

27:18 The *penitent* are those who repent of their sins and come unto the Lord (see Alma 29:10). Those who do receive great joy. Elder Bruce R. McConkie wrote: "Joy is a gift of the Spirit. It comes from the Holy Ghost, [and] is granted to those who gain a remission [forgiveness] of their sins" (*Mormon Doctrine,* 397).

27:20 ***conducted***—led

27:21 It was King Mosiah that set up the process whereby the people voted on important decisions that the government needed to make (see Mosiah 29:26). At this time the chief judge sent out a request to see if the Nephites would vote to allow the Lamanite converts to live with them.

27:22 ***an inheritance***—their own land

27:23 ***on account***—because

27:24 ***portion of their substance to assist***—little of their food and clothing to help

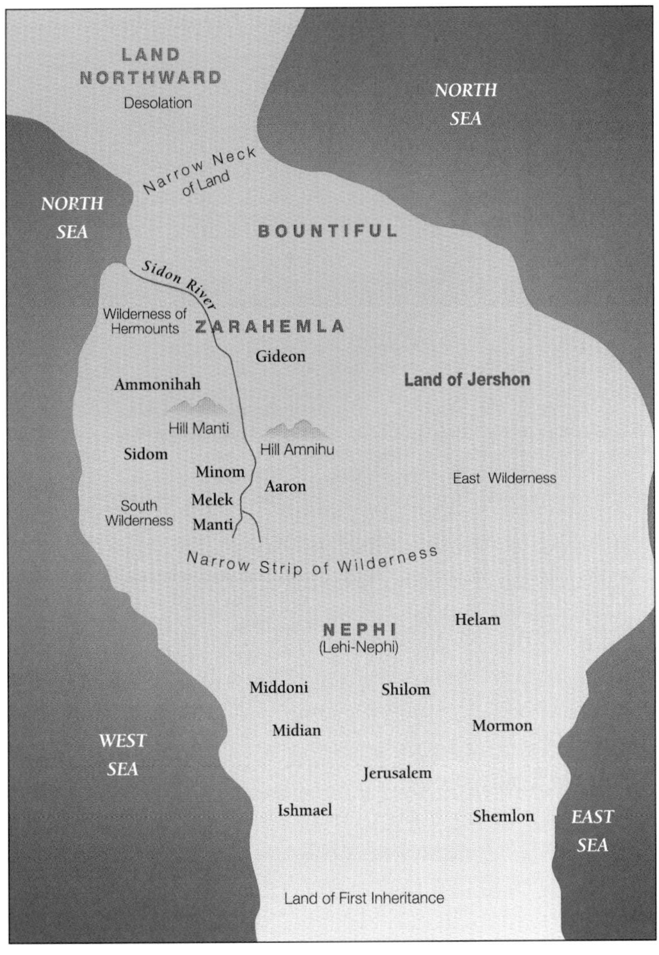


*The Nephites gave the Anti-Nephi-Lehies the land of Jershon.*

26 And it came to pass that it did cause great joy among them. And they went down into the land of Jershon, and took possession of the land of Jershon; and they were called by the Nephites the people of Ammon; therefore they were distinguished by that name ever after.

27 And they were among the people of Nephi, and also numbered among the people who were of the church of God. And they were also distinguished for their zeal towards God, and also towards men; for they were perfectly honest and upright in all things; and they were firm in the faith of Christ, even unto the end.

28 And they did look upon shedding the blood of their brethren with the greatest abhorrence; and they never could be prevailed upon to take up arms against their brethren; and they never did look upon death with any degree of terror, for their hope and views of Christ and the resurrection; therefore, death was swallowed up to them by the victory of Christ over it.

29 Therefore, they would suffer death in the most aggravating and distressing manner which could be inflicted by their brethren, before they would take the sword or cimeter to smite them.

30 And thus they were a zealous and beloved people, a highly favored people of the Lord.

## CHAPTER 28

*Shortly after their moving to the land of Jershon, the people of Ammon are attacked by the Lamanite armies and tens of thousands of Lamanites and Nephites die. Notice how the Nephites fear for their wicked family members who die, while the righteous die with a hope of never-ending happiness.*

### The Lamanites Are Defeated in a Great Battle in Jershon

1 AND now it came to pass that after the people of Ammon were established in the land of Jershon, and a church also established in the land of Jershon, and

---

27:26 ***possession***—control
***distinguished***—known

27:27 The people of Ammon were ideal converts, filled with zeal or enthusiasm for God and their fellowmen. President Hinckley has described true converts as those who "listen to the teachings and testimonies of missionaries and change their lives, leaving the past behind them, and moving forward into a new life" (*Teachings of Gordon B. Hinckley,* 144).

27:28 ***abhorrence***—disgust or hatred
***prevailed upon to take up arms***—talked into using weapons
***swallowed up***—overcome

Are you afraid to die? Why were the people of Ammon not afraid of death? What does this teach us about their faith in Christ?

27:29 ***aggravating and distressing***—painful and disturbing
***inflicted***—brought upon them
***smite***—strike or kill

A cimeter was a weapon used in hunting and in war (see Mosiah 9:16; Helaman 1:14). The Lamanites were particularly skilled in its use (see Enos 1:20).

27:30 ***zealous***—hard-working and enthusiastic

28:1 ***established***—settled

the armies of the Nephites were set round about the land of Jershon, yea, in all the borders round about the land of Zarahemla; behold the armies of the Lamanites had followed their brethren into the wilderness.

2 And thus there was a tremendous battle; yea, even such an one as never had been known among all the people in the land from the time Lehi left Jerusalem; yea, and tens of thousands of the Lamanites were slain and scattered abroad.

3 Yea, and also there was a tremendous slaughter among the people of Nephi; nevertheless, the Lamanites were driven and scattered, and the people of Nephi returned again to their land.

4 And now this was a time that there was a great mourning and lamentation heard throughout all the land, among all the people of Nephi—

5 Yea, the cry of widows mourning for their husbands, and also of fathers mourning for their sons, and the daughter for the brother, yea, the brother for the father; and thus the cry of mourning was heard among all of them, mourning for their kindred who had been slain.

6 And now surely this was a sorrowful day; yea, a time of solemnity, and a time of much fasting and prayer.

7 And thus endeth the fifteenth year of the reign of the judges over the people of Nephi;

## *The Wicked Who Die Are Miserable While the Righteous Receive Great Joy*

8 And this is the account of Ammon and his brethren, their journeyings in the land of Nephi, their sufferings in the land, their sorrows, and their afflictions, and their incomprehensible joy, and the reception and safety of the brethren in the land of Jershon. And now may the Lord, the Redeemer of all men, bless their souls forever.

9 And this is the account of the wars and contentions among the Nephites, and also the wars between the Nephites and the Lamanites; and the fifteenth year of the reign of the judges is ended.

10 And from the first year to the fifteenth has brought to pass the destruction of many thousand lives; yea, it has brought to pass an awful scene of bloodshed.

11 And the bodies of many thousands are laid low in the earth, while the bodies of many thousands are moldering in heaps upon the face of the earth; yea, and many thousands are mourning for the loss of their kindred, because they have reason to fear, according to the promises of the Lord, that they are consigned to a state of endless wo.

12 While many thousands of others truly mourn for the loss of their kindred, yet they rejoice and exult in the hope, and even know, according to the

---

28:2 ***tremendous***—huge

28:4 ***mourning and lamentation***—sadness and crying

28:6 ***solemnity***—seriousness

Anciently, people often fasted when someone died (see 2 Samuel 1:12; Alma 30:2). There are many other worthy purposes of fasting, such as healing the sick (see Matthew 17:18–21), overcoming sin (see Isaiah 58:6), gaining a testimony (see Alma 5:46), and sharing the gospel (see Alma 17:9).

28:7 Alma was the first chief judge. The Nephites began to measure time from the change in their government from kings to judges. For example, the third year of the "reign of the judges" is a phrase that means it has been three years since judges began to govern over the land (see Mosiah 29:44).

28:8 ***incomprehensible***—impossible to understand
***reception***—welcome with friendship

Ammon and his brethren suffered much while on their fourteen-year mission. However, like missionaries today, they rejoiced in seeing their brothers and sisters accept the gospel (see D&C 18:15–16; Alma 17:1–4).

28:9 ***reign***—rule

28:10 ***scene***—view

28:11 ***laid low***—buried
***moldering in heaps***—rotting in piles
***consigned***—sent

Those who have lived a wicked life and die are sent to a place of suffering where they stay until they are resurrected (see Alma 40:14; Moses 7:1).

28:12 ***kindred***—family members
***exult***—have joy

Though we feel sad when loved ones die, the Savior's Atonement gives us cause to rejoice knowing they will live again. The Prophet Joseph Smith said, "The expectation of seeing my friends in the morning of the resurrection cheers my soul. . . . It is like their taking a long journey, and on their return we meet them with increased joy" (*Teachings of the Prophet Joseph Smith,* 296).

promises of the Lord, that they are raised to dwell at the right hand of God, in a state of never-ending happiness.

13 And thus we see how great the inequality of man is because of sin and transgression, and the power of the devil, which comes by the cunning plans which he hath devised to ensnare the hearts of men.

14 And thus we see the great call of diligence of men to labor in the vineyards of the Lord; and thus we see the great reason of sorrow, and also of rejoicing—sorrow because of death and destruction among men, and joy because of the light of Christ unto life.

## CHAPTER 29

*Alma desires that all people repent so they can share in the joy of the gospel. Look for the blessings that come to those who share the gospel with others.*

### Alma Desires to Preach the Gospel

1 O that I were an angel, and could have the wish of mine heart, that I might go forth and speak with the trump of God, with a voice to shake the earth, and cry repentance unto every people!

2 Yea, I would declare unto every soul, as with the voice of thunder, repentance and the plan of redemption, that they should repent and come unto our God, that there might not be more sorrow upon all the face of the earth.

3 But behold, I am a man, and do sin in my wish; for I ought to be content with the things which the Lord hath allotted unto me.

### Men Receive Good or Evil According to Their Desires

4 I ought not to harrow up in my desires, the firm decree of a just God, for I know that he granteth unto men according to their desire, whether it be unto death or unto life; yea, I know that he allotteth unto men, yea, decreeth unto them decrees which are unalterable, according to their wills, whether they be unto salvation or unto destruction.

5 Yea, and I know that good and evil have come before all men; he that knoweth not good from evil is blameless; but he that knoweth good and evil, to him it is given according to his desires, whether he desireth good or evil, life or death, joy or remorse of conscience.

6 Now, seeing that I know these things, why should I desire more than to perform the work to which I have been called?

7 Why should I desire that I were an angel, that I could speak unto all the ends of the earth?

---

28:13 ***cunning***—tricky

Choices bring inequality, or a difference, between those who keep the Lord's commandments and receive His blessings and those who follow Satan and receive his wages (see Alma 5:41–42).

28:14 ***diligence***—effort

Mormon sees a great need for us to labor in the Lord's vineyard (this earth) by sharing the gospel with others. Why do you think it is so important for us to tell others about the Savior's Church?

29:1 Anciently, trumps or trumpets were used to signal special events (see Numbers 29:1), gather people together (see Judges 3:27), or warn of dangers like invading armies (see Jeremiah 4:19–21). Alma's desire to "speak with the trump of God" is symbolic of being able to gather many people at a time to signal the coming of Christ and to warn them of spiritual dangers.

29:3 ***content***—satisfied or happy

29:3 (2-3) Here Alma learns the lesson that "God does not send thunder if a still, small voice is enough, or a prophet if a priest can do the job" (Neal A. Maxwell, in Conference Report, October 1976, 15).

29:4 ***harrow up***—be disturbed
***allotteth***—gives
***decreeth unto them decrees which are unalterable***—gives them commands that cannot change

29:4 (3-4) Alma concluded that he should be happy with what the Lord had given him. Why should we be happy with the blessings God has given us, instead of unhappy over what we do not have?

29:5 ***remorse of conscience***—bitter sadness of mind

How do daily decisions to keep or break the Lord's commandments influence your happiness or sadness?

29:7 ***ends***—people

8 For behold, the Lord doth grant unto all nations, of their own nation and tongue, to teach his word, yea, in wisdom, all that he seeth fit that they should have; therefore we see that the Lord doth counsel in wisdom, according to that which is just and true.

## *Alma Rejoices in Missionary Work*

9 I know that which the Lord hath commanded me, and I glory in it. I do not glory of myself, but I glory in that which the Lord hath commanded me; yea, and this is my glory, that perhaps I may be an instrument in the hands of God to bring some soul to repentance; and this is my joy.

10 And behold, when I see many of my brethren truly penitent, and coming to the Lord their God, then is my soul filled with joy; then do I remember what the Lord has done for me, yea, even that he hath heard my prayer; yea, then do I remember his merciful arm which he extended towards me.

11 Yea, and I also remember the captivity of my fathers; for I surely do know that the Lord did deliver them out of bondage, and by this did establish his church; yea, the Lord God, the God of Abraham, the God of Isaac, and the God of Jacob, did deliver them out of bondage.

12 Yea, I have always remembered the captivity of my fathers; and that same God who delivered them out of the hands of the Egyptians did deliver them out of bondage.

13 Yea, and that same God did establish his church among them; yea, and that same God hath called me by a holy calling, to preach the word unto this people, and hath given me much success, in the which my joy is full.

14 But I do not joy in my own success alone, but my joy is more full because of the success of my brethren, who have been up to the land of Nephi.

15 Behold, they have labored exceedingly, and have brought forth much fruit; and how great shall be their reward!

16 Now, when I think of the success of these my brethren my soul is carried away, even to the separation of it from the body, as it were, so great is my joy.

17 And now may God grant unto these, my brethren, that they may sit down in the kingdom of God; yea, and also all those who are the fruit of their labors that they may go no more out, but that they may praise him forever. And may God grant that it may be done according to my words, even as I have spoken. Amen.

# CHAPTER 30

*Korihor, an anti-Christ, tries to destroy the faith of Church members and leaders. Look for the evidences Church leaders use to show that there really is a God.*

## *The Nephites Live Righteously After the War*

1 BEHOLD, now it came to pass that after the people of Ammon were established in the land of Jershon, yea, and also after the Lamanites were driven out of the land, and their dead were buried by the people of the land—

2 Now their dead were not numbered because of the greatness of their numbers; neither were the dead of the Nephites numbered—but it came to pass after they had buried their dead, and also after the days of fasting, and mourning, and prayer, (and it was in the sixteenth year of the reign of the judges over the people of Nephi) there began to be continual peace throughout all the land.

---

29:9 Elder Richard G. Scott teaches that we can become "an instrument through which the Lord can bless another" (in Conference Report, April 1994, 9). How can you help others feel the joy of repentance?

29:10 ***penitent***—feeling sorry for their sins

29:11 ***captivity***—bondage and slavery

29:15 ***labored exceedingly***—worked very hard

29:16 (15–16) One of the rewards the Lord has promised faithful missionaries is the great joy they will have in heaven with those they have helped to save (see D&C 18:13–16).

29:17 Elder Bruce R. McConkie remarked how "we long to return to [the Lord's] presence, and there, sitting down with Abraham, Isaac, and Jacob, and all the prophets and holy men of old, go no more out forever" (in Conference Report, April 1984, 47).

30:1 ***established***—settled and living safely

30:2 ***mourning***—feeling sad and crying

3 Yea, and the people did observe to keep the
commandments of the Lord; and they were strict in
observing the ordinances of God, according to the
law of Moses; for they were taught to keep the law
of Moses until it should be fulfilled.
4 And thus the people did have no disturbance in
all the sixteenth year of the reign of the judges over
the people of Nephi.
5 And it came to pass that in the commencement
of the seventeenth year of the reign of the judges,
there was continual peace.

## *The Law Allows Korihor to Speak Against the Church and Its Leaders*

6 But it came to pass in the latter end of the seventeenth year, there came a man into the land of
Zarahemla, and he was Anti-Christ, for he began to
preach unto the people against the prophecies
which had been spoken by the prophets, concerning the coming of Christ.
7 Now there was no law against a man's belief; for
it was strictly contrary to the commands of God that
there should be a law which should bring men on
to unequal grounds.
8 For thus saith the scripture: Choose ye this day,
whom ye will serve.
9 Now if a man desired to serve God, it was his
privilege; or rather, if he believed in God it was his
privilege to serve him; but if he did not believe in
him there was no law to punish him.
10 But if he murdered he was punished unto
death; and if he robbed he was also punished; and
if he stole he was also punished; and if he committed adultery he was also punished; yea, for all this
wickedness they were punished.
11 For there was a law that men should be judged
according to their crimes. Nevertheless, there was
no law against a man's belief; therefore, a man was
punished only for the crimes which he had done;
therefore all men were on equal grounds.

## *Korihor Tries to Convince the People Not to Believe in Christ or His Teachings*

12 And this Anti-Christ, whose name was Korihor,
(and the law could have no hold upon him) began
to preach unto the people that there should be no
Christ. And after this manner did he preach, saying:
13 O ye that are bound down under a foolish and
a vain hope, why do ye yoke yourselves with such
foolish things? Why do ye look for a Christ? For no
man can know of anything which is to come.
14 Behold, these things which ye call prophecies,
which ye say are handed down by holy prophets,
behold, they are foolish traditions of your fathers.
15 How do ye know of their surety? Behold, ye
cannot know of things which ye do not see; therefore ye cannot know that there shall be a Christ.
16 Ye look forward and say that ye see a remission of your sins. But behold, it is the effect of a
frenzied mind; and this derangement of your minds
comes because of the traditions of your fathers,
which lead you away into a belief of things which
are not so.

---

30:3 ***observing***—keeping

The law of Moses was fulfilled when the Savior came to earth, suffered for our sins, died, and was resurrected (see Matthew 5:17).

30:4 ***disturbance***—trouble

30:5 ***commencement***—beginning

30:6 An *anti-Christ* is someone who is against Christ, or teaches that there will be no Christ. Other examples of anti-Christs in the Book of Mormon are Sherem and Nehor (see Jacob 7; Alma 1).

30:7 ***strictly contrary to***—entirely against

30:8 It was the prophet Joshua who told the children of Israel that God had blessed them in many ways but that it was up to them to decide whether or not they would serve Him (see Joshua 24:15).

30:9 ***privilege***—right or opportunity

30:13 ***bound***—tied
***vain***—useless and empty
***yoke yourselves with***—believe and follow

30:14 ***traditions***—long-held beliefs and teachings

30:15 ***surety***—truth

30:16 ***remission***—forgiveness
***frenzied***—crazy
***derangement***—confusion or craziness

KORIHOR, BY SCOTT SNOW

*Korihor tried to lead people not to believe in Christ.*

17 And many more such things did he say unto them, telling them that there could be no atonement made for the sins of men, but every man fared in this life according to the management of the creature; therefore every man prospered according to his genius, and that every man conquered according to his strength; and whatsoever a man did was no crime.

18 And thus he did preach unto them, leading away the hearts of many, causing them to lift up their heads in their wickedness, yea, leading away many women, and also men, to commit whoredoms—telling them that when a man was dead, that was the end thereof.

## The People of Jershon Do Not Believe Korihor's Lies

19 Now this man went over to the land of Jershon also, to preach these things among the people of Ammon, who were once the people of the Lamanites.

20 But behold they were more wise than many of the Nephites; for they took him, and bound him, and carried him before Ammon, who was a high priest over that people.

21 And it came to pass that he caused that he should be carried out of the land. And he came over into the land of Gideon, and began to preach unto them also; and here he did not have much success, for he was taken and bound and carried before the high priest, and also the chief judge over the land.

22 And it came to pass that the high priest said unto him: Why do ye go about perverting the ways of the Lord? Why do ye teach this people that there shall be no Christ, to interrupt their rejoicings? Why do ye speak against all the prophecies of the holy prophets?

23 Now the high priest's name was Giddonah. And Korihor said unto him: Because I do not teach the foolish traditions of your fathers, and because I do not teach this people to bind themselves down under the foolish ordinances and performances which are laid down by ancient priests, to usurp power and authority over them, to keep them in ignorance, that they may not lift up their heads, but be brought down according to thy words.

24 Ye say that this people is a free people. Behold, I say they are in bondage. Ye say that those ancient prophecies are true. Behold, I say that ye do not know that they are true.

25 Ye say that this people is a guilty and a fallen people, because of the transgression of a parent. Behold, I say that a child is not guilty because of its parents.

26 And ye also say that Christ shall come. But behold, I say that ye do not know that there shall be a Christ. And ye say also that he shall be slain for the sins of the world—

27 And thus ye lead away this people after the foolish traditions of your fathers, and according to your own desires; and ye keep them down, even as it were in bondage, that ye may glut yourselves with the labors of their hands, that they durst not look up with boldness, and that they durst not enjoy their rights and privileges.

---

30:17 ***fared***—got by
***management of the creature***—control of his own life
***genius***—skill and intelligence

Korihor said that there was no sin, and every person should use his or her intelligence and strength to get ahead of other people. What would the world be like if everybody did what Korihor said? What do Church leaders say we should do for other people with our talents?

30:18 ***commit whoredoms***—be immoral

30:22 ***perverting***—changing or corrupting
***interrupt their rejoicings***—make them sad

30:23 The "ordinances and performances" which Korihor is criticizing here are the commandments and sacrifices of the law of Moses (see Bruce R. McConkie, *The Promised Messiah,* 376).

***usurp***—take
***in ignorance***—without understanding

30:24 ***bondage***—slavery

30:27 ***glut***—feast or get more than you need
***durst***—dare

Elder Henry B. Eyring said, "Korihor was arguing, as men and women have falsely argued from the beginning of time, that to take counsel from the servants of God is to surrender God-given rights of independence. But the argument is false because it misrepresents reality. When we reject the counsel which comes from God, we do not choose to be independent of outside influence. We choose another influence. We reject the protection of a perfectly loving, all-powerful, all-knowing Father in Heaven, whose whole purpose, as that of His Beloved Son, is to give us eternal life, to give us all that He has, and to bring us home again in families to the arms of His love" (in Conference Report, April 1997, 33).

*CONFRONTATION BETWEEN ALMA AND KORIHOR*, BY ROBERT T. BARRETT

*Alma defended the Church and its leaders.*

28 Yea, they durst not make use of that which is their own lest they should offend their priests, who do yoke them according to their desires, and have brought them to believe, by their traditions and their dreams and their whims and their visions and their pretended mysteries, that they should, if they did not do according to their words, offend some unknown being, who they say is God—a being who never has been seen or known, who never was nor ever will be.

29 Now when the high priest and the chief judge saw the hardness of his heart, yea, when they saw that he would revile even against God, they would not make any reply to his words; but they caused that he should be bound; and they delivered him up into the hands of the officers, and sent him to the land of Zarahemla, that he might be brought before Alma, and the chief judge who was governor over all the land.

## Alma Testifies to Korihor of the Truth

30 And it came to pass that when he was brought before Alma and the chief judge, he did go on in the same manner as he did in the land of Gideon; yea, he went on to blaspheme.

---

30:28 **W** ***whims***—foolish wishes

30:29 **W** ***the hardness of his heart***—his stubbornness or unwillingness

***revile***—speak evil

30:30 **W** ***blaspheme***—speak evil of God or falsely claim to be like God

31 And he did rise up in great swelling words
before Alma, and did revile against the priests and
teachers, accusing them of leading away the people
after the silly traditions of their fathers, for the sake
of glutting on the labors of the people.
32 Now Alma said unto him: Thou knowest that
we do not glut ourselves upon the labors of this
people; for behold I have labored even from the
commencement of the reign of the judges until
now, with mine own hands for my support,
notwithstanding my many travels round about the
land to declare the word of God unto my people.
33 And notwithstanding the many labors which I
have performed in the church, I have never
received so much as even one senine for my labor;
neither has any of my brethren, save it were in the
judgment-seat; and then we have received only
according to law for our time.
34 And now, if we do not receive anything for our
labors in the church, what doth it profit us to labor
in the church save it were to declare the truth, that
we may have rejoicings in the joy of our brethren?
35 Then why sayest thou that we preach unto this
people to get gain, when thou, of thyself, knowest
that we receive no gain? And now, believest thou
that we deceive this people, that causes such joy in
their hearts?
36 And Korihor answered him, Yea.
37 And then Alma said unto him: Believest thou
that there is a God?
38 And he answered, Nay.
39 Now Alma said unto him: Will ye deny again
that there is a God, and also deny the Christ? For
behold, I say unto you, I know there is a God, and
also that Christ shall come.
40 And now what evidence have ye that there is
no God, or that Christ cometh not? I say unto you
that ye have none, save it be your word only.
41 But, behold, I have all things as a testimony
that these things are true; and ye also have all
things as a testimony unto you that they are true;
and will ye deny them? Believest thou that these
things are true?
42 Behold, I know that thou believest, but thou art
possessed with a lying spirit, and ye have put off
the Spirit of God that it may have no place in you;
but the devil has power over you, and he doth carry
you about, working devices that he may destroy the
children of God.

### *Korihor Asks for a Sign and Is Cursed*

43 And now Korihor said unto Alma: If thou wilt
show me a sign, that I may be convinced that there
is a God, yea, show unto me that he hath power, and
then will I be convinced of the truth of thy words.
44 But Alma said unto him: Thou hast had signs
enough; will ye tempt your God? Will ye say, Show
unto me a sign, when ye have the testimony of all
these thy brethren, and also all the holy prophets? The
scriptures are laid before thee, yea, and all things

---

30:33 ***performed***—done

A senine was a small piece of Nephite money (see Alma 11:4–19).

30:35 ***gain***—wealth
***deceive***—trick, fool, or lie to

30:40 ***evidence***—proof

30:42 ***possessed with***—controlled by
***devices***—evil plans

Alma explains that Korihor had "put off the Spirit of God." The scriptures teach us that if people continually refuse to listen to the promptings of the Spirit of the Lord, the day will come when they cannot feel them anymore (see 1 Nephi 17:45).

30:43 A *sign* is a physical proof that something is true. Jesus said that wicked people ask to see signs before they will believe (see Matthew 16:4).

30:44 Following his circling the earth as an astronaut, Senator Jake Garn wrote, "It is impossible for me to describe the beauty of the earth. It is a breathtaking, awe-inspiring, spiritual experience to view the earth from space while traveling at twenty-five times the speed of sound. I could also look into the blackness of the vacuum of space and see billions of stars and galaxies millions of light-years away. The universe is so vast as to be impossible to comprehend. But I did comprehend the hand of God in all things. I felt his presence throughout my seven days in space. I know that God created this earth and the universe. . . . I know that God lives and is the Creator of us all" (Jake Garn, as quoted by M. Russell Ballard, in Conference Report, April 1988, 66).

Alma says that all things prove that God lives. What are some things you have seen or heard that help you know that God lives and that Jesus is our Savior?

denote there is a God; yea, even the earth, and all things that are upon the face of it, yea, and its motion, yea, and also all the planets which move in their regular form do witness that there is a Supreme Creator.

45 And yet do ye go about, leading away the hearts of this people, testifying unto them there is no God? And yet will ye deny against all these witnesses? And he said: Yea, I will deny, except ye shall show me a sign.

46 And now it came to pass that Alma said unto him: Behold, I am grieved because of the hardness of your heart, yea, that ye will still resist the spirit of the truth, that thy soul may be destroyed.

47 But behold, it is better that thy soul should be lost than that thou shouldst be the means of bringing many souls down to destruction, by thy lying and by thy flattering words; therefore if thou shalt deny again, behold God shall smite thee, that thou shalt become dumb, that thou shalt never open thy mouth any more, that thou shalt not deceive this people any more.

48 Now Korihor said unto him: I do not deny the existence of a God, but I do not believe that there is a God; and I say also, that ye do not know that there is a God; and except ye show me a sign, I will not believe.

49 Now Alma said unto him: This will I give unto thee for a sign, that thou shalt be struck dumb, according to my words; and I say, that in the name of God, ye shall be struck dumb, that ye shall no more have utterance.

50 Now when Alma had said these words, Korihor was struck dumb, that he could not have utterance, according to the words of Alma.

## The Devil Told Korihor What to Teach

51 And now when the chief judge saw this, he put forth his hand and wrote unto Korihor, saying: Art thou convinced of the power of God? In whom did ye desire that Alma should show forth his sign? Would ye that he should afflict others, to show unto thee a sign? Behold, he has showed unto you a sign; and now will ye dispute more?

52 And Korihor put forth his hand and wrote, saying: I know that I am dumb, for I cannot speak; and I know that nothing save it were the power of God could bring this upon me; yea, and I always knew that there was a God.

53 But behold, the devil hath deceived me; for he appeared unto me in the form of an angel, and said unto me: Go and reclaim this people, for they have all gone astray after an unknown God. And he said unto me: There is no God; yea, and he taught me that which I should say. And I have taught his words; and I taught them because they were pleasing unto the carnal mind; and I taught them, even until I had much success, insomuch that I verily believed that they were true; and for this cause I withstood the truth, even until I have brought this great curse upon me.

54 Now when he had said this, he besought that Alma should pray unto God, that the curse might be taken from him.

55 But Alma said unto him: If this curse should be taken from thee thou wouldst again lead away the hearts of this people; therefore, it shall be unto thee even as the Lord will.

---

30:44 ***denote***—show
***Supreme***—All-powerful

30:45 ***witnesses***—proofs or evidences

30:46 ***grieved***—very sad
***resist***—not listen to

30:47 ***flattering***—good-sounding
***dumb***—unable to speak

30:48 ***the existence of a God***—that there is a God

30:49 ***have utterance***—be able to speak

30:51 ***afflict***—cause something bad to happen to
***dispute***—argue

30:53 ***reclaim***—get back
***have all gone astray after***—are all lost to
***carnal***—worldly
***withstood***—spoke against

The Apostle Paul explained that the devil can even appear as "an angel of light" to deceive or trick people (2 Corinthians 11:14). An angel from God will never ask us to do anything that is wrong or believe anything that is not true.

"That man who rises up to condemn others, finding fault with the Church, saying that they are out of the way, while he himself is righteous, then know assuredly, that that man is on the high road to apostasy; and if he does not repent, will apostatize, as God lives" (*Teachings of the Prophet Joseph Smith,* 156–57).

30:54 ***besought***—begged

### KORIHOR DIES IN AN ACCIDENT

56 And it came to pass that the curse was not taken off of Korihor; but he was cast out, and went about from house to house begging for his food.

57 Now the knowledge of what had happened unto Korihor was immediately published throughout all the land; yea, the proclamation was sent forth by the chief judge to all the people in the land, declaring unto those who had believed in the words of Korihor that they must speedily repent, lest the same judgments would come unto them.

58 And it came to pass that they were all convinced of the wickedness of Korihor; therefore they were all converted again unto the Lord; and this put an end to the iniquity after the manner of Korihor. And Korihor did go about from house to house, begging food for his support.

59 And it came to pass that as he went forth among the people, yea, among a people who had separated themselves from the Nephites and called themselves Zoramites, being led by a man whose name was Zoram—and as he went forth amongst them, behold, he was run upon and trodden down, even until he was dead.

60 And thus we see the end of him who perverteth the ways of the Lord; and thus we see that the devil will not support his children at the last day, but doth speedily drag them down to hell.

## CHAPTER 31

*Alma and his missionary companions find strange teachings and practices among the Zoramite people. Look for how the Zoramites worship and how Alma feels about them.*

### ALMA DECIDES TO PREACH THE GOSPEL TO THE ZORAMITES

1 NOW it came to pass that after the end of Korihor, Alma having received tidings that the Zoramites were perverting the ways of the Lord, and that Zoram, who was their leader, was leading the hearts of the people to bow down to dumb idols, his heart again began to sicken because of the iniquity of the people.

2 For it was the cause of great sorrow to Alma to know of iniquity among his people; therefore his heart was exceedingly sorrowful because of the separation of the Zoramites from the Nephites.

3 Now the Zoramites had gathered themselves together in a land which they called Antionum, which was east of the land of Zarahemla, which lay nearly bordering upon the seashore, which was south of the land of Jershon, which also bordered upon the wilderness south, which wilderness was full of the Lamanites.

4 Now the Nephites greatly feared that the Zoramites would enter into a correspondence with the Lamanites, and that it would be the means of great loss on the part of the Nephites.

5 And now, as the preaching of the word had a great tendency to lead the people to do that which was just—yea, it had had more powerful effect upon the minds of the people than the sword, or anything else, which had happened unto them—therefore Alma thought it was expedient that they should try the virtue of the word of God.

---

30:57 ***published***—spread
***proclamation***—official announcement

30:58 ***converted***—turned

30:59 ***trodden***—stepped on, stomped, or trampled

30:60 ***perverteth***—twists or changes
***support***—care for

The devil will not support those who follow him. Satan has no eternal blessings to offer his followers. What did you learn from this chapter that will help you follow the Lord and avoid deception?

31:1 ***tidings***—news
***perverting***—changing or corrupting
***dumb***—speechless

Alma was very concerned for the Zoramites because they were worshiping idols. One of the Ten Commandments that Moses received on Mount Sinai says that we should not make or worship idols (see Exodus 20:4–5).

31:4 ***correspondence***—discussion and friendship
***means***—cause

31:5 ***just***—fair or right
***expedient***—necessary
***virtue***—purity or power

President Ezra Taft Benson spoke of this verse, saying, "When . . . Alma . . . wrote those words [the Zoramites] were . . . troubled, but his preaching brought about a great reformation which restored peace and happiness. It is so today. This is why we emphasize missionary work as we do. It is the real answer to the world's problems" (*The Teachings of Ezra Taft Benson,* 185).

6 Therefore he took Ammon, and Aaron, and
Omner; and Himni he did leave in the church in
Zarahemla; but the former three he took with him,
and also Amulek and Zeezrom, who were at Melek;
and he also took two of his sons.
7 Now the eldest of his sons he took not with him,
and his name was Helaman; but the names of those
whom he took with him were Shiblon and
Corianton; and these are the names of those who
went with him among the Zoramites, to preach
unto them the word.

## The Zoramites Had Fallen Away from the True Beliefs and Practices of the Church

8 Now the Zoramites were dissenters from the
Nephites; therefore they had had the word of God
preached unto them.
9 But they had fallen into great errors, for they
would not observe to keep the commandments of
God, and his statutes, according to the law of
Moses.
10 Neither would they observe the performances
of the church, to continue in prayer and supplication to God daily, that they might not enter into
temptation.
11 Yea, in fine, they did pervert the ways of the
Lord in very many instances; therefore, for this
cause, Alma and his brethren went into the land to
preach the word unto them.
12 Now, when they had come into the land,
behold, to their astonishment they found that the
Zoramites had built synagogues, and that they did
gather themselves together on one day of the week,
which day they did call the day of the Lord; and
they did worship after a manner which Alma and
his brethren had never beheld;
13 For they had a place built up in the center of
their synagogue, a place for standing, which was
high above the head; and the top thereof would
only admit one person.
14 Therefore, whosoever desired to worship must
go forth and stand upon the top thereof, and stretch
forth his hands towards heaven, and cry with a loud
voice, saying:
15 Holy, holy God; we believe that thou art God,
and we believe that thou art holy, and that thou
wast a spirit, and that thou art a spirit, and that thou
wilt be a spirit forever.
16 Holy God, we believe that thou hast separated
us from our brethren; and we do not believe in the
tradition of our brethren, which was handed down
to them by the childishness of their fathers; but we
believe that thou hast elected us to be thy holy children; and also thou hast made it known unto us
that there shall be no Christ.
17 But thou art the same yesterday, today, and forever; and thou hast elected us that we shall be
saved, whilst all around us are elected to be cast by
thy wrath down to hell; for the which holiness, O
God, we thank thee; and we also thank thee that
thou hast elected us, that we may not be led away
after the foolish traditions of our brethren, which
doth bind them down to a belief of Christ, which
doth lead their hearts to wander far from thee, our
God.
18 And again we thank thee, O God, that we are
a chosen and a holy people. Amen.
19 Now it came to pass that after Alma and his
brethren and his sons had heard these prayers, they
were astonished beyond all measure.
20 For behold, every man did go forth and offer
up these same prayers.
21 Now the place was called by them Rameumptom, which, being interpreted, is the holy stand.
22 Now, from this stand they did offer up, every

---

31:6 Ammon, Aaron, Omner, and Himni were the sons of Mosiah (see Mosiah 27:34). Amulek had been Alma's companion when he taught the people of Ammonihah (see Alma 8:18–32). Zeezrom was the wicked lawyer who believed their words and changed his ways (see Alma 8:18–31; 14:6–7; 15:3–12).

31:9 ***statutes***—laws

31:9 (8–9) Dissenters are people who believed the truth at one time but become wicked and fight against the Church. Why do you think people fall away from the Church? What could they do that would keep their faith strong?

31:10 ***performances***—ordinances and practices
***supplication***—worship

31:11 ***in fine***—finally

31:12 ***astonishment***—surprise
***synagogues***—buildings for worship

31:13 ***admit***—hold

31:16 ***elected***—chosen

31:17 ***whilst***—while
***wrath***—anger

THE RAMEUMPTOM, BY DEL PARSON

*The Zoramites prayed one at a time on a high stand that they called a Rameumptom.*

man, the selfsame prayer unto God, thanking their God that they were chosen of him, and that he did not lead them away after the tradition of their brethren, and that their hearts were not stolen away to believe in things to come, which they knew nothing about.
23 Now, after the people had all offered up thanks after this manner, they returned to their homes, never speaking of their God again until they had assembled themselves together again to the holy stand, to offer up thanks after their manner.

## Alma Prays for Help in Teaching the Zoramites

24 Now when Alma saw this his heart was grieved; for he saw that they were a wicked and a perverse people; yea, he saw that their hearts were set upon gold, and upon silver, and upon all manner of fine goods.
25 Yea, and he also saw that their hearts were lifted up unto great boasting, in their pride.
26 And he lifted up his voice to heaven, and cried, saying: O, how long, O Lord, wilt thou suffer that thy servants shall dwell here below in the flesh, to behold such gross wickedness among the children of men?
27 Behold, O God, they cry unto thee, and yet their hearts are swallowed up in their pride. Behold, O God, they cry unto thee with their mouths, while they are puffed up, even to greatness, with the vain things of the world.
28 Behold, O my God, their costly apparel, and their ringlets, and their bracelets, and their ornaments of gold, and all their precious things which they are ornamented with; and behold, their hearts are set upon them, and yet they cry unto thee and say—We thank thee, O God, for we are a chosen people unto thee, while others shall perish.
29 Yea, and they say that thou hast made it known unto them that there shall be no Christ.
30 O Lord God, how long wilt thou suffer that such wickedness and infidelity shall be among this people? O Lord, wilt thou give me strength, that I may bear with mine infirmities. For I am infirm, and such wickedness among this people doth pain my soul.
31 O Lord, my heart is exceedingly sorrowful; wilt thou comfort my soul in Christ. O Lord, wilt thou grant unto me that I may have strength, that I may suffer with patience these afflictions which shall come upon me, because of the iniquity of this people.
32 O Lord, wilt thou comfort my soul, and give unto me success, and also my fellow laborers who are with me—yea, Ammon, and Aaron, and Omner, and also Amulek and Zeezrom, and also my two sons—yea, even all these wilt thou comfort, O Lord. Yea, wilt thou comfort their souls in Christ.
33 Wilt thou grant unto them that they may have strength, that they may bear their afflictions which

---

31:23 The practice the Zoramites followed of worshiping the Lord only one day a week is, in the words of Elder Neal A. Maxwell, a "fatal flaw" (see *That My Family Should Partake,* 29). The Lord taught that we must not only worship in church each Sabbath day, but "on all days and at all times" (D&C 59:9–11).

31:24 ***grieved***—very sad
***a perverse***—an evil

31:25 ***boasting***—bragging

31:26 ***suffer***—allow
***the flesh***—physical bodies
***gross***—great

31:27 A people whose "hearts are swallowed up in their pride" are people who love the things of the world and not the things of God. Jesus said that we cannot love the things of God and the things of the world at the same time (see Matthew 6:24). What are some things of God that you love? How can you keep from loving the things of the world more than you love the things of God?

***puffed up***—proud
***vain***—useless

31:28 ***apparel***—clothing

31:28 (25–28) President Gordon B. Hinckley cautioned us against pride: "We must be humble before the Lord. He has so declared, and if we will do it, He will hear our prayers and answer them with a blessing upon our heads" ("Messages of Inspiration from President Gordon B. Hinckley," 2).

31:30 ***infidelity***—faithlessness
***infirmities***—weaknesses

31:31 Like Alma, we will find comfort in and through Jesus Christ. He has given us the Holy Ghost, which comforts us and brings us peace (see John 14:16, 26–27; 16:33).

31:33 ***afflictions***—trials and suffering

shall come upon them because of the iniquities of this people.

34 O Lord, wilt thou grant unto us that we may have success in bringing them again unto thee in Christ.

35 Behold, O Lord, their souls are precious, and many of them are our brethren; therefore, give unto us, O Lord, power and wisdom that we may bring these, our brethren, again unto thee.

### *Alma Blesses His Missionary Companions*

36 Now it came to pass that when Alma had said these words, that he clapped his hands upon all them who were with him. And behold, as he clapped his hands upon them, they were filled with the Holy Spirit.

37 And after that they did separate themselves one from another, taking no thought for themselves what they should eat, or what they should drink, or what they should put on.

38 And the Lord provided for them that they should hunger not, neither should they thirst; yea, and he also gave them strength, that they should suffer no manner of afflictions, save it were swallowed up in the joy of Christ. Now this was according to the prayer of Alma; and this because he prayed in faith.

## CHAPTER 32

*Alma teaches the poor the principle of faith. He compares the word of God to a seed that must be planted and nourished through the exercise of faith. See how this process leads to the growth of faith and testimony.*

### *Alma Preaches the Gospel Among the Poor*

1 AND it came to pass that they did go forth, and began to preach the word of God unto the people, entering into their synagogues, and into their houses; yea, and even they did preach the word in their streets.

2 And it came to pass that after much labor among them, they began to have success among the poor class of people; for behold, they were cast out of the synagogues because of the coarseness of their apparel—

3 Therefore they were not permitted to enter into their synagogues to worship God, being esteemed as filthiness; therefore they were poor; yea, they were esteemed by their brethren as dross; therefore they were poor as to things of the world; and also they were poor in heart.

4 Now, as Alma was teaching and speaking unto the people upon the hill Onidah, there came a great multitude unto him, who were those of whom we have been speaking, of whom were poor in heart, because of their poverty as to the things of the world.

5 And they came unto Alma; and the one who was the foremost among them said unto him: Behold, what shall these my brethren do, for they are despised of all men because of their poverty, yea, and more especially by our priests; for they have cast us out of our synagogues which we have labored abundantly to build with our own hands; and they have cast us out because of our exceeding poverty; and we have no place to worship our God; and behold, what shall we do?

---

31:36 ***clapped***—placed

Alma gave his fellow missionaries a priesthood blessing by placing his hands upon them. Ammon did the same thing to his missionary companions in Alma 17:17–18. Today, all missionaries receive a blessing from their priesthood leaders before they go out into the mission field.

31:38 These missionaries felt strong in their work because any trials they had did not compare to the wonderful joy they felt in serving the Savior. When have you felt this kind of joy?

32:2 ***the coarseness of their apparel***—the roughness of their clothing

32:3 ***esteemed***—valued
***dross***—worthless

32:4 (3–4) The rich Zoramites hated the poor people because they were poor in money and poor in heart (meaning humble). The Savior called such humble people "poor in spirit" and said, "Blessed are the poor in spirit who come unto me, for theirs is the kingdom of heaven" (3 Nephi 12:3).

32:5 ***the foremost among***—in front of
***despised***—hated
***abundantly***—very much

6 And now when Alma heard this, he turned him about, his face immediately towards him, and he beheld with great joy; for he beheld that their afflictions had truly humbled them, and that they were in a preparation to hear the word.

## Alma Teaches About Humility

7 Therefore he did say no more to the other multitude; but he stretched forth his hand, and cried unto those whom he beheld, who were truly penitent, and said unto them:

8 I behold that ye are lowly in heart; and if so, blessed are ye.

9 Behold thy brother hath said, What shall we do?—for we are cast out of our synagogues, that we cannot worship our God.

10 Behold I say unto you, do ye suppose that ye cannot worship God save it be in your synagogues only?

11 And moreover, I would ask, do ye suppose that ye must not worship God only once in a week?

12 I say unto you, it is well that ye are cast out of your synagogues, that ye may be humble, and that ye may learn wisdom; for it is necessary that ye should learn wisdom; for it is because that ye are cast out, that ye are despised of your brethren because of your exceeding poverty, that ye are brought to a lowliness of heart; for ye are necessarily brought to be humble.

13 And now, because ye are compelled to be humble blessed are ye; for a man sometimes, if he is compelled to be humble, seeketh repentance; and now surely, whosoever repenteth shall find mercy; and he that findeth mercy and endureth to the end the same shall be saved.

14 And now, as I said unto you, that because ye were compelled to be humble ye were blessed, do ye not suppose that they are more blessed who truly humble themselves because of the word?

15 Yea, he that truly humbleth himself, and repenteth of his sins, and endureth to the end, the same shall be blessed—yea, much more blessed than they who are compelled to be humble because of their exceeding poverty.

16 Therefore, blessed are they who humble themselves without being compelled to be humble; or rather, in other words, blessed is he that believeth in the word of God, and is baptized without stubbornness of heart, yea, without being brought to know the word, or even compelled to know, before they will believe.

## Alma Compares the Word of God to a Seed

17 Yea, there are many who do say: If thou wilt show unto us a sign from heaven, then we shall know of a surety; then we shall believe.

18 Now I ask, is this faith? Behold, I say unto you, Nay; for if a man knoweth a thing he hath no cause to believe, for he knoweth it.

19 And now, how much more cursed is he that knoweth the will of God and doeth it not, than he that only believeth, or only hath cause to believe, and falleth into transgression?

20 Now of this thing ye must judge. Behold, I say unto you, that it is on the one hand even as it is on the other; and it shall be unto every man according to his work.

21 And now as I said concerning faith—faith is not to have a perfect knowledge of things; therefore if ye have faith ye hope for things which are not seen, which are true.

---

32:6 ***afflictions***—trials and sufferings

"Just as soil needs preparation for a seed, so does a human heart for the word of God to take root. Before he told the people to plant the seed, Alma told them that their hearts were prepared. They had been persecuted and cast out of their churches" (Henry B. Eyring, in Conference Report, October 1995, 51).

32:7 ***penitent***—repentant

32:11 (10–11) The scriptures teach that we should worship the Lord "on all days and at all times" (D&C 59:11).

32:13 ***compelled***—forced

32:16 "God will have a humble people. Either we can choose to be humble or we can be compelled to be humble" (Ezra Taft Benson, in Conference Report, April 1989, 6).

32:17 The Book of Mormon tells the stories of two men who asked for a sign. Sherem and Korihor both eventually lost their lives as a result (see Jacob 7:13–20; Alma 30:43–60).

32:21 Alma teaches that when you have faith you hope for things you cannot see which are true. What are some things that you know to be true, even though you have never seen them?

22 And now, behold, I say unto you, and I would
that ye should remember, that God is merciful unto
all who believe on his name; therefore he desireth,
in the first place, that ye should believe, yea, even
on his word.
23 And now, he imparteth his word by angels
unto men, yea, not only men but women also. Now
this is not all; little children do have words given
unto them many times, which confound the wise
and the learned.
24 And now, my beloved brethren, as ye have
desired to know of me what ye shall do because ye
are afflicted and cast out—now I do not desire that
ye should suppose that I mean to judge you only
according to that which is true—
25 For I do not mean that ye all of you have been
compelled to humble yourselves; for I verily believe
that there are some among you who would humble
themselves, let them be in whatsoever circumstances they might.
26 Now, as I said concerning faith—that it was not
a perfect knowledge—even so it is with my words.
Ye cannot know of their surety at first, unto perfection, any more than faith is a perfect knowledge.
27 But behold, if ye will awake and arouse your
faculties, even to an experiment upon my words,
and exercise a particle of faith, yea, even if ye can
no more than desire to believe, let this desire work
in you, even until ye believe in a manner that ye
can give place for a portion of my words.
28 Now, we will compare the word unto a seed.
Now, if ye give place, that a seed may be planted
in your heart, behold, if it be a true seed, or a good
seed, if ye do not cast it out by your unbelief, that
ye will resist the Spirit of the Lord, behold, it will
begin to swell within your breasts; and when you
feel these swelling motions, ye will begin to say
within yourselves—It must needs be that this is a
good seed, or that the word is good, for it beginneth to enlarge my soul; yea, it beginneth to
enlighten my understanding, yea, it beginneth to be
delicious to me.
29 Now behold, would not this increase your
faith? I say unto you, Yea; nevertheless it hath not
grown up to a perfect knowledge.
30 But behold, as the seed swelleth, and
sprouteth, and beginneth to grow, then you must
needs say that the seed is good; for behold it
swelleth, and sprouteth, and beginneth to grow.
And now, behold, will not this strengthen your
faith? Yea, it will strengthen your faith: for ye will
say I know that this is a good seed; for behold it
sprouteth and beginneth to grow.
31 And now, behold, are ye sure that this is a
good seed? I say unto you, Yea; for every seed
bringeth forth unto its own likeness.
32 Therefore, if a seed groweth it is good, but if it
groweth not, behold it is not good, therefore it is
cast away.
33 And now, behold, because ye have tried the
experiment, and planted the seed, and it swelleth
and sprouteth, and beginneth to grow, ye must
needs know that the seed is good.
34 And now, behold, is your knowledge perfect?
Yea, your knowledge is perfect in that thing, and
your faith is dormant; and this because you know,

32:23 ***imparteth***—gives
***confound***—confuse

32:27 ***faculties***—abilities

32:28 (27–28) Elder Robert D. Hales taught, "The first seeds of conversion begin with an awareness of the gospel of Jesus Christ and a desire to know the truth" (in Conference Report, April 1997, 111).

32:34 ***dormant***—inactive or sleeping

*Alma compared the word of God to a seed. If we exercise our faith and plant the seed in our hearts, the seed will sprout and begin to grow.*

PHOTOGRAPH BY EDWIN M. WOOLLEY

for ye know that the word hath swelled your souls, and ye also know that it hath sprouted up, that your understanding doth begin to be enlightened, and your mind doth begin to expand.

35 O then, is not this real? I say unto you, Yea, because it is light; and whatsoever is light, is good, because it is discernible, therefore ye must know that it is good; and now behold, after ye have tasted this light is your knowledge perfect?

36 Behold I say unto you, Nay; neither must ye lay aside your faith, for ye have only exercised your faith to plant the seed that ye might try the experiment to know if the seed was good.

37 And behold, as the tree beginneth to grow, ye will say: Let us nourish it with great care, that it may get root, that it may grow up, and bring forth fruit unto us. And now behold, if ye nourish it with much care it will get root, and grow up, and bring forth fruit.

38 But if ye neglect the tree, and take no thought for its nourishment, behold it will not get any root; and when the heat of the sun cometh and scorcheth it, because it hath no root it withers away, and ye pluck it up and cast it out.

39 Now, this is not because the seed was not good, neither is it because the fruit thereof would not be desirable; but it is because your ground is barren, and ye will not nourish the tree, therefore ye cannot have the fruit thereof.

40 And thus, if ye will not nourish the word, looking forward with an eye of faith to the fruit thereof, ye can never pluck of the fruit of the tree of life.

41 But if ye will nourish the word, yea, nourish the tree as it beginneth to grow, by your faith with great diligence, and with patience, looking forward to the fruit thereof, it shall take root; and behold it shall be a tree springing up unto everlasting life.

42 And because of your diligence and your faith and your patience with the word in nourishing it, that it may take root in you, behold, by and by ye shall pluck the fruit thereof, which is most precious, which is sweet above all that is sweet, and which is white above all that is white, yea, and pure above all that is pure; and ye shall feast upon this fruit even until ye are filled, that ye hunger not, neither shall ye thirst.

43 Then, my brethren, ye shall reap the rewards of your faith, and your diligence, and patience, and long-suffering, waiting for the tree to bring forth fruit unto you.

## CHAPTER 33

*Alma teaches the Zoramites about worshiping God. Look for the principles of prayer, scripture study, and looking to the Savior that are spoken of in this chapter.*

### *ALMA QUOTES THE PROPHET ZENOS ON HOW TO WORSHIP*

1 NOW after Alma had spoken these words, they sent forth unto him desiring to know whether they should believe in one God, that they might obtain this fruit of which he had spoken, or how they should plant the seed, or the word of which he had spoken, which he said must be planted in their hearts; or in what manner they should begin to exercise their faith.

32:35 ***it is discernible***—you notice or sense it

Light is the power and influence that comes from the Lord through the Holy Ghost (see D&C 84:46). To "taste" this light is to feel its influence (see Alma 32:28). We can choose to receive more of this light "until the perfect day" (D&C 50:24).

32:38 ***neglect***—do not take care of

President Benson warned that converts will only survive "under the heat of the day" if their "taproots go down to the fulness of the gospel which the Book of Mormon contains" (Ezra Taft Benson, in Conference Report, April 1975, 96).

32:39 ***is barren***—lacks the necessary foods

32:42 Lehi also ate the fruit of a tree. He said that "it was most sweet," and that it was white "to exceed all the whiteness that I had ever seen," and that "it filled my soul with exceeding great joy" (1 Nephi 8:11–12). When Nephi desired to know what the tree represented, he was shown that it was "the love of God" (1 Nephi 11:22).

Alma teaches that you must feed the truth you receive. What can you do to feed your testimony?

32:43 (28–43) Alma compares the word of God to a seed. Who causes the seed to grow? How can you help a seed grow? Why do you think Alma makes this comparison? What are some of the many different ways comparing the word of God to a seed can help you understand how to gain a testimony?

33:1 ***exercise***—apply

2 And Alma said unto them: Behold, ye have said that ye could not worship your God because ye are cast out of your synagogues. But behold, I say unto you, if ye suppose that ye cannot worship God, ye do greatly err, and ye ought to search the scriptures; if ye suppose that they have taught you this, ye do not understand them.

3 Do ye remember to have read what Zenos, the prophet of old, has said concerning prayer or worship?

4 For he said: Thou art merciful, O God, for thou hast heard my prayer, even when I was in the wilderness; yea, thou wast merciful when I prayed concerning those who were mine enemies, and thou didst turn them to me.

5 Yea, O God, and thou wast merciful unto me when I did cry unto thee in my field; when I did cry unto thee in my prayer, and thou didst hear me.

6 And again, O God, when I did turn to my house thou didst hear me in my prayer.

7 And when I did turn unto my closet, O Lord, and prayed unto thee, thou didst hear me.

8 Yea, thou art merciful unto thy children when they cry unto thee, to be heard of thee and not of men, and thou wilt hear them.

9 Yea, O God, thou hast been merciful unto me, and heard my cries in the midst of thy congregations.

10 Yea, and thou hast also heard me when I have been cast out and have been despised by mine enemies; yea, thou didst hear my cries, and wast angry with mine enemies, and thou didst visit them in thine anger with speedy destruction.

11 And thou didst hear me because of mine afflictions and my sincerity; and it is because of thy Son that thou hast been thus merciful unto me, therefore I will cry unto thee in all mine afflictions, for in thee is my joy; for thou hast turned thy judgments away from me, because of thy Son.

## *Alma Quotes the Words of the Prophets That Testify of Jesus Christ*

12 And now Alma said unto them: Do ye believe those scriptures which have been written by them of old?

13 Behold, if ye do, ye must believe what Zenos said; for, behold he said: Thou hast turned away thy judgments because of thy Son.

14 Now behold, my brethren, I would ask if ye have read the scriptures? If ye have, how can ye disbelieve on the Son of God?

15 For it is not written that Zenos alone spake of these things, but Zenock also spake of these things—

16 For behold, he said: Thou art angry, O Lord, with this people, because they will not understand thy mercies which thou hast bestowed upon them because of thy Son.

17 And now, my brethren, ye see that a second prophet of old has testified of the Son of God, and because the people would not understand his words they stoned him to death.

18 But behold, this is not all; these are not the only ones who have spoken concerning the Son of God.

19 Behold, he was spoken of by Moses; yea, and behold a type was raised up in the wilderness, that whosoever would look upon it might live. And many did look and live.

---

33:2 ***err***—make a mistake

33:3 Zenos was a prophet who lived in Old Testament times before Jeremiah. He was quoted by several Book of Mormon prophets (see 1 Nephi 19:10–17; Jacob 5:1; 3 Nephi 10:16).

33:4 ***merciful***—kind, loving, and forgiving

33:4 (4–11) When and where can we pray to the Lord? When has prayer made a difference in your life?

33:9 ***in the midst of thy congregations***—among all thine other children

33:10 ***despised***—hated

33:11 ***mine afflictions***—my sufferings
***sincerity***—honesty

33:13 ***judgments***—punishments

33:14 In what ways does reading the scriptures help you to believe in Jesus Christ?

33:15 Zenock was also a prophet who lived in Old Testament times before the prophet Jeremiah. He was quoted by other Book of Mormon prophets (see 1 Nephi 19:10; 3 Nephi 10:16).

33:16 ***bestowed upon***—given to

33:19 ***type***—symbol of the Savior

PROPHETS OF ANCIENT ISRAEL, BY SCOTT SNOW

*Prophets of ancient Israel*

20 But few understood the meaning of those
things, and this because of the hardness of their
hearts. But there were many who were so hardened
that they would not look, therefore they perished.
Now the reason they would not look is because
they did not believe that it would heal them.
21 O my brethren, if ye could be healed by
merely casting about your eyes that ye might be
healed, would ye not behold quickly, or would ye
rather harden your hearts in unbelief, and be slothful, that ye would not cast about your eyes, that ye
might perish?
22 If so, wo shall come upon you; but if not so,
then cast about your eyes and begin to believe in
the Son of God, that he will come to redeem his
people, and that he shall suffer and die to atone for

33:21 ***merely casting about your eyes***—only looking
***slothful***—irresponsible or lazy

33:21 (19–21) When the children of Israel were in the wilderness with Moses, the Lord sent poisonous serpents among them to kill the wicked. The *type* that was raised up in the wilderness by Moses was a brass serpent that the Lord told Moses to make so that the people who were bitten could look at it and be healed (see Numbers 21:8). The serpent was a type of Christ—just as the sick people could look at the serpent Moses raised up and live, those who are spiritually sick can look to Christ for eternal life.

33:22 ***wo***—grief, sorrow, and misery

their sins; and that he shall rise again from the
dead, which shall bring to pass the resurrection,
that all men shall stand before him, to be judged at
the last and judgment day, according to their works.
23 And now, my brethren, I desire that ye shall
plant this word in your hearts, and as it beginneth
to swell even so nourish it by your faith. And
behold, it will become a tree, springing up in you
unto everlasting life. And then may God grant unto
you that your burdens may be light, through the joy
of his Son. And even all this can ye do if ye will.
Amen.

## CHAPTER 34

*Amulek teaches the Zoramites the basic principles of the gospel. His teachings include faith in Jesus Christ, repentance, prayer, and the importance of doing good works. As you read this chapter look for those teachings which will help you come unto Christ.*

### Amulek Approves of Alma's Earlier Teaching

1 AND now it came to pass that after Alma had
spoken these words unto them he sat down upon
the ground, and Amulek arose and began to teach
them, saying:
2 My brethren, I think that it is impossible that ye
should be ignorant of the things which have been
spoken concerning the coming of Christ, who is
taught by us to be the Son of God; yea, I know that
these things were taught unto you bountifully
before your dissension from among us.
3 And as ye have desired of my beloved brother
that he should make known unto you what ye
should do, because of your afflictions; and he hath
spoken somewhat unto you to prepare your minds;
yea, and he hath exhorted you unto faith and to
patience—
4 Yea, even that ye would have so much faith as
even to plant the word in your hearts, that ye may
try the experiment of its goodness.
5 And we have beheld that the great question
which is in your minds is whether the word be in
the Son of God, or whether there shall be no Christ.
6 And ye also beheld that my brother has proved
unto you, in many instances, that the word is in
Christ unto salvation.
7 My brother has called upon the words of Zenos,
that redemption cometh through the Son of God,
and also upon the words of Zenock; and also he
has appealed unto Moses, to prove that these things
are true.

### Amulek Testifies of the Atonement of Jesus Christ

8 And now, behold, I will testify unto you of
myself that these things are true. Behold, I say
unto you, that I do know that Christ shall come
among the children of men, to take upon him the
transgressions of his people, and that he shall
atone for the sins of the world; for the Lord God
hath spoken it.
9 For it is expedient that an atonement should be
made; for according to the great plan of the Eternal
God there must be an atonement made, or else all
mankind must unavoidably perish; yea, all are hardened;
yea, all are fallen and are lost, and must perish
except it be through the atonement which it is
expedient should be made.

---

33:23 ***swell***—grow larger
***nourish***—feed and take care of
***burdens***—trials and challenges

33:23 (22–23) What experiences have you had that help you to know that Jesus Christ lives? What can you do to show Heavenly Father that you are thankful for the sacrifice His Son made for you?

34:2 ***be ignorant of***—not know or understand
***bountifully***—in great detail
***dissension***—separating yourselves

34:3 ***afflictions***—suffering and trials
***exhorted***—encouraged or challenged

34:4 Amulek encourages the people to try the same experiment Alma spoke of in Alma 32:27–43.

34:6 ***instances***—times

34:8 ***atone***—willingly suffer the penalty

34:9 ***expedient***—necessary
***unavoidably perish***—surely die

Every person makes mistakes and sins (see Romans 3:23). If Jesus Christ did not pay the penalty for each of our sins, we could never return to live with Heavenly Father (see D&C 1:31–32). Why do you think the Savior did this for everyone? How does knowing this make you feel about Jesus?

10 For it is expedient that there should be a great and last sacrifice; yea, not a sacrifice of man, neither of beast, neither of any manner of fowl; for it shall not be a human sacrifice; but it must be an infinite and eternal sacrifice.

11 Now there is not any man that can sacrifice his own blood which will atone for the sins of another. Now, if a man murdereth, behold will our law, which is just, take the life of his brother? I say unto you, Nay.

12 But the law requireth the life of him who hath murdered; therefore there can be nothing which is short of an infinite atonement which will suffice for the sins of the world.

## The Atonement of Jesus Christ Shall Fulfull the Law of Moses

13 Therefore, it is expedient that there should be a great and last sacrifice, and then shall there be, or it is expedient there should be, a stop to the shedding of blood; then shall the law of Moses be fulfilled; yea, it shall be all fulfilled, every jot and tittle, and none shall have passed away.

14 And behold, this is the whole meaning of the law, every whit pointing to that great and last sacrifice; and that great and last sacrifice will be the Son of God, yea, infinite and eternal.

15 And thus he shall bring salvation to all those who shall believe on his name; this being the intent of this last sacrifice, to bring about the bowels of mercy, which overpowereth justice, and bringeth about means unto men that they may have faith unto repentance.

16 And thus mercy can satisfy the demands of justice, and encircles them in the arms of safety, while he that exercises no faith unto repentance is exposed to the whole law of the demands of justice; therefore only unto him that has faith unto repentance is brought about the great and eternal plan of redemption.

## Amulek Teaches the People to Pray for Mercy and Serve Others

17 Therefore may God grant unto you, my brethren, that ye may begin to exercise your faith unto repentance, that ye begin to call upon his holy name, that he would have mercy upon you;

18 Yea, cry unto him for mercy; for he is mighty to save.

19 Yea, humble yourselves, and continue in prayer unto him.

20 Cry unto him when ye are in your fields, yea, over all your flocks.

21 Cry unto him in your houses, yea, over all your household, both morning, mid-day, and evening.

22 Yea, cry unto him against the power of your enemies.

23 Yea, cry unto him against the devil, who is an enemy to all righteousness.

24 Cry unto him over the crops of your fields, that ye may prosper in them.

25 Cry over the flocks of your fields, that they may increase.

26 But this is not all; ye must pour out your souls in your closets, and your secret places, and in your wilderness.

---

34:10 ***an infinite and eternal sacrifice***—a sacrifice which would pay for all sin for all time

Under the law of Moses animals were sacrificed as a symbol or reminder that Jesus Christ would come into the world, suffer, and die for the sins of all mankind. After the death of Jesus Christ, the law requiring animal sacrifice ended (see LDS Bible Dictionary, s.v. "Sacrifices," 765–67).

34:12 ***suffice***—be enough to pay the price

34:13 Jots and tittles were very small marks used when writing words in Hebrew, similar to periods and commas in English. They are mentioned to show that even the very smallest parts of the law of Moses would be fulfilled by the Atonement of Jesus Christ.

34:14 ***whit***—little bit

34:15 ***intent***—purpose
***the bowels of mercy***—inner feelings of love

34:16 ***exposed***—open

34:16 (15–16) Justice is the law that requires a fair payment every time a law is broken. Mercy is a willingness to make the payment in behalf of another person. Those who do not have faith in Christ must pay for their own sins. But those who have faith can call upon the Lord's mercy to overcome the penalties of sin (see D&C 19:16–18).

34:18 ***cry***—pray

34:26 ***pour out your souls***—pray with all your energy

*CHRIST IN THE GARDEN OF GETHSEMANE, BY ROBERT T. BARRETT*

*Jesus Christ suffered and died to atone for the sins of the world.*

27 Yea, and when you do not cry unto the Lord, let your hearts be full, drawn out in prayer unto him continually for your welfare, and also for the welfare of those who are around you.

28 And now behold, my beloved brethren, I say unto you, do not suppose that this is all; for after ye have done all these things, if ye turn away the needy, and the naked, and visit not the sick and afflicted, and impart of your substance, if ye have, to those who stand in need—I say unto you, if ye do not any of these things, behold, your prayer is vain, and availeth you nothing, and ye are as hypocrites who do deny the faith.

29 Therefore, if ye do not remember to be charitable, ye are as dross, which the refiners do cast out, (it being of no worth) and is trodden under foot of men.

## *We Must Spend Our Lives Preparing to Meet the Lord*

30 And now, my brethren, I would that, after ye have received so many witnesses, seeing that the holy scriptures testify of these things, ye come forth and bring fruit unto repentance.

31 Yea, I would that ye would come forth and harden not your hearts any longer; for behold, now is the time and the day of your salvation; and therefore, if ye will repent and harden not your hearts, immediately shall the great plan of redemption be brought about unto you.

32 For behold, this life is the time for men to prepare to meet God; yea, behold the day of this life is the day for men to perform their labors.

33 And now, as I said unto you before, as ye have had so many witnesses, therefore, I beseech of you that ye do not procrastinate the day of your repentance until the end; for after this day of life, which is given us to prepare for eternity, behold, if we do not improve our time while in this life, then cometh the night of darkness wherein there can be no labor performed.

34 Ye cannot say, when ye are brought to that awful crisis, that I will repent, that I will return to my God. Nay, ye cannot say this; for that same spirit which doth possess your bodies at the time that ye go out of this life, that same spirit will have power to possess your body in that eternal world.

35 For behold, if ye have procrastinated the day of your repentance even until death, behold, ye have become subjected to the spirit of the devil, and he doth seal you his; therefore, the Spirit of the Lord hath withdrawn from you, and hath no place in you, and the devil hath all power over you; and this is the final state of the wicked.

---

34:27 ***welfare***—well-being

Amulek taught the people where to pray, when to pray, and what to pray for. Do you have a special place to pray? How often do you pray and what do you pray for? How has the Lord answered your prayers?

34:28 ***afflicted***—those who are suffering
***impart of your substance***—give or share what you have
***vain***—of no value
***availeth you nothing***—does not help or benefit you
***hypocrites***—those who pretend to be good but are not

34:29 ***charitable***—generous in giving to others what you have
***trodden***—stepped on

"Dross" is the impurities separated out from silver or other metals when they are melted. The "refiners" are the men who work with the metals. Dross is symbolically used to represent the wicked. Like dross, the wicked are separated from the righteous because they are impure or unclean (see LDS Bible Dictionary, s.v. "Refiner," 760).

34:33 ***beseech***—ask
***procrastinate***—put off until later

34:35 ***subjected***—captive
***seal***—make

34:35 (33–35) When we die, our spirits continue to live in the spirit world while we await the resurrection. It will not be easier to repent there because we will have the same desires we do now. "We know not fully on what terms repentance will be obtainable in the hereafter; but to suppose that the soul who has wilfully rejected the opportunity of repentance in this life will find it easy to repent there is contrary to reason. To procrastinate the day of repentance is to deliberately place ourselves in the power of the adversary" (James E. Talmage, *The Articles of Faith,* 115).

36 And this I know, because the Lord hath said he dwelleth not in unholy temples, but in the hearts of the righteous doth he dwell; yea, and he has also said that the righteous shall sit down in his kingdom, to go no more out; but their garments should be made white through the blood of the Lamb.

### Amulek Encourages the People to Obey and Follow the Lord

37 And now, my beloved brethren, I desire that ye should remember these things, and that ye should work out your salvation with fear before God, and that ye should no more deny the coming of Christ;

38 That ye contend no more against the Holy Ghost, but that ye receive it, and take upon you the name of Christ; that ye humble yourselves even to the dust, and worship God, in whatsoever place ye may be in, in spirit and in truth; and that ye live in thanksgiving daily, for the many mercies and blessings which he doth bestow upon you.

39 Yea, and I also exhort you, my brethren, that ye be watchful unto prayer continually, that ye may not be led away by the temptations of the devil, that he may not overpower you, that ye may not become his subjects at the last day; for behold, he rewardeth you no good thing.

40 And now my beloved brethren, I would exhort you to have patience, and that ye bear with all manner of afflictions; that ye do not revile against those who do cast you out because of your exceeding poverty, lest ye become sinners like unto them;

41 But that ye have patience, and bear with those afflictions, with a firm hope that ye shall one day rest from all your afflictions.

## CHAPTER 35

*The teachings of Alma and Amulek make the wicked Zoramites angry. They force all those who believe the gospel to leave. The Zoramites stir up war between the Lamanites and the Nephites. Notice the differences between the way the wicked Zoramites behave and the way the righteous people of Ammon behave.*

### The Converted Zoramites Are Cast Out

1 NOW it came to pass that after Amulek had made an end of these words, they withdrew themselves from the multitude and came over into the land of Jershon.

2 Yea, and the rest of the brethren, after they had preached the word unto the Zoramites, also came over into the land of Jershon.

3 And it came to pass that after the more popular part of the Zoramites had consulted together concerning the words which had been preached unto them, they were angry because of the word, for it did destroy their craft; therefore they would not hearken unto the words.

4 And they sent and gathered together throughout all the land all the people, and consulted with them concerning the words which had been spoken.

5 Now their rulers and their priests and their teachers did not let the people know concerning their desires; therefore they found out privily the minds of all the people.

6 And it came to pass that after they had found out the minds of all the people, those who were in favor of the words which had been spoken by Alma and his brethren were cast out of the land; and they were many; and they came over also into the land of Jershon.

---

34:36 ***dwelleth***—lives
***blood of the Lamb***—Atonement of Jesus Christ

34:38 ***contend***—fight
***bestow upon***—give

34:39 ***exhort***—strongly encourage

34:40 ***bear with***—endure
***revile***—speak evil
***exceeding poverty***—lack of money

35:1 ***withdrew themselves***—went away

35:3 ***consulted***—discussed or talked

The religion of the Zoramites taught that they were better than all other people (see Alma 31:12–18). This religion was very popular with the wealthy Zoramites. Teaching false ideas to be popular and to be paid is called "priestcraft" (see 2 Nephi 26:29).

35:5 ***privily***—secretly

35:6 ***cast out***—forced out

7 And it came to pass that Alma and his brethren
did minister unto them.

### The Zoramites and the Lamanites Begin a War Against the Nephites

8 Now the people of the Zoramites were angry
with the people of Ammon who were in Jershon,
and the chief ruler of the Zoramites, being a very
wicked man, sent over unto the people of Ammon
desiring them that they should cast out of their land
all those who came over from them into their land.
9 And he breathed out many threatenings against
them. And now the people of Ammon did not fear
their words; therefore they did not cast them out,
but they did receive all the poor of the Zoramites
that came over unto them; and they did nourish
them, and did clothe them, and did give unto them
lands for their inheritance; and they did administer
unto them according to their wants.
10 Now this did stir up the Zoramites to anger
against the people of Ammon, and they began to
mix with the Lamanites and to stir them up also to
anger against them.
11 And thus the Zoramites and the Lamanites
began to make preparations for war against the
people of Ammon, and also against the Nephites.
12 And thus ended the seventeenth year of the
reign of the judges over the people of Nephi.
13 And the people of Ammon departed out of the
land of Jershon, and came over into the land of
Melek, and gave place in the land of Jershon for the
armies of the Nephites, that they might contend
with the armies of the Lamanites and the armies of
the Zoramites; and thus commenced a war betwixt
the Lamanites and the Nephites, in the eighteenth
year of the reign of the judges; and an account shall
be given of their wars hereafter.

### Alma Prepares to Counsel His Three Sons

14 And Alma, and Ammon, and their brethren,
and also the two sons of Alma returned to the land
of Zarahemla, after having been instruments in the
hands of God of bringing many of the Zoramites
to repentance; and as many as were brought to
repentance were driven out of their land; but they
have lands for their inheritance in the land of
Jershon, and they have taken up arms to defend
themselves, and their wives, and children, and
their lands.
15 Now Alma, being grieved for the iniquity of his
people, yea for the wars, and the bloodsheds, and
the contentions which were among them; and having been to declare the word, or sent to declare the
word, among all the people in every city; and seeing that the hearts of the people began to wax hard,
and that they began to be offended because of the
strictness of the word, his heart was exceedingly
sorrowful.
16 Therefore, he caused that his sons should be
gathered together, that he might give unto them
every one his charge, separately, concerning the
things pertaining unto righteousness. And we have
an account of his commandments, which he gave
unto them according to his own record.

*The commandments of Alma to his son Helaman. Comprising chapters 36 and 37.**

## CHAPTER 36

*Alma counsels his oldest son, Helaman. As you ponder his words, watch for the promises Alma gives Helaman if he will simply keep the commandments of God.*

---

35:7 ***minister unto***—teach, bless, and comfort

35:9 ***breathed***—spoke
***their inheritance***—them to live on and keep
***administer unto***—care for

35:13 ***contend***—fight
***commenced***—began
***betwixt***—between

35:14 ***instruments***—tools
***arms***—weapons

35:15 ***grieved***—very sad
***contentions***—arguing and fighting
***wax***—grow

Nephi taught that "the guilty taketh the truth to be hard, for it cutteth them to the very center" (1 Nephi 16:2). Why are wicked people offended or made angry when they hear the truth?

35:16 When Alma saw the people getting more and more wicked, he called his family together and taught them to be righteous. What could you do to help protect your family against wickedness?

* The first sentence of this introduction to chapters 36–37 was translated from the Book of Mormon plates.

## Alma Bears Testimony to His Son

1 MY son, give ear to my words; for I swear unto
you, that inasmuch as ye shall keep the commandments of God ye shall prosper in the land.
2 I would that ye should do as I have done, in
remembering the captivity of our fathers; for they
were in bondage, and none could deliver them
except it was the God of Abraham, and the God of
Isaac, and the God of Jacob; and he surely did
deliver them in their afflictions.
3 And now, O my son Helaman, behold, thou art
in thy youth, and therefore, I beseech of thee that
thou wilt hear my words and learn of me; for I do
know that whosoever shall put their trust in God
shall be supported in their trials, and their troubles,
and their afflictions, and shall be lifted up at the last
day.
4 And I would not that ye think that I know of
myself—not of the temporal but of the spiritual, not
of the carnal mind but of God.
5 Now, behold, I say unto you, if I had not been
born of God I should not have known these things;
but God has, by the mouth of his holy angel, made
these things known unto me, not of any worthiness
of myself;

## Alma Tells Helaman His Own Conversion Story

6 For I went about with the sons of Mosiah, seeking to destroy the church of God; but behold, God
sent his holy angel to stop us by the way.
7 And behold, he spake unto us, as it were the
voice of thunder, and the whole earth did tremble
beneath our feet; and we all fell to the earth, for the
fear of the Lord came upon us.
8 But behold, the voice said unto me: Arise. And
I arose and stood up, and beheld the angel.
9 And he said unto me: If thou wilt of thyself be
destroyed, seek no more to destroy the church of
God.
10 And it came to pass that I fell to the earth; and
it was for the space of three days and three nights
that I could not open my mouth, neither had I the
use of my limbs.
11 And the angel spake more things unto me,
which were heard by my brethren, but I did not
hear them; for when I heard the words—If thou
wilt be destroyed of thyself, seek no more to
destroy the church of God—I was struck with such
great fear and amazement lest perhaps I should be
destroyed, that I fell to the earth and I did hear no
more.
12 But I was racked with eternal torment, for my
soul was harrowed up to the greatest degree and
racked with all my sins.
13 Yea, I did remember all my sins and iniquities,
for which I was tormented with the pains of hell;
yea, I saw that I had rebelled against my God, and
that I had not kept his holy commandments.
14 Yea, and I had murdered many of his children,
or rather led them away unto destruction; yea, and
in fine so great had been my iniquities, that the very
thought of coming into the presence of my God did
rack my soul with inexpressible horror.

---

36:1 ***give ear***—listen
***swear***—promise
***prosper***—be blessed and do well

Alma begins and ends his testimony to his son Helaman by promising that the Lord will bless Helaman if he keeps the commandments (see Alma 36:1, 30). What scripture stories have you read which show this promise to be true?

36:2 ***bondage***—slavery

The story of the bondage of their fathers that Alma wanted his son to remember is found in Mosiah 23–24. Alma may have also been teaching his son about the bondage of the children of Israel in Egypt (see Exodus 3–4).

36:3 ***beseech***—ask or plead

Alma tells us to learn to trust God in our youth. Can you think of times when you have put your trust in Heavenly Father and been blessed?

36:4 ***temporal***—physical
***carnal***—worldly

36:5 In the book of Mosiah, King Benjamin teaches what it means to be "born of God" (see Mosiah 3:19; 5:7).

36:10 ***limbs***—arms and legs

36:12 ***racked with eternal torment***—feeling pain and suffering because of my many sins
***harrowed up***—feeling sorrow

36:13 ***tormented***—punished

36:14 ***rack***—fill
***inexpressible horror***—pain and fear so great that I am unable to describe it

ANGEL APPEARS TO ALMA AND THE SONS OF MOSIAH, BY CLARK KELLEY PRICE

*"God sent his holy angel to stop us by the way."*

15 Oh, thought I, that I could be banished and
become extinct both soul and body, that I might not
be brought to stand in the presence of my God, to
be judged of my deeds.
16 And now, for three days and for three nights
was I racked, even with the pains of a damned soul.
17 And it came to pass that as I was thus racked
with torment, while I was harrowed up by the
memory of my many sins, behold, I remembered
also to have heard my father prophesy unto the
people concerning the coming of one Jesus Christ,
a Son of God, to atone for the sins of the world.
18 Now, as my mind caught hold upon this
thought, I cried within my heart: O Jesus, thou Son
of God, have mercy on me, who am in the gall of
bitterness, and am encircled about by the everlasting chains of death.
19 And now, behold, when I thought this, I could
remember my pains no more; yea, I was harrowed
up by the memory of my sins no more.
20 And oh, what joy, and what marvelous light I
did behold; yea, my soul was filled with joy as
exceeding as was my pain!
21 Yea, I say unto you, my son, that there could
be nothing so exquisite and so bitter as were my
pains. Yea, and again I say unto you, my son, that
on the other hand, there can be nothing so exquisite and sweet as was my joy.
22 Yea, methought I saw, even as our father Lehi
saw, God sitting upon his throne, surrounded with
numberless concourses of angels, in the attitude of
singing and praising their God; yea, and my soul
did long to be there.
23 But behold, my limbs did receive their strength
again, and I stood upon my feet, and did manifest
unto the people that I had been born of God.
24 Yea, and from that time even until now, I have
labored without ceasing, that I might bring souls
unto repentance; that I might bring them to taste of
the exceeding joy of which I did taste; that they
might also be born of God, and be filled with the
Holy Ghost.
25 Yea, and now behold, O my son, the Lord doth
give me exceedingly great joy in the fruit of my
labors;
26 For because of the word which he has imparted unto me, behold, many have been born of
God, and have tasted as I have tasted, and have seen
eye to eye as I have seen; therefore they do know
of these things of which I have spoken, as I do
know; and the knowledge which I have is of God.
27 And I have been supported under trials and
troubles of every kind, yea, and in all manner of
afflictions; yea, God has delivered me from prison,
and from bonds, and from death; yea, and I do put
my trust in him, and he will still deliver me.
28 And I know that he will raise me up at the last
day, to dwell with him in glory; yea, and I will
praise him forever, for he has brought our fathers
out of Egypt, and he has swallowed up the
Egyptians in the Red Sea; and he led them by his
power into the promised land; yea, and he has

---

36:15 ***banished***—cast out
***become extinct***—exist no longer

36:18 The phrase "gall of bitterness" is used six times throughout the scriptures, including five times in the Book of Mormon (see Acts 8:23; Mosiah 27:29; Alma 36:18; 41:11; Mormon 8:31; Moroni 8:14). Joseph Fielding Smith said: "None of us is perfect. We all have done things we should not, and when we do things we should not do, we do not feel very good; we are troubled" (*Doctrines of Salvation* 1:129–30).

36:20 "Alma learned the eternal truth that the pain and misery that come from sin can only be erased by repentance. Physical pain ends with death. Spiritual pain, or misery, is everlasting, unless we repent" (Dallin H. Oaks, in Conference Report, October 1991, 103).

36:20 (17–20) When Alma thought about his father's teachings concerning the coming of Jesus Christ, he cried out for forgiveness. Alma was forgiven and filled with peace. How could asking Jesus for forgiveness bring peace to your soul?

36:21 ***exquisite***—intense or extreme

36:22 ***methought***—it seemed to me

36:23 To be "born of God" is to have a change of heart and to decide to put God's desires above everything else in life (see Mosiah 5:2).

36:25 (24–25) Alma's greatest joy was to bring souls to repentance. In modern-day revelation the Lord has promised that we can have that same joy as we share the gospel with others (see D&C 18:15–16).

36:26 ***imparted***—given

36:27 Alma put his trust in the Lord. Proverbs 3:5–6 instructs us to "trust in the Lord with all thine heart and lean not unto thine own understanding. In all thy ways acknowledge him, and he shall direct thy paths."

delivered them out of bondage and captivity from time to time.

29 Yea, and he has also brought our fathers out of the land of Jerusalem; and he has also, by his everlasting power, delivered them out of bondage and captivity, from time to time even down to the present day; and I have always retained in remembrance their captivity; yea, and ye also ought to retain in remembrance, as I have done, their captivity.

30 But behold, my son, this is not all; for ye ought to know as I do know, that inasmuch as ye shall keep the commandments of God ye shall prosper in the land; and ye ought to know also, that inasmuch as ye will not keep the commandments of God ye shall be cut off from his presence. Now this is according to his word.

## CHAPTER 37

*Alma prepares Helaman to take care of the sacred records and to lead the people. Watch for the ways Alma says the scriptures can bless you and your family.*

### *Alma Teaches Helaman About the Importance of the Sacred Records*

1 AND now, my son Helaman, I command you that ye take the records which have been entrusted with me;

2 And I also command you that ye keep a record of this people, according as I have done, upon the plates of Nephi, and keep all these things sacred which I have kept, even as I have kept them; for it is for a wise purpose that they are kept.

3 And these plates of brass, which contain these engravings, which have the records of the holy scriptures upon them, which have the genealogy of our forefathers, even from the beginning—

4 Behold, it has been prophesied by our fathers, that they should be kept and handed down from one generation to another, and be kept and preserved by the hand of the Lord until they should go forth unto every nation, kindred, tongue, and people, that they shall know of the mysteries contained thereon.

5 And now behold, if they are kept they must retain their brightness; yea, and they will retain their brightness; yea, and also shall all the plates which do contain that which is holy writ.

6 Now ye may suppose that this is foolishness in me; but behold I say unto you, that by small and simple things are great things brought to pass; and small means in many instances doth confound the wise.

7 And the Lord God doth work by means to bring about his great and eternal purposes; and by very small means the Lord doth confound the wise and bringeth about the salvation of many souls.

8 And now, it has hitherto been wisdom in God that these things should be preserved; for behold, they have enlarged the memory of this people, yea, and convinced many of the error of their ways, and brought them to the knowledge of their God unto the salvation of their souls.

---

36:29 ***retain***—keep

36:29 (28–29) God's power is great. He delivered the children of Israel from bondage in Egypt and He also helped Lehi's family escape from Jerusalem. In what ways has God helped you to escape or be kept safe?

37:3 The plates of brass were the Old Testament scriptures that Nephi obtained from Laban in Jerusalem. They contained Lehi's genealogy, the five books of Moses, the record of the Jews, and many prophecies of the holy prophets (see 1 Nephi 5:10–14).

37:4 ***generation***—time
***preserved***—protected and saved
***kindred***—family
***tongue***—language

37:5 ***retain***—keep
***writ***—writing

37:6 ***means***—abilities or ways of doing things
***confound***—confuse or silence

37:7 (6–7) What are some "small and simple things" you have done that have blessed people you love?

37:8 ***hitherto***—up to this time
***convinced***—proven to

The scriptures can "enlarge the memory" of people, or help them have a greater understanding of spiritual matters. What have you learned from the Book of Mormon that has helped you to know God better and to want to live with Him again?

9 Yea, I say unto you, were it not for these things
that these records do contain, which are on these
plates, Ammon and his brethren could not have
convinced so many thousands of the Lamanites of
the incorrect tradition of their fathers; yea, these
records and their words brought them unto repentance; that is, they brought them to the knowledge
of the Lord their God, and to rejoice in Jesus Christ
their Redeemer.
10 And who knoweth but what they will be the
means of bringing many thousands of them, yea,
and also many thousands of our stiffnecked
brethren, the Nephites, who are now hardening
their hearts in sin and iniquities, to the knowledge
of their Redeemer?
11 Now these mysteries are not yet fully made
known unto me; therefore I shall forbear.
12 And it may suffice if I only say they are preserved for a wise purpose, which purpose is known
unto God; for he doth counsel in wisdom over all
his works, and his paths are straight, and his course
is one eternal round.

## Helaman Learns What Will Happen to Him If He Breaks the Commandments of God

13 O remember, remember, my son Helaman,
how strict are the commandments of God. And he
said: If ye will keep my commandments ye shall
prosper in the land—but if ye keep not his commandments ye shall be cut off from his presence.
14 And now remember, my son, that God has
entrusted you with these things, which are sacred,
which he has kept sacred, and also which he will
keep and preserve for a wise purpose in him, that he
may show forth his power unto future generations.
15 And now behold, I tell you by the spirit of
prophecy, that if ye transgress the commandments
of God, behold, these things which are sacred shall
be taken away from you by the power of God, and
ye shall be delivered up unto Satan, that he may sift
you as chaff before the wind.
16 But if ye keep the commandments of God, and
do with these things which are sacred according to
that which the Lord doth command you, (for you
must appeal unto the Lord for all things whatsoever ye must do with them) behold, no power of
earth or hell can take them from you, for God is
powerful to the fulfilling of all his words.
17 For he will fulfil all his promises which he shall
make unto you, for he has fulfilled his promises
which he has made unto our fathers.
18 For he promised unto them that he would preserve these things for a wise purpose in him, that he
might show forth his power unto future generations.
19 And now behold, one purpose hath he fulfilled, even to the restoration of many thousands of
the Lamanites to the knowledge of the truth; and he
hath shown forth his power in them, and he will
also still show forth his power in them unto future
generations; therefore they shall be preserved.

---

37:9 ***tradition***—teachings and ways

The story of Ammon and his brothers helping thousands of Lamanites become followers of Christ is found in Alma 17–26.

37:10 ***stiffnecked***—stubborn and rebellious

37:11 ***forbear***—not say

37:12 ***suffice***—be enough

God's "course is one eternal round," meaning that He "changes not" and is "the same yesterday, today, and for ever . . . without variation" (see Joseph Smith, *Lectures on Faith* 3:15).

37:13 ***prosper***—live happily

37:15 ***transgress***—disobey

37:16 ***appeal***—plead

37:19 ***restoration***—bringing back

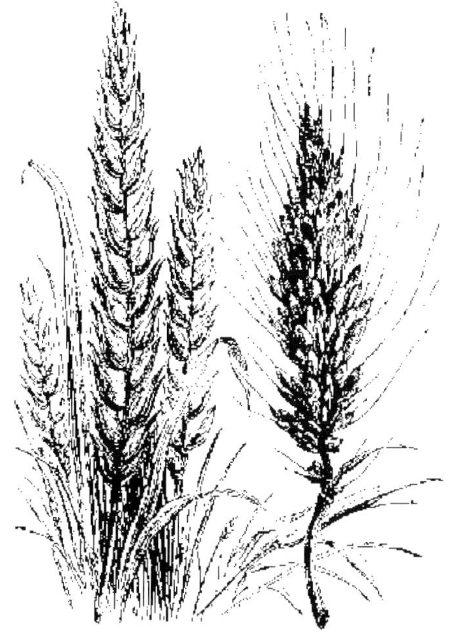

*Chaff is not good to eat. It is sifted, or separated, from grain. Alma prophesied that the wicked will similarly be separated or removed from the righteous.*

20 Therefore I command you, my son Helaman, that ye be diligent in fulfilling all my words, and that ye be diligent in keeping the commandments of God as they are written.

## *Alma Tells Helaman About the Jaredite People Who Made the Twenty-Four Gold Plates*

21 And now, I will speak unto you concerning those twenty-four plates, that ye keep them, that the mysteries and the works of darkness, and their secret works, or the secret works of those people who have been destroyed, may be made manifest unto this people; yea, all their murders, and robbings, and their plunderings, and all their wickedness and abominations, may be made manifest unto this people; yea, and that ye preserve these interpreters.

22 For behold, the Lord saw that his people began to work in darkness, yea, work secret murders and abominations; therefore the Lord said, if they did not repent they should be destroyed from off the face of the earth.

23 And the Lord said: I will prepare unto my servant Gazelem, a stone, which shall shine forth in darkness unto light, that I may discover unto my people who serve me, that I may discover unto them the works of their brethren, yea, their secret works, their works of darkness, and their wickedness and abominations.

24 And now, my son, these interpreters were prepared that the word of God might be fulfilled, which he spake, saying:

25 I will bring forth out of darkness unto light all their secret works and their abominations; and except they repent I will destroy them from off the face of the earth; and I will bring to light all their secrets and abominations, unto every nation that shall hereafter possess the land.

26 And now, my son, we see that they did not repent; therefore they have been destroyed, and thus far the word of God has been fulfilled; yea, their secret abominations have been brought out of darkness and made known unto us.

27 And now, my son, I command you that ye retain all their oaths, and their covenants, and their agreements in their secret abominations; yea, and all their signs and their wonders ye shall keep from this people, that they know them not, lest peradventure they should fall into darkness also and be destroyed.

28 For behold, there is a curse upon all this land, that destruction shall come upon all those workers of darkness, according to the power of God, when they are fully ripe; therefore I desire that this people might not be destroyed.

29 Therefore ye shall keep these secret plans of their oaths and their covenants from this people, and only their wickedness and their murders and their abominations shall ye make known unto them; and ye shall teach them to abhor such wickedness and abominations and murders; and ye shall also teach them that these people were destroyed on account of their wickedness and abominations and their murders.

30 For behold, they murdered all the prophets of the Lord who came among them to declare unto them concerning their iniquities; and the blood of

---

37:20 ***diligent***—persistent or careful

37:21 ***made manifest***—shown

The twenty-four gold plates were found by a group of Nephites (see Mosiah 8:7–9). The plates were among the ruins of a great people who had all been destroyed. These people were the Jaredites, and their story is found in the book of Ether.

The *interpreters* are the Urim and Thummim (see Mosiah 8:13; Joseph Smith—History 1:35).

37:23 Elder Bruce R. McConkie explained that the word *Gazelem* might refer "to the Prophet Joseph Smith who did in fact bring forth part at least of the Ether record. Or it could be that the name Gazelem (Gazelam) is a title having to do with power to translate ancient records and that Alma's reference was to some Nephite prophet who brought the Book of Ether to light in the golden era of Nephite history" (*Mormon Doctrine,* 307).

37:27 ***retain***—keep
***abominations***—acts of great evil
***peradventure***—by chance

37:29 ***abhor***—hate

those whom they murdered did cry unto the Lord their God for vengeance upon those who were their murderers; and thus the judgments of God did come upon these workers of darkness and secret combinations.

31 Yea, and cursed be the land forever and ever unto those workers of darkness and secret combinations, even unto destruction, except they repent before they are fully ripe.

### *Alma Tells Helaman What He Should Teach the People*

32 And now, my son, remember the words which I have spoken unto you; trust not those secret plans unto this people, but teach them an everlasting hatred against sin and iniquity.

33 Preach unto them repentance, and faith on the Lord Jesus Christ; teach them to humble themselves and to be meek and lowly in heart; teach them to withstand every temptation of the devil, with their faith on the Lord Jesus Christ.

34 Teach them to never be weary of good works, but to be meek and lowly in heart; for such shall find rest to their souls.

35 O, remember, my son, and learn wisdom in thy youth; yea, learn in thy youth to keep the commandments of God.

36 Yea, and cry unto God for all thy support; yea, let all thy doings be unto the Lord, and whithersoever thou goest let it be in the Lord; yea, let all thy thoughts be directed unto the Lord; yea, let the affections of thy heart be placed upon the Lord forever.

37 Counsel with the Lord in all thy doings, and he will direct thee for good; yea, when thou liest down at night lie down unto the Lord, that he may watch over you in your sleep; and when thou risest in the morning let thy heart be full of thanks unto God; and if ye do these things, ye shall be lifted up at the last day.

### *The Liahona Led Lehi's Family to the Promised Land*

38 And now, my son, I have somewhat to say concerning the thing which our fathers call a ball, or director—or our fathers called it Liahona, which is, being interpreted, a compass; and the Lord prepared it.

39 And behold, there cannot any man work after the manner of so curious a workmanship. And behold, it was prepared to show unto our fathers the course which they should travel in the wilderness.

40 And it did work for them according to their faith in God; therefore, if they had faith to believe that God could cause that those spindles should point the way they should go, behold, it was done; therefore they had this miracle, and also many other miracles wrought by the power of God, day by day.

---

37:30 ***vengeance***—revenge or punishment

A secret combination is a group of wicked people who secretly join together to lie, cheat, steal, murder, or do whatever else is necessary in order to gain riches, wealth, or power (see Helaman 7:21; 8:27). The first secret combination was between Satan and Cain, who killed his brother Abel to get his flocks (see Moses 5:28–32). "Among today's secret combinations are gangs, drug cartels, and organized crime families" (M. Russell Ballard, in Conference Report, October 1997, 51).

37:33 ***meek***—gentle and humble

How can your faith in Jesus Christ keep you from sinning when you are tempted?

37:34 "As the Savior was in the depths of suffering in the Garden of Gethsemane, he prayed that the bitter cup might pass from him, adding in meekness and lowliness of heart, 'Nevertheless not *my* will, but *thine,* be done' (Luke 22:42; italics added). *A leader in the Lord's kingdom must be meek and lowly of heart* (see Alma 37:34)" (Spencer J. Condie, in Conference Report, April 1990, 36).

37:35 Why does God want His children to learn to keep the commandments while they are young? (see also Alma 41:10–11).

37:36 ***affections***—loving feelings

37:37 "Let prayer, night and morning, as a family and as individuals, become a practice in which children grow while yet young. It will bless their lives forever. No parent in this Church can afford to neglect it" (Gordon B. Hinckley, *Teachings of Gordon B. Hinckley,* 466–67).

37:39 This use of the word "curious" in Joseph Smith's day meant "wrought [or made] with care and art; elegant; neat; finished" (Noah Webster, *American Dictionary of English,* 1828, s.v. "Curious").

***course***—route or way

41 Nevertheless, because those miracles were worked by small means it did show unto them marvelous works. They were slothful, and forgot to exercise their faith and diligence and then those marvelous works ceased, and they did not progress in their journey;

42 Therefore, they tarried in the wilderness, or did not travel a direct course, and were afflicted with hunger and thirst, because of their transgressions.

43 And now, my son, I would that ye should understand that these things are not without a shadow; for as our fathers were slothful to give heed to this compass (now these things were temporal) they did not prosper; even so it is with things which are spiritual.

44 For behold, it is as easy to give heed to the word of Christ, which will point to you a straight course to eternal bliss, as it was for our fathers to give heed to this compass, which would point unto them a straight course to the promised land.

45 And now I say, is there not a type in this thing? For just as surely as this director did bring our fathers, by following its course, to the promised land, shall the words of Christ, if we follow their course, carry us beyond this vale of sorrow into a far better land of promise.

46 O my son, do not let us be slothful because of the easiness of the way; for so was it with our fathers; for so was it prepared for them, that if they would look they might live; even so it is with us. The way is prepared, and if we will look we may live forever.

47 And now, my son, see that ye take care of these sacred things, yea, see that ye look to God and live. Go unto this people and declare the word, and be sober. My son, farewell.

*The commandments of Alma to his son Shiblon.**

## CHAPTER 38

*Alma praises and counsels Shiblon. Look for Alma's advice to his missionary son.*

### *Alma Praises Shiblon for His Faithfulness*

1 MY son, give ear to my words, for I say unto you, even as I said unto Helaman, that inasmuch as ye shall keep the commandments of God ye shall prosper in the land; and inasmuch as ye will not keep the commandments of God ye shall be cut off from his presence.

2 And now, my son, I trust that I shall have great joy in you, because of your steadiness and your faithfulness unto God; for as you have commenced in your youth to look to the Lord your God, even so I hope that you will continue in keeping his commandments; for blessed is he that endureth to the end.

3 I say unto you, my son, that I have had great joy in thee already, because of thy faithfulness and thy diligence, and thy patience and thy long-suffering among the people of the Zoramites.

---

37:41 ***slothful***—lazy

37:42 ***tarried***—stayed
***were afflicted***—suffered

37:43 ***temporal***—earthly

When Alma says that the Liahona is "not without a shadow," he means that there are other things like the Liahona that can give faithful people direction in their lives. What are some things you have that have helped you to choose the right?

37:44 ***eternal bliss***—exaltation

37:45 ***a type in***—something like
***vale of sorrow***—mortal life

How have the words of Christ helped you to move toward being worthy to live with God again?

37:47 ***sober***—serious and reverent

* This introduction was translated from the Book of Mormon plates.

38:1 ***give ear***—listen
***prosper***—live happily

38:2 ***commenced***—begun

Alma had great joy in his son Shiblon's faithfulness. President James E. Faust taught that "steadiness . . . will serve you better than brilliance" (in Conference Report, October 1997, 59).

38:3 ***diligence***—hard work

Alma is very happy with his son Shiblon. How do your actions affect your parents' happiness?

4 For I know that thou wast in bonds; yea, and I also know that thou wast stoned for the word's sake; and thou didst bear all these things with patience because the Lord was with thee; and now thou knowest that the Lord did deliver thee.

5 And now my son, Shiblon, I would that ye should remember, that as much as ye shall put your trust in God even so much ye shall be delivered out of your trials, and your troubles, and your afflictions, and ye shall be lifted up at the last day.

## Alma Remembers His Own Trials

6 Now, my son, I would not that ye should think that I know these things of myself, but it is the Spirit of God which is in me which maketh these things known unto me; for if I had not been born of God I should not have known these things.

7 But behold, the Lord in his great mercy sent his angel to declare unto me that I must stop the work of destruction among his people; yea, and I have seen an angel face to face, and he spake with me, and his voice was as thunder, and it shook the whole earth.

8 And it came to pass that I was three days and three nights in the most bitter pain and anguish of soul; and never, until I did cry out unto the Lord Jesus Christ for mercy, did I receive a remission of my sins. But behold, I did cry unto him and I did find peace to my soul.

9 And now, my son, I have told you this that ye may learn wisdom, that ye may learn of me that there is no other way or means whereby man can be saved, only in and through Christ. Behold, he is the life and the light of the world. Behold, he is the word of truth and righteousness.

## Alma Gives Advice to Missionaries

10 And now, as ye have begun to teach the word even so I would that ye should continue to teach; and I would that ye would be diligent and temperate in all things.

11 See that ye are not lifted up unto pride; yea, see that ye do not boast in your own wisdom, nor of your much strength.

12 Use boldness, but not overbearance; and also see that ye bridle all your passions, that ye may be filled with love; see that ye refrain from idleness.

13 Do not pray as the Zoramites do, for ye have seen that they pray to be heard of men, and to be praised for their wisdom.

*The practice of stoning, as depicted here, was a Jewish custom used to punish those who violated certain laws.*

38:4 Stoning was a way to punish those who violated certain Jewish laws. It was performed by having a group of people gather around the guilty person and throw stones or rocks at him with the intent to kill (see Numbers 15:32–36).

38:5 ***afflictions***—sufferings

38:7 Elder Mark E. Petersen declared that the "scripture clearly teaches that the purpose of the ministry of angels is 'to call men unto repentance . . . by declaring the word of Christ unto the chosen vessels of the Lord, that they may bear testimony of him' (Moroni 7:31)" (in Conference Report, October 1983, 41).

38:8 ***anguish***—sorrow
***remission***—forgiveness

Notice in this verse how Alma could only find inner peace by turning to Jesus Christ. How might turning to Christ bring you peace?

38:10 ***temperate***—restrained or disciplined

38:11 Elder Marvin J. Ashton said, "Boasting is to glorify oneself, to talk in a vain or bragging manner, or to talk especially about one's deeds" (in Conference Report, April 1990, 82).

38:12 ***refrain from idleness***—stay away from laziness

Elder Russell C. Taylor said: "True love comes when you bridle your passions, when you use self-control. You should avoid anything that causes you to lose control of yourself or to lose concern for the welfare of another person" (in Conference Report, April 1989, 54).

14 Do not say: O God, I thank thee that we are better than our brethren; but rather say: O Lord, forgive my unworthiness, and remember my brethren in mercy—yea, acknowledge your unworthiness before God at all times.
15 And may the Lord bless your soul, and receive you at the last day into his kingdom, to sit down in peace. Now go, my son, and teach the word unto this people. Be sober. My son, farewell.

*The commandments of Alma to his son Corianton. Comprising chapters 39 to 42 inclusive.**

## CHAPTER 39

*Alma's third son, Corianton, is guilty of unchastity and had been a bad example for the Church. Look for Alma's counsel to his son on how the Atonement can save people from their sins.*

### Alma Speaks of the Three Most Serious Sins

1 AND now, my son, I have somewhat more to say unto thee than what I said unto thy brother; for behold, have ye not observed the steadiness of thy brother, his faithfulness, and his diligence in keeping the commandments of God? Behold, has he not set a good example for thee?
2 For thou didst not give so much heed unto my words as did thy brother, among the people of the Zoramites. Now this is what I have against thee; thou didst go on unto boasting in thy strength and thy wisdom.
3 And this is not all, my son. Thou didst do that which was grievous unto me; for thou didst forsake the ministry, and did go over into the land of Siron among the borders of the Lamanites, after the harlot Isabel.
4 Yea, she did steal away the hearts of many; but this was no excuse for thee, my son. Thou shouldst have tended to the ministry wherewith thou wast entrusted.
5 Know ye not, my son, that these things are an abomination in the sight of the Lord; yea, most abominable above all sins save it be the shedding of innocent blood or denying the Holy Ghost?
6 For behold, if ye deny the Holy Ghost when it once has had place in you, and ye know that ye deny it, behold, this is a sin which is unpardonable; yea, and whosoever murdereth against the light and knowledge of God, it is not easy for him to obtain forgiveness; yea, I say unto you, my son, that it is not easy for him to obtain a forgiveness.

### Corianton Is Counseled to Repent

7 And now, my son, I would to God that ye had not been guilty of so great a crime. I would not dwell upon your crimes, to harrow up your soul, if it were not for your good.

---

38:14 ***unworthiness***—sins
***acknowledge***—admit to

38:15 ***sober***—serious minded

* This introduction to chapters 39–42, except for the second sentence, was translated from the Book of Mormon plates.

39:1 ***diligence***—care and effort

39:2 ***heed***—obedience
***I have against thee***—you have done wrong
***boasting***—bragging

39:3 ***grievous***—heartbreaking
***forsake the ministry***—leave the mission
***harlot***—wicked and unchaste woman

39:4 ***tended***—paid attention

39:5 ***an abomination***—a great evil

President Gordon B. Hinckley said: "It seems as if the whole world has become obsessed with sex. In a very beguiling and alluring way, it is thrown at you constantly. You are exposed to it on television, in magazines and books, in videos, even in music. Turn your back on it. Shun it. I know that it is easy to say and difficult to do. But each time that you do so, it will be so much the easier the next time. What a wonderful thing it will be if someday you can stand before the Lord and say, 'I am clean' " (in Conference Report, April 1996, 69).

39:6 Denying the Holy Ghost involves denying God after the Holy Ghost has given you a witness that He is real. It is the most serious sin in all eternity and "shall not be forgiven in the world nor out of the world" (D&C 132:27; see also D&C 76:30–38). This sin is called unpardonable since "it is not covered or pardoned by the atonement of Christ" (Joseph Fielding McConkie and others, *Doctrinal Commentary on the Book of Mormon* 3:290).

39:7 ***harrow up***—greatly distress

8 But behold, ye cannot hide your crimes from God; and except ye repent they will stand as a testimony against you at the last day.

9 Now my son, I would that ye should repent and forsake your sins, and go no more after the lusts of your eyes, but cross yourself in all these things; for except ye do this ye can in nowise inherit the kingdom of God. Oh, remember, and take it upon you, and cross yourself in these things.

10 And I command you to take it upon you to counsel with your elder brothers in your undertakings; for behold, thou art in thy youth, and ye stand in need to be nourished by your brothers. And give heed to their counsel.

11 Suffer not yourself to be led away by any vain or foolish thing; suffer not the devil to lead away your heart again after those wicked harlots. Behold, O my son, how great iniquity ye brought upon the Zoramites; for when they saw your conduct they would not believe in my words.

12 And now the Spirit of the Lord doth say unto me: Command thy children to do good, lest they lead away the hearts of many people to destruction; therefore I command you, my son, in the fear of God, that ye refrain from your iniquities;

13 That ye turn to the Lord with all your mind, might, and strength; that ye lead away the hearts of no more to do wickedly; but rather return unto them, and acknowledge your faults and that wrong which ye have done.

14 Seek not after riches nor the vain things of this world; for behold, you cannot carry them with you.

### *Christ's Atonement Is for All Who Repent*

15 And now, my son, I would say somewhat unto you concerning the coming of Christ. Behold, I say unto you, that it is he that surely shall come to take away the sins of the world; yea, he cometh to declare glad tidings of salvation unto his people.

16 And now, my son, this was the ministry unto which ye were called, to declare these glad tidings unto this people, to prepare their minds; or rather that salvation might come unto them, that they may prepare the minds of their children to hear the word at the time of his coming.

17 And now I will ease your mind somewhat on this subject. Behold, you marvel why these things should be known so long beforehand. Behold, I say unto you, is not a soul at this time as precious unto God as a soul will be at the time of his coming?

18 Is it not as necessary that the plan of redemption should be made known unto this people as well as unto their children?

19 Is it not as easy at this time for the Lord to send his angel to declare these glad tidings unto us as unto our children, or as after the time of his coming?

## CHAPTER 40

*Alma continues to teach his son Corianton important gospel principles. He teaches about the spirit world. Look for what happens to the spirits of righteous people when they go to the spirit world.*

### *All Will Be Resurrected Because of the Resurrection of Jesus Christ*

1 NOW my son, here is somewhat more I would say unto thee; for I perceive that thy mind is worried concerning the resurrection of the dead.

---

39:9 " 'The lusts of your eyes'—in our day what does that expression mean? Movies, television programs, and video recordings that are both suggestive and lewd. Magazines and books that are obscene and pornographic" (*The Teachings of Ezra Taft Benson*, 222).

The Joseph Smith Translation helps with the phrase "cross yourself." It says, "And now for a man to take up his cross, is to deny himself all ungodliness, and every worldly lust, and keep my commandments" (JST, Matthew 16:26).

39:10 ***undertakings***—actions
***nourished***—fed spiritually

39:11 ***Suffer***—Allow

Alma wanted Corianton to realize how important it is to be a good example to others. How would you feel if you knew someone had become interested in the gospel because of your good example?

39:12 ***refrain from***—stop

39:13 ***acknowledge***—admit and confess

39:14 ***vain***—empty or useless

39:17 ***beforehand***—before they happen

40:1 ***perceive***—understand or can see
***concerning***—about

2 Behold, I say unto you, that there is no resurrection—or, I would say, in other words, that this mortal does not put on immortality, this corruption does not put on incorruption—until after the coming of Christ.

3 Behold, he bringeth to pass the resurrection of the dead. But behold, my son, the resurrection is not yet. Now, I unfold unto you a mystery; nevertheless, there are many mysteries which are kept, that no one knoweth them save God himself. But I show unto you one thing which I have inquired diligently of God that I might know—that is concerning the resurrection.

4 Behold, there is a time appointed that all shall come forth from the dead. Now when this time cometh no one knows; but God knoweth the time which is appointed.

5 Now, whether there shall be one time, or a second time, or a third time, that men shall come forth from the dead, it mattereth not; for God knoweth all these things; and it sufficeth me to know that this is the case—that there is a time appointed that all shall rise from the dead.

## The Spirit World Has a Place for Both Wicked and Righteous People

6 Now there must needs be a space betwixt the time of death and the time of the resurrection.

7 And now I would inquire what becometh of the souls of men from this time of death to the time appointed for the resurrection?

8 Now whether there is more than one time appointed for men to rise it mattereth not; for all do not die at once, and this mattereth not; all is as one day with God, and time only is measured unto men.

9 Therefore, there is a time appointed unto men that they shall rise from the dead; and there is a space between the time of death and the resurrection. And now, concerning this space of time, what becometh of the souls of men is the thing which I have inquired diligently of the Lord to know; and this is the thing of which I do know.

10 And when the time cometh when all shall rise, then shall they know that God knoweth all the times which are appointed unto man.

11 Now, concerning the state of the soul between death and the resurrection—Behold, it has been made known unto me by an angel, that the spirits of all men, as soon as they are departed from this mortal body, yea, the spirits of all men, whether they be good or evil, are taken home to that God who gave them life.

12 And then shall it come to pass, that the spirits of those who are righteous are received into a state of happiness, which is called paradise, a state of rest, a state of peace, where they shall rest from all their troubles and from all care, and sorrow.

---

40:2 (1–2) Someday our mortal bodies will die. However, Christ was resurrected and opened the way for all of us to be resurrected (see 1 Corinthians 15:20–26). At the resurrection, "the spirit and the body shall be reunited again in its perfect form" (Alma 11:43). A resurrected body is perfect and will live forever (see Alma 40:23).

40:3 ***unfold***—show
***mystery***—truth that cannot be known except through revelation from the Lord
***inquired diligently***—asked with faith

40:4 ***appointed***—set

40:5 ***sufficeth me***—is enough for me

40:6 ***betwixt***—between

40:8 Both the prophet Abraham and the apostle Peter taught that a day to the Lord is one thousand of our years (see Abraham 3:4; 2 Peter 3:8).

40:10 Only God knows when Jesus will come again and continue the first resurrection (see Joseph Smith—Matthew 1:40).

40:11 ***state of***—way of life for
***are departed from***—leave

40:12 Paradise is a place in the spirit world where those who have been righteous go to rest and find peace from their sorrows and troubles. How does knowing this make it easier to be comforted when a loved one dies?

THE ASCENSION, BY ROBERT T. BARRETT

*"Behold he bringeth to pass the resurrection."*

13 And then shall it come to pass, that the spirits of the wicked, yea, who are evil—for behold, they have no part nor portion of the Spirit of the Lord; for behold, they chose evil works rather than good; therefore the spirit of the devil did enter into them, and take possession of their house—and these shall be cast out into outer darkness; there shall be weeping, and wailing, and gnashing of teeth, and this because of their own iniquity, being led captive by the will of the devil.

14 Now this is the state of the souls of the wicked, yea, in darkness, and a state of awful, fearful looking for the fiery indignation of the wrath of God upon them; thus they remain in this state, as well as the righteous in paradise, until the time of their resurrection.

## *Righteous Saints Who Died Before the Time of Christ Will Be Resurrected with Him*

15 Now, there are some that have understood that this state of happiness and this state of misery of the soul, before the resurrection, was a first resurrection. Yea, I admit it may be termed a resurrection, the raising of the spirit or the soul and their consignation to happiness or misery, according to the words which have been spoken.

16 And behold, again it hath been spoken, that there is a first resurrection, a resurrection of all those who have been, or who are, or who shall be, down to the resurrection of Christ from the dead.

17 Now, we do not suppose that this first resurrection, which is spoken of in this manner, can be the resurrection of the souls and their consignation to happiness or misery. Ye cannot suppose that this is what it meaneth.

18 Behold, I say unto you, Nay; but it meaneth the reuniting of the soul with the body, of those from the days of Adam down to the resurrection of Christ.

19 Now, whether the souls and the bodies of those of whom has been spoken shall all be re-united at once, the wicked as well as the righteous, I do not say; let it suffice, that I say that they all come forth; or in other words, their resurrection cometh to pass before the resurrection of those who die after the resurrection of Christ.

20 Now, my son, I do not say that their resurrection cometh at the resurrection of Christ; but behold, I give it as my opinion, that the souls and the bodies are reunited, of the righteous, at the resurrection of Christ, and his ascension into heaven.

## *We Will Receive Perfect Bodies When We Are Resurrected*

21 But whether it be at his resurrection or after, I do not say; but this much I say, that there is a space between death and the resurrection of the body, and a state of the soul in happiness or in misery until the time which is appointed of God that the dead shall come forth, and be reunited, both soul and body, and be brought to stand before God, and be judged according to their works.

22 Yea, this bringeth about the restoration of those things of which has been spoken by the mouths of the prophets.

23 The soul shall be restored to the body, and the body to the soul; yea, and every limb and joint shall be restored to its body; yea, even a hair of the head shall not be lost; but all things shall be restored to their proper and perfect frame.

---

40:13 ***portion***—amount
***their house***—them
***gnashing of teeth***—grinding teeth in pain and sorrow

The devil can only lead us "captive" when we choose not to listen to the voice of the Lord (see Moses 4:4). The Prophet Joseph Smith taught that "the devil has no power over us only as we permit him" (*Teachings of the Prophet Joseph Smith,* 181).

40:14 ***fiery indignation of the wrath***—punishments

40:15 ***termed***—called
***consignation***—being assigned or given

40:18 ***reuniting***—coming together again

40:18 (16–18) Alma explains that when Jesus is resurrected, other righteous Saints who died before Him will be resurrected also. Samuel the Lamanite also prophesied that this would happen (see Helaman 14:25). Matthew later testified that it did happen (see Matthew 27:52–53).

40:20 ***ascension***—rising

40:22 ***restoration***—return

24 And now, my son, this is the restoration of which has been spoken by the mouths of the prophets—
25 And then shall the righteous shine forth in the kingdom of God.
26 But behold, an awful death cometh upon the wicked; for they die as to things pertaining to things of righteousness; for they are unclean, and no unclean thing can inherit the kingdom of God; but they are cast out, and consigned to partake of the fruits of their labors or their works, which have been evil; and they drink the dregs of a bitter cup.

## CHAPTER 41

*Alma continues his message to his son Corianton. He teaches about the resurrection and judgment. Watch for the word* restoration, *its meaning, and how it affects all people.*

### We Are Judged According to Our Works and the Desires of Our Hearts

1 AND now, my son, I have somewhat to say concerning the restoration of which has been spoken; for behold, some have wrested the scriptures, and have gone far astray because of this thing. And I perceive that thy mind has been worried also concerning this thing. But behold, I will explain it unto thee.
2 I say unto thee, my son, that the plan of restoration is requisite with the justice of God; for it is requisite that all things should be restored to their proper order. Behold, it is requisite and just, according to the power and resurrection of Christ, that the soul of man should be restored to its body, and that every part of the body should be restored to itself.
3 And it is requisite with the justice of God that men should be judged according to their works; and if their works were good in this life, and the desires of their hearts were good, that they should also, at the last day, be restored unto that which is good.
4 And if their works are evil they shall be restored unto them for evil. Therefore, all things shall be restored to their proper order, every thing to its natural frame—mortality raised to immortality, corruption to incorruption—raised to endless happiness to inherit the kingdom of God, or to endless misery to inherit the kingdom of the devil, the one on one hand, the other on the other—
5 The one raised to happiness according to his desires of happiness, or good according to his desires of good; and the other to evil according to his desires of evil; for as he has desired to do evil all the day long even so shall he have his reward of evil when the night cometh.
6 And so it is on the other hand. If he hath repented of his sins, and desired righteousness until the end of his days, even so he shall be rewarded unto righteousness.

---

40:25 Jesus taught that after the Resurrection the righteous shall "shine forth as the sun in the kingdom of their Father" (Matthew 13:43). Paul taught that the glory of those who are resurrected to the celestial kingdom can be compared to the brightness of the sun (see 1 Corinthians 15:40–41).

40:26 ***pertaining to***—having to do with
***inherit***—receive
***partake***—eat

"Dregs" are the last remaining parts of a drink. Alma is saying that the wicked will taste the last drop of their punishment.

41:1 ***wrested***—twisted or changed the meaning of
***far astray***—wrong
***perceive***—know or see

41:2 ***requisite***—required
***the justice of God***—God's eternal law that requires punishment for broken laws
***just***—fair

The word *soul* in this verse refers to the spirit after it leaves the body and goes into the spirit world to await the resurrection (see Alma 40:11–14; see also Bruce R. McConkie, *Mormon Doctrine,* 748).

41:2 (1–2) The meaning of the word *restoration* as given by Alma is to "bring back again" (Alma 41:13). Alma uses this word to help explain the resurrection. The resurrection will unite our bodies with our spirits, so that they will never be separated again (see Alma 11:45).

41:4 "*Corruption* means mortality; incorruption means immortality" (Bruce R. McConkie, *Mormon Doctrine,* 163).

***inherit***—receive

7 These are they that are redeemed of the Lord;
yea, these are they that are taken out, that are delivered from that endless night of darkness; and thus they stand or fall; for behold, they are their own judges, whether to do good or do evil.

### Wickedness Never Was Happiness

8 Now, the decrees of God are unalterable; there-
fore, the way is prepared that whosoever will may walk therein and be saved.
9 And now behold, my son, do not risk one more
offense against your God upon those points of doctrine, which ye have hitherto risked to commit sin.
10 Do not suppose, because it has been spoken
concerning restoration, that ye shall be restored from sin to happiness. Behold, I say unto you, wickedness never was happiness.
11 And now, my son, all men that are in a state of
nature, or I would say, in a carnal state, are in the gall of bitterness and in the bonds of iniquity; they are without God in the world, and they have gone contrary to the nature of God; therefore, they are in a state contrary to the nature of happiness.

### Our Choices Will Bring Happiness or Misery in the Next Life

12 And now behold, is the meaning of the word
restoration to take a thing of a natural state and place it in an unnatural state, or to place it in a state opposite to its nature?
13 O, my son, this is not the case; but the mean-
ing of the word restoration is to bring back again evil for evil, or carnal for carnal, or devilish for devilish—good for that which is good; righteous for that which is righteous; just for that which is just; merciful for that which is merciful.
14 Therefore, my son, see that you are merciful
unto your brethren; deal justly, judge righteously, and do good continually; and if ye do all these things then shall ye receive your reward; yea, ye shall have mercy restored unto you again; ye shall have justice restored unto you again; ye shall have a righteous judgment restored unto you again; and ye shall have good rewarded unto you again.
15 For that which ye do send out shall return unto
you again, and be restored; therefore, the word restoration more fully condemneth the sinner, and justifieth him not at all.

## CHAPTER 42

*God provides for us a plan that allows us to return to Him. It is called the plan of redemption. This plan includes the Creation of the world, the Fall of Adam, and the coming of the Savior, who provides the way to return to our Heavenly Father. As you study this chapter, watch for what Alma teaches about these three parts of Heavenly Father's plan.*

---

41:7 The word *night* is a symbol of death. The phrase *night of darkness* refers to the spiritual existence following the death of the mortal body (see Bruce R. McConkie, *Mormon Doctrine,* 537).

41:8 ***decrees***—laws
***are unalterable***—cannot be changed

41:9 ***hitherto***—up to this time

41:10 President Ezra Taft Benson taught, "While a man may take some temporary pleasure in sin, the end result is unhappiness" (in Conference Report, October 1974, 91). Elder Howard W. Hunter explained, "If we think and live righteously, happiness will find its place in our lives" (*The Teachings of Howard W. Hunter,* 74). Why do you think keeping the commandments makes you happier than doing wrong?

41:11 ***carnal***—worldly or evil
***gall of bitterness***—most awful sorrow
***bonds of iniquity***—chains of sin

41:15 ***condemneth the sinner***—finds the sinner guilty
***justifieth him not***—doesn't excuse him

41:15 (13–15) The judgment will be like a harvest. We will gather in what we have planted. If we are merciful, we will receive mercy. If we are kind, we will receive kindness. "How true it is that men get what they earn and keep what they have acquired! . . . What was earned in this life shall remain with each person as his forever" (Bruce R. McConkie, *Doctrinal New Testament Commentary* 3:591; see also D&C 1:10).

## The Fall of Adam Was Important to Heavenly Father's Plan

1 AND now, my son, I perceive there is somewhat more which doth worry your mind, which ye cannot understand—which is concerning the justice of God in the punishment of the sinner; for ye do try to suppose that it is injustice that the sinner should be consigned to a state of misery.

2 Now behold, my son, I will explain this thing unto thee. For behold, after the Lord God sent our first parents forth from the garden of Eden, to till the ground, from whence they were taken—yea, he drew out the man, and he placed at the east end of the garden of Eden, cherubim, and a flaming sword which turned every way, to keep the tree of life—

3 Now, we see that the man had become as God, knowing good and evil; and lest he should put forth his hand, and take also of the tree of life, and eat and live forever, the Lord God placed cherubim and the flaming sword, that he should not partake of the fruit—

4 And thus we see, that there was a time granted unto man to repent, yea, a probationary time, a time to repent and serve God.

5 For behold, if Adam had put forth his hand immediately, and partaken of the tree of life, he would have lived forever, according to the word of God, having no space for repentance; yea, and also the word of God would have been void, and the great plan of salvation would have been frustrated.

6 But behold, it was appointed unto man to die—therefore, as they were cut off from the tree of life they should be cut off from the face of the earth—and man became lost forever, yea, they became fallen man.

7 And now, ye see by this that our first parents were cut off both temporally and spiritually from the presence of the Lord; and thus we see they became subjects to follow after their own will.

8 Now behold, it was not expedient that man should be reclaimed from this temporal death, for that would destroy the great plan of happiness.

9 Therefore, as the soul could never die, and the fall had brought upon all mankind a spiritual death as well as a temporal, that is, they were cut off from the presence of the Lord, it was expedient that mankind should be reclaimed from this spiritual death.

10 Therefore, as they had become carnal, sensual, and devilish, by nature, this probationary state became a state for them to prepare; it became a preparatory state.

11 And now remember, my son, if it were not for the plan of redemption, (laying it aside) as soon as they were dead their souls were miserable, being cut off from the presence of the Lord.

## Jesus Exercises Justice and Mercy in Our Behalf

12 And now, there was no means to reclaim men from this fallen state, which man had brought upon himself because of his own disobedience;

13 Therefore, according to justice, the plan of redemption could not be brought about, only on conditions of repentance of men in this probationary state, yea, this preparatory state; for except it

42:1 **perceive**—understand
**justice**—fairness
**consigned to a state of misery**—given a life of sadness

42:2 **drew out**—put out
**cherubim**—heavenly servants

42:3 **lest**—in case

42:4 **probationary**—testing

42:5 **void**—good for nothing

42:6 **cut off from the face of the earth**—doomed to die

"The fall was a very essential part of the divine plan. Adam and Eve therefore did the very thing that the Lord intended them to do" (Joseph Fielding Smith, *Answers to Gospel Questions* 4:80).

42:7 To be "cut off both temporally and spiritually" is to die physically and be taken spiritually out of God's presence (see Alma 42:9).

**after their own will**—their agency or choice

42:8 **expedient**—helpful or appropriate
**reclaimed**—saved
**temporal**—physical

42:10 **carnal, sensual, and devilish**—people who think and do evil

42:11 **miserable**—very sad

42:13 **preparatory state**—time to prepare

were for these conditions, mercy could not take effect except it should destroy the work of justice. Now the work of justice could not be destroyed; if so, God would cease to be God.

14 And thus we see that all mankind were fallen, and they were in the grasp of justice; yea, the justice of God, which consigned them forever to be cut off from his presence.

15 And now, the plan of mercy could not be brought about except an atonement should be made; therefore God himself atoneth for the sins of the world, to bring about the plan of mercy, to appease the demands of justice, that God might be a perfect, just God, and a merciful God also.

## Sorrow for Sin Is a Part of Repentance

16 Now, repentance could not come unto men except there were a punishment, which also was eternal as the life of the soul should be, affixed opposite to the plan of happiness, which was as eternal also as the life of the soul.

17 Now, how could a man repent except he should sin? How could he sin if there was no law? How could there be a law save there was a punishment?

18 Now, there was a punishment affixed, and a just law given, which brought remorse of conscience unto man.

19 Now, if there was no law given—if a man murdered he should die—would he be afraid he would die if he should murder?

20 And also, if there was no law given against sin men would not be afraid to sin.

21 And if there was no law given, if men sinned what could justice do, or mercy either, for they would have no claim upon the creature?

22 But there is a law given, and a punishment affixed, and a repentance granted; which repentance, mercy claimeth; otherwise, justice claimeth the creature and executeth the law, and the law inflicteth the punishment; if not so, the works of justice would be destroyed, and God would cease to be God.

23 But God ceaseth not to be God, and mercy claimeth the penitent, and mercy cometh because of the atonement; and the atonement bringeth to pass the resurrection of the dead; and the resurrection of the dead bringeth back men into the presence of God; and thus they are restored into his presence, to be judged according to their works, according to the law and justice.

---

42:13 ***cease to be***—stop being

42:14 ***consigned***—committed

42:14 (13–14) Justice is the law that requires a fair payment whenever a law is broken. Mercy is given to those who repent; the Savior makes the payment in their behalf through the Atonement. Those who do not repent are subject to the law of justice, and must pay for their own sins (see D&C 19:16–18).

42:15 "How glorious is the plan of salvation, [planned] before the foundation of the world for the salvation of men. Adam was sent to start the race, and through doing so, it became necessary for him to transgress a law, to bring death, or mortality, into the world. That made it necessary for the coming of Jesus Christ to redeem us from Adam's transgression, or the mortal death, and through the mercy of our Father in heaven, and His Son Jesus Christ, through that atonement we likewise are granted redemption from our own sins on condition of our repentance" (Joseph Fielding Smith, in Conference Report, April 1944, 49).

***appease***—satisfy
***just***—fair

42:16 ***affixed***—made or set

*Mercy cannot rob justice.*

ILLUSTRATION BY LESTER LEE

42:18 ***remorse of conscience***—deep sadness for sin

42:22 ***granted***—allowed
***executeth***—carries out

42:23 ***the penitent***—those who repent
***restored***—brought back

24 For behold, justice exerciseth all his demands, and also mercy claimeth all which is her own; and thus, none but the truly penitent are saved.
25 What, do ye suppose that mercy can rob justice? I say unto you, Nay; not one whit. If so, God would cease to be God.
26 And thus God bringeth about his great and eternal purposes, which were prepared from the foundation of the world. And thus cometh about the salvation and the redemption of men, and also their destruction and misery.

### Those Who Do Not Repent Will Have to Suffer the Consequences of Their Choices

27 Therefore, O my son, whosoever will come may come and partake of the waters of life freely; and whosoever will not come the same is not compelled to come; but in the last day it shall be restored unto him according to his deeds.
28 If he has desired to do evil, and has not repented in his days, behold, evil shall be done unto him, according to the restoration of God.
29 And now, my son, I desire that ye should let these things trouble you no more, and only let your sins trouble you, with that trouble which shall bring you down unto repentance.
30 O my son, I desire that ye should deny the justice of God no more. Do not endeavor to excuse yourself in the least point because of your sins, by denying the justice of God; but do you let the justice of God, and his mercy, and his long-suffering have full sway in your heart; and let it bring you down to the dust in humility.
31 And now, O my son, ye are called of God to preach the word unto this people. And now, my son, go thy way, declare the word with truth and soberness, that thou mayest bring souls unto repentance, that the great plan of mercy may have claim upon them. And may God grant unto you even according to my words. Amen.

## CHAPTER 43

*The Zoramites and other Nephite dissenters join with the Lamanites and battle against the Nephites. Look for reasons why the Lamanites attack the Nephites and reasons why the Nephites have God's help in defending themselves.*

### The Lamanites Attack the Nephites to Bring Them into Bondage

1 AND now it came to pass that the sons of Alma did go forth among the people, to declare the word unto them. And Alma, also, himself, could not rest, and he also went forth.

---

42:24 ***exerciseth***—makes

"*Penitence* [means] sorrow . . . for sins . . . (Alma 32:6–8.) Those who do repent become *truly penitent* in the gospel sense. They are the only ones who are able to know and understand the things of God (Alma 26:21), and to receive that full measure of joy which is available to the saints. (Alma 27:17–18; 29:10.) Mercy shall be granted the penitent in the day of judgment, and *'none but the truly penitent are saved'* " (Bruce R. McConkie, *Mormon Doctrine,* 566).

42:25 ***Nay; not one whit.***—No, not at all.

42:26 ***foundation***—beginning

42:27 This invitation to receive the "waters of life" is an invitation to receive the blessings of Jesus Christ and the Atonement (see Alma 5:34). Jesus spoke of Himself as the "bread of life" (John 6:48) and the "living water" (John 4:10). We remember these symbols of the Lord each week when we partake of the sacrament (see Luke 22:19–20).

***compelled***—forced
***deeds***—actions

42:28 (27–28) In this life we have the moral agency or freedom to choose good or evil (see 2 Nephi 2:27).

42:29 President Ezra Taft Benson taught: "True repentance involves a change of heart and not just a change of behavior (see Alma 5:13). Part of this mighty change of heart is to feel godly sorrow for our sins" (*The Teachings of Ezra Taft Benson,* 71).

42:30 ***endeavor***—try
***long-suffering have full sway***—patience have complete effect

42:31 ***soberness***—seriousness

Alma 49:30 shows that Corianton did what his father, Alma, had commanded; he repented and preached the gospel. Repentance is a wonderful blessing.

43:1 ***declare***—teach

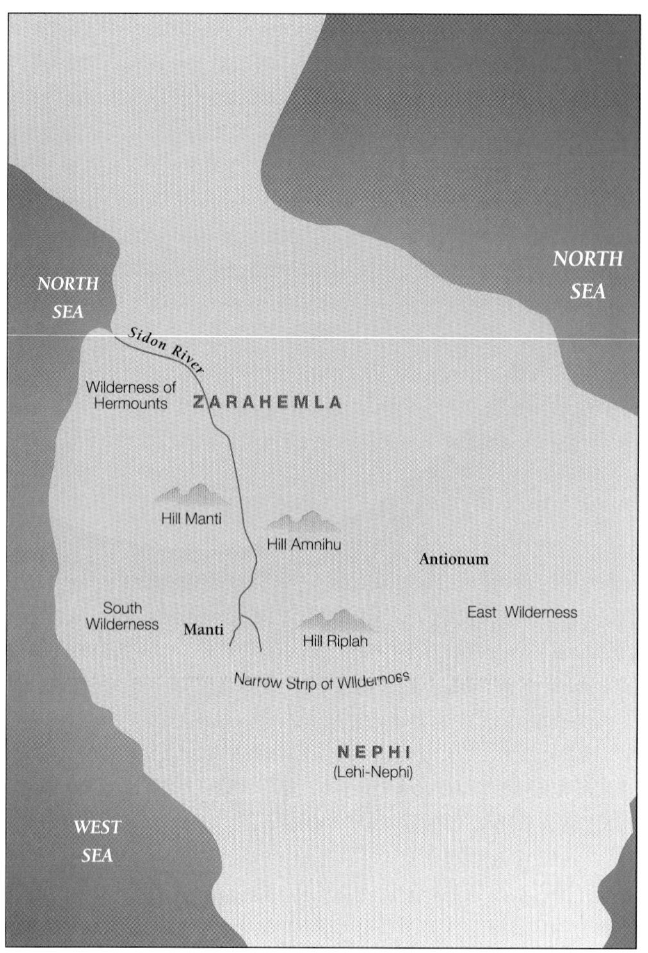


*The armies of Moroni and Zerahemnah battled in these lands.*

2 Now we shall say no more concerning their preaching, except that they preached the word, and the truth, according to the spirit of prophecy and revelation; and they preached after the holy order of God by which they were called.
3 And now I return to an account of the wars between the Nephites and the Lamanites, in the eighteenth year of the reign of the judges.
4 For behold, it came to pass that the Zoramites became Lamanites; therefore, in the commencement of the eighteenth year the people of the Nephites saw that the Lamanites were coming upon them; therefore they made preparations for war; yea, they gathered together their armies in the land of Jershon.
5 And it came to pass that the Lamanites came with their thousands; and they came into the land of Antionum, which is the land of the Zoramites; and a man by the name of Zerahemnah was their leader.
6 And now, as the Amalekites were of a more wicked and murderous disposition than the Lamanites were, in and of themselves, therefore, Zerahemnah appointed chief captains over the Lamanites, and they were all Amalekites and Zoramites.
7 Now this he did that he might preserve their hatred towards the Nephites, that he might bring them into subjection to the accomplishment of his designs.
8 For behold, his designs were to stir up the Lamanites to anger against the Nephites; this he did that he might usurp great power over them, and also that he might gain power over the Nephites by bringing them into bondage.

## The Nephites Fight for Their Families, Freedom, and the Right to Worship the Lord

9 And now the design of the Nephites was to support their lands, and their houses, and their wives, and their children, that they might preserve them from the hands of their enemies; and also that they might preserve their rights and their privileges, yea, and also their liberty, that they might worship God according to their desires.

---

43:2 The words *holy order of God* and sometimes just the word *order* are used in the scriptures to refer to the priesthood of Jesus Christ (see D&C 107:3).

43:3 ***reign***—rule

43:4 ***commencement***—beginning

43:6 ***disposition***—way or nature
***appointed***—chose

The Amalekites, like the Zoramites, were a group of unbelieving and rebellious Nephites.

43:7 ***preserve***—keep
***into subjection***—under his power
***the accomplishment of his designs***—complete his plans

43:8 ***usurp***—take
***bondage***—slavery

43:8 (6–8) What kind of a leader do you think Zerahemnah was? How do you think wicked people are able to gain so much power over other people's lives?

43:9 ***preserve***—save

10 For they knew that if they should fall into the hands of the Lamanites, that whosoever should worship God in spirit and in truth, the true and the living God, the Lamanites would destroy.

11 Yea, and they also knew the extreme hatred of the Lamanites towards their brethren, who were the people of Anti-Nephi-Lehi, who were called the people of Ammon—and they would not take up arms, yea, they had entered into a covenant and they would not break it—therefore, if they should fall into the hands of the Lamanites they would be destroyed.

12 And the Nephites would not suffer that they should be destroyed; therefore they gave them lands for their inheritance.

13 And the people of Ammon did give unto the Nephites a large portion of their substance to support their armies; and thus the Nephites were compelled, alone, to withstand against the Lamanites, who were a compound of Laman and Lemuel, and the sons of Ishmael, and all those who had dissented from the Nephites, who were Amalekites and Zoramites, and the descendants of the priests of Noah.

14 Now those descendants were as numerous, nearly, as were the Nephites; and thus the Nephites were obliged to contend with their brethren, even unto bloodshed.

## Captain Moroni Prepares for the Lamanite Attack

15 And it came to pass as the armies of the Lamanites had gathered together in the land of Antionum, behold, the armies of the Nephites were prepared to meet them in the land of Jershon.

16 Now, the leader of the Nephites, or the man who had been appointed to be the chief captain over the Nephites—now the chief captain took the command of all the armies of the Nephites—and his name was Moroni;

17 And Moroni took all the command, and the government of their wars. And he was only twenty and five years old when he was appointed chief captain over the armies of the Nephites.

18 And it came to pass that he met the Lamanites in the borders of Jershon, and his people were armed with swords, and with cimeters, and all manner of weapons of war.

19 And when the armies of the Lamanites saw that the people of Nephi, or that Moroni, had prepared his people with breastplates and with arm-shields, yea, and also shields to defend their heads, and also they were dressed with thick clothing—

20 Now the army of Zerahemnah was not prepared with any such thing; they had only their swords and their cimeters, their bows and their arrows, their stones and their slings; and they were naked, save it were a skin which was girded about their loins; yea, all were naked, save it were the Zoramites and the Amalekites;

21 But they were not armed with breastplates, nor shields—therefore, they were exceedingly afraid of the armies of the Nephites because of their armor,

---

43:11 (9–11) Why were the Nephites willing to fight against the Lamanites? What would you be willing to defend even at the risk of losing your life?

43:12 ***suffer***—allow
***for their inheritance***—to live in

43:13 ***substance***—food and other supplies
***compelled***—forced
***a compound***—the combined children
***dissented from***—turned against
***descendants***—children, grandchildren, great-grandchildren, and so on

43:14 ***obliged***—forced

43:16 ***command***—leadership

43:20 ***girded about their loins***—tied around their waists

*These ancient Roman breastplates and shields illustrate what may have been used by the Nephites for defense in battles.*

notwithstanding their number being so much greater than the Nephites.
22 Behold, now it came to pass that they durst not come against the Nephites in the borders of Jershon; therefore they departed out of the land of Antionum into the wilderness, and took their journey round about in the wilderness, away by the head of the river Sidon, that they might come into the land of Manti and take possession of the land; for they did not suppose that the armies of Moroni would know whither they had gone.
23 But it came to pass, as soon as they had departed into the wilderness Moroni sent spies into the wilderness to watch their camp; and Moroni, also, knowing of the prophecies of Alma, sent certain men unto him, desiring him that he should inquire of the Lord whither the armies of the Nephites should go to defend themselves against the Lamanites.
24 And it came to pass that the word of the Lord came unto Alma, and Alma informed the messengers of Moroni, that the armies of the Lamanites were marching round about in the wilderness, that they might come over into the land of Manti, that they might commence an attack upon the weaker part of the people. And those messengers went and delivered the message unto Moroni.
25 Now Moroni, leaving a part of his army in the land of Jershon, lest by any means a part of the Lamanites should come into that land and take possession of the city, took the remaining part of his army and marched over into the land of Manti.
26 And he caused that all the people in that quarter of the land should gather themselves together to battle against the Lamanites, to defend their lands and their country, their rights and their liberties; therefore they were prepared against the time of the coming of the Lamanites.
27 And it came to pass that Moroni caused that his army should be secreted in the valley which was near the bank of the river Sidon, which was on the west of the river Sidon in the wilderness.
28 And Moroni placed spies round about, that he might know when the camp of the Lamanites should come.

## The Lamanites Are Caught Between Two Nephite Armies

29 And now, as Moroni knew the intention of the Lamanites, that it was their intention to destroy their brethren, or to subject them and bring them into bondage that they might establish a kingdom unto themselves over all the land;
30 And he also knowing that it was the only desire of the Nephites to preserve their lands, and their liberty, and their church, therefore he thought it no sin that he should defend them by stratagem; therefore, he found by his spies which course the Lamanites were to take.
31 Therefore, he divided his army and brought a part over into the valley, and concealed them on the east, and on the south of the hill Riplah;
32 And the remainder he concealed in the west valley, on the west of the river Sidon, and so down into the borders of the land Manti.
33 And thus having placed his army according to his desire, he was prepared to meet them.
34 And it came to pass that the Lamanites came up on the north of the hill, where a part of the army of Moroni was concealed.
35 And as the Lamanites had passed the hill

---

43:22 ***durst***—dared
***whither***—where

43:24 ***informed***—told
***commence***—begin

43:25 ***lest by any means***—in case somehow

43:26 ***quarter***—part

43:27 ***secreted***—hidden

43:29 ***intention***—desire or plan
***subject***—capture
***establish***—organize or set up

43:30 ***stratagem***—trickery or plan
***course***—way

43:30 (29–30) "In the ensuing battle, Captain Moroni commanded the Nephite armies in war for the first time. He introduced the first known example of military strategy in the Book of Mormon as he entrapped and surrounded the Lamanite–Zoramite army. Moroni also introduced body armor into Nephite warfare for the first time. Yet despite the superiority of Moroni's tactics and equipment, he still relied on the Lord" (Orson Scott Card, "Dissent and Treason," 55).

43:31 ***concealed***—hid

Riplah, and came into the valley, and began to cross
the river Sidon, the army which was concealed on
the south of the hill, which was led by a man
whose name was Lehi, and he led his army forth
and encircled the Lamanites about on the east in
their rear.
36 And it came to pass that the Lamanites, when
they saw the Nephites coming upon them in their
rear, turned them about and began to contend with
the army of Lehi.
37 And the work of death commenced on both
sides, but it was more dreadful on the part of the
Lamanites, for their nakedness was exposed to the
heavy blows of the Nephites with their swords and
their cimeters, which brought death almost at every
stroke.
38 While on the other hand, there was now and
then a man fell among the Nephites, by their
swords and the loss of blood, they being shielded
from the more vital parts of the body, or the more
vital parts of the body being shielded from the
strokes of the Lamanites, by their breastplates, and
their armshields, and their head-plates; and thus the
Nephites did carry on the work of death among the
Lamanites.
39 And it came to pass that the Lamanites became
frightened, because of the great destruction among
them, even until they began to flee towards the
river Sidon.
40 And they were pursued by Lehi and his men;
and they were driven by Lehi into the waters of
Sidon, and they crossed the waters of Sidon. And
Lehi retained his armies upon the bank of the river
Sidon that they should not cross.
41 And it came to pass that Moroni and his army
met the Lamanites in the valley, on the other side
of the river Sidon, and began to fall upon them and
to slay them.
42 And the Lamanites did flee again before them,
towards the land of Manti; and they were met again
by the armies of Moroni.
43 Now in this case the Lamanites did fight
exceedingly; yea, never had the Lamanites been
known to fight with such exceedingly great strength
and courage, no, not even from the beginning.
44 And they were inspired by the Zoramites and
the Amalekites, who were their chief captains and
leaders, and by Zerahemnah, who was their chief
captain, or their chief leader and commander; yea,
they did fight like dragons, and many of the
Nephites were slain by their hands, yea, for they
did smite in two many of their head-plates, and
they did pierce many of their breastplates, and they
did smite off many of their arms; and thus the
Lamanites did smite in their fierce anger.

## *The Nephites Fight for a Better Cause and Rely upon the Lord for Help*

45 Nevertheless, the Nephites were inspired by a
better cause, for they were not fighting for monarchy nor power but they were fighting for their
homes and their liberties, their wives and their children, and their all, yea, for their rites of worship
and their church.
46 And they were doing that which they felt was
the duty which they owed to their God; for the
Lord had said unto them, and also unto their
fathers, that: Inasmuch as ye are not guilty of the
first offense, neither the second, ye shall not suffer yourselves to be slain by the hands of your
enemies.
47 And again, the Lord has said that: Ye shall
defend your families even unto bloodshed.
Therefore for this cause were the Nephites contending with the Lamanites, to defend themselves,
and their families, and their lands, their country,
and their rights, and their religion.

---

43:36 ***contend***—fight

43:38 ***shielded***—protected

The "more vital parts" of your body are your head, chest, and stomach. Wounds to these areas are the most serious and the most likely to result in death.

43:40 ***retained***—kept

43:44 ***smite***—cut
***pierce***—cut through

43:45 ***for monarchy***—for a king or queen

43:46 ***offense***—attack

43:47 (45–47) As the Lord's people, we seek for peace and hate war. However, "it is appropriate and sometimes required to take up arms in defense of one's family, religion, and freedom" (*Encyclopedia of Mormonism,* s.v. "War and Peace," 4:1547).

48 And it came to pass that when the men of Moroni saw the fierceness and the anger of the Lamanites, they were about to shrink and flee from them. And Moroni, perceiving their intent, sent forth and inspired their hearts with these thoughts—yea, the thoughts of their lands, their liberty, yea, their freedom from bondage.

49 And it came to pass that they turned upon the Lamanites, and they cried with one voice unto the Lord their God, for their liberty and their freedom from bondage.

50 And they began to stand against the Lamanites with power; and in that selfsame hour that they cried unto the Lord for their freedom, the Lamanites began to flee before them; and they fled even to the waters of Sidon.

51 Now, the Lamanites were more numerous, yea, by more than double the number of the Nephites; nevertheless, they were driven insomuch that they were gathered together in one body in the valley, upon the bank by the river Sidon.

52 Therefore the armies of Moroni encircled them about, yea, even on both sides of the river, for behold, on the east were the men of Lehi.

53 Therefore when Zerahemnah saw the men of Lehi on the east of the river Sidon, and the armies of Moroni on the west of the river Sidon, that they were encircled about by the Nephites, they were struck with terror.

54 Now Moroni, when he saw their terror, commanded his men that they should stop shedding their blood.

## CHAPTER 44

*Zerahemnah refuses Moroni's peace treaty, and his army is defeated. Find in this chapter how the righteous feel about war and the shedding of blood.*

### Moroni Offers Peace

1 AND it came to pass that they did stop and withdrew a pace from them. And Moroni said unto Zerahemnah: Behold, Zerahemnah, that we do not desire to be men of blood. Ye know that ye are in our hands, yet we do not desire to slay you.

2 Behold, we have not come out to battle against you that we might shed your blood for power; neither do we desire to bring any one to the yoke of bondage. But this is the very cause for which ye have come against us; yea, and ye are angry with us because of our religion.

3 But now, ye behold that the Lord is with us; and ye behold that he has delivered you into our hands. And now I would that ye should understand that this is done unto us because of our religion and our faith in Christ. And now ye see that ye cannot destroy this our faith.

4 Now ye see that this is the true faith of God; yea, ye see that God will support, and keep, and preserve us, so long as we are faithful unto him, and unto our faith, and our religion; and never will the Lord suffer that we shall be destroyed except we should fall into transgression and deny our faith.

---

43:48 ***perceiving***—seeing or understanding

43:54 Moroni stopped the fighting when he saw that he could destroy the Lamanites. What does that tell you about the kind of man he was and why he went to battle?

44:1 ***withdrew a pace***—backed away a step
***of blood***—who kill

44:2 Zerahemnah and his people were angry with Moroni's people because of their religion. Why do you think people get angry over religion? Why is it important to respect other religions?

44:3 Frequently in the Book of Mormon the Lord spares the righteous and delivers their enemies into their hands, or allows the righteous to capture their enemies. Here Moroni follows the Lord's law of proclaiming peace to enemies, even to those who fight against His people (see D&C 98:23–35).

PHOTOGRAPH BY SCOT FACER PROCTOR

*This beautiful valley south of Coban, Guatemala, may be similar to the valley where Moroni and his army met the Lamanites.*

5 And now, Zerahemnah, I command you, in the
name of that all-powerful God, who has strengthened our arms that we have gained power over
you, by our faith, by our religion, and by our rites
of worship, and by our church, and by the sacred
support which we owe to our wives and our children, by that liberty which binds us to our lands
and our country; yea, and also by the maintenance
of the sacred word of God, to which we owe all our
happiness; and by all that is most dear unto us—
6 Yea, and this is not all; I command you by all
the desires which ye have for life, that ye deliver up
your weapons of war unto us, and we will seek not
your blood, but we will spare your lives, if ye will
go your way and come not again to war against us.
7 And now, if ye do not this, behold, ye are in our
hands, and I will command my men that they shall
fall upon you, and inflict the wounds of death in
your bodies, that ye may become extinct; and then
we will see who shall have power over this people;
yea, we will see who shall be brought into bondage.

## Zerahemnah Refuses Peace

8 And now it came to pass that when Zerahemnah
had heard these sayings he came forth and delivered up his sword and his cimeter, and his bow into
the hands of Moroni, and said unto him: Behold,
here are our weapons of war; we will deliver them
up unto you, but we will not suffer ourselves to
take an oath unto you, which we know that we
shall break, and also our children; but take our
weapons of war, and suffer that we may depart into
the wilderness; otherwise we will retain our
swords, and we will perish or conquer.
9 Behold, we are not of your faith; we do not
believe that it is God that has delivered us into your
hands; but we believe that it is your cunning that
has preserved you from our swords. Behold, it is
your breastplates and your shields that have preserved you.
10 And now when Zerahemnah had made an end
of speaking these words, Moroni returned the
sword and the weapons of war, which he had
received, unto Zerahemnah, saying: Behold, we
will end the conflict.
11 Now I cannot recall the words which I have
spoken, therefore as the Lord liveth, ye shall not
depart except ye depart with an oath that ye will
not return again against us to war. Now as ye are in
our hands we will spill your blood upon the
ground, or ye shall submit to the conditions which
I have proposed.
12 And now when Moroni had said these words,
Zerahemnah retained his sword, and he was angry
with Moroni, and he rushed forward that he might
slay Moroni; but as he raised his sword, behold,
one of Moroni's soldiers smote it even to the earth,
and it broke by the hilt; and he also smote
Zerahemnah that he took off his scalp and it fell to
the earth. And Zerahemnah withdrew from before
them into the midst of his soldiers.
13 And it came to pass that the soldier who stood
by, who smote off the scalp of Zerahemnah, took
up the scalp from off the ground by the hair, and
laid it upon the point of his sword, and stretched it
forth unto them, saying unto them with a loud
voice:
14 Even as this scalp has fallen to the earth, which
is the scalp of your chief, so shall ye fall to the earth
except ye will deliver up your weapons of war and
depart with a covenant of peace.

---

44:5 Moroni said that God "strengthened [their] arms," or made his people stronger in war. This means that the Nephites' power came from the Lord. How has the Lord strengthened and helped you to overcome your challenges?

***rites***—ordinances or ceremonies
***binds***—ties

44:6 ***deliver***—surrender

44:7 ***become extinct***—die

44:8 Making or taking oaths is a most serious matter. Elder Bruce R. McConkie wrote that "the taking of oaths was an approved and formal part of the religious lives of the people. . . . These statements, usually made in the name of the Lord, by people who valued their religion and their word above their lives, could be and were relied upon with absolute assurance" *(Doctrinal New Testament Commentary* 3:163).

44:9 ***cunning***—planning

44:11 ***recall***—take back
***submit to the conditions***—follow the plan or offer
***proposed***—suggested

44:12 ***retained***—kept
***hilt***—handle

15 Now there were many, when they heard these words and saw the scalp which was upon the sword, that were struck with fear; and many came forth and threw down their weapons of war at the feet of Moroni, and entered into a covenant of peace. And as many as entered into a covenant they suffered to depart into the wilderness.
16 Now it came to pass that Zerahemnah was exceedingly wroth, and he did stir up the remainder of his soldiers to anger, to contend more powerfully against the Nephites.

## Moroni's Army Defeats Zerahemnah's Army

17 And now Moroni was angry, because of the stubbornness of the Lamanites; therefore he commanded his people that they should fall upon them and slay them. And it came to pass that they began to slay them; yea, and the Lamanites did contend with their swords and their might.
18 But behold, their naked skins and their bare heads were exposed to the sharp swords of the Nephites; yea, behold they were pierced and smitten, yea, and did fall exceedingly fast before the swords of the Nephites; and they began to be swept down, even as the soldier of Moroni had prophesied.
19 Now Zerahemnah, when he saw that they were all about to be destroyed, cried mightily unto Moroni, promising that he would covenant and also his people with them, if they would spare the remainder of their lives, that they never would come to war again against them.
20 And it came to pass that Moroni caused that the work of death should cease again among the people. And he took the weapons of war from the Lamanites; and after they had entered into a covenant with him of peace they were suffered to depart into the wilderness.
21 Now the number of their dead was not numbered because of the greatness of the number; yea, the number of their dead was exceedingly great, both on the Nephites and on the Lamanites.
22 And it came to pass that they did cast their dead into the waters of Sidon, and they have gone forth and are buried in the depths of the sea.
23 And the armies of the Nephites, or of Moroni, returned and came to their houses and their lands.
24 And thus ended the eighteenth year of the reign of the judges over the people of Nephi. And thus ended the record of Alma, which was written upon the plates of Nephi.

*The account of the people of Nephi, and their wars and dissensions, in the days of Helaman, according to the record of Helaman, which he kept in his days. Comprising chapters 45 to 62 inclusive.**

# CHAPTER 45

*This chapter contains Alma's final words to his son Helaman. Helaman is a righteous man who listens to and obeys his father's counsel. Look for what Alma prophesies about the Nephites.*

## Helaman Believes in Jesus Christ and Is Willing to Keep His Commandments

1 BEHOLD, now it came to pass that the people of Nephi were exceedingly rejoiced, because the Lord had again delivered them out of the hands of their enemies; therefore they gave thanks unto the Lord their God; yea, and they did fast much and pray much, and they did worship God with exceedingly great joy.
2 And it came to pass in the nineteenth year of the reign of the judges over the people of Nephi, that Alma came unto his son Helaman and said unto him: Believest thou the words which I spake unto thee concerning those records which have been kept?

---

44:16 ***wroth***—angry

44:17 ***contend***—fight

44:18 ***pierced and smitten***—cut with swords and killed

44:19 Zerahemnah surrenders when he sees that he is about to lose his life. Many lives would have been spared if he had surrendered earlier. How did Zerahemnah's pride hurt his people? How can pride hurt you or others?

44:20 ***cease***—stop

* The first sentence of this introduction to chapters 45–62 was translated from the Book of Mormon plates.

45:1 ***exceedingly rejoiced***—very happy

These people prayed, fasted, and worshiped to show their gratitude to God. What blessings have come to you from the Lord? How have you shown Him that you are thankful?

3 And Helaman said unto him: Yea, I believe.
4 And Alma said again: Believest thou in Jesus Christ, who shall come?
5 And he said: Yea, I believe all the words which thou hast spoken.
6 And Alma said unto him again: Will ye keep my commandments?
7 And he said: Yea, I will keep thy commandments with all my heart.
8 Then Alma said unto him: Blessed art thou; and the Lord shall prosper thee in this land.

## Alma Prophesies of the Destruction of the Nephites

9 But behold, I have somewhat to prophesy unto thee; but what I prophesy unto thee ye shall not make known; yea, what I prophesy unto thee shall not be made known, even until the prophecy is fulfilled; therefore write the words which I shall say.
10 And these are the words: Behold, I perceive that this very people, the Nephites, according to the spirit of revelation which is in me, in four hundred years from the time that Jesus Christ shall manifest himself unto them, shall dwindle in unbelief.
11 Yea, and then shall they see wars and pestilences, yea, famines and bloodshed, even until the people of Nephi shall become extinct—
12 Yea, and this because they shall dwindle in unbelief and fall into the works of darkness, and lasciviousness, and all manner of iniquities; yea, I say unto you, that because they shall sin against so great light and knowledge, yea, I say unto you, that from that day, even the fourth generation shall not all pass away before this great iniquity shall come.
13 And when that great day cometh, behold, the time very soon cometh that those who are now, or the seed of those who are now numbered among the people of Nephi, shall no more be numbered among the people of Nephi.
14 But whosoever remaineth, and is not destroyed in that great and dreadful day, shall be numbered among the Lamanites, and shall become like unto them, all, save it be a few who shall be called the disciples of the Lord; and them shall the Lamanites pursue even until they shall become extinct. And now, because of iniquity, this prophecy shall be fulfilled.

## Alma Gives a Final Blessing to His Children

15 And now it came to pass that after Alma had said these things to Helaman, he blessed him, and also his other sons; and he also blessed the earth for the righteous' sake.
16 And he said: Thus saith the Lord God—Cursed shall be the land, yea, this land, unto every nation, kindred, tongue, and people, unto destruction, which do wickedly, when they are fully ripe; and as I have said so shall it be; for this is the cursing and the blessing of God upon the land, for the Lord cannot look upon sin with the least degree of allowance.

---

45:8 ***prosper***—bless

45:8 (1–8) Alma gives us a great example by interviewing his son Helaman. "This short, informative, and inspiring interview must have pleased Alma greatly. Not only had he communicated heart-to-heart and soul-to-soul with his son, but the son had openly declared his faith and pledged his devotion" (Carlos E. Asay, *Family Pecan Trees: Planting a Legacy of Faith at Home,* 80).

45:8 (6–8) The fifth of the Ten Commandments is: "Honour thy father and thy mother: that thy days may be long upon the land which the Lord thy God giveth thee" (Exodus 20:12). Helaman followed this commandment and was blessed.

45:10 ***perceive***—know
***dwindle in unbelief***—fall away from the truth

45:11 ***pestilences***—terrible diseases
***become extinct***—all die or be killed

45:12 ***lasciviousness***—immorality and unchastity

Alma prophesied that great destructions would come upon the Nephites because they would sin against so much light. This greater light comes when Christ ministers among the people personally. The Lord has said that those who sin against the greater light "shall receive the greater condemnation" (D&C 82:3).

45:14 One disciple who remained faithful to the end of the Nephite civilization was Moroni. Concerning the Lamanites' hatred of the Nephites in his day, he wrote that "they put to death every Nephite that will not deny the Christ. And I, Moroni, will not deny the Christ" (Moroni 1:2–3).

45:15 Have you ever received a priesthood blessing? How did it help you? How do you think Alma's blessings helped his children?

45:16 The Lord cannot look upon sin with "the least degree of allowance." Therefore, every sin has a punishment. But He also says, "He that repents and does the commandments of the Lord shall be forgiven" (D&C 1:32).

17 And now, when Alma had said these words he blessed the church, yea, all those who should stand fast in the faith from that time henceforth.
18 And when Alma had done this he departed out of the land of Zarahemla, as if to go into the land of Melek. And it came to pass that he was never heard of more; as to his death or burial we know not of.
19 Behold, this we know, that he was a righteous man; and the saying went abroad in the church that he was taken up by the Spirit, or buried by the hand of the Lord, even as Moses. But behold, the scriptures saith the Lord took Moses unto himself; and we suppose that he has also received Alma in the spirit, unto himself; therefore, for this cause we know nothing concerning his death and burial.

## Helaman Begins to Teach and Call the People to Repentance

20 And now it came to pass in the commencement of the nineteenth year of the reign of the judges over the people of Nephi, that Helaman went forth among the people to declare the word unto them.
21 For behold, because of their wars with the Lamanites and the many little dissensions and disturbances which had been among the people, it became expedient that the word of God should be declared among them, yea, and that a regulation should be made throughout the church.
22 Therefore, Helaman and his brethren went forth to establish the church again in all the land, yea, in every city throughout all the land which was possessed by the people of Nephi. And it came to pass that they did appoint priests and teachers throughout all the land, over all the churches.
23 And now it came to pass that after Helaman and his brethren had appointed priests and teachers over the churches that there arose a dissension among them, and they would not give heed to the words of Helaman and his brethren;
24 But they grew proud, being lifted up in their hearts, because of their exceedingly great riches; therefore they grew rich in their own eyes, and would not give heed to their words, to walk uprightly before God.

# CHAPTER 46

*Amalickiah tries to overthrow the government and the Church of God. Moroni inspires his people to fight for freedom. Look for why the wicked go to war and how their reasons are so different from the reasons why the righteous go to war.*

## Amalickiah Wants to Be King

1 AND it came to pass that as many as would not hearken to the words of Helaman and his brethren were gathered together against their brethren.
2 And now behold, they were exceedingly wroth, insomuch that they were determined to slay them.
3 Now the leader of those who were wroth against their brethren was a large and a strong man; and his name was Amalickiah.

---

45:19 (17–19) Joseph Fielding Smith wrote, "It is a very reasonable thought to believe that both Moses and Alma, like Elijah and John, were translated to accomplish some work which the Lord had in store for them at some future day" *(Answers to Gospel Questions* 5:38).

45:21 ***dissensions and disturbances***—arguments, disagreements, and fighting
***regulation***—set of rules and laws

45:24 "Most of us think of pride as self-centeredness, conceit, boastfulness, arrogance, or haughtiness. All of these are elements of the sin, but the heart, or core, is still missing. The central feature of pride is enmity—enmity toward God and enmity toward our fellowmen. *Enmity* means 'hatred toward, hostility to, or a state of opposition.' It is the power by which Satan wishes to reign over us" (Ezra Taft Benson, in Conference Report, April 1989, 3).

45:24 (22–24) The people did not heed or obey the words of the priests and teachers in the Church. They would not follow the gospel because of pride. What causes some people to fall away from the Church today? What can you do to help protect yourself from falling away from the gospel of Jesus Christ?

46:2 ***wroth***—angry

4 And Amalickiah was desirous to be a king; and those people who were wroth were also desirous that he should be their king; and they were the greater part of them the lower judges of the land, and they were seeking for power.

5 And they had been led by the flatteries of Amalickiah, that if they would support him and establish him to be their king that he would make them rulers over the people.

6 Thus they were led away by Amalickiah to dissensions, notwithstanding the preaching of Helaman and his brethren, yea, notwithstanding their exceedingly great care over the church, for they were high priests over the church.

7 And there were many in the church who believed in the flattering words of Amalickiah, therefore they dissented even from the church; and thus were the affairs of the people of Nephi exceedingly precarious and dangerous, notwithstanding their great victory which they had had over the Lamanites, and their great rejoicings which they had had because of their deliverance by the hand of the Lord.

8 Thus we see how quick the children of men do forget the Lord their God, yea, how quick to do iniquity, and to be led away by the evil one.

9 Yea, and we also see the great wickedness one very wicked man can cause to take place among the children of men.

10 Yea, we see that Amalickiah, because he was a man of cunning device and a man of many flattering words, that he led away the hearts of many people to do wickedly; yea, and to seek to destroy the church of God, and to destroy the foundation of liberty which God had granted unto them, or which blessing God had sent upon the face of the land for the righteous' sake.

## Captain Moroni Raises the Title of Liberty

11 And now it came to pass that when Moroni, who was the chief commander of the armies of the Nephites, had heard of these dissensions, he was angry with Amalickiah.

12 And it came to pass that he rent his coat; and he took a piece thereof, and wrote upon it—In memory of our God, our religion, and freedom, and our peace, our wives, and our children—and he fastened it upon the end of a pole.

13 And he fastened on his head-plate, and his breastplate, and his shields, and girded on his armor about his loins; and he took the pole, which had on the end thereof his rent coat, (and he called it the title of liberty) and he bowed himself to the earth, and he prayed mightily unto his God for the blessings of liberty to rest upon his brethren, so long as there should a band of Christians remain to possess the land—

14 For thus were all the true believers of Christ, who belonged to the church of God, called by those who did not belong to the church.

---

46:4 Amalickiah was a wicked man who sought for power because of pride. On the other hand, "men and women of Christ magnify their callings without magnifying themselves" (Neal A. Maxwell, in Conference Report, October 1990, 18).

46:5 ***flatteries***—lies and false promises

46:6 ***dissensions***—arguing and fighting

46:7 ***dissented***—fell away
***precarious***—unstable

46:10 ***cunning device***—clever trickery

The Lord promised Lehi that the Americas would be a land of liberty (freedom) for his children as long as they were righteous (see 2 Nephi 1:7–11). Amalickiah's wicked plans to become a king and destroy the Church would have also destroyed the freedom God had given them.

46:10 (8–10) Whenever you see words like "Thus we see," the prophet wants you to notice an important lesson. These verses show us how quickly one wicked man can lead people into sin. Have you seen any examples of this truth in your own community or country? What could you do to avoid being led away into sin by clever but wicked people?

46:12 ***rent***—ripped

"The value of a country rests upon the values of its people. For the people of God, for the people who want peace, for their women and their children, there is only one way, one church, and one Lord" (Charles Didier, in Conference Report, April 1976, 133).

46:13 ***loins***—waist area

Captain Moroni put on his armor in preparation for battle against wicked Amalickiah. The Lord tells us to put on God's "whole armor" to protect us in our fight against evil. For a description of what God's armor is like, see D&C 27:15–18 and Ephesians 6:11–18.

CAPTAIN MORONI AND THE TITLE OF LIBERTY, BY CLARK KELLEY PRICE

*Moroni raises the title of liberty.*

15 And those who did belong to the church were faithful; yea, all those who were true believers in Christ took upon them, gladly, the name of Christ, or Christians as they were called, because of their belief in Christ who should come.

16 And therefore, at this time, Moroni prayed that the cause of the Christians, and the freedom of the land might be favored.

17 And it came to pass that when he had poured out his soul to God, he named all the land which was south of the land Desolation, yea, and in fine, all the land, both on the north and on the south—A chosen land, and the land of liberty.

18 And he said: Surely God shall not suffer that we, who are despised because we take upon us the name of Christ, shall be trodden down and destroyed, until we bring it upon us by our own transgressions.

## The Righteous Covenant to Uphold Their Freedom and the Church of God

19 And when Moroni had said these words, he went forth among the people, waving the rent part of his garment in the air, that all might see the writing which he had written upon the rent part, and crying with a loud voice, saying:

20 Behold, whosoever will maintain this title upon the land, let them come forth in the strength of the Lord, and enter into a covenant that they will maintain their rights, and their religion, that the Lord God may bless them.

21 And it came to pass that when Moroni had proclaimed these words, behold, the people came running together with their armor girded about their loins, rending their garments in token, or as a covenant, that they would not forsake the Lord their God; or, in other words, if they should transgress the commandments of God, or fall into transgression, and be ashamed to take upon them the name of Christ, the Lord should rend them even as they had rent their garments.

22 Now this was the covenant which they made, and they cast their garments at the feet of Moroni, saying: We covenant with our God, that we shall be destroyed, even as our brethren in the land northward, if we shall fall into transgression; yea, he may cast us at the feet of our enemies, even as we have cast our garments at thy feet to be trodden under foot, if we shall fall into transgression.

## Moroni Inspires His People to Fight for Their Freedom, and Amalickiah Flees

23 Moroni said unto them: Behold, we are a remnant of the seed of Jacob; yea, we are a remnant of the seed of Joseph, whose coat was rent by his brethren into many pieces; yea, and now behold, let us remember to keep the commandments of God, or our garments shall be rent by our brethren, and we be cast into prison, or be sold, or be slain.

24 Yea, let us preserve our liberty as a remnant of Joseph; yea, let us remember the words of Jacob, before his death, for behold, he saw that a part of the remnant of the coat of Joseph was preserved and had not decayed. And he said—Even as this remnant of garment of my son hath been preserved, so shall a remnant of the seed of my son be preserved by the hand of God, and be taken unto himself, while the remainder of the seed of Joseph shall perish, even as the remnant of his garment.

25 Now behold, this giveth my soul sorrow; nevertheless, my soul hath joy in my son, because of that part of his seed which shall be taken unto God.

---

46:18 ***suffer***—allow
***despised***—hated
***trodden down***—trampled

46:19 ***garment***—clothing

46:20 ***maintain***—uphold or support

46:21 ***rending their garments in token***—tearing their clothing as a sign
***forsake***—turn away from

46:22 (20–22) What are some of the blessings you have received from keeping the covenants you have made with Heavenly Father?

46:23 ***remnant***—remaining part

The story of Joseph's coat being torn into pieces when he was sold into slavery by his brothers is found in Genesis 37.

46:25 (24–25) This prophecy of Jacob is found only here in the Book of Mormon; it is missing from the Bible. Jacob testified that the preserved part of the coat represented a part of Joseph's descendants that would never be destroyed. President Joseph Fielding Smith taught that the Lamanites are part of the descendants of Joseph that were preserved, and that they "shall eventually partake of the blessings of the Gospel. They shall unite with the remnant which is being gathered from among the nations and they shall be blessed of the Lord forever" (*The Way to Perfection,* 121).

26 Now behold, this was the language of Jacob.
27 And now who knoweth but what the remnant of the seed of Joseph, which shall perish as his garment, are those who have dissented from us? Yea, and even it shall be ourselves if we do not stand fast in the faith of Christ.
28 And now it came to pass that when Moroni had said these words he went forth, and also sent forth in all the parts of the land where there were dissensions, and gathered together all the people who were desirous to maintain their liberty, to stand against Amalickiah and those who had dissented, who were called Amalickiahites.
29 And it came to pass that when Amalickiah saw that the people of Moroni were more numerous than the Amalickiahites—and he also saw that his people were doubtful concerning the justice of the cause in which they had undertaken—therefore, fearing that he should not gain the point, he took those of his people who would and departed into the land of Nephi.
30 Now Moroni thought it was not expedient that the Lamanites should have any more strength; therefore he thought to cut off the people of Amalickiah, or to take them and bring them back, and put Amalickiah to death; yea, for he knew that he would stir up the Lamanites to anger against them, and cause them to come to battle against them; and this he knew that Amalickiah would do that he might obtain his purposes.
31 Therefore Moroni thought it was expedient that he should take his armies, who had gathered themselves together, and armed themselves, and entered into a covenant to keep the peace—and it came to pass that he took his army and marched out with his tents into the wilderness, to cut off the course of Amalickiah in the wilderness.
32 And it came to pass that he did according to his desires, and marched forth into the wilderness, and headed the armies of Amalickiah.
33 And it came to pass that Amalickiah fled with a small number of his men, and the remainder were delivered up into the hands of Moroni and were taken back into the land of Zarahemla.

## *Moroni Establishes Peace Again in the Land*

34 Now, Moroni being a man who was appointed by the chief judges and the voice of the people, therefore he had power according to his will with the armies of the Nephites, to establish and to exercise authority over them.
35 And it came to pass that whomsoever of the Amalickiahites that would not enter into a covenant to support the cause of freedom, that they might maintain a free government, he caused to be put to death; and there were but few who denied the covenant of freedom.
36 And it came to pass also, that he caused the title of liberty to be hoisted upon every tower which was in all the land, which was possessed by the Nephites; and thus Moroni planted the standard of liberty among the Nephites.
37 And they began to have peace again in the land; and thus they did maintain peace in the land until nearly the end of the nineteenth year of the reign of the judges.
38 And Helaman and the high priests did also maintain order in the church; yea, even for the space of four years did they have much peace and rejoicing in the church.

---

46:27 *Stand fast* in Hebrew is *'aman,* which means to be faithful. We get the modern word *amen* from this word (see James Strong, *Dictionary of the Hebrew Bible,* word numbers 539, 543).

46:30 ***expedient***—wise or helpful

46:33 (29–33) Moroni had more courage than Amalickiah because he was fighting for truth and righteousness instead of lies and wickedness. Have you ever felt the courage that comes from knowing you are standing up for the truth?

46:34 ***exercise authority over***—give commands to

46:36 ***hoisted***—raised
***standard***—banner or flag

"We, as Latter-day Saints, should resolve to hold high our modern-day 'title of liberty' in memory of our God and our religion, our fathers and our mothers, our flag, and our country (see Alma 46:12, 36). We can honor through our lives the thousands who died crossing the plains and in the valleys and settlements. The spiritual values for which they died should ever be lodged in our hearts. We will carry the torch of faith which they bequeathed [gave] to us to light the way for those who follow" (Vaughn J. Featherstone, 10).

39 And it came to pass that there were many who
died, firmly believing that their souls were
redeemed by the Lord Jesus Christ; thus they went
out of the world rejoicing.
40 And there were some who died with fevers,
which at some seasons of the year were very frequent in the land—but not so much so with fevers,
because of the excellent qualities of the many
plants and roots which God had prepared to
remove the cause of diseases, to which men were
subject by the nature of the climate—
41 But there were many who died with old age;
and those who died in the faith of Christ are happy
in him, as we must needs suppose.

## CHAPTER 47

*Amalickiah, through lies and murder, gains power among the Lamanites and leads them against the Nephites. As you read, look for the evil plan that Amalickiah uses to gain power, and notice how the wicked acts of one person cause trials for others.*

### Amalickiah Is Given Authority over the Lamanite Army

1 NOW we will return in our record to Amalickiah
and those who had fled with him into the wilderness; for, behold, he had taken those who went
with him, and went up in the land of Nephi among
the Lamanites, and did stir up the Lamanites to
anger against the people of Nephi, insomuch that
the king of the Lamanites sent a proclamation
throughout all his land, among all his people, that
they should gather themselves together again to go
to battle against the Nephites.
2 And it came to pass that when the proclamation
had gone forth among them they were exceedingly
afraid; yea, they feared to displease the king, and
they also feared to go to battle against the Nephites
lest they should lose their lives. And it came to pass
that they would not, or the more part of them
would not, obey the commandments of the king.
3 And now it came to pass that the king was
wroth because of their disobedience; therefore he
gave Amalickiah the command of that part of his
army which was obedient unto his commands, and
commanded him that he should go forth and compel them to arms.

### Amalickiah Plans to Dethrone the King

4 Now behold, this was the desire of Amalickiah;
for he being a very subtle man to do evil therefore
he laid the plan in his heart to dethrone the king of
the Lamanites.
5 And now he had got the command of those parts
of the Lamanites who were in favor of the king; and
he sought to gain favor of those who were not obedient; therefore he went forward to the place which
was called Onidah, for thither had all the Lamanites
fled; for they discovered the army coming, and, supposing that they were coming to destroy them,
therefore they fled to Onidah, to the place of arms.
6 And they had appointed a man to be a king and
a leader over them, being fixed in their minds with
a determined resolution that they would not be
subjected to go against the Nephites.
7 And it came to pass that they had gathered
themselves together upon the top of the mount
which was called Antipas, in preparation to battle.
8 Now it was not Amalickiah's intention to give
them battle according to the commandments of the
king; but behold, it was his intention to gain favor
with the armies of the Lamanites, that he might
place himself at their head and dethrone the king
and take possession of the kingdom.
9 And behold, it came to pass that he caused his
army to pitch their tents in the valley which was
near the mount Antipas.

---

47:1 ***a proclamation***—an order

47:2 ***lest***—in case

The Lamanites did not want to go to battle against the Nephites, but they also did not want to displease the king. Have you ever been in a situation where you wanted to do the right thing but were afraid you might displease someone? Why is it always better to do the right thing than to worry about what others will think of you?

47:3 ***compel them to arms***—force them to fight

47:4 ***subtle***—quietly dishonest or tricky
***laid***—thought of
***dethrone***—remove from the throne or kingship

47:6 ***appointed***—chosen
***resolution***—promise or decision
***subjected***—forced

47:8 ***intention***—plan

10 And it came to pass that when it was night he sent a secret embassy into the mount Antipas, desiring that the leader of those who were upon the mount, whose name was Lehonti, that he should come down to the foot of the mount, for he desired to speak with him.

11 And it came to pass that when Lehonti received the message he durst not go down to the foot of the mount. And it came to pass that Amalickiah sent again the second time, desiring him to come down. And it came to pass that Lehonti would not; and he sent again the third time.

12 And it came to pass that when Amalickiah found that he could not get Lehonti to come down off from the mount, he went up into the mount, nearly to Lehonti's camp; and he sent again the fourth time his message unto Lehonti, desiring that he would come down, and that he would bring his guards with him.

13 And it came to pass that when Lehonti had come down with his guards to Amalickiah, that Amalickiah desired him to come down with his army in the night-time, and surround those men in their camps over whom the king had given him command, and that he would deliver them up into Lehonti's hands, if he would make him (Amalickiah) a second leader over the whole army.

14 And it came to pass that Lehonti came down with his men and surrounded the men of Amalickiah, so that before they awoke at the dawn of day they were surrounded by the armies of Lehonti.

15 And it came to pass that when they saw that they were surrounded, they plead with Amalickiah that he would suffer them to fall in with their brethren, that they might not be destroyed. Now this was the very thing which Amalickiah desired.

16 And it came to pass that he delivered his men, contrary to the commands of the king. Now this was the thing that Amalickiah desired, that he might accomplish his designs in dethroning the king.

## *Amalickiah Gains Control of the Lamanite Army by Lying*

17 Now it was the custom among the Lamanites, if their chief leader was killed, to appoint the second leader to be their chief leader.

18 And it came to pass that Amalickiah caused that one of his servants should administer poison by degrees to Lehonti, that he died.

19 Now, when Lehonti was dead, the Lamanites appointed Amalickiah to be their leader and their chief commander.

20 And it came to pass that Amalickiah marched with his armies (for he had gained his desires) to the land of Nephi, to the city of Nephi, which was the chief city.

21 And the king came out to meet him with his guards, for he supposed that Amalickiah had fulfilled his commands, and that Amalickiah had gathered together so great an army to go against the Nephites to battle.

22 But behold, as the king came out to meet him Amalickiah caused that his servants should go forth to meet the king. And they went and bowed themselves before the king, as if to reverence him because of his greatness.

23 And it came to pass that the king put forth his hand to raise them, as was the custom with the Lamanites, as a token of peace, which custom they had taken from the Nephites.

24 And it came to pass that when he had raised the first from the ground, behold he stabbed the king to the heart; and he fell to the earth.

25 Now the servants of the king fled; and the servants of Amalickiah raised a cry, saying:

26 Behold, the servants of the king have stabbed him to the heart, and he has fallen and they have fled; behold, come and see.

27 And it came to pass that Amalickiah commanded that his armies should march forth and see what had happened to the king; and when they had

---

47:10 W ***embassy***—group of messengers

47:11 W ***durst***—dared

47:15 W ***fall in***—join

47:16 W ***contrary***—directly opposite
***designs***—plans

47:18 W ***by degrees***—in small doses

47:20 W ***chief***—most important

47:22 W ***reverence***—honor or show respect to

come to the spot, and found the king lying in his gore, Amalickiah pretended to be wroth, and said: Whosoever loved the king, let him go forth, and pursue his servants that they may be slain.
28 And it came to pass that all they who loved the king, when they heard these words, came forth and pursued after the servants of the king.
29 Now when the servants of the king saw an army pursuing after them, they were frightened again, and fled into the wilderness, and came over into the land of Zarahemla and joined the people of Ammon.
30 And the army which pursued after them returned, having pursued after them in vain; and thus Amalickiah, by his fraud, gained the hearts of the people.

## Amalickiah, Through Deception, Gains Control of the Entire Lamanite Kingdom

31 And it came to pass on the morrow he entered the city Nephi with his armies, and took possession of the city.
32 And now it came to pass that the queen, when she had heard that the king was slain—for Amalickiah had sent an embassy to the queen informing her that the king had been slain by his servants, that he had pursued them with his army, but it was in vain, and they had made their escape—
33 Therefore, when the queen had received this message she sent unto Amalickiah, desiring him that he would spare the people of the city; and she also desired him that he should come in unto her; and she also desired him that he should bring witnesses with him to testify concerning the death of the king.
34 And it came to pass that Amalickiah took the same servant that slew the king, and all them who were with him, and went in unto the queen, unto the place where she sat; and they all testified unto her that the king was slain by his own servants; and they said also: They have fled; does not this testify against them? And thus they satisfied the queen concerning the death of the king.
35 And it came to pass that Amalickiah sought the favor of the queen, and took her unto him to wife; and thus by his fraud, and by the assistance of his cunning servants, he obtained the kingdom; yea, he was acknowledged king throughout all the land, among all the people of the Lamanites, who were composed of the Lamanites and the Lemuelites and the Ishmaelites, and all the dissenters of the Nephites, from the reign of Nephi down to the present time.
36 Now these dissenters, having the same instruction and the same information of the Nephites, yea, having been instructed in the same knowledge of the Lord, nevertheless, it is strange to relate, not long after their dissensions they became more hardened and impenitent, and more wild, wicked and ferocious than the Lamanites—drinking in with the traditions of the Lamanites; giving way to indolence, and all manner of lasciviousness; yea, entirely forgetting the Lord their God.

---

47:27 ***gore***—blood
***slain***—killed

47:29 "Upon settling in the land of Jershon, the Lamanite converts—or the people of Anti-Nephi-Lehi, as they had chosen to call themselves (see Alma 24:1)—became designated by their Nephite neighbors as Ammonites, or the people of Ammon" (Joseph Fielding McConkie and others, *Doctrinal Commentary on the Book of Mormon* 3:189).

47:30 ***in vain***—without success
***fraud***—lying

47:30 (17–30) Amalickiah, like Cain of the Old Testament, was part of a secret organization that used murder to get gain (see Moses 5:31). These secret organizations are groups of people bound together by oaths to carry out evil purposes of the group (see Helaman 2:4–13).

47:34 ***slew***—killed

47:35 ***cunning***—tricky
***dissenters of the Nephites***—traitors who left the Nephites and joined the Lamanites
***reign***—rule

47:35 (34–35) Elder Joseph B. Wirthlin warned that there are people today who lie and deceive "to get gain or to profit, regardless of the injury, loss, or damage to others." He cautioned: "This attitude is totally contrary to the principles of the gospel. It hinders or thwarts the spiritual progress of anyone afflicted by it" (in Conference Report, April 1988, 94).

47:36 ***impenitent***—unrepentant
***ferocious***—fierce or brutal
***drinking in with***—joining in
***indolence***—laziness
***lasciviousness***—immorality

## CHAPTER 48

*The Nephites and Lamanites continue to prepare for war. Look for what is said about Moroni that would make him easy to follow as a leader.*

### Amalickiah's Desire for Power Causes War Between the Nephites and Lamanites

1 AND now it came to pass that, as soon as
Amalickiah had obtained the kingdom he began to
inspire the hearts of the Lamanites against the people
of Nephi; yea, he did appoint men to speak unto the
Lamanites from their towers, against the Nephites.
2 And thus he did inspire their hearts against the
Nephites, insomuch that in the latter end of the
nineteenth year of the reign of the judges, he having accomplished his designs thus far, yea, having
been made king over the Lamanites, he sought also
to reign over all the land, yea, and all the people
who were in the land, the Nephites as well as the
Lamanites.
3 Therefore he had accomplished his design, for
he had hardened the hearts of the Lamanites and
blinded their minds, and stirred them up to anger,
insomuch that he had gathered together a numerous host to go to battle against the Nephites.
4 For he was determined, because of the greatness
of the number of his people, to overpower the
Nephites and to bring them into bondage.
5 And thus he did appoint chief captains of the
Zoramites, they being the most acquainted with the
strength of the Nephites, and their places of resort,
and the weakest parts of their cities; therefore he
appointed them to be chief captains over his armies.
6 And it came to pass that they took their camp,
and moved forth toward the land of Zarahemla in
the wilderness.

### Moroni Prepares the Nephites for War with the Lamanites

7 Now it came to pass that while Amalickiah had
thus been obtaining power by fraud and deceit,
Moroni, on the other hand, had been preparing the
minds of the people to be faithful unto the Lord
their God.
8 Yea, he had been strengthening the armies of
the Nephites, and erecting small forts, or places of
resort; throwing up banks of earth round about to
enclose his armies, and also building walls of stone
to encircle them about, round about their cities and
the borders of their lands; yea, all round about the
land.
9 And in their weakest fortifications he did place
the greater number of men; and thus he did fortify
and strengthen the land which was possessed by
the Nephites.
10 And thus he was preparing to support their
liberty, their lands, their wives, and their children,
and their peace, and that they might live unto the
Lord their God, and that they might maintain that
which was called by their enemies the cause of
Christians.

### Moroni Rejoices in Liberty and Freedom

11 And Moroni was a strong and a mighty man; he
was a man of a perfect understanding; yea, a man
that did not delight in bloodshed; a man whose soul
did joy in the liberty and the freedom of his country, and his brethren from bondage and slavery;
12 Yea, a man whose heart did swell with thanksgiving to his God, for the many privileges and
blessings which he bestowed upon his people; a
man who did labor exceedingly for the welfare and
safety of his people.

---

48:1 ***obtained***—gotten power over

48:2 ***designs***—plans
***sought***—desired

Nearly one-third of the Book of Mormon is about wars between the Lamanites and Nephites. Why do you think there are so many chapters on war in the Book of Mormon?

48:3 ***hardened the hearts of the Lamanites***—closed the hearts of the Lamanites to the Spirit of the Lord

48:5 ***being the most acquainted with***—knowing best
***resort***—living or hiding

48:7 ***fraud and deceit***—tricks and lies

48:8 ***erecting***—building
***resort***—defense

48:9 ***fortifications***—forts

48:12 ***bestowed upon***—gave

13 Yea, and he was a man who was firm in the
faith of Christ, and he had sworn with an oath to
defend his people, his rights, and his country, and
his religion, even to the loss of his blood.
14 Now the Nephites were taught to defend themselves against their enemies, even to the shedding
of blood if it were necessary; yea, and they were
also taught never to give an offense, yea, and never
to raise the sword except it were against an enemy,
except it were to preserve their lives.
15 And this was their faith, that by so doing God
would prosper them in the land, or in other words,
if they were faithful in keeping the commandments
of God that he would prosper them in the land;
yea, warn them to flee, or to prepare for war,
according to their danger;
16 And also, that God would make it known unto
them whither they should go to defend themselves
against their enemies, and by so doing, the Lord
would deliver them; and this was the faith of
Moroni, and his heart did glory in it; not in the
shedding of blood but in doing good, in preserving
his people, yea, in keeping the commandments of
God, yea, and resisting iniquity.
17 Yea, verily, verily I say unto you, if all men had
been, and were, and ever would be, like unto
Moroni, behold, the very powers of hell would have
been shaken forever; yea, the devil would never
have power over the hearts of the children of men.
18 Behold, he was a man like unto Ammon, the
son of Mosiah, yea, and even the other sons of
Mosiah, yea, and also Alma and his sons, for they
were all men of God.
19 Now behold, Helaman and his brethren were
no less serviceable unto the people than was
Moroni; for they did preach the word of God, and
they did baptize unto repentance all men whosoever would hearken unto their words.
20 And thus they went forth, and the people did
humble themselves because of their words, insomuch
that they were highly favored of the Lord, and thus
they were free from wars and contentions among
themselves, yea, even for the space of four years.
21 But, as I have said, in the latter end of the nineteenth year, yea, notwithstanding their peace
amongst themselves, they were compelled reluctantly to contend with their brethren, the Lamanites.

## The Nephites' Reaction to War Is Revealed

22 Yea, and in fine, their wars never did cease for
the space of many years with the Lamanites,
notwithstanding their much reluctance.
23 Now, they were sorry to take up arms against
the Lamanites, because they did not delight in the
shedding of blood; yea, and this was not all—they
were sorry to be the means of sending so many of
their brethren out of this world into an eternal
world, unprepared to meet their God.

---

48:13 ***an oath***—a sacred promise

48:13 (11–13) Do you know any leaders today like Moroni? What can you do now in your life to become like this great man?

48:14 ***give an offense***—attack first

President David O. McKay explained: "There are, however, two conditions which may justify a truly Christian man to enter—mind you, I say *enter, not begin*—a war: (1) An attempt [by others] to dominate and to deprive another of his free agency, and, (2) Loyalty to his country. Possibly there is a third, viz., defense of a weak nation that is being unjustly crushed by a strong, ruthless one" (in Conference Report, April 1942, 72).

48:15 ***prosper them***—help them succeed

48:16 ***whither***—where
***deliver***—protect
***preserving***—protecting
***resisting iniquity***—not sinning

48:17 Moroni remained faithful, righteous, and strong at a time when death, suffering, and hatred were everywhere. How can you remain faithful and righteous in a world full of temptation and sin?

48:19 ***serviceable***—useful

"Not all of us are going to be like Moroni, catching the acclaim of our colleagues all day every day. Most of us will be quiet, relatively unknown folks who come and go and do our work without fanfare. To those of you who may find that lonely or frightening or just unspectacular, I say, you are 'no less serviceable' than the most spectacular of your associates. You, too, are part of God's army" (Howard W. Hunter, "No Less Serviceable," 64).

48:21 ***compelled***—forced
***reluctantly***—unwillingly

24 Nevertheless, they could not suffer to lay down their lives, that their wives and their children should be massacred by the barbarous cruelty of those who were once their brethren, yea, and had dissented from their church, and had left them and had gone to destroy them by joining the Lamanites.
25 Yea, they could not bear that their brethren should rejoice over the blood of the Nephites, so long as there were any who should keep the commandments of God, for the promise of the Lord was, if they should keep his commandments they should prosper in the land.

## CHAPTER 49

*Amalickiah's army is not able to conquer two Nephite cities. Notice how the Nephites prepare both physically and spiritually to protect themselves from the Lamanites.*

### *The Lamanites Are Afraid to Attack the City of Ammonihah*

1 AND now it came to pass in the eleventh month of the nineteenth year, on the tenth day of the month, the armies of the Lamanites were seen approaching towards the land of Ammonihah.
2 And behold, the city had been rebuilt, and Moroni had stationed an army by the borders of the city, and they had cast up dirt round about to shield them from the arrows and the stones of the Lamanites; for behold, they fought with stones and with arrows.
3 Behold, I said that the city of Ammonihah had been rebuilt. I say unto you, yea, that it was in part rebuilt; and because the Lamanites had destroyed it once because of the iniquity of the people, they supposed that it would again become an easy prey for them.
4 But behold, how great was their disappointment; for behold, the Nephites had dug up a ridge of earth round about them, which was so high that the Lamanites could not cast their stones and their arrows at them that they might take effect, neither could they come upon them save it was by their place of entrance.
5 Now at this time the chief captains of the Lamanites were astonished exceedingly, because of the wisdom of the Nephites in preparing their places of security.

48:24 ***suffer to lay down their lives***—let themselves be killed
***massacred***—murdered
***barbarous***—unfeeling and harsh
***dissented***—gone away

PHOTOGRAPH BY REGNAL GARFF

*Captain Moroni prepared the Nephite cities against the Lamanites. Many remains of walls dating back to this period have been found in southern Mexico.*

ILLUSTRATION BY LESTER LEE

*Anciently, arrowheads were made of various materials, including sharpened stone, wood, bone, and thorns.*

49:2 ***stationed***—placed

49:3 ***prey***—city to take

The city of Ammonihah had previously been destroyed by the Lamanites "in one day" because the wicked people who lived there had rejected the testimonies of Alma and Amulek (see Alma 16:9–11).

49:4 ***ridge***—hill
***take effect***—hurt them

49:5 ***astonished exceedingly***—very surprised
***security***—safety

6 Now the leaders of the Lamanites had supposed, because of the greatness of their numbers, yea, they supposed that they should be privileged to come upon them as they had hitherto done; yea, and they had also prepared themselves with shields, and with breastplates; and they had also prepared themselves with garments of skins, yea, very thick garments to cover their nakedness.
7 And being thus prepared they supposed that they should easily overpower and subject their brethren to the yoke of bondage, or slay and massacre them according to their pleasure.
8 But behold, to their uttermost astonishment, they were prepared for them, in a manner which never had been known among the children of Lehi. Now they were prepared for the Lamanites, to battle after the manner of the instructions of Moroni.
9 And it came to pass that the Lamanites, or the Amalickiahites, were exceedingly astonished at their manner of preparation for war.
10 Now, if king Amalickiah had come down out of the land of Nephi, at the head of his army, perhaps he would have caused the Lamanites to have attacked the Nephites at the city of Ammonihah; for behold, he did care not for the blood of his people.
11 But behold, Amalickiah did not come down himself to battle. And behold, his chief captains durst not attack the Nephites at the city of Ammonihah, for Moroni had altered the management of affairs among the Nephites, insomuch that the Lamanites were disappointed in their places of retreat and they could not come upon them.

## The Lamanites Take an Oath to Attack the City of Noah

12 Therefore they retreated into the wilderness, and took their camp and marched towards the land of Noah, supposing that to be the next best place for them to come against the Nephites.
13 For they knew not that Moroni had fortified, or had built forts of security, for every city in all the land round about; therefore, they marched forward to the land of Noah with a firm determination; yea, their chief captains came forward and took an oath that they would destroy the people of that city.
14 But behold, to their astonishment, the city of Noah, which had hitherto been a weak place, had now, by the means of Moroni, become strong, yea, even to exceed the strength of the city Ammonihah.
15 And now, behold, this was wisdom in Moroni; for he had supposed that they would be frightened at the city Ammonihah; and as the city of Noah had hitherto been the weakest part of the land, therefore they would march thither to battle; and thus it was according to his desires.
16 And behold, Moroni had appointed Lehi to be chief captain over the men of that city; and it was that same Lehi who fought with the Lamanites in the valley on the east of the river Sidon.
17 And now behold it came to pass, that when the Lamanites had found that Lehi commanded the city they were again disappointed, for they feared Lehi exceedingly; nevertheless their chief captains had sworn with an oath to attack the city; therefore, they brought up their armies.
18 Now behold, the Lamanites could not get into their forts of security by any other way save by the entrance, because of the highness of the bank which had been thrown up, and the depth of the ditch which had been dug round about, save it were by the entrance.
19 And thus were the Nephites prepared to destroy all such as should attempt to climb up to enter the fort by any other way, by casting over stones and arrows at them.
20 Thus they were prepared, yea, a body of their strongest men, with their swords and their slings, to smite down all who should attempt to come into their place of security by the place of entrance; and thus were they prepared to defend themselves against the Lamanites.

---

49:6 ***supposed***—thought
***privileged***—able
***hitherto***—before
***garments***—clothes

49:7 ***subject their brethren to the yoke of bondage***—make the Nephites their slaves
***massacre***—murder

49:8 ***uttermost astonishment***—complete surprise

49:11 ***durst***—dared
***altered***—changed

49:13 ***an oath***—a promise

49:15 ***thither***—there

49:16 Lehi had earlier helped to defeat a large army of Lamanites near the river Sidon (see Alma 43–44).

49:18 ***bank***—hill of dirt

## The Lamanites Are Defeated at the City of Noah

21 And it came to pass that the captains of the
Lamanites brought up their armies before the place of
entrance, and began to contend with the Nephites, to
get into their place of security; but behold, they
were driven back from time to time, insomuch that
they were slain with an immense slaughter.
22 Now when they found that they could not
obtain power over the Nephites by the pass, they
began to dig down their banks of earth that they
might obtain a pass to their armies, that they might
have an equal chance to fight; but behold, in these
attempts they were swept off by the stones and
arrows which were thrown at them; and instead of
filling up their ditches by pulling down the banks
of earth, they were filled up in a measure with their
dead and wounded bodies.
23 Thus the Nephites had all power over their enemies; and thus the Lamanites did attempt to destroy
the Nephites until their chief captains were all slain;
yea, and more than a thousand of the Lamanites
were slain; while, on the other hand, there was not
a single soul of the Nephites which was slain.
24 There were about fifty who were wounded,
who had been exposed to the arrows of the
Lamanites through the pass, but they were shielded
by their shields, and their breastplates, and their
head-plates, insomuch that their wounds were
upon their legs, many of which were very severe.

## The Nephites Thank the Lord for His Blessings

25 And it came to pass, that when the Lamanites
saw that their chief captains were all slain they fled
into the wilderness. And it came to pass that they
returned to the land of Nephi, to inform their king,
Amalickiah, who was a Nephite by birth, concerning their great loss.
26 And it came to pass that he was exceedingly
angry with his people, because he had not obtained
his desire over the Nephites; he had not subjected
them to the yoke of bondage.
27 Yea, he was exceedingly wroth, and he did
curse God, and also Moroni, swearing with an oath
that he would drink his blood; and this because
Moroni had kept the commandments of God in
preparing for the safety of his people.
28 And it came to pass, that on the other hand, the
people of Nephi did thank the Lord their God,
because of his matchless power in delivering them
from the hands of their enemies.
29 And thus ended the nineteenth year of the
reign of the judges over the people of Nephi.
30 Yea, and there was continual peace among
them, and exceedingly great prosperity in the
church because of their heed and diligence which
they gave unto the word of God, which was
declared unto them by Helaman, and Shiblon, and
Corianton, and Ammon and his brethren, yea, and
by all those who had been ordained by the holy
order of God, being baptized unto repentance, and
sent forth to preach among the people.

# CHAPTER 50

*Moroni's armies restore peace to the land, and the Nephites prosper. Morianton tries to lead away a portion of the Nephites, but is stopped, and peace returns. Notice the blessings that come from obeying the Lord and living in harmony with His teachings.*

## Moroni's Armies Prepare for Attacks from the Lamanites

1 AND now it came to pass that Moroni did not
stop making preparations for war, or to defend his
people against the Lamanites; for he caused that his
armies should commence in the commencement of
the twentieth year of the reign of the judges, that

---

49:21 ***they were slain with an immense slaughter***—many were killed

49:22 ***pass***—entrance

49:24 ***severe***—serious or dangerous

49:27 ***wroth***—angry

49:30 ***heed***—obedience
***diligence***—care and effort

The holy order of God is the Melchizedek Priesthood (see D&C 107:1–3).

The Nephites lived in peace and happiness because they listened to and obeyed the teachings of their leaders. What have your leaders taught you recently that could bring you peace and safety?

50:1 ***commence***—begin
***reign***—rule

they should commence in digging up heaps of earth round about all the cities, throughout all the land which was possessed by the Nephites.

2 And upon the top of these ridges of earth he caused that there should be timbers, yea, works of timbers built up to the height of a man, round about the cities.

3 And he caused that upon those works of timbers there should be a frame of pickets built upon the timbers round about; and they were strong and high.

4 And he caused towers to be erected that overlooked those works of pickets, and he caused places of security to be built upon those towers, that the stones and the arrows of the Lamanites could not hurt them.

5 And they were prepared that they could cast stones from the top thereof, according to their pleasure and their strength, and slay him who should attempt to approach near the walls of the city.

6 Thus Moroni did prepare strongholds against the coming of their enemies, round about every city in all the land.

## Moroni's Armies Drive Out the Lamanites

7 And it came to pass that Moroni caused that his armies should go forth into the east wilderness; yea, and they went forth and drove all the Lamanites who were in the east wilderness into their own lands, which were south of the land of Zarahemla.

8 And the land of Nephi did run in a straight course from the east sea to the west.

9 And it came to pass that when Moroni had driven all the Lamanites out of the east wilderness, which was north of the lands of their own possessions, he caused that the inhabitants who were in the land of Zarahemla and in the land round about should go forth into the east wilderness, even to the borders by the seashore, and possess the land.

10 And he also placed armies on the south, in the borders of their possessions, and caused them to erect fortifications that they might secure their armies and their people from the hands of their enemies.

11 And thus he cut off all the strongholds of the Lamanites in the east wilderness, yea, and also on the west, fortifying the line between the Nephites and the Lamanites, between the land of Zarahemla and the land of Nephi, from the west sea, running by the head of the river Sidon—the Nephites possessing all the land northward, yea, even all the land which was northward of the land Bountiful, according to their pleasure.

12 Thus Moroni, with his armies, which did increase daily because of the assurance of protection which his works did bring forth unto them, did seek to cut off the strength and the power of the Lamanites from off the lands of their possessions, that they should have no power upon the lands of their possession.

## The Nephites Build Up Their Cities and Prosper

13 And it came to pass that the Nephites began the foundation of a city, and they called the name of the city Moroni; and it was by the east sea; and it was on the south by the line of the possessions of the Lamanites.

14 And they also began a foundation for a city between the city of Moroni and the city of Aaron, joining the borders of Aaron and Moroni; and they called the name of the city, or the land, Nephihah.

---

50:1 Moroni is careful not to allow the Nephites to let down their defenses. President Benson warned, "There is real danger we may let down our guard, as it were; that we may be tempted to join with the world and adopt some of their standards against which we have been warned by the Lord" (*The Teachings of Ezra Taft Benson,* 477).

50:3 ***pickets***—pointed sticks or logs

50:4 ***erected***—built
***security***—safety

50:5 ***pleasure***—desires
***slay***—kill

50:6 A stronghold is a place with strong defenses. It can be a wall, a steep hill, or a fort or similar protective building that an enemy cannot easily enter.

50:6 (1–6) Even though the Nephites are not in immediate danger, Moroni causes his armies to prepare for possible war with their enemies. The scriptures teach that if we are prepared we will not fear (see D&C 38:30). What preparation can you make to protect yourself against evil?

50:10 ***secure***—guard

50:11 ***fortifying***—strengthening

50:12 ***assurance of protection***—confidence

15 And they also began in that same year to build many cities on the north, one in a particular manner which they called Lehi, which was in the north by the borders of the seashore.
16 And thus ended the twentieth year.
17 And in these prosperous circumstances were the people of Nephi in the commencement of the twenty and first year of the reign of the judges over the people of Nephi.
18 And they did prosper exceedingly, and they became exceedingly rich; yea, and they did multiply and wax strong in the land.
19 And thus we see how merciful and just are all the dealings of the Lord, to the fulfilling of all his words unto the children of men; yea, we can behold that his words are verified, even at this time, which he spake unto Lehi, saying:
20 Blessed art thou and thy children; and they shall be blessed, inasmuch as they shall keep my commandments they shall prosper in the land. But remember, inasmuch as they will not keep my commandments they shall be cut off from the presence of the Lord.
21 And we see that these promises have been verified to the people of Nephi; for it has been their quarrelings and their contentions, yea, their murderings, and their plunderings, their idolatry, their whoredoms, and their abominations, which were among themselves, which brought upon them their wars and their destructions.
22 And those who were faithful in keeping the commandments of the Lord were delivered at all times, whilst thousands of their wicked brethren have been consigned to bondage, or to perish by the sword, or to dwindle in unbelief, and mingle with the Lamanites.
23 But behold there never was a happier time among the people of Nephi, since the days of Nephi, than in the days of Moroni, yea, even at this time, in the twenty and first year of the reign of the judges.
24 And it came to pass that the twenty and second year of the reign of the judges also ended in peace; yea, and also the twenty and third year.

## The People of Morianton Rebel Against the Nephites

25 And it came to pass that in the commencement of the twenty and fourth year of the reign of the judges, there would also have been peace among the people of Nephi had it not been for a contention which took place among them concerning the land of Lehi, and the land of Morianton, which joined upon the borders of Lehi; both of which were on the borders by the seashore.
26 For behold, the people who possessed the land of Morianton did claim a part of the land of Lehi; therefore there began to be a warm contention between them, insomuch that the people of Morianton took up arms against their brethren, and they were determined by the sword to slay them.

---

50:17 ***prosperous circumstances***—good times

50:18 ***multiply and wax***—increase and grow

50:19 ***merciful and just***—kind and fair
***verified***—proven true

50:21 ***plunderings***—robbing
***idolatry***—worshiping false gods
***whoredoms***—wickedness and immorality
***abominations***—terrible wickedness

50:22 ***consigned to***—cursed with
***dwindle***—fall away gradually
***mingle***—stay

Elder Dallin H. Oaks taught that these stories "do not mean that the servants of God are delivered from all hardship or that they are always saved from death. Some believers lose their lives in persecutions, and some suffer great hardships as a result of their faith. But the protection promised to the faithful servants of God is a reality today as it was in Bible times" (in Conference Report, October 1992, 54).

50:23 (19–23) Mormon wants to teach what will be of most worth to us, and his use of the words *thus* and *thus we see* make the lessons easier to recognize and understand. Pay close attention to the "thus we see" phrases in the Book of Mormon. Here Mormon wants you to understand that the Lord is keeping His word to Lehi and blessing the Nephites with prosperity when they keep the commandments (see Henry B. Eyring, *To Draw Closer to God,* 146–52).

50:26 The people who possessed or controlled the land of Morianton selfishly wanted more land. Elder Richard G. Scott taught, "By studying the lives recorded in the Book of Mormon, you will see that selfishness is at the root of all sin. It leads to unrighteous acts that bring anguish [sadness] and misery" (in Conference Report, April 1986, 12).

27 But behold, the people who possessed the land of Lehi fled to the camp of Moroni, and appealed unto him for assistance; for behold they were not in the wrong.

28 And it came to pass that when the people of Morianton, who were led by a man whose name was Morianton, found that the people of Lehi had fled to the camp of Moroni, they were exceedingly fearful lest the army of Moroni should come upon them and destroy them.

29 Therefore, Morianton put it into their hearts that they should flee to the land which was northward, which was covered with large bodies of water, and take possession of the land which was northward.

30 And behold, they would have carried this plan into effect, (which would have been a cause to have been lamented) but behold, Morianton being a man of much passion, therefore he was angry with one of his maid servants, and he fell upon her and beat her much.

31 And it came to pass that she fled, and came over to the camp of Moroni, and told Moroni all things concerning the matter, and also concerning their intentions to flee into the land northward.

32 Now behold, the people who were in the land Bountiful, or rather Moroni, feared that they would hearken to the words of Morianton and unite with his people, and thus he would obtain possession of those parts of the land, which would lay a foundation for serious consequences among the people of Nephi, yea, which consequences would lead to the overthrow of their liberty.

33 Therefore Moroni sent an army, with their camp, to head the people of Morianton, to stop their flight into the land northward.

34 And it came to pass that they did not head them until they had come to the borders of the land Desolation; and there they did head them, by the narrow pass which led by the sea into the land northward, yea, by the sea, on the west and on the east.

35 And it came to pass that the army which was sent by Moroni, which was led by a man whose name was Teancum, did meet the people of Morianton; and so stubborn were the people of Morianton, (being inspired by his wickedness and his flattering words) that a battle commenced between them, in the which Teancum did slay Morianton and defeat his army, and took them prisoners, and returned to the camp of Moroni. And thus ended the twenty and fourth year of the reign of the judges over the people of Nephi.

36 And thus were the people of Morianton brought back. And upon their covenanting to keep the peace they were restored to the land of Morianton, and a union took place between them and the people of Lehi; and they were also restored to their lands.

## Pahoran Is Appointed Chief Judge

37 And it came to pass that in the same year that the people of Nephi had peace restored unto them, that Nephihah, the second chief judge, died, having filled the judgment-seat with perfect uprightness before God.

38 Nevertheless, he had refused Alma to take possession of those records and those things which were esteemed by Alma and his fathers to be most sacred; therefore Alma had conferred them upon his son, Helaman.

---

50:30 ***lamented***—mourned
***much passion***—bad temper

50:31 ***intentions to flee***—plans to escape

50:31 (30–31) President Gordon B. Hinckley taught that a "violent temper is such a terrible, corrosive thing. And the tragedy is that it accomplishes no good; it only feeds evil with resentment and rebellion and pain" (in Conference Report, October 1991, 71). What happened because of Morianton's temper? What can happen in your life if you do not control your temper?

50:32 ***consequences***—results

50:35 Morianton uses flattery to convince his people to fight for a selfish cause. Elder James E. Faust pointed out that "Satan is the world's master in the use of flattery, and he knows the great power of speech (see Jacob 7:4)" (in Conference Report, October 1987, 41).

50:36 ***restored***—returned

50:37 ***uprightness***—righteousness

50:38 ***esteemed***—treasured

39 Behold, it came to pass that the son of Nephihah was appointed to fill the judgment-seat, in the stead of his father; yea, he was appointed chief judge and governor over the people, with an oath and sacred ordinance to judge righteously, and to keep the peace and the freedom of the people, and to grant unto them their sacred privileges to worship the Lord their God, yea, to support and maintain the cause of God all his days, and to bring the wicked to justice according to their crime.

40 Now behold, his name was Pahoran. And Pahoran did fill the seat of his father, and did commence his reign in the end of the twenty and fourth year, over the people of Nephi.

## CHAPTER 51

*The Nephites disagree about who should rule their nation. Notice what they fight about and how it nearly causes the destruction of their nation.*

### *A Group of Nephites Known As King-Men Desire a King to Rule over Them*

1 AND now it came to pass in the commencement of the twenty and fifth year of the reign of the judges over the people of Nephi, they having established peace between the people of Lehi and the people of Morianton concerning their lands, and having commenced the twenty and fifth year in peace;

2 Nevertheless, they did not long maintain an entire peace in the land, for there began to be a contention among the people concerning the chief judge Pahoran; for behold, there were a part of the people who desired that a few particular points of the law should be altered.

3 But behold, Pahoran would not alter nor suffer the law to be altered; therefore, he did not hearken to those who had sent in their voices with their petitions concerning the altering of the law.

4 Therefore, those who were desirous that the law should be altered were angry with him, and desired that he should no longer be chief judge over the land; therefore there arose a warm dispute concerning the matter, but not unto bloodshed.

5 And it came to pass that those who were desirous that Pahoran should be dethroned from the judgment-seat were called king-men, for they were desirous that the law should be altered in a manner to overthrow the free government and to establish a king over the land.

6 And those who were desirous that Pahoran should remain chief judge over the land took upon them the name of freemen; and thus was the division among them, for the freemen had sworn or covenanted to maintain their rights and the privileges of their religion by a free government.

7 And it came to pass that this matter of their contention was settled by the voice of the people. And it came to pass that the voice of the people came in favor of the freemen, and Pahoran retained the judgment-seat, which caused much rejoicing among the brethren of Pahoran and also many of the people of liberty, who also put the king-men to silence, that they durst not oppose but were obliged to maintain the cause of freedom.

---

50:39 "Oath-swearing was common among the Book of Mormon peoples. Nephi[1] swore an oath to Zoram assuring him full status in Lehi's family (1 Ne. 4:32–34), and Zoram swore to accompany Nephi and his brothers into the wilderness, after which their 'fears did cease concerning him' (1 Ne. 4:37). Oaths of office were administered to judges (Alma 50:39). In a manner reminiscent of [similar to] biblical and other Near Eastern peoples, the Nephites swore to support Moroni in defensive war, and used their rent garments to represent the punishment they wished upon themselves should they fail" (*Encyclopedia of Mormonism*, s.v. "Oaths," 3:1020).

51:1 ***commencement***—beginning

Morianton and his people claimed as their own a part of the land that belonged to the people of Lehi. This disagreement led to bloodshed between Morianton's people and the Nephite army (see Alma 50:26-36).

51:2 ***altered***—changed

51:3 ***suffer***—allow
***petitions***—pleas or requests

51:4 ***a warm dispute***—an angry argument

51:5 ***dethroned***—removed

51:7 ***retained***—kept
***durst***—dared

51:7 (5–7) King Mosiah warned the Nephites of wicked kings and set up a government in which the people chose their leaders, saying, "It is not common that the voice of the people desireth anything contrary to that which is right" (Mosiah 29:21–26).

8 Now those who were in favor of kings were those of high birth, and they sought to be kings; and they were supported by those who sought power and authority over the people.

## Amalickiah Organizes a Lamanite Army to Fight the Nephites

9 But behold, this was a critical time for such contentions to be among the people of Nephi; for behold, Amalickiah had again stirred up the hearts of the people of the Lamanites against the people of the Nephites, and he was gathering together soldiers from all parts of his land, and arming them, and preparing for war with all diligence; for he had sworn to drink the blood of Moroni.

10 But behold, we shall see that his promise which he made was rash; nevertheless, he did prepare himself and his armies to come to battle against the Nephites.

11 Now his armies were not so great as they had hitherto been, because of the many thousands who had been slain by the hand of the Nephites; but notwithstanding their great loss, Amalickiah had gathered together a wonderfully great army, insomuch that he feared not to come down to the land of Zarahemla.

12 Yea, even Amalickiah did himself come down, at the head of the Lamanites. And it was in the twenty and fifth year of the reign of the judges; and it was at the same time that they had begun to settle the affairs of their contentions concerning the chief judge, Pahoran.

## Captain Moroni Settles a Civil War Against the King-Men

13 And it came to pass that when the men who were called king-men had heard that the Lamanites were coming down to battle against them, they were glad in their hearts; and they refused to take up arms, for they were so wroth with the chief judge, and also with the people of liberty, that they would not take up arms to defend their country.

14 And it came to pass that when Moroni saw this, and also saw that the Lamanites were coming into the borders of the land, he was exceedingly wroth because of the stubbornness of those people whom he had labored with so much diligence to preserve; yea, he was exceedingly wroth; his soul was filled with anger against them.

15 And it came to pass that he sent a petition, with the voice of the people, unto the governor of the land, desiring that he should read it, and give him (Moroni) power to compel those dissenters to defend their country or to put them to death.

16 For it was his first care to put an end to such contentions and dissensions among the people; for behold, this had been hitherto a cause of all their destruction. And it came to pass that it was granted according to the voice of the people.

17 And it came to pass that Moroni commanded that his army should go against those king-men, to pull down their pride and their nobility and level them with the earth, or they should take up arms and support the cause of liberty.

---

51:8 Those of "high birth" were people who claimed to be born into a higher social class (see Alma 51:17–18, 21).

51:9 ***critical***—important and serious
***stirred up***—caused anger to rise in

51:10 ***rash***—foolish

51:11 ***notwithstanding***—in spite of

51:13 ***wroth***—angry

51:14 ***preserve***—save

51:15 ***compel those dissenters***—force the king-men

51:16 ***contentions and dissensions***—fighting and arguing
***hitherto***—up until now
***granted***—allowed

18 And it came to pass that the armies did march forth against them; and they did pull down their pride and their nobility, insomuch that as they did lift their weapons of war to fight against the men of Moroni they were hewn down and leveled to the earth.

19 And it came to pass that there were four thousand of those dissenters who were hewn down by the sword; and those of their leaders who were not slain in battle were taken and cast into prison, for there was no time for their trials at this period.

20 And the remainder of those dissenters, rather than be smitten down to the earth by the sword, yielded to the standard of liberty, and were compelled to hoist the title of liberty upon their towers, and in their cities, and to take up arms in defence of their country.

21 And thus Moroni put an end to those king-men, that there were not any known by the appellation of king-men; and thus he put an end to the stubbornness and the pride of those people who professed the blood of nobility; but they were brought down to humble themselves like unto their brethren, and to fight valiantly for their freedom from bondage.

### Amalickiah and the Lamanites Attack and Capture Many Nephite Cities

22 Behold, it came to pass that while Moroni was thus breaking down the wars and contentions among his own people, and subjecting them to peace and civilization, and making regulations to prepare for war against the Lamanites, behold, the Lamanites had come into the land of Moroni, which was in the borders by the seashore.

23 And it came to pass that the Nephites were not sufficiently strong in the city of Moroni; therefore Amalickiah did drive them, slaying many. And it came to pass that Amalickiah took possession of the city, yea, possession of all their fortifications.

24 And those who fled out of the city of Moroni came to the city of Nephihah; and also the people of the city of Lehi gathered themselves together, and made preparations and were ready to receive the Lamanites to battle.

25 But it came to pass that Amalickiah would not suffer the Lamanites to go against the city of Nephihah to battle, but kept them down by the seashore, leaving men in every city to maintain and defend it.

26 And thus he went on, taking possession of many cities, the city of Nephihah, and the city of Lehi, and the city of Morianton, and the city of Omner, and the city of Gid, and the city of Mulek, all of which were on the east borders by the seashore.

27 And thus had the Lamanites obtained, by the cunning of Amalickiah, so many cities, by their numberless hosts, all of which were strongly fortified after the manner of the fortifications of Moroni; all of which afforded strongholds for the Lamanites.

### Teancum Kills Amalickiah in His Tent

28 And it came to pass that they marched to the borders of the land Bountiful, driving the Nephites before them and slaying many.

29 But it came to pass that they were met by Teancum, who had slain Morianton and had headed his people in his flight.

30 And it came to pass that he headed Amalickiah also, as he was marching forth with his numerous army that he might take possession of the land Bountiful, and also the land northward.

---

51:18 ***hewn down and leveled to the earth***—killed

51:18 (15–18) Elder Ezra Taft Benson, speaking about modern concerns in the United States, warned about this danger: "If our blood-bought freedom is surrendered, it will be because of Americans. . . . 'At what point, then, is the approach of danger to be expected?' asked Abraham Lincoln, and answered, 'If it ever reaches us, it must spring up among us. It cannot come from abroad. If destruction be our lot, we must ourselves be its author and finisher . . .' " (*Teachings of Ezra Taft Benson,* 573).

51:20 ***yielded***—surrendered
***compelled to hoist***—forced to raise

51:21 ***appellation***—title
***professed***—claimed
***valiantly***—bravely

51:22 ***subjecting them to peace and civilization***—bringing them back to a peaceful society
***regulations***—rules

51:23 ***took possession of***—captured

These fortifications, or strongholds, are described in Alma 48:8.

51:27 ***cunning***—trickery or cleverness
***afforded***—became

51:29 ***headed***—cut off

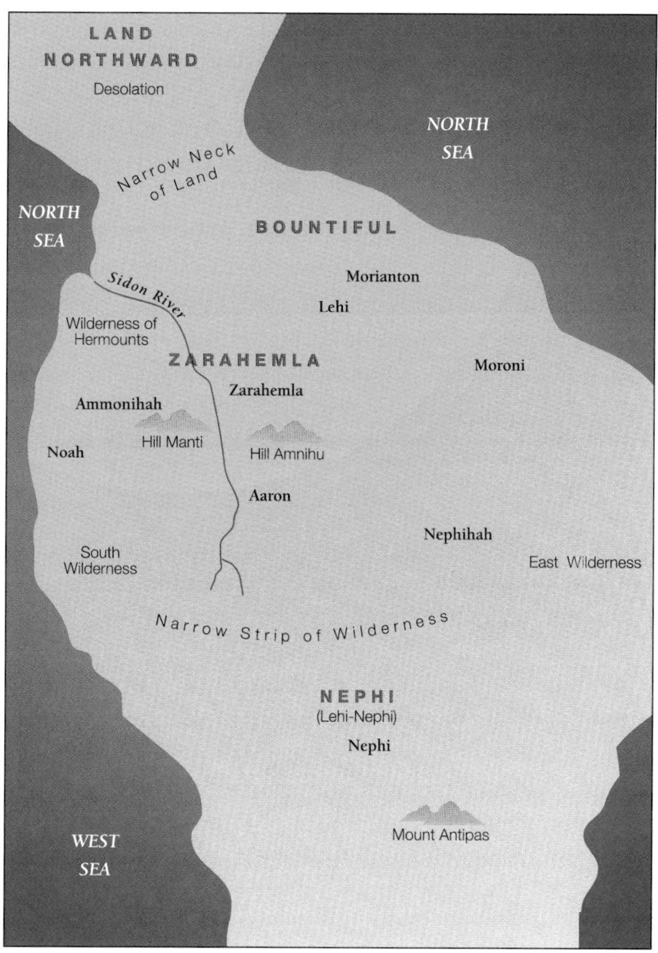


*Amalickiah's army captured many Nephite cities.*

31 But behold he met with a disappointment by
being repulsed by Teancum and his men, for they
were great warriors; for every man of Teancum did
exceed the Lamanites in their strength and in their
skill of war, insomuch that they did gain advantage
over the Lamanites.
32 And it came to pass that they did harass
them, insomuch that they did slay them even
until it was dark. And it came to pass that
Teancum and his men did pitch their tents in the
borders of the land Bountiful; and Amalickiah did
pitch his tents in the borders on the beach by the
seashore, and after this manner were they driven.
33 And it came to pass that when the night had
come, Teancum and his servant stole forth and
went out by night, and went into the camp of
Amalickiah; and behold, sleep had overpowered
them because of their much fatigue, which was
caused by the labors and heat of the day.
34 And it came to pass that Teancum stole privily
into the tent of the king, and put a javelin to his
heart; and he did cause the death of the king immediately that he did not awake his servants.
35 And he returned again privily to his own camp,
and behold, his men were asleep, and he awoke
them and told them all the things that he had done.
36 And he caused that his armies should stand in
readiness, lest the Lamanites had awakened and
should come upon them.
37 And thus endeth the twenty and fifth year of
the reign of the judges over the people of Nephi;
and thus endeth the days of Amalickiah.

## CHAPTER 52

*The Nephites successfully plan a way to win a battle with the Lamanites. See how the Nephites were able to work together and follow their righteous leaders to win the battle.*

### The Lamanites Appoint a New King While the Nephites Prepare for War

1 AND now, it came to pass in the twenty and
sixth year of the reign of the judges over the people
of Nephi, behold, when the Lamanites awoke on
the first morning of the first month, behold, they
found Amalickiah was dead in his own tent; and
they also saw that Teancum was ready to give them
battle on that day.
2 And now, when the Lamanites saw this they
were affrighted; and they abandoned their design in
marching into the land northward, and retreated
with all their army into the city of Mulek, and
sought protection in their fortifications.

---

51:31 ***repulsed***—driven back

51:32 ***harass***—make small, persistent attacks against

51:33 ***stole***—crept
***much fatigue***—tiredness or exhaustion

51:34 ***privily***—privately
***javelin***—spear

Teancum and Moroni were brave soldiers who fought to protect the freedom of their people. Why is it important to have good examples like these men? Who are some examples like these men in our day?

52:2 ***abandoned***—gave up
***design***—plan
***fortifications***—protected cities

3 And it came to pass that the brother of Amalickiah was appointed king over the people; and his name was Ammoron; thus king Ammoron, the brother of king Amalickiah, was appointed to reign in his stead.
4 And it came to pass that he did command that his people should maintain those cities, which they had taken by the shedding of blood; for they had not taken any cities save they had lost much blood.
5 And now, Teancum saw that the Lamanites were determined to maintain those cities which they had taken, and those parts of the land which they had obtained possession of; and also seeing the enormity of their number, Teancum thought it was not expedient that he should attempt to attack them in their forts.
6 But he kept his men round about, as if making preparations for war; yea, and truly he was preparing to defend himself against them, by casting up walls round about and preparing places of resort.
7 And it came to pass that he kept thus preparing for war until Moroni had sent a large number of men to strengthen his army.
8 And Moroni also sent orders unto him that he should retain all the prisoners who fell into his hands; for as the Lamanites had taken many prisoners, that he should retain all the prisoners of the Lamanites as a ransom for those whom the Lamanites had taken.
9 And he also sent orders unto him that he should fortify the land Bountiful, and secure the narrow pass which led into the land northward, lest the Lamanites should obtain that point and should have power to harass them on every side.
10 And Moroni also sent unto him, desiring him that he would be faithful in maintaining that quarter of the land, and that he would seek every opportunity to scourge the Lamanites in that quarter, as much as was in his power, that perhaps he might take again by stratagem or some other way those cities which had been taken out of their hands; and that he also would fortify and strengthen the cities round about, which had not fallen into the hands of the Lamanites.
11 And he also said unto him, I would come unto you, but behold, the Lamanites are upon us in the borders of the land by the west sea; and behold, I go against them, therefore I cannot come unto you.

## The Lamanites Gather Large Armies to Attack the Nephites

12 Now, the king (Ammoron) had departed out of the land of Zarahemla, and had made known unto the queen concerning the death of his brother, and had gathered together a large number of men, and had marched forth against the Nephites on the borders by the west sea.
13 And thus he was endeavoring to harass the Nephites, and to draw away a part of their forces to that part of the land, while he had commanded those whom he had left to possess the cities which he had taken, that they should also harass the Nephites on the borders by the east sea, and should take possession of their lands as much as it was in their power, according to the power of their armies.

---

52:3 ***stead***—place

52:3 (1–3) When a king or military leader was killed, his army often surrendered or ran from the battle (see Alma 49:25). In this case, the army flees to the protected city of Mulek until they can choose a new king.

52:5 ***maintain***—keep
***obtained possession***—gotten control
***enormity of their number***—large size of their army
***expedient***—wise

52:6 ***resort***—safety

Teancum prepares his men to protect and defend themselves in case they are attacked. Heavenly Father has placed us in families to protect us from physical and spiritual dangers. "Our family is our safety place" (Rex D. Pinegar, in Conference Report, April 1990, 8).

52:8 ***retain***—keep
***a ransom***—something they could trade

52:9 ***fortify***—strengthen
***secure***—protect
***harass them***—trouble them with repeated attacks

52:10 ***quarter***—area
***scourge***—beat
***stratagem***—trick or plan

52:13 ***endeavoring***—trying
***forces***—army

14 And thus were the Nephites in those dangerous circumstances in the ending of the twenty and sixth year of the reign of the judges over the people of Nephi.
15 But behold, it came to pass in the twenty and seventh year of the reign of the judges, that Teancum, by the command of Moroni—who had established armies to protect the south and the west borders of the land, and had begun his march towards the land Bountiful, that he might assist Teancum with his men in retaking the cities which they had lost—
16 And it came to pass that Teancum had received orders to make an attack upon the city of Mulek, and retake it if it were possible.
17 And it came to pass that Teancum made preparations to make an attack upon the city of Mulek, and march forth with his army against the Lamanites; but he saw that it was impossible that he could overpower them while they were in their fortifications; therefore he abandoned his designs and returned again to the city Bountiful, to wait for the coming of Moroni, that he might receive strength to his army.
18 And it came to pass that Moroni did arrive with his army at the land of Bountiful, in the latter end of the twenty and seventh year of the reign of the judges over the people of Nephi.

### THE NEPHITE ARMIES RECAPTURE MULEK

19 And in the commencement of the twenty and eighth year, Moroni and Teancum and many of the chief captains held a council of war—what they should do to cause the Lamanites to come out against them to battle; or that they might by some means flatter them out of their strongholds, that they might gain advantage over them and take again the city of Mulek.
20 And it came to pass they sent embassies to the army of the Lamanites, which protected the city of Mulek, to their leader, whose name was Jacob, desiring him that he would come out with his armies to meet them upon the plains between the two cities. But behold, Jacob, who was a Zoramite, would not come out with his army to meet them upon the plains.
21 And it came to pass that Moroni, having no hopes of meeting them upon fair grounds, therefore, he resolved upon a plan that he might decoy the Lamanites out of their strongholds.
22 Therefore he caused that Teancum should take a small number of men and march down near the seashore; and Moroni and his army, by night, marched in the wilderness, on the west of the city Mulek; and thus, on the morrow, when the guards of the Lamanites had discovered Teancum, they ran and told it unto Jacob, their leader.
23 And it came to pass that the armies of the Lamanites did march forth against Teancum, supposing by their numbers to overpower Teancum because of the smallness of his numbers. And as Teancum saw the armies of the Lamanites coming out against him he began to retreat down by the seashore, northward.
24 And it came to pass that when the Lamanites saw that he began to flee, they took courage and pursued them with vigor. And while Teancum was thus leading away the Lamanites who were pursuing them in vain, behold, Moroni commanded that a part of his army who were with him should march forth into the city, and take possession of it.
25 And thus they did, and slew all those who had been left to protect the city, yea, all those who would not yield up their weapons of war.
26 And thus Moroni had obtained possession of the city Mulek with a part of his army, while he marched with the remainder to meet the Lamanites when they should return from the pursuit of Teancum.

---

52:14 ***circumstances***—situations

52:14 (12–14) The Lamanites attempted to take over as much Nephite land as possible by attacking in several locations at once. This is like the trick Satan uses to get people to sin. He tempts them in many different ways (see 2 Nephi 26:22).

52:15 ***established***—put in place

52:19 ***flatter***—lure

52:20 ***embassies***—messengers

52:21 ***resolved***—decided
***decoy***—trick
***strongholds***—protected and guarded cities

52:24 ***vigor***—great energy
***in vain***—without any results

52:25 ***yield***—surrender

### The Surrounded Lamanites Surrender to Moroni

27 And it came to pass that the Lamanites did pursue Teancum until they came near the city Bountiful, and then they were met by Lehi and a small army, which had been left to protect the city Bountiful.
28 And now behold, when the chief captains of the Lamanites had beheld Lehi with his army coming against them, they fled in much confusion, lest perhaps they should not obtain the city Mulek before Lehi should overtake them; for they were wearied because of their march, and the men of Lehi were fresh.
29 Now the Lamanites did not know that Moroni had been in their rear with his army; and all they feared was Lehi and his men.
30 Now Lehi was not desirous to overtake them till they should meet Moroni and his army.
31 And it came to pass that before the Lamanites had retreated far they were surrounded by the Nephites, by the men of Moroni on one hand, and the men of Lehi on the other, all of whom were fresh and full of strength; but the Lamanites were wearied because of their long march.
32 And Moroni commanded his men that they should fall upon them until they had given up their weapons of war.
33 And it came to pass that Jacob, being their leader, being also a Zoramite, and having an unconquerable spirit, he led the Lamanites forth to battle with exceeding fury against Moroni.
34 Moroni being in their course of march, therefore Jacob was determined to slay them and cut his way through to the city of Mulek. But behold, Moroni and his men were more powerful; therefore they did not give way before the Lamanites.
35 And it came to pass that they fought on both hands with exceeding fury; and there were many slain on both sides; yea, and Moroni was wounded and Jacob was killed.
36 And Lehi pressed upon their rear with such fury with his strong men, that the Lamanites in the rear delivered up their weapons of war; and the remainder of them, being much confused, knew not whither to go or to strike.
37 Now Moroni seeing their confusion, he said unto them: If ye will bring forth your weapons of war and deliver them up, behold we will forbear shedding your blood.
38 And it came to pass that when the Lamanites had heard these words, their chief captains, all those who were not slain, came forth and threw down their weapons of war at the feet of Moroni, and also commanded their men that they should do the same.
39 But behold, there were many that would not; and those who would not deliver up their swords were taken and bound, and their weapons of war were taken from them, and they were compelled to march with their brethren forth into the land Bountiful.
40 And now the number of prisoners who were taken exceeded more than the number of those who had been slain, yea, more than those who had been slain on both sides.

## CHAPTER 53

*Wars continue between the Lamanites and the Nephites. Two thousand stripling (young male) warriors offer to help defend the Nephite cities. As you read this chapter, look for what gave the stripling warriors the courage to go to war.*

### The Nephites Make the Lamanite Prisoners Work to Build Up Cities

1 AND it came to pass that they did set guards over the prisoners of the Lamanites, and did compel them to go forth and bury their dead, yea, and also the dead of the Nephites who were slain; and Moroni placed men over them to guard them while they should perform their labors.

---

52:28 ***wearied***—tired

52:30 ***overtake***—catch up with

52:33 ***unconquerable***—unbeatable

The Zoramites were a group of fomer Nephites known by this name because they were the followers of Zoram, an apostate who lived in 74 B.C. (see Alma 30:59).

52:37 ***forbear***—stop

Captain Moroni was a man who did not like to shed blood (see Alma 48:11). He wanted to avoid fighting whenever possible (see also Alma 44:1–3; 48:20–23).

52:39 ***compelled***—forced

52:40 ***exceeded more***—was greater

53:1 ***compel***—force
***slain***—killed

2 And Moroni went to the city of Mulek with Lehi, and took command of the city and gave it unto Lehi. Now behold, this Lehi was a man who had been with Moroni in the more part of all his battles; and he was a man like unto Moroni, and they rejoiced in each other's safety; yea, they were beloved by each other, and also beloved by all the people of Nephi.

3 And it came to pass that after the Lamanites had finished burying their dead and also the dead of the Nephites, they were marched back into the land Bountiful; and Teancum, by the orders of Moroni, caused that they should commence laboring in digging a ditch round about the land, or the city, Bountiful.

4 And he caused that they should build a breastwork of timbers upon the inner bank of the ditch; and they cast up dirt out of the ditch against the breastwork of timbers; and thus they did cause the Lamanites to labor until they had encircled the city of Bountiful round about with a strong wall of timbers and earth, to an exceeding height.

5 And this city became an exceeding stronghold ever after; and in this city they did guard the prisoners of the Lamanites; yea, even within a wall which they had caused them to build with their own hands. Now Moroni was compelled to cause the Lamanites to labor, because it was easy to guard them while at their labor; and he desired all his forces when he should make an attack upon the Lamanites.

6 And it came to pass that Moroni had thus gained a victory over one of the greatest of the armies of the Lamanites, and had obtained possession of the city of Mulek, which was one of the strongest holds of the Lamanites in the land of Nephi; and thus he had also built a stronghold to retain his prisoners.

7 And it came to pass that he did no more attempt a battle with the Lamanites in that year, but he did employ his men in preparing for war, yea, and in making fortifications to guard against the Lamanites, yea, and also delivering their women and their children from famine and affliction, and providing food for their armies.

8 And now it came to pass that the armies of the Lamanites, on the west sea, south, while in the absence of Moroni on account of some intrigue amongst the Nephites, which caused dissensions amongst them, had gained some ground over the Nephites, yea, insomuch that they had obtained possession of a number of their cities in that part of the land.

9 And thus because of iniquity amongst themselves, yea, because of dissensions and intrigue among themselves they were placed in the most dangerous circumstances.

## *The Two Thousand Stripling Warriors Join the Army of the Nephites*

10 And now behold, I have somewhat to say concerning the people of Ammon, who, in the beginning, were Lamanites; but by Ammon and his brethren, or rather by the power and word of God, they had been converted unto the Lord; and they had been brought down into the land of Zarahemla, and had ever since been protected by the Nephites.

53:3 ***commence laboring***—start working

53:4 ***breastwork of timbers***—wall of tall wooden poles
***an exceeding***—a great

53:5 ***an exceeding stronghold***—a very strong, well-protected place

53:6 ***retain***—keep

53:7 ***employ his men***—cause his men to work
***fortifications***—forts
***famine and affliction***—starvation and suffering

53:8 ***intrigue***—evil plans and plotting
***dissensions***—arguments and fighting
***obtained possession***—gained control

53:9 ***iniquity***—wickedness
***circumstances***—conditions

53:9 (8–9) Alma points out again that whenever the Nephites are not united in righteousness, they become weak and are unable to withstand the attacks of their enemies. How does this also apply to families that are not united in righteousness? How does it apply to you personally?

53:10 The people of Ammon were a group of Lamanites who were touched by the Spirit and converted to the gospel through the missionary efforts of Ammon and the other sons of Mosiah during their fourteen-year mission (see Alma 17–26). They were also called the Anti-Nephi-Lehies (see Alma 23:17). After they covenanted to never again take up swords to fight (see Alma 24:15–17), they were driven from their homeland by other Lamanites and finally settled in the land of Jershon (see Alma 27:22).

11 And because of their oath they had been kept
from taking up arms against their brethren; for they
had taken an oath that they never would shed blood
more; and according to their oath they would have
perished; yea, they would have suffered themselves
to have fallen into the hands of their brethren, had
it not been for the pity and the exceeding love
which Ammon and his brethren had had for them.
12 And for this cause they were brought down
into the land of Zarahemla; and they ever had been
protected by the Nephites.
13 But it came to pass that when they saw the
danger, and the many afflictions and tribulations
which the Nephites bore for them, they were
moved with compassion and were desirous to take
up arms in the defence of their country.
14 But behold, as they were about to take their
weapons of war, they were overpowered by the
persuasions of Helaman and his brethren, for they
were about to break the oath which they had made.
15 And Helaman feared lest by so doing they
should lose their souls; therefore all those who had
entered into this covenant were compelled to
behold their brethren wade through their afflictions,
in their dangerous circumstances at this time.
16 But behold, it came to pass they had many
sons, who had not entered into a covenant that they
would not take their weapons of war to defend
themselves against their enemies; therefore they did
assemble themselves together at this time, as many
as were able to take up arms, and they called themselves Nephites.
17 And they entered into a covenant to fight for
the liberty of the Nephites, yea, to protect the land
unto the laying down of their lives; yea, even they
covenanted that they never would give up their liberty, but they would fight in all cases to protect the
Nephites and themselves from bondage.
18 Now behold, there were two thousand of those
young men, who entered into this covenant and
took their weapons of war to defend their country.
19 And now behold, as they never had hitherto
been a disadvantage to the Nephites, they became
now at this period of time also a great support; for
they took their weapons of war, and they would
that Helaman should be their leader.
20 And they were all young men, and they were
exceedingly valiant for courage, and also for
strength and activity; but behold, this was not all—
they were men who were true at all times in whatsoever thing they were entrusted.
21 Yea, they were men of truth and soberness, for
they had been taught to keep the commandments
of God and to walk uprightly before him.
22 And now it came to pass that Helaman did
march at the head of his two thousand stripling soldiers, to the support of the people in the borders of
the land on the south by the west sea.
23 And thus ended the twenty and eighth year of
the reign of the judges over the people of Nephi.

---

53:11 ***oath***—sacred promise
***arms***—weapons

53:13 ***afflictions and tribulations***—difficulties and trials
***bore***—carried or endured
***were moved with compassion***—felt sympathy for them

53:15 ***compelled***—forced

53:18 (15–18) "Making covenants with the Lord is a serious and sacred matter. To those who keep their covenants with Him, the Lord has made clear that His mercy is extended to them" (Leaun G. Otten and C. Max Caldwell, *Sacred Truths of the Doctrine & Covenants* 1:253).

53:19 ***hitherto***—to this point

53:20 ***valiant***—brave

President Howard W. Hunter taught, "If we will be true and faithful to our principles, committed to a life of honesty and integrity, then no king or contest or fiery furnace will be able to compromise us" (in Conference Report, April 1990, 78).

53:21 ***soberness***—seriousness

53:21 (19–21) Notice how the scriptures describe these young men. How would you like the Lord's prophet to describe you in the same way? How would you have to live so that could happen?

53:22 ***stripling***—young male

53:23 ***reign***—rule

53:23 (10–23) President Ezra Taft Benson taught, "In the spiritual battles you are waging, I see you as today's sons of Helaman. Remember well the Book of Mormon account of Helaman's two thousand stripling warriors and how the teachings of their mothers gave them strength and faith. These marvelous mothers taught them to put on the whole armor of God, to place their trust in the Lord, and to doubt not. By so doing, not one of these young men was lost" (*Come, Listen to a Prophet's Voice,* 1–2).

## CHAPTER 54

*Ammoron, the leader of the Lamanite army, and Moroni, the leader of the Nephite army, write letters to each other. Watch for how each leader responds in his letters.*

### AMMORON AND MORONI DISCUSS TRADING PRISONERS

1 AND now it came to pass in the commencement
of the twenty and ninth year of the judges, that
Ammoron sent unto Moroni desiring that he would
exchange prisoners.
2 And it came to pass that Moroni felt to rejoice
exceedingly at this request, for he desired the provisions which were imparted for the support of the
Lamanite prisoners for the support of his own
people; and he also desired his own people for the
strengthening of his army.
3 Now the Lamanites had taken many women
and children, and there was not a woman nor a
child among all the prisoners of Moroni, or the
prisoners whom Moroni had taken; therefore
Moroni resolved upon a stratagem to obtain as
many prisoners of the Nephites from the Lamanites
as it were possible.
4 Therefore he wrote an epistle, and sent it by the
servant of Ammoron, the same who had brought an
epistle to Moroni. Now these are the words which
he wrote unto Ammoron, saying:
5 Behold, Ammoron, I have written unto you
somewhat concerning this war which ye have
waged against my people, or rather which thy
brother hath waged against them, and which ye are
still determined to carry on after his death.
6 Behold, I would tell you somewhat concerning
the justice of God, and the sword of his almighty
wrath, which doth hang over you except ye repent
and withdraw your armies into your own lands, or
the land of your possessions, which is the land of
Nephi.
7 Yea, I would tell you these things if ye were
capable of hearkening unto them; yea, I would tell
you concerning that awful hell that awaits to
receive such murderers as thou and thy brother
have been, except ye repent and withdraw your
murderous purposes, and return with your armies
to your own lands.
8 But as ye have once rejected these things, and
have fought against the people of the Lord, even so
I may expect you will do it again.
9 And now behold, we are prepared to receive
you; yea, and except you withdraw your purposes,
behold, ye will pull down the wrath of that God
whom you have rejected upon you, even to your
utter destruction.
10 But, as the Lord liveth, our armies shall come
upon you except ye withdraw, and ye shall soon be
visited with death, for we will retain our cities and
our lands; yea, and we will maintain our religion
and the cause of our God.
11 But behold, it supposeth me that I talk to you
concerning these things in vain; or it supposeth me
that thou art a child of hell; therefore I will close my
epistle by telling you that I will not exchange prisoners, save it be on conditions that ye will deliver
up a man and his wife and his children, for one
prisoner; if this be the case that ye will do it, I will
exchange.

---

54:1 ***commencement***—beginning
***exchange***—trade

54:2 ***provisions which were imparted***—food and supplies that were being used

54:3 ***resolved upon a stratagem***—decided on a plan

54:4 ***an epistle***—a letter

54:5 ***concerning***—about
***waged***—made

Ammoron's brother who began this war against the Nephites was Amalickiah. He was killed by Teancum (see Alma 52:1–3).

54:6 ***wrath***—anger

54:7 ***hearkening unto***—hearing and following

54:9 ***utter***—complete

54:10 ***retain***—keep

54:11 ***in vain***—with no success

Ammoron was so wicked that he would not repent. He was like those whom Samuel the Lamanite warned that one day it would be "everlastingly too late" to repent because they had spent all the days of their lives in wickedness (see Helaman 13:38).

12 And behold, if ye do not this, I will come against you with my armies; yea, even I will arm my women and my children, and I will come against you, and I will follow you even into your own land, which is the land of our first inheritance; yea, and it shall be blood for blood, yea, life for life; and I will give you battle even until you are destroyed from off the face of the earth.
13 Behold, I am in my anger, and also my people; ye have sought to murder us, and we have only sought to defend ourselves. But behold, if ye seek to destroy us more we will seek to destroy you; yea, and we will seek our land, the land of our first inheritance.
14 Now I close my epistle. I am Moroni; I am a leader of the people of the Nephites.

## Ammoron Demands That the Nephites Surrender

15 Now it came to pass that Ammoron, when he had received this epistle, was angry; and he wrote another epistle unto Moroni, and these are the words which he wrote, saying:
16 I am Ammoron, the king of the Lamanites; I am the brother of Amalickiah whom ye have murdered. Behold, I will avenge his blood upon you, yea, and I will come upon you with my armies for I fear not your threatenings.
17 For behold, your fathers did wrong their brethren, insomuch that they did rob them of their right to the government when it rightly belonged unto them.
18 And now behold, if ye will lay down your arms, and subject yourselves to be governed by those to whom the government doth rightly belong, then will I cause that my people shall lay down their weapons and shall be at war no more.
19 Behold, ye have breathed out many threatenings against me and my people; but behold, we fear not your threatenings.
20 Nevertheless, I will grant to exchange prisoners according to your request, gladly, that I may preserve my food for my men of war; and we will wage a war which shall be eternal, either to the subjecting the Nephites to our authority or to their eternal extinction.
21 And as concerning that God whom ye say we have rejected, behold, we know not such a being; neither do ye; but if it so be that there is such a being, we know not but that he hath made us as well as you.
22 And if it so be that there is a devil and a hell, behold will he not send you there to dwell with my brother whom ye have murdered, whom ye have hinted that he hath gone to such a place? But behold these things matter not.
23 I am Ammoron, and a descendant of Zoram, whom your fathers pressed and brought out of Jerusalem.
24 And behold now, I am a bold Lamanite; behold, this war hath been waged to avenge their wrongs, and to maintain and to obtain their rights to the government; and I close my epistle to Moroni.

---

54:12 ***of our first inheritance***—first given to us

54:12 (11–12) Quoting a First Presidency Message, President Harold B. Lee said, " 'When, therefore, constitutional law, obedient to those principles, calls the manhood of the Church into the armed service of any country to which they owe allegiance, their highest civic duty requires that they meet that call. If, hearkening to that call and obeying those in command over them, they shall take the lives of those who fight against them, that will not make of them murderers, nor subject them to the penalty that God has prescribed for those who kill, beyond the principles to be mentioned shortly: for it would be a cruel God that would punish his children as moral sinners for acts done by them as the innocent instrumentalities of a sovereign whom he had told them to obey and whose will they were powerless to resist.' God is at the helm" ("From the Valley of Despair to the Mountain Peaks of Hope," 5).

54:13 Moroni is a righteous man. He is brave and willing to fight against pride and evil. He seeks to protect and defend his family, religion, and freedom (see Alma 44:5). What can you do to become more like Moroni?

54:16 ***avenge his blood upon you***—get revenge for his death by killing you

54:20 ***authority***—power and rule
***eternal extinction***—absolute death

54:21 When people reject God, Satan rejoices. He tries to "turn . . . hearts away from the truth, that they become blinded" (D&C 78:10).

## CHAPTER 55

*Moroni sees through Ammoron's lies and refuses to trade prisoners. Look for how the Nephites are freed from prison without fighting.*

### Moroni Is Angry at Ammoron's Letter and Refuses to Trade Prisoners

1 NOW it came to pass that when Moroni had received this epistle he was more angry, because he knew that Ammoron had a perfect knowledge of his fraud; yea, he knew that Ammoron knew that it was not a just cause that had caused him to wage a war against the people of Nephi.

2 And he said: Behold, I will not exchange prisoners with Ammoron save he will withdraw his purpose, as I have stated in my epistle; for I will not grant unto him that he shall have any more power than what he hath got.

3 Behold, I know the place where the Lamanites do guard my people whom they have taken prisoners; and as Ammoron would not grant unto me mine epistle, behold, I will give unto him according to my words; yea, I will seek death among them until they shall sue for peace.

### Moroni Uses Trickery to Free the Nephite Prisoners

4 And now it came to pass that when Moroni had said these words, he caused that a search should be made among his men, that perhaps he might find a man who was a descendant of Laman among them.

5 And it came to pass that they found one, whose name was Laman; and he was one of the servants of the king who was murdered by Amalickiah.

6 Now Moroni caused that Laman and a small number of his men should go forth unto the guards who were over the Nephites.

7 Now the Nephites were guarded in the city of Gid; therefore Moroni appointed Laman and caused that a small number of men should go with him.

8 And when it was evening Laman went to the guards who were over the Nephites, and behold, they saw him coming and they hailed him; but he saith unto them: Fear not; behold, I am a Lamanite. Behold, we have escaped from the Nephites, and they sleep; and behold we have taken of their wine and brought with us.

9 Now when the Lamanites heard these words they received him with joy; and they said unto him: Give us of your wine, that we may drink; we are glad that ye have thus taken wine with you for we are weary.

10 But Laman said unto them: Let us keep of our wine till we go against the Nephites to battle. But this saying only made them more desirous to drink of the wine;

11 For, said they: We are weary, therefore let us take of the wine, and by and by we shall receive wine for our rations, which will strengthen us to go against the Nephites.

12 And Laman said unto them: You may do according to your desires.

13 And it came to pass that they did take of the wine freely; and it was pleasant to their taste, therefore they took of it more freely; and it was strong, having been prepared in its strength.

14 And it came to pass they did drink and were merry, and by and by they were all drunken.

15 And now when Laman and his men saw that they were all drunken, and were in a deep sleep, they returned to Moroni and told him all the things that had happened.

---

55:1 ***epistle***—letter
***fraud***—lies
***wage***—carry on

55:2 ***exchange***—trade
***save***—unless

55:3 ***grant unto me mine epistle***—give me what I asked for in my letter
***sue***—plead or beg

55:4 ***a descendant***—of the family

55:5 This Laman is one of the Lamanite king's servants who escaped from Amalickiah and joined the people of Ammon (see Alma 47:20–29).

55:7 ***appointed***—chose

55:8 ***hailed***—called to

55:9 ***weary***—tired

55:11 ***for our rations***—with the food we get

55:12 ***according to your desires***—as you wish

16 And now this was according to the design of
Moroni. And Moroni had prepared his men with
weapons of war; and he went to the city Gid, while
the Lamanites were in a deep sleep and drunken,
and cast in weapons of war unto the prisoners,
insomuch that they were all armed;
17 Yea, even to their women, and all those of their
children, as many as were able to use a weapon of
war, when Moroni had armed all those prisoners;
and all those things were done in a profound
silence.
18 But had they awakened the Lamanites, behold
they were drunken and the Nephites could have
slain them.
19 But behold, this was not the desire of Moroni;
he did not delight in murder or bloodshed, but he
delighted in the saving of his people from destruction; and for this cause he might not bring upon
him injustice, he would not fall upon the Lamanites
and destroy them in their drunkenness.
20 But he had obtained his desires; for he had
armed those prisoners of the Nephites who were
within the wall of the city, and had given them
power to gain possession of those parts which were
within the walls.
21 And then he caused the men who were with
him to withdraw a pace from them, and surround
the armies of the Lamanites.

## Moroni's Army Captures the City of Gid

22 Now behold this was done in the night-time, so
that when the Lamanites awoke in the morning they
beheld that they were surrounded by the Nephites
without, and that their prisoners were armed within.
23 And thus they saw that the Nephites had power
over them; and in these circumstances they found
that it was not expedient that they should fight
with the Nephites; therefore their chief captains
demanded their weapons of war, and they
brought them forth and cast them at the feet of the
Nephites, pleading for mercy.
24 Now behold, this was the desire of Moroni. He
took them prisoners of war, and took possession of
the city, and caused that all the prisoners should be
liberated, who were Nephites; and they did join the
army of Moroni, and were a great strength to his
army.
25 And it came to pass that he did cause the
Lamanites, whom he had taken prisoners, that they
should commence a labor in strengthening the fortifications round about the city Gid.
26 And it came to pass that when he had fortified
the city Gid, according to his desires, he caused that
his prisoners should be taken to the city Bountiful;
and he also guarded that city with an exceedingly
strong force.
27 And it came to pass that they did, notwithstanding all the intrigues of the Lamanites, keep and
protect all the prisoners whom they had taken, and
also maintain all the ground and the advantage
which they had retaken.

## The Nephites Are Protected As They Get Back Their Lands

28 And it came to pass that the Nephites began
again to be victorious, and to reclaim their rights
and their privileges.
29 Many times did the Lamanites attempt to encircle them about by night, but in these attempts
they did lose many prisoners.

---

55:16 ***design***—plan

55:17 ***profound***—deep

55:19 Moroni "did not delight in murder or bloodshed." According to the Prophet Joseph Smith, "When you find a spirit that wants bloodshed,—murder, the same is not of God, but is of the devil" (*Teachings of the Prophet Joseph Smith,* 358).

What do you learn about Moroni's unwillingness to kill the drunken Lamanite guards, even though he is a soldier?

55:20 ***obtained***—received

55:21 ***withdraw a pace***—go back a short distance

55:23 ***expedient***—wise

55:24 ***possession***—control
***liberated***—freed

55:25 ***commence***—begin
***fortifications***—forts

55:26 ***fortified***—strengthened

55:27 ***intrigues***—secret plans and attempts
***maintain***—keep

55:28 ***be victorious***—win battles
***reclaim***—get back

30 And many times did they attempt to administer
of their wine to the Nephites, that they might
destroy them with poison or with drunkenness.
31 But behold, the Nephites were not slow to
remember the Lord their God in this their time of
affliction. They could not be taken in their snares;
yea, they would not partake of their wine, save they
had first given to some of the Lamanite prisoners.
32 And they were thus cautious that no poison
should be administered among them; for if their
wine would poison a Lamanite it would also poison
a Nephite; and thus they did try all their liquors.
33 And now it came to pass that it was expedient
for Moroni to make preparations to attack the city
Morianton; for behold, the Lamanites had, by their
labors, fortified the city Morianton until it had
become an exceeding stronghold.
34 And they were continually bringing new forces
into that city, and also new supplies of provisions.
35 And thus ended the twenty and ninth year of
the reign of the judges over the people of Nephi.

## CHAPTER 56

*Helaman's two thousand stripling warriors courageously fight the Lamanites. Watch for the source of their courage and strength.*

### Helaman Tells of the Converted Lamanites' Covenant

1 AND now it came to pass in the commencement
of the thirtieth year of the reign of the judges, on
the second day in the first month, Moroni received
an epistle from Helaman, stating the affairs of the
people in that quarter of the land.
2 And these are the words which he wrote, saying:
My dearly beloved brother, Moroni, as well in the
Lord as in the tribulations of our warfare; behold, my
beloved brother, I have somewhat to tell you concerning our warfare in this part of the land.
3 Behold, two thousand of the sons of those men
whom Ammon brought down out of the land of
Nephi—now ye have known that these were
descendants of Laman, who was the eldest son of
our father Lehi;
4 Now I need not rehearse unto you concerning
their traditions or their unbelief, for thou knowest
concerning all these things—
5 Therefore it sufficeth me that I tell you that two
thousand of these young men have taken their
weapons of war, and would that I should be their
leader; and we have come forth to defend our
country.
6 And now ye also know concerning the covenant
which their fathers made, that they would not take
up their weapons of war against their brethren to
shed blood.
7 But in the twenty and sixth year, when they saw
our afflictions and our tribulations for them, they
were about to break the covenant which they had
made and take up their weapons of war in our
defence.
8 But I would not suffer them that they should
break this covenant which they had made, supposing that God would strengthen us, insomuch that
we should not suffer more because of the fulfilling
the oath which they had taken.

---

55:30 ***administer***—give

55:31 ***affliction***—trial
***snares***—traps

55:32 ***liquors***—alcoholic drinks

55:34 ***forces***—soldiers

56:1 ***commencement***—beginning
***reign***—rule
***quarter***—part

56:2 ***tribulations***—troubles and misery

56:4 ***rehearse***—repeat

56:5 ***sufficeth***—is enough for

56:8 ***suffer***—allow or let

56:8 (5–8) There are times when it is necessary to take up weapons of war to defend one's country. What do you learn from the stripling warriors about when the Lord allows His children to go to war?

## *Helaman's Two Thousand Stripling Warriors Join Antipus's Army*

9 But behold, here is one thing in which we may have great joy. For behold, in the twenty and sixth year, I, Helaman, did march at the head of these two thousand young men to the city of Judea, to assist Antipus, whom ye had appointed a leader over the people of that part of the land.
10 And I did join my two thousand sons, (for they are worthy to be called sons) to the army of Antipus, in which strength Antipus did rejoice exceedingly; for behold, his army had been reduced by the Lamanites because their forces had slain a vast number of our men, for which cause we have to mourn.
11 Nevertheless, we may console ourselves in this point, that they have died in the cause of their country and of their God, yea, and they are happy.
12 And the Lamanites had also retained many prisoners, all of whom are chief captains, for none other have they spared alive. And we suppose that they are now at this time in the land of Nephi; it is so if they are not slain.
13 And now these are the cities of which the Lamanites have obtained possession by the shedding of the blood of so many of our valiant men;
14 The land of Manti, or the city of Manti, and the city of Zeezrom, and the city of Cumeni, and the city of Antiparah.
15 And these are the cities which they possessed when I arrived at the city of Judea; and I found Antipus and his men toiling with their might to fortify the city.
16 Yea, and they were depressed in body as well as in spirit, for they had fought valiantly by day and toiled by night to maintain their cities; and thus they had suffered great afflictions of every kind.
17 And now they were determined to conquer in this place or die; therefore you may well suppose that this little force which I brought with me, yea, those sons of mine, gave them great hopes and much joy.
18 And now it came to pass that when the Lamanites saw that Antipus had received a greater strength to his army, they were compelled by the orders of Ammoron to not come against the city of Judea, or against us, to battle.
19 And thus were we favored of the Lord; for had they come upon us in this our weakness they might have perhaps destroyed our little army; but thus were we preserved.
20 They were commanded by Ammoron to maintain those cities which they had taken. And thus ended the twenty and sixth year. And in the commencement of the twenty and seventh year we had prepared our city and ourselves for defence.

## *The Nephite Armies Grow in Numbers*

21 Now we were desirous that the Lamanites should come upon us; for we were not desirous to make an attack upon them in their strongholds.
22 And it came to pass that we kept spies out

---

56:9 "These 'stripling warriors', it seems, could have ranged in age from approximately twenty (going by the Mosaic rule) to approximately twenty-two (those who could have been around age seven when the oath was taken) in the twenty-sixth year of the judges" (John A. Tvedtnes, "I Have a Question," 28).

56:10 ***exceedingly***—very much
***slain***—killed
***vast***—large
***mourn***—feel great sadness

56:11 ***console ourselves in this point***—feel better thinking about this

Elder Robert D. Hales taught that "the doctrine of the Atonement [is] that all will be resurrected. . . . While there will be mourning at the temporary separation, there is no sorrow for those who die in the Lord (see Revelation 14:13; D&C 42:46)" (in Conference Report, October 1996, 89).

56:12 ***retained***—kept

56:15 ***toiling***—working

56:16 Elder Rex D. Pinegar noted, "Sometimes hardships come our way or fatigue dims our vision in decision making" (in Conference Report, October 1974, 61). These Nephites soldiers are tired from fighting during the day and working through the night. How does lack of rest affect your spirit?

56:18 ***compelled***—forced

56:19 ***preserved***—saved

56:21 ***desirous***—wanting
***strongholds***—forts

*Helaman leading the stripling warriors*

TWO THOUSAND STRIPLING WARRIORS, BY CLARK KELLEY PRICE

round about, to watch the movements of the Lamanites, that they might not pass us by night nor by day to make an attack upon our other cities which were on the northward.

23 For we knew in those cities they were not sufficiently strong to meet them; therefore we were desirous, if they should pass by us, to fall upon them in their rear, and thus bring them up in the rear at the same time they were met in the front. We supposed that we could overpower them; but behold, we were disappointed in this our desire.

24 They durst not pass by us with their whole army, neither durst they with a part, lest they should not be sufficiently strong and they should fall.

25 Neither durst they march down against the city of Zarahemla; neither durst they cross the head of Sidon, over to the city of Nephihah.

26 And thus, with their forces, they were determined to maintain those cities which they had taken.

27 And now it came to pass in the second month of this year, there was brought unto us many provisions from the fathers of those my two thousand sons.

28 And also there were sent two thousand men unto us from the land of Zarahemla. And thus we were prepared with ten thousand men, and provisions for them, and also for their wives and their children.

29 And the Lamanites, thus seeing our forces increase daily, and provisions arrive for our support, they began to be fearful, and began to sally forth, if it were possible to put an end to our receiving provisions and strength.

### The Nephite Armies Trick the Lamanites

30 Now when we saw that the Lamanites began to grow uneasy on this wise, we were desirous to bring a stratagem into effect upon them; therefore Antipus ordered that I should march forth with my little sons to a neighboring city, as if we were carrying provisions to a neighboring city.

31 And we were to march near the city of Antiparah, as if we were going to the city beyond, in the borders by the seashore.

32 And it came to pass that we did march forth, as if with our provisions, to go to that city.

33 And it came to pass that Antipus did march forth with a part of his army, leaving the remainder to maintain the city. But he did not march forth until I had gone forth with my little army, and came near the city Antiparah.

34 And now, in the city Antiparah were stationed the strongest army of the Lamanites; yea, the most numerous.

35 And it came to pass that when they had been informed by their spies, they came forth with their army and marched against us.

36 And it came to pass that we did flee before them, northward. And thus we did lead away the most powerful army of the Lamanites;

37 Yea, even to a considerable distance, insomuch that when they saw the army of Antipus pursuing them, with their might, they did not turn to the right nor to the left, but pursued their march in a straight course after us; and, as we suppose, it was their intent to slay us before Antipus should overtake them, and this that they might not be surrounded by our people.

38 And now Antipus, beholding our danger, did speed the march of his army. But behold, it was night; therefore they did not overtake us, neither did Antipus overtake them; therefore we did camp for the night.

39 And it came to pass that before the dawn of the morning, behold, the Lamanites were pursuing us. Now we were not sufficiently strong to contend with them; yea, I would not suffer that my little sons should fall into their hands; therefore we did continue our march, and we took our march into the wilderness.

---

56:24 ***durst***—dared

56:27 ***many provisions***—much food and other supplies

"Just as the mothers reared sons of great faith and courage, the fathers sacrificed in delivering provisions to their sons. (Alma 56:27.) Though the stripling warriors' fathers would not bear arms, they gave 'a large portion of their substance' in support of the Nephite armies. (Alma 43:13)" (Spencer J. Condie, "Righteous Oaths, Reproof, and Reconciliation," 86).

56:29 ***sally forth***—send out armies

56:30 ***on this wise***—in this way
***stratagem***—military plan

56:37 ***pursuing***—chasing

40 Now they durst not turn to the right nor to the left lest they should be surrounded; neither would I turn to the right nor to the left lest they should overtake me, and we could not stand against them, but be slain, and they would make their escape; and thus we did flee all that day into the wilderness, even until it was dark.

41 And it came to pass that again, when the light of the morning came we saw the Lamanites upon us, and we did flee before them.

42 But it came to pass that they did not pursue us far before they halted; and it was in the morning of the third day of the seventh month.

43 And now, whether they were overtaken by Antipus we knew not, but I said unto my men: Behold, we know not but they have halted for the purpose that we should come against them, that they might catch us in their snare;

## Helaman's Sons Fight in Righteousness

44 Therefore what say ye, my sons, will ye go against them to battle?

45 And now I say unto you, my beloved brother Moroni, that never had I seen so great courage, nay, not amongst all the Nephites.

46 For as I had ever called them my sons (for they were all of them very young) even so they said unto me: Father, behold our God is with us, and he will not suffer that we should fall; then let us go forth; we would not slay our brethren if they would let us alone; therefore let us go, lest they should overpower the army of Antipus.

47 Now they never had fought, yet they did not fear death; and they did think more upon the liberty of their fathers than they did upon their lives; yea, they had been taught by their mothers, that if they did not doubt, God would deliver them.

48 And they rehearsed unto me the words of their mothers, saying: We do not doubt our mothers knew it.

49 And it came to pass that I did return with my two thousand against these Lamanites who had pursued us. And now behold, the armies of Antipus had overtaken them, and a terrible battle had commenced.

50 The army of Antipus being weary, because of their long march in so short a space of time, were about to fall into the hands of the Lamanites; and had I not returned with my two thousand they would have obtained their purpose.

51 For Antipus had fallen by the sword, and many of his leaders, because of their weariness, which was occasioned by the speed of their march—therefore the men of Antipus, being confused because of the fall of their leaders, began to give way before the Lamanites.

52 And it came to pass that the Lamanites took courage, and began to pursue them; and thus were the Lamanites pursuing them with great vigor when Helaman came upon their rear with his two thousand, and began to slay them exceedingly, insomuch that the whole army of the Lamanites halted and turned upon Helaman.

53 Now when the people of Antipus saw that the Lamanites had turned them about, they gathered together their men and came again upon the rear of the Lamanites.

54 And now it came to pass that we, the people of Nephi, the people of Antipus, and I with my two thousand, did surround the Lamanites, and did slay them; yea, insomuch that they were compelled to deliver up their weapons of war and also themselves as prisoners of war.

---

56:43 ***snare***—trap

56:44 Helaman asks his army if they will go into battle and fight their enemies. Likewise, you are asked to defend or "fight" for the truth. What spiritual preparations can you make in order to defend the truth effectively?

56:47 ***deliver***—save

The young men were taught by their mothers that "if they did not doubt, God would deliver them." President Marion G. Romney called their story "another remarkable demonstration of how the Lord sustains those who put their trust in Him" (in Conference Report, October 1977, 60).

56:48 (47–48) "It seems more than a coincidence to me that when mention is made of all who could be counted as being responsible for the great valor and spirit of these 2,000 young men, the recorder felt impressed to mention only the training by their mothers. Many others might have been mentioned—mothers were" (H. Burke Peterson, in Conference Report, April 1976, 52).

56:50 ***obtained their purpose***—won the battle

HEROES: TAUGHT BY THEIR MOTHERS, BY LIZ LEMON SWINDLE

*"They had been taught by their mothers."*

55 And now it came to pass that when they had surrendered themselves up unto us, behold, I numbered those young men who had fought with me, fearing lest there were many of them slain.

56 But behold, to my great joy, there had not one soul of them fallen to the earth; yea, and they had fought as if with the strength of God; yea, never were men known to have fought with such miraculous strength; and with such mighty power did they fall upon the Lamanites, that they did frighten them; and for this cause did the Lamanites deliver themselves up as prisoners of war.

57 And as we had no place for our prisoners, that we could guard them to keep them from the armies of the Lamanites, therefore we sent them to the land of Zarahemla, and a part of those men who were not slain of Antipus, with them; and the remainder I took and joined them to my stripling Ammonites, and took our march back to the city of Judea.

## CHAPTER 57

*War continues with the Lamanites. The stripling warriors are all wounded, but not one is killed. Look for reasons why they are protected so miraculously.*

### The City of Antiparah Is Taken Without Bloodshed

1 AND now it came to pass that I received an epistle from Ammoron, the king, stating that if I would deliver up those prisoners of war whom we had taken that he would deliver up the city of Antiparah unto us.

2 But I sent an epistle unto the king, that we were sure our forces were sufficient to take the city of Antiparah by our force; and by delivering up the prisoners for that city we should suppose ourselves unwise, and that we would only deliver up our prisoners on exchange.

3 And Ammoron refused mine epistle, for he would not exchange prisoners; therefore we began to make preparations to go against the city of Antiparah.

4 But the people of Antiparah did leave the city, and fled to their other cities, which they had possession of, to fortify them; and thus the city of Antiparah fell into our hands.

5 And thus ended the twenty and eighth year of the reign of the judges.

### The Lamanites in Cumeni Surrender for Lack of Food

6 And it came to pass that in the commencement of the twenty and ninth year, we received a supply of provisions, and also an addition to our army, from the land of Zarahemla, and from the land round about, to the number of six thousand men, besides sixty of the sons of the Ammonites who had come to join their brethren, my little band of two thousand. And now behold, we were strong, yea, and we had also plenty of provisions brought unto us.

7 And it came to pass that it was our desire to wage a battle with the army which was placed to protect the city Cumeni.

8 And now behold, I will show unto you that we soon accomplished our desire; yea, with our strong force, or with a part of our strong force, we did surround, by night, the city Cumeni, a little before they were to receive a supply of provisions.

9 And it came to pass that we did camp round about the city for many nights; but we did sleep upon our swords, and keep guards, that the Lamanites could not come upon us by night and slay us, which they attempted many times; but as many times as they attempted this their blood was spilt.

10 At length their provisions did arrive, and they were about to enter the city by night. And we, instead of being Lamanites, were Nephites; therefore, we did take them and their provisions.

---

57:1 ***an epistle***—a letter

57:2 ***sufficient***—strong enough
***exchange***—trade

57:4 ***fortify***—strengthen

57:6 The story of how the two thousand sons of the Ammonites became Nephite warriors is found in Alma 53:10–22.

57:7 ***wage***—fight

57:9 The Nephites slept with their swords and kept guards to protect themselves from their enemies. How can you always be ready to defend yourself against the spiritual enemies you face? (see 1 Nephi 15:24).

11 And notwithstanding the Lamanites being cut off from their support after this manner, they were still determined to maintain the city; therefore it became expedient that we should take those provisions and send them to Judea, and our prisoners to the land of Zarahemla.

12 And it came to pass that not many days had passed away before the Lamanites began to lose all hopes of succor; therefore they yielded up the city unto our hands; and thus we had accomplished our designs in obtaining the city Cumeni.

## The Lamanites Attack, but the Stripling Warriors Stand Firm

13 But it came to pass that our prisoners were so numerous that, notwithstanding the enormity of our numbers, we were obliged to employ all our force to keep them, or to put them to death.

14 For behold, they would break out in great numbers, and would fight with stones, and with clubs, or whatsoever thing they could get into their hands, insomuch that we did slay upwards of two thousand of them after they had surrendered themselves prisoners of war.

15 Therefore it became expedient for us, that we should put an end to their lives, or guard them, sword in hand, down to the land of Zarahemla; and also our provisions were not any more than sufficient for our own people, notwithstanding that which we had taken from the Lamanites.

16 And now, in those critical circumstances, it became a very serious matter to determine concerning these prisoners of war; nevertheless, we did resolve to send them down to the land of Zarahemla; therefore we selected a part of our men, and gave them charge over our prisoners to go down to the land of Zarahemla.

17 But it came to pass that on the morrow they did return. And now behold, we did not inquire of them concerning the prisoners; for behold, the Lamanites were upon us, and they returned in season to save us from falling into their hands. For behold, Ammoron had sent to their support a new supply of provisions and also a numerous army of men.

18 And it came to pass that those men whom we sent with the prisoners did arrive in season to check them, as they were about to overpower us.

19 But behold, my little band of two thousand and sixty fought most desperately; yea, they were firm before the Lamanites, and did administer death unto all those who opposed them.

20 And as the remainder of our army were about to give way before the Lamanites, behold, those two thousand and sixty were firm and undaunted.

21 Yea, and they did obey and observe to perform every word of command with exactness; yea, and even according to their faith it was done unto them; and I did remember the words which they said unto me that their mothers had taught them.

22 And now behold, it was these my sons, and those men who had been selected to convey the prisoners, to whom we owe this great victory; for it was they who did beat the Lamanites; therefore they were driven back to the city of Manti.

23 And we retained our city Cumeni, and were not all destroyed by the sword; nevertheless, we had suffered great loss.

---

57:11 ***maintain***—control
***expedient***—necessary

57:12 ***succor***—support or help
***yielded***—gave
***designs***—plans or goals

57:13 ***enormity***—huge size or greatness
***obliged***—forced

57:16 ***critical circumstances***—difficult times
***resolve***—decide

57:17 ***inquire***—ask
***season***—time

57:18 ***check***—stop

57:19 ***desperately***—bravely and boldly
***administer death unto***—kill

57:20 ***undaunted***—fearless

57:21 The stripling warriors "gave their mothers credit for teaching them, but they kept the commandments with exactness. This is the great secret. It is so important that we be in condition to serve the Lord, and condition comes only through obedience" (Hartman Rector Jr., "You Shall Receive the Spirit," 106).

57:22 ***convey***—deliver

57:23 ***retained***—continued to hold

## The Stripling Warriors Are Saved by the Power of God

24 And it came to pass that after the Lamanites had fled, I immediately gave orders that my men who had been wounded should be taken from among the dead, and caused that their wounds should be dressed.

25 And it came to pass that there were two hundred, out of my two thousand and sixty, who had fainted because of the loss of blood; nevertheless, according to the goodness of God, and to our great astonishment, and also the joy of our whole army, there was not one soul of them who did perish; yea, and neither was there one soul among them who had not received many wounds.

26 And now, their preservation was astonishing to our whole army, yea, that they should be spared while there was a thousand of our brethren who were slain. And we do justly ascribe it to the miraculous power of God, because of their exceeding faith in that which they had been taught to believe—that there was a just God, and whosoever did not doubt, that they should be preserved by his marvelous power.

27 Now this was the faith of these of whom I have spoken; they are young, and their minds are firm, and they do put their trust in God continually.

## Gid Explains What Happened to the Lamanite Prisoners

28 And now it came to pass that after we had thus taken care of our wounded men, and had buried our dead and also the dead of the Lamanites, who were many, behold, we did inquire of Gid concerning the prisoners whom they had started to go down to the land of Zarahemla with.

29 Now Gid was the chief captain over the band who was appointed to guard them down to the land.

30 And now, these are the words which Gid said unto me: Behold, we did start to go down to the land of Zarahemla with our prisoners. And it came to pass that we did meet the spies of our armies, who had been sent out to watch the camp of the Lamanites.

31 And they cried unto us, saying—Behold, the armies of the Lamanites are marching towards the city of Cumeni; and behold, they will fall upon them, yea, and will destroy our people.

32 And it came to pass that our prisoners did hear their cries, which caused them to take courage; and they did rise up in rebellion against us.

33 And it came to pass because of their rebellion we did cause that our swords should come upon them. And it came to pass that they did in a body run upon our swords, in the which, the greater number of them were slain; and the remainder of them broke through and fled from us.

34 And behold, when they had fled and we could not overtake them, we took our march with speed towards the city Cumeni; and behold, we did arrive in time that we might assist our brethren in preserving the city.

35 And behold, we are again delivered out of the hands of our enemies. And blessed is the name of our God; for behold, it is he that has delivered us; yea, that has done this great thing for us.

36 Now it came to pass that when I, Helaman, had heard these words of Gid, I was filled with exceeding joy because of the goodness of God in preserving us, that we might not all perish; yea, and I trust that the souls of them who have been slain have entered into the rest of their God.

---

57:24 ***dressed***—treated and bandaged

57:25 ***astonishment***—surprise

57:26 ***their preservation was astonishing***—that none of them had been killed was amazing
***spared***—saved
***justly ascribe it***—correctly give the credit

57:28 ***inquire***—ask

57:32 ***rebellion***—opposition and fighting

## CHAPTER 58

*Helaman continues his letter to Moroni (see Alma 56:1). He tells how the city of Manti was taken without a battle. Notice how Helaman and his people turn to the Lord for strength when they are greatly outnumbered by the Lamanites.*

### *Helaman's Army Is Outnumbered and Starving*

1 AND behold, now it came to pass that our next object was to obtain the city of Manti; but behold, there was no way that we could lead them out of the city by our small bands. For behold, they remembered that which we had hitherto done; therefore we could not decoy them away from their strongholds.

2 And they were so much more numerous than was our army that we durst not go forth and attack them in their strongholds.

3 Yea, and it became expedient that we should employ our men to the maintaining those parts of the land which we had regained of our possessions; therefore it became expedient that we should wait, that we might receive more strength from the land of Zarahemla and also a new supply of provisions.

4 And it came to pass that I thus did send an embassy to the governor of our land, to acquaint him concerning the affairs of our people. And it came to pass that we did wait to receive provisions and strength from the land of Zarahemla.

5 But behold, this did profit us but little; for the Lamanites were also receiving great strength from day to day, and also many provisions; and thus were our circumstances at this period of time.

6 And the Lamanites were sallying forth against us from time to time, resolving by stratagem to destroy us; nevertheless we could not come to battle with them, because of their retreats and their strongholds.

7 And it came to pass that we did wait in these difficult circumstances for the space of many months, even until we were about to perish for the want of food.

8 But it came to pass that we did receive food, which was guarded to us by an army of two thousand men to our assistance; and this is all the assistance which we did receive, to defend ourselves and our country from falling into the hands of our enemies, yea, to contend with an enemy which was innumerable.

### *Helaman and His Men Place Their Trust in the Lord*

9 And now the cause of these our embarrassments, or the cause why they did not send more strength unto us, we knew not; therefore we were grieved and also filled with fear, lest by any means the judgments of God should come upon our land, to our overthrow and utter destruction.

10 Therefore we did pour out our souls in prayer to God, that he would strengthen us and deliver us out of the hands of our enemies, yea, and also give us strength that we might retain our cities, and our lands, and our possessions, for the support of our people.

11 Yea, and it came to pass that the Lord our God did visit us with assurances that he would deliver

---

58:1 ***bands***—groups of soldiers
***hitherto***—up to this time
***decoy***—trick

58:2 ***durst***—dared

58:3 ***provisions***—food and other supplies

58:4 ***an embassy***—messengers
***acquaint***—inform

58:6 ***sallying***—rushing
***stratagem***—tricks or plans
***retreats***—places of safety

58:8 ***assistance***—help
***innumerable***—too large to count

58:9 ***embarrassments***—difficulties

58:9 (3–9) Have you ever been disappointed by someone you depended upon? Where did you turn for help? How could the Lord be of help to you in those times?

58:11 ***assurances***—promises

58:11 (10–11) "Just as Helaman discovered in the midst of battle that 'he did speak peace to our souls' (Alma 58:11) . . . all sincere seekers can have that same peace spoken to them. That peace comes from the assurances spoken by a still, small voice. The Holy Ghost is a personage of spirit who generally communicates not through physical senses but by touching the heart and mind; in other words, He speaks through thoughts, impressions, and feelings and does so softly" (Dennis E. Simmons, in Conference Report, April 1997, 42).

us; yea, insomuch that he did speak peace to our souls, and did grant unto us great faith, and did cause us that we should hope for our deliverance in him.

12 And we did take courage with our small force which we had received, and were fixed with a determination to conquer our enemies, and to maintain our lands, and our possessions, and our wives, and our children, and the cause of our liberty.

## The Nephites Take Manti Without Shedding Blood

13 And thus we did go forth with all our might against the Lamanites, who were in the city of Manti; and we did pitch our tents by the wilderness side, which was near to the city.

14 And it came to pass that on the morrow, that when the Lamanites saw that we were in the borders by the wilderness which was near the city, that they sent out their spies round about us that they might discover the number and the strength of our army.

15 And it came to pass that when they saw that we were not strong, according to our numbers, and fearing that we should cut them off from their support except they should come out to battle against us and kill us, and also supposing that they could easily destroy us with their numerous hosts, therefore they began to make preparations to come out against us to battle.

16 And when we saw that they were making preparations to come out against us, behold, I caused that Gid, with a small number of men, should secrete himself in the wilderness, and also that Teomner and a small number of men should secrete themselves also in the wilderness.

17 Now Gid and his men were on the right and the others on the left; and when they had thus secreted themselves, behold, I remained, with the remainder of my army, in that same place where we had first pitched our tents against the time that the Lamanites should come out to battle.

18 And it came to pass that the Lamanites did come out with their numerous army against us. And when they had come and were about to fall upon us with the sword, I caused that my men, those who were with me, should retreat into the wilderness.

19 And it came to pass that the Lamanites did follow after us with great speed, for they were exceedingly desirous to overtake us that they might slay us; therefore they did follow us into the wilderness; and we did pass by in the midst of Gid and Teomner, insomuch that they were not discovered by the Lamanites.

20 And it came to pass that when the Lamanites had passed by, or when the army had passed by, Gid and Teomner did rise up from their secret places, and did cut off the spies of the Lamanites that they should not return to the city.

21 And it came to pass that when they had cut them off, they ran to the city and fell upon the guards who were left to guard the city, insomuch that they did destroy them and did take possession of the city.

22 Now this was done because the Lamanites did suffer their whole army, save a few guards only, to be led away into the wilderness.

23 And it came to pass that Gid and Teomner by this means had obtained possession of their strongholds. And it came to pass that we took our course, after having traveled much in the wilderness towards the land of Zarahemla.

24 And when the Lamanites saw that they were marching towards the land of Zarahemla, they were exceedingly afraid, lest there was a plan laid to lead them on to destruction; therefore they began to retreat into the wilderness again, yea, even back by the same way which they had come.

25 And behold, it was night and they did pitch their tents, for the chief captains of the Lamanites had supposed that the Nephites were weary because of their march; and supposing that they had driven their whole army therefore they took no thought concerning the city of Manti.

---

58:12 "In other words, the Lord put inside these men the will and the power to do what they desired—to begin with a strong resolve and then to see it through. After their prayer was answered, the Nephites went on to secure their liberty" (Gene R. Cook, *Receiving Answers to Our Prayers,* 156).

58:16 ***secrete***—hide

58:17 ***remained, with the remainder***—stayed with the rest

58:19 ***insomuch***—in such a way

58:22 ***suffer***—allow

26 Now it came to pass that when it was night, I caused that my men should not sleep, but that they should march forward by another way towards the land of Manti.
27 And because of this our march in the night-time, behold, on the morrow we were beyond the Lamanites, insomuch that we did arrive before them at the city of Manti.
28 And thus it came to pass, that by this stratagem we did take possession of the city of Manti without the shedding of blood.
29 And it came to pass that when the armies of the Lamanites did arrive near the city, and saw that we were prepared to meet them, they were astonished exceedingly and struck with great fear, insomuch that they did flee into the wilderness.

### The Stripling Warriors Are Protected Because of Their Faith and Obedience

30 Yea, and it came to pass that the armies of the Lamanites did flee out of all this quarter of the land. But behold, they have carried with them many women and children out of the land.
31 And those cities which had been taken by the Lamanites, all of them are at this period of time in our possession; and our fathers and our women and our children are returning to their homes, all save it be those who have been taken prisoners and carried off by the Lamanites.
32 But behold, our armies are small to maintain so great a number of cities and so great possessions.
33 But behold, we trust in our God who has given us victory over those lands, insomuch that we have obtained those cities and those lands, which were our own.
34 Now we do not know the cause that the government does not grant us more strength; neither do those men who came up unto us know why we have not received greater strength.
35 Behold, we do not know but what ye are unsuccessful, and ye have drawn away the forces into that quarter of the land; if so, we do not desire to murmur.
36 And if it is not so, behold, we fear that there is some faction in the government, that they do not send more men to our assistance; for we know that they are more numerous than that which they have sent.
37 But, behold, it mattereth not—we trust God will deliver us, notwithstanding the weakness of our armies, yea, and deliver us out of the hands of our enemies.
38 Behold, this is the twenty and ninth year, in the latter end, and we are in the possession of our lands; and the Lamanites have fled to the land of Nephi.
39 And those sons of the people of Ammon, of whom I have so highly spoken, are with me in the city of Manti; and the Lord had supported them, yea, and kept them from falling by the sword, insomuch that even one soul has not been slain.
40 But behold, they have received many wounds; nevertheless they stand fast in that liberty wherewith God has made them free; and they are strict to remember the Lord their God from day to day; yea, they do observe to keep his statutes, and his judgments, and his commandments continually; and their faith is strong in the prophecies concerning that which is to come.
41 And now, my beloved brother, Moroni, may the Lord our God, who has redeemed us and made us free, keep you continually in his presence; yea, and may he favor this people, even that ye may have success in obtaining the possession of all that which the Lamanites have taken from us, which was for our support. And now, behold, I close mine epistle. I am Helaman, the son of Alma.

## CHAPTER 59

*Moroni, the chief captain of the Nephites, works to protect his people's rights and liberties. He asks for help from Pahoran, the chief judge. Notice how Moroni promotes freedom for his people.*

### The City of Nephihah Falls to the Lamanites

1 NOW it came to pass in the thirtieth year of the reign of the judges over the people of Nephi, after Moroni had received and had read Helaman's epistle, he was exceedingly rejoiced because of the welfare,

58:35 "Those of deep faith do not murmur. They are generously disposed, and they are reluctant to murmur, even while in deep difficulties" (Neal A. Maxwell, in Conference Report, October 1989, 105).

58:36 ***faction***—opposing group

59:1 ***epistle***—letter

HELAMAN AND HIS 2,000 SONS, BY RONALD CROSBY

*"They are strict to remember the Lord their God from day to day."*

yea, the exceeding success which Helaman had had, in obtaining those lands which were lost.
2 Yea, and he did make it known unto all his people, in all the land round about in that part where he was, that they might rejoice also.
3 And it came to pass that he immediately sent an epistle to Pahoran, desiring that he should cause men to be gathered together to strengthen Helaman, or the armies of Helaman, insomuch that he might with ease maintain that part of the land which he had been so miraculously prospered in regaining.
4 And it came to pass when Moroni had sent this epistle to the land of Zarahemla, he began again to lay a plan that he might obtain the remainder of those possessions and cities which the Lamanites had taken from them.
5 And it came to pass that while Moroni was thus making preparations to go against the Lamanites to battle, behold, the people of Nephihah, who were gathered together from the city of Moroni and the city of Lehi and the city of Morianton, were attacked by the Lamanites.
6 Yea, even those who had been compelled to flee from the land of Manti, and from the land round about, had come over and joined the Lamanites in this part of the land.
7 And thus being exceedingly numerous, yea, and receiving strength from day to day, by the command of Ammoron they came forth against the people of Nephihah, and they did begin to slay them with an exceedingly great slaughter.
8 And their armies were so numerous that the remainder of the people of Nephihah were obliged to flee before them; and they came even and joined the army of Moroni.
9 And now as Moroni had supposed that there should be men sent to the city of Nephihah, to the assistance of the people to maintain that city, and knowing that it was easier to keep the city from falling into the hands of the Lamanites than to retake it from them, he supposed that they would easily maintain that city.
10 Therefore he retained all his force to maintain those places which he had recovered.

## Moroni Is Upset with the Government

11 And now, when Moroni saw that the city of Nephihah was lost he was exceedingly sorrowful, and began to doubt, because of the wickedness of the people, whether they should not fall into the hands of their brethren.
12 Now this was the case with all his chief captains. They doubted and marveled also because of the wickedness of the people, and this because of the success of the Lamanites over them.
13 And it came to pass that Moroni was angry with the government, because of their indifference concerning the freedom of their country.

## CHAPTER 60

*Captain Moroni loves his country and his men who have been fighting for freedom. When help doesn't come from the government, he sends a letter of warning to the chief judge, Pahoran. Look for the true principles Moroni teaches about the responsibilities of leaders.*

---

59:3 ***prospered***—blessed

59:4 ***remainder***—rest

59:6 ***compelled***—forced

59:7 ***numerous***—large in number
***slay them with an exceedingly great slaughter***—kill a large number of the people

59:8 ***obliged***—forced

59:9 ***maintain***—protect

59:10 ***retained***—held

59:12 The Nephite military leaders are surprised at the wickedness of their own people and the success of the Lamanites over them. In what ways did the Nephites' wickedness allow for the Lamanites' success? What lesson do you think this could teach to world leaders today?

59:13 ***indifference***—lack of interest

59:13 (4–13) Moroni is a great military genius, but he is caught by surprise by a massive Lamanite attack on Nephihah. Nephihah falls more quickly than expected, and Moroni's brilliant plans to begin recapturing the fallen Nephite cities are foiled. Hugh Nibley points out that these events illustrate the uncertainty and confusion of war: "Everybody surprises everybody else in war; nobody is sure of anything" (*Brother Brigham Challenges the Saints*, 288–89).

## *Moroni Describes His Army's Sufferings*

1 AND it came to pass that he wrote again to the governor of the land, who was Pahoran, and these are the words which he wrote, saying: Behold, I direct mine epistle to Pahoran, in the city of Zarahemla, who is the chief judge and the governor over the land, and also to all those who have been chosen by this people to govern and manage the affairs of this war.

2 For behold, I have somewhat to say unto them by the way of condemnation; for behold, ye yourselves know that ye have been appointed to gather together men, and arm them with swords, and with cimeters, and all manner of weapons of war of every kind, and send forth against the Lamanites, in whatsoever parts they should come into our land.

3 And now behold, I say unto you that myself, and also my men, and also Helaman and his men, have suffered exceedingly great sufferings; yea, even hunger, thirst, and fatigue, and all manner of afflictions of every kind.

4 But behold, were this all we had suffered we would not murmur nor complain.

5 But behold, great has been the slaughter among our people; yea, thousands have fallen by the sword, while it might have otherwise been if ye had rendered unto our armies sufficient strength and succor for them. Yea, great has been your neglect towards us.

6 And now behold, we desire to know the cause of this exceedingly great neglect; yea, we desire to know the cause of your thoughtless state.

## *Moroni Asks the Chief Judge Why No Help Has Come*

7 Can you think to sit upon your thrones in a state of thoughtless stupor, while your enemies are spreading the work of death around you? Yea, while they are murdering thousands of your brethren—

8 Yea, even they who have looked up to you for protection, yea, have placed you in a situation that ye might have succored them, yea, ye might have sent armies unto them, to have strengthened them, and have saved thousands of them from falling by the sword.

9 But behold, this is not all—ye have withheld your provisions from them, insomuch that many have fought and bled out their lives because of their great desires which they had for the welfare of this people; yea, and this they have done when they were about to perish with hunger, because of your exceedingly great neglect towards them.

10 And now, my beloved brethren—for ye ought to be beloved; yea, and ye ought to have stirred yourselves more diligently for the welfare and the freedom of this people; but behold, ye have neglected them insomuch that the blood of thousands shall come upon your heads for vengeance; yea, for known unto God were all their cries, and all their sufferings—

11 Behold, could ye suppose that ye could sit upon your thrones, and because of the exceeding goodness of God ye could do nothing and he would deliver you? Behold, if ye have supposed this ye have supposed in vain.

12 Do ye suppose that, because so many of your brethren have been killed it is because of their wickedness? I say unto you, if ye have supposed this ye have supposed in vain; for I say unto you, there are many who have fallen by the sword; and behold it is to your condemnation;

13 For the Lord suffereth the righteous to be slain that his justice and judgment may come upon the wicked; therefore ye need not suppose that the

---

60:1 ***manage***—lead

60:2 ***condemnation***—reproving or scolding them
***appointed***—chosen

60:3 ***fatigue***—exhaustion

60:5 ***slaughter***—killing
***rendered***—given
***sufficient***—enough
***succor***—help or relief
***neglect***—lack of concern

60:7 ***state of thoughtless stupor***—daze

60:9 ***provisions***—food and supplies
***welfare***—good

60:10 ***stirred yourselves***—worked
***more diligently***—with greater care and effort
***vengeance***—your punishment

60:11 ***supposed in vain***—been mistaken in your thoughts

60:13 ***suffereth***—allows

Sometimes the Lord allows righteous people to be hurt by wicked people so He can judge the wicked for the terrible things they do. Alma and Amulek saw this when they watched the wicked people of Ammonihah throw righteous women and children into a fire (see Alma 14:7–11).

righteous are lost because they are slain; but behold, they do enter into the rest of the Lord their God.

## Moroni Explains How a Lack of Unity Weakens the Nation

14 And now behold, I say unto you, I fear exceedingly that the judgments of God will come upon this people, because of their exceeding slothfulness, yea, even the slothfulness of our government, and their exceedingly great neglect towards their brethren, yea, towards those who have been slain.
15 For were it not for the wickedness which first commenced at our head, we could have withstood our enemies that they could have gained no power over us.
16 Yea, had it not been for the war which broke out among ourselves; yea, were it not for these king-men, who caused so much bloodshed among ourselves; yea, at the time we were contending among ourselves, if we had united our strength as we hitherto have done; yea, had it not been for the desire of power and authority which those king-men had over us; had they been true to the cause of our freedom, and united with us, and gone forth against our enemies, instead of taking up their swords against us, which was the cause of so much bloodshed among ourselves; yea, if we had gone forth against them in the strength of the Lord, we should have dispersed our enemies, for it would have been done, according to the fulfilling of his word.
17 But behold, now the Lamanites are coming upon us, taking possession of our lands, and they are murdering our people with the sword, yea, our women and our children, and also carrying them away captive, causing them that they should suffer all manner of afflictions, and this because of the great wickedness of those who are seeking for power and authority, yea, even those king-men.
18 But why should I say much concerning this matter? For we know not but what ye yourselves are seeking for authority. We know not but what ye are also traitors to your country.
19 Or is it that ye have neglected us because ye are in the heart of our country and ye are surrounded by security, that ye do not cause food to be sent unto us, and also men to strengthen our armies?
20 Have ye forgotten the commandments of the Lord your God? Yea, have ye forgotten the captivity of our fathers? Have ye forgotten the many times we have been delivered out of the hands of our enemies?
21 Or do ye suppose that the Lord will still deliver us, while we sit upon our thrones and do not make use of the means which the Lord has provided for us?
22 Yea, will ye sit in idleness while ye are surrounded with thousands of those, yea, and tens of thousands, who do also sit in idleness, while there are thousands round about in the borders of the land who are falling by the sword, yea, wounded and bleeding?

---

60:14 ***slothfulness***—laziness

60:15 ***commenced at our head***—began with our leaders

60:16 ***contending***—fighting
***hitherto***—before
***dispersed***—scattered

The king-men were wealthy Nephites who wanted a king to rule over the nation (see Alma 51:5). They fought against the righteous Nephites, and many people were hurt and killed (see Alma 51:17–19).

60:17 ***possession***—control

60:17 (16–17) Jesus said that "every kingdom divided against itself" will be destroyed (Matthew 12:25). The division between the king-men and the freemen seriously weakened the Nephite nation and nearly allowed the Lamanites to conquer them.

60:18 ***traitors to***—people who turn against

60:19 ***heart***—middle
***security***—protection

60:20 Moroni reminds Pahoran of the times that the Lord delivered His people from captivity. The scriptures record how Moses led the children of Israel out of Egypt (see Exodus 14:1–31); the Lord led Lehi's family out of Jerusalem to the promised land (see 2 Nephi 1:1–3) and Alma's people to Zarahemla (see Alma 5:4–6).

60:21 The Lord has promised, "I, the Lord, am bound when ye do what I say; but when ye do not what I say, ye have no promise" (D&C 82:10).

60:22 ***in idleness***—and do nothing

23 Do ye suppose that God will look upon you as guiltless while ye sit still and behold these things? Behold I say unto you, Nay. Now I would that ye should remember that God has said that the inward vessel shall be cleansed first, and then shall the outer vessel be cleansed also.

## *Moroni Will Overthrow the Government Leaders Unless They Help His Army*

24 And now, except ye do repent of that which ye have done, and begin to be up and doing, and send forth food and men unto us, and also unto Helaman, that he may support those parts of our country which he has regained, and that we may also recover the remainder of our possessions in these parts, behold it will be expedient that we contend no more with the Lamanites until we have first cleansed our inward vessel, yea, even the great head of our government.

25 And except ye grant mine epistle, and come out and show unto me a true spirit of freedom, and strive to strengthen and fortify our armies, and grant unto them food for their support, behold I will leave a part of my freemen to maintain this part of our land, and I will leave the strength and the blessings of God upon them, that none other power can operate against them—

26 And this because of their exceeding faith, and their patience in their tribulations—

27 And I will come unto you, and if there be any among you that has a desire for freedom, yea, if there be even a spark of freedom remaining, behold I will stir up insurrections among you, even until those who have desires to usurp power and authority shall become extinct.

28 Yea, behold I do not fear your power nor your authority, but it is my God whom I fear; and it is according to his commandments that I do take my sword to defend the cause of my country, and it is because of your iniquity that we have suffered so much loss.

29 Behold it is time, yea, the time is now at hand, that except ye do bestir yourselves in the defence of your country and your little ones, the sword of justice doth hang over you; yea, and it shall fall upon you and visit you even to your utter destruction.

30 Behold, I wait for assistance from you; and, except ye do administer unto our relief, behold, I come unto you, even in the land of Zarahemla, and smite you with the sword, insomuch that ye can have no more power to impede the progress of this people in the cause of our freedom.

31 For behold, the Lord will not suffer that ye shall live and wax strong in your iniquities to destroy his righteous people.

32 Behold, can you suppose that the Lord will spare you and come out in judgment against the Lamanites, when it is the tradition of their fathers that has caused their hatred, yea, and it has been redoubled by those who have dissented from us, while your iniquity is for the cause of your love of glory and the vain things of the world?

---

60:23 ***guiltless***—innocent

A vessel is a container like a cup or bowl. Moroni compares the Nephite nation to a vessel that is unclean on the inside. The inside represents the government of the land. Moroni threatens to clean out the inner vessel, or overthrow the government, to keep the freedom of his country. President Ezra Taft Benson in a similar way explained how each person needs to cleanse his or her inner vessel: "As we cleanse the inner vessel, there will have to be changes made in our own personal lives, in our families, and in the Church" (*Teachings of Ezra Taft Benson*, 72).

60:24 ***recover***—get back
***expedient***—necessary

60:25 ***grant mine epistle***—do the things I have asked in my letter
***operate***—work

60:26 ***tribulations***—trials and difficulties

60:27 ***insurrections***—rebellions
***usurp***—unlawfully take
***extinct***—wiped out

60:28 ***iniquity***—wickedness

60:29 ***bestir yourselves***—take action
***utter***—complete or total

60:30 ***administer unto our relief***—help us
***impede***—stop

60:31 ***wax***—grow

60:32 ***tradition***—teachings or beliefs
***redoubled***—increased
***dissented***—fallen away

33 Ye know that ye do transgress the laws of God, and ye do know that ye do trample them under your feet. Behold, the Lord saith unto me: If those whom ye have appointed your governors do not repent of their sins and iniquities, ye shall go up to battle against them.

34 And now behold, I, Moroni, am constrained, according to the covenant which I have made to keep the commandments of my God; therefore I would that ye should adhere to the word of God, and send speedily unto me of your provisions and of your men, and also to Helaman.

35 And behold, if ye will not do this I come unto you speedily; for behold, God will not suffer that we should perish with hunger; therefore he will give unto us of your food, even if it must be by the sword. Now see that ye fulfil the word of God.

36 Behold, I am Moroni, your chief captain. I seek not for power, but to pull it down. I seek not for honor of the world, but for the glory of my God, and the freedom and welfare of my country. And thus I close mine epistle.

## CHAPTER 61

*Pahoran asks Moroni to send an army to help the righteous Nephites fight the wicked king-men. Watch for signs showing the kind of person Pahoran is.*

### Pahoran Writes That He Has Been Driven Out of Zarahemla

1 BEHOLD, now it came to pass that soon after Moroni had sent his epistle unto the chief governor, he received an epistle from Pahoran, the chief governor. And these are the words which he received:

2 I, Pahoran, who am the chief governor of this land, do send these words unto Moroni, the chief captain over the army. Behold, I say unto you, Moroni, that I do not joy in your great afflictions, yea, it grieves my soul.

3 But behold, there are those who do joy in your afflictions, yea, insomuch that they have risen up in rebellion against me, and also those of my people who are freemen, yea, and those who have risen up are exceedingly numerous.

4 And it is those who have sought to take away the judgment-seat from me that have been the cause of this great iniquity; for they have used great flattery, and they have led away the hearts of many people, which will be the cause of sore affliction among us; they have withheld our provisions, and have daunted our freemen that they have not come unto you.

5 And behold, they have driven me out before them, and I have fled to the land of Gideon, with as many men as it were possible that I could get.

6 And behold, I have sent a proclamation throughout this part of the land; and behold, they are flocking to us daily, to their arms, in the defence of their country and their freedom, and to avenge our wrongs.

7 And they have come unto us, insomuch that those who have risen up in rebellion against us are set at defiance, yea, insomuch that they do fear us and durst not come out against us to battle.

8 They have got possession of the land, or the city, of Zarahemla; they have appointed a king over them, and he hath written unto the king of the Lamanites, in the which he hath joined an alliance with him; in the which alliance he hath agreed to maintain the city of Zarahemla, which maintenance he supposeth will enable the Lamanites to conquer

---

60:34 ***adhere to***—obey

60:34 (33–34) Moroni feels constrained or duty bound by his covenants to write this bold warning to Pahoran. How do the covenants you made at baptism inspire you to keep the commandments?

60:35 ***fulfil***—keep all of

60:36 What does Moroni seek and "seek not" for? What can you learn from Moroni about what is truly important in this life?

61:2 ***afflictions***—trials
***grieves***—saddens

61:3 The freemen were Nephites who wanted to stay free and be governed by elected judges. The king-men were wicked Nephites who wanted to be ruled by a king (see Alma 51:1–8; 60:15–16).

61:4 ***sought***—tried
***great flattery***—pleasing words
***sore***—painful
***daunted***—discouraged

61:6 ***a proclamation***—an official statement
***flocking***—gathering
***avenge***—make right, get even for

61:8 ***possession***—control
***joined an alliance***—made an agreement to fight together
***maintain***—keep
***enable***—make it possible for

the remainder of the land, and he shall be placed king over this people when they shall be conquered under the Lamanites.

## Pahoran Wants the Nephites to Continue to Be Free

9 And now, in your epistle you have censured me, but it mattereth not; I am not angry, but do rejoice in the greatness of your heart. I, Pahoran, do not seek for power, save only to retain my judgment-seat that I may preserve the rights and the liberty of my people. My soul standeth fast in that liberty in the which God hath made us free.
10 And now, behold, we will resist wickedness even unto bloodshed. We would not shed the blood of the Lamanites if they would stay in their own land.
11 We would not shed the blood of our brethren if they would not rise up in rebellion and take the sword against us.
12 We would subject ourselves to the yoke of bondage if it were requisite with the justice of God, or if he should command us so to do.
13 But behold he doth not command us that we shall subject ourselves to our enemies, but that we should put our trust in him, and he will deliver us.

## Pahoran Asks Moroni's Help to Regain the Government

14 Therefore, my beloved brother, Moroni, let us resist evil, and whatsoever evil we cannot resist with our words, yea, such as rebellions and dissensions, let us resist them with our swords, that we may retain our freedom, that we may rejoice in the great privilege of our church, and in the cause of our Redeemer and our God.
15 Therefore, come unto me speedily with a few of your men, and leave the remainder in the charge of Lehi and Teancum; give unto them power to conduct the war in that part of the land, according to the Spirit of God, which is also the Spirit of freedom which is in them.
16 Behold I have sent a few provisions unto them, that they may not perish until ye can come unto me.
17 Gather together whatsoever force ye can upon your march hither, and we will go speedily against those dissenters, in the strength of our God according to the faith which is in us.
18 And we will take possession of the city of Zarahemla, that we may obtain more food to send forth unto Lehi and Teancum; yea, we will go forth against them in the strength of the Lord, and we will put an end to this great iniquity.

---

61:9 ***censured***—scolded
***retain***—keep
***preserve***—protect

61:10 ***resist***—fight against

61:12 ***subject ourselves to the yoke of bondage***—allow ourselves to become slaves
***requisite***—necessary

61:13 (12–13) Pahoran realizes that whatever our trials may be, it is important that we trust in and obey the Lord. President James E. Faust explained, "Let us not presume that because the way is at times difficult and challenging, our Heavenly Father is not mindful of us. He is rubbing off our rough edges and sensitizing [preparing] us for our great responsibilities ahead" ("The Blessings of Adversity," 7).

61:14 ***dissensions***—disagreements

Sometimes members of the Church have to resist people who want them to believe or to do something wrong. How can daily scripture study and personal prayer help you resist the devil's attacks? (see 1 Nephi 15:23–24; Ephesians 6:11–18).

61:15 ***conduct***—lead or direct

61:17 ***dissenters***—people who are fighting against our ways

61:18 Those who go forth "in the strength of the Lord" have the Lord's Spirit and power to help them (see Mosiah 9:17–18; Mormon 2:26). When has the Lord given you strength to do something hard?

19 And now, Moroni, I do joy in receiving your epistle, for I was somewhat worried concerning what we should do, whether it should be just in us to go against our brethren.
20 But ye have said, except they repent the Lord hath commanded you that ye should go against them.
21 See that ye strengthen Lehi and Teancum in the Lord; tell them to fear not, for God will deliver them, yea, and also all those who stand fast in that liberty wherewith God hath made them free. And now I close mine epistle to my beloved brother, Moroni.

## CHAPTER 62

*Moroni joins forces with Pahoran to put down the king-men's rebellion and defeat the Lamanites. Look for the courage of righteous men such as Moroni, Pahoran, and Teancum, and notice their effect on Nephite history.*

### *Moroni's Army Joins Pahoran*

1 AND now it came to pass that when Moroni had received this epistle his heart did take courage, and was filled with exceedingly great joy because of the faithfulness of Pahoran, that he was not also a traitor to the freedom and cause of his country.
2 But he did also mourn exceedingly because of the iniquity of those who had driven Pahoran from the judgment-seat, yea, in fine because of those who had rebelled against their country and also their God.
3 And it came to pass that Moroni took a small number of men, according to the desire of Pahoran, and gave Lehi and Teancum command over the remainder of his army, and took his march towards the land of Gideon.
4 And he did raise the standard of liberty in whatsoever place he did enter, and gained whatsoever force he could in all his march towards the land of Gideon.
5 And it came to pass that thousands did flock unto his standard, and did take up their swords in the defence of their freedom, that they might not come into bondage.
6 And thus, when Moroni had gathered together whatsoever men he could in all his march, he came to the land of Gideon; and uniting his forces with those of Pahoran they became exceedingly strong, even stronger than the men of Pachus, who was the king of those dissenters who had driven the freemen out of the land of Zarahemla and had taken possession of the land.

### *Moroni and Pahoran Defeat Pachus*

7 And it came to pass that Moroni and Pahoran went down with their armies into the land of Zarahemla, and went forth against the city, and did meet the men of Pachus, insomuch that they did come to battle.
8 And behold, Pachus was slain and his men were taken prisoners, and Pahoran was restored to his judgment-seat.
9 And the men of Pachus received their trial, according to the law, and also those king-men who had been taken and cast into prison; and they were executed according to the law; yea, those men of Pachus and those king-men, whosoever would not take up arms in the defence of their country, but would fight against it, were put to death.
10 And thus it became expedient that this law should be strictly observed for the safety of their country; yea, and whosoever was found denying their freedom was speedily executed according to the law.

---

61:19 ***concerning***—about

61:21 Notice that Pahoran, like Nephi, trusts in the power of the Lord to deliver the faithful (see 1 Nephi 1:20). What other examples of the Lord's power to save the faithful can you remember reading about?

62:1 A traitor is "one who betrays his trust" (Noah Webster, *American Dictionary of the English Language,* 1828, s.v. "Traitor").

62:2 ***in fine***—finally
***rebelled***—fought

62:4 The "standard of liberty" was a banner or flag that Captain Moroni raised to rally the Nephites to fight for their freedom, religion, and families (see Alma 46:12).

62:5 ***flock***—gather

62:6 ***dissenters***—rebels

62:8 ***restored***—brought back

62:9 ***executed***—put to death

62:10 ***expedient***—necessary
***strictly***—exactly

11 And thus ended the thirtieth year of the reign of the judges over the people of Nephi; Moroni and Pahoran having restored peace to the land of Zarahemla, among their own people, having inflicted death upon all those who were not true to the cause of freedom.

## Moroni's Army Marches on Nephihah

12 And it came to pass in the commencement of the thirty and first year of the reign of the judges over the people of Nephi, Moroni immediately caused that provisions should be sent, and also an army of six thousand men should be sent unto Helaman, to assist him in preserving that part of the land.
13 And he also caused that an army of six thousand men, with a sufficient quantity of food, should be sent to the armies of Lehi and Teancum. And it came to pass that this was done to fortify the land against the Lamanites.
14 And it came to pass that Moroni and Pahoran, leaving a large body of men in the land of Zarahemla, took their march with a large body of men towards the land of Nephihah, being determined to overthrow the Lamanites in that city.
15 And it came to pass that as they were marching towards the land, they took a large body of men of the Lamanites, and slew many of them, and took their provisions and their weapons of war.
16 And it came to pass after they had taken them, they caused them to enter into a covenant that they would no more take up their weapons of war against the Nephites.
17 And when they had entered into this covenant they sent them to dwell with the people of Ammon, and they were in number about four thousand who had not been slain.
18 And it came to pass that when they had sent them away they pursued their march towards the land of Nephihah. And it came to pass that when they had come to the city of Nephihah, they did pitch their tents in the plains of Nephihah, which is near the city of Nephihah.
19 Now Moroni was desirous that the Lamanites should come out to battle against them, upon the plains; but the Lamanites, knowing of their exceedingly great courage, and beholding the greatness of their numbers, therefore they durst not come out against them; therefore they did not come to battle in that day.

## Moroni's Army Captures Nephihah

20 And when the night came, Moroni went forth in the darkness of the night, and came upon the top of the wall to spy out in what part of the city the Lamanites did camp with their army.
21 And it came to pass that they were on the east, by the entrance; and they were all asleep. And now Moroni returned to his army, and caused that they should prepare in haste strong cords and ladders, to be let down from the top of the wall into the inner part of the wall.
22 And it came to pass that Moroni caused that his men should march forth and come upon the top of the wall, and let themselves down into that part of the city, yea, even on the west, where the Lamanites did not camp with their armies.
23 And it came to pass that they were all let down into the city by night, by the means of their strong cords and their ladders; thus when the morning came they were all within the walls of the city.
24 And now, when the Lamanites awoke and saw that the armies of Moroni were within the walls, they were affrighted exceedingly, insomuch that they did flee out by the pass.
25 And now when Moroni saw that they were fleeing before him, he did cause that his men should march forth against them, and slew many, and surrounded many others, and took them prisoners; and the remainder of them fled into the land of Moroni, which was in the borders by the seashore.
26 Thus had Moroni and Pahoran obtained the possession of the city of Nephihah without the loss of one soul; and there were many of the Lamanites who were slain.

---

62:11 ***inflicted death upon***—put to death
62:12 ***provisions***—food and supplies
62:13 ***a sufficient quantity of***—enough
***fortify***—strengthen
62:19 ***durst***—dared
62:21 ***in haste***—quickly
62:24 ***affrighted exceedingly***—very frightened

27 Now it came to pass that many of the Lamanites that were prisoners were desirous to join the people of Ammon and become a free people.
28 And it came to pass that as many as were desirous, unto them it was granted according to their desires.
29 Therefore, all the prisoners of the Lamanites did join the people of Ammon, and did begin to labor exceedingly, tilling the ground, raising all manner of grain, and flocks and herds of every kind; and thus were the Nephites relieved from a great burden; yea, insomuch that they were relieved from all the prisoners of the Lamanites.
30 Now it came to pass that Moroni, after he had obtained possession of the city of Nephihah, having taken many prisoners, which did reduce the armies of the Lamanites exceedingly, and having regained many of the Nephites who had been taken prisoners, which did strengthen the army of Moroni exceedingly; therefore Moroni went forth from the land of Nephihah to the land of Lehi.

### Teancum and Ammoron Are Killed

31 And it came to pass that when the Lamanites saw that Moroni was coming against them, they were again frightened and fled before the army of Moroni.
32 And it came to pass that Moroni and his army did pursue them from city to city, until they were met by Lehi and Teancum; and the Lamanites fled from Lehi and Teancum, even down upon the borders by the seashore, until they came to the land of Moroni.
33 And the armies of the Lamanites were all gathered together, insomuch that they were all in one body in the land of Moroni. Now Ammoron, the king of the Lamanites, was also with them.
34 And it came to pass that Moroni and Lehi and Teancum did encamp with their armies round about in the borders of the land of Moroni, insomuch that the Lamanites were encircled about in the borders by the wilderness on the south, and in the borders by the wilderness on the east.
35 And thus they did encamp for the night. For behold, the Nephites and the Lamanites also were weary because of the greatness of the march; therefore they did not resolve upon any stratagem in the night-time, save it were Teancum; for he was exceedingly angry with Ammoron, insomuch that he considered that Ammoron, and Amalickiah his brother, had been the cause of this great and lasting war between them and the Lamanites, which had been the cause of so much war and bloodshed, yea, and so much famine.
36 And it came to pass that Teancum in his anger did go forth into the camp of the Lamanites, and did let himself down over the walls of the city. And he went forth with a cord, from place to place, insomuch that he did find the king; and he did cast a javelin at him, which did pierce him near the heart. But behold, the king did awaken his servants before he died, insomuch that they did pursue Teancum, and slew him.
37 Now it came to pass that when Lehi and Moroni knew that Teancum was dead they were exceedingly sorrowful; for behold, he had been a man who had fought valiantly for his country, yea, a true friend to liberty; and he had suffered very many exceedingly sore afflictions. But behold, he was dead, and had gone the way of all the earth.
38 Now it came to pass that Moroni marched forth on the morrow, and came upon the Lamanites, insomuch that they did slay them with a great slaughter; and they did drive them out of the land; and they did flee, even that they did not return at that time against the Nephites.

### The Armies of Moroni Restore Peace in the Land

39 And thus ended the thirty and first year of the reign of the judges over the people of Nephi; and thus they had had wars, and bloodsheds, and famine, and affliction, for the space of many years.
40 And there had been murders, and contentions, and dissensions, and all manner of iniquity among

---

62:29 ***relieved***—freed

62:35 ***resolve***—decide
***stratagem***—military plan

62:36 (35–36) Teancum had fought in many battles to help protect the Nephites and preserve their freedom. He killed the wicked leader Amalickiah almost the same way he killed Ammoron (see Alma 51:34).

62:37 ***valiantly***—bravely
***afflictions***—trials

62:40 ***contentions***—arguing and fighting
***dissensions***—disagreements

the people of Nephi; nevertheless for the righteous' sake, yea, because of the prayers of the righteous, they were spared.
41 But behold, because of the exceedingly great length of the war between the Nephites and the Lamanites many had become hardened, because of the exceedingly great length of the war; and many were softened because of their afflictions, insomuch that they did humble themselves before God, even in the depth of humility.
42 And it came to pass that after Moroni had fortified those parts of the land which were most exposed to the Lamanites, until they were sufficiently strong, he returned to the city of Zarahemla; and also Helaman returned to the place of his inheritance; and there was once more peace established among the people of Nephi.
43 And Moroni yielded up the command of his armies into the hands of his son, whose name was Moronihah; and he retired to his own house that he might spend the remainder of his days in peace.
44 And Pahoran did return to his judgment-seat; and Helaman did take upon him again to preach unto the people the word of God; for because of so many wars and contentions it had become expedient that a regulation should be made again in the church.
45 Therefore, Helaman and his brethren went forth, and did declare the word of God with much power unto the convincing of many people of their wickedness, which did cause them to repent of their sins and to be baptized unto the Lord their God.
46 And it came to pass that they did establish again the church of God, throughout all the land.
47 Yea, and regulations were made concerning the law. And their judges, and their chief judges were chosen.
48 And the people of Nephi began to prosper again in the land, and began to multiply and to wax exceedingly strong again in the land. And they began to grow exceedingly rich.
49 But notwithstanding their riches, or their strength, or their prosperity, they were not lifted up in the pride of their eyes; neither were they slow to remember the Lord their God; but they did humble themselves exceedingly before him.
50 Yea, they did remember how great things the Lord had done for them, that he had delivered them from death, and from bonds, and from prisons, and from all manner of afflictions, and he had delivered them out of the hands of their enemies.
51 And they did pray unto the Lord their God continually, insomuch that the Lord did bless them, according to his word, so that they did wax strong and prosper in the land.
52 And it came to pass that all these things were done. And Helaman died, in the thirty and fifth year of the reign of the judges over the people of Nephi.

## CHAPTER 63

*Many people migrate to new lands. For the first time in more than five hundred years, the record speaks of shipbuilding. Look for why the ships are built and who boards them.*

### *Hagoth Builds Ships That Carry People Northward*

1 AND it came to pass in the commencement of the thirty and sixth year of the reign of the judges over the people of Nephi, that Shiblon took possession of those sacred things which had been delivered unto Helaman by Alma.
2 And he was a just man, and he did walk uprightly before God; and he did observe to do good continually, to keep the commandments of the Lord his God; and also did his brother.

---

62:41 (39–41) "These people all had basically the same experience. The war was the same length for all people; yet out of the same experience some were hardened and some were softened. What made the difference? It was what they thought of God and his Son" (C. Max Caldwell, " 'What Think Ye of Christ?' " 22).

62:42 ***fortified***—strengthened
***exposed***—open

62:43 ***yielded***—gave

62:44 ***a regulation***—rules

62:51 ***wax***—grow

63:1 ***commencement***—beginning
***reign***—rule

The "sacred things" given to Helaman by Alma included the care of the plates of Nephi and the plates of brass (see Alma 37:1–4).

63:2 ***walk uprightly before God***—live righteously

3 And it came to pass that Moroni died also. And thus ended the thirty and sixth year of the reign of the judges.

4 And it came to pass that in the thirty and seventh year of the reign of the judges, there was a large company of men, even to the amount of five thousand and four hundred men, with their wives and their children, departed out of the land of Zarahemla into the land which was northward.

5 And it came to pass that Hagoth, he being an exceedingly curious man, therefore he went forth and built him an exceedingly large ship, on the borders of the land Bountiful, by the land Desolation, and launched it forth into the west sea, by the narrow neck which led into the land northward.

6 And behold, there were many of the Nephites who did enter therein and did sail forth with much provisions, and also many women and children; and they took their course northward. And thus ended the thirty and seventh year.

7 And in the thirty and eighth year, this man built other ships. And the first ship did also return, and many more people did enter into it; and they also took much provisions, and set out again to the land northward.

8 And it came to pass that they were never heard of more. And we suppose that they were drowned in the depths of the sea. And it came to pass that one other ship also did sail forth; and whither she did go we know not.

9 And it came to pass that in this year there were many people who went forth into the land northward. And thus ended the thirty and eighth year.

## Shiblon Passes the Sacred Scriptural Record to Helaman's Son

10 And it came to pass in the thirty and ninth year of the reign of the judges, Shiblon died also, and Corianton had gone forth to the land northward in a ship, to carry forth provisions unto the people who had gone forth into that land.

11 Therefore it became expedient for Shiblon to confer those sacred things, before his death, upon the son of Helaman, who was called Helaman, being called after the name of his father.

12 Now behold, all those engravings which were in the possession of Helaman were written and sent forth among the children of men throughout all the land, save it were those parts which had been commanded by Alma should not go forth.

13 Nevertheless, these things were to be kept sacred, and handed down from one generation to another; therefore, in this year, they had been conferred upon Helaman, before the death of Shiblon.

14 And it came to pass also in this year that there were some dissenters who had gone forth unto the Lamanites; and they were stirred up again to anger against the Nephites.

15 And also in this same year they came down with a numerous army to war against the people of Moronihah, or against the army of Moronihah, in the which they were beaten and driven back again to their own lands, suffering great loss.

16 And thus ended the thirty and ninth year of the reign of the judges over the people of Nephi.

17 And thus ended the account of Alma, and Helaman his son, and also Shiblon, who was his son.

---

ILLUSTRATION BY GARY E. SMITH

*"Hagoth, he being an exceedingly curious man, therefore he went forth and built him an exceedingly large ship."*

63:4 ***departed out of***—left

63:5 ***an exceedingly curious man***—very interested in the world

63:9 (5–9) "President Joseph F. Smith, the president of the Church reported, 'You brethren and sisters from New Zealand, I want you to know that you are from the people of Hagoth'" (President Spencer W. Kimball, as quoted in *Book of Mormon Student Manual: Religion 121 and 122,* 104).

63:12 The parts of the engravings (or metal pages of scripture) that Alma did not want the people to have were the descriptions of secret combinations, murders, and other works of darkness by evil people (see Alma 37:27–32).

63:14 ***dissenters***—people who rebelled

# THE BOOK OF HELAMAN

*Helaman was the son of Helaman (see Alma 63:11), who was the son of Alma the Younger. Helaman lived at a time when many of the Nephites were more wicked than the Lamanites. The Nephites became involved with secret combinations, or secret groups of people with plans to become rich and powerful through evil means. So God sent a great Lamanite prophet named Samuel to call the Nephites to repentance. Helaman begins writing about 52 B.C. and the Book of Helaman covers much of the time leading to Christ's birth.*

*An account of the Nephites. Their wars and contentions, and their dissensions. And also the prophecies of many holy prophets, before the coming of Christ, according to the records of Helaman, who was the son of Helaman, and also according to the records of his sons, even down to the coming of Christ. And also many of the Lamanites are converted. An account of their conversion. An account of the righteousness of the Lamanites, and the wickedness and abominations of the Nephites, according to the record of Helaman and his sons, even down to the coming of Christ, which is called the book of Helaman.**

## CHAPTER 1

*Nephite and Lamanite wars continue and the Nephites suffer greatly. Watch for what causes their suffering.*

### There Is Trouble As a New Chief Judge Is Chosen

1 AND now behold, it came to pass in the commencement of the fortieth year of the reign of the judges over the people of Nephi, there began to be a serious difficulty among the people of the Nephites.
2 For behold, Pahoran had died, and gone the way of all the earth; therefore there began to be a serious contention concerning who should have the judgment-seat among the brethren, who were the sons of Pahoran.
3 Now these are their names who did contend for the judgment-seat, who did also cause the people to contend: Pahoran, Paanchi, and Pacumeni.
4 Now these are not all the sons of Pahoran (for he had many), but these are they who did contend for the judgment-seat; therefore, they did cause three divisions among the people.
5 Nevertheless, it came to pass that Pahoran was appointed by the voice of the people to be chief judge and a governor over the people of Nephi.
6 And it came to pass that Pacumeni, when he saw that he could not obtain the judgment-seat, he did unite with the voice of the people.
7 But behold, Paanchi, and that part of the people that were desirous that he should be their governor, was exceedingly wroth; therefore, he was about to flatter away those people to rise up in rebellion against their brethren.
8 And it came to pass as he was about to do this, behold, he was taken, and was tried according to the voice of the people, and condemned unto death; for he had raised up in rebellion and sought to destroy the liberty of the people.

---

* A Closer Look: This introduction to the book of Helaman was translated from the Book of Mormon plates.

1:1 Word Help: ***commencement***—beginning
***reign***—rule

1:2 Word Help: ***contention***—argument

1:5 Word Help: ***appointed***—chosen

1:7 Word Help: ***exceedingly wroth***—very angry
***flatter away***—use pleasing words to lead
***in rebellion***—to fight

1:7 (6–7) More Light: "If Satan can succeed in creating in us the pastime of arguing, quarreling, and contention, it is easier for him to bind us with heavier sins which can destroy our eternal lives" (Marvin J. Ashton, in Conference Report, October 1991, 99).

= Word Help = A Closer Look
= More Light = Ponder This
Words in pink are explained in the Glossary.

## Wicked People Use Secret Combinations to Get What They Want

9 Now when those people who were desirous that he should be their governor saw that he was condemned unto death, therefore they were angry, and behold, they sent forth one Kishkumen, even to the judgment-seat of Pahoran, and murdered Pahoran as he sat upon the judgment-seat.

10 And he was pursued by the servants of Pahoran; but behold, so speedy was the flight of Kishkumen that no man could overtake him.

11 And he went unto those that sent him, and they all entered into a covenant, yea, swearing by their everlasting Maker, that they would tell no man that Kishkumen had murdered Pahoran.

12 Therefore, Kishkumen was not known among the people of Nephi, for he was in disguise at the time that he murdered Pahoran. And Kishkumen and his band, who had covenanted with him, did mingle themselves among the people, in a manner that they all could not be found; but as many as were found were condemned unto death.

13 And now behold, Pacumeni was appointed, according to the voice of the people, to be a chief judge and a governor over the people, to reign in the stead of his brother Pahoran; and it was according to his right. And all this was done in the fortieth year of the reign of the judges; and it had an end.

## The Lamanites Attack and Defeat the Nephites in Zarahemla

14 And it came to pass in the forty and first year of the reign of the judges, that the Lamanites had gathered together an innumerable army of men, and armed them with swords, and with cimeters and with bows, and with arrows, and with head-plates, and with breastplates, and with all manner of shields of every kind.

15 And they came down again that they might pitch battle against the Nephites. And they were led by a man whose name was Coriantumr; and he was a descendant of Zarahemla; and he was a dissenter from among the Nephites; and he was a large and a mighty man.

16 Therefore, the king of the Lamanites, whose name was Tubaloth, who was the son of Ammoron, supposing that Coriantumr, being a mighty man, could stand against the Nephites, with his strength and also with his great wisdom, insomuch that by sending him forth he should gain power over the Nephites—

---

ILLUSTRATION BY GARY E. SMITH

*Kishkumen "murdered Pahoran as he sat upon the judgment-seat."*

1:10 ***pursued***—chased
***overtake***—catch

1:11 ***swearing***—promising

A covenant is an agreement between two people. In the scriptures it is usually an agreement between God and man. We promise to be obedient to God's commandments, and He promises to bless us (see LDS Bible Dictionary, s.v. "Covenant," 651).

1:12 ***in disguise***—dressed like someone else
***band***—gang

1:12 (9–12) "Beginning in the days of Cain and continuing through all generations, whenever there have been unrighteous and apostate peoples on earth, Satan has revealed unto them his oaths, vows, and *secret combinations*. . . . Murder, plunder, robbery, power, the destruction of freedom, and the persecution of the saints have been the objectives of these societies ever since. (Moses 5:16–59; 6:15; Hela. 6:17–41.)" (Elder Bruce R. McConkie, *Mormon Doctrine*, 698).

1:15 ***a descendant of***—in the family of
***dissenter***—traitor

Zarahemla was the leader of the people in the city of Zarahemla before the Nephites joined them. They were descendants of Mulek, a son of Zedekiah, who escaped death in Jerusalem and was led by the Lord to the Americas (see Omni 1:15; Helaman 6:10; 8:21).

17 Therefore he did stir them up to anger, and he did gather together his armies, and he did appoint Coriantumr to be their leader, and did cause that they should march down to the land of Zarahemla to battle against the Nephites.

18 And it came to pass that because of so much contention and so much difficulty in the government, that they had not kept sufficient guards in the land of Zarahemla; for they had supposed that the Lamanites durst not come into the heart of their lands to attack that great city Zarahemla.

19 But it came to pass that Coriantumr did march forth at the head of his numerous host, and came upon the inhabitants of the city, and their march was with such exceedingly great speed that there was no time for the Nephites to gather together their armies.

20 Therefore Coriantumr did cut down the watch by the entrance of the city, and did march forth with his whole army into the city, and they did slay every one who did oppose them, insomuch that they did take possession of the whole city.

21 And it came to pass that Pacumeni, who was the chief judge, did flee before Coriantumr, even to the walls of the city. And it came to pass that Coriantumr did smite him against the wall, insomuch that he died. And thus ended the days of Pacumeni.

22 And now when Coriantumr saw that he was in possession of the city of Zarahemla, and saw that the Nephites had fled before them, and were slain, and were taken, and were cast into prison, and that he had obtained the possession of the strongest hold in all the land, his heart took courage insomuch that he was about to go forth against all the land.

23 And now he did not tarry in the land of Zarahemla, but he did march forth with a large army, even towards the city of Bountiful; for it was his determination to go forth and cut his way through with the sword, that he might obtain the north parts of the land.

24 And, supposing that their greatest strength was in the center of the land, therefore he did march forth, giving them no time to assemble themselves together save it were in small bodies; and in this manner they did fall upon them and cut them down to the earth.

25 But behold, this march of Coriantumr through the center of the land gave Moronihah great advantage over them, notwithstanding the greatness of the number of the Nephites who were slain.

26 For behold, Moronihah had supposed that the Lamanites durst not come into the center of the land, but that they would attack the cities round about in the borders as they had hitherto done; therefore Moronihah had caused that their strong armies should maintain those parts round about by the borders.

---

PHOTOGRAPH BY SCOT FACER PROCTOR

*Many scriptural passages refer to "going down" to the land of Zarahemla (see Helaman 1:17). It may have been in a lowland area like this jungle in Guatemala.*

1:18 ***sufficient***—enough
***durst***—dared

Notice that the fighting among the Nephites causes them to be unprepared for an attack by the Lamanites. How can we avoid contention in our homes and be better prepared against the evils of the world?

1:19 ***numerous host***—large group of people
***inhabitants of***—people who lived in

1:20 ***watch***—guards
***oppose***—fight against

1:23 ***tarry***—stay

Coriantumr's greed drove him to want more of the Nephite lands than just the city of Zarahemla. But his greed left him open to an attack by Lehi and Moronihah, and Coriantumr was killed in battle. What can you do to avoid greed or selfishness in your life? How could you share more with others?

1:24 ***assemble***—gather
***bodies***—groups

1:26 ***hitherto done***—done before
***maintain***—guard

27 But behold, the Lamanites were not frightened according to his desire, but they had come into the center of the land, and had taken the capital city which was the city of Zarahemla, and were marching through the most capital parts of the land, slaying the people with a great slaughter, both men, women, and children, taking possession of many cities and of many strongholds.

## The Nephite Armies Regain Their Land

28 But when Moronihah had discovered this, he immediately sent forth Lehi with an army round about to head them before they should come to the land Bountiful.
29 And thus he did; and he did head them before they came to the land Bountiful, and gave unto them battle, insomuch that they began to retreat back towards the land of Zarahemla.
30 And it came to pass that Moronihah did head them in their retreat, and did give unto them battle, insomuch that it became an exceedingly bloody battle; yea, many were slain, and among the number who were slain Coriantumr was also found.
31 And now, behold, the Lamanites could not retreat either way, neither on the north, nor on the south, nor on the east, nor on the west, for they were surrounded on every hand by the Nephites.
32 And thus had Coriantumr plunged the Lamanites into the midst of the Nephites, insomuch that they were in the power of the Nephites, and he himself was slain, and the Lamanites did yield themselves into the hands of the Nephites.
33 And it came to pass that Moronihah took possession of the city of Zarahemla again, and caused that the Lamanites who had been taken prisoners should depart out of the land in peace.
34 And thus ended the forty and first year of the reign of the judges.

# CHAPTER 2

*Gadianton becomes the leader of Kishkumen's band. Kishkumen tries to murder Helaman, the new chief judge. Notice what these wicked men wanted and the effect those wicked plans had on the Nephites.*

## Kishkumen Is Killed As He Attempts to Murder Helaman

1 AND it came to pass in the forty and second year of the reign of the judges, after Moronihah had established again peace between the Nephites and the Lamanites, behold there was no one to fill the judgment-seat; therefore there began to be a contention again among the people concerning who should fill the judgment-seat.
2 And it came to pass that Helaman, who was the son of Helaman, was appointed to fill the judgment-seat, by the voice of the people.
3 But behold, Kishkumen, who had murdered Pahoran, did lay wait to destroy Helaman also; and he was upheld by his band, who had entered into a covenant that no one should know his wickedness.
4 For there was one Gadianton, who was exceedingly expert in many words, and also in his craft, to carry on the secret work of murder and of robbery; therefore he became the leader of the band of Kishkumen.
5 Therefore he did flatter them, and also Kishkumen, that if they would place him in the judgment-seat he would grant unto those who belonged to his band that they should be placed in power and authority among the people; therefore Kishkumen sought to destroy Helaman.

---

1:27 ***strongholds***—forts

1:28 ***head***—stop

1:29 ***retreat***—run

1:32 ***plunged the Lamanites into the midst***—placed the Lamanites in the middle
***yield***—give

1:33 Moronihah and his armies allow the Lamanite prisoners to depart in peace. What do you learn from this example about how to treat others?

2:1 ***a contention***—an argument

2:3 ***upheld***—supported

2:4 ***craft***—ability or skill

Gadianton, like other wicked leaders in the Book of Mormon, gains his power by deceiving people with his words. How can you guard against being tricked by wicked people with clever words? (see 2 Nephi 32:3).

2:5 ***flatter***—falsely praise

6 And it came to pass as he went forth towards the judgment-seat to destroy Helaman, behold one of the servants of Helaman, having been out by night, and having obtained, through disguise, a knowledge of those plans which had been laid by this band to destroy Helaman—

7 And it came to pass that he met Kishkumen, and he gave unto him a sign; therefore Kishkumen made known unto him the object of his desire, desiring that he would conduct him to the judgment-seat that he might murder Helaman.

8 And when the servant of Helaman had known all the heart of Kishkumen, and how that it was his object to murder, and also that it was the object of all those who belonged to his band to murder, and to rob, and to gain power, (and this was their secret plan, and their combination) the servant of Helaman said unto Kishkumen: Let us go forth unto the judgment-seat.

9 Now this did please Kishkumen exceedingly, for he did suppose that he should accomplish his design; but behold, the servant of Helaman, as they were going forth unto the judgment-seat, did stab Kishkumen even to the heart, that he fell dead without a groan. And he ran and told Helaman all the things which he had seen, and heard, and done.

## *Gadianton and His Band Flee into the Wilderness*

10 And it came to pass that Helaman did send forth to take this band of robbers and secret murderers, that they might be executed according to the law.

11 But behold, when Gadianton had found that Kishkumen did not return he feared lest that he should be destroyed; therefore he caused that his band should follow him. And they took their flight out of the land, by a secret way, into the wilderness; and thus when Helaman sent forth to take them they could nowhere be found.

12 And more of this Gadianton shall be spoken hereafter. And thus ended the forty and second year of the reign of the judges over the people of Nephi.

13 And behold, in the end of this book ye shall see that this Gadianton did prove the overthrow, yea, almost the entire destruction of the people of Nephi.

14 Behold I do not mean the end of the book of Helaman, but I mean the end of the book of Nephi, from which I have taken all the account which I have written.

# CHAPTER 3

*Many Nephites move away to lands in the north. The Church grows in numbers, but the Church members are persecuted by proud and wicked Nephites. Look for what the Savior's righteous followers do when they are persecuted by wicked people.*

## *Many Nephites and Ammonites Move to the Land Northward*

1 AND now it came to pass in the forty and third year of the reign of the judges, there was no contention among the people of Nephi save it were a little pride which was in the church, which did cause some little dissensions among the people, which affairs were settled in the ending of the forty and third year.

---

2:7 ***conduct***—go with

2:8 A secret combination is a group of wicked people who secretly join together to lie, cheat, steal, murder, or do whatever is necessary to gain riches, wealth, or power (see Helaman 7:21; 8:27). The first secret combination was between Satan and Cain, who killed his brother Abel to get his flocks (see Moses 5:28–32). "Among today's secret combinations are gangs, drug cartels, and organized crime families" (M. Russell Ballard, in Conference Report, October 1997, 51).

2:9 ***exceedingly***—greatly
***design***—plan

2:11 ***wilderness***—wild land where very few people lived

2:13 Like the Nephites of old, we need to guard against the same evil of secret combinations. Elder Bruce R. McConkie warned that "we see evil forces everywhere uniting to destroy the family, to ridicule morality and decency, . . . Gadianton robbers fill the judgment seats in many nations. An evil power seeks to overthrow the freedom of all nations and countries. Satan reigns in the hearts of men; it is the great day of his power" (in Conference Report, April 1980, 99).

2:14 The phrase "the book of Nephi" refers to the plates of Nephi, from which part of the Book of Mormon was translated (see the chart about the Book of Mormon plates in the introduction, xiii)

3:1 ***dissensions***—disagreements
***affairs***—troubles

2 And there was no contention among the people in the forty and fourth year; neither was there much contention in the forty and fifth year.

3 And it came to pass in the forty and sixth, yea, there was much contention and many dissensions; in the which there were an exceedingly great many who departed out of the land of Zarahemla, and went forth unto the land northward to inherit the land.

4 And they did travel to an exceedingly great distance, insomuch that they came to large bodies of water and many rivers.

5 Yea, and even they did spread forth into all parts of the land, into whatever parts it had not been rendered desolate and without timber, because of the many inhabitants who had before inherited the land.

6 And now no part of the land was desolate, save it were for timber; but because of the greatness of the destruction of the people who had before inhabited the land it was called desolate.

7 And there being but little timber upon the face of the land, nevertheless the people who went forth became exceedingly expert in the working of cement; therefore they did build houses of cement, in the which they did dwell.

8 And it came to pass that they did multiply and spread, and did go forth from the land southward to the land northward, and did spread insomuch that they began to cover the face of the whole earth, from the sea south to the sea north, from the sea west to the sea east.

9 And the people who were in the land northward did dwell in tents, and in houses of cement, and they did suffer whatsoever tree should spring up upon the face of the land that it should grow up, that in time they might have timber to build their houses, yea, their cities, and their temples, and their synagogues, and their sanctuaries, and all manner of their buildings.

10 And it came to pass as timber was exceedingly scarce in the land northward, they did send forth much by the way of shipping.

11 And thus they did enable the people in the land northward that they might build many cities, both of wood and of cement.

12 And it came to pass that there were many of the people of Ammon, who were Lamanites by birth, did also go forth into this land.

## *Many Books and Records Are Written and Kept by the Nephites*

13 And now there are many records kept of the proceedings of this people, by many of this people, which are particular and very large, concerning them.

---

3:3 ***inherit***—possess or live in

3:5 ***rendered desolate***—made empty
***inhabitants***—people

3:6 (5–6) The people who lived in the north were called the Jaredites and arrived there shortly after the fall of the tower of Babel. They lived there many hundreds of years (see Omni 1:20–22; Mosiah 8:7–11). You can read about their history and destruction in the book of Ether.

3:7 ***expert***—skilled

3:8 ***multiply***—have many children

3:9 ***suffer***—allow
***synagogues***—buildings used for religious gatherings
***sanctuaries***—places of worship

3:10 ***scarce***—uncommon or rare

3:11 ***enable***—make it possible for

3:12 The people of Ammon, who were once called the Anti-Nephi-Lehies, were converted by Ammon and other missionaries. Their story is found in Alma 17–28.

PHOTOGRAPH BY J.R. FOX

*These ruins in Teotihuacan, northeast of Mexico City, are examples of the use of cement in ancient building.*

3:13 ***proceedings***—history
***particular***—full of details

14 But behold, a hundredth part of the proceedings of this people, yea, the account of the Lamanites and of the Nephites, and their wars, and contentions, and dissensions, and their preaching, and their prophecies, and their shipping and their building of ships, and their building of temples, and of synagogues and their sanctuaries, and their righteousness, and their wickedness, and their murders, and their robbings, and their plundering, and all manner of abominations and whoredoms, cannot be contained in this work.
15 But behold, there are many books and many records of every kind, and they have been kept chiefly by the Nephites.
16 And they have been handed down from one generation to another by the Nephites, even until they have fallen into transgression and have been murdered, plundered, and hunted, and driven forth, and slain, and scattered upon the face of the earth, and mixed with the Lamanites until they are no more called the Nephites, becoming wicked, and wild, and ferocious, yea, even becoming Lamanites.

## Under Helaman's Great Leadership, Many People Join the Church

17 And now I return again to mine account; therefore, what I have spoken had passed after there had been great contentions, and disturbances, and wars, and dissensions, among the people of Nephi.
18 The forty and sixth year of the reign of the judges ended;
19 And it came to pass that there was still great contention in the land, yea, even in the forty and seventh year, and also in the forty and eighth year.
20 Nevertheless Helaman did fill the judgment-seat with justice and equity; yea, he did observe to keep the statutes, and the judgments, and the commandments of God; and he did do that which was right in the sight of God continually; and he did walk after the ways of his father, insomuch that he did prosper in the land.
21 And it came to pass that he had two sons. He gave unto the eldest the name of Nephi, and unto the youngest, the name of Lehi. And they began to grow up unto the Lord.
22 And it came to pass that the wars and contentions began to cease, in a small degree, among the people of the Nephites, in the latter end of the forty and eighth year of the reign of the judges over the people of Nephi.
23 And it came to pass in the forty and ninth year of the reign of the judges, there was continual peace established in the land, all save it were the secret combinations which Gadianton the robber had established in the more settled parts of the land, which at that time were not known unto those who were at the head of government; therefore they were not destroyed out of the land.

---

3:14 ***plundering***—stealing by force
***abominations***—great evils
***whoredoms***—wickedness and immorality

3:15 ***chiefly***—mostly

3:16 ***one generation to another***—father to son or king to king
***ferocious***—cruel

When the Prophet Joseph Smith was translating the Book of Mormon, one of the meanings of the word *transgression* was "the act of passing over or beyond any law or rule of moral duty" (Noah Webster, *An American Dictionary of the English Language*, s.v. "transgression"). In the scriptures *transgression* generally means the breaking of spiritual law. President Joseph Fielding Smith said: "I never speak of the part Eve took in this fall [meaning the Fall of man] as a sin, nor do I accuse Adam of a sin. . . . It is not always a sin to transgress a law. . . . This was a transgression of the law, but not a sin in the strict sense, for it was something that Adam and Eve had to do!" (*Doctrines of Salvation* 1:114, 115).

3:17 ***disturbances***—troubles

3:20 ***equity***—fairness
***statutes***—laws
***prosper***—succeed

What kind of leader was Helaman? Why do you think it is important for our leaders to be righteous?

3:21 Helaman named his sons after two great men in the Book of Mormon (see Helaman 5:6–7). What kind of men were Lehi and Nephi? How might these names have helped Helaman's two sons?

3:22 ***degree***—amount

3:23 ***settled***—lived in

24 And it came to pass that in this same year there
was exceedingly great prosperity in the church,
insomuch that there were thousands who did join
themselves unto the church and were baptized unto
repentance.
25 And so great was the prosperity of the church,
and so many the blessings which were poured out
upon the people, that even the high priests and
the teachers were themselves astonished beyond
measure.
26 And it came to pass that the work of the Lord
did prosper unto the baptizing and uniting to the
church of God, many souls, yea, even tens of
thousands.
27 Thus we may see that the Lord is merciful unto
all who will, in the sincerity of their hearts, call
upon his holy name.
28 Yea, thus we see that the gate of heaven is
open unto all, even to those who will believe on
the name of Jesus Christ, who is the Son of God.
29 Yea, we see that whosoever will may lay hold
upon the word of God, which is quick and powerful, which shall divide asunder all the cunning and
the snares and the wiles of the devil, and lead the
man of Christ in a strait and narrow course across
that everlasting gulf of misery which is prepared to
engulf the wicked—
30 And land their souls, yea, their immortal souls,
at the right hand of God in the kingdom of heaven,
to sit down with Abraham, and Isaac, and with Jacob,
and with all our holy fathers, to go no more out.

## Some Proud and Wicked Nephites Persecute the Members of the Church

31 And in this year there was continual rejoicing
in the land of Zarahemla, and in all the regions
round about, even in all the land which was possessed by the Nephites.
32 And it came to pass that there was peace and
exceedingly great joy in the remainder of the forty
and ninth year; yea, and also there was continual
peace and great joy in the fiftieth year of the reign
of the judges.
33 And in the fifty and first year of the reign of the
judges there was peace also, save it were the pride
which began to enter into the church—not into the
church of God, but into the hearts of the people
who professed to belong to the church of God—
34 And they were lifted up in pride, even to the
persecution of many of their brethren. Now this
was a great evil, which did cause the more humble
part of the people to suffer great persecutions, and
to wade through much affliction.
35 Nevertheless they did fast and pray oft, and did
wax stronger and stronger in their humility, and
firmer and firmer in the faith of Christ, unto the filling their souls with joy and consolation, yea, even

---

3:24 What great blessings have you received or will you receive for being baptized into the Lord's true Church? How do you show your thanks to God?

3:25 ***astonished beyond measure***—greatly surprised

3:28 *Christ* is a Greek word meaning "the Anointed One"; the Hebrew word with the same meaning is *Messiah.* Jesus is the Christ—the one chosen, set apart, and sent by God to save us (see LDS Bible Dictionary, s.v. "Christ," 633).

3:28 (27–28) The Lord is merciful and loving. When are some times you have felt His love in your life?

3:29 ***asunder***—apart
***cunning***—tricks
***snares***—traps
***wiles***—sneaky plans
***engulf***—swallow or surround

The "everlasting gulf of misery" is a phrase that describes the state of unrepentant sinners and how they will feel (see 1 Nephi 15:26–29; Alma 41:10–11).

3:30 ***immortal***—undying or everlasting

3:30 (29–30) Becoming like Christ is a gradual process. Elder Neal A. Maxwell has encouraged: "Again, what manner of individuals ought we to be? Like Christ! . . . That we have a great distance to go should not keep us from continuing the journey" *(Wherefore Ye Must Press Forward,* 31).

3:31 ***possessed***—owned

3:33 ***professed***—claimed

3:34 ***persecution***—mistreatment and abuse
***wade***—struggle to move forward

3:35 ***wax***—grow
***consolation***—comfort

Elder Bruce R. McConkie wrote: "Many specific reasons for fasting are found in the scriptures. . . . It is itself a form of the true worship of God. (Luke 2:37; Acts 9:9; Alma 45:1; 4 Ne. 12.) It is proper to fast for the sick (2 Sam. 12:16); for special blessings (Mosiah 27:22–23); to gain a testimony (Alma 5:46); to gain revelation (Alma 17:3;

to the purifying and the sanctification of their
hearts, which sanctification cometh because of their
yielding their hearts unto God.
36 And it came to pass that the fifty and second
year ended in peace also, save it were the exceedingly great pride which had gotten into the hearts
of the people; and it was because of their exceedingly great riches and their prosperity in the land;
and it did grow upon them from day to day.
37 And it came to pass in the fifty and third year
of the reign of the judges, Helaman died, and his
eldest son Nephi began to reign in his stead. And it
came to pass that he did fill the judgment-seat with
justice and equity; yea, he did keep the commandments of God, and did walk in the ways of his
father.

## CHAPTER 4

*The Nephites again suffer great losses at the hands of the Lamanites. Watch for what the Nephites learn from their sufferings and how those lessons can also apply to our day.*

### Nephite Dissenters Join the Lamanites and Drive the Nephites Out of Zarahemla

1 AND it came to pass in the fifty and fourth year
there were many dissensions in the church, and
there was also a contention among the people,
insomuch that there was much bloodshed.
2 And the rebellious part were slain and driven
out of the land, and they did go unto the king of
the Lamanites.
3 And it came to pass that they did endeavor to
stir up the Lamanites to war against the Nephites;
but behold, the Lamanites were exceedingly afraid,
insomuch that they would not hearken to the words
of those dissenters.
4 But it came to pass in the fifty and sixth year of
the reign of the judges, there were dissenters who
went up from the Nephites unto the Lamanites; and
they succeeded with those others in stirring them
up to anger against the Nephites; and they were all
that year preparing for war.

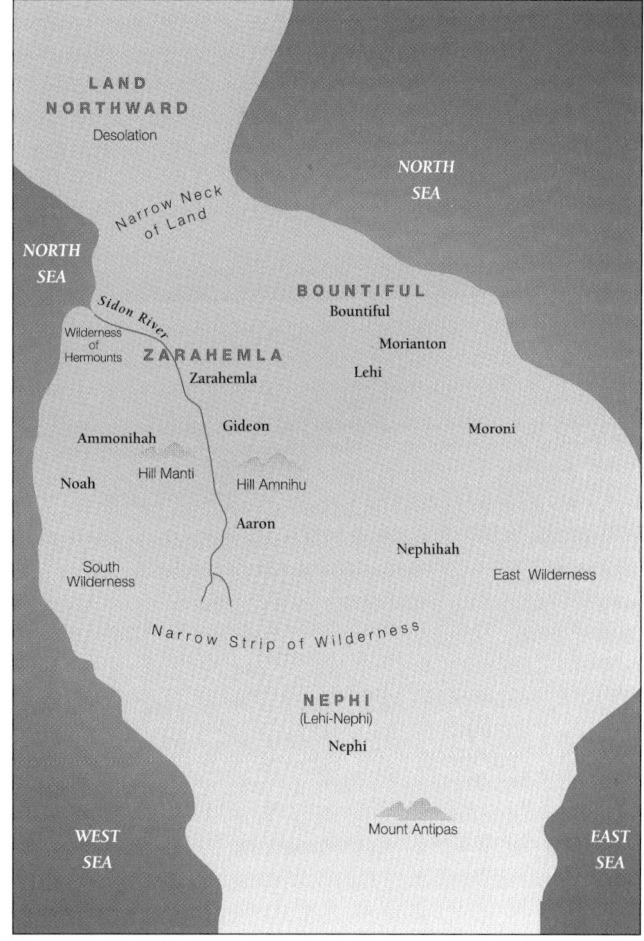


*The Nephites are driven into the land of Bountiful.*

---

3:35 CONT. 3 Ne. 27:1; Ex. 34:28; Deut. 9:9, 18); for the conversion of nonmembers to the truth (Alma 6:6; 17:9); . . . as a means of sanctifying one's soul (Hela. 3: 35); and for guidance along the path leading to salvation. (Omni 26.)" (*Mormon Doctrine,* 276).

"To be *sanctified* is to become clean, pure, and spotless" (Bruce R. McConkie, *Mormon Doctrine,* 675). A person can become sanctified only through the Atonement of Jesus Christ and by obedience to the laws, ordinances, and commandments of the gospel of Jesus Christ.

To yield, or give our hearts, to God is to do whatever He asks or to go through whatever He requires. Jesus is our example because He said to the Father, "Thy will be done, and the glory be thine forever" (Moses 4:2). How can you follow Jesus' example in your own life?

4:3 ***endeavor***—try
***hearken to***—listen to and obey

5 And in the fifty and seventh year they did come down against the Nephites to battle, and they did commence the work of death; yea, insomuch that in the fifty and eighth year of the reign of the judges they succeeded in obtaining possession of the land of Zarahemla; yea, and also all the lands, even unto the land which was near the land Bountiful.

6 And the Nephites and the armies of Moronihah were driven even into the land of Bountiful;

7 And there they did fortify against the Lamanites, from the west sea, even unto the east; it being a day's journey for a Nephite, on the line which they had fortified and stationed their armies to defend their north country.

8 And thus those dissenters of the Nephites, with the help of a numerous army of the Lamanites, had obtained all the possession of the Nephites which was in the land southward. And all this was done in the fifty and eighth and ninth years of the reign of the judges.

## The Nephites Repent but Their Armies Can Only Regain Half of Their Lands

9 And it came to pass in the sixtieth year of the reign of the judges, Moronihah did succeed with his armies in obtaining many parts of the land; yea, they regained many cities which had fallen into the hands of the Lamanites.

10 And it came to pass in the sixty and first year of the reign of the judges they succeeded in regaining even the half of all their possessions.

11 Now this great loss of the Nephites, and the great slaughter which was among them, would not have happened had it not been for their wickedness and their abomination which was among them; yea, and it was among those also who professed to belong to the church of God.

12 And it was because of the pride of their hearts, because of their exceeding riches, yea, it was because of their oppression to the poor, withholding their food from the hungry, withholding their clothing from the naked, and smiting their humble brethren upon the cheek, making a mock of that which was sacred, denying the spirit of prophecy and of revelation, murdering, plundering, lying, stealing, committing adultery, rising up in great contentions, and deserting away into the land of Nephi, among the Lamanites—

13 And because of this their great wickedness, and their boastings in their own strength, they were left in their own strength; therefore they did not prosper, but were afflicted and smitten, and driven

4:5 ***commence***—begin

4:5 (1–5) Whenever the Nephites have "many dissensions," or disagreements, among themselves, the fighting leaves them too weak to defend themselves against the Lamanites (see also Alma 51:16; 53:8–9). How does fighting in your home weaken you and your family?

4:7 ***fortify***—strengthen themselves and their lands

4:12 ***oppression to***—mistreatment of
***smiting***—hitting
***a mock***—light or fun
***plundering***—robbing
***committing adultery***—using the sacred creative powers with someone other than their husband or wife
***deserting away***—running away from their duty

4:12 (11–12) Mormon explains that the Nephites' losses came because of their wickedness. The first sin he mentions is pride. In our day the Lord also warned us to "beware of pride, lest ye become as the Nephites of old" (D&C 38:39).

4:13 ***prosper***—succeed
***afflicted and smitten***—made to suffer and were beaten

### THE NEPHITE CYCLE: MORMON'S WARNING FOR US TODAY

(Helaman 12:1–6, 23–26)

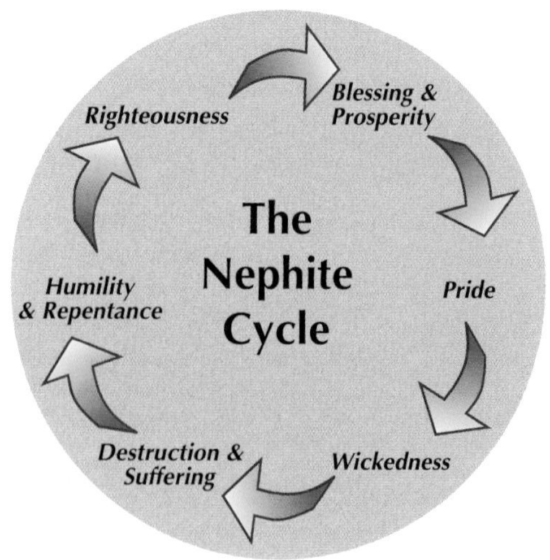

before the Lamanites, until they had lost possession of almost all their lands.

14 But behold, Moronihah did preach many things unto the people because of their iniquity, and also Nephi and Lehi, who were the sons of Helaman, did preach many things unto the people, yea, and did prophesy many things unto them concerning their iniquities, and what should come unto them if they did not repent of their sins.

15 And it came to pass that they did repent, and inasmuch as they did repent they did begin to prosper.

16 For when Moronihah saw that they did repent he did venture to lead them forth from place to place, and from city to city, even until they had regained the one-half of their property and the one-half of all their lands.

17 And thus ended the sixty and first year of the reign of the judges.

18 And it came to pass in the sixty and second year of the reign of the judges, that Moronihah could obtain no more possessions over the Lamanites.

19 Therefore they did abandon their design to obtain the remainder of their lands, for so numerous were the Lamanites that it became impossible for the Nephites to obtain more power over them; therefore Moronihah did employ all his armies in maintaining those parts which he had taken.

## The Nephites Realize That, Because They Had Sinned, They Were as Weak as the Lamanites

20 And it came to pass, because of the greatness of the number of the Lamanites the Nephites were in great fear, lest they should be overpowered, and trodden down, and slain, and destroyed.

21 Yea, they began to remember the prophecies of Alma, and also the words of Mosiah; and they saw that they had been a stiffnecked people, and that they had set at naught the commandments of God;

22 And that they had altered and trampled under their feet the laws of Mosiah, or that which the Lord commanded him to give unto the people; and they saw that their laws had become corrupted, and that they had become a wicked people, insomuch that they were wicked even like unto the Lamanites.

23 And because of their iniquity the church had begun to dwindle; and they began to disbelieve in the spirit of prophecy and in the spirit of revelation; and the judgments of God did stare them in the face.

24 And they saw that they had become weak, like unto their brethren, the Lamanites, and that the Spirit of the Lord did no more preserve them; yea, it had withdrawn from them because the Spirit of the Lord doth not dwell in unholy temples—

25 Therefore the Lord did cease to preserve them by his miraculous and matchless power, for they had fallen into a state of unbelief and awful wickedness; and they saw that the Lamanites were exceedingly more numerous than they, and except they should cleave unto the Lord their God they must unavoidably perish.

26 For behold, they saw that the strength of the Lamanites was as great as their strength, even man for man. And thus had they fallen into this great transgression; yea, thus had they become weak, because of their transgression, in the space of not many years.

---

4:14 ***iniquity***—sins

4:16 ***venture***—try

4:16 (13–16) Whenever the Nephites trusted in their own strength, they were not successful. When they repented and trusted in the Lord, they were successful. What does that teach you about how you can be more successful in overcoming the problems you face in life?

4:21 ***stiffnecked***—stubborn or rebellious
***set at naught***—put aside as worthless

4:22 ***altered and trampled under their feet***—changed and ignored
***corrupted***—full of sin

4:23 ***dwindle***—become weak

4:25 ***cleave unto***—hold on to
***unavoidably***—surely
***perish***—die physically or spiritually, or be destroyed

4:25 (23–25) We learn from the Nephites that wickedness and disobedience weaken faith and testimony. President David O. McKay said, "I have often wondered how many of us are showing our young people *how* they may know, and if we are sufficiently emphasizing the fact that they will never gain a testimony if they indulge in sin" (*Man May Know For Himself,* 13).

## CHAPTER 5

*This chapter contains a miraculous event that shows how the Lord blesses and protects His servants. As you read about Nephi and Lehi's experience, watch for the ways the Lord protected and helped them preach the gospel.*

### Nephi Gives Up the Judgment-Seat to Preach

1 AND it came to pass that in this same year, behold, Nephi delivered up the judgment-seat to a man whose name was Cezoram.

2 For as their laws and their governments were established by the voice of the people, and they who chose evil were more numerous than they who chose good, therefore they were ripening for destruction, for the laws had become corrupted.

3 Yea, and this was not all; they were a stiffnecked people, insomuch that they could not be governed by the law nor justice, save it were to their destruction.

4 And it came to pass that Nephi had become weary because of their iniquity; and he yielded up the judgment-seat, and took it upon him to preach the word of God all the remainder of his days, and his brother Lehi also, all the remainder of his days;

### Helaman Teaches His Sons to Remember Jesus Christ

5 For they remembered the words which their father Helaman spake unto them. And these are the words which he spake:

6 Behold, my sons, I desire that ye should remember to keep the commandments of God; and I would that ye should declare unto the people these words. Behold, I have given unto you the names of our first parents who came out of the land of Jerusalem; and this I have done that when you remember your names ye may remember them; and when ye remember them ye may remember their works; and when ye remember their works ye may know how that it is said, and also written, that they were good.

7 Therefore, my sons, I would that ye should do that which is good, that it may be said of you, and also written, even as it has been said and written of them.

8 And now my sons, behold I have somewhat more to desire of you, which desire is, that ye may not do these things that ye may boast, but that ye may do these things to lay up for yourselves a treasure in heaven, yea, which is eternal, and which fadeth not away; yea, that ye may have that precious gift of eternal life, which we have reason to suppose hath been given to our fathers.

9 O remember, remember, my sons, the words which king Benjamin spake unto his people; yea, remember that there is no other way nor means whereby man can be saved, only through the atoning blood of Jesus Christ, who shall come; yea, remember that he cometh to redeem the world.

10 And remember also the words which Amulek spake unto Zeezrom, in the city of Ammonihah; for he said unto him that the Lord surely should come to redeem his people, but that he should not come to redeem them in their sins, but to redeem them from their sins.

11 And he hath power given unto him from the Father to redeem them from their sins because of repentance; therefore he hath sent his angels to declare the tidings of the conditions of repentance, which bringeth unto the power of the Redeemer, unto the salvation of their souls.

---

5:2 ***established***—supported
***ripening***—getting ready
***corrupted***—full of sin or error

About sixty years earlier, King Mosiah began the practice of governing by the voice of the people. He warned that if the majority of the people ever chose evil over good they would be destroyed (see Mosiah 29:25–27).

5:3 ***stiffnecked***—stubborn or rebellious

5:4 ***iniquity***—sinful actions
***yielded***—gave

Just like Alma who gave up his judgment-seat to preach the gospel (see Alma 4:16–19), Nephi decides that preaching the word of God will have a greater effect upon changing people's hearts than anything else (see Alma 31:5).

5:11 ***tidings of the conditions***—news about the steps

12 And now, my sons, remember, remember that
it is upon the rock of our Redeemer, who is Christ,
the Son of God, that ye must build your foundation;
that when the devil shall send forth his mighty
winds, yea, his shafts in the whirlwind, yea, when
all his hail and his mighty storm shall beat upon
you, it shall have no power over you to drag you
down to the gulf of misery and endless wo, because
of the rock upon which ye are built, which is a sure
foundation, a foundation whereon if men build
they cannot fall.
13 And it came to pass that these were the words
which Helaman taught to his sons; yea, he did
teach them many things which are not written, and
also many things which are written.

## Nephi and Lehi Preach the Gospel

14 And they did remember his words; and therefore they went forth, keeping the commandments
of God, to teach the word of God among all the
people of Nephi, beginning at the city Bountiful;
15 And from thenceforth to the city of Gid; and
from the city of Gid to the city of Mulek;
16 And even from one city to another, until they
had gone forth among all the people of Nephi who
were in the land southward; and from thence into
the land of Zarahemla, among the Lamanites.
17 And it came to pass that they did preach with
great power, insomuch that they did confound
many of those dissenters who had gone over from
the Nephites, insomuch that they came forth and
did confess their sins and were baptized unto
repentance, and immediately returned to the
Nephites to endeavor to repair unto them the
wrongs which they had done.
18 And it came to pass that Nephi and Lehi did
preach unto the Lamanites with such great power
and authority, for they had power and authority
given unto them that they might speak, and they
also had what they should speak given unto them—
19 Therefore they did speak unto the great astonishment of the Lamanites, to the convincing them,
insomuch that there were eight thousand of the
Lamanites who were in the land of Zarahemla and
round about baptized unto repentance, and were
convinced of the wickedness of the traditions of
their fathers.
20 And it came to pass that Nephi and Lehi did
proceed from thence to go to the land of Nephi.

PHOTOGRAPH BY DAVID H. GARNER

*If a house is not built upon a solid foundation, it will fall. Jesus Christ is the Foundation upon which we must build our lives.*

5:12 ***shafts***—tree limbs and debris
***the gulf of misery and endless wo***—hell, where the wicked suffer

Helaman taught his sons to remember Jesus Christ and to build their lives on His foundation. What are you doing to remember Jesus Christ in your life and to improve your relationship with your Heavenly Father?

5:12 (9–12) To *redeem* means to "buy back" or to "set free." Jesus Christ is our Redeemer because He willingly paid the price to buy us back and set us free from the effects of the Fall of Adam and the burden of our own sins (see 1 Corinthians 6:20; D&C 18:11). The price He had to pay was His own blood (see 1 Peter 1:18–19).

5:14 (5–14) The word "remember" is used fifteen times in these verses. President Spencer W. Kimball said: "When you look in the dictionary for the most important word, do you know what it is. It could be 'remember'" ("Circles of Exaltation," 8; see also Alma 5:6).

5:15 ***thenceforth***—there

5:17 ***confound many of those dissenters***—convince many of the traitors
***endeavor***—try

5:18 Nephi and Lehi were great missionaries. As with all the righteous who teach the gospel, the Lord promises that "it shall be given you in the very hour, yea, in the very moment, what ye shall say" (D&C 100:6).

5:19 ***astonishment***—surprise

## Nephi and Lehi Are Put in Prison and Are Miraculously Saved

21 And it came to pass that they were taken by an army of the Lamanites and cast into prison; yea, even in that same prison in which Ammon and his brethren were cast by the servants of Limhi.

22 And after they had been cast into prison many days without food, behold, they went forth into the prison to take them that they might slay them.

23 And it came to pass that Nephi and Lehi were encircled about as if by fire, even insomuch that they durst not lay their hands upon them for fear lest they should be burned. Nevertheless, Nephi and Lehi were not burned; and they were as standing in the midst of fire and were not burned.

24 And when they saw that they were encircled about with a pillar of fire, and that it burned them not, their hearts did take courage.

25 For they saw that the Lamanites durst not lay their hands upon them; neither durst they come near unto them, but stood as if they were struck dumb with amazement.

26 And it came to pass that Nephi and Lehi did stand forth and began to speak unto them, saying: Fear not, for behold, it is God that has shown unto you this marvelous thing, in the which is shown unto you that ye cannot lay your hands on us to slay us.

27 And behold, when they had said these words, the earth shook exceedingly, and the walls of the prison did shake as if they were about to tumble to the earth; but behold, they did not fall. And behold, they that were in the prison were Lamanites and Nephites who were dissenters.

28 And it came to pass that they were overshadowed with a cloud of darkness, and an awful solemn fear came upon them.

29 And it came to pass that there came a voice as if it were above the cloud of darkness, saying: Repent ye, repent ye, and seek no more to destroy my servants whom I have sent unto you to declare good tidings.

30 And it came to pass when they heard this voice, and beheld that it was not a voice of thunder, neither was it a voice of a great tumultuous noise, but behold, it was a still voice of perfect mildness, as if it had been a whisper, and it did pierce even to the very soul—

31 And notwithstanding the mildness of the voice, behold the earth shook exceedingly, and the walls of the prison trembled again, as if it were about to tumble to the earth; and behold the cloud of darkness, which had overshadowed them, did not disperse—

32 And behold the voice came again, saying: Repent ye, repent ye, for the kingdom of heaven is at hand; and seek no more to destroy my servants. And it came to pass that the earth shook again, and the walls trembled.

33 And also again the third time the voice came, and did speak unto them marvelous words which cannot be uttered by man; and the walls did tremble again, and the earth shook as if it were about to divide asunder.

34 And it came to pass that the Lamanites could not flee because of the cloud of darkness which did overshadow them; yea, and also they were immovable because of the fear which did come upon them.

35 Now there was one among them who was a Nephite by birth, who had once belonged to the church of God but had dissented from them.

---

5:21 You can read about Ammon and his brethren's experience with Limhi's people in Mosiah 21.

5:23 ***encircled about***—surrounded
***durst***—dared

5:25 ***dumb with amazement***—speechless and shocked

5:28 ***solemn***—serious

5:29 ***tidings***—news

5:30 ***tumultuous***—loud

"How is inspiration received? Enos stated, 'And while I was thus struggling in the spirit, behold, the voice of the Lord came into my mind' (Enos 1:10). One does not necessarily hear an audible voice. . . . It is the inner voice of the Spirit, which has the capacity to whisper through and pierce all things (see D&C 85:6). . . . Thus the Lord, by revelation, brings inspiration into one's mind as though a voice were speaking" (James E. Faust, in Conference Report, April 1980, 17–18).

5:31 ***disperse***—disappear

5:33 ***divide asunder***—split in pieces

5:34 ***were immovable***—could not move

NEPHI AND LEHI ENCIRCLED BY A PILLAR OF FIRE, BY RONALD CROSBY

*"And when they saw that they were encircled about with a pillar of fire, and that it burned them not, their hearts did take courage."*

36 And it came to pass that he turned him about,
and behold, he saw through the cloud of darkness the faces of Nephi and Lehi; and behold, they did shine exceedingly, even as the faces of angels. And he beheld that they did lift their eyes to heaven; and they were in the attitude as if talking or lifting their voices to some being whom they beheld.
37 And it came to pass that this man did cry unto
the multitude, that they might turn and look. And behold, there was power given unto them that they did turn and look; and they did behold the faces of Nephi and Lehi.
38 And they said unto the man: Behold, what do
all these things mean, and who is it with whom these men do converse?
39 Now the man's name was Aminadab. And
Aminadab said unto them: They do converse with the angels of God.
40 And it came to pass that the Lamanites said
unto him: What shall we do, that this cloud of darkness may be removed from overshadowing us?
41 And Aminadab said unto them: You must
repent, and cry unto the voice, even until ye shall have faith in Christ, who was taught unto you by Alma, and Amulek, and Zeezrom; and when ye shall do this, the cloud of darkness shall be removed from overshadowing you.
42 And it came to pass that they all did begin to
cry unto the voice of him who had shaken the earth; yea, they did cry even until the cloud of darkness was dispersed.

5:36 Others have had a similar experience while speaking with the Lord (see Exodus 34:29–30; 3 Nephi 19:22–26).

5:38  **converse**—talk

43 And it came to pass that when they cast their
eyes about, and saw that the cloud of darkness was
dispersed from overshadowing them, behold, they
saw that they were encircled about, yea every soul,
by a pillar of fire.
44 And Nephi and Lehi were in the midst of them;
yea, they were encircled about; yea, they were as if
in the midst of a flaming fire, yet it did harm them
not, neither did it take hold upon the walls of the
prison; and they were filled with that joy which is
unspeakable and full of glory.
45 And behold, the Holy Spirit of God did come
down from heaven, and did enter into their hearts,
and they were filled as if with fire, and they could
speak forth marvelous words.
46 And it came to pass that there came a voice
unto them, yea, a pleasant voice, as if it were a
whisper, saying:
47 Peace, peace be unto you, because of your
faith in my Well Beloved, who was from the foundation of the world.
48 And now, when they heard this they cast up
their eyes as if to behold from whence the voice
came; and behold, they saw the heavens open; and
angels came down out of heaven and ministered
unto them.
49 And there were about three hundred souls who
saw and heard these things; and they were bidden to
go forth and marvel not, neither should they doubt.
50 And it came to pass that they did go forth, and
did minister unto the people, declaring throughout
all the regions round about all the things which
they had heard and seen, insomuch that the more
part of the Lamanites were convinced of them,
because of the greatness of the evidences which
they had received.
51 And as many as were convinced did lay down
their weapons of war, and also their hatred and the
tradition of their fathers.
52 And it came to pass that they did yield up unto
the Nephites the lands of their possession.

## CHAPTER 6

*Generally, in the Book of Mormon the Nephites are more righteous than the Lamanites. However, now the Lamanites have become more righteous than the Nephites. Look for the ways the Lamanites live the gospel and the ways the Nephites are nearly destroyed for not living it.*

### Many Converted Lamanites Teach the Gospel to the Nephites

1 AND it came to pass that when the sixty and
second year of the reign of the judges had ended,
all these things had happened and the Lamanites
had become, the more part of them, a righteous
people, insomuch that their righteousness did
exceed that of the Nephites, because of their firmness and their steadiness in the faith.
2 For behold, there were many of the Nephites
who had become hardened and impenitent and
grossly wicked, insomuch that they did reject the
word of God and all the preaching and prophesying which did come among them.
3 Nevertheless, the people of the church did have
great joy because of the conversion of the
Lamanites, yea, because of the church of God,
which had been established among them. And they
did fellowship one with another, and did rejoice
one with another, and did have great joy.

---

5:43 (40–43) Aminadab told the Lamanites that they needed to repent and cry (pray) unto the voice to remove the cloud of darkness from them. What kinds of darkness can repentance, prayer, and faith remove from your life?

5:44 ***unspeakable***—beyond description

5:45 (43–45) "The scriptures, and even our church history, record miraculous instances when visible flames encircled the humble followers of Christ—literal manifestations of fire and the Holy Ghost—but more often this fire works quietly and unseen in the hearts of those who have received the gift of the Holy Ghost" (Loren C. Dunn, "Fire and the Holy Ghost," 24).

5:49 ***bidden***—told

5:52 ***yield***—give

6:2 ***hardened***—unwilling to feel the Spirit
***impenitent***—unwilling to repent
***grossly***—awfully

6:3 Nephite members of the Church happily welcomed the Lamanite converts. President Hinckley has asked us to do the same with converts today. To help us he said, "Every [convert] needs three things: a friend, a responsibility, and nurturing with the 'good word of God' (Moro. 6:4). It is our duty and opportunity to provide these things" (*Teachings of Gordon B. Hinckley,* 539).

4 And it came to pass that many of the Lamanites
did come down into the land of Zarahemla, and did
declare unto the people of the Nephites the manner
of their conversion, and did exhort them to faith
and repentance.
5 Yea, and many did preach with exceedingly
great power and authority, unto the bringing down
many of them into the depths of humility, to be the
humble followers of God and the Lamb.
6 And it came to pass that many of the Lamanites
did go into the land northward; and also Nephi and
Lehi went into the land northward, to preach unto
the people. And thus ended the sixty and third year.

## The Nephites and Lamanites Enjoy a Time of Peace and Prosperity

7 And behold, there was peace in all the land,
insomuch that the Nephites did go into whatsoever
part of the land they would, whether among the
Nephites or the Lamanites.
8 And it came to pass that the Lamanites did also
go whithersoever they would, whether it were
among the Lamanites or among the Nephites; and
thus they did have free intercourse one with another, to buy and to sell, and to get gain, according
to their desire.
9 And it came to pass that they became exceedingly rich, both the Lamanites and the Nephites;
and they did have an exceeding plenty of gold, and
of silver, and of all manner of precious metals, both
in the land south and in the land north.
10 Now the land south was called Lehi, and the
land north was called Mulek, which was after the
son of Zedekiah; for the Lord did bring Mulek into
the land north, and Lehi into the land south.
11 And behold, there was all manner of gold in
both these lands, and of silver, and of precious ore
of every kind; and there were also curious workmen, who did work all kinds of ore and did refine
it; and thus they did become rich.
12 They did raise grain in abundance, both in the
north and in the south; and they did flourish
exceedingly, both in the north and in the south.
And they did multiply and wax exceedingly strong
in the land. And they did raise many flocks and
herds, yea, many fatlings.
13 Behold their women did toil and spin, and did
make all manner of cloth, of fine-twined linen and
cloth of every kind, to clothe their nakedness. And
thus the sixty and fourth year did pass away in
peace.
14 And in the sixty and fifth year they did also
have great joy and peace, yea, much preaching and
many prophecies concerning that which was to
come. And thus passed away the sixty and fifth
year.

## The Gadianton Robbers Gain Power Through Secret Combinations

15 And it came to pass that in the sixty and sixth
year of the reign of the judges, behold, Cezoram
was murdered by an unknown hand as he sat upon
the judgment-seat. And it came to pass that in the
same year, that his son, who had been appointed
by the people in his stead, was also murdered. And
thus ended the sixty and sixth year.

---

6:4 ***manner***—story
***exhort***—encourage

6:5 The Lord has instructed missionaries to "go forth in the power of my Spirit, preaching my gospel" (D&C 42:6). The Prophet Joseph Smith taught that "no man can preach the Gospel without the Holy Ghost" (*Teachings of the Prophet Joseph Smith,* 112).

Jesus Christ is "the Lamb of God, which taketh away the sin of the world" (John 1:29).

6:8 ***did have free intercourse***—were free to deal
***get gain***—make money

6:9 ***exceedingly***—very

6:10 "We call the people of Zarahemla Mulekites after the name of Mulek (Helaman 6:10), a son of Zedekiah not named in the Old Testament. Young Mulek and his associates had been led by the Lord across the waters to this north continent" (Sidney B. Sperry, *Book of Mormon Compendium,* 274–75).

6:11 ***curious***—skilled

6:12 ***abundance***—great amounts
***flourish exceedingly***—have great success
***multiply and wax exceedingly strong***—increase in numbers and grow very strong

6:13 ***fine-twined linen***—cloth made from thin thread

6:15 Cezoram became the chief judge of the land when Nephi gave up the position so he could "preach the word of God all the remainder of his days" (Helaman 5:1–4).

16 And in the commencement of the sixty and seventh year the people began to grow exceedingly wicked again.

17 For behold, the Lord had blessed them so long with the riches of the world that they had not been stirred up to anger, to wars, nor to bloodshed; therefore they began to set their hearts upon their riches; yea, they began to seek to get gain that they might be lifted up one above another; therefore they began to commit secret murders, and to rob and to plunder, that they might get gain.

18 And now behold, those murderers and plunderers were a band who had been formed by Kishkumen and Gadianton. And now it had come to pass that there were many, even among the Nephites, of Gadianton's band. But behold, they were more numerous among the more wicked part of the Lamanites. And they were called Gadianton's robbers and murderers.

19 And it was they who did murder the chief judge Cezoram, and his son, while in the judgment-seat; and behold, they were not found.

20 And now it came to pass that when the Lamanites found that there were robbers among them they were exceedingly sorrowful; and they did use every means in their power to destroy them off the face of the earth.

21 But behold, Satan did stir up the hearts of the more part of the Nephites, insomuch that they did unite with those bands of robbers, and did enter into their covenants and their oaths, that they would protect and preserve one another in whatsoever difficult circumstances they should be placed, that they should not suffer for their murders, and their plunderings, and their stealings.

22 And it came to pass that they did have their signs, yea, their secret signs, and their secret words; and this that they might distinguish a brother who had entered into the covenant, that whatsoever wickedness his brother should do he should not be injured by his brother, nor by those who did belong to his band, who had taken this covenant.

23 And thus they might murder, and plunder, and steal, and commit whoredoms and all manner of wickedness, contrary to the laws of their country and also the laws of their God.

24 And whosoever of those who belonged to their band should reveal unto the world of their wickedness and their abominations, should be tried, not according to the laws of their country, but according to the laws of their wickedness, which had been given by Gadianton and Kishkumen.

25 Now behold, it is these secret oaths and covenants which Alma commanded his son should not go forth unto the world, lest they should be a means of bringing down the people unto destruction.

26 Now behold, those secret oaths and covenants did not come forth unto Gadianton from the records which were delivered unto Helaman; but behold, they were put into the heart of Gadianton by that same being who did entice our first parents to partake of the forbidden fruit—

27 Yea, that same being who did plot with Cain, that if he would murder his brother Abel it should not be known unto the world. And he did plot with Cain and his followers from that time forth.

---

6:16 ***commencement***—beginning

6:17 ***stirred up***—awakened

When people "set their hearts," or their love, upon the things of this world they lose their place as the Lord's chosen people (see D&C 121:34–35). Elder Neal A. Maxwell warned that "hearts 'set so much upon the things of this world' are hearts so *set* they must first be broken" ("Why Not Now?" 6).

6:21 ***plunderings***—robberies

6:22 ***distinguish***—tell or identify

6:23 ***whoredoms***—immoral acts

6:24 ***abominations***—evil works

6:25 (22–25) Mormon gives a long list of the Gadianton robbers' evil activities that will eventually destroy the Nephites. Why are secret combinations so dangerous? (see also Glossary: Secret Combinations).

6:26 "That same being" refers to Satan. In the premortal world Lucifer rebelled against God and was cast out of heaven to the earth. He became Satan and he desires to "deceive and to blind men, and to lead them captive at his will" (Moses 4:1–4).

***entice***—tempt

28 And also it is that same being who put it into the hearts of the people to build a tower sufficiently high that they might get to heaven. And it was that same being who led on the people who came from that tower into this land; who spread the works of darkness and abominations over all the face of the land, until he dragged the people down to an entire destruction, and to an everlasting hell.
29 Yea, it is that same being who put it into the heart of Gadianton to still carry on the work of darkness, and of secret murder; and he has brought it forth from the beginning of man even down to this time.
30 And behold, it is he who is the author of all sin. And behold, he doth carry on his works of darkness and secret murder, and doth hand down their plots, and their oaths, and their covenants, and their plans of awful wickedness, from generation to generation according as he can get hold upon the hearts of the children of men.

## The Nephites Become Far More Wicked Than the Lamanites

31 And now behold, he had got great hold upon the hearts of the Nephites; yea, insomuch that they had become exceedingly wicked; yea, the more part of them had turned out of the way of righteousness, and did trample under their feet the commandments of God, and did turn unto their own ways, and did build up unto themselves idols of their gold and their silver.
32 And it came to pass that all these iniquities did come unto them in the space of not many years, insomuch that a more part of it had come unto them in the sixty and seventh year of the reign of the judges over the people of Nephi.
33 And they did grow in their iniquities in the sixty and eighth year also, to the great sorrow and lamentation of the righteous.
34 And thus we see that the Nephites did begin to dwindle in unbelief, and grow in wickedness and abominations, while the Lamanites began to grow exceedingly in the knowledge of their God; yea, they did begin to keep his statutes and commandments, and to walk in truth and uprightness before him.
35 And thus we see that the Spirit of the Lord began to withdraw from the Nephites, because of the wickedness and the hardness of their hearts.
36 And thus we see that the Lord began to pour out his Spirit upon the Lamanites, because of their easiness and willingness to believe in his words.
37 And it came to pass that the Lamanites did hunt the band of robbers of Gadianton; and they did preach the word of God among the more wicked part of them, insomuch that this band of robbers was utterly destroyed from among the Lamanites.
38 And it came to pass on the other hand, that the Nephites did build them up and support them, beginning at the more wicked part of them, until they had overspread all the land of the Nephites, and had seduced the more part of the righteous until they had come down to believe in their works and partake of their spoils, and to join with them in their secret murders and combinations.

---

6:28 Latter-day scriptures teach that there are at least three meanings for the term *hell.* It can describe our suffering here on earth (see Alma 36:18). It can refer to a part of the spirit world where those who have not repented suffer for their sins (see Alma 40:13–14). It is also used to describe the final condition of those who completely turn away from God (see D&C 29:38).

6:30 In verses 17, 21, 26, 28, and 30, we find that the key to influencing people is through their heart. This is one of Satan's greatest tools. Alma taught that when Satan hardens our heart, he can lead us astray; this is what is meant by the "chains of hell" (see Alma 12:9–11).

6:30 (28–30) Secret combinations were also had among the Jaredites and are still among all people (see Ether 8:18–21).

6:31 The Lord has warned that all those who "turn unto their own ways," or turn to idols and false gods instead of to the Lord, "shall surely perish" (Deuteronomy 8:19; see also D&C 1:16).

6:33 ***iniquities***—sins and wickedness

6:34 ***dwindle***—weaken
***statutes***—laws

6:36 President Spencer W. Kimball taught that "the converted Lamanite is devout. Few ever apostatize. Some lose their way as they partake of the worldliness about them, but generally the children of Lehi of the twentieth century have inherited that grace and ability to believe like their ancestors of the long ago" (*The Teachings of Spencer W. Kimball,* 178).

6:37 ***utterly***—completely

6:38 ***seduced***—led astray

39 And thus they did obtain the sole management of the government, insomuch that they did trample under their feet and smite and rend and turn their backs upon the poor and the meek, and the humble followers of God.

40 And thus we see that they were in an awful state, and ripening for an everlasting destruction.

41 And it came to pass that thus ended the sixty and eighth year of the reign of the judges over the people of Nephi.

THE PROPHECY OF NEPHI, THE SON OF HELAMAN—*God threatens the people of Nephi that he will visit them in his anger, to their utter destruction except they repent of their wickedness. God smiteth the people of Nephi with pestilence; they repent and turn unto him. Samuel, a Lamanite, prophesies unto the Nephites. Comprising chapters 7 to 16 inclusive.**

## CHAPTER 7

*Nephi, the son of Helaman, warns the people of Nephi that they will be destroyed if they do not repent. Watch for how the people respond to Nephi's warning.*

### *NEPHI MOURNS OVER THE PEOPLE'S WICKEDNESS*

1 BEHOLD, now it came to pass in the sixty and ninth year of the reign of the judges over the people of the Nephites, that Nephi, the son of Helaman, returned to the land of Zarahemla from the land northward.

2 For he had been forth among the people who were in the land northward and did preach the word of God unto them, and did prophesy many things unto them;

3 And they did reject all his words, insomuch that he could not stay among them, but returned again unto the land of his nativity.

4 And seeing the people in a state of such awful wickedness, and those Gadianton robbers filling the judgment-seats—having usurped the power and authority of the land; laying aside the commandments of God, and not in the least aright before him; doing no justice unto the children of men;

5 Condemning the righteous because of their righteousness; letting the guilty and the wicked go unpunished because of their money; and moreover to be held in office at the head of government, to rule and do according to their wills, that they might get gain and glory of the world, and, moreover, that they might the more easily commit adultery, and steal, and kill, and do according to their own wills—

6 Now this great iniquity had come upon the Nephites, in the space of not many years; and when Nephi saw it, his heart was swollen with sorrow within his breast; and he did exclaim in the agony of his soul:

7 Oh, that I could have had my days in the days when my father Nephi first came out of the land of Jerusalem, that I could have joyed with him in the promised land; then were his people easy to be entreated, firm to keep the commandments of God, and slow to be led to do iniquity; and they were quick to hearken unto the words of the Lord—

---

6:39 When the wicked rule, often the first to suffer are "the poor and the meek, and the humble followers of God." What can you do to bless the lives of people in need?

6:40 (34–40) Mormon uses the phrase "Thus we see" to point out important lessons in the Book of Mormon. The first one is in 1 Nephi 16:29, but most are found scattered throughout the book of Alma (see Alma 28:13–14). However, these few verses contain the phrase more than anywhere else in the Book of Mormon.

* This introduction to chapters 7–16, except for the last sentence, was translated from the Book of Mormon plates.

7:2 ***forth***—traveling

7:3 ***nativity***—birth

7:4 ***usurped***—seized or taken
***aright***—obedient

7:5 ***Condemning***—Punishing
***wills***—desires

7:6 ***iniquity***—wickedness
***swollen***—filled
***agony***—extreme pain

7:6 (4-6) Nephi felt great sadness because of the wickedness of his people. Have you ever been sad because someone you love has not followed Jesus? What can you do to help them?

7:7 ***entreated***—taught

Nephi desired to live in a time and place when the earth was filled with righteousness. What are the advantages of living among good people and having friends that are righteous?

8 Yea, if my days could have been in those days, then would my soul have had joy in the righteousness of my brethren.

9 But behold, I am consigned that these are my days, and that my soul shall be filled with sorrow because of this the wickedness of my brethren.

### Nephi Commands the People to Repent

10 And behold, now it came to pass that it was upon a tower, which was in the garden of Nephi, which was by the highway which led to the chief market, which was in the city of Zarahemla; therefore, Nephi had bowed himself upon the tower which was in his garden, which tower was also near unto the garden gate by which led the highway.

11 And it came to pass that there were certain men passing by and saw Nephi as he was pouring out his soul unto God upon the tower; and they ran and told the people what they had seen, and the people came together in multitudes that they might know the cause of so great mourning for the wickedness of the people.

12 And now, when Nephi arose he beheld the multitudes of people who had gathered together.

13 And it came to pass that he opened his mouth and said unto them: Behold, why have ye gathered yourselves together? That I may tell you of your iniquities?

14 Yea, because I have got upon my tower that I might pour out my soul unto my God, because of the exceeding sorrow of my heart, which is because of your iniquities!

15 And because of my mourning and lamentation ye have gathered yourselves together, and do marvel; yea, and ye have great need to marvel; yea, ye ought to marvel because ye are given away that the devil has got so great hold upon your hearts.

16 Yea, how could you have given way to the enticing of him who is seeking to hurl away your souls down to everlasting misery and endless wo?

17 O repent ye, repent ye! Why will ye die? Turn ye, turn ye unto the Lord your God. Why has he forsaken you?

18 It is because you have hardened your hearts; yea, ye will not hearken unto the voice of the good shepherd; yea, ye have provoked him to anger against you.

19 And behold, instead of gathering you, except ye will repent, behold, he shall scatter you forth that ye shall become meat for dogs and wild beasts.

### The Nephites Are Threatened with Destruction, but the Lamanites Are Promised Mercy

20 O, how could you have forgotten your God in the very day that he has delivered you?

21 But behold, it is to get gain, to be praised of men, yea, and that ye might get gold and silver. And ye have set your hearts upon the riches and the vain things of this world, for the which ye do murder, and plunder, and steal, and bear false witness against your neighbor, and do all manner of iniquity.

22 And for this cause wo shall come unto you except ye shall repent. For if ye will not repent, behold, this great city, and also all those great cities which are round about, which are in the land of our possession, shall be taken away that ye shall have no place in them; for behold, the Lord will not grant unto you strength, as he has hitherto done, to withstand against your enemies.

23 For behold, thus saith the Lord: I will not show unto the wicked of my strength, to one more than the other, save it be unto those who repent of their sins, and hearken unto my words. Now therefore, I would that ye should behold, my brethren, that it shall be better for the Lamanites than for you except ye shall repent.

---

7:9 ***am consigned that these are my days***—accept that I am appointed to live in these days

7:11 ***pouring out his soul***—praying with all of his heart
***mourning***—grief and sorrow

7:15 ***lamentation***—great sorrow
***marvel***—wonder

7:16 ***enticing***—temptations
***hurl***—send
***wo***—sorrow

7:17 ***forsaken***—left

7:18 Alma taught that those who refuse to listen to the voice of the Lord "are not the sheep of the good shepherd. . . . The devil is your shepherd, and ye are of his fold" (Alma 5:38–39).

7:21 ***vain***—empty and useless
***plunder***—rob
***bear false witness***—lie

7:22 ***hitherto***—previously

24 For behold, they are more righteous than you, for they have not sinned against that great knowledge which ye have received; therefore the Lord will be merciful unto them; yea, he will lengthen out their days and increase their seed, even when thou shalt be utterly destroyed except thou shalt repent.

25 Yea, wo be unto you because of that great abomination which has come among you; and ye have united yourselves unto it, yea, to that secret band which was established by Gadianton!

26 Yea, wo shall come unto you because of that pride which ye have suffered to enter your hearts, which has lifted you up beyond that which is good because of your exceedingly great riches!

27 Yea, wo be unto you because of your wickedness and abominations!

28 And except ye repent ye shall perish; yea, even your lands shall be taken from you, and ye shall be destroyed from off the face of the earth.

29 Behold now, I do not say that these things shall be, of myself, because it is not of myself that I know these things; but behold, I know that these things are true because the Lord God has made them known unto me, therefore I testify that they shall be.

## CHAPTER 8

*The judges are angry at Nephi because he testified against their wickedness. Nephi teaches the people that God gives His prophets the power to know the future. Look for how many prophets testified of the coming of the Savior.*

### Wicked Judges Try to Turn the People Against Nephi but Some People Believe He Is a Prophet

1 AND now it came to pass that when Nephi had said these words, behold, there were men who were judges, who also belonged to the secret band of Gadianton, and they were angry, and they cried out against him, saying unto the people: Why do ye not seize upon this man and bring him forth, that he may be condemned according to the crime which he has done?

2 Why seest thou this man, and hearest him revile against this people and against our law?

3 For behold, Nephi had spoken unto them concerning the corruptness of their law; yea, many things did Nephi speak which cannot be written; and nothing did he speak which was contrary to the commandments of God.

4 And those judges were angry with him because he spake plainly unto them concerning their secret works of darkness; nevertheless, they durst not lay their own hands upon him, for they feared the people lest they should cry out against them.

5 Therefore they did cry unto the people, saying: Why do you suffer this man to revile against us? For behold he doth condemn all this people, even unto destruction; yea, and also that these our great cities shall be taken from us, that we shall have no place in them.

6 And now we know that this is impossible, for behold, we are powerful, and our cities great, therefore our enemies can have no power over us.

---

7:24 ***seed***—descendants, meaning children, grandchildren, and so on
***utterly***—completely

Because the Nephites had a greater understanding of the gospel, God expected more from them than He did the Lamanites. The Lord declared, "For of him unto whom much is given much is required; and he who sins against the greater light shall receive the greater condemnation" (D&C 82:3).

7:25 ***abomination***—evil

7:26 ***suffered***—allowed

7:28 (19–28) Nephi told the Nephites the terrible things that would happen to them if they did not repent. Why would it be so difficult to be a prophet? How can you help our prophet today?

7:29 A testimony is a knowledge of truth which comes by the power of the Holy Ghost. What principles of the gospel do you know to be true?

8:1 ***seize upon***—capture
***condemned***—punished

8:2 ***revile***—speak out

8:3 ***corruptness***—wickedness
***contrary to***—against or different from

8:4 ***durst***—dared

8:4 (3–4) Why were the judges angry at the prophet when they knew he was telling the truth? Why does the truth cause some people to get angry?

7 And it came to pass that thus they did stir up the
people to anger against Nephi, and raised contentions among them; for there were some who did
cry out: Let this man alone, for he is a good man,
and those things which he saith will surely come to
pass except we repent;
8 Yea, behold, all the judgments will come upon
us which he has testified unto us; for we know that
he has testified aright unto us concerning our iniquities. And behold they are many, and he knoweth
as well all things which shall befall us as he
knoweth of our iniquities;
9 Yea, and behold, if he had not been a prophet
he could not have testified concerning those things.
10 And it came to pass that those people who
sought to destroy Nephi were compelled because
of their fear, that they did not lay their hands on
him; therefore he began again to speak unto them,
seeing that he had gained favor in the eyes of some,
insomuch that the remainder of them did fear.

## Nephi Tells of Many Prophets Who Testified of Christ

11 Therefore he was constrained to speak more
unto them saying: Behold, my brethren, have ye
not read that God gave power unto one man, even
Moses, to smite upon the waters of the Red Sea,
and they parted hither and thither, insomuch that
the Israelites, who were our fathers, came through
upon dry ground, and the waters closed upon the
armies of the Egyptians and swallowed them up?
12 And now behold, if God gave unto this man
such power, then why should ye dispute among
yourselves, and say that he hath given unto me no
power whereby I may know concerning the judgments that shall come upon you except ye repent?
13 But, behold, ye not only deny my words, but
ye also deny all the words which have been spoken
by our fathers, and also the words which were spoken by this man, Moses, who had such great power
given unto him, yea, the words which he hath spoken concerning the coming of the Messiah.
14 Yea, did he not bear record that the Son of God
should come? And as he lifted up the brazen serpent in the wilderness, even so shall he be lifted up
who should come.
15 And as many as should look upon that serpent
should live, even so as many as should look upon
the Son of God with faith, having a contrite spirit,
might live, even unto that life which is eternal.
16 And now behold, Moses did not only testify of
these things, but also all the holy prophets, from his
days even to the days of Abraham.
17 Yea, and behold, Abraham saw of his coming,
and was filled with gladness and did rejoice.
18 Yea, and behold I say unto you, that Abraham
not only knew of these things, but there were many
before the days of Abraham who were called by the
order of God; yea, even after the order of his Son;
and this that it should be shown unto the people, a
great many thousand years before his coming, that
even redemption should come unto them.

---

8:7 ***contentions***—arguments or fighting

Even though wicked men were arguing against Nephi, some righteous people knew he was a prophet and supported him. How can you show support for the prophet today? What teachings of his are you trying to follow?

8:8 ***aright***—accurately or correctly
***iniquities***—sins

8:10 ***compelled***—held back

8:11 ***constrained***—prompted by the Spirit
***hither and thither***—to one side and the other
***swallowed them up***—drowned them

8:12 ***dispute***—argue

8:13 *Messiah* means "Anointed One." The word *Christ* has the same meaning. Jesus Christ is the promised Messiah—the one chosen, set apart, and sent by God to save us.

8:14 ***bear record***—testify

8:15 ***contrite***—humble and obedient

The Lord also declared that the brazen serpent lifted up by Moses (see Numbers 21:8–9) was an example of His own crucifixion when He said: "And as Moses lifted up the serpent in the wilderness, even so must the Son of man be lifted up: That whosoever believeth in him should not perish, but have eternal life" (John 3:14–15). We must look to Jesus Christ to be saved, because "there shall be no other name given nor any other way nor means whereby salvation can come unto the children of men" (Mosiah 3:17).

8:18 The Melchizedek Priesthood, "the higher priesthood, is defined as the priesthood after the holiest order of God, or the Holy Priesthood after the Order of the Son of God (see Alma 13:18; Hel. 8:18; D&C 107:2–4)" (Boyd K. Packer, "The Holy Temple," 34).

MOSES AND THE BRAZEN SERPENT, BY JUDITH MEHR

*The brass serpent Moses held up for the Israelites was symbolic of Jesus Christ (see Numbers 21:8–9; John 3:14–15).*

19 And now I would that ye should know, that even since the days of Abraham there have been many prophets that have testified these things; yea, behold, the prophet Zenos did testify boldly; for the which he was slain.

20 And behold, also Zenock, and also Ezias, and also Isaiah, and Jeremiah, (Jeremiah being that same prophet who testified of the destruction of Jerusalem) and now we know that Jerusalem was destroyed according to the words of Jeremiah. O then why not the Son of God come, according to his prophecy?

21 And now will you dispute that Jerusalem was destroyed? Will ye say that the sons of Zedekiah were not slain, all except it were Mulek? Yea, and do ye not behold that the seed of Zedekiah are with us, and they were driven out of the land of Jerusalem? But behold, this is not all—

22 Our father Lehi was driven out of Jerusalem because he testified of these things. Nephi also testified of these things, and also almost all of our fathers, even down to this time; yea, they have testified of the coming of Christ, and have looked forward, and have rejoiced in his day which is to come.

23 And behold, he is God, and he is with them, and he did manifest himself unto them, that they were redeemed by him; and they gave unto him glory, because of that which is to come.

### *Nephi Speaks Against the Sins of the Judges and Announces the Chief Judge's Murder*

24 And now, seeing ye know these things and cannot deny them except ye shall lie, therefore in this ye have sinned, for ye have rejected all these things, notwithstanding so many evidences which ye have received; yea, even ye have received all things, both things in heaven, and all things which are in the earth, as a witness that they are true.

25 But behold, ye have rejected the truth, and rebelled against your holy God; and even at this time, instead of laying up for yourselves treasures in heaven, where nothing doth corrupt, and where nothing can come which is unclean, ye are heaping up for yourselves wrath against the day of judgment.

26 Yea, even at this time ye are ripening, because of your murders and your fornication and wickedness, for everlasting destruction; yea, and except ye repent it will come unto you soon.

27 Yea, behold it is now even at your doors; yea, go ye in unto the judgment-seat, and search; and behold, your judge is murdered, and he lieth in his blood; and he hath been murdered by his brother, who seeketh to sit in the judgment-seat.

28 And behold, they both belong to your secret band, whose author is Gadianton and the evil one who seeketh to destroy the souls of men.

## CHAPTER 9

*Nephi miraculously reveals who murdered the chief judge. Watch for the Lord's hand in uncovering this hidden sin.*

### *Five Messengers Are Accused of Murder*

1 BEHOLD, now it came to pass that when Nephi had spoken these words, certain men who were among them ran to the judgment-seat; yea, even

---

8:19 ***slain***—killed

8:20 (19–20) Zenos, Zenock, and Ezias are noted in the Book of Mormon, but are missing from the Bible. Verses 19 and 20 suggest that these men lived somewhere between the time of Abraham (2200 B.C.) and Isaiah (700 B.C.). Their writings were most likely contained on the plates of brass (see LDS Bible Dictionary, s.v. "Lost Books," 725–26).

8:21 (20–21) Jerusalem was destroyed by the Babylonians in about 586 B.C. because the people would not repent (see 2 Kings 25).

8:22 All prophets testify of Jesus Christ. Can you remember hearing our prophet today speak about Jesus Christ? Why do you think the prophets spend so much time teaching and testifying about Jesus Christ?

8:23 ***manifest***—show

8:25 ***corrupt***—spoil or ruin
***heaping up***—gathering
***wrath***—anger

8:26 ***fornication***—use of the sacred creative powers with someone who is not your husband or wife

8:28 ***author***—founder or first leader (see for Helaman 6:26)

9:1 ***judgment-seat***—place where the judge sits

there were five who went, and they said among themselves, as they went:

2 Behold, now we will know of a surety whether this man be a prophet and God hath commanded him to prophesy such marvelous things unto us. Behold, we do not believe that he hath; yea, we do not believe that he is a prophet; nevertheless, if this thing which he has said concerning the chief judge be true, that he be dead, then will we believe that the other words which he has spoken are true.

3 And it came to pass that they ran in their might, and came in unto the judgment-seat; and behold, the chief judge had fallen to the earth, and did lie in his blood.

4 And now behold, when they saw this they were astonished exceedingly, insomuch that they fell to the earth; for they had not believed the words which Nephi had spoken concerning the chief judge.

5 But now, when they saw they believed, and fear came upon them lest all the judgments which Nephi had spoken should come upon the people; therefore they did quake, and had fallen to the earth.

6 Now, immediately when the judge had been murdered—he being stabbed by his brother by a garb of secrecy, and he fled, and the servants ran and told the people, raising the cry of murder among them;

7 And behold the people did gather themselves together unto the place of the judgment-seat—and behold, to their astonishment they saw those five men who had fallen to the earth.

8 And now behold, the people knew nothing concerning the multitude who had gathered together at the garden of Nephi; therefore they said among themselves: These men are they who have murdered the judge, and God has smitten them that they could not flee from us.

9 And it came to pass that they laid hold on them, and bound them and cast them into prison. And there was a proclamation sent abroad that the judge was slain, and that the murderers had been taken and were cast into prison.

10 And it came to pass that on the morrow the people did assemble themselves together to mourn and to fast, at the burial of the great chief judge who had been slain.

11 And thus also those judges who were at the garden of Nephi, and heard his words, were also gathered together at the burial.

12 And it came to pass that they inquired among the people, saying: Where are the five who were sent to inquire concerning the chief judge whether he was dead? And they answered and said: Concerning this five whom ye say ye have sent, we know not; but there are five who are the murderers, whom we have cast into prison.

13 And it came to pass that the judges desired that they should be brought; and they were brought, and behold they were the five who were sent; and behold the judges inquired of them to know concerning the matter, and they told them all that they had done, saying:

14 We ran and came to the place of the judgment-seat, and when we saw all things even as Nephi had testified, we were astonished insomuch that we fell to the earth; and when we were recovered from our astonishment, behold they cast us into prison.

15 Now, as for the murder of this man, we know not who has done it; and only this much we know, we ran and came according as ye desired, and behold he was dead, according to the words of Nephi.

## Nephi Is Accused of Assisting in the Murder of the Chief Judge

16 And now it came to pass that the judges did expound the matter unto the people, and did cry out against Nephi, saying: Behold, we know that this Nephi must have agreed with some one to slay the judge, and then he might declare it unto us, that he might convert us unto his faith, that he might raise himself to be a great man, chosen of God, and a prophet.

17 And now behold, we will detect this man, and he shall confess his fault and make known unto us the true murderer of this judge.

---

9:4 W ***astonished exceedingly***—very surprised

9:5 W ***quake***—shake

9:6 W ***by a garb of secrecy***—who was disguised

9:8 W ***smitten them***—struck them down

9:9 W ***a proclamation***—an official statement

9:12 W ***inquired***—asked

9:14 W ***astonished insomuch***—so surprised

9:17 W ***detect***—reveal the truth about

18 And it came to pass that the five were liberated on the day of the burial. Nevertheless, they did
rebuke the judges in the words which they had spoken against Nephi, and did contend with them one
by one, insomuch that they did confound them.
19 Nevertheless, they caused that Nephi should be
taken and bound and brought before the multitude,
and they began to question him in divers ways that
they might cross him, that they might accuse him to
death—
20 Saying unto him: Thou art confederate; who is
this man that hath done this murder? Now tell us,
and acknowledge thy fault; saying, Behold here is
money; and also we will grant unto thee thy life if
thou wilt tell us, and acknowledge the agreement
which thou hast made with him.
21 But Nephi said unto them: O ye fools, ye uncircumcised of heart, ye blind, and ye stiffnecked
people, do ye know how long the Lord your God will
suffer you that ye shall go on in this your way of sin?
22 O ye ought to begin to howl and mourn,
because of the great destruction which at this time
doth await you, except ye shall repent.
23 Behold ye say that I have agreed with a man
that he should murder Seezoram, our chief judge.
But behold, I say unto you, that this is because I
have testified unto you that ye might know concerning this thing; yea, even for a witness unto you,
that I did know of the wickedness and abominations which are among you.
24 And because I have done this, ye say that I
have agreed with a man that he should do this
thing; yea, because I showed unto you this sign ye
are angry with me, and seek to destroy my life.

## Nephi Gives a Sign to Reveal the Murderer

25 And now behold, I will show unto you another sign, and see if ye will in this thing seek to
destroy me.
26 Behold I say unto you: Go to the house of
Seantum, who is the brother of Seezoram, and say
unto him—
27 Has Nephi, the pretended prophet, who doth
prophesy so much evil concerning this people,
agreed with thee, in the which ye have murdered
Seezoram, who is your brother?
28 And behold, he shall say unto you, Nay.
29 And ye shall say unto him: Have ye murdered
your brother?
30 And he shall stand with fear, and wist not
what to say. And behold, he shall deny unto you;
and he shall make as if he were astonished;
nevertheless, he shall declare unto you that he is
innocent.
31 But behold, ye shall examine him, and ye shall
find blood upon the skirts of his cloak.
32 And when ye have seen this, ye shall say: From
whence cometh this blood? Do we not know that it
is the blood of your brother?
33 And then shall he tremble, and shall look pale,
even as if death had come upon him.
34 And then shall ye say: Because of this fear and
this paleness which has come upon your face,
behold, we know that thou art guilty.
35 And then shall greater fear come upon him;
and then shall he confess unto you, and deny no
more that he has done this murder.

---

9:18 ***liberated***—freed
***rebuke***—correct or chastise
***confound them***—silence them with their words

9:19 ***divers***—different

9:20 ***confederate***—a helper of the murderers

9:21 ***stiffnecked***—stubborn or rebellious

The law of circumcision in the Old Testament was a sign of the covenant made between God and Israel, which set them apart from the world (see Genesis 17:10–11). "Uncircumcised of heart" is a phrase which means that people do not take their covenants to heart and thus do not keep them.

9:22 ***howl and mourn***—cry loudly and feel great sorrow

9:23 The wicked believe they can hide their sins. However, the Lord knows and understands all things (see 2 Nephi 9:20). Nephi's testimony that the Lord revealed to him the chief judge's murder was a witness that the wicked cannot hide their sins from the Lord.

9:30 ***wist***—know

9:31 ***skirts of his cloak***—edges of his robe

36 And then shall he say unto you, that I, Nephi,
know nothing concerning the matter save it were
given unto me by the power of God. And then shall
ye know that I am an honest man, and that I am
sent unto you from God.
37 And it came to pass that they went and did,
even according as Nephi had said unto them. And
behold, the words which he had said were true; for
according to the words he did deny; and also
according to the words he did confess.
38 And he was brought to prove that he himself
was the very murderer, insomuch that the five were
set at liberty, and also was Nephi.
39 And there were some of the Nephites who
believed on the words of Nephi; and there were
some also, who believed because of the testimony
of the five, for they had been converted while they
were in prison.
40 And now there were some among the people,
who said that Nephi was a prophet.
41 And there were others who said: Behold, he is
a god, for except he was a god he could not know
of all things. For behold, he has told us the thoughts
of our hearts, and also has told us things; and even
he has brought unto our knowledge the true murderer of our chief judge.

## CHAPTER 10

*The Lord gives Nephi power to cause famine, move mountains, and even destroy wicked people. Look for reasons why the Lord trusted Nephi with so much power.*

### *The Lord Gives Nephi Power to Do Many Miracles to Help the People Repent*

1 AND it came to pass that there arose a division
among the people, insomuch that they divided
hither and thither and went their ways, leaving Nephi
alone, as he was standing in the midst of them.
2 And it came to pass that Nephi went his way
towards his own house, pondering upon the things
which the Lord had shown unto him.
3 And it came to pass as he was thus pondering—
being much cast down because of the wickedness
of the people of the Nephites, their secret works of
darkness, and their murderings, and their plunderings, and all manner of iniquities—and it came to
pass as he was thus pondering in his heart, behold,
a voice came unto him saying:
4 Blessed art thou, Nephi, for those things which
thou hast done; for I have beheld how thou hast

---

9:36 Moses offered one test of a true prophet: "If the thing follow not, nor come to pass, that is the thing which the Lord hath not spoken" (Deuteronomy 18:22). Some people saw in Nephi's prophecy the possibility for just such a test: "Now we will know of a surety whether this man be a prophet" (Helaman 9:2). As all that Nephi declared was proven to be true, Nephi noted, "Then shall ye know that I am an honest man, and that I am sent unto you from God" (9:36).

9:39 The Lord will use different means to allow the gospel to be taught. President Hinckley said: "Doors now closed to the preaching of the gospel will be opened. The Almighty, if necessary, may have to shake the nations to humble them and cause them to listen to the servants of the living God. Whatever is needed will come to pass" (in Conference Report, October 1997, 92).

9:41 God is the only one who knows our thoughts (see D&C 6:16). When Nephi, filled with the Spirit, revealed the people's thoughts, some believed that he was a god.

10:1 ***hither and thither***—here and there
***midst***—middle

10:2 ***pondering***—thinking deeply

10:3 ***much cast down***—very sad
***plunderings***—stealing things by force

NEPHI CONFOUNDS THE WICKED JUDGES, BY ROBERT T. BARRETT

*Nephi confounds the wicked judges.*

with unwearyingness declared the word, which I
have given unto thee, unto this people. And thou
hast not feared them, and hast not sought thine
own life, but hast sought my will, and to keep my
commandments.
5 And now, because thou hast done this with
such unwearyingness, behold, I will bless thee
forever; and I will make thee mighty in word and
in deed, in faith and in works; yea, even that all
things shall be done unto thee according to thy
word, for thou shalt not ask that which is contrary
to my will.

---

10:4 ***sought thine own life***—done what you wanted to do

10:5 ***deed***—action
***contrary to my will***—against my wishes

Elder Marion G. Romney explained that "the time will come . . . when as a result of righteous living, we shall so enjoy the companionship of the spirit that he will dictate what we ask" (in Conference Report, October 1944, 56; see also D&C 50:29).

10:5 (4–5) "The Lord reminded Nephi of the blessings that would result from the unwearyingness [tireless and persistent way] with which he had labored and taught the people and with which he had kept the commandments of God. With renewed vigor and determination, Nephi turned from his home and returned to his labors to continue as he had commenced" (Rex D. Pinegar, in Conference Report, October 1974, 60).

6 Behold, thou art Nephi, and I am God. Behold,
I declare it unto thee in the presence of mine
angels, that ye shall have power over this people,
and shall smite the earth with famine, and with
pestilence, and destruction, according to the
wickedness of this people.
7 Behold, I give unto you power, that whatsoever
ye shall seal on earth shall be sealed in heaven; and
whatsoever ye shall loose on earth shall be loosed
in heaven; and thus shall ye have power among this
people.
8 And thus, if ye shall say unto this temple it shall
be rent in twain, it shall be done.
9 And if ye shall say unto this mountain, Be thou
cast down and become smooth, it shall be done.
10 And behold, if ye shall say that God shall smite
this people, it shall come to pass.
11 And now behold, I command you, that ye shall
go and declare unto this people, that thus saith the
Lord God, who is the Almighty: Except ye repent ye
shall be smitten, even unto destruction.

## Nephi Tells the People to Repent or They Will Be Destroyed

12 And behold, now it came to pass that when the
Lord had spoken these words unto Nephi, he did
stop and did not go unto his own house, but did
return unto the multitudes who were scattered
about upon the face of the land, and began to
declare unto them the word of the Lord which had
been spoken unto him, concerning their destruction
if they did not repent.
13 Now behold, notwithstanding that great miracle which Nephi had done in telling them concerning the death of the chief judge, they did harden
their hearts and did not hearken unto the words of
the Lord.
14 Therefore Nephi did declare unto them the
word of the Lord, saying: Except ye repent, thus
saith the Lord, ye shall be smitten even unto
destruction.
15 And it came to pass that when Nephi had
declared unto them the word, behold, they did still
harden their hearts and would not hearken unto his
words; therefore they did revile against him, and
did seek to lay their hands upon him that they
might cast him into prison.
16 But behold, the power of God was with him,
and they could not take him to cast him into prison,
for he was taken by the Spirit and conveyed away
out of the midst of them.
17 And it came to pass that thus he did go forth
in the Spirit, from multitude to multitude, declaring the word of God, even until he had declared
it unto them all, or sent it forth among all the
people.
18 And it came to pass that they would not
hearken unto his words; and there began to be contentions, insomuch that they were divided against
themselves and began to slay one another with the
sword.
19 And thus ended the seventy and first year of
the reign of the judges over the people of Nephi.

---

10:6 **smite**—strike or hit
**famine**—a time when there is not enough food
**pestilence**—disease

10:8 **rent in twain**—torn in two parts

10:10 (6–10) Nephi is given the sealing power. Elder Bruce R. McConkie explained: "Whenever the fulness of the gospel is on earth, the Lord has agents to whom he gives power to bind on earth and seal eternally in the heavens (Matt. 16:19; 18:18; Hela. 10:3–10; D. & C. 132:46–49.). . . . All things that are not sealed by this power have an end when men are dead" (*Mormon Doctrine,* 683).

10:12 When the Lord commanded Nephi to tell the people to repent, he immediately did as he was commanded. What do you learn from Nephi about obeying the Lord?

10:13 **harden their hearts**—not feel the Spirit or believe

10:15 **revile against**—criticize

10:16 **conveyed**—moved
**midst**—middle

The Spirit carried Nephi away from danger. The Spirit similarly carried Philip away to continue his missionary work (see Acts 8:39) and Nephi, the son of Lehi, to the top of an "exceedingly high mountain" to see a great vision (see 1 Nephi 11:1).

10:17 **thus**—in this way

10:18 **contentions**—arguments and fighting

## CHAPTER 11

*Nephi asks the Lord to humble the people with a famine instead of war. Notice what the people do when thousands begin to die.*

### The Lord Stops War but Sends a Famine

1 AND now it came to pass in the seventy and
second year of the reign of the judges that the contentions did increase, insomuch that there were
wars throughout all the land among all the people
of Nephi.
2 And it was this secret band of robbers who did
carry on this work of destruction and wickedness.
And this war did last all that year; and in the seventy and third year it did also last.
3 And it came to pass that in this year Nephi did
cry unto the Lord, saying:
4 O Lord, do not suffer that this people shall be
destroyed by the sword; but O Lord, rather let there
be a famine in the land, to stir them up in remembrance of the Lord their God, and perhaps they will
repent and turn unto thee.
5 And so it was done, according to the words of
Nephi. And there was a great famine upon the land,
among all the people of Nephi. And thus in the seventy and fourth year the famine did continue, and
the work of destruction did cease by the sword but
became sore by famine.
6 And this work of destruction did also continue
in the seventy and fifth year. For the earth was smitten that it was dry, and did not yield forth grain in
the season of grain; and the whole earth was smitten, even among the Lamanites as well as among
the Nephites, so that they were smitten that they did
perish by thousands in the more wicked parts of the
land.
7 And it came to pass that the people saw that
they were about to perish by famine, and they
began to remember the Lord their God; and they
began to remember the words of Nephi.
8 And the people began to plead with their chief
judges and their leaders, that they would say unto
Nephi: Behold, we know that thou art a man of
God, and therefore cry unto the Lord our God that
he turn away from us this famine, lest all the words
which thou hast spoken concerning our destruction
be fulfilled.

### Nephi Prays for the Famine to End

9 And it came to pass that the judges did say unto
Nephi, according to the words which had been
desired. And it came to pass that when Nephi saw
that the people had repented and did humble themselves in sackcloth, he cried again unto the Lord,
saying:
10 O Lord, behold this people repenteth; and they
have swept away the band of Gadianton from
amongst them insomuch that they have become
extinct, and they have concealed their secret plans
in the earth.
11 Now, O Lord, because of this their humility wilt
thou turn away thine anger, and let thine anger be
appeased in the destruction of those wicked men
whom thou hast already destroyed.
12 O Lord, wilt thou turn away thine anger, yea,
thy fierce anger, and cause that this famine may
cease in this land.
13 O Lord, wilt thou hearken unto me, and cause
that it may be done according to my words, and

---

11:1 ***reign***—rule
***contentions***—arguing and fighting

11:2 ***band***—gang

11:4 ***suffer***—allow
***stir them up in remembrance of***—cause them to remember

God sometimes uses famines to humble His people (see D&C 43:25). Why do you think famines get people to repent and turn to the Lord?

11:5 Elder A. Theodore Tuttle taught, "A prophet not only prophesies of things that will happen. A prophet, by the exercise of faith, causes things to happen" (in Conference Report, October 1975, 33).

11:6 ***smitten***—cursed

11:8 ***lest***—for fear that

11:9 Sackcloth was "a coarse, dark cloth made of hair of camels and goats and used anciently for making sacks and bags. . . . It was also used for making the rough garments [clothing] worn by mourners" (Bruce R. McConkie, *Mormon Doctrine,* 659). Wearing sackcloth was a symbol of sincere and humble repentance.

11:10 ***have become extinct***—no longer exist
***concealed***—hidden

send forth rain upon the face of the earth, that she may bring forth her fruit, and her grain in the season of grain.

14 O Lord, thou didst hearken unto my words when I said, Let there be a famine, that the pestilence of the sword might cease; and I know that thou wilt, even at this time, hearken unto my words, for thou saidst that: If this people repent I will spare them.

15 Yea, O Lord, and thou seest that they have repented, because of the famine and the pestilence and destruction which has come unto them.

16 And now, O Lord, wilt thou turn away thine anger, and try again if they will serve thee? And if so, O Lord, thou canst bless them according to thy words which thou hast said.

## The Faithful Are Blessed with Peace and Prosperity

17 And it came to pass that in the seventy and sixth year the Lord did turn away his anger from the people, and caused that rain should fall upon the earth, insomuch that it did bring forth her fruit in the season of her fruit. And it came to pass that it did bring forth her grain in the season of her grain.

18 And behold, the people did rejoice and glorify God, and the whole face of the land was filled with rejoicing; and they did no more seek to destroy Nephi, but they did esteem him as a great prophet, and a man of God, having great power and authority given unto him from God.

19 And behold, Lehi, his brother, was not a whit behind him as to things pertaining to righteousness.

20 And thus it did come to pass that the people of Nephi began to prosper again in the land, and began to build up their waste places, and began to multiply and spread, even until they did cover the whole face of the land, both on the northward and on the southward, from the sea west to the sea east.

21 And it came to pass that the seventy and sixth year did end in peace. And the seventy and seventh year began in peace; and the church did spread throughout the face of all the land; and the more part of the people, both the Nephites and the Lamanites, did belong to the church; and they did have exceedingly great peace in the land; and thus ended the seventy and seventh year.

22 And also they had peace in the seventy and eighth year, save it were a few contentions concerning the points of doctrine which had been laid down by the prophets.

23 And in the seventy and ninth year there began to be much strife. But it came to pass that Nephi and Lehi, and many of their brethren who knew concerning the true points of doctrine, having many revelations daily, therefore they did preach unto the people, insomuch that they did put an end to their strife in that same year.

## The Gadianton Robbers Return to Power

24 And it came to pass that in the eightieth year of the reign of the judges over the people of Nephi, there were a certain number of the dissenters from the people of Nephi, who had some years before gone over unto the Lamanites, and taken upon themselves the name of Lamanites, and also a certain number who were real descendants of the Lamanites, being stirred up to anger by them, or by those dissenters, therefore they commenced a war with their brethren.

25 And they did commit murder and plunder; and then they would retreat back into the mountains, and into the wilderness and secret places, hiding

---

11:14 ***pestilence of the sword***—wars

11:16 (14–16) The Lord honored Nephi's request for a famine. Now the prophet is praying for the famine to end. How do you think the Lord will answer this prayer? Why?

11:18 ***esteem***—respect and value

11:19 ***a whit***—even a little bit

Lehi is hardly mentioned, though he was as righteous as Nephi. President Howard W. Hunter counseled us: "If you feel that much of what you do does not make you very famous, take heart. Most of the best people who ever lived weren't very famous, either. Serve and grow, faithfully and quietly" ("No Less Serviceable," 67).

11:22 ***points of doctrine***—teachings
***laid down***—taught

11:23 ***much strife***—many contentions or arguments

11:24 ***dissenters***—people who disagreed and left
***commenced***—began

11:25 ***plunder***—robbery

themselves that they could not be discovered,
receiving daily an addition to their numbers, inasmuch as there were dissenters that went forth unto
them.
26 And thus in time, yea, even in the space of not
many years, they became an exceedingly great
band of robbers; and they did search out all the
secret plans of Gadianton; and thus they became
robbers of Gadianton.
27 Now behold, these robbers did make great
havoc, yea, even great destruction among the
people of Nephi, and also among the people of the
Lamanites.
28 And it came to pass that it was expedient that
there should be a stop put to this work of destruction; therefore they sent an army of strong men into
the wilderness and upon the mountains to search
out this band of robbers, and to destroy them.
29 But behold, it came to pass that in that same
year they were driven back even into their own
lands. And thus ended the eightieth year of the
reign of the judges over the people of Nephi.
30 And it came to pass in the commencement of
the eighty and first year they did go forth again
against this band of robbers, and did destroy many;
and they were also visited with much destruction.
31 And they were again obliged to return out of
the wilderness and out of the mountains unto their
own lands, because of the exceeding greatness of
the numbers of those robbers who infested the
mountains and the wilderness.
32 And it came to pass that thus ended this year.
And the robbers did still increase and wax strong,
insomuch that they did defy the whole armies of
the Nephites, and also of the Lamanites; and they
did cause great fear to come unto the people upon
all the face of the land.
33 Yea, for they did visit many parts of the land,
and did do great destruction unto them; yea, did kill
many, and did carry away others captive into the
wilderness, yea, and more especially their women
and their children.
34 Now this great evil, which came unto the
people because of their iniquity, did stir them up
again in remembrance of the Lord their God.
35 And thus ended the eighty and first year of the
reign of the judges.
36 And in the eighty and second year they began
again to forget the Lord their God. And in the
eighty and third year they began to wax strong in
iniquity. And in the eighty and fourth year they did
not mend their ways.
37 And it came to pass in the eighty and fifth year
they did wax stronger and stronger in their pride,
and in their wickedness; and thus they were ripening again for destruction.
38 And thus ended the eighty and fifth year.

## CHAPTER 12

*We can live again with our Heavenly Father if we live as we should in this life. Notice what Heavenly Father does to encourage His children to live the way they should.*

### God's Children Often Forget the Lord When Their Life Goes Well

1 AND thus we can behold how false, and also the
unsteadiness of the hearts of the children of men;
yea, we can see that the Lord in his great infinite
goodness doth bless and prosper those who put
their trust in him.

---

11:26 The Gadianton robbers are a secret group of wicked people who organize themselves "to murder, and to rob, and to gain power" (Helaman 2:8). Though they had been destroyed once before, Satan influences evil people to learn those wicked ways again.

11:27 ***make great havoc***—cause much damage

11:28 ***expedient***—necessary or essential

11:31 ***obliged***—forced
***infested***—filled or plagued

11:32 ***wax***—grow
***defy***—challenge

11:34 Trials sometimes humble people enough to repent. Alma taught that we are more blessed, however, when we choose to be humble by studying the Lord's words (see Alma 32:12–14). Why do you think it is better to become humble because you love the Lord, rather than having the Lord make you humble by giving you trials?

11:36 ***mend***—correct

12:1 ***also the unsteadiness of***—unsure and uncertain
***infinite***—endless and eternal
***doth bless and prosper***—brings success to

2 Yea, and we may see at the very time when he doth prosper his people, yea, in the increase of their fields, their flocks and their herds, and in gold, and in silver, and in all manner of precious things of every kind and art; sparing their lives, and delivering them out of the hands of their enemies; softening the hearts of their enemies that they should not declare wars against them; yea, and in fine, doing all things for the welfare and happiness of his people; yea, then is the time that they do harden their hearts, and do forget the Lord their God, and do trample under their feet the Holy One—yea, and this because of their ease, and their exceedingly great prosperity.

3 And thus we see that except the Lord doth chasten his people with many afflictions, yea, except he doth visit them with death and with terror, and with famine and with all manner of pestilence, they will not remember him.

4 O how foolish, and how vain, and how evil, and devilish, and how quick to do iniquity, and how slow to do good, are the children of men; yea, how quick to hearken unto the words of the evil one, and to set their hearts upon the vain things of the world!

5 Yea, how quick to be lifted up in pride; yea, how quick to boast, and do all manner of that which is iniquity; and how slow are they to remember the Lord their God, and to give ear unto his counsels, yea, how slow to walk in wisdom's paths!

6 Behold, they do not desire that the Lord their God, who hath created them, should rule and reign over them; notwithstanding his great goodness and his mercy towards them, they do set at naught his counsels, and they will not that he should be their guide.

## *The Earth Is Obedient to the Commands of God*

7 O how great is the nothingness of the children of men; yea, even they are less than the dust of the earth.

8 For behold, the dust of the earth moveth hither and thither, to the dividing asunder, at the command of our great and everlasting God.

---

12:2 ***welfare***—good
***the Holy One***—Jesus Christ
***ease***—easy way of life

12:3 ***chasten***—scold
***afflictions***—trials or sufferings
***famine***—a shortage of food
***pestilence***—terrible diseases

"Afflictions can soften us and sweeten us, and can be a chastening influence. (Alma 62:41.) We often think of chastening as something being done to punish us, such as by a mortal tutor who is angry and peevish with us. Divine chastening, however, is a form of learning as it is administered at the hands of a loving Father" (Neal A. Maxwell, *All These Things Shall Give Thee Experience,* 39).

Why do you think it is so much easier to remember the Lord when we suffer, than when everything is going well? What can you do to remember the Lord even when times are good?

12:4 ***vain***—proud
***do iniquity***—sin
***evil one***—devil

Alma taught his son Corianton that because of the Fall of Adam people "had become carnal, sensual, and devilish, by nature" (Alma 42:9–10). King Benjamin added that each who will change his fallen nature by listening to and obeying the Holy Spirit "becometh a saint through the atonement of Christ the Lord" (Mosiah 3:19).

12:5 ***boast***—brag
***give ear***—listen

12:6 ***mercy***—love and kindness
***do set at naught his counsels***—think His teachings are worthless

12:8 ***hither and thither***—here and there
***dividing asunder***—cutting in two

12:8 (7–8) Mormon "says that man is 'less than the dust of the earth' (Hel. 12:7)—not at all in the sense that man is without value to God, but rather because 'the dust of the earth, moveth hither and thither, to the dividing asunder, at the command of our great and everlasting God.' (Hel. 12:8.) Hills, mountains, seas, earth—all obey his voice. But man does not obey his voice; in willfulness and pride he tramples under foot the words of the Holy One" (Jeffrey R. Holland, "Mormon: The Man and the Book, Part 2," 58).

9 Yea, behold at his voice do the hills and the
mountains tremble and quake.
10 And by the power of his voice they are broken
up, and become smooth, yea, even like unto a valley.
11 Yea, by the power of his voice doth the whole
earth shake;
12 Yea, by the power of his voice, do the foundations rock, even to the very center.
13 Yea, and if he say unto the earth—Move—it is
moved.
14 Yea, if he say unto the earth—Thou shalt go
back, that it lengthen out the day for many hours—
it is done;
15 And thus, according to his word the earth
goeth back, and it appeareth unto man that the sun
standeth still; yea, and behold, this is so; for surely
it is the earth that moveth and not the sun.
16 And behold, also, if he say unto the waters of
the great deep—Be thou dried up—it is done.
17 Behold, if he say unto this mountain—Be thou
raised up, and come over and fall upon that city,
that it be buried up—behold it is done.
18 And behold, if a man hide up a treasure in the
earth, and the Lord shall say—Let it be accursed,
because of the iniquity of him who hath hid it up—
behold, it shall be accursed.
19 And if the Lord shall say—Be thou accursed,
that no man shall find thee from this time henceforth and forever—behold, no man getteth it henceforth and forever.

## Repentance Is the Only Way to Happiness

20 And behold, if the Lord shall say unto a man—
Because of thine iniquities, thou shalt be accursed
forever—it shall be done.
21 And if the Lord shall say—Because of thine
iniquities thou shalt be cut off from my presence—
he will cause that it shall be so.
22 And wo unto him to whom he shall say this,
for it shall be unto him that will do iniquity, and
he cannot be saved; therefore, for this cause, that
men might be saved, hath repentance been
declared.
23 Therefore, blessed are they who will repent
and hearken unto the voice of the Lord their God;
for these are they that shall be saved.
24 And may God grant, in his great fulness, that
men might be brought unto repentance and good
works, that they might be restored unto grace for
grace, according to their works.
25 And I would that all men might be saved. But
we read that in the great and last day there are
some who shall be cast out, yea, who shall be cast
off from the presence of the Lord;
26 Yea, who shall be consigned to a state of endless misery, fulfilling the words which say: They
that have done good shall have everlasting life; and
they that have done evil shall have everlasting
damnation. And thus it is. Amen.

---

12:10 (4–10) "The proud cannot accept the authority of God giving direction to their lives. (See Helaman 12:6.) They pit their perceptions of truth against God's great knowledge, their abilities versus God's priesthood power, their accomplishments against His mighty works. . . . The proud wish God would agree with them. They aren't interested in changing their opinions to agree with God's." (Ezra Taft Benson, in Conference Report, April 1989, 4).

12:15 Many years ago people believed that the sun moved around the earth. The Lord has shown prophets the truth about His creations from the beginning (see Abraham 1:31; 3:1–17).

12:16 ***great deep***—ocean

12:18 (16–18) There are examples of these events in the scriptures. Moses divided the Red Sea (see Exodus 14:21–22). At Christ's death some cities were buried by mountains (see 3 Nephi 9:5–6). Enoch caused mountains to move, rivers to turn out of their place, and islands to appear in the ocean (see Moses 7:13–14). In Helaman 13:33–36 the people have become so wicked that the Lord commands the earth to swallow up their riches.

12:19 ***henceforth and forever***—from now until forever

12:22 ***wo***—grief, sorrow, and misery

12:24 ***grant***—allow
***restored unto grace for grace***—returned to righteousness through the Atonement of the Savior (see also Glossary: Grace)

12:26 ***consigned***—sent
***everlasting damnation***—an end to eternal progress

*The prophecy of Samuel, the Lamanite, to the Nephites. Comprising chapters 13 to 15 inclusive.**

## CHAPTER 13

*Helaman 13–15 records the prophecies of Samuel the Lamanite to the Nephites in Zarahemla. In this chapter, he tells the Nephites of their sins and what will happen if they do not repent. What does Samuel say that could help you be safe in the hard times that are prophesied for our future?*

### Samuel the Lamanite Declares the Word of God to the Nephites

1 AND now it came to pass in the eighty and sixth
year, the Nephites did still remain in wickedness,
yea, in great wickedness, while the Lamanites did
observe strictly to keep the commandments of God,
according to the law of Moses.
2 And it came to pass that in this year there was
one Samuel, a Lamanite, came into the land of
Zarahemla, and began to preach unto the people.
And it came to pass that he did preach, many days,
repentance unto the people, and they did cast him
out, and he was about to return to his own land.
3 But behold, the voice of the Lord came unto
him, that he should return again, and prophesy
unto the people whatsoever things should come
into his heart.
4 And it came to pass that they would not suffer
that he should enter into the city; therefore he went
and got upon the wall thereof, and stretched forth
his hand and cried with a loud voice, and prophesied unto the people whatsoever things the Lord
put into his heart.

### Samuel Predicts the Destruction of the Nephites in Four Hundred Years If They Do Not Repent

5 And he said unto them: Behold, I, Samuel, a
Lamanite, do speak the words of the Lord which he
doth put into my heart; and behold he hath put it
into my heart to say unto this people that the sword
of justice hangeth over this people; and four hundred years pass not away save the sword of justice
falleth upon this people.
6 Yea, heavy destruction awaiteth this people, and
it surely cometh unto this people, and nothing can
save this people save it be repentance and faith on
the Lord Jesus Christ, who surely shall come into
the world, and shall suffer many things and shall be
slain for his people.
7 And behold, an angel of the Lord hath declared
it unto me, and he did bring glad tidings to my soul.
And behold, I was sent unto you to declare it unto
you also, that ye might have glad tidings; but
behold ye would not receive me.
8 Therefore, thus saith the Lord: Because of the
hardness of the hearts of the people of the
Nephites, except they repent I will take away my
word from them, and I will withdraw my Spirit
from them, and I will suffer them no longer, and
I will turn the hearts of their brethren against
them.
9 And four hundred years shall not pass away
before I will cause that they shall be smitten; yea, I
will visit them with the sword and with famine and
with pestilence.
10 Yea, I will visit them in my fierce anger, and
there shall be those of the fourth generation who
shall live, of your enemies, to behold your utter

---

* The first sentence of this introduction was translated from the Book of Mormon plates.

13:1 ***observe strictly***—make every effort

The "eighty and sixth year" of the reign of the judges is about 6 B.C.

The law of Moses includes the laws and ordinances that the children of Israel were commanded to follow from the days of Moses until the time of Jesus Christ (see LDS Bible Dictionary, s.v. "Law of Moses," 722–23).

13:4 ***suffer that he should***—allow him to

13:5 Samuel's prophecy that "the sword of justice falleth upon this people" foretells that the Nephites would be destroyed by wars, famines, and bloodshed. Samuel's message is the same one that Alma foretold to his son Helaman (see Alma 45:10–11).

13:8 (7–8) Samuel shares the glad message of the gospel with the people, but they have hard hearts and will not listen. How should you treat the messages of the Lord's prophets?

13:9 ***smitten***—tormented and afflicted
***famine and with pestilence***—hunger and disease

13:10 (9–10) Moroni, the last prophet to write in the Book of Mormon, saw the fulfillment of Samuel's prophecy of the Nephites' destruction (see Mormon 8:1–7).

destruction; and this shall surely come except ye repent, saith the Lord; and those of the fourth generation shall visit your destruction.

### *It Is Only Because of the Righteous Among Them That Zarahemla Has Not Been Destroyed Already*

11 But if ye will repent and return unto the Lord your God I will turn away mine anger, saith the Lord; yea, thus saith the Lord, blessed are they who will repent and turn unto me, but wo unto him that repenteth not.

12 Yea, wo unto this great city of Zarahemla; for behold, it is because of those who are righteous that it is saved; yea, wo unto this great city, for I perceive, saith the Lord, that there are many, yea, even the more part of this great city, that will harden their hearts against me, saith the Lord.

13 But blessed are they who will repent, for them will I spare. But behold, if it were not for the righteous who are in this great city, behold, I would cause that fire should come down out of heaven and destroy it.

14 But behold, it is for the righteous' sake that it is spared. But behold, the time cometh, saith the Lord, that when ye shall cast out the righteous from among you, then shall ye be ripe for destruction; yea, wo be unto this great city, because of the wickedness and abominations which are in her.

### *The Lord Will Curse the Riches of the Wicked*

15 Yea, and wo be unto the city of Gideon, for the wickedness and abominations which are in her.

16 Yea, and wo be unto all the cities which are in the land round about, which are possessed by the Nephites, because of the wickedness and abominations which are in them.

17 And behold, a curse shall come upon the land, saith the Lord of Hosts, because of the peoples' sake who are upon the land, yea, because of their wickedness and their abominations.

18 And it shall come to pass, saith the Lord of Hosts, yea, our great and true God, that whoso shall hide up treasures in the earth shall find them again no more, because of the great curse of the land, save he be a righteous man and shall hide it up unto the Lord.

19 For I will, saith the Lord, that they shall hide up their treasures unto me; and cursed be they who hide not up their treasures unto me; for none hideth up their treasures unto me save it be the righteous; and he that hideth not up his treasures unto me, cursed is he, and also the treasure, and none shall redeem it because of the curse of the land.

20 And the day shall come that they shall hide up their treasures, because they have set their hearts upon riches; and because they have set their hearts upon their riches, and will hide up their treasures when they shall flee before their enemies; because they will not hide them up unto me, cursed be they and also their treasures; and in that day shall they be smitten, saith the Lord.

21 Behold ye, the people of this great city, and hearken unto my words; yea, hearken unto the words which the Lord saith; for behold, he saith that ye are cursed because of your riches, and also are your riches cursed because ye have set your hearts upon them, and have not hearkened unto the words of him who gave them unto you.

22 Ye do not remember the Lord your God in the things with which he hath blessed you, but ye do always remember your riches, not to thank the Lord your God for them; yea, your hearts are not drawn out unto the Lord, but they do swell with great pride, unto boasting, and unto great swelling, envyings, strifes, malice, persecutions, and murders, and all manner of iniquities.

---

13:11 ***wo***—sorrow and suffering will come

13:14 ***abominations***—great corruption

13:14 (12–14) In these verses Samuel explains that the Lord will not destroy the wicked while the righteous are still living among them. The wicked city of Ammonihah, for example, was not destroyed until the righteous were killed or cast out of the city (see Alma 15:1, 15–16; 16:2–3).

13:17 "Christ is the *Lord of Hosts* (1 Chron. 17:24; Ps. 24:10; Isa. 6:5; Zech. 14:16–17; Mal. 1:14), meaning that he is a man of war (Ex. 15:3), a God of battles (Ps. 24:8), a leader of his saints in days of conflict and carnage" (Bruce R. McConkie, *Mormon Doctrine,* 451).

13:22 ***envyings***—jealousy
***strifes***—fighting
***malice***—hatred
***persecutions***—bad treatment of others
***iniquities***—wickedness

23 For this cause hath the Lord God caused that a curse should come upon the land, and also upon your riches, and this because of your iniquities.

## *The Nephites Cast Out True Prophets and Support False Prophets Instead*

24 Yea, wo unto this people, because of this time which has arrived, that ye do cast out the prophets, and do mock them, and cast stones at them, and do slay them, and do all manner of iniquity unto them, even as they did of old time.

25 And now when ye talk, ye say: If our days had been in the days of our fathers of old, we would not have slain the prophets; we would not have stoned them, and cast them out.

26 Behold ye are worse than they; for as the Lord liveth, if a prophet come among you and declareth unto you the word of the Lord, which testifieth of your sins and iniquities, ye are angry with him, and cast him out and seek all manner of ways to destroy him; yea, you will say that he is a false prophet, and that he is a sinner, and of the devil, because he testifieth that your deeds are evil.

27 But behold, if a man shall come among you and shall say: Do this, and there is no iniquity; do that and ye shall not suffer; yea, he will say: Walk after the pride of your own hearts; yea, walk after the pride of your eyes, and do whatsoever your heart desireth—and if a man shall come among you and say this, ye will receive him, and say that he is a prophet.

28 Yea, ye will lift him up, and ye will give unto him of your substance; ye will give unto him of your gold, and of your silver, and ye will clothe him with costly apparel; and because he speaketh flattering words unto you, and he saith that all is well, then ye will not find fault with him.

29 O ye wicked and ye perverse generation; ye hardened and ye stiffnecked people, how long will ye suppose that the Lord will suffer you? Yea, how long will ye suffer yourselves to be led by foolish and blind guides? Yea, how long will ye choose darkness rather than light?

30 Yea, behold, the anger of the Lord is already kindled against you; behold, he hath cursed the land because of your iniquity.

## *It Is Impossible to Find Happiness by Being Wicked*

31 And behold, the time cometh that he curseth your riches, that they become slippery, that ye cannot hold them; and in the days of your poverty ye cannot retain them.

32 And in the days of your poverty ye shall cry unto the Lord; and in vain shall ye cry, for your desolation is already come upon you, and your destruction is made sure; and then shall ye weep and howl in that day, saith the Lord of Hosts. And then shall ye lament, and say:

33 O that I had repented, and had not killed the prophets, and stoned them, and cast them out. Yea, in that day ye shall say: O that we had remembered the Lord our God in the day that he gave us our

---

13:23 (17–23) The Lord promises to place a "curse" on the riches of the land for the "peoples' sake" (verse 17), meaning for their benefit or blessing. How could the loss of riches be a blessing? In what way is it a blessing when the Lord punishes us for our sins?

13:23 (22–23) Samuel pointed out that one way to tell if we love our treasures more than God is by observing how much gratitude we give to Him for all that He has blessed us with. Elder Milton R. Hunter taught, "Perhaps our lack of gratitude toward God is one of the most common sins among us" (*God's Greatest Gift,* 3).

13:27 President N. Eldon Tanner noted that "the last days are here. . . . Men are refusing sound doctrine . . . and are listening to those who preach to their own liking. As a result, we are suffering many tribulations [trials or sufferings] throughout the world" (in Conference Report, October 1968, 46).

13:28 ***substance***—riches
***costly apparel***—fancy clothes

13:29 ***perverse***—corrupt or evil

The Lord spoke to Joseph Smith about similar stiffnecked, or stubborn, people who were "walking in darkness at noon-day" (D&C 95:5–6). Like the Nephites of Samuel's day, they chose to live in darkness or sin, even though they had the brilliant light of the gospel.

13:30 ***kindled***—burning

13:31 ***poverty***—need or want

13:32 ***lament***—feel great sadness

13:33 This prophecy was fulfilled in 3 Nephi 8:24–25.

riches, and then they would not have become slippery that we should lose them; for behold, our riches are gone from us.
34 Behold, we lay a tool here and on the morrow it is gone; and behold, our swords are taken from us in the day we have sought them for battle.
35 Yea, we have hid up our treasures and they have slipped away from us, because of the curse of the land.
36 O that we had repented in the day that the word of the Lord came unto us; for behold the land is cursed, and all things are become slippery, and we cannot hold them.
37 Behold, we are surrounded by demons, yea, we are encircled about by the angels of him who hath sought to destroy our souls. Behold, our iniquities are great. O Lord, canst thou not turn away thine anger from us? And this shall be your language in those days.
38 But behold, your days of probation are past; ye have procrastinated the day of your salvation until it is everlastingly too late, and your destruction is made sure; yea, for ye have sought all the days of your lives for that which ye could not obtain; and ye have sought for happiness in doing iniquity, which thing is contrary to the nature of that righteousness which is in our great and Eternal Head.
39 O ye people of the land, that ye would hear my words! And I pray that the anger of the Lord be turned away from you, and that ye would repent and be saved.

## CHAPTER 14

*Samuel the Lamanite prophesies of Christ's birth and death. He teaches that the blessings of forgiveness and peace apply to those who have faith in Christ. As you read this chapter watch for these principles and ponder what you can learn from them.*

### Samuel Prophesies of Christ's Birth

1 AND now it came to pass that Samuel, the Lamanite, did prophesy a great many more things which cannot be written.
2 And behold, he said unto them: Behold, I give unto you a sign; for five years more cometh, and behold, then cometh the Son of God to redeem all those who shall believe on his name.
3 And behold, this will I give unto you for a sign at the time of his coming; for behold, there shall be great lights in heaven, insomuch that in the night before he cometh there shall be no darkness, insomuch that it shall appear unto man as if it was day.
4 Therefore, there shall be one day and a night and a day, as if it were one day and there were no night; and this shall be unto you for a sign; for ye shall know of the rising of the sun and also of its setting; therefore they shall know of a surety that there shall be two days and a night; nevertheless the night shall not be darkened; and it shall be the night before he is born.
5 And behold, there shall a new star arise, such an one as ye never have beheld; and this also shall be a sign unto you.
6 And behold this is not all, there shall be many signs and wonders in heaven.
7 And it shall come to pass that ye shall all be amazed, and wonder, insomuch that ye shall fall to the earth.
8 And it shall come to pass that whosoever shall believe on the Son of God, the same shall have everlasting life.

### Samuel Cries Repentance to the Nephites

9 And behold, thus hath the Lord commanded me, by his angel, that I should come and tell this thing unto you; yea, he hath commanded that I should

---

13:38 ***days of probation are***—time of testing is ***procrastinated***—put off or delayed

Why do you think it is impossible to find happiness in sin? How does knowing that help you make better choices in your own life?

14:1 ***prophesy***—tell by the inspiration of the Holy Ghost

14:3 ***insomuch that***—so

14:4 (2–4) Samuel gives a sign that when Christ is born there will be no darkness. Signs are given to strengthen our belief but only after we exercise our faith (see D&C 63:7–10; Helaman 14:12, 28).

14:5 (4–5) Samuel's prophesies were fulfilled exactly as he said (see 3 Nephi 1:15, 21).

14:9 Through modern revelation we learn that God sometimes sends angels to declare the gospel to individuals and call them to repentance (see Moses 5:58; D&C 29:42).

prophesy these things unto you; yea, he hath said
unto me: Cry unto this people, repent and prepare
the way of the Lord.
10 And now, because I am a Lamanite, and have
spoken unto you the words which the Lord hath
commanded me, and because it was hard against
you, ye are angry with me and do seek to destroy
me, and have cast me out from among you.
11 And ye shall hear my words, for, for this intent
have I come up upon the walls of this city, that ye
might hear and know of the judgments of God
which do await you because of your iniquities, and
also that ye might know the conditions of repentance;
12 And also that ye might know of the coming of
Jesus Christ, the Son of God, the Father of heaven
and of earth, the Creator of all things from the
beginning; and that ye might know of the signs of
his coming, to the intent that ye might believe on
his name.
13 And if ye believe on his name ye will repent of
all your sins, that thereby ye may have a remission
of them through his merits.
14 And behold, again, another sign I give unto
you, yea, a sign of his death.
15 For behold, he surely must die that salvation
may come; yea, it behooveth him and becometh
expedient that he dieth, to bring to pass the resurrection of the dead, that thereby men may be
brought into the presence of the Lord.
16 Yea, behold, this death bringeth to pass the resurrection, and redeemeth all mankind from the first
death—that spiritual death; for all mankind, by the
fall of Adam being cut off from the presence of the
Lord, are considered as dead, both as to things temporal and to things spiritual.
17 But behold, the resurrection of Christ
redeemeth mankind, yea, even all mankind, and
bringeth them back into the presence of the Lord.
18 Yea, and it bringeth to pass the condition of
repentance, that whosoever repenteth the same is
not hewn down and cast into the fire; but whosoever repenteth not is hewn down and cast into the
fire; and there cometh upon them again a spiritual
death, yea, a second death, for they are cut off
again as to things pertaining to righteousness.
19 Therefore repent ye, repent ye, lest by knowing these things and not doing them ye shall suffer
yourselves to come under condemnation, and ye
are brought down unto this second death.

## Samuel Gives the Signs of Christ's Death

20 But behold, as I said unto you concerning
another sign, a sign of his death, behold, in that day
that he shall suffer death the sun shall be darkened
and refuse to give his light unto you; and also the
moon and the stars; and there shall be no light
upon the face of this land, even from the time that
he shall suffer death, for the space of three days, to
the time that he shall rise again from the dead.
21 Yea, at the time that he shall yield up the ghost
there shall be thunderings and lightnings for the
space of many hours, and the earth shall shake and

---

14:11 ***iniquities***—sins and wickedness
***conditions***—steps

14:12 ***to the intent***—for the purpose

John also taught that Jesus created all things (see John 1:1–3).

14:15 ***behooveth***—was required of
***expedient***—necessary

14:16 ***temporal***—physical

Spiritual death is to be cut off from the presence of God (see Alma 42:9). The "first death" spoken of by Samuel is a spiritual death. The "temporal" death is the death of our physical body. Both of these deaths come because of the Fall of Adam and both are overcome through the Atonement of Jesus Christ (see 2 Nephi 2:8–10; see also Glossary: Fall of Adam).

14:17 (15–17) Through Christ's Atonement we will all be resurrected and brought back into the presence of the Lord. How can you show your appreciation for the gift of the resurrection?

14:18 ***hewn***—cut
***pertaining to***—having to do with

The "second death" is also a spiritual death and refers to those who refuse to repent of their own sins in this life and once again are cut off from the presence of God. Alma said, "An awful death cometh upon the wicked; for they die as to things pertaining to things of righteousness; for they are unclean, and no unclean thing can inherit the kingdom of God" (Alma 40:26).

14:19 ***lest***—for fear that
***come under condemnation***—be judged guilty of God

14:21 ***yield up the ghost***—die

tremble; and the rocks which are upon the face of this earth, which are both above the earth and beneath, which ye know at this time are solid, or the more part of it is one solid mass, shall be broken up;
22 Yea, they shall be rent in twain, and shall ever
after be found in seams and in cracks, and in broken fragments upon the face of the whole earth,
yea, both above the earth and beneath.
23 And behold, there shall be great tempests, and
there shall be many mountains laid low, like unto a valley, and there shall be many places which are now called valleys which shall become mountains, whose height is great.
24 And many highways shall be broken up, and
many cities shall become desolate.
25 And many graves shall be opened, and shall
yield up many of their dead; and many saints shall appear unto many.
26 And behold, thus hath the angel spoken unto
me; for he said unto me that there should be thunderings and lightnings for the space of many hours.
27 And he said unto me that while the thunder
and the lightning lasted, and the tempest, that these things should be, and that darkness should cover the face of the whole earth for the space of three days.
28 And the angel said unto me that many shall see
greater things than these, to the intent that they might believe that these signs and these wonders should come to pass upon all the face of this land, to the intent that there should be no cause for unbelief among the children of men—
29 And this to the intent that whosoever will
believe might be saved, and that whosoever will not believe, a righteous judgment might come upon them; and also if they are condemned they bring upon themselves their own condemnation.
30 And now remember, remember, my brethren,
that whosoever perisheth, perisheth unto himself; and whosoever doeth iniquity, doeth it unto himself; for behold, ye are free; ye are permitted to act for yourselves; for behold, God hath given unto you a knowledge and he hath made you free.
31 He hath given unto you that ye might know
good from evil, and he hath given unto you that ye might choose life or death; and ye can do good and be restored unto that which is good, or have that which is good restored unto you; or ye can do evil, and have that which is evil restored unto you.

## CHAPTER 15

*Samuel the Lamanite continues his prophecy by explaining why the Nephites suffer trials and the Lamanites receive blessings. Notice how the Lord blesses and corrects His children.*

### THE LORD SCOLDS THE NEPHITES

1 AND now, my beloved brethren, behold, I
declare unto you that except ye shall repent your houses shall be left unto you desolate.
2 Yea, except ye repent, your women shall have
great cause to mourn in the day that they shall give suck; for ye shall attempt to flee and there shall be no place for refuge; yea, and wo unto them which are with child, for they shall be heavy and cannot flee; therefore, they shall be trodden down and shall be left to perish.
3 Yea, wo unto this people who are called the
people of Nephi except they shall repent, when they shall see all these signs and wonders which shall be showed unto them; for behold, they have

---

14:22 ***rent in twain***—torn in pieces
***fragments***—pieces

14:23 ***tempests***—storms
***laid low***—brought down

14:24 ***desolate***—empty and wasted

14:25 Many righteous people in the New World as well as in Jerusalem were resurrected with Christ (see Matthew 27:51–53; 3 Nephi 23:7–13).

14:31 ***restored***—brought back

14:31 (29–31) A righteous judgment will come upon all of us. We will receive happiness if we choose to keep the commandments (see Alma 41:3–4, 13–15).

15:1 ***desolate***—empty

15:2 ***suck***—mother's milk
***refuge***—protection
***with child***—pregnant
***trodden down***—stomped underfoot

15:3 The word *chasten* is defined as "to purify from errors or faults" (Noah Webster, *An American Dictionary of the English Language*, 1828, s.v. "Chasten").

been a chosen people of the Lord; yea, the people of Nephi hath he loved, and also hath he chastened them; yea, in the days of their iniquities hath he chastened them because he loveth them.
4 But behold my brethren, the Lamanites hath he hated because their deeds have been evil continually, and this because of the iniquity of the tradition of their fathers. But behold, salvation hath come unto them through the preaching of the Nephites; and for this intent hath the Lord prolonged their days.

## The Converted Lamanites Are Faithful

5 And I would that ye should behold that the more part of them are in the path of their duty, and they do walk circumspectly before God, and they do observe to keep his commandments and his statutes and his judgments according to the law of Moses.
6 Yea, I say unto you, that the more part of them are doing this, and they are striving with unwearied diligence that they may bring the remainder of their brethren to the knowledge of the truth; therefore there are many who do add to their numbers daily.
7 And behold, ye do know of yourselves, for ye have witnessed it, that as many of them as are brought to the knowledge of the truth, and to know of the wicked and abominable traditions of their fathers, and are led to believe the holy scriptures, yea, the prophecies of the holy prophets, which are written, which leadeth them to faith on the Lord, and unto repentance, which faith and repentance bringeth a change of heart unto them—
8 Therefore, as many as have come to this, ye know of yourselves are firm and steadfast in the faith, and in the thing wherewith they have been made free.
9 And ye know also that they have buried their weapons of war, and they fear to take them up lest by any means they should sin; yea, ye can see that they fear to sin—for behold they will suffer themselves that they be trodden down and slain by their enemies, and will not lift their swords against them, and this because of their faith in Christ.
10 And now, because of their steadfastness when they do believe in that thing which they do believe, for because of their firmness when they are once enlightened, behold, the Lord shall bless them and prolong their days, notwithstanding their iniquity—

## The Lord Will Bless the Lamanites in the Last Days

11 Yea, even if they should dwindle in unbelief the Lord shall prolong their days, until the time shall come which hath been spoken of by our fathers, and also by the prophet Zenos, and many other prophets, concerning the restoration of our brethren, the Lamanites, again to the knowledge of the truth—
12 Yea, I say unto you, that in the latter times the promises of the Lord have been extended to our brethren, the Lamanites; and notwithstanding the many afflictions which they shall have, and notwithstanding they shall be driven to and fro upon the face of the earth, and be hunted, and shall be smitten and scattered abroad, having no place for refuge, the Lord shall be merciful unto them.

---

15:3 Elder Gene R. Cook said, "It's interesting that the Lord says those whom he loves he also chastens. Since he loves all his children, we can assume we will receive some of that chastening. The true purpose of the chastening is that our sins might be forgiven" (*Raising Up a Family to the Lord,* 178; see also D&C 95:1–2).

15:4 ***prolonged***—made longer

15:5 ***circumspectly***—carefully or righteously
***statutes***—laws
***judgments***—declarations and decisions

15:6 One sign that these Lamanites were truly converted was that they freely shared the gospel with those who were not converted (see D&C 88:81). How can you follow their example and share the gospel with your friends and neighbors?

15:7 President Ezra Taft Benson explained the value of the scriptures when he said: "Children, support your parents in their efforts to have daily family scripture study. Pray for them as they pray for you. The adversary does not want scripture study to take place in our homes, and so he will create problems if he can. But we must persist" (in Conference Report, April 1986, 99).

15:9 The Lamanites converted by the sons of Mosiah buried their weapons of war (see Alma 24:17) because "they [feared] to sin." Why should we "fear to sin"?

15:10 ***steadfastness***—unwavering faith

15:11 ***dwindle***—become weak and fall away

13 And this is according to the prophecy, that they shall again be brought to the true knowledge, which is the knowledge of their Redeemer, and their great and true shepherd, and be numbered among his sheep.

14 Therefore I say unto you, it shall be better for them than for you except ye repent.

15 For behold, had the mighty works been shown unto them which have been shown unto you, yea, unto them who have dwindled in unbelief because of the traditions of their fathers, ye can see of yourselves that they never would again have dwindled in unbelief.

16 Therefore, saith the Lord: I will not utterly destroy them, but I will cause that in the day of my wisdom they shall return again unto me, saith the Lord.

17 And now behold, saith the Lord, concerning the people of the Nephites: If they will not repent, and observe to do my will, I will utterly destroy them, saith the Lord, because of their unbelief notwithstanding the many mighty works which I have done among them; and as surely as the Lord liveth shall these things be, saith the Lord.

## CHAPTER 16

*Some people believe the teachings of Samuel the Lamanite and Nephi, but many do not believe even though they see marvelous signs and angels. Look for the reasons people give for not believing that Christ would be born.*

### *Many People Believe the Teachings of Samuel and Nephi and Are Baptized*

1 AND now, it came to pass that there were many who heard the words of Samuel, the Lamanite, which he spake upon the walls of the city. And as many as believed on his word went forth and sought for Nephi; and when they had come forth and found him they confessed unto him their sins and denied not, desiring that they might be baptized unto the Lord.

2 But as many as there were who did not believe in the words of Samuel were angry with him; and they cast stones at him upon the wall, and also many shot arrows at him as he stood upon the wall; but the Spirit of the Lord was with him, insomuch that they could not hit him with their stones neither with their arrows.

3 Now when they saw that they could not hit him, there were many more who did believe on his words, insomuch that they went away unto Nephi to be baptized.

4 For behold, Nephi was baptizing, and prophesying, and preaching, crying repentance unto the people, showing signs and wonders, working miracles among the people, that they might know that the Christ must shortly come—

5 Telling them of things which must shortly come, that they might know and remember at the time of their coming that they had been made known unto them beforehand, to the intent that they might believe; therefore as many as believed on the words of Samuel went forth unto him to be baptized, for they came repenting and confessing their sins.

6 But the more part of them did not believe in the words of Samuel; therefore when they saw that they could not hit him with their stones and their arrows, they cried unto their captains, saying: Take this fellow and bind him, for behold he hath a devil; and because of the power of the devil which is in him we cannot hit him with our stones and our arrows; therefore take him and bind him, and away with him.

7 And as they went forth to lay their hands on him, behold, he did cast himself down from the wall, and did flee out of their lands, yea, even unto his own country, and began to preach and to prophesy among his own people.

---

15:16 ***utterly***—completely

Elder Melvin J. Ballard prophesied: "The work of the Lord [in South America] will grow slowly for a time here just as an oak grows slowly from an acorn. It will not shoot up in a day as does the sunflower that grows quickly and then dies. But thousands will join the Church here. It will be divided into more than one mission and will be one of the strongest in the Church. The work here is the smallest that it will ever be. The day will come when the Lamanites in this land will be given a chance. The South American Mission will be a power in the Church" (as recorded in Vernon Sharp's diary, in *Melvin J. Ballard,* 84).

16:4 ***prophesying***—telling about the future

16:5 ***to the intent***—for the purpose

16:7 ***cast himself***—jump

SAMUEL THE LAMANITE, BY JERRY THOMPSON

The Spirit of the Lord was with Samuel the Lamanite.

8 And behold, he was never heard of more among
the Nephites; and thus were the affairs of the
people.
9 And thus ended the eighty and sixth year of the
reign of the judges over the people of Nephi.
10 And thus ended also the eighty and seventh
year of the reign of the judges, the more part of the
people remaining in their pride and wickedness,
and the lesser part walking more circumspectly
before God.
11 And these were the conditions also, in the
eighty and eighth year of the reign of the
judges.
12 And there was but little alteration in the affairs
of the people, save it were the people began to be
more hardened in iniquity, and do more and more
of that which was contrary to the commandments
of God, in the eighty and ninth year of the reign of
the judges.

## Signs and Wonders Are Seen, but Many People Still Do Not Believe

13 But it came to pass in the ninetieth year of the
reign of the judges, there were great signs given
unto the people, and wonders; and the words of
the prophets began to be fulfilled.
14 And angels did appear unto men, wise men,
and did declare unto them glad tidings of great joy;
thus in this year the scriptures began to be fulfilled.
15 Nevertheless, the people began to harden their
hearts, all save it were the most believing part of
them, both of the Nephites and also of the
Lamanites, and began to depend upon their own
strength and upon their own wisdom, saying:
16 Some things they may have guessed right,
among so many; but behold, we know that all these
great and marvelous works cannot come to pass, of
which has been spoken.

---

16:8 ***affairs***—actions or doings

16:10 ***circumspectly***—righteously and carefully

16:12 ***alteration***—change
***hardened in iniquity***—determined to sin
***contrary to***—against

16:13 ***be fulfilled***—happen as the prophets said

Some of the "great signs" the Nephites saw were prophesied by Samuel the Lamanite. He said there would be great lights in the heaven, that a new star would be seen, and that there would be many "signs and wonders in heaven" (see Helaman 14:2–6).

16:14 Elder David O. McKay taught: "The gospel of Jesus Christ is that good tidings. The term *gospel* means, literally, 'good news,' and such is the news that emanates [comes] from above. There have been but few men in the world's history who have been so in tune with the heavens that they could receive directly from God the Father that good news" (*Gospel Ideals,* 3).

16:15 ***to harden their hearts***—not to believe

17 And they began to reason and to contend
among themselves, saying:
18 That it is not reasonable that such a being as a
Christ shall come; if so, and he be the Son of God,
the Father of heaven and of earth, as it has been
spoken, why will he not show himself unto us as
well as unto them who shall be at Jerusalem?
19 Yea, why will he not show himself in this land
as well as in the land of Jerusalem?
20 But behold, we know that this is a wicked tradition, which has been handed down unto us by our
fathers, to cause us that we should believe in some
great and marvelous thing which should come to
pass, but not among us, but in a land which is far
distant, a land which we know not; therefore they
can keep us in ignorance, for we cannot witness
with our own eyes that they are true.
21 And they will, by the cunning and the myste-
rious arts of the evil one, work some great mystery which we cannot understand, which will keep
us down to be servants to their words, and also
servants unto them, for we depend upon them to
teach us the word; and thus will they keep us in
ignorance if we will yield ourselves unto them, all
the days of our lives.
22 And many more things did the people imagine
up in their hearts, which were foolish and vain; and
they were much disturbed, for Satan did stir them
up to do iniquity continually; yea, he did go about
spreading rumors and contentions upon all the face
of the land, that he might harden the hearts of the
people against that which was good and against
that which should come.
23 And notwithstanding the signs and the wonders which were wrought among the people of the
Lord, and the many miracles which they did, Satan
did get great hold upon the hearts of the people
upon all the face of the land.
24 And thus ended the ninetieth year of the reign
of the judges over the people of Nephi.
25 And thus ended the book of Helaman, according to the record of Helaman and his sons.

---

16:17 ***contend***—argue

16:20 ***tradition***—belief or teaching
***in ignorance***—without the knowledge

16:21 ***cunning***—tricks
***yield***—give up

The "evil one" is Satan (see Bruce R. McConkie, *Mormon Doctrine,* 246).

16:22 ***vain***—of no use
***disturbed***—troubled

"This account of wickedness and contentions among the Nephites prior to the Lord's birth in the meridian of time is duplicated in the wickedness, contentions, and deceptions of our day as we approach the second coming of our Lord and Savior Jesus Christ. Prophecies concerning these days are also being fulfilled and Satan is stirring up the hearts of men to do iniquity continually; and to thwart, if possible, faith in the great event of Christ's second coming to earth, which I testify is sure to come to pass" (Delbert L. Stapley, in Conference Report, October 1961, 22).

16:22 (15–22) Some people use their own reasoning instead of relying on the Spirit to determine whether or not the gospel is true. The prophet Isaiah commanded, "Let the wicked forsake his way, and the unrighteous man his thoughts. . . . For my thoughts are not your thoughts . . . saith the Lord. For as the heavens are higher than the earth, so are my ways higher than your ways, and my thoughts than your thoughts" (Isaiah 55:7–9).

16:22 (16–22) How did these people explain away the prophecies of Samuel that they were seeing fulfilled? What excuses do people use today to explain away the teachings of the prophets? Why do people do that?

16:23 ***notwithstanding***—in spite of
***wrought***—done

# THIRD NEPHI
# THE BOOK OF NEPHI

## THE SON OF NEPHI, WHO WAS THE SON OF HELAMAN

*Third Nephi is sometimes called the "fifth gospel." Like the four Gospels in the Bible (Matthew, Mark, Luke, and John), it is a testimony of the personal ministry of the resurrected Savior, Jesus Christ. An account is included of His appearance at the temple in the land Bountiful as a glorious resurrected being. The time period covered by 3 Nephi is from about A.D. 1 to A.D. 35. Because the Book of Mormon people were so faithful, the Savior was able to teach them many things He wasn't able to teach the Jews in Jerusalem.*

*And Helaman was the son of Helaman, who was the son of Alma, who was the son of Alma, being a descendant of Nephi who was the son of Lehi, who came out of Jerusalem in the first year of the reign of Zedekiah, the king of Judah.**

## CHAPTER 1

*The Nephites see great signs and miracles, yet many refuse to believe. The wicked even plan to kill those who still look for the sign prophesied by Samuel the Lamanite. The sign is given just as Samuel promised, and the believers are saved. As you read this chapter think about how these stories relate to the prophecies the Lord has made for our day.*

### NEPHI, SON OF HELAMAN, GIVES THE RECORDS TO HIS SON NEPHI

1 NOW it came to pass that the ninety and first year had passed away and it was six hundred years from the time that Lehi left Jerusalem; and it was in the year that Lachoneus was the chief judge and the governor over the land.

2 And Nephi, the son of Helaman, had departed out of the land of Zarahemla, giving charge unto his son Nephi, who was his eldest son, concerning the plates of brass, and all the records which had been kept, and all those things which had been kept sacred from the departure of Lehi out of Jerusalem.

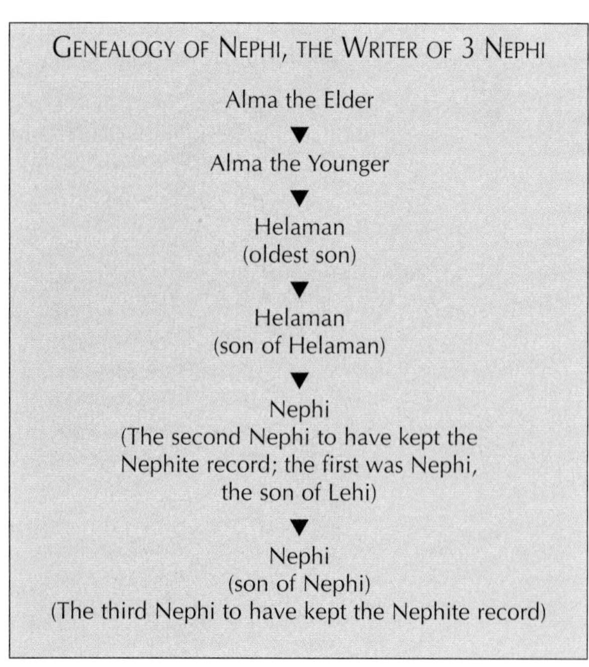


* This introduction to 3 Nephi was translated from the Book of Mormon plates.

1:1 The "ninety and first year" is counted from the beginning of the reign of the judges. This chapter takes place about A.D. 1.

1:2 The plates of brass were the Old Testament scriptures that Nephi obtained from Laban in Jerusalem. They contained Lehi's genealogy, the five books of Moses, the record of the Jews, and many prophecies of the holy prophets (see 1 Nephi 5:10–14).

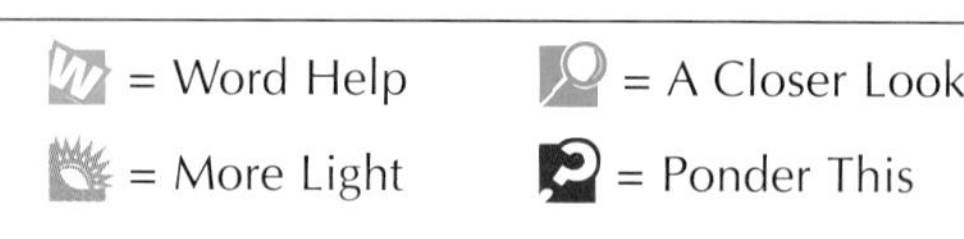

3 Then he departed out of the land, and whither
he went, no man knoweth; and his son Nephi did keep the records in his stead, yea, the record of this people.

## The Wicked Plan to Kill the Righteous in Spite of Great Signs and Miracles

4 And it came to pass that in the commencement
of the ninety and second year, behold, the prophecies of the prophets began to be fulfilled more fully; for there began to be greater signs and greater miracles wrought among the people.
5 But there were some who began to say that the
time was past for the words to be fulfilled, which were spoken by Samuel, the Lamanite.
6 And they began to rejoice over their brethren,
saying: Behold the time is past, and the words of Samuel are not fulfilled; therefore, your joy and your faith concerning this thing hath been vain.
7 And it came to pass that they did make a great
uproar throughout the land; and the people who believed began to be very sorrowful, lest by any means those things which had been spoken might not come to pass.
8 But behold, they did watch steadfastly for that
day and that night and that day which should be as one day as if there were no night, that they might know that their faith had not been vain.
9 Now it came to pass that there was a day set
apart by the unbelievers, that all those who believed in those traditions should be put to death except the sign should come to pass, which had been given by Samuel the prophet.

## The Sign of Christ's Birth Is Given and the Righteous Are Saved

10 Now it came to pass that when Nephi, the son
of Nephi, saw this wickedness of his people, his heart was exceedingly sorrowful.
11 And it came to pass that he went out and
bowed himself down upon the earth, and cried mightily to his God in behalf of his people, yea, those who were about to be destroyed because of their faith in the tradition of their fathers.
12 And it came to pass that he cried mightily unto
the Lord all that day; and behold, the voice of the Lord came unto him, saying:
13 Lift up your head and be of good cheer; for
behold, the time is at hand, and on this night shall the sign be given, and on the morrow come I into the world, to show unto the world that I will fulfil all that which I have caused to be spoken by the mouth of my holy prophets.
14 Behold, I come unto my own, to fulfil all things
which I have made known unto the children of men from the foundation of the world, and to do the will, both of the Father and of the Son—of the Father because of me, and of the Son because of my flesh. And behold, the time is at hand, and this night shall the sign be given.

---

1:3 Nephi, the son of Helaman, like his great-grandfather Alma the Younger, departed out of the land and was not heard from again (see 3 Nephi 2:9). The Nephites believed that Alma was translated or "taken up by the Spirit . . . even as Moses" (Alma 45:19). Nephi may have received the same blessing.

***stead***—place

1:4 ***wrought***—worked

1:6 ***vain***—useless

1:6 (4–6) The wicked refuse to believe the "greater signs and greater miracles" and make fun of those who believe by saying that the time is passed for the signs promised by Samuel to appear. The same kind of doubting will occur in our day when the wicked will say that "Christ delayeth his coming until the end of the earth" (D&C 45:26).

1:8 ***did watch steadfastly***—faithfully watched

1:9 If Samuel's prophecies did not come true, the wicked could say they were right and the believers were wrong, but they were not just interested in being right. They wanted to kill the believers. Why do you think the truth makes the wicked so angry? (see 1 Nephi 16:1–3; Helaman 13:25–28). What truths have the prophets taught in our day that have made some unbelievers angry?

1:14 It is a great comfort to know that the words the Lord gives His prophets will always come true. In a modern revelation the Lord declared, "What I the Lord have spoken, I have spoken, and I excuse not myself; though the heavens and the earth pass away, my word shall not pass away, but shall all be fulfilled, whether by mine own voice or by the voice of my servants, it is the same" (D&C 1:38).

"ON THE MORROW COME I INTO THE WORLD," BY ROBERT T. BARRETT

*"Lift up your head and be of good cheer; . . . on this night shall the sign be given, and on the morrow come I into the world."*

15 And it came to pass that the words which came
unto Nephi were fulfilled, according as they had
been spoken; for behold, at the going down of the
sun there was no darkness; and the people began
to be astonished because there was no darkness
when the night came.
16 And there were many, who had not believed
the words of the prophets, who fell to the earth and
became as if they were dead, for they knew that the
great plan of destruction which they had laid for
those who believed in the words of the prophets
had been frustrated; for the sign which had been
given was already at hand.
17 And they began to know that the Son of God
must shortly appear; yea, in fine, all the people
upon the face of the whole earth from the west to
the east, both in the land north and in the land
south, were so exceedingly astonished that they fell
to the earth.
18 For they knew that the prophets had testified
of these things for many years, and that the sign
which had been given was already at hand; and
they began to fear because of their iniquity and
their unbelief.
19 And it came to pass that there was no darkness
in all that night, but it was as light as though it was
mid-day. And it came to pass that the sun did rise in
the morning again, according to its proper order; and
they knew that it was the day that the Lord should be
born, because of the sign which had been given.
20 And it had come to pass, yea, all things, every
whit, according to the words of the prophets.
21 And it came to pass also that a new star did
appear, according to the word.

1:15 This night with no darkness fulfilled Samuel's prophecy in Helaman 14:3–4.

1:16 ***frustrated***—ruined

1:17 ***astonished***—surprised

1:18 ***iniquity***—wickedness or sins

1:20 ***every whit***—every little part

1:21 This new star fulfilled Samuel's prophecy in Helaman 14:5.

## SATAN SENDS LIES AMONG THE PEOPLE BUT MOST BELIEVE THE SIGNS

22 And it came to pass that from this time forth there began to be lyings sent forth among the people, by Satan, to harden their hearts, to the intent that they might not believe in those signs and wonders which they had seen; but notwithstanding these lyings and deceivings the more part of the people did believe, and were converted unto the Lord.
23 And it came to pass that Nephi went forth among the people, and also many others, baptizing unto repentance, in the which there was a great remission of sins. And thus the people began again to have peace in the land.
24 And there were no contentions, save it were a few that began to preach, endeavoring to prove by the scriptures that it was no more expedient to observe the law of Moses. Now in this thing they did err, having not understood the scriptures.
25 But it came to pass that they soon became converted, and were convinced of the error which they were in, for it was made known unto them that the law was not yet fulfilled, and that it must be fulfilled in every whit; yea, the word came unto them that it must be fulfilled; yea, that one jot or tittle should not pass away till it should all be fulfilled; therefore in this same year were they brought to a knowledge of their error and did confess their faults.
26 And thus the ninety and second year did pass away, bringing glad tidings unto the people because of the signs which did come to pass, according to the words of the prophecy of all the holy prophets.
27 And it came to pass that the ninety and third year did also pass away in peace, save it were for the Gadianton robbers, who dwelt upon the mountains, who did infest the land; for so strong were their holds and their secret places that the people could not overpower them; therefore they did commit many murders, and did do much slaughter among the people.
28 And it came to pass that in the ninety and fourth year they began to increase in a great degree, because there were many dissenters of the Nephites who did flee unto them, which did cause much sorrow unto those Nephites who did remain in the land.
29 And there was also a cause of much sorrow among the Lamanites; for behold, they had many children who did grow up and began to wax strong in years, that they became for themselves, and were led away by some who were Zoramites, by their lyings and their flattering words, to join those Gadianton robbers.

---

1:22 ***notwithstanding***—even with

Satan sent lies among the people to keep them from believing the signs of Jesus' birth. Why didn't Satan want them to believe in the signs? What might he do today to keep you from believing the words of the prophets?

1:23 ***remission***—forgiveness

1:24 ***endeavoring***—trying
***err***—make a mistake

The law of Moses refers to the laws and ordinances that the children of Israel were commanded to follow from the days of Moses until the time of Jesus Christ (see LDS Bible Dictionary, s.v. "Law of Moses," 722–23).

Some Nephites were teaching that because the signs of Christ's birth had come it was no longer necessary to live the law of Moses. They did not understand that all the sacrifices of the law of Moses pointed to the Atonement of Jesus Christ. The law would not be fulfilled until Christ, as the Lamb of God, was sacrificed on the cross (see Alma 34:13–14; 3 Nephi 9:17–20).

1:25 Jots and tittles were very small marks used when writing words in ancient languages, such as Hebrew, and were similar to periods and commas in the English language. Referring to them showed that every single part, even the very smallest parts, of the law of Moses would be fulfilled by the Atonement of Jesus Christ.

1:27 ***infest***—trouble or plague
***slaughter***—killing

1:28 ***dissenters of the Nephites***—Nephites who disagreed with how things were

1:29 ***wax strong***—increase
***flattering words***—false praise

For more information about the Zoramites, see Alma 31–35.

*THE NEW STAR, BY ROBERT T. BARRETT*

*"And it came to pass also that a new star did appear, according to the word."*

30 And thus were the Lamanites afflicted also, and began to decrease as to their faith and righteousness, because of the wickedness of the rising generation.

## CHAPTER 2

*The people become more wicked and begin to doubt the signs and wonders they had seen. The Gadianton robbers threaten to destroy both the Nephites and the Lamanites. Watch for a great miracle that takes place among the righteous Lamanites.*

### The Wicked Reject the Prophecies About Christ

1 AND it came to pass that thus passed away the ninety and fifth year also, and the people began to forget those signs and wonders which they had heard, and began to be less and less astonished at a sign or a wonder from heaven, insomuch that they began to be hard in their hearts, and blind in their minds, and began to disbelieve all which they had heard and seen—

2 Imagining up some vain thing in their hearts, that it was wrought by men and by the power of the devil, to lead away and deceive the hearts of the people; and thus did Satan get possession of the hearts of the people again, insomuch that he did blind their eyes and lead them away to believe that the doctrine of Christ was a foolish and a vain thing.

3 And it came to pass that the people began to wax strong in wickedness and abominations; and they did not believe that there should be any more signs or wonders given; and Satan did go about, leading away the hearts of the people, tempting them and causing them that they should do great wickedness in the land.

4 And thus did pass away the ninety and sixth year; and also the ninety and seventh year; and also the ninety and eighth year; and also the ninety and ninth year;

5 And also an hundred years had passed away since the days of Mosiah, who was king over the people of the Nephites.

6 And six hundred and nine years had passed away since Lehi left Jerusalem.

7 And nine years had passed away from the time when the sign was given, which was spoken of by the prophets, that Christ should come into the world.

8 Now the Nephites began to reckon their time from this period when the sign was given, or from the coming of Christ; therefore, nine years had passed away.

---

1:30 ***afflicted***—mistreated or tormented

1:30 (29–30) The "rising generation" are the young people. In this case "they became for themselves," or they were more interested in themselves than in others. Elder Neal A. Maxwell once explained why selfish people tend to be wicked: "The selfish individual . . . seeks to please not God, but himself. He will even break a covenant in order to fix an appetite" (in Conference Report, October 1990, 15).

2:1 ***astonished***—surprised

"The more hardened a people become, the more serious their sins, the more closed to spiritual experience, the less they are impressed by wonders sent forth from God or inspired acts of his servants" (Joseph Fielding McConkie and others, *Doctrinal Commentary on the Book of Mormon* 4:10–11).

Why does the passing of time seem to dim our memory of sacred and spiritual experiences like our baptismal day, receiving the gift of the Holy Ghost, or receiving answers to our prayers? What are some ways you can always remember these important events?

2:2 ***vain***—useless
***wrought***—worked or done

The name *Christ* is a Greek word meaning "the Anointed One"; the Hebrew word with the same meaning is *Messiah.* Jesus is the Christ—the one chosen, set apart, and sent by God to save us (see LDS Bible Dictionary, s.v. "Christ," 633).

2:3 ***wax strong***—grow
***abominations***—great evils

2:3 (2–3) Satan uses different methods to deceive people. What are some modern-day examples of ways Satan leads people away from the truth?

2:7 The sign of Christ's birth mentioned here is described in the previous chapter, verses 14–21.

2:8 ***reckon***—determine or tell

The Nephites first measured time from when Lehi left Jerusalem (see Jacob 1:1; Enos 1:25). Later years were counted from the beginning of the reign of the judges (see Mosiah 29:44; Alma 1:1).

9 And Nephi, who was the father of Nephi, who had the charge of the records, did not return to the land of Zarahemla, and could nowhere be found in all the land.

10 And it came to pass that the people did still remain in wickedness, notwithstanding the much preaching and prophesying which was sent among them; and thus passed away the tenth year also; and the eleventh year also passed away in iniquity.

### *The Nephites and Righteous Lamanites Unite to Fight Against the Gadianton Robbers*

11 And it came to pass in the thirteenth year there began to be wars and contentions throughout all the land; for the Gadianton robbers had become so numerous, and did slay so many of the people, and did lay waste so many cities, and did spread so much death and carnage throughout the land, that it became expedient that all the people, both the Nephites and the Lamanites, should take up arms against them.

12 Therefore, all the Lamanites who had become converted unto the Lord did unite with their brethren, the Nephites, and were compelled, for the safety of their lives and their women and their children, to take up arms against those Gadianton robbers, yea, and also to maintain their rights, and the privileges of their church and of their worship, and their freedom and their liberty.

13 And it came to pass that before this thirteenth year had passed away the Nephites were threatened with utter destruction because of this war, which had become exceedingly sore.

### *The Skin of Converted Lamanites Becomes White Like the Nephites' Skin*

14 And it came to pass that those Lamanites who had united with the Nephites were numbered among the Nephites;

15 And their curse was taken from them, and their skin became white like unto the Nephites;

16 And their young men and their daughters became exceedingly fair, and they were numbered among the Nephites, and were called Nephites. And thus ended the thirteenth year.

17 And it came to pass in the commencement of the fourteenth year, the war between the robbers and the people of Nephi did continue and did become exceedingly sore; nevertheless, the people of Nephi did gain some advantage of the robbers, insomuch that they did drive them back out of their lands into the mountains and into their secret places.

18 And thus ended the fourteenth year. And in the fifteenth year they did come forth against the people of Nephi; and because of the wickedness of the people of Nephi, and their many contentions and dissensions, the Gadianton robbers did gain many advantages over them.

19 And thus ended the fifteenth year, and thus were the people in a state of many afflictions; and the sword of destruction did hang over them, insomuch that they were about to be smitten down by it, and this because of their iniquity.

---

2:11 ***contentions***—fighting
***lay waste***—destroy
***carnage***—bloodshed
***expedient***—necessary

2:12 ***compelled***—forced

In the last days we will see a similar situation. The righteous will be gathered to Zion for safety, "and it shall be the only people that shall not be at war one with another" (D&C 45:69).

2:13 ***utter***—complete

2:15 "The mark of God's curse, the dark skin (see 1 Nephi 2:23; 2 Nephi 5:21–23) was taken away. This was consistent with the prophetic word which declared that when the Lamanites are restored to the knowledge of Jesus Christ and his gospel, 'their scales of darkness shall begin to fall from their eyes; and many generations shall not pass away among them, save they shall be a pure and delightsome people' (2 Nephi 30:6)" (Joseph Fielding McConkie and others, *Doctrinal Commentary on the Book of Mormon* 4:12).

2:16 ***fair***—beautiful

2:17 ***sore***—terrible or intense

2:18 ***dissensions***—strong disagreements

Notice that there were great miracles and great wickedness happening at about the same time (see verses 14–16, 18). Is that also true of our day? What do you think you can do to make sure you experience the great miracles, not the great wickedness?

2:19 ***afflictions***—trials or sufferings
***smitten***—beaten or struck

## CHAPTER 3

*The Gadianton robbers threaten a war against the Nephites. Look for how the Nephites prepare to meet their enemies and for who is chosen to lead their armies and why.*

### The Robber Giddianhi Demands That the Nephites Surrender

1 AND now it came to pass that in the sixteenth
year from the coming of Christ, Lachoneus, the governor of the land, received an epistle from the leader and the governor of this band of robbers; and these were the words which were written, saying:
2 Lachoneus, most noble and chief governor of
the land, behold, I write this epistle unto you, and do give unto you exceedingly great praise because of your firmness, and also the firmness of your people, in maintaining that which ye suppose to be your right and liberty; yea, ye do stand well, as if ye were supported by the hand of a god, in the defence of your liberty, and your property, and your country, or that which ye do call so.
3 And it seemeth a pity unto me, most noble
Lachoneus, that ye should be so foolish and vain as to suppose that ye can stand against so many brave men who are at my command, who do now at this time stand in their arms, and do await with great anxiety for the word—Go down upon the Nephites and destroy them.
4 And I, knowing of their unconquerable spirit,
having proved them in the field of battle, and knowing of their everlasting hatred towards you because of the many wrongs which ye have done unto them, therefore if they should come down against you they would visit you with utter destruction.
5 Therefore I have written this epistle, sealing it
with mine own hand, feeling for your welfare, because of your firmness in that which ye believe to be right, and your noble spirit in the field of battle.
6 Therefore I write unto you, desiring that ye
would yield up unto this my people, your cities, your lands, and your possessions, rather than that they should visit you with the sword and that destruction should come upon you.
7 Or in other words, yield yourselves up unto us,
and unite with us and become acquainted with our secret works, and become our brethren that ye may be like unto us—not our slaves, but our brethren and partners of all our substance.
8 And behold, I swear unto you, if ye will do this,
with an oath, ye shall not be destroyed; but if ye will not do this, I swear unto you with an oath, that on the morrow month I will command that my armies shall come down against you, and they shall not stay their hand and shall spare not, but shall slay you, and shall let fall the sword upon you even until ye shall become extinct.
9 And behold, I am Giddianhi; and I am the gov-
ernor of this the secret society of Gadianton; which society and the works thereof I know to be good; and they are of ancient date and they have been handed down unto us.

---

3:1 The "coming of Christ" in this verse refers to the Savior's birth (see 3 Nephi 1:19).

***an epistle***—a letter

3:2 ***firmness***—strength or determination

3:3 ***pity***—shame
***vain***—prideful
***anxiety***—eagerness

3:4 ***utter***—complete

3:5 ***welfare***—safety or well-being

3:6 ***yield up***—surrender

3:7 ***become acquainted with***—learn about or accept
***substance***—possessions

3:8 ***an oath***—a solemn promise
***slay***—kill
***extinct***—completely destroyed

The wicked always fight against righteousness. This battle began in the premortal life and continues today (see D&C 29:36–37).

3:9 Giddianhi wrote that the secret oaths were ancient. It was Satan, the father of lies, who gave these secret oaths to Cain when they conspired to kill Abel (see Moses 5:29; Helaman 6:26–30).

10 And I write this epistle unto you, Lachoneus,
and I hope that ye will deliver up your lands and
your possessions, without the shedding of blood,
that this my people may recover their rights and
government, who have dissented away from you
because of your wickedness in retaining from them
their rights of government, and except ye do this, I
will avenge their wrongs. I am Giddianhi.

## Lachoneus Refuses to Surrender and Asks His People to Repent and Pray for Help

11 And now it came to pass when Lachoneus
received this epistle he was exceedingly astonished,
because of the boldness of Giddianhi demanding
the possession of the land of the Nephites, and also
of threatening the people and avenging the wrongs
of those that had received no wrong, save it were
they had wronged themselves by dissenting away
unto those wicked and abominable robbers.
12 Now behold, this Lachoneus, the governor, was
a just man, and could not be frightened by the
demands and the threatenings of a robber; therefore he did not hearken to the epistle of Giddianhi,
the governor of the robbers, but he did cause that
his people should cry unto the Lord for strength
against the time that the robbers should come down
against them.
13 Yea, he sent a proclamation among all the
people, that they should gather together their
women, and their children, their flocks and their
herds, and all their substance, save it were their
land, unto one place.
14 And he caused that fortifications should be
built round about them, and the strength thereof
should be exceedingly great. And he caused that
armies, both of the Nephites and of the Lamanites,
or of all them who were numbered among the
Nephites, should be placed as guards round about
to watch them, and to guard them from the robbers
day and night.
15 Yea, he said unto them: As the Lord liveth,
except ye repent of all your iniquities, and cry unto
the Lord, ye will in nowise be delivered out of the
hands of those Gadianton robbers.
16 And so great and marvelous were the words
and prophecies of Lachoneus that they did cause
fear to come upon all the people; and they did
exert themselves in their might to do according to
the words of Lachoneus.

## Gidgiddoni Is Chosen as Chief Captain over the Nephite Armies

17 And it came to pass that Lachoneus did appoint
chief captains over all the armies of the Nephites, to
command them at the time that the robbers should
come down out of the wilderness against them.
18 Now the chiefest among all the chief captains
and the great commander of all the armies of the
Nephites was appointed, and his name was
Gidgiddoni.
19 Now it was the custom among all the Nephites
to appoint for their chief captains, (save it were in
their times of wickedness) some one that had the
spirit of revelation and also prophecy; therefore,
this Gidgiddoni was a great prophet among them,
as also was the chief judge.
20 Now the people said unto Gidgiddoni: Pray
unto the Lord, and let us go up upon the mountains
and into the wilderness, that we may fall upon the
robbers and destroy them in their own lands.

---

3:10 ***dissented***—turned
***retaining***—keeping or holding back

Notice how the wicked Giddianhi pretended to praise Lachoneus and then used threats to try to get Lachoneus to agree to his demands. Has anyone ever tried to get you to do something wrong by pretending to be your friend or by threatening you? How does knowing that those methods are wicked give you the strength to stand up to that kind of person?

3:12 ***hearken to***—listen to and obey

When Lachoneus was threatened by evil, he had faith and prayed to the Lord for help. How can faith and prayer help you when you are tempted or threatened by wickedness? Notice what else Lachoneus did to protect his people in verses 13–17. How is that like what our modern prophets are doing to protect us from the evils in our day?

3:13 ***a proclamation***—an announcement

3:14 ***fortifications***—barriers or walls

3:16 ***exert themselves***—work hard

3:17 ***wilderness***—wild land with very few people

3:20 ***fall upon***—go to war against

21 But Gidgiddoni saith unto them: The Lord forbid; for if we should go up against them the Lord would deliver us into their hands; therefore we will prepare ourselves in the center of our lands, and we will gather all our armies together, and we will not go against them, but we will wait till they shall come against us; therefore as the Lord liveth, if we do this he will deliver them into our hands.

### The Nephites Gather Together, Repent, and Prepare for War

22 And it came to pass in the seventeenth year, in the latter end of the year, the proclamation of Lachoneus had gone forth throughout all the face of the land, and they had taken their horses, and their chariots, and their cattle, and all their flocks, and their herds, and their grain, and all their substance, and did march forth by thousands and by tens of thousands, until they had all gone forth to the place which had been appointed that they should gather themselves together, to defend themselves against their enemies.

23 And the land which was appointed was the land of Zarahemla, and the land which was between the land Zarahemla and the land Bountiful, yea, to the line which was between the land Bountiful and the land Desolation.

24 And there were a great many thousand people who were called Nephites, who did gather themselves together in this land. Now Lachoneus did cause that they should gather themselves together in the land southward, because of the great curse which was upon the land northward.

25 And they did fortify themselves against their enemies; and they did dwell in one land, and in one body, and they did fear the words which had been spoken by Lachoneus, insomuch that they did repent of all their sins; and they did put up their prayers unto the Lord their God, that he would deliver them in the time that their enemies should come down against them to battle.

26 And they were exceedingly sorrowful because of their enemies. And Gidgiddoni did cause that they should make weapons of war of every kind, and they should be strong with armor, and with shields, and with bucklers, after the manner of his instruction.

## CHAPTER 4

*The Nephites unite against the Gadianton robbers and defeat them. Notice how the Lord protects His people when they turn to Him.*

### The Gadianton Robbers Are Unable to Steal from the United Nephites

1 AND it came to pass that in the latter end of the eighteenth year those armies of robbers had prepared for battle, and began to come down and to sally forth from the hills, and out of the mountains, and the wilderness, and their strongholds, and their secret places, and began to take possession of the lands, both which were in the land south and which were in the land north, and began to take possession of all the lands which had been deserted by the Nephites, and the cities which had been left desolate.

---

3:21 ***The Lord forbid***—May it not be so

3:22 ***appointed***—selected

3:24 (23–24) The land Desolation is where the bones of the Jaredites were found by Limhi's people (see Mosiah 8:7–9). The Nephites considered this land cursed because it was here the Jaredites were destroyed for not obeying Jesus Christ (see Ether 2:9).

3:25 ***fortify***—strengthen

3:26 (22–26) In these verses the Nephites gathered together to protect and strengthen one another in righteousness. Lachoneus and Gidgiddoni understood that repentance and spiritual preparation were as essential as military preparation (see verses 25–26). The Lord has also commanded the Latter-day Saints to gather in stakes to receive help and protection (see D&C 115:6). Our temples also help strengthen faithful Church members (see D&C 109:24–26).

PHOTOGRAPH BY EDWIN M. WOOLLEY

*These ancient weapons may be similar to the kinds used by the Nephites and Lamanites.*

4:1 ***sally***—rush
***desolate***—empty

2 But behold, there were no wild beasts nor game
in those lands which had been deserted by the
Nephites, and there was no game for the robbers
save it were in the wilderness.
3 And the robbers could not exist save it were in
the wilderness, for the want of food; for the
Nephites had left their lands desolate, and had gathered their flocks and their herds and all their substance, and they were in one body.
4 Therefore, there was no chance for the robbers
to plunder and to obtain food, save it were to come
up in open battle against the Nephites; and the
Nephites being in one body, and having so great a
number, and having reserved for themselves provisions, and horses and cattle, and flocks of every
kind, that they might subsist for the space of seven
years, in the which time they did hope to destroy
the robbers from off the face of the land; and thus
the eighteenth year did pass away.

## Nephite Armies Defeat the Gadianton Robbers in Battle

5 And it came to pass that in the nineteenth year
Giddianhi found that it was expedient that he
should go up to battle against the Nephites, for
there was no way that they could subsist save it
were to plunder and rob and murder.
6 And they durst not spread themselves upon the
face of the land insomuch that they could raise
grain, lest the Nephites should come upon them
and slay them; therefore Giddianhi gave commandment unto his armies that in this year they should
go up to battle against the Nephites.
7 And it came to pass that they did come up to
battle; and it was in the sixth month; and behold,
great and terrible was the day that they did come
up to battle; and they were girded about after the
manner of robbers; and they had a lamb-skin about
their loins, and they were dyed in blood, and their
heads were shorn, and they had head-plates upon
them; and great and terrible was the appearance of
the armies of Giddianhi, because of their armor,
and because of their being dyed in blood.
8 And it came to pass that the armies of the
Nephites, when they saw the appearance of the
army of Giddianhi, had all fallen to the earth, and
did lift their cries to the Lord their God, that he
would spare them and deliver them out of the
hands of their enemies.
9 And it came to pass that when the armies of
Giddianhi saw this they began to shout with a loud
voice, because of their joy, for they had supposed
that the Nephites had fallen with fear because of
the terror of their armies.
10 But in this thing they were disappointed, for
the Nephites did not fear them; but they did fear
their God and did supplicate him for protection;
therefore, when the armies of Giddianhi did rush

PHOTOGRAPH BY SCOT FACER PROCTOR

*Horses are mentioned throughout the Book of Mormon until A.D. 26. Some feel that the word* horse *in the Book of Mormon is used to refer to deer or some other domesticated animal; however, horse bones predating Columbus have been found on the Yucatan Peninsula.*

4:2 ***game***—animals to eat

4:3 ***substance***—supplies for living

4:4 ***plunder***—steal
***provisions***—food and other supplies

4:4 (3–4) The Nephites were safe from the attacks of their enemies because they were gathered together and unified. Elder Howard W. Hunter taught, "Within this Church there is a constant need for unity, for if we are not one, we are not his (see D&C 38:27)." He has also said that "one of the things that has made the Church strong is the great principle of unity" (*The Teachings of Howard W. Hunter,* 194, 195).

4:5 ***expedient***—necessary
***subsist***—live

4:6 ***durst***—dared

4:7 ***girded***—clothed
***shorn***—shaved

4:10 ***supplicate***—pray to

4:10 (7–10) Many times evil can look frightening. The Nephites did not give in to fear but instead turned to the Lord in prayer for strength. What should you do when you are frightened?

upon them they were prepared to meet them; yea, in the strength of the Lord they did receive them.

11 And the battle commenced in this the sixth month; and great and terrible was the battle thereof, yea, great and terrible was the slaughter thereof, insomuch that there never was known so great a slaughter among all the people of Lehi since he left Jerusalem.

12 And notwithstanding the threatenings and the oaths which Giddianhi had made, behold, the Nephites did beat them, insomuch that they did fall back from before them.

13 And it came to pass that Gidgiddoni commanded that his armies should pursue them as far as the borders of the wilderness, and that they should not spare any that should fall into their hands by the way; and thus they did pursue them and did slay them, to the borders of the wilderness, even until they had fulfilled the commandment of Gidgiddoni.

14 And it came to pass that Giddianhi, who had stood and fought with boldness, was pursued as he fled; and being weary because of his much fighting he was overtaken and slain. And thus was the end of Giddianhi the robber.

15 And it came to pass that the armies of the Nephites did return again to their place of security. And it came to pass that this nineteenth year did pass away, and the robbers did not come again to battle; neither did they come again in the twentieth year.

16 And in the twenty and first year they did not come up to battle, but they came up on all sides to lay siege round about the people of Nephi; for they did suppose that if they should cut off the people of Nephi from their lands, and should hem them in on every side, and if they should cut them off from all their outward privileges, that they could cause them to yield themselves up according to their wishes.

17 Now they had appointed unto themselves another leader, whose name was Zemnarihah; therefore it was Zemnarihah that did cause that this siege should take place.

18 But behold, this was an advantage to the Nephites; for it was impossible for the robbers to lay siege sufficiently long to have any effect upon the Nephites, because of their much provision which they had laid up in store,

19 And because of the scantiness of provisions among the robbers; for behold, they had nothing save it were meat for their subsistence, which meat they did obtain in the wilderness;

20 And it came to pass that the wild game became scarce in the wilderness insomuch that the robbers were about to perish with hunger.

21 And the Nephites were continually marching out by day and by night, and falling upon their armies, and cutting them off by thousands and by tens of thousands.

22 And thus it became the desire of the people of Zemnarihah to withdraw from their design, because of the great destruction which came upon them by night and by day.

23 And it came to pass that Zemnarihah did give command unto his people that they should withdraw themselves from the siege, and march into the furthermost parts of the land northward.

24 And now, Gidgiddoni being aware of their design, and knowing of their weakness because of the want of food, and the great slaughter which had been made among them, therefore he did send out his armies in the night-time, and did cut off the way of their retreat, and did place his armies in the way of their retreat.

25 And this did they do in the night-time, and got on their march beyond the robbers, so that on the morrow, when the robbers began their march, they were met by the armies of the Nephites both in their front and in their rear.

26 And the robbers who were on the south were also cut off in their places of retreat. And all these things were done by command of Gidgiddoni.

27 And there were many thousands who did yield themselves up prisoners unto the Nephites, and the remainder of them were slain.

---

4:11 ***commenced***—began
***slaughter***—killing

4:13 ***pursue***—follow

4:16 ***hem***—surround or confine
***yield***—give

4:19 ***scantiness***—lack or shortage

4:22 ***design***—plan

### Victorious Nephites Praise God for Their Success

28 And their leader, Zemnarihah, was taken and hanged upon a tree, yea, even upon the top thereof until he was dead. And when they had hanged him until he was dead they did fell the tree to the earth, and did cry with a loud voice, saying:
29 May the Lord preserve his people in righteousness and in holiness of heart, that they may cause to be felled to the earth all who shall seek to slay them because of power and secret combinations, even as this man hath been felled to the earth.
30 And they did rejoice and cry again with one voice, saying: May the God of Abraham, and the God of Isaac, and the God of Jacob, protect this people in righteousness, so long as they shall call on the name of their God for protection.
31 And it came to pass that they did break forth, all as one, in singing, and praising their God for the great thing which he had done for them, in preserving them from falling into the hands of their enemies.
32 Yea, they did cry: Hosanna to the Most High God. And they did cry: Blessed be the name of the Lord God Almighty, the Most High God.
33 And their hearts were swollen with joy, unto the gushing out of many tears, because of the great goodness of God in delivering them out of the hands of their enemies; and they knew it was because of their repentance and their humility that they had been delivered from an everlasting destruction.

## CHAPTER 5

*The Nephites enjoy a time of righteousness. Notice the blessings that come to those who try to live the gospel.*

### The Nephites Repent and the Secret Combinations Are Destroyed

1 AND now behold, there was not a living soul among all the people of the Nephites who did doubt in the least the words of all the holy prophets who had spoken; for they knew that it must needs be that they must be fulfilled.
2 And they knew that it must be expedient that Christ had come, because of the many signs which had been given, according to the words of the prophets; and because of the things which had come to pass already they knew that it must needs be that all things should come to pass according to that which had been spoken.
3 Therefore they did forsake all their sins, and their abominations, and their whoredoms, and did serve God with all diligence day and night.
4 And now it came to pass that when they had taken all the robbers prisoners, insomuch that none did escape who were not slain, they did cast their prisoners into prison, and did cause the word of God to be preached unto them; and as many as would repent of their sins and enter into a covenant that they would murder no more were set at liberty.

---

4:29 A secret combination is a group of wicked people who secretly join together to lie, cheat, steal, murder or do whatever is necessary to gain riches, wealth, or power (see Helaman 7:21; 8:27). The first secret combination was between Satan and Cain, who killed his brother Abel to get his flocks (see Moses 5:28–32). "Among today's secret combinations are gangs, drug cartels, and organized crime families" (M. Russell Ballard, in Conference Report, October 1997, 51).

4:33 Repentance and humility saved these Nephites. Speaking of our day President Gordon B. Hinckley said, "While we must have science, while we must have education, while we must have arms, we must also have righteousness if we are to merit the protection of God" (*Teachings of Gordon B. Hinckley,* 40).

4:33 (31–33) These righteous Nephites expressed thankfulness for their protection by singing, crying, and praising God. How can you show your gratitude to Heavenly Father for the many ways He helps you?

5:3 ***forsake***—give up
***abominations, and their whoredoms***—great wickedness, and immorality
***all diligence***—great care and effort

5:4 ***slain***—killed
***at liberty***—free

A covenant is an agreement between two people. In the scriptures it is usually an agreement between God and man. We agree to be obedient to God's commandments, and He promises to bless us (see LDS Bible Dictionary, s.v. "Covenant," 651).

Speaking of the power of the word of God to change lives, President Ezra Taft Benson said: "When individual members and families immerse themselves in the scriptures regularly and consistently . . . testimonies will increase. Commitment will be strengthened. Families will be fortified. Personal revelation will flow" ("The Power of the Word," 81; see also Alma 31:5).

5 But as many as there were who did not enter
into a covenant, and who did still continue to have
those secret murders in their hearts, yea, as many as
were found breathing out threatenings against their
brethren were condemned and punished according
to the law.
6 And thus they did put an end to all those
wicked, and secret, and abominable combinations,
in the which there was so much wickedness, and so
many murders committed.
7 And thus had the twenty and second year
passed away, and the twenty and third year also,
and the twenty and fourth, and the twenty and fifth;
and thus had twenty and five years passed away.

## The Prophet Mormon Explains the Record He Is Making

8 And there had many things transpired which, in
the eyes of some, would be great and marvelous;
nevertheless, they cannot all be written in this
book; yea, this book cannot contain even a hundredth part of what was done among so many
people in the space of twenty and five years;
9 But behold there are records which do contain
all the proceedings of this people; and a shorter but
true account was given by Nephi.
10 Therefore I have made my record of these
things according to the record of Nephi, which was
engraven on the plates which were called the plates
of Nephi.
11 And behold, I do make the record on plates
which I have made with mine own hands.
12 And behold, I am called Mormon, being called
after the land of Mormon, the land in which Alma
did establish the church among the people, yea, the
first church which was established among them
after their transgression.
13 Behold, I am a disciple of Jesus Christ, the Son
of God. I have been called of him to declare his
word among his people, that they might have everlasting life.
14 And it hath become expedient that I, according
to the will of God, that the prayers of those who
have gone hence, who were the holy ones, should
be fulfilled according to their faith, should make a
record of these things which have been done—
15 Yea, a small record of that which hath taken
place from the time that Lehi left Jerusalem, even
down until the present time.
16 Therefore I do make my record from the
accounts which have been given by those who were
before me, until the commencement of my day;
17 And then I do make a record of the things
which I have seen with mine own eyes.
18 And I know the record which I make to be a
just and a true record; nevertheless there are many
things which, according to our language, we are not
able to write.
19 And now I make an end of my saying, which
is of myself, and proceed to give my account of the
things which have been before me.

---

5:5 ***condemned***—found guilty

5:8 ***transpired***—happened

5:9 ***proceedings***—activities

5:10 ***engraven***—written by being cut or impressed into metal

5:11 (8–11) Mormon made an abridgement (meaning a shorter version) of the record of Nephi. He tells us throughout the plates of Mormon that he cannot even tell us a hundredth part, or a very small part, of all the doings of the Nephites (see Helaman 3:13–14).

5:12 ***establish***—start

In Noah Webster's 1828 *American Dictionary of the English Language* the word *transgression* is defined as "passing over or beyond any law or rule of moral duty" (s.v. "transgression"). In the scriptures *transgression* generally means the breaking of spiritual law.

5:13 Mormon said he was a disciple, or follower, of Jesus Christ. He was called to preach God's word. What has the Lord asked you to do as a disciple of Jesus Christ?

5:14 ***gone hence***—died

Mormon tells us that his record fulfills the faith and prayers of "holy ones," or prophets and other righteous individuals who lived before him. They also prayed for the Book of Mormon to go to the Lamanites and to the world (see D&C 10:46–50).

5:16 ***commencement***—beginning

5:18 ***just***—fair

5:19 ***proceed***—move on

PLATES OF MORMON, BY TED HENNINGER

*"It hath become expedient that I [Mormon], according to the will of God, . . . should make a record of these things which have been done."*

20 I am Mormon, and a pure descendant of Lehi.
I have reason to bless my God and my Savior Jesus
Christ, that he brought our fathers out of the land
of Jerusalem, (and no one knew it save it were himself and those whom he brought out of that land)
and that he hath given me and my people so much
knowledge unto the salvation of our souls.

## Mormon Prophesies of the Scattering and Gathering of Israel

21 Surely he hath blessed the house of Jacob, and
hath been merciful unto the seed of Joseph.
22 And insomuch as the children of Lehi have
kept his commandments he hath blessed them and
prospered them according to his word.
23 Yea, and surely shall he again bring a remnant
of the seed of Joseph to the knowledge of the Lord
their God.
24 And as surely as the Lord liveth, will he gather
in from the four quarters of the earth all the remnant of the seed of Jacob, who are scattered abroad
upon all the face of the earth.
25 And as he hath covenanted with all the house
of Jacob, even so shall the covenant wherewith he

5:20 ***a pure descendant***—in the direct family line

5:21 ***merciful***—loving and forgiving
***seed***—descendants, meaning children, grandchildren and so on

The Lord changed Jacob's name to "Israel" (see Genesis 32:28; see also Glossary: Israel). Therefore, the house of Jacob is the same as the house of Israel. Joseph was the birthright son of Jacob. The birthright son was the one who received the greatest physical and spiritual blessings from his father (see Genesis 37:3).

5:23 ***remnant***—remaining part

hath covenanted with the house of Jacob be fulfilled in his own due time, unto the restoring all the house of Jacob unto the knowledge of the covenant that he hath covenanted with them.
26 And then shall they know their Redeemer, who is Jesus Christ, the Son of God; and then shall they be gathered in from the four quarters of the earth unto their own lands, from whence they have been dispersed; yea, as the Lord liveth so shall it be. Amen.

## CHAPTER 6

*For several years the people are righteous and they are blessed. They become proud of their riches and Satan gains great power over them. They kill the prophets and begin again uniting in secret combinations. Look for the terrible consequences that begin with the sin of pride.*

### The Nephites Prosper in Peace

1 AND now it came to pass that the people of the Nephites did all return to their own lands in the twenty and sixth year, every man, with his family, his flocks and his herds, his horses and his cattle, and all things whatsoever did belong unto them.
2 And it came to pass that they had not eaten up all their provisions; therefore they did take with them all that they had not devoured, of all their grain of every kind, and their gold, and their silver, and all their precious things, and they did return to their own lands and their possessions, both on the north and on the south, both on the land northward and on the land southward.
3 And they granted unto those robbers who had entered into a covenant to keep the peace of the land, who were desirous to remain Lamanites, lands, according to their numbers, that they might have, with their labors, wherewith to subsist upon; and thus they did establish peace in all the land.
4 And they began again to prosper and to wax great; and the twenty and sixth and seventh years passed away, and there was great order in the land; and they had formed their laws according to equity and justice.
5 And now there was nothing in all the land to hinder the people from prospering continually, except they should fall into transgression.
6 And now it was Gidgiddoni, and the judge, Lachoneus, and those who had been appointed leaders, who had established this great peace in the land.
7 And it came to pass that there were many cities built anew, and there were many old cities repaired.
8 And there were many highways cast up, and many roads made, which led from city to city, and from land to land, and from place to place.
9 And thus passed away the twenty and eighth year, and the people had continual peace.

### The Nephites Become Lifted Up in Pride

10 But it came to pass in the twenty and ninth year there began to be some disputings among the people; and some were lifted up unto pride and boastings because of their exceedingly great riches, yea, even unto great persecutions;

---

5:26 ***dispersed***—scattered

To *redeem* means to "buy back" or to "set free." Jesus Christ is our Redeemer because He willingly paid the price to buy us back and set us free from the effects of the Fall of Adam and from the burden of our own sins (see 1 Corinthians 6:20; D&C 18:11). The price He had to pay was His own blood (see 1 Peter 1:18–19).

5:26 (24–26) Because of disobedience the house of Israel had been scattered over all the earth (see 1 Nephi 22:3–4). Mormon testifies that the Lord will also gather them again in the last days, both spiritually and physically. When they come to "know their Redeemer, who is Jesus Christ . . . then shall they be gathered in from the four quarters of the earth unto their own lands" (verse 26).

6:2 ***provisions***—food supplies
***devoured***—eaten

6:3 ***subsist upon***—live on
***establish***—bring about

6:4 ***wax***—grow
***equity and justice***—fairness

6:5 ***hinder***—keep

The prophet Mormon explained that only disobedience could stop these people from prospering. How might sin affect the blessings you want most in life?

6:10 ***disputings***—arguments
***boastings***—bragging
***great persecutions***—hurting others

11 For there were many merchants in the land, and also many lawyers, and many officers.

12 And the people began to be distinguished by ranks, according to their riches and their chances for learning; yea, some were ignorant because of their poverty, and others did receive great learning because of their riches.

13 Some were lifted up in pride, and others were exceedingly humble; some did return railing for railing, while others would receive railing and persecution and all manner of afflictions, and would not turn and revile again, but were humble and penitent before God.

14 And thus there became a great inequality in all the land, insomuch that the church began to be broken up; yea, insomuch that in the thirtieth year the church was broken up in all the land save it were among a few of the Lamanites who were converted unto the true faith; and they would not depart from it, for they were firm, and steadfast, and immovable, willing with all diligence to keep the commandments of the Lord.

15 Now the cause of this iniquity of the people was this—Satan had great power, unto the stirring up of the people to do all manner of iniquity, and to the puffing them up with pride, tempting them to seek for power, and authority, and riches, and the vain things of the world.

16 And thus Satan did lead away the hearts of the people to do all manner of iniquity; therefore they had enjoyed peace but a few years.

17 And thus, in the commencement of the thirtieth year—the people having been delivered up for the space of a long time to be carried about by the temptations of the devil whithersoever he desired to carry them, and to do whatsoever iniquity he desired they should—and thus in the commencement of this, the thirtieth year, they were in a state of awful wickedness.

18 Now they did not sin ignorantly, for they knew the will of God concerning them, for it had been taught unto them; therefore they did wilfully rebel against God.

19 And now it was in the days of Lachoneus, the son of Lachoneus, for Lachoneus did fill the seat of his father and did govern the people that year.

## The Wicked Kill the Prophets and Set Up Secret Combinations to Destroy the People of God

20 And there began to be men inspired from heaven and sent forth, standing among the people in all the land, preaching and testifying boldly of the sins and iniquities of the people, and testifying unto them concerning the redemption which the Lord would make for his people, or in other words, the resurrection of Christ; and they did testify boldly of his death and sufferings.

---

6:12 The Book of Mormon warns us that one of the signs of pride is ranking people according to their wealth and education. President Ezra Taft Benson adds that "the record of the Nephite history just prior to the Savior's visit reveals many parallels to our own day as we anticipate the Savior's second coming. The Nephite civilization had reached great heights. They were prosperous and industrious. . . . But, as so often happens, the people rejected the Lord. Pride became commonplace" (in Conference Report, April 1987, 3).

***poverty***—lack of money

6:13 ***railing***—insulting language
***afflictions***—sufferings
***revile***—say unkind things
***penitent***—repentant

6:14 ***inequality***—unfairness
***steadfast***—determined
***diligence***—care and effort

6:15 ***iniquity***—wickedness
***vain***—empty or useless

6:16 (10–16) After quoting these verses, President N. Eldon Tanner noted that we "learn that among the causes of iniquity are pride, wealth, unrighteous dominion, class distinctions, selfishness, lusts for power, and the like. It is demonstrated to us that the righteous remain so by faith, by constant communication with God, by devotion to their leaders, by being humble and submissive to the mind and will of the Lord" ("The Inevitable Choice," 5).

6:17 ***commencement***—beginning

6:18 (17–18) The wickedness of the Nephites in this period was more serious because they knew the truth and still chose to sin. King Benjamin said that such people were in "open rebellion against God" (Mosiah 2:36–37).

6:19 ***fill the seat***—rule in the place

21 Now there were many of the people who were exceedingly angry because of those who testified of these things; and those who were angry were chiefly the chief judges, and they who had been high priests and lawyers; yea, all those who were lawyers were angry with those who testified of these things.
22 Now there was no lawyer nor judge nor high priest that could have power to condemn any one to death save their condemnation was signed by the governor of the land.
23 Now there were many of those who testified of the things pertaining to Christ who testified boldly, who were taken and put to death secretly by the judges, that the knowledge of their death came not unto the governor of the land until after their death.
24 Now behold, this was contrary to the laws of the land, that any man should be put to death except they had power from the governor of the land—
25 Therefore a complaint came up unto the land of Zarahemla, to the governor of the land, against these judges who had condemned the prophets of the Lord unto death, not according to the law.
26 Now it came to pass that they were taken and brought up before the judge, to be judged of the crime which they had done, according to the law which had been given by the people.
27 Now it came to pass that those judges had many friends and kindreds; and the remainder, yea, even almost all the lawyers and the high priests, did gather themselves together, and unite with the kindreds of those judges who were to be tried according to the law.
28 And they did enter into a covenant one with another, yea, even into that covenant which was given by them of old, which covenant was given and administered by the devil, to combine against all righteousness.
29 Therefore they did combine against the people of the Lord, and enter into a covenant to destroy them, and to deliver those who were guilty of murder from the grasp of justice, which was about to be administered according to the law.
30 And they did set at defiance the law and the rights of their country; and they did covenant one with another to destroy the governor, and to establish a king over the land, that the land should no more be at liberty but should be subject unto kings.

## CHAPTER 7

*The government is destroyed and the people divide into tribes. Nephi continues to preach with power among the people. Look for ways the Lord blesses His followers even though they are living in a time of great wickedness.*

### *The Government of Judges Is Destroyed and the People Divide into Tribes*

1 NOW behold, I will show unto you that they did not establish a king over the land; but in this same year, yea, the thirtieth year, they did destroy upon the judgment-seat, yea, did murder the chief judge of the land.
2 And the people were divided one against another; and they did separate one from another into tribes, every man according to his family and his kindred and friends; and thus they did destroy the government of the land.
3 And every tribe did appoint a chief or a leader over them; and thus they became tribes and leaders of tribes.
4 Now behold, there was no man among them save he had much family and many kindreds and friends; therefore their tribes became exceedingly great.

---

6:21 Why do people sometimes get angry when they are told they are doing wrong? How should you respond when your parents or Church leaders correct you?

6:24 ***contrary***—against

6:27 ***kindreds***—relatives
***unite***—join

6:28 For more information about this covenant "administered by the devil," see Glossary: Secret Combinations.

6:29 ***grasp***—hold

6:30 ***set at defiance***—challenge

7:1 ***establish***—set

7:2 ***kindred***—relatives

7:3 ***appoint***—choose

5 Now all this was done, and there were no wars as yet among them; and all this iniquity had come upon the people because they did yield themselves unto the power of Satan.

6 And the regulations of the government were destroyed, because of the secret combination of the friends and kindreds of those who murdered the prophets.

7 And they did cause a great contention in the land, insomuch that the more righteous part of the people had nearly all become wicked; yea, there were but few righteous men among them.

8 And thus six years had not passed away since the more part of the people had turned from their righteousness, like the dog to his vomit, or like the sow to her wallowing in the mire.

## The Secret Combinations Flee to the North As the Other Tribes Unite to Defend Themselves

9 Now this secret combination, which had brought so great iniquity upon the people, did gather themselves together, and did place at their head a man whom they did call Jacob;

10 And they did call him their king; therefore he became a king over this wicked band; and he was one of the chiefest who had given his voice against the prophets who testified of Jesus.

11 And it came to pass that they were not so strong in number as the tribes of the people, who were united together save it were their leaders did establish their laws, every one according to his tribe; nevertheless they were enemies; notwithstanding they were not a righteous people, yet they were united in the hatred of those who had entered into a covenant to destroy the government.

12 Therefore, Jacob seeing that their enemies were more numerous than they, he being the king of the band, therefore he commanded his people that they should take their flight into the northernmost part of the land, and there build up unto themselves a kingdom, until they were joined by dissenters, (for he flattered them that there would be many dissenters) and they become sufficiently strong to contend with the tribes of the people; and they did so.

13 And so speedy was their march that it could not be impeded until they had gone forth out of the reach of the people. And thus ended the thirtieth year; and thus were the affairs of the people of Nephi.

14 And it came to pass in the thirty and first year that they were divided into tribes, every man according to his family, kindred and friends; nevertheless they had come to an agreement that they would not go to war one with another; but they were not united as to their laws, and their manner of government, for they were established according to the minds of those who were their chiefs and their leaders. But they did establish very strict laws that one tribe should not trespass against another, insomuch that in some degree they had peace in the land; nevertheless, their hearts were turned from the Lord their God, and they did stone the prophets and did cast them out from among them.

---

7:5 ***yield themselves unto***—give in to

7:6 ***regulations***—rules

7:7 ***contention***—argument or fight

7:8 Notice that it had taken less than six years for the people to turn from a righteous and blessed people to a people whose wickedness destroyed their government (see 3 Nephi 6:4). Why do you think Mormon uses the examples of the dog and the pig in this verse to describe a group that had repented but then returned to its wicked ways?

7:10 ***band***—group of people
***chiefest***—most influential

When a person speaks against the Lord's servants, he is on very dangerous ground. President Brigham Young said, "One of the first steps to apostasy is to find fault with your Bishop; and when that is done, unless repented of a second step is soon taken, and by and by the person is cut off from the Church, and that is the end of it" (*Discourses of Brigham Young,* 86).

7:11 ***notwithstanding***—even though

7:12 ***take their flight***—run away
***dissenters***—people who were unhappy living in the tribes
***flattered them***—told them what they wanted to believe
***contend***—fight

7:13 ***impeded***—slowed down or prevented

7:14 ***manner***—kind
***trespass against***—harm
***degree***—small way
***stone***—throw rocks at to hurt or kill

## Nephi Preaches with Great Power and Many People Become Angry at Him

15 And it came to pass that Nephi—having been visited by angels and also the voice of the Lord, therefore having seen angels, and being eye-witness, and having had power given unto him that he might know concerning the ministry of Christ, and also being eye-witness to their quick return from righteousness unto their wickedness and abominations;
16 Therefore, being grieved for the hardness of their hearts and the blindness of their minds—went forth among them in that same year, and began to testify, boldly, repentance and remission of sins through faith on the Lord Jesus Christ.
17 And he did minister many things unto them; and all of them cannot be written, and a part of them would not suffice, therefore they are not written in this book. And Nephi did minister with power and with great authority.
18 And it came to pass that they were angry with him, even because he had greater power than they, for it were not possible that they could disbelieve his words, for so great was his faith on the Lord Jesus Christ that angels did minister unto him daily.
19 And in the name of Jesus did he cast out devils and unclean spirits; and even his brother did he raise from the dead, after he had been stoned and suffered death by the people.
20 And the people saw it, and did witness of it, and were angry with him because of his power; and he did also do many more miracles, in the sight of the people, in the name of Jesus.

## Many People Believe Nephi and Are Baptized

21 And it came to pass that the thirty and first year did pass away, and there were but few who were converted unto the Lord; but as many as were converted did truly signify unto the people that they had been visited by the power and Spirit of God, which was in Jesus Christ, in whom they believed.
22 And as many as had devils cast out from them, and were healed of their sicknesses and their infirmities, did truly manifest unto the people that they had been wrought upon by the Spirit of God, and had been healed; and they did show forth signs also and did do some miracles among the people.
23 Thus passed away the thirty and second year also. And Nephi did cry unto the people in the commencement of the thirty and third year; and he did preach unto them repentance and remission of sins.
24 Now I would have you to remember also, that there were none who were brought unto repentance who were not baptized with water.
25 Therefore, there were ordained of Nephi, men unto this ministry, that all such as should come unto them should be baptized with water, and this as a witness and a testimony before God, and unto the people, that they had repented and received a remission of their sins.

---

7:15 ***ministry***—life and teachings
***abominations***—great evils

7:16 ***grieved***—very sorry
***the hardness of their hearts***—their unwillingness to obey the commandments or feel the Spirit
***the blindness of their minds***—their unwillingness to understand things clearly
***remission***—forgiveness

7:17 ***minister***—teach
***suffice***—be enough

7:18 ***minister unto***—give aid or service to

7:19 Elder Bruce R. McConkie said, "By faith the dead are sometimes raised, meaning that the spirit is called back to inhabit again the mortal body. Such persons pass through the natural or temporal death twice" (*Mormon Doctrine,* 185–86).

7:20 ***witness of***—tell other people about

7:20 (18–20) There are few people in history with faith as great as Nephi's. Observe how his faith blessed his own life as well as the lives of those around him. How can your faith grow to be like the faith of this great prophet? (see Alma 32:21–42).

7:21 ***signify***—testify

7:22 ***infirmities***—weaknesses
***manifest***—show or testify
***wrought upon***—changed or blessed

7:23 ***cry***—speak loudly
***commencement***—beginning

7:25 ***ordained of***—given priesthood power by

7:25 (24–25) Jesus explained that a person must be baptized before he or she can enter the kingdom of heaven (see John 3:3–5). Before people can be baptized they must "humble themselves before God," be willing to "take upon them the name of Jesus Christ," and be determined to serve Him to the end (D&C 20:37).

26 And there were many in the commencement of this year that were baptized unto repentance; and thus the more part of the year did pass away.

## CHAPTER 8

*As this chapter begins it has been 34 years (A.D. 34) since the sign was given of the birth of Jesus Christ. The signs of Christ's crucifixion come just as Samuel the Lamanite said they would. Look for where the destruction is the worst and why.*

### *The People Begin to Doubt and Argue About the Signs of Christ's Crucifixion*

1 AND now it came to pass that according to our record, and we know our record to be true, for behold, it was a just man who did keep the record—for he truly did many miracles in the name of Jesus; and there was not any man who could do a miracle in the name of Jesus save he were cleansed every whit from his iniquity—

2 And now it came to pass, if there was no mistake made by this man in the reckoning of our time, the thirty and third year had passed away;

3 And the people began to look with great earnestness for the sign which had been given by the prophet Samuel, the Lamanite, yea, for the time that there should be darkness for the space of three days over the face of the land.

4 And there began to be great doubtings and disputations among the people, notwithstanding so many signs had been given.

### *A Great Storm Arises and There Is a Great Earthquake; Many Cities Are Destroyed*

5 And it came to pass in the thirty and fourth year, in the first month, on the fourth day of the month, there arose a great storm, such an one as never had been known in all the land.

6 And there was also a great and terrible tempest; and there was terrible thunder, insomuch that it did shake the whole earth as if it was about to divide asunder.

7 And there were exceedingly sharp lightnings, such as never had been known in all the land.

---

8:1 ***just***—righteous
***every whit***—completely

"Those, therefore, exercising the authority of the priesthood not only must do so in faith but in worthiness, having eliminated all the iniquity from their souls. Joseph Smith taught that 'the power, glory, and blessings of the priesthood could continue with those who received ordination only as their righteousness continued.' The priesthood, then, to be effective can only be exercised in righteousness and faith. Worthy men endowed with the Holy Priesthood, administering to those of faith, have power given them of God to heal the sick." (Delbert L. Stapley, *The Power of Faith*, Brigham Young University Speeches of the Year, 4 February 1958, 9; see also D&C 121:34–37).

8:2 ***reckoning***—counting

8:3 ***earnestness***—seriousness or intentness

8:4 ***disputations***—arguments
***notwithstanding***—even though

8:5 "The Lord uses the weather sometimes to discipline his people for the violation of his laws. . . . Perhaps the day has come when we should take stock of ourselves and see if we are worthy to ask or if we have been breaking the commandments, making ourselves unworthy of receiving the blessings" (Spencer W. Kimball, in Conference Report, April 1977, 4–5).

PHOTOGRAPH BY EDWIN M. WOOLLEY

*Volcanoes abound in Central America, making the land unstable with eruptions and frequent earthquakes.*

8:6 ***tempest***—violent windstorm
***divide asunder***—be broken in parts

8:7 These terrible destructions took place at the time Jesus Christ was crucified in Jerusalem. Why do you think Heavenly Father allowed these events to take place at this time? What does that teach you about Heavenly Father's love for His Son?

8 And the city of Zarahemla did take fire.

9 And the city of Moroni did sink into the depths of the sea, and the inhabitants thereof were drowned.

10 And the earth was carried up upon the city of Moronihah, that in the place of the city there became a great mountain.

11 And there was a great and terrible destruction in the land southward.

12 But behold, there was a more great and terrible destruction in the land northward; for behold, the whole face of the land was changed, because of the tempest and the whirlwinds, and the thunderings and the lightnings, and the exceedingly great quaking of the whole earth;

13 And the highways were broken up, and the level roads were spoiled, and many smooth places became rough.

14 And many great and notable cities were sunk, and many were burned, and many were shaken till the buildings thereof had fallen to the earth, and the inhabitants thereof were slain, and the places were left desolate.

15 And there were some cities which remained; but the damage thereof was exceedingly great, and there were many in them who were slain.

16 And there were some who were carried away in the whirlwind; and whither they went no man knoweth, save they know that they were carried away.

17 And thus the face of the whole earth became deformed, because of the tempests, and the thunderings, and the lightnings, and the quaking of the earth.

18 And behold, the rocks were rent in twain; they were broken up upon the face of the whole earth, insomuch that they were found in broken fragments, and in seams and in cracks, upon all the face of the land.

## For Three Days a Thick Darkness Covers the Land

19 And it came to pass that when the thunderings, and the lightnings, and the storm, and the tempest, and the quakings of the earth did cease—for behold, they did last for about the space of three hours; and it was said by some that the time was greater; nevertheless, all these great and terrible things were done in about the space of three hours—and then behold, there was darkness upon the face of the land.

20 And it came to pass that there was thick darkness upon all the face of the land, insomuch that the inhabitants thereof who had not fallen could feel the vapor of darkness;

21 And there could be no light, because of the darkness, neither candles, neither torches; neither could there be fire kindled with their fine and exceedingly dry wood, so that there could not be any light at all;

22 And there was not any light seen, neither fire, nor glimmer, neither the sun, nor the moon, nor the stars, for so great were the mists of darkness which were upon the face of the land.

---

8:12 (11–12) The destruction was more terrible in the land northward where the Nephites lived than it was in the south where the Lamanites lived. When Samuel the Lamanite prophesied of these destructions he warned the Nephites that it would be worse for them because they had become more wicked than the Lamanites (see Helaman 15:3–6).

8:14 ***notable***—important
***inhabitants thereof were slain***—people who lived there were killed

8:17 ***deformed***—changed

8:18 ***rent in twain***—torn in two

The breaking of the rocks into pieces was just as Samuel the Lamanite had predicted (see Helaman 14:21–22).

8:18 (12–18) "Since the earth has been in its present fallen or telestial state, it has been subject to earthquakes. These are part of the Lord's plan; they come by his power and fulfil his purposes. . . . Among the Nephites the quakings and destructions at the time of the crucifixion were so extensive that the whole face of the land was changed and the wicked and rebellious were destroyed. (3 Ne. 8; 9:1–14; 10:9–10.) Earthquakes are given as one of the signs of the times; they foreshadow the Second Coming. (Matt. 24:7; Mark 13:8; Luke 21:11; D. & C. 45:33; 87:6)" (Bruce R. McConkie, *Mormon Doctrine,* 211–12).

8:19 In Jerusalem there was also darkness for about three hours and an earthquake at the Crucifixion of Jesus (see Matthew 27:45, 51).

8:20 ***vapor***—thick fog or cloud

8:21 The thick darkness was just as Samuel the Lamanite prophesied (see Helaman 14:20). Contrast this thick darkness with the miraculous light that signified the Savior's birth (see 3 Nephi 1:15–19).

GOLGOTHA, BY SCOTT SNOW

*Great destruction took place on the American continent when Jesus Christ was crucified in Jerusalem.*

23 And it came to pass that it did last for the space of three days that there was no light seen; and there was great mourning and howling and weeping among all the people continually; yea, great were the groanings of the people, because of the darkness and the great destruction which had come upon them.
24 And in one place they were heard to cry, saying: O that we had repented before this great and terrible day, and then would our brethren have been spared, and they would not have been burned in that great city Zarahemla.
25 And in another place they were heard to cry and mourn, saying: O that we had repented before this great and terrible day, and had not killed and stoned the prophets, and cast them out; then would our mothers and our fair daughters, and our children have been spared, and not have been buried up in that great city Moronihah. And thus were the howlings of the people great and terrible.

## CHAPTER 9

*The terrible storms, earthquakes, and fires end. In the darkness the voice of the Lord tells of the cities that were destroyed. Watch for who is spared from destruction and who is not. Notice also what those who are saved still must do to be blessed by the Lord.*

### The Lord Destroys Nephite Cities and Their Inhabitants Because of Wickedness

1 AND it came to pass that there was a voice heard among all the inhabitants of the earth, upon all the face of this land, crying:
2 Wo, wo, wo unto this people; wo unto the inhabitants of the whole earth except they shall repent; for the devil laugheth, and his angels rejoice, because of the slain of the fair sons and daughters of my people; and it is because of their iniquity and abominations that they are fallen!
3 Behold, that great city Zarahemla have I burned with fire, and the inhabitants thereof.
4 And behold, that great city Moroni have I caused to be sunk in the depths of the sea, and the inhabitants thereof to be drowned.
5 And behold, that great city Moronihah have I covered with earth, and the inhabitants thereof, to hide their iniquities and their abominations from before my face, that the blood of the prophets and the saints shall not come any more unto me against them.
6 And behold, the city of Gilgal have I caused to be sunk, and the inhabitants thereof to be buried up in the depths of the earth;
7 Yea, and the city of Onihah and the inhabitants thereof, and the city of Mocum and the inhabitants thereof, and the city of Jerusalem and the inhabitants thereof; and waters have I caused to come up in the stead thereof, to hide their wickedness and abominations from before my face, that the blood of the prophets and the saints shall not come up any more unto me against them.
8 And behold, the city of Gadiandi, and the city of Gadiomnah, and the city of Jacob, and the city of Gimgimno, all these have I caused to be sunk, and made hills and valleys in the places thereof; and the inhabitants thereof have I buried up in the depths of the earth, to hide their wickedness and abominations from before my face, that the blood of the prophets and the saints should not come up any more unto me against them.

---

8:23 ***mourning***—sorrowing

8:25 ***stoned***—thrown rocks at
***howlings***—crying and sorrowing

The prophets have declared that in the last days, before the Second Coming of Jesus Christ, the people will again become very wicked. In that day, there will also be many natural disasters upon the face of the earth (see D&C 45:39–42). However, the Lord has promised to protect His faithful Saints (see D&C 109:22).

8:25 (24–25) Notice that after the destruction the people wish they had repented. Why do you think some people won't repent until something terrible happens? What are some changes you might want to make in your life before the Savior comes again?

9:1 ***inhabitants***—people

9:2 ***Wo***—Sorrow and suffering

9:3 The destruction of Zarahemla by fire was prophesied by Samuel the Lamanite in Helaman 13:13–14. What does that tell you about the ability of the Lord's prophets to see the future? What does that teach you about the warnings the Lord's prophet is giving us today?

9:5 ***abominations***—great evils

9:7 ***stead***—place

9 And behold, that great city Jacobugath, which was inhabited by the people of king Jacob, have I caused to be burned with fire because of their sins and their wickedness, which was above all the wickedness of the whole earth, because of their secret murders and combinations; for it was they that did destroy the peace of my people and the government of the land; therefore I did cause them to be burned, to destroy them from before my face, that the blood of the prophets and the saints should not come up unto me any more against them.
10 And behold, the city of Laman, and the city of Josh, and the city of Gad, and the city of Kishkumen, have I caused to be burned with fire, and the inhabitants thereof, because of their wickedness in casting out the prophets, and stoning those whom I did send to declare unto them concerning their wickedness and their abominations.
11 And because they did cast them all out, that there were none righteous among them, I did send down fire and destroy them, that their wickedness and abominations might be hid from before my face, that the blood of the prophets and the saints whom I sent among them might not cry unto me from the ground against them.
12 And many great destructions have I caused to come upon this land, and upon this people, because of their wickedness and their abominations.

## The Lord Pleads with Those Who Are Left to Repent and Be Healed

13 O all ye that are spared because ye were more righteous than they, will ye not now return unto me, and repent of your sins, and be converted, that I may heal you?
14 Yea, verily I say unto you, if ye will come unto me ye shall have eternal life. Behold, mine arm of mercy is extended towards you, and whosoever will come, him will I receive; and blessed are those who come unto me.
15 Behold, I am Jesus Christ the Son of God. I created the heavens and the earth, and all things that in them are. I was with the Father from the beginning. I am in the Father, and the Father in me; and in me hath the Father glorified his name.
16 I came unto my own, and my own received me not. And the scriptures concerning my coming are fulfilled.
17 And as many as have received me, to them have I given to become the sons of God; and even so will I to as many as shall believe on my name, for behold, by me redemption cometh, and in me is the law of Moses fulfilled.
18 I am the light and the life of the world. I am Alpha and Omega, the beginning and the end.

---

9:9 The Lord says that Jacobugath was the most wicked city because it was the center of secret combinations. The people involved in these secret combinations were once known as the Gadianton robbers. The story of their beginnings is found in Helaman 6:15–30.

9:13 The Lord asks the more righteous, who survived, to repent of their sins and be converted. What will He do for them if they repent?

9:14 The mission of the Church is to invite all people to come unto Christ that they may have eternal life. This is a consistent theme in the Book of Mormon. Among the last words written in the book is Moroni's plea for readers to "come unto Christ, and be perfected in him" (Moroni 10:32).

9:15 ***glorified***—given glory to

Under our Heavenly Father's direction, Jesus Christ created all of the worlds (see Moses 1:33).

9:18 The Greek alphabet begins with the letter *alpha* and ends with the letter *omega.* Jesus Christ is "the beginning and the end, the light and the life of the world" (D&C 45:7).

Can you imagine being in complete darkness for three days? How would this experience affect your understanding of Jesus' words when, in the midst of this darkness, He said, "I am the light and the life of the world"?

CHRIST IS THE CREATOR, BY ROBERT T. BARRETT

*"Behold, I am Jesus Christ the Son of God.*
*I created the heavens and the earth, and all things that in them are."*

19 And ye shall offer up unto me no more the
shedding of blood; yea, your sacrifices and your
burnt offerings shall be done away, for I will accept
none of your sacrifices and your burnt offerings.
20 And ye shall offer for a sacrifice unto me a broken heart and a contrite spirit. And whoso cometh
unto me with a broken heart and a contrite spirit,
him will I baptize with fire and with the Holy
Ghost, even as the Lamanites, because of their faith
in me at the time of their conversion, were baptized
with fire and with the Holy Ghost, and they knew
it not.
21 Behold, I have come unto the world to bring
redemption unto the world, to save the world from
sin.
22 Therefore, whoso repenteth and cometh unto
me as a little child, him will I receive, for of such is
the kingdom of God. Behold, for such I have laid
down my life, and have taken it up again; therefore
repent, and come unto me ye ends of the earth, and
be saved.

## CHAPTER 10

*After three days of darkness morning comes, and sorrow is replaced by joy and hope. Notice how even in our darkest hours the Lord still reaches out to us.*

### The Voice of Christ Breaks the Silence and He Promises to Gather His People

1 AND now behold, it came to pass that all the
people of the land did hear these sayings, and did
witness of it. And after these sayings there was
silence in the land for the space of many hours;
2 For so great was the astonishment of the people
that they did cease lamenting and howling for the
loss of their kindred which had been slain; therefore there was silence in all the land for the space
of many hours.
3 And it came to pass that there came a voice
again unto the people, and all the people did hear,
and did witness of it, saying:
4 O ye people of these great cities which have fall-
en, who are descendants of Jacob, yea, who are of
the house of Israel, how oft have I gathered you as
a hen gathereth her chickens under her wings, and
have nourished you.
5 And again, how oft would I have gathered you
as a hen gathereth her chickens under her wings,
yea, O ye people of the house of Israel, who have
fallen; yea, O ye people of the house of Israel, ye
that dwell at Jerusalem, as ye that have fallen; yea,
how oft would I have gathered you as a hen gathereth her chickens, and ye would not.

---

9:20 Before the time of Christ the Saints sacrificed animals to remind them of the Savior's coming sacrifice (see LDS Bible Dictionary, s.v. "Sacrifices," 765–66).

After the Savior gave His own life, He required His Saints to have "a broken heart and a contrite spirit," which means to be humble and willing to do whatever He asks.

9:21 Jesus Christ came into the world to save us from sin, "for all have sinned, and come short of the glory of God" (Romans 3:23).

9:22 Jesus said He laid His life down for those who come to Him as little children. How can your mother and father come to Jesus Christ as children? What is the difference between being "childlike" and being "childish"? How does repenting make even adults more childlike? (see Mosiah 3:19).

10:2 ***astonishment***—surprise
***cease lamenting and howling***—quit mourning and wailing
***kindred***—relatives

10:4 ***descendants***—children, grandchildren, and so on
***nourished***—cared for or fed

The name *Israel* means "one who prevails with God," or "let God prevail." It is used several ways in the scriptures. It may refer to (1) the man Jacob, whose name was changed to Israel; (2) the family, children, or tribes of Israel (the scriptures often use the phrase "house of Israel" in this sense); (3) the land of Israel; or (4) the true believers in Christ, no matter what their family or where they live (see LDS Bible Dictionary, s.v. "Israel," 708).

10:5 "The Savior has always been the protector of those who would accept His protection. . . . There seems to be no end to the Savior's desire to lead us to safety. And there is constancy in the way He shows us the path. He calls by more than one means so that His message will reach those willing to accept it. And those means always include sending the message by the mouths of His prophets whenever people have qualified to have the prophets of God among them. Those authorized servants are always charged with warning the people, telling them the way to safety" (Henry B. Eyring, in Conference Report, April 1997, 31–32).

6 O ye house of Israel whom I have spared, how
oft will I gather you as a hen gathereth her chickens under her wings, if ye will repent and return
unto me with full purpose of heart.
7 But if not, O house of Israel, the places of your
dwellings shall become desolate until the time of
the fulfilling of the covenant to your fathers.
8 And now it came to pass that after the people
had heard these words, behold, they began to weep
and howl again because of the loss of their kindred
and friends.

## The More Righteous People Are Saved from Destruction

9 And it came to pass that thus did the three days
pass away. And it was in the morning, and the darkness dispersed from off the face of the land, and the
earth did cease to tremble, and the rocks did cease
to rend, and the dreadful groanings did cease, and
all the tumultuous noises did pass away.
10 And the earth did cleave together again, that it
stood; and the mourning, and the weeping, and the
wailing of the people who were spared alive did
cease; and their mourning was turned into joy, and
their lamentations into the praise and thanksgiving
unto the Lord Jesus Christ, their Redeemer.
11 And thus far were the scriptures fulfilled which
had been spoken by the prophets.
12 And it was the more righteous part of the
people who were saved, and it was they who
received the prophets and stoned them not; and it
was they who had not shed the blood of the saints,
who were spared—
13 And they were spared and were not sunk and
buried up in the earth; and they were not drowned
in the depths of the sea; and they were not burned
by fire, neither were they fallen upon and crushed
to death; and they were not carried away in the
whirlwind; neither were they overpowered by the
vapor of smoke and of darkness.

## Mormon Explains That All These Destructions Were Prophesied

14 And now, whoso readeth, let him understand;
he that hath the scriptures, let him search them, and
see and behold if all these deaths and destructions
by fire, and by smoke, and by tempests, and by
whirlwinds, and by the opening of the earth to
receive them, and all these things are not unto the
fulfilling of the prophecies of many of the holy
prophets.
15 Behold, I say unto you, Yea, many have testified of these things at the coming of Christ, and
were slain because they testified of these things.
16 Yea, the prophet Zenos did testify of these
things, and also Zenock spake concerning these
things, because they testified particularly concerning us, who are the remnant of their seed.

---

10:6 ***spared***—allowed to live

10:7 ***dwellings shall become desolate***—homes shall be empty

10:9 ***dispersed***—disappeared
***rend***—break
***tumultuous***—loud and violent

10:10 ***cleave***—join
***mourning***—sorrowing
***wailing***—moaning or loud crying
***lamentations***—expressions of sorrow

President Howard W. Hunter testified that "Jesus is the only true source of lasting joy, that our only peace is in him. . . . May we be more devoted and disciplined followers of Christ. May we cherish him in our thoughts and speak his name with love. May we kneel before him with meekness and mercy" (*That We Might Have Joy,* 10).

10:10 (9–10) Just as Jesus took the physical darkness from the land, He can take the darkness out of our lives. Even though these people suffered great loss, what happened to their sorrow? Have there been difficult times in your life when Jesus has helped you? Have you, like the Nephites, remembered to praise and thank Him?

10:13 ***whirlwind***—tornado

10:13 (12–13) Nephi testified that "the righteous need not fear; for thus saith the prophet, they shall be saved" (1 Nephi 22:17).

10:14 ***tempests***—terrible storms

Quoting this verse, Elder L. Lionel Kendrick taught: "It is not enough to read the scriptures. Random reading results in reduced retention. We must search for specifics. We must seek for truth and increased understanding of its application in our lives" (in Conference Report, April 1993, 15).

17 Behold, our father Jacob also testified concerning a remnant of the seed of Joseph. And behold,
are not we a remnant of the seed of Joseph? And
these things which testify of us, are they not written
upon the plates of brass which our father Lehi
brought out of Jerusalem?
18 And it came to pass that in the ending of the
thirty and fourth year, behold, I will show unto you
that the people of Nephi who were spared, and also
those who had been called Lamanites, who had
been spared, did have great favors shown unto
them, and great blessings poured out upon their
heads, insomuch that soon after the ascension of
Christ into heaven he did truly manifest himself
unto them—
19 Showing his body unto them, and ministering
unto them; and an account of his ministry shall be
given hereafter. Therefore for this time I make an
end of my sayings.

*Jesus Christ did show himself unto the people of Nephi, as the multitude were gathered together in the land Bountiful, and did minister unto them; and on this wise did he show himself unto them. Comprising chapters 11 to 26 inclusive.**

## CHAPTER 11

*The Savior visits the Book of Mormon people and teaches them His doctrine. As you read this chapter, try to picture yourself as one of the people who saw and heard the Savior and imagine what a glorious experience that would be!*

### The Resurrected Christ Appears to the People at the Temple in Bountiful

1 AND now it came to pass that there were a great
multitude gathered together, of the people of
Nephi, round about the temple which was in the
land Bountiful; and they were marveling and won-
dering one with another, and were showing one to
another the great and marvelous change which had
taken place.
2 And they were also conversing about this Jesus
Christ, of whom the sign had been given concerning his death.
3 And it came to pass that while they were thus
conversing one with another, they heard a voice as
if it came out of heaven; and they cast their eyes
round about, for they understood not the voice
which they heard; and it was not a harsh voice, neither was it a loud voice; nevertheless, and notwithstanding it being a small voice it did pierce them
that did hear to the center, insomuch that there was
no part of their frame that it did not cause to quake;
yea, it did pierce them to the very soul, and did
cause their hearts to burn.
4 And it came to pass that again they heard the
voice, and they understood it not.
5 And again the third time they did hear the voice,
and did open their ears to hear it; and their eyes
were towards the sound thereof; and they did look
steadfastly towards heaven, from whence the sound
came.
6 And behold, the third time they did understand
the voice which they heard; and it said unto them:

---

10:17 ***remnant of the seed of Joseph***—part of the family of Joseph

10:18 ***manifest***—show

10:19 (18–19) How would seeing Jesus Christ be a reward for remaining faithful in difficult times?

* This introduction to chapters 11–26, excluding the last sentence, was translated from the Book of Mormon plates.

11:1 The Nephites were gathered at the temple in Bountiful prior to hearing the voice of the Lord. Why do you think they gathered there? What spiritual blessings bring families to temples today?

***marveling***—amazed

11:2 ***conversing***—talking

11:2 (1–2) You can read about the signs of Christ's death, foretold by Samuel the Lamanite, in Helaman 14:20–28.

11:3 ***a harsh***—an unpleasant
***frame***—body

The burning they felt in their hearts was the Holy Ghost testifying to them that what they were hearing was from God (see Luke 24:32; D&C 9:8).

11:5 ***steadfastly***—constantly

7 Behold my Beloved Son, in whom I am well
pleased, in whom I have glorified my name—hear
ye him.
8 And it came to pass, as they understood they cast
their eyes up again towards heaven; and behold,
they saw a Man descending out of heaven; and he
was clothed in a white robe; and he came down and
stood in the midst of them; and the eyes of the
whole multitude were turned upon him, and they
durst not open their mouths, even one to another,
and wist not what it meant, for they thought it was
an angel that had appeared unto them.
9 And it came to pass that he stretched forth his
hand and spake unto the people, saying:
10 Behold, I am Jesus Christ, whom the prophets
testified shall come into the world.
11 And behold, I am the light and the life of the
world; and I have drunk out of that bitter cup
which the Father hath given me, and have glorified
the Father in taking upon me the sins of the world,
in the which I have suffered the will of the Father
in all things from the beginning.
12 And it came to pass that when Jesus had spoken these words the whole multitude fell to the
earth; for they remembered that it had been prophesied among them that Christ should show himself
unto them after his ascension into heaven.
13 And it came to pass that the Lord spake unto
them saying:
14 Arise and come forth unto me, that ye may
thrust your hands into my side, and also that ye
may feel the prints of the nails in my hands and in
my feet, that ye may know that I am the God of
Israel, and the God of the whole earth, and have
been slain for the sins of the world.
15 And it came to pass that the multitude went
forth, and thrust their hands into his side, and did
feel the prints of the nails in his hands and in his
feet; and this they did do, going forth one by one
until they had all gone forth, and did see with their
eyes and did feel with their hands, and did know of
a surety and did bear record, that it was he, of
whom it was written by the prophets, that should
come.
16 And when they had all gone forth and had witnessed for themselves, they did cry out with one
accord, saying:
17 Hosanna! Blessed be the name of the Most
High God! And they did fall down at the feet of
Jesus, and did worship him.

### *Jesus Teaches the Nephite Disciples About Baptism*

18 And it came to pass that he spake unto
Nephi (for Nephi was among the multitude)
and he commanded him that he should come
forth.

---

11:7 On rare occasions Heavenly Father has appeared to introduce His Son (see Matthew 3:17; 17:5; Joseph Smith—History 1:17). "This introduction is unique in that it adds the phrase, 'in whom I have glorified my name.' No doubt this has reference to Christ's fulfillment of the atoning sacrifice that makes immortality and eternal life possible for mankind—which is the 'work and glory' of the Father (see Moses 1:39)" (Joseph Fielding McConkie and others, *Doctrinal Commentary on the Book of Mormon* 4:52).

11:7 (3–7) "The Spirit does not get our attention by shouting or shaking us with a heavy hand. Rather it whispers. It caresses so gently that if we are preoccupied we may not feel it at all" (Boyd K. Packer, "The Candle of the Lord," 53).

At first the Nephites didn't understand the voice of the Lord. What did they do that helped them understand His voice? What could you do to open your ears and eyes to the things the Lord wants to tell you?

11:8 ***durst***—dared
***wist***—knew

11:11 Jesus Christ is the source of all light, life, and truth (see D&C 88:6–13).

Notice that Jesus chose to introduce Himself as one who was obedient to the Father in all things. Why do you think obedience is so important to the Lord? What blessings might come to you if you were obedient to Heavenly Father in all things?

11:12 ***ascension***—rising

11:14 ***slain***—killed

11:16 ***with one accord***—all together

11:17 The word *Hosanna* means "Save, we pray" (*Smith's Bible Dictionary,* s.v. "Hosanna"). It is a word of praise to the Lord and a request for salvation.

11:17 (15–17) How did this sacred experience affect the people? If you had been a part of this group, how would you have felt to be so close to the Savior?

*"The multitude went forth, and thrust their hands into his side, and did feel the prints of the nails in his hands and in his feet."*

THAT YE MAY KNOW, BY GARY KAPP

19 And Nephi arose and went forth, and bowed
himself before the Lord and did kiss his feet.
20 And the Lord commanded him that he should
arise. And he arose and stood before him.
21 And the Lord said unto him: I give unto you
power that ye shall baptize this people when I am
again ascended into heaven.
22 And again the Lord called others, and said unto
them likewise; and he gave unto them power to baptize. And he said unto them: On this wise shall ye baptize; and there shall be no disputations among you.
23 Verily I say unto you, that whoso repenteth of
his sins through your words, and desireth to be
baptized in my name, on this wise shall ye baptize
them—Behold, ye shall go down and stand in the
water, and in my name shall ye baptize them.
24 And now behold, these are the words which ye
shall say, calling them by name, saying:

11:19 Elder Bruce R. McConkie taught: "I am one of his witnesses, and in a coming day I shall feel the nail marks in his hands and in his feet and shall wet his feet with my tears. But I shall not know any better then than I know now that he is God's Almighty Son, that he is our Savior and Redeemer, and that salvation comes in and through his atoning blood and in no other way" (in Conference Report, April 1985, 12).

11:22 ***On this wise***—In this way
***disputations***—arguments

25 Having authority given me of Jesus Christ, I
baptize you in the name of the Father, and of the
Son, and of the Holy Ghost. Amen.
26 And then shall ye immerse them in the water,
and come forth again out of the water.
27 And after this manner shall ye baptize in my
name; for behold, verily I say unto you, that the
Father, and the Son, and the Holy Ghost are one;
and I am in the Father, and the Father in me, and
the Father and I are one.
28 And according as I have commanded you thus
shall ye baptize. And there shall be no disputations
among you, as there have hitherto been; neither
shall there be disputations among you concerning
the points of my doctrine, as there have hitherto
been.
29 For verily, verily I say unto you, he that hath
the spirit of contention is not of me, but is of the
devil, who is the father of contention, and he stirreth up the hearts of men to contend with anger,
one with another.
30 Behold, this is not my doctrine, to stir up the
hearts of men with anger, one against another; but
this is my doctrine, that such things should be done
away.

## *Jesus Christ Declares His Doctrine*

31 Behold, verily, verily, I say unto you, I will
declare unto you my doctrine.
32 And this is my doctrine, and it is the doctrine
which the Father hath given unto me; and I bear
record of the Father, and the Father beareth record
of me, and the Holy Ghost beareth record of the
Father and me; and I bear record that the Father
commandeth all men, everywhere, to repent and
believe in me.
33 And whoso believeth in me, and is baptized,
the same shall be saved; and they are they who
shall inherit the kingdom of God.
34 And whoso believeth not in me, and is not
baptized, shall be damned.
35 Verily, verily, I say unto you, that this is my
doctrine, and I bear record of it from the Father;
and whoso believeth in me believeth in the Father
also; and unto him will the Father bear record of
me, for he will visit him with fire and with the Holy
Ghost.
36 And thus will the Father bear record of me, and
the Holy Ghost will bear record unto him of the
Father and me; for the Father, and I, and the Holy
Ghost are one.
37 And again I say unto you, ye must repent,
and become as a little child, and be baptized in
my name, or ye can in nowise receive these
things.
38 And again I say unto you, ye must repent, and
be baptized in my name, and become as a little
child, or ye can in nowise inherit the kingdom of
God.

---

11:26 ***immerse***—fully cover

11:27 Speaking on how the Father, Son, and Holy Ghost are one, Elder Bruce R. McConkie said: "Three glorious persons comprise the Godhead. . . . They are the Father, the Son, and the Holy Ghost. Each one possesses the same divine nature, knows all things, and has all power. Each one has the same character, the same perfections, and the same attributes. . . . Because of this perfect unity, they are spoken of as being one God" (*A New Witness for the Articles of Faith,* 58).

11:28 ***doctrine***—teachings

11:29 ***contention***—arguing or fighting

11:30 (29–30) "Contention is a tool of the adversary. Peace is a tool of our Savior. What a wonderful tribute we pay people when we describe them as being gentle, firm, and calm! Contention stops progress. Love brings eternal progression. Where contention prevails, there can be no united effort in any purposeful direction" (Marvin J. Ashton, *The Measure of Our Hearts,* 20).

11:32 ***record***—testimony

11:33 ***inherit the kingdom of God***—be allowed to live in heaven

11:34 ***damned***—shut out from the presence of the Lord

11:37 ***nowise***—no way

11:38 (37–38) Elder James E. Talmage said: "Christ would not have had His chosen representatives become childish; far from it, they had to be men of courage, fortitude, and force; but He would have them become childlike. The distinction is important. Those who belong to Christ must become like little children in obedience, truthfulness, trustfulness, purity, humility, and faith" (*Jesus the Christ,* 359; see also Mosiah 3:19).

39 Verily, verily, I say unto you, that this is my
doctrine, and whoso buildeth upon this buildeth
upon my rock, and the gates of hell shall not prevail against them.
40 And whoso shall declare more or less than this,
and establish it for my doctrine, the same cometh of
evil, and is not built upon my rock; but he buildeth
upon a sandy foundation, and the gates of hell
stand open to receive such when the floods come
and the winds beat upon them.
41 Therefore, go forth unto this people, and
declare the words which I have spoken, unto the
ends of the earth.

## CHAPTER 12

*Jesus begins teaching the Nephites by giving them a sermon similar to one called the "Sermon on the Mount" in the New Testament (compare 3 Nephi 12–14 with Matthew 5–7). There are several important differences in the Book of Mormon version that add to our understanding of the gospel. Watch for them as you read these chapters.*

### Jesus Teaches the Beatitudes

1 AND it came to pass that when Jesus had spoken these words unto Nephi, and to those who had
been called, (now the number of them who had
been called, and received power and authority to
baptize, was twelve) and behold, he stretched forth
his hand unto the multitude, and cried unto them,
saying: Blessed are ye if ye shall give heed unto the
words of these twelve whom I have chosen from
among you to minister unto you, and to be your
servants; and unto them I have given power that
they may baptize you with water; and after that ye
are baptized with water, behold, I will baptize you
with fire and with the Holy Ghost; therefore blessed
are ye if ye shall believe in me and be baptized,
after that ye have seen me and know that I am.
2 And again, more blessed are they who shall
believe in your words because that ye shall testify
that ye have seen me, and that ye know that I am.
Yea, blessed are they who shall believe in your
words, and come down into the depths of humility
and be baptized, for they shall be visited with fire
and with the Holy Ghost, and shall receive a remission of their sins.
3 Yea, blessed are the poor in spirit who come
unto me, for theirs is the kingdom of heaven.
4 And again, blessed are all they that mourn, for
they shall be comforted.
5 And blessed are the meek, for they shall inherit
the earth.
6 And blessed are all they who do hunger and
thirst after righteousness, for they shall be filled
with the Holy Ghost.
7 And blessed are the merciful, for they shall
obtain mercy.
8 And blessed are all the pure in heart, for they
shall see God.

---

11:39 Latter-day scriptures teach that there are at least three meanings for the term *hell*. It can describe our suffering here on earth (see Alma 36:18). It can refer to a part of the spirit world where those who have not repented suffer for their sins (see Alma 40:13–14). It is also used to describe the final condition of those who completely turn away from God (see D&C 29:38).

"His law require[s] all mankind, regardless of station in life, to repent and be baptized in His name and receive the Holy Ghost as the sanctifying power to cleanse themselves from sin. Compliance with these laws and ordinances will enable each individual to stand guiltless before Him at the day of judgment. Those who so comply are likened to one who builds his house on a firm foundation so that even 'the gates of hell shall not prevail against them' (3 Nephi 11:39)" (Ezra Taft Benson, in Conference Report, October 1983, 6).

12:1 ***cried***—spoke or called out
***give heed unto***—listen to and obey
***minister unto***—serve

12:2 ***remission***—forgiveness

12:2 (1–2) The Book of Mormon and the Joseph Smith Translation of the Bible show that most of this beautiful sermon is meant for those who are willing to follow Jesus Christ and His chosen servants and who strive to keep His commandments (see JST—Matthew 5:1–2).

12:3 ***poor in spirit***—humble

12:4 ***mourn***—sorrow or grieve

12:5 ***meek***—gentle and forgiving
***inherit***—receive

12:7 ***merciful***—kind and forgiving

12:8 We are promised that if we repent of our sins and overcome our weaknesses we will someday have the privilege of seeing God (see D&C 67:10; 93:1).

CHRIST ORDAINING THE TWELVE, BY GARY KAPP

*Jesus Christ called and ordained twelve Apostles in America, just as He had done in Israel.*

9 And blessed are all the peacemakers, for they
shall be called the children of God.
10 And blessed are all they who are persecuted
for my name's sake, for theirs is the kingdom of
heaven.
11 And blessed are ye when men shall revile you
and persecute, and shall say all manner of evil
against you falsely, for my sake;
12 For ye shall have great joy and be exceedingly
glad, for great shall be your reward in heaven; for
so persecuted they the prophets who were before
you.

---

12:10 **persecuted**—mistreated

12:11 **revile**—say bad things about

12:11 (1–11) The word *blessed* is used many times in these verses. President Harold B. Lee taught that "blessedness is defined as being higher than happiness. 'Happiness comes from without and is dependent on circumstances; blessedness is an inward fountain of joy in the soul itself, which no outward circumstances can seriously affect.' (Dummelow's Commentary)" (*Decisions For Successful Living*, 56–57).

12:12 (10–12) Those who try to live like the Savior will sometimes be made fun of or even hurt by others. What would Jesus want you to do if this happens to you?

## JESUS COMPARES THE LAW OF MOSES WITH THE GOSPEL

13 Verily, verily, I say unto you, I give unto you to be the salt of the earth; but if the salt shall lose its savor wherewith shall the earth be salted? The salt shall be thenceforth good for nothing, but to be cast out and to be trodden under foot of men.

14 Verily, verily, I say unto you, I give unto you to be the light of this people. A city that is set on a hill cannot be hid.

15 Behold, do men light a candle and put it under a bushel? Nay, but on a candlestick, and it giveth light to all that are in the house;

16 Therefore let your light so shine before this people, that they may see your good works and glorify your Father who is in heaven.

17 Think not that I am come to destroy the law or the prophets. I am not come to destroy but to fulfil;

18 For verily I say unto you, one jot nor one tittle hath not passed away from the law, but in me it hath all been fulfilled.

19 And behold, I have given you the law and the commandments of my Father, that ye shall believe in me, and that ye shall repent of your sins, and come unto me with a broken heart and a contrite spirit. Behold, ye have the commandments before you, and the law is fulfilled.

20 Therefore come unto me and be ye saved; for verily I say unto you, that except ye shall keep my commandments, which I have commanded you at this time, ye shall in no case enter into the kingdom of heaven.

21 Ye have heard that it hath been said by them of old time, and it is also written before you, that thou shalt not kill, and whosoever shall kill shall be in danger of the judgment of God;

22 But I say unto you, that whosoever is angry with his brother shall be in danger of his judgment. And whosoever shall say to his brother, Raca, shall be in danger of the council; and whosoever shall say, Thou fool, shall be in danger of hell fire.

23 Therefore, if ye shall come unto me, or shall desire to come unto me, and rememberest that thy brother hath aught against thee—

24 Go thy way unto thy brother, and first be reconciled to thy brother, and then come unto me with full purpose of heart, and I will receive you.

25 Agree with thine adversary quickly while thou art in the way with him, lest at any time he shall get thee, and thou shalt be cast into prison.

26 Verily, verily, I say unto thee, thou shalt by no means come out thence until thou hast paid the uttermost senine. And while ye are in prison can ye pay even one senine? Verily, verily, I say unto you, Nay.

---

12:13 ***savor***—flavor and strength
***trodden***—stepped on

" 'When men are called unto mine everlasting gospel, and covenant with an everlasting covenant, they are accounted as the salt of the earth and the savor of men; *They are called to be the savor of men*' (D&C 101:39–40; italics added). The word savor . . . denotes taste, pleasing flavor, interesting quality, and high repute" (Carlos E. Asay, in Conference Report, April 1980, 60).

12:15 ***bushel***—basket or bowl

12:16 (14–16) President Gordon B. Hinckley taught that "others seeing our good works can be led to glorify our Father in Heaven and emulate [copy] in their own lives the examples they have observed in ours" ("A City upon a Hill," 5).

12:17 "The law" in this verse refers to the law of Moses as found in the first five books of the Old Testament, which were written by Moses (see Glossary: Law of Moses). The term "the prophets" refers to the words of the prophets in the Old Testament.

12:18 Jots and tittles were very small marks used when writing words in ancient languages, such as Hebrew, similar to periods and commas in the English language. They are referred to here to show that every single part, even the very smallest part, of the law of Moses was fulfilled by the Atonement of Jesus Christ.

12:19 ***contrite***—humble and repentant

12:22 ***Raca***—Fool
***in danger of the council***—likely to be judged and punished

12:23 ***aught***—anything

12:24 ***be reconciled to***—become friends again with

12:25 ***adversary***—enemy

12:26 ***thence***—from there
***paid the uttermost senine***—paid all that the law requires

27 Behold, it is written by them of old time, that
thou shalt not commit adultery;
28 But I say unto you, that whosoever looketh on
a woman, to lust after her, hath committed adultery
already in his heart.
29 Behold, I give unto you a commandment, that ye
suffer none of these things to enter into your heart;
30 For it is better that ye should deny yourselves
of these things, wherein ye will take up your cross,
than that ye should be cast into hell.
31 It hath been written, that whosoever shall put
away his wife, let him give her a writing of divorcement.
32 Verily, verily, I say unto you, that whosoever
shall put away his wife, saving for the cause of fornication, causeth her to commit adultery; and whoso
shall marry her who is divorced committeth adultery.
33 And again it is written, thou shalt not forswear
thyself, but shalt perform unto the Lord thine oaths;
34 But verily, verily, I say unto you, swear not at
all; neither by heaven, for it is God's throne;
35 Nor by the earth, for it is his footstool;
36 Neither shalt thou swear by thy head, because
thou canst not make one hair black or white;
37 But let your communication be Yea, yea; Nay,
nay; for whatsoever cometh of more than these is evil.
38 And behold, it is written, an eye for an eye, and
a tooth for a tooth;
39 But I say unto you, that ye shall not resist evil,
but whosoever shall smite thee on thy right cheek,
turn to him the other also;
40 And if any man will sue thee at the law and
take away thy coat, let him have thy cloak also;
41 And whosoever shall compel thee to go a mile,
go with him twain.
42 Give to him that asketh thee, and from him that
would borrow of thee turn thou not away.
43 And behold it is written also, that thou shalt
love thy neighbor and hate thine enemy;
44 But behold I say unto you, love your enemies,
bless them that curse you, do good to them that
hate you, and pray for them who despitefully use
you and persecute you;
45 That ye may be the children of your Father
who is in heaven; for he maketh his sun to rise on
the evil and on the good.
46 Therefore those things which were of old time,
which were under the law, in me are all fulfilled.
47 Old things are done away, and all things have
become new.
48 Therefore I would that ye should be perfect
even as I, or your Father who is in heaven is perfect.

---

12:27 ***adultery***—use of the sacred creative powers with someone who is not your husband or wife

12:28 ***lust after her***—desire her in a sinful way

12:31 ***put away***—divorce

Elder Bruce R. McConkie explained, "In this day divorces are permitted in accordance with civil statues, and the divorced persons are permitted by the Church to marry again without the stain of immorality which under a higher system would attend such a course" (*Doctrinal New Testament Commentary* 1:547).

12:32 ***fornication***—use of the sacred creative powers between people who are not married

12:33 ***forswear thyself***—break your promise
***thine oaths***—your promises

12:34 ***swear not at all***—do not make promises in the name of someone or something that is honored

12:38 Under the law of Moses, if a wrong was done to someone, a punishment or price equal to the hurtful act was to be paid by the guilty person (see Leviticus 24:20).

12:39 ***smite***—hit

12:40 ***coat***—inner garment (like a shirt)
***cloak***—outer garment (like a robe)

12:41 ***compel***—make or force
***twain***—two

12:44 ***despitefully use***—abuse

12:46 The word *law* in this verse refers to the law of Moses (see Glossary: Law of Moses).

12:47 (21–47) Jesus asks His followers to live a higher law. He compares parts of the law of Moses with His higher law when He uses words like "ye have heard" and "it is written" in verses 21, 27, 31, 33, 38, and 43.

12:48 "In both His Old and New World ministries, the Savior commanded, 'Be ye therefore perfect.' A footnote explains that the Greek word translated as *perfect* means 'complete, finished, fully developed.' Our Heavenly Father wants us to use this mortal probation to 'fully develop' ourselves, to make the most of our talents and abilities" (Joseph B. Wirthlin, in Conference Report, April 1998, 15).

We can become perfect only with the help of Jesus Christ (see Moroni 10:32–33). What have you learned from this chapter that could help you be more perfect?

## CHAPTER 13

*Jesus continues teaching the Nephites about His gospel (see the introduction to 3 Nephi 13 and compare Matthew 6). Look for what Jesus teaches about doing the right things for the right reasons.*

### Jesus Teaches About Giving

1 VERILY, verily, I say that I would that ye should do alms unto the poor; but take heed that ye do not your alms before men to be seen of them; otherwise ye have no reward of your Father who is in heaven.

2 Therefore, when ye shall do your alms do not sound a trumpet before you, as will hypocrites do in the synagogues and in the streets, that they may have glory of men. Verily I say unto you, they have their reward.

3 But when thou doest alms let not thy left hand know what thy right hand doeth;

4 That thine alms may be in secret; and thy Father who seeth in secret, himself shall reward thee openly.

### Jesus Teaches About Prayer and Fasting

5 And when thou prayest thou shalt not do as the hypocrites, for they love to pray, standing in the synagogues and in the corners of the streets, that they may be seen of men. Verily I say unto you, they have their reward.

6 But thou, when thou prayest, enter into thy closet, and when thou hast shut thy door, pray to thy Father who is in secret; and thy Father, who seeth in secret, shall reward thee openly.

7 But when ye pray, use not vain repetitions, as the heathen, for they think that they shall be heard for their much speaking.

8 Be not ye therefore like unto them, for your Father knoweth what things ye have need of before ye ask him.

9 After this manner therefore pray ye: Our Father who art in heaven, hallowed be thy name.

10 Thy will be done on earth as it is in heaven.

11 And forgive us our debts, as we forgive our debtors.

12 And lead us not into temptation, but deliver us from evil.

13 For thine is the kingdom, and the power, and the glory, forever. Amen.

14 For, if ye forgive men their trespasses your heavenly Father will also forgive you;

15 But if ye forgive not men their trespasses neither will your Father forgive your trespasses.

16 Moreover, when ye fast be not as the hypocrites, of a sad countenance, for they disfigure their faces that they may appear unto men to fast. Verily I say unto you, they have their reward.

17 But thou, when thou fastest, anoint thy head, and wash thy face;

---

13:1 ***do alms***—give gifts or do kind deeds
***take heed***—be careful

13:2 ***sound a trumpet***—blow a horn
***hypocrites***—people who pretend to be good when they are not
***synagogues***—churches

13:4 (3–4) Would you rather be blessed by Heavenly Father for doing good secretly or be praised by men for doing good where everyone can see?

13:6 "The marvelous thing about prayer is that it is personal, it's individual. . . . Ask the Lord for all of the important things that mean so much to you in your lives. He stands ready to help. Don't ever forget it" (*Teachings of Gordon B. Hinckley,* 468).

13:7 ***use not vain repetitions***—do not say the same words over and over without any thought or feeling
***heathen***—people who do not believe in the true and living God

13:8 If Heavenly Father already knows what you need, why does He still want to hear from you in prayer?

13:9 ***hallowed***—sacred and holy

13:11 ***debts***—mistakes and sins
***our debtors***—those who sin against us

13:14 ***trespasses***—sins

13:15 (14–15) In modern revelation the Lord declared that those who refuse to forgive the sins of others are guilty of the greater sin (see D&C 64:9).

13:16 ***fast***—go without food or drink for spiritual reasons
***countenance***—appearance
***disfigure their faces***—make their faces look sad

13:17 ***anoint thy head***—put oil on your head for a healthy look

18 That thou appear not unto men to fast, but unto thy Father, who is in secret; and thy Father, who seeth in secret, shall reward thee openly.

## The Disciples of Christ Seek First the Kingdom of God

19 Lay not up for yourselves treasures upon earth, where moth and rust doth corrupt, and thieves break through and steal;

20 But lay up for yourselves treasures in heaven, where neither moth nor rust doth corrupt, and where thieves do not break through nor steal.

21 For where your treasure is, there will your heart be also.

22 The light of the body is the eye; if, therefore, thine eye be single, thy whole body shall be full of light.

23 But if thine eye be evil, thy whole body shall be full of darkness. If, therefore, the light that is in thee be darkness, how great is that darkness!

24 No man can serve two masters; for either he will hate the one and love the other, or else he will hold to the one and despise the other. Ye cannot serve God and Mammon.

## Jesus Gives Special Instructions to His Twelve Disciples

25 And now it came to pass that when Jesus had spoken these words he looked upon the twelve whom he had chosen, and said unto them: Remember the words which I have spoken. For behold, ye are they whom I have chosen to minister unto this people. Therefore I say unto you, take no thought for your life, what ye shall eat, or what ye shall drink; nor yet for your body, what ye shall put on. Is not the life more than meat, and the body than raiment?

26 Behold the fowls of the air, for they sow not, neither do they reap nor gather into barns; yet your heavenly Father feedeth them. Are ye not much better than they?

27 Which of you by taking thought can add one cubit unto his stature?

28 And why take ye thought for raiment? Consider the lilies of the field how they grow; they toil not, neither do they spin;

29 And yet I say unto you, that even Solomon, in all his glory, was not arrayed like one of these.

30 Wherefore, if God so clothe the grass of the

---

13:18 (16–18) Fasting, like prayer and good deeds, must be done with the desire to please the Lord. If you do these things to be praised by others, or with an unwilling heart, you cannot receive our Heavenly Father's full blessings (see Moroni 7:6).

13:19 ***corrupt***—ruin

13:21 (20–21) Our treasures are whatever we spend our time, money, and thoughts on. Which of your "treasures" can you take with you to heaven?

13:22 ***single***—focused

13:24 ***Mammon***—worldly riches

Elder Bruce R. McConkie said: "We cannot survive spiritually with one foot in the Church and the other in the world. We must make the choice. It is either the Church or the world. There is no middle ground" (in Conference Report, October 1974, 44; see also 2 Nephi 10:16; Alma 5:41).

13:25 ***minister unto***—serve
***meat***—food
***raiment***—clothes

13:26 ***sow***—plant
***reap***—harvest

PHOTOGRAPH BY DAVID H. GARNER

*Heavenly Father cares for all His creations and will certainly provide for us.*

13:27 ***one cubit***—about eighteen inches
***stature***—height

13:28 ***toil***—work

13:29 Solomon was a great and wealthy king of ancient Israel (see 1 Kings 10:4–7).

***arrayed like***—dressed as well as

field, which today is, and tomorrow is cast into the oven, even so will he clothe you, if ye are not of little faith.
31 Therefore take no thought, saying, What shall we eat? or, What shall we drink? or, Wherewithal shall we be clothed?
32 For your heavenly Father knoweth that ye have need of all these things.
33 But seek ye first the kingdom of God and his righteousness, and all these things shall be added unto you.
34 Take therefore no thought for the morrow, for the morrow shall take thought for the things of itself. Sufficient is the day unto the evil thereof.

## CHAPTER 14

*Jesus teaches the multitude how to make righteous choices. Notice the promises given to those who choose wisely.*

### *Judge Others the Way You Would Like God to Judge You*

1 AND now it came to pass that when Jesus had spoken these words he turned again to the multitude, and did open his mouth unto them again, saying: Verily, verily, I say unto you, Judge not, that ye be not judged.
2 For with what judgment ye judge, ye shall be judged; and with what measure ye mete, it shall be measured to you again.
3 And why beholdest thou the mote that is in thy brother's eye, but considerest not the beam that is in thine own eye?
4 Or how wilt thou say to thy brother: Let me pull the mote out of thine eye—and behold, a beam is in thine own eye?
5 Thou hypocrite, first cast the beam out of thine own eye; and then shalt thou see clearly to cast the mote out of thy brother's eye.
6 Give not that which is holy unto the dogs, neither cast ye your pearls before swine, lest they trample them under their feet, and turn again and rend you.

### *Jesus Teaches About Prayer and the Golden Rule*

7 Ask, and it shall be given unto you; seek, and ye shall find; knock, and it shall be opened unto you.
8 For every one that asketh, receiveth; and he that seeketh, findeth; and to him that knocketh, it shall be opened.
9 Or what man is there of you, who, if his son ask bread, will give him a stone?
10 Or if he ask a fish, will he give him a serpent?
11 If ye then, being evil, know how to give good gifts unto your children, how much more shall your Father who is in heaven give good things to them that ask him?

---

13:31 ***Wherewithal***—With what

13:34 ***Sufficient is the day unto the evil thereof***—There is enough trouble in one day

14:2 (1–2) The Lord has declared that if we are harsh and unforgiving in our judgment of others, He will not be merciful in His judgment of us (see D&C 1:10; 64:9–11).

14:3 ***considerest***—see

14:5 (3–5) A mote is a small speck or a splinter. A beam refers to a large rafter that supports the roof (see the LDS Edition of the King James Bible, Matthew 7:3, notes b and c).

14:6 The Joseph Smith Translation explains that the pearls represent the mysteries, or sacred truths, of the gospel. These truths should not be shared with people who are not spiritually prepared (see JST, Matthew 7:9–11).

***rend***—tear

14:11 (7–11) "Our Father in heaven is not an umpire who is trying to count us out. He is not a competitor who is trying to outsmart us. He is not a prosecutor who is trying to convict us. He is a loving Father who wants our happiness and eternal progress and who will help us all he can if we will but give him in our lives an opportunity to do so with obedience and humility, and faith and patience" (Richard L. Evans, as quoted in N. Eldon Tanner, "The Power of Prayer," in *Prayer,* 123).

12 Therefore, all things whatsoever ye would that men should do to you, do ye even so to them, for this is the law and the prophets.
13 Enter ye in at the strait gate; for wide is the gate, and broad is the way, which leadeth to destruction, and many there be who go in thereat;
14 Because strait is the gate, and narrow is the way, which leadeth unto life, and few there be that find it.

## True Prophets Are Known by Their Good Works

15 Beware of false prophets, who come to you in sheep's clothing, but inwardly they are ravening wolves.
16 Ye shall know them by their fruits. Do men gather grapes of thorns, or figs of thistles?
17 Even so every good tree bringeth forth good fruit; but a corrupt tree bringeth forth evil fruit.
18 A good tree cannot bring forth evil fruit, neither a corrupt tree bring forth good fruit.
19 Every tree that bringeth not forth good fruit is hewn down, and cast into the fire.
20 Wherefore, by their fruits ye shall know them.

## Jesus's Promise to Those Who Hear and Obey

21 Not every one that saith unto me, Lord, Lord, shall enter into the kingdom of heaven; but he that doeth the will of my Father who is in heaven.
22 Many will say to me in that day: Lord, Lord, have we not prophesied in thy name, and in thy name have cast out devils, and in thy name done many wonderful works?
23 And then will I profess unto them: I never knew you; depart from me, ye that work iniquity.
24 Therefore, whoso heareth these sayings of mine and doeth them, I will liken him unto a wise man, who built his house upon a rock—
25 And the rain descended, and the floods came, and the winds blew, and beat upon that house; and it fell not, for it was founded upon a rock.
26 And every one that heareth these sayings of mine and doeth them not shall be likened unto a foolish man, who built his house upon the sand—
27 And the rain descended, and the floods came, and the winds blew, and beat upon that house; and it fell, and great was the fall of it.

# CHAPTER 15

*Jesus explains what to do about the law of Moses and speaks of those who are His sheep. Look for why Jesus did not tell the people in Jerusalem about the Nephites.*

## Jesus Explains How the Law of Moses Is Fulfilled in Him

1 AND now it came to pass that when Jesus had ended these sayings he cast his eyes round about on the multitude, and said unto them: Behold, ye have heard the things which I taught before I ascended to my Father; therefore, whoso remembereth these

---

14:12 This is sometimes called the "Golden Rule." What changes have you noticed in others when you are nice to them?

"The law" in this verse refers to the law of Moses as found in the first five books of the Old Testament, which were written by Moses (see Glossary: Law of Moses). The term "the prophets" refers to the words of the prophets in the Old Testament.

14:13 ***strait***—narrow and difficult
***broad***—wide

14:15 ***in sheep's clothing***—appearing harmless
***ravening***—mean and hungry

14:17 ***corrupt***—rotten

14:19 ***hewn***—cut

14:20 The Lord gives us a great key to making good choices about others—"by their fruits [words and actions] ye shall know them." What kind of fruits would a person have who is a true follower of Jesus Christ?

14:21 Not everyone who calls Jesus "Lord" will be admitted into heaven; we must also do what He says. What are some of the commandments that you could do a better job of obeying?

14:25 Jesus Christ is the "rock" on whom we should build our house (see Helaman 5:12). Elder Russell M. Nelson testified that Jesus is "'the chief corner stone' upon which the organization of His church is based (Ephesians 2:20). We know Him to be the Rock from whom revelation comes to His authorized agents (see 1 Corinthians 10:4; Helaman 5:12) and to all who worthily seek Him (see D&C 88:63)" (in Conference Report, April 1990, 19).

***founded***—built

15:1 ***cast his eyes***—looked
***ascended***—went up

sayings of mine and doeth them, him will I raise up at the last day.
2 And it came to pass that when Jesus had said these words he perceived that there were some among them who marveled, and wondered what he would concerning the law of Moses; for they understood not the saying that old things had passed away, and that all things had become new.
3 And he said unto them: Marvel not that I said unto you that old things had passed away, and that all things had become new.
4 Behold, I say unto you that the law is fulfilled that was given unto Moses.
5 Behold, I am he that gave the law, and I am he who covenanted with my people Israel; therefore, the law in me is fulfilled, for I have come to fulfil the law; therefore it hath an end.
6 Behold, I do not destroy the prophets, for as many as have not been fulfilled in me, verily I say unto you, shall all be fulfilled.
7 And because I said unto you that old things have passed away, I do not destroy that which hath been spoken concerning things which are to come.
8 For behold, the covenant which I have made with my people is not all fulfilled; but the law which was given unto Moses hath an end in me.
9 Behold, I am the law, and the light. Look unto me, and endure to the end, and ye shall live; for unto him that endureth to the end will I give eternal life.
10 Behold, I have given unto you the commandments; therefore keep my commandments. And this is the law and the prophets, for they truly testified of me.

## The Nephites Are Some of the Other Sheep Jesus Promised to Visit

11 And now it came to pass that when Jesus had spoken these words, he said unto those twelve whom he had chosen:
12 Ye are my disciples; and ye are a light unto this people, who are a remnant of the house of Joseph.
13 And behold, this is the land of your inheritance; and the Father hath given it unto you.

---

15:1 Jesus promised that if we keep the commandments He gave in 3 Nephi 12–14 He will raise us up to be with Him at the last day. Think about what you learned in those chapters. Are you willing to do all those things for the privilege of living with Jesus again?

15:2 ***perceived***—understood
***marveled***—were amazed
***would concerning***—wanted to do about

15:5 Elder Joseph Fielding Smith taught: "All revelation since the fall has come through Jesus Christ, who is the Jehovah of the Old Testament. In all of the scriptures, where God is mentioned and where he has appeared, it was Jehovah [Jesus Christ] who talked with Abraham, with Noah, Enoch, Moses and all the prophets. He is the God of Israel, the Holy One of Israel" (*Doctrines of Salvation* 1:27).

15:8 The Lord has made other covenants with his people besides the law of Moses. For example, He made covenants with Enoch, Noah, and Abraham (see Moses 7:50–52; JST, Genesis 9:21–25; Abraham 2:9–11). The Lord will keep every covenant He has made with His children.

15:8 (4–8) The prophet Alma explained that all the sacrifices of the law of Moses were to teach the people of a future final sacrifice, "and that great and last sacrifice will be the Son of God" (Alma 34:14). After Jesus gave Himself as that final sacrifice, there would be "a stop to the shedding of blood; then shall the law of Moses be fulfilled" (Alma 34:13).

15:9 ***endure***—stay righteous

"As the great *Lawgiver,* He gave laws and commandments for the benefit of all our Heavenly Father's children. Indeed, His law fulfilled all previous covenants with the house of Israel. . . . His law required all mankind, regardless of station in life, to repent and be baptized in His name and receive the Holy Ghost as the sanctifying power to cleanse themselves from sin. Compliance with these laws and ordinances will enable each individual to stand guiltless before Him at the day of judgment" (Ezra Taft Benson, in Conference Report, October 1983, 6).

15:10 "The law" in this verse refers to the law of Moses as found in the first five books of the Old Testament, which were written by Moses (see Glossary: Law of Moses). The term "the prophets" refers to the words of the prophets in the Old Testament.

15:12 ***disciples***—followers
***remnant of the house***—part of the family

When he read the plates of brass Lehi learned he was of the family of Joseph, who was sold into Egypt (see 1 Nephi 5:14).

15:13 ***land of your inheritance***—land promised to you

14 And not at any time hath the Father given me
commandment that I should tell it unto your
brethren at Jerusalem.
15 Neither at any time hath the Father given me
commandment that I should tell unto them concerning the other tribes of the house of Israel,
whom the Father hath led away out of the land.
16 This much did the Father command me, that I
should tell unto them:
17 That other sheep I have which are not of this
fold; them also I must bring, and they shall hear my
voice; and there shall be one fold, and one shepherd.
18 And now, because of stiffneckedness and
unbelief they understood not my word; therefore I
was commanded to say no more of the Father concerning this thing unto them.
19 But, verily, I say unto you that the Father hath
commanded me, and I tell it unto you, that ye were
separated from among them because of their iniquity; therefore it is because of their iniquity that
they know not of you.
20 And verily, I say unto you again that the other
tribes hath the Father separated from them; and it is
because of their iniquity that they know not of
them.
21 And verily I say unto you, that ye are they of
whom I said: Other sheep I have which are not of
this fold; them also I must bring, and they shall hear
my voice; and there shall be one fold, and one
shepherd.
22 And they understood me not, for they supposed
it had been the Gentiles; for they understood not
that the Gentiles should be converted through their
preaching.
23 And they understood me not that I said they
shall hear my voice; and they understood me not
that the Gentiles should not at any time hear my
voice—that I should not manifest myself unto them
save it were by the Holy Ghost.
24 But behold, ye have both heard my voice, and
seen me; and ye are my sheep, and ye are numbered among those whom the Father hath given
me.

## CHAPTER 16

*Jesus is the Good Shepherd for all of Heavenly Father's children. In addition to the Jews in Palestine and the Nephites in the Americas, Jesus promises to visit other lost sheep of the house of Israel. Notice how the gospel, in the latter days, will go to the Gentiles and from them to all the house of Israel.*

### *Jesus Christ Speaks of Other People He Will Visit*

1 AND verily, verily, I say unto you that I have
other sheep, which are not of this land, neither of
the land of Jerusalem, neither in any parts of that
land round about whither I have been to minister.
2 For they of whom I speak are they who have
not as yet heard my voice; neither have I at any
time manifested myself unto them.

---

15:17 ***fold***—flock

15:18 ***stiffneckedness***—stubbornness

15:20 ***tribes***—groups of people or families

15:22 ***be converted***—become believers

*Gentiles* is a word that means "nations." It refers to those not of the family of Israel or who do not believe in the God of Israel. In the Book of Mormon it also refers to those who come from Gentile nations, which are all nations outside the land of Israel (see LDS Bible Dictionary, s.v. "Gentile," 679).

15:23 ***manifest***—show

15:24 These faithful people knew the Lord and were numbered as His sheep. How would it make you feel to be counted as one of Jesus' sheep? What do you need to do to make that possible?

15:24 (17–24) Jesus explained to the Jews in Israel that He had other sheep (followers) besides them, but the Jews did not understand what He meant (see John 10:11–16). They did not understand that to be Jesus' "sheep" they must hear His voice and follow Him (see John 10:27). Some of the ways we learn to hear the Savior's voice are in prayer, through reading the scriptures (see D&C 18:34–36), and by listening to His prophets (see D&C 1:38).

16:1 ***whither***—where

16:2 ***manifested***—shown

THE LOST LAMB, BY DEL PARSON

*"There shall be one fold, and one shepherd."*

3 But I have received a commandment of the
Father that I shall go unto them, and that they shall
hear my voice, and shall be numbered among my
sheep, that there may be one fold and one shepherd; therefore I go to show myself unto them.

## *In the Latter Days, the Gospel Shall Go First to the Gentiles and Then to the Children of Israel*

4 And I command you that ye shall write these
sayings after I am gone, that if it so be that my
people at Jerusalem, they who have seen me and
been with me in my ministry, do not ask the Father
in my name, that they may receive a knowledge of
you by the Holy Ghost, and also of the other tribes
whom they know not of, that these sayings which
ye shall write shall be kept and shall be manifested unto the Gentiles, that through the fulness
of the Gentiles, the remnant of their seed, who
shall be scattered forth upon the face of the earth
because of their unbelief, may be brought in, or
may be brought to a knowledge of me, their
Redeemer.
5 And then will I gather them in from the four
quarters of the earth; and then will I fulfil the
covenant which the Father hath made unto all the
people of the house of Israel.
6 And blessed are the Gentiles, because of their
belief in me, in and of the Holy Ghost, which witnesses unto them of me and of the Father.
7 Behold, because of their belief in me, saith the
Father, and because of the unbelief of you, O house
of Israel, in the latter day shall the truth come unto
the Gentiles, that the fulness of these things shall be
made known unto them.
8 But wo, saith the Father, unto the unbelieving of
the Gentiles—for notwithstanding they have come
forth upon the face of this land, and have scattered
my people who are of the house of Israel; and my
people who are of the house of Israel have been
cast out from among them, and have been trodden
under feet by them;
9 And because of the mercies of the Father unto
the Gentiles, and also the judgments of the Father
upon my people who are of the house of Israel,
verily, verily, I say unto you, that after all this, and
I have caused my people who are of the house of
Israel to be smitten, and to be afflicted, and to be
slain, and to be cast out from among them, and to
become hated by them, and to become a hiss and
a byword among them—

16:3 ***fold***—flock

"Leaving his Nephite kinsmen, our Lord, risen and glorified, went to minister unto the lost tribes of Israel. (3 Ne. 16:1–5; 17:4.) Where he went and what he did we do not know. Did he visit one group or many? Did twenty-five hundred or thirty thousand more Israelites see his face? Someday we shall know. As of now we know in principle that these other Israelites were prepared and worthy, as all men must be who stand in the divine presence" (Bruce R. McConkie, *The Promised Messiah,* 610).

16:3 (1–3) The Lord told His disciples in the land of Jerusalem that He had "other sheep" to visit (see John 10:16). In 3 Nephi 15:21, Jesus explained that the Book of Mormon people were the "other sheep" He was talking about. Jesus explains here that there are still "other sheep," besides the Nephites, that He must visit.

16:4 ***remnant of their seed***—descendants of their children

16:5 President Ezra Taft Benson asked: "Now, what is the instrument that God has designed for this gathering? It is the same instrument that is designed to convince the world that Jesus is the Christ, that Joseph Smith is His prophet, and that The Church of Jesus Christ of Latter-day Saints is true. . . . It is the Book of Mormon" (in Conference Report, April 1987, 107–8).

16:6 One of the primary purposes of the Holy Ghost is to bear witness of the "Father and the Son" (see D&C 42:17).

16:8 ***wo***—sorrow and misery
***notwithstanding***—even though
***trodden***—stomped

16:9 ***mercies***—love and kindness
***a hiss and a byword***—jeered and taunted

10 And thus commandeth the Father that I should
say unto you: At that day when the Gentiles shall
sin against my gospel, and shall reject the fulness of
my gospel, and shall be lifted up in the pride of
their hearts above all nations, and above all the
people of the whole earth, and shall be filled with
all manner of lyings, and of deceits, and of mis-
chiefs, and all manner of hypocrisy, and murders,
and priestcrafts, and whoredoms, and of secret
abominations; and if they shall do all those things,
and shall reject the fulness of my gospel, behold,
saith the Father, I will bring the fulness of my
gospel from among them.
11 And then will I remember my covenant which
I have made unto my people, O house of Israel,
and I will bring my gospel unto them.
12 And I will show unto thee, O house of Israel,
that the Gentiles shall not have power over you; but
I will remember my covenant unto you, O house of
Israel, and ye shall come unto the knowledge of the
fulness of my gospel.
13 But if the Gentiles will repent and return unto
me, saith the Father, behold they shall be numbered
among my people, O house of Israel.
14 And I will not suffer my people, who are of the
house of Israel, to go through among them, and
tread them down, saith the Father.
15 But if they will not turn unto me, and hearken
unto my voice, I will suffer them, yea, I will suffer
my people, O house of Israel, that they shall go
through among them, and shall tread them down,
and they shall be as salt that hath lost its savor,
which is thenceforth good for nothing but to be cast
out, and to be trodden under foot of my people, O
house of Israel.
16 Verily, verily, I say unto you, thus hath the
Father commanded me—that I should give unto
this people this land for their inheritance.
17 And then the words of the prophet Isaiah shall
be fulfilled, which say:
18 Thy watchmen shall lift up the voice; with the
voice together shall they sing, for they shall see eye
to eye when the Lord shall bring again Zion.
19 Break forth into joy, sing together, ye waste
places of Jerusalem; for the Lord hath comforted his
people, he hath redeemed Jerusalem.
20 The Lord hath made bare his holy arm in the
eyes of all the nations; and all the ends of the earth
shall see the salvation of God.

## CHAPTER 17

*It is near the end of Jesus' first day with the righteous people gathered at the temple in Bountiful. Notice how these people treat Jesus compared to how He was treated in His mortal ministry. Watch for the wonderful miracles and blessings that the Lord is able to do for them because of their faith in Him.*

---

16:10 ***deceits***—tricks and lies
***hypocrisy***—pretending to be good when they actually are not
***whoredoms***—wickedness and immorality

Priestcrafts are when men teach their own ideas for money and praise and do not care about God or His people (see 2 Nephi 26:29).

16:13 If the Gentiles will repent and come unto Christ they will be accepted by God just as if they were of the house of Israel (see 2 Nephi 26:33).

16:14 ***suffer***—allow
***tread them down***—destroy them

16:16 ***inheritance***—special place to live

16:18 A watchman is a man who stands on a tower and warns others when danger comes. "The Church is led by a prophet of God, who, as chief watchman on the towers of Zion, has the courage and inspiration to speak out against current evils" (Ezra Taft Benson, in Conference Report, October 1968, 17).

The term *Zion* is used several ways in the scriptures. Zion is defined as "the pure in heart" (D&C 97:21). Sometimes Zion has reference to a geographical location. Enoch's city was called Zion (see Moses 7:18–19). Jackson County, Missouri, is also referred to as Zion (see D&C 58:49–50), and the city of New Jerusalem, which is to be built in Jackson County, will be called Zion (see D&C 45:66-67). Joseph Smith referred to Zion, in a broader sense, as all of North and South America (see *History of the Church* 6:318–19; see also LDS Bible Dictionary, s.v. "Zion," 792–93).

16:20 ***made bare his holy arm***—shown His power

At the Second Coming the whole world will see Jesus Christ come in His power and glory. What makes you excited about the Second Coming?

CHRIST HEALING THE SICK, BY GARY KAPP

*"Have ye any that are lame, or blind, or halt, or maimed, or leprous, or that are withered, or that are deaf, or that are afflicted in any manner? Bring them hither and I will heal them."*

## Jesus Commands the People to Go to Their Homes and Prepare for Tomorrow

1 BEHOLD, now it came to pass that when Jesus had spoken these words he looked round about again on the multitude, and he said unto them: Behold, my time is at hand.
2 I perceive that ye are weak, that ye cannot understand all my words which I am commanded of the Father to speak unto you at this time.
3 Therefore, go ye unto your homes, and ponder upon the things which I have said, and ask of the Father, in my name, that ye may understand, and prepare your minds for the morrow, and I come unto you again.

---

17:1 When Jesus said, "My time is at hand," He was telling the people that it was time for Him to leave (see 3 Nephi 17:4).

17:2 ***perceive***—see or understand

17:3 To ponder is to think seriously about something. Elder Gene R. Cook taught: "When it comes to prayer and revelation, our minds need to be active and engaged if we hope to receive answers from the Lord. If we simply wait passively for something to come into our empty minds, we'll wait a long time. . . . Pondering and studying things out in our minds is part of that process" (*Receiving Answers to Our Prayers,* 38).

4 But now I go unto the Father, and also to show myself unto the lost tribes of Israel, for they are not lost unto the Father, for he knoweth whither he hath taken them.

## Jesus Heals All the Sick and Afflicted

5 And it came to pass that when Jesus had thus spoken, he cast his eyes round about again on the multitude, and beheld they were in tears, and did look steadfastly upon him as if they would ask him to tarry a little longer with them.

6 And he said unto them: Behold, my bowels are filled with compassion towards you.

7 Have ye any that are sick among you? Bring them hither. Have ye any that are lame, or blind, or halt, or maimed, or leprous, or that are withered, or that are deaf, or that are afflicted in any manner? Bring them hither and I will heal them, for I have compassion upon you; my bowels are filled with mercy.

8 For I perceive that ye desire that I should show unto you what I have done unto your brethren at Jerusalem, for I see that your faith is sufficient that I should heal you.

9 And it came to pass that when he had thus spoken, all the multitude, with one accord, did go forth with their sick and their afflicted, and their lame, and with their blind, and with their dumb, and with all them that were afflicted in any manner; and he did heal them every one as they were brought forth unto him.

10 And they did all, both they who had been healed and they who were whole, bow down at his feet, and did worship him; and as many as could come for the multitude did kiss his feet, insomuch that they did bathe his feet with their tears.

## Jesus Prays and Blesses the Little Children

11 And it came to pass that he commanded that their little children should be brought.

12 So they brought their little children and set them down upon the ground round about him, and Jesus stood in the midst; and the multitude gave way till they had all been brought unto him.

13 And it came to pass that when they had all been brought, and Jesus stood in the midst, he commanded the multitude that they should kneel down upon the ground.

14 And it came to pass that when they had knelt upon the ground, Jesus groaned within himself, and said: Father, I am troubled because of the wickedness of the people of the house of Israel.

15 And when he had said these words, he himself also knelt upon the earth; and behold he prayed unto the Father, and the things which he prayed cannot be written, and the multitude did bear record who heard him.

16 And after this manner do they bear record: The eye hath never seen, neither hath the ear heard, before, so great and marvelous things as we saw and heard Jesus speak unto the Father;

17 And no tongue can speak, neither can there be written by any man, neither can the hearts of men conceive so great and marvelous things as we both saw and heard Jesus speak; and no one can conceive of the joy which filled our souls at the time we heard him pray for us unto the Father.

18 And it came to pass that when Jesus had made an end of praying unto the Father, he arose; but so great was the joy of the multitude that they were overcome.

---

17:4 The "lost tribes of Israel" are the ten tribes of Israel who, because of wickedness, were "led away" and "scattered" (1 Nephi 22:4; see also LDS Bible Dictionary, s.v. "Israel, Kingdom of," 708).

***whither***—where

17:5 ***steadfastly***—steadily or constantly
***tarry***—stay

17:6 ***bowels***—emotions or heart

17:9 ***with one accord***—all together
***their dumb***—those unable to speak

17:9 (5–9) Because of the faith of the people, Jesus heals all their sick. The words *lame, halt, maimed,* and *withered* mean those whose bodies are injured or deformed. A person who is *leprous* suffers from a serious skin disease. Nephi saw this day of miracles in vision and said, "The Son of righteousness shall appear unto them; and he shall heal them" (2 Nephi 26:9).

17:14 ***groaned***—sighed or moaned

17:15 ***bear record***—testify

17:17 ***conceive***—understand

17:18 ***overcome***—physically weak because of the power of the Spirit

BEHOLD YOUR LITTLE ONES, BY DEL PARSON

*"He took their little children, one by one, and blessed them."*

19 And it came to pass that Jesus spake unto them, and bade them arise.

20 And they arose from the earth, and he said unto them: Blessed are ye because of your faith. And now behold, my joy is full.

21 And when he had said these words, he wept, and the multitude bare record of it, and he took their little children, one by one, and blessed them, and prayed unto the Father for them.

22 And when he had done this he wept again;

23 And he spake unto the multitude, and said unto them: Behold your little ones.

24 And as they looked to behold they cast their eyes towards heaven, and they saw the heavens open, and they saw angels descending out of heaven as it were in the midst of fire; and they came down and encircled those little ones about, and they were encircled about with fire; and the angels did minister unto them.

25 And the multitude did see and hear and bear record; and they know that their record is true for they all of them did see and hear, every man for himself; and they were in number about two thousand and five hundred souls; and they did consist of men, women, and children.

## CHAPTER 18

*Jesus teaches the people about the sacrament and prayer. Look for how Jesus also sets an example for them to follow.*

### *Jesus Begins the Sacrament Among the Nephites*

1 AND it came to pass that Jesus commanded his disciples that they should bring forth some bread and wine unto him.

2 And while they were gone for bread and wine, he commanded the multitude that they should sit themselves down upon the earth.

3 And when the disciples had come with bread and wine, he took of the bread and brake and blessed it; and he gave unto the disciples and commanded that they should eat.

4 And when they had eaten and were filled, he commanded that they should give unto the multitude.

5 And when the multitude had eaten and were filled, he said unto the disciples: Behold there shall one be ordained among you, and to him will I give power that he shall break bread and bless it and give it unto the people of my church, unto all those who shall believe and be baptized in my name.

6 And this shall ye always observe to do, even as I have done, even as I have broken bread and blessed it and given it unto you.

7 And this shall ye do in remembrance of my body, which I have shown unto you. And it shall be a testimony unto the Father that ye do always remember me. And if ye do always remember me ye shall have my Spirit to be with you.

8 And it came to pass that when he said these words, he commanded his disciples that they should take of the wine of the cup and drink of it, and that they should also give unto the multitude that they might drink of it.

9 And it came to pass that they did so, and did drink of it and were filled; and they gave unto the multitude, and they did drink, and they were filled.

10 And when the disciples had done this, Jesus said unto them: Blessed are ye for this thing which ye have done, for this is fulfilling my commandments, and this doth witness unto the Father that ye are willing to do that which I have commanded you.

---

17:19 ***bade them arise***—asked them to stand

17:24 ***encircled***—surrounded
***minister unto***—bless and comfort

17:24 (21–24) "Jesus loves and blesses children. They are the companions of angels. They shall be saved. Of such is the kingdom of heaven" (Bruce R. McConkie, "The Salvation of Little Children," 3). What is it about little children that brings Jesus so much joy?

17:25 ***consist of***—include

18:2 ***multitude***—many people

18:5 ***ordained***—given authority

18:6 ***observe to do***—follow

18:9 "Let us qualify ourselves for our Savior's promise that by partaking of the sacrament we will 'be filled' (3 Ne. 20:8; see also 3 Ne. 18:9), which means that we will be 'filled with the Spirit' (3 Ne. 20:9). That Spirit—the Holy Ghost—is our comforter, our direction finder, our communicator, our interpreter, our witness, and our purifier—our infallible guide and sanctifier for our mortal journey toward eternal life" (Dallin H. Oaks, in Conference Report, October 1996, 82).

THAT YE DO ALWAYS REMEMBER ME, BY GARY KAPP

*Jesus institutes the sacrament among His disciples in America.*

11 And this shall ye always do to those who
repent and are baptized in my name; and ye shall
do it in remembrance of my blood, which I have
shed for you, that ye may witness unto the Father
that ye do always remember me. And if ye do
always remember me ye shall have my Spirit to be
with you.
12 And I give unto you a commandment that ye
shall do these things. And if ye shall always do these
things blessed are ye, for ye are built upon my rock.
13 But whoso among you shall do more or less
than these are not built upon my rock, but are built
upon a sandy foundation; and when the rain
descends, and the floods come, and the winds
blow, and beat upon them, they shall fall, and the
gates of hell are ready open to receive them.

---

18:11 (7–11) "When we partake of the sacrament, we witness unto God the Eternal Father that we 'do always remember' his Son (D&C 20:77, 79; 3 Ne. 18:7, 11). Each Sabbath day millions of Latter-day Saints make this promise. What does it mean to 'always remember' our Savior? To remember means to keep in memory. In the scriptures, it often means to keep a person in memory, together with associated emotions like love, loyalty, or gratitude" (Dallin H. Oaks, in Conference Report, April 1988, 33).

We take the sacrament to remember Jesus Christ's sacrifice for us. Whenever we remember Him, He promises that His Spirit will be with us. How can you remember Jesus more often in your life?

18:13 ***foundation***—groundwork or support
***descends***—falls

14 Therefore blessed are ye if ye shall keep my
commandments, which the Father hath commanded me that I should give unto you.

## Jesus Teaches the Multitude to Pray

15 Verily, verily, I say unto you, ye must watch
and pray always, lest ye be tempted by the devil,
and ye be led away captive by him.
16 And as I have prayed among you even so shall
ye pray in my church, among my people who do
repent and are baptized in my name. Behold I am
the light; I have set an example for you.
17 And it came to pass that when Jesus had spoken these words unto his disciples, he turned again
unto the multitude and said unto them:
18 Behold, verily, verily, I say unto you, ye must
watch and pray always lest ye enter into temptation;
for Satan desireth to have you, that he may sift you
as wheat.
19 Therefore ye must always pray unto the Father
in my name;
20 And whatsoever ye shall ask the Father in my
name, which is right, believing that ye shall receive,
behold it shall be given unto you.
21 Pray in your families unto the Father, always in
my name, that your wives and your children may
be blessed.
22 And behold, ye shall meet together oft; and
ye shall not forbid any man from coming unto
you when ye shall meet together, but suffer them
that they may come unto you and forbid them
not;
23 But ye shall pray for them, and shall not cast
them out; and if it so be that they come unto you oft
ye shall pray for them unto the Father, in my name.
24 Therefore, hold up your light that it may shine
unto the world. Behold I am the light which ye shall
hold up—that which ye have seen me do. Behold
ye see that I have prayed unto the Father, and ye all
have witnessed.
25 And ye see that I have commanded that none
of you should go away, but rather have commanded that ye should come unto me, that ye
might feel and see; even so shall ye do unto the
world; and whosoever breaketh this commandment
suffereth himself to be led into temptation.

## Jesus Gives Commandments to the Disciples

26 And now it came to pass that when Jesus had
spoken these words, he turned his eyes again upon
the disciples whom he had chosen, and said unto
them:

---

18:15 ***captive***—prisoner

18:18 ***sift you***—pick you out

President Ezra Taft Benson said, "If you will earnestly seek guidance from your Heavenly Father, morning and evening, you will be given the strength to shun any temptation" ("To 'The Rising Generation,' " 8).

18:20 When we pray for things that are right for us, we can have confidence and faith that those blessings will be given to us (see D&C 46:30).

18:22 ***forbid***—stop

18:23 ***cast***—throw

18:24 After quoting this verse, Elder Jeffrey R. Holland stated: "The praying Christ. That is the example to which we are to point others. The Christ of humility. The Christ of spiritual communion. The Christ who is dependent upon his Father. The Christ who asks for blessings upon others. The Christ who calls down the powers of heaven. The Christ who submits, yields, and obeys the will of the Father. The Christ who is one with the Father in at least one way that we may be united with him as well—through prayer. That is the light we are to show to the world. It is the image of Christ praying such unspeakable things" ("For a Wise Purpose," 19).

*Jesus taught us to pray in our families.*

PHOTOGRAPH BY JOHN LUKE

27 Behold verily, verily, I say unto you, I give unto
you another commandment, and then I must go
unto my Father that I may fulfil other commandments which he hath given me.
28 And now behold, this is the commandment
which I give unto you, that ye shall not suffer any
one knowingly to partake of my flesh and blood
unworthily, when ye shall minister it;
29 For whoso eateth and drinketh my flesh and
blood unworthily eateth and drinketh damnation
to his soul; therefore if ye know that a man is unworthy to eat and drink of my flesh and blood ye
shall forbid him.
30 Nevertheless, ye shall not cast him out from
among you, but ye shall minister unto him and shall
pray for him unto the Father, in my name; and if it
so be that he repenteth and is baptized in my name,
then shall ye receive him, and shall minister unto
him of my flesh and blood.
31 But if he repent not he shall not be numbered
among my people, that he may not destroy my
people, for behold I know my sheep, and they are
numbered.
32 Nevertheless, ye shall not cast him out of your
synagogues, or your places of worship, for unto
such shall ye continue to minister; for ye know not
but what they will return and repent, and come
unto me with full purpose of heart, and I shall heal
them; and ye shall be the means of bringing salvation unto them.
33 Therefore, keep these sayings which I have
commanded you that ye come not under condemnation; for wo unto him whom the Father condemneth.
34 And I give you these commandments because
of the disputations which have been among you.
And blessed are ye if ye have no disputations
among you.
35 And now I go unto the Father, because it is
expedient that I should go unto the Father for your
sakes.
36 And it came to pass that when Jesus had made
an end of these sayings, he touched with his hand
the disciples whom he had chosen, one by one,
even until he had touched them all, and spake unto
them as he touched them.
37 And the multitude heard not the words which
he spake, therefore they did not bear record; but
the disciples bare record that he gave them power
to give the Holy Ghost. And I will show unto you
hereafter that this record is true.
38 And it came to pass that when Jesus had

---

18:27 Jesus said the Father had given Him other commandments to fulfill. What can you learn about keeping God's commandments from the Savior's example?

18:28 ***my flesh and blood***—the sacrament
***minister***—serve

18:29 ***eateth and drinketh damnation to his soul***—cuts himself off from God's presence, stopping his progress

We should make sure we are always worthy to partake of the sacrament. That is why Paul told the Corinthian Saints that they should "examine themselves" each time to see if they thought they were worthy to partake (see 1 Corinthians 11:26–30).

18:31 "Forgiveness of sins is one of the most glorious principles God ever gave to man. Just as repentance is a divine principle, so also is forgiveness. Were it not for this principle, there would be no point in crying repentance. But because of this principle the divine invitation is held out to all of us—come, repent of your sins, and be forgiven!" (Spencer W. Kimball, "God Will Forgive," 7).

18:32 ***synagogues***—churches

President Ezra Taft Benson taught us how to "continue to minister" to those who are less active: "The lost or less-active must be found and contacted. . . . They must feel of our love. They must be taught the gospel. They must feel the power of the Holy Ghost through the teachers. They must be included in our fellowship" (*Teachings of Ezra Taft Benson,* 234).

18:33 ***come not under condemnation***—are not found guilty
***wo***—sorrow

18:34 ***disputations***—arguments

18:35 ***expedient***—necessary

18:37 ***bear record***—testify

The gift of the Holy Ghost allows us to have the Holy Ghost with us if we are worthy. How helpful do you think it would be to have this powerful being, who is actually a God, as your constant companion?

18:37 (36–37) The words that Jesus spoke to His disciples are recorded in Moroni 2:1–3.

touched them all, there came a cloud and overshadowed the multitude that they could not see Jesus.

39 And while they were overshadowed he departed from them, and ascended into heaven. And the disciples saw and did bear record that he ascended again into heaven.

## CHAPTER 19

*Word of the Savior's appearance in Bountiful quickly spreads throughout the land. An "exceedingly great number" travel all night to see the Savior appear again the next day. See how well their long night's journey is rewarded.*

### *The Twelve Disciples Organize, Teach, and Pray with the People*

1 AND now it came to pass that when Jesus had ascended into heaven, the multitude did disperse, and every man did take his wife and his children and did return to his own home.

2 And it was noised abroad among the people immediately, before it was yet dark, that the multitude had seen Jesus, and that he had ministered unto them, and that he would also show himself on the morrow unto the multitude.

3 Yea, and even all the night it was noised abroad concerning Jesus; and insomuch did they send forth unto the people that there were many, yea, an exceedingly great number, did labor exceedingly all that night, that they might be on the morrow in the place where Jesus should show himself unto the multitude.

4 And it came to pass that on the morrow, when the multitude was gathered together, behold, Nephi and his brother whom he had raised from the dead, whose name was Timothy, and also his son, whose name was Jonas, and also Mathoni, and Mathonihah, his brother, and Kumen, and Kumenonhi, and Jeremiah, and Shemnon, and Jonas, and Zedekiah, and Isaiah—now these were the names of the disciples whom Jesus had chosen—and it came to pass that they went forth and stood in the midst of the multitude.

5 And behold, the multitude was so great that they did cause that they should be separated into twelve bodies.

6 And the twelve did teach the multitude; and behold, they did cause that the multitude should kneel down upon the face of the earth, and should pray unto the Father in the name of Jesus.

7 And the disciples did pray unto the Father also in the name of Jesus. And it came to pass that they arose and ministered unto the people.

8 And when they had ministered those same words which Jesus had spoken—nothing varying from the words which Jesus had spoken—behold, they knelt again and prayed to the Father in the name of Jesus.

9 And they did pray for that which they most desired; and they desired that the Holy Ghost should be given unto them.

10 And when they had thus prayed they went down unto the water's edge, and the multitude followed them.

### *The Savior Appears and Commands His Disciples to Pray*

11 And it came to pass that Nephi went down into the water and was baptized.

12 And he came up out of the water and began to baptize. And he baptized all those whom Jesus had chosen.

---

18:39 ***ascended***—went up

19:1 ***did disperse***—left

19:2 ***noised abroad***—told everywhere
***ministered unto***—taught and blessed
***on the morrow***—the next day

Notice that everything Jesus did from 3 Nephi 11:1 to 19:2 happened in one day.

19:3 ***and insomuch did they send forth***—and they spread the news to such a degree

19:4 Just as Jesus chose twelve leaders (called Apostles) in Judea during His mortal ministry, He also chose twelve leaders (called disciples) to lead His Church in the Americas.

***midst of the multitude***—middle of the people

19:5 ***separated***—divided
***bodies***—groups

13 And it came to pass when they were all baptized and had come up out of the water, the Holy
Ghost did fall upon them, and they were filled with
the Holy Ghost and with fire.
14 And behold, they were encircled about as if it
were by fire; and it came down from heaven, and
the multitude did witness it, and did bear record;
and angels did come down out of heaven and did
minister unto them.
15 And it came to pass that while the angels were
ministering unto the disciples, behold, Jesus came
and stood in the midst and ministered unto them.
16 And it came to pass that he spake unto the
multitude, and commanded them that they should
kneel down again upon the earth, and also that his
disciples should kneel down upon the earth.
17 And it came to pass that when they had all
knelt down upon the earth, he commanded his disciples that they should pray.
18 And behold, they began to pray; and they did
pray unto Jesus, calling him their Lord and their
God.

## The Savior Prays for His Disciples

19 And it came to pass that Jesus departed out of
the midst of them, and went a little way off from
them and bowed himself to the earth, and he said:
20 Father, I thank thee that thou hast given the
Holy Ghost unto these whom I have chosen; and it
is because of their belief in me that I have chosen
them out of the world.
21 Father, I pray thee that thou wilt give the Holy
Ghost unto all them that shall believe in their
words.
22 Father, thou hast given them the Holy Ghost
because they believe in me; and thou seest that
they believe in me because thou hearest them, and
they pray unto me; and they pray unto me because
I am with them.
23 And now Father, I pray unto thee for them, and
also for all those who shall believe on their words,
that they may believe in me, that I may be in them
as thou, Father, art in me, that we may be one.
24 And it came to pass that when Jesus had thus
prayed unto the Father, he came unto his disciples,
and behold, they did still continue, without ceasing,
to pray unto him; and they did not multiply many
words, for it was given unto them what they should
pray, and they were filled with desire.
25 And it came to pass that Jesus blessed them as
they did pray unto him; and his countenance did
smile upon them, and the light of his countenance
did shine upon them, and behold they were as

---

19:13 (11–13) President Joseph Fielding Smith explained: "When Christ appeared to the Nephites on this continent, he commanded them to be baptized, although they had been baptized previously for the remission of their sins. . . . Then we read that the Savior commanded Nephi and the people to be baptized again, because he had organized anew the Church under the gospel. Before that it had been organized under the law [meaning the law of Moses]" (*Doctrines of Salvation* 2:336).

19:14 ***bear record***—testify

19:18 The scriptures teach that we are to pray to Heavenly Father in the name of Jesus Christ (see 2 Nephi 32:9; 3 Nephi 19:6). This time the people prayed to Jesus because He was with them (see verse 22). According to Elder Bruce R. McConkie: "Jesus was present before them as the symbol of the Father. Seeing him, it was as though they saw the Father; praying to him, it was as though they prayed to the Father. It was a special and unique situation that as far as we know has taken place only once on earth during all the long ages of the Lord's hand-dealings with his children" (*The Promised Messiah,* 561).

19:23 (19–23) Here Jesus prays that He, His Father, and those who believe in Him "may be one." He offered a similar prayer just before His suffering in Gethsemane (see John 17:20–21). "On both occasions Jesus was praying for a oneness in purpose for all the disciples as the Father and he were one in purpose—not in essence or substance" (Roy W. Doxey, "I Have a Question," 12).

19:24 ***ceasing***—stopping

This verse teaches us more about something Jesus taught in the Sermon on the Mount. To the Jews He said, "When ye pray, use not vain repetitions" (Matthew 6:7). Vain repetition is to repeat the same words over and over again without any thought or feeling.

19:25 ***countenance***—face

19:25 (24–25) "Perfect prayers are those which are inspired, in which the Spirit reveals the words which should be used. (3 Ne. 19:24.) 'And if ye are purified and cleansed from all sin, ye shall ask whatsoever you will in the name of Jesus and it shall be done. But know this, it shall be given you what you shall ask.' (D. & C. 50:29–30.)" (Bruce R. McConkie, *Mormon Doctrine,* 586).

CHRIST PRAYING FOR THE NEPHITES, BY GARY KAPP

*"Jesus departed out of the midst of them, and went a little way off from them and bowed himself to the earth."*

white as the countenance and also the garments of Jesus; and behold the whiteness thereof did exceed all the whiteness, yea, even there could be nothing upon earth so white as the whiteness thereof.

26 And Jesus said unto them: Pray on; nevertheless they did not cease to pray.

27 And he turned from them again, and went a little way off and bowed himself to the earth; and he prayed again unto the Father, saying:

28 Father, I thank thee that thou hast purified those whom I have chosen, because of their faith, and I pray for them, and also for them who shall believe on their words, that they may be purified in me, through faith on their words, even as they are purified in me.

29 Father, I pray not for the world, but for those whom thou hast given me out of the world, because of their faith, that they may be purified in me, that I may be in them as thou, Father, art in me, that we may be one, that I may be glorified in them.

30 And when Jesus had spoken these words he came again unto his disciples; and behold they did pray steadfastly, without ceasing, unto him; and he did smile upon them again; and behold they were white, even as Jesus.

31 And it came to pass that he went again a little way off and prayed unto the Father;

32 And tongue cannot speak the words which he prayed, neither can be written by man the words which he prayed.

33 And the multitude did hear and do bear record; and their hearts were open and they did understand in their hearts the words which he prayed.

34 Nevertheless, so great and marvelous were the words which he prayed that they cannot be written, neither can they be uttered by man.

35 And it came to pass that when Jesus had made an end of praying he came again to the disciples, and said unto them: So great faith have I never seen among all the Jews; wherefore I could not show unto them so great miracles, because of their unbelief.

36 Verily I say unto you, there are none of them that have seen so great things as ye have seen; neither have they heard so great things as ye have heard.

## CHAPTER 20

*Jesus teaches the Nephites the importance of the covenant the Lord made with Abraham and his children of the house of Israel. Look for what Jesus says He has done and will do for the house of Israel because of that covenant.*

### JESUS MIRACULOUSLY PROVIDES BREAD AND WINE FOR THE PEOPLE

1 AND it came to pass that he commanded the multitude that they should cease to pray, and also his disciples. And he commanded them that they should not cease to pray in their hearts.

---

19:29 "How do we glorify Jesus? How do we say thank you for the Atonement? How do we state gratitude for the ordinances and the covenants? How do we express appreciation for his teachings? Of course, we do it by loving God, by loving our neighbor, by living the commandments, and also by being one. We adapt to the Master's teachings. We place him and others with us into one: 'One Lord, one faith, one baptism,' as Paul taught (Ephesians 4:5)" (Hugh W. Pinnock, in Conference Report, April 1987, 77).

19:30 ***steadfastly***—faithfully

19:34 ***uttered***—spoken

19:34 (19–34) The people prayed, the twelve disciples prayed, and then the Savior prayed for them all. What does this teach you about the importance of prayer? What blessings were received by this people as a result of their faith and prayers?

19:34 (32–34) Joseph Smith had a similar spiritual experience during his vision of the three degrees of glory. He was told that some of what he saw could not be written because "they are only to be seen and understood by the power of the Holy Spirit, which God bestows on those who love him, and purify themselves before him" (D&C 76:115–16).

19:35 The term *Jew* often refers to a descendant from the tribe of Judah. However, the Book of Mormon also uses the term *Jew* to refer to any Israelite from the land or kingdom of Judah, even if not descended from the tribe of Judah (see LDS Bible Dictionary, s.v. "Jew," 713). In addition, the Book of Mormon uses the term *Jews* to refer to the entire house of Israel (see *Book of Mormon Student Manual, Religion 121 and 122,* 15).

19:36 (35–36) Why did the Nephites see and hear things that the Jews never did? Why does this make you want to increase your faith?

20:1 ***multitude***—many people
***cease***—stop

2 And he commanded them that they should arise and stand up upon their feet. And they arose up and stood upon their feet.

3 And it came to pass that he brake bread again and blessed it, and gave to the disciples to eat.

4 And when they had eaten he commanded them that they should break bread, and give unto the multitude.

5 And when they had given unto the multitude he also gave them wine to drink, and commanded them that they should give unto the multitude.

6 Now, there had been no bread, neither wine, brought by the disciples, neither by the multitude;

7 But he truly gave unto them bread to eat, and also wine to drink.

8 And he said unto them: He that eateth this bread eateth of my body to his soul; and he that drinketh of this wine drinketh of my blood to his soul; and his soul shall never hunger nor thirst, but shall be filled.

9 Now, when the multitude had all eaten and drunk, behold, they were filled with the Spirit; and they did cry out with one voice, and gave glory to Jesus, whom they both saw and heard.

## *Jesus Teaches How the Covenant with Israel Will Be Fulfilled*

10 And it came to pass that when they had all given glory unto Jesus, he said unto them: Behold now I finish the commandment which the Father hath commanded me concerning this people, who are a remnant of the house of Israel.

11 Ye remember that I spake unto you, and said that when the words of Isaiah should be fulfilled—behold they are written, ye have them before you, therefore search them—

12 And verily, verily, I say unto you, that when they shall be fulfilled then is the fulfilling of the covenant which the Father hath made unto his people, O house of Israel.

13 And then shall the remnants, which shall be scattered abroad upon the face of the earth, be gathered in from the east and from the west, and from the south and from the north; and they shall be brought to the knowledge of the Lord their God, who hath redeemed them.

14 And the Father hath commanded me that I should give unto you this land, for your inheritance.

15 And I say unto you, that if the Gentiles do not

---

20:9 ***glory***—praise

20:9 (6–9) This was the second time Jesus gave the sacrament to the people. This time He provided the bread and wine miraculously and taught an important lesson. After they had been fed, Jesus said that those who partake of the sacrament "shall never hunger nor thirst, but shall be filled" (verse 8). Jesus wasn't talking about being filled with food. In verse 9 we learn that they were "filled with the Spirit."

20:9 (8–9) Elder George Albert Smith said, "We partake of physical food—that is, we partake of bread and water etc., to nourish the physical body. It is just as necessary that we partake of the emblems of the body and blood of our risen Lord to increase our spiritual strength" (in Conference Report, April 1908, 34).

20:10 ***remnant***—part or remainder

20:11 What do you think is the difference between *reading* the scriptures and *searching* them?

20:12 (11–12) The Lord declared that when the words of Isaiah are fulfilled, the covenant which the Father made with the house of Israel will also be fulfilled. "Why? Isaiah taught Israel concerning her covenants with the Lord. Isaiah was the last great prophet who spoke to all of Israel while they were still one people in the Holy Land. He taught the Israelites how the Lord had worked with their ancestors and why they were his covenant people. He reminded them of how they were breaking their covenants and why the Lord's punishment would come upon them. In short, he was the greatest teacher of Israel since Moses, and the last prophetic witness before the scattering" (Victor Ludlow, *Isaiah: Prophet, Seer, and Poet,* 13).

20:13 ***scattered abroad***—dispersed or spread out among the nations

20:14 (13–14) "In the day of gathering the Lehite remnants of Joseph are to receive the land of America as their inheritance. (3 Ne. 20:13–14.)" (Bruce R. McConkie, *The Millennial Messiah,* 294).

repent after the blessing which they shall receive,
after they have scattered my people—
16 Then shall ye, who are a remnant of the house
of Jacob, go forth among them; and ye shall be in
the midst of them who shall be many; and ye shall
be among them as a lion among the beasts of the
forest, and as a young lion among the flocks of
sheep, who, if he goeth through both treadeth
down and teareth in pieces, and none can deliver.
17 Thy hand shall be lifted up upon thine adversaries, and all thine enemies shall be cut off.
18 And I will gather my people together as a man
gathereth his sheaves into the floor.
19 For I will make my people with whom the
Father hath covenanted, yea, I will make thy horn
iron, and I will make thy hoofs brass. And thou
shalt beat in pieces many people; and I will consecrate their gain unto the Lord, and their substance
unto the Lord of the whole earth. And behold, I am
he who doeth it.
20 And it shall come to pass, saith the Father, that
the sword of my justice shall hang over them at that
day; and except they repent it shall fall upon them,
saith the Father, yea, even upon all the nations of
the Gentiles.
21 And it shall come to pass that I will establish
my people, O house of Israel.
22 And behold, this people will I establish in this
land, unto the fulfilling of the covenant which I made
with your father Jacob; and it shall be a New Jerusalem.
And the powers of heaven shall be in the midst of
this people; yea, even I will be in the midst of you.
23 Behold, I am he of whom Moses spake, saying:
A prophet shall the Lord your God raise up unto
you of your brethren, like unto me; him shall ye
hear in all things whatsoever he shall say unto you.
And it shall come to pass that every soul who will
not hear that prophet shall be cut off from among
the people.
24 Verily I say unto you, yea, and all the prophets
from Samuel and those that follow after, as many as
have spoken, have testified of me.

## *Israel Will Be Gathered Again When They Accept Jesus Christ*

25 And behold, ye are the children of the
prophets; and ye are of the house of Israel; and
ye are of the covenant which the Father made
with your fathers, saying unto Abraham: And in
thy seed shall all the kindreds of the earth be
blessed.
26 The Father having raised me up unto you first,
and sent me to bless you in turning away every one
of you from his iniquities; and this because ye are
the children of the covenant—
27 And after that ye were blessed then fulfilleth
the Father the covenant which he made with
Abraham, saying: In thy seed shall all the kindreds
of the earth be blessed—unto the pouring out of
the Holy Ghost through me upon the Gentiles,
which blessing upon the Gentiles shall make them
mighty above all, unto the scattering of my people,
O house of Israel.

---

20:16 ***midst***—middle
***treadeth***—stomps or tramples

20:16 (15–16) Quoting the prophet Micah, the Lord warned that if the Gentiles do not repent after scattering Israel and after receiving so many blessings, then a numerous Israel within their midst will, like a young lion, tread them down and tear them to pieces (see Micah 4:12–13; 5:8–9).

20:17 ***adversaries***—opponents or foes

20:18 ***sheaves***—bundles of cut stalks

20:19 ***I will make thy horn iron***—I will give you the power to tear in pieces
***I will make thy hoofs brass***—I will give you the power to tread down
***consecrate***—dedicate

20:21 ***establish***—strengthen

20:22 Elder Bruce R. McConkie stated that this verse had reference to "the Lehite civilization who were of the house of Joseph," who the Lord would establish in America. Elder McConkie further indicated that "apparently the whole land—'shall be a New Jerusalem,'" and that "Jesus is speaking of the New Jerusalem during its millennial existence, for it is then that he shall dwell on earth among the righteous" (*The Millennial Messiah,* 303).

20:23 Moses had prophesied that the coming Messiah would be a prophet like unto Moses himself (see Deuteronomy 18:15–22; Acts 3:22–26; 7:37).

20:26 ***iniquities***—sins

20:27 (25–27) "Every person who embraces the gospel becomes of the house of Israel. In other words, they become members of the chosen lineage, or Abraham's children through Isaac and Jacob unto whom the promises were made" (Joseph Fielding Smith, *Doctrines of Salvation* 3:246).

28 And they shall be a scourge unto the people of
this land. Nevertheless, when they shall have
received the fulness of my gospel, then if they shall
harden their hearts against me I will return their
iniquities upon their own heads, saith the Father.
29 And I will remember the covenant which I
have made with my people; and I have covenanted
with them that I would gather them together in
mine own due time, that I would give unto them
again the land of their fathers for their inheritance,
which is the land of Jerusalem, which is the
promised land unto them forever, saith the Father.
30 And it shall come to pass that the time cometh,
when the fulness of my gospel shall be preached
unto them;
31 And they shall believe in me, that I am Jesus
Christ, the Son of God, and shall pray unto the
Father in my name.
32 Then shall their watchmen lift up their voice,
and with the voice together shall they sing; for they
shall see eye to eye.
33 Then will the Father gather them together
again, and give unto them Jerusalem for the land of
their inheritance.
34 Then shall they break forth into joy—Sing
together, ye waste places of Jerusalem; for the
Father hath comforted his people, he hath
redeemed Jerusalem.
35 The Father hath made bare his holy arm in the
eyes of all the nations; and all the ends of the earth
shall see the salvation of the Father; and the Father
and I are one.
36 And then shall be brought to pass that which is
written: Awake, awake again, and put on thy
strength, O Zion; put on thy beautiful garments, O
Jerusalem, the holy city, for henceforth there shall
no more come into thee the uncircumcised and the
unclean.
37 Shake thyself from the dust; arise, sit down, O
Jerusalem; loose thyself from the bands of thy neck,
O captive daughter of Zion.
38 For thus saith the Lord: Ye have sold yourselves
for naught, and ye shall be redeemed without money.
39 Verily, verily, I say unto you, that my people
shall know my name; yea, in that day they shall
know that I am he that doth speak.
40 And then shall they say: How beautiful upon
the mountains are the feet of him that bringeth
good tidings unto them, that publisheth peace; that
bringeth good tidings unto them of good, that publisheth salvation; that saith unto Zion: Thy God
reigneth!
41 And then shall a cry go forth: Depart ye, depart
ye, go ye out from thence, touch not that which is
unclean; go ye out of the midst of her; be ye clean
that bear the vessels of the Lord.

---

20:28 ***scourge***—torment and affliction

20:29 "Jerusalem will be restored in its former place, be sanctified, and become a city of holiness, graced with a new temple (Zech. 2:12; 12:6; Ether 13:5, 11; 3 Ne. 20:29–36; D&C 77:15). Elder Orson Hyde, an apostle, journeyed to Jerusalem in 1841 to dedicate the land 'for the building up of Jerusalem again . . . and for rearing a Temple in honor of [the Lord's] name' (HC 4:456)" (*Encyclopedia of Mormonism,* vol. 2, s.v. "Jerusalem," 723).

20:32 "This prophecy [originally] uttered by Isaiah does not refer to the watchmen who were set about Jerusalem in the towers of its walls to warn of approaching enemies, but to all the holy prophets who in times past have raised their voices to declare the coming of the Lord, the Messiah, and like *watchmen* notify the people of Jerusalem of the wonderful reception due Him Who is their King, and to warn them of the error of His rejection" (George Reynolds and Janne M. Sjodahl, *Commentary on the Book of Mormon* 7:167).

20:33 "Although according to Elder Wilford Woodruff a certain number of the Jews will 'gather to their own land in unbelief' (in *Journal of Discourses,* 15:277–78), the Book of Mormon makes it clear that the greater part will gather only after they have come to believe in Jesus as the Messiah. That places the burden squarely on the shoulders of the Latter-day Saints, who alone are empowered to teach the fulness of the gospel" (David B. Galbraith, D. Kelley Ogden, and Andrew C. Skinner, *Jerusalem, the Eternal City,* 358).

20:36 ***garments***—clothing

The Lord has revealed that the term "put on thy strength, O Zion" means to "put on the authority of the priesthood" (see D&C 113:7–8).

*Uncircumcised* refers to someone of another nation who has not entered into the Abrahamic covenant. Often it is associated with being unclean (see Genesis 17:14).

20:41 (40–41) Abinadi taught that this prophecy referred to the prophets (see Mosiah 15:13), but most especially "the founder of peace, yea, even the Lord, who has redeemed his people; yea, him who has granted salvation unto his people" (Mosiah 15:18).

42 For ye shall not go out with haste nor go by
flight; for the Lord will go before you, and the God
of Israel shall be your rearward.
43 Behold, my servant shall deal prudently; he
shall be exalted and extolled and be very high.
44 As many were astonished at thee—his visage
was so marred, more than any man, and his form
more than the sons of men—
45 So shall he sprinkle many nations; the kings
shall shut their mouths at him, for that which had
not been told them shall they see; and that which
they had not heard shall they consider.
46 Verily, verily, I say unto you, all these things
shall surely come, even as the Father hath commanded me. Then shall this covenant which the
Father hath covenanted with his people be fulfilled;
and then shall Jerusalem be inhabited again with
my people, and it shall be the land of their inheritance.

## CHAPTER 21

*The Lord will gather His people in the last days. Look for what happens when we either accept or reject the restored gospel.*

### *The Gathering of Israel Is a Sign of the Lord's Second Coming*

1 AND verily I say unto you, I give unto you a
sign, that ye may know the time when these things
shall be about to take place—that I shall gather in,
from their long dispersion, my people, O house of
Israel, and shall establish again among them my
Zion;
2 And behold, this is the thing which I will give
unto you for a sign—for verily I say unto you that
when these things which I declare unto you, and
which I shall declare unto you hereafter of myself,
and by the power of the Holy Ghost which shall be
given unto you of the Father, shall be made known
unto the Gentiles that they may know concerning
this people who are a remnant of the house of
Jacob, and concerning this my people who shall be
scattered by them;
3 Verily, verily, I say unto you, when these things
shall be made known unto them of the Father, and
shall come forth of the Father, from them unto you;
4 For it is wisdom in the Father that they should
be established in this land, and be set up as a free
people by the power of the Father, that these things

---

20:44 ***visage***—appearance

20:45 (43–45) The servant mentioned here is Jesus Christ. But "as with many prophecies, the divine word has a dual fulfillment. In this setting we may properly say that Joseph Smith . . . was marred. . . . And it may yet well be that there will be other Latter-day servants to whom also it will apply" (Bruce R. McConkie, *The Mortal Messiah* 4:354).

21:1 A sign can be a signal that an important promised event is about to happen. "The coming forth of the Book of Mormon signals the beginning of the Father's work—the work of the gathering of Israel—in the last days" (Joseph Fielding McConkie and others, *Doctrinal Commentary on the Book of Mormon* 4:147).

The Lord's covenant people, Israel, are scattered throughout the earth. This scattering took place when the Lord's people forgot Him and His ways (see Deuteronomy 4:27; 28:64; Jeremiah 16:13; Hosea 9:17).

21:2 ***remnant***—remainder

21:3 President Ezra Taft Benson taught that the things that will be made known are the Book of Mormon and the Doctrine and Covenants because they "are bound together as revelations from Israel's God to gather and prepare His people for the second coming of the Lord" (in Conference Report, April 1987, 104).

21:4 President Ezra Taft Benson testified: "God raised up the founding fathers of the United States of America and established the inspired Constitution (see D&C 101:77–80). This was the required prologue [beginning] for the restoration of the gospel (see 3 Nephi 21:4)" (in Conference Report, October 1988, 103).

Why do you think the Lord restored His Church in America? How is freedom of worship a blessing?

might come forth from them unto a remnant of your
seed, that the covenant of the Father may be fulfilled which he hath covenanted with his people, O
house of Israel;
5 Therefore, when these works and the works
which shall be wrought among you hereafter shall
come forth from the Gentiles, unto your seed which
shall dwindle in unbelief because of iniquity;
6 For thus it behooveth the Father that it should
come forth from the Gentiles, that he may show
forth his power unto the Gentiles, for this cause that
the Gentiles, if they will not harden their hearts, that
they may repent and come unto me and be baptized in my name and know of the true points of
my doctrine, that they may be numbered among my
people, O house of Israel;
7 And when these things come to pass that thy
seed shall begin to know these things—it shall be a
sign unto them, that they may know that the work
of the Father hath already commenced unto the fulfilling of the covenant which he hath made unto the
people who are of the house of Israel.
8 And when that day shall come, it shall come to
pass that kings shall shut their mouths; for that
which had not been told them shall they see; and
that which they had not heard shall they consider.

## Those Who Reject the Restoration of the Gospel Will Be Cut Off

9 For in that day, for my sake shall the Father
work a work, which shall be a great and a marvelous work among them; and there shall be among
them those who will not believe it, although a man
shall declare it unto them.
10 But behold, the life of my servant shall be in
my hand; therefore they shall not hurt him,
although he shall be marred because of them. Yet I
will heal him, for I will show unto them that my
wisdom is greater than the cunning of the devil.
11 Therefore it shall come to pass that whosoever
will not believe in my words, who am Jesus Christ,
which the Father shall cause him to bring forth unto
the Gentiles, and shall give unto him power that he
shall bring them forth unto the Gentiles, (it shall be
done even as Moses said) they shall be cut off from
among my people who are of the covenant.
12 And my people who are a remnant of Jacob
shall be among the Gentiles, yea, in the midst of
them as a lion among the beasts of the forest, as a
young lion among the flocks of sheep, who, if he
go through both treadeth down and teareth in
pieces, and none can deliver.
13 Their hand shall be lifted up upon their adversaries, and all their enemies shall be cut off.
14 Yea, wo be unto the Gentiles except they
repent; for it shall come to pass in that day, saith
the Father, that I will cut off thy horses out of the
midst of thee, and I will destroy thy chariots;
15 And I will cut off the cities of thy land, and
throw down all thy strongholds;
16 And I will cut off witchcrafts out of thy land,
and thou shalt have no more soothsayers;
17 Thy graven images I will also cut off, and thy
standing images out of the midst of thee, and thou
shalt no more worship the works of thy hands;

---

21:5 ***wrought***—done
***dwindle***—fall away

21:6 ***behooveth***—is necessary for

21:7 ***commenced***—begun

21:9 The restoration of the gospel is called a marvelous work and a wonder. Why do you think the gospel is so marvelous and wonderful?

21:10 ***cunning***—tricks

Here Jesus was speaking of Joseph Smith. Even though his enemies rejected, injured, and finally killed him, they could not "hurt" him in God's eyes or stop the work of God that he began (see D&C 135:1–3).

21:12 ***midst***—middle
***treadeth down***—step on and smash down

21:13 ***adversaries***—enemies

21:14 Horses and chariots were symbols of war and power in the ancient world (see J. C. Cooper, *An Illustrated Encyclopaedia of Traditional Symbols,* s.v. "chariot," "horse").

21:17 "Turning to false gods will not bring peace. Turning to the gods of mythology, heathen gods, graven images . . . has only increased selfishness, greed, and lust, and has intensified contention, conflict, and strife. What men must do to find peace is discover and emulate [follow] the true and living God" (Marion G. Romney, in Conference Report, April 1970, 67–68).

MY SERVANT JOSEPH, BY LIZ LEMON SWINDLE

*Speaking of the Prophet Joseph Smith, the Lord told the Nephites, "The life of my servant shall be in my hand."*

18 And I will pluck up thy groves out of the midst of thee; so will I destroy thy cities.
19 And it shall come to pass that all lyings, and deceivings, and envyings, and strifes, and priestcrafts, and whoredoms, shall be done away.
20 For it shall come to pass, saith the Father, that at that day whosoever will not repent and come unto my Beloved Son, them will I cut off from among my people, O house of Israel;
21 And I will execute vengeance and fury upon them, even as upon the heathen, such as they have not heard.

## The Gentiles Will Help Build the New Jerusalem and Gather Scattered Israel

22 But if they will repent and hearken unto my words, and harden not their hearts, I will establish my church among them, and they shall come in unto the covenant and be numbered among this the remnant of Jacob, unto whom I have given this land for their inheritance;
23 And they shall assist my people, the remnant of Jacob, and also as many of the house of Israel as shall come, that they may build a city, which shall be called the New Jerusalem.
24 And then shall they assist my people that they may be gathered in, who are scattered upon all the face of the land, in unto the New Jerusalem.
25 And then shall the power of heaven come down among them; and I also will be in the midst.
26 And then shall the work of the Father commence at that day, even when this gospel shall be preached among the remnant of this people. Verily I say unto you, at that day shall the work of the Father commence among all the dispersed of my people, yea, even the tribes which have been lost, which the Father hath led away out of Jerusalem.
27 Yea, the work shall commence among all the dispersed of my people, with the Father to prepare the way whereby they may come unto me, that they may call on the Father in my name.

---

21:18 Anciently "the groves" were places where people worshiped false gods and committed sins in their worship (see Exodus 34:13; Deuteronomy 7:5; 12:3; Judges 3:7).

21:19 ***deceivings***—trickery
***envyings***—jealousies
***strifes***—arguments
***whoredoms***—wickedness and immorality

Priestcrafts are when men teach their own ideas for money and praise, not caring about God or His people (see 2 Nephi 26:29).

21:21 The Lord said He will bring judgment and anger upon those nations that refuse to obey Him. This "comes as a just and proper reward for the deeds done in the flesh; it is the Lord's way of recompensing [paying] the wicked for their rejection of his truths and the persecutions they have heaped upon his people" (Bruce R. McConkie, *The Millennial Messiah,* 501).

21:21 (11–21) The Lord listed many harmful things that He will destroy at the last day because He loves us. Until that day comes, what is the best way for you to remain safe from these things?

21:22 (14–22) Even the Gentiles can be included with the house of Israel, and receive all the same blessings, if they are humble and repent. What does this tell you about your Heavenly Father? What must you do to please Him?

21:23 Elder Bruce R. McConkie wrote: "Zion, the New Jerusalem, on American soil! And we hasten to add, so also shall there be Zions in all lands and New Jerusalems in the mountains of the Lord in all the earth. But the American Zion shall be the capital city, the source whence the law shall go forth to govern all the earth. It shall be the city of the Great King. His throne shall be there, and from there he shall reign gloriously over all the earth" (*The Millennial Messiah,* 301–2).

21:24 (23–24) "The Gentiles, if repentant, are to be permitted to assist the house of Israel in building the city to be called the New Jerusalem" (James E. Talmage, *The Articles of Faith,* 355).

21:25 This verse refers to a time when the Lord will "come down among them" and "be in the midst" during the Millennium. The Prophet Joseph Smith wrote: "Christ and the resurrected Saints will reign over the earth during the thousand years. They will not probably dwell upon the earth, but will visit it when they please, or when it is necessary to govern it" *(Teachings of the Prophet Joseph Smith,* 268).

21:26 ***commence***—begin
***dispersed***—scattered

"The great day of the return of the Ten Tribes, the day when the assembling hosts shall fulfill the prophetic promises, shall come after our Lord's return" (Bruce R. McConkie, *The Millennial Messiah,* 323; see also D&C 133:23–34).

28 Yea, and then shall the work commence, with
the Father among all nations in preparing the way
whereby his people may be gathered home to the
land of their inheritance.
29 And they shall go out from all nations; and they
shall not go out in haste, nor go by flight, for I will
go before them, saith the Father, and I will be their
rearward.

## CHAPTER 22

*The Savior quotes Isaiah 54. In the last days Zion will be built and dwell in peace and righteousness. Look for the blessings the Lord promises to His people in the last days.*

### The Lord's Church Shall Grow and Nothing Will Stop It

1 AND then shall that which is written come to
pass: Sing, O barren, thou that didst not bear; break
forth into singing, and cry aloud, thou that didst not
travail with child; for more are the children of the
desolate than the children of the married wife, saith
the Lord.
2 Enlarge the place of thy tent, and let them
stretch forth the curtains of thy habitations; spare
not, lengthen thy cords and strengthen thy stakes;
3 For thou shalt break forth on the right hand and
on the left, and thy seed shall inherit the Gentiles
and make the desolate cities to be inhabited.
4 Fear not, for thou shalt not be ashamed; neither
be thou confounded, for thou shalt not be put to
shame; for thou shalt forget the shame of thy youth,
and shalt not remember the reproach of thy youth,
and shalt not remember the reproach of thy wid-
owhood any more.
5 For thy maker, thy husband, the Lord of Hosts is
his name; and thy Redeemer, the Holy One of
Israel—the God of the whole earth shall he be
called.

### The Lord Will Again Gather and Protect His Children in the Last Days

6 For the Lord hath called thee as a woman forsaken and grieved in spirit, and a wife of youth,
when thou wast refused, saith thy God.
7 For a small moment have I forsaken thee, but
with great mercies will I gather thee.

---

21:29 ***rearward***—rear guard

21:29 (28–29) All of us have a part to play in the great work of gathering God's children from all over the earth. You must first repent and join Jesus Christ's true church and be numbered with the house of Israel (see 3 Nephi 21:20–22). After you have come unto Christ you must then warn others to do the same so that they too may be gathered (see D&C 84:76; 88:81–82).

22:1 Elder Bruce R. McConkie explained that in 3 Nephi 22, Isaiah was talking about "the stability, growth, and eventual destiny of the Church," and that "this great latter-day kingdom has been set up for the last time, never again to be destroyed, . . . to remain among men to prepare a people for the second coming of the Son of man" (in Conference Report, October 1958, 115).

***O barren***—scattered Israel
***thou that didst not bear***—you who did not have children
***thou that didst not travail with child***—you who did not suffer the pains of birth
***the desolate***—those who were left alone, without family

22:2 ***habitations***—living places

Elder Joseph Fielding Smith explained: "Isaiah speaks of Zion as a tent, or tabernacle, having in mind the Tabernacle which was built and carried in the wilderness in the days of Moses, and the cords are the binding cables that extend from the tent, or tabernacle, to the stakes which are fastened in the ground. Now, the Lord revealed that Zion was to be built and surrounding her would be the stakes helping to bind and keep her in place" (*Church History and Modern Revelation* 2:88).

22:3 ***inherit***—receive
***desolate***—empty

22:4 ***confounded***—stopped
***reproach***—shame or disgrace

22:5 There are six names for the Savior in this verse. What do you learn about the Savior from each of these names?

"Christ is the *Lord of Hosts* (1 Chron. 17:24; Ps. 24:10; Isa. 6:5; Zech. 14:16–17; Mat. 1:14), meaning that he is a man of war (Ex. 15:3), a God of battles (Ps. 24:8), a leader of his saints in days of conflict and carnage" (Bruce R. McConkie, *Mormon Doctrine*, 451).

22:6 ***forsaken***—left behind or abandoned
***grieved***—saddened

8 In a little wrath I hid my face from thee for a
moment, but with everlasting kindness will I have
mercy on thee, saith the Lord thy Redeemer.
9 For this, the waters of Noah unto me, for as I
have sworn that the waters of Noah should no more
go over the earth, so have I sworn that I would not
be wroth with thee.
10 For the mountains shall depart and the hills be
removed, but my kindness shall not depart from
thee, neither shall the covenant of my peace be
removed, saith the Lord that hath mercy on thee.
11 O thou afflicted, tossed with tempest, and not
comforted! Behold, I will lay thy stones with fair
colors, and lay thy foundations with sapphires.
12 And I will make thy windows of agates, and
thy gates of carbuncles, and all thy borders of pleasant stones.
13 And all thy children shall be taught of the Lord;
and great shall be the peace of thy children.
14 In righteousness shalt thou be established; thou
shalt be far from oppression for thou shalt not fear,
and from terror for it shall not come near thee.
15 Behold, they shall surely gather together
against thee, not by me; whosoever shall gather
together against thee shall fall for thy sake.
16 Behold, I have created the smith that bloweth
the coals in the fire, and that bringeth forth an
instrument for his work; and I have created the
waster to destroy.
17 No weapon that is formed against thee shall
prosper; and every tongue that shall revile against
thee in judgment thou shalt condemn. This is the
heritage of the servants of the Lord, and their righteousness is of me, saith the Lord.

## CHAPTER 23

*Jesus commands the people to search the words of the prophets, especially Isaiah. Look for what was missing from their scriptures that Jesus commands them to add.*

---

22:8 ***wrath***—anger

22:9 ***sworn***—promised

After the flood in the days of Noah, the Lord promised Noah that He would never again destroy the earth with water (see Genesis 9:11).

22:10 ***depart***—go away

22:11 ***afflicted***—mistreated
***tempest***—storm

22:13 "Peace. What a marvelous, desirable blessing to bring to the souls of our children. If they are at peace within themselves and secure in their knowledge of Heavenly Father and His eternal plan for them, they will be able to cope better with the unrest in the world around them and be prepared better for reaching their divine potential" (M. Russell Ballard, "Great Shall Be the Peace of Thy Children," 60).

22:14 ***established***—organized, founded or set up
***oppression***—persecution
***terror***—great fear

22:16 "Joseph was surely the smith who forged the instrument by which the Lord's people continue to prepare individually and collectively for the Savior's return—and that instrument is The Church of Jesus Christ of Latter-day Saints" (Gerald N. Lund, "A Prophet for the Fulness of Times," 54).

22:17 ***prosper***—succeed
***revile***—say bad things
***condemn***—punish
***heritage***—blessing

President Ezra Taft Benson reminded the Saints that "opposition is not new to the Church. We have had opposition in the past, and we shall continue to have opposition in the future. Do not become discouraged by what others say or do. Stay on the strait and narrow path. You do this by holding fast to the iron rod—the words of God as contained in the scriptures and as given by His living servants on this earth" ("The Heritage of the Servants of the Lord," 5).

22:17 (10–17) Isaiah describes the blessings of wealth, peace, and protection the Lord will give His obedient children in the last days. Which of all those blessings seem the most exciting to you? What will you have to do to be able to receive such blessings?

22:17 (15–17) The Church will have enemies but nothing will stop it from doing all that God planned for it. The Prophet Joseph Smith said, "The Standard of Truth has been erected; no unhallowed hand can stop the work from progressing . . . but the truth of God will go forth boldly, nobly, and independent, till it has penetrated every continent, visited every clime, swept every country, and sounded in every ear, till the purposes of God shall be accomplished, and the Great Jehovah shall say the work is done" (*History of the Church* 4:540).

## *Everything Isaiah Taught About the House of Israel Will Be Fulfilled*

1 AND now, behold, I say unto you, that ye ought
to search these things. Yea, a commandment I give
unto you that ye search these things diligently; for
great are the words of Isaiah.
2 For surely he spake as touching all things concerning my people which are of the house of Israel;
therefore it must needs be that he must speak also
to the Gentiles.
3 And all things that he spake have been and shall
be, even according to the words which he spake.
4 Therefore give heed to my words; write the
things which I have told you; and according to the
time and the will of the Father they shall go forth
unto the Gentiles.
5 And whosoever will hearken unto my words
and repenteth and is baptized, the same shall be
saved. Search the prophets, for many there be that
testify of these things.

## *Jesus Commands the Missing Words of Samuel the Lamanite to Be Added to the Nephites' Scriptures*

6 And now it came to pass that when Jesus had said
these words he said unto them again, after he had
expounded all the scriptures unto them which they
had received, he said unto them: Behold, other scriptures I would that ye should write, that ye have not.
7 And it came to pass that he said unto Nephi:
Bring forth the record which ye have kept.
8 And when Nephi had brought forth the records,
and laid them before him, he cast his eyes upon
them and said:
9 Verily I say unto you, I commanded my servant
Samuel, the Lamanite, that he should testify unto
this people, that at the day that the Father should
glorify his name in me that there were many saints
who should arise from the dead, and should appear
unto many, and should minister unto them. And he
said unto them: Was it not so?
10 And his disciples answered him and said: Yea,
Lord, Samuel did prophesy according to thy words,
and they were all fulfilled.
11 And Jesus said unto them: How be it that ye
have not written this thing, that many saints did
arise and appear unto many and did minister unto
them?
12 And it came to pass that Nephi remembered
that this thing had not been written.
13 And it came to pass that Jesus commanded that
it should be written; therefore it was written according as he commanded.
14 And now it came to pass that when Jesus had
expounded all the scriptures in one, which they
had written, he commanded them that they should
teach the things which he had expounded unto
them.

---

23:1 ***diligently***—carefully and with great effort

"If our eternal salvation depends upon our ability to understand the writings of Isaiah as fully and truly as Nephi understood them—and who shall say such is not the case!—how shall we fare in that great day when with Nephi we shall stand before the pleasing bar of Him who said: 'Great are the words of Isaiah'? . . . The risen Lord commanded the Nephites and all the house of Israel, including us, and, for that matter, all the nations of the gentiles, to 'search . . . diligently . . . the words of Isaiah'" (Bruce R. McConkie, "Ten Keys to Understanding Isaiah," 78).

23:3 (1–3) The Lord commanded us to search Isaiah's words diligently. He said they apply to Israel as well as to the Gentiles and that every word Isaiah wrote has or will come to pass. What can you do to better understand Isaiah's writings?

23:4 ***give heed to***—obey

23:6 ***expounded***—explained in detail

23:8 ***cast his eyes***—looked

23:9 ***minister unto***—serve and bless

23:13 It was important to the Savior that the resurrection of people in America be recorded, "especially in a book that was to come forth in our time, a time when, as foreseen, many doubt the reality of the resurrection!" (Neal A. Maxwell, *We Talk of Christ, We Rejoice in Christ,* 165).

23:14 "Each time the records come forth they are brought together in one with such scriptures as have survived among men, making possible the correction and the understanding of the latter. Being the source and author of all, Jesus Christ among the Nephites 'expounded all the scriptures in one, which they had written,' and 'he commanded them that they should teach the things which he had expounded unto them.' (3 Ne. 23:14.) This was after he had personally examined all the records, corrected defects, and brought them up to date" (Hugh Nibley, "A Strange Thing in the Land: The Return of the Book of Enoch, Part 4," 66).

BRING FORTH THE RECORD, BY ROBERT T. BARRETT

"Bring forth the record which ye have kept."

## CHAPTER 24

*The Lord gives the words of Malachi to the Nephites. Jesus Christ will be the Judge when He comes again. Notice what Malachi teaches about the importance of tithing.*

### The Lord Will Send His Messenger to Prepare Us for the Second Coming

1 AND it came to pass that he commanded them that they should write the words which the Father had given unto Malachi, which he should tell unto them. And it came to pass that after they were written he expounded them. And these are the words which he did tell unto them, saying: Thus said the Father unto Malachi—Behold, I will send my messenger, and he shall prepare the way before me, and the Lord whom ye seek shall suddenly come to his temple, even the messenger of the covenant, whom ye delight in; behold, he shall come, saith the Lord of Hosts.

2 But who may abide the day of his coming, and who shall stand when he appeareth? For he is like a refiner's fire, and like fuller's soap.

---

24:1 ***expounded***—explained

Malachi was a prophet who lived about two hundred years after Lehi left Jerusalem. Not only did Jesus quote from this important Old Testament prophet, but so did Moroni when teaching Joseph Smith (see Joseph Smith—History 1:36–39; see also LDS Bible Dictionary, s.v. "Malachi," 728).

The "messenger" sent to prepare the way before the Savior's Second Coming could refer to any or all of the following: John the Baptist; Peter, James, and John (see Joseph Smith—History 1:68–74); the Prophet Joseph Smith (see D&C 1:17–30); or the restored gospel of Jesus Christ (see D&C 45:9).

24:2 ***abide***—endure or survive

3 And he shall sit as a refiner and purifier of silver; and he shall purify the sons of Levi, and purge them as gold and silver, that they may offer unto the Lord an offering in righteousness.
4 Then shall the offering of Judah and Jerusalem be pleasant unto the Lord, as in the days of old, and as in former years.
5 And I will come near to you to judgment; and I will be a swift witness against the sorcerers, and against the adulterers, and against false swearers, and against those that oppress the hireling in his wages, the widow and the fatherless, and that turn aside the stranger, and fear not me, saith the Lord of Hosts.

## Israel Will Be Blessed for Paying Tithes and Offerings

6 For I am the Lord, I change not; therefore ye sons of Jacob are not consumed.
7 Even from the days of your fathers ye are gone away from mine ordinances, and have not kept them. Return unto me and I will return unto you, saith the Lord of Hosts. But ye say: Wherein shall we return?
8 Will a man rob God? Yet ye have robbed me. But ye say: Wherein have we robbed thee? In tithes and offerings.
9 Ye are cursed with a curse, for ye have robbed me, even this whole nation.
10 Bring ye all the tithes into the storehouse, that there may be meat in my house; and prove me now herewith, saith the Lord of Hosts, if I will not open you the windows of heaven, and pour you out a blessing that there shall not be room enough to receive it.
11 And I will rebuke the devourer for your sakes, and he shall not destroy the fruits of your ground; neither shall your vine cast her fruit before the time in the fields, saith the Lord of Hosts.
12 And all nations shall call you blessed, for ye shall be a delightsome land, saith the Lord of Hosts.

---

24:3 ***purge***—make clean or purify

24:3 (2–3) A "refiner" is a person who uses intense heat to separate precious metals from the impure materials they are mixed with (see LDS Bible Dictionary, s.v. "Refiner," 760). The "fuller" made clothing clean and white by washing it in strong soap (see LDS Bible Dictionary, s.v. "Fuller," 676).

Elder Jeffrey R. Holland explained: "The Savior's return will be a cleansing, refining experience by fire. The righteous will endure and be purified by this flame of truth, while the wicked will be burned as stubble, unable to withstand its unquenchable demands" (*Christ and the New Covenant,* 294).

24:4 ***former***—past

24:5 The Lord will be very strict with those who have not repented of these very serious sins. These are the kinds of sins that would lead someone to the telestial kingdom (see D&C 76:103).

24:6 ***consumed***—destroyed

24:7 The Lord says if we return to Him then He will return to us. Why would you want to have the Lord close to you?

24:10 ***prove***—test or try

24:10 (6–10) The *sons of Jacob* is another name for the house of Israel (see Glossary: Israel). They had strayed from the Lord's covenants and are invited to return to Him. "One of the steps, however, in this restoration was the invitation the Lord would extend unto Israel to return to him in the payment of their tithes and offerings" (LeGrand Richards, *A Marvelous Work and a Wonder,* 390).

24:10 (8–10) After quoting these verses, Elder Dallin H. Oaks stated: "Here we see that the law of tithing is not a remote Old Testament practice but a commandment directly from the Savior to the people of our day. The Lord reaffirmed that law in modern revelation, commanding his people to pay 'one-tenth of all their interest annually' and declaring that 'this shall be a standing law unto them forever' (D&C 119:4)" (in Conference Report, April 1994, 43).

24:11 ***rebuke the devourer***—keep back the destroyer
***cast***—drop

24:11 (10–11) President Gordon B. Hinckley said, "I will always be grateful for a father and a mother who, as far back as I can remember, taught us to pay our tithing. . . . Even as small children we were doing our duty as the Lord had outlined that duty, and . . . we were assisting his church in the great work it had to accomplish" ("The Sacred Law of Tithing," 4).

24:12 (10–12) The Lord promises many blessings to those who pay an honest tithing, but we do not pay tithing to get rich. President Gordon B. Hinckley explained that the "Lord will open the windows of heaven according to our need, and not according to our greed" (in Conference Report, April 1982, 60).

### *A Book of Remembrance Is Written for the Righteous*

13 Your words have been stout against me, saith the Lord. Yet ye say: What have we spoken against thee?
14 Ye have said: It is vain to serve God, and what doth it profit that we have kept his ordinances and that we have walked mournfully before the Lord of Hosts?
15 And now we call the proud happy; yea, they that work wickedness are set up; yea, they that tempt God are even delivered.
16 Then they that feared the Lord spake often one to another, and the Lord hearkened and heard; and a book of remembrance was written before him for them that feared the Lord, and that thought upon his name.
17 And they shall be mine, saith the Lord of Hosts, in that day when I make up my jewels; and I will spare them as a man spareth his own son that serveth him.
18 Then shall ye return and discern between the righteous and the wicked, between him that serveth God and him that serveth him not.

## CHAPTER 25

*When Jesus comes again all the wicked will be destroyed and the righteous will be saved. Before He comes, Jesus will send Elijah the prophet to bring the power to join families together forever. Look for what will happen to the hearts of the people because of Elijah's visit.*

### *The Wicked Will Be Burned but the Righteous Will Be Saved at the Second Coming*

1 FOR behold, the day cometh that shall burn as an oven; and all the proud, yea, and all that do wickedly, shall be stubble; and the day that cometh shall burn them up, saith the Lord of Hosts, that it shall leave them neither root nor branch.
2 But unto you that fear my name, shall the Son of Righteousness arise with healing in his wings; and ye shall go forth and grow up as calves in the stall.
3 And ye shall tread down the wicked; for they shall be ashes under the soles of your feet in the day that I shall do this, saith the Lord of Hosts.

---

24:13 ***stout***—harsh or unkind

24:14 ***vain***—useless
***mournfully***—sadly

24:17 ***spare***—save

24:17 (14–17) Some people today are like the Jews of Malachi's day who were upset because the wicked seemed to do as well as those who kept the commandments. Elder Neal A. Maxwell responded, "Yet is it not true that 'the triumphing of the wicked is short, and the joy of the hypocrite but for a moment?' (Job 20:5.) The Lord Himself confirmed that those who follow the ways of man have 'joy in their works [but] for a season' (3 Nephi 27:11)" (*Men and Women of Christ,* 117).

24:18 ***discern***—see the difference

25:1 "Stubble" is dry grain stalks left in the field after the grain has been harvested (see Noah Webster, *An American Dictionary of the English Language,* 1828, s.v. "stubble").

The phrase "it shall leave them neither root nor branch" means the opposite of turning the "heart of the fathers to the children, and the heart of the children to their fathers" (3 Nephi 25:6). The righteous will be joined in eternal families while the wicked will be cut off from their fathers and grandfathers (their roots) and also cut off from their children and grandchildren (their branches).

When the angel Moroni came to the Prophet Joseph Smith, he quoted this prophecy about the Second Coming a little differently from the way it reads here and in Malachi. He changed "the day that cometh shall burn them up" to "they that come shall burn them" (see Joseph Smith—History 1:37), meaning that the presence of the Lord is so bright and glorious that the wicked will burn in His presence, while the righteous are protected (see D&C 64:23–24; Moses 1:11).

25:2 ***the Son of Righteousness***—Jesus Christ

At the Second Coming, Jesus will "arise with healing in his wings." This is a reference to the healing effects of the resurrection (see *Encyclopedia of Mormonism,* s.v. "Malachi, Prophecies of," 2:851). Those who "fear [His] name" (meaning the righteous) will be resurrected first (see D&C 76:50–65). The wicked will have to wait for the last resurrection (see D&C 76:81–86).

4 Remember ye the law of Moses, my servant,
which I commanded unto him in Horeb for all
Israel, with the statutes and judgments.
5 Behold, I will send you Elijah the prophet before
the coming of the great and dreadful day of the Lord;
6 And he shall turn the heart of the fathers to the
children, and the heart of the children to their
fathers, lest I come and smite the earth with a curse.

## CHAPTER 26

*Jesus continues to teach and bless the people, especially the children. Even little babies are able to speak wonderful things. Look for what Jesus said would have to happen in our day before we would be able to receive the same blessings.*

### *Jesus Reveals All Things from the Beginning of the World to the Final Judgment*

1 AND now it came to pass that when Jesus had
told these things he expounded them unto the multitude;
and he did expound all things unto them,
both great and small.
2 And he saith: These scriptures, which ye had not
with you, the Father commanded that I should give
unto you; for it was wisdom in him that they should
be given unto future generations.
3 And he did expound all things, even from the
beginning until the time that he should come in his
glory—yea, even all things which should come
upon the face of the earth, even until the elements
should melt with fervent heat, and the earth should
be wrapt together as a scroll, and the heavens and
the earth should pass away;
4 And even unto the great and last day, when all
people, and all kindreds, and all nations and tongues
shall stand before God, to be judged of their works,
whether they be good or whether they be evil—
5 If they be good, to the resurrection of everlasting
life; and if they be evil, to the resurrection of
damnation; being on a parallel, the one on the one
hand and the other on the other hand, according to
the mercy, and the justice, and the holiness which
is in Christ, who was before the world began.

### *Mormon Writes Only a Small Part of Jesus' Teachings*

6 And now there cannot be written in this book
even a hundredth part of the things which Jesus did
truly teach unto the people;
7 But behold the plates of Nephi do contain the
more part of the things which he taught the people.
8 And these things have I written, which are a
lesser part of the things which he taught the people;
and I have written them to the intent that they may
be brought again unto this people, from the
Gentiles, according to the words which Jesus hath
spoken.
9 And when they shall have received this, which
is expedient that they should have first, to try their
faith, and if it shall so be that they shall believe
these things then shall the greater things be made
manifest unto them.

---

25:4 Mount Horeb is another name for Mount Sinai, where Moses received the "statutes and judgments" or the Ten Commandments (see LDS Bible Dictionary, s.v. "Horeb," 704).

25:5 ***the coming of the great and dreadful day of the Lord***—the Second Coming of Jesus Christ

Elijah, the promised prophet, has already come. On April 3, 1836, he appeared to the Prophet Joseph Smith in the Kirtland Temple and revealed the keys of the priesthood power used to seal (meaning join or unite) families together forever (see D&C 110:13).

25:6 After Elijah revealed the power to join families together forever, parents and children began to take a greater interest in their families. The faithful are especially interested in finding the names of family members who have died and in doing ordinance work (such as baptisms for the dead) for them in the temples (see James E. Talmage, *The Articles of Faith,* 151–52).

26:1 ***expounded***—explained

26:2 ***generations***—children, grandchildren, and so on

26:3 ***elements***—mountains and rocks

26:4 ***kindreds***—families

26:5 ***on a parallel***—separated
***mercy***—kindness or compassion
***justice***—fairness

26:8 ***to the intent***—for the purpose

26:9 ***expedient***—necessary
***made manifest***—shown

ELIJAH RESTORING THE KEYS, BY ROBERT T. BARRETT

*When the prophet Elijah appeared to Joseph Smith and Oliver Cowdery in the Kirtland Temple in 1836, he "turn[ed] the heart of the fathers to the children, and the heart of the children to their fathers."*

10 And if it so be that they will not believe these things, then shall the greater things be withheld from them, unto their condemnation.

11 Behold, I was about to write them, all which were engraven upon the plates of Nephi, but the Lord forbade it, saying: I will try the faith of my people.

12 Therefore I, Mormon, do write the things which have been commanded me of the Lord. And now I, Mormon, make an end of my sayings, and proceed to write the things which have been commanded me.

### *Jesus Blesses the Children; They Speak Marvelous Things*

13 Therefore, I would that ye should behold that the Lord truly did teach the people, for the space of three days; and after that he did show himself unto them oft, and did break bread oft, and bless it, and give it unto them.

14 And it came to pass that he did teach and minister unto the children of the multitude of whom hath been spoken, and he did loose their tongues, and they did speak unto their fathers great and marvelous things, even greater than he had revealed unto the people; and he loosed their tongues that they could utter.

15 And it came to pass that after he had ascended into heaven—the second time that he showed himself unto them, and had gone unto the Father, after having healed all their sick, and their lame, and opened the eyes of their blind and unstopped the ears of the deaf, and even had done all manner of cures among them, and raised a man from the dead, and had shown forth his power unto them, and had ascended unto the Father—

16 Behold, it came to pass on the morrow that the multitude gathered themselves together, and they both saw and heard these children; yea, even babes did open their mouths and utter marvelous things; and the things which they did utter were forbidden that there should not any man write them.

### *The Twelve Disciples Teach and Baptize*

17 And it came to pass that the disciples whom Jesus had chosen began from that time forth to baptize and to teach as many as did come unto them; and as many as were baptized in the name of Jesus were filled with the Holy Ghost.

18 And many of them saw and heard unspeakable things, which are not lawful to be written.

19 And they taught, and did minister one to another; and they had all things common among them, every man dealing justly, one with another.

20 And it came to pass that they did do all things even as Jesus had commanded them.

21 And they who were baptized in the name of Jesus were called the church of Christ.

---

26:10 ***unto their condemnation***—that will keep them from progressing

26:11 ***forbade it***—did not permit it
***try***—test

26:12 (9–12) Jesus explained that He gives us truth a little at a time. "For [God] will give unto the faithful line upon line, precept upon precept; and I will try you and prove you herewith" (D&C 98:12). Only if we are obedient to what we know will we be given more. It is a test of our faith to see if we will be obedient even though we do not know everything (see also Alma 12:9–11).

26:13 ***break bread oft, and bless it***—provide the sacrament

26:14 ***minister unto***—bless and serve
***utter***—speak

26:15 ***ascended***—gone up

26:16 (14–16) Why do you think the Savior taught the children and then loosed their tongues for them to teach their fathers such great and marvelous truths? Would this be a miracle soon forgotten? How would it bring families closer together? How would it help parents see the greatness of their children? How would these children feel about the Lord?

26:18 ***unspeakable things***—things that cannot be talked about

26:19 The phrase "had all things common among them" means that they shared all of their possessions equally, so that no one was poor. This is called the law of consecration and is one of the signs of a Christlike or Zion people (see 4 Nephi 1:2–3; D&C 42:30; Moses 7:18).

***dealing justly***—being honest and fair

## CHAPTER 27

*In this chapter Jesus continues to teach the Nephites about His church and gospel. As you ponder these words, ask yourself what the difference is between the Church organization and the gospel upon which it is built.*

### Jesus Names His Church

1 AND it came to pass that as the disciples of
Jesus were journeying and were preaching the
things which they had both heard and seen, and
were baptizing in the name of Jesus, it came to
pass that the disciples were gathered together and
were united in mighty prayer and fasting.
2 And Jesus again showed himself unto them, for
they were praying unto the Father in his name; and
Jesus came and stood in the midst of them, and said
unto them: What will ye that I shall give unto you?
3 And they said unto him: Lord, we will that thou
wouldst tell us the name whereby we shall call this
church; for there are disputations among the people
concerning this matter.
4 And the Lord said unto them: Verily, verily, I say
unto you, why is it that the people should murmur
and dispute because of this thing?
5 Have they not read the scriptures, which say ye
must take upon you the name of Christ, which is
my name? For by this name shall ye be called at the
last day;
6 And whoso taketh upon him my name, and
endureth to the end, the same shall be saved at the
last day.
7 Therefore, whatsoever ye shall do, ye shall do it
in my name; therefore ye shall call the church in my
name; and ye shall call upon the Father in my name
that he will bless the church for my sake.
8 And how be it my church save it be called in my
name? For if a church be called in Moses' name
then it be Moses' church; or if it be called in the
name of a man then it be the church of a man; but
if it be called in my name then it is my church, if it
so be that they are built upon my gospel.

### Jesus Explains His Gospel

9 Verily I say unto you, that ye are built upon my
gospel; therefore ye shall call whatsoever things ye
do call, in my name; therefore if ye call upon the
Father, for the church, if it be in my name the
Father will hear you;
10 And if it so be that the church is built upon my
gospel then will the Father show forth his own
works in it.
11 But if it be not built upon my gospel, and is
built upon the works of men, or upon the works of
the devil, verily I say unto you they have joy in their
works for a season, and by and by the end cometh,
and they are hewn down and cast into the fire, from
whence there is no return.
12 For their works do follow them, for it is
because of their works that they are hewn down;
therefore remember the things that I have told you.
13 Behold I have given unto you my gospel, and
this is the gospel which I have given unto you—that
I came into the world to do the will of my Father,
because my Father sent me.

---

27:1 ***disciples***—followers

27:2 ***midst***—middle

27:3 ***disputations***—arguments

27:4 ***murmur***—complain

27:5 We covenant with Heavenly Father to take upon ourselves the name of Jesus Christ when we are baptized (see D&C 20:37).

27:8 According to President Marion G. Romney, "this statement gives us the twofold test: Christ's church (1) must bear his name, and (2) must be built upon his gospel. That there should be no uncertainty about the name in this last dispensation, the Lord said to Joseph Smith: '. . . thus shall my church be called in the last days, even *The Church of Jesus Christ of Latter-day Saints.*' (D&C 115:4. Italics added.) . . . The restored church thus meets the Savior's twofold test: it bears his name and it is built upon his gospel" (in Conference Report, October 1972, 78).

27:9 "Signs always follow true believers; miracles always abound in the true church; the power of God is always manifest in the congregations of the saints" (Bruce R. McConkie, *A New Witness for the Articles of Faith,* 139).

27:11 ***joy in their works for a season***—success for a while
***hewn***—cut

27:12 (11–12) "Churches built on false gospels are false churches. They have no saving power" (Bruce R. McConkie, *A New Witness for the Articles of Faith,* 141).

14 And my Father sent me that I might be lifted up upon the cross; and after that I had been lifted up upon the cross, that I might draw all men unto me, that as I have been lifted up by men even so should men be lifted up by the Father, to stand before me, to be judged of their works, whether they be good or whether they be evil—

15 And for this cause have I been lifted up; therefore, according to the power of the Father I will draw all men unto me, that they may be judged according to their works.

16 And it shall come to pass, that whoso repenteth and is baptized in my name shall be filled; and if he endureth to the end, behold, him will I hold guiltless before my Father at that day when I shall stand to judge the world.

17 And he that endureth not unto the end, the same is he that is also hewn down and cast into the fire, from whence they can no more return, because of the justice of the Father.

18 And this is the word which he hath given unto the children of men. And for this cause he fulfilleth the words which he hath given, and he lieth not, but fulfilleth all his words.

19 And no unclean thing can enter into his kingdom; therefore nothing entereth into his rest save it be those who have washed their garments in my blood, because of their faith, and the repentance of all their sins, and their faithfulness unto the end.

20 Now this is the commandment: Repent, all ye ends of the earth, and come unto me and be baptized in my name, that ye may be sanctified by the reception of the Holy Ghost, that ye may stand spotless before me at the last day.

21 Verily, verily, I say unto you, this is my gospel; and ye know the things that ye must do in my church; for the works which ye have seen me do that shall ye also do; for that which ye have seen me do even that shall ye do;

22 Therefore, if ye do these things blessed are ye, for ye shall be lifted up at the last day.

## Jesus Teaches the Importance of Keeping Records

23 Write the things which ye have seen and heard, save it be those which are forbidden.

24 Write the works of this people, which shall be, even as hath been written, of that which hath been.

25 For behold, out of the books which have been written, and which shall be written, shall this people be judged, for by them shall their works be known unto men.

26 And behold, all things are written by the Father; therefore out of the books which shall be written shall the world be judged.

27 And know ye that ye shall be judges of this people, according to the judgment which I shall give unto you, which shall be just. Therefore, what manner of men ought ye to be? Verily I say unto you, even as I am.

---

27:16 ***endureth to the end***—stays faithful until death

27:19 ***unclean***—sinful
***washed their garments in my blood***—become clean through the Atonement of Jesus Christ

27:20 "To be *sanctified* is to become clean, pure, and spotless" (Bruce R. McConkie, *Mormon Doctrine*, 675). A person can only become sanctified through the Atonement of Jesus Christ and by obedience to the laws, ordinances, and commandments of the gospel of Jesus Christ.

27:21 (13–21) "On several occasions the Savior has defined what his gospel is—faith in his atoning sacrifice, repentance of sins, baptism by immersion, receiving the Holy Ghost, and enduring to the end. . . . President Ezra Taft Benson explained that when the Lord spoke of the Book of Mormon as containing the 'fulness of the gospel,' he did not mean that 'it contains every teaching, every doctrine ever revealed. Rather, it means that in the Book of Mormon we will find the fulness of those doctrines required for our salvation. And they are taught plainly and simply so that even children can learn the ways of salvation and exaltation' (*Ensign*, Nov. 1986, 6)" (Richard O. Cowan, *Answers to Your Questions About the Doctrine and Covenants*, 24).

27:23 ***save it be***—except for

27:26 We will be judged out of the records that are kept on earth and in heaven (see D&C 128:7–8).

27:27 "Christ, then, has set us the example of what we should be like and what we should do. While many men have admirable qualities, there is only one man who ever walked the earth who was without sin. . . . Christ is God the Son and possesses every virtue in its perfection. Therefore, the only measure of true greatness is how close a man can become like Jesus. That man is greatest who is most like Christ, and those who love him most will be most like him" (Ezra Taft Benson, in Conference Report, October 1972, 53).

CHRIST REVIEWING THE RECORD, BY GARY KAPP

*Jesus Christ taught the importance of keeping records.*

## Jesus Leaves to Go to the Father

28 And now I go unto the Father. And verily I say
unto you, whatsoever things ye shall ask the Father
in my name shall be given unto you.
29 Therefore, ask, and ye shall receive; knock,
and it shall be opened unto you; for he that asketh,
receiveth; and unto him that knocketh, it shall be
opened.
30 And now, behold, my joy is great, even unto
fulness, because of you, and also this generation;
yea, and even the Father rejoiceth, and also all the
holy angels, because of you and this generation; for
none of them are lost.
31 Behold, I would that ye should understand; for
I mean them who are now alive of this generation;
and none of them are lost; and in them I have fulness of joy.

27:29 (28–29) "No message in scripture is repeated more often than the invitation, even the command, to pray—to ask" (Boyd K. Packer, in Conference Report, October 1994, 76).

27:30 ***generation***—group of people

32 But behold, it sorroweth me because of the fourth generation from this generation, for they are led away captive by him even as was the son of perdition; for they will sell me for silver and for gold, and for that which moth doth corrupt and which thieves can break through and steal. And in that day will I visit them, even in turning their works upon their own heads.

33 And it came to pass that when Jesus had ended these sayings he said unto his disciples: Enter ye in at the strait gate; for strait is the gate, and narrow is the way that leads to life, and few there be that find it; but wide is the gate, and broad the way which leads to death, and many there be that travel therein, until the night cometh, wherein no man can work.

## CHAPTER 28

*The Savior gives His disciples what they desire. Look for the special blessing that He gives three of His disciples.*

### Jesus Blesses Nine of His Twelve Disciples to Find Rest in His Heavenly Kingdom

1 AND it came to pass when Jesus had said these words, he spake unto his disciples, one by one, saying unto them: What is it that ye desire of me, after that I am gone to the Father?

2 And they all spake, save it were three, saying: We desire that after we have lived unto the age of man, that our ministry, wherein thou hast called us, may have an end, that we may speedily come unto thee in thy kingdom.

3 And he said unto them: Blessed are ye because ye desired this thing of me; therefore, after that ye are seventy and two years old ye shall come unto me in my kingdom; and with me ye shall find rest.

### Jesus Promises Three Disciples That They Will Not Taste Death

4 And when he had spoken unto them, he turned himself unto the three, and said unto them: What will ye that I should do unto you, when I am gone unto the Father?

5 And they sorrowed in their hearts, for they durst not speak unto him the thing which they desired.

6 And he said unto them: Behold, I know your thoughts, and ye have desired the thing which John, my beloved, who was with me in my ministry, before that I was lifted up by the Jews, desired of me.

7 Therefore, more blessed are ye, for ye shall never taste of death; but ye shall live to behold all the doings of the Father unto the children of men, even until all things shall be fulfilled according to the will of the Father, when I shall come in my glory with the powers of heaven.

8 And ye shall never endure the pains of death; but when I shall come in my glory ye shall be changed in the twinkling of an eye from mortality to immortality; and then shall ye be blessed in the kingdom of my Father.

---

27:32 ***sorroweth me***—makes me sad
***corrupt***—destroy

"It is possible for people to get so far in the dark through rebellion and wickedness that the spirit of repentance leaves them. It is a gift of God, and they get beyond the power of repentance. How well Mormon speaks of that, in reference to the people who turned away with their eyes open, who turned against the truth some 200 years following the coming of Christ. . . . They sinned wilfully, and therefore salvation cannot come to them. It was offered to them, and they would not have it. They rejected it. They fought it and preferred to take the course of rebellion" (Joseph Fielding Smith, *Doctrines of Salvation* 2:194–95).

28:1 Note that the Lord spoke to His disciples "one by one" and asked what they desired of Him. Why do you think He did that? What does this teach you about His concern for each individual?

28:3 "The rest of the Lord, in eternity, is to inherit eternal life, to gain the fulness of the Lord's glory. (D&C 84:24.)" (Bruce R. McConkie, *Mormon Doctrine,* 633).

28:5 ***sorrowed in their hearts***—were sad
***durst***—dared

28:6 ***lifted up***—crucified

John, like these three Nephite disciples, was promised that he would not die but would live until the Savior's Second Coming (see John 21:20–23).

*To the Three Nephites, Jesus Christ said, "More blessed are ye, for ye shall never taste of death; but ye shall live to behold all the doings of the Father unto the children of men."*

9 And again, ye shall not have pain while ye shall
dwell in the flesh, neither sorrow save it be for the
sins of the world; and all this will I do because of
the thing which ye have desired of me, for ye have
desired that ye might bring the souls of men unto
me, while the world shall stand.
10 And for this cause ye shall have fulness of joy;
and ye shall sit down in the kingdom of my Father;
yea, your joy shall be full, even as the Father hath
given me fulness of joy; and ye shall be even as I
am, and I am even as the Father; and the Father and
I are one;
11 And the Holy Ghost beareth record of the
Father and me; and the Father giveth the Holy
Ghost unto the children of men, because of
me.

---

28:9 (7–9) Elder Bruce R. McConkie said, "It is from the Book of Mormon account relative to the Three Nephites that we gain our greatest scriptural knowledge about translated beings" (*The Millennial Messiah,* 647; see also 3 Nephi 28:20, 30, 39–40).

28:10 "Despite all we can do, we cannot have a fulness of joy in this world or through our own efforts (see D&C 101:36). Only in Christ can our joy be full" (Dallin H. Oaks, in Conference Report, October 1991, 103).

28:11 The Holy Ghost's "mission is to bear witness to men of the existence of God and the truth of the gospel of Jesus Christ, and also to fill men with knowledge and power and to inspire them to works leading to happiness" (John A. Widtsoe, *Evidences and Reconciliations,* 77).

12 And it came to pass that when Jesus had spoken these words, he touched every one of them with his finger save it were the three who were to tarry, and then he departed.

## The Three Disciples Are Translated

13 And behold, the heavens were opened, and they were caught up into heaven, and saw and heard unspeakable things.
14 And it was forbidden them that they should utter; neither was it given unto them power that they could utter the things which they saw and heard;
15 And whether they were in the body or out of the body, they could not tell; for it did seem unto them like a transfiguration of them, that they were changed from this body of flesh into an immortal state, that they could behold the things of God.
16 But it came to pass that they did again minister upon the face of the earth; nevertheless they did not minister of the things which they had heard and seen, because of the commandment which was given them in heaven.

## Mormon Writes of the Ministry of the Three Disciples

17 And now, whether they were mortal or immortal, from the day of their transfiguration, I know not;
18 But this much I know, according to the record which hath been given—they did go forth upon the face of the land, and did minister unto all the people, uniting as many to the church as would believe in their preaching; baptizing them, and as many as were baptized did receive the Holy Ghost.
19 And they were cast into prison by them who did not belong to the church. And the prisons could not hold them, for they were rent in twain.
20 And they were cast down into the earth; but they did smite the earth with the word of God, insomuch that by his power they were delivered out of the depths of the earth; and therefore they could not dig pits sufficient to hold them.
21 And thrice they were cast into a furnace and received no harm.
22 And twice were they cast into a den of wild beasts; and behold they did play with the beasts as a child with a suckling lamb, and received no harm.
23 And it came to pass that thus they did go forth among all the people of Nephi, and did preach the gospel of Christ unto all people upon the face of the land; and they were converted unto the Lord, and were united unto the church of Christ, and thus the people of that generation were blessed, according to the word of Jesus.
24 And now I, Mormon, make an end of speaking concerning these things for a time.
25 Behold, I was about to write the names of those who were never to taste of death, but the Lord forbade; therefore I write them not, for they are hid from the world.
26 But behold, I have seen them, and they have ministered unto me.

---

28:12 ***tarry***—stay or remain

28:14 ***utter***—speak

28:14 (13–14) Other prophets have had similar experiences, such as Paul (see 2 Corinthians 12:1–4), Joseph Smith and Sidney Rigdon (see D&C 76), and John (see Revelation 4:1–4).

28:16 (15–16) "Mormon called this change upon the Three Nephites a 'transfiguration,' and they did have a transfiguring experience. However, the more traditional understanding of the status of these three is that they were 'translated' beings. A person who is transfigured is one who is temporarily taken into a higher, heavenly experience, as were Peter, James, and John, and then returned to a normal telestial status. As noted above, these three Nephites, as part of their translation experience, were also transfigured, caught up into heaven, where they 'saw and heard unspeakable things' " (Jeffrey R. Holland, *Christ and the New Covenant,* 305–6).

28:19 ***rent in twain***—torn in two

28:22 ***suckling***—baby

28:22 (18–22) Notice how these disciples are protected and delivered by the Lord. Why do you think that they have this protection? How has the Lord protected you in your life?

28:25 The Lord does not reveal the names of these three special disciples. This is in harmony with the Lord's teaching that our alms [service] should be done in secret (see 3 Nephi 13:1–4).

27 And behold they will be among the Gentiles, and the Gentiles shall know them not.
28 They will also be among the Jews, and the Jews shall know them not.
29 And it shall come to pass, when the Lord seeth fit in his wisdom that they shall minister unto all the scattered tribes of Israel, and unto all nations, kindreds, tongues and people, and shall bring out of them unto Jesus many souls, that their desire may be fulfilled, and also because of the convincing power of God which is in them.
30 And they are as the angels of God, and if they shall pray unto the Father in the name of Jesus they can show themselves unto whatsoever man it seemeth them good.
31 Therefore, great and marvelous works shall be wrought by them, before the great and coming day when all people must surely stand before the judgment-seat of Christ;
32 Yea even among the Gentiles shall there be a great and marvelous work wrought by them, before that judgment day.
33 And if ye had all the scriptures which give an account of all the marvelous works of Christ, ye would, according to the words of Christ, know that these things must surely come.
34 And wo be unto him that will not hearken unto the words of Jesus, and also to them whom he hath chosen and sent among them; for whoso receiveth not the words of Jesus and the words of those whom he hath sent receiveth not him; and therefore he will not receive them at the last day;
35 And it would be better for them if they had not been born. For do ye suppose that ye can get rid of the justice of an offended God, who hath been trampled under feet of men, that thereby salvation might come?
36 And now behold, as I spake concerning those whom the Lord hath chosen, yea, even three who were caught up into the heavens, that I knew not whether they were cleansed from mortality to immortality—
37 But behold, since I wrote, I have inquired of the Lord, and he hath made it manifest unto me that there must needs be a change wrought upon their bodies, or else it needs be that they must taste of death;
38 Therefore, that they might not taste of death there was a change wrought upon their bodies, that they might not suffer pain nor sorrow save it were for the sins of the world.
39 Now this change was not equal to that which shall take place at the last day; but there was a change wrought upon them, insomuch that Satan could have no power over them, that he could not tempt them; and they were sanctified in the flesh, that they were holy, and that the powers of the earth could not hold them.
40 And in this state they were to remain until the judgment day of Christ; and at that day they were to receive a greater change, and to be received into the kingdom of the Father to go no more out, but to dwell with God eternally in the heavens.

## CHAPTER 29

*The Book of Mormon is a witness that Heavenly Father loves His children and keeps His covenants. Look for what it means to be covenant people.*

### The Coming Forth of the Book of Mormon Is a Sign That God Will Keep His Promise to Gather Israel

1 AND now behold, I say unto you that when the Lord shall see fit, in his wisdom, that these sayings shall come unto the Gentiles according to his word, then ye may know that the covenant which the Father hath made with the children of Israel, concerning their restoration to the lands of their inheritance, is already beginning to be fulfilled.

---

28:31 ***wrought***—done

28:35 ***trampled***—stepped on

28:40 (36–40) "Translated beings live in a state of mortality, but changes are 'wrought upon their bodies' so that they will not taste of death. (3 Ne. 28:36–40.)" (Bruce R. McConkie, *Mormon Doctrine,* 514).

29:1 ***restoration to the lands of their inheritance***—return to the lands promised to them by the Lord

"These sayings" are the Book of Mormon. Since 1830 when the Book of Mormon was first printed, the Lord has been gathering scattered Israel. Eventually the members of the tribe of Joseph will gather to the Americas, and the rest of the tribes of Israel will gather to the land of Israel (see Ether 13:4–11).

2 And ye may know that the words of the Lord,
which have been spoken by the holy prophets,
shall all be fulfilled; and ye need not say that the
Lord delays his coming unto the children of Israel.
3 And ye need not imagine in your hearts that the
words which have been spoken are vain, for
behold, the Lord will remember his covenant which
he hath made unto his people of the house of Israel.

### People Who Reject God's Work in the Last Days Will Be Cursed

4 And when ye shall see these sayings coming
forth among you, then ye need not any longer
spurn at the doings of the Lord, for the sword of his
justice is in his right hand; and behold, at that day,
if ye shall spurn at his doings he will cause that it
shall soon overtake you.
5 Wo unto him that spurneth at the doings of the
Lord; yea, wo unto him that shall deny the Christ
and his works!
6 Yea, wo unto him that shall deny the revelations
of the Lord, and that shall say the Lord no longer
worketh by revelation, or by prophecy, or by gifts,
or by tongues, or by healings, or by the power of
the Holy Ghost!
7 Yea, and wo unto him that shall say at that day,
to get gain, that there can be no miracle wrought by
Jesus Christ; for he that doeth this shall become like
unto the son of perdition, for whom there was no
mercy, according to the word of Christ!
8 Yea, and ye need not any longer hiss, nor spurn,
nor make game of the Jews, nor any of the remnant
of the house of Israel; for behold, the Lord remembereth his covenant unto them, and he will do unto
them according to that which he hath sworn.
9 Therefore ye need not suppose that ye can turn
the right hand of the Lord unto the left, that he may
not execute judgment unto the fulfilling of the
covenant which he hath made unto the house of
Israel.

## CHAPTER 30

*The Lord commands the prophet Mormon to write a message to the Gentiles living in the last days. Look for how the Gentiles can become members of the house of Israel.*

### The Gentiles Living in the Latter Days Are Invited to Turn Away from Wickedness and to Come unto Christ

1 HEARKEN, O ye Gentiles, and hear the words of
Jesus Christ, the Son of the living God, which he
hath commanded me that I should speak concerning you, for, behold he commandeth me that I
should write, saying:

---

29:2 ***delays***—puts off or postpones

29:3 ***vain***—useless

Mormon testified that the coming forth of the Book of Mormon is a sign to us that the Lord will fulfill all His promises. What are some of the promises the Lord has made to you? What does it mean to you to know that the Lord never breaks a promise?

29:4 ***spurn at***—reject or mock
***overtake***—catch up with

29:5 ***Wo***—Sorrow or suffering
***deny***—refuse or reject

29:7 Elder Bruce R. McConkie explained that perdition means "no hope whatever of any degree of salvation" or "wholly given . . . up to iniquity" (*Mormon Doctrine,* 566).

29:7 (6–7) "No, revelation has not ceased and will not cease. This kingdom of God has been set up for the rest of time, never to be torn down nor given to another people. It is a continuous program and will grow instead of diminish. . . . Revelation and other miracles will never cease unless faith ceases. Where there is adequate faith, these things will continue" (Spencer W. Kimball, "Gospel Forum: Continuing Revelation," 21).

29:8 ***hiss***—mock
***spurn***—reject
***remnant***—part or remainder
***sworn***—promised

29:9 ***execute***—carry out

"God's covenant will be kept with all of his covenant people. No one will be able to 'turn the right hand of the Lord unto the left' on this matter. And the call to the Gentiles, for which Christ's visit to the Nephites published in the Book of Mormon is the ultimate latter-day declaration, is for them to claim the same covenant and promises" (Jeffrey R. Holland, *Christ and the New Covenant,* 308).

2 Turn, all ye Gentiles, from your wicked ways; and repent of your evil doings, of your lyings and deceivings, and of your whoredoms, and of your secret abominations, and your idolatries, and of your murders, and your priestcrafts, and your envyings, and your strifes, and from all your wickedness and abominations, and come unto me, and be baptized in my name, that ye may receive a remission of your sins, and be filled with the Holy Ghost, that ye may be numbered with my people who are of the house of Israel.

---

30:2 ***whoredoms***—wickedness and immorality
***abominations***—acts of great evil
***idolatries***—worshiping of false gods
***envyings***—jealousies
***strifes***—arguments and fights
***remission***—forgiveness

Priestcrafts are when men teach their own ideas for money and praise, and do not care about God or His people (see 2 Nephi 26:29).

The Lord promised the Gentiles that if they will repent and come unto Him, they will "be filled with the Holy Ghost." The Prophet Joseph Smith said that when the Holy Ghost comes upon a Gentile it will "purge out the old blood, and make him actually of the [house of Israel]" (*Teachings of the Prophet Joseph Smith,* 150).

# FOURTH NEPHI
# THE BOOK OF NEPHI

## WHO IS THE SON OF NEPHI—ONE OF THE DISCIPLES OF JESUS CHRIST

*The book of 4 Nephi continues the story of the Nephites after Jesus Christ appeared and ministered to them. This remarkable book contrasts the great happiness that comes from keeping the Lord's commandments and the great sorrow that results from pride and selfishness. The events of 4 Nephi cover the time from A.D. 36 to A.D. 321.*

*An account of the people of Nephi, according to his record.**

### CHAPTER 1

*The Book of Mormon people enjoy peace and great blessings for almost two hundred years. Watch for how pride and greed destroy these blessings.*

#### *EVERYONE IS CONVERTED TO THE CHURCH OF CHRIST*

1 AND it came to pass that the thirty and fourth
year passed away, and also the thirty and fifth, and
behold the disciples of Jesus had formed a church
of Christ in all the lands round about. And as many
as did come unto them, and did truly repent of their
sins, were baptized in the name of Jesus; and they
did also receive the Holy Ghost.
2 And it came to pass in the thirty and sixth year,
the people were all converted unto the Lord, upon
all the face of the land, both Nephites and
Lamanites, and there were no contentions and disputations
among them, and every man did deal
justly one with another.
3 And they had all things common among them;
therefore there were not rich and poor, bond and
free, but they were all made free, and partakers of
the heavenly gift.
4 And it came to pass that the thirty and seventh
year passed away also, and there still continued to
be peace in the land.
5 And there were great and marvelous works
wrought by the disciples of Jesus, insomuch that
they did heal the sick, and raise the dead, and
cause the lame to walk, and the blind to receive
their sight, and the deaf to hear; and all manner of
miracles did they work among the children of men;
and in nothing did they work miracles save it were
in the name of Jesus.

---

* This introduction to the book of 4 Nephi was translated from the Book of Mormon plates.

1:1 ***formed***—organized

*Christ* is a Greek word meaning "the Anointed One"; the Hebrew word with the same meaning is *Messiah*. Jesus is the Christ—the one chosen, set apart, and sent by God to save us (see LDS Bible Dictionary, s.v. "Christ," 633).

1:2 ***contentions and disputations***—fights and arguments

1:3 The "heavenly gift" is the gift of the Holy Ghost. Elder Neal A. Maxwell taught that once we receive this gift "we will be guided constantly by the Holy Ghost. The important thing is for us to make the basic decision to knock and to ask so that we can be brought into the light" (*That My Family Should Partake*, 26).

1:4 Elder John A. Widtsoe said that when we live the gospel there will be more peace in the world. "That makes me responsible for the peace of the world, and makes you individually responsible for the peace of the world" (in Conference Report, October 1943, 113).

1:5 ***wrought***—done or performed

The disciples of Christ, "in the name of Jesus," performed the same miracles as Jesus did when He was on earth (see Matthew 11:5; Luke 7:22).

= Word Help = A Closer Look
= More Light = Ponder This
Words in pink are explained in the Glossary.

6 And thus did the thirty and eighth year pass away, and also the thirty and ninth, and forty and first, and the forty and second, yea, even until forty and nine years had passed away, and also the fifty and first, and the fifty and second; yea, and even until fifty and nine years had passed away.

7 And the Lord did prosper them exceedingly in the land; yea, insomuch that they did build cities again where there had been cities burned.

8 Yea, even that great city Zarahemla did they cause to be built again.

9 But there were many cities which had been sunk, and waters came up in the stead thereof; therefore these cities could not be renewed.

10 And now, behold, it came to pass that the people of Nephi did wax strong, and did multiply exceedingly fast, and became an exceedingly fair and delightsome people.

11 And they were married, and given in marriage, and were blessed according to the multitude of the promises which the Lord had made unto them.

12 And they did not walk any more after the performances and ordinances of the law of Moses; but they did walk after the commandments which they had received from their Lord and their God, continuing in fasting and prayer, and in meeting together oft both to pray and to hear the word of the Lord.

13 And it came to pass that there was no contention among all the people, in all the land; but there were mighty miracles wrought among the disciples of Jesus.

## The New Generation Remains Faithful

14 And it came to pass that the seventy and first year passed away, and also the seventy and second year, yea, and in fine, till the seventy and ninth year had passed away; yea, even an hundred years had passed away, and the disciples of Jesus, whom he had chosen, had all gone to the paradise of God, save it were the three who should tarry; and there were other disciples ordained in their stead; and also many of that generation had passed away.

15 And it came to pass that there was no contention in the land, because of the love of God which did dwell in the hearts of the people.

16 And there were no envyings, nor strifes, nor tumults, nor whoredoms, nor lyings, nor murders, nor any manner of lasciviousness; and surely there could not be a happier people among all the people who had been created by the hand of God.

17 There were no robbers, nor murderers, neither were there Lamanites, nor any manner of -ites; but they were in one, the children of Christ, and heirs to the kingdom of God.

---

1:10 ***wax***—grow
***an exceedingly***—a very
***delightsome***—blessed or happy

1:11 (10–11) President Ezra Taft Benson taught that "in the Book of Mormon we find a pattern for preparing for the Second Coming" (in Conference Report, October 1986, 5). Just as the appearance of Jesus Christ to the Nephites was followed by a time of peace when the people were married and had many children, the same will be true of the period following the Second Coming of Christ (see D&C 45:58).

1:12 ***performances***—practices

The law of Moses included the laws and ordinances that the children of Israel were commanded to follow from the days of Moses until the time of Jesus Christ (see LDS Bible Dictionary, s.v. "Law of Moses," 722–23).

1:13 (12–13) Bishop Robert L. Simpson explained that "there were significant changes made at the time of Christ's mission in mortality. The law of sacrifice, for example, was replaced by a higher law. . . . So complete and sincere were the people in obeying his commandments 'that there was no contention among all the people, in all the land' (4 Ne. 13.) Wouldn't it be thrilling to enjoy such a condition today!" ("The Law of the Fast," 48).

1:16 ***strifes***—arguments and fighting
***tumults***—riots or disorderly groups of people
***whoredoms***—wickedness and immorality
***lasciviousness***—focusing on immorality

These people were happy because they were keeping God's commandments. The Prophet Joseph Smith said that "happiness is the object and design of our existence; and will be the end thereof, if we pursue the path that leads to it; and this path is virtue, uprightness, faithfulness, holiness, and keeping all the commandments of God" (*Teachings of the Prophet Joseph Smith,* 255–56).

1:17 Elder Russell M. Nelson used this verse to teach that we should "delete from our personal vocabularies names . . . that separate" (in Conference Report, April 1995, 44). How does labeling people influence our feelings toward them?

18 And how blessed were they! For the Lord did bless them in all their doings; yea, even they were blessed and prospered until an hundred and ten years had passed away; and the first generation from Christ had passed away, and there was no contention in all the land.
19 And it came to pass that Nephi, he that kept this last record, (and he kept it upon the plates of Nephi) died, and his son Amos kept it in his stead; and he kept it upon the plates of Nephi also.
20 And he kept it eighty and four years, and there was still peace in the land, save it were a small part of the people who had revolted from the church and taken upon them the name of Lamanites; therefore there began to be Lamanites again in the land.
21 And it came to pass that Amos died also, (and it was an hundred and ninety and four years from the coming of Christ) and his son Amos kept the record in his stead; and he also kept it upon the plates of Nephi; and it was also written in the book of Nephi, which is this book.
22 And it came to pass that two hundred years had passed away; and the second generation had all passed away save it were a few.

## *The People Are Lifted Up in Pride and Become Wicked*

23 And now I, Mormon, would that ye should know that the people had multiplied, insomuch that they were spread upon all the face of the land, and that they had become exceedingly rich, because of their prosperity in Christ.
24 And now, in this two hundred and first year there began to be among them those who were lifted up in pride, such as the wearing of costly apparel, and all manner of fine pearls, and of the fine things of the world.
25 And from that time forth they did have their goods and their substance no more common among them.
26 And they began to be divided into classes; and they began to build up churches unto themselves to get gain, and began to deny the true church of Christ.
27 And it came to pass that when two hundred and ten years had passed away there were many churches in the land; yea, there were many churches which professed to know the Christ, and yet they did deny the more parts of his gospel, insomuch that they did receive all manner of wickedness, and did administer that which was sacred unto him to whom it had been forbidden because of unworthiness.
28 And this church did multiply exceedingly because of iniquity, and because of the power of Satan who did get hold upon their hearts.
29 And again, there was another church which denied the Christ; and they did persecute the true church of Christ, because of their humility and their belief in Christ; and they did despise them because of the many miracles which were wrought among them.
30 Therefore they did exercise power and authority over the disciples of Jesus who did tarry with them, and they did cast them into prison; but by the power of the word of God, which was in them, the prisons were rent in twain, and they went forth doing mighty miracles among them.
31 Nevertheless, and notwithstanding all these miracles, the people did harden their hearts, and did seek to kill them, even as the Jews at Jerusalem sought to kill Jesus, according to his word.

---

1:20 The Lord declared that "if ye are not one ye are not mine" (D&C 38:27). Notice how losing even a small number of Church members began to bring down this peaceful society.

1:24 "I guess one of the greatest mysteries of mortality is why mankind fails to learn from history. Why do those who profess to be true followers of Christ so often become victims of the enticements [temptations] of the world?" (L. Tom Perry, in Conference Report, October 1992, 19).

1:25 As soon as the people were lifted up in pride, they stopped sharing what they had with each other. President Ezra Taft Benson taught that "selfishness is one of the more common faces of pride" (in Conference Report, April 1989, 5).

1:30 ***rent in twain***—broken in pieces

1:31 The term *Jews* often refers to a descendant from the tribe of Judah. However, the Book of Mormon also uses the term *Jew* to refer to any Israelite from the land or kingdom of Judah, even if not descended from the tribe of Judah (see LDS Bible Dictionary, s.v. "Jew," 713). In addition, the Book of Mormon uses the term *Jews* to refer to the entire house of Israel (see *Book of Mormon Student Manual, Religion 121 and 122,* 15).

The disciples of Jesus performed wonderful miracles, but the people kept trying to kill them. Why don't miracles convince people if they don't first believe in Jesus Christ?

32 And they did cast them into furnaces of fire, and they came forth receiving no harm.

33 And they also cast them into dens of wild beasts, and they did play with the wild beasts even as a child with a lamb; and they did come forth from among them, receiving no harm.

34 Nevertheless, the people did harden their hearts, for they were led by many priests and false prophets to build up many churches, and to do all manner of iniquity. And they did smite upon the people of Jesus; but the people of Jesus did not smite again. And thus they did dwindle in unbelief and wickedness, from year to year, even until two hundred and thirty years had passed away.

35 And now it came to pass in this year, yea, in the two hundred and thirty and first year, there was a great division among the people.

## *The People Divide into Tribes and Introduce Secret Combinations*

36 And it came to pass that in this year there arose a people who were called the Nephites, and they were true believers in Christ; and among them there were those who were called by the Lamanites—Jacobites, and Josephites, and Zoramites;

37 Therefore the true believers in Christ, and the true worshipers of Christ, (among whom were the three disciples of Jesus who should tarry) were called Nephites, and Jacobites, and Josephites, and Zoramites.

38 And it came to pass that they who rejected the gospel were called Lamanites, and Lemuelites, and Ishmaelites; and they did not dwindle in unbelief, but they did wilfully rebel against the gospel of Christ; and they did teach their children that they should not believe, even as their fathers, from the beginning, did dwindle.

39 And it was because of the wickedness and abomination of their fathers, even as it was in the beginning. And they were taught to hate the children of God, even as the Lamanites were taught to hate the children of Nephi from the beginning.

40 And it came to pass that two hundred and forty and four years had passed away, and thus were the affairs of the people. And the more wicked part of the people did wax strong, and became exceedingly more numerous than were the people of God.

41 And they did still continue to build up churches unto themselves, and adorn them with all manner of precious things. And thus did two hundred and fifty years pass away, and also two hundred and sixty years.

42 And it came to pass that the wicked part of the people began again to build up the secret oaths and combinations of Gadianton.

43 And also the people who were called the people of Nephi began to be proud in their hearts, because of their exceeding riches, and become vain like unto their brethren, the Lamanites.

44 And from this time the disciples began to sorrow for the sins of the world.

45 And it came to pass that when three hundred years had passed away, both the people of Nephi and the Lamanites had become exceedingly wicked one like unto another.

46 And it came to pass that the robbers of Gadianton did spread over all the face of the land; and there were none that were righteous save it were the disciples of Jesus. And gold and silver did they lay up in store in abundance, and did traffic in all manner of traffic.

47 And it came to pass that after three hundred and five years had passed away, (and the people did still remain in wickedness) Amos died; and his brother, Ammaron, did keep the record in his stead.

---

1:34 ***smite***—hit
***dwindle***—fall away

1:38 ***wilfully***—purposefully or knowingly

1:40 ***wax***—grow

1:42 A secret combination is a group of wicked people who secretly join together to lie, cheat, steal, murder, or do whatever is necessary to gain riches, wealth, or power (see Helaman 7:21; 8:27). The first secret combination was between Satan and Cain, who killed his brother Abel to get his flocks (see Moses 5:28–32). "Among today's secret combinations are gangs, drug cartels, and organized crime families" (M. Russell Ballard, in Conference Report, October 1997, 51).

1:43 ***vain***—foolish or proud

1:46 ***traffic***—trade

Who do you think was more happy—the Gadianton robbers or the righteous disciples of Jesus? What makes the followers of Jesus happy?

48 And it came to pass that when three hundred and twenty years had passed away, Ammaron, being constrained by the Holy Ghost, did hide up the records which were sacred—yea, even all the sacred records which had been handed down from generation to generation, which were sacred—even until the three hundred and twentieth year from the coming of Christ.
49 And he did hide them up unto the Lord, that they might come again unto the remnant of the house of Jacob, according to the prophecies and the promises of the Lord. And thus is the end of the record of Ammaron.

1:48 ***constrained***—prompted

1:49 ***the remnant***—those who are left

# THE BOOK OF MORMON

*This small book is the prophet Mormon's own writings about the things that happened in his day (see the illustration "The Plates of the Book of Mormon" on page xiv). The first seven chapters are Mormon's account of the wars and destruction of his people, the Nephites. These events occurred between about A.D. 322 and 385. The last two chapters were written by Mormon's son, Moroni, who finished this book after his father was killed.*

## CHAPTER 1

*Mormon begins to record the history of the Nephites in his day. It is a time of wickedness and war. Notice what kind of young man Mormon is and how different he is from the people around him.*

### *Mormon, as a Child, Is Given Responsibility for the Sacred Records*

1 AND now I, Mormon, make a record of the
things which I have both seen and heard, and call
it the Book of Mormon.
2 And about the time that Ammaron hid up the
records unto the Lord, he came unto me, (I being
about ten years of age, and I began to be learned
somewhat after the manner of the learning of my
people) and Ammaron said unto me: I perceive that
thou art a sober child, and art quick to observe;
3 Therefore, when ye are about twenty and four
years old I would that ye should remember the
things that ye have observed concerning this
people; and when ye are of that age go to the land
Antum, unto a hill which shall be called Shim; and
there have I deposited unto the Lord all the sacred
engravings concerning this people.
4 And behold, ye shall take the plates of Nephi
unto yourself, and the remainder shall ye leave in
the place where they are; and ye shall engrave on
the plates of Nephi all the things that ye have
observed concerning this people.
5 And I, Mormon, being a descendant of Nephi,
(and my father's name was Mormon) I remembered
the things which Ammaron commanded me.

### *War Begins Between the Nephites and the Lamanites*

6 And it came to pass that I, being eleven years
old, was carried by my father into the land southward, even to the land of Zarahemla.
7 The whole face of the land had become covered
with buildings, and the people were as numerous
almost, as it were the sand of the sea.
8 And it came to pass in this year there began to
be a war between the Nephites, who consisted of
the Nephites and the Jacobites and the Josephites
and the Zoramites; and this war was between the
Nephites, and the Lamanites and the Lemuelites and
the Ishmaelites.
9 Now the Lamanites and the Lemuelites and the
Ishmaelites were called Lamanites, and the two par-
ties were Nephites and Lamanites.
10 And it came to pass that the war began to be
among them in the borders of Zarahemla, by the
waters of Sidon.

---

1:2 ***perceive***—see
***sober***—serious and dependable
***quick to observe***—teachable, thoughtful, and aware of what is happening around you

1:3 ***observed***—seen and learned
***deposited***—buried or hidden
***engravings***—writings cut, etched, or impressed into metal

1:5 ***a descendant***—of the family or a direct relative

MORMON, AGE 10, BY SCOTT SNOW

*Mormon was "a sober child, and . . . quick to observe."*

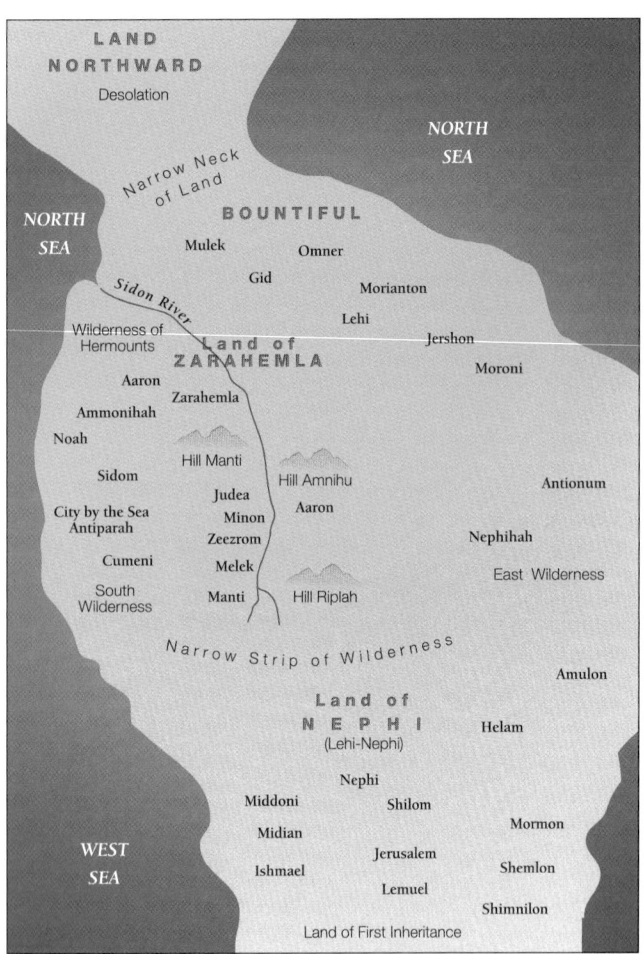


*As an eleven-year-old, Mormon moved with his father to the land of Zarahemla.*

11 And it came to pass that the Nephites had gathered together a great number of men, even to exceed the number of thirty thousand. And it came to pass that they did have in this same year a number of battles, in which the Nephites did beat the Lamanites and did slay many of them.

12 And it came to pass that the Lamanites withdrew their design, and there was peace settled in the land; and peace did remain for the space of about four years, that there was no bloodshed.

## *Because of the Wickedness of the People, the Three "Beloved Disciples" Are Taken Away, and Mormon Is Forbidden to Preach*

13 But wickedness did prevail upon the face of the whole land, insomuch that the Lord did take away his beloved disciples, and the work of miracles and of healing did cease because of the iniquity of the people.

14 And there were no gifts from the Lord, and the Holy Ghost did not come upon any, because of their wickedness and unbelief.

15 And I, being fifteen years of age and being somewhat of a sober mind, therefore I was visited of the Lord, and tasted and knew of the goodness of Jesus.

16 And I did endeavor to preach unto this people, but my mouth was shut, and I was forbidden that I should preach unto them; for behold they had wilfully rebelled against their God; and the beloved disciples were taken away out of the land, because of their iniquity.

17 But I did remain among them, but I was forbidden to preach unto them, because of the hardness of their hearts; and because of the hardness of their hearts the land was cursed for their sake.

---

1:11 ***to exceed***—more than

1:12 ***withdrew their design***—gave up their plan

1:13 ***prevail***—continue and grow
***iniquity***—wickedness

The "beloved disciples" spoken of here are the three Nephite disciples of Jesus Christ who were promised they would not die but be allowed to remain on the earth to teach and bless people (see 3 Nephi 28:4–12).

1:14 Mormon tells us that the Holy Ghost and spiritual gifts were no longer given to the people in his day because of their wickedness and lack of faith. The Prophet Joseph Smith learned that we do not have to be perfect to receive spiritual gifts, but we do have to be trying to keep the commandments (see D&C 46:9).

1:15 Imagine what this experience meant to the fifteen-year-old Mormon. He lived in a time of great wickedness and yet he was able to live righteously enough to be visited by the Savior! In what ways would you like to be more like Mormon?

1:16 ***endeavor***—try

These people "wilfully rebelled" against God, which means they knew what was right and chose to do wrong anyway. King Benjamin told us that such people take themselves so far away from the Spirit of the Lord that they can no longer be helped by the Lord (see Mosiah 2:36–37). The Prophet Joseph Smith learned that people who refuse to repent lose even the light or spiritual understanding they once had (see D&C 1:33).

18 And these Gadianton robbers, who were among the Lamanites, did infest the land, insomuch that the inhabitants thereof began to hide up their treasures in the earth; and they became slippery, because the Lord had cursed the land, that they could not hold them, nor retain them again.
19 And it came to pass that there were sorceries, and witchcrafts, and magics; and the power of the evil one was wrought upon all the face of the land, even unto the fulfilling of all the words of Abinadi, and also Samuel the Lamanite.

## CHAPTER 2

*The Nephite nation is near destruction, and Mormon fears for the people. As you read, think about Mormon's feelings for the Nephites during this terrible time.*

### At Age Sixteen, Mormon Leads the Nephite Armies

1 AND it came to pass in that same year there began to be a war again between the Nephites and the Lamanites. And notwithstanding I being young, was large in stature; therefore the people of Nephi appointed me that I should be their leader, or the leader of their armies.
2 Therefore it came to pass that in my sixteenth year I did go forth at the head of an army of the Nephites, against the Lamanites; therefore three hundred and twenty and six years had passed away.
3 And it came to pass that in the three hundred and twenty and seventh year the Lamanites did come upon us with exceedingly great power, insomuch that they did frighten my armies; therefore they would not fight, and they began to retreat towards the north countries.
4 And it came to pass that we did come to the city of Angola, and we did take possession of the city, and make preparations to defend ourselves against the Lamanites. And it came to pass that we did fortify the city with our might; but notwithstanding all our fortifications the Lamanites did come upon us and did drive us out of the city.
5 And they did also drive us forth out of the land of David.
6 And we marched forth and came to the land of Joshua, which was in the borders west by the seashore.
7 And it came to pass that we did gather in our people as fast as it were possible, that we might get them together in one body.
8 But behold, the land was filled with robbers and with Lamanites; and notwithstanding the great destruction which hung over my people, they did not repent of their evil doings; therefore there was blood and carnage spread throughout all the face of the land, both on the part of the Nephites and also on the part of the Lamanites; and it was one complete revolution throughout all the face of the land.
9 And now, the Lamanites had a king, and his name was Aaron; and he came against us with an army of forty and four thousand. And behold, I withstood him with forty and two thousand. And it came to pass that I beat him with my army that he fled before me. And behold, all this was done, and three hundred and thirty years had passed away.

---

1:18 ***did infest***—were everywhere in
***inhabitants thereof***—people who lived there
***retain***—keep

1:18 (17–18) As the people became wicked many began to hide their treasures in the earth. How do you think they felt about their treasures compared to how they felt about God? Why do you think the Lord "cursed the land" so that they could not find their treasures again?

1:19 ***sorceries, and witchcrafts, and magics***—all kinds of evils inspired by the devil
***wrought***—worked

2:1 ***notwithstanding***—even though
***stature***—size and height

2:2 (1–2) Mormon was only sixteen years of age when he became the leader of the Nephite armies. This shows that the Lord can use young people to accomplish His work. What can you do to be an example and leader for your family and friends?

2:3 ***retreat***—withdraw or go back

2:4 ***fortify the city***—strengthen and protect the city by building defenses

2:8 ***carnage***—death and destruction
***complete revolution***—full-scale war

## Mormon Is Saddened by the Wickedness of His People

10 And it came to pass that the Nephites began to
repent of their iniquity, and began to cry even as
had been prophesied by Samuel the prophet; for
behold no man could keep that which was his own,
for the thieves, and the robbers, and the murderers,
and the magic art, and the witchcraft which was in
the land.
11 Thus there began to be a mourning and a
lamentation in all the land because of these things,
and more especially among the people of Nephi.
12 And it came to pass that when I, Mormon,
saw their lamentation and their mourning and
their sorrow before the Lord, my heart did begin
to rejoice within me, knowing the mercies and the
long-suffering of the Lord, therefore supposing
that he would be merciful unto them that they
would again become a righteous people.
13 But behold this my joy was vain, for their sorrowing was not unto repentance, because of the
goodness of God; but it was rather the sorrowing of
the damned, because the Lord would not always
suffer them to take happiness in sin.
14 And they did not come unto Jesus with broken
hearts and contrite spirits, but they did curse God,
and wish to die. Nevertheless they would struggle
with the sword for their lives.
15 And it came to pass that my sorrow did return
unto me again, and I saw that the day of grace was
passed with them, both temporally and spiritually;
for I saw thousands of them hewn down in open
rebellion against their God, and heaped up as dung
upon the face of the land. And thus three hundred
and forty and four years had passed away.

## Mormon Continues to Lead the Nephites in Battle

16 And it came to pass that in the three hundred
and forty and fifth year the Nephites did begin to
flee before the Lamanites; and they were pursued
until they came even to the land of Jashon, before
it was possible to stop them in their retreat.
17 And now, the city of Jashon was near the land
where Ammaron had deposited the records unto
the Lord, that they might not be destroyed. And
behold I had gone according to the word of
Ammaron, and taken the plates of Nephi, and did
make a record according to the words of Ammaron.
18 And upon the plates of Nephi I did make a full
account of all the wickedness and abominations;
but upon these plates I did forbear to make a full
account of their wickedness and abominations, for
behold, a continual scene of wickedness and abominations has been before mine eyes ever since I
have been sufficient to behold the ways of man.
19 And wo is me because of their wickedness; for
my heart has been filled with sorrow because of
their wickedness, all my days; nevertheless, I know
that I shall be lifted up at the last day.

---

2:10 ***iniquity***—sins
***magic art, and the witchcraft***—evils inspired by the devil

2:11 ***lamentation***—wailing and sorrow

2:13 ***vain***—useless
***the damned***—those without hope of salvation

We must be truly sorry for our sins in order to repent of them (see 2 Corinthians 7:10). This is called "godly sorrow." President Ezra Taft Benson taught: "Godly sorrow is a gift of the Spirit. It is a deep realization that our actions have offended our Father and our God. It is the sharp and keen awareness that our behavior caused the Savior . . . to endure agony and suffering" (*The Teachings of Ezra Taft Benson,* 72).

Alma taught his son Corianton that "wickedness never was happiness" (Alma 41:10).

2:14 ***contrite***—truly repentant

2:15 ***day of grace***—opportunity to repent
***temporally***—physically
***hewn***—cut
***dung***—manure

Nearly three hundred years earlier Samuel the Lamanite told the people they had put off the day of their repentance until it was too late (see Helaman 13:38). We must prepare to meet God while we are alive and not wait until we die and face the time "wherein there can be no labor performed" (see Alma 34:32–34).

2:17 ***deposited***—buried or hidden

2:18 ***abominations***—sinful behavior

2:19 ***wo***—sorrow

2:19 (17–19) Even though there was wickedness all around, Mormon was able to remain righteous. Can you identify one thing Mormon did that you could also do to successfully rise above the evil that surrounds you?

20 And it came to pass that in this year the people
of Nephi again were hunted and driven. And it
came to pass that we were driven forth until we had
come northward to the land which was called
Shem.
21 And it came to pass that we did fortify the city
of Shem, and we did gather in our people as much
as it were possible, that perhaps we might save
them from destruction.
22 And it came to pass in the three hundred and
forty and sixth year they began to come upon us
again.
23 And it came to pass that I did speak unto my
people, and did urge them with great energy, that
they would stand boldly before the Lamanites and
fight for their wives, and their children, and their
houses, and their homes.
24 And my words did arouse them somewhat to
vigor, insomuch that they did not flee from before
the Lamanites, but did stand with boldness against
them.
25 And it came to pass that we did contend with
an army of thirty thousand against an army of fifty
thousand. And it came to pass that we did stand
before them with such firmness that they did flee
from before us.
26 And it came to pass that when they had fled we
did pursue them with our armies, and did meet
them again, and did beat them; nevertheless the
strength of the Lord was not with us; yea, we were
left to ourselves, that the Spirit of the Lord did not
abide in us; therefore we had become weak like
unto our brethren.
27 And my heart did sorrow because of this the
great calamity of my people, because of their
wickedness and their abominations. But behold, we
did go forth against the Lamanites and the robbers
of Gadianton, until we had again taken possession
of the lands of our inheritance.
28 And the three hundred and forty and ninth year
had passed away. And in the three hundred and
fiftieth year we made a treaty with the Lamanites
and the robbers of Gadianton, in which we did get
the lands of our inheritance divided.
29 And the Lamanites did give unto us the land
northward, yea, even to the narrow passage which
led into the land southward. And we did give unto
the Lamanites all the land southward

## CHAPTER 3

*Mormon is saddened because of the wickedness of his people. He refuses to lead them into battle and pleads with them to repent. Look for what Mormon teaches about the final Judgment.*

### Mormon Asks His People to Repent

1 AND it came to pass that the Lamanites did not
come to battle again until ten years more had
passed away. And behold, I had employed my
people, the Nephites, in preparing their lands and
their arms against the time of battle.
2 And it came to pass that the Lord did say unto
me: Cry unto this people—Repent ye, and come
unto me, and be ye baptized, and build up again
my church, and ye shall be spared.
3 And I did cry unto this people, but it was in vain;
and they did not realize that it was the Lord that had
spared them, and granted unto them a chance for
repentance. And behold they did harden their hearts
against the Lord their God.

---

2:26 Mormon sorrowed for his people because they didn't have the Spirit of the Lord in their lives. Why would losing the Spirit be so terrible?

2:27 ***calamity***—disaster

2:28 ***a treaty***—an agreement or promise

3:1 ***employed***—put to work
***arms***—weapons

3:2 ***Cry unto***—Preach to or tell

3:3 ***in vain***—useless

These people did not understand and were not grateful for the Lord's blessings. We have been commanded to give thanks unto God for every blessing we receive (see D&C 46:32). How can you show gratitude to God?

MORMON PREACHING TO THE NEPHITES, BY ROBERT T. BARRETT

*"I did cry unto this people, but it was in vain."*

## The Nephites Prepare for and Win Other Battles

4 And it came to pass that after this tenth year had
passed away, making, in the whole, three hundred
and sixty years from the coming of Christ, the king
of the Lamanites sent an epistle unto me, which
gave unto me to know that they were preparing to
come again to battle against us.
5 And it came to pass that I did cause my people
that they should gather themselves together at the
land Desolation, to a city which was in the borders,
by the narrow pass which led into the land southward.
6 And there we did place our armies, that we
might stop the armies of the Lamanites, that they
might not get possession of any of our lands; therefore we did fortify against them with all our force.
7 And it came to pass that in the three hundred
and sixty and first year the Lamanites did come
down to the city of Desolation to battle against us;
and it came to pass that in that year we did beat
them, insomuch that they did return to their own
lands again.
8 And in the three hundred and sixty and second
year they did come down again to battle. And we
did beat them again, and did slay a great number of
them, and their dead were cast into the sea.

---

3:4 *Christ* is a Greek word meaning "the Anointed One"; the Hebrew word with the same meaning is *Messiah.* Jesus is the Christ—the one chosen, set apart, and sent by God to save us (see LDS Bible Dictionary, s.v. "Christ," 633).

***an epistle***—a letter

3:6 ***fortify against***—strengthen ourselves and prepare for

3:8 ***slay***—kill

9 And now, because of this great thing which my people, the Nephites, had done, they began to boast in their own strength, and began to swear before the heavens that they would avenge themselves of the blood of their brethren who had been slain by their enemies.

10 And they did swear by the heavens, and also by the throne of God, that they would go up to battle against their enemies, and would cut them off from the face of the land.

## Mormon Refuses to Lead Because of His People's Wickedness

11 And it came to pass that I, Mormon, did utterly refuse from this time forth to be a commander and a leader of this people, because of their wickedness and abomination.

12 Behold, I had led them, notwithstanding their wickedness I had led them many times to battle, and had loved them, according to the love of God which was in me, with all my heart; and my soul had been poured out in prayer unto my God all the day long for them; nevertheless, it was without faith, because of the hardness of their hearts.

13 And thrice have I delivered them out of the hands of their enemies, and they have repented not of their sins.

14 And when they had sworn by all that had been forbidden them by our Lord and Savior Jesus Christ, that they would go up unto their enemies to battle, and avenge themselves of the blood of their brethren, behold the voice of the Lord came unto me, saying:

15 Vengeance is mine, and I will repay; and because this people repented not after I had delivered them, behold, they shall be cut off from the face of the earth.

16 And it came to pass that I utterly refused to go up against mine enemies; and I did even as the Lord had commanded me; and I did stand as an idle witness to manifest unto the world the things which I saw and heard, according to the manifestations of the Spirit which had testified of things to come.

## Mormon Invites the Gentiles and Latter-day Israel to Come unto Christ

17 Therefore I write unto you, Gentiles, and also unto you, house of Israel, when the work shall commence, that ye shall be about to prepare to return to the land of your inheritance;

---

3:9 To boast in one's own strength is to be full of pride. President Ezra Taft Benson taught: "Pride is the universal sin, the great vice. . . . The [cure] for pride is humility—meekness, submissiveness (see Alma 7:23). It is the broken heart and contrite spirit" (in Conference Report, April 1989, 6).

***swear***—promise or make a solemn oath
***avenge themselves of***—get even for

3:10 The Nephites began to swear, or to make wicked promises or oaths in God's name. Jesus Christ explained that this was an evil practice (see 3 Nephi 12:34 and Matthew 5:34–37).

3:11 ***utterly***—completely
***abomination***—sinful behavior

3:12 To have a pure and perfect love for people is to have "charity," which is a gift of God (see Moroni 7:45–47).

How difficult was it for Mormon to love his people when he knew they were wicked? What can you learn from Mormon's example about continuing to love others even when they are not keeping the commandments?

3:13 ***thrice***—three times

3:15 To take "vengeance" on someone is to punish them for their actions. The Lord, however, has commanded us to forgive all people (see D&C 64:9–11).

3:17 ***house***—family
***commence***—begin

*Gentiles* is a word that means "nations." It refers to those not of the family of Israel or who do not believe in the God of Israel. In the Book of Mormon it also refers to those who come from gentile nations, which are all nations outside the land of Israel (see LDS Bible Dictionary, s.v. "Gentile," 679).

The name *Israel* means "one who prevails with God," or "let God prevail." It is used several ways in the scriptures. It may refer to (1) the man Jacob, whose name was changed to Israel; (2) the family, children, or tribes of Israel (the scriptures often use the phrase "house of Israel" in this sense); (3) the land of Israel; or (4) the true believers in Christ, no matter what their family or where they live (see LDS Bible Dictionary, s.v. "Israel," 708).

18 Yea, behold, I write unto all the ends of the
earth; yea, unto you, twelve tribes of Israel, who
shall be judged according to your works by the
twelve whom Jesus chose to be his disciples in the
land of Jerusalem.
19 And I write also unto the remnant of this
people, who shall also be judged by the twelve
whom Jesus chose in this land; and they shall be
judged by the other twelve whom Jesus chose in
the land of Jerusalem.
20 And these things doth the Spirit manifest unto
me; therefore I write unto you all. And for this
cause I write unto you, that ye may know that ye
must all stand before the judgment-seat of Christ,
yea, every soul who belongs to the whole human
family of Adam; and ye must stand to be judged of
your works, whether they be good or evil;
21 And also that ye may believe the gospel of
Jesus Christ, which ye shall have among you; and
also that the Jews, the covenant people of the Lord,
shall have other witness besides him whom they
saw and heard, that Jesus, whom they slew, was the
very Christ and the very God.
22 And I would that I could persuade all ye ends
of the earth to repent and prepare to stand before
the judgment-seat of Christ.

## CHAPTER 4

*The Nephites and Lamanites become more wicked. The Lamanites begin to destroy the Nephites. Watch for what happens to the Nephites because they turn away from the Lord.*

### *The Nephites Become More Wicked and the Lamanites Begin to Conquer Them*

1 AND now it came to pass that in the three hundred and sixty and third year the Nephites did go
up with their armies to battle against the Lamanites,
out of the land Desolation.
2 And it came to pass that the armies of the
Nephites were driven back again to the land of
Desolation. And while they were yet weary, a fresh
army of the Lamanites did come upon them; and
they had a sore battle, insomuch that the Lamanites
did take possession of the city Desolation, and did
slay many of the Nephites, and did take many prisoners.
3 And the remainder did flee and join the inhabitants of the city Teancum. Now the city Teancum
lay in the borders by the seashore; and it was also
near the city Desolation.
4 And it was because the armies of the Nephites
went up unto the Lamanites that they began to be
smitten; for were it not for that, the Lamanites could
have had no power over them.
5 But, behold, the judgments of God will overtake
the wicked; and it is by the wicked that the wicked
are punished; for it is the wicked that stir up the
hearts of the children of men unto bloodshed.
6 And it came to pass that the Lamanites did make
preparations to come against the city Teancum.
7 And it came to pass in the three hundred and
sixty and fourth year the Lamanites did come
against the city Teancum, that they might take possession of the city Teancum also.

---

3:18 The Savior told His Apostles that they would help judge the twelve tribes of Israel (see Matthew 19:28).

3:20 All people, after they die, will be brought before the Lord and be judged for the choices they have made on earth. How does it make you feel to know that Jesus Christ will judge you? Why is He the perfect judge?

3:21 The word *Jew* often refers to a descendant from the tribe of Judah. However, the Book of Mormon also uses the term *Jew* to refer to any Israelite from the land or kingdom of Judah, even if not descended from the tribe of Judah (see LDS Bible Dictionary, s.v. "Jew," 713). In addition, the Book of Mormon uses the term *Jews* to refer to the entire house of Israel (see *Book of Mormon Student Manual, Religion 121 and 122,* 15).

4:1 In this chapter Mormon refuses to lead the Nephites in battle. They had become very proud and would not repent. Instead of just defending themselves, they attacked the Lamanites out of anger and vengeance (see Mormon 3:9–11).

4:2 ***weary***—tired
***sore***—terrible

4:4 ***smitten***—beaten

4:5 ***overtake***—conquer or overpower

4:5 (4–5) In the days of Captain Moroni, the Lord protected the Nephites because they were "faithful unto [God]" (Alma 44:3–4). However, because the people in the days of Mormon were wicked, they did not receive the Lord's protection.

8 And it came to pass that they were repulsed and
driven back by the Nephites. And when the
Nephites saw that they had driven the Lamanites
they did again boast of their own strength; and they
went forth in their own might, and took possession
again of the city Desolation.
9 And now all these things had been done, and
there had been thousands slain on both sides, both
the Nephites and the Lamanites.
10 And it came to pass that the three hundred and
sixty and sixth year had passed away, and the
Lamanites came again upon the Nephites to battle;
and yet the Nephites repented not of the evil they
had done, but persisted in their wickedness continually.
11 And it is impossible for the tongue to describe,
or for man to write a perfect description of the
horrible scene of the blood and carnage which
was among the people, both of the Nephites and
of the Lamanites; and every heart was hardened,
so that they delighted in the shedding of blood
continually.
12 And there never had been so great wickedness
among all the children of Lehi, nor even among all
the house of Israel, according to the words of the
Lord, as was among this people.
13 And it came to pass that the Lamanites did take
possession of the city Desolation, and this because
their number did exceed the number of the
Nephites.
14 And they did also march forward against the
city Teancum, and did drive the inhabitants forth
out of her, and did take many prisoners both
women and children, and did offer them up as sacrifices unto their idol gods.
15 And it came to pass that in the three hundred
and sixty and seventh year, the Nephites being
angry because the Lamanites had sacrificed their
women and their children, that they did go against
the Lamanites with exceedingly great anger, insomuch that they did beat again the Lamanites, and
drive them out of their lands.
16 And the Lamanites did not come again against
the Nephites until the three hundred and seventy
and fifth year.
17 And in this year they did come down against
the Nephites with all their powers; and they were
not numbered because of the greatness of their
number.

## The Nephites Begin to Flee Before the Lamanite Armies

18 And from this time forth did the Nephites
gain no power over the Lamanites, but began to
be swept off by them even as a dew before the
sun.
19 And it came to pass that the Lamanites did
come down against the city Desolation; and there
was an exceedingly sore battle fought in the land
Desolation, in the which they did beat the
Nephites.
20 And they fled again from before them, and they
came to the city Boaz; and there they did stand
against the Lamanites with exceeding boldness,
insomuch that the Lamanites did not beat them until
they had come again the second time.
21 And when they had come the second time, the
Nephites were driven and slaughtered with an
exceedingly great slaughter; their women and their
children were again sacrificed unto idols.
22 And it came to pass that the Nephites did again
flee from before them, taking all the inhabitants
with them, both in towns and villages.

---

4:8 ***repulsed***—stopped

Again the Nephites "boast of their own strength." The Lord has said, "Thou shalt thank the Lord thy God in all things" (D&C 59:7), and "in nothing doth man offend God, or against none is his wrath kindled, save those who confess not his hand in all things" (D&C 59:21).

4:10 ***persisted***—continued

4:11 ***carnage***—killing

4:12 Mormon describes in chilling detail the awful wickedness committed by the Lamanites and the Nephites in a letter to his son, Moroni (see Moroni 9:6–11, 18–20).

4:13 ***did exceed***—was more than

4:14 ***offer them up***—kill them

4:18 The moisture that is sometimes on the ground in the early morning is called dew. When the sunlight hits the dew, it quickly dries up and disappears. In a similar way, the Nephites were quickly disappearing off the land.

4:21 ***slaughtered***—brutally killed

23 And now I, Mormon, seeing that the Lamanites were about to overthrow the land, therefore I did go to the hill Shim, and did take up all the records which Ammaron had hid up unto the Lord.

## CHAPTER 5

*Mormon leads his people in battle. He writes of their wickedness and the sad future of the Lamanites. Try to sense his sadness and loss of hope for his once righteous people.*

### *Mormon Sadly Leads the Nephites into Battle Again*

1 AND it came to pass that I did go forth among the Nephites, and did repent of the oath which I had made that I would no more assist them; and they gave me command again of their armies, for they looked upon me as though I could deliver them from their afflictions.

2 But behold, I was without hope, for I knew the judgments of the Lord which should come upon them; for they repented not of their iniquities, but did struggle for their lives without calling upon that Being who created them.

3 And it came to pass that the Lamanites did come against us as we had fled to the city of Jordan; but behold, they were driven back that they did not take the city at that time.

4 And it came to pass that they came against us again, and we did maintain the city. And there were also other cities which were maintained by the Nephites, which strongholds did cut them off that they could not get into the country which lay before us, to destroy the inhabitants of our land.

5 And it came to pass that whatsoever lands we had passed by, and the inhabitants thereof were not gathered in, were destroyed by the Lamanites, and their towns, and villages, and cities were burned with fire; and thus three hundred and seventy and nine years passed away.

6 And it came to pass that in the three hundred and eightieth year the Lamanites did come again against us to battle, and we did stand against them boldly; but it was all in vain, for so great were their numbers that they did tread the people of the Nephites under their feet.

7 And it came to pass that we did again take to flight, and those whose flight was swifter than the Lamanites' did escape, and those whose flight did not exceed the Lamanites' were swept down and destroyed.

PHOTOGRAPH BY EDWIN M. WOOLLEY

*This is the Hill Vigia in Central America. Ammaron hid the records in a hill.*

4:23 ***overthrow***—take control of

When Mormon was only ten years old, Ammaron told him that sacred records were hidden in the hill Shim. Ammaron commanded Mormon that when he became old enough, Mormon was to get the plates and write upon them all the things that he had seen in his lifetime (see Mormon 1:2–5).

5:1 ***repent of the oath***—turn from the promise
***assist***—help
***afflictions***—troubles or problems

5:4 ***strongholds***—protected and guarded cities

5:6 ***in vain***—useless
***tread***—crush

5:7 ***take to flight***—retreat
***did not exceed***—was not quicker than

## The Book of Mormon Will Come Forth to Bring People to Christ

8 And now behold, I, Mormon, do not desire to
harrow up the souls of men in casting before them
such an awful scene of blood and carnage as was
laid before mine eyes; but I, knowing that these
things must surely be made known, and that all
things which are hid must be revealed upon the
house-tops—
9 And also that a knowledge of these things must
come unto the remnant of these people, and also
unto the Gentiles, who the Lord hath said should
scatter this people, and this people should be
counted as naught among them—therefore I write
a small abridgment, daring not to give a full account
of the things which I have seen, because of the
commandment which I have received, and also that
ye might not have too great sorrow because of the
wickedness of this people.
10 And now behold, this I speak unto their seed,
and also to the Gentiles who have care for the
house of Israel, that realize and know from whence
their blessings come.
11 For I know that such will sorrow for the
calamity of the house of Israel; yea, they will sorrow for the destruction of this people; they will
sorrow that this people had not repented that they
might have been clasped in the arms of Jesus.
12 Now these things are written unto the remnant
of the house of Jacob; and they are written after this
manner, because it is known of God that wickedness will not bring them forth unto them; and they
are to be hid up unto the Lord that they may come
forth in his own due time.
13 And this is the commandment which I have
received; and behold, they shall come forth according to the commandment of the Lord, when he shall
see fit, in his wisdom.
14 And behold, they shall go unto the unbelieving
of the Jews; and for this intent shall they go—that
they may be persuaded that Jesus is the Christ, the
Son of the living God; that the Father may bring
about, through his most Beloved, his great and eternal purpose, in restoring the Jews, or all the house
of Israel, to the land of their inheritance, which the
Lord their God hath given them, unto the fulfilling
of his covenant;
15 And also that the seed of this people may more
fully believe his gospel, which shall go forth unto
them from the Gentiles; for this people shall be
scattered, and shall become a dark, a filthy, and a
loathsome people, beyond the description of that
which ever hath been amongst us, yea, even that
which hath been among the Lamanites, and this
because of their unbelief and idolatry.

---

5:8 ***harrow up***—trouble or disturb
***carnage***—death and destruction

If we choose to not repent of our sins, they will eventually be known by everyone, as if they were "spoken upon the housetops" (D&C 1:3).

5:9 ***naught***—nothing

Mormon knew an abridgment, or record, needed to be written of his people. The abridgment he made is what we now know as the book of Mormon (see Mormon 1:1).

5:9 (8–9) The destruction was so sickening to Mormon that it was difficult for him to write about it. "Mormon was torn not only by what he saw but also by what he must—and must not—write" (Jeffrey R. Holland, *Christ and the New Covenant,* 320).

5:10 ***seed***—descendants, meaning children, grandchildren and so on

5:11 ***calamity***—misery or misfortune

If these Nephites had given up their sins and repented they could have been "clasped [embraced or hugged] in the arms of Jesus." What sins would you be willing to give up to receive this blessing?

5:14 A covenant is an agreement between two people. In the scriptures it is usually an agreement between God and man. We promise to be obedient to God's commandments, and He promises to bless us (see LDS Bible Dictionary, s.v., "Covenant," 651).

The title page in the Book of Mormon also tells us that the book was written to convince "the Jew and Gentile that Jesus is the Christ." How has the Book of Mormon helped your testimony of Jesus Christ grow?

5:15 ***loathsome***—disgusting

5:15 (12–15) Mormon knows that his record will be hidden for many years before it is made available to the descendants of Lehi (see Enos 1:16), as well as to the Jews (see 2 Nephi 29:13).

16 For behold, the Spirit of the Lord hath already
ceased to strive with their fathers; and they are
without Christ and God in the world; and they are
driven about as chaff before the wind.
17 They were once a delightsome people, and
they had Christ for their shepherd; yea, they were
led even by God the Father.
18 But now, behold, they are led about by Satan,
even as chaff is driven before the wind, or as a vessel is tossed about upon the waves, without sail or
anchor, or without anything wherewith to steer her;
and even as she is, so are they.
19 And behold, the Lord hath reserved their blessings, which they might have received in the land,
for the Gentiles who shall possess the land.
20 But behold, it shall come to pass that they shall
be driven and scattered by the Gentiles; and after
they have been driven and scattered by the
Gentiles, behold, then will the Lord remember the
covenant which he made unto Abraham and unto
all the house of Israel.
21 And also the Lord will remember the prayers of
the righteous, which have been put up unto him for
them.
22 And then, O ye Gentiles, how can ye stand
before the power of God, except ye shall repent
and turn from your evil ways?
23 Know ye not that ye are in the hands of God?
Know ye not that he hath all power, and at his great
command the earth shall be rolled together as a
scroll?
24 Therefore, repent ye, and humble yourselves
before him, lest he shall come out in justice against
you—lest a remnant of the seed of Jacob shall go
forth among you as a lion, and tear you in pieces,
and there is none to deliver.

## CHAPTER 6

*As the Nephites gather for their final battles, Mormon hides the records in the Hill Cumorah. Watch for what leads to the destruction of the Nephite nation and how it could have been prevented.*

### The Nephites Gather to Cumorah for Their Last Battles

1 AND now I finish my record concerning the
destruction of my people, the Nephites. And it
came to pass that we did march forth before the
Lamanites.
2 And I, Mormon, wrote an epistle unto the king
of the Lamanites, and desired of him that he would
grant unto us that we might gather together our
people unto the land of Cumorah, by a hill which
was called Cumorah, and there we could give them
battle.
3 And it came to pass that the king of the
Lamanites did grant unto me the thing which I
desired.
4 And it came to pass that we did march forth to
the land of Cumorah, and we did pitch our tents
round about the hill Cumorah; and it was in a land
of many waters, rivers, and fountains; and here we
had hope to gain advantage over the Lamanites.
5 And when three hundred and eighty and four
years had passed away, we had gathered in all the
remainder of our people unto the land Cumorah.
6 And it came to pass that when we had gathered
in all our people in one to the land of Cumorah,
behold I, Mormon, began to be old; and knowing it
to be the last struggle of my people, and having been
commanded of the Lord that I should not suffer the

---

5:16 **chaff**—the worthless part of a head of wheat

5:18 **vessel**—ship

5:18 (17–18) The Book of Mormon is a story of a people who were blessed when they worshiped Jesus Christ and kept His commandments but who fell into misery when they sinned (see *Teachings of Gordon B. Hinckley,* 406–7). Why are you happier when you keep the commandments?

5:20 Both President Spencer W. Kimball and President Ezra Taft Benson taught that this verse had application to the afflictions, deaths, and inequities suffered by the American Indians over the years (see Spencer W. Kimball, *Faith Precedes the Miracle,* 341; Ezra Taft Benson, *This Nation Shall Endure,* 160–61).

6:2 **an epistle**—a letter
**grant**—allow or permit

6:4 **pitch**—set up

6:5 **remainder**—rest

6:6 **suffer**—allow or permit

records which had been handed down by our
fathers, which were sacred, to fall into the hands of
the Lamanites, (for the Lamanites would destroy
them) therefore I made this record out of the plates
of Nephi, and hid up in the hill Cumorah all the
records which had been entrusted to me by the
hand of the Lord, save it were these few plates
which I gave unto my son Moroni.
7 And it came to pass that my people, with their
wives and their children, did now behold the armies
of the Lamanites marching towards them; and with
that awful fear of death which fills the breasts of all
the wicked, did they await to receive them.
8 And it came to pass that they came to battle
against us, and every soul was filled with terror
because of the greatness of their numbers.
9 And it came to pass that they did fall upon my
people with the sword, and with the bow, and with
the arrow, and with the ax, and with all manner of
weapons of war.
10 And it came to pass that my men were hewn
down, yea, even my ten thousand who were with
me, and I fell wounded in the midst; and they passed
by me that they did not put an end to my life.
11 And when they had gone through and hewn
down all my people save it were twenty and four
of us, (among whom was my son Moroni) and we
having survived the dead of our people, did behold
on the morrow, when the Lamanites had returned
unto their camps, from the top of the hill Cumorah,
the ten thousand of my people who were hewn
down, being led in the front by me.
12 And we also beheld the ten thousand of my
people who were led by my son Moroni.
13 And behold, the ten thousand of Gidgiddonah
had fallen, and he also in the midst.
14 And Lamah had fallen with his ten thousand; and
Gilgal had fallen with his ten thousand; and Limhah
had fallen with his ten thousand; and Jeneum had
fallen with his ten thousand; and Cumenihah, and
Moronihah, and Antionum, and Shiblom, and
Shem, and Josh, had fallen with their ten thousand
each.
15 And it came to pass that there were ten more
who did fall by the sword, with their ten thousand
each; yea, even all my people, save it were those
twenty and four who were with me, and also a
few who had escaped into the south countries,
and a few who had deserted over unto the
Lamanites, had fallen; and their flesh, and bones,
and blood lay upon the face of the earth, being
left by the hands of those who slew them to
molder upon the land, and to crumble and to
return to their mother earth.

## Mormon Mourns the Death of His People

16 And my soul was rent with anguish, because of
the slain of my people, and I cried:
17 O ye fair ones, how could ye have departed
from the ways of the Lord! O ye fair ones, how
could ye have rejected that Jesus, who stood with
open arms to receive you!

---

6:6 ***entrusted***—given or committed

6:7 The faithful stripling soldiers who followed Helaman "did not fear death" (Alma 56:47) as they went into battle because they were righteous. On the other hand, the Nephites in Mormon's day had an "awful fear of death" because they had not kept the Lord's commandments.

6:8 ***terror***—fear or horror

6:8 (7–8) Everyone born on the earth will die someday. We just don't know exactly when our time to die will come. When we die we will have the opportunity to stand before God to be judged on what we did in this life. What could you do now to make that meeting with your Father in Heaven wonderful instead of frightening?

6:10 ***hewn***—cut
***midst***—middle

6:11 ***on the morrow***—the next day

6:13 ***fallen***—been wounded or killed

6:15 ***slew***—killed
***molder***—decay or rot

6:16 About 230,000 Nephite men were killed, and that number does not seem to include the women and children or any Lamanite deaths. More than four hundred fifty years earlier, Alma prophesied that because of their wickedness, the Nephites would either be destroyed or they would have to join the Lamanites (see Alma 45:13–14). The Nephites had become so wicked that they would not repent or even pray to God for help (see Mormon 5:1–2).

***anguish***—sorrow and grief

6:17 ***fair***—beautiful or precious

18 Behold, if ye had not done this, ye would not
have fallen. But behold, ye are fallen, and I mourn
your loss.
19 O ye fair sons and daughters, ye fathers and
mothers, ye husbands and wives, ye fair ones, how
is it that ye could have fallen!
20 But behold, ye are gone, and my sorrows cannot bring your return.
21 And the day soon cometh that your mortal
must put on immortality, and these bodies which
are now moldering in corruption must soon
become incorruptible bodies; and then ye must
stand before the judgment-seat of Christ, to be
judged according to your works; and if it so be that
ye are righteous, then are ye blessed with your
fathers who have gone before you.
22 O that ye had repented before this great
destruction had come upon you. But behold, ye are
gone, and the Father, yea, the Eternal Father of
heaven, knoweth your state; and he doeth with you
according to his justice and mercy.

## CHAPTER 7

*Mormon has compassion on the Lamanites even though they destroyed his people. He invites the Lamanites of our day to repent and believe in Christ to be saved from their sins. Watch for what he says we can do to be saved as well.*

### MORMON EXPLAINS WHAT THE LAMANITES MUST DO TO BE SAVED

1 AND now, behold, I would speak somewhat
unto the remnant of this people who are spared, if
it so be that God may give unto them my words,
that they may know of the things of their fathers;
yea, I speak unto you, ye remnant of the house of
Israel; and these are the words which I speak:
2 Know ye that ye are of the house of Israel.
3 Know ye that ye must come unto repentance, or
ye cannot be saved.
4 Know ye that ye must lay down your weapons
of war, and delight no more in the shedding of
blood, and take them not again, save it be that God
shall command you.
5 Know ye that ye must come to the knowledge of
your fathers, and repent of all your sins and iniquities, and believe in Jesus Christ, that he is the Son of
God, and that he was slain by the Jews, and by the
power of the Father he hath risen again, whereby he
hath gained the victory over the grave; and also in
him is the sting of death swallowed up.
6 And he bringeth to pass the resurrection of the
dead, whereby man must be raised to stand before
his judgment-seat.
7 And he hath brought to pass the redemption of
the world, whereby he that is found guiltless before
him at the judgment day hath it given unto him to

---

6:21 ***your mortal must put on immortality***—you will be resurrected
***moldering in corruption***—decaying or rotting
***incorruptible bodies***—bodies that are immortal or not subject to physical death or decay

6:22 Mormon knows that his people will face a fair judgment when they stand before their "Eternal Father of heaven." President J. Reuben Clark Jr. testified: "I believe that in his justice and mercy he will give us the maximum reward for our acts, give us all that he can give, and in the reverse, I believe that he will impose upon us the minimum penalty which it is possible for him to impose" (in Conference Report, October 1953, 84).

6:22 (17–22) Samuel the Lamanite also prophesied this terrible destruction, but he said it could be avoided if the Nephites would be willing to repent (see Helaman 13:8–10). Great destructions have also been prophesied for the last days (see D&C 29:14–21). What has the Lord told us that we must do to avoid the same awful fate as the Nephites?

7:1 ***remnant of this people***—Lamanites and their descendents

7:3 One reason why we cannot be saved without repentance is that we all sin (see 1 John 1:8), and no unclean thing can live with God (see 1 Nephi 10:21). Repentance makes it possible for us to be forgiven of our sins (see Alma 7:14).

7:4 ***delight no more in the shedding of blood***—take no more enjoyment in killing

7:5 ***iniquities***—wickedness
***slain***—killed

7:6 ***whereby***—by which

7:6 (5–6) Has someone you loved passed away? Did you feel the "sting" of their death? How does knowing that Jesus conquered death and has provided resurrection for everyone help to take away that sting?

7:7 ***guiltless***—innocent or not guilty

dwell in the presence of God in his kingdom, to
sing ceaseless praises with the choirs above, unto
the Father, and unto the Son, and unto the Holy
Ghost, which are one God, in a state of happiness
which hath no end.

## *The Book of Mormon Testifies of the Bible, and Both Books Testify of Jesus Christ*

8 Therefore repent, and be baptized in the name
of Jesus, and lay hold upon the gospel of Christ,
which shall be set before you, not only in this
record but also in the record which shall come unto
the Gentiles from the Jews, which record shall
come from the Gentiles unto you.
9 For behold, this is written for the intent that ye
may believe that; and if ye believe that ye will
believe this also; and if ye believe this ye will know
concerning your fathers, and also the marvelous
works which were wrought by the power of God
among them.
10 And ye will also know that ye are a remnant of
the seed of Jacob; therefore ye are numbered
among the people of the first covenant; and if it so
be that ye believe in Christ, and are baptized, first
with water, then with fire and with the Holy Ghost,
following the example of our Savior, according to
that which he hath commanded us, it shall be well
with you in the day of judgment. Amen.

# CHAPTER 8

*Mormon's ministry ends, and Moroni, as a prophet, sees the future of the Book of Mormon. Pay attention to Moroni's warnings for our day.*

## *Mormon Is Killed and Moroni Is Left Alone*

1 BEHOLD I, Moroni, do finish the record of my
father, Mormon. Behold, I have but few things to write,
which things I have been commanded by my father.
2 And now it came to pass that after the great and
tremendous battle at Cumorah, behold, the
Nephites who had escaped into the country southward were hunted by the Lamanites, until they
were all destroyed.

---

7:7 ***dwell***—live
***ceaseless***—never ending

Redemption means to be "bought back" or "set free." Jesus Christ is our Redeemer because He willingly paid the price to buy us back and set us free from the effects of the Fall of Adam and from the burden of our own sins (see 1 Corinthians 6:20 and D&C 18:11). The price He had to pay was His own blood (see 1 Peter 1:18–19).

7:7 (6–7) Jesus Christ will someday judge all people for what they have thought, said, and done (see Mosiah 4:30; John 5:22). The righteous will live with God in happiness.

7:8 ***lay hold upon***—accept or grasp
***this record***—the Book of Mormon
***the record which shall come unto the Gentiles from the Jews***—the Bible

7:9 The word *this* in this verse means the Book of Mormon. Except for the first time it is used, the word *that* in this verse means the Bible.

The Book of Mormon and the Bible testify of each other. If you believe one, you will believe the other. Nephi said the Book of Mormon would convince people of the truthfulness of the Bible. The Bible and Book of Mormon will grow together to the confounding (putting down) of false doctrine and will establish peace (see 2 Nephi 3:11–12).

***for the intent***—for the purpose
***wrought***—done

7:10 ***a remnant***—those who are left

How many conditions of this verse apply to you? Do you believe in Christ? Do you follow His example? How will it be "well with you in the day of judgment" if you have done these things?

PHOTOGRAPH BY DAVID H. GARNER

*The Nephites' final battle took place at a hill called Cumorah.*

3 And my father also was killed by them, and I even remain alone to write the sad tale of the destruction of my people. But behold, they are gone, and I fulfil the commandment of my father. And whether they will slay me, I know not.

4 Therefore I will write and hide up the records in the earth; and whither I go it mattereth not.

5 Behold, my father hath made this record, and he hath written the intent thereof. And behold, I would write it also if I had room upon the plates, but I have not; and ore I have none, for I am alone. My father hath been slain in battle, and all my kinsfolk, and I have not friends nor whither to go; and how long the Lord will suffer that I may live I know not.

6 Behold, four hundred years have passed away since the coming of our Lord and Savior.

7 And behold, the Lamanites have hunted my people, the Nephites, down from city to city and from place to place, even until they are no more; and great has been their fall; yea, great and marvelous is the destruction of my people, the Nephites.

8 And behold, it is the hand of the Lord which hath done it. And behold also, the Lamanites are at war one with another; and the whole face of this land is one continual round of murder and bloodshed; and no one knoweth the end of the war.

9 And now, behold, I say no more concerning them, for there are none save it be the Lamanites and robbers that do exist upon the face of the land.

10 And there are none that do know the true God save it be the disciples of Jesus, who did tarry in the land until the wickedness of the people was so great that the Lord would not suffer them to remain with the people; and whether they be upon the face of the land no man knoweth.

11 But behold, my father and I have seen them, and they have ministered unto us.

## *The Book of Mormon Will Come to Light*

12 And whoso receiveth this record, and shall not condemn it because of the imperfections which are in it, the same shall know of greater things than these. Behold, I am Moroni; and were it possible, I would make all things known unto you.

13 Behold, I make an end of speaking concerning this people. I am the son of Mormon, and my father was a descendant of Nephi.

14 And I am the same who hideth up this record unto the Lord; the plates thereof are of no worth, because of the commandment of the Lord. For he truly saith that no one shall have them to get gain; but the record thereof is of great worth; and whoso shall bring it to light, him will the Lord bless.

15 For none can have power to bring it to light save it be given him of God; for God wills that it shall be done with an eye single to his glory, or the welfare of the ancient and long dispersed covenant people of the Lord.

---

8:3 (1–3) The Book of Mormon begins with Nephi obeying his father's command (see 1 Nephi 3:7) and ends with Moroni obeying his father's command. Obedience to righteous parents is an important message of the Book of Mormon. How should you treat the righteous instructions of your parents?

8:4 ***whither***—where

8:5 ***intent***—purpose
***ore***—rock or mineral from which metal is obtained
***kinsfolk***—relatives

Moroni remained alone for the last years of his life. Are there times in your life when you have felt alone because you chose to do what is right? How has the Lord blessed you for doing what is right?

8:7 ***marvelous***—astonishing

8:10 When the people's wickedness becomes so great, often the Lord does not allow the righteous to remain with them. When the wicked are left without the righteous, they are ready to be destroyed (see Genesis 18:27–33; 2 Nephi 26:3; Alma 10:22–23).

8:11 Elder Joseph B. Wirthlin, speaking about Moroni, said that as "a result of his perseverance and righteousness, he was ministered to by the Three Nephites" (in Conference Report, October 1987, 8).

8:12 ***imperfections***—mistakes or faults

8:14 Moroni told Joseph Smith "that Satan would try to tempt me . . . to get the plates for the purpose of getting rich. This he forbade me, saying that I must have no other object in view [purpose] in getting the plates but to glorify God, and must not be influenced by any other motive [desire] than that of building his kingdom; otherwise I could not get them" (Joseph Smith—History 1:46).

8:15 ***dispersed***—scattered

We also can help bring the Book of Mormon to light by sharing it with others. How can you share the Book of Mormon with others? What does it mean to have your eye single to the glory of God?

MORONI BURYING THE PLATES, BY CLARK KELLEY PRICE

*Moroni buried the gold plates and other sacred objects in the Hill Cumorah.*

16 And blessed be he that shall bring this thing to light; for it shall be brought out of darkness unto light, according to the word of God; yea, it shall be brought out of the earth, and it shall shine forth out of darkness, and come unto the knowledge of the people; and it shall be done by the power of God.

## Moroni Counsels Future Readers to Search the Book of Mormon

17 And if there be faults they be the faults of a man. But behold, we know no fault; nevertheless God knoweth all things; therefore, he that condemneth, let him be aware lest he shall be in danger of hell fire.

18 And he that saith: Show unto me, or ye shall be smitten—let him beware lest he commandeth that which is forbidden of the Lord.

19 For behold, the same that judgeth rashly shall be judged rashly again; for according to his works shall his wages be; therefore, he that smiteth shall be smitten again, of the Lord.

---

8:16 ***this thing***—the Book of Mormon

Joseph Smith is the one who brought the Book of Mormon to light. He said: "Through the medium of the Urim and Thummim I translated the record by the gift, and power of God" ("Church History," 707).

8:17 ***faults***—problems or mistakes
***condemneth***—criticizes

Latter-day scriptures teach that there are at least three meanings for the term *hell.* It can describe our suffering here on earth (see Alma 36:18). It can refer to a part of the spirit world where those who have not repented suffer for their sins (see Alma 40:13–14). It is also used to describe the final condition of those who completely turn away from God (see D&C 29:38).

8:19 ***rashly***—harshly or carelessly

8:19 (18–19) Do you know people who won't believe something until they see it with their own eyes? Why do you think the Lord wants us to accept some truths—such as the existence of the gold plates—on faith?

20 Behold what the scripture says—man shall not smite, neither shall he judge; for judgment is mine, saith the Lord, and vengeance is mine also, and I will repay.

21 And he that shall breathe out wrath and strifes against the work of the Lord, and against the covenant people of the Lord who are the house of Israel, and shall say: We will destroy the work of the Lord, and the Lord will not remember his covenant which he hath made unto the house of Israel—the same is in danger to be hewn down and cast into the fire;

22 For the eternal purposes of the Lord shall roll on, until all his promises shall be fulfilled.

23 Search the prophecies of Isaiah. Behold, I cannot write them. Yea, behold I say unto you, that those saints who have gone before me, who have possessed this land, shall cry, yea, even from the dust will they cry unto the Lord; and as the Lord liveth he will remember the covenant which he hath made with them.

24 And he knoweth their prayers, that they were in behalf of their brethren. And he knoweth their faith, for in his name could they remove mountains; and in his name could they cause the earth to shake; and by the power of his word did they cause prisons to tumble to the earth; yea, even the fiery furnace could not harm them, neither wild beasts nor poisonous serpents, because of the power of his word.

25 And behold, their prayers were also in behalf of him that the Lord should suffer to bring these things forth.

26 And no one need say they shall not come, for they surely shall, for the Lord hath spoken it; for out of the earth shall they come, by the hand of the Lord, and none can stay it; and it shall come in a day when it shall be said that miracles are done away; and it shall come even as if one should speak from the dead.

## Moroni Sees Our Day

27 And it shall come in a day when the blood of saints shall cry unto the Lord, because of secret combinations and the works of darkness.

28 Yea, it shall come in a day when the power of God shall be denied, and churches become defiled and be lifted up in the pride of their hearts; yea, even in a day when leaders of churches and teachers shall rise in the pride of their hearts, even to the envying of them who belong to their churches.

29 Yea, it shall come in a day when there shall be heard of fires, and tempests, and vapors of smoke in foreign lands;

30 And there shall also be heard of wars, rumors of wars, and earthquakes in divers places.

---

8:20 ***vengeance***—punishment

8:21 ***wrath and strifes***—anger and arguments
***hewn***—cut

8:23 (22–23) Elder Henry B. Eyring explained that "we make promises with God and He makes promises with us. He always keeps His promises offered through His authorized servants, but it is the crucial [important] test of our lives to see if we will make and keep our covenants with Him" (in Conference Report, October 1996, 40).

8:25 (24–25) Heavenly Father listens to and answers our prayers. President Harold B. Lee taught that "the fundamental and soul-satisfying step in our eternal quest [journey] is to come in a day when each does know, for himself, that God answers his prayers" (in Conference Report, April 1969, 133).

8:27 A secret combination is a group of wicked people who secretly join together to lie, cheat, steal, murder, or do whatever else is necessary in order to gain riches, wealth, or power (see Helaman 7:21; 8:27). The first secret combination was between Satan and Cain, who killed his brother Abel to get his flocks (see Moses 5:28–32). "Among today's secret combinations are gangs, drug cartels, and organized crime families" (M. Russell Ballard, in Conference Report, October 1997, 51).

8:28 President Ezra Taft Benson warns us that "in the scriptures there is no such thing as righteous pride. It is always considered as a sin. We are not speaking of a wholesome view of self-worth, which is best established by a close relationship with God. But we are speaking of pride as the universal sin. . . . The two groups in the Book of Mormon that seemed to have the greatest difficulty with pride are the 'learned, and the rich' (2 Nephi 28:15)" (in Conference Report, April 1986, 5–6).

***defiled***—unclean or corrupted
***envying***—being jealous

8:29 ***tempests***—violent storms

8:30 ***divers***—many

31 Yea, it shall come in a day when there shall be great pollutions upon the face of the earth; there shall be murders, and robbing, and lying, and deceivings, and whoredoms, and all manner of abominations; when there shall be many who will say, Do this, or do that, and it mattereth not, for the Lord will uphold such at the last day. But wo unto such, for they are in the gall of bitterness and in the bonds of iniquity.

32 Yea, it shall come in a day when there shall be churches built up that shall say: Come unto me, and for your money you shall be forgiven of your sins.

33 O ye wicked and perverse and stiffnecked people, why have ye built up churches unto yourselves to get gain? Why have ye transfigured the holy word of God, that ye might bring damnation upon your souls? Behold, look ye unto the revelations of God; for behold, the time cometh at that day when all these things must be fulfilled.

34 Behold, the Lord hath shown unto me great and marvelous things concerning that which must shortly come, at that day when these things shall come forth among you.

35 Behold, I speak unto you as if ye were present, and yet ye are not. But behold, Jesus Christ hath shown you unto me, and I know your doing.

36 And I know that ye do walk in the pride of your hearts; and there are none save a few only who do not lift themselves up in the pride of their hearts, unto the wearing of very fine apparel, unto envying, and strifes, and malice, and persecutions, and all manner of iniquities; and your churches, yea, even every one, have become polluted because of the pride of your hearts.

37 For behold, ye do love money, and your substance, and your fine apparel, and the adorning of your churches, more than ye love the poor and the needy, the sick and the afflicted.

38 O ye pollutions, ye hypocrites, ye teachers, who sell yourselves for that which will canker, why have ye polluted the holy church of God? Why are ye ashamed to take upon you the name of Christ? Why do ye not think that greater is the value of an endless happiness than that misery which never dies—because of the praise of the world?

39 Why do ye adorn yourselves with that which hath no life, and yet suffer the hungry, and the needy, and the naked, and the sick and the afflicted to pass by you, and notice them not?

40 Yea, why do ye build up your secret abominations to get gain, and cause that widows should mourn before the Lord, and also orphans to mourn

---

8:31 "The people of God have always been commanded to abstain from language that is profane or vulgar" said Elder Dallin H. Oaks. He also noted, "Today, our young people hear such expressions from boys and girls in their grade schools, from actors on stage and in the movies, from popular novels, and even from public officials and sports heroes. Television and videotapes bring profanity and vulgarity into our homes. . . . Surely this is one fulfillment of the Book of Mormon prophecy that in the last days 'there shall be great pollutions upon the face of the earth' " (in Conference Report, April 1986, 66).

***whoredoms***—wickedness and immorality
***abominations***—sins

"Gall of bitterness" represents the suffering of the wicked (see Acts 8:23).

8:33 ***perverse***—rebellious
***stiffnecked***—stubborn
***transfigured***—changed or corrupted

8:35 President Ezra Taft Benson testified that God inspired Mormon, who compiled and abridged most of the Book of Mormon, to include those things that we would need in our day. President Benson asked, "If they saw our day and chose those things which would be of greatest worth to us, is not that how we should study the Book of Mormon? We should constantly ask ourselves, 'Why did the Lord inspire Mormon (or Moroni or Alma) to include that in his record? What lesson can I learn from that to help me live in this day and age?' " (in Conference Report, October 1986, 5).

8:36 ***apparel***—clothing
***malice***—desire to harm others

8:37 ***adorning***—decorating

Moroni warned of spending more money, time, and attention on ourselves than we do in serving others. Why should you serve others? How does helping others make you feel?

8:38 ***ye hypocrites***—you who pretend to be better than you really are
***canker***—corrupt or destroy

8:40 (37–40) Elder Henry B. Eyring testified "that the Savior always organizes His disciples to care for the poor and the needy among them" (in Conference Report, April 1996, 86).

before the Lord, and also the blood of their fathers and their husbands to cry unto the Lord from the ground, for vengeance upon your heads?
41 Behold, the sword of vengeance hangeth over you; and the time soon cometh that he avengeth the blood of the saints upon you, for he will not suffer their cries any longer.

## CHAPTER 9

*Moroni finishes his father's account by pleading with unbelievers to repent so they can enjoy the blessings of Christ's gifts and powers. Look for reasons why you can rely on the Lord.*

### Moroni Invites Unbelievers in the Last Days to Repent

1 AND now, I speak also concerning those who do not believe in Christ.
2 Behold, will ye believe in the day of your visitation—behold, when the Lord shall come, yea, even that great day when the earth shall be rolled together as a scroll, and the elements shall melt with fervent heat, yea, in that great day when ye shall be brought to stand before the Lamb of God—then will ye say that there is no God?
3 Then will ye longer deny the Christ, or can ye behold the Lamb of God? Do ye suppose that ye shall dwell with him under a consciousness of your guilt? Do ye suppose that ye could be happy to dwell with that holy Being, when your souls are racked with a consciousness of guilt that ye have ever abused his laws?
4 Behold, I say unto you that ye would be more miserable to dwell with a holy and just God, under a consciousness of your filthiness before him, than ye would to dwell with the damned souls in hell.
5 For behold, when ye shall be brought to see your nakedness before God, and also the glory of God, and the holiness of Jesus Christ, it will kindle a flame of unquenchable fire upon you.
6 O then ye unbelieving, turn ye unto the Lord; cry mightily unto the Father in the name of Jesus, that perhaps ye may be found spotless, pure, fair, and white, having been cleansed by the blood of the Lamb, at that great and last day.

### Moroni Testifies That God Has Always Performed Miracles and Given Revelations

7 And again I speak unto you who deny the revelations of God, and say that they are done away, that there are no revelations, nor prophecies, nor gifts, nor healing, nor speaking with tongues, and the interpretation of tongues;
8 Behold I say unto you, he that denieth these things knoweth not the gospel of Christ; yea, he has not read the scriptures; if so, he does not understand them.

---

8:41 ***avengeth***—pays back or punishes you for

9:2 ***in the day of your visitation***—at the Second Coming

When the Lord comes again, the earth will be renewed and be as it was in the garden of Eden (see 2 Nephi 8:3). This will require great changes in the appearance of the earth. The Doctrine and Covenants indicates that "the earth shall tremble, and reel to and fro" (D&C 45:48). It was revealed to Joseph Smith that the elements will melt with fervent (very hot) heat. This "fervent heat" will burn "every corruptible thing . . . and all things shall become new" (D&C 101:24–25).

9:3 ***the Lamb of God***—Jesus Christ
***a consciousness***—an awareness
***that holy Being***—Jesus Christ
***racked***—tormented
***abused***—broken

9:4 ***miserable***—unhappy
***the damned souls***—those shut out from the presence of God

9:5 ***your nakedness before God***—that nothing is hidden from God
***kindle a flame of unquenchable fire***—start a fire that can't be put out

King Benjamin warned that wicked people will experience "an awful view of their own guilt and abominations" and inherit "a state of misery and endless torment" which will be "as a lake of fire and brimstone, whose flames are unquenchable" (Mosiah 3:25, 27).

9:5 (3–5) Moroni taught that sinners would be more comfortable dwelling with other sinners in hell than with the righteous in heaven. Why will keeping the commandments help you feel more comfortable in the presence of Jesus Christ?

9:7 ***tongues***—languages

9 For do we not read that God is the same yesterday, today, and forever, and in him there is no variableness neither shadow of changing?
10 And now, if ye have imagined up unto yourselves a god who doth vary, and in whom there is shadow of changing, then have ye imagined up unto yourselves a god who is not a God of miracles.
11 But behold, I will show unto you a God of miracles, even the God of Abraham, and the God of Isaac, and the God of Jacob; and it is that same God who created the heavens and the earth, and all things that in them are.
12 Behold, he created Adam, and by Adam came the fall of man. And because of the fall of man came Jesus Christ, even the Father and the Son; and because of Jesus Christ came the redemption of man.
13 And because of the redemption of man, which came by Jesus Christ, they are brought back into the presence of the Lord; yea, this is wherein all men are redeemed, because the death of Christ bringeth to pass the resurrection, which bringeth to pass a redemption from an endless sleep, from which sleep all men shall be awakened by the power of God when the trump shall sound; and they shall come forth, both small and great, and all shall stand before his bar, being redeemed and loosed from this eternal band of death, which death is a temporal death.
14 And then cometh the judgment of the Holy One upon them; and then cometh the time that he that is filthy shall be filthy still; and he that is righteous shall be righteous still; he that is happy shall be happy still; and he that is unhappy shall be unhappy still.
15 And now, O all ye that have imagined up unto yourselves a god who can do no miracles, I would ask of you, have all these things passed, of which I have spoken? Has the end come yet? Behold I say unto you, Nay; and God has not ceased to be a God of miracles.
16 Behold, are not the things that God hath wrought marvelous in our eyes? Yea, and who can comprehend the marvelous works of God?
17 Who shall say that it was not a miracle that by his word the heaven and the earth should be; and by the power of his word man was created of the dust of the earth; and by the power of his word have miracles been wrought?
18 And who shall say that Jesus Christ did not do many mighty miracles? And there were many mighty miracles wrought by the hands of the apostles.

---

9:9 ***variableness***—inconsistency
***shadow***—hint

Modern revelation tells us that God doesn't "vary from that which he hath said, therefore his paths are straight" (D&C 3:2). That is one of the reasons why we can have absolute confidence and faith in Him.

9:12 "The fall of Adam is one of the most important occurrences in the history of man. Before the fall, Adam and Eve had physical bodies but no blood. There was no sin, no death, and no children among any of the earthly creations." The Fall brought mortality and "both physical and spiritual death into the world upon all mankind (Hel. 14:16–17). . . . It was a necessary step in the progress of man, and provisions for a Savior had been made even before the fall had occurred. Jesus Christ came to atone for the fall of Adam and also for man's individual sins" (LDS Bible Dictionary, s.v. "Fall of Adam," 670).

9:13 ***this eternal band of death, which death is a temporal death***—the death of our physical bodies

9:13 (12–13) Elder Bruce R. McConkie told how the Creation, the Fall of Adam, and the Atonement of Jesus Christ all work together: "Creation is father to the Fall; and by the Fall came mortality and death; and by Christ came immortality and eternal life. If there had been no fall of Adam, by which cometh death, there could have been no atonement of Christ, by which cometh life" (in Conference Report, April 1985, 12).

9:14 Mormon taught that the Judgment will bring to us rewards for how we chose to live. The Prophet Joseph Smith taught that an important reason we are living is to have happiness (see *Teachings of the Prophet Joseph Smith,* 255). What kinds of experiences make you happy?

9:14 (13–14) Because of the Atonement of Jesus Christ, all people will be resurrected and brought back to God's presence to be judged (see Helaman 14:15–18).

9:15 ***ceased to be***—stopped being

9:16 ***wrought***—brought about or caused to happen
***comprehend***—understand

19 And if there were miracles wrought then, why has God ceased to be a God of miracles and yet be an unchangeable Being? And behold, I say unto you he changeth not; if so he would cease to be God; and he ceaseth not to be God, and is a God of miracles.

## Miracles and Signs Come to Those Who Believe in Christ

20 And the reason why he ceaseth to do miracles among the children of men is because that they dwindle in unbelief, and depart from the right way, and know not the God in whom they should trust.

21 Behold, I say unto you that whoso believeth in Christ, doubting nothing, whatsoever he shall ask the Father in the name of Christ it shall be granted him; and this promise is unto all, even unto the ends of the earth.

22 For behold, thus said Jesus Christ, the Son of God, unto his disciples who should tarry, yea, and also to all his disciples, in the hearing of the multitude: Go ye into all the world, and preach the gospel to every creature;

23 And he that believeth and is baptized shall be saved, but he that believeth not shall be damned;

24 And these signs shall follow them that believe—in my name shall they cast out devils; they shall speak with new tongues; they shall take up serpents; and if they drink any deadly thing it shall not hurt them; they shall lay hands on the sick and they shall recover;

25 And whosoever shall believe in my name, doubting nothing, unto him will I confirm all my words, even unto the ends of the earth.

26 And now, behold, who can stand against the works of the Lord? Who can deny his sayings? Who will rise up against the almighty power of the Lord? Who will despise the works of the Lord? Who will despise the children of Christ? Behold, all ye who are despisers of the works of the Lord, for ye shall wonder and perish.

## Moroni Teaches That It Is Wise to Keep the Commandments

27 O then despise not, and wonder not, but hearken unto the words of the Lord, and ask the Father in the name of Jesus for what things soever ye shall stand in need. Doubt not, but be believing, and begin as in times of old, and come unto the Lord with all your heart, and work out your own salvation with fear and trembling before him.

28 Be wise in the days of your probation; strip yourselves of all uncleanness; ask not, that ye may consume it on your lusts, but ask with a firmness unshaken, that ye will yield to no temptation, but that ye will serve the true and living God.

29 See that ye are not baptized unworthily; see that ye partake not of the sacrament of Christ unworthily; but see that ye do all things in worthiness, and do it in the name of Jesus Christ, the Son of the living God; and if ye do this, and endure to the end, ye will in nowise be cast out.

---

9:19 (18–19) Bruce R. McConkie wrote: "Miracles wrought by the power of God are the perfect proof of pure religion. They are always . . . found in the true Church" (*Doctrinal New Testament Commentary* 2:374).

9:20 ***dwindle in unbelief***—lose their faith
***depart***—turn away

9:22 ***tarry***—not die

9:24 The Lord promised His believers in the New Testament this same special gift of protection. "The use of this miraculous gift was to preserve life, in case any believer should accidentally be bitten by a poisonous serpent as Paul was (see Acts 28); or should unintentionally swallow a deadly poison, as the sons of the prophets did (see II Kings 4)" (Orson Pratt, *Orson Pratt's Works,* 85).

9:25 ***confirm***—prove

9:25 (21–25) Why is it so hard not to have doubts? What blessings come to those who do not doubt but have faith?

9:26 ***despise***—hate or ignore
***perish***—die spiritually

9:27 ***hearken unto***—listen to and obey

9:28 Our "probation" is the time God has given us to live on earth to be tested and tried (see Abraham 3:24–25). During this time of trial we must cleanse our lives of sin because sin makes us spiritually unclean.

***ask not, that ye may consume it on your lusts***—pray not for things that will only satisfy your physical desires
***yield***—give in

9:29 ***nowise***—no way

30 Behold, I speak unto you as though I spake from
the dead; for I know that ye shall have my words.
31 Condemn me not because of mine imperfection, neither my father, because of his imperfection,
neither them who have written before him; but
rather give thanks unto God that he hath made
manifest unto you our imperfections, that ye may
learn to be more wise than we have been.

## Moroni Tells About the Language of the Book of Mormon

32 And now, behold, we have written this record
according to our knowledge, in the characters
which are called among us the reformed Egyptian,
being handed down and altered by us, according to
our manner of speech.
33 And if our plates had been sufficiently large we
should have written in Hebrew; but the Hebrew
hath been altered by us also; and if we could have
written in Hebrew, behold, ye would have had no
imperfection in our record.
34 But the Lord knoweth the things which we
have written, and also that none other people
knoweth our language; and because that none
other people knoweth our language, therefore he
hath prepared means for the interpretation thereof.
35 And these things are written that we may rid
our garments of the blood of our brethren, who
have dwindled in unbelief.
36 And behold, these things which we have desired
concerning our brethren, yea, even their restoration
to the knowledge of Christ, are according to the
prayers of all the saints who have dwelt in the land.
37 And may the Lord Jesus Christ grant that their
prayers may be answered according to their faith;
and may God the Father remember the covenant
which he hath made with the house of Israel; and
may he bless them forever, through faith on the
name of Jesus Christ. Amen.

---

9:31 ***made manifest***—shown

9:32 ***altered***—changed or modified

9:34 The "means" the Lord prepared for interpreting or translating languages are known in the Book of Mormon as seer stones (see Mosiah 28:13–16) and in the Bible as the Urim and Thummim (see LDS Bible Dictionary, s.v. "Urim and Thummim," 786–87).

9:35 The Lord has said, "It becometh every man who hath been warned to warn his neighbor" (D&C 88:81). In other words, those who have been taught the gospel are required to share it with others. This is how Moroni could "rid [his] garments of the blood of [his] brethren." Once he taught them the gospel, he was no longer responsible for their lack of belief (see also Jacob 1:19).

9:37 Moroni desired the Lord to answer the prayers of many Book of Mormon Saints that the Lamanites would someday come to know Jesus Christ. The Lord heard those prayers and brought forth the Book of Mormon in 1830 (see D&C 10:42–52).

# THE BOOK OF ETHER

*The Book of Ether is the record of a group of people called the Jaredites. The Lord led them away from the Tower of Babel to the American continent over two thousand years before the time of Christ. The book is named for the last great Jaredite prophet, who witnessed the destruction of his people and wrote the record (see Ether 1:6; 15:33–34). The book of Ether was written on twenty-four plates of gold that were found by the people of Limhi (see Mosiah 8:7–9). Those plates were translated by King Mosiah II (see Mosiah 28:11). Moroni then made an abridgment (a shortened version) of King Mosiah's translation, called it the book of Ether, and included it as part of the Book of Mormon (see Ether 1:1–5).*

*The record of the Jaredites, taken from the twenty-four plates found by the people of Limhi in the days of king Mosiah.**

## CHAPTER 1

*The Lord changes the people's language at the Tower of Babel and scatters them. Watch for why the Jaredites' language was not changed and why the Lord led them to a promised land.*

### MORONI BEGINS HIS ABRIDGMENT OF THE JAREDITE RECORD

1 AND now I, Moroni, proceed to give an account of
those ancient inhabitants who were destroyed by the
hand of the Lord upon the face of this north country.
2 And I take mine account from the twenty and
four plates which were found by the people of
Limhi, which is called the Book of Ether.
3 And as I suppose that the first part of this record,
which speaks concerning the creation of the world,
and also of Adam, and an account from that time
even to the great tower, and whatsoever things transpired among the children of men until that time, is
had among the Jews—
4 Therefore I do not write those things which transpired from the days of Adam until that time; but
they are had upon the plates; and whoso findeth
them, the same will have power that he may get the
full account.
5 But behold, I give not the full account, but a part
of the account I give, from the tower down until
they were destroyed.

---

* This introduction to the book of Ether was translated from the Book of Mormon plates.

1:1 ***proceed***—begin
***an account***—a history
***ancient inhabitants***—people who lived a long time ago

As Moroni wrote about the Jaredites, he helped fulfill his father's commandment. Mormon had said that "it is expedient [necessary] that all people should know the things which are written in this account" (Mosiah 28:19).

1:3 The "great tower" mentioned here is the Tower of Babel (see Genesis 11:1–9). It was built in the land of Shinar, which is commonly believed to be in ancient Babylonia or modern-day Iraq (see LDS Bible Dictionary, s.v. "Shinar, Plain of," 774).

The term *Jew* often refers to a descendant from the tribe of Judah. However, the Book of Mormon also uses the term *Jew* to refer to any Israelite from the land or kingdom of Judah, even if not descended from the tribe of Judah (see LDS Bible Dictionary, s.v. "Jew," 713). In addition, the Book of Mormon sometimes uses the term *Jews* to refer to the entire house of Israel (see *Book of Mormon Student Manual, Religion 121 and 122,* 15).

***transpired***—happened

= Word Help = A Closer Look
= More Light = Ponder This
Words in pink are explained in the Glossary.

## Moroni Lists Ether's Genealogy (Family Line)

6 And on this wise do I give the account. He that
wrote this record was Ether, and he was a descendant of Coriantor.
7 Coriantor was the son of Moron.
8 And Moron was the son of Ethem.
9 And Ethem was the son of Ahah.
10 And Ahah was the son of Seth.
11 And Seth was the son of Shiblon.
12 And Shiblon was the son of Com.
13 And Com was the son of Coriantum.
14 And Coriantum was the son of Amnigaddah.
15 And Amnigaddah was the son of Aaron.
16 And Aaron was a descendant of Heth, who was
the son of Hearthom.
17 And Hearthom was the son of Lib.
18 And Lib was the son of Kish.
19 And Kish was the son of Corom.
20 And Corom was the son of Levi.
21 And Levi was the son of Kim.
22 And Kim was the son of Morianton.
23 And Morianton was a descendant of Riplakish.
24 And Riplakish was the son of Shez.
25 And Shez was the son of Heth.
26 And Heth was the son of Com.
27 And Com was the son of Coriantum.
28 And Coriantum was the son of Emer.
29 And Emer was the son of Omer.
30 And Omer was the son of Shule.
31 And Shule was the son of Kib.
32 And Kib was the son of Orihah, who was the
son of Jared;

## The Brother of Jared Asks the Lord Not to Change Their Language

33 Which Jared came forth with his brother and
their families, with some others and their families,
from the great tower, at the time the Lord confounded the language of the people, and swore in
his wrath that they should be scattered upon all
the face of the earth; and according to the word of
the Lord the people were scattered.
34 And the brother of Jared being a large and
mighty man, and a man highly favored of the Lord,
Jared, his brother, said unto him: Cry unto the Lord,
that he will not confound us that we may not
understand our words.
35 And it came to pass that the brother of Jared
did cry unto the Lord, and the Lord had compassion
upon Jared; therefore he did not confound the language of Jared; and Jared and his brother were not
confounded.
36 Then Jared said unto his brother: Cry again
unto the Lord, and it may be that he will turn away
his anger from them who are our friends, that he
confound not their language.
37 And it came to pass that the brother of Jared
did cry unto the Lord, and the Lord had compassion
upon their friends and their families also, that they
were not confounded.

## The Brother of Jared Prays to Be Led to a Choice Land

38 And it came to pass that Jared spake again
unto his brother, saying: Go and inquire of the
Lord whether he will drive us out of the land, and
if he will drive us out of the land, cry unto him
whither we shall go. And who knoweth but the
Lord will carry us forth into a land which is choice
above all the earth? And if it so be, let us be faithful unto the Lord, that we may receive it for our
inheritance.
39 And it came to pass that the brother of Jared
did cry unto the Lord according to that which had
been spoken by the mouth of Jared.
40 And it came to pass that the Lord did hear the
brother of Jared, and had compassion upon him,
and said unto him:
41 Go to and gather together thy flocks, both male
and female, of every kind; and also of the seed of
the earth of every kind; and thy families; and also
Jared thy brother and his family; and also thy
friends and their families, and the friends of Jared
and their families.

1:6 ***was a descendant of***—came from the family line of

Verses 6–32 teach us about Ether's family. Why do you think it is important to know who our ancestors are? Who are your grandparents and great-grandparents?

1:33 ***confounded***—changed or confused
***swore in his wrath***—promised in his anger

1:35 ***compassion***—mercy

1:38 ***inquire of***—ask
***whither***—where
***inheritance***—homeland

THE BROTHER OF JARED OFFERING A SACRIFICE, BY GARY KAPP

*The brother of Jared prayed that the Lord would not confound (change) the language of his family.*

42 And when thou hast done this thou shalt go at
the head of them down into the valley which is
northward. And there will I meet thee, and I will go
before thee into a land which is choice above all
the lands of the earth.
43 And there will I bless thee and thy seed, and
raise up unto me of thy seed, and of the seed of thy
brother, and they who shall go with thee, a great
nation. And there shall be none greater than the
nation which I will raise up unto me of thy seed,
upon all the face of the earth. And thus I will do unto
thee because this long time ye have cried unto me.

## CHAPTER 2

*The Jaredites prepare to come to the promised land. Notice what the Lord says the people who live on this land must do to remain free from bondage and to keep possession of the land.*

### *The Jaredites Prepare for Their Journey*

1 AND it came to pass that Jared and his brother,
and their families, and also the friends of Jared and
his brother and their families, went down into the
valley which was northward, (and the name of the
valley was Nimrod, being called after the mighty
hunter) with their flocks which they had gathered
together, male and female, of every kind.
2 And they did also lay snares and catch fowls of
the air; and they did also prepare a vessel, in which
they did carry with them the fish of the waters.
3 And they did also carry with them deseret,
which, by interpretation, is a honey bee; and thus
they did carry with them swarms of bees, and all
manner of that which was upon the face of the
land, seeds of every kind.

### *The Lord Directs the Jaredites to the Promised Land*

4 And it came to pass that when they had come
down into the valley of Nimrod the Lord came down
and talked with the brother of Jared; and he was in
a cloud, and the brother of Jared saw him not.
5 And it came to pass that the Lord commanded
them that they should go forth into the wilderness,
yea, into that quarter where there never had man
been. And it came to pass that the Lord did go
before them, and did talk with them as he stood in
a cloud, and gave directions whither they should
travel.

---

1:42 ***go at the head of***—lead
***go before***—lead

1:43 Notice the great blessings the Lord gave the brother of Jared and his people because of his faithful prayers. What does this teach us about Heavenly Father's willingness to bless us? How faithful have you been in praying for the blessings you need?

PHOTOGRAPH BY G. R. SIMS

*This sample of ancient hieroglyphics includes a honeybee. The Jaredite word for* bee *was* deseret.

2:1 Nimrod was a noted hunter in Babylon. He was a great-grandson of Noah. Some traditions tie him with the building of the ancient city of Nineveh (see LDS Bible Dictionary, s.v. "Nimrod," 738).

2:2 ***lay snares***—set traps
***vessel***—boat

2:3 President Joseph F. Smith explained that in earlier days the state of Utah was called Deseret (honey bee). Like a bee in a beehive, every Church member "should be in a position to add something to the wealth of the whole. Everyone should be increasing, improving, and advancing in some way, and accomplishing something for his or her good and for the good of the whole" (in Conference Report, October 1898, 23).

2:4 The Lord also appeared in a cloud to the children of Israel as they journeyed toward a promised land (see Exodus 13:21; 16:10; Numbers 11:25).

2:5 ***wilderness***—wild land with very few people
***quarter***—area
***whither***—where

6 And it came to pass that they did travel in the wilderness, and did build barges, in which they did cross many waters, being directed continually by the hand of the Lord.

7 And the Lord would not suffer that they should stop beyond the sea in the wilderness, but he would that they should come forth even unto the land of promise, which was choice above all other lands, which the Lord God had preserved for a righteous people.

## *Jesus Will Protect Those Living in the Promised Land Who Serve Him*

8 And he had sworn in his wrath unto the brother of Jared, that whoso should possess this land of promise, from that time henceforth and forever, should serve him, the true and only God, or they should be swept off when the fulness of his wrath should come upon them.

9 And now, we can behold the decrees of God concerning this land, that it is a land of promise; and whatsoever nation shall possess it shall serve God, or they shall be swept off when the fulness of his wrath shall come upon them. And the fulness of his wrath cometh upon them when they are ripened in iniquity.

10 For behold, this is a land which is choice above all other lands; wherefore he that doth possess it shall serve God or shall be swept off; for it is the everlasting decree of God. And it is not until the fulness of iniquity among the children of the land, that they are swept off.

11 And this cometh unto you, O ye Gentiles, that ye may know the decrees of God—that ye may repent, and not continue in your iniquities until the fulness come, that ye may not bring down the fulness of the wrath of God upon you as the inhabitants of the land have hitherto done.

12 Behold, this is a choice land, and whatsoever nation shall possess it shall be free from bondage, and from captivity, and from all other nations under heaven, if they will but serve the God of the land, who is Jesus Christ, who hath been manifested by the things which we have written.

13 And now I proceed with my record; for behold, it came to pass that the Lord did bring Jared and his brethren forth even to that great sea which divideth the lands. And as they came to the sea they pitched their tents; and they called the name of the place Moriancumer; and they dwelt in tents, and dwelt in tents upon the seashore for the space of four years.

---

2:6 ***barges***—boats

2:7 ***suffer***—allow

Elder Spencer W. Kimball said: "This America is no ordinary country. It is a choice land, 'choice above all other lands.' (1 Nephi 2:20.) It has a tragic and bloody past, but a glorious and peaceful future if its inhabitants really learn to serve their God" (in Conference Report, October 1961, 30).

2:8 ***sworn***—promised
***possess***—live in

2:9 ***decrees***—commands
***iniquity***—sin

2:10 (8–10) Those who live on this land must keep the commandments to be protected and blessed. President Joseph Fielding Smith explained, "They must serve him; they will have to keep his commandments; at least they will have to have some semblance of righteousness or when the fulness of wickedness comes, he certainly will remove them" (*Doctrines of Salvation* 3:320).

2:11 ***hitherto***—previously

*Gentiles* is a word that means "nations." It refers to those not of the family of Israel or who do not believe in the God of Israel. In the Book of Mormon it also refers to those who come from gentile nations, which are all nations outside the land of Israel (see LDS Bible Dictionary, s.v. "Gentile," 679).

2:12 *Christ* is a Greek word meaning "the Anointed One"; the Hebrew word with the same meaning is *Messiah.* Jesus is the Christ—the one chosen, set apart, and sent by God to save us (see LDS Bible Dictionary, s.v. "Christ," 633).

2:13 ***proceed***—continue

The Prophet Joseph Smith was asked to bless and name Elder Reynolds Cahoon's baby. As he did so he gave the boy the name of *Mahonri Moriancumer.* When he finished, the Prophet explained, "The name I have given your son is the name of the Brother of Jared; the Lord has just shown [or revealed] it to me" (as quoted in Bruce R. McConkie, *Mormon Doctrine,* 463).

14 And it came to pass at the end of four years that the Lord came again unto the brother of Jared, and stood in a cloud and talked with him. And for the space of three hours did the Lord talk with the brother of Jared, and chastened him because he remembered not to call upon the name of the Lord.

15 And the brother of Jared repented of the evil which he had done, and did call upon the name of the Lord for his brethren who were with him. And the Lord said unto him: I will forgive thee and thy brethren of their sins; but thou shalt not sin any more, for ye shall remember that my Spirit will not always strive with man; wherefore, if ye will sin until ye are fully ripe ye shall be cut off from the presence of the Lord. And these are my thoughts upon the land which I shall give you for your inheritance; for it shall be a land choice above all other lands.

## *The Jaredites Build Barges According to the Instructions of the Lord*

16 And the Lord said: Go to work and build, after the manner of barges which ye have hitherto built. And it came to pass that the brother of Jared did go to work, and also his brethren, and built barges after the manner which they had built, according to the instructions of the Lord. And they were small, and they were light upon the water, even like unto the lightness of a fowl upon the water.

17 And they were built after a manner that they were exceedingly tight, even that they would hold water like unto a dish; and the bottom thereof was tight like unto a dish; and the sides thereof were tight like unto a dish; and the ends thereof were peaked; and the top thereof was tight like unto a dish; and the length thereof was the length of a tree; and the door thereof, when it was shut, was tight like unto a dish.

18 And it came to pass that the brother of Jared cried unto the Lord, saying: O Lord, I have performed the work which thou hast commanded me, and I have made the barges according as thou hast directed me.

19 And behold, O Lord, in them there is no light; whither shall we steer? And also we shall perish, for in them we cannot breathe, save it is the air which is in them; therefore we shall perish.

20 And the Lord said unto the brother of Jared: Behold, thou shalt make a hole in the top, and also in the bottom; and when thou shalt suffer for air thou shalt unstop the hole and receive air. And if it be so that the water come in upon thee, behold, ye shall stop the hole, that ye may not perish in the flood.

21 And it came to pass that the brother of Jared did so, according as the Lord had commanded.

22 And he cried again unto the Lord saying: O Lord, behold I have done even as thou hast commanded me; and I have prepared the vessels for my people, and behold there is no light in them. Behold, O Lord, wilt thou suffer that we shall cross this great water in darkness?

23 And the Lord said unto the brother of Jared: What will ye that I should do that ye may have light in your vessels? For behold, ye cannot have windows, for they will be dashed in pieces; neither shall ye take fire with you, for ye shall not go by the light of fire.

24 For behold, ye shall be as a whale in the midst of the sea; for the mountain waves shall dash upon you. Nevertheless, I will bring you up again out of

---

2:14 The Lord talked with the brother of Jared for three hours and chastened or corrected him for not praying. Why do you think it is important to remember to pray? How often do you pray?

2:15 ***fully ripe***—completely ready

2:16 ***hitherto***—previously
***after the manner***—in the same way

2:19 ***perish***—die

2:23 ***dashed***—broken

After the brother of Jared asked how they were going to have light in the barges, the Lord told him to study it out in his mind. This is similar to what the Lord taught Oliver Cowdery about translating the Book of Mormon (see D&C 9:7–9).

This story of the brother of Jared's visit with the Lord about the barges is a great example of how the Lord gives us direction in our lives. We must study things out for ourselves and then ask Him for direction on the decisions that we think are best. What can you learn about receiving answers to prayer from this story?

2:24 ***midst***—middle

The Lord warned the brother of Jared that the journey to the promised land would be rough and challenging. The Lord allows us to have trials and struggles to help us grow spiritually. What challenges do you have? What can you learn from this story about preparing for and dealing with those challenges?

the depths of the sea; for the winds have gone forth out of my mouth, and also the rains and the floods have I sent forth.

25 And behold, I prepare you against these things; for ye cannot cross this great deep save I prepare you against the waves of the sea, and the winds which have gone forth, and the floods which shall come. Therefore what will ye that I should prepare for you that ye may have light when ye are swallowed up in the depths of the sea?

## CHAPTER 3

*The brother of Jared sees the premortal Jesus Christ and has a vision of this earth's destiny and people. Look for the reasons the brother of Jared received this sacred opportunity.*

### The Brother of Jared Asks the Lord to Touch the Sixteen Stones

1 AND it came to pass that the brother of Jared, (now the number of the vessels which had been prepared was eight) went forth unto the mount, which they called the mount Shelem, because of its exceeding height, and did molten out of a rock sixteen small stones; and they were white and clear, even as transparent glass; and he did carry them in his hands upon the top of the mount, and cried again unto the Lord, saying:

2 O Lord, thou hast said that we must be encompassed about by the floods. Now behold, O Lord, and do not be angry with thy servant because of his weakness before thee; for we know that thou art holy and dwellest in the heavens, and that we are unworthy before thee; because of the fall our natures have become evil continually; nevertheless, O Lord, thou hast given us a commandment that we must call upon thee, that from thee we may receive according to our desires.

3 Behold, O Lord, thou hast smitten us because of our iniquity, and hast driven us forth, and for these many years we have been in the wilderness; nevertheless, thou hast been merciful unto us. O Lord, look upon me in pity, and turn away thine anger from this thy people, and suffer not that they shall go forth across this raging deep in darkness; but behold these things which I have molten out of the rock.

4 And I know, O Lord, that thou hast all power, and can do whatsoever thou wilt for the benefit of man; therefore touch these stones, O Lord, with thy finger, and prepare them that they may shine forth in darkness; and they shall shine forth unto us in the vessels which we have prepared, that we may have light while we shall cross the sea.

5 Behold, O Lord, thou canst do this. We know that thou art able to show forth great power, which looks small unto the understanding of men.

### The Brother of Jared Sees the Spirit Body of Jesus Christ

6 And it came to pass that when the brother of Jared had said these words, behold, the Lord stretched forth his hand and touched the stones one by one with his finger. And the veil was taken from off the eyes of the brother of Jared, and he saw the finger of the Lord; and it was as the finger of a man, like unto flesh and blood; and the brother of Jared fell down before the Lord, for he was struck with fear.

7 And the Lord saw that the brother of Jared had fallen to the earth; and the Lord said unto him: Arise, why hast thou fallen?

---

3:1 ***molten***—melt
***transparent***—clear

3:2 ***encompassed about***—surrounded

"The fall of Adam is one of the most important occurrences in the history of man. Before the fall, Adam and Eve had physical bodies but no blood. There was no sin, no death, and no children among any of the earthly creations." The Fall brought mortality and "both physical and spiritual death into the world upon all mankind (Hel. 14:16–17). . . . It was a necessary step in the progress of man, and provisions for a Savior had been made even before the fall had occurred. Jesus Christ came to atone for the fall of Adam and also for man's individual sins" (LDS Bible Dictionary, s.v. "Fall of Adam," 670).

3:3 ***smitten***—punished
***in pity***—tenderly

3:4 ***benefit***—good

3:6 The spirit of a person looks like that person's physical body (see D&C 77:2). The spirit finger of the premortal Jesus looked so much like a physical finger that the brother of Jared thought he was seeing the physical body of Jesus.

THE BROTHER OF JARED, BY DEL PARSON

*The brother of Jared*

8 And he saith unto the Lord: I saw the finger of the Lord, and I feared lest he should smite me; for I knew not that the Lord had flesh and blood.

9 And the Lord said unto him: Because of thy faith thou hast seen that I shall take upon me flesh and blood; and never has man come before me with such exceeding faith as thou hast; for were it not so ye could not have seen my finger. Sawest thou more than this?

10 And he answered: Nay; Lord, show thyself unto me.

11 And the Lord said unto him: Believest thou the words which I shall speak?

12 And he answered: Yea, Lord, I know that thou speakest the truth, for thou art a God of truth, and canst not lie.

13 And when he had said these words, behold, the Lord showed himself unto him, and said: Because thou knowest these things ye are redeemed from the fall; therefore ye are brought back into my presence; therefore I show myself unto you.

14 Behold, I am he who was prepared from the foundation of the world to redeem my people. Behold, I am Jesus Christ. I am the Father and the Son. In me shall all mankind have life, and that eternally, even they who shall believe on my name; and they shall become my sons and my daughters.

15 And never have I showed myself unto man whom I have created, for never has man believed in me as thou hast. Seest thou that ye are created after mine own image? Yea, even all men were created in the beginning after mine own image.

16 Behold, this body, which ye now behold, is the body of my spirit; and man have I created after the body of my spirit; and even as I appear unto thee to be in the spirit will I appear unto my people in the flesh.

## Moroni Explains Why the Brother of Jared Could See Jesus Christ

17 And now, as I, Moroni, said I could not make a full account of these things which are written, therefore it sufficeth me to say that Jesus showed himself unto this man in the spirit, even after the manner and in the likeness of the same body even as he showed himself unto the Nephites.

18 And he ministered unto him even as he ministered unto the Nephites; and all this, that this man might know that he was God, because of the many great works which the Lord had showed unto him.

19 And because of the knowledge of this man he could not be kept from beholding within the veil; and he saw the finger of Jesus, which, when he saw, he fell with fear; for he knew that it was the finger of the Lord; and he had faith no longer, for he knew, nothing doubting.

---

3:13 To *redeem* means to "buy back" or to "set free." Jesus Christ is our Redeemer because He willingly paid the price to buy us back and set us free from the effects of the Fall of Adam and from the burden of our own sins (see 1 Corinthians 6:20 and D&C 18:11). The price He had to pay was His own blood (see 1 Peter 1:18–19).

3:14 ***from the foundation of the world***—before the earth was created

Jesus Christ is called "Father" for several reasons. One reason is because He offers us a new life when we choose to follow Him. When we have faith in Him, repent, are baptized, and receive the gift of the Holy Ghost, we can be born again. Through the power of the Atonement we can "be called the children of Christ, his sons, and his daughters; for behold, . . . he hath spiritually begotten [us]" (Mosiah 5:7).

3:15 ***image***—appearance or likeness

The brother of Jared had great faith in Jesus Christ. What do you learn from this story about the importance of having faith? What can you do to help your faith grow?

3:17 ***make a full account***—tell the entire story
***sufficeth***—is enough for

3:18 ***ministered unto***—served and taught

3:19 ***beholding within the veil***—seeing spiritual things

3:19 (15–19) Elder Joseph Fielding Smith explained this unusual experience of the brother of Jared: "The Savior stood before the Brother of Jared plainly, distinctly, and showed him his whole body and explained to him that he was a spirit. . . . His appearances to earlier prophets had not been with that same fulness" (*Doctrines of Salvation* 1:37). This sacred appearance came because of the brother of Jared's faith, which was so great that "he could not be kept from beholding within the veil" (Ether 3:19).

THE COUNCIL IN HEAVEN, BY ROBERT T. BARRETT

*"I am he who was prepared from the foundation of the world to redeem my people. Behold, I am Jesus Christ."*

20 Wherefore, having this perfect knowledge of
God, he could not be kept from within the veil;
therefore he saw Jesus; and he did minister unto him.

## *The Lord Shows the Brother of Jared All Things*

21 And it came to pass that the Lord said unto the
brother of Jared: Behold, thou shalt not suffer these
things which ye have seen and heard to go forth
unto the world, until the time cometh that I shall
glorify my name in the flesh; wherefore, ye shall
treasure up the things which ye have seen and
heard, and show it to no man.
22 And behold, when ye shall come unto me, ye
shall write them and shall seal them up, that no one
can interpret them; for ye shall write them in a language that they cannot be read.
23 And behold, these two stones will I give unto
thee, and ye shall seal them up also with the things
which ye shall write.
24 For behold, the language which ye shall write
I have confounded; wherefore I will cause in my
own due time that these stones shall magnify to the
eyes of men these things which ye shall write.
25 And when the Lord had said these words, he
showed unto the brother of Jared all the inhabitants
of the earth which had been, and also all that
would be; and he withheld them not from his sight,
even unto the ends of the earth.
26 For he had said unto him in times before, that
if he would believe in him that he could show unto
him all things—it should be shown unto him; therefore the Lord could not withhold anything from
him, for he knew that the Lord could show him all
things.
27 And the Lord said unto him: Write these things
and seal them up; and I will show them in mine
own due time unto the children of men.
28 And it came to pass that the Lord commanded
him that he should seal up the two stones which he
had received, and show them not, until the Lord
should show them unto the children of men.

# CHAPTER 4

*Moroni is commanded to seal up the brother of Jared's record. Look for the commandments the Savior gives in this chapter.*

## *The Brother of Jared's Record Is to Be Hid Until After Christ's Death*

1 AND the Lord commanded the brother of Jared
to go down out of the mount from the presence of
the Lord, and write the things which he had seen;
and they were forbidden to come unto the children
of men until after that he should be lifted up upon
the cross; and for this cause did king Mosiah keep
them, that they should not come unto the world
until after Christ should show himself unto his
people.

---

3:21 ***suffer***—allow

Speaking of the need to keep sacred things private, Elder Boyd K. Packer said: "I have come to believe also that it is not wise to continually talk of unusual spiritual experiences. They are to be guarded with care and shared only when the Spirit itself prompts you to use them to the blessing of others" ("The Candle of the Lord," 53).

3:22 ***seal***—lock
***interpret***—read and understand

It appears that the brother of Jared used the Adamic language, or the language of God (see Joseph Fielding Smith, *The Way to Perfection,* 69).

3:23 The "two stones" given to the brother of Jared by the Lord are called the Urim and Thummim. "Joseph Smith received the same Urim and Thummim had by the Brother of Jared for it was the one expressly provided for the translation of the Jaredite and Nephite records" (Bruce R. McConkie, *Mormon Doctrine,* 818; see also D&C 10:1; 17:1).

3:24 ***confounded***—made unreadable

3:25 ***inhabitants***—people

3:28 (25–28) The brother of Jared was shown a vision of all things from the beginning to the end. He was told to "seal up" this vision. This vision is located in what is called the "sealed" portion of the Book of Mormon (see 2 Nephi 27:7, 10).

4:1 The Lord commanded the brother of Jared to "write the things which he had seen." We are given a similar commandment. President Spencer W. Kimball urged "every person in the Church to keep a diary or a journal from youth up, all through his life" (in Conference Report, October 1977, 4).

Does anyone in your family keep a journal or family history? How could those records bless members of your family in future years? What kinds of information should you write in a journal?

MORONI BURYING THE RECORD, BY CLARK KELLEY PRICE

*The writings of the brother of Jared were sealed up by Moroni as commanded.*

2 And after Christ truly had showed himself unto his people he commanded that they should be made manifest.

## MORONI IS COMMANDED TO SEAL UP THE BROTHER OF JARED'S RECORD

3 And now, after that, they have all dwindled in unbelief; and there is none save it be the Lamanites, and they have rejected the gospel of Christ; therefore I am commanded that I should hide them up again in the earth.
4 Behold, I have written upon these plates the very things which the brother of Jared saw; and there never were greater things made manifest than those which were made manifest unto the brother of Jared.
5 Wherefore the Lord hath commanded me to write them; and I have written them. And he commanded me that I should seal them up; and he also hath commanded that I should seal up the interpretation thereof; wherefore I have sealed up the interpreters, according to the commandment of the Lord.
6 For the Lord said unto me: They shall not go forth unto the Gentiles until the day that they shall repent of their iniquity, and become clean before the Lord.

---

4:2 ***made manifest***—shown

4:3 ***dwindled***—become weakened or fallen away

4:4 The brother of Jared actually saw the spirit body of Jesus Christ (see Ether 3:13–16). This is among the greatest manifestations ever shown to man.

4:6 The people were not to have this sacred record until they were "clean before the Lord." Why do you think we must be clean to receive sacred communications from the Lord? What are you doing to be clean? How do the commandments like the Word of Wisdom help you to be clean?

7 And in that day that they shall exercise faith in
me, saith the Lord, even as the brother of Jared did,
that they may become sanctified in me, then will I
manifest unto them the things which the brother of
Jared saw, even to the unfolding unto them all my
revelations, saith Jesus Christ, the Son of God, the
Father of the heavens and of the earth, and all
things that in them are.

## Jesus Christ Commands All People to Repent, Come unto Him, and Be Saved

8 And he that will contend against the word of the
Lord, let him be accursed; and he that shall deny
these things, let him be accursed; for unto them will
I show no greater things, saith Jesus Christ; for I am
he who speaketh.
9 And at my command the heavens are opened
and are shut; and at my word the earth shall shake;
and at my command the inhabitants thereof shall
pass away, even so as by fire.
10 And he that believeth not my words believeth
not my disciples; and if it so be that I do not speak,
judge ye; for ye shall know that it is I that speaketh,
at the last day.
11 But he that believeth these things which I have
spoken, him will I visit with the manifestations of
my Spirit, and he shall know and bear record. For
because of my Spirit he shall know that these things
are true; for it persuadeth men to do good.
12 And whatsoever thing persuadeth men to do
good is of me; for good cometh of none save it be
of me. I am the same that leadeth men to all good;
he that will not believe my words will not believe
me—that I am; and he that will not believe me will
not believe the Father who sent me. For behold, I
am the Father, I am the light, and the life, and the
truth of the world.
13 Come unto me, O ye Gentiles, and I will show
unto you the greater things, the knowledge which
is hid up because of unbelief.
14 Come unto me, O ye house of Israel, and it
shall be made manifest unto you how great things
the Father hath laid up for you, from the foundation
of the world; and it hath not come unto you,
because of unbelief.
15 Behold, when ye shall rend that veil of unbelief which doth cause you to remain in your awful
state of wickedness, and hardness of heart, and
blindness of mind, then shall the great and marvelous things which have been hid up from the
foundation of the world from you—yea, when ye
shall call upon the Father in my name, with a broken heart and a contrite spirit, then shall ye know

---

4:7 "To be *sanctified* is to become clean, pure, and spotless" (Bruce R. McConkie, *Mormon Doctrine,* 675). A person can become sanctified only through the Atonement of Jesus Christ and by obedience to the laws, ordinances, and commandments of the gospel of Jesus Christ.

4:8 ***contend***—fight
***accursed***—cursed or punished

4:9 This verse reveals some of God's powers. The LDS Bible Dictionary teaches that God is the "supreme Governor of the universe and the Father of mankind," and that He is "omnipotent," meaning all-powerful (s.v. "God," 681).

4:11 ***persuadeth***—convinces

4:12 Moroni's father, Mormon, taught that "the Spirit of Christ is given to every man, that he may know good from evil." Every thing that leads us to Christ is of God, and every thing that leads us away from Christ is of the devil (see Moroni 7:16–19).

When was the last time you had to make a choice between good and evil? How did you know which choice to make? How did that choice help you come unto Christ? Why do you think it is important to follow a path leading to Jesus Christ?

4:14 The name *Israel* means "one who prevails with God," or "let God prevail." It is used several ways in the scriptures. It may refer to (1) the man Jacob, whose name was changed to Israel; (2) the family, children, or tribes of Israel (the scriptures often use the phrase "house of Israel" in this sense); (3) the land of Israel; or (4) the true believers in Christ, no matter what their family or where they live (see LDS Bible Dictionary, s.v. "Israel," 708).

***foundation of the world***—premortal life or before the earth was created

4:14 (13–14) While He lived on earth, Jesus Christ invited all people to come unto Him and promised that He would give us "rest" or comfort and peace (see Matthew 11:28).

4:15 ***rend that veil of unbelief***—tear away your unbelief
***with a broken heart and a contrite spirit***—in humility and truly repentant

that the Father hath remembered the covenant which he made unto your fathers, O house of Israel.
16 And then shall my revelations which I have caused to be written by my servant John be unfolded in the eyes of all the people. Remember, when ye see these things, ye shall know that the time is at hand that they shall be made manifest in very deed.
17 Therefore, when ye shall receive this record ye may know that the work of the Father has commenced upon all the face of the land.
18 Therefore, repent all ye ends of the earth, and come unto me, and believe in my gospel, and be baptized in my name; for he that believeth and is baptized shall be saved; but he that believeth not shall be damned; and signs shall follow them that believe in my name.
19 And blessed is he that is found faithful unto my name at the last day, for he shall be lifted up to dwell in the kingdom prepared for him from the foundation of the world. And behold it is I that hath spoken it. Amen.

## CHAPTER 5

*The future translator of the Book of Mormon (Joseph Smith) is told he may show the gold plates to three people. Look for why it is helpful to have three witnesses.*

### *Three Witnesses Will Testify of the Gold Plates*

1 AND now I, Moroni, have written the words which were commanded me, according to my memory; and I have told you the things which I have sealed up; therefore touch them not in order that ye may translate; for that thing is forbidden you, except by and by it shall be wisdom in God.
2 And behold, ye may be privileged that ye may show the plates unto those who shall assist to bring forth this work;
3 And unto three shall they be shown by the power of God; wherefore they shall know of a surety that these things are true.

---

4:15 A covenant is an agreement between two people. In the scriptures it is usually an agreement between God and man. We promise to be obedient to God's commandments, and He promises to bless us (see LDS Bible Dictionary, s.v. "Covenant," 651).

4:16 These revelations of John can be found in the book of Revelation. John is one of Jesus Christ's original Twelve Apostles.

4:17 ***commenced***—begun

4:18 "Life is made up of choices. There are two ways of doing things, the right way and the wrong way. Every responsible individual stands almost daily at the crossroads and must choose which way he will travel" (Delbert L. Stapley, in Conference Report, April 1968, 29).

4:19 (18–19) Those who have faith, repent, are baptized, and continue faithfully to the end can return to live with Heavenly Father again. Do you want to return to heaven? Are you willing to do the things that Jesus Christ asks of you?

5:1 Moroni tells Joseph Smith that part of the gold plates are sealed. Elder Joseph Fielding Smith explained: "Revelations are hidden in the sealed part of the record given to Joseph Smith, who was commanded by the Lord not to break the seals, for they were not for this generation of wickedness" (*The Way to Perfection*, 339).

5:2 ***privileged***—allowed
***assist***—help

*The Three Witnesses to the Book of Mormon were Oliver Cowdery, David Whitmer, and Martin Harris.*

ENGRAVING BY JUNIUS F. WELLS

4 And in the mouth of three witnesses shall these
things be established; and the testimony of three,
and this work, in the which shall be shown forth
the power of God and also his word, of which the
Father, and the Son, and the Holy Ghost bear
record—and all this shall stand as a testimony
against the world at the last day.
5 And if it so be that they repent and come unto
the Father in the name of Jesus, they shall be
received into the kingdom of God.
6 And now, if I have no authority for these things,
judge ye; for ye shall know that I have authority
when ye shall see me, and we shall stand before
God at the last day. Amen.

## CHAPTER 6

*The Jaredites arrive in the promised land. The story of the Jaredites' journey can be likened to our own lives. Their arrival in the promised land can be compared to our entrance into the celestial kingdom. Watch for other items in the story that can be likened to our own experiences.*

### *The Jaredites Arrive in the Promised Land*

1 AND now I, Moroni, proceed to give the record
of Jared and his brother.
2 For it came to pass after the Lord had prepared
the stones which the brother of Jared had carried up
into the mount, the brother of Jared came down out
of the mount, and he did put forth the stones into the
vessels which were prepared, one in each end thereof; and behold, they did give light unto the vessels.
3 And thus the Lord caused stones to shine in
darkness, to give light unto men, women, and children, that they might not cross the great waters in
darkness.
4 And it came to pass that when they had prepared all manner of food, that thereby they might
subsist upon the water, and also food for their
flocks and herds, and whatsoever beast or animal
or fowl that they should carry with them—and it
came to pass that when they had done all these
things they got aboard of their vessels or barges,
and set forth into the sea, commending themselves
unto the Lord their God.

---

5:4 ***established***—made known, set forth, or verified

5:4 (3–4) It is the Lord's way of teaching to provide more than one testimony or witness to important truths (see 2 Corinthians 13:1; 2 Nephi 11:3; 27:12).

The "three" people who were chosen to be witnesses of the gold plates were Oliver Cowdery, David Whitmer, and Martin Harris. They "were shown the Gold Plates by the Angel Moroni, and they heard the voice of God bear record that the translation was correct" (Bruce R. McConkie, *Mormon Doctrine,* 841; see also D&C 17; *History of the Church* 1:54–55). Their testimonies appear at the beginning of every copy of the Book of Mormon (see the title page of the Book of Mormon and D&C 17).

5:6 Moroni, as well as other prophets, will stand at the Judgment as a witness of the Book of Mormon's truthfulness (see 2 Nephi 33:11; Moroni 10:27).

Why is it better to have more than one person testify of the truth? In what ways can you be a witness of the Book of Mormon?

6:1 ***proceed***—continue

6:2 ***vessels***—boats or barges

6:3 These stones can represent Jesus Christ who is the "light and the life of the world" (D&C 11:28; 12:9; 34:2; 39:2; 45:7). The Savior can help us in every difficult and dark time of life.

6:4 ***manner***—kinds
***subsist***—live
***commending***—giving

President Spencer W. Kimball, speaking on preparedness said: "Maintain a year's supply. The Lord has urged that his people save for the rainy days, prepare for the difficult times, and put away for emergencies, a year's supply or more of bare necessities so that when comes the flood, the earthquake, the famine, the hurricane, the storms of life, our families can be sustained through the dark days" (*The Teachings of Spencer W. Kimball,* 374).

*JAREDITE BARGES, BY GARY E. SMITH*

*Eight barges carried the Jaredites to the promised land.*

5 And it came to pass that the Lord God caused
that there should be a furious wind blow upon the
face of the waters, towards the promised land; and
thus they were tossed upon the waves of the sea
before the wind.
6 And it came to pass that they were many times
buried in the depths of the sea, because of the
mountain waves which broke upon them, and also
the great and terrible tempests which were caused
by the fierceness of the wind.
7 And it came to pass that when they were buried
in the deep there was no water that could hurt
them, their vessels being tight like unto a dish, and
also they were tight like unto the ark of Noah;
therefore when they were encompassed about by
many waters they did cry unto the Lord, and he
did bring them forth again upon the top of the
waters.
8 And it came to pass that the wind did never
cease to blow towards the promised land while
they were upon the waters; and thus they were driven forth before the wind.

---

6:5 **furious**—violent or powerful

6:6 **tempests**—storms

6:7 **encompassed about**—surrounded

The Lord also helped Noah prepare the ark (boat) that would protect and save his family (see Genesis 6–8).

9 And they did sing praises unto the Lord; yea, the
brother of Jared did sing praises unto the Lord, and
he did thank and praise the Lord all the day long;
and when the night came, they did not cease to
praise the Lord.
10 And thus they were driven forth; and no monster of the sea could break them, neither whale that
could mar them; and they did have light continually, whether it was above the water or under the
water.
11 And thus they were driven forth, three hundred
and forty and four days upon the water.
12 And they did land upon the shore of the
promised land. And when they had set their feet
upon the shores of the promised land they bowed
themselves down upon the face of the land, and did
humble themselves before the Lord, and did shed
tears of joy before the Lord, because of the multitude of his tender mercies over them.

## The Jaredites Want a King

13 And it came to pass that they went forth upon
the face of the land, and began to till the earth.
14 And Jared had four sons; and they were called
Jacom, and Gilgah, and Mahah, and Orihah.
15 And the brother of Jared also begat sons and
daughters.
16 And the friends of Jared and his brother were
in number about twenty and two souls; and they
also begat sons and daughters before they came to
the promised land; and therefore they began to be
many.
17 And they were taught to walk humbly before
the Lord; and they were also taught from on high.
18 And it came to pass that they began to spread
upon the face of the land, and to multiply and to till
the earth; and they did wax strong in the land.
19 And the brother of Jared began to be old, and
saw that he must soon go down to the grave;
wherefore he said unto Jared: Let us gather together our people that we may number them, that
we may know of them what they will desire of us
before we go down to our graves.
20 And accordingly the people were gathered
together. Now the number of the sons and the
daughters of the brother of Jared were twenty and
two souls; and the number of sons and daughters
of Jared were twelve, he having four sons.
21 And it came to pass that they did number their
people; and after that they had numbered them,
they did desire of them the things which they
would that they should do before they went down
to their graves.
22 And it came to pass that the people desired of
them that they should anoint one of their sons to be
a king over them.
23 And now behold, this was grievous unto them.
And the brother of Jared said unto them: Surely this
thing leadeth into captivity.

---

6:9 In our day the Lord declared: "For my soul delighteth in the song of the heart; yea, the song of the righteous is a prayer unto me, and it shall be answered with a blessing upon their heads" (D&C 25:12).

The Jaredites thanked the Lord "all the day long" for their blessings. What blessings have you received from the Lord? How often do you thank Him for those blessings?

6:10 ***monster of the sea***—large sea animal or creature
***mar***—damage or injure

6:12 "The Prophet Joseph is reported to have said at one time that one of the greatest sins for which the Latter-day Saints would be guilty would be the sin of ingratitude. I presume most of us have not thought of that as a serious sin. There is a great tendency for us in our prayers—in our pleadings with the Lord—to ask for additional blessings. Sometimes I feel we need to devote more of our prayers to expressions of gratitude and thanksgiving for blessings already received" (*The Teachings of Ezra Taft Benson,* 363).

6:15 ***begat***—was the father of

6:17 The teaching of gospel principles at home and at church is important in our gaining knowledge, or light and truth. But the power of teaching comes not from parents or leaders alone, but by the power of the Holy Ghost. "Earthly gospel instruction and learning prepares the heart and mind to be 'taught from on high' by revelation" (Joseph Fielding McConkie and others, *Doctrinal Commentary on the Book of Mormon* 4:289).

6:18 ***till the earth***—plant and farm
***wax***—grow

6:22 The term "anoint" means to put someone into an office or position by pouring oil on his or her head (see Noah Webster, *An American Dictionary of the English Language,* 1828, s.v. "Anoint").

6:23 ***grievous***—disturbing

24 But Jared said unto his brother: Suffer them
that they may have a king. And therefore he said
unto them: Choose ye out from among our sons a
king, even whom ye will.
25 And it came to pass that they chose even the
firstborn of the brother of Jared; and his name was
Pagag. And it came to pass that he refused and
would not be their king. And the people would that
his father should constrain him, but his father
would not; and he commanded them that they
should constrain no man to be their king.
26 And it came to pass that they chose all the
brothers of Pagag, and they would not.
27 And it came to pass that neither would the sons
of Jared, even all save it were one; and Orihah was
anointed to be king over the people.
28 And he began to reign, and the people began
to prosper; and they became exceedingly rich.
29 And it came to pass that Jared died, and his
brother also.
30 And it came to pass that Orihah did walk
humbly before the Lord, and did remember how
great things the Lord had done for his father, and
also taught his people how great things the Lord
had done for their fathers.

## CHAPTER 7

*Wickedness and rebellion cause many wars and divide the country. Peace is restored when the people listen to the prophets and repent. Notice what happens when family members seek for power over each other.*

### Corihor Rebels and Places His Father in Captivity

1 AND it came to pass that Orihah did execute
judgment upon the land in righteousness all his
days, whose days were exceedingly many.
2 And he begat sons and daughters; yea, he begat
thirty and one, among whom were twenty and
three sons.
3 And it came to pass that he also begat Kib in his
old age. And it came to pass that Kib reigned in his
stead; and Kib begat Corihor.
4 And when Corihor was thirty and two years old
he rebelled against his father, and went over and
dwelt in the land of Nehor; and he begat sons and
daughters, and they became exceedingly fair;
wherefore Corihor drew away many people after
him.
5 And when he had gathered together an army he
came up unto the land of Moron where the king
dwelt, and took him captive, which brought to pass
the saying of the brother of Jared that they would
be brought into captivity.
6 Now the land of Moron, where the king dwelt,
was near the land which is called Desolation by the
Nephites.
7 And it came to pass that Kib dwelt in captivity, and his people under Corihor his son, until
he became exceedingly old; nevertheless Kib
begat Shule in his old age, while he was yet in
captivity.

---

6:24 ***Suffer them that they may***—Allow them to

6:25 ***constrain***—require or force

6:27 ***save***—except

6:28 ***reign***—rule
***exceedingly***—very

6:30 Orihah remembered the Lord. What great things has the Lord done for you? Why do you think it would be important to remember those things?

7:1 ***execute judgment***—rule

7:2 ***begat***—was the father of

7:3 ***reigned***—ruled
***stead***—place

7:4 ***drew away***—influenced or attracted

7:5 Jared's prophecy of this captivity is recorded in Ether 6:23. This captivity was brought on because of Corihor's wickedness. President David O. McKay warned that "wars spring from wickedness of unrighteous leaders" (in Conference Report, April 1969, 5).

***captive***—prisoner
***captivity***—bondage and slavery

### *Shule Frees His Father, Who Then Gives Shule the Kingdom*

8 And it came to pass that Shule was angry with
his brother; and Shule waxed strong, and became
mighty as to the strength of a man; and he was also
mighty in judgment.
9 Wherefore, he came to the hill Ephraim, and
he did molten out of the hill, and made swords
out of steel for those whom he had drawn away
with him; and after he had armed them with
swords he returned to the city Nehor, and gave
battle unto his brother Corihor, by which means
he obtained the kingdom and restored it unto his
father Kib.
10 And now because of the thing which Shule had
done, his father bestowed upon him the kingdom;
therefore he began to reign in the stead of his
father.
11 And it came to pass that he did execute judgment in righteousness; and he did spread his kingdom upon all the face of the land, for the people
had become exceedingly numerous.
12 And it came to pass that Shule also begat many
sons and daughters.
13 And Corihor repented of the many evils which
he had done; wherefore Shule gave him power in
his kingdom.

### *Rebellion and War Result in Two Rival Kingdoms*

14 And it came to pass that Corihor had many
sons and daughters. And among the sons of Corihor
there was one whose name was Noah.
15 And it came to pass that Noah rebelled against
Shule, the king, and also his father Corihor, and
drew away Cohor his brother, and also all his
brethren and many of the people.
16 And he gave battle unto Shule, the king, in
which he did obtain the land of their first inheritance; and he became a king over that part of the
land.
17 And it came to pass that he gave battle again
unto Shule, the king; and he took Shule, the king,
and carried him away captive into Moron.
18 And it came to pass as he was about to put him
to death, the sons of Shule crept into the house of
Noah by night and slew him, and broke down the
door of the prison and brought out their father, and
placed him upon his throne in his own kingdom.
19 Wherefore, the son of Noah did build up his
kingdom in his stead; nevertheless they did not gain
power any more over Shule the king, and the
people who were under the reign of Shule the king
did prosper exceedingly and wax great.
20 And the country was divided; and there were
two kingdoms, the kingdom of Shule, and the
kingdom of Cohor, the son of Noah.

### *King Shule Is a Righteous King; the People Follow the Prophets and Repent*

21 And Cohor, the son of Noah, caused that his
people should give battle unto Shule, in which
Shule did beat them and did slay Cohor.
22 And now Cohor had a son who was called
Nimrod; and Nimrod gave up the kingdom of
Cohor unto Shule, and he did gain favor in the eyes
of Shule; wherefore Shule did bestow great favors
upon him, and he did do in the kingdom of Shule
according to his desires.
23 And also in the reign of Shule there came
prophets among the people, who were sent from
the Lord, prophesying that the wickedness and idolatry of the people was bringing a curse upon the
land, and they should be destroyed if they did not
repent.

---

7:8 ***waxed***—became

The word *judgment* in this verse means "the spirit of wisdom . . . enabling a person to discern [choose] between right and wrong, good and evil" (Noah Webster, *An American Dictionary of the English Language,* 1828, s.v. "Judgment").

7:9 ***molten***—melt ore

7:10 ***bestowed upon***—gave

7:13 Corihor repented and Shule forgave him even though Corihor had taken their father prisoner. The Lord has commanded us to forgive all people (see D&C 64:10). What lesson do you learn about forgiving others from Shule's example?

7:16 ***of their first inheritance***—where they first lived

7:23 ***idolatry***—worship of false gods

24 And it came to pass that the people did revile
against the prophets, and did mock them. And it
came to pass that king Shule did execute judgment
against all those who did revile against the prophets.
25 And he did execute a law throughout all the
land, which gave power unto the prophets that they
should go whithersoever they would; and by this
cause the people were brought unto repentance.
26 And because the people did repent of their
iniquities and idolatries the Lord did spare them,
and they began to prosper again in the land. And it
came to pass that Shule begat sons and daughters
in his old age.
27 And there were no more wars in the days of
Shule; and he remembered the great things that the
Lord had done for his fathers in bringing them
across the great deep into the promised land;
wherefore he did execute judgment in righteousness all his days.

## CHAPTER 8

*This chapter gives an example of the destructive power of secret combinations. Watch for the warning Moroni gives us about secret combinations in our day.*

### Jared's Desire for Power Leads to Great Suffering in His Family

1 AND it came to pass that he begat Omer, and
Omer reigned in his stead. And Omer begat Jared;
and Jared begat sons and daughters.
2 And Jared rebelled against his father, and came
and dwelt in the land of Heth. And it came to pass
that he did flatter many people, because of his cunning words, until he had gained the half of the
kingdom.
3 And when he had gained the half of the kingdom he gave battle unto his father, and he did carry
away his father into captivity, and did make him
serve in captivity;
4 And now, in the days of the reign of Omer he
was in captivity the half of his days. And it came to
pass that he begat sons and daughters, among
whom were Esrom and Coriantumr;
5 And they were exceedingly angry because of the
doings of Jared their brother, insomuch that they
did raise an army and gave battle unto Jared. And
it came to pass that they did give battle unto him by
night.
6 And it came to pass that when they had slain the
army of Jared they were about to slay him also; and
he plead with them that they would not slay him,
and he would give up the kingdom unto his father.
And it came to pass that they did grant unto him his
life.
7 And now Jared became exceedingly sorrowful
because of the loss of the kingdom, for he had set
his heart upon the kingdom and upon the glory of
the world.

---

7:24 ***revile***—say unkind things
***mock***—make fun of or ridicule

7:25 ***execute***—make

7:26 ***iniquities***—sins

7:27 Shule was a righteous king who remembered the Lord and the blessings he and his people had received. How does remembering the Lord's blessings help you stay close to Him?

8:1 ***begat***—was the father of
***reigned***—ruled
***stead***—place

8:2 ***flatter***—give false praise to
***cunning words***—lies

8:3 ***captivity***—slavery

8:6 ***plead with***—begged

8:7 ***sorrowful***—sad

Jesus taught that "where your treasure is, there will your heart be also" (Matthew 6:21). Rather than setting his heart on spiritual things, Jared set his heart on the "glory of the world." What was wrong with this? What do you desire the most in your heart?

8:7 (3–7) Jared's wicked desire for power and glory caused much war, death, and sorrow. Elder Jeffrey R. Holland said: "We declare to all the world that for real and abiding peace to come, we must strive to be more like that exemplary Son of God. . . . In seeking true peace, some of us need to improve what has to be improved, confess what needs to be confessed, forgive what has to be forgiven, and forget what should be forgotten in order that [peace] can come to us. If there is a commandment we are breaking, and as a result it is breaking us and hurting those who love us, let us call down the power of the Lord Jesus Christ to help us, to free us, to lead us through repentance to that peace 'which passeth all understanding' " (in Conference Report, October 1996, 114).

## Jared and His Daughter Start a Secret Combination

8 Now the daughter of Jared being exceedingly expert, and seeing the sorrows of her father, thought to devise a plan whereby she could redeem the kingdom unto her father.

9 Now the daughter of Jared was exceedingly fair. And it came to pass that she did talk with her father, and said unto him: Whereby hath my father so much sorrow? Hath he not read the record which our fathers brought across the great deep? Behold, is there not an account concerning them of old, that they by their secret plans did obtain kingdoms and great glory?

10 And now, therefore, let my father send for Akish, the son of Kimnor; and behold, I am fair, and I will dance before him, and I will please him, that he will desire me to wife; wherefore if he shall desire of thee that ye shall give unto him me to wife, then shall ye say: I will give her if ye will bring unto me the head of my father, the king.

11 And now Omer was a friend to Akish; wherefore, when Jared had sent for Akish, the daughter of Jared danced before him that she pleased him, insomuch that he desired her to wife. And it came to pass that he said unto Jared: Give her unto me to wife.

12 And Jared said unto him: I will give her unto you, if ye will bring unto me the head of my father, the king.

13 And it came to pass that Akish gathered in unto the house of Jared all his kinsfolk, and said unto them: Will ye swear unto me that ye will be faithful unto me in the thing which I shall desire of you?

14 And it came to pass that they all sware unto him, by the God of heaven, and also by the heavens, and also by the earth, and by their heads, that whoso should vary from the assistance which Akish desired should lose his head; and whoso should divulge whatsoever thing Akish made known unto them, the same should lose his life.

15 And it came to pass that thus they did agree with Akish. And Akish did administer unto them the oaths which were given by them of old who also sought power, which had been handed down even from Cain, who was a murderer from the beginning.

16 And they were kept up by the power of the devil to administer these oaths unto the people, to keep them in darkness, to help such as sought power to gain power, and to murder, and to plunder, and to lie, and to commit all manner of wickedness and whoredoms.

17 And it was the daughter of Jared who put it into his heart to search up these things of old; and Jared put it into the heart of Akish; wherefore, Akish administered it unto his kindred and friends, leading them away by fair promises to do whatsoever thing he desired.

---

8:8 ***exceedingly expert***—very smart
***devise***—make
***redeem***—return or deliver

8:9 ***fair***—beautiful

Jared's daughter knew of secret combinations because of her people's records. Alma told his son Helaman to keep the descriptions of all the secret combinations out of the record of the Nephites because it could bring about the destruction of their nation (see Alma 37:21, 27; see also Glossary: Secret combinations).

8:10 During Christ's life, the daughter of another wicked person danced in order to fulfill a wicked plan. Her dance led to the death of John the Baptist (see Mark 6:22–25).

8:12 (11–12) President Spencer W. Kimball taught: "Much better is it to avoid the steps which lead to unforgivable sin. Thus as a preventive measure against murder one should avoid anger and hatred, avarice [unrighteous desires] and greed, and any of the other impulses which can spark the act" (*The Miracle of Forgiveness,* 131).

8:13 ***kinsfolk***—relatives
***swear***—promise

8:14 ***vary from the assistance***—fail to give the help
***divulge***—tell

8:15 ***administer***—plan and carry out
***oaths***—secret promises

8:16 ***plunder***—rob
***whoredoms***—immorality

8:16 (15–16) The first secret combination was between Satan and Cain, who killed his brother Abel to get his flocks (see Moses 5:28–32).

8:17 ***put it into his heart***—gave him the idea

## Moroni Warns Against Secret Combinations

18 And it came to pass that they formed a secret
combination, even as they of old; which combination is most abominable and wicked above all, in
the sight of God;
19 For the Lord worketh not in secret combinations, neither doth he will that man should shed
blood, but in all things hath forbidden it, from the
beginning of man.
20 And now I, Moroni, do not write the manner of
their oaths and combinations, for it hath been made
known unto me that they are had among all people,
and they are had among the Lamanites.
21 And they have caused the destruction of this
people of whom I am now speaking, and also the
destruction of the people of Nephi.
22 And whatsoever nation shall uphold such
secret combinations, to get power and gain, until
they shall spread over the nation, behold, they shall
be destroyed; for the Lord will not suffer that the
blood of his saints, which shall be shed by them,
shall always cry unto him from the ground for
vengeance upon them and yet he avenge them not.
23 Wherefore, O ye Gentiles, it is wisdom in God
that these things should be shown unto you, that
thereby ye may repent of your sins, and suffer not
that these murderous combinations shall get above
you, which are built up to get power and gain—and
the work, yea, even the work of destruction come
upon you, yea, even the sword of the justice of the
Eternal God shall fall upon you, to your overthrow
and destruction if ye shall suffer these things to be.
24 Wherefore, the Lord commandeth you, when
ye shall see these things come among you that ye
shall awake to a sense of your awful situation,
because of this secret combination which shall be
among you; or wo be unto it, because of the blood
of them who have been slain; for they cry from the
dust for vengeance upon it, and also upon those
who built it up.
25 For it cometh to pass that whoso buildeth it up
seeketh to overthrow the freedom of all lands,
nations, and countries; and it bringeth to pass the
destruction of all people, for it is built up by the
devil, who is the father of all lies; even that same
liar who beguiled our first parents, yea, even that
same liar who hath caused man to commit murder
from the beginning; who hath hardened the hearts
of men that they have murdered the prophets, and
stoned them, and cast them out from the beginning.
26 Wherefore, I, Moroni, am commanded to write
these things that evil may be done away, and that
the time may come that Satan may have no power
upon the hearts of the children of men, but that
they may be persuaded to do good continually, that
they may come unto the fountain of all righteousness and be saved.

## CHAPTER 9

*Several different kings rule over the Jaredites. Some of them come to power in an evil manner or through murder. Others receive the power to rule in a righteous manner. Look for what happens to the Jaredites when they don't listen to the counsel of their prophets.*

---

8:18 ***abominable***—terrible and evil

8:19 ***shed blood***—murder

8:21 Secret combinations not only destroyed the Jaredites and the Nephites, but "the Lord has warned that secret combinations will be present in [the last days] (D&C 38:29; Ether 8:20–25). They threaten freedom everywhere. However, Latter-day Saints believe that secret combinations and their practices can be overcome, but only through righteous living and full support of honest government" (*Encyclopedia of Mormonism,* s.v. "Secret Combinations," 3:1291).

8:22 ***suffer***—allow
***vengeance***—punishment
***avenge***—punish

8:23 ***sword of the justice***—fair punishments

8:24 ***wo***—sorrow

8:25 ***buildeth it up***—supports it
***beguiled***—deceived and tempted

8:26 Moroni wrote this message so that we could be protected from secret combinations and so that Satan would not have power over us. What did you learn from this chapter that would help you avoid secret combinations?

## The Jaredites and Their Kings Suffer Because of Wickedness

1 AND now I, Moroni, proceed with my record. Therefore, behold, it came to pass that because of the secret combinations of Akish and his friends, behold, they did overthrow the kingdom of Omer.

2 Nevertheless, the Lord was merciful unto Omer, and also to his sons and to his daughters who did not seek his destruction.

3 And the Lord warned Omer in a dream that he should depart out of the land; wherefore Omer departed out of the land with his family, and traveled many days, and came over and passed by the hill of Shim, and came over by the place where the Nephites were destroyed, and from thence eastward, and came to a place which was called Ablom, by the seashore, and there he pitched his tent, and also his sons and his daughters, and all his household, save it were Jared and his family.

4 And it came to pass that Jared was anointed king over the people, by the hand of wickedness; and he gave unto Akish his daughter to wife.

5 And it came to pass that Akish sought the life of his father-in-law; and he applied unto those whom he had sworn by the oath of the ancients, and they obtained the head of his father-in-law, as he sat upon his throne, giving audience to his people.

6 For so great had been the spreading of this wicked and secret society that it had corrupted the hearts of all the people; therefore Jared was murdered upon his throne, and Akish reigned in his stead.

7 And it came to pass that Akish began to be jealous of his son, therefore he shut him up in prison, and kept him upon little or no food until he had suffered death.

8 And now the brother of him that suffered death, (and his name was Nimrah) was angry with his father because of that which his father had done unto his brother.

9 And it came to pass that Nimrah gathered together a small number of men, and fled out of the land, and came over and dwelt with Omer.

10 And it came to pass that Akish begat other sons, and they won the hearts of the people, notwithstanding they had sworn unto him to do all manner of iniquity according to that which he desired.

11 Now the people of Akish were desirous for gain, even as Akish was desirous for power; wherefore, the sons of Akish did offer them money, by which means they drew away the more part of the people after them.

12 And there began to be a war between the sons of Akish and Akish, which lasted for the space of many years, yea, unto the destruction of nearly all the people of the kingdom, yea, even all, save it were thirty souls, and they who fled with the house of Omer.

13 Wherefore, Omer was restored again to the land of his inheritance.

## Emer, a Righteous King, Sees the Lord

14 And it came to pass that Omer began to be old; nevertheless, in his old age he begat Emer; and he anointed Emer to be king to reign in his stead.

15 And after that he had anointed Emer to be king he saw peace in the land for the space of two years, and he died, having seen exceedingly many days, which were full of sorrow. And it came to pass that Emer did reign in his stead, and did fill the steps of his father.

---

9:1 ***proceed***—continue
***overthrow***—defeat

9:3 ***thence***—there

9:4 ***by the hand of wickedness***—through a wicked plan

9:5 ***sought the life of***—wanted to kill
***applied unto***—asked for the help of

This oath or promise was called the "oath of the ancients" because it began long before, when Satan and Cain promised to keep secret their plan to murder Abel (see Moses 5:29–32).

9:6 ***corrupted***—turned evil
***stead***—place

9:11 ***drew***—turned

9:12 (5–12) Notice how the lack of family love caused death and sorrow for these Jaredites. What caused these family members to not love one another? Why do you think it is important that family members love one another?

16 And the Lord began again to take the curse
from off the land, and the house of Emer did prosper exceedingly under the reign of Emer; and in the
space of sixty and two years they had become
exceedingly strong, insomuch that they became
exceedingly rich—
17 Having all manner of fruit, and of grain, and of
silks, and of fine linen, and of gold, and of silver,
and of precious things;
18 And also all manner of cattle, of oxen, and
cows, and of sheep, and of swine, and of goats, and
also many other kinds of animals which were useful for the food of man.
19 And they also had horses, and asses, and there
were elephants and cureloms and cumoms; all of
which were useful unto man, and more especially
the elephants and cureloms and cumoms.
20 And thus the Lord did pour out his blessings
upon this land, which was choice above all other
lands; and he commanded that whoso should possess the land should possess it unto the Lord, or
they should be destroyed when they were ripened
in iniquity; for upon such, saith the Lord: I will pour
out the fulness of my wrath.
21 And Emer did execute judgment in righteousness all his days, and he begat many sons and
daughters; and he begat Coriantum, and he
anointed Coriantum to reign in his stead.
22 And after he had anointed Coriantum to reign
in his stead he lived four years, and he saw peace
in the land; yea, and he even saw the Son of
Righteousness, and did rejoice and glory in his day;
and he died in peace.

## *The Lord Sends Prophets to Warn the People*

23 And it came to pass that Coriantum did walk in
the steps of his father, and did build many mighty
cities, and did administer that which was good unto
his people in all his days. And it came to pass that
he had no children even until he was exceedingly
old.
24 And it came to pass that his wife died, being an
hundred and two years old. And it came to pass
that Coriantum took to wife, in his old age, a young
maid, and begat sons and daughters; wherefore he
lived until he was an hundred and forty and two
years old.
25 And it came to pass that he begat Com, and
Com reigned in his stead; and he reigned forty and
nine years, and he begat Heth; and he also begat
other sons and daughters.
26 And the people had spread again over all the
face of the land, and there began again to be an
exceedingly great wickedness upon the face of the
land, and Heth began to embrace the secret plans
again of old, to destroy his father.
27 And it came to pass that he did dethrone his
father, for he slew him with his own sword; and he
did reign in his stead.
28 And there came prophets in the land again,
crying repentance unto them—that they must prepare the way of the Lord or there should come a
curse upon the face of the land; yea, even there
should be a great famine, in which they should be
destroyed if they did not repent.

PHOTOGRAPH BY EDWIN M. WOOLLEY

*When the people were righteous the Lord removed the curse from the land, and the people "became exceedingly rich—having all manner of . . . gold, and of silver, and of precious things." This jewelry was found near Monte Alban, in Central America.*

9:18 ***swine***—pigs

9:19 ***cureloms and cumoms***—unknown animals used by the Jaredites

9:22 Emer was such a righteous man that he saw "the Son of Righteousness," or Jesus Christ. Many other prophets have also seen Him (see Ether 3:13; 2 Nephi 11:2–3). The Prophet Joseph Smith saw Him in our day (see D&C 76:22–24; 110:1–4; Joseph Smith—History 1:17).

9:26 ***embrace***—accept and love

9:27 ***dethrone***—take the kingdom from
***slew***—killed

29 But the people believed not the words of the prophets, but they cast them out; and some of them they cast into pits and left them to perish. And it came to pass that they did all these things according to the commandment of the king, Heth.

## *The People Suffer a Famine and a Plague of Poisonous Snakes*

30 And it came to pass that there began to be a great dearth upon the land, and the inhabitants began to be destroyed exceedingly fast because of the dearth, for there was no rain upon the face of the earth.

31 And there came forth poisonous serpents also upon the face of the land, and did poison many people. And it came to pass that their flocks began to flee before the poisonous serpents, towards the land southward, which was called by the Nephites Zarahemla.

32 And it came to pass that there were many of them which did perish by the way; nevertheless, there were some which fled into the land southward.

33 And it came to pass that the Lord did cause the serpents that they should pursue them no more, but that they should hedge up the way that the people could not pass, that whoso should attempt to pass might fall by the poisonous serpents.

34 And it came to pass that the people did follow the course of the beasts, and did devour the carcasses of them which fell by the way, until they had devoured them all. Now when the people saw that they must perish they began to repent of their iniquities and cry unto the Lord.

35 And it came to pass that when they had humbled themselves sufficiently before the Lord he did send rain upon the face of the earth; and the people began to revive again, and there began to be fruit in the north countries, and in all the countries round about. And the Lord did show forth his power unto them in preserving them from famine.

## CHAPTER 10

*Many different kings continue to reign over the Jaredites. Some are righteous and some are not. Notice what happens to the people when their leaders are righteous compared to the times when their leaders are wicked.*

---

9:29 ***perish***—die

Pits were deep holes dug into the earth to store grain or collect water. They were often deep enough to use as prisons. For example, the prophet Jeremiah was imprisoned in a pit (see Jeremiah 38:6).

9:29 (28–29) The Lord has said if we don't listen to and obey the prophets we "shall be cut off from among the people" (D&C 1:14). That is, if we disobey God's prophets, we lose God's blessings and the fellowship of other Church members. How did the Jaredites lose God's blessings? How can you better follow the prophet?

9:30 ***dearth***—drought or famine, which is a lack of water or food
***inhabitants***—people

9:31 The Lord punished the wicked Jaredites by sending poisonous snakes to plague them. This is similar to how the Lord "straitened," or disciplined, the children of Israel (see 1 Nephi 17:41).

9:34 ***course***—trail
***devour the carcasses of them***—eat the meat off the dead animals

9:35 ***sufficiently***—enough
***revive***—gain their strength
***preserving***—saving

To be humble is to be willing to follow God, instead of only doing what you want. It is better to choose to be humble than to be forced to be humble (see Alma 32:14–16). Why were the Jaredites humble at this time? What can you do to be more humble in your life?

*"There came forth poisonous serpents . . . upon the face of the land, and did poison many people."*

## Shez Remembers the Lord and Rebuilds the Kingdom in Righteousness

1 AND it came to pass that Shez, who was a descendant of Heth—for Heth had perished by the famine, and all his household save it were Shez—wherefore, Shez began to build up again a broken people.

2 And it came to pass that Shez did remember the destruction of his fathers, and he did build up a righteous kingdom; for he remembered what the Lord had done in bringing Jared and his brother across the deep; and he did walk in the ways of the Lord; and he begat sons and daughters.

3 And his eldest son, whose name was Shez, did rebel against him; nevertheless, Shez was smitten by the hand of a robber, because of his exceeding riches, which brought peace again unto his father.

4 And it came to pass that his father did build up many cities upon the face of the land, and the people began again to spread over all the face of the land. And Shez did live to an exceedingly old age; and he begat Riplakish. And he died, and Riplakish reigned in his stead.

## Riplakish Makes His People Pay Heavy Taxes

5 And it came to pass that Riplakish did not do that which was right in the sight of the Lord, for he did have many wives and concubines, and did lay that upon men's shoulders which was grievous to be borne; yea, he did tax them with heavy taxes; and with the taxes he did build many spacious buildings.

6 And he did erect him an exceedingly beautiful throne; and he did build many prisons, and whoso would not be subject unto taxes he did cast into prison; and whoso was not able to pay taxes he did cast into prison; and he did cause that they should labor continually for their support; and whoso refused to labor he did cause to be put to death.

7 Wherefore he did obtain all his fine work, yea, even his fine gold he did cause to be refined in prison; and all manner of fine workmanship he did cause to be wrought in prison. And it came to pass that he did afflict the people with his whoredoms and abominations.

8 And when he had reigned for the space of forty and two years the people did rise up in rebellion against him; and there began to be war again in the land, insomuch that Riplakish was killed, and his descendants were driven out of the land.

## The People Prosper Most When Their Kings Are Righteous

9 And it came to pass after the space of many years, Morianton, (he being a descendant of Riplakish) gathered together an army of outcasts, and went forth and gave battle unto the people; and he gained power over many cities; and the war became exceedingly sore, and did last for the space of many years; and he did gain power over all the land, and did establish himself king over all the land.

---

10:1 ***a descendant of***—of the family of or a direct relative of
***perished***—died

10:2 The story of how the Lord brought Jared and his brother "across the deep" (over the ocean) is found in Ether 6.

Shez built a "righteous kingdom" because he "remembered" the blessings given to the righteous. How much death and destruction could be avoided if all people "remembered" the Lord's blessings? How has remembering your blessings helped give you courage to obey?

10:3 ***smitten***—hurt or killed

10:4 ***reigned***—ruled
***stead***—place

10:5 In the Old Testament, a concubine was a woman who belonged to a man in a relationship similar to but not equal to that of a legal wife. There were laws protecting concubines (Exodus 21:7–10; Deuteronomy 21:10–14), but they usually had very little authority in the family. Generally, a concubine's main purpose was to bear children (see *Easton's Bible Dictionary,* s.v. "Concubine").

***grievous to be borne***—very hard to bear

10:6 ***erect***—build or make

10:7 ***refined***—melted down and made pure
***wrought***—done
***whoredoms***—wickedness and immorality

10:9 ***exceedingly sore***—terrible or intense

10 And after that he had established himself king
he did ease the burden of the people, by which he
did gain favor in the eyes of the people, and they
did anoint him to be their king.
11 And he did do justice unto the people, but not
unto himself because of his many whoredoms;
wherefore he was cut off from the presence of the
Lord.
12 And it came to pass that Morianton built up
many cities, and the people became exceedingly
rich under his reign, both in buildings, and in gold
and silver, and in raising grain, and in flocks, and
herds, and such things which had been restored
unto them.
13 And Morianton did live to an exceedingly great
age, and then he begat Kim; and Kim did reign in
the stead of his father; and he did reign eight years,
and his father died. And it came to pass that Kim
did not reign in righteousness, wherefore he was
not favored of the Lord.
14 And his brother did rise up in rebellion against
him, by which he did bring him into captivity; and
he did remain in captivity all his days; and he begat
sons and daughters in captivity, and in his old age
he begat Levi; and he died.
15 And it came to pass that Levi did serve in captivity
after the death of his father, for the space of
forty and two years. And he did make war against
the king of the land, by which he did obtain unto
himself the kingdom.
16 And after he had obtained unto himself the
kingdom he did that which was right in the sight of
the Lord; and the people did prosper in the land;
and he did live to a good old age, and begat sons
and daughters; and he also begat Corom, whom he
anointed king in his stead.
17 And it came to pass that Corom did that which
was good in the sight of the Lord all his days; and
he begat many sons and daughters; and after he
had seen many days he did pass away, even like
unto the rest of the earth; and Kish reigned in his
stead.
18 And it came to pass that Kish passed away also,
and Lib reigned in his stead.
19 And it came to pass that Lib also did that which
was good in the sight of the Lord. And in the days
of Lib the poisonous serpents were destroyed.
Wherefore they did go into the land southward, to
hunt food for the people of the land, for the land
was covered with animals of the forest. And Lib also
himself became a great hunter.

### *The People Are Blessed and Prospered Because They Are Righteous*

20 And they built a great city by the narrow neck
of land, by the place where the sea divides the
land.
21 And they did preserve the land southward for
a wilderness, to get game. And the whole face of
the land northward was covered with inhabitants.
22 And they were exceedingly industrious, and
they did buy and sell and traffic one with another,
that they might get gain.

10:10 For more information on the word *anoint,* see for Ether 6:22.

10:12 (11–12) Morianton was not righteous, but he was a successful king because he treated his people fairly and they prospered. That kind of success is only temporary, however, for Jesus taught that the wicked will have "joy in their works for a season, and by and by the end cometh, and they are hewn down and cast into the fire" (3 Nephi 27:11).

10:14 ***captivity***—prison or bondage

10:15 ***obtain unto himself***—get or gain

10:16 ***did prosper***—were blessed or became rich

10:21 ***game***—meat
***covered with inhabitants***—filled with people

10:22 ***industrious***—hardworking
***traffic***—trade

*Some scholars believe this hieroglyph can be translated as "it came to pass."*

PHOTOGRAPH BY EDWIN M. WOOLLEY

23 And they did work in all manner of ore, and they did make gold, and silver, and iron, and brass, and all manner of metals; and they did dig it out of the earth; wherefore, they did cast up mighty heaps of earth to get ore, of gold, and of silver, and of iron, and of copper. And they did work all manner of fine work.

24 And they did have silks, and fine-twined linen; and they did work all manner of cloth, that they might clothe themselves from their nakedness.

25 And they did make all manner of tools to till the earth, both to plow and to sow, to reap and to hoe, and also to thrash.

26 And they did make all manner of tools with which they did work their beasts.

27 And they did make all manner of weapons of war. And they did work all manner of work of exceedingly curious workmanship.

28 And never could be a people more blessed than were they, and more prospered by the hand of the Lord. And they were in a land that was choice above all lands, for the Lord had spoken it.

### *War Begins Again and Secret Bands of Robbers Infest the Land*

29 And it came to pass that Lib did live many years, and begat sons and daughters; and he also begat Hearthom.

30 And it came to pass that Hearthom reigned in the stead of his father. And when Hearthom had reigned twenty and four years, behold, the kingdom was taken away from him. And he served many years in captivity, yea, even all the remainder of his days.

31 And he begat Heth, and Heth lived in captivity all his days. And Heth begat Aaron, and Aaron dwelt in captivity all his days; and he begat Amnigaddah, and Amnigaddah also dwelt in captivity all his days; and he begat Coriantum, and Coriantum dwelt in captivity all his days; and he begat Com.

32 And it came to pass that Com drew away the half of the kingdom. And he reigned over the half of the kingdom forty and two years; and he went to battle against the king, Amgid, and they fought for the space of many years, during which time Com gained power over Amgid, and obtained power over the remainder of the kingdom.

33 And in the days of Com there began to be robbers in the land; and they adopted the old plans, and administered oaths after the manner of the ancients, and sought again to destroy the kingdom.

34 Now Com did fight against them much; nevertheless, he did not prevail against them.

## CHAPTER 11

*The Jaredites continue in their great wickedness even though prophets warn them that they will be destroyed if they do not repent. Look for what causes the Jaredites to repent for a short time.*

### *Wicked Jaredites Kill the Prophets and Are Cursed with a Great Destruction*

1 AND there came also in the days of Com many prophets, and prophesied of the destruction of that great people except they should repent, and turn unto the Lord, and forsake their murders and wickedness.

2 And it came to pass that the prophets were rejected by the people, and they fled unto Com for protection, for the people sought to destroy them.

3 And they prophesied unto Com many things; and he was blessed in all the remainder of his days.

4 And he lived to a good old age, and begat Shiblom; and Shiblom reigned in his stead. And the brother of Shiblom rebelled against him, and there began to be an exceedingly great war in all the land.

---

10:24 ***fine-twined linen***—good cloth

10:27 ***curious workmanship***—high quality or very well made

10:28 These people prospered and were very happy because they worked hard (see verse 22) and "did that which was good in the sight of the Lord" (Ether 10:19). How has working hard and staying close to the Lord brought blessings into your family's life? Why is it important to always follow the Lord?

10:33 ***adopted***—used
***administered oaths***—made promises or covenants

For more information on these "old plans" and ancient secret "oaths" used by these robbers, see for Ether 8:21 and 9:5.

11:1 ***forsake***—stop

11:2 ***rejected***—ignored or turned against
***sought***—tried

11:4 ***reigned in his stead***—ruled in his place

5 And it came to pass that the brother of Shiblom caused that all the prophets who prophesied of the destruction of the people should be put to death;

6 And there was great calamity in all the land, for they had testified that a great curse should come upon the land, and also upon the people, and that there should be a great destruction among them, such an one as never had been upon the face of the earth, and their bones should become as heaps of earth upon the face of the land except they should repent of their wickedness.

7 And they hearkened not unto the voice of the Lord, because of their wicked combinations; wherefore, there began to be wars and contentions in all the land, and also many famines and pestilences, insomuch that there was a great destruction, such an one as never had been known upon the face of the earth; and all this came to pass in the days of Shiblom.

## *The Jaredites Repent for a Short Time and Then Become Wicked Again Even Though Prophets Warn Them*

8 And the people began to repent of their iniquity; and inasmuch as they did the Lord did have mercy on them.

9 And it came to pass that Shiblom was slain, and Seth was brought into captivity, and did dwell in captivity all his days.

10 And it came to pass that Ahah, his son, did obtain the kingdom; and he did reign over the people all his days. And he did do all manner of iniquity in his days, by which he did cause the shedding of much blood; and few were his days.

11 And Ethem, being a descendant of Ahah, did obtain the kingdom; and he also did do that which was wicked in his days.

12 And it came to pass that in the days of Ethem there came many prophets, and prophesied again unto the people; yea, they did prophesy that the Lord would utterly destroy them from off the face of the earth except they repented of their iniquities.

13 And it came to pass that the people hardened their hearts, and would not hearken unto their words; and the prophets mourned and withdrew from among the people.

14 And it came to pass that Ethem did execute judgment in wickedness all his days; and he begat Moron. And it came to pass that Moron did reign in his stead; and Moron did that which was wicked before the Lord.

15 And it came to pass that there arose a rebellion among the people, because of that secret combination which was built up to get power and gain; and there arose a mighty man among them in iniquity, and gave battle unto Moron, in which he did overthrow the half of the kingdom; and he did maintain the half of the kingdom for many years.

16 And it came to pass that Moron did overthrow him, and did obtain the kingdom again.

17 And it came to pass that there arose another mighty man; and he was a descendant of the brother of Jared.

18 And it came to pass that he did overthrow Moron and obtain the kingdom; wherefore, Moron dwelt in captivity all the remainder of his days; and he begat Coriantor.

19 And it came to pass that Coriantor dwelt in captivity all his days.

---

11:6 ***calamity***—trouble
***heaps***—large piles

11:7 For help with the term *wicked combinations,* see Glossary: Secret combinations.

***pestilences***—terrible diseases

11:8 ***iniquity***—sins

Even though the Jaredites have been very wicked, the Lord forgives them when they repent. In Mosiah 26:30, the Lord says, "Yea, and as often as my people repent will I forgive them their trespasses [sins] against me."

11:11 ***a descendant of***—of the family of or a direct relative of

11:12 ***utterly***—completely

11:13 ***hearken unto***—listen to and obey
***mourned and withdrew from among***—were very sad and left

When the prophets left, the people cut themselves off from the revelation and vision that prophets receive. The Bible warns of what will happen when there is no vision: "Where there is no vision, the people perish [or die]" (Proverbs 29:18).

11:14 ***execute***—do or perform
***begat***—was the father of

11:15 ***maintain***—keep

20 And in the days of Coriantor there also came many prophets, and prophesied of great and marvelous things, and cried repentance unto the people, and except they should repent the Lord God would execute judgment against them to their utter destruction;

21 And that the Lord God would send or bring forth another people to possess the land, by his power, after the manner by which he brought their fathers.

22 And they did reject all the words of the prophets, because of their secret society and wicked abominations.

23 And it came to pass that Coriantor begat Ether, and he died, having dwelt in captivity all his days.

## CHAPTER 12

*Moroni tells how Ether pleaded with his people to believe in Jesus Christ. Moroni also tells of many of the miracles that have happened as a result of faith. Watch for all the examples Moroni uses to teach the power that faith can have in our lives.*

### Ether Strongly Asks His People to Have Faith

1 AND it came to pass that the days of Ether were in the days of Coriantumr; and Coriantumr was king over all the land.

2 And Ether was a prophet of the Lord; wherefore Ether came forth in the days of Coriantumr, and began to prophesy unto the people, for he could not be restrained because of the Spirit of the Lord which was in him.

3 For he did cry from the morning, even until the going down of the sun, exhorting the people to believe in God unto repentance lest they should be destroyed, saying unto them that by faith all things are fulfilled—

4 Wherefore, whoso believeth in God might with surety hope for a better world, yea, even a place at the right hand of God, which hope cometh of faith, maketh an anchor to the souls of men, which would make them sure and steadfast, always abounding in good works, being led to glorify God.

5 And it came to pass that Ether did prophesy great and marvelous things unto the people, which they did not believe, because they saw them not.

### Moroni Tells How Faith Blesses the Lives of Saints

6 And now, I, Moroni, would speak somewhat concerning these things; I would show unto the world that faith is things which are hoped for and not seen; wherefore, dispute not because ye see not, for ye receive no witness until after the trial of your faith.

---

11:20 ***utter***—complete

11:21 ***possess***—have or control

11:21 (20–21) When prophets ask us to repent, they are asking us to return to the ways of the Lord so that we can be happy. What have you heard our prophet teach that you think is "great and marvelous"? What blessings have you received when you have followed the prophet's counsel?

11:22 This secret society is also called a secret combination (see Ether 8:20). Years later this same land would be plagued with a similar group known as the Gadianton robbers (see Helaman 6:16–33; 4 Nephi 1:42, 46; Mormon 1:18).

12:2 ***restrained***—stopped from expressing his feelings

12:3 ***cry***—speak loudly
***exhorting***—encouraging
***fulfilled***—accomplished

12:4 ***steadfast***—faithful
***abounding in***—doing many

What does an anchor do for a ship? How can hope be an "anchor" to you? If you were anchored to Jesus Christ, how do you think it would help you?

12:6 ***dispute***—argue

12:6 (5–6) Some people say, "I'll believe it when I see it." But Moroni taught that the witness or testimony comes "after the trial of [our] faith," or after our faith is tested (see verses 7, 12, 17–18, 30–31). Why do you think God wants us to believe before blessing us? Have you ever had a "witness," or answer, to prayer after a trial of your faith?

Elder Spencer W. Kimball said: "Remember that Abraham, Moses, Elijah, and others could not see clearly the end from the beginning. They also walked by faith and without sight. . . . Remember that there were no clouds in the sky, no evidence of rain . . . when Noah [built] the ark. . . . There was no ram in the thicket when Isaac and his father left for Moriah for the sacrifice" (in Conference Report, October 1952, 51).

7 For it was by faith that Christ showed himself unto our fathers, after he had risen from the dead; and he showed not himself unto them until after they had faith in him; wherefore, it must needs be that some had faith in him, for he showed himself not unto the world.
8 But because of the faith of men he has shown himself unto the world, and glorified the name of the Father, and prepared a way that thereby others might be partakers of the heavenly gift, that they might hope for those things which they have not seen.
9 Wherefore, ye may also have hope, and be partakers of the gift, if ye will but have faith.
10 Behold it was by faith that they of old were called after the holy order of God.
11 Wherefore, by faith was the law of Moses given. But in the gift of his Son hath God prepared a more excellent way; and it is by faith that it hath been fulfilled.
12 For if there be no faith among the children of men God can do no miracle among them; wherefore, he showed not himself until after their faith.
13 Behold, it was the faith of Alma and Amulek that caused the prison to tumble to the earth.
14 Behold, it was the faith of Nephi and Lehi that wrought the change upon the Lamanites, that they were baptized with fire and with the Holy Ghost.
15 Behold, it was the faith of Ammon and his brethren which wrought so great a miracle among the Lamanites.
16 Yea, and even all they who wrought miracles wrought them by faith, even those who were before Christ and also those who were after.
17 And it was by faith that the three disciples obtained a promise that they should not taste of death; and they obtained not the promise until after their faith.
18 And neither at any time hath any wrought miracles until after their faith; wherefore they first believed in the Son of God.
19 And there were many whose faith was so exceedingly strong, even before Christ came, who could not be kept from within the veil, but truly saw with their eyes the things which they had beheld with an eye of faith, and they were glad.
20 And behold, we have seen in this record that one of these was the brother of Jared; for so great was his faith in God, that when God put forth his finger he could not hide it from the sight of the brother of Jared, because of his word which he had spoken unto him, which word he had obtained by faith.
21 And after the brother of Jared had beheld the finger of the Lord, because of the promise which the brother of Jared had obtained by faith, the Lord could not withhold anything from his sight; wherefore he showed him all things, for he could no longer be kept without the veil.

---

12:8 ***be partakers of the heavenly gift***—receive forgiveness of sins and the companionship of the Holy Ghost

12:10 Modern revelation tells us that this "holy order" is "the Holy Priesthood, after the Order of the Son of God," or the Melchizedek Priesthood (D&C 107:3).

12:11 The law of Moses included the laws and ordinances that the children of Israel were commanded to follow from the days of Moses until the time of Jesus Christ (see LDS Bible Dictionary, s.v. "Law of Moses," 722–23).

12:14 ***wrought***—worked

Baptism with fire and the Holy Ghost cleanses us from sin. Elder Bruce R. McConkie said, "The Holy Ghost is a sanctifier, and those who receive the baptism of fire have sin and evil burned out of their souls as though by fire" (Bruce R. McConkie, *The Mortal Messiah* 2:50).

12:17 The Lord promised these three disciples that they would live until He came again at the Second Coming. They received this promise in 3 Nephi 28:6–10.

12:19 ***exceedingly***—very
***from within***—outside

12:20 ***obtained***—received

12:21 ***without***—outside

The brother of Jared's faith was so strong that he saw the Lord. Other prophets like Moses, Nephi, Jacob, and Isaiah have had the same privilege (see Moses 1:1–2; 2 Nephi 11:2–3).

22 And it is by faith that my fathers have obtained
the promise that these things should come unto
their brethren through the Gentiles; therefore the
Lord hath commanded me, yea, even Jesus Christ.

## Moroni Is Concerned About His Ability to Write the Book of Mormon

23 And I said unto him: Lord, the Gentiles will
mock at these things, because of our weakness in
writing; for Lord thou hast made us mighty in word
by faith, but thou hast not made us mighty in writing; for thou hast made all this people that they
could speak much, because of the Holy Ghost
which thou hast given them;
24 And thou hast made us that we could write but
little, because of the awkwardness of our hands.
Behold, thou hast not made us mighty in writing
like unto the brother of Jared, for thou madest him
that the things which he wrote were mighty even as
thou art, unto the overpowering of man to read
them.
25 Thou hast also made our words powerful and
great, even that we cannot write them; wherefore,
when we write we behold our weakness, and
stumble because of the placing of our words; and
I fear lest the Gentiles shall mock at our words.
26 And when I had said this, the Lord spake unto
me, saying: Fools mock, but they shall mourn; and
my grace is sufficient for the meek, that they shall
take no advantage of your weakness;
27 And if men come unto me I will show unto
them their weakness. I give unto men weakness
that they may be humble; and my grace is sufficient
for all men that humble themselves before me; for
if they humble themselves before me, and have
faith in me, then will I make weak things become
strong unto them.

## We Must Have Faith, Hope, and Charity to Be Saved

28 Behold, I will show unto the Gentiles their
weakness, and I will show unto them that faith,
hope and charity bringeth unto me—the fountain of
all righteousness.
29 And I, Moroni, having heard these words, was
comforted, and said: O Lord, thy righteous will be
done, for I know that thou workest unto the children of men according to their faith;
30 For the brother of Jared said unto the mountain
Zerin, Remove—and it was removed. And if he had
not had faith it would not have moved; wherefore
thou workest after men have faith.
31 For thus didst thou manifest thyself unto thy
disciples; for after they had faith, and did speak in
thy name, thou didst show thyself unto them in
great power.
32 And I also remember that thou hast said that
thou hast prepared a house for man, yea, even
among the mansions of thy Father, in which man
might have a more excellent hope; wherefore man
must hope, or he cannot receive an inheritance in
the place which thou hast prepared.

---

12:22 The Lord promised Nephite prophets that "these things," or the Book of Mormon, would one day be taken to the Lamanites by the Gentiles (see Enos 1:13, 16).

12:22 (10–22) All these verses speak of the accomplishments of people with faith. Hebrews chapter 11 contains a list similar to this one.

12:23 ***mock at***—make fun of

12:24 ***awkwardness***—lack of skill
***overpowering***—convincing

12:26 ***sufficient for the meek***—enough for the humble

Grace is divine help given by God through the Atonement of Jesus Christ. It provides us with the power needed to repent, keep the commandments, and become like God (see LDS Bible Dictionary, s.v. "Grace," 697; see also 2 Nephi 25:23).

12:27 (26–27) Moroni worried that his lack of writing skills would make others laugh at the Lord's sacred message. Has the Book of Mormon been inspiring to you? What can the Lord do with your weaknesses if you are humble and have faith in Him? Why would you like to overcome your weaknesses?

12:28 Jesus Christ is the fountain of all righteousness. Everything that is good and everything that leads us to do good comes from Him (see Moroni 7:16).

12:31 ***manifest***—show or make known

12:32 ***an inheritance***—a reward

A mansion is a large house. Jesus taught that in His "Father's house are many mansions" (John 14:2), meaning that there are many kingdoms of glory in heaven.

33 And again, I remember that thou hast said that
thou hast loved the world, even unto the laying
down of thy life for the world, that thou mightest
take it again to prepare a place for the children of
men.
34 And now I know that this love which thou hast
had for the children of men is charity; wherefore,
except men shall have charity they cannot inherit
that place which thou hast prepared in the mansions of thy Father.
35 Wherefore, I know by this thing which thou
hast said, that if the Gentiles have not charity,
because of our weakness, that thou wilt prove
them, and take away their talent, yea, even that
which they have received, and give unto them who
shall have more abundantly.
36 And it came to pass that I prayed unto the Lord
that he would give unto the Gentiles grace, that
they might have charity.
37 And it came to pass that the Lord said unto me:
If they have not charity it mattereth not unto thee,
thou hast been faithful; wherefore, thy garments
shall be made clean. And because thou hast seen
thy weakness thou shalt be made strong, even unto
the sitting down in the place which I have prepared
in the mansions of my Father.
38 And now I, Moroni, bid farewell unto the
Gentiles, yea, and also unto my brethren whom I
love, until we shall meet before the judgment-seat
of Christ, where all men shall know that my garments are not spotted with your blood.
39 And then shall ye know that I have seen Jesus,
and that he hath talked with me face to face, and
that he told me in plain humility, even as a man telleth another in mine own language, concerning
these things;
40 And only a few have I written, because of my
weakness in writing.
41 And now, I would commend you to seek this
Jesus of whom the prophets and apostles have written, that the grace of God the Father, and also the
Lord Jesus Christ, and the Holy Ghost, which
beareth record of them, may be and abide in you
forever. Amen.

## CHAPTER 13

*Ether, the mighty Jaredite prophet, sees the latter days and prophesies concerning his people. Notice how the people treat Ether and try to imagine how that makes Heavenly Father feel.*

### Ether Prophesies That the New Jerusalem Will Be Built in the Americas

1 AND now I, Moroni, proceed to finish my record
concerning the destruction of the people of whom
I have been writing.
2 For behold, they rejected all the words of Ether;
for he truly told them of all things, from the beginning of man; and that after the waters had receded
from off the face of this land it became a choice
land above all other lands, a chosen land of the
Lord; wherefore the Lord would have that all men
should serve him who dwell upon the face thereof;
3 And that it was the place of the New Jerusalem,
which should come down out of heaven, and the
holy sanctuary of the Lord.

12:34 Mormon explains that charity "is the pure love of Christ," and that we must seek after it (Moroni 7:47).

12:38 ***bid farewell***—say good-bye

12:38 (37–38) Moroni's garments were clean of others' blood (sins) because he shared the gospel with them. If you do your best to teach the gospel to others, your garments will also be clean (or the Lord will not hold you responsible) even if they do not believe the message (see Jacob 1:19).

12:41 ***abide***—remain or stay

All of the prophets in the Book of Mormon, as well as modern prophets today, tell us to "seek . . . Jesus." What can you do a little better in your life to seek Jesus?

13:1 ***proceed***—continue

13:2 ***receded***—moved back
***face***—surface

President David O. McKay explained that the Americas are "a land of liberty unto those who keep the commandments of God" (in Conference Report, October 1968, 5).

13:3 Eventually, the New Jerusalem will be built upon the American continent (see Articles of Faith 1:10; D&C 84:3–4). The New Jerusalem will be a place of peace, refuge, and safety for God's covenant people (see D&C 42:36; 45:66–69).

***sanctuary***—place of worship

*JERUSALEM, BY ROBERT T. BARRETT*

*Ether prophesied that after Jerusalem would be destroyed it would "be built up again, and become a holy city of the Lord."*

4 Behold, Ether saw the days of Christ, and he spake concerning a New Jerusalem upon this land.

5 And he spake also concerning the house of Israel, and the Jerusalem from whence Lehi should come—after it should be destroyed it should be built up again, a holy city unto the Lord; wherefore, it could not be a new Jerusalem for it had been in a time of old; but it should be built up again, and become a holy city of the Lord; and it should be built unto the house of Israel—

6 And that a New Jerusalem should be built upon this land, unto the remnant of the seed of Joseph, for which things there has been a type.

7 For as Joseph brought his father down into the land of Egypt, even so he died there; wherefore, the Lord brought a remnant of the seed of Joseph out of the land of Jerusalem, that he might be merciful unto the seed of Joseph that they should perish not, even as he was merciful unto the father of Joseph that he should perish not.

8 Wherefore, the remnant of the house of Joseph shall be built upon this land; and it shall be a land of their inheritance; and they shall build up a holy city unto the Lord, like unto the Jerusalem of old; and they shall no more be confounded, until the end come when the earth shall pass away.

---

13:6 ***remnant of the seed***—remainder of the family

A type is one of the ways the Lord teaches us His truths. Noah Webster's *An American Dictionary of the English Language,* 1828, defines a type as "a figure of something to come; . . . , Abraham's sacrifice [of Isaac] and the paschal lamb, were types of Christ" (s.v. "Type").

13:7 (6–7) Genesis 37–46 contains the story of Joseph who was sold into Egypt, protected and blessed by the Lord, and able to help save his family during a time of famine. The story of Joseph is a "type" of the story of Lehi's family. Lehi's family was directed to a promised land, protected, and prospered. It will be the people who are from the family of Joseph and Lehi who will help spiritually save others in the latter days (see also JST, Genesis 48:5–11).

13:8 ***confounded***—defeated or destroyed

9 And there shall be a new heaven and a new earth; and they shall be like unto the old save the old have passed away, and all things have become new.

10 And then cometh the New Jerusalem; and blessed are they who dwell therein, for it is they whose garments are white through the blood of the Lamb; and they are they who are numbered among the remnant of the seed of Joseph, who were of the house of Israel.

11 And then also cometh the Jerusalem of old; and the inhabitants thereof, blessed are they, for they have been washed in the blood of the Lamb; and they are they who were scattered and gathered in from the four quarters of the earth, and from the north countries, and are partakers of the fulfilling of the covenant which God made with their father, Abraham.

12 And when these things come, bringeth to pass the scripture which saith, there are they who were first, who shall be last; and there are they who were last, who shall be first.

## Ether Is Rejected and Cast Out, and His People Continue Their War

13 And I was about to write more, but I am forbidden; but great and marvelous were the prophecies of Ether; but they esteemed him as naught, and cast him out; and he hid himself in the cavity of a rock by day, and by night he went forth viewing the things which should come upon the people.

14 And as he dwelt in the cavity of a rock he made the remainder of this record, viewing the destructions which came upon the people, by night.

15 And it came to pass that in that same year in which he was cast out from among the people there began to be a great war among the people, for there were many who rose up, who were mighty men, and sought to destroy Coriantumr by their secret plans of wickedness, of which hath been spoken.

16 And now Coriantumr, having studied, himself, in all the arts of war and all the cunning of the world, wherefore he gave battle unto them who sought to destroy him.

17 But he repented not, neither his fair sons nor daughters; neither the fair sons and daughters of Cohor; neither the fair sons and daughters of Corihor; and in fine, there were none of the fair sons and daughters upon the face of the whole earth who repented of their sins.

18 Wherefore, it came to pass that in the first year that Ether dwelt in the cavity of a rock, there were many people who were slain by the sword of those secret combinations, fighting against Coriantumr that they might obtain the kingdom.

19 And it came to pass that the sons of Coriantumr fought much and bled much.

PHOTOGRAPH BY REGNAL GARFF

*A cavity of a rock is a cave or a hole in the earth.*

13:10 Having garments made white through the blood of the lamb means being made clean from sin through the Atonement and blood of Jesus Christ, who is the "Lamb of God" (John 1:29).

13:11 The "four quarters of the earth" means the entire earth. In the last days, God's children will be gathered from all around the earth and will become His covenant people by joining The Church of Jesus Christ of Latter-day Saints. How did your family find the Church and gather to it? Why are you thankful that you have made covenants with the Lord?

13:13 ***esteemed him as naught***—gave him no honor or respect

13:16 ***arts***—learning
***cunning***—evil plans

13:17 None of these people chose to repent. Why do you think it would be difficult to live among a people who refused to repent? Why is it important to repent of our sins?

ETHER HIDING IN THE CAVE, BY GARY SMITH

*"As [Ether] dwelt in the cavity of a rock he made the remainder of this record, viewing the destructions which came upon the people, by night."*

## Ether Prophesies of the Destruction of His People

20 And in the second year the word of the Lord
came to Ether, that he should go and prophesy unto
Coriantumr that, if he would repent, and all his
household, the Lord would give unto him his kingdom and spare the people—
21 Otherwise they should be destroyed, and all
his household save it were himself. And he should
only live to see the fulfilling of the prophecies
which had been spoken concerning another people
receiving the land for their inheritance; and
Coriantumr should receive a burial by them; and
every soul should be destroyed save it were
Coriantumr.
22 And it came to pass that Coriantumr repented
not, neither his household, neither the people; and
the wars ceased not; and they sought to kill Ether,
but he fled from before them and hid again in the
cavity of the rock.
23 And it came to pass that there arose up Shared,
and he also gave battle unto Coriantumr; and he did
beat him, insomuch that in the third year he did
bring him into captivity.
24 And the sons of Coriantumr, in the fourth year,
did beat Shared, and did obtain the kingdom again
unto their father.
25 Now there began to be a war upon all the face
of the land, every man with his band fighting for
that which he desired.
26 And there were robbers, and in fine, all manner of wickedness upon all the face of the land.
27 And it came to pass that Coriantumr was
exceedingly angry with Shared, and he went against
him with his armies to battle; and they did meet in
great anger, and they did meet in the valley of
Gilgal; and the battle became exceedingly sore.
28 And it came to pass that Shared fought against
him for the space of three days. And it came to pass
that Coriantumr beat him, and did pursue him until
he came to the plains of Heshlon.
29 And it came to pass that Shared gave him
battle again upon the plains; and behold, he did
beat Coriantumr, and drove him back again to the
valley of Gilgal.
30 And Coriantumr gave Shared battle again in the
valley of Gilgal, in which he beat Shared and slew
him.
31 And Shared wounded Coriantumr in his thigh,
that he did not go to battle again for the space of
two years, in which time all the people upon the
face of the land were shedding blood, and there
was none to restrain them.

## CHAPTER 14

*Thousands die because of wickedness. Notice how bloodshed and civil war cause a cursing upon the land.*

### Coriantumr Fights Against Secret Combinations

1 AND now there began to be a great curse upon
all the land because of the iniquity of the people, in
which, if a man should lay his tool or his sword
upon his shelf, or upon the place whither he would
keep it, behold, upon the morrow, he could not
find it, so great was the curse upon the land.

---

13:20 Even though the Jaredites had committed many sins, the Lord would have forgiven them if they had repented. God has promised: "He that repents and does the commandments of the Lord shall be forgiven" (D&C 1:31–32).

13:21 ***receive a burial***—be buried

13:25 ***band***—followers or soldiers

13:27 ***sore***—terrible

Elder ElRay L. Christiansen warned us that anger "destroys wisdom and sound judgment. When we become upset, reason is [overcome], and anger rushes in. To make decisions while [angry] is as unwise and foolish as it is for a captain to put out to sea in a raging storm. Only injury and wreckage result from [angry] moments" (in Conference Report, April 1971, 27).

13:28 ***pursue***—chase

13:31 ***restrain***—stop

You can see how Ether's prophecies began to be fulfilled by reading about the wars and suffering in verses 21–31. What can you learn from this about the importance of following a prophet? How do you think this story would have been different if the people had repented as Ether asked them to?

14:1 ***iniquity***—sins or wickedness
***morrow***—next day

2 Wherefore every man did cleave unto that which was his own, with his hands, and would not borrow neither would he lend; and every man kept the hilt of his sword in his right hand, in the defence of his property and his own life and of his wives and children.

3 And now, after the space of two years, and after the death of Shared, behold, there arose the brother of Shared and he gave battle unto Coriantumr, in which Coriantumr did beat him and did pursue him to the wilderness of Akish.

4 And it came to pass that the brother of Shared did give battle unto him in the wilderness of Akish; and the battle became exceedingly sore, and many thousands fell by the sword.

5 And it came to pass that Coriantumr did lay siege to the wilderness; and the brother of Shared did march forth out of the wilderness by night, and slew a part of the army of Coriantumr, as they were drunken.

6 And he came forth to the land of Moron, and placed himself upon the throne of Coriantumr.

7 And it came to pass that Coriantumr dwelt with his army in the wilderness for the space of two years, in which he did receive great strength to his army.

8 Now the brother of Shared, whose name was Gilead, also received great strength to his army, because of secret combinations.

## Lib Murders Gilead and Takes His Throne

9 And it came to pass that his high priest murdered him as he sat upon his throne.

10 And it came to pass that one of the secret combinations murdered him in a secret pass, and obtained unto himself the kingdom; and his name was Lib; and Lib was a man of great stature, more than any other man among all the people.

11 And it came to pass that in the first year of Lib, Coriantumr came up unto the land of Moron, and gave battle unto Lib.

12 And it came to pass that he fought with Lib, in which Lib did smite upon his arm that he was wounded; nevertheless, the army of Coriantumr did press forward upon Lib, that he fled to the borders upon the seashore.

13 And it came to pass that Coriantumr pursued him; and Lib gave battle unto him upon the seashore.

14 And it came to pass that Lib did smite the army of Coriantumr, that they fled again to the wilderness of Akish.

15 And it came to pass that Lib did pursue him until he came to the plains of Agosh. And Coriantumr had taken all the people with him as he fled before Lib in that quarter of the land whither he fled.

16 And when he had come to the plains of Agosh he gave battle unto Lib, and he smote upon him until he died; nevertheless, the brother of Lib did come against Coriantumr in the stead thereof, and the battle became exceedingly sore, in the which Coriantumr fled again before the army of the brother of Lib.

---

14:2 ***cleave***—hold
***hilt***—handle

14:2 (1–2) So many were stealing from each other that people would not lend or borrow and were using their swords to defend their possessions. Years later, the Nephites became just as wicked (see Helaman 13:16–18; Mormon 1:18–19).

14:3 ***pursue***—follow or chase

14:4 ***exceedingly sore***—terrible or intense

14:5 The term "lay siege" means to surround a place to force surrender or starvation of the people inside (see Isaiah 29:3).

***slew***—killed

14:10 ***stature***—size or height

14:12 ***press***—continue

14:14 ***smite***—strike

14:15 ***quarter***—area

14:16 ***smote***—struck
***stead***—place

## Coriantumr Battles Shiz As Death and Destruction Cover the Land

17 Now the name of the brother of Lib was called Shiz. And it came to pass that Shiz pursued after Coriantumr, and he did overthrow many cities, and he did slay both women and children, and he did burn the cities.
18 And there went a fear of Shiz throughout all the land; yea, a cry went forth throughout the land—Who can stand before the army of Shiz? Behold, he sweepeth the earth before him!
19 And it came to pass that the people began to flock together in armies, throughout all the face of the land.
20 And they were divided; and a part of them fled to the army of Shiz, and a part of them fled to the army of Coriantumr.
21 And so great and lasting had been the war, and so long had been the scene of bloodshed and carnage, that the whole face of the land was covered with the bodies of the dead.
22 And so swift and speedy was the war that there was none left to bury the dead, but they did march forth from the shedding of blood to the shedding of blood, leaving the bodies of both men, women, and children strewed upon the face of the land, to become a prey to the worms of the flesh.
23 And the scent thereof went forth upon the face of the land, even upon all the face of the land; wherefore the people became troubled by day and by night, because of the scent thereof.
24 Nevertheless, Shiz did not cease to pursue Coriantumr; for he had sworn to avenge himself upon Coriantumr of the blood of his brother, who had been slain, and the word of the Lord which came to Ether that Coriantumr should not fall by the sword.
25 And thus we see that the Lord did visit them in the fulness of his wrath, and their wickedness and abominations had prepared a way for their everlasting destruction.
26 And it came to pass that Shiz did pursue Coriantumr eastward, even to the borders by the seashore, and there he gave battle unto Shiz for the space of three days.
27 And so terrible was the destruction among the armies of Shiz that the people began to be frightened, and began to flee before the armies of Coriantumr; and they fled to the land of Corihor, and swept off the inhabitants before them, all them that would not join them.
28 And they pitched their tents in the valley of Corihor; and Coriantumr pitched his tents in the valley of Shurr. Now the valley of Shurr was near the hill Comnor; wherefore, Coriantumr did gather his armies together upon the hill Comnor, and did sound a trumpet unto the armies of Shiz to invite them forth to battle.
29 And it came to pass that they came forth, but were driven again; and they came the second time, and they were driven again the second time. And it came to pass that they came again the third time, and the battle became exceedingly sore.
30 And it came to pass that Shiz smote upon Coriantumr that he gave him many deep wounds; and Coriantumr, having lost his blood, fainted, and was carried away as though he were dead.

---

14:17 Notice that women and children were also killed. Wickedness sometimes even affects innocent people. This is part of the test of mortality. Elder Spencer W. Kimball taught, "Even the righteous will not always be healed, and even those of great faith will die when it is according to the purpose of God" ("Tragedy or Destiny," 211).

14:18 ***sweepeth the earth***—destroys people and cities

14:19 ***flock***—gather

14:21 ***carnage***—slaughter

14:22 ***strewed***—scattered or spread

14:23 ***scent***—stink or smell

14:24 ***sworn to avenge himself***—promised to get revenge

14:25 ***wrath***—anger
***abominations***—great evils

Whenever you see the words "thus we see" in the Book of Mormon, the author is probably telling his reader why he included this story in the record (see also Alma 30:60). The great destruction came because the people chose wickedness. If they had chosen righteousness they would have had peace (see Ether 2:8–12).

31 Now the loss of men, women and children on both sides was so great that Shiz commanded his people that they should not pursue the armies of Coriantumr; wherefore, they returned to their camp.

## CHAPTER 15

*Millions of people are killed as the Jaredites destroy themselves in battle. Look for how the warnings the Lord gave the Jaredites are fulfilled.*

### Coriantumr Sorrows over the Deaths of So Many People

1 AND it came to pass when Coriantumr had recovered of his wounds, he began to remember the words which Ether had spoken unto him.
2 He saw that there had been slain by the sword already nearly two millions of his people, and he began to sorrow in his heart; yea, there had been slain two millions of mighty men, and also their wives and their children.
3 He began to repent of the evil which he had done; he began to remember the words which had been spoken by the mouth of all the prophets, and he saw them that they were fulfilled thus far, every whit; and his soul mourned and refused to be comforted.
4 And it came to pass that he wrote an epistle unto Shiz, desiring him that he would spare the people, and he would give up the kingdom for the sake of the lives of the people.

### The People Are Filled with Anger, and War Continues

5 And it came to pass that when Shiz had received his epistle he wrote an epistle unto Coriantumr, that if he would give himself up, that he might slay him with his own sword, that he would spare the lives of the people.
6 And it came to pass that the people repented not of their iniquity; and the people of Coriantumr were stirred up to anger against the people of Shiz; and the people of Shiz were stirred up to anger against the people of Coriantumr; wherefore, the people of Shiz did give battle unto the people of Coriantumr.
7 And when Coriantumr saw that he was about to fall he fled again before the people of Shiz.
8 And it came to pass that he came to the waters of Ripliancum, which, by interpretation, is large, or to exceed all; wherefore, when they came to these waters they pitched their tents; and Shiz also pitched his tents near unto them; and therefore on the morrow they did come to battle.
9 And it came to pass that they fought an exceedingly sore battle, in which Coriantumr was wounded again, and he fainted with the loss of blood.
10 And it came to pass that the armies of Coriantumr did press upon the armies of Shiz that they beat them, that they caused them to flee before them; and they did flee southward, and did pitch their tents in a place which was called Ogath.

### For Four Years Ether Watches the People Gather into Two Armies

11 And it came to pass that the army of Coriantumr did pitch their tents by the hill Ramah; and it was that same hill where my father Mormon did hide up the records unto the Lord, which were sacred.
12 And it came to pass that they did gather together all the people upon all the face of the land, who had not been slain, save it was Ether.

---

14:31 The loss of lives was so great that the people returned to their camp. Why do you think the people wouldn't simply repent and stop fighting? Why do people keep doing wrong even when it makes them unhappy?

15:1 The prophecy Ether gave to Coriantumr concerning the destruction of this people is found in Ether 13:20–21.

15:3 ***whit***—little bit
***mourned***—felt bad or grieved

Coriantumr's decision to not follow Ether's counsel caused the deaths of many people, and he felt terrible. How would you feel if someone suffered because you did not obey?

15:4 ***an epistle***—a letter

15:6 ***were stirred up to***—began to feel

Elder M. Russell Ballard taught that "much adversity is man-made. Men's hearts turn cold, and the spirit of Satan controls their actions. . . . The Savior said, 'The love of men shall wax cold, and iniquity shall abound' (D&C 45:27)" (in Conference Report, April 1995, 30).

15:8 ***morrow***—next day

15:9 ***exceedingly sore***—terrible or intense

15:12 ***slain***—killed

13 And it came to pass that Ether did behold all the doings of the people; and he beheld that the people who were for Coriantumr were gathered together to the army of Coriantumr; and the people who were for Shiz were gathered together to the army of Shiz.

14 Wherefore, they were for the space of four years gathering together the people, that they might get all who were upon the face of the land, and that they might receive all the strength which it was possible that they could receive.

### Ether Sees the War Continue Until All the Jaredites Are Destroyed Except Coriantumr

15 And it came to pass that when they were all gathered together, every one to the army which he would, with their wives and their children—both men, women and children being armed with weapons of war, having shields, and breastplates, and head-plates, and being clothed after the manner of war—they did march forth one against another to battle; and they fought all that day, and conquered not.

16 And it came to pass that when it was night they were weary, and retired to their camps; and after they had retired to their camps they took up a howling and a lamentation for the loss of the slain of their people; and so great were their cries, their howlings and lamentations, that they did rend the air exceedingly.

17 And it came to pass that on the morrow they did go again to battle, and great and terrible was that day; nevertheless, they conquered not, and when the night came again they did rend the air with their cries, and their howlings, and their mournings, for the loss of the slain of their people.

18 And it came to pass that Coriantumr wrote again an epistle unto Shiz, desiring that he would not come again to battle, but that he would take the kingdom, and spare the lives of the people.

19 And behold, the Spirit of the Lord had ceased striving with them, and Satan had full power over the hearts of the people; for they were given up unto the hardness of their hearts, and the blindness of their minds that they might be destroyed; wherefore they went again to battle.

20 And it came to pass that they fought all that day, and when the night came they slept upon their swords.

21 And on the morrow they fought even until the night came.

22 And when the night came they were drunken with anger, even as a man who is drunken with wine; and they slept again upon their swords.

23 And on the morrow they fought again; and when the night came they had all fallen by the sword save it were fifty and two of the people of Coriantumr, and sixty and nine of the people of Shiz.

24 And it came to pass that they slept upon their swords that night, and on the morrow they fought again, and they contended in their might with their swords and with their shields, all that day.

25 And when the night came there were thirty and two of the people of Shiz, and twenty and seven of the people of Coriantumr.

26 And it came to pass that they ate and slept, and prepared for death on the morrow. And they were large and mighty men as to the strength of men.

27 And it came to pass that they fought for the space of three hours, and they fainted with the loss of blood.

28 And it came to pass that when the men of Coriantumr had received sufficient strength that they could walk, they were about to flee for their lives; but behold, Shiz arose, and also his men, and he swore in his wrath that he would slay Coriantumr or he would perish by the sword.

29 Wherefore, he did pursue them, and on the morrow he did overtake them; and they fought again with the sword. And it came to pass that when they had all fallen by the sword, save it were Coriantumr and Shiz, behold Shiz had fainted with the loss of blood.

---

15:16 ***howling***—loud, sad crying
***lamentation***—cry of sorrow

15:19 ***striving with***—working with or influencing

15:22 What happened to the Jaredites because of their anger? What happens to you when you get angry?

15:28 ***sufficient***—enough
***perish***—die

30 And it came to pass that when Coriantumr had
leaned upon his sword, that he rested a little, he
smote off the head of Shiz.
31 And it came to pass that after he had smitten
off the head of Shiz, that Shiz raised upon his hands
and fell; and after that he had struggled for breath,
he died.
32 And it came to pass that Coriantumr fell to the
earth, and became as if he had no life.
33 And the Lord spake unto Ether, and said unto
him: Go forth. And he went forth, and beheld that the words of the Lord had all been fulfilled; and he finished his record; (and the hundredth part I have not written) and he hid them in a manner that the people of Limhi did find them.
34 Now the last words which are written by Ether
are these: Whether the Lord will that I be translated, or that I suffer the will of the Lord in the flesh, it mattereth not, if it so be that I am saved in the kingdom of God. Amen.

---

15:30 ***smote***—cut

15:33 The prophecies and promises the Lord spoke through the prophet Ether were all fulfilled (see also D&C 1:38). What are some of the prophecies and promises the Lord has given through His prophets in our day? What should you do to prepare for those things?

15:34 Ether's final desire was to be saved in the kingdom of God. He did not care whether he died or was translated, as long as he was able to go to heaven. Ether knew that eternal life "is the greatest of all the gifts of God" (D&C 14:7).

# THE BOOK OF MORONI

*Moroni, the last Nephite prophet, wrote the last book in the Book of Mormon. Moroni's book includes some important instructions, letters from his father, and his final testimony and farewell. He wrote this record while wandering and finished it before he buried the gold plates in the Hill Cumorah in about A.D. 421 (see Moroni 10:1–2). Ponder Moroni's promise on how you can receive your own testimony of the truth of the Book of Mormon.*

## CHAPTER 1

*Moroni is the only righteous Nephite left after the terrible wars. He writes this last book while hiding from the Lamanites. Watch for whom he is writing and why.*

### MORONI'S FINAL WORDS ARE TO THE LAMANITES

1 NOW I, Moroni, after having made an end of abridging the account of the people of Jared, I had supposed not to have written more, but I have not as yet perished; and I make not myself known to the Lamanites lest they should destroy me.

2 For behold, their wars are exceedingly fierce among themselves; and because of their hatred they put to death every Nephite that will not deny the Christ.

3 And I, Moroni, will not deny the Christ; wherefore, I wander whithersoever I can for the safety of mine own life.

4 Wherefore, I write a few more things, contrary to that which I had supposed; for I had supposed not to have written any more; but I write a few more things, that perhaps they may be of worth unto my brethren, the Lamanites, in some future day, according to the will of the Lord.

## CHAPTER 2

*Christ gives the twelve disciples power to give the gift of the Holy Ghost. Look for how the twelve disciples were to use this power.*

### JESUS GIVES HIS TWELVE NEPHITE DISCIPLES THE POWER TO GIVE THE GIFT OF THE HOLY GHOST

1 THE words of Christ, which he spake unto his disciples, the twelve whom he had chosen, as he laid his hands upon them—

---

1:1 **abridging**—editing and shortening
**perished**—died

The story of the people of Jared is told in the book of Ether.

1:2 **exceedingly fierce**—terrible

1:3 **whithersoever**—wherever

1:3 (2–3) President Ezra Taft Benson taught that those who love the Savior "not only would . . . die for [Him], but more important they want to live for Him" (in Conference Report, October 1985, 6).

*Christ* is a Greek word meaning "the Anointed One"; the Hebrew word with the same meaning is *Messiah.* Jesus is the Christ—the one chosen, set apart, and sent by God to save us (see LDS Bible Dictionary, s.v. "Christ," 633).

1:4 **contrary**—opposite

Why would Moroni write "a few more things" that "may be of worth" to the descendants of those who had killed his family? What does this tell you about Moroni? In what ways do you think his testimony of Jesus Christ influenced his love for the Lamanites?

1:4 (1–4) Imagine that you are all alone. You do not have a home. Your friends and family have been killed, and their murderers now seek your life. Where would you turn for help in a situation like this? Why do you think the Lord saved Moroni from being killed in the wars?

2:1 **disciples**—followers

According to the fifth article of faith, "we believe that a man must be called of God, by prophecy, and *by the laying on of hands* by those who are in authority, to preach the Gospel and administer in the ordinances thereof" (emphasis added).

Words in pink are explained in the Glossary.

2 And he called them by name, saying: Ye shall
call on the Father in my name, in mighty prayer;
and after ye have done this ye shall have power
that to him upon whom ye shall lay your hands, ye
shall give the Holy Ghost; and in my name shall ye
give it, for thus do mine apostles.
3 Now Christ spake these words unto them at the
time of his first appearing; and the multitude heard
it not, but the disciples heard it; and on as many as
they laid their hands, fell the Holy Ghost.

## CHAPTER 3

*The priesthood can only be given by one who has authority from God. Notice the way the Nephites ordained people to the priesthood in their day.*

### Moroni Explains How the Nephites Ordained Men to the Priesthood

1 THE manner which the disciples, who were
called the elders of the church, ordained priests and
teachers—
2 After they had prayed unto the Father in the name
of Christ, they laid their hands upon them, and said:
3 In the name of Jesus Christ I ordain you to be a
priest, (or, if he be a teacher) I ordain you to be a
teacher, to preach repentance and remission of sins
through Jesus Christ, by the endurance of faith on
his name to the end. Amen.
4 And after this manner did they ordain priests
and teachers, according to the gifts and callings of
God unto men; and they ordained them by the
power of the Holy Ghost, which was in them.

## CHAPTER 4

*Moroni records the way the sacrament bread is to be blessed. See what Church members covenant to do when they partake of the bread.*

### Jesus Christ Gave Instructions on How to Bless the Sacrament Bread

1 THE manner of their elders and priests administering the flesh and blood of Christ unto the church;
and they administered it according to the commandments of Christ; wherefore we know the manner to be true; and the elder or priest did minister
it—
2 And they did kneel down with the church, and
pray to the Father in the name of Christ, saying:
3 O God, the Eternal Father, we ask thee in the
name of thy Son, Jesus Christ, to bless and sanctify
this bread to the souls of all those who partake of
it; that they may eat in remembrance of the body of
thy Son, and witness unto thee, O God, the Eternal
Father, that they are willing to take upon them the
name of thy Son, and always remember him, and
keep his commandments which he hath given
them, that they may always have his Spirit to be
with them. Amen.

---

2:3 When is a person given the gift of the Holy Ghost? How has the Holy Ghost helped you? What can you do to feel His influence?

2:3 (1–3) The description of Christ's giving the Melchizedek Priesthood to His Nephite disciples in the Americas is found in 3 Nephi 18:36–38.

3:1 ***manner***—way
***ordained***—gave priesthood power to

3:3 ***remission***—forgiveness
***the endurance of faith on his name to the end***—having faith in Christ until the end of your life

3:4 Joseph Smith stated: "We believe in the gift of the Holy Ghost being enjoyed now, as much as it was in the Apostles' days; we believe that it [the gift of the Holy Ghost] is necessary to make and to organize the Priesthood, that no man can be called to fill any office in the ministry without it; we also believe in prophecy, in tongues, in visions, and in revelations, in gifts, and in healings; and that these things cannot be enjoyed without the gift of the Holy Ghost" (*Teachings of the Prophet Joseph Smith,* 243).

Why do you think it is important that men have the power of the Holy Ghost when they serve in priesthood callings?

4:1 ***manner***—way
***minister***—serve

4:3 ***sanctify***—make holy
***witness***—show

In the prayer on the sacrament bread, we promise that we will remember the body of the Savior. What do you remember about the Savior's body when you partake of the sacrament bread? What blessings can come to you because of Christ's Atonement?

## CHAPTER 5

*Moroni records the sacrament prayer for the wine. Notice ways this prayer is similar to and different from the prayer on the bread in Moroni 4.*

### Jesus Christ Taught the Nephites How to Bless the Wine

1 THE manner of administering the wine—
Behold, they took the cup, and said:
2 O God, the Eternal Father, we ask thee, in the
name of thy Son, Jesus Christ, to bless and sanctify
this wine to the souls of all those who drink of it,
that they may do it in remembrance of the blood of
thy Son, which was shed for them; that they may
witness unto thee, O God, the Eternal Father, that
they do always remember him, that they may have
his Spirit to be with them. Amen.

## CHAPTER 6

*Moroni teaches about baptism and church membership. Look for how similar the Church Jesus organized among the Nephites is to His Church today.*

### Moroni Teaches About Baptism

1 AND now I speak concerning baptism. Behold,
elders, priests, and teachers were baptized; and
they were not baptized save they brought forth fruit
meet that they were worthy of it.
2 Neither did they receive any unto baptism save
they came forth with a broken heart and a contrite
spirit, and witnessed unto the church that they truly
repented of all their sins.
3 And none were received unto baptism save they
took upon them the name of Christ, having a determination to serve him to the end.
4 And after they had been received unto baptism,
and were wrought upon and cleansed by the power
of the Holy Ghost, they were numbered among the
people of the church of Christ; and their names
were taken, that they might be remembered and
nourished by the good word of God, to keep them
in the right way, to keep them continually watchful
unto prayer, relying alone upon the merits of Christ,
who was the author and the finisher of their faith.

### Moroni Writes About Church Practices

5 And the church did meet together oft, to fast and
to pray, and to speak one with another concerning
the welfare of their souls.
6 And they did meet together oft to partake of
bread and wine, in remembrance of the Lord Jesus.
7 And they were strict to observe that there should
be no iniquity among them; and whoso was found
to commit iniquity, and three witnesses of the
church did condemn them before the elders, and if

---

5:1 ***manner of administering***—way to bless

The authority to use water rather than wine in the sacrament was given to the Prophet Joseph Smith by the Savior in August 1830 (see D&C 27:1–4 and the section heading).

5:2 ***sanctify***—make holy

The Sacrament prayers promise that if we always remember the Lord, His Spirit will always be with us. What can you do to always remember the Lord?

6:1 ***brought forth fruit meet***—showed by their works

6:2 ***contrite***—truly repentant

6:3 (1–3) People who are baptized also promise "to come into the fold of God, and to be called his people, . . . to bear one another's burdens, . . . to mourn with those that mourn . . . and to stand as witnesses of God . . . even until death" (Mosiah 18:8–9).

6:4 ***wrought upon***—changed
***nourished***—spiritually fed
***merits***—grace or Atonement

The scriptures help to "keep us in the right way," or to keep the commandments. How do the scriptures help you keep the commandments?

President Gordon B. Hinckley said, "Every [new member] needs three things: a friend, a responsibility, and nurturing with 'the good word of God' (Moroni 6:4)" (in Conference Report, April 1997, 66).

6:5 ***welfare***—well-being or health

6:6 Elder David B. Haight said, "Our most valuable worship experience in the sacrament meeting is the sacred ordinance of the sacrament, for it provides the opportunity to focus our minds and hearts upon the Savior and His sacrifice" (in Conference Report, October 1989, 75).

they repented not, and confessed not, their names were blotted out, and they were not numbered among the people of Christ.
8 But as oft as they repented and sought forgiveness, with real intent, they were forgiven.
9 And their meetings were conducted by the church after the manner of the workings of the Spirit, and by the power of the Holy Ghost; for as the power of the Holy Ghost led them whether to preach, or to exhort, or to pray, or to supplicate, or to sing, even so it was done.

## CHAPTER 7

*Moroni includes the teachings of his father, Mormon, who explains some of the most basic but important principles of the gospel. Look for what Mormon taught about faith, hope, and charity.*

### Mormon Speaks to the Peaceable Followers of Christ

1 AND now I, Moroni, write a few of the words of my father Mormon, which he spake concerning faith, hope, and charity; for after this manner did he speak unto the people, as he taught them in the synagogue which they had built for the place of worship.
2 And now I, Mormon, speak unto you, my beloved brethren; and it is by the grace of God the Father, and our Lord Jesus Christ, and his holy will, because of the gift of his calling unto me, that I am permitted to speak unto you at this time.
3 Wherefore, I would speak unto you that are of the church, that are the peaceable followers of Christ, and that have obtained a sufficient hope by which ye can enter into the rest of the Lord, from this time henceforth until ye shall rest with him in heaven.
4 And now my brethren, I judge these things of you because of your peaceable walk with the children of men.

### We Must Serve with Real Intent

5 For I remember the word of God which saith by their works ye shall know them; for if their works be good, then they are good also.
6 For behold, God hath said a man being evil cannot do that which is good; for if he offereth a gift, or prayeth unto God, except he shall do it with real intent it profiteth him nothing.
7 For behold, it is not counted unto him for righteousness.
8 For behold, if a man being evil giveth a gift, he doeth it grudgingly; wherefore it is counted unto him the same as if he had retained the gift; wherefore he is counted evil before God.
9 And likewise also is it counted evil unto a man, if he shall pray and not with real intent of heart; yea, and it profiteth him nothing, for God receiveth none such.
10 Wherefore, a man being evil cannot do that which is good; neither will he give a good gift.

---

6:7 ***blotted out***—removed

6:8 ***sought***—asked for

6:9 ***exhort***—strongly encourage or urge
***supplicate***—ask humbly

7:1 ***synagogue***—church

7:2 Grace is divine help given by God through the Atonement of Jesus Christ. It provides us with the power needed to repent, keep the commandments, and become like God (see LDS Bible Dictionary, s.v. "Grace," 697; see also 2 Nephi 25:23).

7:3 What do you think it means to be a peaceable follower of Christ? How are you trying to better follow the Savior?

***a sufficient***—enough
***henceforth***—on

In the eternal sense, to enter into "the rest of the Lord" is to "behold the face of God" by entering into "the fulness of his glory" (D&C 84:23–24). However, President Joseph F. Smith taught that we may "enter into the rest of the Lord today, by coming to an understanding of the truths of the gospel" (*Gospel Doctrine,* 126).

7:4 The Lord revealed how we can have a "peaceable walk." He said, "Walk in the meekness of my Spirit, and you shall have peace in me" (D&C 19:23).

7:6 ***with real intent***—sincerely
***profiteth him nothing***—brings him no blessings

7:8 ***grudgingly***—unwillingly or because he was forced to
***retained***—kept

11 For behold, a bitter fountain cannot bring forth
good water; neither can a good fountain bring forth
bitter water; wherefore, a man being a servant of
the devil cannot follow Christ; and if he follow
Christ he cannot be a servant of the devil.

## Mormon Teaches How We Can Know Good from Evil

12 Wherefore, all things which are good cometh
of God; and that which is evil cometh of the devil;
for the devil is an enemy unto God, and fighteth
against him continually, and inviteth and enticeth to
sin, and to do that which is evil continually.
13 But behold, that which is of God inviteth and
enticeth to do good continually; wherefore, every
thing which inviteth and enticeth to do good, and
to love God, and to serve him, is inspired of God.
14 Wherefore, take heed, my beloved brethren,
that ye do not judge that which is evil to be of
God, or that which is good and of God to be of
the devil.
15 For behold, my brethren, it is given unto you
to judge, that ye may know good from evil; and the
way to judge is as plain, that ye may know with a
perfect knowledge, as the daylight is from the dark
night.
16 For behold, the Spirit of Christ is given to every
man, that he may know good from evil; wherefore,
I show unto you the way to judge; for every thing
which inviteth to do good, and to persuade to
believe in Christ, is sent forth by the power and gift
of Christ; wherefore ye may know with a perfect
knowledge it is of God.
17 But whatsoever thing persuadeth men to do
evil, and believe not in Christ, and deny him, and
serve not God, then ye may know with a perfect
knowledge it is of the devil; for after this manner
doth the devil work, for he persuadeth no man to
do good, no, not one; neither do his angels; neither
do they who subject themselves unto him.
18 And now, my brethren, seeing that ye know
the light by which ye may judge, which light is the
light of Christ, see that ye do not judge wrongfully;
for with that same judgment which ye judge ye
shall also be judged.

---

7:11 Mormon compares people who serve for wrong reasons to a bitter or dirty fountain of water. Would you want to drink from a dirty fountain? What can you do to make sure you serve the way Jesus would want you to?

7:11 (5–11) Elder Dallin H. Oaks taught: "People serve one another for different reasons, and some reasons are better than others. . . . Our service should be for the love of God and the love of fellowmen rather than for personal advantage or any other lesser motive" (in Conference Report, October 1984, 14, 16).

7:12 ***enticeth***—tries to persuade us

Elder David B. Haight stated: "Teach your loved ones to distinguish between Satan and our Savior. Teach your loved ones that 'all things which are good cometh of God; and that which is evil cometh of the devil; for the devil is an enemy unto God, . . . and inviteth and enticeth to sin.' (Moro. 7:12.) Not explaining these eternal truths of the gospel in the warm atmosphere of your home could be the difference between exaltation and darkness. At a crucial moment in a youth's life, the humble testimony of mother and father could be recalled and make the difference in a critical decision" (in Conference Report, April 1973, 85).

7:13 What are some things that help you feel closer to God? What are some things that take you away from Him? How can knowing the difference between these two help you make better choices?

7:14 ***take heed***—be careful

7:16 The Spirit of Christ is sometimes called the Light of Christ. It is given to each person born into the world and is often referred to as our conscience (see D&C 84:46; 93:2). President Joseph F. Smith said that this Spirit of Christ "strives with . . . men, and will continue to strive with them [if they will resist the enticings of Satan], until it brings them to a knowledge of the truth and the possession of the greater light and testimony of the Holy Ghost" (*Gospel Doctrine,* 67–68).

7:17 Satan rebelled against Heavenly Father's plan in the premortal life (see Moses 4:3). From that time until now, he and those who follow him tempt us to turn from God. Lehi taught that Satan wants everyone to be miserable as he is (see 2 Nephi 2:18).

7:18 The New Testament teaches, "Judge not, that ye be not judged" (Matthew 7:1). However, the Prophet Joseph Smith's inspired translation says, "Judge not unrighteously" (JST, Matthew 7:1). In these verses Mormon teaches how we can judge righteously.

19 Wherefore, I beseech of you, brethren, that ye should search diligently in the light of Christ that ye may know good from evil; and if ye will lay hold upon every good thing, and condemn it not, ye certainly will be a child of Christ.

20 And now, my brethren, how is it possible that ye can lay hold upon every good thing?

### *Mormon Speaks About Faith in Jesus Christ*

21 And now I come to that faith, of which I said I would speak; and I will tell you the way whereby ye may lay hold on every good thing.

22 For behold, God knowing all things, being from everlasting to everlasting, behold, he sent angels to minister unto the children of men, to make manifest concerning the coming of Christ; and in Christ there should come every good thing.

23 And God also declared unto prophets, by his own mouth, that Christ should come.

24 And behold, there were divers ways that he did manifest things unto the children of men, which were good; and all things which are good cometh of Christ; otherwise men were fallen, and there could no good thing come unto them.

25 Wherefore, by the ministering of angels, and by every word which proceeded forth out of the mouth of God, men began to exercise faith in Christ; and thus by faith, they did lay hold upon every good thing; and thus it was until the coming of Christ.

26 And after that he came men also were saved by faith in his name; and by faith, they become the sons of God. And as surely as Christ liveth he spake these words unto our fathers, saying: Whatsoever thing ye shall ask the Father in my name, which is good, in faith believing that ye shall receive, behold, it shall be done unto you.

27 Wherefore, my beloved brethren, have miracles ceased because Christ hath ascended into heaven, and hath sat down on the right hand of God, to claim of the Father his rights of mercy which he hath upon the children of men?

28 For he hath answered the ends of the law, and he claimeth all those who have faith in him; and they who have faith in him will cleave unto every good thing; wherefore he advocateth the cause of the children of men; and he dwelleth eternally in the heavens.

29 And because he hath done this, my beloved brethren, have miracles ceased? Behold I say unto you, Nay; neither have angels ceased to minister unto the children of men.

30 For behold, they are subject unto him, to minister according to the word of his command, showing themselves unto them of strong faith and a firm mind in every form of godliness.

31 And the office of their ministry is to call men unto repentance, and to fulfil and to do the work of the covenants of the Father, which he hath made unto the children of men, to prepare the way among the children of men, by declaring the word of Christ unto the chosen vessels of the Lord, that they may bear testimony of him.

32 And by so doing, the Lord God prepareth the way that the residue of men may have faith in Christ, that the Holy Ghost may have place in their hearts, according to the power thereof; and after this manner bringeth to pass the Father, the covenants which he hath made unto the children of men.

---

7:19 ***lay hold upon***—receive

7:22 ***minister unto***—serve or teach
***manifest***—known

7:24 ***divers***—many or various

7:26 (23–26) Since the days of Adam, ministering angels, prophets, scriptures, and the Savior Himself have declared the same message: "There shall be no other name given nor any other way nor means whereby salvation can come unto the children of men, only in and through the name of Christ" (Mosiah 3:17).

7:28 ***cleave unto***—hold onto
***advocateth***—pleads

7:29 ***ceased***—stopped

7:31 ***vessels***—servants

A covenant is an agreement between two people. In the scriptures it is usually an agreement between God and man. We promise to be obedient to God's commandments, and He promises to bless us (see LDS Bible Dictionary, s.v. "Covenant," 651).

7:31 (29–31) Angels have not stopped appearing to mankind. One example is the appearance of the angel Moroni to the Prophet Joseph Smith on September 21, 1823 (see Joseph Smith—History 1:29–32).

7:32 ***residue***—remainder

*JESUS OF NAZARETH*, BY ROBERT T. BARRETT

*"All things which are good cometh of Christ."*

33 And Christ hath said: If ye will have faith in me
ye shall have power to do whatsoever thing is
expedient in me.
34 And he hath said: Repent all ye ends of the
earth, and come unto me, and be baptized in my
name, and have faith in me, that ye may be saved.
35 And now, my beloved brethren, if this be the
case that these things are true which I have spoken
unto you, and God will show unto you, with power
and great glory at the last day, that they are true,
and if they are true has the day of miracles ceased?
36 Or have angels ceased to appear unto the children of men? Or has he withheld the power of the
Holy Ghost from them? Or will he, so long as time
shall last, or the earth shall stand, or there shall be
one man upon the face thereof to be saved?
37 Behold I say unto you, Nay; for it is by faith
that miracles are wrought; and it is by faith that
angels appear and minister unto men; wherefore, if
these things have ceased wo be unto the children
of men, for it is because of unbelief, and all is vain.
38 For no man can be saved, according to the
words of Christ, save they shall have faith in his
name; wherefore, if these things have ceased, then
has faith ceased also; and awful is the state of man,
for they are as though there had been no redemption made.
39 But behold, my beloved brethren, I judge
better things of you, for I judge that ye have faith
in Christ because of your meekness; for if ye have
not faith in him then ye are not fit to be numbered
among the people of his church.

## Mormon Speaks About Hope

40 And again, my beloved brethren, I would
speak unto you concerning hope. How is it that ye
can attain unto faith, save ye shall have hope?
41 And what is it that ye shall hope for? Behold I
say unto you that ye shall have hope through the
atonement of Christ and the power of his resurrection, to be raised unto life eternal, and this because
of your faith in him according to the promise.
42 Wherefore, if a man have faith he must needs
have hope; for without faith there cannot be any
hope.
43 And again, behold I say unto you that he cannot have faith and hope, save he shall be meek,
and lowly of heart.

## Charity Is the Pure Love of Christ

44 If so, his faith and hope is vain, for none is
acceptable before God, save the meek and lowly in
heart; and if a man be meek and lowly in heart, and
confesses by the power of the Holy Ghost that Jesus
is the Christ, he must needs have charity; for if he
have not charity he is nothing; wherefore he must
needs have charity.
45 And charity suffereth long, and is kind, and
envieth not, and is not puffed up, seeketh not her
own, is not easily provoked, thinketh no evil, and
rejoiceth not in iniquity but rejoiceth in the truth,
beareth all things, believeth all things, hopeth all
things, endureth all things.

---

7:33 ***expedient***—necessary

7:37 ***vain***—useless

Miracles can only be wrought, or worked, by faith. What miracles have you seen in your life? Why do you believe God causes miracles to happen?

7:37 (32–37) "Faith . . . must be centered in Jesus Christ in order to produce salvation. To have faith is to have confidence in something or someone. . . . Where there is true faith there are miracles, visions, dreams, healings, and all the gifts of God that he gives to his saints" (LDS Bible Dictionary, s.v. "Faith," 669–70).

7:38 Redemption means to "buy back" or to "set free." Jesus Christ is our Redeemer because He willingly paid the price to buy us back and set us free from the effects of the Fall of Adam and from the burden of our own sins (see 1 Corinthians 6:20 and D&C 18:11). The price He had to pay was His own blood (see 1 Peter 1:18–19).

In what spiritual condition would makind be without the Atonement of Jesus Christ? How has the Atonement blessed your life?

7:39 ***fit***—worthy

7:42 As used in the Book of Mormon, hope is more than just wishful thinking; it is the knowledge that we can be resurrected and return to live with God (see Jeffrey R. Holland, *Christ and the New Covenant*, 334–35).

7:45 ***envieth not***—is not jealous
***puffed up***—full of pride
***provoked***—made angry

46 Wherefore, my beloved brethren, if ye have not charity, ye are nothing, for charity never faileth. Wherefore, cleave unto charity, which is the greatest of all, for all things must fail—
47 But charity is the pure love of Christ, and it endureth forever; and whoso is found possessed of it at the last day, it shall be well with him.
48 Wherefore, my beloved brethren, pray unto the Father with all the energy of heart, that ye may be filled with this love, which he hath bestowed upon all who are true followers of his Son, Jesus Christ; that ye may become the sons of God; that when he shall appear we shall be like him, for we shall see him as he is; that we may have this hope; that we may be purified even as he is pure. Amen.

## CHAPTER 8

*Mormon explains the power of the Atonement and why little children should not be baptized. Watch for how the Savior's love blesses little children.*

### MORONI RECORDS A LETTER FROM HIS FATHER

1 AN epistle of my father Mormon, written to me, Moroni; and it was written unto me soon after my calling to the ministry. And on this wise did he write unto me, saying:
2 My beloved son, Moroni, I rejoice exceedingly that your Lord Jesus Christ hath been mindful of you, and hath called you to his ministry, and to his holy work.
3 I am mindful of you always in my prayers, continually praying unto God the Father in the name of his Holy Child, Jesus, that he, through his infinite goodness and grace, will keep you through the endurance of faith on his name to the end.

### LITTLE CHILDREN ARE SAVED BY JESUS CHRIST AND DO NOT NEED BAPTISM

4 And now, my son, I speak unto you concerning that which grieveth me exceedingly; for it grieveth me that there should disputations rise among you.
5 For, if I have learned the truth, there have been disputations among you concerning the baptism of your little children.
6 And now, my son, I desire that ye should labor diligently, that this gross error should be removed from among you; for, for this intent I have written this epistle.
7 For immediately after I had learned these things of you I inquired of the Lord concerning the matter. And the word of the Lord came to me by the power of the Holy Ghost, saying:
8 Listen to the words of Christ, your Redeemer, your Lord and your God. Behold, I came into the world not to call the righteous but sinners to repentance; the whole need no physician, but they that are sick; wherefore, little children are whole, for they are not capable of committing sin; wherefore the curse of Adam is taken from them in me, that it hath no power over them; and the law of circumcision is done away in me.

---

7:47 "If we must have charity, then we must know what it is. The phrase 'love of Christ' might have meaning in three dimensions: (1) love *for* Christ; (2) love *from* Christ; (3) love *like* Christ" (C. Max Caldwell, in Conference Report, October 1992, 39).

7:47 (45–47) The greatest and most perfect act of charity ever shown was when Jesus Christ gave up His own life for each of us. What else did Jesus do that showed His love for us? Why do you think you would be a better person if you were filled with charity?

7:48 ***bestowed upon***—given to

What does this scripture say we need to do to be filled with the love of Heavenly Father? How sincere are your prayers? What do you pray for?

President Joseph Fielding Smith taught that "when Christ comes, those who have kept the commandments and stand before him, will see themselves like they see him, a Son of God" (*Doctrines of Salvation* 2:37).

8:1 ***ministry***—service of the Lord

8:3 ***infinite***—never-ending
***through the endurance of***—as you continue to have

8:4 ***grieveth me***—makes me sad
***disputations***—arguments

8:6 ***gross***—shameful or serious

8:6 (4–6) Mormon wrote to correct those who were teaching false doctrine about little children. President Harold B. Lee taught: "The doctrines of the Church are not ours but His whose Church this is! . . . Failure to keep the doctrines given by Christ pure and simple would cause much human misery here and in eternity" (*The Teachings of Harold B. Lee,* 438).

CHRIST WITH THE CHILDREN, BY ROBERT T. BARRETT

*Mormon taught that "little children are alive in Christ" and should not be baptized until they reach the age of accountability.*

9 And after this manner did the Holy Ghost
manifest the word of God unto me; wherefore,
my beloved son, I know that it is solemn mockery before God, that ye should baptize little children.
10 Behold I say unto you that this thing shall ye
teach—repentance and baptism unto those who are
accountable and capable of committing sin; yea,
teach parents that they must repent and be baptized, and humble themselves as their little children,
and they shall all be saved with their little children.
11 And their little children need no repentance,
neither baptism. Behold, baptism is unto repentance to the fulfilling the commandments unto the
remission of sins.
12 But little children are alive in Christ, even from
the foundation of the world; if not so, God is a partial God, and also a changeable God, and a
respecter to persons; for how many little children
have died without baptism!

---

8:9 **W** ***mockery***—disrespect or insult

8:12 **W** ***partial God***—God who has favorites or an unfair God

8:12 (8–12) Elder Boyd K. Packer taught that today some believe "little children are conceived in sin and enter mortality in a state of natural corruption. That doctrine is false! Each time a child is born, the world is renewed in innocence" (in Conference Report, October 1986, 20).

13 Wherefore, if little children could not be saved
without baptism, these must have gone to an endless hell.
14 Behold I say unto you, that he that supposeth
that little children need baptism is in the gall of bitterness and in the bonds of iniquity; for he hath
neither faith, hope, nor charity; wherefore, should
he be cut off while in the thought, he must go
down to hell.
15 For awful is the wickedness to suppose that
God saveth one child because of baptism, and the
other must perish because he hath no baptism.
16 Wo be unto them that shall pervert the ways of
the Lord after this manner, for they shall perish
except they repent. Behold, I speak with boldness,
having authority from God; and I fear not what man
can do; for perfect love casteth out all fear.
17 And I am filled with charity, which is everlasting love; wherefore, all children are alike unto me;
wherefore, I love little children with a perfect love;
and they are all alike and partakers of salvation.
18 For I know that God is not a partial God, neither a changeable being; but he is unchangeable
from all eternity to all eternity.
19 Little children cannot repent; wherefore, it is
awful wickedness to deny the pure mercies of God
unto them, for they are all alive in him because of
his mercy.
20 And he that saith that little children need baptism denieth the mercies of Christ, and setteth at
naught the atonement of him and the power of his
redemption.
21 Wo unto such, for they are in danger of death,
hell, and an endless torment. I speak it boldly; God
hath commanded me. Listen unto them and give
heed, or they stand against you at the judgment-seat
of Christ.
22 For behold that all little children are alive in
Christ, and also all they that are without the law.
For the power of redemption cometh on all them
that have no law; wherefore, he that is not condemned, or he that is under no condemnation,
cannot repent; and unto such baptism availeth
nothing—
23 But it is mockery before God, denying the mercies of Christ, and the power of his Holy Spirit, and
putting trust in dead works.
24 Behold, my son, this thing ought not to be; for
repentance is unto them that are under condemnation and under the curse of a broken law.

---

8:14 (13–14) Latter-day scriptures teach that there are at least three meanings for the term *hell.* It can describe our suffering here on earth (see Alma 36:18). It can refer to a part of the spirit world where those who have not repented suffer for their sins (see Alma 40:13–14). It is also used to describe the final condition of those who completely turn away from God (see D&C 29:38).

8:14 The phrase "gall of bitterness and bonds of iniquity" is used four times in the Book of Mormon (see Mosiah 27:29; Alma 41:11; Mormon 8:31; Moroni 8:14). Gall was a bitter and sometimes poisonous herb or drink. The word is used first in the Old Testament to describe those who turn away from God (see Deuteronomy 29:18). The phrase *bonds of iniquity* refers to the cords or chains of wickedness and sin (see Proverbs 5:22; Isaiah 58:6).

8:16 ***pervert***—change or distort

8:16 (15–16) To perish is to die physically or spiritually, or to be destroyed.

8:20 ***naught***—nothing

8:20 (19–20) "[Little children] are saved through the atonement and because they are free from sin. They come from God in purity; no sin or taint attaches to them in this life; and they return in purity to their Maker. . . . 'Little children are redeemed from the foundation of the world through mine Only Begotten,' the Lord says. (D&C 29:46.)" (Bruce R. McConkie, "The Salvation of Little Children," 4–5).

8:21 ***torment***—pain

8:22 ***availeth***—gains

"Are all little children saved automatically in the celestial kingdom? To this question the answer is a thunderous *yes,* which echoes and re-echoes from one end of heaven to the other. Jesus taught it to his disciples. Mormon said it over and over again. . . . Joseph Smith's Vision of the Celestial Kingdom contains this statement: 'And I also beheld that all children who die before they arrive at the years of accountability are saved in the celestial kingdom of heaven.' [D&C 137:10]" (Bruce R. McConkie, "The Salvation of Little Children," 4).

8:24 ***under condemnation***—judged guilty

## MORONI EXPLAINS THE FRUITS OF REPENTANCE

25 And the first fruits of repentance is baptism; and baptism cometh by faith unto the fulfilling the commandments; and the fulfilling the commandments bringeth remission of sins;
26 And the remission of sins bringeth meekness, and lowliness of heart; and because of meekness and lowliness of heart cometh the visitation of the Holy Ghost, which Comforter filleth with hope and perfect love, which love endureth by diligence unto prayer, until the end shall come, when all the saints shall dwell with God.
27 Behold, my son, I will write unto you again if I go not out soon against the Lamanites. Behold, the pride of this nation, or the people of the Nephites, hath proven their destruction except they should repent.
28 Pray for them, my son, that repentance may come unto them. But behold, I fear lest the Spirit hath ceased striving with them; and in this part of the land they are also seeking to put down all power and authority which cometh from God; and they are denying the Holy Ghost.
29 And after rejecting so great a knowledge, my son, they must perish soon, unto the fulfilling of the prophecies which were spoken by the prophets, as well as the words of our Savior himself.
30 Farewell, my son, until I shall write unto you, or shall meet you again. Amen.

# CHAPTER 9

*The second epistle of Mormon to his son Moroni.*

*In Mormon's second letter to his son Moroni he describes the wickedness of both the Nephites and Lamanites as they enjoy torturing and killing each other. Notice the difference in Mormon's sad description of his people and his hope for his righteous son Moroni.*

## MORMON DESCRIBES THE EVIL ACTS OF THE NEPHITES AND LAMANITES

1 MY beloved son, I write unto you again that ye may know that I am yet alive; but I write somewhat of that which is grievous.
2 For behold, I have had a sore battle with the Lamanites, in which we did not conquer; and Archeantus has fallen by the sword, and also Luram and Emron; yea, and we have lost a great number of our choice men.
3 And now behold, my son, I fear lest the Lamanites shall destroy this people; for they do not repent, and Satan stirreth them up continually to anger one with another.
4 Behold, I am laboring with them continually; and when I speak the word of God with sharpness they tremble and anger against me; and when I use no sharpness they harden their hearts against it; wherefore, I fear lest the Spirit of the Lord hath ceased striving with them.

---

8:26 (25–26) Notice what Mormon said leads to baptism. How is this like the Fourth Article of Faith? Once you've been baptized how can faith and repentance continue to bless you?

8:28 ***striving***—working

Mormon asked Moroni to pray for the Nephites because he feared that the Spirit would quit striving or working with them. President Joseph Fielding Smith said: "The Spirit of the Lord will not argue with men, nor abide in them, except they yield obedience" (*Answers to Gospel Questions* 3:29).

9:1 ***grievous***—very sad or serious

9:2 ***sore***—terrible

9:4 Mormon feared that because of his people's wickedness they had lost the Light of Christ (their conscience). Elder Bruce R. McConkie taught that the Light of Christ strives or works with all people "unless and until they rebel against light and truth, at which time the striving ceases, and in that sense the Spirit is withdrawn" (*The Promised Messiah,* 209).

THE NEPHITES' LAST BATTLE, BY GARY SMITH

*Mormon wrote in an epistle to his son Moroni, "I have had a sore battle with the Lamanites, in which we did not conquer."*

5 For so exceedingly do they anger that it seemeth me that they have no fear of death; and they have lost their love, one towards another; and they thirst after blood and revenge continually.

6 And now, my beloved son, notwithstanding their hardness, let us labor diligently; for if we should cease to labor, we should be brought under condemnation; for we have a labor to perform whilst in this tabernacle of clay, that we may conquer the enemy of all righteousness, and rest our souls in the kingdom of God.

7 And now I write somewhat concerning the sufferings of this people. For according to the knowledge which I have received from Amoron, behold, the Lamanites have many prisoners, which they took from the tower of Sherrizah; and there were men, women, and children.

8 And the husbands and fathers of those women and children they have slain; and they feed the women upon the flesh of their husbands, and the children upon the flesh of their fathers; and no water, save a little, do they give unto them.

---

9:5 ***thirst after blood***—desire to shed blood or kill

Mormon's wicked people had lost their love for each other. "The absence of affection and the loss of love—whether in a family or a nation—appear to mark points of almost no return" (Neal A. Maxwell, *That My Family Should Partake,* 105).

9:6 ***labor diligently***—work hard
***brought under condemnation***—punished

Though others were not repenting, Mormon encouraged his son to live faithfully and teach others to do so. Even if those around you make wrong choices, how can you follow Mormon and Moroni's examples and choose the right?

9 And notwithstanding this great abomination of the Lamanites, it doth not exceed that of our people in Moriantum. For behold, many of the daughters of the Lamanites have they taken prisoners; and after depriving them of that which was most dear and precious above all things, which is chastity and virtue—

10 And after they had done this thing, they did murder them in a most cruel manner, torturing their bodies even unto death; and after they have done this, they devour their flesh like unto wild beasts, because of the hardness of their hearts; and they do it for a token of bravery.

## Mormon Feels Sorrow for a Once Great People

11 O my beloved son, how can a people like this, that are without civilization—

12 (And only a few years have passed away, and they were a civil and a delightsome people)

13 But O my son, how can a people like this, whose delight is in so much abomination—

14 How can we expect that God will stay his hand in judgment against us?

15 Behold, my heart cries: Wo unto this people. Come out in judgment, O God, and hide their sins, and wickedness, and abominations from before thy face!

16 And again, my son, there are many widows and their daughters who remain in Sherrizah; and that part of the provisions which the Lamanites did not carry away, behold, the army of Zenephi has carried away, and left them to wander whithersoever they can for food; and many old women do faint by the way and die.

17 And the army which is with me is weak; and the armies of the Lamanites are betwixt Sherrizah and me; and as many as have fled to the army of Aaron have fallen victims to their awful brutality.

18 O the depravity of my people! They are without order and without mercy. Behold, I am but a man, and I have but the strength of a man, and I cannot any longer enforce my commands.

19 And they have become strong in their perversion; and they are alike brutal, sparing none, neither old nor young; and they delight in everything save that which is good; and the suffering of our women and our children upon all the face of this land doth exceed everything; yea, tongue cannot tell, neither can it be written.

20 And now, my son, I dwell no longer upon this horrible scene. Behold, thou knowest the wickedness of this people; thou knowest that they are without principle, and past feeling; and their wickedness doth exceed that of the Lamanites.

21 Behold, my son, I cannot recommend them unto God lest he should smite me.

## Mormon Expresses Hope for His Righteous Son Moroni

22 But behold, my son, I recommend thee unto God, and I trust in Christ that thou wilt be saved; and I pray unto God that he will spare thy life, to witness the return of his people unto him, or their utter destruction; for I know that they must perish except they repent and return unto him.

23 And if they perish it will be like unto the Jaredites, because of the wilfulness of their hearts, seeking for blood and revenge.

24 And if it so be that they perish, we know that

---

9:9 ***depriving them of***—taking from them

"Chastity and virtue" refer to a person's purity and moral cleanliness. President Spencer W. Kimball taught that chastity is "our most valuable possession" (in Conference Report, October 1979, 6).

9:10 ***devour***—eat up greedily
***token***—sign or badge

9:11 ***civilization***—law and order

9:14 ***stay***—stop

9:17 ***betwixt***—between
***brutality***—cruelty

9:18 ***depravity***—corruption or wickedness

9:19 ***perversion***—wickedness

9:20 The Nephites' sins had made them "past feeling," unable to feel the Lord's Spirit (see 1 Nephi 17:45). President Kimball explained that "when we move away from the Lord there seems to grow upon us a film of worldliness, which insulates us from his influence" (*Faith Precedes the Miracle,* 209).

9:22 Why do you think Mormon praised his son for staying faithful? How hard do you think it was for Moroni to be faithful in a world where so many were wicked?

many of our brethren have deserted over unto the Lamanites, and many more will also desert over unto them; wherefore, write somewhat a few things, if thou art spared and I shall perish and not see thee; but I trust that I may see thee soon; for I have sacred records that I would deliver up unto thee.
25 My son, be faithful in Christ; and may not the things which I have written grieve thee, to weigh thee down unto death; but may Christ lift thee up, and may his sufferings and death, and the showing his body unto our fathers, and his mercy and long-suffering, and the hope of his glory and of eternal life, rest in your mind forever.
26 And may the grace of God the Father, whose throne is high in the heavens, and our Lord Jesus Christ, who sitteth on the right hand of his power, until all things shall become subject unto him, be, and abide with you forever. Amen.

## CHAPTER 10

*Moroni ends the Book of Mormon with an invitation to readers to receive many wonderful spiritual blessings in their lives. Look for all the blessings you can receive.*

### Prayerful Readers Can Know If the Book of Mormon Is True

1 NOW I, Moroni, write somewhat as seemeth me good; and I write unto my brethren, the Lamanites; and I would that they should know that more than four hundred and twenty years have passed away since the sign was given of the coming of Christ.
2 And I seal up these records, after I have spoken a few words by way of exhortation unto you.
3 Behold, I would exhort you that when ye shall read these things, if it be wisdom in God that ye should read them, that ye would remember how merciful the Lord hath been unto the children of men, from the creation of Adam even down unto the time that ye shall receive these things, and ponder it in your hearts.
4 And when ye shall receive these things, I would exhort you that ye would ask God, the Eternal Father, in the name of Christ, if these things are not true; and if ye shall ask with a sincere heart, with real intent, having faith in Christ, he will manifest the truth of it unto you, by the power of the Holy Ghost.
5 And by the power of the Holy Ghost ye may know the truth of all things.

### The Gifts of the Spirit Are Given to People Who Believe

6 And whatsoever thing is good is just and true; wherefore, nothing that is good denieth the Christ, but acknowledgeth that he is.
7 And ye may know that he is, by the power of the Holy Ghost; wherefore I would exhort you that ye deny not the power of God; for he worketh by power, according to the faith of the children of men, the same today and tomorrow, and forever.
8 And again, I exhort you, my brethren, that ye deny not the gifts of God, for they are many; and they come from the same God. And there are different ways that these gifts are administered; but it is the same God who worketh all in all; and they are given by the manifestations of the Spirit of God unto men, to profit them.
9 For behold, to one is given by the Spirit of God, that he may teach the word of wisdom;
10 And to another, that he may teach the word of knowledge by the same Spirit;

---

9:25 Christ can "lift us up" and give us hope when we are discouraged (see Matthew 11:28–30; James 4:10). His Atonement will, in the end, "lift" the righteous to eternal life (see Alma 13:29; D&C 106:7–8).

9:26 ***subject unto him***—under his power

10:2 ***seal***—lock or close
***exhortation***—strong encouragement

10:3 ***these things***—the Book of Mormon
***ponder***—seriously think about

10:4 ***intent***—desire
***manifest***—show

10:5 (4–5) Moroni 10:4–5 is known as Moroni's promise. Millions of people have had their prayers answered concerning the Book of Mormon. Have you prayed to know if the Book of Mormon is true?

10:6 ***just***—fair
***denieth***—refuses to accept
***acknowledgeth***—admits

10:8 ***are administered***—work or are given
***profit***—bless or help

11 And to another, exceedingly great faith; and to
another, the gifts of healing by the same Spirit;
12 And again, to another, that he may work
mighty miracles;
13 And again, to another, that he may prophesy
concerning all things;
14 And again, to another, the beholding of angels
and ministering spirits;
15 And again, to another, all kinds of tongues;
16 And again, to another, the interpretation of languages and of divers kinds of tongues.
17 And all these gifts come by the Spirit of Christ;
and they come unto every man severally, according
as he will.
18 And I would exhort you, my beloved brethren,
that ye remember that every good gift cometh of
Christ.
19 And I would exhort you, my beloved brethren,
that ye remember that he is the same yesterday,
today, and forever, and that all these gifts of which
I have spoken, which are spiritual, never will be
done away, even as long as the world shall stand,
only according to the unbelief of the children of
men.

## We Must Have Faith, Hope, and Charity

20 Wherefore, there must be faith; and if there
must be faith there must also be hope; and if there
must be hope there must also be charity.
21 And except ye have charity ye can in nowise
be saved in the kingdom of God; neither can ye be
saved in the kingdom of God if ye have not faith;
neither can ye if ye have no hope.
22 And if ye have no hope ye must needs be in
despair; and despair cometh because of iniquity.
23 And Christ truly said unto our fathers: If ye
have faith ye can do all things which are expedient
unto me.

## All People Will See Moroni at the Judgment and Know His Words Are True

24 And now I speak unto all the ends of the
earth—that if the day cometh that the power and
gifts of God shall be done away among you, it shall
be because of unbelief.
25 And wo be unto the children of men if this be
the case; for there shall be none that doeth good
among you, no not one. For if there be one among
you that doeth good, he shall work by the power
and gifts of God.
26 And wo unto them who shall do these things
away and die, for they die in their sins, and they
cannot be saved in the kingdom of God; and I
speak it according to the words of Christ; and I lie
not.

---

10:13 ***prophesy***—tell what will happen in the future

10:14 ***beholding***—seeing

The Prophet Joseph Smith explained the difference between angels and ministering spirits: "There are two kinds of beings in heaven, namely: Angels, who are resurrected personages, having bodies of flesh and bones. . . . Secondly: the spirits of just men made perfect, they who are not resurrected, but inherit the same glory" (D&C 129:1, 3).

10:15 ***tongues***—languages

10:16 ***interpretation***—translation or understanding of
***divers***—several or many

10:17 ***severally***—individually

10:18 (8–18) Elder Bruce R. McConkie once wrote of these gifts of God: "By the grace of God . . . certain special spiritual blessings called *gifts of the Spirit* are bestowed upon men. . . . Because they are freely available to all the obedient, they are called gifts. They are signs and miracles reserved for the faithful and none else. . . . And these are by no means all of the gifts. In the fullest sense, they are infinite [endless] in number" (*Mormon Doctrine,* 314–15). These gifts are also listed in 1 Corinthians 12:1–11 and D&C 46:8–29.

10:18 (9–18) Which of the gifts of the Spirit listed in these verses have you been given? What does God want you to do with your spiritual gifts?

10:20 Mormon said charity is "the pure love of Christ" (Moroni 7:47) and "everlasting love" (Moroni 8:17).

10:21 ***nowise***—no way

10:22 ***despair***—sorrow or misery

10:23 In the Old and the New Testament the Lord tells people that all things are possible to those who believe (see Genesis 18:14 and Mark 9:23).

10:25 ***wo***—sorrow or misery

27 And I exhort you to remember these things; for the time speedily cometh that ye shall know that I lie not, for ye shall see me at the bar of God; and the Lord God will say unto you: Did I not declare my words unto you, which were written by this man, like as one crying from the dead, yea, even as one speaking out of the dust?

28 I declare these things unto the fulfilling of the prophecies. And behold, they shall proceed forth out of the mouth of the everlasting God; and his word shall hiss forth from generation to generation.

29 And God shall show unto you, that that which I have written is true.

## Moroni Invites All People to Come unto Christ and Be Perfected in Him

30 And again I would exhort you that ye would come unto Christ, and lay hold upon every good gift, and touch not the evil gift, nor the unclean thing.

31 And awake, and arise from the dust, O Jerusalem; yea, and put on thy beautiful garments, O daughter of Zion; and strengthen thy stakes and enlarge thy borders forever, that thou mayest no more be confounded, that the covenants of the Eternal Father which he hath made unto thee, O house of Israel, may be fulfilled.

32 Yea, come unto Christ, and be perfected in him, and deny yourselves of all ungodliness; and if ye shall deny yourselves of all ungodliness, and love God with all your might, mind and strength, then is his grace sufficient for you, that by his grace ye may be perfect in Christ; and if by the grace of God ye are perfect in Christ, ye can in nowise deny the power of God.

33 And again, if ye by the grace of God are perfect in Christ, and deny not his power, then are ye sanctified in Christ by the grace of God, through the shedding of the blood of Christ, which is in the covenant of the Father unto the remission of your sins, that ye become holy, without spot.

34 And now I bid unto all, farewell. I soon go to rest in the paradise of God, until my spirit and body shall again reunite, and I am brought forth triumphant through the air, to meet you before the pleasing bar of the great Jehovah, the Eternal Judge of both quick and dead. Amen.

---

10:27 ***bar of God***—judgment
***declare***—speak

10:28 ***proceed***—go
***hiss forth***—go forth, signal, or call

10:28 (27–28) The Book of Mormon was written by people who are now dead. It was buried in the "dust," or ground, until 1823, when the angel Moroni showed Joseph Smith where to find it. God gave Joseph the power to translate it. So the coming forth of the Book of Mormon in the latter days fulfills this prophecy (see Joseph Smith—History 1:29–67 and Moses 7:62).

10:30 ***lay***—take

10:31 ***garments***—clothes
***confounded***—confused or ashamed
***fulfilled***—kept

Zion is used in several ways in the scriptures. Zion is defined as "the pure in heart" (D&C 97:21). Sometimes Zion has reference to a specific place. Enoch's city was called Zion (see Moses 7:19).

The name *Israel* means "one who prevails with God," or "let God prevail." It is used several ways in the scriptures. It may refer to (1) the man Jacob, whose name was changed to Israel; (2) the family, children, or tribes of Israel (the scriptures often use the phrase "house of Israel" in this sense); (3) the land of Israel; or (4) the true believers in Christ, no matter what their family or where they live (see LDS Bible Dictionary, s.v. "Israel," 708).

10:32 ***sufficient***—enough

10:33 "To be *sanctified* is to become clean, pure, and spotless" (Bruce R. McConkie, *Mormon Doctrine,* 675). A person can become sanctified only through the Atonement of Jesus Christ and by obedience to the laws, ordinances, and commandments of the gospel of Jesus Christ.

***remission***—forgiveness

10:33 (32–33) The Book of Mormon can help us "come unto Christ and be perfected in him." President Ezra Taft Benson taught the Saints, "There is a power in the book which will begin to flow into your lives the moment you begin a serious study of the book. You will find greater power to resist temptation. You will find the power to avoid deception. You will find the power to stay on the straight and narrow path" (in Conference Report, October 1986, 6).

10:34 ***bid***—say
***reunite***—come back together
***triumphant***—victorious
***quick***—the living

*MORONI BURYING THE PLATES*, BY TOM LOVELL

*Moroni buried the gold plates in the Hill Cumorah in* A.D. *421.*

# Glossary

***Christ.*** A Greek word meaning "the Anointed One"; the Hebrew word with the same meaning is *Messiah.* Jesus is the Christ—the one chosen, set apart, and sent by God to save us (see LDS Bible Dictionary, s.v. "Christ," 633).

***Covenant.*** A covenant is an agreement between two people. In the scriptures it is usually an agreement between God and man. We promise to be obedient to God's commandments, and He promises to bless us (see LDS Bible Dictionary, s.v. "Covenant," 651).

***Engrave, Engraven.*** To engrave is to write by cutting, etching, or impressing into metal.

***Fall, Fall of Adam, Fall of man.*** "The fall of Adam is one of the most important occurrences in the history of man. Before the fall, Adam and Eve had physical bodies but no blood. There was no sin, no death, and no children among any of the earthly creations." The Fall brought mortality and "both physical and spiritual death into the world upon all mankind (Hel. 14:16–17). . . . It was a necessary step in the progress of man, and provisions for a Savior had been made even before the fall had occurred. Jesus Christ came to atone for the fall of Adam and also for man's individual sins" (LDS Bible Dictionary, s.v. "Fall of Adam," 670).

***Genealogy of my forefathers, Genealogy of his fathers.*** The names and history of my (his) father, grandfathers, and other ancestors.

***Gentiles.*** A word that means "nations." It refers to those not of the family of Israel or who do not believe in the God of Israel. In the Book of Mormon it also refers to those who come from gentile nations, which are all nations outside the land of Israel (see LDS Bible Dictionary, s.v. "Gentile," 679).

***Grace.*** Divine help given by God through the Atonement of Jesus Christ. It provides us with the power needed to repent, keep the commandments, and become like God (see LDS Bible Dictionary, s.v. "Grace," 697; see also 2 Nephi 25:23).

***Hell.*** Latter-day scriptures teach that there are at least three meanings for the term *hell.* It can describe our suffering here on earth (see Alma 36:18). It can refer to a part of the spirit world where those who have not repented suffer for their sins (see Alma 40:13–14). It is also used to describe the final condition of those who completely turn away from God (see D&C 29:38).

***Hearken to, Hearken unto.*** Listen to and obey.

***Isles, Isles of the sea.*** "Refers not only to islands but also to the continents of the earth (2 Ne. 10:20). It may also mean any place not immediately accessible to Israel by land" (Donald W. Parry and others, *Understanding Isaiah,* 425).

***Israel, House of Israel.*** The name *Israel* means "one who prevails with God" or "let God prevail." It is used several ways in the scriptures. It may refer to (1) the man Jacob, whose name was changed to Israel; (2) the family, children, or tribes of Israel (the scriptures often use the phrase "house of Israel" in this sense); (3) the land of Israel; or (4) the true believers in Christ, no matter what their family or where they live (see LDS Bible Dictionary, s.v. "Israel," 708).

***Jew.*** The term *Jew* often refers to a descendant from the tribe of Judah. However, the Book of Mormon also uses the term *Jew* to refer to any Israelite from the land or kingdom of Judah, even if not descended from the tribe of Judah (see LDS Bible Dictionary, s.v. "Jew," 713). In addition, the Book of Mormon sometimes uses the term *Jews* to refer to the entire house of Israel (see *Book of Mormon Student Manual, Religion 121 and 122,* 15).

***Law of Moses.*** The laws and ordinances that the children of Israel were commanded to follow from the days of Moses until the time of Jesus Christ (see LDS Bible Dictionary, s.v. "Law of Moses," 722–23).

***Lord of Hosts.*** "Christ is the *Lord of Hosts* (1 Chron. 17:24; Ps. 24:10; Isa. 6:5; Zech. 14:16–17; Mal. 1:14), meaning that he is a man of war (Ex. 15:3), a God of battles (Ps. 24:8), a leader of his saints in days of conflict and carnage" (Bruce R. McConkie, *Mormon Doctrine,* 451).

***Messiah.*** Means "Anointed One." The word *Christ* has the same meaning. Jesus Christ is the promised Messiah—the one chosen, set apart, and sent by God to save us.

***Murmur.*** To grumble and complain.

***Perish.*** To die physically or spiritually, or to be destroyed.

***Plates of brass.*** The plates of brass were the Old Testament scriptures that Nephi obtained from Laban in Jerusalem. They contained Lehi's genealogy, the five books of Moses, the record of the Jews, and many prophecies of the holy prophets (see 1 Nephi 5:10–14).

***Redeem, Redeemer, Redemption.*** To *redeem* means to "buy back" or to "set free." Jesus Christ is our Redeemer because He willingly paid the price to buy us back and set us free from the effects of the Fall of Adam and from the burden of our own sins (see 1 Corinthians 6:20 and D&C 18:11). The price He had to pay was His own blood (see 1 Peter 1:18–19).

***Sanctification, Sanctify.*** "To be *sanctified* is to become clean, pure, and spotless" (Bruce R. McConkie, *Mormon Doctrine,* 675). A person can become sanctified only through the Atonement of Jesus Christ and by obedience to the laws, ordinances, and commandments of the gospel of Jesus Christ.

***Secret combinations.*** A secret combination is a group of wicked people who secretly join together to lie, cheat, steal, murder, or do whatever else is necessary in order to gain riches, wealth, or power (see Helaman 7:21; 8:27). The first secret combination was between Satan and Cain, who killed his brother Abel to get his flocks (see Moses 5:28–32). "Among today's secret combinations are gangs, drug cartels, and organized crime families" (M. Russell Ballard, in Conference Report, October 1997, 51).

***Seed.*** Descendants, meaning children, grandchildren, and so on.

***Transgress, Transgression.*** When the Prophet Joseph Smith was translating the Book of Mormon, one of the meanings of the word *transgression* was "the act of passing over or beyond any law or rule of moral duty" (Noah Webster, *An American Dictionary of the English Language,* s.v. "Transgression"). In the scriptures *transgression* generally means the breaking of spiritual law. President Joseph Fielding Smith said: "I never speak of the part Eve took in this fall [meaning the Fall of man] as a sin, nor do I accuse Adam of a sin. . . . It is not always a sin to transgress a law. . . . This was a transgression of the law, but not a sin in the strict sense, for it was something that Adam and Eve had to do!" (*Doctrines of Salvation* 1:114, 115).

***Wilderness.*** Wild land with very few people.

***Zion.*** Used in several ways in the scriptures. Zion is defined as "the pure in heart" (D&C 97:21). Sometimes Zion has reference to a specific place. Enoch's city was called Zion (see Moses 7:19). Jackson County, Missouri, is also referred to as Zion (see D&C 58:49–50), and the city of New Jerusalem, which is to be built in Jackson County, will be called Zion (see D&C 45:66–67). Joseph Smith referred to Zion, in a broader sense, as all of North and South America (see *History of the Church* 6:318–19; see also LDS Bible Dictionary, s.v. "Zion," 792).

# Sources Cited


Asay, Carlos E. *Family Pecan Trees: Planting a Legacy of Faith at Home*. Salt Lake City: Deseret Book Co., 1992.

———. *In the Lord's Service: A Guide to Spiritual Development*. Salt Lake City: Deseret Book Co., 1990.

Ashton, Marvin J. *The Measure of Our Hearts*. Salt Lake City: Deseret Book Co., 1991.

Ballard, M. Russell. "Great Shall Be the Peace of Thy Children." *Ensign* 24 (April 1994): 59–61.

———. *Our Search for Happiness: An Invitation to Understand The Church of Jesus Christ of Latter-day Saints*. Salt Lake City: Deseret Book Co., 1993.

Benson, Ezra Taft. *Come, Listen to a Prophet's Voice*. Salt Lake City: Deseret Book Co., 1990.

———. "The Heritage of the Servants of the Lord." *Ensign* 22 (October 1992): 2–5.

———. "Keys to Successful Member-Missionary Work." *Ensign* 20 (September 1990): 2–7.

———. "A Mighty Change of Heart." *Ensign* 19 (October 1989): 2–5.

———. "The Power of the Word." *Ensign* 16 (May 1986): 79–82.

———. *The Teachings of Ezra Taft Benson*. Salt Lake City: Bookcraft, 1988.

———. "To the Rising Generation." *New Era* 16 (June 1986): 4–8.

———. *A Witness and a Warning*. Salt Lake City: Deseret Book Co., 1998.

*Book of Mormon Student Manual, Religion 121 and 122*. Salt Lake City: The Church of Jesus Christ of Latter-day Saints, 1989.

Brewster, Hoyt W., Jr. *Doctrine and Covenants Encyclopedia*. Salt Lake City: Bookcraft, 1988.

———. *Isaiah Plain & Simple: The Message of Isaiah in the Book of Mormon*. Salt Lake City: Deseret Book Co., 1995.

Caldwell, C. Max. " 'What Think Ye of Christ?' " *Ensign* 14 (February 1984): 18–22.

Card, Orson Scott. "Dissent and Treason." *Ensign* 7 (September 1977): 53–58.

Clark, James R., ed. *Messages of the First Presidency of The Church of Jesus Christ of Latter-day Saints*. 6 vols. Salt Lake City: Bookcraft, 1965–75.

Clarke, Adam. *The Holy Bible . . . with a Commentary and Critical Notes*. 6 vols. New York: Abingdon-Cokesbury Press, n.d.

Clarke, J. Richard. "Confession, a Requirement of Forgiveness." In *Repentance*. Salt Lake City: Deseret Book Co., 1990.

*Collected Discourses*. Compiled and edited by Brian H. Stuy. 5 vols. Burbank, Calif. and Woodland Hills, Utah: B. H. S. Publishing, 1987–92.

Condie, Spencer J. "Righteous Oaths, Reproof, and Reconciliation." In *Studies in Scripture, vol. 8: Alma to Moroni*. Edited by Kent P. Jackson. Salt Lake City: Deseret Book Co., 1988, 80–91.

Conference Reports of The Church of Jesus Christ of Latter-day Saints. Salt Lake City: The Church of Jesus Christ of Latter-day Saints, 1899–.

Cook, Gene R. *Raising up a Family to the Lord*. Salt Lake City: Deseret Book Co., 1993.

———. *Receiving Answers to Our Prayers*. Salt Lake City: Deseret Book Co., 1996.

Cooper, J. C. *An Illustrated Encyclopaedia of Traditional Symbols*. London: Thames and Hudson, 1978.

Cowan, Richard O. *Answers to Your Questions About the Doctrine and Covenants*. Salt Lake City: Deseret Book Co., 1996.

Doxey, Roy W. "I Have a Question." *Ensign* 15 (August 1985): 11–13.

Dunn, Loren C. "Fire and the Holy Ghost." *Ensign* 26 (June 1996): 22–26.

Easton, M. G. *Illustrated Bible Dictionary*. New York: 1893.

*Encyclopedia of Mormonism*. Edited by Daniel H. Ludlow. 5 vols. New York: Macmillan, 1992.

Eyring, Henry B. *To Draw Closer to God*. Salt Lake City: Deseret Book Co., 1997.

Faust, James E. "The Blessings of Adversity." *Ensign* 28 (February 1998): 2–7.

Featherstone, Vaughn J. "Following in Their Footsteps." *Ensign* 27 (July 1997): 8–11.

*For the Strength of Youth* [pamphlet]. Salt Lake City: The Church of Jesus Christ of Latter-day Saints, 1990.

Galbraith, David B., D. Kelley Ogden, and Andrew C. Skinner. *Jerusalem, the Eternal City*. Salt Lake City: Deseret Book Co., 1996.

*Gospel Principles*. Salt Lake City: Deseret Book Co., 1978.

Hanks, Marion D. "An Attitude: The Weightier Matters." *Ensign* 11 (July 1981): 67–72.

Hinckley, Gordon B. "A City upon a Hill." *Ensign* 20 (July 1990): 2–5.

———. *Be Thou an Example*. Salt Lake City: Deseret Book Co., 1996.

———. "Messages of Inspiration from President Gordon B. Hinckley." *Church News,* 3 October 1998, 2.

———. "The Sacred Law of Tithing." *Ensign* 19 (December 1989): 2–5.

———. "Messages of Inspiration from President Hinckley." *Church News,* 6 December 1997, 2.

———. *Teachings of Gordon B. Hinckley*. Salt Lake City: Deseret Book Co., 1997.

"His Atoning Sacrifice." *Church News,* 23 March 1991, 16.

Holland, Jeffrey R. *Christ and the New Covenant: The Messianic Message of the Book of Mormon*. Salt Lake City: Deseret Book Co., 1997.

———. "Daddy, Donna, and Nephi." *Ensign* 6 (September 1976): 7–11.

———. " 'For a Wise Purpose.' " *Ensign* 26 (January 1996): 12–19.

———. "Mormon: The Man and the Book, Part 2," *Ensign* 8 (April 1978): 57–59.

———. *"A Standard unto My People."* An address given at the 1994 Book of Mormon Symposium, 9 August 1994.

Hunter, Howard W. "No Less Serviceable." *Ensign* 22 (April 1992): 64–67.

———. *The Teachings of Howard W. Hunter.* Edited by Clyde J. Williams. Salt Lake City: Bookcraft, 1998.

———. *That We Might Have Joy*. Salt Lake City: Deseret Book Co., 1994.

Hunter, Milton R. *God's Greatest Gift*. Brigham Young University Speeches of the Year, 15 December 1964.

*Hymns of The Church of Jesus Christ of Latter-day Saints*. Salt Lake City: The Church of Jesus Christ of Latter-day Saints, 1985.

Johnson, Lynn Nations. Review of *To Mothers & Fathers from the Book of Mormon,* by Blaine Yorgason and Brenton Yorgason. *Review of Books on the Book of Mormon* 4 (1992): 258–61.

Journal History of The Church of Jesus Christ of Latter-day Saints, Church Historical Department, The Church of Jesus Christ of Latter-day Saints, Salt Lake City, Utah.

*Journal of Discourses*. 26 vols. London: Latter-day Saints' Book Depot, 1854–1886.

Kimball, Spencer W. "Circles of Exaltation." An address given at Brigham Young University, 28 June 1968.

———. *Faith Precedes the Miracle*. Salt Lake City: Deseret Book Co., 1972.

———. "God Will Forgive." *Ensign* 12 (March 1982): 2–7.

———. "Gospel Forum: Continuing Revelation." *Ensign* 1 (February 1971): 20–21.

———. *The Teachings of Spencer W. Kimball*. Edited by Edward L. Kimball. Salt Lake City: Bookcraft, 1982.

———. "Tragedy or Destiny." *Improvement Era* 69 (March 1966): 211.

Lee, Harold B. *Decisions for Successful Living*. Salt Lake City: Deseret Book Co., 1973.

———. "From the Valley of Despair to the Mountain Peaks of Hope." *New Era* 1 (August 1971): 4–9.

———. *Stand Ye in Holy Places: Selected Sermons and Writings of President Harold B. Lee*. Salt Lake City: Deseret Book Co., 1974.

———. *The Teachings of Harold B. Lee*. Edited by Clyde J. Williams. Salt Lake City: Bookcraft, 1996.

Ludlow, Daniel H. *A Companion to Your Study of the Book of Mormon*. Salt Lake City: Deseret Book Co., 1976.

Ludlow, Victor L. *Isaiah: Prophet, Seer, and Poet*. Salt Lake City: Deseret Book Co., 1982.

Lund, Gerald N. "A Prophet for the Fulness of Times." *Ensign* 27 (January 1997): 50–54.

Maxwell, Neal A. *All These Things Shall Give Thee Experience*. Salt Lake City: Deseret Book Co., 1979.

———. *Meek and Lowly*. Salt Lake City: Deseret Book Co., 1987.

———. *Men and Women of Christ*. Salt Lake City: Bookcraft, 1991.

———. *The Neal A. Maxwell Quote Book*. Edited by Cory H. Maxwell. Salt Lake City: Bookcraft, 1997.

———. *"Not My Will, But Thine."* Salt Lake City: Bookcraft, 1988.

———. *That My Family Should Partake*. Salt Lake City: Deseret Book Co., 1974.

———. *Things as They Really Are*. Salt Lake City: Deseret Book Co., 1978.

———. *We Talk of Christ, We Rejoice in Christ*. Salt Lake City: Deseret Book Co., 1984.

———. *We Will Prove Them Herewith*. Salt Lake City: Deseret Book Co., 1982.

———. "Why Not Now?" *New Era* 5 (April 1975): 5–6.

———. *Wherefore, Ye Must Press Forward*. Salt Lake City: Deseret Book Co., 1977.

McConkie, Bruce R. *Doctrinal New Testament Commentary*. 3 vols. Salt Lake City: Bookcraft, 1965–73.

———. *The Millennial Messiah*. Salt Lake City: Deseret Book Co., 1982.

———. *Mormon Doctrine*. 2d ed. Salt Lake City: Bookcraft, 1966.

———. *The Mortal Messiah*. 4 vols. Salt Lake City: Deseret Book Co., 1979–81.

———. *A New Witness for the Articles of Faith*. Salt Lake City: Deseret Book Co., 1985.

———. *The Promised Messiah*. Salt Lake City: Deseret Book Co., 1978.

———. "The Salvation of Little Children." *Ensign* 7 (April 1977): 3–7.

———. "Ten Keys to Understanding Isaiah." *Ensign* 3 (October 1973): 78–83.

McConkie, Joseph Fielding, Robert L. Millet, and Brent L. Top (vol. 4). *Doctrinal Commentary on the Book of Mormon*. 4 vols. Salt Lake City: Bookcraft, 1987–92.

McKay, David O. *Gospel Ideals*. Salt Lake City: Bookcraft, 1998.

———. *Man May Know for Himself: Teachings of President David O. McKay*. Compiled by Clare Middlemiss. Salt Lake City: Deseret Book Co., 1967.

Nibley, Hugh. *An Approach to the Book of Mormon*. Vol. 6 of *The Collected Works of Hugh Nibley*. Salt Lake City and Provo, Utah: Deseret Book Co. and Foundation for Ancient Research and Mormon Studies, 1988.

———. *Brother Brigham Challenges the Saints*. Vol. 13 of *The Collected Works of Hugh Nibley*. Salt Lake City and Provo, Utah: Deseret Book Co. and Foundation for Ancient Research and Mormon Studies, 1994.

———. *Lehi in the Desert/The World of the Jaredites/There Were Jaredites*. Vol. 5 of *The Collected Works of Hugh Nibley*. Salt Lake City and Provo, Utah: Deseret Book Co. and Foundation for Ancient Research and Mormon Studies, 1988.

———. "A Strange Thing in the Land: The Return of the Book of Enoch, Part 4." *Ensign* 6 (March 1976): 62–66.

Nyman, Monte S. *"Great Are the Words of Isaiah."* Salt Lake City: Bookcraft, 1980.

Oaks, Dallin H. *The Lord's Way*. Salt Lake City: Deseret Book Co., 1991.

———. *Pure in Heart*. Salt Lake City: Bookcraft, 1988.

*Old Testament: 1 Kings–Malachi, Religion 302 Student Manual*. Salt Lake City: The Church of Jesus Christ of Latter-day Saints, 1982.

Otten, Leaun G., and C. Max Caldwell. *Sacred Truths of the Doctrine and Covenants*. 2 vols. Salt Lake City: Deseret Book Co., 1993.

Packer, Boyd K. "The Candle of the Lord." *Ensign* 13 (January 1983): 51–56.

———. "The Holy Temple." *Ensign* 25 (February 1995): 32–36.

———. *Our Father's Plan*. Salt Lake City: Deseret Book Co., 1984.

———. *The Play and the Plan*. CES fireside address for college-age adults, 7 May 1995, in Kirkland, Washington.

———. *"That All May Be Edified."* Salt Lake City: Bookcraft, 1982.

Parry, Donald W., Jay A. Parry, and Tina M. Peterson. *Understanding Isaiah*. Salt Lake City: Deseret Book Co., 1998.

Perry, L. Tom. *Living With Enthusiasm*. Salt Lake City: Deseret Book Co., 1996.

*Random House Webster's College Dictionary*. 2d ed. New York: Random House, 1997.

Rector, Hartman, Jr. "You Shall Receive the Spirit." *Ensign* 4 (January 1974): 1987–92.

Reynolds, George, and Janne M. Sjodahl. *Commentary on the Book of Mormon*. 7 vols. Salt Lake City: Deseret Book Co., 1955–61.

Richards, LeGrand. *A Marvelous Work and a Wonder*. Rev. and enl. ed. Salt Lake City: Deseret Book Co., 1976.

Romney, Marion G. *Learning for the Eternities*. Compiled by George J. Romney. Salt Lake City: Deseret Book Co., 1977.

Scott, Richard G. "The Power of the Book of Mormon in My Life." *Ensign* 14 (October 1984): 6–11.

Simpson, Robert L. "The Law of the Fast." *Improvement Era* 70 (December 1967): 48–50.

Smith, Joseph. "Church History." *Times and Seasons* 3 (1 March 1842): 706–10.

———. *History of The Church of Jesus Christ of Latter-day Saints*. Edited by B. H. Roberts. 2d ed., rev. 7 vols. Salt Lake City: The Church of Jesus Christ of Latter-day Saints, 1932–51.

———. *Teachings of the Prophet Joseph Smith*. Selected by Joseph Fielding Smith. Salt Lake City: Deseret Book Co., 1938.

———, comp. *Lectures on Faith*. Salt Lake City: Deseret Book Co., 1985.

Smith, Joseph Fielding. *Answers to Gospel Questions*.

Compiled by Joseph Fielding Smith, Jr. 5 vols. Salt Lake City: Deseret Book Co., 1957–66.

———. *Church History and Modern Revelation.* 2 vols. Salt Lake City: The Church of Jesus Christ of Latter-day Saints, 1953.

———. *Doctrines of Salvation.* Compiled by Bruce R. McConkie. 3 vols. Salt Lake City: Bookcraft, 1954–56.

———. *Religious Truths Defined: A Comparison of Religious Faiths with the Restored Gospel.* Salt Lake City: Bookcraft, 1959.

———. *The Way to Perfection.* Salt Lake City: Deseret Book Co., 1972.

———, comp. *Life of Joseph F. Smith.* 2d ed. Salt Lake City: Deseret Book Co., 1938.

Smith, William. *Smith's Bible Dictionary.* Grand Rapids, Michigan: Zondervan, 1948.

Sperry, Sidney B. *Book of Mormon Compendium.* Salt Lake City: Bookcraft, 1968.

Strong, James. *The Exhaustive Concordance of the Bible.* Nashville, Tenn.: Abingdon Press, 1973.

Talmage, James E. *The Articles of Faith.* 12th ed. Salt Lake City: The Church of Jesus Christ of Latter-day Saints, 1924.

———. *Jesus the Christ.* 3rd ed. Salt Lake City: The Church of Jesus Christ of Latter-day Saints, 1916.

Tanner, N. Eldon. "The Inevitable Choice." *Ensign* 7 (September 1977): 2–5.

———. "The Power of Prayer." In *Prayer.* Salt Lake City: Deseret Book Co., 1977.

Tvedtnes, John A. "I Have a Question." *Ensign* 22 (September 1992): 28.

Webster, Noah. *An American Dictionary of the English Language.* 1828. Reprint, San Francisco, Calif.: Foundation for American Christian Education, 1967.

Widtsoe, John A. *Evidences and Reconciliations.* Arranged by G. Homer Durham. Collector's edition. Salt Lake City: Bookcraft, 1987.

Whitney, Orson F. *Saturday Night Thoughts.* Salt Lake City: Deseret News Press, 1921.

Young, Brigham. *Discourses of Brigham Young.* Compiled by John A. Widtsoe. Salt Lake City: Deseret Book Co., 1941.

# Illustration and Photo Credits

All maps by Tom Child.

Photographs and illustrations on the following pages are © Intellectual Reserve—xii, xvii, xx, 2, 4, 19, 25, 34, 36, 39, 45, 47, 52, 55, 57, 60, 71, 76, 80, 85, 95, 137, 160, 174, 183, 188, 190, 191, 194, 207, 208, 215, 265, 315, 336, 350, 357, 364, 450, 452, 474, 494, 510, 518, 608, 665

Illustration, page 183: courtesy Museum of Church History and Art
Illustration, page 619: courtesy Jim and Paula Conway
Illustration, page 621: courtesy Don Boulter
Illustration, page 641: courtesy Robert Garff
Illustration, page 660: courtesy Blaine Hudson Printing

ISBN 1-57008-684-2

EAN

SKU 3909368 U.S. $49.95

UPC

SKU 3909368 U.S. $49.95